HOME RULE IN AMERICA

HOME RULE IN AMERICA

A FIFTY-STATE HANDBOOK

DALE KRANE
University of Nebraska, Omaha

PLATON N. RIGOS
University of South Florida

MELVIN B. HILL JR.
University of Georgia

CQ PRESS

A Division of Congressional Quarterly Inc.
Washington, D.C.

CQ Press

A Division of Congressional Quarterly Inc.

1255 22nd Street, N.W., Suite 400

Washington, D.C. 20037

(202) 822-1475; (800) 638-1710

www.cqpress.com

Cover designer: Kachergis Book Design
Book design and composition: Kachergis Book Design, Pittsboro, North Carolina

Printed and bound in the United States of America.

05   04   03   02   01   6   5   4   3   2

(∞) The paper used in this publication meets the minimum requirements of the
American National Standards for Information Services—Permanence of Paper
for Printed Library Materials, ANSI Z39.48–1992.

Library of Congress Cataloging-in-Publication Data

Krane, Dale.

    Home rule in America : a fifty-state handbook / Dale Krane, Platon N.
Rigos, Melvin B. Hill Jr.

       p.   cm.

    Includes bibliographical references.

    ISBN 1-56802-281-6

    1. Municipal home rule—United States—States. 2. Local government—Law
and legislation—United States—States. I. Rigos, Platon N. II. Hill,
Melvin B., Jr. III. Title.

    KF5305.Z95 K73   2001

    320.8'0973—dc21   00-045450

CONTENTS

Foreword / vii
Preface / ix
List of Contributors / xv

Introduction / 1

Alabama / 23

Alaska / 33

Arizona / 41

Arkansas / 49

California / 58

Colorado / 69

Connecticut / 78

Delaware / 86

Florida / 94

Georgia / 103

Hawaii / 112

Idaho / 120

Illinois / 128

Indiana / 139

Iowa / 148

Kansas / 156

Kentucky / 166

Louisiana / 173

Maine / 183

Maryland / 191

Massachusetts / 203

Michigan / 212

Minnesota / 224

Mississippi / 231

Missouri / 241

Montana / 248

Nebraska / 258

Nevada / 269

New Hampshire / 277

New Jersey / 285

New Mexico / 295

New York / 303

North Carolina / 312

North Dakota / 322

Ohio / 330

Oklahoma / 341

Oregon / 348

Pennsylvania / 356

Rhode Island / 367

South Carolina / 375

South Dakota / 383

Tennessee / 391

Texas / 399

Utah / 408

Vermont / 417

Virginia / 427

Washington / 436

West Virginia / 445

Wisconsin / 453

Wyoming / 462

Appendix / 471
Glossary / 493

FOREWORD

A long-standing topic of discussion and debate among government reformers, public officials, and civic groups is the relationship between local government units and state government. Since the 1980s, state and local public interest groups, study commissions, and academicians have produced studies of the "state of state-local relations"; generally they have concluded that there is considerable room for improvement.

Recommendations from these studies for remedial action have focused on six general areas: (1) greater local government home rule, discretionary authority, or empowerment; (2) increased state financial aid to localities, especially to compensate for federal funding cuts resulting from the elimination of general revenue sharing and other federal-local grant programs; (3) relief from unfunded state mandates; (4) local tax reform and assistance with equalizing expenditures for public education; (5) sorting out functional responsibilities followed by the state's assumption of greater financial and administrative responsibilities in such areas as courts, corrections, mental health, and transportation; and (6) creation of intergovernmental advisory bodies to facilitate public official communications, identify friction points, and recommend solutions. Although each of these actions could go a long way toward improving state-local relations, empowerment of local governments is the foundation.

In view of the prevailing "Dillon's Rule" interpretation that local governments are creations or "creatures" of the states, empowerment depends on constitutional amendment or statutory action at the state level. Some of the early studies of home rule, conducted by the U.S. Advisory Commission on Intergovernmental Relations (ACIR), called on the states to "unshackle" their local governments and give them greater discretionary authority over their structures, functions, personnel, and finances. In many states, the response has been slow and painful.

A 1981 ACIR report by Joseph F. Zimmerman, *Measuring Local Discretionary Authority*, found wide variation across the country in the extent to which state constitutions and legislatures had granted discretionary authority to various types of general-purpose local governments. Using an index of discretionary authority, Zimmerman surveyed state officials and organizations representing local governments and found that state legislatures generally were more willing to give home rule to cities than counties and that state legislatures were less willing to empower localities in the area of finances than in the areas of functional responsibilities, form of government, and personnel policies.

Other studies of state constitutional actions, statutory enactments, court decisions, and opinions of state attorneys general affecting local governments have been conducted over the past two decades by one of the authors of this book, Melvin Hill, and by other scholars. However, the Zimmerman index has remained the definitive reading of local discretionary authority.

A number of recent trends have called attention to the need for better understanding of the legal, political, fiscal, and operational dynamics of state-local relations. These trends include the modernization of institutional capacity and civic governance processes at the state and local levels, the devolution of authority by the national government, the "reinventing government" movement, and globalization. These trends underscore the need for effective partnerships between state and local governments that strike a balance between "Dillon's Rule" traditions and the need for flexibility and discretion in local practice.

The authors of this book continue the tradition of empirical research across the fifty states begun by Zimmerman, Hill, and other scholars. *Home Rule in America* offers the definitive contemporary assessment of the "state of state-local relations" and a concise state-by-state "snapshot" of the current status of home rule. In addition to updating and refining state constitutional and statutory activities affecting local governments, this new national study provides important perspectives on discretionary authority not revealed by legalistic analyses or public official surveys. It is a welcome addition to the literature of federalism and intergovernmental relations by experts in the field.

CARL W. STENBERG
Dean and Professor
University of Baltimore

PREFACE

Municipal independence in the United States is therefore a natural consequence of this very principle of the sovereignty of the people.
— *Alexis de Tocqueville,* Democracy in America[1]

Home rule, or "municipal independence" as de Tocqueville called it, is not a household concept. It does not strike most citizens as a pressing problem or even as something that ought to command their attention. As long as the garbage is collected, potholes in the neighborhood streets are filled, and firefighters or police respond promptly when called, the typical citizen gives little thought to the degree of discretionary authority available to local government officials. Consider the following questions about any locality in the United States:

• May it sell a public asset, such as a hospital, with or without a vote of the local citizens?

• May it use locally raised revenues to capitalize an economic development corporation in a predominantly minority neighborhood? Or in any neighborhood?

• May it establish and operate an airfield? May it buy or sell services, such as electricity, natural gas, or water?

• May it borrow money? Impose a new tax? Open a casino? Surprisingly, a city or county may be unable to execute these rather ordinary activities because state statutes do not permit it to do so.

Usually, a pressing problem or a contentious issue must arise before citizens discover their locality does not possess the power to act unless permission is first obtained from the state government. Witness the recent attempts by some large cities to sue handgun manufacturers for their role in the violent deaths that plague the country. Members of the state legislatures who opposed controls on firearms passed legislation that prohibited cities in the states from suing the handgun manufacturers. As a consequence, no matter how passionately the local residents wanted their cities to go forward with lawsuits, the cities were prohibited from doing so. The simple lesson learned from this example is that whatever the officials of a local government may do ultimately rests on the authority granted to them by state governments.

Many people are astonished to learn that the U.S. Constitution makes no mention of cities, counties, or any other type of local jurisdiction, such as a school district or public authority. The type, number, form, and function of local governments in the United States are dictated by the constitutions and statutory laws of the fifty American states. Because the legal system of each state determines the powers that cities may exercise,[2] local governments are often called creatures of the state.

Although the fifty states function with very similar governmental structures, their laws differ in interesting and often significant areas; one in particular is the degree of autonomy or discretionary authority local governments possess. The term "home rule," which emerged during the Progressive movement of the late 1800s, referred to proposals to amend state constitutions or pass state laws that would increase the power of local governments and decrease the power of state legislatures over local governments. Typically, these proposals sought either to restrict the ability of state legislatures to pass what is termed "local" or "special privilege" legislation—acts aimed at a single community, or to permit localities to write a charter specifying a locally chosen form of government, such as a city manager government. Over time, a number of states passed legislation that went beyond these two basic approaches to granting local governments more discretionary authority.

We take the position in this volume that passage of any statute or constitutional provision that enhances the authority and opportunities for a local jurisdiction to control its own affairs can be considered as an effort to grant an additional degree of "home rule."[3] Given that the fifty states vary in their cultural, economic, historic, political, and social features, it is not surprising that they also vary in the way they control local governments. Local governments in some states are not much more than appendages of the state government, whereas other states have granted local governments extensive authority to make their own policy decisions.

It is curious, given the importance of this topic, that the level of knowledge about local government autonomy in the United States is so scant. One author recently suggested that there is a "blind spot" in the professional research on this topic by noting "relatively few scholars know much about the constitutional, political, and fiscal ties that bind states and localities, and even fewer have much information about the complex interactions between state and local governments engaged in the delivery of public goods and services."[4] This reference volume is intended to reduce this "blind spot" in our knowledge about the powers that state governments have granted or not granted to their local governments.

Organization of the Volume

Home Rule In America is organized in three main sections: an introductory essay on the development of home rule in the United States and the research that has been conducted on the topic; individual chapters on the fifty states; and a fifty-state comparative appendix containing several charts and tables along with accompanying explanatory text. Also included at the end of the volume is a glossary of important terms. Each state chapter opens with a single summary paragraph that encapsulates the current status of home rule in that state. This structure makes it possible for the reader to gain a brief, but accurate sense of local government autonomy in any one of the fifty states. Each state chapter follows the same topical organization; thus, a reader interested in a particular topic will be able to find that information in the same general location in each state chapter.[5] The chapter organization facilitates not only the quick location of particular items in different states but also comparisons among the fifty states.

The outline of topics, shown in the box on p. xi, is rather extensive, and in many cases, authors of state chapters had to tailor their presentation of topics to fit within these established limits. As a consequence, some topics receive differential treatment from state to state, depending on an author's judgment about the importance of a given topic to the overall status of local government autonomy in the state. Certainly, different persons examining this outline could offer suggestions for the addition or deletion of specific items. One principal consideration that shaped the outline was the desire to add topics that had been omitted in previous efforts to study home rule, for example, economic development authority and citizens' control over local government officials. Another important consideration that structured this outline was the utility of collecting much of the same information that had been gathered in the few previous studies of home rule. This collection of data would permit not only analysis of changes in local government status, but also a comparison of research that relied solely on legal documents with research that used documents, interviews, and expert observation.

The editors asked the authors of the state chapters to write for a general audience rather than a legal or an academic one. As a consequence, we believe the volume will be accessible and informative to a variety of readers. For example, citizens who are active or interested in the affairs of their local community will acquire a sense of what authority their local officials may or may not possess. Journalists assigned to city hall or the county court-

house will find many of their questions about local government operations answered here. Local officials will gain not only an overview of the parameters on local government in their state, but also a convenient source of information for the practices found in other states. Similarly, attorneys who serve local governments will benefit from the legal references accompanying each state chapter as well as from the descriptions of local authority that transcend a solely legal focus. Students and scholars will be able to use the material on each state for a wide range of projects; in particular, the information greatly facilitates comparative studies of neighboring states and of all fifty states.

Much as geologic strata are formed by slow processes as well as by sudden upheavals, so too are the institutional forms and practices of government. The Introduction reviews the long history of home rule, with attention to the events and motives that led to important changes in the authority of local governments. The editors invite the readers to review this historical overview before turning their attention to any of the individual states. In particular, a review of legal theory bearing on local government authority is presented; and readers who are not familiar with the basic legal issues may find some of their questions answered in this general treatment of home rule.

The reader should be aware of what is not included in this volume. There are no descriptions, except tangentially, of political parties, interest groups, election results, or general political behavior. Nor do the state chapters present details about the design and implementation of state government programs, except where such detail illuminates the question of local authority. The principal focus of the volume is on municipal and county governments. Special districts and public authorities are also described, but usually in relation to the powers of city or county governments. Because school districts typically operate under significant state control and completely separate constitutional and statutory authority, and because school districts have not been part of the debates about home rule, this volume does not include many details about them. Finally, we deliberately excluded any treatment of home rule in the District of Columbia, which is governed by the U.S. Congress.

Origins of the Volume

Home Rule in America has its roots in a 1978 work entitled *State Laws Governing Local Government Structure and Administration,* conducted under the direction of Melvin B. Hill Jr., who at the time was a legal research associate in the Carl Vinson Institute of Government at the University of Georgia. This study compiled all the state laws affecting the structure and operation of local governments placed them in six specific categories: form of government, altering boundaries and responsibilities, local elections, administrative operations and procedures, financial man-

STANDARD OUTLINE FOR STATE CHAPTERS

Opening Paragraph. A synopsis of the main points about the character of the state and the status of home rule in the state.

I. Governmental Setting
An introduction to the state, including a review of the basic governmental structures, historical evolution, political culture, and distinctive features of local government—particularly how these unique aspects shape home rule and local government autonomy in the state.

II. Home Rule
A. Historical Development (of home rule)
B. Definition of Home Rule
  1. *Legal*
  2. *Operational*
C. Structural Features (of home rule)
  1. *Local or special privilege legislation*
  2. *Classes of cities*
  3. *Charters and forms of government*
  4. *Incorporation, boundary setting, and annexation*
  5. *Status of counties*
  6. *Other legal/constitutional features, such as extraterritoriality*

III. Functions of Local Government
A. Functional Responsibilities
  1. *Functions and tasks assigned to cities*
  2. *Functions and tasks assigned to counties*
  3. *Actual practice*
  4. *Creation of special districts and public authorities*
  5. *Interlocal cooperation, including commonly used mechanisms*
B. Administrative Discretion (permitted local governments)
  1. *Personnel management*
  2. *Administrative procedures, rules, and systems*
  3. *Contracting/purchasing authority and bidding procedures*
  4. *Planning, zoning, and land use controls*
C. Economic Development (activities permitted local governments)
  1. *Creation of community development organizations, enterprise zones, etc.*
  2. *Economic (re)development banks and funds*
  3. *Industrial park and other facility (re)development*
  4. *Other*

IV. Fiscal Autonomy of Local Governments
A. Local Revenues
  1. *Minimum tax base*
  2. *Number and types permitted to localities*
  3. *Local control over rates and valuation*
  4. *Tax caps or limitations*
  5. *Borrowing and debt limits*
  6. *Other*
B. Local Expenditures (tables and charts may be provided)
  1. *Forms and types of expenditures*
  2. *Forms of budgets and auditing/accounting*
  3. *Expenditure limits*
  4. *Balanced budget requirement?*
  5. *Bankruptcy and receivership*
  6. *Other*
C. State Government Grants-in-Aid to Localities
  1. *Number, types, and amounts*
  2. *State rules and controls*
  3. *Local discretion over administration and spending*
  4. *Local political leverage*
  5. *Other*
D. Unfunded Mandates (imposed by the state)
  1. *Number and types*
  2. *State oversight mechanisms*
  3. *Degree of local compliance*

V. Citizen Access to Local Government
A. Local Elections (and conduct by local governments)
  1. *Degree of local control over elections*
  2. *Local rules on candidates, parties, and media*
B. Citizen Controls Over the Actions of Local Officials
  1. *Impeachment and recall*
  2. *Initiative and referendum*
  3. *Open meetings and open records*

VI. State-Local Relations
A brief summary of evolution and current status of home rule; trends and issues affecting the near-future for local governments; and author's final points.

VII. Notes

agement, and personnel management. To many citizens these may not be terribly exciting topics, but decisions taken in these areas are the "nuts and bolts" of local government operations.

Shortly after publication in 1978, Platon N. Rigos, who was studying annexation and incorporation issues as well as their role as variables in expenditure studies, contacted Professor Hill and asked him whether exchanging information with other scholars might not improve the accuracy of annexation indexes, since information in law books does not always describe the actual practice in many areas of state–local relations.

In 1993 the U.S. Advisory Commission on Intergovernmental Relations (ACIR), just before Congress eliminated it, published an updated version of the 1978 report.[6] Professor Hill also directed this new study. Although that ACIR document was helpful in identifying the legal foundation for local governments in six functional areas, as a survey of the law it did not provide a complete picture of what was actually happening in local governments in the respective states.

Following the publication of the 1993 ACIR volume, Professor Rigos convened a panel at the annual meeting of the American Political Science Association. The panel sought to explore in a more detailed fashion local government authority and home rule issues in a few states. Early participants in the conversations included David Morgan, Beverly Cigler, Robert Stein, and Russ Getter. A follow-up session was held in 1994 at the national conference of the American Society for Public Administration. Among the new scholars invited to join the dialogue was Dale Krane, who proposed to expand the project from one of a limited focus on a few select states to a fifty-state compilation. Additional conversations led to the decision to move forward with a national study. Professors Rigos, Krane, and Hill recruited a network of scholars in all fifty states to profile the current status of home rule in each state. Professor Krane became the overall project manager and senior editor.

Professor Rigos took the lead in organizing sessions devoted to home rule issues at various professional conferences. At considerable cost to himself, he attended as many as four conferences a year in developing a network of scholars interested in local government. These experts were asked to write an essay about the status of local government authority in their state and to present the essay at a series of conference panels arranged by Professors Rigos and Krane. The conference papers were used to prepare a list of topics germane to home rule. Advice on the project was sought from a group of scholars distinguished for their work in local government and intergovernmental relations, including David Berman, Al Sokolow, and Joseph Zimmerman. From these dialogues, the project organizers developed an outline that all authors were asked to follow in preparing the chapters on the fifty states.

As scholars around the country agreed to participate in the national project, they were sent a copy of the standard outline and asked to conduct original research related to the topics listed in the outline, and to adhere to the outline in writing their particular chapter. Each of the state chapters has the same organization and presentation of topics. At the same time, each chapter is unique in that it describes one of the fifty states and reflects the author's perspective on home rule in that state. Most chapters were written between 1996 and 1999. Although a modest number of details may have changed since a particular chapter was written, we believe in general that the overall picture of local government authority presented in each chapter accurately represents the current status of home rule in the state.

Many chapters include information not previously available, not easily obtainable, or not collected for use in census documents or statistical abstracts. Some of the material presented in the state chapters was developed from interviews with or surveys of local government officials. Information was also gleaned from government documents, such as reports to the state legislature or issued by a state auditor, or from newsletters produced by the state association of municipal or county officials. Many of the state authors have engaged in nearly heroic efforts to unearth information about their state that was not previously available. More than one author has commented that the most recent book in the library on home rule for a particular state was written before World War II!

Many state chapters include hard-to-obtain budget data; a few of these are presented in charts and tables. Although some of the fiscal data are several years old, it is important to remember that it takes considerable time to collect budget data across even a single state. In some cases, no official entity may be responsible for collecting this type of information, or it may not be collected or recorded in a regular or systematic manner.

Professors Hill and Krane attempted to survey the opinions of the state authors about home rule and local government authority as well as to obtain certain specific pieces of information. Because the survey was not compulsory, it did not reach its goal of fifty states. It was a valuable effort because in many cases the survey helped state authors begin their research and organize their material. The survey also assisted us in thinking more precisely about the variations in home rule provisions across the country.

Acknowledgments

We would like to express our deep appreciation and gratitude to the eighty-one state chapter authors who agreed to devote their time to this project. Without their willingness to engage in original research, the state chapters would not contain the wealth of information they exhibit. We would especially like to recognize two state chapter authors who were good friends to many on this project, but who sadly died this year: Janet W. Patton, author of the Kentucky chapter, and Charles J. Spindler, author of the Alabama chapter.

During the course of the project, many of the state chapters were presented as papers at various professional conferences, including those of the Urban Affairs Association; the American Political Science Association, especially its Section on Federalism and Intergovernmental Relations; the Southwest Social Science Association; and the American Society for Public Administration, especially its Section on Intergovernmental Administration and Management. We also thank the conference organizers and the officers of these associations for their willingness to let us arrange a number of working sessions at the various meetings.

We also must note the contributions by staff at our respective institutions, in particular Sue Bishop, secretary in the Department of Public Administration at the University of Nebraska, Omaha, and Carolyn Wynes, former secretary to the director of the Carl Vinson Institute of Government at the University of Georgia.

The editorial team at CQ Press, at times, may have thought that this volume would never be completed, but their advice, counsel, and, most of all, patience helped us bring this work to publication. CQ Press's executive editor David Tarr has been our principal guide, and without his wisdom we would not have been able to manage the many elements of this project. Jayne Plymale, Jerry Orvedahl, Sandy Chizinsky, and Jon Preimesberger deserve special thanks as well for their yeoman editorial efforts with the original drafts. Our thanks also go to our good friend and colleague Carl Stenberg for his contribution of the foreword.

We believe this reference volume provides a detailed picture of local government autonomy and discretionary authority at the beginning of the twenty-first century. As such, it describes the culmination of almost four hundred years of experience with local governments, since the initial colonies that became the United States were settled. Simultaneously, the volume will serve as a foundation and a catalyst for future studies of local government authority and as a benchmark against which to compare changes in state–local relationships as they continue to evolve. Above all, we hope that this volume will increase the reader's appreciation for the importance of home rule issues and local government discretion as they relate to the future of each reader's own community. We welcome comments and observations from our readers.

DALE KRANE
PLATON N. RIGOS
MELVIN B. HILL JR.

Notes

1. Alexis de Tocqueville, *Democracy in America,* Vol. 1 (New York: Vintage Books, 1945), 67.

2. Gerald E. Frug, *City Making: Building Communities Without Building Walls* (Princeton: Princeton University Press, 1999), 4.

3. A similar usage of the term *home rule* can be found in Vincent Ostrom, Robert Bish, and Elinor Ostrom, *Local Government in the United States* (San Francisco: ICS Press, 1988), 34.

4. Russell L. Hanson, *The Interaction of State and Local Governments,* Chap. 1 in *Governing Partners: State-Local Relations in the United States,* ed. Russell L. Hanson (Boulder, Colo.: Westview Press, 1998), 3.

5. A particular item is sometimes addressed in subsection of a state chapter different from that indicated in the standard outline for the state chapters. Authors were permitted freedom to present items within subsections in the order that worked best for their own style of writing. Authors were not allowed to present a specific item outside of a major section of the outline.

6. U.S. Advisory Commission on Intergovernmental Relations, *State Laws Governing Local Government Structure and Administration* (Washington, D.C.: U.S. Government Printing Office, March 1993), M-186.

LIST OF CONTRIBUTORS

Alabama

Charles J. Spindler
Auburn University

Alaska

Clive S. Thomas
University of Alaska Southeast

Anthony T. Nakazawa
Alaska Cooperative Extension

Carl E. Shepro
University of Alaska Anchorage

Arizona

David R. Berman
Arizona State University

Tanis J. Salant
University of Arizona

Arkansas

Margaret F. Reid
University of Arkansas

Will Miller
University of Arkansas

California

Alvin D. Sokolow
University of California, Davis

Peter M. Detwiler
Consultant, California State Senate

Colorado

Jason Stilwell
Assistant town manager, Superior, Colorado

Robert W. Gage
University of Colorado at Denver

Connecticut

Richard C. Kearney
East Carolina University

Delaware

Jeffrey A. Raffel
University of Delaware

Jerome R. Lewis
University of Delaware

Deborah A. Auger
University of Delaware

Kathryn G. Denhardt
University of Delaware

Florida

Platon N. Rigos
University of South Florida

John J. Bertalan
Hillsborough Community College

Richard C. Feiock
Florida State University

Georgia

Melvin B. Hill Jr.
University of Georgia

Hawaii

Anne Feder Lee
Freelance writer

Norman Meller
Professor emeritus, University of Hawaii

Idaho

James B. Weatherby
Boise State University

Illinois

Richard Wandling
Eastern Illinois University

Indiana

William Blomquist
Indiana University at Indianapolis

Iowa

Paul Coates
Iowa State University

Jack Whitmer
Iowa State University

Tom Bredeweg
League of Iowa Cities

Kansas

H. Edward Flentje
Wichita State University

Kentucky

Janet W. Patton
Eastern Kentucky University

Louisiana

Richard Engstrom
University of New Orleans

Robert K. Whelan
University of New Orleans

Maine

G. Thomas Taylor
University of Maine

Kenneth T. Palmer
University of Maine

Maryland

Andrée Reeves
University of Alabama—Huntsville

Patricia S. Florestano
Maryland Higher Education Commission

Massachusetts

Meredith Ramsay
University of Massachusetts, Boston

Michigan

Kenneth VerBurg
Professor emeritus, Michigan State University

Minnesota

Philip H. Wichern
Freelance writer

Mississippi

Annie Johnson Benifield
Tomball College

Missouri

E. Terrence Jones
University of Missouri—St. Louis

Donald Phares
University of Missouri—St. Louis

Montana

Kenneth L. Weaver
Montana State University

Nebraska

Dale Krane
University of Nebraska, Omaha

Nevada

Robert P. Morin
California State University, Chico

Erik B. Herzik
University of Nevada, Reno

New Hampshire

John F. Camobreco
Christopher Newport University

Mark V. Ebert
Arizona State University—West

New Jersey

Ernest C. Roeck Jr.
Rutgers University—New Brunswick

Alma Joseph
Rutgers University—Newark

Michele Collins
Rutgers University—Newark

New Mexico

John G. Bretting
University of Texas, San Antonio

New York

Jeffrey M. Stonecash
Maxwell School, Syracuse University

North Carolina

James H. Svara
North Carolina State University

North Dakota

Mary Grisez Kweit
University of North Dakota

Robert W. Kweit
University of North Dakota

Ohio

Jack L. Dustin
Wright State University

Oklahoma

David R. Morgan
Professor emeritus, University of Oklahoma

Robert England
Oklahoma State University

Michael W. Hirlinger
Oklahoma State University

James T. Laplant
Valdosta State University

Oregon

Carolyn N. Long
Washington State University, Vancouver

Pennsylvania

Beverly Cigler
Penn State University—Harrisburg

Richard D. White Jr.
Louisiana State University

Rhode Island

Elmer E. Cornwell
Brown University

South Carolina

Cole Blease Graham Jr.
University of South Carolina

South Dakota

Timothy J. Schorn
University of South Dakota

David Aronson
University of South Dakota

Buffie K. Main
Graduate student, University of South Dakota

Kenneth J. Tauke
U.S. Military Academy

Tennessee

Lon S. Felker
Eastern Tennessee State University

Michael P. Marchioni
Eastern Tennessee State University

Platon N. Rigos
University of South Florida

Texas

Charldean Newell
University of North Texas

Victor S. DeSantis
Bridgewater State College

Utah

F. Ted Hebert
University of Utah

Mark G. Bedel
Office of Planning and Budget, State of Utah

Vermont

Paul S. Gillies
Tarrant, Marks, & Gillies

Virginia

Keeok Park
University of La Verne

Washington

Meredith A. Newman
Washington State University, Vancouver

Nicholas P. Lovrich
Washington State University, Pullman

West Virginia

Kenneth A. Klase
West Virginia University

Wisconsin

Stephen E. C. Hintz
University of Wisconsin, Oshkosh

Wyoming

Robert A. Schuhmann
University of Wyoming

INTRODUCTION

HOME RULE IN AMERICA

These [conditions] are, indeed, almost sufficient to account for that lack of civic patriotism shown by even well-intentioned municipal citizens, and without which as a basis, no city can be well governed. They are the small sphere of local autonomy assigned by law to our cities, and the continual interference in city affairs of the central commonwealth legislature.

Frank Goodnow, *Municipal Home Rule: A Study in Administration*, 1895[1]

Local self-government is one of the most cherished and fiercely contested ideas in the pantheon of principles by which Americans organize their system of governance. The struggle for local control over public decisions has characterized the American experiment in democratic government, from the earliest congregations that formed local towns in New England to today's clashes over "gated communities" and urban sprawl. The intensity of attitudes about local government reflects the multiple purposes that localities serve in our lives—local governments are at once accessible forums for political participation, marketplaces where we work or do business, and, most crucially, the homes of our families and neighbors, who make up our "place" in the world. Yet, after nearly 400 years of experience with local government, beginning with Jamestown, a right of home rule does not exist; rather, legal theory in the United States declares local government to be the agent, creature, and delegate of state government.[2] Their legal inferiority means that "local governments exercise limited, expressly delegated authority, . . ." and if there is any "reasonable doubt concerning the existence of power [it] is resolved by the courts against the municipality."[3] Instead of exercising self-government, local governments may act only in the areas and in the ways specified by state government.

The debates over the position and power of local governments began early in U.S. history, and they have continued unabated in terms of both the nature of the problem and the remedies proposed. Popular sovereignty rests on the basic principles of representation: that each individual is the best judge of personal self-interest and that government action ought to follow the collective expressed views of the individuals who are affected by the public decision. The case for local self-government simply extends this logic to the level of the local community, or as the nineteenth-century French observer Alexis de Tocqueville phrased the relationship: "Municipal independence in the United States is therefore a natural consequence of this very principle of the sovereignty of the people."[4] Home rule, then, requires that the elected officials of a local jurisdiction, not the state government, make basic decisions about the structure, functions, authority, and methods of public action for the locality.

However, local governments function within a larger society, and on matters that extend beyond a single community, each locality must act within the legal framework of the overarching state and nation. That is, on those issues that cannot be contained within one community, that spill over to other communities, or that require actions that cut across multiple localities, local preferences must be adapted to those of the larger society. Whether the issue is mosquito control, landfill location, or drug trafficking, local officials are expected to accommodate local interests to those of the larger society. At the same time, while higher level authorities may command cooperation from lower level jurisdictions, state or national officials need to interact responsibly in a reciprocal fashion with local officials and citizens. Where the line between an appropriate sphere of local action and the authority of state government is drawn has been a source of continuous conflict in state capitals. An action that state officials see as a legitimate exercise of state power to establish a uniform strategy toward a particular problem, such as water quality standards, local officials may perceive to be an unnecessary and overly expensive intrusion in local affairs. Conversely, local actions undertaken to ensure a certain style of life, for example, restricting the types of housing units permitted within a community, may be viewed by state officials as a serious obstacle to the recruitment of new industry to the state or, worse, as a not so subtle form of discrimination.

Table 1. The Case for and against Home Rule

The case for home rule	*The case against home rule*
Local citizens can select the form of government they prefer. If citizens want to consolidate or reorganize their public institutions, they can do so without obtaining permission from state officials.	Home rule would allow local officials to act in an arbitrary and capricious fashion. Local officials could favor political friends and disfavor political enemies. Violations of due process and equal treatment would likely increase.
Local communities are diverse, and home rule allows local citizens to solve their problems in their own fashion, thus decentralization fosters local experimentation, flexibility, innovation, and responsiveness.	Home rule will result in a lack of uniformity among units of government; services, structures, and actions that are available or permitted in one locality will be absent in another. Without statewide regulations, inequities in the provision and delivery of public services would be more common.
Home rule reduces the time that a state legislature devotes to "local affairs." Scholars have estimated that in some states, local bills constitute as much as 20 to 25 percent of the legislature's workload.	Local citizens whose preferences are not met or served by the local government will increase their appeals to the state legislature, and thus the state legislature will spend more time on local affairs.
Home rule units with control of their finances place the responsibility for public expenditures and taxation where it belongs—on the elected officials of the local jurisdiction, and not on distant state officials.	Home rule units with control over their finances may undercut the revenue base of the state government. If each locality is responsible for its own finances, income inequalities among local jurisdictions would leave some communities unable to solve their own problems.
With home rule, local officials can exercise greater discretion in the daily operations of the locality. Any change or new activity does not require preapproval by the state legislature before it is initiated or implemented. State officials do not "second guess" local officials.	Home rule units with the authority to make and administer their own public policies would make it very difficult for the state government to address problems that cut across jurisdictional boundaries or require the action of multiple jurisdictions. Units that make their own policy might be deprived of the greater expertise and technical resources available at the state level and might lose the cost savings associated with centralization of administrative activities at the state level.
"Liberal construction" of home rule provisions reduces court interference in local policy making and administration.	No legal wording is immune from challenge, and any "liberal construction" language is certain to provoke lawsuits.

Source: Adapted from David L. Martin, *Running City Hall: Municipal Administration in America,* 2d ed. (Tuscaloosa: University of Alabama Press, 1990), 22–25.

There is an extensive body of argument over where the line between local autonomy and state control should appropriately be drawn. Rather than devoting additional space to these debates over the pros and cons of home rule, we have distilled them into a set of points (see Table 1). These debates are an integral part of the history of the now 150-year effort to achieve home rule for local governments. More of this history will be provided later in this chapter, but at this point, it is important to note that at the end of the nineteenth century reformers lamented the legally inferior position of cities and campaigned to convince state governments to grant "home rule" to localities. Now, at the beginning of the twenty-first century, another set of reformers deplores the "powerlessness" of American cities, and calls for decentralization and more local authority are more frequent.

In general terms, the ideal of home rule is defined as the ability of a local government to act and make policy in all areas that have not been designated to be of statewide interest through general law, state constitutional provisions, or initiatives and referenda. The ideal notion admits to the possibility that state government actions may severely limit local autonomy and discretion—state-imposed limits on the annual increase in local property taxes are a well known example. Under the hypothesis that local governments are closer to the people and enjoy the support of local citizens, one would postulate that local governments, to be effective as well as democratic, ought to possess a broad range of discretionary authority. The state should limit local autonomy only if local decisions significantly interfere with the choices or rights of another community or shift nontrivial costs to other communities or to the state government. It may also limit local choice to protect the rights and liberties of minorities or protected classes of persons; that is, a state may prohibit local governments from using their autonomy to maintain inequitable conditions or policies. Consequently, responsible behavior by local officials is a key part of the home rule ideal; however, as with many other aspects of political behavior, what is considered to be responsible will prompt sharp differences of opinion.

Although possessing substantial freedom from state government control is vital for the development of dynamic communities, analyses that focus solely on the degree of decentralization in the state-local relationship miss another critical set of local government attributes. Local legitimacy depends greatly on the capacity of local government officials to respond to local citizen demands for public goods and services and to administer local policy choices effectively. Home rule includes more than just the degree of autonomy or local discretion granted to local jurisdictions; it also includes the capacity of the local government to perform effectively. Without sufficient authority to make decisions and to administer the policies chosen, local governments will have little if any autonomy. Similarly, home rule depends not only on the ability of local governments to satisfy local policy demands but also on the degree to which local officials are accountable to local citizens and not just to state government on matters of statewide policy. State government possesses a variety of administrative, fiscal, and legal controls over local government actions; however, for local citizens to hold local officials accountable, state governments must also provide local citizens with the tools by which they may act to ensure the responsiveness of local officials.

Contemporary discussions of governmental reform in America have paid little attention to the venerable topic of home rule. For many people, home rule is a quaint, outmoded, and failed concept. Even where it has been associated with successful developments in the evolution of U.S. local governments, those successes are seen as part of the past.[5] So why resurrect an antique idea and suggest that it has value for today's debates over the nature of governance and civic life? We suggest that a renewed interest in home rule bears directly on six significant aspects of local government and state-local relations—service provision, policy tools, interstate variation, trends shaping local governments, federalism, and democracy. One could make a persuasive case that the fundamental ideas embodied in the concept of home rule can contribute to the debates over the future direction of local government and that a broad base of information about the discretionary authority of local governments will aid in the analysis of their condition.

The Contemporary Significance of Home Rule

Basic Service Providers

What local governments may or may not do is a worthy topic because people live and confront the problems of daily life at the community level. People have established and operated cities, towns, and villages throughout history for the individual and collective benefits to be achieved by living in an organized community with powers of government. Writing about municipal problems over a century ago, Frank Goodnow, the preeminent authority on administrative law in the late 1800s and early 1900s, noted that cities, particularly American cities, were "an organ for the satisfaction of local needs."[6] The fundamental purpose of local governments in the United States, as textbooks explain, is the provision of basic services to the community household. The performance of local governments in the delivery and distribution of public goods and services—such as police and fire protection, streets and parks, water and sewerage, waste collection and disposal, land use and transportation, public health and welfare—directly conditions the quality of life in every locality. This relationship between local service provision and quality of life fuels many local political struggles, and the range of discretionary action available to local officials substantially affects their ability to make choices about service provision and delivery.

Americans have not been hesitant to create local governments, as Table 2 illustrates. The 1997 Census of Governments lists the total number of local jurisdictions in the United States as 87,453. Local governments come in a wide variety of types—for example, boroughs, cities, counties, special districts, school districts, townships, villages. Across the country, each type of local government often manifests itself in several forms—for example, a board or commission, but no single executive, governs some counties; other counties operate with an executive and a legislative body; and in still others, a single executive governs the county. Further, different state governments assign different responsibilities to different local governments—for example, in some states, municipalities are responsible for K-12 education, whereas in others, independent school districts are responsible. Similarly, state governments vary in the way they assign fiscal authority to local governments—a city in one state may possess the power to levy a particular type of tax, while a city in a neighboring state may not be able to levy the same tax. This variation in type, form, and authority from state to state creates considerable differences in local capacity to address problems and to satisfy local needs.

The Toolkit of Local Government

The degree and types of discretionary authority possessed by local governments constitute the "toolkit" with which local officials may act to satisfy local needs. The assignment of functional responsibilities (for example, public health and safety) and the

Table 2. Number of U.S. Local Government Units, by Type, 1997

Type of local government	Number
County	3,043
Municipality	19,372
Town/township	16,629
Special district (for example, flood control, library)	34,683
School district	13,726
Total	87,453

Source: U.S. Bureau of Census, "Preliminary Estimates," *1997 Census of Governments* (Washington, D.C.: U.S. Government Printing Office, 1998).

delegation of formal instruments (among them, planning and zoning) to a particular type of local jurisdiction (like a county or municipality), in effect, establishes the machinery of local government. Individual public officials come and go with the fortunes of electoral results, but what any one official or body of officials may accomplish is bounded by state constitutional provisions, statutes, and related judicial interpretations.

An important question about any organization is "who does what?" As the economy and culture have become more complex, so have the combinations of responsibilities and tools assigned to various local governments. The complexity of these combinations has become so great that the authors of one major study of local government autonomy declared: "Today, in any one state, the scope of home rule or local autonomy is often difficult to discern."[7] One has to attend only a few city council or county board meetings to notice that the questions of what the jurisdiction may do and how it may act, using which types of instruments, are a principal preoccupation of local officials and a major parameter affecting the choices they make.

The diversity and sophistication of the "policy tools" available to local government officials determine, to a great extent, the capacity of local government to act on behalf of the community's residents. John Gargan, an authority on state and local government administration, formulates the relationship between home rule and local governing capacity by emphasizing two dimensions: the ability to meet requirements and the ability to do what is expected.[8] These two "abilities," in turn, are shaped by the local government's capacity in three general areas: policy management, resource management, and program management.[9] More generally, "governance capacity" refers to the ability of a government to design and implement collective choices; thus, any discussion of the capacity of a local government presumes some degree of independence from superior tiers of government.

Interstate Variation in Local Government Status

Renewed attention to home rule is a convenient and useful focus by which to examine interstate variation in the relationship between local governments and state governments. For more than 130 years, prevailing legal doctrine, as expressed in *Clinton v. Cedar Rapids,* has considered local governments to be subordinate "creatures of the state." In the last thirty years, state governments have taken actions that have had the effect of undercutting this view of local governments as "creatures of the state." Many state governments, for example, have granted broader powers to localities by reversing the traditional legal view so that cities may exercise all powers that have not been forbidden to them.[10] Furthermore, many state governments have enlarged the functional areas of activity within which local governments may make policy; economic development and

transportation are good examples. State governments have also permitted general-purpose governments (cities and counties) to establish new forms of organization, including public authorities, public corporations, and special districts, which enhance the capacity of local governments to resolve problems such as blight and poverty. To support this wider range of responsibilities, many state governments have even expanded the types of taxes (for example, sales, income, and entertainment) that cities and counties may levy.

At the same time, however, state governments have taken actions that have had the effect of reducing the extent of local government discretionary authority. The primary examples can be found in the area of fiscal policy. The growth of state revenues has outstripped that of local governments, many of whom do not possess the economic base by which to sustain themselves. This fiscal disparity has prompted state governments to increase the amount and forms of state financial aid to local governments, and, of course, following the axiom that the person who has the gold makes the rules, increased state aid to localities has led to increased centralization at the state level. This trend has been exacerbated by the revolt against local property taxes that began in California and has spread throughout the country. As a consequence of protests over taxes, many state governments have imposed limits on local government revenues or expenditures or both.[11] These fiscal constraints on local governments have also been accompanied by the growth in state regulatory power over the traditional service functions of local governments. Some state regulations have been relatively noncontroversial, such as training standards for police officers and fire fighters, whereas other regulations have been flashpoints of conflict between state and local governments, such as school curricula or land-use controls. Connecticut, Massachusetts, and Rhode Island have gone so far as to effectively abolish county governments.

The point is quite simple: even though state courts typically hold the state-local relationship to be unitary and hierarchical, the political reality is that the relationship is more complicated. The contradictory trends by which state governments have simultaneously expanded certain areas of local government discretion while imposing constraints in other areas contributes to the complications of the state-local relationship. In order to understand the current status of local governments, one must take into account the interstate variation in these contradictory trends. That is, the degree of independence possessed by local governments varies from state to state, and any effort to understand home rule must take into account that variation.

Multiple Trends Affecting Local Governments

A number of important macrotrends have been reshaping the world of large and small local governments, and the interstate variation in the powers and responsibilities of local government greatly determines how a local government can respond to these larger trends.[12] Perhaps the most important change affecting all local governments is the now thirty-year-old era of federal devolution. Since the presidency of Richard Nixon (1969–1974), national government policy has sought to reduce the amount of national fiscal aid to states and localities, return responsibility for a number of public programs (education, health, and welfare, among them) to state government, and reduce the number of national regulations imposed on state and local government.[13] Scholars continue to debate just how much devolution has occurred,[14] but it is clear that "federal assistance to cities is much diminished since the late 1970s" and "a much smaller portion of federal aid is devoted to urban programs than was true just a decade and half ago."[15] The reductions in federal grants-in-aid to places (aid to persons actually increased) have resulted in a condition best described as "fend-for-yourself federalism."[16] Some view this reduction of national support for local jurisdictions as a long overdue readjustment of power and responsibilities between national and state governments, whereas others argue that the reduction in aid is an abdication of national responsibility for the problems besetting urban areas.

Although the "devolution revolution" sought to shift power away from Washington, D.C., to the states, the necessity of "fending for oneself" also pushed the responsibility for administering and financing (and, in some cases, designing) major public programs to subnational governments.[17] The movement to transfer program responsibility did not stop at state capitals, but continued on to county courthouses and city halls. Jonathan Walters, in an essay on county government, notes:

In this era of squeeze-down federalism, one thing is emerging quite clearly: From welfare to corrections, health care to the environment, counties have in many ways become the backstop of American government. In fact, a huge amount of responsibility for some of society's toughest, costliest, most thankless jobs has either been handed or simply devolved to county governments, and the results can be overwhelming.[18]

Even though aggregate state aid to local governments increased from $83 billion in 1980 to $218 billion in 1994, it decreased as a portion of total state spending from a high in the late 1970s and early 1980s, when it was 33 percent, to approximately 28 percent in the mid-1990s.[19] Much of this decline can be attributed to the stagnant economic conditions that prevailed through the mid-1980s and early 1990s.[20]

State aid to localities has not kept pace with the programmatic obligations that have been transferred to local governments, and local governments have responded by seeking authority to obtain revenues by means other than the property tax.[21] The devolution of programs to substate governments has forced them not only to seek authority to use new sources of revenues but to acquire more capacity to cope with increased service burdens.[22] To obtain more capacity, local governments must request more discretionary authority from their state legislatures.

The decline in fiscal resources received from the national government has made it harder for localities to cope with a wide range of problems, from suburbanization and sprawl to racial and class isolation to the lack of connectedness of neighborhoods within metropolitan areas. American cities, especially those that house the majority of the nation's citizens, have been in a constant state of flux since their founding. The movement to the suburbs, the rebirth of central business districts, and the "gentrification" of decayed inner neighborhoods are only the more recent forms of change. No one doubts that many of the toughest socioeconomic urban problems have been exacerbated by local policy decisions. Although the motives underlying gated communities are not likely to disappear in the future, the attitude that economically successful and viable cities require the integration of marginalized areas and persons into the life of the community has emerged in the form of human capital strategies, public-private-nonprofit partnerships, and community or "problem-oriented" policing. DeWitt John, Alexis Halley, and R. Scott Fosler capture this shift to a policy orientation, which they label as "civic governance" with the following description:

Civic governance employs a situational, broad approach to the public's business. The efforts that we describe . . . illustrate the engagement of a wide variety of public, nonprofit, and private leaders at the local level in implementing custom-designed, broad approaches to addressing broad social problems. They seek to tap a community's social capital: the relationships and shared understandings that emerge when people live and work closely with one another and learn to span professional and bureaucratic barriers in order to work together. These are, in a word, *civic* efforts to do the public's business. [italics in original].[23]

John, Halley, and Fosler argue that civic governance requires the formation of a *shadow community* of persons that transcends the existing institutional fragmentation of American life. At some point, though, new policy directions will have to be legitimized by formal actions of the community's public officials.[24] However, even if local officials are part of the shadow community and are supportive of its aims, if they are hamstrung by a lack of discretionary authority, new policy directions may well require the approval of state government officials and may well be thwarted at that level.

The public demand to make government work better and cost less constitutes another powerful current making waves in local governments from metropolises to villages.[25] The "reinventing government" movement—with its emphasis on "customer-driven government," "decentralization," "letting managers manage," "shared power," and "value-added management"—presupposes that local governments possess extensive autonomy and capacity. Obviously, any reform that rests on moving policy making from higher levels of government to lower levels depends for its success on the capacity of the lower units of government. As part of reinventing government, then, cities and counties will have to be given sufficient institutional and governmental authority to undertake existing and emerging roles.[26] For example, local government action based on market-oriented strategies such as contracting out, user charges, or vouchers may not be permitted under state law. Similarly, local government action that involves partnerships with for-profit enterprises or nonprofit organizations may also require state government permission. Thus, advocates of reinvention will have to pay attention to the home rule status of local governments.

The rapid and sweeping advances in telecommunications, information technologies, and high-speed transportation that have produced an increasingly globalized economy constitute another macrotrend that is forcing significant changes in the organization and operation of governments around the world.[27] Of all the prescriptions proposed to cope with globalization, perhaps the most widely recommended is "to think globally, but act locally." Certainly, much effort has been put into helping officials and citizens alike "think globally," but once local plans are aligned with global changes, the local population must possess the capacity and discretion "to act locally." Neal Peirce, one of the country's most distinguished observers of state and local government, captures this relationship between globalization and local governments when he points out that "Across America and across the globe, citistates are emerging as a critical focus of economic activity, of governance, of social organization for the 1990s and the century to come."[28] The trends of globalization, Peirce explains, "accentuate the rise of the citistate and the eclipse of the nation-state," and local governing entities are increasing in importance because globalization is "simultaneously pushing power *up,* to the international level, and *down,* to the local level" [italics in original].[29] Susan Clarke and Gary Gaile, in their major study of economic development activities of U.S. cities, assert that the efforts of local officials to transform their local economies to cope with globalization "entailed not only rethinking local economic development strategies but also redesigning local institutions. Cities faced the need to structure decision contexts in ways that would enable them to mobilize local interests."[30] Again, the conclusion is clear: home rule, or the degree of discretionary authority available to local governments, is vital to successful economic growth policies.

Peirce also argues that local development cannot be handled on a municipality-by-municipality basis—the only viable approach is regional, hence the idea of a citistate that extends beyond a central city and its suburbs to encompass an interconnected economic region that can effectively compete in the world market.[31] His prescription for a regional approach to economic growth is paralleled by similar prescriptions to address other types of problems—ranging from suburban sprawl and environmental protection to transportation and crime control—at a regional level. However it is labeled—collaborative, functional, or structural—regionalism rests partly on the willingness of local officials to cooperate with officials in nearby jurisdictions and partly on the authority of local officials to act across jurisdictional lines.[32] However, how can regional efforts be forged when, as in some states, local governments possess few, if any, policy tools for cooperating intergovernmentally? If the state legislature has not authorized interjurisdictional action, then regional solutions will be stymied.

American Federalism

Constitutionally, a complex set of separated institutions and intertwined principles compose the federal government of the United States of America. Two key features of U.S. federalism are the placement of the state governments on a coordinate plane with the national government, and the hierarchical and unitary relationship between state and local governments.[33] But, as Howard McBain observed, "our national constitution, in reserving 'all other powers' to the states, prescribes no machinery for the exercise of these powers . . . As it is, however, the states have been left to their own devices in this matter."[34] The "silence" of the U.S. Constitution on the position and powers of local governments relative to state government leaves decisions about these issues in the hands of the states. It is conceivable that a state could confer to its cities the power over their own affairs in much the same way as the power over state affairs is reserved to the states in the U.S. Constitution.[35] Obviously, changes in the amount and types of local discretion permitted by state governments directly affects state-local relationships (at least in that state) as well as affects the larger character of American federalism.

Much academic discourse on American federalism continues to use the traditional approaches of history and law. However, since the mid-1950s, scholars have developed a theoretical approach to federalism based on public finance economics. This school of thought contends that local governments behave as competitive economic markets in that local officials manipulate the level and mix of public goods and services that the locality provides and the prices (that is, taxes) it charges. By offering different levels of services and taxes, local governments seek to attract certain types of citizens (and businesses) and to create a particular style of community life. This competition is made possible because individual citizens who are dissatisfied with a local government's policies (the mix of services and taxes) can "vote with their feet" by moving to another jurisdiction in order to maximize the services received for the taxes paid.[36] A large number of scholars over the years have been attracted to this "public choice" theory and have produced a variety of arguments and evidence in support of this competitive model of local government.[37]

The public choice model of federalism rests on several assumptions: local government officials are responsive to the preferences of the local citizenry, local governments possess adequate powers by which to respond to citizen preferences, and local government activities are the product of local citizen choices as reflected through the policy decisions of local officials and do not reflect the policy decisions of some other body of government (that is, state government).[38] But why is home rule important for this theoretical argument? First, public choice theory depends on local government autonomy—without autonomy, the model collapses.[39] Second, this theory serves as one of the main justifications for many of the proposals to reform government, including privatization, the reinvention movement, and entrepreneurial public management as put forward by David Osborne and Ted Gaebler.[40] If local governments must now "compete or die," then they desperately need the tools by which to compete, that is, substantial discretionary authority. Consequently, many of the reforms that are being attempted in American government, if they indeed enhance the authority and autonomy of local government, have the potential to alter our federal arrangements.

Democracy and Popular Sovereignty

The relationship of local self-government to the American sense of democracy is even older than its previously discussed connection with American federalism. In the earliest settlements, which would become the thirteen original states, individual freedom was tied intimately to being a legal inhabitant who could participate in the town meeting. Today, at the beginning of the twenty-first century, this same view remains a key value by which the quality of contemporary democracy is judged. Lively debates have arisen about the character of civic life, the relationship of citizens to public officials, and the value of elected representatives.[41] Much of this debate revolves around remedies for reducing the level of citizen distrust of government officials.[42] One important theme in this debate suggests that existing, electorally based forms of representation have failed and need to be replaced by more direct citizen involvement in policy making.[43]

Phrased somewhat differently, the argument is that "top-down" forms of governance seldom succeed, and only through authentically mutual relationships, where government officials and citizens engage in joint decision making, will it be possible to raise the level of citizen satisfaction with and trust in public officials.[44] Of course, it is at the local government level that such joint decision making is both possible and probable. Proposals to create forums for "community conversations," so that democracy is truly deliberative, not only hark back to the practices and

virtues of town governance in colonial America but presume that once a community decides to act, it possesses the authority and the capacity to carry out its decisions. The missing piece in the communitarian vision is the same missing piece in the "public choice" economic model of local government—home rule. A municipal government that is not under the control of its local population renders even extensive civic discourse futile. One can encourage "maximum feasible participation" by citizens, but unless the government has the authority to act, the discourse between citizens, elected officials, and public servants is in vain.

In brief, then, home rule, or the range of discretionary authority and action available to local government officials, is a matter of vital importance to any discussion of government and democracy in the United States. All of the prescriptions for reforming the public sector— returning to "local control," fostering "self-sufficiency," encouraging and rewarding "experimentation" and "innovation," and "empowering" citizens—require that the ideas encapsulated in the venerable concept of home rule be dusted off and put into practice. Since local government autonomy and capacity are critical elements of these reform proposals, the legal theory of local government as a "creature of the state" cannot continue as a feature of the intergovernmental framework, especially when state governments themselves are making changes in what local governments may or may not do.

A Brief History of Home Rule in the United States

The Colonial and Constitutional Eras

"The municipal organization [as well as county organization] which first obtained in this country was, like most of our governmental institutions, an importation from England rather than an indigenous growth."[45] In Anglo-American history, the *Carta Civibus Londonarum* (the municipal charter of the City of London) from the year 1100 serves as the basic pattern for the grant of rights and liberties to the residents of a municipality. English borough charters gave communities the status of a corporation, granted various commercial privileges, established the right to select local officials, and often provided immunity from certain royal taxes.[46] The growing conflict between the Crown, the nobles, and the emerging economic elites in English towns became intertwined with the power struggle between the king and the Parliament. Although Charles II won the court case in which he challenged the corporate status of London, just six years later, in 1688, the Glorious Revolution ended royal power and reaffirmed the immunity of corporate charters from royal revocation.[47]

The English colonists transported the forms and structures of English local government to North America just as they brought with them other aspects of late medieval English culture. They had established townships and counties by the mid-1630s, long before any other institutions of government came into being. The creation of towns conferred several benefits on the property owners and residents of the community. Towns had the authority to perform some roles and offer various services, such as roads and grain inspection, regulate the value of land, develop commercial spaces, and impose and enforce settlement laws. These "settlement" laws permitted town residents to select who could live in the community and who could be excluded; the residents of these first localities actually voted in town meetings on the admission of new inhabitants.[48]

Most towns and cities in colonial America did not adopt or possess corporate charters. Instead, localities saw themselves as "bodies politic," governed by meetings of the town's freemen, with numerous officers and committeemen responsible for various aspects of town affairs, who were required to serve when elected to these posts—in fact, they could be fined for failure to serve.[49] The relative isolation of the scattered settlements in the vast colonial territory reinforced the sense of local control. America's nearly 150-year colonial period served to incubate local governments and local politics so that by the time of independence "the custom and practice of local self-governance was strong and pervasive."[50]

The War for Independence was fueled by the spirit of an inherent right to local self-government, and it is this persistent belief that drives the desire for home rule. Roscoe Martin captures this ethos well: "The hard-won fruits of rebellion were considered to be local gains, and any enterprise not associated with the immediate local community was regarded with suspicion. . . . They had the right to control their own affairs, which to the greatest degree possible were to be vested in the seeable, touchable government of the small community."[51] Curiously, though, this strong localist belief did not enter into the U.S. Constitution. Most, if not all, of the issues debated at the Constitutional Convention involved the establishment of a new national government and the relation of that national government to the state governments, which by that time exercised substantial powers. The existing state-local relations, in which local communities elected representatives to the state legislature, were left undisturbed by the convention delegates, hence the lack of any specific constitutional language on local governments. This omission set the stage for ". . . a reversal of the teachings of colonial history; for by it the anterior governments, the local communities, were made secondary, and the derivative governments, the states, became primary."[52]

The Pre–Civil War Era

The next developmental phase crucial to the scope of local government authority in the United States emerged out of battles over three apparently different questions, which ultimately became fused into a series of court decisions that established the legal theory of state-local relations that exists to the present day. The first of these issues was the distinction between private and public corporations. Medieval English law and early American law made no distinction among various types of corporate associations, whether a church, a business enterprise, or a municipal corporation. All corporations possessed rights and powers, but they were neither an individual nor the state (in the governance sense), so the question of their relation to government increasingly presented legal puzzles as economic development accelerated and as more towns and cities came into being.[53]

The spread of Jacksonian ideas of popular democracy forced state legislatures to create a wider range of economic opportunities by opening the door to incorporation to more and more persons, not just the wealthy. Many cities as well as private companies obtained capital or income from commerce and trade. State legislatures were the issuers of corporate charters, and they were not always honest or prudent with the grants of benefits, privileges, and rights contained in the corporate charters.[54] Localities could buy and sell services or invest and earn money. Some individuals began to argue that such authority was a threat to private property because local governments could use the power of taxation to raise capital to compete against private firms.

The expansion of incorporation led to the pivotal issue of the protection of private property, especially an investor's property, and culminated in a decisive ruling by the U.S. Supreme Court in the 1819 case of *Trustees of Dartmouth College v. Woodward*. The Court ruled, based on Article I, section 10 of the U.S. Constitution, that "no state shall impair the obligation of a contract," and thus erected one of the principal pillars of the American system of contract law. But the Court also addressed the distinction between private and public corporations by defining public corporations as ones that exist for

. . . public political purposes only, such as towns, cities, parishes, and counties; and in many respects, they are so, although they involve some private interests; but strictly speaking, public corporations are such only as are founded by the government for public purposes, where the whole interests belong also to the government."[55]

Furthermore, the Court ruled that a municipal charter was not a contract between the state and the city, rather, it was an ordinary act of legislation.[56]

The *Dartmouth* ruling was more than a little ambiguous, since Justice Story noted that cities, although public corporations, did possess certain property rights. This ambiguity remained until James Kent published *Commentaries on American Law* in 1836, an influential early text on law.[57] Kent had been a university professor, then a state legislator, and then a judge. In his *Commentaries,* Kent argued that

public corporations are such as created by the government for political purposes, as counties, cities, towns and villages; they are invested with subordinate legislative powers to be exercised for local purposes connected with the public good, and such powers are subject
to the control of the legislature of the state.[58]

Kent's assertion that public corporations, encompassing all
forms of local government, are "subject to the control of the
legislature of the state" was a precursor to the legal theory of local government that would later be known as the "creatures of
the state" theory. Gerald Frug, the distinguished scholar of local
government law, has argued that Kent's declaration that local
governments were subordinate to state governments ignored
nearly 200 years of local government preeminence, most especially the fact that state legislators were representatives chosen
by their localities. As Frug states:

Indeed, the subordination of cities to the state turned the political
world as it then existed upside down. New England towns had controlled state legislatures since prior to the Revolution, and the move
in other sections of the country to end aristocratic city governance
in favor of democracy was not made with the intention of establishing state control over cities. Nor was subservience of cities to
the state inevitable. The proper relationship of city to state was a
hotly contested political issue.[59]

The status of cities was a hotly contested issue in the early
nineteenth century not just because of concerns that public corporations might compete with private ones, but because local
government offices might fall into the hands of political leaders
representing the swelling ranks of immigrants arriving from Europe. Long-time "Yankee" residents in the larger, older cities,
and residents of smaller, more rural communities began to fear
the growing votes of the newly arrived urban ethnic groups.
Long before members of the virulent, anti-immigrant, anti-
Catholic political faction the "Know-Nothings" won the governorship and most of the state legislature in Massachusetts in
1854, Thomas Jefferson opined that "the mobs of the great cities
add just so much to the support of pure government, as sores do
to the strength of the human body."[60]

Great economic and social change also characterized the early nineteenth century, as railroads and other forms of steam
power accelerated the Industrial Revolution and the mechaniza-
tion of agriculture. Westward migration opened new territories
for development and exploitation. In the larger communities,
new technologies made possible the installation of water and
sewer systems as well as gas lighting and trolleys. Construction
contracts for municipal utilities were lucrative sources of income and patronage.[61] The all-too-familiar story of Boss Rule
and the spoils system led many people to perceive of cities as the
home of mobs, foreigners, racial minorities, and sinners. Malap-
portioned state legislatures dominated by rural interests sought
to constrain the evils they perceived as associated with city life.

Frug suggests that these fears were in part behind Kent's reasoning that local governments should be made subject to the control of the state legislature.[62]

The third major issue that would shape the nature of local
government authority erupted out of widespread corruption
and scandals associated with abuses of the public purse. Between the War of 1812 and the beginning of the Civil War in
1861, state governments, not the national government, aggressively built infrastructure, particularly railroads, canals, and
turnpikes. States were driven not just by their own inhabitants
to improve transportation from farm to market, but also by the
desire to attract new residents and commercial activities. Interstate rivalries led many state governments to borrow substantial
sums, and when the panic of 1837 occurred, the ensuing economic depression forced many states to default on their loans.
The collapse of the market for state bonds brought to light rampant corruption and incompetence, which had contributed to
the crisis. Revulsion over the illegalities led to large majorities in
favor of the imposition of debt limits on state government borrowing, and by 1857, nineteen states amended their constitutions
to restrict state borrowing and the use of state government credit for the benefit of private corporations.[63]

Curiously, while debt limits were imposed on state governments, local governments were left unrestricted, so enterprising
investors turned to municipal corporations as sources of capital.
Some state governments began to use local governments as sur-
rogates for state economic development projects. At the same
time, local governments themselves competed more actively to
attract business opportunities. This shift in the locus of economic development activity led to another round of corruption and
scandal.

The ill-defined legal status of municipal corporations contributed significantly to the financial machinations that characterized the pre–Civil War era. Ambitious officials in many localities borrowed large amounts of money to foster local economic
growth.[64] These borrowed funds were spent not only to build local infrastructure, but often to attract manufacturing plants or
to lure railroads. When these investments failed, some municipalities repudiated their debt by terminating the city charter,
that is, literally voting the city out of existence![65] The investment behavior of local governments prompted a debate among
state judges as to the proper types of municipal economic activities. An important question was whether the use of municipal
bonds for assisting railroads or manufacturers constituted a legitimate "public purpose" or was an improper intervention into
private enterprise.

Dillon's Rule

State and federal courts settled this debate over the proper
use of municipal bonds. The precedent-setting court decision
was promulgated by the Iowa Supreme Court in the 1868 case of

City of Clinton v. Cedar Rapids and Missouri Railroad Company.[66] Judge John F. Dillon, disturbed by wasteful municipal investment practices, based his ruling on the idea that strong state government control of municipalities would minimize the mingling of public and private functions, which Dillon saw as detrimental.[67] Dillon, who was the nation's premier authority on municipal law, saw the solution to the burgeoning financial misconduct in making all functions of local governments "public" functions, and so he decreed:

The true view is this: Municipal Corporations owe their origin to, and derive their powers and rights wholly from the legislature. It breathes into them the breath of life, without which they cannot exist. As it creates, so it may destroy. If it may destroy, it may abridge and control. Unless there is some constitutional limitation on the right, the legislature might by a single act, if we can suppose it capable of so great a folly and so great a wrong, sweep from existence all of the municipal corporations in the State, and the corporations could not prevent it . . . They are, so to phrase it, mere tenants at will of the legislature.[68]

Like Kent, Dillon was also the author of a law text, and in his *Commentaries on the Law of Municipal Corporations,* Dillon explained his position in greater detail:

It is a general and undisputed proposition of law that a municipal corporation possesses and can exercise the following powers and no others: First, those granted in express words; second, those necessarily or fairly implied in or incident to the powers expressly granted; third, those essential to the declared objects and purposes of the corporation—not simply convenient but indispensable. Any fair, reasonable doubt concerning the existence of the power is resolved by the courts against the corporation and the power is denied.[69]

Dillon focused his opinion on the immediate issue of municipal bonds, but from a larger perspective, Dillon also followed the line of reasoning established in the *Dartmouth* case, which separated private from public corporations. It is also clear that Dillon followed in the footsteps of Kent's "creatures of the state" theory of local governments.

The logic Dillon used in his *Commentaries* has come to be labeled by legal scholars, judges, and city and county attorneys as "Dillon's Rule." It should also be noted that Dillon's Rule applies to local governments the reasoning of an older doctrine, the Ultra Vires Rule, "which holds that political subdivisions possess only those powers expressly conferred by charter or law and no other powers."[70] Michael Libonati, a distinguished law professor, traces the roots of Dillon's Rule to an 1816 Massachusetts case, *Stetson v. Kemp,* which concerned an interpretation of a 1785 statute that conferred on all towns the status of a "body politic and corporate" and vested the towns with the power to legislate for managing and ordering the "prudential affairs" of the town.[71] Justice Isaac Parker, writing the majority opinion for the state supreme court, declared that towns are "the creatures of

legislation" and may exercise "only the powers expressly granted to them."[72]

In 1903 and again in 1923, the U.S. Supreme Court upheld Dillon's Rule, and it has remained the dominant legal rule in state-local relations in the United States since its promulgation. It is important to note, however, that Dillon's Rule expressed only one side of what was a short-lived but important debate over the appropriate extent of local government authority in the United States. Judge Dillon based his dictum on the view that the state legislature was the embodiment of popular sovereignty and exercised supreme authority within state governments. Other judges, such as Thomas Cooley in Michigan, challenged Dillon's position by ruling that the Tenth Amendment's reservation of powers to the states and to the people, albeit ambiguous, nevertheless reserved the right of local self-government to the people.[73] Courts in Indiana, Kentucky, Texas, and even Iowa supported "Cooley's Rule," which became an important component of the home rule movement.[74] However, once the U.S. Supreme Court upheld the state-dominant position and rejected Judge Cooley's defense of an inherent right of local self-government, its decision enshrined Dillon's Rule and permitted state courts to narrow the general grants of authority to municipalities.

In the context of national government supremacy and the stranglehold of Dillon's Rule, the meaning of home rule has become relatively standardized around the country. Although the term carries the aura of vigorous local autonomy and self-determination, it has generally been interpreted to mean that local governments—cities, counties, and other types—have only as much freedom and authority to govern their affairs as the state, through its constitution, statutory laws, and the judicial interpretation of those laws, chooses to give them. Home rule never means total freedom from state involvement in local matters; it never means complete autonomy; it never means sovereignty. Unfortunately, Dillon's Rule has been misinterpreted to mean that state government should grant a narrow range of authority to local governments. This reading of Judge Dillon's opinion is incorrect because his ruling vested the power over local government in the hands of the state legislature, but he left open the issue of how much authority the legislature might choose to grant. Under Dillon's Rule, state legislatures could grant a broad range of discretionary authority to their local governments, and, in fact, many have done so, as described in this volume.[75]

The Home Rule Movement

In the decades just before and after the Civil War, reformers sought to end the problems caused by "local privilege" legislation and to end or minimize state legislative interference in municipal operations. Rather than subjecting municipalities to state legislative control, these reformers sought state constitutional grants that would permit cities to write and amend their own charters. This reform strategy was known as the home rule movement and originally was conceived as a means for ending the interference of local state legislative delegations in municipal affairs.[76] Over time, the movement became associated with the larger idea of broad grants of local government autonomy.

In the 1840s and 1850s local delegates to state legislatures used their position to write state statutes that permitted them to manipulate municipal activity. The explosion of "local privilege" or "special privilege" legislation and the general practice of enacting innumerable and detailed state laws on every aspect of local government activity led to complaints over the chaos in state codes under which cities were governed. In effect, "local privilege" legislation produced two, often warring, political masters: the city council and the local state legislative delegation. Unfortunately, this practice led to widespread abuse, forms of which included the deliberate creation and extinction of municipal corporations as a tactic to avoid accumulated debt, patronage-based awarding of utility franchises,[77] and "the rape of the cities by the so-called 'robber barons' of the late nineteenth century."[78]

An even more insidious interference in local affairs came in the form of "ripper laws," so named for the fact that the state legislature transferred control of certain activities of municipal government to state-appointed officials. For example, in 1857 the New York legislature initiated a series of statutes designed to transfer important parts of the government of New York City to the control of state-appointed commissions; the first of these created the Metropolitan Police District. Passage of this law led to protests, riots, and bloodshed.[79]

Ohio acted in 1851 to prohibit special legislation, and many other states, but not all, followed its example. Iowa followed suit in 1858 and enacted an even more expansive statute that not only protected municipalities from special privilege legislation, but also extended home rule charters to cities that had been incorporated before statehood. Because state courts generally refused to provide any protection to municipalities under either the contract clause or the guarantees of due process and equal treatment, reformers had few options but to seek constitutional provisions that ended these abuses.

After the Civil War, those who sought to provide cities with constitutional protections from state legislative abuse understood that it would be impossible to confer substantive powers on cities without also conferring on them the power to write their own charters. When Missouri wrote its 1875 constitution, it included the first-ever state constitutional provision to permit the drafting of municipal charters. Howard McBain, in his seminal work *The Law and the Practice of Municipal Home Rule,* published in 1916, declared that the Missouri action "marked the most important step that had ever been taken in the United States in the direction of securing home rule to cities through

the medium of a constitutional provision."[80] Several other states soon followed Missouri's lead and gave positive grants of authority to municipalities via various forms of general enabling laws and the option for home rule charters. The list includes: California (1879), Washington State (1889), Minnesota (1896), Colorado (1902), Virginia (1902), Oregon (1906), Oklahoma (1907), Michigan (1908), Arizona (1912), Ohio (1912), Nebraska (1912), and Texas (1912). The constitutional language in these thirteen states shared the common feature of establishing home rule through the use of a locally drafted charter which was to be ratified by local voters (or in one case, the city council).

Advocates of home rule benefited from an association with the Populist and Progressive reformers who sprung up on the Great Plains after the Civil War. The aggrieved farmers who made up the Populist movement attacked a wide range of private and public abuses of power, and in the process spawned a series of important changes in government at all levels—for example, the secret ballot, direct election of U.S. senators, a public fund deposit law, initiative, referendum, recall, and the end of free railroad passes for elected officials.[81] Whereas the Populists were primarily agrarians, the Progressives, who came a bit later, were primarily urban dwellers, but the two movements shared a similar reform impulse: breaking the alliance between big business and party officials. In particular, the Progressives sought to constrain the abuses of boss rule, state legislative interference in local governments, and the spoils system. With their emphasis on efficiency, economy, and professionalism, the Progressives pushed for "good government," defined as making it more "business-like." At the local government level, the Progressives urged the adoption of city-commission and city-manager forms of government, unified executive budgets, regional planning, and a merit-based civil service system.[82]

The First Half of the Twentieth Century

The Progressive Movement, with its emphasis on business-like government, became the vehicle for further efforts to reform government after World War I, and the home rule idea continued to spread. In the 1920s "good government" associations such as the National Municipal League disseminated model constitutional provisions that included home rule concepts. This modest campaign continued for the next three decades with incremental advances. A good example of this effort is H. S. Gilbertson's book *The County: The "Dark Continent" of American Politics,* which leveled damning indictments at county and township governments.[83] Gilbertson called for the reform of county governments and urged other states to emulate the 1911 California County Home Rule Constitutional Amendment and the 1912 Los Angeles County Charter. Richard Childs, one of the most influential of the Progressive reformers in the National Municipal League, was impressed by the success of the league's

Model City Charter in spreading the adoption of the city manager form of government. In 1930, along with others, Childs proposed the "Principles of a Model County Government" as well as a Model County Manager Law.[84]

After the U.S. Supreme Court in 1923 upheld Dillon's Rule for a second time, the home rule movement waned, coming to a standstill by the middle of the Great Depression. By 1937, only twenty-one states had opted for some form of home rule charter authority. States adopting home rule were Maryland (1915), Pennsylvania (1923), New York (1923), Nevada (1924), Wisconsin (1924), Utah (1932), Ohio (1933), and West Virginia (1936).

The home rule movement, in its campaign for municipal and county charters, broached the crucial question: What powers should be granted to local jurisdictions? If the purpose of a home rule charter is threefold—"(1) to prevent [state] legislative interference with local government, (2) to enable cities [and counties] to adopt the kind of government they desire, and (3) to provide cities [and counties] with sufficient powers to meet the increasing needs for local services"[85]—then the fundamental question in home rule becomes where should the line between "local affairs" and "state government interests" be drawn? New York State addressed this question in 1923 when it adopted a constitutional amendment that included a lengthy list of items regarded as essentially "local," which thus were placed under local control. Other states, such as Utah, also adopted this strategy of enumerating "local affairs," because they thought this approach would clarify the line between state and local interests and, as a consequence, would reduce the number of lawsuits that were filed immediately after the adoption of a home rule charter.

It is easy to understand the attraction of this strategy, which parallels the enumeration clause in the U.S. Constitution. This period was still under the influence of the doctrine of "dual federalism," which held that national and state governments possessed separate spheres of authority and that neither plane of government should be permitted to interfere with the other's responsibilities. The National Municipal League supported this "dual federalism" approach by arguing for the concept of *Imperium in Imperio,* or the establishment of a state within a state. The device of a constitutional list of specified local government powers, because of the legal rule of exclusion, would not only enumerate the areas of local activity but would also reserve to state governments those activities not on the list, and thus the list was believed to be a clear statement that could be adhered to by state legislators and state judges.[86] The *Imperium* approach suffers from the inflexibility of constitutions. Once the list of state versus local powers becomes part of the state constitution, it is very difficult to amend. As a result, state courts, through their decisions in lawsuits challenging state or local exercise of some power, become the arbiters of the scope of local authority.

However, just as sorting out national versus state interests has been a quixotic quest, so also has been the effort to do so be-

tween states and localities. Table 3 provides a list of functions sorted by their assignment to local interest, state interest, or concurrent jurisdiction and typifies the logic of the enumeration approach to home rule. State courts soon found themselves embroiled in numerous lawsuits asking for rulings as to whether some activity such as public health, street repair, or liquor licenses were matters of local or state interest. The frustration of finding a clear line was expressed by the Wisconsin Supreme Court in a 1936 ruling on home rule: "When is an enactment of the legislature of state wide concern? We find no answer to this question in any decision of any court in this country."[87] Despite the logical difficulties of this strategy, vestiges of it continue to the present day, and the matters that state courts consider to be "local affairs" vary from state to state.

Last Half of the Twentieth Century

The American Municipal Association, forerunner to the National League of Cities, hired Jefferson B. Fordham in 1952 to analyze state-local relations and to make recommendations for a new approach. Fordham was professor and dean of the College of Law at Ohio State University and was the author of *Local Government Law: Text, Cases, & Other Materials.*[88] His book, according to the American Bar Association, "revolutionized the teaching of this field."[89] Fordham's report suggested a European-style "devolution of powers" plan in which a state legislature would grant local discretionary authority via the adoption of a municipal charter. The charter, under the Fordham plan, would allow municipalities to supersede special state laws and many general laws applicable to municipal corporations. In its essence, the Fordham "devolution of powers" plan proposed a reversal of Dillon's Rule:

A municipal corporation which adopts a home rule charter rule may exercise any power or perform any function which the legislature has power to devolve upon a non-home rule charter municipal corporation and which is not denied to that municipal corporation by its home rule charter, is not denied to all home rule charter municipal corporations by statute and is within such limitations as may be established by the statute.[90]

Instead of exercising only those powers explicitly granted to them, municipalities under Fordham's plan could act unless explicitly prohibited by state law. Twelve states adopted the plan, but, as with the original home rule movement, enthusiasm waned for the "devolution of powers" model.[91] This model of home rule authority is sometimes referred to as "legislative home rule."[92]

County home rule also showed signs of life after World War II. In 1945 Missouri made home rule charters available to its largest counties, and Washington enacted county home rule in 1948. By the end of the 1960s, county home rule had been established in fifteen states. Beginning in the 1970s, the movement to reform county government focused on other features of county government, such as county executives and city-county consolidation; nevertheless, adoption of county home rule picked up pace, and by 1996, 37 states (of the 47 states with viable counties) provided for some form of county home rule. Few counties took advantage of the new authority; only 129 of the nation's 3,043 counties have adopted some type of home rule charter, and 68 of the 85 have been in place since 1959.[93]

Despite the enlargement of local government discretion by state legislatures during the last half of the twentieth century, the actions of state legislatures have often been negated by state courts that have been reluctant to drop the catechism of Dillon's Rule. Crabbed judicial interpretations have continued to construe local government power very narrowly, even when the legislature has indicated that it has a contrary intent. "Even in *imperio* states, where local ordinances are supposed to govern in municipal matters," Richard Briffault asserts, "the difficulties state courts experience in defining exclusive areas of local interest erode the legal protection of autonomy."[94] Consequently, in many states, a narrow interpretation of Dillon's Rule prevails, and "this means that a city cannot operate a peanut stand at the city zoo without first getting the state legislature to pass an enabling law, unless, perchance, the city's charter or some previously enacted law unmistakably covers the sale of peanuts."[95]

State constitutional provisions, statutes, court decisions, and advisory rulings by state attorneys general and by other state officers (auditors, for example) continue to define, refine, and redefine the parameters of local government authority in each state. For example, Illinois, when it rewrote its constitution in 1970, modified the devolution-of-powers model by moving in the direction of the enumeration strategy that had been tried during the "good government" era. That is, the Illinois Constitution set forth complex decision rules related to the establishment of home rule; the writing and adoption of charters; the specific areas of local affairs, including powers to regulate health, safety, morals, and welfare; and powers to tax and incur debt. Equally important, the Illinois Constitution went to the heart of Dillon's Rule by telling state legislators and judges how to interpret the list of local powers—"the powers and functions of home rule units shall be construed liberally." By contrast, non–home rule units and limited-purpose governments (such as special districts, townships) "shall have only powers granted by law."[96]

The Illinois approach is significant because it has established what might be labeled as a new model of home rule—the "liberal construction" model. By reaching back to the "sorting out" strategy and then wrapping the list of local powers within the cloak of reasonably clear language that state courts and the legislature must follow, Illinois tried to clarify the conditions under

Table 3. Distribution of the Functions of City Government, circa 1936

Local interest paramount

Structure of city government
Salaries of city officials
Terms of city officials
Qualifications of city officials
Methods of awarding contracts
Ordinance procedure
Regulation of prosecutions for violations of charter and ordinances
Street cleaning
Street lighting
Fire protection
Recreation
Water supply
Ownership and operation of utilities
Zoning[a]
Housing
Construction and maintenance of local streets

State interest paramount

Municipal debt limits
Taxation for state purposes
Regulation of prosecutions for violation of state constitution and laws
Organization and jurisdiction of higher courts
Annexation of territory
Regulation of privately owned utilities
Consolidation of city with other local units of government
Elections

Concurrent jurisdiction necessary

Police power[b]
Health
Education
Poor relief
Sanitation
Correction
City and regional planning
Construction and maintenance of through streets

Controversial subjects

Organization and jurisdiction of local courts
Eminent domain[c]
Settlement of claims against the city
Taxation for local purposes

Source: Austin F. MacDonald, *American City Government and Administration* (New York: Thomas Y. Crowell Publishers, 1936), 103.

a. Zoning: The division of a city into districts or zones for the purpose of applying different regulations to the property within each district.

b. Police power: The power to make reasonable regulations for the health, safety, morals, and general welfare of the people.

c. Eminent domain: The power to take private property, by paying just compensation, for a public or quasi-public purpose.

which the state government could preempt a local government charter. The language on preemption is instructive:

Home rule units may exercise and perform concurrently with the State any power or function of a home rule unit to the extent that the General Assembly by law does not specifically limit the concurrent exercise or declare the state's exercise to be exclusive.[97]

If the state does not declare a function the exclusive domain of the state, the state constitution requires a three-fifths vote in the legislature to prohibit a home rule unit's use of its local powers.[98] Illinois has served as an example for other states who copied the "liberal construction" language in recent revisions of their constitutions.

The language in the Alaska constitution is very direct: "A liberal construction shall be given to the powers of local government units . . . and [a] home rule borough or city may exercise all legislative powers not prohibited by law or by charter."[99] Another example of the "liberal construction" idea can be found in the New Jersey constitution.[100] The New Jersey supreme court has followed the liberal construction language and permitted a broader interpretation of municipal functional responsibilities. The New Jersey Constitution addresses local privilege legislation in a unique way by requiring a concurrent majority of the local governing body and the state legislature to pass a special act in the legislature.[101]

Year 2000

Professor Timothy Mead, in a recent review of legal factors constraining or facilitating local government initiative, summarized the current status of home rule in America.[102] First, according to Mead, "Dillon's Rule has been accepted as the essential legal doctrine of state-local relations." Second, while some states, such as North Carolina and Alaska, have granted local governments extensive authority and discretion, "it remains the case that local powers are *granted,* not inherent" [italics in original]. Third, "home rule, in one of its variants, is the practice in forty-five states," and the states may be classified in two forms: *imperium in imperio* and legislative home rule. The imperium model, which Mead found in nineteen states, rests on the enumeration strategy, in which certain powers are delegated to municipal governments or are designated as "matters of local concern." Whether delegated or designated as matters of local concern, the powers are the exclusive preserve of local government. Legislative home rule, used in twenty-six states by Mead's count, is based on the "devolution of powers" idea that local governments ought "to be able to exercise any power that the legislature is constitutionally able to grant or is not prohibited by either the U.S. or state constitution." Mead concluded his review by stating: "From virtually any perspective, local governments are legally powerless in the face of judgments by other levels of government."[103]

Daniel Elazar, a world renown authority on federalism, addressed the topic of home rule in one of his last essays before his death in 1999. He pointed out that "if home rule has not brought all the benefits its champions sought, it did represent a major step in the transformation (or restoration) of local government as a recognized partner in its own right within the federal system."[104] Elazar went on to observe that "the old demand for separation of functions by plane of government—the traditional basis for home rule—has surfaced once again," and he attributed this renewed interest in home rule to the "devolution" revolution. We agree with Elazar, but we would expand the list of forces prompting a renewed interest in home rule to include the intense policy debates over economic growth, metropolitan sprawl, fiscal and quality of life inequities, and globalization. These issues were mentioned earlier as part of the discussion of the significance of home rule to governance in present-day America. Common to the various remedies offered in all four of these political-economic issue areas are proposals to change the nature of local government and especially the scope of local government discretionary authority, which is the heart of home rule. One prominent example of this emphasis on local government autonomy and discretionary authority is David Rusk's book *Inside Game, Outside Game: Winning Strategies for Saving Urban America.* Rusk maintains that "inside strategies"—strategies to improve city government by changing its internal structure and powers—turn on local empowerment of "citistates."[105] The creation of strong, "empowered" governments, according to Rusk, requires revisiting and rethinking the restrictive reins that Dillon's Rule has placed on local governments.[106] So, 150 years after the birth of the home rule movement, its goals and objectives have been incorporated into the current policy discussions over how best to reform American government. Whether this renewed interest in home rule and increased discretionary authority for local governments leads to enhanced autonomy for local governments and alters the nature of state-local relationships is still an open question.

Research on Home Rule

The goals of the home rule movement were to protect local governments from undue interference by state government and to create a sphere within which local government officials could make decisions without first having to seek authority or permission from the state government. Once states began to establish home rule, scholars began to inventory the various types of home rule provisions. Most of the research on home rule, from the earliest studies, made in the late 1800s, to those of the present day, has been descriptive, classificatory, and often historical. As Howard McBain explained in his seminal research published 1916:

Broadly construed the term "municipal home rule" has reference to any power of self-government that may be conferred upon a city, whether the grant of such power be referable to statute or constitution. In American usage, however, the term has become associated with those powers that are vested in cities by constitutional provisions, and more especially provisions that extend to cities the authority to frame and adopt their own charters.[107]

This conceptualization of home rule, narrowly focused on the authority of a local government to draft its own charter, continues to be cited in textbooks on state and local government; McBain's key idea—"any power of self-government"—often is not cited.

State codes place the powers of general-purpose governments into three categories—governmental, corporate, and proprietary. Governmental powers usually refer to ordinance-making authority and the use of police powers and taxation. Corporate powers include the ability to enter into contracts and to buy and sell property, but it also means the jurisdiction can sue and be sued. Proprietary powers permit a local government to engage in commercial activities, for example, owning and operating a utility. Which of these powers are granted to which type of local government varies from state to state—in some states, municipalities possess all three. Although states typically have not provided counties with corporate or proprietary power, some states have acted to do so in recent years, especially for urbanized counties.

Another feature of home rule scholarship is the effort to categorize states by the presence or absence of home rule and the legal basis on which it is grounded. This type of scheme classifies the fifty states according to the legal distinctions of Dillon's Rule, *imperium in imperio,* and devolution of powers models. Mead's classification, mentioned in the previous section, is a typical example. J. Devereux Weeks and Paul Hardy provide another commonly cited example:

1. non–home rule governments—Dillon's Rule prevails;
2. home rule charter governments—the original home rule idea that a city should exercise those powers expressly granted in their locally adopted charter; and
3. home-rule grant governments—Fordham's "devolution of powers" plan[108]

Their rather straightforward taxonomy of home rule does not make explicit the amount of discretionary authority available to local governments and is problematic because local discretionary authority varies significantly from state to state. Furthermore, "it is not possible to use them [threefold legal distinctions] to classify the 50 states because no one type applies to all general-purpose local governments in any state, and many states have a legal system that blends two or three of the types."[109]

In addition, a classification based solely on the availability and type of charter options does not take into account other important dimensions of local government authority, such as choice in form of government, functional responsibilities, and fiscal actions.[110] The traditional definitional approach to home rule, therefore, provides little, if any, basis for the development of systematic knowledge about the discretionary authority of local government and the consequences of variation in that authority. E. Blaine Liner makes the basic point that "complexity is given" when one examines state-local systems of governance and the degree of local government autonomy in the fifty American states.[111] He suggests a two-by-two classification scheme of public goods and services, where one axis is the presence or absence of local control and the other axis is local versus state funding. The problem with Liner's scheme is that these decisions are seldom either-or; rather, they typically are decisions of degree, as in the percentage of local versus state funding for a given public service. Steven Gold follows a somewhat parallel path in his attempt to analyze how state-local systems differ. Gold identifies four major attributes along which states may vary: local government structures, local autonomy, fiscal centralization, and local revenue systems.[112] Gold, in effect, argues for the use of Joseph Zimmerman's well known "index of local discretionary authority" in combination with other common measures of fiscal centralization as the best means for gauging the variation in state-local systems.

Building from his earlier work on state-local relations, Joseph Zimmerman, under the auspices of the Advisory Commission on Intergovernmental Relations (ACIR), published a major study of local discretionary authority in 1981.[113] His research is one of the few attempts to define home rule more broadly than charter-writing authority and to conduct a national study of local discretion. In his report, Zimmerman developed for the first time a quantified measure of local discretion, gathered data from the fifty states, and rank ordered the states by degree of local discretion (or its inverse, state control). Zimmerman scored the discretionary authority of general-purpose units of local government—cities, counties, towns, villages, townships, and boroughs—in four areas: structure, functions, personnel, and fiscal policy. He derived the index in part from constitutional and statutory statements, which he rank ordered ordinally from 1 (greatest freedom from state control) to 5 (smallest degree of freedom). He assigned a separate score to each state on each of the four dimensions. In addition, Zimmerman sent a mail questionnaire to knowledgeable persons in each state, who were asked to rate (on the five-point scale) the degree of discretion available to cities and counties for each of the four components. Although the original Zimmerman Index scores reflect the situation in the late 1970s, and although the scores represent potential authority rather than the authority actually exercised, the index remains to this date the best available measure of local government discretion.

Since Zimmerman's national study in 1981, two other national studies of home rule have been conducted, both published by ACIR in 1993. Michael Libonati authored a report entitled *Local*

Government Autonomy: Needs for State Constitutional, Statutory, and Judicial Clarification.[114] Based on an in-depth analysis of court cases and the reading of state constitutions and statutes, Libonati's monograph provides a highly detailed legal history and sourcebook on local government autonomy and home rule. The report is also a convenient introduction to the legal research on home rule that is published in law journals.

The other ACIR document, *State Laws Governing Local Government Structure and Administration,* was compiled by Melvin B. Hill Jr.[115] This report contains substantial information on seventy-five separate items categorized under six topics: form of government, altering boundaries and responsibilities, local elections, administrative operations and procedures, financial management, and personnel management. For each of the fifty states, Hill denotes with a code whether each of the seventy-five items—for example, "home rule authority granted counties" or "classes of cities provided for"— is present in state law.

Specifically, Hill categorizes home rule first by whether it is established by state constitution or by general law, and second by whether the home rule granted is structural, broad functional, or limited functional. For example, the ACIR report classifies all states other than Alabama and Vermont as granting some form of home rule authority to cities, and the report indicates that thirty-seven states provide home rule to counties. *Structural home rule,* or some local autonomy in selecting a form of government, is available to municipalities in forty states and to counties in twenty-four states. *Broad home rule,* or a great deal of local autonomy in carrying out local government functions with broad local powers and wide discretion, exists for cities in twenty-eight states and for counties in twenty-one states. *Limited home rule,* or little local autonomy with greatly circumscribed local powers and discretion, is the situation for cities in seventeen states and for counties in fourteen states.

Although this ACIR report on local government structure is a conveniently organized survey of state laws, it was limited to a survey of the legal language of state constitutions and statutes, and in some cases the legal language did not reflect actual practice. For example, the ACIR study indicates that Nebraska cities have been granted home rule authority by the state constitution. From a strict legal perspective, this is correct, since the Nebraska Constitution permits any city with a population of 5,000 to "frame a charter for its own government," and cities of more than 100,000 people may adopt their statutory charter as a home rule charter. However, of the state's twenty-eight municipalities of 5,000+ population, only three have ever adopted home rule, and one of those three later voted to rescind its charter. Further, the two cities with home rule charters possess at best an illusory form of home rule because (1) almost any new action they take requires approval of the state legislature, and (2) state court rulings have left no matter outside the bounds of state action. Thus, on the basis of actual practice, it is more ac-

curate to assert that "home rule does not really exist in Nebraska."[116]

This one example, which can be replicated in other states, should alert persons interested in home rule and local government discretionary authority of the danger of relying on narrow legal definitions of home rule. The Nebraska illustration also points to the danger of equating the language of constitutions and statutes with the behavior of state and local officials in regard to the degree of discretionary authority actually exercised by local governments in a given state. The gap between theory and practice is as great in local government law as it is in political science and public administration. It is especially tempting to rely on the legal language now that it is so easily accessed via the Internet.[117]

A solely legal approach to home rule disregards important behavioral aspects of state-local relations. Using the language of state constitutions or state codes as the primary, and often only, source of information about home rule presumes that local officials are inert or passive in respect to state laws or constitutional provisions; but this is not the case. Alberta Sbragia, as part of a study of urban governments as borrowers and investors, describes how local governments, although limited by legislation and court rulings, have managed to "circumvent" institutional limits.[118] Many commonplace instruments of local government action, such as revenue bonds, tax exemptions, tax increment financing as well new forms of local government (public authorities and special districts, among others) were created by general-purpose local governments in their effort to behave as entrepreneurs in pursuit of their cities' interests. The "politics of circumvention," as Sbragia calls it, suggests that any analysis of local government autonomy must include both the positive grants of discretionary authority, and how officials use this discretion as well as the constraints on local discretion and how local officials circumvent the restrictions. After all, local government officials are resourceful individuals who will pursue the interests of their locality by searching for room to maneuver within the current institutional arrangements. Deil Wright pointed out this important feature of American intergovernmental relations more than a decade ago.[119] What is striking about previous discussions of local government autonomy is the absence of any mention of the distinction between legal language and actual practice.

The current status of home rule and local government discretionary authority in the fifty states has been influenced strongly by the trends mentioned in the opening section of this chapter as well as by the modernization of state governments that occurred primarily between 1970 and 1990. The transformation of most state governments from their antiquated structures, political patronage arrangements, widespread administrative mismanagement, and inequitable forms of representation to more streamlined organizations, merit-based personnel systems, broad-based representation, and diversified forms of revenue contributed to an enhanced governing capacity at both the state and local levels.[120] This modernization of state government is a major argument in support of devolution.

Another important trend affecting the development of home rule is the continuing move by state governments to expand local government discretionary authority into new policy areas such as public-private interaction and land-use controls. At the same time, new forms of restrictions, especially in the area of local finances and the conduct of public business, also continue to be established. For example, some states have acted to address the issue of local government bankruptcy, and other states have imposed a variety of accounting and budgetary practices. State legislatures have also responded to demands for more transparency in government by passing laws establishing "open meetings," "open records," and codes of ethical conduct. Just as the national government has imposed unfunded mandates on the states, so also have state governments imposed them on their localities. All of these newer forms of discretionary authority and newer forms of restricted authority need to be identified and systematically examined.

In short, the available information about the types and extent of discretionary authority possessed by U.S. local governments is woefully incomplete, and one important reason for this situation is the almost exclusive reliance in home rule research on the limited definition of home rule as charter-writing authority and the use of legal documents as the source of information about the status of home rule in a state. The chapters written for this volume address the definitional issue first by reviewing the legal definition in the state constitution and state code, and second by providing a sense of the extent to which the legal definition of home rule is congruent with the actual practice of state-local relations. The authors of the fifty state chapters are able to make this comparison because they conducted original research using sources beyond the usual legal documents. These other sources include interviews with state or local officials, government reports and academic studies, newsletters and magazines produced by state associations of municipal or county officials, and the expert opinion of knowledgeable observers. Furthermore, the types of discretionary authority catalogued within each chapter were not limited to the four conventional categories of structure, function, personnel, and finance. As noted in the preface, the topics on the standard outline for the state chapters include several items that have not been included in previous studies of home rule. Because of the broader base of information used to prepare the state chapters, this handbook on home rule in America comes closer to the standard set by McBain's 1916 definition—"any power of self-government that may be conferred upon a city [or county]."

The Implications of a Renewed Interest in Home Rule

The chapters on home rule in the fifty states presented in this volume are an initial step toward a systematic collection of information about the discretionary authority available to local governments. The existence of a comprehensive survey of home rule has several important implications for scholarly research, administrative practice, and the development of theory about state-local relations as well as for practical political purposes and our nation's philosophy of government.

Scholarly Research

Obviously, a body of relatively standard information on state-local relations facilitates comparison of the fifty states. Without national data that is relatively uniform, it would be difficult not only to develop an accurate classification of home rule provisions but also to measure the degree of local discretion (or state control), and without a valid measure of local discretion, one cannot begin to answer the question: Does home rule make a difference? The professional literature on government in general and local government specifically has long hypothesized that institutional features (for example, city manager form; county plural executive form) make a significant difference in policy outputs and administrative performance. But these types of questions cannot be answered until a body of evidence on home rule is available. Science proceeds from the first steps of description to classification by similarities and differences before it can move on to more complex analyses of causes and consequences. The information contained in the state chapters are building blocks for comparative analysis, because these chapters detail what exists—for example, which states permit annexation without a vote of the residents of the area to be annexed, or which states have expanded the types of taxes a local government may levy.

Administrative Practice

As we noted earlier, one of the forces prompting a renewed interest in home rule is the ongoing effort to devolve public policy decision making and program administration from the national government to state and local governments. It has long been an article of faith in public administration circles that any effort to devolve new functions and responsibilities to local governments can be successful only if local governments possess sufficient capacity to perform the devolved functions. A necessary element of local capacity is discretionary authority. Similarly, the campaign to "reinvent" government by making it more entrepreneurial began with an emphasis on local governments, and like devolution, reinvention presupposes that local governments possess extensive autonomy and capacity. Because local government capacity is a linchpin in many proposals to reform government and its administration in the United States, local discretionary authority cannot be passed over as an antiquated feature of local governments.

A national study of home rule aids the reform process by establishing a systematic body of knowledge that profiles the extent and types of local discretion. Without an empirical baseline on the current degree of local authority, it will be difficult to monitor progress, identify trends, and offer sound prescriptions for change. The place to start is with a basic descriptive study such as provided in this volume.

Another reform effort currently under way in public administration is the identification and dissemination of "best practices." The fifty state essays and the associated comparative charts at the end of this volume provide a convenient inventory of the different practices and provisions adopted by various states. We anticipate that this information will be extremely useful to policy makers and public administrators, as they have easy access to the practices found in other states. These officials can decide to what extent an area of discretionary authority permitted in another state would be helpful in resolving issues or problems in their state.

Theory

Social science theories about the behavior of local government officials and about the functions and operations of local governments as institutions have made significant strides in recent decades. A large number of public finance economists, political scientists, and urban government scholars have become advocates of an economic approach to the study of local government. Based on their assumption that local governments behave in a manner similar to firms in a competitive marketplace, "public choice" theorists emphasize the pursuit of individual self-interest as it relates to issues such as a person's selection of residence, the level of taxes a county decides to levy, the quality of services offered by a jurisdiction, and interjurisdictional cooperation. A key assumption in public choice theory is that local officials possess and exercise a broad range of discretionary authority so that they can respond to citizen preferences.[121] However, if local governments in many American states do not possess broad powers, then a key assumption of "public choice" theory is incorrect, and the applicability of the theory becomes suspect.

A more recent theoretical alternative—"agency theory"—has attracted the attention of students of local governments. Related to institutional economics, agency theory views social relationships as analogous to contracts between a buyer, or "principal," and the provider of a service, or "agent." As with any contract, a variety of so-called transaction costs are associated with making and enforcing the contract. These ideas have been applied to analysis of the relationships between state and local governments (for example, grants-in-aid) as well as interjurisdictional interaction (for example, city-county consolidation).[122] An important premise of the theory of institutional economics that underlies agency theory is that institutions and organizations can be treated as distinct variables because they are more than the mere aggregation of the behavior of the individuals who compose them. Since legal theory holds that local governments are agents of state government (the "principal"), then agency theory can be readily applied to home rule questions. For example, different patterns of powers and responsibilities between states and localities ought to be characterized by different combinations of transaction costs. More fundamentally, if local governments are powerless, then it is hard to treat them as agents who can make choices in regard to their own interests. Just as with public choice theory, the application of agency theory to the study of local government depends on the degree and the types of discretionary authority available to local governments.

Practical Politics

The questions of home rule and local self-government are normally debated in the arcane arenas of law journals and political science books. But every so often, they rise to the forefront of local political discussion and action. The degree to which local officials in a city, a township, or a county may act in accord with the wishes of the local residents is constrained by the state government. As local citizens begin to understand that their particular policy preference is not permitted (or is prohibited) by state government, the issues of "municipal independence" and the degree of home rule available to local governments in the state become pressing practical problems.

In February 2000, Virginia legislators rejected proposals to give local officials in that state the power to control local development by imposing limits on home construction and by imposing charges on developers in order to raise funds to construct the infrastructure—new roads and schools—needed to serve the rapidly expanding population. The proposed new authority to control development was supported by a coalition of twenty-four communities in Northern Virginia. Loudoun County, one of these communities, is the third fastest growing county in the nation and was faced with financing the construction of twenty-three new schools in six years. Opposing the limits on development, as one might easily guess, were lobbyists for the home building, real estate, and utility industries as well as businesses who were concerned about ensuring affordable housing as part of the effort to attract new workers in a tight labor market. Although there are more details about this political battle, an important one is the small amount of local discretionary authority that Virginia local governments possess, as compared with that possessed by their counterparts in Maryland. By contrast, Maryland law allows a county to stop home construction in places where schools and other infrastructure is insufficient.[123]

This commonplace example from Virginia not only dramatizes the significance of home rule but also underscores the practical political nature of home rule in present-day relationships between U.S. states and their localities. First, the Virginia case demonstrates the legally subordinate, "creatures of the state" position of local governments within current American jurisprudence. From a practical perspective, no matter what the residents of these Virginia localities wanted as the solution to their local problems, they could act only in ways established by the state government, and since the state government decided not to permit the proposed solution, the localities are, to use Frug's term, "powerless."

Second, this situation in Virginia illustrates the substantial changes that have occurred in the actual discretionary authority exercised by local governments. As the modernization and reform of American states have advanced since the late 1960s, state governments have delegated more and different forms of discretionary authority to local governments. The explosive population growth in Northern Virginia has resulted, in part, from local communities using their discretionary authority in economic development to attract additional business enterprises. One unsympathetic state legislator rejected the limits on development by stating, "I will believe a county is serious about trying to control growth when they stop trying to attract it."[124]

Third, the example displays the growing "partnership" of state and local governments in numerous policy areas. In Maryland, where county government has the authority to stop home construction, the state government is moving forward with a "smart growth" plan designed to steer new development into areas with established infrastructure. In Virginia, some of the state legislators from more rural areas in the south and west of the state opposed growth limits in the northern part because new development anywhere in the state would augment state revenues, and thus make it possible for the state to spend more money in less affluent areas.

Despite the devolution of powers or more liberal construction of home rule in some states, local governments in the majority of U.S. states are still treated as "creatures of the state," even though local governments have increasingly become partners in state and local policy making and administration. From a legal perspective, city and county attorneys and state court judges refer to "powers expressly granted" to local governments; at the same time, mayors, city managers, and county supervisors refer to the choices they have to make and the "powers [they] exercise." This difference in the language used by the different officials reflects the reality of state-local relations in which the legal basis of local government increasingly is disconnected from its actual practice.

Philosophy of Government

Citizens and scholars who have an interest in the quality of democracy and its relationship to the quality of civil society in our communities cannot ignore home rule and its related issues. The desire for local self-government is embodied in that most revolutionary of phrases—"We, the People"—and the capacity for self-government is grounded in the consent of the people, or so American theories of democracy argue. Much of the outcry over the loss of citizen trust in government and in public officials bemoans the decline of citizen participation, even at the local level, and the deterioration of a shared sense of community. Innumerable commentators have offered many different causes for the decline of active citizenship. One reason that keeps reappearing is the lack of incentives to participate—that is, citizens do not participate because they believe that participation has no meaning or value and that decision makers often disregard their views. Calls to encourage more citizen participation and to create a "deliberative democracy" have to confront the question of home rule. A local government that is not under the control of its own citizens, or a local government that lacks much discretionary authority to act in accord with citizen preferences, renders any civic deliberations futile. Without some degree of "municipal independence," to recall de Tocqueville's term, an active citizenry will be stymied if the local government does not possess sufficient capacity to pursue the goals chosen through "community conversations." We opened this chapter with a quotation from Frank Goodnow's 1895 study of municipal home rule in which he links the "lack of civic patriotism" to "the small sphere of local autonomy." It is instructive to note that Goodnow's reasoning has reappeared in the contemporary debates over community and governance.

We conclude this extended essay at the place where we began—the old and venerable idea of home rule, after more than a century, is still an important and lively topic with implications for several aspects of public affairs. Numerous policy questions at the local level turn on whether local officials possess sufficient discretionary authority to address local needs and problems. Questions such as those that we listed in the introduction fall precisely within the domain of home rule. Because we believe that the ideas inherent in home rule need further discovery and explication, we launched this national project to profile the scope and status of home rule and local government autonomy in the fifty states. A broad base of information about home rule, we believe, will allow discussions of local government, civil society, and democracy to proceed on a more informed basis. We concur with Victor DeSantis and Tari Renner when they state that "home-rule authority, whether at the county or municipal level, is undoubtedly one of the more understudied areas of local government."[125] We also agree with them that studying home rule is no easy task—as we can testify from the work of the more than eighty scholars who have participated in this project. However, we are also convinced that further research on what to many is an outdated concept will yield considerable fruit in terms of improving our knowledge about state-local relations and how those relations shape the work of local governments and the quality of life for "We the People."

Notes

1. Frank J. Goodnow, *Municipal Home Rule: A Study in Administration* (New York: MacMillan, 1895), 8.

2. Richard Briffault, "Our Localism: Part I—The Structure of Local Government Law," *Columbia Law Review* 90 (January 1990), 112.

3. Council of State Governments, *State-Local Relations: Report of the Committee on State-Local Relations* (Chicago: Council of State Governments, 1946), 142.

4. Alexis de Tocqueville, *Democracy in America*, Vol. 1 (New York: Vintage Books, Random House, 1945), 67.

5. Daniel J. Elazar, "State-Local Relations: Union and Home Rule." In *Governing Partners: State-Local Relations in the United States*, ed. Russell L. Hanson (Boulder: Westview Press, 1998), 37–38.

6. Frank J. Goodnow, *Municipal Problems* (New York: MacMillan, 1903), 63.

7. U.S. Advisory Commission on Intergovernmental Relations, *Local Government Autonomy: Needs for State Constitutional, Statutory, and Judicial Clarification* (Washington, D.C.: ACIR, A-127, October 1993), 2.

8. John J. Gargan, "Local Government Governing Capacity: Challenges for the New Century." In *Handbook of Local Government Administration*, ed. John J. Gargan (New York: Marcel Dekker, 1997), 520–525.

9. John J. Gargan, "Consideration of Local Government Capacity," *Public Administration Review* 41 (November–December 1981), 650.

10. David C. Nice, "The Intergovernmental Setting of State-Local Relations." In *Governing Partners: State-Local Relations in the United States*, ed. Russell L. Hanson (Boulder: Westview Press, 1998), 28.

11. Jeffrey M. Stonecash, "The Politics of State-Local Fiscal Relations." In *Governing Partners: State-Local Relations in the United States*, ed. Russell L. Hanson (Boulder: Westview Press, 1998).

12. Beverly A. Cigler, "Emerging Trends in State-Local Relations." In *Governing Partners: State-Local Relations in the United States*, ed. Russell L. Hanson (Boulder: Westview Press, 1998), 54–64.

13. Dale Krane, "Devolution as an Intergovernmental Reform Strategy." In *Strategies for Managing Intergovernmental Policies and Networks*, ed. Robert W. Gage and Myrna P. Mandell (New York: Praeger, 1990); Timothy Conlan, *New Federalism: Intergovernmental Reform from Nixon to Reagan* (Washington, D.C.: Brookings Institution, 1988).

14. David B. Walker, "Devolution: A Big Deal or Only One Dynamic in the System?" Paper presented at the 1997 annual meeting of the New England Political Science Association, New London, Conn., May 3.

15. Peter Eisinger, "City Politics in an Era of Federal Devolution," *Urban Affairs Review* 33 (January 1998), 310–311.

16. John Shannon, "The Return to Fend-for-Yourself Federalism: The Reagan Mark," *Intergovernmental Perspective* 13 (summer–fall 1987), 34–37.

17. Richard Nathan, "The Devolution Revolution: An Overview," *Rockefeller Institute Bulletin*, 1996.

18. Jonathan Walters, "Cry, the Beleaguered County," *Governing*, August 1996, 33.

19. David R. Berman, "State-Local Relations: Authority, Finance, and Regional Cooperation," *The Municipal Yearbook 1998* (Washington, D.C.: International City/County Management Association, 1998), 68.

20. Ibid.

21. Clifford P. McCue, "Local Government Revenue Diversification: A Portfolio Analysis and Evaluation." In *Handbook of Comparative Public Budgeting and Financial Management*, ed. Thomas D. Lynch and Lawrence L. Martin (New York: Marcel Dekker, 1993).

22. Peter Eisinger, "City Politics in an Era of Federal Devolution," *Urban Affairs Review* 33 (January 1998), 318–322.

23. DeWitt John, Alexis A. Halley, and R. Scott Fosler, "Remapping Federalism: The Rediscovery of Civic Governance in the United States." In *Globalization and Decentralization: Institutional Contexts, Policy Issues, and Intergovernmental Relations in Japan and the United States*, ed. Jong S. Jun and Deil S. Wright (Washington, D.C.: Georgetown University Press, 1996), 89.

24. Ibid., 102–104.

25. Bill Clinton and Albert Gore, *The Blair House Papers* (Washington, D.C.: National Performance Review, January 1997), vii.

26. Beverly A. Cigler, "Emerging Trends in State-Local Relations." In *Governing Partners: State-Local Relations in the United States*, ed. Russell L. Hanson (Boulder: Westview Press, 1998), 53–74.

27. Jong S. Jun and Deil S. Wright, "Globalization and Decentralization: An Overview." In *Globalization and Decentralization: Institutional Contexts, Policy Issues, and Intergovernmental Relations in Japan and the United States*, ed. Jong S. Jun and Deil S. Wright (Washington, D.C.: Georgetown University Press, 1996), 1–18.

28. Neal R. Peirce, *Citistates: How Urban America Can Prosper in a Competitive World* (Washington, D.C.: Seven Locks Press, 1993), 1.

29. Ibid., 2.

30. Susan E. Clarke and Gary L. Gaile, *The Work of Cities* (Minneapolis: University of Minnesota Press, 1998), 211.

31. Peirce, *Citistates*, 32–35.

32. Federico Pena, "Reflections on the Role of Regions" (Washington, D.C.: National Academy of Public Administration). The Staats Lecture delivered June 5, 1998, at Boulder, Colo.

33. Dale Krane, "Federalism." In *International Encyclopedia of Public Policy and Administration*, Vol. 2, ed. Jay M. Shafritz (Boulder: Westview Press, 1998), 865–877.

34. Howard L. McBain, *The Law and the Practice of Municipal Home Rule* (New York: Columbia University Press, 1916), 656.

35. Ibid.

36. Charles M. Tiebout, "A Pure Theory of Local Expenditures," *Journal of Political Economy* 64 (October 1956), 416–424.

37. Albert Breton, "The Existence and Stability of Interjurisdictional Competition." In *Competition Among States and Local Governments: Efficiency and Equity in American Federalism*, ed. Daphne A. Kenyon and John Kincaid (Washington, D.C.: Urban Institute Press, 1991); Thomas R. Dye, *American Federalism: Competition Among Governments* (Lexington: D.C. Heath, 1990); Paul E. Peterson, *City Limits* (Chicago: University of Chicago Press, 1981); Vincent Ostrom, Charles M. Tiebout, and Robert Warren, "The Organization of Government in Metropolitan Areas," *American Political Science Review* 55 (December 1961), 831–842.

38. Gordon Clark, "A Theory of Local Autonomy," *Annals of the Association of American Geographers* 74 (June 1984), 201–203.

39. Jeffrey Chapman, "Local Government, Fiscal Autonomy and Fiscal Stress: The Case of California," paper presented at the sixtieth national conference of the American Society for Public Administration, Orlando, Fla., April 10–14, 1999; Clark, "A Theory of Local Autonomy."

40. David Osborne and Ted Gaebler, *Reinventing Government: How the Entrepreneurial Spirit Is Transforming the Public Sector from Schoolhouse to Statehouse, City Hall to the Pentagon* (Reading: Addison-Wesley, 1992).

41. Richard Box, *Citizen Governance: Leading American Communities into the 21st Century* (Thousand Oaks: Sage Publications, 1998); Susan J. Tolchin, *The Angry American Voter: How Voter Rage Is Changing the Nation* (Boulder: Westview Press, 1996); Amitai Etzioni, *The Spirit of Community* (New York: Crown, 1993).

42. Brian O'Connell, *Civil Society: The Underpinnings of American Democracy* (Hanover, N.H.: Tufts University, University Press of New England, 1999); Craig Rimmerman, *The New Citizenship: Unconventional Politics, Activism, and Service* (Boulder: Westview Press, 1997).

43. Ralph Hummel and Camilla Stivers, "Government Isn't Us: The Possibility of Democratic Knowledge in Representative Government." In *Government Is Us: Public Administration in an Anti-Government Era*, ed. Cheryl K. King and Camilla Stivers (Thousand Oaks: Sage Publications, 1998), 28–48; Charles C. Euchner, *Extraordinary Politics: How Protest and Dissent Are Changing American Democracy* (Boulder: Westview Press, 1996).

44. William Simonsen and Mark D. Robbins, *Citizen Participation in Resource Allocation* (Boulder: Westview Press, 2000); David D. Chrislip and Carl E. Larson, *Collaborative Leadership: How Citizens and Civic Leaders Can Make a Difference* (San Francisco: Jossey-Bass Books, 1994).

45. Goodnow, *Municipal Home Rule*, 2. This section on the history of home rule is a substantially expanded and revised version of an earlier draft that was part of an essay entitled "Local Government Autonomy and Discretion in the United States," which was published in *The Challenge to New Governance in the*

Twenty-First Century: Achieving Effective Central-Local Relations (Tokyo, Japan: National Institute for Research Advancement, 1999), 267–298.

46. Harold F. Alderfer, *American Local Government and Administration* (New York: MacMillan, 1956), 147.

47. Gerald E. Frug, "The City as a Legal Concept," *Harvard Law Review* 93 (April 1980), 1090–1094.

48. Nancy Burns, *The Formation of American Local Governments: Private Values in Public Institutions* (New York: Oxford University Press, 1994).

49. Vincent Ostrom, Robert Bish, and Elinor Ostrom, *Local Government in the United States* (San Francisco: ICS Press, 1988), 22.

50. U.S. Advisory Commission on Intergovernmental Relations, *Local Government Autonomy*, 29.

51. Roscoe Martin, *The Cities and the Federal System* (New York: Atherton, 1965), 28–29.

52. Ibid., 29.

53. Gerald E. Frug, *Citymaking: Building Communities without Building Walls* (Princeton: Princeton Universton University Press, 1999), 36–40.

54. W. Brooke Graves, *American Intergovernmental Relations: Their Origins, Historical Development, and Current Status* (New York: Charles Scribner's Sons, 1964), 106.

55. 17 U.S. (4 Wheat) 518 (1819) at 668–669.

56. McBain, *The Law and the Practice of Municipal Home Rule*, 19.

57. Frug, "The City as a Legal Concept," 1104.

58. 2 James Kent, *Commentaries on American Law* 275 (3d ed. 1836).

59. Frug, *Citymaking*, 43.

60. Quoted in Frug, *Citymaking*, 44.

61. Alberta M. Sbragia, *Debt Wish: Entrepreneurial Cities, U.S. Federalism, and Economic Development* (Pittsburgh: University of Pittsburgh Press, 1996), ch. 4; Ostrom, Bish, and Ostrom, *Local Government in the United States*, 27.

62. Frug, *Citymaking*, 44.

63. Sbragia, *Debt Wish*, 19–43.

64. Ibid., ch 3.

65. Burns, *The Formation of American Local Governments*, 49.

66. 24 Iowa 455 at 461.

67. Sbragia, *Debt Wish*, 89–90.

68. City of Clinton v. Cedar Rapids and Missouri River Railroad Co. (1868).

69. John Dillon, *Commentaries on the Law of Municipal Corporations* (Boston: Little, Brown, 1911), 48.

70. Joseph F. Zimmerman, *State-Local Relations: A Partnership Approach*, 2d ed. (Westport: Praeger Publishers, 1995), 17.

71. 13 Mass. 272, 284 (1816).

72. Quoted in U.S. Advisory Commission on Intergovernmental Relations, *Local Government Autonomy*, 31–32.

73. *People v. Hurlburt*, 24 Michigan 44, 1871.

74. Zimmerman, *State-Local Relations*, 19–20.

75. Sarah F. Liebschutz and Joseph F. Zimmerman, "Fiscal Dependence and Revenue Enhancement Opportunities for Local Governments in the United States." In *Future Challenges of Local Autonomy in Japan, Korea, and the United States: Shared Responsibilities between National and Sub-national Governments*, ed. Fukashi Horie and Masaru Nishio (Tokyo, Japan: National Institute for Research Advancement, 1997), 187–188.

76. Sbragia, *Debt Wish*, 90.

77. McBain, *The Law and the Practice of Municipal Home Rule*, 6; Burns, *The Formation of American Local Governments*, 49–50.

78. Ostrom, Bish, and Ostrom, *Local Government in the United States*, 32.

79. McBain, *The Law and the Practice of Municipal Home Rule*, 7.

80. Ibid., 113.

81. James C. Olson and Ronald C. Naugle, *History of Nebraska*, 3d ed. (Lincoln: University of Nebraska Press, 1997), 224–236.

82. Ibid., 89.

83. H. S. Gilbertson, *The County: The "Dark Continent" of American Politics* (New York: National Short Ballot Association, 1917).

84. Graves, *American Intergovernmental Relations*, 793–797.

85. American Municipal Association, as quoted in Alderfer, *American Local Government and Administration*, 136–137.

86. Zimmerman, *State-Local Relations*, 27.

87. Quoted in A. B. Winter, "Nebraska Home Rule: The Record and Some Recommendations," *Nebraska Law Review* 59, no. 3 (1980), 623.

88. Jefferson B. Fordham, *Local Government Law: Text, Cases, & Other Materials* (Brooklyn: Foundation Press, 1949).

89. *www.abanet.org/media/aproo/fordham2000.html*

90. American Municipal Association, *Model Constitutional Provisions for Municipal Home Rule* (Chicago: AMA, 1953), 19.

91. Zimmerman, *State-Local Relations*, 29–34.

92. The terminology used for the devolution of powers model can be somewhat confusing. Usually, a state that opts for this approach begins with a constitutional provision; devolution of powers usually requires the state legislature to enact enabling language. Because the devolution model at least partially restores the role of the state legislature as the primary body that draws the line between state and local matters, many analysts refer to this model as "legislative home rule." Sometimes it is also labeled the "residual powers" model.

93. Dawn Cowan and Tanis J. Salant, *County Charter Government in the West* (Tucson: Office of Government Programs, University of Arizona, April 1999), 5; National Civic League, *Model County Charter* (Denver: NCL, 1990), xii–xix.

94. Briffault, "Our Localism," 16.

95. Edward C. Banfield and James Q. Wilson, *City Politics* (New York: Vintage Books, Random House, 1963), 65.

96. U.S. Advisory Commission on Intergovernmental Relations, *Local Government Autonomy*, 46–47.

97. Ibid., 47.

98. Ibid., 47.

99. See chapter on Alaska in this volume.

100. See chapter on New Jersey in this volume.

101. U.S. Advisory Commission on Intergovernmental Relations, *Local Government Autonomy*, 45.

102. Timothy D. Mead, "Federalism and State Law: Legal Factors Constraining and Facilitating Local Initiatives." In *Handbook of Local Government Administration*, ed. John J. Gargan (New York: Marcel Dekker, 1997), 31–45.

103. Ibid., 42.

104. Elazar, "State-Local Relations," 38.

105. David Rusk, *Inside Game, Outside Game: Winning Strategies for Saving Urban America* (Washington, D.C.: Brookings Institution, 1999).

106. Carl W. Stenberg, "Structuring Local Government Units and Relationships," Symposium on the Future of Local Government in Michigan (*http://mml.org/foundation/structuring_relationships.htm*).

107. McBain, *The Law and the Practice of Municipal Home Rule*, v.

108. J. Devereux Weeks and Paul T. Hardy, "The Legal Aspects of Local Government." In *Small Cities and Counties: A Guide to Managing Services*, ed. James M. Banovetz (Washington, D.C.: International City/County Management Association, 1984), 27.

109. Joseph F. Zimmerman, "State Dominance or Local Autonomy." In *The Politics of Subnational Governance*, 2d ed., ed. Deirdre A. Zimmerman and Joseph F. Zimmerman (Lanham, Md.: University Press of America, 1991), 51.

110. E. Blaine Liner, "Sorting Out State-Local Relations." In *A Decade of Devolution: Perspectives on State-Local Relations*, ed. E. Blaine Liner (Washington, D.C.: Urban Institute Press, 1989); Steven D. Gold, *Reforming State-Local Relations: A Practical Guide* (Washington, D.C.: National Conference of State Legislatures, 1989).

111. Liner, "Sorting Out State-Local Relations," 13.

112. Gold, *Reforming State-Local Relations*, 11.

113. U.S. Advisory Commission on Intergovernmental Relations, *Measuring Local Discretionary Authority* (Washington, D.C.: USAICR, November 1981).

114. U.S. Advisory Commission on Intergovernmental Relations, *Local Government Autonomy*.

115. U.S. Advisory Commission on Intergovernmental Relations, *State Laws Governing Local Government Structure and Administration* (Washington, D.C.: ACIR, M-186, March 1993).

116. Winter, "Nebraska Home Rule," 626.

117. An over-reliance on legal sources easily accessible through the Internet can lead researchers to fall for the "Lexis-Nexis" fallacy—that is, assuming that

the legally defined situation can be equated to the actual political situation. The existence of a statute does not ensure that it will be enforced or obeyed. A researcher must determine the actual practice, and that usually entails more than merely downloading text from databases such as Lexis-Nexis.

118. Sbragia, *Debt Wish,* 9–16.

119. Deil S. Wright, *Understanding Intergovernmental Relations,* 3d ed. (Pacific Grove: Brooks/Cole, 1988), 14–26.

120. Mavis M. Reeves, "Look Again at State Capacity: The Old Gray Mare Ain't What She Used to Be," *American Review of Public Administration* 16 (spring 1982), 74–89.

121. Tiebout, "A Pure Theory of Local Expenditures"; Ostrom, Tiebout, and Warren, "The Organization of Government in Metropolitan Areas"; Mark Schneider, *The Competitive City: The Political Economy of Suburbia* (Pittsburgh: University of Pittsburgh Press, 1989).

122. John E. Chubb, "The Political Economy of Federalism," *American Political Science Review* 79 (December 1985), 994–1015; David Lowery, "A Transactions Costs Model of Metropolitan Governance: Allocation versus Redistribution in Urban America," *Journal of Public Administration Research and Theory* 10 (January 2000), 49–78.

123. Justin Blum, "Virginia Kills Plans to Let Localities Slow Growth," *The Washington Post* (February 9, 2000), A01.

124. Ibid.

125. Victor S. DeSantis and Tari Renner, "Governing the County: Authority, Structure, and Elections." In *County Governments in an Era of Change,* ed. David R. Berman (Westport: Greenwood Press, 1993), 21.

ALABAMA

Charles J. Spindler

As the nation moves into the twenty-first century, Alabama's constitution, politics, and government structure remain mired in the past. Operating under a constitution adopted in 1901, Alabama still uses outmoded rules to frame the relationship between state and local government. Few states restrict local government to the extent found in Alabama. Alabama is only one of two states that deny home rule to cities, and only three Alabama counties have a limited form of home rule. The constitution also restricts local governments' ability to raise taxes. Local government finances are further constrained, with approximately ninety cents of every tax dollar earmarked.

Governmental Setting

In recent years, a political culture termed the "New South" has emerged in southern states such as Florida, Tennessee, South Carolina, and Georgia. The New South builds new political coalitions based on better race relations, economic growth, and improvements in education, social services, and health care. The promise of the New South however is largely unrealized in Alabama. Instead, Alabama remains traditionalistic, "authorizing and expecting those at the top of the social structure to take a special and dominant role in government."[1] Chain gangs, mandatory school prayer, and the governor's disavowal of the Bill of Rights are among the state's efforts to preserve the status quo.

Race, religion, and class are entangled in nearly every aspect of politics in Alabama. Although race relations are better today, the past still affects state politics. In 1901 the state constitution established racial segregation and the disenfranchisement of blacks and poor whites as official state policies. Segregated facilities were the norm until they were declared unconstitutional by the U.S. Supreme Court in *Brown v. Board of Education of Topeka* (1954). In 1956 Alabama disavowed any responsibility to provide education to its citizens, hoping to avoid desegregating public schools. In the same year, blacks protested segregation on city buses in the Montgomery bus boycott.

At his first inauguration in 1963, Gov. George Wallace promised "segregation now, segregation tomorrow, segregation forever." Wallace then stood on the steps of the University of Alabama to block integration. In the same year, the brutal treatment of nonviolent civil rights demonstrators at the hands of Birmingham police chief Eugene "Bull" Connor brought national attention to Alabama. In 1965 the voter registration march from Selma to Montgomery was turned back with tear gas and beatings; President Lyndon Johnson then ordered the Alabama National Guard to escort the marchers. It was not until 1974 that the public schools in Montgomery were forced by a federal judge to integrate. These points of racial conflict in Alabama illustrate the pernicious and deep-seated efforts of a traditionalistic political culture.

Religion also significantly influences Alabama politics and policies. Alabama was settled principally by Scots-Irish with Puritan religious beliefs. Alabama is part of the Bible Belt of religious conservatism, which includes the "religious right," Sunday blue laws, dry counties, and mandatory school prayer. In a political pose reminiscent of George Wallace, Gov. Forrest "Fob" James declared in 1997 that he would use state troopers and the National Guard to stop anyone trying to remove prayer and religious displays from circuit courtrooms. James also attempted to reinstate school prayer, along with corporal punishment, as a means of restoring respect and traditional values in public schools. More recently, Gov. Don Siegelman has attempted to legislate politeness in the schools by requiring students to address their teachers as "ma'am" and "sir."[2]

Alabama has been marked by class division since the time of its settlement. The state is still a polarized society, divided between the rich and powerful and the poor and politically impotent. Prior to the Civil War, Alabama politics was dominated by a narrow economic elite that drew its power from a plantation economy based on slavery. Political power was denied the masses until Reconstruction following the Civil War. The power of the landed aristocracy was threatened by Reconstruction, which promised to expand suffrage. Most white voters joined the Democratic Party and supported "white supremacy."

Toward the end of the nineteenth century, Black Belt[3] agricultural elites joined forces with urban industrial elites to create a political coalition known as the "Big Mules." This coalition worked together for "low taxes, a school system that provided minimal education . . . a small electorate, and racial segregation."[4] The constitution of 1901 institutionalized the economic and political interests of the Big Mule coalition. Although political power today is diffused among interest groups representing teachers, lawyers, farmers, and insurance interests, the constitution of 1901 is still in effect.

From the Civil War and Reconstruction until 1986, Alabama remained essentially a single-party state under the control of the Democrats. Democratic dominance was broken in 1986, when Republican Guy Hunt was elected governor as a result of a split in the Democratic vote. The election of Fob James, a former Democrat turned Republican, in 1996 makes it clear the Democrats have lost their hold on the governor's seat.

The outcomes of Alabama's traditionalistic political culture are almost painfully obvious. There is a wide gap between rich and poor, and Alabama is one of the nation's poorest states. Median household income in Alabama was lower in 1995 than in 1990, and in 1995 Alabama ranked forty-eighth nationally in household income. Alabama ranked third among the states in total poverty in 1994; 20.1 percent of the population had incomes below the poverty level. Yet, for the same year, only 6.8 percent of Alabama's population received public assistance. Alabama ranked fourth nationwide in infant mortality in 1994 and third in births to teenage mothers in 1996.[5]

Educational attainment (or the lack thereof) is closely related to poverty and health.[6] In 1990 one-third of the population over twenty-five years of age had not completed high school, and the dropout rate was 12.6 percent.[7] Only 10.1 percent of the population over twenty-five earned bachelor's degrees; only Arkansas, Indiana, Mississippi, and West Virginia had fewer college graduates.

In May 1990 the Alabama Coalition for Equity—a group of twenty-two Alabama public schools—filed suit against the state, alleging discrimination in the distribution of state school money and disparities among local governments' abilities to fund education. The American Civil Liberties Union joined the School Equity and Funding lawsuit (as it was known in 1991) to represent affected public school children. In August 1991 Circuit Judge Eugene Reese struck down the 1956 amendment to the state constitution, ruling that it was racially discriminatory. In April 1993 Judge Reese found that "the quality of educational opportunities available to a child in the public schools of Alabama depends upon the fortuitous circumstances of where that child happens to reside and attend school." Wealthier jurisdictions had a higher tax base and could spend more for better facilities and salaries, which translated into more state assistance. To settle the School Equity and Funding lawsuit, Alabama would have had to spend an additional $500 million to equalize funding be-

tween wealthy and poor districts. Governor James resolved the suit, without raising taxes, by transferring funding from higher education to K–12.

Alabama's population is relatively small and stable. In 1994 the state population was 4,219,000.[8] Of the population, approximately 73 percent is white, 26 percent is black, and less than 1 percent is Native American.

Home Rule in Alabama

Historical Development

Home rule may be defined as the authority of local governments to determine "the organization, procedures and powers of their own governments [with] maximum freedom from control by either the legislature or state administrative officers."[9] Home rule typically is granted through state constitutional provisions; it is a concept that must be realized in practice as well as in law. That is, the legislature may grant home rule status to cities and/or counties but impose significant mandates or other requirements that effectively curtail or eliminate home rule.

Alabama has no constitutional provisions for home rule; it is only through constitutional amendment that three urban counties enjoy legal recognition of a limited form of home rule. The Alabama Constitution of 1901 imposes significant restrictions on state and local governments and remains in effect today, unless amended by legislation. The ability of cities and counties to deal with local problems depends on the state legislature.

Alabama's restrictive constitution enumerates specific powers and prohibitions and does not make broad grants of authority. Originally, the power of the state legislature was curtailed by limiting the legislative session to fifty days once every four years, later amended to a biennial session of thirty-six days. The power of the governor was diffused with the creation of the offices of lieutenant governor and commissioners of agriculture and industry.

Tax and revenue limitations first imposed under the constitution of 1875 were continued under the 1901 constitution, with additional limitations on the creation of new state debt. Similar tax and revenue restrictions were imposed on local governments. The constitution of 1901 also created a highly politicized government. At the state level, many executive branch departments have elected heads, and all state judges are elected. At the county level, almost all offices are elected, including those of tax assessor and county coroner.

Definition of Home Rule

In keeping with the traditionalistic political culture, there is no constitutional provision for home rule for cities or counties. Alabama's courts have interpreted Dillon's Rule[10] as the standard for construing local governmental authority: incorporated cities derive all powers from the state legislature.[11] Alabama counties are regarded as legal subdivisions of the state.

Alabama's constitution is the longest in the United States and has become essentially a legislative document with more that 600 amendments. Most amendments to the constitution are local in nature. Local amendments apply to less than the state as a whole; general legislation applies to the entire state. Without home rule powers, cities and counties must appeal to their local legislative delegation for special legislation to amend the constitution to address local needs. In one respect, "Alabama does have a form of home rule, since the legislature enacts virtually any local legislation that the local delegation supports."[12] This description does not meet the commonly accepted definition of home rule.

Originally, the 1901 constitution limited the power of the legislature to enact local laws by prohibiting the introduction of local legislation that applied to any political subdivision less than the state as a whole. Soon after the constitution was adopted, judicial interpretation held that general legislation based on population classifications was permissible, even it applied to a limited number of governments. Recent estimates suggest that approximately 70 percent of Alabama's constitutional amendments apply to a single city or county:

About half the local amendments authorize local governments to raise property tax millage rates for a broad range of purposes. Over 35 authorize specific counties to remove certain officials from the fee system and place them on salaries. Over 100 of the amendments provide relief from the tax and debt limits placed on counties and municipalities.[13]

The possibility of home rule was raised briefly in the 1970s by the Alabama Constitutional Commission. In 1979 Governor James proposed a new constitution based largely on the recommendations of the commission; however, the proposal contained no provision for home rule for cities. Some have suggested that "the absence of home rule does allow local officials to deflect citizen complaints about local services with the response that the community government is not empowered to do whatever the citizen wishes to see done."[14]

Structural Features

Both the state house and senate have standing committees to consider local legislation. Local legislation is presented by a legislative committee composed of legislators from the affected cities or counties. Under the custom of legislative courtesy, the legislature normally supports bills that have the unanimous approval of the local legislative committee. The legislative committee becomes the legislative authority for local government. The result of this process is an uncodified, uncoordinated mass of laws governing cities and counties.

In 1978 the state supreme court ruled that legislation that applied to less than the entire state was unconstitutional. The court found that arbitrary population classifications used by the legislature were unconstitutional and again interpreted the literal language of the constitution to prohibit local acts.[15] The state legislature responded immediately, passing an amendment that expanded the definition of general law to include law that applied to the state as a whole, as well as to one or more municipalities on the basis of eight population classes:

Class 1	300,000 population and more
Class 2	175,000–299,999
Class 3	100,000–174,999
Class 4	50,000–99,999
Class 5	25,000–49,999
Class 6	12,000–24,999
Class 7	6,000–11,999
Class 8	cities under 6,000 population

Three forms of municipal government are provided for in the Code of Alabama (1975, as amended): mayor-council, commission, and council-manager. The council-manager form was authorized under the Council Manager Act of 1982 for Class 2–8 municipalities. There are other permutations of municipal government, the result of special legislation—for example, the creation of a mayor-commission-manager form for Class 5 municipalities. Almost all municipalities operate under the mayor-council form. In Class 7 and 8 municipalities, the mayor and council jointly perform legislative functions, and the mayor generally does not have a veto.

Municipal incorporation requires a minimum population of 300. A petition for incorporation must be signed by not less than 15 percent of the qualified electors residing within the limits of the proposed city.[16] An unincorporated community lying within or partly within the boundaries of a county with a population of 600,000 or more can incorporate if certain conditions are met:

1. the territory proposed for incorporation has a total population of less than 1,000; or
2. the proposed incorporation is within three miles of a

    a. Class 1, 4, or 5 municipality, unless the incorporated population is 10,000 or more;

    b. Class 4 or 5 municipality, unless the population is 3,000 or more; or

    c. Class 6, 7, or 8 municipality, unless the population is 1,500 or more.

Any city may be annexed to and merged into a contiguous city or town. Both cities must adopt a resolution to appoint a consolidation commission, or a petition for annexation must be signed and presented by one-third of the qualified electors residing in each city. A six-member consolidation commission is created, and each mayor appoints two members. An election on the question of consolidation must be held and approved by a majority of the electors of each city.[17] (Constitutionally, there are no provisions for the initiative or referendum; only referendum-like procedures governing incorporation, annexation, and consolidation are available.)

Two cities or towns whose boundaries touch may consolidate and merge with a third that is not contiguous to either but whose boundary is within one mile or less of either city. A petition requesting a referendum on consolidation must be signed by 10 percent of the qualified voters in each of the municipalities. If the majority of the electors in each municipality favors consolidation, the municipalities and other territory are consolidated. The consolidated municipality has all the rights, powers, and duties conferred under general or special law. The municipal property of each consolidated municipality vests in the consolidated municipality.[18]

Municipalities in Alabama can annex property in four ways. Most annexations occur in Alabama through local acts. This legislative procedure does not require referendum or approval by the property owners. The second method requires the city council to pass a resolution in support of annexation. A certified copy of the resolution is given to the probate judge. Each qualified elector in the proposed area must appear before the judge and consent to the proposed annexation in writing. In absence of unanimous consent, an election is held; if the majority of electors favors annexation, and the owners of at least 60 percent of the property favor it, annexation can proceed.

The third method of annexation is through special statute and is available only to cities with populations of 25,000 or more. The electors residing in the area must vote on annexation; there is no provision for the consent of the landowners. The drawback to this method is that city tax is exempted for ten years, which precludes privilege licenses. The final method permits annexation where there is unanimous consent by all of the property owners in the annexed area. A referendum or petition is submitted to the governing body, which then votes on the proposal.

The designation of county government has varied over time, including "court of county commissioners," "board of revenues," "board of finance," and "commission of roads and bridges." Since 1970 the official name has been county commission.[19] Alabama counties have two basic types of governing bodies. In most counties, a commission chairman is either elected at large or selected by the other commissioners from among themselves. In a few counties, the probate judge sits as ex officio chairman of the commission. Most counties are divided into districts, and commissioners are elected from districts. In a small number of counties, commissioners are elected at large.

The size of the county commission ranges from three to seven members. State law sets the minimum salaries for commissioners and the commission chair. State law also sets a four-year term, but local legislation permits six-year terms in some coun-

ties. Other constitutionally elected officers at the county level include sheriff, probate judge, coroner, board of education, tax assessor, and tax collector.

Three urban counties in Alabama—St. Clair, Jefferson, and Mobile—have limited home rule powers enacted through special legislation. These are the most populous, urban counties in Alabama. The grant of home rule power is very limited but includes authorization to increase taxes. DeKalb County was granted home rule by the local legislative delegation, but the grant was rescinded following a dispute with the commission.

Changes in county boundaries may be made with a two-thirds vote of both houses of the Alabama legislature. The following conditions must also be met:

1. Every new county must contain at least 600 square miles of territory; existing counties cannot be reduced to less than 600 square miles.

2. The population must be large enough to entitle the county to one representative.

3. No county boundary within seven miles of an existing courthouse can be altered or created.

4. A majority of the electorate must approve the removal or change of any county seat.

5. No county seat may be changed or located by local legislation.

Functions of Local Government

There is a basic legal distinction between municipalities and counties in Alabama. A county is considered an involuntary association created as an arm of the state with responsibilities delegated by the state; counties have no corporate powers. A city is a voluntary association created by the community and its citizens. In Alabama, counties and cities have only those functions allowed by statute or special legislation. There is no uniform administrative structure or functional responsibilities for Alabama municipalities and counties. "No two cities or counties are governed entirely alike. While the [l]egislature governs local units by general legislation, there are hundreds of local acts passed at each regular legislative session . . . which makes generalizations hazardous and almost impossible."[20] At present, there is no consistent source that codifies constitutional amendments, local legislative acts, and local government ordinances and resolutions.

Functional Responsibilities

The powers and functions of local government are generally enumerated in the constitution rather than given under broad grant of authority. Functions are divided into government functions (such as law enforcement) and corporate functions (such as operation of a waterworks system). The power and authority to repair streets is considered a corporate function, whereas zoning is a government function. Constitutionally, municipal and county functions are separated.

Counties were established by the state to perform state functions, including collecting taxes, building roads, enforcing laws, and holding elections. State law also requires counties to provide buildings to house the state courts, sheriff, jail, and other county offices. The county commission is responsible for establishing precinct lines, designating polling places, and maintaining voting machines. Counties also assess and collect ad valorem taxes on property. Some county functions are administered for corresponding state departments, for example, pubic health and welfare. Although county officials frequently complain about unfunded state mandates, counties—as arms of the state government—receive significant amounts of state-shared revenues.

Additional functions have developed through local legislation and constitutional amendments that vary from county to county. County public works functions include solid waste disposal; operation of utilities, industrial parks, and airports; and provision of community development activities. Counties provide funds for the sheriff's office and jail, which is required under the constitution, as well as other public safety functions such as youth services, fire protection, ambulance, and 911 service. Public health functions include operation of the county board of health, county hospitals, libraries, parks and recreation, animal control, and public housing. Only Jefferson County has received legislative approval for land use and zoning under special act, but all counties have authority to review and approve subdivisions; only the largest counties are actively involved in this area.

Municipalities exercise similar governmental and corporate functions. Corporate functions include operating municipal utilities such as electricity, gas, water, and sewer services. Alabama cities can also operate transportation services, including bus lines and airports. As agents of the state, cities perform governmental functions such as fire protection, health and sanitation, taxation, and administration of justice and welfare. In both governmental and corporate functions, municipalities are legally under the direct control of the state legislature.

A municipal "police jurisdiction" extends three miles beyond the corporate limits for Class 1–7 cities and one and one-half miles for Class 8 cities. The planning jurisdiction extends for five miles. Municipalities can regulate businesses within their police jurisdiction (for example, slaughter house regulation). Within the police jurisdiction, a municipality can levy taxes at one-half the city rate, but the revenues must be used to pay for services within the jurisdiction. Alabama municipalities can own facilities (such as airports) beyond the city limits. Municipalities are required by state law to establish a planning commission and enforce planning, zoning, and subdivision regulations.

In addition to the 67 counties and 438 cities in Alabama, there are 487 special districts or public authorities that provide services such as housing and community development; soil and natural resource conservation; and utilities, airports, and other functions.[21] Local authorities and special districts are created almost entirely through local legislation and are financed through appropriations or fee-for-service arrangements. Municipalities do not need to create authorities or special districts for most city functions; most are created by counties. For example, cities provide water and sewer services under a municipal department, whereas counties must create a water authority. Municipal authorities typically include hospital authorities and industrial development authorities.

Most cities and counties in Alabama operate on a small scale. Cooperative ventures are one way in which both can join together to undertake a specific responsibility and divide up costs. There is regular cooperation between cities and counties on contracts for road paving. In addition, county personnel may perform contract work for cities in their jurisdiction.

Jail facilities are shared on a limited basis. A joint jail authority arrangement exists between Tuscaloosa County and the cities of Tuscaloosa and Northport. Municipalities also pay their county for the use of county jail space. Some cities and counties are building joint jail facilities under a contractual agreement that specifies responsibilities and the division of costs, such as that which exists between Mobile County and the City of Mobile.

Under the Alabama Solid Waste Management Act of 1989, each county is required to develop a solid waste management plan. Municipalities often join their county's plan, sharing costs on a per capita basis. Several counties and cities have cooperative agreements to collect data and operate a geographic information system (GIS). For example, the City of Huntsville, Hunts-ville Utilities, and Madison County operate a joint GIS system.

There are several examples of interlocal cooperation for tourism and industrial development. In 1991 the City of Huntsville and Madison County merged tourism development agencies. There are also several instances of joint city-county industrial authorities.

Administrative Discretion

There is no overriding authority in county government because of the number of constitutional elected officers, including sheriff, probate judge, coroner, tax assessor, tax collector, and members of the board of education. There is no provision in the Code of Alabama authorizing the county commission to oversee personnel functions. A unified personnel system is impossible when each constitutional officer seeks to maintain direct control over personnel. Analysis of court cases shows that counties have no authority over the sheriff's department, even if the county has a personnel board, which is typical in larger municipalities. Administrative discretion for municipalities and counties is limited to establishing processes for purchasing, budgeting, and other administrative procedures. Personnel, supplies, and equipment are a substantial part of local government expenditures. Statewide cooperative retirement and health insurance programs are available to local government employees.

All school systems participate in the Teachers' Retirement System of Alabama, and many counties, municipalities, and special districts elect to participate. Under a 1991 law, municipalities and certain special districts can elect to have employees, officers, and retirees covered under the State Employees' Insurance Board. State-local cooperative mechanisms also include local government purchasing through a division of the state Department of Finance.

Before 1972, public employee membership in labor unions was prohibited by the Solomon Act. Any public employee who joined a labor union lost all rights under the state merit system, including employment rights. The Solomon Act was declared unconstitutional in 1972. Firefighters have received a statutory right to join a union, and teachers are also granted some statutory rights. Alabama has a "right to work" law that prohibits both public and private employers from requiring employees to join a labor union or refrain from joining, but there are no statutes covering collective bargaining rights of public employees. Public employees do not have the right to strike or withhold services from their employer.

Municipal and county land-use policies, housing, and economic development activities are governed by the constitution. Alabama's municipalities have been permitted to form planning commissions and engage in land-use regulation since 1935. Counties generally do not have land-use regulation powers. Municipalities have had authority to adopt building codes since 1969. Counties with over 30,000 population can adopt building codes after publication of intent in a county newspaper for four weeks and notice at the county court house.

Economic Development

Under the 1901 constitution, municipalities and counties were prohibited from lending credit or money to any individual, association, or stockholder. Most counties and municipalities have since received authority through special legislation to

1. acquire real property;
2. sell, lease, or give away such property;
3. promote industrial, commercial, and agricultural development;
4. become a stockholder in corporations;
5. lend credit and grant public monies;
6. sell bonds to acquire property;
7. levy a special tax to pay indebtedness; and
8. create a public corporation (namely an industrial development authority) for the above purposes.

Local authorities are created almost entirely through local legislation. Counties create most local authorities to carry out functions not authorized by general or special legislation. Authorities and special districts include hospital authorities, airport authorities, electrical and water authorities and boards, civic center authorities, water conservation corporations, development authorities, municipal utility boards, soil and water conservation districts, water management districts, boards of health, and taxing and assessment districts.

Special districts are created at the local level when there is a general act providing that authority. Municipalities do not need to create special districts for most functions. For example, cities provide water service under a municipal department, whereas counties must create a water authority.

Fiscal Autonomy of Local Governments

Local Revenues

Local government revenues are divided into (1) general revenues and (2) utility, liquor store, and employee retirement system revenues. Liquor store and retirement system revenues are marginal sources of revenue for Alabama municipal and county governments. General revenues include intergovernmental revenues and own-source revenues. Intergovernmental revenues are received from the federal, state, and other local governments. State-shared revenues include state-collected gasoline tax, wine and beer taxes, and motor vehicle license tag fees. Own-source revenues include the general property tax, general and selective sales taxes, income tax, privilege licenses, and user fees and assessments.

Privilege licenses are levied for conducting a business, profession, or occupation; "occupational licenses" are a flat income tax levied by municipalities on all persons working in the city. User fees are charges for services such as garbage collection, building inspection, and utility usage. Assessments and fines are nontax sources of revenue.

Alabama's constitution allows a maximum county tax rate of 24.1 mills, allocated to roads, bridges, and public highways; public schools; hospitals; and libraries, among other purposes.[22] A maximum municipal property tax rate of 13 mills is set for general and library purposes.[23] Constitutional amendments applicable to specific counties and classes of municipalities permit property taxes to be levied in excess of the generally prescribed limits.

The adoption of constitutional Amendment 373 in 1978, the so-called Lid Bill, restricted the ability of local governments to raise taxes. To raise or decrease taxes, the local governing body must take three steps: (1) the proposal must be presented at a public hearing; (2) it must be approved by an act of the legislature; and (3) a special election must be held in the local jurisdiction, and the issue must be approved by a majority of the voters.

Counties normally are limited in their indebtedness to 5 percent of assessed property value, and cities are limited to 20 percent; local legislation permits numerous exceptions. Local governments enter into long-term debt with three types of instruments: general-obligation bonds, revenue bonds, and warrants. General-obligation bonds must be authorized by a majority vote of the municipality or county electorate. Section 104 of the constitution prohibits the state legislature from enacting special legislation to avoid this requirement. Unlike general-obligation bonds, revenue bonds are not counted against constitutional debt limits and do not require public approval. Warrants can be used for any general purpose of government; they are counted against the legal debt limit but do not require public approval. Warrants are issued in anticipation of revenue and constitute "an order to pay when in funds." To avoid the constitutional debt limit, many jurisdictions have formed special boards or authorities that can borrow without having the liability count against the city or county.[24] Most revenue bonds are issued by special boards and authorities.

Municipalities and counties must depend on local legislation to increase tax limits. There are approximately 100 local constitutional amendments that authorize counties to raise property taxes. Municipalities have no cap on locally authorized sales, business, and tobacco taxes; they can tax general sources without state approval. The only general authority that counties have to increase taxes without state approval is the sales tax dedicated to education.

All municipalities are authorized a 5 mill tax on real and personal properties based on the assessed value for state and county taxation. No referendum is required for this tax. Municipalities may impose ad valorem taxes up to 12.5 mills if the amount over 5 mills is authorized in a special referendum.

There are four classes of property in Alabama, each subject to state limitations on assessments. Class I property covers utility-owned property, and assessment is limited to 30 percent of fair market value. Class II includes general business, industry, personal and undeveloped property, and property not specifically enumerated in the other classes. Assessment is limited to 20 percent of fair market value. Class III includes agricultural forest, residential property, and historic sites; assessment is limited to 10 percent of fair market value. Class IV includes private automobiles and trucks; assessment is limited to 15 percent of fair market value. Most municipalities and counties collect sales and gross receipts license taxes through the state Department of Revenue. Local governments also employ selective sales taxes, or levies on specific commodities or services. Often called excise taxes, selective sales taxes include taxes on alcoholic beverages, tobacco products, public utilities, and motor fuels.

On average, more than 60 percent of municipal revenues are derived from a combination of utility revenues, general sales taxes and fees, and licenses and assessments (see Figure 1).[25] Property taxes are a small portion of total revenues (approximately 5 percent). Municipalities in Alabama are not dependent

Fig. 1 Municipal Government Revenues in Alabama, 1991–1992

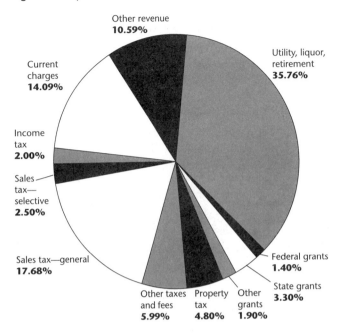

Source: U.S. Department of Commerce, Economics and Statistics Administration, Bureau of the Census, *Census of Governments,* vol. 4 (Washington, D.C.: U.S. Government Printing Office, 1995), table 5.

Fig. 2 County Government Revenues in Alabama, 1991–1992

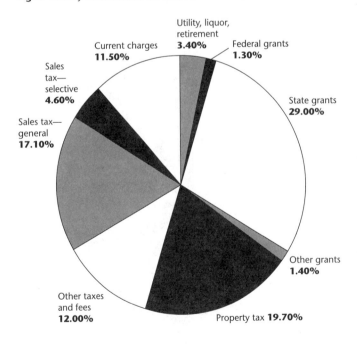

Source: U.S. Department of Commerce, Economics and Statistics Administration, Bureau of the Census, *Census of Governments,* vol. 3 (Washington, D.C.: U.S. Government Printing Office, 1995), table 4.

on federal or state grants-in-aid to the extent that Alabama counties are.

As arms of the state, Alabama counties are heavily dependent on state intergovernmental revenue. Almost 30 percent of total county revenues comprise state intergovernmental revenues and grants (see Figure 2). Like municipalities, counties depend on the general sales tax; unlike municipalities, however, counties derive a large portion of total revenues (nearly 20 percent) from the property tax.[26]

Local Expenditures

On average, utilities, environment and housing, and public safety functions constitute approximately 60 percent of total municipal expenditures (see Figure 3). Most municipal expenditures are for utility construction and operations, followed by environment and housing, which includes sewerage and solid waste, parks and recreation, and housing and community development.[27]

Transportation (primarily roads and bridges), social services (including welfare and public health), and public safety account for nearly 60 percent of total county expenditures (see Figure 4).[28] Counties spend considerably less than municipalities do on environment (including sewerage and solid waste) and housing functions as a proportion of total expenditures. Proportionately more is spent for government administration in counties than in

Fig. 3 Municipal Government Expenditures in Alabama, 1991–1992

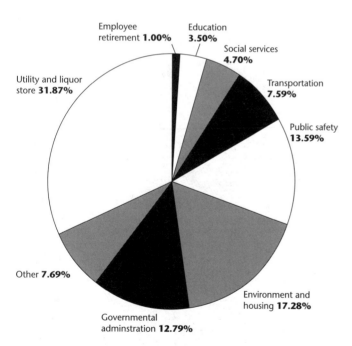

Source: U.S. Department of Commerce, Economics and Statistics Administration, Bureau of the Census, *Census of Governments,* vol. 4 (Washington, D.C.: U.S. Government Printing Office, 1995), table 9.

Fig. 4 County Government Expenditures in Alabama, 1991–1992

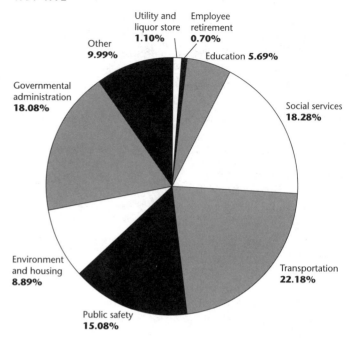

Source: U.S. Department of Commerce, Economics and Statistics Administration, Bureau of the Census, *Census of Governments,* vol 4 (Washington, D.C.: U.S. Government Printing Office, 1995), table 8.

municipalities. Counties are responsible for a broad range of state-related administrative services such as welfare, public health, tax collection, and elections.

In 1919 the state legislature adopted a law requiring a county budget system. When this law proved unworkable, the legislature enacted the County Financial Control Act of 1935, which is the basis for county budgeting operations. The act requires counties to prepare and adopt estimates of income, expenditures, and appropriate funds for certain purposes. The act prohibits appropriations in excess of income, a balanced budget requirement.

Counties are required to publish a statement of receipts, expenditures, and indebtedness semiannually, and county records are reviewed by the state Department of Examiners of Public Accounts. A 1939 act requires each county and municipality to submit a copy of its budget to the finance department, along with a statement of financial condition. However, the department has no power to revise or reject local budgets. Municipalities are required to have an annual audit by an outside auditor and to pass a balanced budget.

The constitution does not prohibit municipalities or counties from declaring bankruptcy. No cities have declared bankruptcy since Reconstruction. Greene County, in September 1996, became the first county in Alabama history to file for bankruptcy, following two audits by state examiners showing $1.76 million in unpaid debts and back taxes. A bankruptcy judge gave Greene County four months to develop a plan to pay the debts. In October 1996, after noting that the county owed more than $500,000 in unpaid taxes, the Internal Revenue Service placed a lien on its checking account. The county commission chairman and a county aide were indicted on theft and ethics charges. A citizen's group sued the Greene County commission, seeking to force the bankrupt county to return $1.7 in misappropriated funds to taxpayers.[29]

State Government Grants-in-Aid to Localities

Alabama imposes more taxes than it allocates for current state services; these revenues are used to pay for local services. There are several state-shared revenues, the largest being the state gasoline tax. There is a separate seven-cent and four-cent gasoline tax. Other state-shared taxes include state sales tax, corporate franchise tax, excise tax on financial institutions, state inspection fees on motor fuels and motor oil, motor vehicle licenses tax and title fees, state alcoholic beverage commission (ABC) profits, table wine tax, uniform beer tax, tax on state ABC sales, privilege tax on oil and gas production, coal severance tax, and interest on the Alabama Trust Fund. Most of these revenues are earmarked at the state level. Counties depend more heavily on state resources than do municipalities.

Alabama has the most extensive earmarking of governmental revenues among the fifty states.[30] Nearly 90 percent of Alabama's tax revenues are earmarked by the state.[31] All of the state income tax goes to education; education and highways account for about 90 percent of the state's allocated tax revenues.

Unfunded Mandates

State mandates are commonly defined as constitutional, statutory, or administrative actions that either limit or put requirements on local governments. Mandates can effectively impede home rule powers of local governments. The constitution does not grant general governing authority but does impose heavy mandates and restrictions on local governments. Some mandates have been amended through general and local legislation. The result is not greater local independence but a greater reliance on the state legislature to solve the problems of local government.

According to the statutes, the state legislative fiscal office is required to estimate the fiscal effect of any general bill that "creates, eliminates or affects a state or local program, service, function or revenue source and which requires the expenditure of county or municipal funds, or decreases or increases revenue collections by any county or municipality." This estimate is attached to the bill before a vote takes place.

Counties are more constrained than municipalities are in raising revenues to fund mandates. Consequently, counties tend to oppose state mandates vigorously, even though they receive significant state revenues to carry out their functions.

Access to Local Government

Local Elections

Voter registration is handled by county boards of registrars. State law prohibits voter registration within ten days of an election, except in counties with more than 60,000 population.

Citizen Controls over Actions of Local Officials

County commissioners may be removed from office only by impeachment, which may be legislative or judicial in character. Where the probate judge serves as commission chairman, the state Judicial Inquiry Commission directs impeachment proceedings.

More generally, the state constitution has no provisions for the initiative or referendum, though there are initiative- and referendum-like procedures governing incorporation, annexation, and consolidation. For example, in annexation, electors petition the city requesting annexation; the city must then vote on the request. In consolidation, a petition may be submitted requesting consolidation; the electorates of both cities then vote on the proposal.

All meetings of county commissions and municipal governing boards are required by law to be open to the public. The only exception is a meeting in which the good name or character of a person is discussed.

State-Local Relations

Alabama's municipalities and counties are not likely to receive home rule powers soon. Yet the state is badly in need of an effective means of shoring up local government authority. One more amendment to the constitution is not the answer. Until the constitution is thoroughly revised or a new one written through constitutional convention, local governments are at the mercy of state legislatures for authority not provided under general law. Several reforms are necessary:

• Establish home rule for cities and an integrated county government structure and centralized administrative authority for counties, at a minimum.
• Expand local tax discretion, especially for counties.
• Eliminate state sales tax exemptions to reduce tax expenditures, increase revenues, and make the system easier to understand, administer, and enforce.
• Permit counties to levy an income tax—an authority already granted to municipalities.

Alabama's counties and municipalities are led by dedicated men and women working in an environment of fiscal constraint, zealous legislative oversight and control, and growing expectations of citizens. However, the constitution and basic laws governing cities and counties are nearly a century old, and Alabama's local governments are stuck in the past. Although the demands on local government have changed dramatically since adoption of the 1901 constitution, the capacity of local government to respond to those demands has not changed.

Notes

1. Daniel J. Elazar, "Introduction," in *Alabama Government and Politics,* ed. James D. Thomas and William H. Stewart (Lincoln: University of Nebraska Press, 1988), xx.

2. Adam Cohen, "Governor with a Mission," *Time,* 4 September 1995; "Alabama Governor Fights Prayer Ruling," *ACLU News,* 6 February 1997.

3. "Black Belt" refers to the rich loamy soil that attracted planters and supported development of a plantation economy in the South. Today, the term often comprises the nonmetropolitan counties with 30 percent or more black population that stretch across ten southern states, from Virginia through Tennessee and the Carolinas, across Georgia, Florida, Alabama, Mississippi, Louisiana, and Arkansas.

4. Anne Permaloff and Carl Grafton, *Political Power in Alabama: The More Things Change . . .* (Athens: University of Georgia Press, 1995).

5. *Statistical Abstract of the United States* (Washington, D.C.: U.S. Department of Commerce, 1997), tables 722, 741, 604, 126, 98.

6. Charles J. Spindler, "Education in Alabama," *Public Sector* 15, no. 1 (June 1993): 1–8.

7. *Statistical Abstract of the United States,* table 247.

8. *Statistical Abstract of the United States,* table 34.

9. Rodney L. Mott, *Home Rule for America's Cities* (Chicago: American Municipal Association, 1949), 1.

10. John F. Dillon, *Commentaries on the Law of Municipal Corporations,* 5th ed. (Boston: J. Cockroft, 1911), 448.

11. *Mobile v. Mobile etc. R. Co.,* 38 So. 127.

12. Thomas and Stewart, eds. *Alabama Government and Politics,* 150.

13. Albert P. Brewer and Charles D. Cole, *Brewer and Cole: Alabama Constitutional Law* (Birmingham, Ala.: Samford University, 1992), viii.

14. Thomas and Stewart, eds. *Alabama Government and Politics,* 147.

15. *Peddycoat v. City of Birmingham* 354 So. 2d 808, 814 (1978).

16. Alabama Statute, section 11-41-1.

17. Alabama Statute, section 11-42-120.

18. Alabama Statute, section 11-42-150.

19. Alabama Constitution, amendment 375.

20. William V. Holloway and Charles W. Smith Jr., *Government and Politics in Alabama* (University, Ala.: University Supply Store, 1942), 131.

21. *Statistical Abstract of the United States,* table 475.

22. Alabama Constitution, sections 215, 269 (as amended by amendment 11); amendments 3, 59, 72, 202, 269.

23. Alabama Constitution, amendments 216, 56, 269.

24. David L. Martin, *Alabama's State and Local Governments,* 2d. ed. (University, Ala.: University of Alabama Press, 1985), 207.

25. U.S. Department of Commerce, Economics and Statistics Administration, Bureau of the Census, *Census of Governments (1992),* vol. 4 (Washington, D.C.: U.S. Government Printing Office, 1995), table 5.

26. U.S. Department of Commerce, Economics and Statistics Administration, Bureau of the Census, *Census of Governments (1992),* vol. 3 (Washington, D.C.: U.S. Government Printing Office, 1995), table 4.

27. U.S. Department of Commerce, Economics and Statistics Administration, Bureau of the Census, *Census of Governments (1992),* vol. 4, table 9.

28. U.S. Department of Commerce, Economics and Statistics Administration, Bureau of the Census, *Census of Governments (1992),* vol. 3, table 8.

29. Bill Pryon, Alabama Attorney General (press release, 24 October 1997); Gita M. Smith, "Alabama County Leaders Charged with Election Fraud," *Atlanta Constitution,* 31 January 1997, C-1.

30. Public Affairs Research Council of Alabama (PARCA), "How Alabama's Taxes Compare," *PARCA Report* 37 (summer 1999): 3.

31. Martha A. Fabricus and Ronald K. Snell, *Earmarking State Taxes,* 2d ed. (Denver: National Conference of State Legislatures, 1990), 38–39 (table 6).

ALASKA

Clive S. Thomas, Anthony T. Nakazawa, and Carl E. Shepro

Local governments in Alaska have two distinctive characteristics: simplicity and degree of formal local autonomy. Municipalities spring from one uniform local government concept, which takes either a regional form called a borough or the city. The state constitution grants boroughs and first-class cities authority to adopt home rule powers.

There are two blemishes on this image of local control, however. First, approximately 60 percent of the land in Alaska and approximately 90 small rural Alaska Native villages are outside the jurisdiction of any municipality. Some claim inherent local autonomy (sovereignty) based on "Indian Country," but the state refuses to recognize their legitimacy and has challenged them before the U.S. courts.[1] Second, local governments rely on state revenues derived from oil development for operating and capital construction costs. This dependence remains even though the revenues have declined.[2] Thus, local control in Alaska depends on political considerations, especially at the state level, despite the strong constitutional provisions.

Governmental Setting

Alaska, the largest state in the union geographically, is the second smallest in population, with approximately 650,000 people. Natural boundaries divide the state into regions, effectively isolating the regions (and most communities within them) from one another. Juneau, the state capital located in the southeast region, is accessible to most Alaskans only by air, although the Alaska Marine Highway (ferry system) serves the region.

Alaska appears to be a two-party competitive state in gubernatorial elections, with emerging Republican domination of the legislature. However, partisan identification is excessively weak, due in part to demographic changes since the oil boom. The demographic changes reflect Alaska's economic dependence on natural resource extraction, especially oil, since the 1970s. One authority estimates an annual population turnover of approximately 25 percent.[3] The result is strong interest group participation in Alaska politics—especially on the part of the petroleum industry.

The political culture of Alaska is individualistic; government is viewed as a business whose major role is to maintain the operation of the marketplace,[4] and political pragmatism is seen to dominate. Alaska has also been characterized as a frontier[5] political culture, where "can do" attitudes prevail. Major interest groups are encouraged to operate to their best advantage. Although petroleum interests currently exercise significant influence, historically fishing, gold mining, and timber interests have

dominated at various times. In addition to the Alaska Municipal League, National Education Association–Alaska, and Alaska Public Employee's Union,[6] environmental groups such as the Sierra Club have had a significant presence, and the "Christian right" has exerted influence on the current Republican-led legislature.[7]

Alaska governments have been influenced by Alaska's long colonial and territorial history (1867–1959), resulting in strong anti–federal government sentiment, anti–absentee owner attitudes, and a perception that provisions for strong state and local government would be necessary for the U.S. Congress to support statehood. The influence of Progressive reform politics is equally apparent. For example, the design of the state legislature incorporated the latest theories about strong, professional legislative government: small size (a forty-member House of Representatives and twenty-member senate), uniform rules, annual sessions with no time limits, requirements for joint sessions, and generous legislative pay. The executive branch was similarly designed. It featured a single executive (governor and lieutenant governor running as a team) and gubernatorial powers, including but not limited to appointment and removal of all agency heads, ability to reorganize the executive branch, and veto powers.[8] The judicial branch featured a unified judicial system, with all courts under the direction of the state supreme court, no local courts, and use of a modified Missouri plan of judicial selection and retention.

Other Progressive influences include requirements for calling a constitutional convention every ten years and provisions for the initiative (with limitations on legitimate subjects), referendum, and recall. Unique to the constitution is the Natural Resource Article, requiring that natural resources be reserved for use by all residents of the state. This article is the source of the current conflict among the State of Alaska, Alaska Native groups, and the federal government concerning the subsistence provision in the Alaska National Interests Land Conservation Act (ANILCA).

Finally, a congressional prohibition against counties during the territorial period (from 1912 until statehood in 1959) enabled some innovation in local government. All forms of special districts and special-purpose governments were eliminated, and the uniform local government concept was substituted, allowing only two basic forms of municipality: the borough and the city. An incorporated borough had mandatory powers of education, taxation, and planning and zoning. If no organized borough existed, first-class cities had those mandatory powers. School districts were fiscally subordinate to the legislative body of the municipality, and the state had the responsibility of providing education when no borough or first-class city existed.[9]

The entire state was to be divided into boroughs, but only sixteen predominately urban boroughs have been formed, leaving a large part of the state without the regional form of municipal government. In addition, many Alaska Native villages did not incorporate, and some that did have dissolved their municipal governments. Thus, local government services in much of the state are provided by a "complex nonsystem of governments"[10] made up of federally recognized "Indian" councils, state-chartered business corporations mandated by the Alaska Native Claims Settlement Act (ANCSA), and a variety of state and federal government agencies.

Home Rule in Alaska

Historical Development

Development of home rule was strongly influenced by the state's colonial history and by a perceived need to demonstrate to the U.S. Congress that Alaskans were not afraid of strong government. Alaska had little experience with local government during the colonial period, and the army and navy were the only "government" until passage of the First Organic Act in 1884. This act did not provide for local control but extended the mining laws of the Oregon Territory to Alaska, which made Alaska a mining district, not a territory. Permanent settlers in Sitka, then the capital, attempted to create local government, but these "Sitka experiments" were failures. Congress only made provisions for local government in the early 1900s, allowing incorporation of second-class cities with populations over 300 and severely limiting their taxing authorities. The dual system of education—where non-Native children were educated in territori-

al schools supported by local tax dollars and Alaska Native children attended federal Bureau of Education day schools—was also established at this time. The Second Organic Act of 1912 conferred territorial status on Alaska, enabling formation of a small territorial legislature with significant limitations; for example, all acts of the legislature were subject to congressional veto. It also featured a presidentially appointed governor and a prohibition against counties that protected owners of resource extractive industries from local taxation. These factors significantly influenced the development of home rule in the new state.[11]

Definition of Home Rule

The Alaska Constitution contains a broad grant of home rule power unusual among state constitutions.[12] The key provisions are "a liberal construction shall be given to the powers of local government units" and "[a] home rule borough or city may exercise all legislative powers not prohibited by law or by charter."[13] Consequently, any borough or first-class city may form a home rule government.[14] The constitutional phrase "[a] liberal construction shall be given to the powers of local government units" gives municipalities the benefit of the doubt in disputes with the legislature over their power to act.[15] Further, the constitution states that all local government powers are vested in boroughs and cities; the state's ability to delegate taxing powers beyond those units is restricted. Finally, the broad grant of power to home rule municipalities contained in section 11 was intended to make home rule powers as expansive as possible. A major provision in the constitution prohibits the adoption of local or special-privilege legislation.

Structural Features

No structures existed to influence the delegates writing about local government at the constitutional convention in 1955. Rather than adopt a traditional county structure, the delegates opted for one they believed would provide maximum local self-government with a minimum of local government units—that is, the uniform local government concept that provides for two forms, the regional and dominant borough and the city. There are three classes of boroughs and cities: home rule, first-class, and second-class. Although the state legislature passed a 1968 act allowing the incorporation of Haines as a third-class borough, it abolished the act in 1985, leaving Haines the only such government. Three areas have adopted charters that dissolved all city structures within their borders, creating unified home rule municipalities.

Formation of boroughs is required by the constitution.[16] All organized boroughs[17] are constitutionally required to perform three areawide powers: education, planning and zoning, and taxation, with the exception of Haines Borough, which is not required to provide planning and zoning. The addition of other borough-wide powers depends on the classification of borough.

Table 1. Comparison Summary of Boroughs in Alaska

Characteristic	Type of borough			
	Second class[a]	First class[b]	Home rule[c]	Unified home rule[d]
Home rule upgrade possible?	Yes	Yes	Not applicable	Not applicable
Mandatory areawide powers	Tax assessment and collection, education, planning, and land-use control	Tax assessment and collection, education, planning, and land-use control	Tax assessment and collection, education, planning, and land-use control	Tax assessment and collection, education, planning, and land-use control
Addition of areawide powers	Transfer by all cities or by areawide referendum	Transfer by all cities or by areawide referendum; transportation systems, pollution control, day care licensing, and animal control may be assumed by ordinance	Charter provision	Charter provision
Non-areawide powers	None mandatory; can add by transfer by a city or limited powers may be assumed by ordinance; remainder of powers requires a referendum vote of residents outside city limits	None mandatory; may assume any non-areawide powers by ordinance	Charter provision	Charter provision
Service areas	Established, operated, altered, or abolished by Assembly; exercise of power requires a referendum vote of service area residents	Established, operated, altered, or abolished by Assembly; exercise of power by Assembly ordinance	Established, operated, altered, or abolished by Assembly; exercise of power by charter	Established, operated, altered, or abolished by Assembly; exercise of power by charter
Borough executive	Mayor, with veto power	Mayor, with veto power	Mayor, with veto power	Mayor, with veto power
Legislative body	Assembly	Assembly	Assembly	Assembly
Education body	School board	School board	School board	School board

Note: Population is not a factor in determining the classification of a borough. The major unstated requirement is that there be a revenue base to support the mandated powers of education, planning and zoning, and taxation.

a. Addition of any areawide or non-areawide powers requires a referendum vote by the citizens. If a non-areawide power is being added—and this is not done by a transfer of powers from a city to the borough—the residents outside the city must approve the adoption of new powers. Service areas are established by the Assembly upon referendum vote by affected residents. Cities within the borough retain their jurisdiction and identity. This is the most "democratic" of the borough levels, because the Assembly cannot add powers unilaterally. Most of the original nine boroughs adopted a second-class status upon their incorporation to restrain the power of this new level of government.

b. Adoption of new powers does not require a referendum vote, but any new powers may be assumed by Assembly ordinance. Service areas are established by the Assembly through ordinance. Cities within the borough remain separate in terms of jurisdiction and identity.

c. Adoption of new powers is by charter provision. Service areas are established by the Assembly through charter revision. Cities within the borough retain their jurisdiction and identity.

d. All powers are exercised by the borough; all local jurisdictions under the borough are dissolved, and their powers are assumed by the borough. All powers are exercised by the Assembly by charter provision. Adoption of this, the highest form of borough government, usually is accomplished to "streamline" government at the local level.

Table 2. First- and Second-Class City Powers in Alaska

Powers	First class	Second class
Education[a]	Mandatory	Not allowed
Planning, platting, land use[b]	Mandatory	Optional
Property tax limits	30 mills	20 mills (with voter OK)
City council	6 members	7 members
Mayoral election and term	At large, 3 years	By council, 1 year
Mayoral eligibility for office	Any voter	City council member
Mayoral powers	Votes in tie	Votes in all matters
Mayoral veto power	Yes	No
Power of eminent domain	Statutory procedure	Ratified by voters
Home rule	May adopt charter	May not adopt charter[c]

a. For cities in the Unorganized Borough only.

b. For cities in the Unorganized Borough only. Home rule, first-class, and second-class cities within an organized borough may be delegated planning, platting, and land-use powers by the borough.

c. Second-class cities with populations of at least 3,500 that exceed thirty-five square miles in area may adopt a home rule charter.

Home rule boroughs must have provisions in, or amend, their charters, whereas second-class boroughs must conduct an areawide referendum to add a power. First-class boroughs may add some areawide powers by ordinance; others require a referendum. Services that are not areawide may be provided when residents desiring the service form a "service area." Members of the service area agree to pay an increase in borough taxes, and the borough pays the service provider's fees. Most service areas in Alaska are volunteer fire departments outside cities and road maintenance areas.

Mayors are the chief executives of boroughs, and most exercise veto power. The legislative body is the Assembly. The school district and its elected board do not qualify as special districts because they are fiscally accountable to the Assembly. Boroughs vary with regard to structure (see Table 1). Thus, on the one hand, one finds "weak" mayor, council-manager forms with five-member assemblies elected at large (for example, the second-class Bristol Bay Borough) and on the other, "strong" mayor forms with an eleven-member assembly elected by district (for example, the unified home rule municipality of Anchorage).

Home rule cities in Alaska are also required to adopt a charter governing the city. The best-known home rule city in the Unorganized Borough is Valdez, the terminus of the Aleyska Pipeline bringing oil from Prudhoe Bay for shipment to the contiguous states. In the Unorganized Borough, Valdez is required to perform the education, planning and zoning, and taxing functions. In comparison, Fairbanks, as a home rule city in the Fairbanks North Star Borough, is not required to provide education or planning and zoning. The borough, as the superior form of government, must do so.

The powers exercised by a first-class city are similarly dependent on location: if it is outside an organized borough, it is required to provide for education and planning and zoning and to tax its residents to pay for the services. If the city is located within an organized borough, the powers of education and planning and zoning are exercised by the borough. Second-class cities, regardless of their location, do not exercise education powers.

First-class cities are governed by an elected "strong" mayor and a six-member city council (see Table 2). Second-class cities have a "weak" mayor–council system: the seven-member city council is elected and then selects one of its number as mayor. Second-class cities are required to have a city manager, or, if this position is beyond budgetary capabilities, the city clerk acts as the city administrator.[18]

Property taxes in first-class cities are limited to 30 mills and do not require voter approval. In second-class cities, property taxes are limited to 20 mills, with voter approval required to implement. Planning and zoning are mandatory for first-class cities outside organized boroughs but are optional for second-class cities in the same areas. The processes of incorporation, expansion, annexation, and/or dissolution of municipalities are controlled by the state through a constitutionally mandated Local Boundary Commission. Recommendations by the commission are subject to a legislative veto.[19]

Functions of Local Government

Functional Responsibilities

All local government functions and tasks in Alaska are performed either by the borough or the city. However, actions by the legislative and executive branches have imposed effective limits on the exercise of that power. Although the constitution makes the state responsible for establishing and maintaining a system of public schools for all children, education remains a local power in Alaska. Organized boroughs, regardless of classification, have the mandatory power of education, and the school district is subordinate to the borough. First-class cities located outside an organized borough also have the mandatory power of education. In both instances, local governments must tax their citizens in order to pay part of the costs of education. In the case of second-class cities outside organized boroughs, the state legislature established regional education attendance areas (REAAs) in the mid-1970s to provide for education.[20] Because of the lack of a tax base in most of rural Alaska, REAAs have been supported entirely by state funds; each REAA is accountable to the legislature for the use of the funds.

The judiciary in Alaska is part of state government; no local courts exist. Similarly, the Alaska Department of Corrections is in charge of the entire penal system, with local jails functioning only as holding facilities. The constitution vests the responsibility for public health and public welfare with the state, in two brief sections of Article VII.

In addition to the mandatory powers of education, taxation and planning, and zoning, incorporated boroughs can assume a variety of functions, ranging from the seventeen performed by the North Slope Borough to the minimum required functions performed by the third-class Haines Borough.[21]

The creation of special districts is specifically prohibited, and all that existed at statehood were to be integrated with boroughs and/or cities. Interlocal cooperation between cities and boroughs is addressed by the constitution, which provides a mechanism to avoid the conflict and jurisdictional rivalry that exists under the inefficiency and rigidity of municipal governments elsewhere.[22] Intergovernmental cooperation has also taken the form of participation by municipalities in the Alaska Municipal League to advance their interests in the legislative process. Regional associations of mayors, city managers, school boards, city clerks, and others are examples of intergovernmental cooperation.

Administrative Discretion

Municipal public employees are covered under the provisions of the Public Employee Retirement System (PERS), and teachers in the local school districts and the University of Alaska participate in the Teachers Retirement System (TRS). In addition, merit systems are required of local governments. Local governments negotiate labor contracts separately with the public employee unions. State law governs administrative procedures at all levels of government in Alaska, although municipalities and other government entities such as the University of Alaska can exempt themselves from these procedures.

Economic Development

Development activities are mandated by Article VIII of the constitution, the Natural Resources Article, which states in part that "it is the policy of the State to encourage the settlement of its land and the development of its resources by making them available for maximum use consistent with the public interest."[23] Local governments have little option but to seek development as a means of financing local improvements. The Mandatory Borough Act of 1963 encouraged development by "permit[ting] or-

ganized boroughs to select 10 percent of the vacant, unappropriated, and unreserved state lands located within their boundaries."[24] These lands have been used by predominantly urban boroughs to provide incentives for the development of privately built and financed housing subdivisions and for the construction of office, retail space, and multiple family buildings. They are also used in exchange for private lands in order to construct public facilities. Municipalities may establish development authorities within their boundaries to finance and provide direction for economic development if they so desire.

The state plays a role in local development activities in at least two major ways. First, because special districts are prohibited, airports in Alaska are state facilities. Although local jurisdictions do participate in planning and development decisions, the state has ultimate decision-making authority. Second, a state entity, the Alaska Economic and Industrial Development Corporation (AEIDC), exercises a great deal of influence over development activities by virtue of its ability to grant or withhold monies from individual projects.

Fiscal Autonomy of Local Governments

Local Revenues

In addition to state and federal transfers, local governments in Alaska have two major revenue sources: property and sales taxes. Alaska statutes limit local property taxes that fund the operating expenses of government to 30 mills, but there is no limit for revenues used to repay bonded indebtedness.[25] The constitution prohibits local governments from contracting debt, "unless authorized for capital improvements by its governing body and ratified by a majority vote of those qualified to vote and voting on the question."[26] There is no limitation on the amount of debt a municipality can contract. The 30-mill limit is not a ceiling imposed by the constitution, as is the case in many states. Instead this is a legislative limit, initiated in 1972 in an attempt to keep the newly created North Slope Borough from imposing high property taxes on the oil industry. Because special privilege legislation is constitutionally prohibited, the limit applies to all municipalities.

Although all general obligation bonds must be approved by a vote of the people in a municipality, home rule and first-class municipalities may issue revenue bonds that do not require an election. However, these municipalities have the option of amending their charters or ordinances, respectively, to insert such a requirement.[27] They may also establish tax and spending limitations, both of which have been adopted by the unified home rule municipality of Anchorage. Approved by the voters in 1983, taxes (other than those for debt service) are limited to the amount levied in the previous year and are increased or decreased by a complex formula.[28]

Because most municipalities have relied on state revenues

generated by North Slope oil, few currently levy taxes at the maximum levels allowed by statutes or charters. The largest Alaska municipality in terms of population, Anchorage, levies a property tax but because of citizen resistance has yet to implement a sales tax. In contrast, the largest municipal government in the United States in terms of area, the North Slope Borough, levies both a property and a sales tax. The borough also has the largest bonded indebtedness in the state because of its large and ongoing capital construction program. Most of the smaller urban municipalities are located between these two in terms of reliance on local taxes. In the Unorganized Borough, where employment opportunities are scarce, many live a subsistence lifestyle, and the tax base is almost nonexistent.

Property and sales taxes are seldom used, except by first-class cities. Most communities rely on state revenue sharing and safe community funding (formerly municipal assistance) revenues provided by the state. In fiscal 1995 the latter program provided approximately $34 million and the former, $28 million to Alaska local governments. These figures are down significantly from the peak years of the early 1980s, but the programs still provide an important source of revenues for small rural communities. Anchorage's portion of local revenues relative to other sources was 87 percent during this period;[29] that for the North Slope Borough and the City of Valdez—the two highest-spending municipalities in the state—was even higher.

Local Expenditures

The largest local government expenditures in Alaska are for public services, especially education. Because of the inequities in tax base between rural, predominantly Alaska Native villages and urban, predominantly non-Native municipalities and the absence of boroughs and/or first-class cities, the state provides 100 percent of the funding for the regional education attendance areas that serve rural communities. State funding for all school districts is set in the foundation funding formula, which provides an amount to each school site based on a complicated formula involving student population, the location of the school, value of assessed property, and other factors.

Although support for the minimum levels of education is provided to all schools, rural districts receive larger payments than do urban ones. Urban districts collect local contributions to enable delivery of programs above this minimum. Some urban residents are dissatisfied with the system, and there have been court challenges based on perceived inequities in education expenditures. The courts have upheld the funding system, but the legislature has considered bills that require REAAs to impose a 4.5-mill property tax to support education.[30]

State Government Grants-in-Aid to Localities

Alaska provides four basic forms of aid to localities. In addition to the foundation formula funding for education, state revenue sharing, and municipal assistance (safe community funding), capital construction grants are provided to localities.

Revenue sharing began in 1969 to encourage local governments to provide services formerly provided by the state. The program initially provided per capita amounts to local governments—until the legislature substituted a formula program based on population, tax base, and rate of local taxation and provided a minimum revenue sharing payment of $25,000 for smaller municipalities.[31]

Municipal assistance was initiated by the legislature in 1980 to provide local tax relief.[32] This important revenue source for local governments reduced local taxes, some substantially more than others. The state also repealed the individual income tax in 1980, the same year it enacted the Permanent Fund Dividend Program that provides each resident with an annual payment for living in Alaska. From being the most heavily taxed residents in the nation, Alaskans thus became the least taxed.[33] Other state taxes are shared with local governments, chief among them being the raw fish tax, which constitutes an important source of revenues for local governments where fishing is a primary activity.

State spending has had a significant roller-coaster effect on local governments. In 1976 a total of $14 million in revenue sharing was distributed to local governments in Alaska. During the peak year of 1982, it rose to $56 million and fell to $28 million in 1995. Eleven million dollars in municipal assistance revenues were distributed in 1980, rising to $87 million in 1982 and falling to $34 million in 1995. Shared taxes remained relatively steady during this period.

Similarly, state spending for capital construction has varied since 1980, when grants first were made directly to municipalities. In that year, $24 million was allocated, rising to $497 million in 1982 and falling to $34 million in 1995. Unlike the other grant funds, they revert to the general fund unless capital construction funds are spent on the projects for which they are granted.

Local governments' continued dependency on diminished state funding rather than on local taxes indicates that, in effect, the state is directing localities. The local political leverage available during the peak of oil production has disappeared, and many decisions about the nature and direction of local government spending are now being made by the legislature.

Unfunded Mandates

Although some contend that increased petroleum revenues during the 1980s did not lead to state control over local government policies and spending,[34] there are certain areas where state funding of programs (especially capital construction projects) resulted in unfunded mandates. Because capital construction grants do not include operating expenses, municipalities are effectively forced to operate facilities they might otherwise not construct. In many small, rural, predominantly Alaska Native villages, major public buildings such as schools, community centers, and "washaterias" (that is, combination self-service laundries and shower facilities) were constructed during the boom period. Because there is no tax base in many of these communities, localities cannot afford to maintain the facilities. Few state programs explicitly contain unfunded mandates. However, local officials are concerned that, although current legislative actions to reduce state expenditures purport to reestablish local decision-making authority, the result will be more costs to local government.

Access to Local Government

Local Elections

State law governs the conduct of all elections in Alaska. The lieutenant governor supervises the entire election process, and there are election supervisors in each judicial district. The process includes registering voters, ensuring that candidates are qualified, preparing ballots, overseeing the vote, tallying votes, and certifying election results.

Municipal elections are conducted according to state requirements, with a degree of local autonomy. Municipal elections are nonpartisan. A blanket primary features an official ballot that is used to narrow the field for the general election. Municipal elections are held separately from state elections.

State laws govern the role played by political parties in the election process. State campaign finance laws, administered by the Alaska Public Offices Commission (APOC), govern the kind and amount of campaign contributions and expenditures that are permissible, including the placement and sponsorship of campaign signs. The media are also regulated by APOC. Media campaigns in Alaska are limited, however, and statewide media campaigns extending outside the larger incorporated municipalities are rare.

Citizen Controls over Actions of Local Officials

Local government officials are subject to recall under the state municipal code and the general provisions of Article XI, section 8 of the constitution.[35] Although recall efforts take place occasionally, unsuccessful recall attempts usually do not receive a lot of media coverage. The direct democracy provisions of the initiative and referendum are also available to citizens.[36] The initiative process is used regularly in most municipalities; the referendum is used less frequently. All three measures are administered by the borough clerk or city clerk, who oversees the ballot process. In all Alaska municipalities, meetings and records are open.

State-Local Relations

The Alaska Constitution contains provisions for municipal home rule that are among the most supportive found in all the states. Because there are no special districts, and local powers are located in either the borough or the city, these provisions are reinforced. Thus, there is no competition within municipalities for taxing or political authority—at least in theory.

However, the formal provision for municipal home rule has not necessarily resulted in true local control and autonomy. Much of the state is unincorporated. Alaska Native villages, many of which have federally recognized tribal councils, predominate in the Unorganized Borough. The state refuses to recognize the legitimacy of these communities and actively fights their attempts to exercise local control or autonomy, thereby exacerbating the urban–rural, non-Native–Native rift.

Moreover, many municipalities and unincorporated areas rely heavily on state revenues for funds, which have declined as a result of budgetary constraints and slumps in oil prices. At the urging of the legislature during the peak of the oil glut, local property and sales taxes were reduced and public services were added—paid for in large part by state revenue sharing and municipal assistance funds. These funding sources have since been cut significantly by the legislature, and local governments are finding it difficult (if not impossible) to either raise taxes or to cut services to previous levels. Similarly, communities that accepted generous capital construction grants to build public facilities in good times now find themselves encumbered by substantial operating costs and unable to raise taxes to pay those costs.

Local governments' dependency has fostered an expectation that the state will fund services. Furthermore, the prevailing antitax attitude and reliance on petroleum-derived revenues from the state has resulted in citizens' detachment from their local governments. This alienation prompts local officials to lobby more intensely for state funds to maintain and operate their governments. Thus, decisions about the nature and direction of policies affecting localities are not made by localities themselves—a trend that will likely continue, at least until there is a change in the political leadership of the legislature and a corresponding change in policy and state-local relations. Until then, home rule and the local autonomy it implies will continue to suffer.

Notes

1. *State of Alaska v. Native Village of Venetie Tribal Government,* et al. U.S. 96-1577 (1997).

2. Gerald A. McBeath and Thomas A. Morehouse, *Alaska Politics and Government* (Lincoln: University of Nebraska Press, 1994), 51–74.

3. Ibid., 58–59; and Thomas A. Morehouse, "Alaska's Political and Economic Future" (public lecture, University of Alaska, Anchorage, April 1994).

4. Gerald A. McBeath and Thomas A. Morehouse, eds., *Alaska State Government and Politics* (Fairbanks: University of Alaska Press, 1987), 58.

5. Lee J. Cuba, *Identity and Community on the Alaskan Frontier* (Philadelphia: Temple University Press, 1987), xv–xvi.

6. Clive S. Thomas, "Interest Groups and Lobbying in Alaska," in *Alaska State Government and Politics,* ed. McBeath and Morehouse, 161–186.

7. Carl E. Shepro, "Alaska," in *State Party Profiles: A Fifty- State Guide to Development, Organization, and Resources,* ed. Andrew M. Appleton and Daniel S. Ward (Washington, D.C.: Congressional Quarterly, 1997), 8–16.

8. Gordon S. Harrison, *Alaska's Constitution: A Citizen's Guide,* 3d ed. (Juneau: Alaska Leg Harrison Legislative Research Agency, 1992), 3–7, 51–106; and McBeath and Morehouse, *Alaska Politics and Government,* 167.

9. Constitution of the State of Alaska, articles VIII, VII; and Harrison, *Alaska's Constitution,* 143–167.

10. David S. Case, *Alaska Natives and American Laws* (Fairbanks: University of Alaska Press, 1984), 371.

11. Thomas A. Morehouse, Gerald A. McBeath, and Linda Leask, *Alaska's Urban and Rural Governments* (Lanham, Md.: University Press of America, 1984), 15–21.

12. Harrison, *Alaska's Constitution,* 201–202.

13. Constitution of the State of Alaska, Article X, section 11.

14. Department of Community and Regional Affairs (DCRA), *Alaska Local Government Handbook,* 3d ed. (Juneau: State of Alaska, DCRA, August 1987), 1–12.

15. Harrison, *Alaska's Constitution,* 194.

16. Constitution of the State of Alaska, Article X, section 2; Article II, section 19; Article X, section 1.

17. The constitution envisioned the entire state being organized into boroughs, those that incorporated and those that had not yet done so. To date, the legislature has not acted to create "unorganized boroughs," but it is currently considering such action to force local support of education.

18. Alaska Statutes, title 29.

19. Morehouse, McBeath, and Leask, *Alaska's Urban and Rural Governments,* 32–33.

20. McBeath and Morehouse, *Alaska Politics and Government,* 273.

21. Morehouse, McBeath, and Leask, *Alaska's Urban and Rural Governments,* 52–53.

22. Harrison, *Alaska's Constitution,* 204–205.

23. Constitution of the State of Alaska, Article VIII, section 1.

24. Thomas A. Morehouse and Victor Fischer, *Borough Government in Alaska: A Study of State-Local Relations* (Fairbanks: Institute of Social, Economic, and Government Research, 1971), 75.

25. Alaska Statutes (AS 29.45.090–100).

26. Constitution of the State of Alaska, Article IX, section 9.

27. Alaska Statutes (AS 29.47.190).

28. Municipality of Anchorage Comprehensive Annual Financial Report.

29. Municipality of Anchorage Comprehensive Annual Financial Report (1996).

30. HB 165.

31. Morehouse, McBeath and Leask, *Alaska's Urban and Rural Governments,* 76.

32. Ibid., 77.

33. McBeath and Morehouse, *Alaska Politics and Government,* 64–66.

34. Morehouse, McBeath, and Leask, *Alaska's Urban and Rural Governments,* 104–106.

35. Alaska Statutes (AS 29.26.240–350).

36. Constitution of the State of Alaska, sections 1–7.

ARIZONA

David R. Berman and Tanis J. Salant

Compared with municipalities elsewhere, those in Arizona have had considerable freedom in terms of structure and operations to address a conventional set of local problems and needs. Legal traditions, culture, and political factors have helped to shape and preserve a degree of independence. Counties have enjoyed less autonomy, although recently the state's two largest counties have been given an opportunity to adopt home rule charters. Local governments in Arizona have an unusual amount of discretionary authority, but like local governments elsewhere, they must live with numerous state-imposed limitations on their powers. They attempt to fight off unwanted controls but also look to the state for financial assistance.

Governmental Setting

Arizona is one of the fastest growing states in the nation. It trailed only Nevada in growth, from some 750,000 people in 1950 to 3.7 million people in 1990. By 1996, population had increased to about 4.5 million. Phoenix, the largest city in the state, had 1.2 million and was the sixth most populated city in the country. The state is more than 85 percent urban. Most Arizonans (nearly 60 percent) live in Maricopa County (Phoenix). An additional 20 percent of the population lives in Pima County (Tucson), another largely urban county. The remainder of the population is scattered among thirteen other counties. Overall, the state has a relatively low population density of 32.3 persons per square mile, compared, for example, with about 191 in California. Settlements are widely scattered over the state's 113,642 square miles.

Arizona has an above-average percentage of Hispanics and Native Americans. The former constitute about 20 percent of the population, whereas the latter make up 6 percent. Arizona trails only Oklahoma in the number of Native Americans. The percentage of Arizonans who are sixty-five or older is just slightly above the national average, but the elderly population is growing rapidly. Arizona's growth has been fueled by migration, mostly from California but also from the South (especially Texas) and the Midwest. The 1990 census revealed that three of every four people living in Arizona were born outside the state and that 20 percent of the people living in the state had been there for five years or less. The population is highly transient; some 10,000 people either enter or leave the state each month. This population flux has made Arizona politics more unpredictable than it has been before.

Rapid growth has brought demands for education, transportation, and other services and problems, such as urban sprawl and air pollution, which have strained the public sector. The state has experienced a long-term improvement in per capita personal income but still ranks only thirty-sixth among the states. Growth and quality-of-life issues are paramount in city council races, especially in metropolitan areas.

In 1912, when Arizona gained statehood, the state was dominated by reform-minded Democrats who, rebelling against the railroad and mining interests, produced a highly progressive state constitution. By the 1930s through the early 1960s, however, Arizona was primarily a traditional, one-party southern state. It was Democratic, conservative, and supportive of the goals of the leading economic interests, which were commonly identified as the "three Cs" of copper, cattle, and cotton. Changes brought about largely by post–World War II migration and the economic development of the state resulted in a more competitive party system and a more pluralistic interest group system in which banks, utilities, and new industries (particularly in the fast-growing Phoenix area) became more important. Over the past several years, Republicans have generally controlled the legislature and have an edge over Democrats in voter registration. Although perhaps less conservative than in the past, Arizona continues to be among the more conservative states. It has relatively low levels of citizen participation in politics, and governments provide relatively low levels of service.[1]

There are 87 incorporated cities and towns and 15 county governments in Arizona. These general-purpose governments provide residents with direct and constitutionally mandated services. Special-purpose governments number 268 special districts and 227 school districts; the total number of local governments in Arizona is 597. Most special districts deal with a single function, such as fire protection, irrigation, sewage, or water supply. The 21 Indian tribes in Arizona maintain sovereign status with respect to state and local law, but they can and frequently do enter numerous intergovernmental agreements and pacts with both the state and local governments. The major areas of concern for cities and towns have been police and fire protection, transportation improvements, sewage and solid waste management, parks and recreation, housing and community services, and zoning and planning. Cities and towns have little responsibility in the areas of education, welfare, and health and hospitals. Independent school districts provide elementary and secondary education services at the local level, and counties administer local welfare and health and hospital programs.

Like other Progressives, the framers of the Arizona Constitution felt that cities should be free to exercise local functions without state legislative interference. Accordingly, they made a liberal grant of municipal home rule and by prohibiting special legislation sought to enhance local authority and democracy. At the municipal level, Arizona's professional management is distinctive in that the council-manager form is commonly used. Arizona's fifteen county governments have enjoyed less legal autonomy. They have traditional commission-type governing boards (boards of supervisors) and seven elected constitutional officers: assessor, attorney, clerk of court, recorder, sheriff, school superintendent, and treasurer. All fifteen counties, however, employ a professional manager or administrator who is appointed by the governing board.

Home Rule in Arizona

Historical Development

The Progressive movement deeply influenced Arizona's system of municipal government. The state's first and only constitution was framed in 1910 by reformers caught up in the spirit of the Progressive movement. The constitution prohibited the legislature from passing special or local legislation on matters such as the incorporation of municipalities, the amendment of municipal charters, the assessment and collection of taxes, the conduct of elections, and "when a general law can be made applicable." The drafters of the constitution added a provision that gives any municipality with 3,500 or more people the right to "frame a charter for its own government consistent with, and subject to, the Constitution and the laws of the State."[2] Thus, municipal home rule in Arizona was firmly established by an express and self-executing constitutional provision rather than, as in many other states, by legislation.

The only other major development in the history of home rule in Arizona was a 1992 constitutional amendment authorizing home rule in counties with more than 500,000 people—a category that currently includes only Maricopa and Pima Counties. Charter counties, under the law, may exercise all powers over local concerns of the county consistent with, and subject to, the constitution and laws of the state. County charters enable citizens to restructure governing boards, appoint or consolidate certain constitutional offices, and levy additional sales taxes. City-county or county-county consolidations, however, are not allowed. Charter counties, moreover, must still provide the same state-mandated services and perform the same state-mandated functions as noncharter counties. Thus far, voters have rejected proposed charters for Maricopa and Pima Counties.

Definition of Home Rule

Local governments in Arizona, with or without charters, are the legal creatures of the state and, as such, are subject to various state controls. The courts, moreover, have tended to follow Judge John F. Dillon's well-known dictum (known as Dillon's Rule) that the powers of municipal governments are limited to what is expressly stated or necessarily implied in the state constitution, state laws, or city charters.[3]

The Arizona Supreme Court has recognized that charters give cities a certain independence from the state on matters of local concern but, like state courts elsewhere, have found it difficult to distinguish between matters of local and state concern. Arizona courts have varied greatly in how they have construed home rule powers in particular cases. Courts have declared that state laws on police pensions, overtime pay, and traffic safety, for example, preempt the regulatory authority of charter governments. On the other hand, plumbing codes and regulations on local elections are deemed local matters within the regulatory authority of charter governments.[4]

Some observers have questioned the value of having a home rule charter. In the mid-1960s, for example, one study suggested "the advantages of charter cities over non-charter cities are quite limited."[5] The authors found this to be particularly true in the area of finance and taxation. Having a charter had proved to be of no advantage when it came to debt and other state regulations; both charter and noncharter cities had to abide by the same restrictions. In regard to taxation, the state supreme court had ruled that no municipality (charter or noncharter) had the power to levy a fuel tax.[6] Many lawyers felt that cities could not levy a sales tax without having a charter giving them such power, but noncharter cities found that they could do so without judicial interference.

Although charters fall short of expectations in terms of conferring powers and immunities, local officials and scholars have valued charter government because it allows citizens in various communities the opportunity to shape local government structures that best fit their needs. Moreover, it gives municipalities more power to initiate action (relieving them from having to go to the legislature for authority) and helps restrict state interference in local affairs. Municipal charters permit citizens to determine structural features such as the number and length of terms of officials, the manner of mayoral selection, organization of city departments, and the requirement for voter approval to levy certain taxes. Home rule cities can also limit the powers that they themselves exercise.[7]

Structural Features

The framers of the Arizona Constitution intended the ban on special and local legislation to deter "the granting of special privileges to particular cities on terms different from those required of other municipalities."[8] The framers worried that some municipalities would use their influence in the legislature, even resorting to corrupt methods, to secure special favors.[9] The Arizona legislature had been guilty of such abuses in its territorial years (1850–1912), and in response, Congress had passed the Harrison Act in 1886, which banned special legislation. The framers wrote a broader and more stringent protection into the state constitution.

The constitutional provisions regarding special and local legislation have not altogether prevented the legislature from passing laws affecting individual or select groups of municipalities or counties. However, they have offered some protection against the more extreme cases in which the legislature has favored particular jurisdictions over others or imposed burdens on particular governments while ignoring others. State courts have acknowledged that lawmakers have the power to classify local governments according to population for purposes of legislation and may use a classification, even though it includes only one local government. In several cases, courts have dismissed challenges to legislation affecting one or only a few selected local governments by finding that the classification system employed had a rational relationship to a legitimate legislative end.[10]

State courts, however, have occasionally declared that passing an equal protection or rational basis type of test is not enough. For example, in 1989 the state supreme court held that a deannexation law which was limited to a few cities within only one county and for a limited time violated the ban against local or special laws. The court found that the law "subverts the explicit mandates" of the constitution and "contravenes the admonition against imposing greater burdens on some while granting privileges to others."[11]

Arizona has three general types or classes of municipal governments: towns that operate under the general law; cities that operate under the general law; and home rule, or charter, cities. State law allows a community with 1,500–3,000 people to incorporate as a town. A community with more than 3,000 people may incorporate as a city or change status from a town to a city with voter approval. Cities with populations of more than 3,500 may frame and adopt their own home rule charters.

Cities without charters and towns operate under the general laws of the state. This means that they must look to the state for general or specific authorizations to pass laws. Charter cities have more discretion to initiate action without specific authorization and (theoretically, at least) more freedom from state intervention. The basic form of government provided by state law for cities and towns operating under the general law is called the "common council" form. Under it, voters elect a council of seven members for two-year terms on an at-large basis.[12] The law requires the council to appoint certain officials such as a city or town clerk. In the basic form, the council selects one of its members to be mayor. State law, however, allows cities and towns to elect the mayor directly for a two- or four-year term, if the voters approve the alternative. Council members are permitted to have overlapping terms, pending voter approval.

State law further allows cities and towns operating under the general law to adopt a council-manager form of government simply by passing an ordinance. Currently, the only difference between cities operating under the general law and towns is that the former have the option of electing council people from wards, pending voter approval. Cities and towns typically function under the council-manager form of government. The mayor is usually elected citywide but may be elected from among council members.

Charters are initiated, developed, and adopted at the local level; the governor reviews the charters to make sure they do not conflict with the constitution or state laws. Gubernatorial approval, thus far, has been a mere formality. Slightly fewer than half of the forty-two municipalities with 3,500 or more people, including all of the major cities, have taken advantage of the opportunity to adopt their own charters.[13] More cities have not sought home rule status because the legislature has gradually given general law cities greater discretion, making charters less necessary. By allowing cities to elect mayors directly rather than from among council members, the legislature appears to have eliminated a particularly strong incentive for cities to secure charter status.[14]

Municipal governments also exercise certain controls over local boundaries. Arizona, for example, has a unique "anti-incorporation" law that prohibits new incorporations within six miles of an existing municipality of 5,000 or more population or within three miles of a municipality of less than 5,000 population. There are two exceptions to this rule: when the existing municipal governing body refuses to annex an area within 120 days after a valid annexation petition is filed, or when the governing body gives permission for incorporation.

Historically, Arizona has made annexation rather easy. Arizona lawmakers in the mid-1980s, however, made the annexation process more difficult in reaction to intense competition among municipalities for valuable land. The law gives control to property owners in the area to be annexed. Petitions must be signed by the owners of more than half of the value of the property and by more than one-half of the property owners in the area to be annexed; petitions must be filed with the county recorder. Once petitions are filed, public hearings are held, and the council then adopts an ordinance annexing the property. That Arizona proscribes this variation of the popular determination model probably makes it relatively difficult for cities to expand through annexation; however, the process is not as onerous as it would be if the state required general elections in the area to be annexed.

Under Arizona law, any municipality may exercise powers in regard to planning, zoning, and subdivision regulations in unincorporated territory within three miles of its boundaries. Further, municipalities may enter into intergovernmental agreements with the county, tribes, and others for a joint development plan for land use, traffic circulation, recreation, transportation and transit, public services, public safety, and economic development. Municipalities may also own property or facilities beyond their city limits.

In Arizona, as elsewhere, counties have had more difficulty than municipalities in securing independence from the state. Courts and legislators have historically regarded counties as administrative arms of the state government rather than governments (such as cities or towns) that were created on a voluntary basis by people in a particular geographical area to serve their own needs. Home rule—in the broad political sense as well as the legal sense—has been reserved for cities: "as a political subdivision of the state, the County possesses only those powers that have been expressly, or by necessary implication, delegated to it by the legislature or the constitution."[15] As the rival general-purpose governments, counties have had to secure authority from the legislature to adopt even the most routine ordinances. Even though counties with greater than 500,000 population have been allowed to adopt their own home rule charters since 1992, none have done so thus far.

Functions of Local Government

Functional Responsibilities

Some of the basic services that cities provide are police protection, maintenance and construction of local streets, fire protection, garbage and trash collection, water, sewer, parks and recreation, financial administration, and misdemeanor adjudication. Property assessment, tax collection, disbursement and management, recordation, prosecution, misdemeanor and felony adjudication, adult and juvenile probation and detention,

indigent defense, health care, restaurant inspection, roads, bridges and flood control, and long-term health care are among county-provided services. Cities and counties may also provide planning and zoning, libraries, economic development, animal control, housing, and airports. Both counties and municipalities have broad authority to enter into intergovernmental agreements with other local governments and with tribal governments. Counties and municipalities can also form regional units of authority to address multijurisdictional issues, such as planning, water quality, and narcotics interdiction.

Both municipalities and counties have the authority to form special districts. Of the twenty-nine types of special districts in Arizona, the most prevalent pertain to community facilities, fire, county improvement, special roads and jails, stadiums, public libraries, groundwater replenishment, and active water management areas. Sports authorities may fund sports complexes. Counties, cities, and towns may exercise joint power in formal agreements with one another or with another governmental agency. Formal contracts and agreements are part of a broader network of informal as well as formal cooperative arrangements among local officials in metropolitan areas and throughout the state.

Voluntary regional councils of governments (COGs) have been a principal means of enhancing coordination among local governments in Arizona.. Since the early 1970s six COGs in various parts of the state have helped promote uniformity in the planning and programming of various activities, some of which are required by federal transportation and other programs. The Maricopa Association of Governments (MAG), for example, has pursued an aggressive regional agenda. It is currently spearheading a campaign for a unified vision of what the valley should be like in 2025 that governments in the valley may endorse.

In practice, cooperation among local governments is sometimes frustrated by long-standing rivalries between local units or because various units perceive their own problems as unique or are suspicious of one another's special agenda. Local officials also actively compete for resources such as land, population, industry, and taxes. Moreover, the emphasis on the sales tax as a source of municipal revenues may lead to wasteful competition for the location of shopping centers in the region as a whole. This kind of competition may inadvertently benefit opportunistic businesses shopping around for a location.

Administrative Discretion

The state has delegated a considerable amount of discretion to municipal and county governments to adopt new functions and manage their internal operations. Regarding personnel matters, local governments decide on collective bargaining, affirmative action, and the political rights of public employees. State law does not require local governments to have a merit system, affirmative action, residency requirements, or a retirement system, but workers' compensation is mandated. State law is also silent regarding contracting and purchasing standards for local governments and procedures for adoption of municipal and county ordinances and/or resolutions. However, there are certain posting and publication requirements.

State law does not require codification of municipal or county ordinances or resolutions, nor does it impose a code of ethics on local officials. However, conflicts of interest are prohibited, nepotism is banned, and each municipality is required to adopt standards of financial disclosure for elected officials. State law also regulates the content of a city or town council's agenda, authorizes the initiative and referendum on local ordinances, and makes numerous regulations regarding local elections. In the area of financial administration, state control over local activities is considerable; state laws limit expenditures, debt, and property taxation. Many of these restrictions took the form of constitutional amendments in 1980, at a time when the legislature was trying to head off a taxpayers' rebellion.

Municipalities and counties are required by state law to adopt comprehensive, long-range land-use plans and zoning ordinances to implement these plans. They are also required to impose additional controls on land use through subdivision regulations. Historically, however, Arizona's statutes regarding land-use plans have not been well implemented. There is no state review or "planning police" to enforce the state law. Developers have lobbied city councils or county boards to change plans put together by commissions or to override the more restrictive decisions made by boards of adjustment. Because of the inconsistency in land-use control among Arizona's municipalities and counties, developers have been able to shop around and gravitate to areas with the fewest controls or lowest impact fees (if any) on proposed projects.

Recently, the legislature has addressed some of the criticisms of local planning. Under the "Growing Smarter" law that went into effect in 1998, cities, towns, and counties have to adopt or renew land-use plans for ten-year periods, and amendments to general growth plans require a two-thirds vote of city council or county board of supervisors members (rather than, as in the past, a majority of members). The law states that each governing body must "adopt written procedures to provide effective, early, and continuous public participation in the development and major amendment of general plans." The new law also requires cities and towns to adopt general plans with appropriate zone standards and with specific points or elements, such as protection of open space, strategies for efficient transportation, and well-timed expansion of infrastructure (for example, sewers). Although the legislation mandates some important changes in existing practices, there is no state agency to monitor compliance.

Economic Development

Municipalities and counties have broad authority for providing development activities. Nearly all have created departments of economic development, and many make cash contributions to local or regional economic development organizations (counties are limited to $500,000 per year) and chambers of commerce. The formation of enterprise zones is also permitted, as are industrial parks and other facility developments, such as airports and ball parks. Local governments also form industrial developmental authorities (IDAs) to promote industrial development and create jobs. Other financing mechanisms for facility development include lease-purchase agreements with private developers and tax increment financing. Nonprofit agencies may be formed to finance construction.

Fiscal Autonomy of Local Governments

Local Revenues

U.S. census figures indicate that local governments in Arizona raise 64 percent of the total revenues they spend. Thirty-three percent of the total revenue comes from the state, and about 3 percent comes from the federal government. The most popular source of tax revenue is the property tax, followed by the sales tax. Further analysis, using fiscal 1998 budgets for the state's largest cities, suggests that municipalities rely primarily on the local sales tax, enterprise and user fees, and state-shared revenues for 26 percent, 25 percent, and 20 percent of their revenues, respectively.[16] For counties, the property tax (real and secondary) and state-shared revenues are the principal source of income, accounting for 37 percent and 36 percent, respectively.

Property tax limits are imposed on both cities and counties. State law also establishes the method of property tax assessment for local governments. Under a 1980 constitutional amendment, an increase in the amount of revenue from the primary property tax is limited to 2 percent from one year to another, plus an amount concomitant with annexations or new construction.[17] State law allows local governments to approve property tax revenue increases in excess of these limits through override elections.

Although limitations on property taxes have made life more difficult for local decision makers, municipalities have been able to reduce their dependence on this source by shifting to other revenue sources. Of particular importance to municipalities has been the local sales tax, which is now the leading source of tax revenue for several cities. All cities and towns can levy a sales tax, but some of the charter cities require voter approval of any increase. Arizona appears somewhat unique in that cities and towns have authority not only to set their own sales tax rates but also their own sales tax bases. They can, for example, tax food purchased for home consumption, even though the state exempts these types of purchases. Use of this discretion has been somewhat controversial, because it complicates matters for the many businesses operating in more than one jurisdiction.[18]

Currently, the Arizona Department of Revenue collects the local sales tax for seventy-one of the eighty-seven cities and towns, at no charge to the municipalities.[19] Twelve counties also levy this tax. To help make growth pay for itself, many jurisdictions in Arizona (as elsewhere) have adopted impact fees on new developments, whereby developers and new owners pay for at least part of the cost of providing infrastructure (such as roads) necessary for the new development.

State limitations on the ability of local governments to borrow money are expressed in the constitution as a percentage of assessed property value in a jurisdiction.[20] Localities cannot exceed these sums without public approval. State law also requires a referendum for all bond issues, not simply general-obligation bonds. In 1980 the percentage of the taxable property that could be used for borrowing for cities and towns was raised from 4 percent to 6 percent for the base debt and from 15 percent to 20 percent for certain specified purposes (for example, water, electricity, sewer, and recreational facilities). However, because the voters approved a property tax reform plan proposed by the legislature that severely reduced the value of the taxable property in local jurisdictions, percentage adjustments did little to increase the total dollar borrowing capacities of local governments. Local governments in Arizona may not become indebted by more than 6 percent of the taxable property in the jurisdiction without the consent of a majority of property taxpayers. The absolute limit is 15 percent.

Local Expenditures

By far the largest category of expenditure for all local governments is education. The second largest category for municipalities is police and fire (21 percent); for counties, it is health and welfare (42 percent). The state requires counties, cities, and towns to adopt an annual operating budget. State law specifies the budget format and requires at least one public hearing before budget adoption, in addition to other procedural requirements. In effect, local governments must adopt a balanced budget.[21]

Since 1980 the state has limited expenditures of local governments to fiscal 1979–1980 levels, as adjusted annually to reflect changes in population and the cost of living. The law exempts certain expenditures, such as bond principal and interest payments. Expenditures in excess of the limitation must receive voter approval. In practice, this formula has an adverse effect on municipalities that have experienced rapid growth and that, as a result, have greatly increased infrastructure and other expenditures since 1980. Cities and towns, however, may (with voter ap-

proval) adopt an alternative expenditure limit, by making a permanent base adjustment based on current spending, for example. About half of the state's cities and towns have convinced voters to come up with an alternative system. Regardless, every city and town must comply with a uniform reporting system detailed in state law and file a report after each fiscal year showing compliance with the state or local expenditure limit. Arizona local governments are not authorized to declare bankruptcy under Arizona law. They can, however, be ordered to disincorporate.

State Government Grants-in-Aid to Localities

As a result of the efforts of local officials and the organizations that represent them, the state has more than two dozen programs giving various types of aid to local governments. These range from narrowly targeted categorical grants to unrestricted shared revenues. The state distributes restricted highway-user revenues (largely taxes on gasoline) to counties, cities, and towns by a complicated formula that accounts for population and origin of sales. The law earmarks the money for street and related projects. Cities and towns in Arizona receive much of their general or unrestricted aid from their share of the state income tax and state sales tax revenues; these programs were made possible by the initiative process in the wake of a legislative decision not to share state revenues with municipalities. In recent years, municipalities have had to struggle to retain their share of the revenues.

Arizona also shares with local governments revenues from the vehicle license tax and the state lottery. In 1998 the amount of shared revenue was $665 million from the sales tax, $435 million from the gas tax, $291 million from the income tax, $109 million from the vehicle license tax, and $33 million from the lottery. The U.S. Bureau of the Census estimated in 1996 that Arizona local governments received about $4.3 billion in state assistance from state government, equal to $961 per capita. Of this, 52 percent was allocated for education, 20 percent for general local government support, 11 percent for public welfare, and 10 percent for highways.

Unfunded Mandates

Most of the mandates that impose large costs on Arizona municipalities are federal mandates regarding environmental matters. Local officials, however, are concerned about current state mandates and the possibility that the legislature will try to shift more costs their way as it tries to reduce spending and meet demands, for example, to equalize education expenditures. Thus far, municipal and county officials have not been able to rally legislators to support a constitutional amendment that allows local officials to ignore state mandates unless the state provides money to pay for the mandates. This opposition may stem from a perception among legislators that counties and municipalities are simply legal creatures of the state that can be dealt with as the legislature sees fit.[22] Counties continue to chafe under state mandates in the area of health care, which often translates into increased costs for county health departments.

Access to Local Government

Local Elections

State law in Arizona establishes dates and candidate qualifications for local elections. There are no statutes limiting expenditures of candidates for local office; however, local candidates are required to disclose campaign finances. For local elections, state law sets voter qualifications and requires local governments to provide for absentee voting and write-in votes. Voter registration procedures are established by law; one registration suffices for all elections.

Citizen Controls over Actions of Local Officials

As part of the state's Progressive heritage, the constitution makes instruments of "direct democracy"—the initiative, referendum, and recall—applicable to local government. Among the three types, the recall is most common. According to a survey by the League of Arizona Cities, twenty-five of the state's eighty-seven incorporated cities or towns held recall elections in 1988–1993. Of the seventy-five officials recalled to the ballot, thirty-one (or about 41 percent) were recalled from office. Most of the recall elections took place in small jurisdictions.[23] Recall petitions must have a number of signatures equal to 25 percent of the votes cast for the office in question in the preceding general election. This moderately high percentage is deceptive, however, because most recalls have taken place in small communities with minimal voter turnout.[24]

State law requires all local government meetings at which official action is taken to be open to the public, but there is no state requirement that local government records be open to public inspection at reasonable hours. Except in special circumstances, the date, time, and place of meetings of local officials must be publicly disclosed, and an agenda must be provided for public inspection at least twenty-four hours in advance of such meetings. To keep officials accountable and to counter problems of an ethical nature, other state controls prevent nepotism and conflicts of interest (for example, when elected officials participate in decisions that benefit them directly economically); financial disclosure requirements are included among such controls.

State-Local Relations

The role of state government in the affairs of local governments in Arizona is broad. The constitution, statutes, courts, administrative orders, and significant state revenue sharing make the state an important determinant in local decision making. Considering the wide range of state controls, one can hardly describe local governments as autonomous entities that are insulated from state politics. Nor can it be said that they are self-sufficient in terms of financial resources or indeed, that local officials think that self-sufficiency is a particularly desirable objective. In nearly every legislative session in Arizona, local officials and lobbyists who represent cities, towns, and counties try to ward off state controls. The same forces, however, have often demanded certain types of state intervention, particularly financial assistance.

There is a considerable gap between the potential power of the state and the actual amount of control it exercises over local governments. State intervention in local affairs is mitigated by constitutional, cultural, and political constraints that work against the exercise of state authority. Arizona municipalities, in practice, have much freedom, particularly when it comes to structural and personnel matters and most aspects of their internal operations. Constitutional provisions help explain the relatively high level of discretionary authority and low level of state interference.

Some have observed an unusually strong tradition of local self-government in Arizona, described by one author as a "natural negative reaction" in the state "to state-imposed solutions of local problems."[25] Local officials invite state aid but resist as many state controls as possible and seem to be relatively successful in both regards. However, the distinction between state and local functions is becoming somewhat blurred, and local units have had to struggle to exert influence on state policy.

Notes

1. See generally David Berman, *Arizona and Politics: The Quest for Autonomy, Democracy, and Development* (Lincoln: University of Nebraska Press, 1998).

2. Arizona State Constitution, Article 4, part 2, section 19; Article 13, section 2.

3. See David A. Bingham, *Constitutional Municipal Home Rule in Arizona* (Tucson: Department of Public Administration and Division of Economic and Business Research, University of Arizona, October 1978).

4. John D. Leshy, *The Arizona State Constitution: A Reference Guide* (Westport, Conn.: Greenwood Press, 1993), 265–266.

5. Arizona Academy, *Gearing Arizona's Communities to Orderly Growth* (Phoenix: Arizona Academy, 1965), 14–15.

6. *City of Phoenix v. Popkin*, 93 Arizona 12 (1963).

7. Bingham, *Constitutional Municipal Home Rule in Arizona*.

8. *Udall v. Severn*, 52 Arizona 65 (1938).

9. John R. Murdock, *Constitutional Development of Arizona* (privately printed, 1933), 101–102.

10. On justifications for various classifications, see *Udall v. Severn*, 52 Arizona 65 (1938), *Luhrs v. City of Phoenix*, 52 Arizona 438 (1938), *State v. Loughran*, 143 Arizona 345 (1985), and *Picture Rocks Fire District v. Pima County*, 152 Arizona 442 (1986).

11. *Petitioners for Deannexation v. Goodyear*, 160 Arizona 467 (1989); Leshy, *Arizona State Constitution*, 265.

12. Before 1972 a community needed only 500 people to incorporate. Towns that were incorporated before 1972 with fewer than 1,500 people had five council members elected at large for two-year terms. Since then, they have had the option of adding two more council members once their population exceeds 1,500.

13. Leshy, *Arizona State Constitution,* 265.

14. Interview with Cathy Connolly, Arizona League of Cities and Towns, 25 June 1995.

15. *Maricopa County v. Maricopa County Municipal Water Conservation District No. 1,* 171 Arizona 325 (1992).

16. The estimates are based on the budgets of Phoenix, Tucson, Mesa, Scottsdale, Tempe, Glendale, and Flagstaff, which combined have 72 percent of the incorporated population.

17. Cities also have an unlimited secondary property tax that is levied to pay the principal and interest on bonded indebtedness.

18. Helen F. Ladd and Dana West, "General Sales Taxes," in *State and Local Finance for the 1990s: A Case Study of Arizona,* ed. Therese J. McGuire and Dana Wolf Naimak (Tempe: School of Public Affairs, Arizona State University, 1991), 117–148. These authors note that the authority of localities to define their own tax bases "arises from Arizona's strong tradition of local home rule and the fact that sales taxes were initially collected at the local level" (139–140).

19. Arizona Department of Revenue, *1994 Annual Report* (Tucson: Arizona Department of Revenue, 1994), 7.

20. Arizona State Constitution, Article 9, section 8.

21. Arizona Revised Statutes, 42302. See also *City of Tucson v. Tucson Sunshine Climate Club,* 64 Arizona 1 (1946). Regarding Phoenix and Tucson, see Carol W. Lewis, "Budgetary Balance: The Norm, Concept, and Practice in Large U.S. Cities," *Public Administration Review* (November–December 1994): 515–524.

22. Mary Jo Pitzl, "Cities, Towns Rail Against Big Brother," *Arizona Republic,* 20 February 1995, A1, A2.

23. "Summary of City/Town Recall Election Information" (report prepared by the League of Arizona Cities and Towns, August 1993).

24. On percentages and procedures required elsewhere, see Charles M. Price, "Electoral Accountability: Local Recalls," *National Civic Review* 77 (March–April 1988): 118–123.

25. John Stuart Hall, "State-Local Relations in Arizona: Change, Within Limits," in *A Decade of Devolution: Perspectives on State-Local Relations,* ed. E. Blaine Liner (Washington, D.C.: Urban Institute Press, 1989), 155. An elaboration on these points is found in David R. Berman, "Municipal Home Rule in Arizona: Law, Politics, and the Progressive Heritage" (paper prepared for presentation at the 1995 annual meeting of the American Political Science Association, Chicago).

ARKANSAS

Margaret F. Reid and Will Miller

The rural character of Arkansas is rapidly changing as the state's largest cities continue to be population growth magnets. Constitutional and institutional arrangements in the state, however, have responded only incrementally to these changes. Arkansas does not give its cities functional home rule but rather closely circumscribed structural home rule. Counties were given a form of structural home rule in the early 1970s. Yet, given their limited administrative capacities and their extreme institutional fragmentation, effective governance of the counties has lagged far behind that of the state's larger cities.

Governmental Setting

A general frustration with the quality of state government, the lack of continuing and predictable interactions with state officials, and the infrequency with which the state legislature convenes (Arkansas has a biennial legislature) provide the general context for an assessment of constitutional provisions pertaining to local governmental autonomy. The tremendous changes that have occurred in Arkansas, both politically and economically, during the past four decades are most visible in the state's larger local communities.

The state's historically disenfranchised electorate is slowly discovering its clout.[1] Since the mid-1980s, urban areas have become a fertile recruiting ground for the Republican Party. Although the historic stranglehold of the Democratic Party has not been broken, Republicans have been able to make inroads in some parts of the state, especially its more affluent northwestern quarter. Politics in Arkansas, rather than being simply a party affair, is profoundly personalized in nature.[2] In an analysis of Arkansas, three issues stand out: (1) the lack of formal independence of the municipal governments, (2) the fiscal and managerial challenges before local public administrators and elected officials as the state moves from a largely rural to an urban lifestyle, and (3) the inherent tension between elite rule and popular rule at both state and local levels.

The state constitution in many ways reflects citizens' antipathy toward and mistrust in government. The current constitution was adopted in 1874 in the wake of the Reconstruction period following the Civil War and is predominantly a negative document:[3] it prohibits more than it enables. The constitution fragments power at all levels of government by requiring the separate election of many public officers, by (originally) reducing

terms in office from four to two years (the governor's four-year term was reinstated only in 1984 with Amendment 63), by limiting the legislative session to sixty days over a biennium (Article 5, section 5), and by requiring constitutional amendments for a wide range of issues.[4] More than 150 amendments to change the constitution have been submitted since its adoption.[5] Recent constitutional reform efforts (1970, 1980, and 1995) have failed largely because of citizens' indifference or because of continued distrust in government. Thus, constitutional change has been incremental, resulting in a rather unwieldy, convoluted document.

The executive powers of the governor are weak in some areas and considerable in others (Article 6). Institutionally, the governor's powers are severely curtailed, gubernatorial power is fragmented, and the salary of the governor is one of the lowest in the nation. Historically, the actual powers of individual governors have been quite substantial.[6] Because Arkansas's legislature meets only biennially, the governor is afforded opportunities for political visibility that legislative activities and actors otherwise would receive. The governor is probably the most well-known elected official in the state and, in a small state like Arkansas, enjoys considerable political visibility. The governor is also the most visible representative of his party and has influence over the state's economic affairs. The general public's distrust of political institutions has made it difficult for reform-oriented governors to initiate and successfully complete administrative or constitutional changes.

Arkansas citizens select their governors with greater care and attention than they do their representatives. The rural bias of the legislature has been a considerable disadvantage for the emerging urban areas. Moreover, the legislature's age composition, male-female ratio, and level of educational attainment are not representative of its constituency. Arkansas's African American population is concentrated in a few southeastern counties and in some of the larger cities of central and eastern Arkansas. Overall, the state has lost a large share of its black population, which has declined steadily from 27 percent (1920) to 22 percent (1950) and 16 percent (1980). That the legislative clout of this demographic group and that of the rapidly growing Hispanic population in the northwestern and central parts of the state has been negligible may be a source of future conflict.[7]

Legislative rules have fostered the static appearance of the Arkansas legislature.[8] Until a term-limits provision was passed in 1996, seniority was a decisive criterion for committee assignments. The lack of ambition of most Arkansas legislators to move to other elected offices outside the state has made this legislative body one of the least progressive in the United States.

Home Rule in Arkansas

Historical Development

The Arkansas Constitution has treated its local governments in a restrictive fashion. Mirroring both the general distrust of government as manifested in the constitution of 1874 and the predominantly rural characteristics of the state, local governments were given limited powers. Counties were the locus of local political power. As in many other states, counties were originally established as administrative branches of state government through which the state could enforce its laws, conduct elections, collect taxes, and provide needed services.

The most significant current development is the increased willingness of the state's larger municipalities—the Little Rock metropolitan area, Fort Smith, Hot Springs, Fayetteville–Springdale–Rogers metropolitan statistical area (MSA), Jonesboro, and Pine Bluff—to pressure the legislature for greater governing powers. The move to propose home rule was deferred when municipalities were forced to focus on defeating a popular push for property rights reforms and a concerted effort by a group of northwest Arkansans to abolish the property tax altogether. A proposed constitutional amendment to abolish all property taxes failed in 1998, only after it was determined that some of the signatures on the petition had been collected illegally and were struck, reducing the number of signatures below the legally required threshold.

Definition of Home Rule

Functional home rule in Arkansas is, in its most general sense, a grant of power from the state legislature that determines the corporate functions of counties and municipalities. The municipal charter reserves the right of the legislature to modify, amend, or even revoke the charter. The 1974 amendment to the constitution (Amendment 55) provided counties with broad functional home rule.[9] The constitution states that counties are entitled to "exercise local legislative authority not denied by the Constitution or by law." Furthermore, the Arkansas County Government Code (Act 742) specifies that the quorum court (that is, the body with legislative authority) should have between nine and fifteen members. The primary administrative responsibilities lie with (at most, nine) county elected offices. Most counties elect the county judge (chief operating officer), county clerk, sheriff, tax collector, treasurer, and assessor. In 1981 the added local-option one-cent sales tax further enhanced counties' financial position.

Cities in Arkansas, on the other hand, have never been given broad home rule powers.[10] Article 12 and Amendment 14 (1926) represent the constitutional foundation for a grant of authority to local governments to conduct their affairs.[11] Upon approval by the electorate, cities of a certain size can adopt a charter that spells out the types of services to be provided, the amount of taxes to be levied, the method of election of city council members, and the general form of government.[12] Any changes to the charter require approval by citizens during a regular or special election. Changes in rules and procedures are statutory in nature and do not require voters' approval. First- and second-class cities are given additional powers to regulate streets, alleys, and sidewalks and trades, businesses, and hotels.[13]

The constitution invests cities with the traditional powers to form administrative agencies (such as finance, planning and zoning, and public works) to maintain infrastructure, preserve the general health and welfare, and own and operate facilities. Cities may own airports, river ports, sewer plants, or communications facilities (radio, TV, or cable). In addition, "the territorial jurisdiction of the legislative body of the city having a planning commission" can extend five miles beyond corporate limits. If municipalities are in close proximity, a line equidistant from their respective boundaries shall constitute the mutual boundary.[14] Much of the Arkansas Code of 1987 and subsequent amendments deal with fiscal and economic powers of counties and cities.

Structural Features

Arkansas has 490 incorporated[15] cities and towns, 75 counties, 324 school districts, and approximately 584 special districts.[16] Except for the mayor's position in larger urban areas, elected posts in the smaller communities are rarely contested. In small rural communities, it is often difficult to find willing candidates for local elected posts. Most towns and cities in Arkansas use the mayor-council form of government. Only nine cities use the manager-council arrangement or an administrator-council form.[17] All towns and cities elect their mayors and other public offices for four-year terms. Aldermen in cities under 50,000 in population are elected for two years; in cities over 50,000, aldermen are elected for four-year terms.[18] On paper, Arkansas mayors would appear "weak," yet the reality has shown that mayors wield considerable executive powers if they so choose to do so. The Arkansas state legislature does not use "local privilege" or other forms of special legislation to alter the authority, function, or operation of its local governments.

To annex or not to annex is a question that often is determined by weighing the benefits derived by smaller towns or unincorporated areas when joining a larger community and by the perceived cost associated with an "urban" lifestyle.[19] In Arkansas, two possibilities exist for a municipality to change or expand its territory: incorporation or annexation.[20] Incorporation allows an assembly of buildings to be declared a town, a municipal corporation. The new town must file a petition with the county court. If the new entity is within five miles of an existing town, the consent of that municipality must be sought.

Like many other states, Arkansas gives municipalities considerable latitude to expand boundaries outside existing ones (annexation). Several methods are available. The election method requires consent by voters in both the area to be annexed and the annexing community. If two cities vie for the area to be annexed, the voters of the contested area provide the deciding vote.

The ordinance method is applicable when an unincorporated area is completely surrounded by a municipality. It requires a vote of the local legislature to make the decision final. In the petition method, property owners who want their land to be annexed by the city file a petition with the county court. If no lawsuit is filed, the annexation is confirmed, and the city council passes an ordinance or resolution to declare the land annexed.

Annexation also occurs when a smaller and a larger community decide to merge their territories. In a mainly rural state, counties have traditionally assumed an important role as an arm of state government, even though more recently this role has been eclipsed by the state's larger cities. Counties, as in most other states, have been instrumental in constructing roads and highways and in providing public health services through county health departments and various social services.

Functions of Local Government

Functional Responsibilities

Functional home rule in Arkansas in its most general sense is a grant of power from the state legislature that determines the corporate functions of municipalities. The Arkansas Code specifies that a municipality may exercise grants of powers to preserve public health, develop standards and rules and regulations needed to govern its own affairs, and levy appropriate taxes to provide services or acquire needed property.[21] The municipal charter reserves the right of the legislature to modify, amend, or even revoke the charter. The constitution invests cities with the power to maintain agencies (such as fire and police departments) and infrastructure, to preserve the general health and welfare (through water and sewer, public health), to own and operate facilities (such as recreational facilities and parks), and to raise funds to support the municipal corporation.

Counties are likewise authorized to own and operate public facilities such as ports and harbors or transportation terminals. Levies associated with these facilities must be authorized by state law. Additional monies for improvements have been added over the years, extending the ability of municipalities and counties to perform capital improvements and to issue bonds in the pursuit of their economic activities.[22]

Municipalities and counties are further authorized to create public authorities, such as housing authorities, to provide for sanitary and safe accommodations for persons of low income. As a public entity, an authority can raise funds through the issuance of bonds and has the right to use eminent domain to condemn private property.

Arkansas statutes permit the creation of a variety of special districts or authorities that assume governmental functions to meet needs that cannot be addressed by a single community. Act 26 (1955), for example, allowed for joint planning commissions. Examples of such commissions are Metroplan (for two central counties around Little Rock), the Northwest Arkansas Planning Commission, the Southwest Regional Planning Commission, and the Southeast Planning Commission.[23] Conservation districts are established by the state Soil and Water Conservation Commission on petition of landowners and after local referendum. The conservation district board may require contributions in money, services, and materials; accept donations and gifts; levy special benefit assessments; and issue bonds.

Fire protection districts (1939 and 1979 laws) are formed by ordinance of, or petition to, the county governing body; in the latter instance, voter approval is necessary. An elected board of commissioners governs each district. The districts may levy benefit assessments and borrow money. Districts established under the 1979 law may also issue general obligation bonds upon voter approval.

Arkansas statutes authorize municipal, county, consolidated (two or more cities), and regional (two or more counties) housing authorities. Under general law, housing authorities are created when a resolution is adopted by the governing body of the city or county. The executive head of the municipality appoints the housing commissioners of a municipal housing authority; the governing body of the county appoints the commissioners of a county housing authority. Housing authorities may determine rents and receive assistance and grants from both the state and the federal government. Housing authorities may also issue bonds and carry out urban renewal activities. Legislation passed in 1976 grants municipalities and counties all powers given to housing authorities. Housing authorities administered by county or municipal governing bodies ex officio are not counted as separate governments.

A variety of improvement districts have been formed by municipalities and counties to protect citizens against natural forces (such as dam and lake districts and irrigation, drainage, or watershed districts); joint county and municipal solid waste disposal authorities have also been created. A board of directors, appointed by the participating governments, governs each authority. An authority may fix and collect charges and issue bonds. Some authorities of these types are categorized as resource recovery authorities. Others seek improvements in towns and cities, such as parks, arts centers, or museums.

On petition of property owners and after public hearing, municipal improvement districts may be established by the governing body of any city or town. A board of commissioners appointed by the municipal governing body governs each district. The board may fix rates and rents, levy benefit assessments, and issue bonds. Similar provisions apply to consolidated municipal utility districts. Property owners improvement districts (1983 and 1987 laws) are another example. Districts to fund improvements such as streets, sewers, and water utilities are created by petition of landowners to the municipal governing body. The districts may levy special assessments and issue bonds. Districts under the 1983 law may also levy ad valorem taxes. During the 1999 legislative session, municipal management districts were added (Act 230). They are in effect improvement districts with the purpose of enhancing the economic health and viability of the municipality.

The fragmentation of urban areas is a well-documented phenomenon.[24] Arkansas's urban areas are becoming strained because of sprawl, environmental degradation, and incursion of economic activities into rural areas that were once unaffected by these developments. Although the Arkansas Constitution is silent on this issue, the Arkansas Code clearly encourages interlocal agreements.[25] The Interlocal Cooperation Act (1967) allows "local governmental units to make the most efficient use of their powers by enabling them to cooperate with other localities on the basis of mutual advantage and thereby provide services and facilities . . . that will accord best with geographic, economic, population, and other factors."

Sanctioned interlocal activities include contracting with other governmental units for services, constructing facilities, or otherwise interacting in a formal or informal manner. The act does not specify or prohibit specific activities as long as they adhere to the statutory grants of authority to the units involved. An example is the Joint County and Municipal Waste Disposal Act (1979), which creates a sanitation authority of several cooperating counties and cities for the purpose of identifying the best site for solid waste disposal.[26] Other types of activities might include the building of new airports, regional jails, or juvenile detention centers; the creation of port authorities; or the establishment of economic development agreements.

Administrative Discretion

Despite the limited grants of powers to local governments, Arkansas cities and counties possess considerable latitude in how they fund—and especially administer—their own affairs. The rural nature of the state, the absence of very large cities, and the predominance of the mayor-council form are main factors limiting professionalization at all levels of government. Counties in the most rapidly growing areas of the state (central and northwestern parts) find themselves scrambling to meet new demands.

Civil service provisions have existed for sixty years and have been upgraded and strengthened for cities with 20,000–75,000 population—those cities that are most likely to struggle with increased responsibilities. These provisions elaborate on the hiring and firing of nonuniformed and uniformed employees, establish restraints on the political activities of employees, and address other areas of conduct.[27] Because of weak or nonexistent human resource departments, however, many smaller towns and cities have underdeveloped procedures that regulate hiring, firing, and promoting. Training efforts to upgrade managerial competencies of supervisors and employee skills have increased considerably. The Arkansas Public Administration Consortium (APAC) has developed a nationally recognized partnership among its three public administration programs to provide training opportunities for state employees. APAC has begun a municipal training program directed toward local and county administrative personnel, county judge executives, and planning commissioners. Other state agencies have also conducted training when needed. Individual communities might offer selected training opportunities through their chambers of commerce or other local organizations.

Purchases not exceeding $5,000 can be made without council approval in first-class cities. Larger purchases require the invitation of competitive bidding, with bids going to the "lowest responsible bidder."[28] The Arkansas Municipal League has also been pressing for changes in municipal accounting practices to simplify and standardize its provisions across the state (Act 218).

Arkansas municipalities must establish planning commissions and adopt zoning ordinances. The smaller or rural counties have only recently begun to do so, often despite strong resistance by residents. City and county master plans are required by the state constitution to guide development. These plans and the granting of variances are often subject to dispute, especially in areas that have experienced rapid shifts from rural to urban conditions. These rural areas had few if any written planning documents. The larger counties and all but the smallest cities have instituted planning procedures to promote orderly growth and preserve undeveloped rural land. Such efforts are often opposed by property owners who feel that only they should determine how their land will be used.

Citizens who disagree with variances granted by the municipality may appeal to the chancery or county courts. Counties are increasingly cooperating with larger municipalities on planning efforts to save both citizens and developers the aggravation associated with incompatible planning and zoning regulations. In addition, any two or more cities of the first class may establish a commission to exercise the planning powers, duties, and functions for the combined area of both cities.[29]

In recent years, the use of eminent domain and other municipal planning activities have come under attack by those who rely on Article 22 of the constitution, which states that "the right of property is before and higher than any constitutional sanction; and private property shall not be taken, appropriated or damaged for public use, without just compensation." However, the next section assures the state's "ancient right of eminent domain and taxation." Title 18 of the Arkansas Code reaffirms the powers of municipal corporations to take and condemn private property for the construction of "lawful purposes." Nevertheless, the issue remains vigorously debated as urbanized areas encroach upon rural areas. The 1999 legislative session witnessed another effort to impose stringent "takings" legislation that would have severely curtailed municipal planning activities. Such efforts were less favorably received than they were just a few years ago and were soundly defeated.

Economic Development

Many Arkansas statutes are devoted to encouraging and regulating economic development activities. Community development corporations (CDCs), industrial parks, planning and development districts, enterprise zones, and improvement districts have been utilized as developmental vehicles in many of Arkansas's larger communities.[30]

The Arkansas Economic Development Commission (AEDC) is the primary state agency for economic development activity. Set up in 1967 as "emergency legislation" under the Industrial Revenue Bond Guaranty Law, the commission guarantees county and municipal revenue bonds that are issued for economic development purposes.[31] Legislation in 1997 changed the name of the AEDC from "Industrial Development" to "Economic Development" to better reflect the changing nature of the state's economy. Moreover, the amount that the AEDC can guarantee was increased from $2 million to $4 million for amortization payments of tax-exempt industrial revenue bonds and Arkansas Development Finance Authority bonds issued for construction to secure and develop the economy of the state. For each loan they secure, county and city governments pay a one-time premium payment into the Revenue Bond Guaranty Reserve Account to maintain this account. During the 1999 legislative session, AEDC funding was reappropriated, and additional monies were provided for incentives to companies to locate new or expanded facilities (Act 421).

The trend has been to use revenue bonds (especially those designed for economic development purposes), because they do not require a public vote. Arkansas allows cities and counties to form "industrial development compacts" to issue revenue bonds. Municipalities often argue that revenue bond debt is not really "public" debt and that the cities serve only as conduits. The commission is required to use the funds on deposit in the Revenue Bond Guaranty Reserve Account to meet amortization payments as guaranteed, if there is a failure to make bond payments. This guaranty, however, is not a general obligation of the commission or the state. Often, the potential debt is defined so that it is not a "constitutional debt." The legislation states that "in no event shall the guaranty constitute an indebtedness of the commission or of the State of Arkansas within the meaning of any constitutional or statutory limitation."[32] During the 1999 legislative session, the Arkansas Municipal League supported the introduction of tax increment financing (TIF) as a financial tool not previously available to municipalities. The introduction of TIF will require a constitutional amendment.

Enterprise zones were authorized in 1993 (pursuant of the Enterprise Zone Act of 1989) and established a series of distress criteria to be verified by the Department of Economic Development for the governor's approval. However, counties and cities can petition the department to have an area decertified if none of the businesses in the zone have applied for tax credits. Enterprise zone provisions were authorized through June 1999 and were renewed indefinitely during the 1999 session (Act 1130).

Fiscal Autonomy of Local Governments

Local Revenues

The west–south central region of the United States tends to have lower per capita revenues than the national median.[33] Arkansas cities tend to be lower still. Arkansas ranks forty-ninth in state and local taxes and fifty-first (counting the District of Columbia) in total state and local revenue per capita. No municipal corporation may levy a tax on real or personal property greater than 5 mills on each dollar of assessed property value. Sales taxes are the major source of city and county operating revenue; more than 99.5 percent of sales in Arkansas are subject to local sales tax.[34] Cities and towns are authorized a total of four cents in sales tax, subject to voter approval. Two cents are authorized for operating expenses, one cent for capital improvements, and one cent for park improvements. Counties are authorized to use three cents: two cents for operating and one cent for capital improvements.

There are sales taxes on food and medicine. The Arkansas Municipal League and other municipal advocacy organizations thus far have prevented efforts to remove these taxes. Small rural cities would be the most negatively affected if food and medicine were not taxed because these cities have little sales other than food. Lobbying efforts to introduce new exemptions from sales taxes for the most part have been defeated.

Tax comparisons across states can be misleading. When per capita comparisons are used, Arkansas relies less on the property tax than do many other states. Arkansas cities are authorized to use an income tax, but no Arkansas city currently levies it. The Arkansas Municipal League favors phasing out the state income tax, provided that other means can be found to replace lost revenue. (Neighboring states such as Texas and Tennessee have no or very low state income tax levels.[35])

Local governments in Arkansas receive more than half of their resources from own sources, such as taxes and fees, and the remainder comes from state and federal sources. Of the 53 percent in own-source revenues, only 30 percent is generated from taxes, with the property tax being the largest revenue raiser. Own-source revenues comprise fees and charges—a clear departure from traditional revenue-raising patterns with their heavy reliance on more "visible" sources such as property and sales taxes.

Recently, efforts to eliminate the local property tax have been a concern in the legislature. A series of measures to fend off attempts at constitutional tax reform have been proposed and an orderly appraisal system for property (Act 385) has been designed. Moreover, a constitutional amendment has been advanced that would provide for up to $300 in property tax reductions on homes in exchange for a half-cent increase in the state sales tax.

Sales tax exemptions currently deprive the state of about $800 million in revenue.[36] Several newly passed acts (1137, 1289) require that municipalities must submit to the Department of Finance and Administration proposed ordinances levying city or county sales and use taxes. This measure is designed to prevent any illegal exactions. Arkansas has joined a number of other states to push for the collection of sales taxes on mail order or Internet sales that adversely affect local merchants and businesses.

A final revenue-related measure will require a constitutional amendment. House Joint Resolution 1012 will grant municipalities and counties authority for tax increment financing and short-term lease purchase authority of up to 5 percent of the assessed value of a municipality (and 2.5 percent for counties) to be paid for a period of up to five years.

County revenues are derived primarily from real and property taxes. State revenue "turnbacks"—which are local revenues collected by the state and then returned to the local communities according to a population-based formula—such as highways, roads, and forest and public land sales, make up about one-third of total revenues. Remaining revenues come from fees, charges, fines, and licenses. Arkansas counties may impose an income tax, but none currently do so. In 1999 a provision was passed allowing county voters to use the initiative process to force the quorum court to put a sales tax proposal before the

voters. The state legislature also agreed to increase turnbacks by 10 percent, contingent on a robust state economy.

Arkansas cities and counties are allowed by constitutional amendment to issue bonds.[37] Earlier in its history, the state mandated a public vote on any new bonds—a provision that still applies to bonds for nonindustrial capital improvements. There has been an increasing trend not to put revenue bonds before a public vote, especially bonds that are designed for economic development purposes within a city.

The state's supreme court also has played an active role in the evolving definition of what is appropriate debt. There is a continual need to reconcile the older constitutional language of restraint with the newer legislative intent for local governments to stimulate development. To avoid 1974 constitutional provisions against the use of public money for private purposes (such as railroads), a relatively recent state supreme court decision found that economic development was a "public purpose."[38]

Court interpretations often have supported municipal desires. For example, one lawsuit filed by a worker on an economic development site attempted to force a private contractor to the pay minimum wage, which is required on public projects. The court found that the legislature did not intend for such provisions to cover economic development projects.[39] That these projects have been determined to be public in purpose and yet, in some respects, private has allowed cities to take advantage of both perspectives.

This interaction among substate governments, the legislature, and the supreme court is characteristic of Arkansas politics. The state supreme court has intervened in situations in which cities have overcommitted themselves. The Arkansas Constitution forbids cities from incurring expenses that exceed their revenues in any given year. When a city has not been able to pay a large debt, the court has declared that debt unconstitutional and void. The city is then forbidden to repay it. The constitution further dictates that the state never assumes responsibility for that debt.[40] A notable intergovernmental exception is the state supreme court's ruling that obligations to the federal government must be paid, even when expenses exceed revenues.[41]

Local Expenditures

Most local expenditures in Arkansas are channeled into education, health, and public welfare projects. Requirements for municipal fiscal management are written into the state constitution. The regulations broach various topics, from the mayor's annual report to the use of prenumbered checks and receipts for all city business. First-class cities are required to have an independent certified public accountant verify their financial affairs. There is no requirement for other types of cities.[42]

County expenditures may not be budgeted for more than 90 percent of estimated revenue. No county funds may be spent without the express approval of the quorum court. Counties expend up to one-third of their revenues on roads and rural services; approximately another third goes to rural law enforcement and jail operations. About 10–15 percent is spent on courts and judicial administration, and the remainder is allocated for general administration, building maintenance, health and social services, elections, and emergency services.

In 1999 Arkansas joined many other states in adopting new policies on electric utility deregulation. Ensuring that deregulation does not erode local revenue sources has been a concern. Deregulation also allows municipally owned utilities to opt in or out of competition.

State Government Grants-in-Aid to Localities

Arkansas municipalities receive only a small fraction of their revenues from the federal government, with the majority of federal funds going to individuals as entitlements.[43] More than 40 percent of local revenues come from turnbacks from the state. In 1996, 23.2 percent of state expenditures were intergovernmental.[44] Sales taxes are collected at the state level and then are returned to local coffers. Several local governments in the rapidly growing northwestern part of the state have commissioned a special census to attest to population increases in the hope that their turnbacks from the state will be augmented (turnbacks are tied to the size of the local population).

Unfunded Mandates

Of greatest concern to local government officials are maintaining fire and police pension funds and fringe benefits; ensuring that the onus for enforcement of gun control laws is on local government officials; and streamlining car tag renewal procedures (a 1997 law removed many of the procedures that triggered complaints from citizens and local officials).[45] The Arkansas Municipal League and others have requested that the state perform tasks considered by many communities to be costly and burdensome, such as maintaining records as called for by the Sex and Child Offender Registration Act of 1997. Freedom of Information Act language also needs to be clarified to avert undue burdens on city and county offices.

Counties are required to provide for the administration of justice through courts. Although salaries are paid by the state, other court expenses must be paid by counties. Counties also must build jail facilities that are in compliance with federal and state restrictions (such as limitations on the number of inmates per cell) and must ensure separate facilities for women and juveniles and access to various services. The salaries of the county health administrators are paid by the state; however, counties are responsible for building health facilities. Special districts and school districts are also required to meet standards defined at higher levels of government, but without added compensation to meet these requirements.

Access to Local Government

Local Elections

State laws provide guidelines for conducting local elections, registering voters, qualifying candidates for public office, balloting, and validating election results. In cities of 50,000 or more population, municipal elections are held every four years. These elections are supervised, and results are tabulated by the county board of election commissioners. Mayoral candidates must receive a majority of the votes to be declared a winner. In the city manager form of government, the mayor is elected by the directors of the city board. Terms for the mayor may be as short as one year. Directors in city manager governments can be removed by citizen petition.[46]

There have been some moves to make the political process more accessible to citizens. Title 7 of the Arkansas Code details recent changes in election and campaign procedures, such as how precinct boundaries are drawn, when candidates must file, and the nature of campaign contributions. In another reform, the supreme court found that forcing political parties in Arkansas to pay for primary elections was unconstitutional; the intention of this decision was to facilitate the participation of third parties and their candidates. In 1999 numerous bills were passed that clarified issues pertaining to election laws, such as oath procedure, voting forms (write-in votes are prohibited), residency requirements, filing deadlines, and political activities of public employees (see Acts 640, 641, 642, 650, 653, 658, 752).

Citizen Controls over Actions of Local Officials

Amendment 7 (which was declared adopted by the state supreme court in 1925) specifically mentions two methods by which the people can enact legislation and reject actions taken by the legislative body: initiative and referendum. The amendment does not prohibit the use of these methods for activities other than those not permitted by law. Initiatives or referendums seeking to change the tax code or introduce activities are not permissible under the city charter. Similar procedures apply to county government.

The recall procedure may be used to remove the mayor or any city director from office. A petition must be filed with the city clerk and must be signed by a number of qualified electors equal to 35 percent of the total number of votes cast for that office in the preceding election. A majority vote is needed to remove the individual from office. In the manager-administrator form of government, the city manager can be removed by a vote of the board.

All boards and commissions must comply with the Freedom of Information Act (FOIA) (Act 93 of 1967) and must conform to the Administrative Procedures Act (Act 434 of 1976). The latter is designed to hold agencies accountable through the adoption of uniform rules and procedures that must be reviewed by the legislative council and the attorney general. All actions of boards and commissions must be published in the *Arkansas Register.* Continued problems with the implementation of FOIA prompted the Arkansas legislature, in 1999, to create an Electronic Records Study Commission to recommend changes to the next legislature.

The Arkansas Ethics Commission was established in 1991 "to serve as the compliance and enforcement agency under Arkansas's standards of conduct and disclosure laws concerning candidates for public office, state and local public officials, lobbyists and committees, and individuals involved with initiatives, referendums and other matters referred to the voters." Under the strong leadership of its director, Bob Brooks, the commission interprets this mandate to mean that legislators and other elected officials are prohibited from receiving any gifts. Specific guidelines for gifts have been criticized by some legislators who feel that the commission's approach is excessive.[47]

State-Local Relations

Economically, Arkansas is a state of extremes. Concentrations of affluence and abject poverty continue to characterize various regions of the state. Urbanization has largely benefited the more affluent areas and the metropolitan regions but has done little to upgrade towns tied to agriculture (for example, rice, cotton, and forest products). Governments in growing cities and counties are overwhelmed by the responsibilities associated with increased population but are only slowly effecting administrative and fiscal changes.

The state's largest cities are attempting to achieve more local control and may adopt a new strategy to obtain home rule, but constitutional and statutory changes have been incremental. Unresolved or confused interpretations of contradictory legal and fiscal issues have resulted in cities being sued. City officials are not likely to embark on new endeavors when the likelihood of litigation is high.

Changes confronting counties are even more daunting, since professional county management is a rarity in Arkansas. County officials are unprepared for the growing number of tasks that are pushed into their legislative chambers. At the same time, some rural residents resist the efforts of counties that comprise larger cities to impose planning, zoning, and other regulations. They perceive these regulations as infringements on their lifestyle.

Citizens do not trust their state and local governments to adopt sweeping changes. In the face of long-standing elite rule and self-serving legislatures reinforced by one-party control, this attitude is not entirely surprising. Reactions by local governments to pressures to change have ranged from acting defensively to circumventing citizens' concerns to allowing only token input by the electorate. Predictably, increasing numbers of citizens are clamoring for true participation, greater transparency of local decision-making processes, and greater accountability of local officials.

Despite considerable changes in Arkansas's political landscape over the past two decades, constitutional limitations on local governments likely have been an impediment. Failed efforts to revise the state constitution comprehensively also have kept local governments from enjoying a broader interpretation of their powers. The reticence of the legislature and the rural-urban split in the state make efforts to grant this new power an uphill struggle. Moreover, state and local governments are insufficiently prepared for the tasks resulting from federal devolution. In the absence of home rule, the state is likely either to mandate changes without relinquishing its traditional controls on local administration or to seek private-sector solutions to bypass local governments altogether.

Notes

1. Among recent rejections at the polls were then-governor Jim Guy Tucker's sponsorship of a bond issue to fund highway improvements in the state and a call for a convention to revamp the antiquated constitution. (Governor Tucker was convicted for his involvement in the Whitewater affair and resigned his office in May 1996.)

2. D. Blair, *Arkansas Politics and Government* (Lincoln: University of Nebraska Press, 1988).

3. For a survey of Arkansas constitutions, see R. A. Leflar, "A Survey of Arkansas Constitutions," in *Arkansas: Colony and State,* ed. L. DuVall (Little Rock: Rose Publishing, 1973), 188.

4. Recent amendments to the Arkansas Constitution dealing with local matters include Amendment 62 (1984), authorizing the issuance of local capital improvement bonds; Amendment 64 (1986), clarifying the types of cases that municipal courts can adjudicate; and Amendment 65 (1986), clarifying the issuance of revenue bonds.

5. Blair, *Arkansas Politics and Government,* 124. As of May 1996, seventy-one amendments had been approved. The amendment adopted in 1993 removed ad valorem property taxes on personal household goods, except for motor vehicles. A survey of state laws governing local affairs by the U.S. Advisory Commission on Intergovernmental Relations (ACIR) ranks Arkansas in the upper range between 1978 and 1990. ACIR, *State Laws Governing Local Government Structure and Administration* (Washington, D.C.: ACIR, 1993), 59.

6. Examples include Jeff Davis (1901–1907) and the fabled Orval Faubus (1955–1967), who received national attention when he ordered the National Guard to stop nine black students from entering Little Rock's Central High School in 1957.

7. Blair, *Arkansas Politics and Government,* chapter 9. For a more detailed analysis, see also chapter 4.

8. Ibid., 166.

9. ACIR, *State Laws Governing Local Government Structure and Administration,* 20.

10. Ibid.

11. Amendment 14 prohibits local legislation if a law is proposed that would apply only to selected subdivisions of the state—that is, if it is not general in nature. That a statute may affect some jurisdictions differently than it does others does not make it a priori "local." See *City of Little Rock v. Waters,* 303 Ark. 363, 797 S.W.2nd 426 (1990). For further clarification, see Arkansas Municipal League (AML), *Handbook for Arkansas Municipal Officials,* 2 vols. (Little Rock: AML, 1996), 61. Titles 14 and 26 of the Arkansas Code deal with the various provisions

contained in the laws and statutes, specifically 14-42-301–311; 14-43-601–611; and 26-73-101–109.

12. First-class cities are all cities over 2,500 population. However, cities of 1,500 and larger can become first-class cities by passing a municipal ordinance. Second-class cities are all other cities with 500–2,500 population and those under 500 that have voted to be second-class cities. Arkansas Code 14-42, 14-43, 14-44, 14-45. Incorporated towns are all other incorporated places.

13. Arkansas Code 14-54-104–105.

14. Arkansas Code 14-56-413.

15. Arkansas Municipal League (AML), *Guidebook for Municipal Officials of Mayor-Council Cities* (Little Rock: AML, 1997), 5.

16. State Policy Research, *States in Profile* (McConnellsburg, Pa.: U.S. Data on Demand, 1995), table E-16. The total is 1,473 units, which ranks Arkansas twenty-second among the fifty states. Given the small size of the state, however, the relative rank is probably higher.

17. For specifics relating to city-manager and city-administrator forms of government, see Arkansas Code 14-47 and 14-48.

18. Arkansas Code 14-43 and 14-44.

19. In the wake of problems some cities encountered in instituting growth policies, the 1999 legislative session approved several acts to clarify annexation or de-annexation (detachment) issues (Acts 1128, 779, 988). Several cities have proposed to annex land in their natural growth zone. The city of Arkadelphia, for example, has annexed territory that effectively doubled its size.

20. The Arkansas Municipal League's flyer, "Municipal Annexation, Incorporation and Other Boundary Changes" (Little Rock: AML, 1993), presents a concise overview. The relevant state statutes are Arkansas Code 14-38-101–108 and 14-38-114 (incorporation); 14-40-301–303 (annexation—election method); 14-40-501–503 (annexation—ordinance method); 14-40-601–603 (annexation—petition method).

21. Arkansas Code 14-42-307 and 14-43-601.

22. Arkansas Constitution, amendments 62 and 65.

23. See also League of Women Voters (LOWV), *Government in Arkansas* (Little Rock: LOWV, 1993), 63.

24. See, for example, P. Kantor, with S. David, *The Dependent City: The Changing Political Economy of Urban America* (Glenview, Ill.: Foresman, 1988); M. Gottdiener, *The Decline of Urban Politics: Political Theory and the Crisis of the Local State* (Newbury Park, Calif.: Sage, 1987); and Brian D. Jacobs, *Fractured Cities* (New York: Routledge, 1992).

25. Arkansas Code 25-20.

26. Arkansas Code 14-233.

27. Arkansas Code 14-50ff.

28. Arkansas Code 14-58-303.

29. Arkansas Code 14-56.

30. Arkansas Code 14-48-131.

31. Arkansas Code 15- 4.

32. Arkansas Code 14-165, 14-164-522.

33. Using the ACIR's Tax Capacity Index, Arkansas ranked next to last in its region (it scored a seventy-eight, with the region averaging eighty-six). Similarly, on the Tax Effort Index, Arkansas lagged behind the other states in the region, with a score of eighty-two compared with the region's ninety. See ACIR, *Significant Features of Fiscal Federalism,* vol. 2 (Washington, D.C.: ACIR, 1994), 182–183.

34. See Arkansas Municipal League (AML), *City and County Sales Tax: Information and Statistics* (Little Rock: AML, 1995). The ACIR's annual survey of states reports that of all municipal revenues, Arkansas uses the sales tax to a greater degree than any other source. Indeed, when compared with other states, Arkansas ranks in the bottom third in its use of the property tax, even though in nominal terms the property tax generates more income than the sales tax. See ACIR, *Significant Features of Fiscal Federalism,* vol. 2, 203.

35. ACIR, *Significant Features of Fiscal Federalism,* vol. 2, 203.

36. Arkansas Municipal League, "Policies and Goals" (Little Rock: Arkansas Municipal League, 1999), 8.

37. Arkansas Constitution, amendment 62.

38. *Wayland v. Snapp,* 232 Ark. 57, 334 S.W.2d 633 (1960). The *Handbook for Arkansas Municipal Officials* (North Little Rock: AML, 1996) comments that the phrase "public purpose" is a vague one. For example in the *City of Fayetteville v. Phillips* (306 Ark. 87, 811 S.W.2nd 308 [1991]), the court argued that tax exemption for public property under construction may not be summarily denied based on the taxing authority's belief that the property might be used for nonpublic purposes. In a 1995 case, the court developed a test for exemption (*City of Little Rock v. McIntosh,* 319 Ark. 87, 892 S.W.2nd 462 [1995]). Whether or not the property is public property and is being used exclusively for public purposes determines its exemption status.

39. *Daniels v. City of Fort Smith,* 268 Ark. 157, 594 S.W.2d 238 (1980).

40. Arkansas Constitution, Article 12.

41. *Cravens v. United States,* 163 F. Supp. 309 (W.D. Ark. 1958).

42. Arkansas Code 14-58-60.

43. ACIR, *Significant Features of Fiscal Federalism,* vol. 2, 203.

44. U.S. Bureau of the Census, *Annual Survey of Government Finances* (Washington, D.C.: U.S. Government Printing Office, 1996).

45. Information is based on interviews with or comments by public officials at 1996 Arkansas Municipal League and Arkansas Public Management Association meetings during debates about unfunded mandates.

46. Arkansas Code 14-40–48.

47. The Arkansas Ethics Commission's authorities and responsibilities are set out in Arkansas Code Annotated sections 7-6-217–218. The initiated act defines gifts as anything worth more than $100 that might be given to an official. The new proposal, section 303(a), specifies further that "no public servants shall receive a gift for the performance of the duties and responsibilities of his or her office or position." There were appropriate exceptions in the law. Few cities have adopted citywide ethics codes to guide the conduct of appointed officials. See http://www.arkansasethics.com/mission_statement.htm and http://www.arkansasethics.com/proposedgifts.pdf.

CALIFORNIA

Alvin D. Sokolow and Peter M. Detwiler

Since the adoption in 1879 of California's current constitution, cities and counties in this state have enjoyed considerable home rule. They have organizational flexibility, a wide latitude to spend and regulate, and the ability to experiment with programs and procedures. Much of this discretion, however, is now compromised by constraints on local government revenue authority—a result of the gradual abandonment of the property tax as a local revenue source and the domination of state fiscal rules. Home rule for local governments in California consequently resembles a "hollow sphere," a superficial outer skin of structural and programmatic discretion hiding a weakened fiscal core. Clearly, revenue issues dominate the ongoing story of state-local relations in California.

Governmental Setting

Local governments in California operate in an environment of continual population increase, reform tradition, and now a growing distrust of public institutions. The result is a fundamental contradiction: a highly professional and efficient public sector that nevertheless is fiscally constrained by ballot-driven forces and is hard-pressed to keep up with a rapidly expanding and extraordinarily diverse population, which is projected to reach 63 million by 2040.[1]

Historical patterns of continued growth and constitutional change have affected local government performance in this state. In the past two decades, another element, Proposition 13, has been added to the state-local context. Proposition 13, the famous property tax cut approved by voters in 1978, set a precedent for the substantial transfer to the state of revenues that once were considered local—that is, from county, city, special-district, and school governments.

Since statehood in 1850, California's population increase has averaged about 41 percent per decade. The state contains the nation's second and fifth largest consolidated metropolitan areas, the urban agglomerations surrounding Los Angeles and San Francisco, respectively. In the past two decades, the most rapid growth has been in the desert regions east and north of Los Angeles, the foothills of the Sierra Nevada, and the agriculturally rich Central Valley.

As a result of such extensive growth, land use, service delivery, and finance issues top local government agendas. Community policy controversies focus on the challenges of paying for urbanization; preserving agricultural land, open space, and other natural resources; and allocating a limited water supply to serve the competing demands of population growth, agriculture, and the environment. To finance development and expanded public services in a post–Proposition 13 era, cities and counties impose heavy fees on new housing and compete with neighboring jurisdictions for sales tax–generating commercial development. Moreover, both state and local governments face the difficult task of absorbing and serving many new residents who are non–English speaking, relatively poor, and in need of K–12 education, social services, and other expensive programs.

In the state's first century, the second (and current) constitution was adopted, in 1879, and Progressive reforms were added in 1911. The adoption of the 1879 constitution established a firm basis for local government home rule, with broad grants of power to cities and counties. Progressive reforms introduced the tools of "direct democracy" (that is, the initiative, referendum, and recall) to California state and local government, which greatly reduced the significance of political parties and established nonpartisan local elections.

Compared with the frequently corrupt governments of its first sixty years, California state and local governance since the adoption of Progressive reforms has been relatively honest. In recent years, however, the political process has been tainted by the large sums spent in legislative lobbying and election campaigns at the state level and by pressures on local governments to gain favorable land-use decisions. In the late 1980s and early 1990s, several state legislators, legislative staff members, and a lobbyist were convicted on federal bribery and related charges as a result of a series of FBI "sting" operations. More recently, another FBI operation in the Fresno area resulted in the convictions of several developers and city council members for exchanging favorable land-use decisions for campaign contributions.[2]

Professionalism and innovation in government also characterize California's public sector. At the state level, there is a comprehensive civil service system that has been in place since the 1930s, a governor with extensive executive powers, and a legislature that has been full time and well staffed since 1967. Despite the imposition of term limits in 1996, political careerism exists among legislators and executive branch officials: these officeholders can readily move to other positions, including congressional seats and local government offices.

Professionalism also prevails in the way California's local governments are administered. Almost 80 percent of all cities follow the classic manager-council model of government, with "strong" managers, small councils (five-members) elected at large, "weak" mayors selected from the council, no other elected officials, and merit employment systems. About four-fifths of county governments also employ professional chief executive officers, who have limited powers that are shared among elected county officials, such as the sheriff, district attorney, and treasurer.

As innovators, California local governments pioneered the development of collective bargaining arrangements with employees, comprehensive general planning for cities and counties, redevelopment financing, and joint powers and other intergovernmental operating agreements. The employment of the first genuine city "manager" has been attributed to a California community. Four years before the more publicized action of Staunton, Virginia, the small city of Ukiah on the north coast of California in 1904 employed an "executive officer" who had appointment power over all employees.[3]

The professionalism and representative democracy of California state and local government is often countered by the expression of direct democracy. Increasingly, California voters bypass or second guess their elected representatives by putting measures on the ballot and approving them. Indeed, the most significant statewide policy changes enacted since the 1970s primarily have been products of the initiative, including Proposition 13 and other revenue restrictions on state and local government, expenditure limitations, political reform, environmental protection, guaranteed funding for K–12 education, rail transit and parkland spending, and limitations on insurance rates and terms. Initiatives at the local level also have been more frequent in recent years, especially voter challenges to city and county growth policies and practices.

The public-sector landscape of California is populated by about 4,400 distinct units of local government, according to the U.S. Census of Governments. Almost two-thirds are special districts, and school districts compose another quarter of the total. In terms of numbers of special districts and school districts, California ranks second in the nation (after Illinois and Texas, re-

spectively).[4] In numbers of general-purpose governments, municipalities, and counties, however, the state is in the middle nationally.

In this most populous state, individual cities and counties serve relatively large populations. In 1999 California had 139 municipalities with estimated populations of more than 50,000 apiece (more than one-quarter of the total), but only 60 with less than 5,000. Of the 58 counties, 22 (including the city-county of San Francisco) served estimated populations of 250,000 or more.

Home Rule in California

Historical Development

It was California's 1879 constitution—the second adopted and the one still in use today, although much amended—that established the framework for local government autonomy. Under the 1849 constitution, written the year before formal statehood, local government affairs were largely subject to the whim of the state legislature. Most of the seventy-one cities incorporated between 1850 and 1879 were created by special act. The first counties were created in the same way, as were later counties that spun off from existing ones. A more pernicious aspect of the caprice with which local government affairs were handled was the state legislature's frequent interference with local powers and finances. For example, individual cities were required to pay certain debts, levy taxes for particular purposes, and issue bonds for financing public improvements such as railroad construction.[5]

Reacting to the unpopularity of legislative interference, the delegates to the 1879 constitutional convention wrote a local government article with strong home rule language.[6] The article's key provisions included prohibitions on special legislation and legislative imposition of taxes on cities for municipal purposes; broad regulatory power for cities; requirements that the legislature prescribe "uniform procedures" for city formation and powers; and charter authority for cities with a population greater than 100,000 (which at that time only applied to San Francisco).

The scope of home rule was expanded in later years through amendments to the 1879 constitution and new statutes (see Box 1). Overall, the trend in the century after the 1879 constitution was toward greater local government autonomy in structural, programmatic, and fiscal areas. However, Proposition 13 in 1978 drastically reversed this direction in fiscal matters, introducing the current period of diminished revenue authority for California local governments.[7]

Recent home rule–related developments include legislative and constitutional efforts to reform a state-local government system that many critics regard as fiscally dysfunctional and unmanageable by elected officials. The state's political leaders in the early 1990s created the California Constitutional Revision

BOX 1. CHRONOLOGY OF HOME RULE ACTIONS IN CALIFORNIA

1849   First constitution adopted. Provided for legislative control of local affairs.

1879   Second and current constitution adopted. Prohibited special legislation, gave cities broad regulatory powers, required uniform procedures for city legislation, permitted charters to larger cities.

1892   Constitutional amendment extended charter authority to smaller cities.

1903   Los Angeles voters add initiative, referendum, and recall to the city's charter, preceding statewide adoption of these measures eight years later.

1907   Subdivision Map Act gave cities and counties their first planning and land-use powers.

1911   Constitutional amendments extended charter authority to counties, gave cities corporate power, and provided for initiative, referendum, and recall.

1917   Legislation gave cities and counties zoning powers.

1937   Legislation required cities and counties to adopt master plans.

1953   Brown Act required open meetings of all local legislative bodies.

1956   Bradley-Burns Act gave a share of the state sales tax to cities and counties.

1961   George-Brown Act required local governments to "meet and confer" with employee representatives, the beginning of collective bargaining.

1965   Knox-Nisbet Act established boundary controls for local government formations and annexations through Local Agency Formation Commissions at the county level.

1955–
1971   Legislation required cities and counties to add specific elements to their general plans, including land use, circulation, housing, and open space elements.

1970   California Environmental Quality Act required local governments to assess the environmental impacts of development projects.

1972   Legislation required state to reimburse localities for mandated program costs.

1978   Proposition 13 (constitutional amendment adopted by initiative) limited property tax rate and growth of assessed valuation.

1979   Proposition 4 (constitutional amendment adopted by initiative) put appropriation limits on state and local governments.

1987   Legislation allowed countywide sales tax increases for particular purposes.

1992–
1993   Legislation shifted $4 billion in property taxes from cities, counties, and special districts to schools.

1995   California Supreme Court affirms two-thirds voter requirement for local "special" taxes.

1996   Proposition 218 (constitutional amendment adopted by initiative) required voter approval of all local taxes and imposed limits on assessments and fees.

Commission to address a variety of organizational and fiscal issues. The commission's final report in 1996 recommended several measures to improve political accountability, reform the state's budget procedures, focus accountability for the K–12 schools, and straighten out state-local roles and relationships.[8] Distracted by impending elections and lacking political leadership, neither the legislature nor Gov. Pete Wilson took the commission's work seriously, and its recommendations were shelved. Since that time, more than a half-dozen other advisory panels, study commissions, and task forces have covered much of the same policy ground. Whether these renewed efforts are political window dressing or serious reform efforts remains to be seen.

Definition of Home Rule

"Home rule" is a term that does not appear in the California Constitution nor in the nineteen-volume Government Code, the compilation of state statutes affecting the organization and basic powers of state and local government. But the concept is much discussed in law reviews and among municipal attorneys. One source defines home rule as "the authority to take desired action at the local government's initiative without seeking legislative authority each time the local government wants to act."[9] The California Supreme Court has generously interpreted constitutional provisions for local governments, rarely if ever favoring state control in situations of ambiguity.

Much of the pertinent case law has examined the scope of

"municipal affairs," the key constitutional term that identifies the legislative powers of charter cities. As interpreted by the California judiciary over the years, municipal affairs include the creation of boards and commissions, methods of enacting ordinances, and regulation of gambling. Conversely, matters of "statewide concern," and thus not subject to local discretion, include annexation procedures, regulation of traffic, licensing of professionals, and taxation of financial corporations.[10]

Even before statehood, Californians have behaved at times as if community control of public affairs were an inherent right that did not depend on state law. During the four years of transition between the end of Mexican rule in 1846 and statehood in 1850, when California had U.S. military governors, several communities formed ad hoc governing institutions such as elected legislative assemblies and charters. These temporary arrangements were later superseded by the actions of the legislature working under the first constitution. Nevertheless, a strong belief in local control still prevails, particularly in smaller communities, and is often expressed in negative reactions to the imposition of state and federal authority.

Structural Features

The formal extent of local government autonomy is rooted in two key provisions of the current (1879) constitution, giving all cities and counties created by both general law as well as charter basic regulatory and service delivery powers. According to Article XI, Section 7:

A county or city may make and enforce within its limits all local, police, sanitary, and other ordinances and regulations not in conflict with general laws.[11]

Further, Section 9 states the following:

A municipal corporation may establish, purchase, and operate public works to furnish its inhabitants with light, water, power, heat, transportation, or means of communication.[12]

Termed, respectively, the "police" and "corporate" powers, these broad grants of authority have been interpreted to permit a wide array of legislative and programmatic functions. In the regulatory area, for example, counties and cities have considerable discretion to control land-use and development matters, extending beyond basic building, subdivision, and zoning ordinances to include caps on a community's overall growth rate and requiring changes in specific projects to reduce environmental impacts.

Under the constitutional constraint on special legislation, acts applied to individual local governments are prohibited if the legislature can make a general law apply.[13] Nevertheless, the legislature can enact bills that affect only a specific county or city, provided that the legislation invokes the community's need for special legislation. Legislative ingenuity sometimes applies general statutory language to individual governments in setting salary schedules for local officials, combining offices in specific counties, and limiting a particular city's zoning power, for example.

Statutory classification schemes can bypass the ban on special acts. Each of California's fifty-eight counties is still categorized in a separate population class, although the use of county classes has fallen out of favor. A classification scheme for cities and towns that contained six population categories was abandoned by the legislature in the 1950s. Years of statutory exceptions and rapid population growth made the classification scheme obsolete. Now all 473 municipalities are treated the same, regardless of the title of "city" or "town."

Because constitutional provisions assign virtually the same powers to cities and counties, there are few programmatic differences between these two general-purpose governments. Within their unincorporated areas, California counties have essentially the same regulatory and service delivery powers as do cities within their incorporated boundaries. The principal difference is counties' nonlocal role as agents of state government for a number of functions; counties' discretion is limited in ways not shared by municipalities.

With rare exception, the police powers of cities and counties are mutually exclusive. Cities cannot regulate activities outside their boundaries, and, conversely, county governments use their police powers to regulate activities only within the unincorporated areas. An exception is that cities may project the extension of their boundaries and urban development into unincorporated areas through general plan boundaries, for example, which typically extend beyond incorporated limits, and through the prezoning of land slated for annexation. Cities and counties regularly own and use public property in each others' jurisdictions. Cities operate airports, dams, landfills, and wastewater disposal sites outside city limits, and counties locate their courthouses, jails, and offices inside cities.

The constitution does allow individual cities and counties to adopt charters.[14] However, because local functions inferred from the constitutional police and corporate powers are so extensive, there is little distinction between general-law and charter status for both cities and counties. Charter governments have somewhat more leeway in personnel matters (including increased discretion to contract for services) and in purchasing procedures, but there are few other substantial differences in terms of fiscal, regulatory, and programmatic powers—the result of a generous legislature.

More significant is the organizational flexibility allowed under charter status. Communities adopting new charters do so for primarily structural reasons. For example, charter counties can elect their legislative bodies other than by district. Charter cities can have "strong" mayors. Currently, 13 counties and 100 cities operate under charters, about one-fifth of the total number of each type. Charters can be written and proposed to the voters either by elected charter commissions or by city and county governing boards. The initiative process can be used to instigate this process and to propose revisions.

At times, proposals to adopt or revise charters become major issues in individual jurisdictions. Elections to revise existing charters are more common; revisions often address the details in language that seem to favor one political interest over another. In June 1999, Los Angeles voters approved major changes in the city charter that increased the mayor's powers and established neighborhood councils and area planning commissions, but voters rejected an increase in the city council from fifteen to twenty-one or twenty-five members.[15] The charter contained more than 600 pages and had been exposed to more than 400 amendments since 1925.[16]

California has a strong though decentralized system for controlling new local government formations and boundary changes. Local Agency Formation Commissions (LAFCOs) are quasi-independent agencies[17] that were created by 1965 legislation in response to extensive urban sprawl and interjurisdictional boundary wars in metropolitan areas. LAFCOs are organized in all counties except San Francisco and comprise five or more members representing county and city governments and the public. The commissions review and pass on all proposals for city incorporations, special-district formations, annexations to cities and districts, and dissolutions and detachments. LAFCOs examine the proposals and feasibility studies that document service delivery and fiscal consequences. Moreover, they can deny proposals, approve them outright, or submit them for final voter approval. In 1972 the responsibilities of LAFCOs were significantly expanded to include designating city and special-district "spheres of influences," which essentially are long-term growth areas for individual governments.

Functions of Local Government

Functional Responsibilities

California's fifty-eight counties remain the administrative arms of the state government, operating the public assistance (welfare, social services, general relief), public protection (prosecution, trial courts, jails, probation), and health (public health, indigent care, mental health, drug and alcohol abuse) programs. Without exception, each county commits the bulk of its annual spending to state-mandated programs. Counties also deliver local services and provide local facilities to their unincorporated communities, including law enforcement, land-use planning and regulation, roads, parks, and waste collection. As well, counties perform countywide or regional functions, such as administering the property tax system, running solid waste facilities, operating air pollution control programs, and managing library systems.

By contrast, California's 473 cities focus almost exclusively on providing local services and facilities. The number of municipal services varies widely, with "full-service cities" providing police, fire, street lighting, streets, transit, water, sewers, drainage, parks and recreation, land-use planning, building regulation, and economic development. Some municipalities administer few basic services themselves but instead contract with the county government or other agencies for services such as law enforcement, public works, and recreation programs.

Special districts are largely a California invention. Starting with the Wright Act in 1887, special districts have become an important feature of the state's political landscape. Although two-thirds of the 3,400 special districts have their own independent governing bodies, and most districts deliver only a single service, there are tremendous variations in size, function, and governance.[18]

For a state as large and diverse as California, it is not surprising that public officials rely on special arrangements to promote cooperation or create new programs to focus on specific problems overlooked by traditional local governments. More than 650 joint powers agencies serve as confederations of public agencies to finance facilities, deliver services, or coordinate programs. In addition, local officials have created nearly 250 public corporations as institutional vehicles to finance local infrastructure projects. Unlike other states, however, California has created few public authorities to promote particular projects. Less formal are the numerous memoranda of understanding (MOUs) that are agreed to between or among local governments, covering such matters as revenue sharing, community growth, and service delivery.

Administrative Discretion

Although general-law counties and cities and all special districts must adhere to state statutes, there is a surprising amount of discretion for local officials. Cities and counties are relatively free to organize their own internal structures, and most opt for administration by managers or other professional chief administrators.

Cities and counties can adopt their own local ordinances, following statutory procedures. Most formally codify their ordinances to expedite administration and enforcement. Except when the state government has intervened, such as in alcoholic beverage control, city and county ordinances can create local regulations, require permits, and provide for enforcement.

In many cases, state law prescribes the procedures that cities and counties must follow but leaves the substance of those decisions up to locally elected officials. Planning and regulation of land use is one important example of this feature of intergovernmental relations. State law requires every city and county to adopt a comprehensive master plan, called a general plan, containing seven mandatory elements covering topics such as land use, transportation, and housing. Most major local land-use decisions (for example, zoning, subdivisions, public works, and use permits) must be consistent with these general plans. Despite this rigorous statutory structure, cities and counties have considerable flexibility in applying the planning mandates; in effect, they establish their own local land-use policies and practices.

State law spells out the purchasing and contracting procedures that general-law cities and counties must follow. The statutes set specific dollar-amount thresholds that trigger requirements to invite bids, award contracts to the lowest responsible bidder, and negotiate contract terms. For general-law cities, the threshold is $5,000, but the threshold for counties varies according to population. A bewildering array of bidding thresholds applies to the state's myriad special districts. Not bound by these statutory requirements, charter cities and counties are free to adopt their own local procedures for purchasing and contracting.

Economic Development

Many economic development options are available to California communities. To address urban blight, cities and counties can create community redevelopment agencies which have the extraordinary powers of property tax increment financing and eminent domain. In 1997–1998 the 403 redevelopment agencies operated 796 separate redevelopment project areas and spent $3.4 billion.[19] Redevelopment remains popular with local officials as the main way to attract and retain private investment to older areas and as a means of funding infrastructure improvements. Redevelopment projects, however, are controversial among schools and counties, for example, because they ordinarily do not share in the increase in property tax revenues.

Communities can also use "enterprise zones" to attract private investment. Based on several different laws passed in the 1980s and early 1990s, the state government now offers thirty-nine enterprise zones, eight military base recovery areas, and the Los Angeles Revitalization Zone, which was formed after the 1992 riots. Businesses locating and expanding in these areas benefit from sales tax credits when purchasing new machinery and from tax credits for hiring qualified employees, business expense deductions, net interest deductions, and net operating losses.

A more traditional form of public support for private development is infrastructure financing. Local general-obligation bonds require two-thirds voter approval, but voter approval is not always required for revenue bonds.

Local officials are continually seeking creative ways to attract new businesses, including waiving developer fees, subsidizing public works, and discounting land sales. However, property tax rebates are not generally possible (except for certain types of machinery). In 1993 the legislature limited the application of sales tax–revenue rebates.

Fiscal Autonomy of Local Governments

Local Revenues

When California voters amended the constitution with Proposition 13 in June 1978, they put new restrictions on the two major components of the ad valorem property tax: the rate and the assessed valuation base. Proposition 13

• capped the total property tax rate in an area (the aggregate of all rates set by local governments) at 1 percent of market value, excepting increases for general-obligation debt that are approved by two-thirds voter majorities;

• rolled back real property assessed values to their 1975 levels;

• banned future increases in assessed value except for (1) the rate of inflation limited to 2 percent a year, (2) the added value of new construction, and (3) reassessment to current market value when ownership changes; and

• required two-thirds voter majorities to levy "special" taxes.

Proposition 13 did more than just cut property tax yields; it also fundamentally undermined the fiscal and, therefore, the political independence of local governments, principally by capping the total tax rate. Locally elected officials' control over—and political accountability for—determining the rate and, hence, the yield of the property tax was diminished. Before 1978 city councils, county boards of supervisors, and other elected governing bodies annually set their own property tax rates. That discretion and variability no longer exists because the maximum 1 percent rate is fixed statewide. Even local voters cannot approve higher rates for operating (nondebt) purposes since there is no constitutional provision for this. Because of these restrictions and continued state control, the California property tax can no longer be considered a *local* revenue source. Rather, it can best be described as shared state-local revenue dominated by state government objectives.

The state's rules for allocating revenues from the property tax, a power given to the legislature by Proposition 13, can change in any year. In 1979, a year after the passage of the initiative, legislators attempted to alleviate initial local revenue losses by shifting significant amounts of property tax revenues from K–12 schools and community colleges to cities and counties, thus increasing direct state aid to the schools. That policy, however, was reversed when the state encountered serious budget problems in the 1990s. In 1992 and 1993 the legislature and the governor transferred about $3.6 billion in property taxes away from counties, cities, redevelopment agencies, and special districts to the schools as a means of reducing state budget obligations to local education. This was a permanent reallocation; as a result, the combined county-city share of total property tax collections statewide was reduced from 47 percent to 32 percent, whereas schools' share was increased from 35 percent to 52 percent. The tax shift ever since has been a sore point in state-local

Fig. 1 Revenue Sources for California Cities, 1996–1997 (in millions)

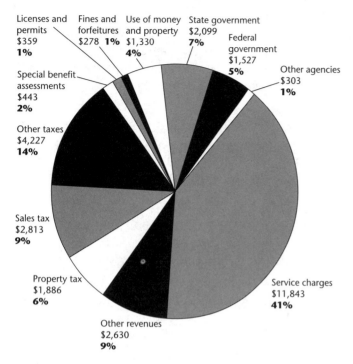

Licenses and permits
$359
1%

Fines and forfeitures
$278 **1%**

Use of money and property
$1,330
4%

State government
$2,099
7%

Federal government
$1,527
5%

Other agencies
$303
1%

Special benefit assessments
$443
2%

Other taxes
$4,227
14%

Sales tax
$2,813
9%

Property tax
$1,886
6%

Other revenues
$2,630
9%

Service charges
$11,843
41%

Source: State of California Cities Annual Report, 1996–1997, Kathleen Connell, state controller.

Fig. 2 Revenue Sources for California Counties, 1996–1997 (in millions)

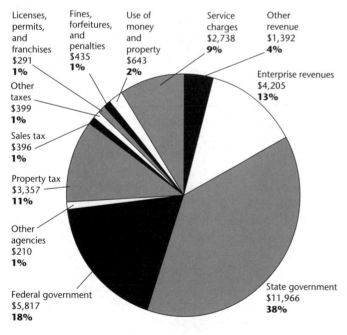

Licenses, permits, and franchises
$291
1%

Fines, forfeitures, and penalties
$435
1%

Use of money and property
$643
2%

Service charges
$2,738
9%

Other revenue
$1,392
4%

Other taxes
$399
1%

Enterprise revenues
$4,205
13%

Sales tax
$396
1%

Property tax
$3,357
11%

Other agencies
$210
1%

Federal government
$5,817
18%

State government
$11,966
38%

Source: State of California Counties Annual Report, 1996–1997, Kathleen Connell, state controller.

relations, and counties and cities continually seek legislation to restore the old allocation.

California local governments have other revenue sources, but none compares to the primacy of the property tax before Proposition 13, in either revenue yield or local discretionary significance. In 1996–1997 California counties and cities received total revenues of $31.8 billion and $28.8 billion, respectively. When special-district and redevelopment agency revenues are also included, the total for all nonschool local governments was $80 billion.

Figures 1 and 2 show the distribution of revenue sources for cities and counties in 1996–1997. For cities, service charges were the largest revenue component, followed by other taxes (business license, utility use, hotel occupancy, and so forth) and the retail sales tax. The county revenue picture was dominated by state and federal aid, followed by enterprise revenue (income from hospitals, airports, refuse facilities, transportation systems) and property taxes. Special districts have a smaller number of revenue sources, principally small shares of the property tax, enterprise income, and federal-state grants for particular purposes.

As a result of Proposition 13 and the 1992–1993 reallocation, the property tax share of local budgets has declined since 1977–1978 for both cities and counties. At the same time, city budgets rely more on service charges and a variety of smaller revenue sources, whereas counties have become more dependent on state aid. California cities have been especially aggressive in tapping diverse forms of revenue and shifting service delivery and infrastructure costs from their general funds to specific types of consumers, including utility and recreation users and new home buyers.

Along with property tax limits, Proposition 13 ushered in an era of increased voter control over local government revenue actions. The 1978 initiative requires two-thirds voter approval for special taxes, defined as earmarked taxes. A later statutory initiative (Proposition 62 in 1986) required a majority voter approval for general taxes. More recently, in 1996, voters passed Proposition 218, which limits local governments' use of fees and assessments by requiring a majority of property owners to approve new or increased revenues in these categories and by applying the restriction to charter as well as general-law cities. This measure was authored by Proposition 13 supporters concerned about local government evasions of the 1978 property tax restriction.

A striking product of California's fiscal stress, and a mark of how conflicts among and between local governments have escalated, is the so-called fiscalization of land use.[20] Fiscalization refers to the growing tendency of city and county governments to make growth and land-use decisions primarily according to revenue consequences. Diminished property tax revenues, combined with decreased state and federal aid, force many cities to aggressively seek the economic gains of land development, especially as reflected in increased sales tax revenues. The result is intensive competition among neighboring communities for desirable development—a competition that features new city incorporations, municipal annexations, and suburban redevelopment. County governments lose land and revenue base to municipal annexations and incorporations, although they must still pay for social service, criminal justice, and other mandated programs. Counties respond by opposing municipal annexations or seeking revenue-sharing arrangements with their cities.

In this interlocal competition for land and revenue, there are a few "winners" and many "losers"; the winners develop major shopping centers and retail malls for auto dealers. Cities and some counties tend to pursue commercial development and upscale housing that generate revenues without demanding expensive services. This emphasis on sales and other business tax opportunities avoids the limited property tax benefits of most housing and even manufacturing. California's fiscal rules actually stimulate competition for growth-related taxes and lead to revenue disparities since sales tax and other tax receipts are based on point of sale.

Like other states, California imposes statutory limits (1.5–15 percent of assessed valuation of property) on long-term debt. Incurring general-obligation debt, payable from property tax revenues, is further complicated by the two-thirds voter requirement. Local governments can bypass this obstacle in certain circumstances by engaging in other forms of borrowing that do not require voter approval, such as revenue bonds, special assessment bonds, and lease purchase arrangements.

Local government investment practices in California are more closely scrutinized now as a result of the stunning declaration of bankruptcy by Orange County in December 1994. Risky investment practices by the elected county treasurer led to the loss of $1.64 billion in public funds. The county treasurer had pooled public funds from the county government and 200 other local agencies into an investment program totaling $20.6 billion. When interest rates rose, the "reverse repurchase agreements" dropped greatly in value. Unable to pay its debt, the county filed for Chapter 9 bankruptcy, setting off controversy, recrimination, and political reactions. This was the largest municipal bankruptcy ever in the United States. By late 1995, Orange County adopted a court-approved recovery plan and was on the road to fiscal recovery.[21]

Local Expenditures

California's (nonschool) local governments spent more than $60 billion in 1996–1997, with counties accounting for $32.1 billion and cities spending $28.8 billion. Figures 3 and 4 chart the distribution of expenditure categories for cities and counties in 1996–1997.

Counties must adopt annual balanced budgets and follow detailed statutory procedures. Although most cities adopt annual budgets, the practice is a custom, not a state mandate. Most special districts must adopt annual budgets under state-enabling

Fig. 3 Expenditures by California Cities, 1996–1997 (in millions)

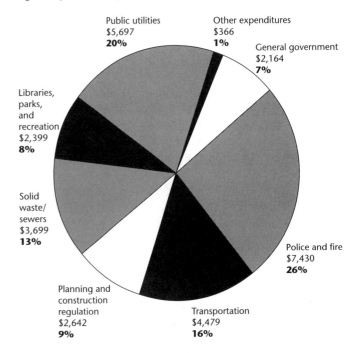

Source: State of California Cities Annual Report, 1996–1997, Kathleen Connell, state controller.

Fig. 4 Expenditures by California Counties, 1996–1997 (in millions)

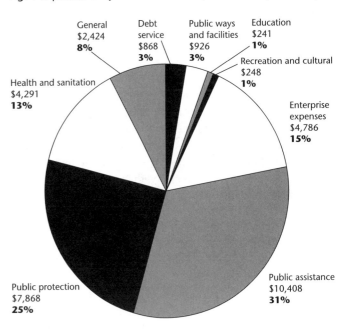

Source: State of California Counties Annual Report, 1996–1997, Kathleen Connell, state controller.

acts. Redevelopment agencies must also adopt annual balanced budgets. Since its adoption in 1879, the state constitution has prohibited cities and counties from committing more than their annual revenue without first obtaining two-thirds voter approval. This constitutional ban on deficit spending keeps local officials' attention focused on the balance between their revenues and their expenditures. Curiously, the constitutional ban does not mention special districts or redevelopment agencies.

A 1979 voter initiative (Proposition 4) amended the California Constitution to require local and state governments to set and operate under appropriations limits. Although amended several times in the 1980s to accommodate transportation and school spending programs, the constitutional language generally limits a local government's spending to its 1978–1979 level, adjusted for population growth and inflation since that time. If local officials want to exceed their spending cap, they must obtain majority voter approval for the higher limit every four years.

State Government Grants-in-Aid to Localities

About 70 percent of California's state budget (total budgeted spending of $77.5 billion for 1999–2000) is appropriated as "local assistance" funds,[22] which are mostly grants and other transfers to counties and school districts for their programs, including programs mandated by the state. More than four-fifths of all local assistance funds are for education and health and welfare. Other than the public education system, counties are the major recipients of state fiscal support because they are the administrative arms for state programs in health, welfare, and other areas.

Unfunded Mandates

For more than twenty-five years, local officials and state legislators have wrangled over the state government's continued imposition of mandates on local programs. In 1972 legislators passed a self-imposed ban on new, unfunded state mandates. Subsequent legislatures routinely ignored this restriction, adopting waivers that justified new mandates. A 1979 voter initiative gave the mandate restriction constitutional status.

Definitions of state-mandated local programs vary because of their political implications. One survey in the mid-1990s reported that counties must comply with more than 250 mandated programs.[23] Some of the mandates require local officials to follow specific procedures (open meetings laws, competitive bidding requirements), others require local officials to implement programs (general relief, local general plans), and still others affect substantive decisions (specific service levels, maintenance-of-effort requirements).

Rather than directly funding new state mandates, the legislature created a process whereby local officials may claim reimbursements for their costs. The legislative counsel identifies the bills that create or expand state mandates, and the state Department of Finance estimates the costs. After the bills' enactment

and initial implementation, local officials file reimbursement claims with the quasi-judicial Commission on State Mandates, which adjudicates test claims, issues decisions, defines guidelines for reimbursement, and recommends the appropriation of funds.

Access to Local Government

Local Elections

California's electoral process is largely dictated in the state's Elections Code. County governments administer most aspects of state and local elections. Oversight is provided by the California secretary of state. County clerks (or in larger counties, separate election departments) register voters and maintain the official registration records, receive candidacy petitions, organize the polls and employ poll workers, count ballots, and certify the results. All local as well as judicial elections are nonpartisan.

Cities and counties have considerable discretion in regulating campaign finance. The California Political Reform Act of 1974, the principal statute controlling campaign finance and candidate disclosures, allows cities and counties to adopt their own, more stringent ordinances. Nearly 100 jurisdictions have adopted ordinances limiting individual contributions per candidate, preventing contributions from certain sources (for example, corporations, labor unions, and political action committees), imposing disclosure requirements, and restricting the carryover of campaign funds from one election cycle to another.[24]

Citizen Controls over the Actions of Local Officials

The 1911 constitutional amendment to include the initiative, referendum, and recall applied to local as well as state government. These tools of "direct democracy" are now well-established practices in the politics of many communities. The initiative and recall, more so than the referendum, are frequently employed by organized groups of citizens to challenge the actions of their local government officials. Most initiatives attempt to counter city and county land-use and development policies by seeking to slow down growth or stop particular projects.[25] California courts have determined that the initiative does not extend to administrative acts of local governments, but rather it is limited to legislative or policy matters. Recalls are much harder to classify because they cover a wide range of citizen grievances pertaining to particular elected officials and their actions, including issues dealing with salary increases, dismissal of popular employees, alleged "arrogance," tax increases, and specific spending decisions. All elected officials in California are recallable.

An open question is how a state's empowerment of citizens with these tools contributes to home rule. Since they are employed by citizens in an adversarial capacity against some or all of their local government officials, the initiative, referendum, and recall appear to work against representative democracy.

The Progressive movement's insistence on political accountability and responsiveness also shows up in state laws affecting open meetings and public records. The Brown Act, dating from the mid-1950s, requires most meetings of local governments to be open and public. Local officials must post their agendas seventy-two hours before their meetings, allow time for public comment, and permit access by the press and other media. Closed sessions are possible only in limited circumstances.[26]

Similarly, the California Public Records Act ensures public access to most government documents, restricting disclosure only of specified files.[27] Along with the statutory requirements for public notice and hearing, these statutes create a political culture of relative openness in California's local governments.

State-Local Relations

After a century of home rule, California's communities still struggle to define where state control ends and local autonomy begins. Successive waves of growth, reaction, and reform have created a political landscape in which older institutional forms coexist with the latest political trends. One prominent example is structural fragmentation of California's county governments—a product of nineteenth-century thinking imported from older parts of the nation—that coexists uneasily with the latest innovations in public finance to attract private investment.

Given California's growing and diverse population, marked by Hispanic and Asian political majorities in certain communities, it is difficult to predict how local governments will be affected by emerging political movements. Whatever forces eventually come to dominate the politics of individual localities and regions, it is clear that without substantial statewide structural change, the capacity of local governments will be constrained by diminished autonomy.

The discretion available to local elected officials and their professional administrators forms what has been described as a "hollow sphere." On the surface, California's local governments have many of the trappings of home rule, including constitutional standing, charter authority, flexible statutory authority, and a political tradition that honors local control. However, local officials lack the power to set their own property tax rates, face increasingly expensive entitlement programs, operate under both collective bargaining and merit system limits, and must cope with state-mandated procedural requirements. Taken together, these factors erode the reality of local control, even though the surface image of home rule appears to be intact.

California's recent experiences with state-local relations suggest that revenue authority, and especially control over the property tax, is critical to local government discretion. More than revenue productivity, communities' ability to set property tax rates epitomizes local autonomy and enhances representative democracy. When local elected officials control the rate, local government budgets can respond to community priorities and pressures.

The abandonment of local control over the property tax caused by Proposition 13 effectively established state mastery over a traditional fixture of community autonomy. Few other states have deprived localities of such revenue authority.[28] The 1978 shift not only fundamentally altered the ways in which California local governments operate, both fiscally and in terms of policy,[29] but it also substantially revised the state-local relationship, making local governments beholden to frequent state changes in the fiscal rules.

Notes

1. California Department of Finance, press release, 17 December 1998.

2. Peter H. King, "Fresno Scandal Shines Light on Business as Usual," *Sacramento Bee*, 27 March 1998, A3.

3. Randy H. Hamilton, "Ukiah, 1904: A Modest Footnote to the History of the Council-Manager Form of Municipal Government In the United States," working paper 89-2 (Berkley: Institute of Governmental Studies, University of California, 1989).

4. For a view of the relative fragmentation of the California system of local government, see Paul G. Lewis, *Deep Roots: Local Government Structure in California* (San Francisco: Public Policy Institute of California, 1998).

5. Peter M. Detwiler, "Creatures of Statute, Children of Trade: The Legal Origins of California Cities," appendix to *History and Perspectives* (Sacramento: California Constitutional Revision Commission, 1996).

6. Undoubtedly the delegates were influenced by the new Missouri Constitution, which four years earlier had become the first in the nation to sharply limit legislative control over cities and permit locally adopted charters. California was thus the second state to affirm in constitutional language home rule for its local governments.

7. California Legislative Analyst's Office, "Major Milestones: Twenty-five Years of the State-Local Fiscal Relationship," *California Update* (December 1997).

8. California Constitutional Revision Commission, *Final Report and Recommendations to the Governor and the Legislature* (Sacramento: California Constitutional Revision Commission, 1996).

9. Sho Sato, "Municipal Affairs in California," *California Law Review* 60 (June 1972): 34.

10. League of California Cities, *The California Municipal Law Handbook* (Sacramento: League of California Cities, 1994).

11. Constitution of California, Article XI, section 7.

12. Constitution of California, Article XI, section 9.

13. Constitution of California, Article IV, section 16.

14. Constitution of California, Article X, sections 3–6.

15. Jim Newton, "Voters Approve New City Charter by Wide Margin," *Los Angeles Times*, 9 June 1999, A1, A19.

16. Kevin F. McCarthy, Steven P. Erie, and Robert E. Reichardt, *Meeting the Challenge of Charter Reform* (Santa Monica: Rand, 1998), 3–4, 10–12, 58–83.

17. Senate Local Government Committee, *It's Time to Draw the Line: A Citizen's Guide to Local Agency Formation Commissions in California* (Sacramento: California State Legislature, August 1996).

18. April Manatt, *What's So Special About Special Districts? A Citizen's Guide to Special Districts in California* (Sacramento: Senate Committee on Local Government, 1993).

19. Kathleen Connell, *Community Redevelopment Agencies Annual Report, Fiscal Year 1997–98* (Sacramento: California State Controller, 1999).

20. Dean J. Misczynski, "The Fiscalization of Land Use," chap. 5 in *California*

Policy Choices, vol. 3, ed. John Kirlin and Donald Winkler (Sacramento: School of Public Administration, University of Southern California, 1986).

21. Mark Baldassare, *When Government Fails: The Orange County Bankruptcy* (Berkeley: University of California Press, 1998).

22. Gray Davis, appendix to *Governor's Budget Summary, 1999–2000* (Sacramento: California Governor, 1999).

23. California State Association of Counties, *Counties at the Crossroads* (Sacramento: California State Association of Counties, 1994).

24. California Commission on Campaign Financing, *Financing California's Local Elections: Money and Politics in the Golden State* (Los Angeles: Center for Responsive Government, 1989), 71–94.

25. Madelyn Glickfield and Ned Levine, *The New Land Use Regulation "Revolution": Why California's Local Jurisdictions Enact Growth Control and Management Measures* (Cambridge, Mass.: Lincoln Institute of Land Policy, 1991).

26. Ted Fourkas, *Open & Public II: A User's Guide to the Ralph M. Brown Act* (Sacramento: California First Amendment Coalition, 1994).

27. Christopher Kahn, *Your Guide to Public Information: The California Public Records Act* (Sacramento: Senate Local Government Committee, 1990).

28. Alvin D. Sokolow, "The Changing Property Tax and State-Local Relations," *Publius* 28 (winter 1998): 165–187.

29. For a comprehensive examination of the long-term implications of Proposition 13, see Jeffrey I. Chapman, *The Continuing Redistribution of Fiscal Stress: The Long Run Consequences of Proposition 13* (Cambridge, Mass.: Lincoln Institute of Land Policy, 1998).

COLORADO

Jason Stilwell and Robert W. Gage

The authors thank Sam Mamet, associate director of the Colorado Municipal League, for his assistance and encouragement; Martin R. McCullough, attorney for the City of Westminster, Colorado; Kathleen E. Haddock, attorney for the Town of Superior, Colorado; and Maryann McGeady, legal council to various special districts and partner in the firm McGeady and Sisneros, for her help on the functional responsibilities section.

Home rule in Colorado has produced substantial authority for local governments, with minimal state interference. In matters of purely local concern, ordinances adopted by home rule municipalities supersede conflicting state statutes. In matters of mixed statewide and local concern, state statutes and municipal ordinances may coexist if they do not conflict; if they do, the courts hold the state statute supreme. In matters of purely statewide concern, state law entirely preempts municipal legislation. Home rule is a grant of authority from the people, not the state. Thus, the state is not able to remove a home rule municipality's authority.

Governmental Setting

Colorado became a territory in 1861 and entered the Union on August 1, 1876, as the thirty-eighth state and the eighth largest.[1] Between 1980 and 1994, the state population grew from 2,889,735 to 3,655,647.[2] The population continues to grow at annual rates over 2 percent.

The original constitution, adopted in 1876, still governs Colorado.[3] The constitution has been amended more than 130 times since its adoption. Some of the more notable amendments are suffrage for women (1902), the first home rule amendment (1902), the initiative and referendum (1910), and more recently the 1992 Taxpayer's Bill of Rights, which imposes a number of limitations on local governments.

The state's chief executive, the governor, may serve no more than two four-year terms. The state legislature is the General Assembly, a bicameral body made up of thirty-five senators serving four-year terms and sixty-five members of the House serving two-year terms. The state supreme court, the highest state tribunal, includes a chief justice and six associates, who serve ten-year terms.

At the local level, the state consists of 63 counties and 269 municipalities, with Denver (the state capital) being the most populous city.[4] Municipalities consist of both towns and cities that can operate under either state statute or a home rule charter. Towns with populations of 2,000 and less operate under a government comprising a mayor and board of trustees. Statutory cities operate with either the "weak" mayor–council form of government or the council-manager type. Home rule cities and towns operate under a variety of governmental forms that generally approximate the council-manager form. As of August 31, 1996, Colorado had 76 home rule cities and towns.[5] Denver utilizes the "strong" mayor and "weak" council form. The council-manager form of government is widespread in Colorado; 145 of a total 269 municipalities maintain such a system.

Colorado's generally conservative political culture stems from the state's widely Republican and Anglo-American population. Colorado maintains blue laws prohibiting certain activities on Sundays and strictly limits taxing and spending. Two less conservative enclaves, Boulder and Denver, are influenced by university environments and larger populations.

State and local government in Colorado is distinctive as a result of constituent control. Residents in Colorado have great influence in controlling the actions of their governments. As a result, local governments focus in particular on local issues while working cooperatively, in contrast to other states, such as Oregon and Florida, where there is more of a state focus.

Home Rule in Colorado

Historical Development

In the nineteenth century, the Colorado Supreme Court accepted Judge Dillon's interpretation of municipalities as administrative arms of the state.[6] Dillon's Rule holds that municipal corporations have and can exercise only those powers expressly granted, those necessarily or fairly implied therefrom, and those that are essential and indispensable to their corporate statutes.[7]

The "legislature's supremacy encompasses all activities, governmental and proprietary; no action of a municipality is valid unless some relatively specific grant of authority can be found in a statutory or constitutional provision."[8] Thus, "cities and counties have only as much authority and freedom to govern their own affairs as the state, through its constitution and statutory laws, chooses to give them."[9] The twentieth century brought with it a lessening of acceptance of Dillon's Rule.

Municipal home rule was first adopted in 1902 "for the purpose of creating the consolidated City and County of Denver and establishing that city's independence from state legislative control of its internal affairs."[10] The popular mood surrounding the legislative treatment of Denver became one of dissatisfaction in the early 1900s.[11] During that period, the legislature had the authority and power to "create a municipal corporation by enacting a special law granting a corporate charter. By the terms of the grant, the legislature could control the form of organization and scope of powers of any particular city."[12]

This dissatisfaction was the spark of the home rule movement. The movement resulted in Colorado citizens approving Article XX as an amendment to the Colorado Constitution. Section 1 of Article XX, approved in 1902, granted home rule power to Denver. Overall, this article "consolidated the City and County of Denver into one entity, granted the new entity the right to adopt a home rule charter, and provided in section 6 for the adoption of home rule charters by certain other Colorado cities."[13]

In 1912, with approval of Article XX, section 6, all cities were granted the opportunity to adopt home rule powers, which relieved them "from their dependence on legislative action for their form of organization and powers from the resultant interference in municipal affairs such dependence made possible."[14] Today, the home rule doctrine is one of the most well established and stable bodies of case law in Colorado and has been the subject of more than 200 appellate decisions.[15]

Definition of Home Rule

Article XX of the Colorado Constitution delineates home rule for cities and towns. The first five sections of Article XX establish guidelines and parameters for Denver becoming a combined home rule city-county. Section 6 primarily concerns the "people of each city or town" in Colorado.[16] By contrast, the Colorado General Assembly, in Title 31 of the Colorado Revised Statutes, delineates and authorizes powers and authorities to non–home rule (statutory) cities and towns.

Article XX, section 6 grants cities and towns the permanent power to make, amend, or add a charter that is designed to be the city or town's organic law extending to all of its local and municipal matters. The charter shall supersede, within the territorial limits, any conflicting law of the state. Section 6 grants home rule cities and towns all powers necessary to administrate

local and municipal matters. Specifically included in these powers is the power to legislate upon, provide, regulate, conduct, and control the following:

1. The creation and terms of municipal officers, agencies, and employments; the definition, regulation, and alteration of the powers, duties, qualifications, and terms or tenure of all municipal officers, agents, and employees;

2. The creation of police courts; the definition and regulation of the jurisdiction, powers and duties thereof, and the election or appointment of police magistrates;

3. The creation of municipal courts; the definition and regulation of the jurisdiction, powers and duties thereof, and the election or appointment of the officers;

4. All matters pertaining to municipal elections in such city or town and to electoral votes therein on measures submitted under the charter or ordinances;

5. The issuance, refunding, and liquidation of all kinds of municipal obligations, including bonds and other obligations of park, water, and local improvement districts;

6. The consolidation and management of park or water districts in such cities or towns or within their jurisdiction;

7. The assessment of property in such city or town for municipal taxation and the levy and collection of taxes thereon for municipal purposes and special assessments for local improvements;

8. The imposition, enforcement, and collection of fines and penalties for the violation of any of the provisions of the charter or of any ordinance adopted in pursuance of the charter.

A home rule municipality does not need a specific grant of authority to act. The municipality has the authority to act in local and municipal matters unless there is a specific limitation in Colorado's constitution or in the local charter.[17] Because home rule municipalities derive their authority to act from the constitution, the terms of their charter limit the general constitutional authority. Failure to comply with a charter limitation renders an action invalid.

In 1971 the Colorado General Assembly passed the Municipal Home Rule Act.[18] With it, the General Assembly established rules and guidelines for all municipalities to implement Article XX. The various provisions in Article XX for establishing home rule were to continue to apply until superseded by statute. Adoption of the Municipal Home Rule Act superseded the procedural requirements for adopting and amending home rule charters.

The subsection titled "Status of Counties" more thoroughly explains Colorado's county home rule. Article XIV of the Colorado Constitution concerns counties and delineates county home rule authority. Section 16 states that a county's registered electors may adopt home rule to establish governmental structure. Moreover, the county "shall provide all mandatory county functions, services, and facilities and shall exercise all mandatory powers as may be required by statute." Section 16 also empowers a home rule county to provide such permissive functions, services, and facilities and to exercise such permissive powers as may be authorized by statute applicable to all home rule counties, except as may be otherwise prohibited or limited by charter or the state constitution.

Many Colorado local government attorneys understand home rule to mean the "right for a municipality to govern itself rather than be bound by the statutes adopted by the state legislature in local and municipal matters,"[19] or the "power to determine your own destiny."[20] Colorado municipalities view home rule as a method by which to increase autonomy over daily administration and to broaden opportunities. Municipalities can use home rule to increase autonomy by eliminating state statutory restrictions. For example, home rule cities may enact their own procedures for budget approval, zoning hearings, and local elections. Municipalities can also use a home rule charter to broaden opportunities such as implementing alternative ways to generate revenue. For example, statutory requirements prohibit cities from levying taxes on admissions to public places; by charter, home rule municipalities may implement such taxes.[21]

Structural Features

Colorado cities and towns have very similar powers and authorities; the primary difference between the two is population size. The Municipal Home Rule Act of 1971 establishes a simplified procedure for reclassifying a town with a population greater than 2,000 as a city or a city with a population less than or equal to 2,000 as a town.[22] The act allows the town or city simply to reclassify itself upon adoption of its home rule charter. By so doing, the municipality need not comply with the more detailed procedures for reclassification found in Colorado's statutes.[23]

Citizens in a home rule municipality may establish the form of government they desire. In Colorado, these forms vary from the "strong" mayor form used by Denver to a semi–town meeting form.[24] For example, local governments can determine the size of the council, whether voters elect council members at large or from districts, the terms of office, procedures for filling council vacancies, and the council's powers. Council size varies (from four to eight members and a mayor); the typical size is six council members and a mayor. Adopting home rule does not require any change in the form of government, but the form must be specified. Many home rule municipalities have made only minor changes in their form of government upon charter adoption.

The state legislature established the Municipal Annexation Act of 1965 to

- encourage natural and well-ordered development of municipalities;

- distribute fairly and equitably the costs of municipal services among beneficiaries;
- extend municipal government, services, and facilities to eligible areas that form a part of the whole community;
- simplify governmental structure in urban areas;
- provide an orderly system for extending municipal regulations to newly annexed areas;
- reduce friction among contiguous or neighboring municipalities; and
- increase the ability of municipalities in urban areas to provide their citizens with the services they require.[25]

The act encourages municipal growth over development of new municipalities. As such, growth in Colorado has been a bane for municipalities. Likewise, large cities historically have annexed adjacent smaller municipalities.

Municipal annexation rules are shaped by the Poundstone Amendments. Poundstone I,[26] passed in 1974, aimed to control Denver's annexations. Denver, as a home rule municipality, was capable of annexing territory in the same manner as other municipalities under the Annexation Act and was vigorously pursuing new annexations.[27] Poundstone I did not prohibit Denver's annexations but did require that annexations first be approved by a majority vote of a six-member Boundary Control Commission composed of one commissioner from each of the boards of county commissioners in the three surroundings counties plus three elected officials of Denver. Further, no land located in any county (excluding the three surrounding counties) could be annexed without unanimous approval by the county commissioners of the county in which that land was located. Poundstone I effectively eliminated Denver's ability to annex property.

The approval of Poundstone II in 1980[28] affected all Colorado municipalities. The amendment requires that one of three conditions be met before a municipality may proceed with annexation: (1) a majority of voters in the annexation area approve the annexation, (2) the annexing municipality receives a petition of annexation signed by more than half of the landowners in the area considered for annexation, or (3) the area is entirely surrounded or solely owned by the annexing municipality. The effect of Poundstone II was to make annexations more difficult for municipalities. In 1987 Senate Bill 45 revised many provisions of the 1965 act, one of which added new distance limitations to annexations, including a three-mile limit on annexations in any one year.

In 1981 the Colorado General Assembly enacted the Colorado County Home Rule Powers Act designed to expand the powers of home rule counties. The act in particular expanded the ordinance and finance powers of home rule counties[29] and permits counties to restructure under a home rule charter. Of Colorado's sixty-three counties, only Pitkin and Weld have adopted home rule charters. Weld County maintained most of the constitutional and statutory structural provisions. The home rule charter primarily promoted changes in the areas of tax limitation and administrative restructuring.

County home rule clearly is not as prevalent in Colorado as is municipal home rule. County and city home rule differ legally, which may be why fewer counties than municipalities adopt home rule. State law provides counties with only structural, not functional home rule. Structural home rule "allows the county to change the structure of county government, but does not allow counties any more significant authority than statutory counties presently have."[30] Colorado law allows municipalities to adopt both structural and functional home rule. Functional home rule enables a municipality to modify its functions.

The courts have supported extraterritorial actions by home rule cities and towns. The most influential decision in terms of local government survival and growth concerned water. A 1975 case held that Article XX specifically defined the selling of water by a municipality both within and without its territorial boundaries to be a proper exercise of its powers.[31] Other noteworthy holdings are that a city may condemn private property outside its boundaries for its local public use[32] and that a home rule jurisdiction is not required to obtain the consent of an incorporated town before acquiring title and possessions of rights-of-way through such town by condemnation proceedings.[33]

Functions of Local Government

Functional Responsibilities

Colorado cities provide a broad range of services, including public safety, road maintenance, recreation, parks, code enforcement, libraries, and animal control. To a lesser extent, Colorado cities provide ambulance, housing, transportation, gas and electric, sanitation, and health services. State law establishes parameters regarding these services and lists specific functions regarding the exercise of municipal powers, ordinance making, taxation and finance, bonds, planning and zoning, public improvements, fire and police, sanitation, utilities, and water and sewage.

The constitutional amendment adopted by voters that limits taxing and spending affects both cities and counties. The Taxpayer's Bill of Rights (TABOR), adopted in 1992, ties government spending to growth. TABOR essentially caps government spending at the growth rate and requires the government to rebate any excess money to the taxpayers. It is likely that TABOR will significantly affect provision of governmental services when Colorado's growth rate slows.

Although many areas of Colorado are outside the boundaries of an established municipality, all areas are included in sixty-three counties. Thus, counties provide the essential services, coordinate elections, maintain roadways and land records, record and monitor motor vehicles, and provide sheriff and detention services and social services. Specific counties also oper-

ate airports, provide park and recreation facilities, and operate ski resorts.

Colorado courts have held that a Colorado county is nothing more than an agency of the state in the general administration of state policy and that its powers are solely governmental.[34] Also, a county, unlike a municipal corporation, does not in its own right possess a complete local government (that is, executive, legislative, and judicial powers).[35]

Although localities have significant influence over their development, limited finances often constrain implementation. Land-use planning is local in nature; however, local government must act either regionally or with state assistance in most instances. For example, local governments are free to plan their transportation needs, but because of the enormous costs of all but the very small transportation projects, localities must rely on state transportation funding or federal funding. Thus, a project must compete with other projects to realize funding. The result is that a locality can rarely guarantee funding for any transportation project. Especially in the area of transportation funding, "regardless of the amount of discretionary authority granted by the state constitution . . . the key determinant of the ability of a local government to exercise fully the grant of powers is adequate finance."[36]

Special districts originated in Colorado to meet demands that county governments were unable to meet, particularly infrastructure expansion. Title 32 special districts (known as such from the state statute authorizing them) came into being because counties did not have the ability, until recently, to provide water and sewer service. With the state's push to "have growth pay its way," cities began to team with special districts more frequently.

Today, Colorado has more than 1,000 special districts. Three of the most prominent types of special districts are fire protection, utility provider, and metropolitan districts. Metropolitan districts provide multiple services or have more than one power. Typically, metropolitan districts provide water and sewer service.

Article 1, part 2 of Title 32, known as the Special District Control Act, establishes the procedures necessary for the coordination and creation of special-district governments and for the logical extension of special-district services throughout the state. The original act focused on the creation of special districts in the county; subsequent amendments have given municipalities more authority. However, Title 32 gives special districts the authority of independent governments, even within the boundaries of a home rule city.

One key aspect regarding the authority of Colorado special districts concerns condemnation powers.[37] The condemnation powers of special districts are stronger than those of home rule municipalities. Special-district condemnation authority is limited only in the area of water rights. State law empowers a special district to serve areas outside its boundaries and to condemn "property necessary to the exercise of the powers granted" inside and outside its borders.[38] The history of these powers derives primarily from counties' desire to expand service to county residents without increasing either the county's burden to provide these services or the authority of municipalities.

Interlocal relations in Colorado are both competitive and cooperative. There is a strong sense of competitiveness in the areas of nonresidential development and, concurrently, preservation. Competition is strong among localities to lure the next large generator of sales tax. Moreover, there is competition (although not so much on a statewide basis) to preserve undeveloped land. In the Denver metropolitan area, it is not unprecedented to have a county purchase land from within the borders of a municipality or a neighboring county to preserve as open space.

In other areas, there is significant cooperation among the localities. Localities seem to realize that they need each other to realize savings from economies of scale and to control challenges that extend beyond any particular locality's borders. Areas of greatest cooperation are air quality, emergency services, and regional transportation. Other areas that are experiencing increased interlocal cooperation are wastewater treatment, growth control, and open-space preservation. The state has kept legislation mandating interlocal cooperation to a minimum, largely because of Colorado's strong home rule powers. Existing mandates are not of great significance; local governments have, in all areas of local concern, great individual authority to establish interlocal relations.

Administrative Discretion

Home rule cities and towns can rely on the broad constitutional language of Article XX as the source of authority to act. When authority is in question, the actions of home rule municipalities more so than non–home rule (statutory) municipalities are likely to be upheld.[39] For example, the courts have held that local charters allow home rule municipalities to provide greater monetary compensation to victims of torts committed by the municipality's police officers than that authorized by statute.[40] Moreover, a home rule municipality may assume greater liability for the actions of its employees than the liability permitted by state statute.[41]

Article XX, section 6 of the Colorado Constitution grants to home rule municipalities very broad authority to legislate upon, provide, regulate, conduct, and control the creation and terms of municipal officers, agencies, and employments.[42] The courts have also supported broad authority for home rule cities and towns to define, regulate, and alter the powers, duties, qualifications, and terms or tenure of all municipal officers, agents, and employees. Similarly, the courts have ruled that a city's power to determine the limits of its public officers' authority, by charter or amendment to its charter, is exclusive since such matters are purely of local concern.[43]

By comparison, the determination of whether an employee is entitled to unemployment compensation benefits is a matter of statewide concern, and state statutes supersede ordinances of home rule cities.[44] The court has held that self-insuring for employee health and other benefits and residency of municipal employees are matters of local concern subject to legislation by charter provision or ordinance of the home rule city.[45] State law prohibits statutory cities from imposing residency requirements for city employees. A home rule provision conflicting with this law preempts the state law.

The investment of funds by a home rule municipality is a "local and municipal matter" under the home rule article of the state constitution.[46] Home rule municipalities may establish their own procedures for and restrictions on the investment of public funds; state statute does not limit authorized investments.

Colorado has a state agency to assist localities in their administrative procedures. The mission statement of the Department of Local Affairs is "Help Colorado Communities Achieve Their Goals." The department has a division of local governments that "works with municipalities, counties, and special districts to define and identify their needs and to develop their capacity for appropriate responses. The division also provides technical data, information, and program assistance and training."[47]

Home rule provides local governments the authority to modify a number of their administrative procedures. Home rule municipalities may include in their charters provisions for electing the clerk or treasurer, fine and fee schedule adjustments and modifications, and exclusions from certain statutory or constitutional requirements.

Colorado home rule provisions generally allow a home rule municipality more freedom and responsibility to act in the area of contracting and purchasing than do state statutes. However, the exact limits of localities' powers have not been completely tested or defined. Thus, some powers to act in the areas of contracting and purchasing—and indeed, other relatively new areas—may be subject to question.

Economic Development

Colorado has strong local control of land use. Individual municipalities, for the most part, are able to plan, implement, and manage their land-use patterns. This local control is precipitated by the control localities have over other areas that affect growth, such as water and transportation planning.

The general independence and broad authority of Colorado local governments endures in the development arena. Colorado counties and municipalities have flexibility to finance, acquire, own, lease, improve, and dispose of property to promote industry and develop economic activity.

One tool provided by state statute to local governments to facilitate development is the urban renewal authority. Under this statute, local governments may create an urban renewal authority that has expanded powers to encourage development, including tax-increment financing, condemnation authority, and debt financing. Second, the County and Municipal Development Revenue Bond Act provides broad authorization for development financing. A third tool used by local governments to encourage development is the general improvement district (GID) and business improvement district (BID).[48] These improvement districts expand financing opportunities for large commercial developments such as industrial parks. A GID or BID can be used to finance large-cost infrastructure items, including roads, utilities, and other public improvements.

Fiscal Autonomy of Local Governments

Local Revenues

The property tax has been a primary source of tax revenue for many municipalities. However, in communities that have enacted a sales-and-use tax, the property tax often provides a declining portion of local revenue. Pursuant to its home rule powers, Denver adopted the first municipal sales tax in Colorado in 1948. In 1967 authority to levy sales tax was granted to statutory municipalities. Since then, Colorado municipalities have become less dependent on property taxes. Property tax revenue as a share of municipal tax revenue now makes up 10 percent of municipal tax revenue.[49] By comparison, municipal property tax

Fig. 1 Colorado Municipal Revenue Sources, 1997 (in millions of dollars)

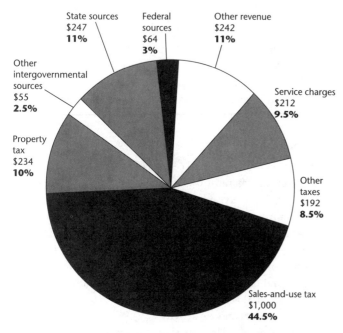

Source: Colorado Municipal League, *Financial Condition of Colorado Municipalities* (Denver: Colorado Municipal League, 1997), 79.

Note: Dollar amounts and percentages have been rounded.

revenue was 35.8 percent of municipal tax revenue in 1972. Since 1992, Colorado's property tax rate has been nearly one-third the national average.[50] The remainder of local government revenue comes from service charges and intergovernmental revenues (see Figure 1 for 1997 composite municipal revenue sources).

In recent years the general sales tax has become the major source of revenue for Colorado municipalities.[51] Sales tax revenue in 1990 made up 67 percent of municipal tax revenue, compared with only 28 percent nationwide. Of Colorado municipalities, 201 levy a sales tax. Rates range from 1 to 5 percent. There are statutory limits on the sales tax rate a municipality may impose. Case law is insufficient to determine if these limits apply to home rule municipalities. Home rule offers local governments the opportunity to expand their revenue base by employing selective sales taxes. Home rule charters can include tax levies precluded under the Colorado Revised Statutes, such as sales taxes on car rentals, restaurant meals, admissions to events, and lodging.

Many municipalities view sales-and-use tax revenue as a way to lessen their reliance on external finances. Competition is steep among Colorado local municipalities to secure sales-and-use tax revenue. Colorado local governments are increasingly expanding their economic development departments and devising new ways to provide incentives to large tax generators.

Colorado has three revenue limitation provisions that can affect local governments. The Gallagher Amendment minimizes residential property taxes by limiting property values. The result is that commercial property taxes increase. Although it does not limit the amount of property tax revenue that a local government may collect, the amendment could have a residual effect on property tax revenues for local governments by dissuading businesses from locating in Colorado. The statutory limit caps annual mill levy increases at 5.5 percent. However, this limitation is less restrictive than the mill levy provisions in the Taxpayer's Bill of Rights (TABOR).

Local Expenditures

The Local Government Budget Law of Colorado[52] frames the municipal expenditure process. It requires certain local governments to adopt an annual budget and outlines expenditure record keeping. The budget is the only plan legally required of all statutory local governments. Expenditure categories are administration, operations, maintenance, debt service, and capital projects.

Expenditure amounts vary widely among Colorado municipalities, primarily because of the myriad services municipal governments in Colorado provide. Many special districts in the state provide municipal-type services such as water, sewer, fire, parks, and recreation. Moreover, some cities operate gas and electric utilities and other atypical municipal services. In cities with municipal gas and electric utilities, these utilities are the largest expense categories. In other cities, the largest expenditure categories are water and sewer services. Among most municipalities, the largest expenditure is related to public safety.

Because Colorado cities provide a varying array of municipal functions, it is difficult to generalize about fiscal allocation. However, according to the Department of Local Affairs, 36.3 percent of general-fund expenditures in Colorado cities (excluding Denver) was spent on public safety, 22.7 percent on general government, and 17.3 percent on culture and recreation.[53]

Financial limitations imposed on local governments in Colorado are revenue limitations. The Taxpayer's Bill of Rights is the most recent amendment limiting revenue. State statutes establish guidelines for local government budgeting, such as the requirement that local governments maintain a balanced budget.[54]

State Government Grants-in-Aid to Localities

Intergovernmental revenues are an important municipal revenue source.[55] However, intergovernmental revenue has steadily declined over the past twenty years. In 1973 federal and state aid made up 29.7 percent of general revenues for municipalities; by 1993, that figure had dropped to 13.3 percent.

The state aid trend in particular is misleading. From 1983 to 1993, state aid to municipalities slightly increased from 9.2 percent to 10.7 percent. However, two-thirds of state aid to municipalities goes to Denver. In 1993, $138.9 million of the $223.6 million went to Denver, which (although listed as a municipality) provides relatively expensive state-supported programs, such as social services, because of its city-county designation. Denver and Broomfield are the only combined city-county governments in Colorado.

The state shares four revenues with municipal governments: the highway users tax (motor fuel tax), cigarette tax (flat, per pack tax), conservation trust (lottery funds), and motor vehicle registration fees. Only the cigarette tax is not earmarked for a specific use. Two of the shared revenues, the highway users tax and motor vehicle registration fees, are calculated based on the number of vehicles and miles of streets in a community. These revenues must be spent on new transportation-related construction, safety, maintenance, and capacity improvements, not for administrative purposes. The conservation trust fund is allocated by population and must be spent on parks, wildlife, outdoor recreation, environmental education, open space, and natural areas.

Unfunded Mandates

Unfunded Colorado program requirements are not of great concern to municipalities. Throughout Colorado's history, local governments have had relative sovereignty and have been able to spend general revenues to best advantage.

In the broader sense of unfunded mandates, municipal governments must by law maintain a clerk, treasurer, and judge. Municipalities that do not do so have made titular modifications with existing employees or employ people who are required to perform minimum tasks in return for a small stipend. Home rule governments have greater flexibility to eliminate such statutory requirements in their charters.

Access to Local Government

Local Elections

Control over elections is a local and municipal matter; citizens in a home rule municipality may therefore establish their own election procedures. Subsequent court rulings have supported this authority conferred by Article XX, section 6. *People ex. rel. Tate v. Prevost* held that by adopting the home rule amendment, the people have declared that municipal elections are local and municipal matters, over which they have the power to legislate.[56]

A home rule municipality may establish its own date of election (either in odd- or even-numbered years) and the particular time of year in which the city holds an election.[57] The citizens may determine when newly elected officials will assume office, which may be any time after the election.

Many home rule municipalities have adopted a version of the Municipal Election Code. These are the state statutes governing municipal elections. Although it does not apply to a home rule municipality, the code does provide that a home rule municipality may adopt it in whole or in part.[58] Often, home rule cities and towns modify the code to coincide with the particular interests and concerns of the citizens of the home rule community. The Colorado General Assembly cannot divest a home rule city of its plenary power over municipal elections.[59]

Lawmakers designed Article XX, section 6 to vest home rule cities with the authority to opt for partisan elections if they so desired. The courts have questioned the area of law regarding partisan elections for home rule municipalities. The case of *Hoper v. Denver* held that the article was not intended to limit a home rule city to nonpartisan elections.[60]

Citizen Controls over Actions of Local Officials

Home rule places the responsibility for the quality of municipal government more firmly in the hands of the municipality's citizens and officials by reducing reliance on the state legislature for authority to act. The people of Colorado reserve the powers of initiative, referendum, and recall of officials, pursuant to the constitution. The Municipal Home Rule Act of 1971 requires a home rule charter to contain initiative and referendum measures and provides for the recall of officers.[61]

State law gives municipal voters the rights of initiative and referendum.[62] The language in Article V, section 1 is not that of maximal limitation: "The initiative and referendum powers reserved to the people by this section are hereby further reserved to the legal voters of every city, town, and municipality as to all local, special, and municipal legislation of every character."

In regard to ordinance legislation, the home rule charter may provide that ordinances are subject to referendum. A city charter can provide that all ordinances, with exceptions, are subject to a referendum provision.[63]

Colorado law requires most state and local government meetings to be open to the public and most records to be public.[64] Three Colorado Supreme Court decisions, however, have exempted Colorado's home rule municipalities from the open meetings and open records requirements.[65] Thus, "open government at the local level in Colorado depends largely on the provisions in the home rule charters of the major cities and towns in the state."[66]

State-Local Relations

The long tradition of home rule in Colorado has brought some clarity with regard to the rights, duties, and authorities of and relationships among governmental entities. However, there are broad trends that may affect the authority of municipalities in the future. In Colorado, as in other states, federal mandates are precipitating a trend toward regionalism. For example the Intermodal Surface Transportation Efficiency Act requires local governments to coordinate transportation planning and construction through the local council of governments. Nevertheless, the regionalism trend has not deterred interest in home rule, because statutory local governments continue to examine home rule implementation. Given the apparent trend toward regionalism, home rule in Colorado remains an alternative by which to strengthen local autonomy and control.

In terms of Colorado's intergovernmental relations, growth has augmented transportation infrastructure challenges. Transportation issues often pit the state against local governments, with counties and regional entities in between. Growth has also exacerbated attempts to preserve open space, the fight for water, and shifts in revenue; the latter will likely result in future conflicts.

As a result of reduced federal dollars and a diminished state budget, the state is considering tapping further into local government revenue. Options include augmenting the sales tax ratio,[67] requiring local governments to pay more for transportation infrastructure improvements, and increasing funding for education. Although intergovernmental relations have been harmonious, these fiscal modifications, if realized, will undoubtedly increase conflict among all levels of government in Colorado.

Notes

1. There was interest in joining the United States earlier, but Colorado lacked the required 60,000 population until the mid-1870s.

2. Colorado Demographic Service, *Colorado Population Counts and Estimates, 1980–1994* (Denver: Demographic Section, Colorado Division of Local Government, 1995).

3. See Roger A. Walton, *Colorado: A Practical Guide to Its Government and Politics* (Ft. Collins: Publishers Consultants, 1984).

4. Denver is included as one of the sixty-three counties. Denver and Broomfield are the only jurisdictions in the state that have combined city-county governments. (Broomfield will become a combined city-county government in 2001.)

5. Colorado Municipal League, *1996–1997 CML Directory: Municipal and County Officials in Colorado* (Denver: Colorado Municipal League, 1996), 80.

6. The court first accepted Dillon's Rule in 1893, with the case of *Phillips v. City of Denver*, 19 Colo. 179, 34 P. 902 (1893).

7. David J. McCarthy Jr., *Local Government Law*, 3d ed. (St. Paul, Minn.: West, 1990), 18.

8. Howard C. Klemme, "Powers of Home Rule Cities in Colorado," *University of Colorado Law Review* 36 (1964): 323.

9. Dale Krane, Russell L. Smith, and Platon N. Rigos, "Responsibility, Responsiveness in Local Government and the Meaning of Home Rule" (facsimile, 2 February 1995), 4.

10. *People ex. rel. Elder v. Sours*, 31 Colo. 369, 387, 74 P. 167 (1903), as cited in Klemme, "Powers of Home Rule Cities in Colorado," 321.

11. Colorado Municipal League, *Home Rule Handbook* (Denver: Colorado Municipal League, 1991), 2.

12. Klemme, "Powers of Home Rule Cities in Colorado," 323.

13. Colorado Municipal League, *Home Rule Handbook*, 2.

14. Klemme, "Powers of Home Rule Cities in Colorado," 324.

15. Martin R. McCullough, "A Primer on Municipal Home Rule in Colorado," *Colorado Lawyer* 18 (1989): 443.

16. Colorado Constitution, Article XX, section 6.

17. Colorado Municipal League, *Home Rule Handbook*, 2.

18. Colorado Revised Statutes (1994), 31-2-201.

19 Kathy Haddock, "Answers to Your Questions about Home Rule" (memorandum, Town of Superior, Colorado, 18 June 1993), 1.

20. Charles Houghton, as quoted in Ruth Zirkle, "Home Rule Could Give Cripple Creek Edge," *Ute Pass Courier*, 13 December 1990, A3.

21. *Deluxe Theaters, Inc. v. City of Englewood*, 198 Colo. 85, 596 P.2d 771 (1979).

22. Colorado Municipal League, *Home Rule Handbook*, 14.

23. Colorado Revised Statutes (1994), 31-2-216.

24. Susan K. Griffiths, "Advantages and Disadvantages of Home Rule" (memorandum, City of Louisville, Colorado, 11 April 1980), 2.

25. Colorado Revised Statutes (1994), 31-12-102.

26. Colorado Constitution, Article XX, section 1.

27. Colorado Municipal League, *Home Rule Handbook*, 19.

28. Colorado Constitution, Article II, section 30.

29. Thomas O. David, "County Home Rule: A Blueprint for the Future," *Commentator* (May–June 1992): 15.

30. J. Paul Brown, "Reflections on the La Plata County Home Rule Battle," *Commentator* (May–June 1992): 22.

31. *Colorado Open Space Council v. City & County of Denver*, 190 Colo. 122, 543 P.2d 1258 (1975).

32. *Fishel v. City and County of Denver*, 106 Colo. 576, 108 P.2d 236 (1940).

33. *Town of Glendale v. City and County of Denver*, 137 Colo. 188, 322 P.2d 1053 (1958).

34. *Stermer v. Board of Commissioners of La Plata County*, 38 P. 839 (Colo. App. 1899).

35. *Colburn v. Board of Commissioners of El Paso County*, 61 P. 241 (Colo. App. 1900).

36. Advisory Commission on Intergovernmental Relations (ACIR), *Measuring Local Discretionary Data* (Washington, D.C.: ACIR, November 1981), 16.

37. The powers of special districts are enumerated in Colorado Revised Statutes (1994), 32-1-1001.

38. Ibid., 32-1-1004(4).

39. Griffiths, "Advantages and Disadvantages of Home Rule," 8.

40. *DeLong v. City and County of Denver,* 195 Colo. 27, 576 P.2d 537 (1978).

41. *Frick v. Abell,* 602 P.2d 852 (Colo. 1980).

42. Griffiths, "Advantages and Disadvantages of Home Rule," 7.

43. *International Brotherhood of Police Officers v. City and County of Denver,* 185 Colo. 50, 521 P.2d 916 (1974).

44. *Colorado Springs v. Industrial Commission,* 720 P.2d 601 (Colo. App. 1985); affirmed 749 P.2d 412 (Colo. 1988).

45. *City and County of Denver v. State,* 788 P.2d 764 (Colo. 1990).

46. McCullough, "A Primer on Municipal Home Rule in Colorado," 444.

47. See State of Colorado, Department of Local Affairs, Division of Local Government Web page: http://www.dlg.oem2.state.co.us/index.htm.

48. Colorado Revised Statutes (1994), 31-25-101, 29-3-101, 31-25-1201.

49. Colorado Municipal League, *1995 Municipal Taxes* (Denver: Colorado Municipal League, 1995), 19, 33; and *1998 Municipal Taxes* (1998), 7.

50. Tax Foundation, *Facts and Figures on Government Finance* (New York: Tax Foundation, 1993), 307.

51. Colorado Municipal League, *1995 Municipal Taxes,* 31.

52. Colorado Revised Statutes (1994), 29-1-101.

53. State of Colorado, Department of Local Affairs, Division of Local Government, *Thirtieth Annual Local Government Financial Compendium* (Denver: Division of Local Government, March 1997), 350.

54. Colorado Revised Statutes (1994), 29-1-103(2).

55. Colorado Municipal League, *1995 Municipal Taxes,* 115.

56. *People* ex. rel. *Tate v. Prevost,* 55 Colo. 199, 134 P. 129 (1913).

57. McCullough, "A Primer on Municipal Home Rule in Colorado," 444.

58. Colorado Municipal League, *Home Rule Handbook,* 33. See also Colorado Revised Statutes (1994), 31-10-1539(2).

59. *Gosliner v. Denver Election Commission,* 191 Colo. 328, 552 P.2d 1010 (1976).

60. *Hoper v. City and County of Denver,* 173 Colo. 390, 479 P.2d 967 (1971).

61. Colorado Revised Statutes (1994), 31-2-212.

62. *Burks v. City of Lafayette,* 142 Colo. 61, 349 P.2d 692 (1960).

63. *City of Fort Collins v. Dooney,* 178 Colo. 25, 496 P.2d 316 (1972).

64. See the Colorado Sunshine Act, Colorado Revised Statutes (1994), 24-6-401, 29-9-101.

65. See *Associated Students of the University of Colorado v. Board of Regents,* 543 P.2d 59 (Colo. 1975); *Gosliner v. Denver Election Commission,* 552 P.2d 1010 (Colo. 1976); and *Uberoi v. University of Colorado,* 686 P.2d 785 (Colo. 1984).

66. Sam Archibald, "Home Rule Municipalities and Colorado's Open Records and Meetings Laws," *Colorado Lawyer* 18 (1989): 1125.

67. Currently the state collects a 3 percent sales-and-use tax. The maximum allowable rate is 7 percent, although there are a number of specially earmarked taxes excluded from this cap. Municipalities may charge a tax rate that when combined with the state's tax totals the cap, not including excluded taxes. The governor has discussed modifying the ratio to provide the state with a larger share.

CONNECTICUT

Richard C. Kearney

Conventional wisdom holds that local autonomy prevails in Connecticut. However, the 169 local governments in the Nutmeg State are increasingly constricted in their actions by state government mandates, preemption, and financial constraints. There remains a sense that local authority is grander than it actually is, probably because local governments in Connecticut are much smaller and more accessible than those in most other states. Yet during the 1990s, a struggle ensued between forces arguing in favor of continued local autonomy and those prodding local governments toward greater cooperation.

Governmental Setting

The state context of local government in Connecticut is strong two-party competition, a rapidly changing economic system, and a political culture with the prevailing belief that government exists to advance the public interest while protecting individualism. In 1994 Republican John G. Rowland replaced Independent Lowell Weicker as chief executive; Weicker had followed a two-term Democrat, William O'Neill. The General Assembly was controlled by the Democrats in 1998 (but by only a one-vote margin in the senate), and Rowland retained the governorship. Connecticut rates high in measures of policy liberalism. It is a strong union state, particularly in the public sector, where collective bargaining sets wages, benefits, and working conditions for nearly all state and local employees.

The economic situation changed rapidly after the late 1980s, when a lengthy economic boom finally peaked. Connecticut's economy had relied heavily on defense-related manufacturing, finance, and insurance. All of these sectors suffered greatly during the economic readjustments accompanying the recession of 1990–1991 and shed employment significantly for nearly five years. Nonetheless, in 2000 Connecticut remained the wealthiest state in terms of per capita personal income, and employment was growing once again.

Contributing to the sense of economic crisis was the huge state indebtedness of nearly $3 billion in 1990–1991 (second only to that of California on a per capita basis), which produced a political battle over Governor Weicker's proposal for a state income tax.[1] The state personal income tax was enacted in 1991; in its wake were broken promises and political careers and a vocal group of angry citizens.

As Connecticut lost jobs in the hundreds and thousands at a time, an unlikely savior appeared. The Mashantucket Pequot casino at Ledyard has been a success, generating more than 25,000 jobs. The Pequots, the native population of the state, have also exhibited a remarkable political sophistication. For example, in 1995 more than $135 million in slot machine revenues was shared with the state, in return for a ban on slot machines off the reservation. A second Native American casino began operations on a Mohegan reservation near Ledyard in 1997, boosting state revenues to an estimated $230 million annually. This money is quite important to local governments, which received $85 million of it yearly as state-shared revenue in 1994–1997.

Connecticut towns provide the services that are associated with counties in most other states.[2] The absence of large units of government, in conjunction with the narrow geographic reach of the local property tax, has contributed to the development and perpetuation of pockets of urban poverty. The problems of fiscal "donut holes," with huge fiscal disparities between cities and their wealthy suburban enclaves, is evident in the three major cities (Hartford, New Haven, and Bridgeport). The economic imbalance exceeds such disparities in all other states. New Haven's per capita income in 1990 was only 67.7 percent of that of its suburbs; Bridgeport's was 66.6 percent; and Hartford's, 53.7 percent. Yet those cities' property tax rates are the highest in the state, substantially exceeding the statewide average.[3] These cities import workers during the day for high-paying jobs, then jettison them at night to their homes in the suburbs. Meanwhile, population declined in the cities during the 1990s. Hartford, New Haven, Bridgeport, and Waterbury made a national list of the "ten fastest-shrinking U.S. cities" for the years 1990–1994.[4]

Home Rule in Connecticut

Historical Development

Connecticut has a long and proud history of local autonomy. The towns of Hartford, Wethersfield, and Windsor were founded in the 1630s, several years before the adoption of Connecticut's—and America's—first written constitution, the Fundamental Orders of 1639. The towns were subject only to the authority of a General Court and the British Crown. Indeed, it was the association of the three original towns that created the State of Connecticut.

An early form of home rule was devised by the General Court in 1639. The court specified the powers that were already being exercised informally by several towns and broadened them to include grants of land and selection of town officials as well as making "such orders as may be for the well ordering of their own Towns, being not repugnant to any law here established."[5] Further affirmations of home rule may be found in the code of 1650 and the revised codes of 1672.

Citizens take pride in and identify with their towns, each of which is popularly believed to have its own identity. The town in which one lives represents a form of self-expression. Historian Charles McClean Andrews, in discussing the earliest Connecticut River towns, wrote that

the valley towns were within their own boundaries as exclusive as a feudal knight within his castle. . . . This principle of town separation; the maintenance of its privileges as against all intruders; the jealousy with which it watched over all grants to the individual inhabitants, taking the greatest care that not one jot or title of town rights or town possessions should be lost or given up, characterizes everywhere the New England towns.[6]

The twentieth-century home rule movement in Connecticut was embodied in a 1915 statute that authorized municipalities to adopt charters without obtaining legislative permission. The statute, however, required 60 percent of the registered voters in a jurisdiction to approve the proposed charter, a percentage that proved to be extremely difficult to obtain. It was repealed in 1929. Eventually, the legislature lowered the voter approval percentage to 26 percent of the electorate,[7] but only a handful of towns opted for charter adoption even under the 26 percent rule. Most towns continued to be governed through numerous special acts of the General Assembly, and the selectmen–town meeting form of government prevailed.

Definition of Home Rule

Connecticut has constitutional home rule, but practically speaking, statutory law determines and defines the relationships between the state and its localities. Statutory law enumerates specific local powers, including eighty-seven basic municipal powers in the Home Rule Act and numerous other, more specif-ic powers; all other powers are implicitly reserved to the state. In other words, Dillon's Rule is alive and well in Connecticut; that is, local governments may exercise only those powers explicitly granted to them by the state and those clearly implied by these explicit powers. The Connecticut Supreme Court has strictly interpreted home rule powers and rejected those that do not have a clear statutory basis, that contradict or frustrate state policy, or that are preempted by state law. "Implied" powers are generally "restricted to actions that are essential to carry out specifically delegated powers."[8] The state supreme court's rulings on home rule have been criticized as being exceedingly narrow, arbitrary, and contradictory.[9]

Structural Features

There are some anomalous features of local government in Connecticut that distinguish it from other states. For one thing, Connecticut has no functional counties. Although eight counties had been established by 1785, they never were vested with significant authority. In 1960 Connecticut became the first state to abolish its counties. The state took over all county property and functions under the authority of Public Act 152, which simply but effectively eliminated county government by deleting the word *county* from all statutes. The state continues to delineate counties on official maps, and there remains a single elected county official—the high sheriff—whose major function is to transfer prisoners from one place to another.

Another feature of Connecticut local government is that there are no independent school districts. School boards report and submit their annual budgets to the town's legislative body. The town and school budgets are approved separately. In practice, school boards function nearly independently. During the tight fiscal climate of the 1990s, conflicts between school boards and town councils grew, and in some cases, relations deteriorated significantly.

The local government picture becomes more muddled when other units of local government are considered. Some are officially designated in their local charters as municipalities (for example, Hartford, New Haven, Bridgeport), but they retain the legal status of towns. Some municipalities are situated within towns (for example, Putnam, Groton, Willimantic), as are boroughs and villages. Boroughs and villages are special taxing and service districts with an elected official called the borough warden. Only a handful of boroughs remain today.

The 1957 Home Rule Act broadened the scope of home rule substantially by permitting local governments to select among six different types of chief executives and several types of legislative bodies.[10] Charter adoption or revision could thus be initiated by citizen petition or by two-thirds vote of the local legislative body.

The act sets forth a means for consolidating the town with

other political subdivisions within its geographical boundaries. It also prohibits the General Assembly from enacting special legislation concerning the organization, form of government, or powers of a municipality unless requested to do so by the affected municipality. This prohibition generally has been complied with; only a modest number of special acts have been passed since 1957.

Home rule was constitutionalized in 1969 in Article 10, section 1, which reaffirmed and strengthened the ban on special acts applying to local governments. Such acts pertained to the maximum terms of office of town officials, the borrowing of power, the validation of acts, and the formation, consolidation, or dissolution of a local government.

The most recent home rule legislation was adopted in 1981. The Municipal Powers Act extended to all towns (whether or not they operated under charters) the full range of powers listed in the 1957 act. (The 1957 act applied only to charter municipalities; other municipalities continued functioning under special acts.) Another 1981 act clarified charter adoption and revision procedures and, in an important move, declared that such charters shall not be inconsistent with the constitution or general statutes. More than 102 towns have organized under local charters; the remainder function under the general statutes. Both charter and noncharter towns and cities also operate partly under special acts of the legislature that were enacted before the 1965 constitutional revisions, which prohibited new acts while grandfathering existing ones.

Town forms of government include mayor-council, council-manager, or selectmen–town meeting. (For the latter, the legislative body may be called the board of selectmen, board of directors, board of aldermen, or board of burgesses.) Variations exist, including representative town meeting and mayor-manager-council. The majority of towns (that is, 109), most of which have populations less than 25,000, operate under the selectmen–town meeting form. Twenty-nine have mayor-council forms, and 31 have council-manager systems.[11]

The selectmen form is typically characterized by three or five elected board members who make policy decisions on town services and other operations. A first selectman (also elected) functions as chief executive. Important issues, such as the town budget and ordinances, are decided in a town meeting in which any adult town resident or property owner may speak and vote. These gatherings—considered by some to be cumbersome anachronisms and by others to be valued vestiges of "direct democracy"—are held at regularly scheduled times and on special occasions to consider pressing issues. Governing authority of the selectmen is shared not only with residents in the town meeting but also with elected boards of education, boards of finance, and planning and zoning boards.

In addition to a legislative body, all municipalities must have a chief executive officer. This may be the first selectman; an appointed chief administrative officer; an elected mayor; an elected borough warden; a town, city, or borough manager; or a chief administrative officer appointed by a mayor.

There are no unincorporated areas in Connecticut, because all territory is situated within one of the 169 towns. Virtually all forms of extraterritoriality are therefore precluded. Counting regional school districts and 368 special-purpose districts, there is a total of 563 local governments in the state. Although annexation and incorporation are nonissues in Connecticut, the statutes do provide for units of local government to consolidate.

In localities where town meetings still prevail, "regionalism" is considered to be undesirable state intervention into local affairs. The heavy hand of the state is detested, unless of course it allocates significant sums of money to the towns. As one writer put it, "The towns occupy an emotional place in the hearts and minds of . . . citizens, and any threat to diminish their powers results in an opposition stronger than that which accompanies any seeming threat to so-called states' rights in the South."[12]

Functions of Local Government

Functional Responsibilities

The Connecticut towns (referred to in statute as "municipalities") perform all of the functions that are the responsibility of municipalities and counties in other states. They conduct elections, build and repair roads, engage in planning and zoning, provide law enforcement and fire protection, and generally deliver a full range of services.

Among the state services made available to local governments are state purchasing services for interested towns and the resident state trooper program for small towns without their own police force. With respect to the latter, the town contributes to the costs of supporting the compensation of a trooper who is assigned to the town or shared with nearby towns. The resident trooper exercises full responsibilities and powers of a chief law enforcement officer.

Among the myriad specified municipal powers is the authority to create special-purpose districts. Twenty or more voters may petition for a special-purpose district, which must be approved in a town meeting or by referendum. Charter towns may establish special-services districts through local ordinance. The territorial limits of the district constitute a separate taxing district.[13]

Interlocal cooperation assumes several forms. Although "regionalism" has negative connotations in Connecticut, towns do engage in "voluntary" endeavors. Examples of such interlocal and interregional cooperation are increasing. Reports by the Connecticut Advisory Commission on Intergovernmental Relations indicate that cooperative ventures grew from 59 in 1990 to

700 in 1996. Regional health districts, economic development coalitions, cooperative purchasing programs, and many other cooperative relationships are being developed.

Through a vote of their respective legislative bodies, two or more towns may form a municipal district for any purpose that is permitted by statute to be performed by an individual town. Municipal district affairs are managed by a board appointed by the legislative body of the cooperating towns. "Metropolitan districts" are also permitted and comprise metropolitan areas consisting of cities of 25,000 or more population and any town or other unit of government within fifteen miles.

Interlocal agreements may be established by any unit of local government to address specific tasks. Most agreements are funded by general-fund appropriations from the participating towns or through fees and charges. In some cases, however, the state has created an incentive structure to promote interlocal cooperation. Examples include regional planning agencies, councils of government, and regional education service centers. Regional planning agencies and councils of government are most prevalent, but as is typical in other states, they have very limited power and authority over fiscal and service-provision matters.

Administrative Discretion

Connecticut is a strong collective bargaining state. Local governments are highly organized by unions across all functions, including the level of department heads in some towns. Binding arbitration is compulsory for contract-related and grievance-related impasses in local governments, including those in public education, which is covered by a separate arbitration law. Strikes are illegal.

State law imposes personnel training requirements on police officers but not on firefighters. Fire departments are predominantly volunteer except in the larger towns and cities. There are 115 volunteer fire departments; 37 departments combine paid and volunteer firefighters.[14]

State law does not require towns to establish a merit system of employment, to establish a municipal retirement system, or to participate in the state retirement system. State law does provide for optional merit system structures and processes. Likewise, there are no mandated pay plans (such as comparable worth) nor are specific benefits required for local government workers concerning health care, family leave, or day care. Statute does establish a Municipal Employees Retirement Fund that towns have the option of adopting for elected, appointed, and civil service employees.

However, there is a prevailing wage mandate that riles local officials. This statute requires that workers on public works projects valued at $400,000 or more for new construction or $100,000 or more for repairs and renovations be paid the prevailing wage, which in Connecticut is essentially union scale. This mandate,

patterned on the federal Davis-Bacon Act, was originally intended to protect construction workers from cut-rate wage competition but now effectively protects unionized firms from wage markets. Nine states have repealed their prevailing wage laws since 1980, but given continued union strength, Connecticut is unlikely to be the tenth. The costs are significant; the prevailing wage is estimated to increase the cost of public works projects by 30 percent compared with private-sector construction.[15]

Local governments enjoy a great deal of immunity from state mandates in the area of administrative procedures, rules, and systems (such as purchasing standards). Open meetings and public availability of records—both of which must be maintained—are the exception. Sovereign immunity for local government torts has been waived by the state.

Local planning and land-use authority is strong and is vested by state law in planning and zoning boards or in the local legislative body.[16] Where planning and zoning boards exist, their decisions are not subject to review by other units of town government—only by the state courts. Wetlands are also subject to strong local regulation through planning and zoning boards, conservation commissions, or special wetlands commissions. Local wetlands decisions are also subject to state oversight.

Economic Development

Any town or city may establish through ordinance an economic development commission. The commission, which may be either appointed or elected, may conduct research and make recommendations to local officials concerning development opportunities and strategies; further, it may coordinate local development activities. Two or more towns may join together in creating regional economic development commissions. For example, the Capitol Region Growth Council covers a large geographic area around Hartford.

Towns may establish convention and visitors' commissions to coordinate and promote usage of town-owned facilities designed to attract tourists. Historic districts may be established to preserve and protect local buildings and places. Towns may also establish foreign trade zones, subject to review and approval by the state. Local redevelopment agencies are permitted under state law and are granted the power to contract with federal agencies for grant-in-aid purposes.[17]

In Connecticut, "distressed municipalities" receive special state financial aid and payments in lieu of taxes for local businesses. Distressed municipalities may designate an area as an enterprise zone, subject to approval of the commissioner of economic development and in conformance with certain census tract criteria. (Connecticut was the first state, in 1981, to permit enterprise zones.) Seventeen enterprise zones had been created by 2000, along with three enterprise zone corridors, in which multiple, contiguous small towns form a multitown enterprise zone. Firms locating within enterprise zones are granted various tax abatements and deferrals and other financial inducements. Because enterprise zones have not been systematically evaluated, their performance is unknown.

Little money has been offered to localities for economic development purposes. In practice, the local government role in economic development is of minor importance.

Fiscal Autonomy of Local Governments

Local Revenues

In Connecticut, local governments have little fiscal autonomy. They are not permitted to assess local sales or income taxes. Fees and charges for local government services, licenses, and permits are generally allowed, but they account for only about 13 percent of total local revenues.

Of greatest importance to towns and municipalities is the property tax, which brings in about 57 percent of local revenues, the second highest percentage of all states, behind New Hampshire. (The remainder of revenues consists of state and federal grants and payments.) At $1,413 per capita (in 1999), the individual property tax burden is the fourth highest in the country. Both real property and personal property (such as machinery, equipment, vehicles, and boats) are taxed by local governments based on assessments performed and rates set by the locality. No property tax limit or other restrictions are imposed by the state. Revaluation of real property, under recent statute, must take place every four years.

State property is excluded from local taxation. The state, however, does provide some compensation through payment in lieu of taxes, thus reimbursing towns for property taxes paid on state land and buildings and certain private property as well. There is a partial exemption of property taxes for veterans also ($3,000 of assessed valuation annually).

Few debt limits are imposed on towns and cities. They are required not to have a deficit in their operating budgets at the end of the fiscal year, and debt is limited to a set percentage of the fair market value of assets in the town's sinking fund (the limitation varies by type or purpose of the debt). State law specifies the purposes for which local debt may be incurred, such as capital improvements, infrastructure, and economic development purposes. Authority is granted for local governments to issue municipal bonds, with no restrictions as to terms, types, or tax status. Short-term borrowing is permitted without prior state approval.

Local Expenditures

The state requires towns and cities to adopt an annual operating budget and to follow generally accepted accounting principles. However, local governments must conduct independent

Table 1. Expenditures for Three Connecticut Cities, 1996 (in percent)

Function	Hartford (pop. 135,750)	Middletown (pop. 43,620)	New Canaan (pop. 18,622)
General government	3%	4%	3%
Police	8	9	7
Fire	5	0	3
Planning and development	1	2	1
Public works	8	6	9
Health and social services	10	5	1
Libraries	1	2	3
Education	48	53	61
Parks and recreation	1	3	3
Debt service	4	7	4
Fringe benefits	8	6	4
Miscellaneous	3	3	0

Source: Connecticut Policy and Expenditure Council (CPEC), "Analysis of 1996 Connecticut Municipal Budgets" (Hartford: CPEC, 1997).

postaudits and file them with the state. There is no specific statutory requirement for a balanced budget, but it is generally mandated by state policy. Table 1 shows the distribution of expenditures for three towns with varying population sizes.

A uniform fiscal year must be adopted and complied with by all local governments. They must also hold annual budget hearings, and the budget must be published. All municipal accounts must be audited annually by an independent public accountant selected by the town and approved by the state Office of Policy and Management. Towns must also provide for the independent audit of school districts within their jurisdiction. Audit results must be published in the annual report of the town.

On June 6, 1991, Connecticut's largest city, Bridgeport, became the largest general-purpose government to seek bankruptcy under Chapter 9 of the U.S. Bankruptcy Code. The city had fallen into financial crisis in 1988, when it lost access to bond markets because of substantial debts, revenue shortfalls, and a lengthy period of fiscal mismanagement.[18] The state responded by guaranteeing $35 million in municipal bonds and establishing a financial review board to oversee the city's operations and expenditures. When the financial situation continued to deteriorate, the mayor sought to file for bankruptcy. The state objected to the city's bankruptcy petition and eventually prevailed in the federal courts.[19]

In 1992, when the town of West Haven faced serious financial problems, the state headed off another Bridgeport-type crisis by expressly prohibiting that locality from seeking bankruptcy, in exchange for guaranteeing West Haven bonds.[20] Bridgeport has since recovered from potential fiscal collapse. In September 1995 the financial review board was dissolved, and the city was once again able to sell bonds in the municipal bond markets without state guarantees.

State Government Grants-in-Aid to Localities

State aid to towns and cities amounted to $1.838 billion in fiscal 1996 (26 percent of total local revenues), which included $1.364 billion for grants for education and $55.4 million in grants for state property and certain exempted private property.

The state enacted legislation in 1994 to take over general assistance from local governments. The takeover was completed in 1998, with full reimbursement to towns and cities for general assistance.

Unfunded Mandates

The popular notion of local autonomy in Connecticut is undermined by the more than 700 mandates imposed by the state on localities. The Connecticut Advisory Commission on Intergovernmental Relations published a 1995 compendium of statutory mandates on local governments that identified the mandates and estimated the costs of each of them. The mandates vary from the mundane and minor (for example, the requirement that local officials use alkaline paper for permanent records) to the extraordinary and expensive (for example, a mandate that local governments must provide heart disease and hypertension benefits for police and firefighters, costing up to $17 million per year). Mandates relating to support of the public schools are estimated to cost $2.5 billion annually, about 36 percent of total local operating budgets.[21]

Not surprisingly, most state mandates can be connected to special interests that reap the benefits. Among the most successful "rent seeking" special interest groups[22] are public employee unions, professions, industries, and individual firms. Collective bargaining and arbitration mandates, requirements that local boards of education hire medical advisors and school nurses, and a variety of property tax breaks for industries and firms are just a few examples.

State mandates are widely reviled by local officials in Connecticut. The Connecticut Conference of Municipalities seldom misses an opportunity to point out that about half of all local government expenditures in the state are in response to mandated services or benefits, leaving "half of all local budgets beyond [the] control"[23] of localities themselves. Receiving special opprobrium are the heart and hypertension mandate, the prevailing wage mandate, and compulsory arbitration for teachers and town employees.

Outcries about mandates prompted the state legislature in 1983 to enact a statutory requirement for municipal fiscal notes to identify potential costs and impacts on local revenues of proposed state legislation and regulations.[24] Fiscal impact statements must be attached to any bill or conference committee report that would create or expand a state mandate to cities and towns. Any bill or amendment creating or enlarging a mandate is referred to the (joint) appropriations committee for a determination of whether a reimbursement should accompany the mandate. Connecticut is one of at least forty-two states requiring a fiscal estimate of mandates and one of at least eighteen states requiring the legislature to consider reimbursement of mandate costs to local governments.

Legislation enacted in 1993[25] responded to local government concerns. The new legislation required a one-year delay in implementing new state mandates that cause localities to appropriate funds so that the General Assembly could weigh relevant information on mandate costs and benefits. This same law calls on the Connecticut Advisory Commission on Intergovernmental Relations to submit an annual report to the legislature that lists all town and municipal mandates. However, the various statutory limitations on mandates have been ignored or given little serious attention by many legislators.

Despite the negativity surrounding mandates, most local officials consider them to be rational, understandable, and not particularly burdensome. The number of mandates is impressively large, but the percentage that meaningfully affects local fiscal affairs and expenditures is small.

Access to Local Government

Local Elections

Local election procedures generally are specified in state law.[26] Procedures to fill vacancies in elected offices are established by the state. Referendums and associated procedures and requirements are provided for in local charters. Towns determine the date of a referendum, but the state mandates that referendums not be held until thirty or more days after public notice. Polls are required to be open from noon until 8:00 P.M., but local governments may open polling places as early as 6:00 A.M., and most do. The legislative body determines where elections will be held. The state Elections Enforcement Commission investigates alleged irregularities in local elections and may assess fines on violators.

Town clerks and registrars are required to follow certain procedures concerning voter registration, determination of eligible electors, maintenance of the registry list, and absentee voting.

All municipalities must hold elections biennially on a date specified in state law. Special elections to fill vacancies may be called by local legislative bodies or convened upon application of twenty registered voters of the jurisdiction.

Towns and cities may hold at-large or district elections. The specific elective offices are set by charter and must comply with state provisions. Terms of office must be two years for most municipal officials and two or four years for elected chief executive officers, town clerks, and registrars. State law also sets restrictions on election of boards of education, including the number and terms of members.

Voting machines are required for all local elections. The order of names on the ballot, by political party, is determined through a state formula. Duties of election officials are specified, as is the process of voting.

State law stipulates permissible campaign expenditures and requires a campaign treasurer to file various statements. Individual contributions for municipal elections are limited to $250 per candidate. Contributions to a political party are limited to $5,000 per calendar year. Political action committees are limited to contributions of $250. State law prohibits at least twenty-four election practices.[27]

Political parties must file party rules with the secretary of state. Party-endorsed candidates are selected in a caucus, party convention, or town committee. State law is fairly restrictive regarding party primary procedures and requirements. Provisions are made for minor parties and petitioning parties. All local elections are partisan.

Citizen Controls over Actions of Local Officials

Recall or impeachment of local officials is not authorized. Initiative and referendum are provided for under all forms of local government. Procedures for adopting local ordinances are determined at the town level in the charter, not mandated by the state. In the selectmen form of government, the town budget must be submitted to a vote of citizens in a town meeting. In recent years, this has resulted in a sort of mini–taxpayer revolt; antitax forces have mustered their numbers in town meetings and voted down operating budgets numerous times in a single fiscal year, thereby forcing the boards of selectmen to revise and lower spending proposals until the figures are deemed satisfactory by a majority of town meeting voters.

Open meetings and open records are required by the state.

State-Local Relations

In many important respects, local autonomy is a popular myth in Connecticut. Inexorable pressures weigh against any expansion of local autonomy, including economic and social demands for regionalism and the irrepressible tendency of the state legislature to issue mandates that circumscribe local discretion and home rule. Proposals for regionalism provoke opposition from local government traditionalists, especially when presented as mandates or requirements from the state. Towns and cities are greatly restricted in their ability to raise revenues through any tax except that on property. Dillon's Rule reigns in the state courts and in municipal practice.

Nonetheless, 360 years of history and the unusual structures and processes of local government—such as the selectmen form of town government, the absence of counties, and the prevalence of town meetings to enact policy and budgets—lend credence to local authority and home rule. Compared with other states, Connecticut towns enjoy a great deal of local discretion and authority in structure, personnel, financial management, and functions.[28] Citizens identify personally with the respective towns in which they live and commonly associate towns with certain characteristics and traditions.

If, as has been suggested,[29] a city's elasticity is its destiny, Connecticut's cities are doomed to continued loss of population and tax base. In a legal sense, it is nearly impossible for Connecticut cities to expand their taxing jurisdictions into the suburbs and thereby capture some of the surrounding wealth and population. Voluntary interlocal cooperation is on the rise, but by its very nature it is limited in what it can accomplish. If there is a "solution" to the crisis of the cities, it will require strong state actions that will most certainly diminish autonomy and discretion for all local governments in Connecticut.

Notes

1. Carol W. Lewis, "Connecticut: Surviving Tax Reform," in *The Fiscal Crisis of the States,* ed. Steven Gold (Washington, D.C.: Georgetown University Press, 1996), 14–31.

2. The General Assembly abolished counties in 1960.

3. Connecticut Conference of Municipalities (CCM), *Indicators of Need in Connecticut Municipalities* (New Haven: CCM, 1994), 70–71.

4. Mike Swift, "People Leaving Hartford in Record Numbers," *Hartford Courant,* 2 October 1995, 1, 10.

5. Charles McClean Andrews, quoted in Thomas W. Jodziewicz, "'Vox Populi': Fairfield and Early Connecticut's Dual Localism," *New England Quarterly* (4 December 1985): 583.

6. Ibid., 580.

7. See Janice C. Griffith, "Connecticut's Home Rule: The Judicial Resolution of State and Local Conflicts," *University of Bridgeport Law Review* 4 (1983): 177–263.

8. Connecticut Advisory Commission on Intergovernmental Relations, *Home Rule in Connecticut* (Hartford: Connecticut Advisory Commission on Intergovernmental Relations, January 1987), 16, 20–22.

9. Griffith, "Connecticut's Home Rule"; Timothy S. Hollister, "The Myth and the Reality of Home Rule Powers in Connecticut," *Connecticut Bar Journal* 59 (1985): 388–403.

10. Connecticut Advisory Commission on Intergovernmental Relations, *Home Rule in Connecticut,* 11.

11. Frank B. Connolly, *Local Government in Connecticut* (Storrs, Conn.: Institute of Public Service, 1992), 6.

12. Rosaline Levenson, *County Government in Connecticut: Its History and Demise* (Storrs, Conn.: Institute of Public Service, 1981), 20.

13. Connecticut Advisory Commission on Intergovernmental Relations, *A Compendium of Statutory Mandates on Municipalities in Connecticut* (Hartford: Connecticut Advisory Commission on Intergovernmental Relations, 1995), 4.

14. Connolly, *Local Government in Connecticut,* 30.

15. Connecticut Advisory Commission on Intergovernmental Relations, *Compendium of Statutory Mandates on Municipalities in Connecticut,* Appendix A.

16. General Statutes of Connecticut, 7-195–201.

17. General Statutes of Connecticut, 8-126, 8-138, 8-143–144.

18. See Carol W. Lewis, "Municipal Bankruptcy and the States," *Urban Affairs Quarterly* 30 (September 1994): 3–26.

19. The state's position was, first, that Bridgeport did not meet the eligibility criteria for debtor status under federal law and, second, that state law did not explicitly permit municipalities to petition for bankruptcy relief. The state prevailed on the first objection but lost on the second. The court determined that Bridgeport did not meet the criteria for protection under federal bankruptcy law because the city was receiving tax revenues sufficient to cover most of its operating expenses. Moreover, Bridgeport was not legally impeded to raise property taxes further in order to increase revenues; therefore, Bridgeport was not "insolvent." The bankruptcy court's reasoning on the separate issue of state law was that "a state's political silence is tantamount to authorizing municipalities to file under Chapter 9." It would appear, then, that federal bankruptcy protection is potentially available to local governments in all states except Georgia, which is the only one to specifically prohibit it.

20. Lewis, "Municipal Bankruptcy and the States," 21.

21. Connecticut Advisory Commission on Intergovernmental Relations, *Compendium of Statutory Mandates on Municipalities in Connecticut,* Appendix A.

22. William Hoyt and Eugenia Toma, "State Mandates and Interest Group Lobbying," *Journal of Public Economics* 38 (1989).

23. Connecticut Conference of Municipalities, 1994.

24. General Statutes of Connecticut, 2-24, 2-24a, 4-170b.

25. Public Act 93-434.

26. General Statutes of Connecticut, 9-164, 9-153.

27. General Statutes of Connecticut, 9-354–362.

28. U.S. Advisory Commission on Intergovernmental Relations (ACIR), *State and Local Roles in the Federal System* (Washington, D.C.: ACIR, 1982).

29. David Rusk, *Cities Without Suburbs* (Washington, D.C.: Woodrow Wilson Center Press, 1993). Rusk lists Hartford, New Haven, and Bridgeport as having "zero elasticity."

DELAWARE

Jeffrey A. Raffel, Jerome R. Lewis, Deborah A. Auger, and Kathryn G. Denhardt

The authors wish to thank Roy Lopata, for detailed and stimulating comments on an earlier draft of this paper; Arno Loessner, for critical information about public finance in Delaware; Bill Boyer, for substantive and editorial suggestions; and Sarah Keifer, for diligent and focused research assistance.

In Delaware the roles and functions assumed by state and local government have not been the result of any formal, structured process of sifting through and sorting out respective responsibilities. Home rule coexists with state-level functions. Rather than opting for a systematic approach of specifying in state law the areas in which localities have autonomy, Delaware instead has favored an ad hoc strategy for contending with intergovernmental tensions or concerns. Where significant state-local conflicts surface, there has been a history of state responsiveness and pragmatic problem solving on a case-by-case basis. Delaware's small size, political intimacy, and an at least fundamentally accommodating political demeanor on the part of the state have made local acceptance of this ad hoc approach possible. Sustaining this strategy in the face of significant, newly emerging local tensions over planning and land-use issues will be critical for the state.

Governmental Setting

Being first to ratify the U.S. Constitution garnered Delaware the appellation of "the First State," but this historical moniker remains apt for other reasons in contemporary times. Delaware has retained a kind of primacy as a target of study, valued for embodying, in miniature form, qualities representative of a broad cross section of American states. Both northern and southern in character by virtue of its location along the Mason-Dixon Line, Delaware also serves as an economic, social, and political composite of the conditions and qualities prevailing in the nation.

Demographically heterogeneous, Delaware roughly parallels the nation in its racial and social composition. In terms of its economy, Delaware's core industries range from chicken farming to corporate headquarters, from chemical manufacturing to beachfront tourism. It has endured the kind of globally induced economic ups and downs experienced by other states. Politically, Delaware has evolved through periods of governmental reforms and resistance that have marked modernization efforts in other states. Moreover, it has been shaped by the same urban-rural, upstate-downstate cleavages that have tended to dominate state politics nationally.

In terms of its intergovernmental relations, though, Delaware's small geographic scale (highway signs welcome travelers to "the Small Wonder") and streamlined governmental configuration have led to the emergence of ad hoc relations between state and local government. Although state-local issues have not been paramount in the past two decades, planning may become a major issue in the near future. The state's home rule provisions, small size and population, lack of contentious partisanship conflict, concentration of functions at the state level, and ability to respond to problems and opportunities have tempered state-local issues.

Delaware is rightly considered small: its population is only 743,603,[1] ranking forty-sixth in the nation, and its size at 1,982 square miles is forty-ninth among the states. The state capital, Dover, is but an hour's drive from the southern and northern ends of the state, which is 96 miles long and 35 miles wide. The state's tourism industry stresses beautiful beaches, tax-free shopping, and elegant estates.

Since the 1980s, Delaware's financial condition has been excellent. Although Gov. Pete DuPont (1977–1984) declared the state to be almost bankrupt when he first took office, he helped establish a "rainy day" fund for sudden shortfalls in revenue. Through the Financial Development Center Act, Delaware became a leading banking and credit card processing center. The state is also considered a haven for corporations, with favorable tax laws and a court system accustomed to handling corporate litigation. Moreover, the state has maintained its place as the home of America's chemical industry. Thus, the political culture of the state can be described as decidedly probusiness.

Because of its financial soundness and small size, the state has assumed responsibilities that traditionally have been the purview of local governments. Although devolution has been the trend elsewhere, county and municipal governments in Delaware have permitted the state to take on considerable responsibility (from both a policy and a funding perspective) for education, welfare, roads, public health, and corrections. Delaware is a "strong" governor state; the governor has line-item veto power, and the executive branch sets the policy agenda. The legislature is part time and maintains a small staff. Cooperation across party lines is common.

The states vary widely in terms of numbers of local political jurisdictions; in 1995 Hawaii had 4, whereas Illinois had 6,700.[2] Delaware, befitting its small size, is at the low end of the scale. The state has three counties: urbanized New Castle County, with 482,807 people, in the north; small-town–oriented Kent County, with a population of 124,089, in the middle of the state; and Sussex County to the south, a rural region that is also home to Delaware's beach resorts, with a population of 136,707.[3] Delaware has three major cities: Wilmington (population 73,000), a city with urban problems typical of eastern and midwestern cities, including population losses, financial strains, and some racial divisions; Dover, the small-town state capital, with a population of 29,000; and Newark, home of the University of Delaware, with a population of 27,500. There are 57 other local governments in the state, plus 19 school districts and 201 special districts (mostly utility districts).

Delaware is a very competitive state in terms of partisan electoral politics. Voters regularly split their tickets, and a sizable number indicate their independent status by registering as "declines" (that is, they decline to declare a party affiliation). The longstanding electoral competitiveness of the two parties is reflected in Delaware's two senators, Democrat Joe Biden and Republican Bill Roth, each of whom has served for more than twenty years. The state has voted for the winner (whether Democrat or Republican) in almost all of the presidential elections in this century. The current governor, Democrat Thomas Carper, took office in January 1993, but his two immediate predecessors were Republicans (Mike Castle and Pete du Pont); their immediate predecessor was Democrat Sherman Tribbitt. The state's General Assembly is split: as the millenium turned, the Republicans controlled the state house (26 to 15) and the Democrats held a majority in the senate (13 to 8).

The state received much attention in 1994, when Carper, then a U.S. representative, "switched seats" with Governor Castle. Not only was this an interesting political feature story, but the election of these two popular politicians across party lines and offices illustrated the personal rather than partisan nature of Delaware politics. Although partisan squabbles certainly do occur in the General Assembly, cooperation across party lines plays a stronger role in shaping government in Delaware than in many other states.[4] Political observers have concluded that upstate-downstate cleavages are more significant in the state than

party differences. Because this competitive political environment features small legislative districts, politicians are responsive to local needs.

Home Rule in Delaware

Historical Development

The state code provisions for home rule were passed by the General Assembly in 1953. Since 1964, the General Assembly has continued to provide Delaware's counties with more authority. Like several other small states that are limited in population or area (such as Rhode Island, Vermont, Maine, and Hawaii), Delaware has few restrictions on local government. One study in the early 1990s found Delaware to be the fourth least restrictive state.[5] The limited size of the state makes it possible for local governments to handle issues on a personal and specific or ad hoc basis. Thus, the state has broad functional rather than limited home rule. Special legislation has been used sparingly in Delaware. Examples of such legislation include limits on the authority of the City of Wilmington to annex, set a wage tax, and restructure schools.

Definition of Home Rule

Title 22 and Chapter 8 of the Delaware Code Annotated discuss municipalities and home rule, respectively. The focus of the chapter is "municipal corporations," which include "all cities, towns, and villages . . . which possess legislative, administrative and police powers for the general exercise of municipal functions."[6] This code permits all municipal corporations in the state with at least 1,000 persons to amend their charters and "to assume all powers which, under the Constitution of the State, it would be competent for the General Assembly to grant by specific enumeration and which are not denied by statute." Court decisions have reaffirmed the power of municipalities to enact ordinances to designate crimes and resulting punishments, to condemn public property, and to enact housing codes.

Structural Features

The state does not have a classification system for municipal corporations. The *Annual Directory* of the Delaware League of Local Governments[7] lists the villages of Arden, Ardencroft, and Ardentown; the towns of Bellefonte, Bethany Beach, and Bridgeville; and the cities of Delaware City, Harrington, and Lewes. The designation of village, town, or city seems arbitrary: the three villages cited are all under 1,000 in population and lack home rule. By contrast, the three towns all have over 1,000 population but include one home rule municipality (Bellefonte) and two without home rule. The three cities include one non–home rule (Lewes) and two home rule governments. Section 102 of the Delaware Code also provides for local governments that are not incorporated:

unincorporated towns of at least 300 inhabitants may elect three commissioners who may regulate the streets, lanes and alleys of the town, on complaint of any citizen, examine any chimney, stovepipe, fixture or other matter dangerous to the town, . . . prohibit firing of guns or pistols, the making of bonfires or setting off of fireworks or any dangerous sport or practice, and prevent or suppress any noisy and turbulent assemblages within the town after night or on the Sabbath Day.

Under the code, twelve municipalities have home rule and can change their charters through referendum or by direct action of the General Assembly. In the case of referendum, such changes can be negated by a two-thirds vote of each chamber of the General Assembly.[8]

Annexations are governed by the state code. Annexation rules differ among Delaware municipalities. In some instances, municipalities may annex adjoining or adjacent territory, but only after gaining the approval of a majority of voters in the area to be annexed. In other municipalities, such as Newark, the owner of a contiguous property must submit a request for annexation and receive approval by a majority vote of the city council. If 20 percent of other adjoining landowners lodge a written protest, however, the annexing party must receive six out of seven affirmative council member votes.

Newark and Dover, for example, have successfully expanded their borders by annexing residential and commercial land. (More than fifty annexations have been approved for Newark since 1970.) A special provision for "large municipalities in the state" (that is, those with more than 50,000 population) has severely limited the annexation process for Wilmington by requiring that the county's legislative body and chief executive officer in which the property is to be annexed (in this case, New Castle County) approve the plan. Generally, municipalities do not exercise any form of extraterritoriality, although Wilmington owns Hoopes Reservoir, several miles from the city's borders.

According to the Delaware Superior Court's *State v. Warwick* decision,[9] "Under Delaware constitutional and statutory provision counties, while containing defined territorial areas, are in legal significance nothing more than political subdivisions of Delaware and are not designated under the law as bodies corporate." The state code specifies the general powers and duties of county government and states that the counties shall "have full and complete jurisdiction over all matters and things now or hereafter vested by law in the county governments of the respective counties." The only book written exclusively about Delaware politics and government in the past three decades concludes that "throughout the state's basic document the county looms large"; counties are cited in the state constitution in the description of grand juries, voting qualifications, and constitutional conventions.[10] The boundaries of the three counties remain essentially what they were in colonial times.

Until 1965, each of the counties was administered through a levy court, primarily a taxing body. These levy courts did not have ordinance power and had few administrative powers. Reacting to pressure from populous and urbanized New Castle County, the General Assembly overhauled the county's governmental structure in 1964. New Castle County now has a county council, six members of which are elected by district, and a president who is elected at large; all officials serve for four years. The county executive also is elected in a countywide race and serves for four years. Until 1997, when county offices were moved to an airport office park outside the city boundaries, Wilmington served as the county seat.

New Castle County is an active government involved in redevelopment, planning, subsidized housing, sewer construction and maintenance, solid waste collection, parks and recreation, public safety (primarily police), and library services.[11] In fact, under the activist administration of Mel Slawik, a former social worker and the county executive in the mid-1970s, the county went so far as to initiate an advisory body to help implement a federal school desegregation order—certainly an unusual activity for a county government.

The major task of the county council is to enact the county's budget and set the tax rate. The county council has taken an active role in planning and zoning decisions because suburban sprawl has become the biggest issue in the jurisdiction. The county executive appoints the chief administrative officer, who is primarily responsible for developing the annual budget. The powers of the county executive are so numerous that "the office is without a doubt the second most powerful and influential political position in the state."[12] However, only one county executive has sought and won reelection to a second term, and none has run and won a higher office in the state.

The General Assembly expanded the levy court in Kent County in 1967 from three to seven members. Six members are elected by district for four-year terms; one member is elected at large. The members of the levy court are active in the administration of the county; however, no strong administrator analogous to the county executive of New Castle County exists. The seat of Kent County is Dover.

In December 1995 the Wilmington *News Journal* stated editorially that "Kent County Levy Court needs a change in name and a home rule charter" to "relieve the county of having to go hat-in-hand to the General Assembly every time it needs to do something important." Echoing the sentiments of one Kent County commissioner, the *News Journal* noted that the levy court could not fix its own tax rate or issue its own bonds and that it needed to have "the powers to run an increasingly urban, industrial community with all the problems of any growing county on the Eastern seaboard." In 1970 the state legislature reorganized the government of Sussex County by enlarging the legislative body to five members and renaming it a county council. Members are elected by district, choose a president from among their members, and appoint an administrator. The county administrator supervises the work of the administrative departments and acts as an executive assistant to the council. The county seat is the small town of Georgetown.

Functions of Local Government

Functional Responsibilities

Section 301 of the Delaware Code Annotated specifies the role of municipalities with respect to zoning regulations, parking authorities, planning commissions, and municipal electric companies. Municipalities may regulate and restrict building and land use but must appoint a zoning commission and board of adjustment to do so. They may institute a parking authority and a planning commission according to code specifications. The code authorizes municipally owned or operated electric utilities.

Although not explicit, the code does mention a number of permitted county functions by way of specifying various restrictions and limits. The functions noted include taxation, ambulance, fire protection, and police services. Moreover, counties may award contracts for public works. Section 330 prohibits counties from regulating firearms.

In practice, the activity level of the state's local governments varies tremendously. New Castle County, for example, is an active, multifunctional government. Wilmington city, like its home county, has an active government with a parking authority, major redevelopment and housing subsidiaries, and the usual departments such as public works and licensing and inspection. Wilmington provides water, cleans and plows local streets, has a local police force, and provides its residents with a parks and recreation program. Even the small city of Newark has a planning commission, parking authority, housing authority, all the standard municipal public works functions, and a community development revenue-sharing advisory committee, which allocates city funds to social service agencies. Dover, like Newark, is a full-service city.

In southern Delaware, the major functions of local government vary. In Sussex County, which has twenty-five municipalities, beach resorts such as Rehoboth emphasize public safety and have well-developed parking, sewer, water supply, and recreational facilities. Inland municipalities stress economic development, focusing their energies on fending off Wal-Mart–type challenges that threaten downtown areas and transitioning from an agriculture to a service economy. Some towns such as Harrington and Clayton have industrial parks that are intended to shift the economy from agriculture to manufacturing and small business.

Although Delaware has almost 200 special-district governments, virtually all provide for drainage of agricultural land. The major cities (Wilmington, Dover, and Newark) have housing authorities, and state law allows cities and towns to form municipal electric companies, county councils to create park districts, and municipalities to establish water and sewer as well as redevelopment authorities. The authorities that have played a major role in Delaware, however, have been subordinate agencies of the state, including the Delaware Solid Waste Authority and the Delaware Transportation Authority.

There are several examples of ad hoc interlocal cooperation in the state. Until recently, the offices of the City of Wilmington and New Castle County were housed on separate floors of the same building. These two jurisdictions also have shared computing services for many years. Although Delaware is one of only a few states without legislation authorizing interlocal agreements, it does have a law allowing cooperative purchasing.[13] The Delaware Electric Cooperative includes several small towns that band together to buy and resell power. Wilmington's sewer treatment plant processes all of the sewage in New Castle County, including that from other municipalities like Newark. The Water Resources Agency provides for cooperative water system planning among Wilmington, New Castle County, and Newark; the board includes the chief executives of these jurisdictions.

In the 1970s an ad hoc commission on intergovernmental relations was established to investigate potential cooperative efforts and consolidations. The Intergovernmental Task Force made a number of recommendations, mostly calling for the establishment of systematic, cooperating, interjurisdictional committees in areas such as police, computing, and purchasing. The initial flurry of work to implement these ideas has long since dissipated.[14] The state does not have a law regulating consolidation of governments.

Financial problems of local governments in Delaware have been solved a number of times by shifting governmental functions. Under economic pressure for several decades, Wilmington has shed some of its parks and courts; the state recently took over its port; and the city "shopped around" its wastewater treatment plant to the county before deciding to privatize its operation. In addition to their duties as notaries public, counties have relinquished their prison and welfare functions to the state. The state also plays the largest role in funding public schools. In Delaware, then, many of the most contentious issues are reconciled at the state rather than the local level.

One recent issue with regard to state-local relations and economic development was the transfer of the Wilmington port from the city to the state. The port was an important economic generator in the city, but the need for new capital expenditures outstripped the city's ability to raise money. Although the state bond fund had helped in the past, the city and state agreed to transfer the responsibility and funding for the port to the state. Similarly, New Castle County recently transferred its airport to the Delaware River and Bay Authority to avoid annual losses and to realize needed capital investment.

Administrative Discretion

There are few state-imposed constraints on the administrative discretion permitted local governments in Delaware. For example, a code provision permits each county government to adopt a merit personnel system but does not require or restrict such a system. Police must receive a minimum of training in cities and counties, collective bargaining is permitted, and binding arbitration is required; otherwise, the code is silent on personnel matters. Counties are required to formally bid for contracts over $10,000. The fiscal year must be specified, and an annual audit by a CPA is required. Counties do have discretion with regard to the type of accounts they may keep. Delaware is the only state that makes workers' compensation optional rather than mandatory for each municipality.[15]

The General Assembly occasionally gets involved in local issues of administration or governance. For example, in January 1996 the state senate voted to increase the minimum salary of New Castle County's executive to $87,500 from $67,000. By state law the General Assembly sets the minimum salary for this office, but the council is allowed to establish a higher salary.[16] The salary question later complicated the transition to a new county executive.

Economic Development

Economic development is an important function of state and local government in Delaware. Both Wilmington and New Castle County have active economic development corporations. The Wilmington Economic Development Corporation has played a major role in developing downtown, and the New Castle County Economic Development Corporation has spearheaded efforts to develop the commercial appeal of the county airport. Wilmington recently adopted a business zone to increase services for the major downtown commercial area. The state has a "main street" development program aimed at municipalities, but only $50,000 has been appropriated annually for this function; thus, the amount appropriated to the eight qualifying towns is limited. However, cities and towns such as Newark (which helped to form the Newark Business Association) and Laurel (which has its own development corporation) have been making efforts in this area.

Much of the groundwork for intergovernmental cooperation for economic development was laid during the state's struggle to implement the federal court order to desegregate the public schools of New Castle County. The merging of the City of Wilmington School District with the ten surrounding suburban school districts required the governor, New Castle County's executive, and Wilmington's mayor to cooperate in managing the state, county, and city police; to coordinate their communications; and to project a unified stance toward the unpopular court order.[17] Cooperation not only continued through two administrations and across party lines but also prevailed in successful efforts to retain the headquarters of chemical giant Hercules, Inc., and to attract banks and credit card operations following the passage of the Financial Center Development Act. In 1996, at the request of the city, the state assumed responsibility for the Port of Wilmington, an indication of the generally cooperative nature of state-local relations and the state's healthy financial status.

State and local relations in the area of land-use planning are somewhat more strained, particularly in the period of intensive growth pressures since 1995. Traditionally, the state has been a minor player in planning decisions. Delaware had a state planner in the 1960s and 1970s but abolished the position in the early 1980s; it was not revived until 1996. The three counties all have planning arms and view planning decisions as their own. However, the state plays the chief role in transportation and road construction, and local planning decisions are not always in synchrony with the state's capital improvement expenditures. The Land Use Planning Act (LUPA) of 1994 mandates intergovernmental consultation on decisions that will affect or be affected by other levels of government, but this has not resolved planning problems. The governor and a nonprofit policy institute closely allied with the chamber of commerce initiated a statewide "Land Use Summit" in 1997. The shared vision for growth in Delaware and strengthened intergovernmental coordination, which were the goals of the summit, have not yet been realized.

In the mid-1970s the county executive of New Castle County was convicted of perjury in an investigation of corruption in the county development process. More recently an FBI "sting" operation resulted in the conviction of the state's secretary of transportation in a development kickback and rezoning scheme involving the New Castle County planning process. A reform-minded county executive elected in 1996 declared a six-month moratorium on all zoning decisions, during which time a new comprehensive plan and zoning ordinances were drafted and proposed. These changes were intended to address growth pressures as well as to tighten up a process that was seen as too friendly to developers. The buildup of the major commercial developments along the county's Concord Pike has angered many citizens, as has the prospect of continued commercial growth near the highly successful Christiana Mall and traffic problems around the expanding Route 40 corridor. As a result of these conflicts, several civic association activists have been elected to office in New Castle County.

Fiscal Autonomy of Local Governments

Local Revenues

The state is, of course, "wealthier" than local governments in Delaware, with 85 percent of the fiscal pie. The major state revenues are from the state income tax and franchise fees. There is no state (or local) sales tax, a condition that not only is popular with the state's residents but also has led to commercially successful shopping centers that attract interstate customers.

Municipalities derive most of their revenues from property taxes, but electrical utility revenues are very important to Newark. In 1996 Newark received more than half its revenue from utility sales and only 15 percent from property taxes. Dover relied primarily on the property tax (41 percent of total revenues) in fiscal 1997–1998. In fiscal 1999 Wilmington received almost half of its funds (47 percent) from a wage tax; property taxes made up 29 percent of the city's revenue.

The state has adopted limited restrictions on local government finances in Delaware. The state code provides for a process for setting assessments and reassessments for municipalities; for example, the code stipulates when assessments can take place and how property owners shall be notified. The state restricts Wilmington from borrowing in excess of 16 percent of its real estate–assessed valuation; excluded from this calculation are bonds issued for the water system, sewer system, and parking authority. Municipalities are limited to a bonded indebtedness of 15 percent of assessed value subject to taxation. However, the thrust of the state's laws in local finance are enabling rather than restrictive. For example, the state permits municipalities to enact local laws or ordinances that exclude residents who are over sixty-five years of age from paying local property tax.

In 1970 the General Assembly passed a law allowing "any municipality of this State with a population in excess of 50,000 persons" to levy a wage or earned income tax. By such definition, only Wilmington was allowed to establish such a tax. The rate was initially set at a maximum of 1.5 percent, then lowered to 1.25 percent after the federal school desegregation court order, which combined school districts in Wilmington and ten suburban areas and resulted in a decreased school property tax for the city.[18] The city's support for the desegregation order and subsequent busing decisions disturbed suburban residents and created tax collection problems. Although public school taxes were tied to the federal court order, they continued to be collected through the county government. To minimize the political impact, the tax bills were reformatted to make clear that the school tax, although collected by the county, was not a county tax.

Local Expenditures

The state has not enacted any expenditure limit of property tax restriction analogous to Proposition 13 in California. However, property taxes in the state are modest. The rates for the counties are all under $.50 per $100 of assessed valuation—$0.265 for Kent, $0.455 for New Castle, and $0.445 for Sussex. (These figures do not include school taxes and additional or substitutions of municipal taxes.) Because Sussex County has not had an assessment since 1974—and New Castle County and Kent County have not since 1983 and 1987, respectively—there is some pressure for periodic reassessment within and across counties. There

are no state laws restricting the declaration of bankruptcy by cities or municipalities.

There is no typical pattern of expenditures by function (for example, police, parks and recreation, and sewers) for Delaware municipalities. Because local governments use different accounting systems, it is difficult to summarize expenditure patterns.

State Government Grants-in-Aid to Localities

The state has a number of programs to assist localities financially.[19] The grant-in-aid program has received the most publicity. Each year the General Assembly appropriates funds that are used directly by the legislature to provide relatively unencumbered grants. The amount is not insubstantial (typically about 2 percent of the state's overall budget), but the dilemma for municipalities is that they must compete against the state's increasingly prominent nonprofit sector for grants on a by-project basis. To the discontent of localities—and despite the fact that the General Assembly established funding formulas for categories of grants-in-aid—nonprofit organizations continue to receive the most funding, mostly to support local volunteer firefighting groups and nonprofit senior centers across the state.

The municipal street aid bill distributes funds to municipalities for local roads, of which there are few. The state Department of Transportation is responsible for 3,876 miles of roads; municipal roads account for 661 miles of road, and a separate category of suburban development streets accounts for 1,093 miles. The fund was originally set by formula but was capped at $3 million and has not changed for several years. The Suburban Street Aid Fund contributes $16.7 million; each legislator may spend approximately $250,000 annually for "suburban streets" projects in his or her own district. This very direct role of legislators in allocating street funds for specific projects might be unthinkable in other states but reflects the hands-on approach to politics and policy in Delaware.

The annual bond bill includes funds for various projects advocated by cities and towns throughout the state. In 1995 the state received a one-time award of $220 million in escheat funds and about $35 million in annual receipts; these are funds from stocks that have not been claimed by their owners. Twenty-one local government agencies shared over $1 million of these funds. Allocations included $100,000 for a new municipal building in Bethany Beach, $100,000 for a development project sponsored by the Downtown Dover Development Corporation, a similar amount for an emergency services command center in Kent County, and $85,000 to partially fund a residential rehabilitation program in Wilmington. Funds designated for nonprofit agencies were distributed to a wide range of organizations, from historical societies to community action agencies.

There is dissatisfaction with the ad hoc way in which aid is allocated by the state to localities. During the 1998 legislative session, a movement emerged to establish a permanent state revenue-sharing program for municipalities and counties. (Delaware remains one of only three states that lack some form of local revenue-sharing arrangement.) The General Assembly passed a modest law that allowed municipalities to increase their share of the property transfer tax by an additional 0.5 percent (thus reducing the state's cut from 2 to 1.5 percent).

Delaware's nineteen school districts receive two-thirds of their revenues from the state—one of the highest proportions in the nation. Division I funding provides each district with salaries based on a September 30 pupil enrollment count. Division II provides for other school costs (except for debt service and transportation), including utility costs and books. Division III provides equalization funds to districts with lower per pupil assessed valuation; the state also provides transportation funds to each district. The result of this complex funding system is school districts that have a relatively narrow range of expenditures per pupil, within a few hundred dollars for all but one regular (that is, nonvocational) district in the state. The consensus is that Delaware's schools are well funded and equitably funded. Recent school finance issues include whether or not local referendums to approve property tax hikes for the local share of school district revenues should be required (these are frequently defeated), whether or not state (and local) funds are being well spent, and what to do about inequities in the assessed valuation-to-market ratio across Delaware's three counties.

Unfunded Mandates

There is no clear line of demarcation between the obligations of state government and those of local governments in Delaware. For example, the maintenance of roads and streets in communities seems to have little to do with whether they are technically "state" roads or "local" streets and more to do with long-established practices. If a community has the infrastructure to do so, it tends to maintain state roads within its boundaries as well as local streets. In other communities, the state maintains the roads and the community is responsible only for lighting or storm water drainage. In this environment, it is rare for state government to pass along unfunded mandates without making accommodations with state agencies.

Access to Local Government

Local Elections

State law details voter and candidate qualifications for local elections, absentee and write-in ballots, and voter registration.[20] The Delaware Code Annotated specifies the nature of elections for revising charters but does not state when municipal elections must take place. Municipal elections are scheduled for every month of the year, mostly in March and April, depending on the city. Municipalities determine the dates and times of meetings, number of representatives, and method of election of their councils. The state code regulates the administration of the oath of office and organizational meetings of the governing bodies of the counties.

Citizen Controls over Actions of Local Officials

Delaware has no state law covering impeachment of local officials or local initiative and referendum. However, the state's "sunshine law" does require that whenever a quorum of a legislative body convenes, the meetings must be open to the public and publicized in advance. In 1996 the state Department of Justice advised the City of Newark's council and mayor that their meetings with University of Delaware officials over lunch in groups of two or three violated the law.

State-Local Relations

In this small state—where financial times have been relatively good, elections are competitive, party leadership changes frequently, and bipartisanship is more common than not—state-local relations have tended not to dominate the headlines. Although many of Delaware's municipalities enjoy home rule as provided for by law, the state's three counties vary in terms of autonomy. Despite some restrictions, municipalities and counties have not been burdened with tax caps, administrative directives, or other onerous constraints.

But there are some issues on the horizon. For example, rural Sussex County continues to grow as a resort and retirement area, and there is a concomitant need for home rule and county government "modernization." The way in which land-use planning is handled by the counties and the state will probably be the most controversial state-local issue of the future. If the past is prologue, compromises between state and local leaders will result in a responsive, mutually agreeable policy of land-use control.

Notes

1. This population estimate, for 1998, is from the Center for Applied Demography and Survey Research, University of Delaware (http://www.cadsr.udel.edu/application/population.asp).

2. Joseph F. Zimmerman, *State-Local Relations: A Partnership Approach* (Westport, Conn.: Praeger, 1995).

3. Population estimates for 1998 from the Center for Applied Demography and Survey Research, University of Delaware.

4. Celia Cohen, "Political Civility Put Delaware on Primary Map," *Wilmington News Journal*, 3 March 1996.

5. Advisory Commission on Intergovernmental Relations (ACIR), *State Laws Governing Local Government Structure and Administration* (Washington, D.C.: ACIR, 1993).

6. Delaware Code Annotated (revised 1989, 1994 cumulative supplement), chapter 8, subchapter 1, section 801.

7. Delaware League of Local Governments, *Annual Directory* (Dover: Delaware League of Local Governments, 1995–1996).

8. Antoinette T. Eaton and Peter Ross, *A Guide for Delaware Municipal Charter Review* (Newark: University of Delaware, 1990).

9. *State of Delaware v. Warwick*, 108 A2nd 85 (1954).

10. Paul Dolan and James Soles, *Government of Delaware* (Newark: University of Delaware, 1976).

11. Ibid.

12. Ibid., 246.

13. ACIR, *State Laws Governing Local Government Structure and Administration*.

14. Jeffrey A. Raffel, "My Days in Dover, Weeks in Wilmington, and Nights in Newark," *University of Delaware News* XLVII, no. 3 (1981): 15–21.

15. ACIR, *State Laws Governing Local Government Structure and Administration*.

16. Nancy Kesler, "Senate Votes Pay Raise to NCCo Leader," *Wilmington News Journal,* 17 January 1996.

17. Jeffrey A. Raffel, *The Politics of School Desegregation: The Metropolitan Remedy in Delaware* (Philadelphia: Temple University Press, 1980).

18. Ibid.

19. However, Zimmerman ranks Delaware near the bottom of states in noneducational per capita state aid to localities (see Zimmerman, *State-Local Relations*). State programs are detailed in Cabinet Council on State Planning Issues, *Delaware State Assistance Handbook for Local Governments* (Dover: Cabinet Council on State Planning Issues, 1995).

20. ACIR, *State Laws Governing Local Government Structure and Administration*.

FLORIDA

Platon N. Rigos, John J. Bertalan, and Richard C. Feiock

City and county home rule in Florida is constricted by a powerful state legislature, the practice of "special legislation," very restricted tax opportunities, and difficult annexation laws. Although Florida's thirty-two-year-old constitution authorizes home rule for all of its municipalities and 15 percent of the state's sixty-seven counties, the meaning of home rule is dubious. Home rule for counties, which is less ambiguous and more empowering than for municipalities, is enjoyed by two-thirds of the state's population who live in the largest counties, two of which essentially function as cities (Miami–Dade County and Jacksonville–Duval County). Special legislation continues to affect the meaning of home rule in cities and counties. Florida's history of rampant land development—boom and bust periods that forced many communities into or close to bankruptcy—has left a residue of distrust of local government authority and tax limitations. The result is home rule powers that are less than what they appear to be on paper.

Governmental Setting

In every decade since the beginning of the twentieth century, Florida's population has increased by 30 percent or more, making it the fourth largest state in the nation.[1] This rapid growth and fast urbanization[2] have been spurred partly by low taxes (no income tax and a large property tax homestead exemption) and the availability of entry-level, low-income jobs. Florida's winter population swells with "snow birds"—retirees with two residences, one in the North and another in Florida—who inhabit the state from about November through April. Consequently, this population explosion has created local service burdens in a state that has restricted state and local powers and resources.

Because the ban against the income tax is in the state constitution, only an amendment by popular vote can remove it—a telling political fact and fiscal constraint in Florida. Every politician knows that to suggest an income tax is tantamount to suggesting a cut in social security. The state's own resource pool is therefore limited, and there is little to be allocated to local governments to help them meet their obligations and enjoy true home rule.

A primary and unique feature of Florida state government is the relative institutional weakness of the chief executive, the governor, who shares power with a number of elected executive officers.[3] The "cabinet" is a constitutionally defined group of six state political executives presided over by the governor. The cabinet serves as a collective decision-making body for the state in many policy areas.[4] The 1968 constitution strengthened the governor's control of the executive branch and created an executive budget for the first time in the state's history, but it did not remove the cabinet.[5]

The legislature has traditionally been, and still remains, a formidable force in policy making. Florida was a Democratic, prosegregationist and antiblack, one-party state from 1877 to the 1960s. As in many southern states, county officials were the primary local political actors. The legislature was dominated until the 1960s by a group of conservative and rural legislators from the northern part of the state. Counties of 4,000 population had just as much representation as counties of 500,000. Highly urbanized areas received little state support, and major roads and universities were located in the rural north. Malapportionment was finally declared unconstitutional in the 1960s. At the same time, retirees from the Midwest and refugees from Cuba arrived in ever larger numbers, and Florida gravitated toward the Republican Party. Republicans currently dominate both upper and lower houses of the legislature and the governorship.

Florida became a state in 1845 and is governed by its sixth constitution. Midwestern migrants have brought with them a predilection for small cities, reformed government, and fragmentation. An individualistic culture[6] has been imposed on top of a southern traditionalistic culture, resulting in, at the local level, state paternalism, antitax attitudes, and a large county role.

In traditionalistic cultures, a certain elite seeks to maintain power. At the local level, this elite has been called the "old boys' network" or "the courthouse gang," as in other southern states, and has always been well linked to the state government through county officials. The resulting state-county coalition produced the state paternalism that exists today. Activists who are impatient with municipal officials often criticize this system.

Home Rule in Florida

In legal terms, a home rule ideal can be defined as the ability of local government to act and make policy in all areas that are not of statewide interest. Preferably, responsible home rule means complete discretion to make policies—as long as they have local approval, do not interfere with the rights of another community, do not shift costs to the state government or other jurisdictions, do not infringe on the rights of minorities, and do not create irreversible damage to the environment. As of 1995, Florida had 392 municipalities,[7] 67 counties,[8] 67 school districts, and 963 special districts. Before 1968, all counties were merely administrative divisions of the state. The school districts are governed separately but have coterminous boundaries with the counties. This unification dates back to 1939.[9] Most large counties in Florida have adopted home rule.

Historical Development

Understanding home rule in Florida is impossible without a thorough understanding of the process of special legislation.[10] Special legislation—which together with county politics, dominated local affairs throughout the nineteenth century and still plays a prominent role to this day—is any legislation that applies to a specific jurisdiction or geographic area and imposes the will of a majority of the entire legislature on that area. As such, special legislation is arbitrary, favorable to one local government or punitive to another. Special-act legislation can provide convenient excuses for local decision makers not to act or to pass the buck. Special legislation means that, despite constitutional home rule provisions, municipalities still have to ask the legislature to ratify their charters. Yet special legislation in Florida never has been as punitive toward cities as it has been in northern states. It is not and never has been resented.

Definition of Home Rule

The right to home rule for cities and counties is declared but not explained in the 1968 constitution.[11] Before 1968, Florida cities received "a form of home rule" as each incorporated under special law. Now home rule powers are specified in state statutes.[12] Twenty attempts have since been made to adopt county home rule; of fourteen counties, only nine have been successful.[13] Home rule in Florida essentially means that cities and counties have certain customary areas of responsibility, but the legislature can at any time intervene to impart a new meaning.

The 1973 and 1974 legislatures continued the pattern of support for home rule in Florida by enacting the Municipal Home Rule Charter Law of 1973 and repealing many population classification statutes. Although the grant of home rule authority in the constitution of 1968 was self-executing, "[in] reality the full exercise of home rule power" has required "implementing statutes to overcome the resistance of city and county attorneys, the courts and elements of the executive branch."[14] Several municipalities formed charter review commissions to examine their special-act charters and adapt them to the needs of the new era.

Structural Features

In the twentieth century, through what is called "local bill courtesy," special legislation came to mean that whatever the local legislative delegation decided in local hearings was (and still is) quickly adopted by the entire state legislature. It can be argued that this process protects local autonomy because locally elected officials make decisions.

Special legislation can be used for positive purposes, such as increasing coordination among cities and counties through new local agencies, and for innovative approaches to public policy, such as functional transfers. Special legislation is particularly useful in coordinating cooperation between various cities and the county to provide services.[15] On the other hand, local officials (executives and council persons) support local legislation because they can evade the need to build a consensus for locally solvable problems. They can use the delegation to initiate controversial policies such as the creation of downtown development districts or county authorities.[16] Issues appearing before the legislative delegation have less visibility, and the responsibility can be shifted if something goes wrong.

Charters are drafted to meet the exact requirements of each municipality and county. Florida does not restrict the type of government a general-purpose unit can have. Even though the initial charters must pass the scrutiny of the county legislative delegation, the community is free to amend them once they have been in effect. Some cities use the manager-council package, whereas others retain a "weak" mayor system. Many others have the commission system with a hired professional city manager. Large cities, for the most part, have adopted the "strong" mayor council system. Most municipal elections (even in large strong mayor cities) are nonpartisan and at large. County elections are partisan.

State laws on incorporation and annexation shape the operational meaning of home rule. Less restrictive annexation rules are vital to keeping cities in good fiscal health; they add tax base and allow for better home rule. The land boom of the 1920s created a first wave of incorporations, but the crash in land value in 1926 and the Great Depression stopped this first wave. Many newly created municipalities incurred huge debts and struggled to remain solvent. A second wave of incorporations took place after 1945, when GIs stationed in Florida during World War II sought to settle in new cities. A third wave took place after 1962 but was already running out of steam by the early 1970s, when the freshly reapportioned legislature changed the rules of incorporation and made it very difficult to create new cities.[17] Only a dozen or so have been created since then.

Current incorporation rules are very restrictive. Before 1974, incorporation standards in Florida were simple. Agreement among a thousand "freeholders" (that is, citizens who owned lands in the affected area) was sufficient to create a municipality. The creation of even smaller municipalities was possible through special legislation. In some cases, municipal corporations were created purely for the convenience of developers, industrialists, and wealthy homeowners seeking to build tax havens. The legislature of 1974 acted with reformist zeal by changing the law to make incorporation difficult. The new standards required new municipalities to meet three conditions:

1. a minimum population of 1,500 in counties with fewer than 50,000 people, or a minimum population of 5,000 in counties with 50,000 or more total population;

2. a minimum average density of 1.5 persons per acre; and

3. a minimum distance of two miles from all other existing municipalities within the county.[18]

After satisfying these minimum requirements, a community still needs a special act of the legislature to become incorporated. A local incorporation act must include a municipal charter that prescribes a form of government and clearly defines the legislative and executive functions of government. In practice, however, one or more of these requirements often are waived.

Home rule charters are not self-executing. Even though charters can vary in functional and structural scope, the final shape is determined not by the citizens or local officials but by the local legislative delegation in hearings held at the county courthouse. Only when a bill is passed by the legislature can a referendum be held to give the local citizens a say. On the other hand, an incorporation bid backed by major interests in the county with support of the local delegation can override all of these rigid rules. This is how very small cities have emerged in northern counties recently.[19]

Annexation statutes[20] make it difficult for existing cities to annex large amounts of territory in a short time. A majority of the citizens in the area to be annexed and in the municipality must approve. Majority approval does not happen often. In so-called voluntary annexations, municipalities try to convince a few territories to join them by getting 100 percent of the homeowners to agree. In some cases, however, annexation happens quickly when the voluntary annexation[21] involves a large swath of land owned by one corporation or individual. Rules about voluntary annexation specifically forbid the creation of "enclaves," "islands," or "fingers," yet they are routinely ignored, even in interpretations by the state attorney general. In voluntary annexation, cities bargain with owners and developers of as yet unsettled territory.[22] Finally, annexation is possible through special acts, even against the wishes of the local population.[23]

Most county governments use the five-member commission system, with no separation of powers. Commissioners, elected officials (such as the sheriff and clerk of the circuit court), and county administrator-managers make policy. The status of counties in Florida is enhanced by the ability to obtain home rule. The 1968 constitution describes a very specific procedure for acquiring home rule and becoming a charter county, but many counties have often adopted the concept of a county administrator through special laws.[24] Charters do not allow counties to invalidate city ordinances or require higher standards of service, except in Dade and Volusia Counties.[25]

Charter counties have the right to reorganize their governmental system. Many advocates of county reform had hoped that counties would eventually streamline their administrative structure upon receiving home rule, but this has not happened. The political power of local county constitutional officers has restricted the meaning of county home rule. None of the counties (except for Dade) have been able to change their structure of government (and the role of the "constitutional officers") through home rule.[26] Constitutional officers have such political clout that they may effectively veto how "home rule charters are crafted."[27] These executive county officers also support the continuation of special legislation as a flexible, quick tool for internal management needs. Special laws allow them to bypass board of county commissioners' concerns.

Functions of Local Government

Functional Responsibilities

In Florida the extent to which a jurisdiction controls the range of functions needed to serve most of its citizens' needs is highly regulated. Not only are some functions given to specific units, but special districts are often created to compete with cities and counties. This lack of flexibility is mitigated only by numerous laws and provisions that encourage interlocal cooperation.

Cities provide police, fire, and street lighting and cleaning. Water and sewer operations and parking facilities are important revenue-producing functions. A few cities (Homestead, Lakeland, Orlando, and Tallahassee) own electric utilities, which create additional revenue. The only redistributive function that is linked to a municipality is housing, which helps poorer families and is operated by a city department or housing authority. Many city governments have established revolving funds to encourage housing rehabilitation and affordable housing.[28] Many cities have launched risky economic development activities such as arenas, convention centers, and stadiums.

Florida's counties have always played an important role in providing local services. In a rural state with few large cities, the county was not only an arm of the state government but also a significant local service provider. From their inception, Florida's counties have been active in highway development, welfare, health, sanitation, and some hospital services. The state's Department of Children and Family Services administrates welfare and is organized through multicounty districts. Counties, however, are allowed some discretion in implementing welfare services. Some major counties have ventured into water and sewer provision in urbanized areas. Florida counties are large enough (700–1,000 square miles) to handle areawide functions. County fire departments and county parks have absorbed volunteer fire units, and recreation programs have become common. Planning needs and federal environmental and transportation laws mean that counties have more responsibilities than cities.

Job training has been a poorly organized function, divided among state, county, and many types of specially created units. Highways and major thoroughfares in major cities are county responsibilities, but funding also comes from the state. The state highway department works in consultation with metropolitan planning organizations (MPOs) on all transportation issues, from highways to mass transit. City governments have representation on MPOs.[29]

In Florida, city-county consolidations and other metropolitan reorganization efforts are possible and have been attempted a dozen times.[30] County home rule (since 1968) made the procedures easier. The successful cases—Miami–Dade County in the 1950s[31] and Jacksonville–Duval County in 1967[32]—are well known (see Boxes 1 and 2). In 1978 Hillsborough County (Tampa) invented the municipal services taxing unit to fund county services in unincorporated areas.[33] Tampa had alleged "double taxation," claiming that its citizens were paying both a city tax and a county tax to fund municipal services in unincorporated areas.[34] Other urban counties quickly adopted the municipal services taxing unit in order to remain important urban service providers.

In 1998, through Florida's relatively unique constitutional revision commission (which meets every twenty years), the electorate adopted ten amendments. Among these, one specified that the cost of running local courts would be assumed by the state. However, it is too early to determine if this "reverse mandate" will be implemented meaningfully or if some funds will be merely redirected from another part of state aid.

Because it is easy to form special districts in Florida, they have proliferated. Special districts are created by a few developers, who then register with the county government and begin incurring debt through bond issues; this has led to some corrupt practices. In populated areas, the debt is retired through property taxes. Special districts are not completely unaccountable; the state began regulating them in the early 1980s by adding them to the Florida comptroller's survey of local government finance.

Some small districts provide mosquito abatement, water provision, and fire fighting and prevention. They also operate roads and bridges. Some even supply hospital services. Large districts and authorities are created by state legislation and operate spe-

BOX 1. MIAMI–DADE COUNTY

Dade County is considered to be a modified two-tier system of government because the county is the sole provider of services in the unincorporated areas. Twenty-six municipalities, with two levels of government, still provide services. Dade County has abolished the office of sheriff and other constitutional officers; these offices are now under a county manager.

Dade County's system of government was adopted in 1957 through an amendment to the Florida Constitution that brought about a home rule charter with features that even present-day home rule counties are not allowed to have. Among such features, the charter empowers the county to "set reasonable minimum standards for all governmental units in the county for the performance of any service or function." Where minimum standards are set, the cities are denied the option of forgoing a service or setting a lower standard; they must either meet the standards or transfer the service to the county. "Metro," as the Dade County government is known, also has the power to abolish special districts.

There are also "elastic clauses" in the charter that in turn give the county the authority to do everything necessary to carry out the work of a central metropolitan government and go beyond the specified powers. Municipalities are not allowed to expand and annex. Incorporation, however, is possible, as evidenced in 1990 by the new city of Biscayne.

Dade County's responsibilities are much wider than those of most counties. Many functions performed by special districts and authorities are part of the Dade County government. The airport and port of Miami are examples. Mass transit and hospitals are also directly controlled by the county government and not by independent authorities, as in most county areas. Dade County is a very large government, employing more than 21,000 workers.

Because Dade County has a historic record of bureaucratic competence, it is able to set performance standards that are difficult for smaller cities to meet. Unlike Dade County, most urbanizing county standards exceed municipal standards in only a few services. Municipal standards are almost invariably set well above county standards.

cial functions such as stadiums, ports, airports, and tollways. They are governed by boards that have gubernatorial appointees and local ex-officio representatives who can levy taxes or impose user fees.

One variety of special district, the community development district, can be created by municipalities and counties within their own borders. Such districts levy an additional tax to cater to the needs of residents in newly settled wealthy areas. These districts are not independent, and their taxes accrue to the city. The authority for local governments in Florida to enter interlocal agreements derives from the Florida Interlocal Cooperation Act of 1969.[35] Interlocal agreements may specify how collection of funds and payments are to be structured. Interlocal agreements take different forms. Many simply allow one gov-

BOX 2. JACKSONVILLE-DUVAL COUNTY

Adopted in 1967 by local popular vote and then constitutionalized, the Jacksonville consolidation charter features a strong mayor who appoints all executive officials except the county sheriff. The charter also provides for a twenty-one member council elected by district and two distinct areas of property taxation (one for the urban core and one for the outlying, previously unincorporated areas). All county-elected constitutional officers, including a sheriff, were retained. Preexisting cities (six small units) have been allowed but may not expand.

The new system has been popular with most voters. Jacksonville had been in such a mess (polluted river, discredited schools, local politicians suing each other) that the contrast could not be more pronounced. One study has shown, however, that the level of spending in police, total expenditures, and taxes over fourteen years—when compared with those in Tampa—had not been affected by the consolidation.[1] On the other hand, unification has allowed the consolidated government to get more federal aid, recruit businesses, and attract a National Football League franchise.

1. E. Benton and D. Gamble, "City-County Consolidation and Economies of Scale," *Social Science Quarterly* (March 1985): 190–198.

ernment to operate as a service provider in another city or in parts of the unincorporated areas and to bill users directly. In other cases, an intergovernmental agreement will entail the payment of a sum by one government for services rendered (for example, planning) to another. Some interlocal agreements are crafted to allow for emergency services (such as fire, police, and ambulances) to be brought to a municipality that needs additional resources.[36] Most agreements are by one government to another. However, some agreements can include more than one government acting in concert, in an area such as transportation, for example. Moreover, new units may be created to administer the agreement.[37] Planning is the principal product of interlocal cooperation.[38]

Administrative Discretion

Despite expensive state-imposed unfunded mandates regarding personnel salaries, growth management, and tax and debt limitations, local governments may decide how to zone, fund, and develop areas and set construction and service standards. The right of public employees to strike is not recognized. Some collective bargaining is allowed and takes place within restrictive parameters. Unions play a very limited role; they are most useful in the resolution of grievances and the protection of employees in the workplace. Affirmative action programs are in effect throughout Florida.

Municipal training for services other than police is rare, and even police training is done only in the very largest cities. Junior college training has replaced some of the academies. On occa-

sion, governments will pay to send workers to local community colleges and universities, but this practice is not as common today as it was in the 1970s, when the federal Comprehensive Employment Training Act was in effect and planning grants were available. The 1985 Growth Management Act established a minimal amount of funds for implementation seminars. The demands of federal programs, fast growth, new universities, and northern newcomers have prompted localities to increase employee training to a level not unlike that of other large states.

Florida statutes require that a well-defined, competitive bidding system be used in purchasing and contracting for local governments.[39] Minority business purchasing programs are optional (but codified) and have been enacted in most urban counties.[40] Local ordinances determine which purchases are made by the legislative body and which are made by the purchasing director.[41]

Florida's fast-paced growth had by the end of the 1960s created poorly planned and zoned cities that threatened the state's fragile environment.[42] The excesses of poor zoning and the tendency of counties to issue building permits readily brought about a major effort to curb growth that is one of the most advanced in the country. Under the Environmental Land and Water Management Act of 1972 and related legislation, Florida began regulating large developments through the "development of regional impact" process and the concept of "area of state critical concern."

The Local Government Comprehensive Planning Act of 1975 required all cities and counties to create plans for review by regional planning agencies and the Department of Community Affairs. Because of a lack of financial support, the act was instrumental only in creating an infrastructure for better planning.

The 1985 Growth Management Act and its successors of 1986 and 1991 have created costly and restrictive mandates but have brought about the kind of responsible local planning behavior that many other states lack. All local plans—municipal, countywide, and regionwide—must conform with the state plan and be approved by the Department of Community Affairs. Plans must also be compatible with those of neighboring local governments. The requirement for concurrency is "the most demanding substantive requirement."[43] Local governments set service levels for six main functions in each government's capital improvement plan. The capital improvement plan must show that the county or cities are fiscally capable of supporting the projected service levels. Such plans can and have been rejected as overly ambitious. Once a level of service is set, a local government cannot allow any new development to dilute it or weaken it. Development orders cannot be issued if they will affect the level of service negatively.

Florida's planning system has been a success because of the concept of concurrency (that is, ensuring the availability of infrastructure concurrent with growth) and because rules and plans have been diligently implemented by subsequent state administrations. The Department of Community Affairs has been fairly strict in implementing the Growth Management Act, even under a Republican administration. The courts have refused all challenges that have been brought by some counties.

In the latest confrontation over the effective implementation of plans, Gov. Jeb Bush's cabinet has come down hard on Collier County, on the southwest coast, where local commissioners had begun to allow runaway growth and overbuilding. Their power was taken from them, and the state assumed direct supervision over the issuance of building permits. Planning enjoys a high level of consensus and has ceased to be the source of conflicts and corruption that it was in the past.

Economic Development

The state traditionally has granted authority to local governments to pursue economic development goals. The Revenue Bond Act of 1957 and the Florida Industrial Development Financing Act give broad authority to local governments to issue revenue bonds for economic development purposes. Counties are authorized by statute to expend public monies to attract and retain business and to pursue their economic development goals. Authorized activities include developing and improving infrastructure, issuing bonds for capital projects and industrial plants, leasing and conveying real property, and making grants to private enterprises for the expansion of business or the attraction of new business.

The state has sought to direct the development activities of local governments and encourage public-private cooperation through the Florida Enterprise Zone Act. The state provides many development incentives to employers within areas designated as enterprise zones, including tax credits and corporate and sales tax exemptions. Zones are designated by the Florida Department of Community Affairs and are based on economic need and the willingness of local governments to commit resources to provide development incentives.

Although municipalities and redevelopment agencies have substantial authority to promote growth, the authority of county governments is more significant. Chapter 125 of the Florida Statutes gives counties the power to approve or disapprove the issuance of industrial revenue bonds by all entities within their borders. Cities and counties may also permit the creation of tax increment–financing devices and enterprise zones.

Fiscal Autonomy of Local Governments

Local Revenues

Local revenues are derived from the property tax,[44] the local-option sales tax, other forms of hidden sales taxes, state grants-in-aid, occupational licenses, and tourist taxes. In Florida, property tax restrictions for each city and county are written in the constitution.[45] School districts are also subject to a smaller mill-age limitation (about 6.5 mills) and receive grants-in-aid through a complicated state redistributive revenue-sharing formula.[46] City councils and county commissions set the property tax rate, but the county property appraiser appraises all property, and the county tax collector notifies individuals and corporations of what taxes they owe. Citizens may appeal property valuations.

The most potent fiscal restriction on local government is the homestead exemption. Since 1982, the homestead exemption has reduced the taxable value of homes by $25,000.[47] It was set at $5,000 as early as 1942 to attract settlers from elsewhere and quickly became a cherished right for all Floridians. The new higher level has not been an overwhelming burden in fast-growing, urbanizing counties. The finances of rural counties, on the other hand, have been strained, forcing some to tax at the limit of 10 mills. A number of proposals (in the form of legislation and referendums) to limit the impact of this tax provision have failed.

In 1992 the revenue-levying capacity of local government was constrained further by a limitation that allowed only a 3 percent increase in the appraisal of property value. The limit, which is reminiscent of California's Proposition 13, was approved in a constitutional amendment and was known as the "Save Our Homes" initiative.

Any local sales tax must first be approved by the legislature, which has the option of requiring a local referendum. The right to levy some special sales taxes if approved by citizens in a referendum was granted to large urban counties in the early 1990s.[48] Only home rule municipalities may derive sales tax from telephone service and electricity and private water consumption. Cable service is also taxed by municipalities. All of these so-called franchise fees taxes are a substantial source of revenue for existing cities and help cities maintain low levels of property taxation.

Counties are given the right to tax tourist facilities (for example, hotels and restaurants), and the proceeds are shared with the municipalities in the county. Counties can impose a criminal justice facilities sales tax and a convention development tax. All governments may levy a discretionary infrastructure tax and two forms of local gas taxes,[49] but only counties have chosen to use them.[50]

Florida is one of many states that allow the levying of local impact fees for most local services. A court decision in Dunedin[51] established how such fees would fund fire protection.[52] As growth-control tools that provide additional revenue,[53] impact fees have strengthened cities, counties, and school districts, which have rushed to implement them.

Restrictions on indebtedness make borrowing through general-obligation bonds difficult. The issuance of general-obligation bonds requires the acquiescence of the electorate. Most cities prefer to issue debt in the form of revenue bonds, which do not require a referendum but must be backed by a money-making enterprise, such as a water or sewer plant. It does not matter for what purpose the new revenue is used.

Local Expenditures

The comptroller's office has categorized expenditures since the 1970s. Until recently, these data were available annually in a publication from the comptroller's office. In 1992–1993, the last year for which we have published data,[54] an average large city such as Orlando spent 19.8 percent of its budget on general governmental services; 15.2 percent on public safety (police and fire); and 18 percent on the physical environment (public works). Only 9.6 percent was allocated to transportation (streets and street lighting). The economic environment (a category that includes developmental activities) took 6 percent of the budget for Orlando. Receiving only 0.5 percent was human services, which is financed mostly by the state. The culture and recreation category amounted to about 8.5 percent of Orlando's budget.

Legally, cities and counties are required to present balanced line-item budgets. Short-term borrowing through revenue anticipation notes is possible in Florida but is not used to keep the budget in balance. This type of borrowing has been closely monitored by the comptroller's office in the Department of Banking and Finance. Many cities have experimented with performance-based budgets and zero-based budgets. Florida state government instituted a uniform accounting system for all local governments in the early 1970s. Detailed budgetary information has been readily available since the 1980s.

State Government Grants-in-Aid to Localities

State grants-in-aid amount to as little as 10.9 percent of the budget for Orlando and 5.5 percent for Miami.[55] Grants-in-aid account for only 5–10 percent of counties' budgets. Local governments are apportioned one cent, respectively, from the cigarette and the gasoline tax. Since 1985 one-half of the sixth cent of state sales tax has been given automatically to cities and counties. All state grant-in-aid is audited by the comptroller's office. Not since the early 1980s have federal grants-in-aid been a prominent feature of budgets in most small- to medium-sized cities. Larger cities and counties have been able to qualify for community development block grants and comprehensive employment training act grants.

Unfunded Mandates

Like other states, Florida has its share of unfunded mandates. According to a study by Florida's Advisory Council on Intergovernmental Relations—now the Legislative Committee on Intergovernmental Relations (LCIR)—the burden of mandates is heavy. The Florida League of Cities has been vociferous about state-imposed mandates. The biggest complaint has been about "assumption mandates," which allow police and fire protection personnel to retire on a disability pension after twenty years; the "assumption" is that because of the stress of these occupations these public servants are susceptible to heart disease.[56] So contentious are these mandates that a statewide referendum was held in 1991 to address "unfunded mandates"; however, the language of the referendum was tepid and allowed for loopholes.

Mandates pertaining to minimum salary and retirement level usually do not mean much in metropolitan areas, where salary levels exceed the state minimum, but they can be burdensome on rural counties and small towns. Environmental mandates (hazardous waste disposal), some of which have federal roots, are particularly expensive for counties.

Access to Local Government

Local Elections

Most municipal elections (even in large "strong" mayor cities) are nonpartisan and at large. Most cities and counties prefer the at-large system, with residency requirements. Some have now adopted a mixed system of at-large and by-district elections as a response to demands by minority groups for greater representation. County elections are fought on a partisan basis. Only one home rule county (Volusia) so far has adopted nonpartisan elections. Even though electoral practice is closely regulated and is the same across the state, local councils have the right to slate special referendums. Charters vary regarding other procedures. St. Petersburg, for instance, nominates candidates through a by-district system, which allows minority candidates to be nominated. The final election remains at large. In this way, some moderate minority leaders have been elected.

Citizen Controls over Actions of Local Officials

Florida has been at the forefront of movements to expand financial disclosure of campaign expenditures of persons running for office. Florida is even more well known for "government in the sunshine," which calls for public meetings and records to be open to all, including the media, except in very special cases. All laws adopted to regulate disclosure for state legislators apply equally to local government.

Theoretically, cities and counties can impeach and recall local officials, but they rarely do so because the procedures are complicated and difficult. Removal of indicted officials by the state governor is possible. The governor quickly appoints new officials. Takeover of municipal functions is also legally possible but rarely practiced.

At first glance, initiatives and referendums seem to be relatively straightforward under Florida law.[57] However, certain requirements for these procedures often bring the courts to bear. The wording of initiatives and referendums is subject to review. A requirement that each one must address a single issue often invalidates a proposal. Signatures are challenged. The state has allowed municipal charters that severely restrict some forms of initiative. In St. Petersburg, for example, a prohibition on initiatives dealing with capital projects was never challenged by the state.

Provisions pertaining to recall are far more restrictive.[58] A little-known state statute imposes a specific and complicated procedure for recalling local officials of home rule cities and counties. Two petition drives are required, and the official who is subject to recall is given the right to respond to the first. The second petition must reach a threshold of as much as 15 percent of qualified votes to be on the ballot. Recall of local officials is rarely successful.[59]

State-Local Relations

The restricted number of functions granted to city and county government in Florida minimizes local ability to serve citizens. The ease with which special districts may be created reinforces these functional restrictions. Fiscal and financial limitations on revenue raising most affect local responsibility. Regardless of grants-in-aid and mandates, revenue-raising limitations are so severe that local governments often act irresponsibly by incurring large revenue-bond debt.

For communities that have reached the size of 5,000 inhabitants and a density of 1.5 persons per acre, service problems and planning problems may be so severe that the prospect of incorporation seems less promising.[60] Unless it is a very tax-rich enclave, a small city has little hope of reversing patterns of urban sprawl, traffic jams, mixed land use, and poor police response that have been tolerated by inattentive county governments.

Florida local governments must depend on national economic growth and some voluntary annexation to expand their tax bases. Contemporary trends that create more complexities and call for state help have reinforced the paternalism of the past; more mandates have been issued, and there have been attempts to stop or reverse metropolitan fragmentation.

In Florida, the legislature has been accustomed to having its way in state and local policy making. Special legislation, even with all of its modern adjustments, has negatively affected local government autonomy. State legislators have often presented and enacted statutes that local officials or citizens have opposed. For example, measures that weaken a local public employee union's right to strike have been enacted.

Most local officials do not even bother to scrutinize proposed measures. State legislators are immune to small constituencies, such as neighborhood groups, and have favored powerful downtown redevelopment interests. Local officials who support special legislation may do so for personal and pragmatic reasons, but they are diminished in stature as a class of policymaker.

Old boundary laws have created great variations in capacity among municipalities. One city in Florida had a median income

of $150,000, whereas others had no more than $16,000 in 1990. Some of the poorest communities are in rural areas.

Among average Floridians, there remains a fear that local governments will act in childish, irresponsible ways. The state will be well into the twenty-first century before cities seriously consider efforts to abolish special legislation or the millage cap. The same can be said of the income tax restriction, which, if lifted, might allow the state better means to help its local governments.

Notes

1. Florida had nearly 13,000,000 people in 1990.

2. Florida has at least five major metropolitan areas, Miami, Fort Lauderdale–Hollywood, Tampa–St. Petersburg–Clearwater, Orlando, and Jacksonville.

3. Governors are usually leaders in administrative reform, and as state governments have given more powers to governors, governors have given more leeway to local governments. See Ann O'M. Bowman and Richard Kearney, *State and Local Government,* 3d ed. (New York: Houghton Mifflin, 1996), 139–176.

4. Amendments adopted in November 1998 propose to shrink the cabinet to include four executives, the governor, the lieutenant-governor, the commissioner of agriculture, and the attorney general.

5. J. Robinson and R. M. Storm, "Plural Executives: Functions of the Governor and Cabinet," in *Government and Politics in Florida,* 2d ed., ed. R. J. Huckshorn (Gainesville: University of Florida Press, 1998), 105–123.

6. See D. Elazar, *American Federalism: A View from the States,* 3d ed. (New York: Harper & Row, 1968).

7. Most municipalities had incorporated without home rule but did so through special acts and special charters. The 1968 constitution gave all municipalities home rule. Classifications of cities do not exist any more in Florida. See Allen Morris, *Florida Handbook, 1995–1996* (Tallahassee: Peninsular, 1996).

8. Even though classified as a city, Jacksonville-Duval is considered a county for certain purposes because it has county officers.

9. See Michael Gannon, "A History of Florida to 1990," in *Government and Politics in Florida,* ed. R. J. Huckshorn (Gainesville: University of Florida Press, 1991), 7–59.

10. Also called local bills, local legislation, or special-privilege legislation in other states. Local bills were common in all states in the nineteenth century.

11. Florida Constitution, Article VIII, section 1 addresses county home rule; section 2 covers municipalities.

12. Florida Statutes, chapter 166, section 021. The 1969 and 1971 legislative sessions eliminated population acts that limited home rule authority. See J. De-Grove and R. Turner, "Local Government in Florida: Coping with Massive and Sustained Growth," in *Government and Politics in Florida,* 217.

13. The nine counties that successfully attempted home rule were Miami–Dade, Jacksonville–Duval, Broward (Ft. Lauderdale), Volusia (Daytona), Sarasota, Pinellas (St. Petersburg), Hillsborough (Tampa), Orange (Orlando), and Charlotte (Punta Gorda).

14. See DeGrove and Turner, "Local Government in Florida," 216–240.

15. For example, if the central city library needs to be transferred to the county to remain financially solvent, this transfer can be done with a local bill. If the central city needs the county's cooperation in creating an airport, this too can be done by establishing a special district (an authority) where the city and county have ex officio representation.

16. Although the City of St. Petersburg used the Pinellas Sport Authority to underwrite bonds to build its stadium, the sheer neglect of popular will took other forms. See P. N. Rigos and D. F. Paulson, "Urban Development, Policy Failure and Regime Change in a Manager-Council City: The Case of St. Petersburg, FL," *Urban Affairs Review* 32 (1996): 244–263.

17. Miami and the surrounding area boomed, and many new municipalities were created, both in Dade and Broward (Ft. Lauderdale) counties. See P. N. Rigos, "Incorporation and the Greed-Exclusion Theory" (paper presented at the annual meeting of the American Political Science Association, Washington D.C., 1 September 1993).

18. Florida Statutes, chapter 165, section 041.

19. The cities of Noma (Holmes County), Jacob (Jackson County), and Midway (Gadsden County) were created in 1977, 1983, and 1986, respectively, even though all had less than the required 1,000 population as called for by the 1974 statute.

20. Florida Statutes, chapter 171, sections 011–091.

21. Florida Statutes, chapter 171, section 044. Because large tracts of land in the state often are owned by one person, voluntary annexation is not unusual.

22. Higher densities to allow for future developments or special services may be bargained for, which may make the area more attractive to high-income homeowners or investors. Wealthy enclaves may thus emerge just as easily within cities as they otherwise might through incorporation, but residents will pay slightly higher taxes.

23. Tampa achieved its present size under a special act in 1953 by annexing the then-city of Port Tampa.

24. Florida Constitution, Article VIII, sections 1d, 1c.

25. County ordinances prevail only when the county charter makes specific provisions for such preemption and the people throughout the county approve the adoption of the charter. See J. DeGrove, "Analysis of Home Rule and Intergovernmental Relations: The Case of Florida" in *Partnership Within the States*, ed. Stephanie Cole (Philadelphia: Institute of Government and Public Affairs, Center for the Study of Federalism, Temple University, 1976).

26. Dade County (Miami) acquired its charter as an amendment to the pre-1968 constitution (see Florida Constitution, Article VIII, sections 6e, 6f).

27. Florida Constitution, Article VIII, section 1c.

28. Orlando, for example, has made an impressive effort to provide affordable housing. See R. Turner, "Growth Politics and Downtown Development," *Urban Affairs Quarterly* 28 (September 1993): 3–21.

29. Metropolitan planning organizations have existed in Florida since 1975 but have emerged as new units of metropolitan coordination since the enactment of the federal Intermodal Surface Transportation Efficiency Act (ISTEA) of 1991.

30. The city-county of Tallahassee–Leon tried three times to consolidate; Gainesville–Alachua County tried twice; and Okeechobee City–Okeechobee County and Tampa–Hillsborough County both tried three times.

31. See Edward Sofen, *The Miami Metropolitan Experiment* (Bloomington: Indiana University Press, 1963).

32. See Richard A. Martin, *Consolidation: Jacksonville–Duval County*, 2d ed. (Jacksonville, Fla.: Crawford, 1972).

33. Miami–Dade County was the first, in 1973, to impose a utility tax on its unincorporated areas.

34. See D. Paulson and P. N. Rigos, "The Resolution of City-Council Taxation Inequities: The Double Taxation Experience in Florida," *Urban Interest* (fall 1982): 76–89.

35. Florida Statutes, chapter 163, section 01(2).

36. See E. J. Benton, D. Picot Floyd, P. Menzel, P. Paluch, and P. Rigos, *Interlocal Agreements and Local Government D.R.I. Certification* (Tallahassee: Florida Institute of Government, 1987).

37. Florida Statutes, chapter 163, section 01(7)(a).

38. Many urban counties have joint city planning commissions with powers to plan and review zoning decisions of other municipalities and county ordinances according to a comprehensive plan.

39. Florida Statutes, chapter 287, section 055 applies specifically to municipalities.

40. Florida Statutes, chapter 287, section 093 states that any local government may "set aside up to 10 percent or more of the total amount . . . for the purpose of entering into contracts with minority business enterprises."

41. In a typical urban county, purchases of more than $50,000 are made by the board of county commissioners.

42. J. DeGrove and R. Turner, "Local Government: Coping with Massive and Sustained Growth," in *Government and Politics in Florida*, 2d ed., 243.

43. DeGrove and Turner, "Local Government in Florida," 228–230.

44. See Florida Constitution, Article VII, section 1.

45. Florida Constitution, Article VII, section 9. The "millage" cap is set at 10 mills, that is, $10.00 per $1,000 of property valuation.

46. The formula includes, among other factors, the number of pupils in school and the appraised valuation of the county.

47. S. MacManus, "Financing Florida Governments," in *Government and Politics in Florida*, 241–283.

48. MacManus, "Financing Florida Governments," 260.

49. Florida Statutes, chapter 212, section 055(2); chapter 336, section 021.

50. See MacManus, "Financing Florida Governments," 262–265.

51. *Contractors & Builders Association v. Dunedin*, 329, So.2nd 314 (Florida 1976). See also *Hollywood Inc. v. Broward County* (1983, 4th District Court of Appeals).

52. Impact fees have been levied on educational construction, transportation, police services, and even parks and recreation.

53. See DeGrove and Turner, "Local Government in Florida," 213–240. See also James Nicholas, "Capital Improvement Finance and Impact Fees after the Growth Management Act of 1985," in Monograph 86-5, ed. J. DeGrove and Julian Jurgensmeyer (Cambridge, Mass.: Lincoln Land Policy, 1986), 175–182.

54. Department of Banking and Finance, Office of the Comptroller, State of Florida, *Local Government Financial Report, Fiscal Year 1992–93* (Tallahassee).

55. Department of Banking and Finance, *Local Government Financial Report, Fiscal Year 1992–93*.

56. For a thorough study of mandates, see S. MacManus, E. J. Benton, and D. C. Menzel, "Personal Mandate Cost Study: Florida Municipalities; A Survey" (report of the Florida Institute of Government, February 1993).

57. See Florida Advisory Council on Intergovernmental Relations, *Initiatives and Referenda: Issues in Citizen Lawmaking* (Tallahassee: Office of the Secretary of the Senate, State of Florida, January 1986).

58. Florida Statutes, chapter 100, section 361.

59. In St. Petersburg in the late 1980s, a movement to recall council members responsible for outlandish investment decisions was so thoroughly stymied in the courts that a sports facility was built despite citizens' objections. See Rigos and Paulson, "Urban Development, Policy Failure and Regime Change in a Manager-Council City," 244–263.

60. See P. N. Rigos and C. J. Spindler, "The Role of Incorporation and Annexation Laws in State Growth Management Policies: The Case of Florida" (paper presented at the annual meeting of the Southeast Conference for Public Administration, Jackson, Miss., 6 October 1989).

GEORGIA

Melvin B. Hill Jr.

For their helpful review and comments, the author thanks the late Ed Sumner, general counsel of the Georgia Municipal Association; Jim Grubiak, general counsel of the Association County Commissioners of Georgia; and Dr. Arnold Fleischmann, associate professor of political science at the University of Georgia. Also thanks to Haoran Lu, Carl Vinson Institute of Government, University of Georgia, for his assistance with the local government revenue and expenditure data, and Steed Robinson of the Georgia Department of Community Affairs and George Rogers of the Georgia Department of Industry, Trade and Tourism, for their helpful suggestions on the development activities section.

On January 2, 1788, Georgia became the first state in the South and the fourth colony among the original thirteen colonies to ratify the proposed U.S. Constitution. As a member of the Confederacy, it suffered directly the trials and tribulations of the Civil War and its aftermath. Its strong independent streak and suspicion toward governmental authority are reflected in its governmental structure even today, with a state government comprising eight elected executive officers and 236 legislators and a local governmental structure characterized by historic fragmentation and diffusion in authority and operation. Efforts to delegate "home rule" power to local governments generally have been ambiguous; thus, local governments have both broad and limited home rule authority. The most radical change in the intergovernmental system in Georgia occurred in 1972, when the voters approved a constitutional amendment (Amendment 19) giving counties the same authority to provide a wide range of urban- and municipal-type services as cities. This change further blurred the legal distinction between county and municipal governments, resulting in duplication, overlap, and competition in the delivery of local government services.

Governmental Setting

Georgia has been described as a state caught between its deeply rooted traditions and the stunning changes of the past forty years—namely, governmental restructuring, declining rural influence, the growing political clout of African Americans and Republicans, and the rise of new interest groups.[1] The contrast can be seen in basic statistics. Georgia is the largest state east of the Mississippi and nationally ranks tenth in total population, fifth in African American population (fourth in percentage of African American residents), fourth in population growth, and sixth in percent increase of population in 1990–1997.[2] Georgia also boasts one of the nation's largest state economies, one that is increasingly tied to the global economy through its hub of Atlanta. Yet indicators on education and poverty levels in Georgia still paint a bleak picture.[3]

Atlanta acts as the engine driving the state's economic development. Strategic decisions made by the state government to support the expansion of Hartsfield International Airport (one of the busiest in the United States), the construction of the Metropolitan Area Rapid Transit Authority (MARTA) rail system, and the World Congress Center in downtown Atlanta all pro-

pelled the capital's growth. The "Atlanta factor" has caused discord in other parts of the state, however. The state's response to the feud over "two Georgias" (that is, Atlanta and everywhere else) has been to "spread the wealth" by promoting stronger programs statewide. A collaborative 1998 initiative by the Georgia Department of Community Affairs and the Georgia Department of Industry, Trade, and Tourism to encourage better planning and to promote rural development through the establishment of eleven regional offices is a recent case in point.[4]

Certainly race continues to affect politics in Georgia. Racial progress is reflected in the composition of state and local governing bodies. The state now has the fifth highest number and the fourth highest percentage of African American elected officials in the nation. In local government, African American representation and influence have been growing significantly. Many inner cities in Georgia are now predominantly African American. Atlanta's majority African American population has elected African American mayors since 1973 (when Maynard Jackson was elected), and most of the city council is African American. In 1995 Savannah elected its first African American mayor. This trend has added a new dimension to the old urban-rural schism and created a whole new one—namely, the urban-suburban standoff, which has prompted calls for local government reorganization, particularly in Fulton County, the county home of Atlanta.[5]

Besides race, party has become a major force in Peach State politics. For most of the twentieth century, Georgia, like other southern states, was a Democratic stronghold. That is not the picture today. In the 1996 general election, the Republicans came closer than ever before to taking over the General Assembly, gaining 74 of the 180 house seats and 22 of the 56 senate seats.[6] In the 1998 general election, the Republicans lost one seat in the house and gained none in the senate, but Georgia will never again be considered a one-party state.

That race and party are interrelated in Georgia is highlighted by decisions about representation. Consolidating African American populations into single voting districts during the decennial reapportionment process to enhance minority voting strength has had the concomitant effect of boosting Republican votes in predominantly white suburbs. Reapportionment has therefore inadvertently contributed to Georgia's elected officials becoming both more diverse and more Republican.

Like most Americans, Georgians have a love-hate relationship with government. On one hand, the most popular target for ridicule and criticism in any election is the government itself. Perceived government waste, inefficiency, incompetence, overspending, cronyism, and duplication and overlap of services are fodder for nonincumbents of either party. Nevertheless, Georgians have a way of springing to the defense of the status quo, particularly when it comes to altering cherished traditions. Whether or not they decide to vote, Georgians like their elections, even if they do not know any of the candidates. Examples abound of Georgians rejecting proposed constitutional amendments that would have had the effect of abolishing an elected office.[7]

Even though Georgians defend their right to vote, the state ranks only forty-eighth in voter participation.[8] Maybe the sheer number of elected officials is dissuasive; at last count, Georgians elected 274 individuals to statewide offices and scores of people to local offices in each county. In addition, there are 550 cities (or incorporated places), each with an elected mayor (or chairman) and council (or commission) of three to eighteen members. To bring some order to the planning process, there are sixteen regional development centers, whose leadership is selected by the city and county membership.

Distrust of nonelected government officials is pervasive. The council-manager plan, for example, in which the council or commission appoints a manager on the basis of his or her education and experience (that is, competence), has not fared well historically in Georgia. Direct accountability and control implied by electoral power are preferred over professional management. Only 13 percent of Georgia cities have the council-manager form of government.[9] In 1997 voters in Norcross, a growing suburb outside Atlanta, voted to end the council-manager form and adopt a mayor-council form.[10] Counties have been governed historically either by a board of commissioners or by a sole county commissioner. There is some evidence that this pattern is changing, particularly in larger urban counties. The January 1997 issue of *Georgia County Government* reported that 95 of the state's 159 counties have county managers or administrators working directly for the board of commissioners.

Historically, elected officials—especially county commissioners and mayors and city council members—have not been keen to work together closely. This "go it alone" stance divided the two principal associations representing local government interests, the Association County Commissioners of Georgia and the Georgia Municipal Association, such that each developed separate legislative agendas, often with competing objectives. Beginning in the early 1980s, the two associations realized that they could accomplish more working together than they could separately and crafted a joint legislative agenda. In 1990 the two bodies coalesced on a historic and unprecedented proposal to establish mandatory training requirements for newly elected county commissioners, mayors, and council members. In the 1997 legislative session, they passed a monumental bill mandating that counties and cities improve efficiency by developing a common delivery strategy for local government services within each county to eliminate overlapping and unnecessary service competition and duplication. In 1998 the two associations decided for the first time ever to convene their annual fall policy conferences jointly.[11]

This spirit of cooperation has prompted more intergovernmental cooperation over the past several years, usually through contracts for service delivery in specific functional areas. This so-called functional consolidation of services on a case-by-case basis has had much more success than full-scale consolidation, even though the latter has attracted most of the press coverage. In fact, only three full-scale consolidations of city and county governments have occurred in Georgia: Columbus–Muscogee County, Athens–Clarke County, and Augusta–Richmond County.

Home Rule in Georgia

Historical Development

Home rule for cities is granted by the General Assembly pursuant to express constitutional authority. Home rule for counties is granted directly by the constitution.

When cities were first established in Georgia, power was delegated to them exclusively by local legislation of the General Assembly. Each municipal charter set forth the boundaries, form of government, and specific powers of that political unit. If a particular power was not listed in the charter, it could not be exercised by the city. Additional city powers could be obtained only by an amendment to the city's charter through local legislation of the General Assembly.

As population grew and the number of local governmental units increased, the General Assembly sought to give certain powers to all local municipal units by general law. Its first attempt to do this through the Municipal Home Rule Law of 1951[12] was unsuccessful. In *Phillips v. City of Atlanta*,[13] the Georgia Supreme Court struck down the home rule law as violating the constitutional command that "the legislative power of the State shall be vested in a General Assembly which shall consist of a Senate and House of Representatives."[14] The court found that the constitutional provision authorizing the General Assembly to provide for "uniform systems of county and municipal government, and provide for optional plans for both" was not specific enough to allow delegation of legislative powers by general law.[15]

A constitutional amendment to rectify the constitutional deficiencies cited in *Phillips* was imminent. Proposed by the state legislature at its November 1953 session and subsequently ratified by the people in 1954, this amendment provided as follows:

The General Assembly may provide by law for the self-government of municipalities and to that end is expressly given the authority to delegate its power so that matters pertaining to municipalities may be dealt with without the necessity of action by the General Assembly.[16]

Although this post-*Phillips* amendment was ratified in 1954, it was not until 1962 that any general law on it was enacted. In that year the General Assembly adopted legislation granting home rule power to cities in seven specific areas. Among them were the powers to

- establish municipal offices, agencies, and employments;
- establish merit systems, retirement systems, and insurance plans for all municipal employees;
- contract with any state department or agency or any other political subdivision for joint services or the exchange of services or for the joint use of facilities or equipment; and
- grant franchises to make contracts with railroads, electric light or power companies, gas companies, water companies, and other public utilities for the use and occupancy of the streets of the city.[17]

To exercise any other power, however, specific authority still had to be found in the city charter.

The Municipal Home Rule Act of 1965 was the next major legislative enactment following the 1954 amendment. Originally included as part of the proposed constitution of 1964, but subsequently adopted by the state legislature as general law, the act represented an attempt by the General Assembly to delegate more authority to its municipal corporations than had been given previously.[18] This desire to delegate was understandable, because the General Assembly was flooded with requests for amendments to charters and local acts of counties at every legislative session. In fact, even today it is not uncommon for there to be more than 1,000 local acts passed in any given session.

County home rule followed a different legal path from that of municipal home rule. Because the 1954 amendment to the Georgia Constitution had granted the General Assembly the authority to delegate powers only to cities, counties could receive a similar grant of home rule authority only through a new constitutional amendment. Despite its similarity to the Municipal Home Rule Act, the grant of home rule authority to counties in 1966 was a direct one from the constitution itself,[19] whereas the home rule grant to cities was to the legislature first and then to the cities through a statutory grant of authority.

County home rule authorization opened the door to amendments to the state statute by the county government itself, either through a local ordinance or resolution or through a public referendum called for by a certain percentage of the population of the county. The constitutional provision also listed eight exceptions to the grant of home rule power for counties, encompassing a wide range of local activities.[20]

The final aspect of home rule in Georgia relates to local constitutional amendments. An anomaly exists in Georgia law and history that, at least until 1983, allowed local amendments to the state constitution relating to individual cities and counties to be introduced and passed in the General Assembly in the same manner as local legislation. (That is, if a majority of the local delegation from the particular city or county to be affected approved the amendment, it would be passed by the entire legislature as a matter of "legislative courtesy.") The proposed amendment would be subject to referendum approval by the qualified voters of that city or county at the next election. If approved, it would have the same weight as any other constitutional amendment (freedom of speech, for example).

This procedure was used so often and so indiscriminately that at the time of the referendum on the proposed 1983 constitution at the 1982 general election, the Georgia Constitution included 908 local amendments.[21] Thus, to understand the law governing a city or county, an attorney had to review not only the charter or local act of the jurisdiction setting up its boundaries and form of government but also any local amendment that might have been passed. Any such amendment would take precedence over the charter or general law provision or even a prior constitutional provision. This precedence ended in 1993, however, because the 1983 constitution prohibited future local constitutional amendments, including amendments of existing local amendments.

Definition of Home Rule

Although "enabling," the grants of home rule authority in both the municipal and county home rule provisions were not intended to be all-inclusive so that local governments would never have to refer to the General Assembly for legislative authorization. Expressly excluded from municipal home rule authority were actions affecting the composition and form of the municipal governing authority, any form of taxation beyond that authorized by law or by the constitution, the exercise of the power of eminent domain, and other matters.[22] Expressly excluded from county home rule authority were actions affecting any elective county office, the salaries thereof, or the personnel thereof, except the personnel subject to the jurisdiction of the county governing authority; action affecting the composition, form, procedure for election or appointment, compensation, and expenses and allowances of the county governing authority; action adopting any form of taxation beyond that authorized by law and by the constitution; and other matters.[23]

The operative clause of the home rule provisions grant to each municipality and county legislative power to adopt "clearly reasonable ordinances, resolutions, or regulations relating to its property, affairs, local government." Several questions arise: How broadly should one interpret the general phrase "property, affairs, and local government"? And what is "clearly reasonable"? Must actions taken pursuant to the home rule provisions meet a higher standard of reasonableness than other local government actions? To date, the courts have given no definitive answers.

In fact, there seems to be a continuing conservative bent in the Georgia courts to interpret any grant of local government power very strictly. This strict "constructionism" is reinforced by city and county attorneys, who are generally conservative and who prefer to see clear authorization in writing. The same attitude also pervades interpretations by judges who generally have little familiarity with local government law. Perhaps because of these ingrained biases on the part of attorneys and judges—or perhaps because of the legal ambiguity surrounding the scope of local government authority—the General Assembly, through local legislation, remains the dominant force in Georgia local government law.

Structural Features

There are only two types of general-purpose local governments in Georgia: cities and counties. State law does not provide for classes of cities or counties.

As mentioned, local legislation is predominant in Georgia, despite repeated efforts by the legislature to delegate away much local government authority. Incorporation of cities is still a matter for the state legislature. Certain minimal standards must be met before incorporation; for example, new city limits must be more than three miles from an existing city, there must be a total resident population of at least 200 persons in the area proposed to be incorporated, and the new city must provide at least three of eleven specified services.[24] Most municipal charter amendments (other than annexations) and most changes in local

acts establishing county governing authorities are likewise implemented by the state legislature rather than by a "home rule" amendment to the charter or local act by the local governing authority itself, despite the clear authorization for such action.

Form of government is also a matter for the state legislature. (It is a power exempted from the general home rule authorization for cities and counties, even though it is one of the most important issues for a local government.) "Form of government" refers to the formal assignment of authority among local government officials and determines the respective roles of these officials in policy making and administration. County governments in Georgia generally fit into one of five structural categories: traditional commission, sole commissioner, elected executive, commission-administrator, or commission-manager form of government. City government generally falls into one of four forms: "weak" mayor, "strong" mayor, commission, or council-manager. The distinction between a strong or weak mayor form is not always clear and often reflects the personality of the incumbent as much as the legal differences. These two forms taken together, however, account for about 85 percent of the cities in Georgia; the council-manager form accounts for only about 13 percent.[25]

Municipal annexation can be accomplished by a local act of the legislature amending the city charter, but usually it is handled by the municipalities themselves under one of three annexation methods authorized by general law: the "100 percent method" allows owners of adjacent land to petition to join the city; the "60 percent method" allows 60 percent of the owners representing 60 percent of the adjacent land to petition to join the city; and the "initiative and referendum method" allows adjacent or contiguous "urban areas" to be annexed if approved in a referendum by a majority of the voters in the area to be annexed.[26]

Although interlocal service agreements are encouraged, constitutional provisions relating to local government service delivery stipulate that a city or county may not provide any service in another jurisdiction without that jurisdiction's approval.[27] Most city charters have a provision authorizing service delivery "within and without the boundaries of the city," especially for extension of water and sewer services, without requiring that all parties agree to the service. In light of a bill passed at the 1997 legislative session mandating negotiations between cities and counties on service delivery arrangements, intergovernmental service agreements are likely to become a standard feature of city and county relationships.[28]

Functions of Local Government

Functional Responsibilities

Counties and cities in Georgia differ in one fundamental way: counties, unlike cities, are considered administrative arms of state government for purposes of many important public functions, such as property tax assessment and administration, elections, public health and social services (welfare), and the operation of the courts. Like cities, however, counties are considered "local governments" for other purposes, such as public works, parks and recreation, and water supply and solid waste disposal. This bifurcated nature of county government has been a source of confusion to the public over which unit of government (city or county) is responsible for what local government service.

The confusion was confounded in 1972, when the people of Georgia ratified a constitutional amendment (Amendment 19) that authorized counties to provide the same type of municipal services that historically cities had provided, such as police, fire, and solid waste.[29] This amendment was a revolutionary enactment in the history of local government in Georgia. Permissive in nature and seemingly innocuous, it originally received overwhelming approval by the people. Nevertheless, "municipalizing" county government effectively blurred the distinction between counties and cities to the point that today there is almost no practical difference from a legal standpoint in the authority of each to provide "urban"-type services. Counties continue to serve as administrative subunits of state government, however, for purposes of the court system, tax collection, health-related matters, welfare, and other historic state responsibilities.

State law does encourage intergovernmental cooperation and contracting. In fact, the constitution authorizes cities and counties to contract with each other for any service or activity that they are each authorized to provide.[30]

In terms of the creation of special districts, Amendment 19 also gives cities and counties the authority to create special districts for the provision of local government services within such districts and to levy and collect special fees, assessments, or taxes within such districts to support such services.[31]

Administrative Discretion

Local governments have wide discretion in handling their own affairs, particularly with respect to internal organization, administration, and procedures. Authorization for contracting and purchasing comes initially from the municipal charter or from the local act of the county, but discretion is broad, subject to conditions and limitations in specific instances.[32] Planning, zoning, and land-use control are powers that are specifically given to cites and counties by the constitution. The General Assembly's authority in this area is limited to establishing procedures governing the exercise of planning and zoning powers.[33]

In the area of personnel, cities have more latitude than counties because of the status and historical role of county constitutional officers. The elected county commission is referred to as the "county governing authority," but in actuality its ability to "govern" is greatly circumscribed, particularly in the area of personnel. Case law interpretation of their powers gives elected

county officers—including the sheriff, clerk of superior court, judge of probate court, tax commissioner, tax receiver and/or tax collector, and, in most counties, the coroner and the surveyor—almost unfettered control over their own employees. In fact, the employees of these officers are covered by the county merit system only if the county officer permits it.[34] The problem is especially acute in the area of liability. Under current Georgia law, the board of county commissioners is financially liable for the misdeeds of personnel of county officers (that is, personnel over whom the board has no direct supervision or control).

Municipal personnel management authority, on the other hand, is more discretionary. Cities are at-will employers, unless they adopt a personnel system giving employees some expectation of continued employment, for example, thereby triggering due process requirements. Of course, cities must comply with federal law on civil rights, the Americans with Disabilities Act, and so forth; otherwise, they may decide what type of personnel or civil service systems to establish, if any.

Economic Development

The state has a vested interest in promoting strong economic and community development by cities and counties and has taken many steps to empower local governments in this area. Historically, it has favored regional development activities. In the early 1960s, area planning and development commissions were established statewide. These units worked with cities and counties within their respective jurisdictions to promote environmentally compatible development and orderly growth. In 1989, as a result of recommendations of the governor's Growth Strategies Commission, these commissions became "regional development centers," focusing more on economic and community development than on planning per se.[35]

Special attention has been paid to rural economic development in Georgia. The Rural Economic Development Law, in 1981, was an early example. The establishment of the Office of Rural Development and the State Advisory Committee on Rural Development were later initiatives.[36]

The state has used its tax code to encourage business development. The Georgia Business Expansion Support Act of 1994 (known as the BEST program) is an example.[37] Under this program, a statewide job tax credit is made available for certain types of businesses and industries; the amount of the credit ranges from $500 to $3,000, depending on which "tier" the county falls into. Higher credits are available for job creation in less developed communities. Regional economic development activities are encouraged by an additional $500 job tax credit for businesses located in the jurisdiction of a multicounty joint development authority.[38]

Much if not most of the economic development activity in Georgia results from interaction among the Georgia Department of Industry, Trade, and Tourism, local chambers of commerce, local development authorities, and local government officials. State law provides for the establishment of a development authority in each county and city in the state. Downtown development authorities are authorized in the central business districts of cities.[39]

Property tax exemptions can assist in attracting new businesses. The commonly used constitutional freeport exemption, for example, which exempts a manufacturer's inventory from ad valorem taxation, must be first approved by the governing authority and then by a majority of qualified voters voting in the city or county affected. "Homestead exemptions" can be granted by local legislation of the General Assembly under the same voting conditions.[40]

A constitutional amendment approved in 1984 authorized the creation of "community improvement districts" by any county or city. Such districts allow for a higher level of service delivery in specified areas of the local government and are funded by taxes, fees, or assessments agreed to by the property owners affected.[41]

Fiscal Autonomy of Local Governments

Local Revenues

In the area of revenue, Georgia could be said to have both broad and limited home rule authority for local governments. On the one hand, for those revenue sources they are authorized to adopt, local governments have wide discretion and therefore broad home rule authority. Property taxes continue to be the primary source of local government revenue in Georgia, especially for counties (see Figure 1). Other sources include sales taxes, excise taxes, service charges, licenses or permits, and intergovernmental revenues. Of course, the weight of each of these varies with the type of local government. Local governments are free to decide on whatever mix they want, and the limitations are practical more than legal. Discretion regarding new sources of revenue, however, is very narrow, because neither counties nor cities can adopt any new type of taxation without specific legislative approval. This matter is exempted from the home rule authorization of both cities and counties.

The process of tax assessment and administration is closely monitored and regulated by the state. General law dictates, for example, that tangible real and personal property be assessed at 40 percent of its fair market value. The tax rate is stated in terms of mills, with 10 mills equal to 1 percent of a property's assessed valuation. Municipal ad valorem tax (millage) rates are set by the city governing authority before the city tax digest is approved by the Georgia Department of Revenue. Similarly, the county tax rates are set by the county governing authority and are submitted to the department. Although the constitution sets a 20-mill cap on property tax for schools, there is no such constitutional or general law limitation on property tax for local gov-

Fig. 1 Revenue Composition of Georgia Local Government

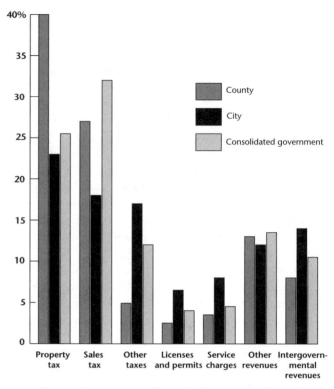

Source: "Report of Local Government Finances for Georgia Municipalities and Counties" (Georgia Department of Community Affairs, 1998).

ernment operations.[42] The principal deterrent to increases in this tax by cities and counties is the wrath of voters at the next election.

In terms of local government debt, the Georgia Constitution limits indebtedness to 10 percent of the assessed value of all taxable property located within the local government jurisdiction.[43] It also provides that no new debt may be incurred without the approval of the bond issue by a majority of qualified voters voting in the county or city affected. A strict interpretation of this provision by the Georgia courts made it almost impossible for local governments to enter into multiyear installment purchases or leases, since any obligation in excess of a year was considered "debt" by the courts.[44] (This limitation did not apply to revenue bonds since the full faith and credit of the jurisdiction was not being pledged for those types of instruments but only the projected revenues from the operation or facility financed.) A 1988 law opened the door to multiyear agreements of this type, however, provided that certain specified conditions and requirements are met.[45]

Local Expenditures

Local governments have almost unlimited discretion in terms of the expenditures of local funds. Before the adoption of the 1983 constitution, spending by counties and cites was limited to

Table 1. Direct Intergovernmental Revenues from State and Local Sources in Georgia, FY 1997–1998

Source of revenue	State			Local		
	County	City	Consolidated government	County	City	Consolidated government
Payment in lieu of taxes	0	0	0	$591,035	$1,532,491	$99,270
General public purpose grants	0	0	0	0	0	0
Capital outlay grants	0	0	0	0	0	0
Fuel oil and road mileage	0	0	0	0	0	0
Road, street, and bridge funds	$46,972,495	$10,601,006	$1,893,551	94,416	2,371,861	0
Water/wastewater grants	1,539,585	3,361,530	0	1,134,125	378,521	0
Solid waste grants	1,005,399	585,456	0	177,715	0	0
Revenues of county board of health	7,450,264	0	0	36,979	0	0
Crime and corrections grants	16,867,164	3,115,174	794,003	1,100,589	1,026,891	52,756
Community development block grants	15,091,022	20,432,159	329,605	4,020	1,243,191	0
Public welfare grants	17,927,113	1,113,693	258,505	1,145,676	88,576	0
Real estate transfer taxes	9,629,481	3,555,200	519,927	0	0	0
Physical health & mental health grants	136,777,631	0	19,821,538	0	0	0
Other	58,559,398	21,461,063	6,806,229	23,867,646	31,609,810	1,121,082
Total	$311,819,552	$64,225,281	$30,423,358	$28,152,201	$38,251,341	$1,273,108

Source: "Report of Local Government Finances for Georgia Municipalities and Counties" (Georgia Department of Community Affairs, 1998).

Fig. 2 Operating Expenditure Pattern of Georgia Local Government

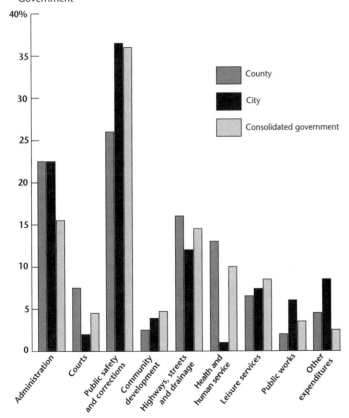

Source: "Report of Local Government Finances for Georgia Municipalities and Counties" (Georgia Department of Community Affairs, 1998).

fourteen enumerated purposes. Under the 1983 constitution, expenditures are allowed for any "public service or function."[46] Public safety and corrections is the largest expenditure for all types of local governments (see Figure 2). The next largest expenditure categories for counties are health and human services, administration, highway streets and drainage, the courts, and leisure services. For cities, the categories include administration, highway streets and drainage, leisure services, public works, and others expenditures. The law gives local governments wide discretion over the types of services they offer, primarily because of Amendment 19, and most local governments take full advantage of this authorization.

Discretion over budgetary matters is limited for both cities and counties. Minimum budget, accounting, and auditing requirements for local governments are imposed by general law, including establishment of a fiscal year for local government operations, an annual balanced budget, a uniform chart of accounts, annual local government finances reports, and other matters.[47] Through these various controls, the state tries to ensure that local governments remain solvent and well run because there is no provision in state law for dealing with bankruptcy by a city or county. If a bankruptcy were to happen, the state would no doubt fall back on its residual powers and exert its inherent power to act for the public welfare.

State Government Grants-in-Aid to Localities

State government grants and aid account for a significant percentage of local governments' budgets, although much aid is targeted to specific purposes, such as roads (see Table 1). Grants-in-aid are a major source of revenue for counties—more so than for cities—because counties function as subunits of state government as well as local governments.

Unfunded Mandates

The subject of unfunded mandates has been an important one in Georgia, as in most other states. Local governments believe that they are often saddled with responsibilities for major government functions without enough revenue to carry out those responsibilities. In 1983 a commission was established to look closely at this subject, and new conditions now make it more difficult for state government merely to impose requirements on local government without providing either the resources directly or the opportunity to generate the resources needed to carry out the responsibility. Although the exact impact of these conditions is not clear, the state legislature is more sensitized to the issue of unfunded mandates than it was previously.

Access to Local Government

Local Elections

Local elections are governed by state law and monitored by the secretary of state. Both county and municipal elections are regulated by the Georgia Election Code. State law authorizes the creation of joint county-municipal boards of elections and registration. Cities may authorize counties to carry out the election function. However, many cities prefer to keep their own voter registration lists and conduct their own elections.[48]

Citizen Controls over Actions of Local Officials

Other than elections themselves, the most direct method of citizen control over the action of local officials is recall. The Recall Act of 1989 provides the grounds and procedures for the recall of local elected officials.[49] Recall provisions are seldom used, however, since elections are held relatively frequently, and most people believe that they can exercise this right to change course at the next general election.

Provision for initiative and referendum is found in the municipal and county home rule laws, which authorize the amendment of local charters on petition of a minimum percentage of the voters who voted in the last general election. Some refer to this right as a "sleeping giant," since citizens can, but often do not, change certain charter provisions if they organize effectively to do so.

In terms of open meetings and open records, local governments are subject to a rather strict "sunshine" law. Meetings and records must be open except in certain instances as specified in state law.[50]

State-Local Relations

The state has investigated ways in which the structure and operation of local governments could be improved. Most attempts have encountered serious political obstacles, especially when the recommendations have been bold or significant. The report of the governor's Local Governance Commission in 1992, "A Platform for Local Government Change in Georgia," called for radical restructuring of local government, particularly regarding the elected constitutional officers in county government. Even the governor eventually distanced himself from the recommendations of his own commission because the recommendations were so controversial. The 1995 Georgia Future Communities Commission delayed the release of its final report because of opposition to some of its preliminary recommendations from certain local government groups. Two laws recommended by this commission were passed at the l997 legislative session, however: one relating to the establishment of a uniform chart of accounts to help standardize local financial data and one requiring the development of a local government service delivery strategy.[51]

The status of county and municipal home rule in Georgia is as it has been for a long time—namely, mixed. State legislators want local governments to have discretion in dealing with local affairs—but not too much. Local government officials want to have more discretion over their own business, but they seem reluctant to take advantage of many of the prerogatives they already have, particularly when it comes to amending their own charters or local acts.

The relationship between state and local governments in Georgia could best be characterized as guarded. From the state government perspective, local governments are often seen as another lobby group rather than as true partners in the intergovernmental system. Moreover, state lawmakers often like to exert their power over local officials, since it is one of the major arrows in their quiver.

From the local government perspective, state lawmakers are often perceived as aloof and out of touch with local constituents, as thinking they know more about the local situation than they actually do. And there is some justification for this concern. Instead of coming from a traditional local government background, today's state legislators more likely hail from business or private practice. Although suspicion often underlies surface camaraderie, local government associations have generally promoted enhanced cooperation among state and local government officials.

Notes

1. Arnold Fleischmann and Carol Pierannunzi, *Politics in Georgia* (Athens: University of Georgia Press, 1997), xi.

2. Douglas C. Bachtel, *Passport to Georgia: A Statistical Journey* (Athens: College of Family and Consumer Sciences, University of Georgia, 1996).

3. Fleischmann and Pierannunzi, *Politics in Georgia*, xi.

4. Jim Higdon, "Fuel for Rural Development," *Georgia County Government* (May–June 1998): 30–34.

5. Many residents of North Fulton County have been calling for the reestablishment of Milton County (which had been merged with Campbell County and Fulton County in 1932) to give them autonomy from the rest of Fulton County. Unfortunately for them, the Georgia Constitution limits the number of counties to 159 (the current number). Although unlikely, the only way that Milton County could be reestablished would be for two other counties to merge.

6. Fleischmann and Pierannunzi, *Politics in Georgia*, 89.

7. The position of state school superintendent was a recent case in point. Several years ago, to promote greater professionalism of candidates for the position and a more harmonious relationship between the board and the superintendent, the governor proposed converting the office to an appointed one under the State Board of Education (for which the state school superintendent serves as executive director). Although the governor actively campaigned for the proposal's passage, the people said "no." In 1996 the conflicts between the appointed board and the elected superintendent became so serious that the governor asked all of the appointed board members to resign so that he could try again. Initially, only three agreed to do so.

8. Bachtel, *Passport to Georgia*.

9. J. Devereux Weeks and Paul T. Hardy, eds., *Handbook for Georgia Mayors and Councilmembers*, 3d ed. (Athens: Carl Vinson Institute of Government, University of Georgia, 1993), 19.

10. *Atlanta Constitution*, 18 June 1997, C3.

11. Official Code of Georgia Annotated (O.C.G.A.), section 36-45-5 et seq. and the Georgia County Leadership Act; section 36-20-1 et seq. (see the Georgia Municipal Training Act); section 36-70-1 et seq., HB 489, 1997 Georgia General Assembly.

12. Georgia Laws 116.

13. Georgia 72, 77 S.E.2d 723 (1953).

14. Georgia Constitution, Article III, section I, paragraph I.

15. For a detailed and well-documented discussion of the legislative history of home rule in Georgia, see Perry Sentell, "Home Rule Benefits or Homemade Problems for Georgia Local Government Law," 8 *Georgia State Bar Journal* 317 (1968), and "'Home Rule': Its Impact on Georgia Local Government Law," 8 *Georgia State Bar Journal* 277 (1972), both reprinted in Perry Sentell, *Studies in Georgia Local Government Law*, 2d ed. (Charlottesville, Va.: Michie, 1973). Note that although the Municipal Home Rule Law of 1951 was declared invalid by the *Phillips* decision in 1953, it was not expressly repealed by the General Assembly until 1976. See Georgia Laws 1976, 259.

16. Georgia Constitution, Article IX, section II, paragraph II.

17. The exact text of this list can be found in Georgia Laws 1962, 140. It now appears (after several amendments since 1962) in O.C.G.A., section 36-34-2.

18. O.C.G.A., section 36-35-3, originally enacted 1965 Georgia Laws 298.

19. Georgia Constitution, Article IX, section II, paragraph I(a).

20. The eight exceptions to the constitutional grant of county home rule authority are found in Georgia Constitution, Article IX, section II, paragraph I(c), (1)–(8).

21. See Melvin B. Hill Jr., *The Georgia State Constitution, A Reference Guide* (Westport, Conn.: Greenwood Press, 1994), 22.

22. O.C.G.A., section 36-35-6.

23. Georgia Constitution, Article IX, section II, paragraph I(c).

24. See O.C.G.A., sections 36-31-1–5, 36-30-7.1. This latter law, passed in 1993, had the effect of repealing city charters of "inactive municipalities."

25. Weeks and Hardy, eds., *Handbook for Georgia Mayors and Councilmembers*, 5, 13, 19.

26. See O.C.G.A., sections 36-36-20–21; 36-36-30–40; 36-36-50–61.

27. Georgia Constitution, Article IX, section II, paragraph III (b).

28. See O.C.G.A., sections 36-66-3 and 36-70-1, HB 489, 1997 Georgia General Assembly.

29. Georgia Constitution, Article IX, section II, paragraph III. This provision is referred to as Amendment 19 because it was the nineteenth constitutional amendment on the ballot at the 1972 general election.

30. See especially Georgia Constitution, Article IX, section III, paragraph I.

31. Georgia Constitution, Article IX, section II, paragraph VI.

32. See Weeks and Hardy, eds., *Handbook for Georgia Mayors and Councilmembers*, 170, 204.

33. See Georgia Constitution, Article IX, section II, paragraph IV; Hill, *The Georgia State Constitution*, 195.

34. See O.C.G.A., section 36-1-21.

35. See O.C.G.A., section 50-8-30 et seq.

36. See O.C.G.A., sections 50-8-120 et seq., 50-8-140 et seq.

37. See O.C.G.A., section 48-7-40 et seq.

38. The Job Tax Credit Program provides tax credits to businesses that create jobs. In the least developed counties (1st–53d, Tier 1), eligible businesses creating at least an average of five full-time jobs earn a $2,500 per job credit. See O.C.G.A., section 48-70-40 et seq. This program is administered by the Georgia Department of Community Affairs and is described in some detail in the department's Web site: http://www.dca.state.ga.us/economic/economic2.html.

39. See the Development Authorities Law (O.C.G.A., section 36-62-1 et seq.) and the Downtown Development Authorities Law (O.C.G.A., section 36-42-1 et seq.).

40. Georgia Constitution, Article VII, section II, paragraphs III, II(a)(2).

41. Georgia Constitution, Article IX, section II, paragraph II(a)(2); section VII.

42. See O.C.G.A., sections 48-5-7 et seq., 48-5-273.

43. Georgia Constitution, Article IX, section I.

44. *City Council of Dawson v. Dawson Water Works Company*, 106 Ga. 696, 32 S.E.2d 907, 1899.

45. See O.C.G.A., section 36-60-13.

46. Georgia Constitution, Article IX, section IV, paragraph II.

47. See O.C.G.A., section 36-81-1 et seq. Note that section 36-81-10 states that "it is the specific intent of the General Assembly in adopting this article that local units of government shall continue to have and to exercise their home rule powers as provided by law."

48. See O.C.G.A., section 21-2-1 et seq. The former Georgia Municipal Election Code was merged into this code, effective January 1, 1999. O.C.G.A., sections 21-2-40, 21-2-45.

49. See O.C.G.A., section 21-4-1 et seq.

50. See the open and public meetings provisions in O.C.G.A., sections 50-14-1–6 and the inspection of public records provisions in O.C.G.A., sections 50-18-70–73.

51. O.C.G.A., section 36-81-1 et seq., HB 491, 1997 Georgia General Assembly; section 36-70-1 et seq., HB 489, 1997 Georgia General Assembly.

HAWAII

Anne Feder Lee and Norman Meller

The authors thank Duke Bainum, Mary George, Lowell Kalapa, Mona Nakayama, Mark Oto, Newton Sue, and Carol Whitesell for their assistance.

Whereas mainland states are complex in terms of both numbers and variety of overlapping local jurisdictions, local government in Hawaii comprises only four counties[1] and sixteen soil conservation districts.[2] The state constitution nominally assures structural home rule to the counties by allowing them to determine their own legislative and administrative structures and organizations when adopting their charters through popular vote. In so doing, the constitution denies the state legislature any power of review over those aspects of home rule. Offsetting what at first glance might appear to be a grant of local autonomy, the division of functions in Hawaii is far more heavily weighted toward the state than it is elsewhere; so local government plays a relatively narrow role in Hawaii. Like most local governments in the United States, Hawaii's counties depend on statutory authority to perform their functions. That Hawaii is both different from and similar to other states is explained by the state's unique history, played out against its multi-island geography.

Governmental Setting

Centralization and the existence of very few units of government characterize the governmental setting in Hawaii. These are the legacies of a long-standing history of a strong central government, a lengthy period when an oligopoly dominated the economy, and one-party control of the elected offices.

When Kamehameha I, in 1810, succeeded in establishing a monarchical government encompassing all of Hawaii, in effect he built a single jurisdiction. The configuration of today's counties can be directly traced to the administration he created to tend to the needs of the various islands. The state's strong executive has its roots in the monarchy and the territorial experience.

The transition from monarchy to territorial status did little to change the centralized nature of government services. After annexation by the United States in 1900, and at the behest of the U.S. Congress, the territorial legislature in 1905 established four counties: Hawaii, Maui (including the islands of Kahoolawe, Maui, Molokai, and Lanai), Oahu, and Kauai (including the islands of Kauai and Niihau). Two years later, the county of Oahu was converted into the city-county of Honolulu.[3] However, counties were not permitted to become major providers of governmental services.

The state constitution, which became effective with statehood in 1959, mandated the existence of the counties. Although the legislature was authorized to "create other political subdivisions," it has never believed that Hawaii needed additional forms of local government, such as townships or municipalities, nor has the legislature ever felt the need to expand the number of counties. Thus, centralization has continued.

Until the mid-1900s, sugar was the dominant economic interest in Hawaii. The five large corporations that controlled sugar and indirectly, almost all other aspects of the economy constituted not only an economic but a political oligopoly as well. For years, the bulk of Hawaii's taxable income and wealth was located on Oahu, either by virtue of the commercial activity occurring on the island or because the economically and politically powerful institutions of the oligopoly were headquartered there. Given their limited economic bases, counties of neighboring islands were in a poor position to seek local autonomy. Although the city-county of Honolulu was better able to fund the growing array of services sought by its citizenry, it could not be allowed to attain full self-government lest it disturb the allocation patterns being observed by the central government.

Hawaii has had little experience of viable party competition because the Republican Party dominated politics from about 1902 to the 1950s; since 1962, the Democratic Party has been equally dominant. One party dominance, regardless of the party, has contributed to the continuation of centralization because no viable competitive forces have successfully urged decentralization, and there have been no particular reasons to shift administration to the counties.

Although the four counties have sought expanded powers

and additional self-government since their creation, the legislature has only grudgingly complied. As the need for governmental services grew in the islands, given the limited scope of permitted local government, the power of the central government over local matters has correspondingly increased.

Home Rule in Hawaii

Historical Development

When the territorial legislature created the four counties, it also established the governmental structure for each and specified its powers and duties. Before statehood, Honolulu city-county adopted a charter following statutorily prescribed procedures, as did the other counties subsequent to statehood. Although the constitution expressly allowed counties to frame and adopt their own charters, this power was nevertheless subject to "such limits and under such procedures as may be prescribed by general law."[4] In 1968 the state supreme court ruled that such a county charter "is no more than a statutory charter" and that nothing in the constitution prohibited the legislature from amending a county charter, even after it had been adopted by the voters.[5]

In response, the delegates to the 1968 constitutional convention proposed and the electorate ratified several significant amendments that moved Hawaii closer to home rule. County charters were not to be conditional upon legislative ratification. In addition, a "superior clause" was added, stating that charter provisions dealing with executive, legislative, and administrative structure and organization were granted a status superior to that of any statutory provision the legislature may adopt (that is, county charters were protected against legislative interference in those areas).[6]

The new language, however, also included a provision stating that this superior status was subject to the authority of the legislature to enact general laws allocating and reallocating powers and functions. The effect of this exception has enabled the legislature to interfere with charter provisions by transferring a power or function from the counties to the state, or vice versa. Court rulings have tended to support the position that this constitutional section allows counties in Hawaii only limited freedom from legislative control.

In 1978 the constitution was further amended to transfer the real property tax to the counties.[7] Underlying this change was a recognition that state government no longer had any need for the revenues derived from the property tax; so the counties could administer this tax. All of the other fiscal powers the counties enjoy are still dependent on legislative authorization.

Although the constitution has always limited the legislature from enacting mandates requiring a subdivision to pay any previously accrued claim, an additional provision was added in 1978 in response to complaints by county officials. Now, if the state mandates a new program or an increase in the level of service under an existing program, the state must "share" in the cost with the political subdivisions.[8]

As reflected in constitutional changes—and starting with the original language denying the legislature the ability to grant powers or to impose duties on the counties—the historical development of county home rule has been incremental. The counties first obtained the right to frame their own charters. Next, they freed themselves from legislative review and also made charter provisions regarding organization that preempted state law. Finally, counties gained functional authority directly from the constitution, as evidenced by the assignment of the property tax to the counties.

From the perspective of those who desire "enhanced home rule," all of this represents progress. However, although county charters are declared superior to statutory law with respect to their provisions covering executive, legislative, and administrative structure and organization, that status has been somewhat muted by the residual power of the state to enact general laws allocating and reallocating powers and functions. Moreover, counties must look to the legislature for their grants of functional authority.

Barring further enhancement of home rule is Article VIII (local government), which expressly states that it does not limit the power of the legislature to enact laws of statewide concern.[9] The Hawaii Supreme Court has declared that to give effect to this provision, the power of the legislature to enact laws of statewide concern regarding local self-government cannot be diminished.[10] Supplementing this ruling, the court has also held that "on functions of statewide interest and concern, the general rule is that if the counties are not given specific authority to take over the function, the counties cannot thwart the State from performing its duty."[11]

Definition of Home Rule

There are both constitutional and statutory provisions with relevance to what is commonly called home rule, but that phrase does not appear in either provision. Hawaii's courts have ruled that the counties have received only limited freedom from legislative control and that "complete home rule" would be total protection against legislative intrusion.[12]

In practice, home rule in Hawaii means that the counties enjoy self-government or autonomy over matters that the legislature has not determined to be of statewide concern. Although the constitution and statutes do grant what might be described as "partial home rule," those powers do not afford the counties as much autonomy as many local government officials would like. Practical discourse, therefore, revolves around increasing such autonomy, through what some call "enhanced home rule."

Structural Features

Although Hawaii's legislature no longer uses local privilege or special legislation in its dealings with the counties, much the same purpose is achieved by classifying the counties in statutory provisions. Distinctions are made between counties with less than and more than 100,000 population. Counties with less than and more than 500,000 population are also distinguished.

For many years, the 100,000-population cutoff separated only the city-county of Honolulu from the other counties, but with the growth of population in the counties of Hawaii and Maui, today the cutoff serves only to distinguish Kauai County from the other three. The 500,000-population classification continues to separate the city-county of Honolulu from the others. A few statutes still include specific county designations, a carryover from when the legislature could adopt special and local laws. Because the legislature can pass general statutes applicable only to the counties, there is some question about whether merely repealing such a designated county provision does not contravene this requirement.[13]

Because Honolulu city-county is so much larger, both in terms of population and governmental capacity, some distinction in law between it and the other counties would seem to be appropriate. However, this differential treatment has also been based on a sense of obligation toward the smaller, poorer counties and tension caused by the fact that Honolulu encompasses 70–80 percent of the entire state's population. The fact that the other three counties used to be called "outer islands" and are now referred to by the euphemism of "neighbor islands" underscores the disparity in political and economic power of Honolulu vis-à-vis the other counties. Even though reapportionment has expanded Honolulu's legislative delegation to reflect its population dominance, there remains within the city-county the feeling that the state legislature is disproportionately friendly to the requests of the neighbor islands.

Now that the counties are chartered, all of them have opted to install a mayor-council form of government with broad supervisory powers and a "strong" mayor. The prosecutor is the only other elected official. However, there are variances among them with respect to such matters as mayoral term of office, number of council members, and partisanship in elections of officers. Similarly, their internal structures of government vary, reflecting different county activities.

Statutes harking back to prestatehood days still specify procedures for the chartering of counties.[14] They provide for establishing charter commissions and for voter ratification of charters as well as amendments and revisions.

Functions of Local Government

Functional Responsibilities

Although called counties, Hawaii's units of local government are somewhat unique in the American context. Many functions usually carried out by political subdivisions in other states are instead performed by the state government. For example, the state government administers public education, prison incarceration, airports, harbors, and most public health functions. Initially, the district courts were a county responsibility but were then transferred to the state; the entire judiciary is now part of the state government. At the same time, however, Hawaii's counties resemble cities in other states by virtue of the municipal services they provide, such as fire and police protection, garbage collection, water and sewage, and street construction, lighting, and maintenance.

Hawaii's constitution eschews outlining functional authority for counties but instead leaves it to the discretion of the legislature to allocate to or share concurrent powers with counties. By statute, counties are given authority to protect health, life, and property; to preserve order and security; to prevent and remove nuisances; to regulate particular business activities; and to perform myriad specific functions that range from the appropriate (such as acquiring and controlling appliances for the cleaning of streets and the flushing of sewers) to the seemingly ridiculous (such as making appropriations for the entertainment of visiting dignitaries). Alcohol beverage control represents one of the few functions formerly administered by the central government that has been transferred to the counties. Counties may make contracts, acquire and dispose of property, exercise the power of eminent domain, fix fees for services, enforce all claims on behalf of the county, and do everything necessary and proper to execute all powers vested in the counties or their officers.

In some cases, exercise of the powers granted to the counties requires state consent; for example, before development bonds are issued, they must first be certified by a state agency. In other cases, the counties must perform a function under express threat of state assumption should they fail to do so (for example, control of underground water). Counties risk losing powers when they resort to the legislature for specific authority; for instance, granting a county the ability to regulate housing rentals may implicitly preclude its ability to regulate nonhousing rentals. Asking the legislature for authorization to act may also be a form of reassurance that such state authorization exists. With each request, however, the number of statutorily specified county powers grows. Because it is easier politically to obtain specific legislative approval than to secure broad grants of power, the statutory detail of county functions likely will continue to expand.

Normally (but not always) when the legislature adopts a statute on a function of government, its provisions preempt application of a county ordinance on the same subject. In the field of human services, all the counties provide social services to some degree so that they share responsibilities with the state. The legislature may express an intent for a county ordinance to coexist, or even to prevail, as when the fire safety rules of a county are more stringent than those adopted by state statute.[15]

Given the noncontiguous character of the counties (all are bounded by water), interlocal cooperation focuses primarily on maintenance of county solidarity as, for example, through collective bargaining negotiations and lobbying of the state government. State statute permits county officials to engage in intergovernmental cooperative purchasing of supplies, services, and construction. One county is rarely called upon to provide services for another. The city-county of Honolulu, however, maintains the real property tax maps and records for all four counties.

With legislative approval, the counties may cooperate with political subdivisions outside the state on matters affecting public health, safety, and general welfare. Less formal cooperation between county officials and their peers outside Hawaii occurs more frequently, without recourse to legislative legitimization.

Administrative Discretion

When the delegates to the convention in 1968 proposed the addition of the "superior clause" to the constitution, giving the counties control over their internal organization, they deliberately refrained from using the model language then being recommended by the American Municipal Association. Hawaii previously had adopted an overarching civil service law for the state and all the counties and similarly had prescribed the administrative procedures that were to be observed by all government officials and agencies within the state. The delegates pointedly omitted the words "personnel" and "procedures" from the powers that were constitutionally granted to chartered counties that were freed of legislative intrusion. In this way, they sought to assure that civil service and other matters relating to county personnel as well as oversight of administrative procedures would remain within the purview of the legislature.[16]

Under its charter, each county appoints a civil service commission that administers the personnel needs of the county. All county actions regarding the classification of positions and the hiring, training, transfer, promotion, and disciplining of county employees generally are covered by state civil service law. State policy favors equal pay for equal work (that is, all positions within one grade are paid the same), which results in anomalies. Thus, a firefighter in the predominantly rural county of Kauai receives the same remuneration as one hired by the metropolitan city-county of Honolulu or by the state to work at the international airports. To ensure equality of pay, position classifications are periodically reviewed and brought into line. In theory, this uniformity of classification and pay is in conflict with home rule, but the legislature that mandated it found that the law

"would bring about practical uniformity and still retain the basic concept of home rule."[17]

Pursuant to constitutional authorization, the state and the counties collectively negotiate labor contracts with the several governmental employee unions. To facilitate these negotiations, state law categorizes governmental employees and permits bargaining on differential wage and benefit issues. In negotiations, the state representative presents the combined governments' position. Each county is afforded one vote; the state, four. Thus, for agreement to be reached with a union, at least one of the counties must concur with the state.

The state retirement system covers both state and county employees. The counties are required to make annual payments into the system. Health and welfare plans established under state law cover all employees equally, whether county or state.

Because it can pass general laws applicable to the counties, the legislature has fixed the salaries of members of elected county councils, distinguishing between counties with less than and more than 100,000 population. County councils have the power to set the salaries of county department heads, deputies, and assistants when no provision is otherwise made by statute. The salary of any first deputy or first assistant to the head of any county department may not exceed 95 percent of the salary of such department head.[18] This attempt by the legislature to micromanage county government demonstrates the limitations of counties' "home rule" powers.

County charters (not state law) detail the specific procedures for the passing of county ordinances, but statutes do touch on some related aspects. For example, ordinances, amendments, resolutions, and bills must be published or advertised in newspapers of general circulation within the county concerned. Once ordinances are enacted, all counties with populations in excess of 100,000 must arrange them as a comprehensive ordinance code to be published every ten years. In addition, supplements to update the codes must be produced at least once a year.[19]

The administrative actions of both state and county officers and agencies are governed by state statute. A uniform information practices act applicable to the state and the counties requires governmental records to be open but also makes provision for the protection of personal records.[20] A state office oversees all agencies' compliance in both granting and denying access to records.

Each county may adopt its own rules with respect to public contracting and purchases, but the rules must be consistent with the requirements of the state public procurement code.[21] Under that law, a five-member board on which at least one county employee sits adopts rules governing the public procurement, management, control, and disposal of all goods, services, and construction. The counties must provide a process whereby citizens may object to county solicitations and county awards. A state hearing officer may void a county contract if procurement rules are not followed. Wage and hour provisions for all county public works are controlled by state law.

Economic Development

By ordinance, counties may create assessment districts, float district bonds to pay the costs of improvements (the benefits of which are to be shared by the landowners of the district), and then assess landowners to repay the bonds. This form of financing has been eclipsed by general public funding. Beyond this, the counties have been granted fairly broad authority to engage in economic and community development activities. They may use locally generated revenues for the purposes of developing industrial parks, establishing enterprise zones, renewing blighted areas, and making infrastructure improvements. Counties may float both economic development bonds and general-obligation bonds for solid waste processing and generation of electricity.

By statute, the state, as well as counties, may finance low- and moderate-income housing.[22] All of the counties have incorporated housing and community development agencies within their administrative structures. They have engaged in urban renewal projects for housing, commercial space, public parking, and infrastructure support.

Because the state has assumed responsibility for developmental matters of local concern, the scope of county development activities has been correspondingly constricted. The state's superior financial resources may be one reason for the intrusion. Another reason is the state has more public lands at its disposal for siting and exchanging private property slated for development, thus reducing out-of-pocket costs. Moreover, the legislature can override county zoning limitations and building codes by creating development authorities.

Under Hawaii's unique statewide zoning system, the state Land Use Commission effectively controls what land may be developed and how it may be used by categorizing all land as urban, rural, agricultural, or "conservation." Only about 4 percent of state land area is considered "urban"; only within this class do counties control development. Through boundary amendments—particularly for urban uses, special permits (such as those for golf courses in agricultural areas), and land reclassifications—the commission may facilitate or discourage particular projects, whether publicly or privately financed. More generally, the commission has been able to implement the state administration policy on development issues over which the counties have no veto; for example a prescribed percentage of all units in new housing projects must be "affordable."

It has been strongly contended that because of rapid urbanization, the counties ought to have more say about land-use matters. Such empowerment was only narrowly defeated at the last constitutional convention in 1978. Any such change would materially affect county development activities. The politics (both partisan and personal) of land decisions, as well as the state's intrusion into what otherwise would be the developmental domain of the county, constitutes fertile ground for conjecture in Hawaii.[23]

Fiscal Autonomy of Local Governments

Local Revenues

Hawaii's constitution sets no limits on the ability of the legislature to establish or revise local taxing policies, except those to do with the property tax. Counties may levy and utilize revenues from a property tax; motor vehicle tax (such as the wheel tax); entertainment and tourism tax (for example, room or ticket tax); and taxes on business, commerce, and industry (for example, licenses). Other revenues include liquid fuel taxes; motor vehicle weight taxes; liquor licenses and fees; parking meter fees; fines, forfeitures, and penalties; departmental earnings; and other licenses and fees, such as camping and building permits.

Before the change mandated by the 1978 constitutional convention transferred the real property tax to the counties, the central government administered the tax, assessing property and collecting revenues. Counties had authority to vary the yield of the property tax by setting rates within their jurisdiction. Even though the monies were returned to the counties, the state charged an administrative fee. Each side blamed the other for the burden of property taxes.

Now, however, the counties are solely responsible for assessment, rate setting, and collection, and they are clearly accountable to the voters. This situation has given rise to some complaints that the counties—which are reluctant to raise assessments or increase rates for fear of voter retaliation—have not fully taken responsibility for this new authority but instead continue to look to the legislature for other sources of income. Nevertheless, real property tax revenues make up a significant proportion of county revenues. For example, about half of total revenues in the counties of Maui and Hawaii come from property taxes.

Another major source of revenue for the counties comes from the transient accommodation tax (TAT), often referred to as the hotel room tax, which was instituted by the legislature in 1986. The state began sharing TAT revenues with the counties in 1991. A statutory formula currently in use allocates 44.8 percent of total TAT revenues to the counties, with each county receiving a different but statutorily set percentage of that amount.[24]

All of the revenues from gas and electricity franchise taxes, the county fuel tax, and the county motor vehicle weight tax that counties receive are earmarked for county highways. Although counties are authorized to raise revenues through the sale of county services to other jurisdictions or organizations, Honolulu city-county is probably the only county in a position to do so because of its much larger size; it provides real property tax services to the other counties, but this is not a major source

Table 1. Distribution of County Revenues in Hawaii, FY 1995 (in percent)

Source of revenue	County			
	Honolulu	Maui	Hawaii	Kauai
Liquid fuel tax	4.7%	3.9%	3.5%	2.0%
Motor vehicle weight tax	2.5	2.0	1.5	1.4
Real property tax	44.2	49.8	57.7	22.4
Other taxes	1.8	2.0	2.0	1.1
Federal grants	5.2	3.6	9.1	32.3
State grants	4.3	16.2	16.5	32.2
Departmental earnings	24.7	18.6	5.5	6.5
Other revenue	12.6	3.9	4.2	2.1

Source: *Government in Hawaii 1996, A Handbook of Financial Statistics* (Honolulu: Tax Foundation of Hawaii, 1996), 31.

Table 2. Distribution of County Expenditures in Hawaii, FY 1995 (in percent)

Function	County			
	Honolulu	Maui	Hawaii	Kauai
General government	10.0%	6.8%	11.7%	30.8%
Public saftey	19.6	19.4	35.5	11.4
Highways	3.0	4.6	3.3	3.1
Health, sanitation	16.2	8.4	7.0	2.5
Recreation	6.2	5.9	7.3	2.9
Debt retirement	15.2	7.7	7.9	4.4
Retirement and pensions	5.5	4.8	6.9	3.6
Cash capital improvements	1.1	24.1	1.3	24.4
Other	23.3	18.3	19.2	18.9

Source: *Government in Hawaii 1996, A Handbook of Financial Statistics* (Honolulu: Tax Foundation of Hawaii, 1996), 48.

of revenue. All of the counties obtain limited revenues from business, commerce, and industry licenses. Table 1 indicates the distribution of county revenues for fiscal 1995, the last year for which total cumulative data are available.

Under Article VII, section 12 of the constitution, the legislature may prescribe the manner in which political subdivisions issue general-obligation bonds, bonds stemming from special improvement statutes, and revenue bonds. The legislature may also authorize political subdivisions to issue special-purpose revenue bonds, provided that the county governing body finds issuance to be in the public interest. Hawaii is one of the few states that do not require a referendum for the approval of a local government bond issue. Long-term borrowing is not constitutionally restricted to the financing of capital improvements, although that is primarily its purpose.

There are no constitutional or statutory caps, lids, or limits on the amount of revenue that may be raised by the counties. However, there is a constitutional limit on bonded indebtedness based on the assessed value of real property within the county (a maximum of 15 percent).[25] This percentage no longer poses an effective monetary constraint, given the explosion of property values in Hawaii.

Besides the general-obligation bonds, the legislature has authorized the counties to incur specific forms of debt by issuing tax incremental bonds, economic development bonds, revenue bonds, and pollution-control special-purpose revenue bonds.[26]

Local Expenditures

Table 2 shows the distribution of county expenditures by function for fiscal 1995. There are no statutory limits on the amount of money a county may spend, but there are indirect limitations; for example, there is a maximum amount of bonded indebtedness that may be incurred. Moreover, counties are unable to impose new taxes on their own initiative, and the state earmarks certain tax revenues for county highways. In addition,

county spending is constrained by purchasing procedures and standards established in the state-prescribed public procurement code.

The constitution requires the state legislative auditor to audit the transactions, accounts, programs, and performance of all departments, offices, and agencies of the state and its political subdivisions.[27] In practice, each county passes legislation to hire an outside auditor to conduct that county's audit. These audit reports are transmitted to the state legislative auditor, but this is done by tradition; the language of the constitutional provision is vague on this procedure. State law establishes a common fiscal year. An accounting system installed under a 1923 act—and later modified by the state comptroller "in the best interest of the state and counties"[28]—provides a common basis for maintaining governmental fiscal reporting and accountability.

By adhering to certain statutory directions, Hawaii's counties may invest their funds and exercise control over the choice of investments.[29] Although there is no state-imposed requirement for balanced budgets, the counties themselves have stipulated balanced budgets in their charters.

State Government Grants-in-Aid to Localities

A significantly large share of state-to-county grant-in-aid has been derived from the transient accommodation tax. For example, for fiscal 1995 the total allocated to the four counties was $77.6 million. This figure does not represent the entire sum of monies collected by the state from the TAT but rather that portion which is allocated to the counties. County officials have discretion over how the funds received from the TAT will be expended and can determine which activities or projects will be funded and who the eligible recipients will be.

For fiscal 1995, the second largest allocation for the counties was for emergency medical services ($31.0 million) and the third largest was the wastewater loan program ($22 million). The fourth and fifth largest allocations were, respectively, $3.5 million for the prosecution of crimes (career criminal program and the victim witness program) and $2.5–$3 million for the program on aging.[30] For these allocations, the counties have only limited discretion over fund expenditures.

Unfunded Mandates

Unfunded mandates were a matter of concern at the last constitutional convention in 1978. A proposed amendment ratified by the voters requires the state to share in the cost of any new program or increase in the level of service under an existing program.[31] What this constitutional provision means remains unresolved however. Some in the executive branch have interpreted it to mean that the state must pay completely for any newly mandated program or increase in services. At the county level, there does not seem to be any current controversy regarding mandates, perhaps because the state so often assumes responsibility for major projects.

Access to Local Government

Local Elections

State law governs the conduct of all elections, both state and county, providing for the registration of voters, the qualifying of candidates, the preparation of ballots, the casting and tallying of ballots, and the certification of election results. The clerks in each county are responsible for maintaining and purging the electoral rolls and performing other delegated election duties. For combined elections, the state and counties share expenses; otherwise, the counties fund their own elections.

The provisions of county charters and ordinances relevant to elections serve to supplement and implement the overarching state election laws. For example, because the statutes do not specify voter recall of any official, the county must determine the eligibility of a recall petition naming one of the county's officers. The vote would be considered a county special election under state statute.

State laws that govern the qualifying of political parties for participation in partisan elections, and those that specify the nature and amount of permissible contributions and expenditures, are administered by state agencies and applied equally to political activity at the state and county levels. Although county sign laws are permitted, county attempts to regulate political signs have been held to violate the U.S. constitutional guarantee of freedom of speech.[32]

Citizen Controls over Actions of Local Officials

Hawaii has been reluctant to provide direct citizen participation at the state level through the initiative, referendum, or recall. County charters, however, do include these forms of "direct democracy" (although neither the city-county of Honolulu nor Maui County permits the use of the referendum to challenge county council action). Aside from the recall, several county charters also provide for impeachment as a means to hold county officials accountable. The exercise of the recall power has not been an idle threat, although since 1992 there has been only one effort to recall a Honolulu council member.[33]

A failed attempt by Honolulu city-county to use charter-provided initiative power in 1989 demonstrates the lack of home rule by counties in Hawaii. The adoption of a restrictive local zoning ordinance by initiative was invalidated because it was held to violate the state zoning statute. Moreover, the superior clause added to the constitution in 1968, which exempted county executive, legislative, and administrative structure and organization from state control, was held to be inapplicable.[34]

State law requires all public meetings and records, whether state or county, to be open. Some designated matters are exempt and may be considered at closed meetings.

State-Local Relations

Within a few years of Hawaii becoming a territory and until the end of World War II, the Republican Party dominated island politics, with the exception of Honolulu city-county. The platform of the Democratic Party long advocated home rule for the counties, but as a minority party the Democrats were relatively ineffective in achieving that objective. Because the membership of the territorial legislature was disproportionate, the centralization that had characterized government in Hawaii would not be materially modified for several years.

After World War II, the Republicans relinquished control over the central and county governments, and the legislature was reapportioned to reflect Hawaii's population more accurately. Although it was assumed that the Democratic Party would move to reverse centralization, it did not do so because it focused on expanding existing state functions and adding new ones. Because the neighbor islands lacked fiscal resources, some of the services they could not afford were transferred to the state.

The legislative approach to county government has long been characterized by close supervision and review, reflecting a lack of confidence in the ability of local governments to manage their own affairs.[35] Neither reversal of political party fortunes nor legislative redistricting has been sufficient to shake the ingrained structure and practices of Hawaii's political culture. The appeal for home rule has received greater attention in the state constitutional conventions than in the legislative halls.

The desire for more governmental decision making at the local level, which remains palpable in Hawaii, is evidence of dissatisfaction with the current processes of government. But rather than turn to the counties for educational reform, for example, the state Department of Education has allowed schools to experiment with different curriculums, modified yearly schedules, dress codes for students, physical plant maintenance, and various methods designed to attract parents to become more involved in school activities. In another scenario, however, it appears that through privatization and other means, state hospitals located in the various counties will be removed from the monolithic state health administration and be made more responsive to local needs and desires. In short, devolution and state contracting for services may hold more promise than grants of greater home rule to the counties.

Notes

1. The fifth "county" of Kalawao, which comprises the Hansen Disease Settlement on the island of Molokai, is administered by the state Department of Health.

2. The soil and water conservation districts are institutionally housed in the state Department of Land and Natural Resources. Each district is headed by a board of five directors, two of whom are appointed by the director of the department. The districts receive assistance from the U.S. Soil Conservation Service.

3. Although the U.S. Bureau of the Census classifies "cities and counties" as cities, Honolulu city-county is treated as any other county in Hawaii (Hawaii Revised Statutes, 1-22, 50-2). Besides Oahu, Honolulu city-county includes islands separated by hundreds of miles, because by law every island (such as French Frigate Shoals) not within the other counties is included within the city-county of Honolulu.

4. Hawaii Constitution, Article VIII, section 2.

5. *Fasi v. City and County of Honolulu*, 50 H. 277, 439 P.2d. 206 (1968).

6. Hawaii Constitution, Article VIII, section 2.

7. Hawaii Constitution, Article VIII, section 3.

8. Hawaii Constitution, Article VIII, section 5.

9. Hawaii Constitution, Article VIII, section 6.

10. *City and County of Honolulu v. Ariyoshi*, 67 H. 412, 689 P.2d. 757 (1984), 416.

11. *Kunimoto v. Kawakami*, 56 H. 582, 545 P.2d. 684 (1976), 585.

12. *Hawaii Government Employees' Association v. County of Maui*, 59 H. 65, 576 P.2d. 1029 (1978), 85.

13. Op. Att'y Gen. 62-11, 1962; Op. Att'y Gen. 87-1, 1987.

14. Hawaii Revised Statutes, Chapter 50.

15. Hawaii Revised Statutes, 132-3. With state approval, a county may adopt a less stringent fire code.

16. Elizabeth Kent, "The Erosion of Home Rule in Hawaii: *City and County of Honolulu v. Ariyoshi*," *University of Hawaii Law Review* 7 (1985): 507, 508.

17. Judy Stalling, "Article VII: Local Government," *Constitutional Convention Studies 1968* (Honolulu: Legislative Reference Bureau, 1968), 41.

18. Hawaii Revised Statutes, 46-23, 46-24.

19. Hawaii Revised Statutes, 46-2, 46-2.1, 46-2.2.

20. Hawaii Revised Statutes, 91-2; Chapters 91, 92.

21. Hawaii Revised Statutes, Chapter 103D.

22. Statutory provisions granted to counties include Act 48 of 1985 (development agreements); Act 267 of 1985 (tax increment financing for redevelopment agency); Act 78 of 1986 (enterprise zones); Act 226 of 1992 (community facilities special tax districts); and Act 282 of 1992 (impact fees for public improvements). When providing the counties with housing development powers, the legislature made it clear that its intention was to have the counties supplement, but not replace or reduce, state housing programs.

23. See, for example, George Cooper and Gavan Daws, *Land and Power in Hawaii, The Democratic Years* (Honolulu: Benchmark Books, 1985).

24. Hawaii Revised Statutes, 237D-6.5. As of 1999, the percentage of the portion of the TAT revenues going to the counties is 44.1 percent for Honolulu city-county, 18.6 percent for Hawaii county, 14.5 percent for Kauai county, and 22.8 percent for Maui county. These percentages were established independent of where the TAT was derived.

25. Hawaii Constitution, Article VII, section 13.

26. Hawaii Revised Statutes, Chapters 46, 48, 49, 48E.

27. Hawaii Constitution, Article VII, section 10.

28. Hawaii Revised Statutes, 40-2.

29. Hawaii Revised Statutes, 46-50.

30. Figures obtained through personal communication with the staff of Sen. Donna Ikeda, chair of the Senate Committee on Ways and Means, 19 July 1996.

31. Hawaii Constitution, Article VIII, section 5.

32. *Runyon v. Fasi*, 762 F. Supp. 280 (D. Haw. 1991).

33. The recall effort was unsuccessful because there were not enough signatures on the recall petition, which precluded the appearance of the question on the ballot.

34. *Kaiser Hawaii Kai Development Co. v. City and County of Honolulu*, 70 H. 480, 777 P.2d. 244 (1989).

35. Stalling, "Article VII," 3.

IDAHO

James B. Weatherby

Idaho is a rural, conservative state with more than 1,000 local governments serving only 1.2 million people. Although Idahoans strongly prefer local governments, they consistently have elected legislators who typically have given local governments little meaningful discretionary authority, especially in fiscal discretion. Cities and counties rely heavily on the property tax as their major tax source. Recent growth in the state, which is among the highest in the nation, has not necessarily moderated the state's politics. But it may be causing the legislature to loosen some of the restraints on local fiscal powers and to seriously reexamine the consequences of tight state control.

Governmental Setting

Idaho is a sectional state with three distinct regions and, according to some, three capitals: Boise, Idaho; Spokane, Washington; and Salt Lake City, Utah. Northern Idaho is geographically isolated from southern Idaho. Northern Idaho residents are more likely to identify with eastern Washington than with Boise and southern Idaho. Spokane is the trade and communication center for inland areas, which includes much of northern Idaho. Southeastern Idaho is more closely tied to northern Utah and Salt Lake City both religiously and economically.

Sectionalism historically has played a major role in this state. North and south are divided by time zones, mountains, rivers, religions, and cultures. Idaho is said to be a mix of individualistic and moralistic political cultures.[1] Northern Idaho has been influenced by the mining and timber industries that have given its politics more of an individualistic, laissez-faire orientation. Southern Idaho, with its rather large settlement of Mormons and midwestern farmers, has been more community oriented, better suited to the moralistic tradition that emphasizes civic participation as a duty and community over individual needs.[2]

By most standards, Idaho is conservative.[3] Even with the significant recent emigration from other western states (particularly California, Oregon, and Washington), the state remains very conservative; new residents seek a conservative refuge in Idaho, or the dominant culture has influenced them. Early in the state's history, voters strongly supported populist and Progressive Party candidates. The Democrats did well in the state earlier in the twentieth century. In the past several decades, however, the Republican Party clearly has dominated Idaho politics, even though the Democrats have had their stars (among them Sen. Frank Church and Govs. Cecil Andrus and John Evans). The

Democrats held the governor's office for twenty-four years (1971–1995), and, from 1950 until 1994, they had at least one of their own on the four-member congressional delegation.

Home rule in Idaho is more myth than reality, more the province of reelection rhetoric than concrete state policies. Part of this lack of discretionary authority can be explained by the dominance of major corporations in the state's past and current politics.[4] These corporations prefer to deal with one set of elected officials at the state level rather than hundreds at the local government level. Centralization of basic local government policy making is a major characteristic of state and local government relations in Idaho, especially in terms of local fiscal discretion.

The politics and impact of growth have played a major role in state-local government relations in Idaho. On a percentage basis, Idaho was among the nation's leaders in the 1990s in both population and economic growth. Much of Idaho's recent history has been influenced by property tax policy debates and proposals. The property tax has been a source of controversy for more than three decades. Idahoans' responses to public opinion polls on the subject have been relatively consistent: the property tax is hated and is seen as the least fair tax. Rapid growth, especially in Idaho's urban areas, has annually pushed assessed valuations higher and often resulted in major property tax increases. The fear of runaway increases in valuation and taxation has led to continued support for property tax relief and stricter property tax limitation measures.[5]

In a state with limited local discretionary authority, the legislature is the dominant player in state and local government relations and is annually visited by local officials seeking more authority or additional funding. No competent local governing body would engage in long-range planning without considering what the legislature might do to or for them. Generally, however, Idaho legislators have been beneficent rulers of local government. State-shared revenues have become more important in recent years, and gradually, some revenue constraints are being relaxed, allowing for mechanisms such as development impact and franchise fees.

Idaho's governor enjoys fairly strong executive powers, little of which is shared with other state-elected officials. Governors can succeed themselves but are now limited to two terms under the term limits initiative passed in 1994. Several have initiated policy affecting local government issues that relate to planning and zoning legislation, state revenue sharing, and implementation of the 1 percent initiative of 1978.

The state constitution has been amended many times but never has been completely revised. Most of the amendments of particular relevance to local governments concern local bonding authority. In the past four decades, all of the amendments have slightly increased local discretion, and none have provided further limitations. Even though Idaho voters have significant lawmaking authority through the initiative process, they cannot amend the constitution by initiative. Their only direct role is through ratification of a constitutional amendment proposed by the legislature or a constitutional convention.

Home Rule in Idaho

Historical Development

There have been intermittent efforts in Idaho's history to enact either constitutional or legislative home rule for cities. Municipal officials in the 1950s worked to pass a constitutional amendment to grant cities charter-making authority. Their efforts were highlighted in the 1955 *Municipal Yearbook* of the International City Managers Association. The Idaho Municipal League launched the most vigorous effort to adopt home rule; its "1955 proposal was defeated in the state senate by the narrow margin of a single vote."[6]

In the 1976 session a residual powers statutory home rule provision was enacted that granted cities authority to exercise powers and engage in programs not prohibited by or in conflict with the state constitution and the general laws of the state of Idaho.[7] Even though House Bill 422 was hotly debated and unnerving to many legislators, it did not deliver the substantial new municipal powers its sponsors intended. Cities were not freed from the need to find express authority in the state statutes or constitution for everything they wanted or needed to do. Rather than validating this rather symbolic attempt to expand municipal powers, the Idaho Supreme Court has reaffirmed Dillon's Rule in Idaho; that is, cities may engage only in services and programs that are expressly granted to them by the state legislature.[8] This narrow interpretation of local government powers is still exhibited in Idaho court decisions today.

Definition of Home Rule

Home rule in Idaho may be an oxymoron. Idaho cities and counties have been found to have the least amount of local discretionary authority, primarily because there is a lack of local fiscal discretionary authority.[9] There is no provision for general home rule powers in the Idaho Constitution. However, cities and counties enjoy a direct grant of constitutional home rule police powers. Idaho case law has supported the self-executing nature of this provision.[10] The constitution provides in Article 12, section 2, that "[a]ny county or incorporated city or town may make and enforce, within its limits, all such local police, sanitary and other regulations as are not in conflict with its charter or with the general laws."[11]

This broad grant of authority means that cities and counties do not need to look to the state legislature as a source of authority to extend their police powers as they would under the general rule or Dillon's Rule.[12] According to one municipal law expert, they have the

power to restrict and regulate, within the boundaries of the constitution, the conduct and property of individuals for the protection and promotion of the public health, safety, morals, and welfare. The police power includes the power to zone and regulate property as well as to enact other local regulatory ordinances to provide for the public health and safety by operating fire departments and sewer systems, to regulate traffic and other uses of the streets, etc.[13]

There are limitations, however. Local police policies and ordinances cannot be in conflict with state laws. Cities and counties are not given "a general grant of authority in all areas of municipal concerns," nor are they given taxing authority or proprietary powers.[14]

Structural Features

Of the 1,023 local governmental entities in Idaho in 1995, 200 were cities and 44 were counties. There were also 22 different types of special districts. The most significant perhaps were the 112 school districts, governed by an elected school board typically composed of five members and administered by a superintendent. There were 101 highway districts, 135 fire protection districts, 180 cemetery districts, 49 highway districts, 32 sewer districts, 46 sewer and water districts, 23 water districts, and many others.[15] Most of these special districts are created by citizens' petition and an election validating the creation of the district. They have their own independently elected boards or commissions that set policy, including budgeting and property tax levies.

There is a constitutional prohibition against the passage of special or local legislation.[16] However, there have been successful measures that have somewhat circumvented this prohibition. For example, in 1987 cities with more than 100,000 population were given tax increment financing authority. (Boise is the only such city in the state.) Since 1988, however, when the "small cities" bill was enacted for cities with less than 100,000 population, all cities have had that authority.[17]

Until 1996, only certain local governments in counties with more than 200,000 population (Ada County is the only such county) could impose development impact fees. After several attempts by local officials in the past several legislative sessions to expand this authority statewide, the 1996 legislature extended the authority to all cities, counties, and highway districts in the state.[18] The City of Boise (in Ada County) has imposed a parks fee; the Ada County Highway District has imposed a street fee; and Boise's close neighbor, Meridian, imposes a general facilities impact fee.

Another example of special or local legislation is the resort cities' local option taxation authority. "Resort" cities with fewer than 10,000 people may, subject to voter approval, impose local option sales, liquor-by-the-drink, and/or hotel-motel taxes. These taxes are a major source of revenue for these cities, including the two cities in the internationally renowned ski resort area of Sun Valley.[19]

Despite the use of special legislation, however limited, there is no classification in Idaho of incorporated places. The classification scheme that provided for villages and cities of the first and second class was abolished with the recodification of the municipal statutes in 1967. All incorporated places are cities by definition. Warm River, with eight people, is as much a city as Boise, with more than 160,000 people; both have basically the same authority and restrictions.

Some aspects of the municipal reform movement have influenced Idaho city government, but others have not. City officials run at large in nonpartisan elections. Only three of the state's 200 cities use the council-manager form of government. Idahoans, reflecting their populist heritage, prefer to vote for many of their local governmental officials, even though most cities in neighboring states use the council-manager form. Idaho city officials recognize the need for professional city assistance; about twenty of Idaho's largest cities have a city administrator, who performs many of the functions of a city manager.

Only two cities have been incorporated in the past twenty-five years, even though there has been significant expansion in the number of other local taxing districts. The municipal incorporation process is relatively straightforward, with fairly significant limitations. Areas petitioning the county commissioners to be incorporated must be located one mile or more from the limits of an existing city. The number of miles beyond the city limits that require consent of the city council is determined on a per capita basis. For example, a city of 10,000 people has veto power over proposed incorporations within two miles of its boundaries. A city of 25,000 has control up to four miles.[20]

Although their fiscal powers are restricted, Idaho cities have significant annexation powers.[21] Subject only to general density, contiguity, and area of city impact requirements, Idaho cities

may unilaterally annex adjacent territories by ordinance. There are no referendum requirements, and there is no appeal process short of litigation.

Cities and counties are treated differently in the Idaho Constitution. County government structure is set forth in considerable detail, whereas there are very few references to cities. County governments have been constrained since statehood (in 1890) by the constitutional provisions requiring a uniform "one size fits all" structure. All counties since statehood have been and are governed by a three-member board of county commissioners and an entire slate of constitutionally elected row officers, including clerk, treasurer, assessor, sheriff, coroner, and prosecuting attorney.

In 1994 Idaho voters approved a constitutional amendment allowing the legislature to authorize optional forms of county government. In 1996 the Idaho legislature implemented the constitutional amendment by enacting two measures that grant significant flexibility to local voters to change their county form of government. One provides for a county executive, county manager, or variations on the existing commission form. The other allows for a charter commission that could make major changes to the structure of county government.[22]

Cities may own property or facilities beyond their boundaries for proprietary purposes, including airports and water, sewer, and other facilities. Moreover, a city may annex facilities that are not contiguous to the city. Cities are mandated by the Local Planning Act of 1975 to negotiate "areas of city impact" outside city limits. As part of this negotiation process, cities and counties determine whose developmental regulations will apply within the "urban fringe area" and how far that authority extends into the unincorporated area of the county. As a matter of practice, once the area of the impact is established by mutual agreement, the county adopts the new zoning regulations as part of the county ordinance.

There is also a much earlier provision in the Idaho Code that extends legislative (primarily plat review authority) and police powers beyond cities' jurisdictional limits. Recent attorneys general opinions have held that this section of the code (50-1306) is probably unconstitutional and in violation of Article 12, section 2 of the Idaho Constitution that gives a city police powers only "within its limits."

Functions of Local Government

Functional Responsibilities

Cities are municipal corporations, voluntarily organized to benefit the citizenry they are created to serve. Accordingly, Idaho cities are not mandated to provide any particular types of services or levels of service. However, most provide an entire package of municipal services including street maintenance and police, fire, water, sewer, and sanitation services.

Counties serve two basic functions. In their traditional role as administrative arms of state government, they perform functions such as property tax and court administration and law enforcement. Moreover, they maintain vital statistics, record land-ownership and debt records, and administer certain welfare programs. Counties also provide general government services such as public works, planning, parks, recreation, and solid waste disposal.

The Intergovernmental Cooperation Act of 1968, or joint exercise of powers statute, is an important tool that promotes mutual aid agreements, the sharing of equipment and facilities, and contracting for important local government functions such as law enforcement. Most of the contracting is among local governments—that is, cities, counties, highway districts, and fire protection districts. The act provides that all of the parties entering into such cooperative agreements must be able to do separately what they agree to do cooperatively. For example, in the investment of public funds, many smaller local governments participate in the state treasurer's investment pool rather than trying to invest the monies themselves.[23]

Administrative Discretion

Despite the fact that local control is limited in Idaho, local governments enjoy considerable discretion regarding administrative matters. Ordinance-making authority is largely left to local discretion, with the exception of public hearings requirements for the enactment of certain ordinances.

With the exception of the collective bargaining requirement for firefighters and school teachers, there are few other state personnel mandates. There are, for example, no merit system standards, no residency requirements for local employees, no salary schedules, and no binding arbitration mandates.

Cities and counties are required to undertake comprehensive planning, adopt zoning ordinances, and negotiate areas of city impact. These are principally procedural requirements; the substance of policy making is left to the local governmental entities, and there are no explicit penalty provisions for noncompliance.

Some of the decisions in the budgeting process are determined locally. There are no expenditure limits on local government budgets, but there are property tax limits. State law and the constitution, however, require that budgets be balanced and that a summary of the revenues and expenditures for the previous year as well as the new fiscal year be published for comparison purposes in the public hearing notice for the budget. Cities and counties are required to have annual audits that must be filed with the legislative services office, but there is virtually no state oversight beyond collecting the documents.

Competitive bid limits for public works contracts have always been a source of controversy and frustration to local officials. Since 1975, competitive bidding has been required for purchases exceeding $5,000. Despite significant declines in purchasing power since 1975, the requirement has changed little over the years. Cities and counties argue with the public works contractors association about how much local government capital improvement should be done by the local governments' own employees and how much should be contracted out to the private sector. Cities and counties are required to contract with the lowest responsible bidder. If the bids are comparable in quality, preference must be given to the bidder having a significant economic presence in Idaho.[24] Most professional services (legal, auditing, engineering, and so forth) are excluded from such limitations.

Cities have significant planning and zoning powers and are not subject to stringent state growth management mandates. The passage of the Local Planning Act in Idaho in 1975 mandated planning and required cities and counties to take into account a number of socioeconomic factors in addition to physical land-use planning considerations. Negotiations determine whose developmental regulations will apply in the affected area. This joint planning requirement is designed to provide a smooth transition for areas that could conceivably be annexed by a city.[25]

Economic Development

In terms of economic development, Idaho's local governments appear to be disadvantaged by having only a limited number of incentives. Not only is their use of the property tax severely restricted by state law, but there is no authority for local governments in other states to offer enterprise zones or tax exemptions that might enhance economic development prospects. Local governments can issue industrial revenue bonds (IRB) as a result of a 1982 constitutional amendment to Article VIII, section 4, which prohibited cities and counties from lending or pledging credit. Cities may create tax increment financing (TIF) districts as part of their urban renewal agency function. Industrial revenue bond and tax increment financing may be created without a vote of the people; both have been used to attract industry to the state.[26]

Local governments may also issue general-obligation bonds to be redeemed by property tax levies or revenue bonds to be repaid by project incomes. For improvement purposes, cities may also impose an assessment fee on downtown businesses, a majority of which must assent to the creation of such a district. The purpose of the district is to promote economic activity and beautification of central business districts.

Fiscal Autonomy of Local Governments

Local Revenues

Local governments rely on three major revenue sources: property taxes, fees and service charges, and intergovernmental aid (there are four major state aid programs). Some cities have experimented with innovative fee systems, but they have not fared well in taxpayer lawsuits. Under the cities' statutory home rule authority and constitutional police powers, there have been attempts to impose innovative financing schemes such as fire flow fees for fire protection and street maintenance fees on all properties, including tax-exempt properties. These fees have been struck down by the Idaho Supreme Court. Echoing Dillon's Rule, the supreme court ruled in *Brewster v. Pocatello* that even though the fee schedule was well conceived there was no specific statutory authority for such an innovation.[27]

Most of the fees and service charges benefit enterprise funds such as water, sewer, and sanitation. Such fees constitute a significant portion of most municipal budgets but have little relationship to the funding of general governmental operations and services. There are some fees for recreation, libraries, and some capital improvements.

The Idaho state and local government tax structure is relatively balanced with fairly equal reliance on three major revenue sources: state income tax, state sales tax, and local property tax. At the local level, however, there is only the property tax. The property tax funds most of the operating budgets of cities and counties

Some historic limitations on levy rates have been adjusted over the years, but others have remained in place since the early days of statehood. In most cases, these limits are high enough that annual adjustments in assessed valuation make them largely irrelevant as deterrents to property tax increases.

In addition to the individual statutory levy limits, a 3 percent cap was imposed in 1995 on the property tax portion of local governments' operating budgets. Growth in the tax base allows for additional budgetary expansion and is perceived by local officials as a means of obtaining expanded levying authority. Growth is calculated by adding to the 3 percent limitation an amount equal to the percentage increase in the local government's tax base. This expansion is based on increases resulting from either new construction or annexation of adjacent properties into the taxing district. However, "artificial" increases stemming from reappraisal or inflation cannot be used for budget expansion purposes.[28]

Idaho is a low-debt state. Few general-obligation bonds are issued because most bonds are constitutionally required to be approved by a two-thirds majority vote.[29] Also, total general-obligation bonded indebtedness may not exceed 2 percent of the assessed market value. Those bonds that do pass are for school buildings and sometimes pass only after having been submitted to the voters in several elections. Revenue bonds have a much better chance of passage. They are redeemed from the revenues of a given enterprise (such as an airport, water, or sewer facility), and most are subject to a simple majority approval requirement.

There is, however, significant ambiguity in the constitutional requirement that general-obligation bonds must receive a two-thirds vote of approval. Some bonds are issued without a vote because the constitution also provides an exception for "the ordinary and necessary expenses authorized by the general laws of the state."[30] An increasing number of improvements are being financed under this constitutional provision. Bonds may also be issued without a vote for tax increment financing, local improvement districts, and industrial revenue purposes.

Local Expenditures

There is no state-level collection of local expenditure data. Budgets are scrutinized for property tax–levying purposes, but the financial reports and audits do not receive the same kind of analysis. Municipal services are supported primarily by property taxes, intergovernmental aid (state and federal), and user fees and service charges. The largest share of city budgets is allocated to streets, police and fire protection, parks and recreation, and utility operations (for water, sewer, sanitation, and so forth.).

Like cities, counties do not have educational responsibilities but have many of the functions typical of America's counties. As with cities, the property tax is the major source of county revenue, along with intergovernmental aid and fees. Significant portions of county expenditures support health and hospital, county road, public welfare, and law enforcement services.

Since 1976, the city and county fiscal year has begun on October 1. The fiscal year was changed from a calendar year to better align the taxing and spending cycles. Under the old system, local governments budgeted their expenditures in one year and received the revenues in the next to "fund" their prior year's expenditures. The passage of the Cash Basis Act of 1976 mandated the change and allowed cities and counties to carry over fund balances to maintain their operations on a cash basis.[31]

Cities and counties are required to adopt balanced budgets, hold public hearings, and enact appropriation ordinances before the beginning of the fiscal year. Monies may be expended only for public purposes. There are constitutional prohibitions against making expenditures that benefit private groups and individuals, including nonprofit associations.[32] However, the Idaho Supreme Court has ruled that dues to local government associations are legal.[33]

Appropriation ordinances must be passed before the beginning of the fiscal year. The amount of the ordinance cannot be greater than the proposed budget. Copies of the ordinance are submitted to the secretary of state's office. These ordinances may be amended during the fiscal year when unanticipated increases in state or federal grants, additional revenues in enterprise funds, or any other non–property tax revenues are received. The process for amending the appropriation ordinance is the same as that for budget adoption. Cities may exceed budgeted amounts for emergencies caused by a casualty, accident, or act of nature.[34]

State Government Grants-in-Aid to Localities

Cities and counties receive substantial state assistance from the state sales tax, highway user revenues, and state liquor profits. The total amount from these sources was $133,186,000 in fiscal 1995, or 44.5 percent of total city and county property tax revenues ($299,224,000). Among cities and counties in eleven western states, Idaho cities ranked sixth in percentage reliance on state aid, and Idaho counties ranked seventh. There are essentially no strings attached to state aid; it can be used as other local revenues are used; and there is little state monitoring. Highway distribution account monies are the exception. They are dedicated for local transportation purposes, and their expenditures must be annually reported to the Idaho Transportation Department. Cities and counties received approximately $40 million annually from this source.

State-shared revenue from two programs is allocated to cities and counties from state sales tax revenues. The city-county revenue-sharing program is funded by 7.75 percent of total sales tax collections earmarked for that purpose. Current allocations are approximately $50 million (more than double the amount of federal revenue-sharing dollars that Idaho cities and counties received in the early 1980s). Revenue-sharing dollars are equally divided between cities and counties. The city portion is allocated on a market valuation and per capita basis and represents approximately 17 percent of what cities generate in local property taxes. Each county receives a flat $35,000 allocation, and the balance is distributed among all counties on a per capita basis. This amounts to about 14 percent of counties' total property tax revenues.[35]

The inventory replacement program is also funded by sales tax revenues; it was established with the creation of the sales tax in 1965. The package deal that was struck between the affected business interests and state policy makers stipulated that if the sales tax were enacted, the local property taxes on business inventories would be repealed. To replace the lost property tax revenues, a percentage of sales tax revenues was dedicated for replacement purposes. Currently, local governments receive 6 percent of total sales tax collections from this program. The amount to cities and counties is approximately $20 million annually.[36]

A fairly significant source of state-shared revenues to local government comes from the profits of the state-controlled liquor dispensary. Cities and counties receive a portion of the 15 percent state liquor surcharge after certain allocations are made to state agencies. Currently, they receive approximately $10 million annually.

Unfunded Mandates

Putting a stop to unfunded federal and state mandates was a major priority of both local government associations in the 1990s. Most of the mandates that frustrate city officials are federal mandates, although it is sometimes difficult to determine which level of government sets the mandates, particularly when it comes to environmental mandates. County governments struggle with some of the same mandates as cities, in addition to their traditional state-mandated functions as administrative arms of state government.

Labor relations mandates are significant. Cities that have full-time paid firefighters are required to engage in collective bargaining with firefighter unions. School districts have the same requirement with teacher organizations. This mandate has led to strikes, mediation, and fact finding efforts. However, Idaho law does not require mandatory binding arbitration. Idaho local budgets are set by elected officials, not outside arbitrators. No such collective bargaining mandates are extended to other local government employees.

Other than the bargaining mandates, local governments are not required to adopt personnel policies, but they must adhere to the state's Ethics in Government Act of 1990, which defines conflict of interest and requires full disclosure.[37] Ethics legislation limits gifts to public officials, prohibits officials from using their position for personal gain, and does not allow officials to hold incompatible offices.

Local governments must participate in the State Workers Compensation Program and must maintain their participation in the Idaho Public Employees Retirement System once they have elected to participate. They are not required to join, however.

Access to Local Government

Local Elections

Public opinion surveys in Idaho show that local governments are the most trusted and are considered to be the most responsive. Some of this favorable ranking may be attributed to the fairly open process at the local level. State mandates that require open meetings and access to public records may help improve the local government image.

With the exception of school districts, all local government elections are held as part of the state consolidated election schedule. The intent of this consolidation is to promote turnout and the visibility of all elections. Before the passage of this legislation in 1993, a local election could have been held almost any time during the calendar year. How candidates may qualify and the procedures for voter registration and campaign finance reporting for larger cities and counties are clearly set forth in statute. Idaho is one of only a handful of states that provides for same-day voter registration; individuals may register at the polls on election day.

Citizen Controls over Actions of Local Officials

Typical of those of most western states, Idaho's constitution and statutes authorize initiative, referendum, and recall elections. The initiative and referendum are rarely used at the local level. The recall provisions are used fairly often, even though amendments in the early 1980s made it increasingly difficult for citizens to recall a local official. All of these "direct democracy" tools require signatures on a petition exceeding 20 percent of the total number of registered voters at the last general election. Initiatives and referendums require only a simple majority for passage. A successful recall effort needs majority approval plus more votes approving recall than the official being recalled received at his or her last election.

Idaho's Open Meeting Laws define what an official meeting is and state that elected officials have no authority to make decisions outside these lawfully held meetings. There are notice requirements for both regular and special meetings and restrictions on the types of subjects a governing body may use to justify an executive session.[38] Open records legislation require "that all public records in Idaho are open at all reasonable times for inspection (and copying) except as expressly provided otherwise by statute."[39] Requests for most information must be responded to within three working days.

State-Local Relations

Public opinion surveys document Idahoans' high trust and confidence levels in local government. But their legislators have not always shared this trust and confidence in local government; especially in terms of taxation powers, home rule is more myth than reality. Operationally speaking, however, Idaho cities are similar to or are even less burdened by state controls than home rule cities in some other states. Special legislation is used typically to expand municipal powers. Other than certain procedural requirements, there are no major mandates for growth management. There are few restrictions on municipal annexation authority. Personnel mandates are minimal.

Growth is transforming the state's physical landscape and may very well change its intergovernmental landscape. Slowly and perhaps inexorably, rigid fiscal restrictions are being relaxed. There is serious legislative discussion about the importance of encouraging more state and local partnerships, the need to strengthen local governments, and the value of creating a forum for the discussion of intergovernmental issues.

One wildcard in the future of state-local relations is the state initiative process. The frequency and continuing support for statewide property tax limitation initiatives could undermine much of the limited local control governments enjoy today. There is a real irony here: although the state representative body is slowly granting more local discretion, one of the tools of "direct democracy" could take it away in one fell swoop.

Notes

1. Daniel Elazar, *American Federalism: A View from the States*, 2d ed. (New York: Harper & Row, 1984).

2. James Weatherby, "The 1994 Idaho Election: The Pendulum Swings Farther to the Right" (paper presented at the annual meeting of the American Political Science Association, Chicago, 3 September 1995), 13.

3. See the *Idaho Policy Survey, 1995* (Boise: Survey Research Center, Boise State University, 1995).

4. Because Boise is headquarters for major national and international corporations, it is also the center of state and local governmental power. The Boise valley may be the only metropolitan area in the country under one million population that is home to four major national or international corporations: Alberstons, Inc.; Boise Cascade Corporation; J. R. Simplot; and Morrison Knudsen. It is also home for Micron Technology, Zilog, T. J. International, and a major division of Hewlett-Packard.

5. See *Idaho Policy Surveys* conducted by Boise State University's Survey Research Center from 1989 to 1996.

6. James Weatherby, Michael C. Moore, and Lorna Jorgensen, *Idaho Municipal Source Book* (Boise: Association of Idaho Cities and Public Affairs Program, Boise State University, 1993), 3.

7. Idaho Code, section 50-301.

8. Weatherby, Moore, and Jorgensen, *Idaho Municipal Source Book.*

9. See James Weatherby and Stephanie L. Witt, *The Urban West: Managing Growth and Decline* (New York: Praeger, 1994). This lack of local discretionary authority was documented in a 1980 survey sponsored by the U.S. Advisory Commission on Intergovernmental Relations (ACIR). In a ranking of the degree of autonomy exercised by cities and counties throughout the country, Joseph Zimmerman found that Idaho cities and counties had the least discretionary authority of all. See *State and Local Roles in the Federal System* (Washington, D.C.: ACIR, 1982).

10. Michael C. Moore, "The Idaho Constitution and Local Governments—Selected Topics," *Idaho Law Review* 31 (1995): 417–460. See also *Rowe v. City of Pocatello*, 70 Idaho 343 (1950); and *State v. Robbins*, 59 Idaho 279 (1938).

11. Idaho Constitution, Article 12, section 2. That there is not a comma between *local* and *police* in this excerpt implies that this is only a police home rule authority rather than a thoroughgoing home rule authority. Some have misread this. In the late 1970s, John Evans, then lieutenant governor, made a speech to the annual conference of the Association of Idaho Cities. In reaction to the speech, a chief deputy attorney general wrote that Idaho cities and counties do indeed have home rule authority. In his letter, he quoted Article 12, section 2, including a comma between *local* and *police*. His letter sparked a controversy that led to one of the most extensive formal opinions of an attorney general and a statutory home rule bill for Idaho cities in 1976.

12. Dillon's Rule is named after Iowa State Supreme Court Justice John Dillon, who wrote in a mid–nineteenth century case that cities could engage only in those services and programs that were expressly granted to them by the state legislature. In short, cities were creatures of the state. They possessed no implied powers beyond those specifically accorded to them by their state (*City of Clinton v. Cedar Rapids and Missouri River Railroad Co.*, 1868.)

13. Michael C. Moore, "Cities—Their Nature and Powers," in *Idaho Municipal Source Book*, ed. Weatherby, Moore, and Jorgensen, 6.

14. Michael C. Moore, "Municipal Home Rule in Idaho," *Idaho Law Review* 12 (1976): 168.

15. *1995 Annual Report* (Boise: Idaho State Tax Commission, State of Idaho, 1995).

16. Idaho Constitution, Article 3, section 19.

17. Even though Boise was granted the authority first, the authority for small cities is much broader. Consequently, Boise had its legislation repealed in 1990 and amended so that the city could share in the benefits of the small cities bill. (Apparently there are benefits to having a trailer bill that is roughly patterned after sweeping new legislative authority. The first bill is sometimes more closely scrutinized than the second.)

18. Idaho Session Laws, Chapter 366 (HB 789).

19. Idaho Code, sections 50-1043–1049.

20. Idaho Code, section 50-101.

21. Idaho Code, Title 50, Chapter 2.

22. See House Concurrent Resolution 17 of the 1994 Idaho Session Laws, 1498–1499, and Chapters 129 and 283 in the 1996 Idaho Session Laws.

23. Idaho Code, Title 67, Chapter 23; section 63-2328.

24. Idaho Code, section 50-341.

25. See Idaho's Local Planning Act in title 67, Chapter 65 of the Idaho Code.

26. Idaho Code, Title 50, Chapters 27 and 29.

27. *Brewster v. Pocatello,* 115 Idaho 502 (1988).

28. Idaho Code, section 63-2220A.

29. Idaho Constitution, Article 8, section 3.

30. Ibid.

31. James Weatherby, "The Cash Basis Act of 1976: Triumph of City-County Cooperation," *Western City Magazine* (1976), 16–17.

32. Idaho Constitution, Article 8, section 4; Article 12, section 4.

33. The planning for the new fiscal year typically begins in the spring, when the budget request forms are sent out to the departments. The budget is put together in late spring and early summer, with formal public hearings held in late July and August. Some of the larger entities like the City of Boise and Ada County hold additional hearings and broadcast their budget presentations on the local access channel. Budgets are typically prepared in line-item format. However, some of the larger cities and counties have utilized program budgeting formats and incorporated strategic planning in their budgeting processes.

34. Idaho Code, sections 50-1003, 50-1106.

35. Idaho Code, section 63-3638(e).

36. Idaho Code, section 63-3638(g).

37. Idaho Code, Title 59, Chapter 7.

38. Idaho Code, section 67-2341.

39. Idaho Code, section 9-338(1).

ILLINOIS

Richard Wandling

Although home rule has been available since 1971 to Illinois municipalities and counties, either automatically on the basis of population or by referendum, only about 10 percent of municipalities and just one county have home rule. Home rule units have a broad grant of powers, but constitutional and statutory limits exist. State government may preempt home rule authority, and it has done so on local sales tax authority and numerous times on local licensing powers. The legislature has not authorized a local income tax for home rule units. Although they have a measure of flexibility in certain areas, the remainder of Illinois's 7,000-plus local governments are subject to Dillon's Rule; that is, they may engage only in services and programs that are expressly granted to them by the state legislature. Non–home rule units have experienced incursions on their fiscal autonomy as a result of property tax caps first enacted by the legislature in 1991. The unfunded mandates issue has produced some tense state-local relations, in part because the legislature has repeatedly exempted the state from reimbursement responsibilities.

Governmental Setting

Illinois is the sixth most populous state and is among the leading states on wealth measures such as per capita income. Its diverse economy includes strong sectors in service, manufacturing, and agriculture. Although the competitiveness of its mining industry in its southern region has declined noticeably, the state continues to be among the nation's leading agricultural states, particularly in corn and soybeans. Chicago, still the state's flagship city, is the home of four major financial exchanges, including the high-profile Board of Trade. Moreover, the Chicago metropolitan area is one of the country's top exporters.

Almost two-thirds of Illinois's residents live in the six counties of the metropolitan Chicago region (Cook, DuPage, Lake, Will, Kane, and McHenry Counties). Although declining in population, Chicago remains the population anchor of this region, with 2.7 million residents; most of Illinois's cities with populations over 50,000 (eighteen out of twenty-four) are found in this six-county region.[1] The closest rivals to Chicago's population standing in the state are in the 100,000–145,000 population range; that is, the rapidly growing suburban areas of Aurora and Naperville, along with the downstate cities of Peoria, Rockford, and Springfield. The Chicago area also contributes significantly to the ethnic and racial diversity of Illinois, and diversity is making inroads into the traditionally homogeneous suburban counties.[2]

Illinois achieved statehood in 1818, and its formative political development owes much to four groups of nineteenth-century settlers: Appalachians in southern Illinois; New Englanders in the northern part of the state; former residents of Pennsylvania, Ohio, and Indiana who located to central Illinois; and large numbers of immigrants who facilitated the rapid growth of Chicago. Although relations among these groups were not always smooth, an underlying outlook on the legitimate role of government took root. Politics came to be seen as an arena in which to respond to, mediate, or broker sometimes competing definitions of self-interest, whether the participants be individuals, businesses, or even regions of the state.[3] This self-interested orientation toward politics and government correlated with an important Illinois value—an emphasis on local control.

Debate over great issues tends to be muted in Illinois, and state public policy is not known for being entrepreneurial or innovative. Pragmatic questions about the distribution of benefits and costs tend to dominate public discourse. The "who benefits?" and "who pays?" concerns have been particularly evident in efforts to resolve regional differences.[4] Three key regions in Illinois are the City of Chicago; the Chicago-area suburbs, particularly those in the five "collar" counties; and the geographically spacious area popularly known as Downstate.

During Illinois's history, each of the three regions has been at the center of power in the state. The most recent power shift has been from Democratic-dominated Chicago to the suburban "collar" counties, particularly DuPage County, the state's Republican Party stronghold. James Nowlan, one of the state's most insightful political analysts, notes that Illinois has a long history of regional conflicts that have focused on three pragmatic issues—roads and public improvements, schools, and taxes.[5] Yet, no one region has the political clout to dominate policy making; coalition building among regions and other interests is necessary.

The Illinois state legislature (the General Assembly) consists of full-time professionals known for addressing issues from the standpoint of partisanship, regional interests, and constituency demands. The Democratic and Republican Parties are competitive, and divided control of state government is the rule. The General Assembly's majority and minority leaders have centralized power, aided by large campaign funds used to influence "targeted" legislative races.[6] These campaign funds are fortified by generous donations from powerful interest groups that operate in an environment of highly permissive campaign finance law.[7] Although a campaign finance reform movement has emerged, significant changes are unlikely. Interest groups and their lobbyists are important in the legislative process. The concerns of local governments are represented through organizations such as the Illinois Municipal League, Metro Counties of Illinois, Township Officials of Illinois, and the Suburban Mayors Action Coalition.

The Illinois governor introduces the budget and may shape legislation through a generous set of veto powers, including line-item, amendatory, and reduction vetoes. Gubernatorial success, however, normally means bargaining and negotiating—"deal making," in Illinois parlance—with the legislature's leaders. Illinois governors can shape bureaucratic policy making by appointing top administrators of 22 administrative code departments and making appointments to about 300 boards and commissions, about 30 of which are very important in state governance. The executive branch, however, has built-in centrifugal forces, since voters choose the state's attorney general, secretary of state, comptroller, and treasurer.

Although Illinois's judiciary reflects the reform model of a unified court system, the legislature and public are content to elect the state's circuit, appellate, and supreme court judges through partisan elections. A coalition of law school deans and professors and "good government" advocates has been frustrated in its quest for merit plan selection. With respect to its policy-making role, Illinois courts tend to avoid high-profile issues and have been characterized as "generally conservative and nonactivist" in Progressive causes such as school funding; the courts have not been as reluctant toward highly politicized issues such as redistricting, however.[8]

Home Rule in Illinois

Historical Development

Illinois adopted its fourth and present constitution in 1970. Under the 1970 constitution's predecessor, the long-lived 1870 constitution, local government debt was limited to no more than 5 percent of total assessed valuation. A requirement to have uniform tax assessment precluded special service areas. Creating new local government units became a favored approach to meet service demands and bypass debt and assessment limitations.[9] Municipalities during this period were heavily regulated by state law, and state courts adopted a narrow Dillon's Rule interpretation of local powers.[10] Sentiment for home rule, however, was evident early in the twentieth century, when Progressives and Chicago officials lobbied for home rule at Illinois's failed 1920 constitutional convention.[11] In the 1950s, Chicago formed a Home Rule Commission that issued a landmark report emphasizing statutory changes to improve Chicago's governmental structure along with its service, police, and revenue powers.[12]

The 1970 constitution contains a "local government" article (Article VII) that addresses home rule powers. Although home rule came late to Illinois, the home rule section was described at its adoption as "one of the most liberal found in any state constitution."[13] Under the 1970 constitution, automatic home rule is granted to municipalities with populations greater than 25,000. The grant is less extensive for counties; home rule status is available only to counties that have a popularly elected chief executive. When the new constitution took effect in 1971, only Cook County had such an officer; thus, it joined the original sixty-seven municipalities with automatic home rule status.[14]

Municipalities with populations of 25,000 or less may elect through referendum to exercise home rule powers. Counties other than Cook County were given the opportunity to become home rule counties through the County Executive Act of 1971, which gave county voters the opportunity to adopt home rule by adopting the county executive form of government. Finally, any home rule unit—whether county or municipality—may elect by referendum to abandon home rule status.

As of 1998, Illinois had 142 home rule municipalities, 100 of which were located within the six-county metropolitan Chicago area. Seventy-eight municipalities have achieved home rule by referendum, and only 4 municipalities have voted to abandon home rule. The Illinois Municipal League, the flagship association for Illinois cities and villages, has played an active role in supporting home rule municipalities through its Committee of Home Rule Attorneys, which has published numerous editions of its report on home rule legislative and judicial developments.[15]

Cook County remains Illinois's only home rule county. During the 1970s, nine counties held referendums (two of the counties did so twice) to become home rule units by adopting the county executive form of government, but all referendums failed.[16] More recently, as a result of a 1985 change in the County Executive Act, Will County voted in 1988 by referendum to adopt the county executive form without home rule status.[17] Will County remains the state's only county with the county executive form of government.

Definition of Home Rule

Home rule units are given a broad grant of powers in the Illinois Constitution. Home rule units are assumed to possess powers unless otherwise limited by the constitution or statutory law.[18] Municipal attorneys in home rule jurisdictions do not have to search the statutes to identify and confirm the authority to act. In fact, one legal expert points to Chicago's confidence in its authority by noting that the "apparent philosophy in Chicago city government is that everything is home rule."[19]

The Illinois Constitution (Article VII, section 6) directs state courts to be generous toward home rule authority by asserting that "powers and functions of home rule units shall be construed liberally." In the first decade of home rule, the Illinois Supreme Court established a pattern of supporting home rule in landmark rulings, although the court has not always ruled in favor of home rule units.[20] Today, legal issues affecting home rule municipalities, along with non–home rule cities and villages, are monitored by the Illinois Municipal League's legal department, which files *amicus curiae* briefs and informs league members of judicial developments.

Non–home rule municipalities and counties remain subject to Dillon's Rule, but they share some general powers with home rule units. General powers granted by the constitution include (1) the power of special assessment subject to legislative restrictions; (2) the right to adopt, alter, or repeal governmental forms by referendum and to make provisions for government officers; and (3) the power to establish special service areas. Although only one out of ten Illinois municipalities and only one county are designated home rule, these jurisdictions include at least two-thirds of Illinois's residents.[21] This makes home rule governments a force to be reckoned with in the state legislature. The formation in 1994 of the Illinois Municipal League Non–Home Rule Committee represents an acknowledgment of this demographic and political reality.

Home rule units face both specific and general constitutional limits on the exercise of their powers. That home rule units must seek authority from the state legislature to license for revenue and to tax income, earnings, or occupations exemplifies a specific limit. The general limits on home rule powers often are referred to as the "preemption" provisions. Major ways by which the legislature may preempt home rule include:

1. The tax power is subject to state limitation or denial with a three-fifths vote of the elected membership of both houses.

2. The state may declare a matter to be its exclusive jurisdiction by a simple majority of the elected membership of both legislative houses, as long as the exclusive jurisdiction claim does not concern a taxing power or powers concurrently exercised with municipal governments.

3. The General Assembly may place limits on debt incurred by home rule units beyond thresholds specified for three population categories.[22]

Since 1977, laws that limit or deny home rule powers must explicitly identify their preemptive intent. The Home Rule Note Act of 1992 requires that bills that deny or limit the powers of home rule units include an estimate of their impact. One of the legislature's most prominent examples of preemption concerns municipal licensing of businesses and professions. There are at least forty areas of preemption of municipal licensing powers, and the state municipal league views the numerous preemptions of licensing powers as a "great threat" to local autonomy.[23] "Partial preemption" also has become an issue as a result of a 1993 Illinois Supreme Court ruling permitting preemption of home rule units on the basis of population classification.[24]

Structural Features

Illinois leads the nation in number of local governments. In 1996 the Illinois comptroller's office counted 7,239 local governments in Illinois (102 counties, 1,284 municipalities, 1,433 townships, 1,399 township road and bridge districts, and 3,021 special districts).[25] This situation has been viewed as the "nation's largest experiment in decentralized government" or, less generously, as the "local government quagmire" or even the "crazy quilt of government."[26]

The major statutory municipal government structures are the city aldermanic, village trustee, commission, and manager forms, with the city aldermanic and village trustee forms clearly being the most common. Municipalities have discretion over type of structure, and they may modify a particular form. For example, the council-manager form permits a variety of options on how council members are elected. At the same time, statutory constraints exist; for example, the number of aldermen is based on population, and there is a 200,000 population ceiling on the commission form.

By statute, counties may choose among three forms of government: township organization counties, commission counties, and the county executive form. The township form is most common and is found in eighty-five counties, including Cook County.[27] Township counties with populations less than 3,000,000 (all but Cook County) are governed by county boards with memberships in the five to twenty-nine range. Within this range, however, counties may decide on number of board members; choose between at-large and district-based elections, or some combination thereof; and may even establish multimember districts.

Cook County may be viewed as a separate form of county government, primarily because it is uniquely identified in the statutes as the Board of Commissioners of Cook County. The seventeen commission counties, which are governed by three commissioners elected on an at-large basis, are found mostly in the southern region of Illinois and reflect the southern tradition of strong county government without townships.[28] The county executive form is available to any county but Cook, but only suburban Will County has adopted it.

The 1870 constitution prohibited special legislation concerning municipal incorporation and charters. With the passage of the Cities and Villages Act of 1872, municipalities thereafter would be established and governed according to general statutes rather than charters. Today, these general statutes are found in the municipal code of the Illinois Compiled Statutes.[29] The 1970 constitution exhorts the state legislature to avoid special legislation if general laws can be written, but the courts determine the applicability of general legislation.

The municipal code has a Chicago article, and numerous sections on Cook County are found in the counties code; however, local governments are most often differentiated by population. For example, with regard to fees and compensation of county and township officials, there are three classes of county.[30] One of the most common classifications refers to municipalities above or below the 500,000 or 1,000,000 population markers, which historically was a strategy to differentiate Chicago from remaining municipalities. For municipalities smaller than Chicago and counties other than Cook, the quantity and variety of classifications by population will challenge even the most mathematically inclined reader of the Illinois Compiled Statutes.

Population classification is used sometimes to address specific local issues. For example, a 1996 amendment stated that counties with populations of "more than 800,000 but less than 3,000,000" could establish forest preserve districts. Although seemingly broad, this classification is designed to refer only to one county, DuPage, whose officials lobbied for the amendment.[31] With the emergence of DuPage County as an important Republican power base in Illinois, further self-serving classification by population can be expected.

Moreover, classifications sometimes resemble special legislation and perhaps local privilege legislation. An example is a provision that grants counties with 3,000,000 or more population (that is, Cook County) the authority to grant a general homestead exemption of up to $4,500 as opposed to $3,500 in the remaining counties.

Incorporation of cities and villages is subject to statutory requirements that consider factors such as territorial contiguity, population size, and location relative to incorporated municipalities.[32] The statutes include provisions on creating, altering, and uniting counties, but these provisions are mere formalities, because county boundaries have been the same since 1859.[33] Municipal incorporation depends on local initiative involving petitions and ballot propositions. However, the state has extraterritoriality requirements designed to promote incorporation that respects the autonomy of nearby municipalities.

Annexation of a settled unincorporated area requires approval by a majority of the area's residents; annexation of one municipality to another requires majority votes by referendum in both municipalities. According to most home rule attorneys, home rule municipalities do not have greater annexation powers than their non–home rule counterparts.[34] In addition, home rule municipalities have no inherent extraterritorial powers. That authority must be granted by the legislature; however, home rule municipalities do not require statutory authorization for extraterritorial "proprietary" acts (that is, acquiring land outside municipal boundaries).[35] Counties, however, have only limited jurisdiction over municipalities that exercise powers within their boundaries and defined extraterritorial jurisdictions, such as the one and one-half mile distance beyond corporate boundaries for municipal zoning.

Functions of Local Government

Functional Responsibilities

Municipalities have much discretion over which powers to exercise or services to provide.[36] Major areas of statutorily authorized responsibilities include police and fire protection, planning and zoning, public health, building regulations, streets and public ways, business and professional licensing, water and sewer systems, and economic development. Once invoked by a city or village, such power becomes subject to all statutorily prescribed procedures and restrictions. Home rule municipalities, however, are not limited to the statutes and may deviate from statutory procedures. To invoke its home rule authority, a municipality need only enact an ordinance, and the ordinance itself need not make reference to its home rule underpinnings.[37]

Chicago's declining political clout is an interesting example of the relationship between state politics and local autonomy. Although suburban Rosemont in Cook County may gain a casino, Chicago experienced years of frustration in its similar quest. In 1996 a Republican-controlled state government attempted to seize a small, municipally run lakeside airport, Meigs Field, from a Democratic Chicago administration that announced plans for its conversion to recreational use. The same governor and legislature, however, actually strengthened municipal influence over the city's schools by giving increased powers to the mayor, including the authority to appoint the school system's chief executive officer.

Illinois counties have a number of constitutionally and statutorily required functions. Important responsibilities include judicial administration, law enforcement, property tax administration, and elections supervision. Within township counties, townships have state-mandated responsibilities in general assistance, road and bridge maintenance, and property tax assessment.[38] Counties, however, are not completely constrained by state laws; a number of services and regulatory activities are either completely or mostly optional, such as county zoning or regional planning.

Contrary to the intent of the 1970 constitution's framers, special-district creation continues unabated. The most common types of special districts in Illinois are fire protection, park, library, and sanitary districts.[39] Special districts also include authorities for areas such as airports, civic centers, and regional development. Special districts and authorities also rank among Illinois's most well-known and powerful local governments, such as the Chicago area's Metropolitan Water Reclamation District, Metropolitan Pier and Exposition Authority, and Regional Transportation Authority.

Generous constitutional language supports and even explicitly encourages the state to promote intergovernmental cooperation. In 1973 the legislature enacted the Intergovernmental Cooperation Act, which established the statutory framework for intergovernmental agreements, contracts, and alternative forms of governing bodies. An Illinois Commission on Intergovernmental Cooperation survey of intergovernmental agreements found that public safety agreements were the most common for both municipalities and counties. Townships reported transportation agreements as their most frequently used form of intergovernmental cooperation.[40]

Administrative Discretion

The statutes assert that state government's approach is to affirmatively authorize rather than deny local government powers. Local officials and employees are provided important liability protections associated with policy-related discretion.[41] Municipalities may seize property through eminent domain, contract with the private sector, shape growth through annexation agreements, and own public utilities. Likewise, counties may adopt a county zoning ordinance, establish a department of public works, or contract with a sanitary district for sewerage service. Each grant of power, however, may be accompanied by specific guidelines or limitations.

Municipal discretion in personnel management is a mixed situation. Nonmanager municipalities may hire a city administrator, and municipalities may adopt a civil service system. Adoption and abandonment of a civil service system, however, must be done by referendum. Police and fire department employees are covered by civil service regulations only if they are not under the jurisdiction of a preexisting board of police and fire commissioners. Home rule municipalities, however, may deviate from statutory civil service guidelines and are not bound by state statutes on matters such as composition of the local board of police and fire commissioners.[42]

Counties face a complex situation. Any county besides Cook may adopt the county executive form; county boards may hire a county administrator. On the other hand, county board efforts to develop uniform personnel policies are constrained by the authority given to elected county officials (such as the auditor, clerk, and recorder) to control the "internal operations" of their respective offices. Furthermore, explicit statutory authority to adopt elements of a civil service system is available to only the very largest counties.[43]

Since 1984, local governments have been under the jurisdiction of the Illinois Public Labor Relations Act, which established public employees' rights to collective bargaining and imposed a "duty to bargain" on local governments with thirty-five or more employees.[44] Home rule authority was preempted—an action that still stirs debate. Both municipalities and counties have broad authority to enter into contracts.[45] The contracting process, however, is subject to procedures such as the Local Government Prompt Payment Act's deadlines for bill approval and payment to vendors. Competitive bidding requirements for municipalities and counties also exist, although local officials often avoid them. Constraints on contractual procedures are counterbalanced by flexible bidding requirements.

All municipalities and counties are authorized to establish local or regional organizations and planning processes. Planning, however, is not a strong priority. The six-county Chicago region faces intergovernmental coordination difficulties, traffic congestion, storm water runoff, and unplanned development. Although the Northeastern Illinois Planning Commission (NIPC) is statutorily empowered to provide for "sound and orderly development of the northeastern Illinois counties area," it feels obligated to defer to local control, and its authority is limited mostly to advisory activities.[46]

Economic Development

Both home rule and non–home rule units may engage in development activities, although flexibility may be limited for any local government that participates in a state program. The Illinois Supreme Court has tended to affirm relatively expansive uses of public funds for local economic development.[47] Both municipalities and counties may create community development corporations, and municipalities may form neighborhood redevelopment corporations. The general contracting powers of local governments also enable them to participate in public-private development organizations, and state law encourages the creation of county- or regional-level industrial development agencies.

Since 1982, Illinois has had an enterprise zone program for both municipalities and counties. As of 1996, there were ninety-one enterprise zones, and none had been added since 1993 because of a statutory cap. Although state approval for these zones was required, the actual granting of local incentives is a matter of local discretion.[48] Furthermore, to the extent that state monitoring occurs, the local zone ordinance is the controlling factor.[49]

Home rule municipalities may offer residential development abatements to fight urban decay, and all municipalities may grant abatements on property covered by annexation agreements. Subject to some limitations, all taxing districts may abate any portion of property taxes on commercial and industrial property. Performance conditions may also be attached, such as those stipulating "jobs to be retained, created, or lost because of the incentives."[50]

Municipalities and counties have a variety of development financing tools. Illinois's most high profile and controversial local development finance tool is its tax increment financing (TIF) program. In 1986 sales tax TIF districts were awarded to over 100 municipalities that had the creative foresight to apply for approval by the state's Department of Revenue during a limited period. The legislature was not pleased to fund the sales tax TIFs and consequently devised a funding formula designed to limit state support.[51] Property tax–based TIFs, however, involve much more local discretion, but the use of this discretion has been criticized, particularly by school district officials concerned about lost property tax revenues.[52]

Additional development tools are available. Municipalities and counties have extensive powers regarding land assembly, public improvements, and industrial park development. Municipalities may designate and administer commercial "business districts," and both municipalities and counties may establish small-business incubators. Counties may levy a tax to promote economic development; as of 1995, municipalities may abate sales taxes through economic incentive agreements.

Fiscal Autonomy of Local Governments

Local Revenues

The primary local revenue source in Illinois is the heavily regulated property tax; over 6,000 units of local government use the property tax.[53] Most assessment in the state is done by elected township assessors, but the state's revenue department equalizes property by issuing multipliers to individual counties. Equalization is required because Illinois has many taxing districts that overlap counties. Taxpayer objections are processed through a local board of review; appeals are heard by the state's independent Property Tax Appeal Board.[54] In 1995 the General Assembly took away Cook County's unique authority to handle taxpayer objections and appeals; however, the county does retain its unique property classification system.[55]

Home rule units have much discretion over revenue sources and rates, including revenues not expressly authorized in the statutes; however, important constraints exist. Home rule units may not impose an income tax unless authorized by statute; despite authorization, the legislature is not likely to support such a measure. Licensing for revenue and taxing occupations by home rule units is dependent on statutory authority.[56]

Local sales tax authority has been preempted, an action that has been characterized as a "dangerous precedent."[57] In response to growing criticism of local control over sales taxation, a statewide 6.25 percent rate was implemented effective January 1990, with 5 percent allocated to the state and the remaining 1.25 percent to municipalities and counties. Home rule units lost the authority to tailor their sales taxes to local circumstances, but they were permitted to levy supplemental "home rule" sales taxes in 0.25 increments. These "home rule" taxes, however, are to be collected and distributed by the state's Department of Revenue, along with the 1.25 percent portion of the state sales tax. Home rule authority over excise taxes on items such as alcohol, cigarettes, and restaurant food was not preempted by the state.[58]

Non–home rule units are subject to property tax–rate limits and referendum requirements that differ by levy. Some levies with rate limits, such as the municipal and county "corporate" levies, may be increased through referendums.[59] Responsiveness is promoted through the Truth in Taxation Law, which requires public disclosure and a public hearing for any taxing body (including home rule units) that proposes a levy greater than 105 percent of the property taxes extended in the preceding year.

Local fiscal autonomy was further limited in 1991 by property tax caps. Although it exempts home rule units, the Property Tax Extension Limitation Act limits property taxes to 5 percent per year or to that year's inflation rate based on the Consumer Price Index, whichever is less. A referendum is required for proposed extensions beyond the legislated caps. Initially, the act applied only to the "collar" counties surrounding Cook County, but following a state-submitted advisory referendum in Cook County, it was extended in 1995 to include Cook County. In 1996 remaining counties were given the authority to hold referendums on property tax caps. Eighteen out of nineteen counties supported caps in the November 1996 election, generally by less than anticipated margins.[60] Since then, the success rate has been ten referendums passed and eight defeated, an indication that voters are aware of the potentially damaging effects of property tax caps.[61]

The constitution prohibits all counties and municipalities from incurring property tax–based debt beyond 40 years. Other debt limits for non–home rule counties and municipalities are set by law, and limits on home rule debt authority are possible. The legislature is given a general power to limit a home rule county's debt; it may limit a municipality's debt not payable from property taxes by a three-fifths vote of the elected membership of both houses. The General Assembly also may set home rule municipal debt limits based on property taxes and impose referendum approval requirements. A debt limit of 8.625 percent of the assessed valuation of property has been imposed on all non–home rule municipalities. General-obligation bond indebtedness usually requires referendum approval. Statutes must be examined case by case to determine if referendum requirements exist for the many types of revenue bonds. Home rule municipalities are not subject to debt limits and referendum requirements.[62]

County boards may issue debt of up to 5.75 percent of the taxable property of the county in order to "perform any of the duties imposed upon them by law." With some exceptions, this general-obligation debt requires approval by referendum, for which the statutory language for each specific revenue bond must be examined. Under the Local Government Debt Limitation Act, counties with populations of less than 500,000, along with townships, face a general statutory debt limit of 2.875 percent of the value of taxable property. This limit, however, does not apply to counties for purposes such as building a court house or jail or providing adequate rooms and accommodations for the county board and certain county officers.

Local Expenditures

The Illinois comptroller's office in 1996 reported the following spending breakdown for municipalities, excluding Chicago: public safety (30 percent), public works and transportation (19 percent), general government (18 percent), debt service (11 percent), development (8 percent), and other (14 percent). Comparable figures were reported for Chicago. The comptroller's office reported the following distribution for county spending: general government (24 percent), public works and transportation (20 percent), health and welfare (15 percent), public safety (14 percent), judiciary (8 percent), corrections (4 percent), debt service (4 percent), development (1 percent), and other (10 percent). For townships, 71 percent of spending was for general government purposes; 16 percent went to health and welfare; and the remaining 13 percent was spent on activities such as public works, development, and debt service.[63]

Local budgeting is both flexible and restrictive. The state does not require that fiscal years be uniform, but a large measure of uniformity has existed in practice. All local governments, however, must comply with broad procedural guidelines regarding the yearly appropriations measure and property tax levy.[64] Responsiveness and responsibility are encouraged through public input requirements, such as public inspection and public hearings before municipal adoption of appropriation ordinances or budgets.

With the exception of Chicago, Illinois municipalities are required only to adopt an appropriation ordinance; however, they may implement a "budget officer" option by a two-thirds vote. Budget reformers no doubt take some solace in the outreach and technical assistance efforts of the Illinois Department of Commerce and Community Affairs (DCCA) to encourage municipalities without the budget officer system to develop an operational budget. Other local governments are required by law to adopt budgets, not just appropriation ordinances.[65] All local governments, however, have been required since July 31, 1998, to have a written investment policy for public funds.

The constitution requires that all units of local government use systems of accounting, auditing, and reporting as provided by the General Assembly. By law, most local governments are required to have audits conducted each year by certified public accountants and submit annual financial reports (AFRs) to the state comptroller's office.[66] These audits focus on financial integrity and compliance with the law and are not required to consider factors such as performance and effectiveness.[67] The Fiscal Responsibility Report Card Act requires the comptroller annually to brief each county clerk and members of the General Assembly on information contained in the AFRs.

Although the comptroller is authorized to enforce compliance with reporting and auditing laws, groups such as the Taxpayers' Federation of Illinois have criticized state government for its limited oversight role.[68] Furthermore, Illinois has been cited as having a "minimum of state agency control," which leads to the neglect of local performance standards and taxpayer accountability.[69] Of course, local autonomy is the flip side of this critique, and it is questionable whether Illinois's political culture would support strong state oversight over local financial administration.

There are no general expenditure increase limits, but property tax caps for non–home rule local governments may achieve the same effect. Although balanced budgets are not formally required of municipalities and counties, there are requirements that promote fiscal caution, such as prior appropriations to support expenditures, and relatively difficult requirements related to additional or supplemental appropriations. Home rule units, however, may spend money without meeting the prior appropriation requirement.[70]

In 1990 the General Assembly enacted the Local Government Financial Planning and Supervision Act and the Financially Distressed City Law. A general state policy on bankruptcy or receivership, however, has not been established. East St. Louis, known nationally for its poverty-related problems, was the exclusive focus. With $34 million in state loans, the East St. Louis Financial Advisory Authority seized control of the city's budgeting and financial administration for at least a ten-year period as a result of mounting debts and increasingly serious financial mismanagement.[71]

State Government Grants-in-Aid to Localities

The Illinois Department of Revenue collects and distributes revenues earmarked for local governments. For FY 1997, it reported $4,909,862,005 paid to local governments, which was approximately 21 percent of the taxes collected by the department.[72] The major forms of local assistance are sales taxes, personal property replacement taxes, motor fuel taxes, and income tax sharing; sales tax revenues provide the most support overall to local governments.

Because the state preempts local authority over the sales tax, the 1.25 percent portion of the state sales tax should not be considered a local own-source revenue. With the exception of certain categories of excise taxes, all sales taxes are collected and distributed by the Department of Revenue, even the home rule option sales tax. On the basis of point of origin of sale, revenues are distributed by the department to counties, municipalities, and certain special districts, such as the Chicago area's Regional Transportation Authority and the Metro-East Mass Transit District of Madison and St. Clair Counties. Local governments also receive part of a state-administered use tax on out-of-state purchases.

The General Assembly in 1979 adopted the Personal Property Replacement Income Tax, a tax mostly on corporate income that compensates local governments for revenues lost as a result of the elimination of personal property tax. Counties, municipalities, townships, and special districts are allocated revenues based on previous personal property tax collections, with Cook County local governments receiving slightly over half of the distributed revenues. The state revenue department collects the state motor fuel tax, and the Department of Transportation distributes funds to municipalities, counties, townships, and road districts. Although a large measure of local discretion is permitted with the other state-distributed revenues, motor fuel funds may be spent only on road or street construction and maintenance and related expenditures.

The state's Local Government Distributive Fund transfers one-tenth of net state income taxes to municipalities and counties on a per capita basis. Through June 1994, the allocation was one-twelfth, coupled with local government and school district sharing of an income tax surcharge instituted in 1989, and one-eleventh during the period of July 1, 1994, to June 30, 1995.[73] The fund's beneficiaries and allocation were the subjects of much debate in the late 1980s and early 1990s. Since then, political battles have been fought over proposals to address long-standing inequities in per pupil school funding and deterioration of school buildings and other infrastructure, culminating in legislation enacted in 1997. Taxes on cigarettes, telephone use, and gambling distracted from more difficult issues concerning the role of the state income tax and local property taxes in school funding. In addition, a complex school construction grant formula undermined much of the political goodwill that had been generated by the belated, although modest, funding reform.[74]

Unfunded Mandates

Illinois first adopted a fiscal note act in 1965. The subsequent State Mandates Act of 1981 established a framework for evaluating the effects of state-imposed mandates on local governments and providing reimbursement for costs incurred. Reimbursement is to be provided for service, tax exemption, and personnel mandates; those to do with due process and local government organization or structure are excluded.

State government implementation of the act, however, has angered local governments. Numerous reimbursement exemptions have been added to the law, and the state has yet to reimburse local governments for mandate costs incurred beyond appropriated dollars.[75] Although a mandate reimbursement review process exists—involving the Department of Commerce and Community Affairs (DCCA) and the independent State Mandates Board of Review—the process is a mere formality. In fact, a 1996 state attorney general opinion asserted that the DCCA is not required to review local government reimbursement applications in the absence of state appropriations; the agency is required only to rule on whether or not a mandate is at issue and its statewide cost of implementation.[76]

The unfunded mandates issue crystallized in the early 1990s. The state legislature in 1992 submitted to the voters an advisory referendum calling for a constitutional amendment prohibiting new unfunded mandates; not surprisingly, the amendment received strong support.[77] Legislative inaction on the referendum results angered the Illinois Municipal League, which led an unsuccessful campaign in 1995–1996 to convince the General Assembly to ballot an unfunded mandates amendment. Since then, the league has adopted a lower profile strategy of lobbying on bills with unfunded mandate provisions. Other local governments also are concerned; the Metro Counties Association, for example, has focused on unfunded mandates related to criminal justice and the judicial system.

Access to Local Government

Local Elections

The county clerk is the "election authority" for almost all local jurisdictions; a few local governments such as DuPage County and Chicago have boards of election commissioners. Local election authority includes overseeing voter registration, preparing ballots, operating polling sites, and tallying results. Elections for all local offices are held according to a timetable established in a consolidated elections statute.[78] Although local elections are administered locally, county clerks and other election officials must implement a complex state election code and comply with the broad oversight authority of the State Board of Elections. In addition, all local governments are starting to implement a heavily criticized Gift Ban Act that requires the formation of local ethics commissions while preempting home rule authority.[79]

County and township elections are partisan, and municipalities may conduct partisan elections unless limited by state law. Chicago illustrates the role of state politics in local elections practices. Until 1995, state law required Chicago's fifty aldermen to be selected in nonpartisan elections; the high profile mayoral race, however, was conducted as an overt partisan election. In that year, the Republican-controlled legislature passed legislation mandating nonpartisan elections for the mayor's office, one of the Democratic Party's most powerful positions in the state.

Citizen Controls over Actions of Local Officials

Although the term "impeachment" is not used, the statutes contain various provisions that call for removal of officials from office on the grounds of misconduct or the failure to perform duties; the courts figure prominently in removal processes. Chicago is permitted the option of recall elections, although it has not adopted this form of citizen control. Otherwise, recall elections are not provided for statutorily. Home rule units may enact recall procedures by ordinance but not by referendum.[80]

Initiative and referendum opportunities are plentiful throughout the statutes, covering topics such as form of municipal or county government, bonding authority, extension of property tax–rate limits, and special-district creation. Residents of municipalities, counties, and townships may have an advisory referendum put on the ballot after securing the signatures of 10 percent of the jurisdiction's registered voters. With certain exceptions, however, the statutes limit the number of public questions on the ballot to three per election. Illinois thus permits local participatory democracy but within limits.

Underlying Illinois's Open Meetings Act is the philosophy that the "people have a right to be informed" of the business of governmental bodies, including local governments.[81] Twenty-two exceptions to conducting open meetings, which are intended to be interpreted strictly, are established.[82] Home rule units are bound by the act but may enact stricter provisions. Responsive local government is promoted with a Freedom of Information Act, the "exclusive state statute on freedom of information," unless there are stricter provisions in the statutes.[83] A number of exemptions exist, mostly in the interest of personal privacy, but the courts have interpreted these strictly.[84]

State-Local Relations

Since home rule was established in the 1970 constitution, the number of home rule municipalities has increased from the original 67 to over 140. The state's most populous county (Cook) retains its home rule status. Comprising over two-thirds of the state's population, Illinois's home rule units are electorally and politically capable. Most important, there is no imminent or even distant threat of repeal of the constitution's home rule provisions.

However, the more than 1,100 municipalities and 101 counties, along with all townships and special districts, that do not enjoy home rule status cannot act unless empowered by the statutes. The secretary of state's office reports that even though about 25 municipalities supported home rule referendums in the 1990s, at least thirty referendums were defeated.[85] Furthermore, the 101 non–home rule counties are unlikely to vote for home rule status, even though they face fiscal pressures and state-mandated responsibilities.

Home rule units themselves have experienced the contradictory impulses in the state. Although the courts and legislature usually have respected the prerogatives of home rule units, incursions have occurred. Major limitations on home rule include (1) numerous preemptions of local powers regarding the licensing of professions and occupations, (2) partial preemption that differentiates among home rule municipalities by population classification, and (3) constraints on home rule revenue powers—the two most important being state preemption of local

authority with respect to sales taxation and the legislature's denial of the local income tax to all local governments.

Notes

1. "U.S. Census Bureau Population Estimates for NIPC Area Counties, 1990–98," Available from the Northeastern Illinois Planning Commission Web site http://www.nipc.cog.il.us/cnty9098.html; Susan R. Harter, ed. "Estimated Population of Illinois Cities," *1998 Illinois Statistical Abstract* (Urbana-Champaign: Bureau of Economic and Business Research, University of Illinois at Urbana-Champaign, 1998), 16–21; U.S. Bureau of the Census, "Resident Population-States: 1970 to 1997," *Statistical Abstract of the United States: 1998* (Washington, D.C.: U.S. Bureau of the Census, 1998), 28.

2. The Metro Chicago Information Center reports the following distribution of Chicago's voting age population in 1996: Whites, 40.3 percent; African Americans, 34.6 percent; Latinos, 20.6 percent; and Others, 4.4 percent. In James H. Lewis, D. Garth Taylor, and Paul Kleppner, *Metro Chicago Political Atlas: 97–98* (Springfield: University of Illinois at Springfield), 10.

3. Daniel J. Elazar, *Cities of the Prairie: The Metropolitan Frontier and American Politics* (New York: Basic Books Inc., 1970). Frederick M. Wirt, "The Changing Social Bases of Regionalism: Peoples, Cultures, and Politics in Illinois," in *Diversity, Conflict and State Politics: Regionalism in Illinois*, ed. Peter F. Nardulli (Urbana: University of Illinois Press, 1989); Samuel K. Gove and James D. Nowlan, *Illinois Politics and Government: The Expanding Metropolitan Frontier* (Lincoln: University of Nebraska Press, 1996); Harold Henderson, "Who We Are," *Illinois Issues* 24 (May 1998): 12–19.

4. Peter Nardulli, "Understanding and Reassessing Geo-Political Cleavages in State Politics," in *Diversity, Conflict and State Politics: Regionalism in Illinois*.

5. James D. Nowlan, "From Lincoln to Forgottonia," *Illinois Issues* 24 (September 1998): 27–30.

6. James L. Merriner, "The Four Tops: When It Comes to Campaign Cash, Illinois Legislative Leaders Call the Shots," *Comparative State Politics* 17 (December 1996): 5–14.

7. Kent D. Redfield, *Cash Clout: Political Money in Illinois Legislative Elections* (Springfield: University of Illinois at Springfield, 1995).

8. Gove and Nowlan, *Illinois Politics and Government*, 148–149.

9. Alice L. Ebel, "Local Government Outside Cook County," in *Con-Con: Issues for the Illinois Constitution Convention*, ed. Samuel K. Gove and Victoria Ranney (Urbana: University of Illinois Press, 1970); Joseph F. Small, "Urban Government," in *Con-Con*; Thomas R. Kitsos, "State Constitutional Revision and the Urban Crisis: The Sixth Illinois Constitutional Convention" (Ph.D. dissertation, University of Illinois at Urbana-Champaign, 1972).

10. Ebel, "Local Government Outside Cook County," in *Con-Con*; Sixth Illinois Constitution Committee on Local Government, "Committee on Local Government Committee Report: Proposed Article on Local Government" (1970); Stephanie Cole, "Illinois Home Rule in Historical Perspective," in *Home Rule in Illinois*, ed. Stephanie Cole and Samuel K. Gove (Urbana: Institute of Government and Public Affairs, University of Illinois at Urbana-Champaign, 1973); Stephanie Cole, "Home Rule in Illinois: The Constitutional Provisions," in *Illinois Issues Annual*, ed. Caroline A. Gheraardini (Springfield, Ill.: Legislative Studies Center, 1975).

11. Elazar, *Cities of the Prairie*; Gove and Nowlan, *Illinois Politics and Government*.

12. Chicago Home Rule Commission, *Modernizing a City Government* (Chicago: University of Chicago Press, 1954). See also James Banovetz and Thomas Kelty, "Illinois Home Rule and Taxation: A New Approach to Local Government Enabling Authority," *Northern Illinois University Law Review* 8 (1988): 709–730.

13. Samuel K. Gove, "Foreword," in *Home Rule in Illinois*.

14. James M. Banovetz and Thomas Kelty, "Home Rule: The Aftermath of a Revolution," *Illinois Issues* 11 (August–September 1985): 52–57.

15. See Illinois Municipal League Committee of Home Rule Attorneys, "Report of the Illinois Municipal League Committee of Home Rule Attorneys: 1970 Illinois Constitution" (Springfield: Illinois Municipal League, 1987).

16. David R. Beam, Alex Pattakos, and David Tobias, *County Home Rule in Illinois* (DeKalb: Center for Governmental Studies, Northern Illinois University, 1977).

17. Tom Andreoli, "Will County Executive: New Office Takes Hold Under Adelman," *Illinois Issues* 16 (August–September 1990): 44–46.

18. Illinois Municipal League Committee of Home Rule Attorneys, "Report of the Illinois Municipal League Committee of Home Rule Attorneys: 1970 Illinois Constitution" (Springfield: Illinois Municipal League, 1987).

19. Kurt P. Froelich, "Home Rule and Intergovernmental Cooperation," in *Municipal Law and Practice*, vol. 3, ed. Stewart H. Diamond (Springfield: Illinois Institute for Continuing Legal Education, 1994): 24–76.

20. James M. Banovetz and Thomas W. Kelty, "The Watchdogs of Home Rule," *Illinois Issues* 11 (October 1985): 17–22; "Supreme Court Decisions Affecting Home Rule Powers, 1972–85," *Home Rule in Illinois: Image and Reality* (Springfield, Ill.: Illinois Issues, 1987), 34–37.

21. This point is often made to underline the population-based importance of home rule in Illinois. See Gove and Nowlan, *Illinois Politics and Government*, 156.

22. Kurt P. Froelich notes that the term preemption is not constitutional language: "The ability of the general assembly to take away the power and authority of home rule is often called preemption, although that specific term is not used in the constitution." See "Illinois Home Rule," in *Illinois Local Government: A Handbook*, ed. James F. Keane and Gary Koch (Carbondale: Southern Illinois University Press, 1990), 233.

23. Stewart H. Diamond and the attorneys of Ancel, Glink, Diamond, Cope and Bush, P.C., *1998–1999 Illinois Municipal Handbook* (Springfield: Illinois Municipal League, 1998), 234–237.

24. Beth Anne Janicki, "Illinois Supreme Court Renders Decisions Impacting Municipal Franchise Agreements and Preemptions of Home Rule Authority," *Illinois Municipal Review* 72 (October 1993): 23–24. In *Nevitt v. Langfelder* (157 Ill.2d 116), the court ruled in favor of the Public Employee Disability Act's preemption of home rule units with less than one million population, which as a result excluded Chicago.

25. State of Illinois Comptroller, *Local Government Finance Series* (Springfield: State of Illinois, 1996), 3–5. The comptroller's office excludes school districts because they are not part of the Illinois Constitution's definition of local governments. Township road and bridge districts are included in the count because they oversee local spending of state-administered and -allocated motor fuel taxes. The comptroller maintains the central registry of local governments.

26. Gove and Nowlan, *Illinois Politics and Government*, 150; Dick Simpson and Linda Moll, *The Crazy Quilt of Government: Units of Government in Cook County, 1993* (Chicago: Office of Publication Services of the University of Illinois at Chicago, 1993).

27. Within Cook County, Chicago and the town of Cicero do not have township government. See State of Illinois Comptroller, *Local Government Finance Series*, 35.

28. Clyde F. Snider and Irving Howards, *County Government in Illinois* (Carbondale: Southern Illinois University, 1960).

29. Diamond et al., *1998–1999 Illinois Municipal Handbook*, 2.

30. According to 55 Illinois Compiled Statutes 5/4-1004, the three classes are: (1) counties of the first class, 25,000 or fewer residents, (2) counties of the second class, 25,001–1,000,000 residents, and (3) counties of the third class, over 1,000,000 residents.

31. 70 Illinois Compiled Statutes 805/3c; Ted Gregory, "Democratic Firm Hired as Forest Lobby," *Chicago Tribune*, 22 February 1995.

32. Terrance Barnicle, "Cities-vs-Villages," in *Municipal Forms of Government*, ed. Patrick A. Lucansky (Springfield: Illinois Municipal League, 1994).

33. Snider and Howards, *County Government in Illinois*, 15.

34. Diamond et al., *1998–1999 Illinois Municipal Handbook*, 253.

35. *Carbondale v. Van Natta* (61 Ill.2d. 483).

36. A former executive director of the Illinois Municipal League writes, "Illinois statutes require municipal governments to do little or nothing. Cities are not required to have streets, police, or fire protection, zoning, drinking water, or employees." See Steve Sargent, "Municipal Government," in *Illinois Local Government*, 58.

37. Diamond et al., *1998–1999 Illinois Municipal Handbook*, 250–252.

38. Robin A. Johnson and Norman Walzer, "Township Services," *County and Township Official* (June 1996): 16–17.

39. Illinois Commission on Intergovernmental Cooperation, *Legislator's Guide to Local Governments in Illinois: Special Districts* (Springfield: State of Illinois, August 1992).

40. Illinois Commission on Intergovernmental Cooperation, *Intergovernmental Cooperation Handbook* (Springfield: State of Illinois, October 1995).

41. 50 Illinois Compiled Statutes 35/1; 745 Illinois Compiled Statutes 10/2-201.

42. *Stryker v. Village of Oak Park* (62 Ill.2d. 523); James Baird and Ronald J. Kramer, "Municipal Personnel Practices," in *Municipal Law and Practice in Illinois*, vol. 1, 4-23-4-28.

43. Cook County has the authority to establish a position classification agency, and since 1895 it has had a statutorily mandated civil service commission. The statutes also provide for the Cook County Sheriff's Merit Board. A personnel policy commission may be created by counties with 350,000–1,000,000 population.

44. 5 Illinois Compiled Statutes 315/2 et seq.

45. The breadth of the powers is seen in the following statutory language: Municipalities as "bodies politic and corporate" have the power to "contract and be contracted with" (65 Illinois Compiled Statutes 5/2-2-12); counties have the power to "make all contracts and do all other acts in relation to the property and concerns of the county necessary to the exercise of corporate powers" (55 Illinois Compiled Statutes 5/5-1005).

46. Northeastern Illinois Planning Commission, *Strategic Plan for Land Resource Management* (Chicago: Northeastern Illinois Planning Commission, 1992), 7.

47. See *Salem v. McMackin* (53 Ill.2d. 347); *Urbana v. Paley* (68 Ill.2d. 62); and *Canton v. Crouch* (79 Ill.2d. 356).

48. Illinois Department of Commerce and Community Affairs, "Illinois Enterprise Zone Program Annual Report, Fiscal Year 1996" (Springfield: State of Illinois, 1996).

49. State monitoring of enterprise zones has been an issue in the past. A 1991 study by the Illinois Taxpayers' Federation—the state's most prominent revenue watchdog association—asserted that "no systematic monitoring of the tax cost of the enterprise zones occurs at the state or local level." See Kent D. Redfield and John F. McDonald, *Enterprise Zones in Illinois* (Springfield: Illinois Tax Foundation, 1991), 24.

50. 30 Illinois Compiled Statutes 760/5.

51. Michael D. Klemens, "TIFS: What Cost to the State Treasury?" *Illinois Issues* 16 (June 1990): 18–27; Diane Oltman Ayers, "TIF Districts: Tiff Over Turf on Sales Tax Growth," *Illinois Issues* 18 (November 1992): 20–24.

52. Ed Wojcicki, "TIF for TAT, Can We Fix the State's Tax Increment Financing Laws?" *Illinois Issues* 23 (May 1997): 11; State Capitol Bureau, "Legislation to Reform TIF Districts Sent to Governor's Desk," *Springfield Journal Register*, 20 May 1999.

53. Loleta A. Didrickson, State of Illinois Comptroller, "Property Taxes in Illinois," *Illinois Municipal Review* 75 (August 1996): 15–16.

54. 35 Illinois Compiled Statutes 200/5-5 et seq.; David Young, "Cook County Taxpayers to Get a Break," *Chicago Tribune*, 9 December 1996.

55. Cook County takes advantage of a law that enables counties with populations greater than 200,000 to classify property (35 Illinois Compiled Statutes 200/9-145). Otherwise, property is assessed at one-third market value; there are separate standards for farmland. By local ordinance, Cook County has nine separate classes of property, with each having its own assigned percentage of market value for assessed valuation.

56. Local officials who devise taxes that might be interpreted as revenue from licensing or an occupational tax must be prepared to face court challenges.

In 1981 a Chicago tax crafted as a service tax on purchasers of business and professional services was ruled an occupations tax and therefore unconstitutional without explicit statutory authority. This case is instructive, because the Home Rule Attorneys Committee of the Illinois Municipal League warned that Chicago should not proceed with the tax in view of potential damage to home rule that could result from a negative ruling. See *Commercial National Bank of Chicago v. Chicago* (89 Ill.2d. 45); Banovetz and Kelty, "Illinois Home Rule and Taxation," 728.

57. Stewart H. Diamond and the attorneys of Ancel, Glink, Diamond, Cope and Bush, P.C., *1996–1997 Illinois Municipal Handbook* (Springfield: Illinois Municipal League, 1996), 281.

58. Illinois Department of Revenue, "1997 Annual Report" (Springfield: State of Illinois, 1997), 57–58.

59. The number of levies is large. To illustrate, through 1996 there were 73 separate levies for the operating and capital budgeting needs of non–home rule municipalities and an additional 26 for debt service. See Illinois Department of Commerce and Community Affairs, Office of Local Government Management Services, "Municipal Revenue Sources-Document #1," *Municipal Finance Series* (Springfield: State of Illinois, 1996).

60. Anthony Man, "Surprise, Surprise: Voters Like the Idea of Capping Property Taxes, But by Underwhelming Margins," *Illinois Issues* 22 (December 1996): 9.

61. Based on "Property Tax Extension Limitation Law County Referendum Results" of the Policy and Communications Office (Springfield: Illinois Department of Revenue) through the April 1999 election.

62. Stewart H. Diamond and the attorneys of Ancel, Glink, Diamond, Cope and Bush, P.C., *1994–1995 Illinois Municipal Handbook* (Springfield: Illinois Municipal League, 1993).

63. Municipal, county, and township spending information comes from the Comptroller's Office's *Local Government Finance Series* (1996). The figures are based on a database generated from the collection of annual financial reports (AFRs).

64. John J. Zimmerman, *Levying Taxes in Illinois Municipalities* (Springfield: Illinois Municipal League, 1995).

65. Jay Hedges, director, Illinois Department of Commerce and Community Affairs, "Illinois Municipal Appropriation and Tax Laws Changed," *Illinois Municipal Review* 67 (October 1988): 9–10.

66. For municipalities and counties, reporting and auditing requirements are found in the Illinois Municipal Auditing Law (65 Illinois Compiled Statutes 5/8-8-1 et seq.) and the County Auditing Law (55 Illinois Compiled Statutes 5/6-31001 et seq.). Townships and certain special districts are subject to the Governmental Account Audit Act (50 Illinois Compiled Statutes 310/0.01 et seq.).

67. Terrance Barnicle, Thomas P Bayer, and Janet N. Petsche, "Finance and Tax," in *Municipal Law and Practice in Illinois,* 12–53.

68. Tara McClellan, "Annual Financial Reports: Unused and Unusable," *Illinois Tax Facts* 44 (October 1990): 1–7; Ronald D. Picur, *Local Government Fiscal Practices in Illinois* (Springfield: Taxpayers' Federation of Illinois, 1991), 156.

69. Gove and Nowlan, *Illinois Politics and Government,* 150, 157–159.

70. Diamond et al., *1996–1997 Illinois Municipal Handbook,* 282.

71. John Racine, "East St. Louis: What Can, Should State Do?" *Illinois Issues* 16 (March 1990): 12–15.

72. Illinois Department of Revenue, "1997 Annual Report," 54.

73. Ibid., 63.

74. Jennifer Davis, "Slicing the Bread: More Dough (and Rules) for Schools," *Illinois Issues* 24 (January 1998): 8; Jennifer Davis, "Lawmakers Approved Funds for School Building. April Fool!" *Illinois Issues* 24 (April 1998): 6; State of Illinois Comptroller, "Cover Story: Back to School," in *Fiscal Focus* (October–November 1998): 1, 6–7, 12.

75. Illinois Commission on Intergovernmental Cooperation, *Catalog of State Assistance to Local Governments* (Springfield: State of Illinois, 1997), 52–53.

76. Illinois Attorney General Opinion (96-018, 4 March 1996).

77. The 1992 advisory referendum asked: "Should the Illinois General Assembly, in order to stop increasing property taxes because of unfunded mandates on local government, approve a Resolution for a State Constitutional Amendment prohibiting the General Assembly and Governor from adopting new unfunded State mandates that impose additional costs on units of local government?" This question passed with 80.6 percent of the vote. See Thomas G. Fitzsimmons, "A Call to Action," *Illinois Municipal Review* 73 (April 1994): 7–9.

78. The original Consolidated Elections Act of 1980 was further refined in a 1997 law that brought together school district elections with other local governments while eliminating the fall election held in odd years (for example, the Fall 1999 school district elections).

79. Ed Wojcicki, "Gift Ban Act May Give Local Governments a Headache," *Illinois Issues* 25 (May 1999): 9; Burney Simpson, "Implementation of Ethics Law Draws Confusion and Criticism," *Illinois Issues* 25 (July–August 1999): 11.

80. Diamond et al., *1996–1997 Illinois Municipal Handbook,* 282.

81. 5 Illinois Compiled Statutes 120/1.

82. Attorney General, *Guide to the Illinois Open Meetings Act* (Springfield: State of Illinois, 1995), 10–11.

83. 5 Illinois Compiled Statutes 140/1.

84. Diamond et al., *1996–1997 Illinois Municipal Handbook,* 151.

85. Index Department, Secretary of State, "Home Rule Referendums Index by Year" (Springfield: State of Illinois, reported election results through 1998).

INDIANA

William Blomquist

Although Indiana adopted a home rule statute in 1980, the history of state-local relations before and since then demonstrates that local governments enjoy limited autonomy. State regulations of local fiscal affairs are highly detailed. Despite the fact that Indiana's home rule law contains the usual statement that local governments may exercise all powers not prohibited, the list of prohibitions is extensive and growing. During the 1990s, the Indiana General Assembly enacted preemption statutes removing several subjects from local jurisdiction.

Governmental Setting

Indiana's political and governmental system avoided most early twentieth-century reform moves. The state still exhibits many pre-reform characteristics. State and local government structure in Indiana reflects Jacksonian more than Progressive-era influence; many offices are filled by election, and terms of office are kept short. There are term limits for the executive branch. Reform measures such as the initiative, recall, and non-partisan elections for local offices have not been adopted, and others such as merit personnel systems and home rule came to Indiana later than in most other states. Party organizations remain comparatively strong, and partisanship is the organizing principle of elections and campaigns, the legislative process, and executive branch staffing.

Indiana's political culture has been described as individualistic. The principal purpose of political activity is to win; the object of winning is to control the offices of government, and few are surprised if one uses those offices to reward one's supporters. In addition, Indiana has long been described as the most "southern" of northern states. One of the characteristics it shares with more traditional southern state politics is the relative strength of the state legislature compared with the other two branches of state government and with any form of local government.

Indiana remained a "Dillon's Rule" state into the 1970s (that is, cities had only those powers expressly given to them by the state). Moreover, the state received low ratings on the scales used in the U.S. Advisory Commission on Intergovernmental Relations (ACIR) 1981 report on local autonomy. Subsequent efforts to establish home rule have been offset by tax-limitation and preemption trends.

Home Rule in Indiana

Historical Development

The state-local legal relationship followed Dillon's Rule through nearly all of Indiana's history. In the post–World War II period, the General Assembly twice failed to bring before the voters constitutional amendments that would have granted municipalities home rule (including charter) authority.

In 1969 the General Assembly adopted the Unigov law, probably the most dramatic development in local government in Indiana in the past half-century. The law merged the governments of the city of Indianapolis and Marion County and absorbed seventeen other municipalities within the county into the new consolidated city (but excluded four others). Contemporaneous newspaper accounts and the recollections of those involved in Indianapolis government and politics at the time indicate that consolidation was probably not supported by a majority of central-city residents or of those residing in the surrounding suburbs within the county; however, there was no referendum.[1] Unigov came about solely through state legislation.

Another important event was the 1973 enactment of a property tax limitation statute that imposed numerous restrictions on levies by municipalities and special districts while granting income taxing authority to counties. Indiana has very detailed rules on local finances—even stipulating the day on which township boards may approve their operating budgets—and the 1973 act added new ones.

A state government that tells township boards when to meet and pass their budgets does not exhibit a strong tradition of local autonomy. In its 1981 report, *Measuring Local Discretionary Authority*, the ACIR assessed the legal relationship between the state and local governments in Indiana as fitting the Dillon's Rule classification; Indiana is one of only five states to receive that rating. Indiana ranked fortieth among forty-nine states in discretionary authority allowed to cities, with particularly low marks in the categories of governmental structure and finances.

There have been efforts to relax the grip of Dillon's Rule on local governments in Indiana. In 1971 the General Assembly passed the Powers of Cities Act, under which Indiana cities and towns were permitted to enact any and all ordinances "necessary and desired" for the regulation of local affairs, except those that were prohibited by the federal or state constitutions or statutes, or those that were preempted by state laws that either contained an express statement of preemption or were clearly intended to preempt local legislation.

This legislation failed to make its intended impression on Indiana courts, which continued to apply Dillon's Rule and "implied preemption" reasoning to cases in which municipal powers were challenged. In 1973 the legislature tried to clarify its intention by amending the 1971 law, stating that cities could exercise powers "to the extent that such power is not by express provision vested" in another unit or agency. Two years later,[2] the Indiana Court of Appeals again applied the implied-preemption reasoning of a 1939 Indiana Supreme Court precedent rather than the statutory guidance of the 1973 law.

Responding to its own frustration as well as that of local officials, the General Assembly in 1978 established the Local Government Study Commission. The commission met for three years and produced several recommendations, many of which were enacted in 1980 and 1981. The Home Rule Act of 1980 applies to counties, cities, and towns but not to townships, special districts, or school corporations. It contains a policy declaration that Dillon's Rule shall no longer apply in Indiana and that municipalities and counties have all powers not expressly forbidden to them or expressly reserved to another governmental body.

When it adopted the Home Rule Act in 1980, the Indiana General Assembly recodified local government laws into a new Title 36 of the Indiana Code. Supporters predicted that it would simplify and clarify local government law in Indiana. Moreover, they hoped it would enhance the visibility and symbolic importance of local governments in state lawmaking and interpretation.[3] Unfortunately, Title 36 is neither brief nor comprehensive: its ten articles cover more than 1,000 pages of the Indiana Code. Nor does it gather into one convenient source all, or even most, state laws regulating or restricting local government activities. Extensive portions of Title 5 ("state and local administration") and Title 6 ("taxation") impose requirements on local governments, and many provisions of the other thirty-three titles (such as "elections," "public safety," and "environment") specify local actions or procedures.

Definition of Home Rule

Home rule in Indiana is defined entirely in terms of the reversal of Dillon's Rule.[4] The 1980 Home Rule Act declared that "the rule of law that any doubt as to the existence of a power of a unit shall be resolved against its existence is abrogated" and "the policy of the state is to grant units all the powers that they need for the effective operation of government as to local affairs." Cities, towns, and counties are declared to have all powers granted to them by statute and "all other powers necessary or desirable in the conduct of [their] affairs, even though not granted by statute," unless "expressly denied by the Indiana Constitution or by statute" or "expressly granted to another entity."[5]

In light of the language of the Home Rule Act and the events leading up to its passage, legislative adoption of home rule in Indiana appears to have been primarily an effort to instruct the courts on proper interpretation rather than to extend local autonomy. Communities have not gained control over either their governmental structures, which the state constitution and statutes prescribe in detail, or their fiscal matters. In 1993 the ACIR categorized Indiana as having "limited functional home rule."

State law contains a lengthy and growing list of restrictions on local government powers.[6] In the Home Rule Act itself, municipalities and counties are denied the power to

1. impose any tax, except as expressly granted by statute;
2. impose a license or other fee greater than that reasonably related to the administrative cost of exercising a regulatory power;
3. impose a service charge greater than that reasonably related to the cost of providing the service;
4. invest money, except as expressly authorized by statute;
5. prescribe a penalty of imprisonment for violation of a municipal ordinance;
6. prescribe a fine of more than $2,500 for violation of an ordinance;
7. regulate conduct that is regulated by a state agency, except as expressly granted by statute;
8. impose duties on another local jurisdiction, unless expressly granted by statute;
9. condition or limit their civil liability, except as expressly granted by statute;
10. prescribe the laws governing civil actions between private persons; or
11. order or conduct an election, except as expressly provided by statute.[7]

This list prompted one commentator to conclude, "Ironically, Title 36, intending to grant extensive powers to local units, may have reduced those powers thus impairing their ability to function as integral units of state government."[8]

Furthermore, instances of local or special legislation abound, despite a prohibition in the Indiana Constitution.[9] Constitutional challenges to special legislation have been unavailing; courts have allowed the legislature to determine whether or not a law applies generally rather than locally. A statute authorizing riverboat gaming in 1993, which required some counties to hold referendums while allowing other counties to proceed without one, was written so "creatively" that it prompted a (unsuccessful) constitutional challenge.[10] A special legislation enactment in 1997 prompted another fruitless challenge. The statute created a separate public improvement bond bank for "a city with a population of more than four thousand two hundred (4,200) but less than five thousand (5,000) located in a county having a population of more than thirty-eight thousand five hundred (38,500) but less than thirty-nine thousand (39,000)"—which could only describe Lawrenceburg.[11]

Structural Features

Indiana law prescribes local government structure and does not authorize optional forms of local government for counties or municipalities. In Indiana, as in most states, the number of state laws regulating local government structure and administration grew between 1978 and 1990.[12]

Indiana cities are categorized as first class (250,000 or more population), second class (35,000–250,000), or third class (less than 35,000).[13] Only one city (Indianapolis) falls into the first-class designation, and the Unigov law prescribes its governmental form. For second- and third-class cities, state law establishes the form of government (mayor-council);[14] the size of the council (twenty-nine members for a first-class city, nine for a second-class city, and seven for a third-class city); the number of members elected by district or at large; the length of and limits on terms of elected officials; the dates of municipal elections; the kinds of departments and boards that may exist within the executive branch; and whether there should be a separately elected clerk or clerk-treasurer (second-class cities have the former; third-class cities, the latter). For second- and third-class cities, the law specifies whether there should be a department of development, an advisory plan commission, and/or a board of zoning appeals.

Indiana law allows town governments somewhat greater structural flexibility than it allows cities. Towns are governed by boards of no fewer than three and no more than seven members elected from wards or at large. Towns do not have mayors, but they do have elected clerk-treasurers; towns may appoint town marshals. Town boards may choose to employ a town manager. The structure of departments and commissions is left to the discretion of town boards instead of being specified, as it is for cities.

Towns normally are expected to have fewer than 2,000 residents. Towns with more than 2,000 residents may elect to become third-class cities, but there is no statutory or constitutional requirement that they do so. There is a trade-off to becoming a city: although visibility and prestige are increased, structural flexibility is reduced. Not surprisingly, some communities that are larger than many third-class cities have chosen to retain town status (most notably, Speedway and Merrillville).

The structure of county government in Indiana is as closely prescribed as that of city government. However, because the prescriptions appear in the Indiana Constitution, they are even less amenable to change. Marion County's structure differs slightly because the legislature has discovered ways to make some constitutionally required officers satisfy more than one capacity.[15]

State law provides for the incorporation of new municipalities as towns. A community wishing to become a third- or second-class city would incorporate first as a town and then (perhaps simultaneously) elect to become a city. Incorporation requires that a petition be put before the county commissioners. The petition must include the signatures of at least fifty landowners within the area to be incorporated, a survey and description of the area's boundaries, an enumeration of its residents and landowners, an estimate of the assessed valuation of real property, and a plan describing the municipal services that will be provided within the area upon or after its incorporation. State law directs that no new town may be incorporated within three miles of an existing municipality, or within four miles of the city of Indianapolis, without an ordinance of consent from the existing municipality.[16]

As in most states, municipal annexation in Indiana is fairly difficult. Territory can be annexed only if "contiguous," defined as at least one-eighth of the boundaries of the territory coinciding with the boundaries of the annexing municipality. Furthermore, the territory must meet one of the following requirements: the density of resident population is at least three persons per acre, 60 percent of the territory is subdivided, or the territory is zoned for commercial or industrial use. If none of these requirements is met, the municipality may still proceed with an annexation ordinance if at least one-fourth of the territory is contiguous to the municipality "and the territory sought to be annexed is needed and can be used by the municipality for its development in the reasonably near future."[17] In all cases, state law requires municipalities that attempt to annex territory within three miles of the corporate boundaries of another municipality to obtain an ordinance of consent from their neighbor.

State law prescribes the manner of publication of a municipality's annexation plan, the procedures for remonstrance and appeal against a proposed annexation, and the manner of filing and recording of the annexation ordinance if the annexation is completed. Annexation actions may be initiated by a municipality itself or through a petition of property owners in an area seeking annexation. The annexing municipality's council must adopt fiscal and service plans detailing the municipal services that will be provided to the territory, the timetable, and the means of financing the service extensions. The law describes the required contents of these plans. Moreover, it stipulates that the timetable for extending noncapital services (for example, police and fire protection) cannot be longer than one year after the effective date of the annexation; for capital improvements, the timetable cannot be longer than three years.

The territorial jurisdiction of counties and municipalities is restricted by statute to the area inside their corporate boundaries. Extraterritorial exercise of jurisdiction is permitted only as authorized by statute. However, some statutory grants can be quite broad, such as that which authorizes municipalities to exercise eminent domain powers and to acquire, improve, and dispose of property within four miles outside their corporate boundaries.[18]

Functions of Local Government

Functional Responsibilities

With respect to local government powers and functions, Indiana law does not discern between municipalities and counties. Like most of Title 36, the language on "general corporate powers" refers to "units," which may be counties, cities, or towns.

On the other hand, county government has always been the primary form of local government in Indiana. Thus, state law and practice presume that the general array of local government functions and powers (that is, public safety, public health and sanitation, transportation, recreation, public assistance) are provided by counties, except within the jurisdiction of municipalities that exercise those functions and powers. Once incorporated, cities and towns may exercise most local government functions and powers within their jurisdiction. Any power or function not exercised by a municipality within its jurisdiction defaults to the county.[19]

A few functions are reserved to counties, most notably voter registration and the conduct of elections, including municipal ones. The administration of courts and the prosecution of violations of state law generally are county functions, although some cities have retained municipal courts and city prosecutor offices. Some locally provided services are expressly delegated to other units; for example, local school corporations created by the legislature are responsible for local schooling, and townships administer emergency relief.

In part because Indiana follows the southern practice of defaulting local government functions to counties, it has not created special-purpose local governments as aggressively as has its neighbor Illinois, for example. In addition to school corporations, special districts have been created throughout Indiana for soil and water conservation and for solid waste management. Other special districts (library, airport authority) have been created ad hoc in response to specific local concerns.

State law authorizes interlocal agreements (including those providing for fiscal, administrative, or operations assistance) and the exercise of joint powers among municipalities, counties, or solid waste management districts.[20] Service delivery contracts, mutual aid agreements, joint ownership of facilities, and risk pooling for insurance coverage are forms of interlocal agreement.

Administrative Discretion

State rules govern local legislative processes, including the adoption of ordinances; the authority to engage in contracting, planning, and zoning; and the receipt, investment, and payment of public funds. State laws instruct local government executive officers on matters such as how frequently to meet with department heads and how many days may elapse before complaints about license holders must be heard.[21]

Indiana law governs purchases involving any expenditure of public funds by any local governmental body, and the Indiana Code contains numerous rules covering local government purchasing and contracting authority and procedures. In addition to a general statute covering most local governments,[22] there are separate sets of rules governing various categories of special-purpose districts and authorities such as hospital authorities, housing authorities, library boards, and municipally owned utilities.

There are fewer state restrictions on local government personnel matters, including compensation.[23] Despite this grant of authority, however, compensation increases are limited because personnel costs represent the majority of local government operating budgets, and the state limits the growth of those operating budgets. State law does not prohibit political activity by municipal employees, require municipalities to adopt an employee grievance process, or require local officials to engage in collective bargaining with representatives of public employee unions. Wider local latitude over personnel matters reflects Indiana's prevailing approach to employment practices generally, rather than a particular generosity toward local governments per se.

State law requires some municipalities (usually those with more than 10,000 people) to adopt a merit system covering certain positions, provide some form of retirement plan option and some form of group health insurance, and cover municipal employees under the state's worker compensation program. Indiana local governments may participate in the state-managed pension fund, the Public Employees Retirement Fund (PERF). Governments may apply for (or withdraw from) membership in PERF and decide which jobs they wish to cover.[24]

Although they regulate and limit local government functions, state activities do provide support services. Several state agencies provide training and technical assistance for municipal officials and personnel.[25] The Indiana Department of Transportation's Division of Local Assistance helps local governments develop projects and procure federal funding. Right-of-way agreements are processed by the Division of Land Acquisition. The

Board of Firefighting Personnel Standards and Education certifies firefighter training and education programs and fire department instructors. The Law Enforcement Training Board establishes minimum training standards. The board also provides executive-level training for police chiefs and basic training and continuing education for law enforcement officers.

Economic Development

Counties, cities, and towns in Indiana are authorized to engage in planning, zoning, land-use regulation, and code enforcement. A city, town, or county may form a redevelopment commission to oversee the recovery of blighted areas. Two or more counties may also establish a regional planning commission to coordinate economic development activities for the region.[26] State legislation enacted in 1992, however, prohibited the establishment of enterprise zones, economic development districts, and allocation areas after December 31, 1995.

The Indiana Department of Commerce provides technical assistance on community development issues and municipal finance. Department of Commerce staff also work with visitor and trade bureaus, regional planning commissions, and local economic development organizations.

Fiscal Autonomy of Local Governments

Local fiscal autonomy in Indiana is an oxymoron. Every aspect of local public finance—from revenue sources to annual budgets to financial accounting to indebtedness—is covered by state requirements, review, and/or limits.

Local Revenues

The state has restricted local property taxes, through limits on rates or on the total levy or both, since 1932. The degree to which those state-imposed limits continued to abide varied a great deal, however. In its 1966 report, the Indiana Commission on State Tax and Financing Policy alleged that not only were property tax rate limits erratically obeyed and enforced, but they also belied "a form of distrust of either the tax officials or of the local electorate by the state legislature."

Despite this critique, Indiana created an even more extensive system of property tax limits in 1973 (well before California's much publicized Proposition 13). These changes limited all three aspects of property tax revenues for municipalities—that is, tax rates, the rate of increase in assessed valuation of property, and the rate of increase in the total property tax levy. Property taxes can be raised beyond state controls only if civil units successfully appeal to the State Board of Tax Commissioners or if local school corporations hold a successful referendum.

Indiana's history of property tax controls helps to explain the prominent position of the state Board of Tax Commissioners. Also called the state tax board, it was created in 1891 and is the oldest state tax commission of its kind in the nation. It has always had the formal charge of overseeing the assessment and taxation of real property in Indiana, but its control over local finances has grown as the state has increased its controls. The board consists of three members appointed by the governor for renewable terms. However, its staff is much more extensive and is now organized into divisions comprising numerous field representatives as well as personnel in Indianapolis.

Legislation governing property assessment, adopted in 1949, expanded the powers of the state Board of Tax Commissioners. The board could determine assessment practices and require county and township assessors to follow those regulations. In 1961 the board was given the authority to equalize assessments between taxing districts and classes of property.[27] The board can order real property reassessed on taxpayer petition; it orders approximately 6,000 parcels to be reassessed every year. In 1991 the board ordered that an entire county be reassessed.[28] It also issues guidelines for the use of property tax exemptions and deductions, conservancy districts, and special taxing districts.

When it adopted the 1973 property tax freeze, the state supplied two options to compensate for the revenue losses. The first option made localities more financially dependent on the state: the state's general sales tax was increased from two to four cents per dollar, with most of the increased revenue earmarked for local governments for property tax replacement. The second option made municipalities more dependent on counties. Counties were granted the option of adopting an adjusted gross income tax, the revenue from which was intended for local units within the county for property tax replacement.[29] Although counties must distribute income tax revenues to other local governments within their borders, the counties have kept the lion's share of income tax revenues. As of 1994, 61 percent of local income tax revenues in Indiana were retained by counties, whereas municipalities received 27.5 percent.

The state tried to ensure that adoption of an income tax option would not increase overall tax burdens. Counties that adopted the income tax were subject to a freeze on property tax *revenues* (that is, all increases in local revenues had to come from the income tax or other sources). Counties that did not adopt the income tax were subject to a freeze on property tax *rates* (that is, future growth in property tax revenues would have to come from growth in assessed valuation rather than rate increases).

The state has authorized other county local-option taxes: the innkeeper's tax (1972), admissions tax (1980), the county wheel tax (1980), and food and beverage tax (1981).[30] Municipalities may request approval from the General Assembly to impose the innkeeper's, admissions, or food and beverage tax, but only counties may impose the wheel tax. Table 1 shows the results of a statewide review of local government revenues in Indiana.

State controls on local taxes have succeeded in keeping the local tax burden low in Indiana,[31] but this has been achieved at

Table 1. Distribution of Local Governmental Revenues in Indiana, 1991

Source of revenue	Counties		Municipalities	
	$ per capita	Percent	$ per capita	Percent
Intergovernmental	$88	22%	$119	22%
Property taxes	82	21	136	26
Other taxes	40	10	25	5
Fees and charges	149	38	98	18
Utilities	0	0	92	17
Other revenues	36	9	61	11
Total	395	100	531	100

Source: Indiana University Center for Urban Policy and the Environment (1994).

the expense of local control and with greater local dependence on state government funding. Undaunted, Indiana legislators in the 1998 and 1999 sessions debated eliminating local property taxes as a basis for funding public school operations and replacing them with state appropriations. The measure did not pass in either session.

With respect to borrowing, the Indiana Constitution limits local bonded indebtedness to no more than 2 percent of a jurisdiction's assessed valuation; the maximum life of bond issues is also limited. State law provides a process whereby taxpayers may block bond issues. Issuance of general-obligation bonds is subject to review by the state Board of Tax Commissioners, which may approve, reduce, or reject a proposed bond issue.

Because general-obligation bonds are restricted, several local governments have turned to lease-purchase agreements. These agreements do not require the prior approval of the tax commissioners' board and do not count against the constitutional 2 percent debt limitation. However, local governments that wish to execute lease-purchase agreements must publish notice of them. If ten or more resident taxpayers sign a petition objecting to the lease on the basis that it is "unnecessary or unwise," the board will hold a hearing and make a final administrative determination.[32]

Local Expenditures

Table 2 shows the results of a statewide review of local government expenditures in Indiana. The real story of state-local fiscal relations in Indiana is demonstrated not by revenue-expenditure balance sheets, however, but by the state's virtually unparalleled control of local government budgeting. The state has used property tax controls to implement annual state-level review and approval of every local government budget in Indiana. The Board of Tax Commissioners and its staff exercise the state's discretion in reviewing and approving local government budgets. State law and board rules specify in remarkable detail the procedures to be followed, forms to be filled out, and dead-

lines to be met in the preparation of local government budgets.[33] The Indiana Association of Cities and Towns' guidelines for helping municipal officials through the budget-preparation process cover twenty-four single-spaced pages.

The municipal budget process begins with the publication of the estimated budget for the coming fiscal year. This public notice must contain the estimated budget, the tax levy required, the proposed property tax rate, and the time and place for a public hearing on the budget. Once advertised, the amounts for the budget, tax rate, and tax levy constitute a legal ceiling on each of those items—none can be increased. The public hearing on the budget must be completed at least seven days before the municipality's legislative body formally approves the budget, tax rate, and tax levy. Towns and third-class cities must approve their budgets by the last Monday in August. First- and second-class cities must approve their budgets by their last September meeting.

Field examiners for the tax commissioner's board then hold informal hearings on the approved budgets of local units of government in each respective county. The field examiners make recommendations to the board, which issues final budget orders by January 15. Each final budget order includes the state-allowed budget amount and the state-allowed tax rate.

If municipal officials discover that during the course of the fiscal year the state-allowed budget amount will be insufficient, an "additional appropriation" is necessary. To make additional appropriations, a municipality must advertise on two separate occasions the request for the appropriation. The city or town council must then hold a public hearing. If the council approves the additional appropriation, the appropriation is transmitted to the state Board of Tax Commissioners. If the additional spending will occur in a fund that receives property taxes, the board must also hold a public hearing on it. Ultimately, the additional appropriation must be approved by the board.

Once the fiscal year begins, municipal officials may transfer

Table 2. Distribution of Local Governmental Expenditures in Indiana, 1991

Category of expenditure	Counties		Municipalities	
	$ per capita	Percent	$ per capita	Percent
Intergovernmental	$28	7%	—	—
Administrative	82	21	$93	17%
Streets and highways	44	11	32	6
Public safety	—	—	80	15
Welfare	44	11	—	—
Health and hospitals	140	36	—	—
Utilities	—	—	173	32
Other	51	13	158	29
Total	389	100	536	100

Source: Indiana University Center for Urban Policy and the Environment (1994).

money from one major budget classification to another within a department or office. State law requires, however, that the transfer be approved at a regular public meeting and by proper ordinance. State law also used to require that the tax commissioners' board be notified of the transfer, but the public hearing and ordinance provisions now suffice.[34]

Indiana does not have a statute or regulation providing for, prohibiting, or otherwise governing the matter of municipal bankruptcies, nor is there a precedent for such a situation. State law and regulations control the municipal budgeting process so completely that a municipality is unlikely to implement inadequately funded budgets to the point of financial calamity.

All local government expenditures are subject to review by the state Board of Accounts. The board establishes a uniform system of accounting and record-keeping procedures for all governments within the state, and it conducts audits. Fiscal reports of local governments, reports of their street departments' purchases and activities, and records of public employees are filed with the board and are examined by field supervisors. The accounts board audits the financial systems used by local governments, issues financial reports, and often performs tests to check the accuracy of municipalities' accounting. When there are allegations of misconduct, the board performs specific audit work. A recent addition to the Indiana Code authorizes governmental bodies to use electronic or digital signatures to authorize purchases and conduct transactions.[35]

State Government Grants-in-Aid to Localities

In addition to locally raised revenue and their distributions from the state's Property Tax Replacement Fund, municipalities receive distributions from other state and county taxes. These include a motor vehicle excise tax, a gasoline tax, tobacco taxes, alcoholic beverage taxes, inheritance taxes, and a financial institutions tax. Distributions totaled $2.33 billion in 1995–1997 ($1.15 billion for fiscal 1995–1996, $1.18 billion for fiscal 1996–1997) and represent virtually all state financial assistance to local governments in Indiana. All other state distributions to local governments amounted to $159 million, or 0.6 percent of the state's $25.3 billion in expenditures during the 1995–1997 biennium.

State grants to localities included support for victims' assistance programs, Drug-Free Indiana funds, community health center start-up costs, disaster and other emergency preparedness, and wastewater and hazardous materials treatment. A state revolving-loan fund—administered by the Indiana Department of Environmental Management and capitalized with federal and state funds—makes low-interest loans available for developing or upgrading wastewater collection and treatment systems. Another revolving-loan fund for local infrastructure improvement projects was authorized by the General Assembly in 1996, but no funds were appropriated. Revenue transfers work in both directions in Indiana. For example, the state funds much of its share

of the basic family-assistance program (formerly Aid to Families with Dependent Children, now Temporary Assistance to Needy Families) with county property-tax revenues.

Unfunded Mandates

Unfunded mandates are not prohibited by constitution or statute in Indiana. There is no mandate-reimbursement requirement, nor must local impact statements be attached to bills that are introduced in the General Assembly. Partly because there are no mandate restrictions, data on state mandates to local governments are not collected on an ongoing basis. A commission appointed by the legislature in 1993 to study local government finances recommended barring any state mandate that would increase local government expenditures, unless the state provided funds or a funding mechanism. Such an amendment was introduced in the 1994 legislative session but not approved.

A 1997 survey by the Indiana Advisory Commission on Intergovernmental Relations asked local government officials, "Which mandates/responsibilities most significantly affect your local government's ability to meet the needs of your community?" The survey respondents were asked to distinguish between state and federal mandates and to rank their answers according to impact. The top six areas of responsibility were (in descending order of impact) tax controls, welfare funding, corrections, court funding, health, and pension.

Access to Local Government

Local Elections

State law specifies when county and municipal primary and general elections may be held and what the requirements are for candidate qualification and voter eligibility. Municipal elections in Indiana are held in the odd-numbered years preceding a presidential election year. Elections for county government offices occur in general election years, with some offices filled during presidential election years and the others in congressional election years.

The state Election Commission regulates what voting equipment may be used and collects and maintains the canvassers' precinct election results. State law requires counties to pay all expenses associated with voter registration and the conduct of elections. Counties may charge municipalities for the costs of any extra personnel or supplies needed for a municipal primary or general election; counties may not charge for the ongoing or overhead costs of the county voter registration and election functions. Furthermore, counties may not charge towns for the costs of primary or general elections that occur in the same year as a county election.[36]

Nominees of the major parties for county and municipal offices are decided in primary elections, except in towns of less than 3,500 population. Candidates running for major-party nominations for local offices who wish their name to appear on the primary ballot are required by law to file a formal declaration of candidacy during a 30-day period 74–104 days before the primary election.[37]

Candidates for local offices (except for offices paying less than $5,000 per year) are required by state law to form campaign committees and to file campaign finance reports by certain deadlines specified by statute. State law limits contributions from corporations and labor unions to candidates for local government offices. County election boards are mandated to use the state's system for filing, coding, and cross-indexing campaign finance data; to make the reports and statements available for public inspection and copying; and to monitor candidate report filings and to publicly identify delinquent reporting.[38]

State law does not provide for local initiative, referendum, or recall elections, at least not when instigated by local officials or citizens. The state reserves the right to order local officials to conduct referendums on issues when the legislature chooses, as was the case with the 1993 statute ordering certain referendums on riverboat gambling. State law requires approval by the tax commissioners' board (but not local voter approval through referendum) of general-obligation bonds issued by municipalities—another example of Indiana's preference for state over popular control.

Citizen Controls over Actions of Local Officials

Indiana's open-meeting and open-records laws are phrased in expansive language and apply to local government bodies of all sorts, such as agencies, boards, commissions, authorities, and councils.[39] The open-meeting mandate includes a requirement that notice be provided of the time, location, and agenda of the meeting.

The 1993 ACIR survey of state rules governing localities indicated that municipal officials in Indiana are not subject to a state-imposed code of ethics. State laws do, however, define and prohibit conflicts of interest, reckless misuse of public resources, and other ethical violations by local officials, their appointees, and consultants and contractors doing business with local governments. According to state law, any local official convicted of a felony may be removed from office as a part of the sentence for his or her conviction. Moreover, allegations of malfeasance in office against any local official may be presented to the grand jury of the county. Jury trials are conducted in the same manner as trials for misdemeanors, and the verdict determines if the official will be retained or removed from office.[40]

State-Local Relations

Local officials in Indiana have expressed frustration about their relationship with state government. Lack of a regular fo-

rum in which state and local representatives can communicate has been particularly disappointing. The establishment of the Governor's Local Government Advisory Council in 1989 raised the hopes of local officials, but the advisory council languished; meetings were not held and vacancies went unfilled. The creation of the Indiana Advisory Commission on Intergovernmental Relations in 1995 is the most recent effort to address local officials' concerns. Its activities and staffing have been modest.

Local officials' disappointment with the state executive branch has been exacerbated by legislative actions during the 1990s. Trends toward preemptions, special legislation, and fiscal controls have accelerated rather than abated. In 1992 the General Assembly replaced local governments' authority to regulate the use or application of pesticides with that of a pesticide review board. Municipalities were prohibited from regulating the sounding of a warning whistle or bell at railroad crossings. In 1993 they were barred from enacting rent-control ordinances. New gun-control ordinances could not be enforced, except with respect to firearms on municipally owned public property, as per a 1994 statute. Another 1994 law prohibited municipalities from regulating the placement or use of satellite dishes smaller than twenty-four inches in diameter.[41] A petition-and-remonstrance procedure for challenging local government bond issues was created in 1995 and has resulted in litigation. A 1996 bill barring municipalities from adopting further cigarette-smoking restrictions passed the General Assembly, was vetoed by the governor, but nevertheless was passed in the 1997 legislative session. Another 1996 statute, applicable to all classes of city, states that police officers and firefighters do not have to reside within the jurisdictions they protect.

In the words of a commentator writing after the adoption of the 1980 Home Rule Act, Indiana's "unspoken assumption is that the state legislature is the sole safe bursar of governmental power," and "'communal freedom' in de Tocqueville's sense has not yet come to form part of Indiana's mores."[42] Recent trends toward more restrictions on local government finances and preemptions of functional areas reinforce those conclusions.

Notes

1. Indeed, one state legislator who supported Unigov admitted to a local newspaper that he opposed a referendum because Unigov would not pass if one were held.

2. *City of Richmond v. S.M.O., Inc.,* 165 Ind. App. 641, 333 N.E.2d 797 (1975).

3. Susan B. Rivas, "The Indiana Home Rule Act: A Second Chance for Local Self-Government," *Indiana Law Review* 16, no. 3 (1983): 684; Leslie Bender, "Home Rule, Revisited," *Journal of Legislation* 10, no. 1 (winter 1983): 232.

4. David Nice states that this is a "devolution of authority" statute rather than "home rule" proper. See Nice, *Federalism: The Politics of Intergovernmental Relations* (New York: St. Martins Press, 1987), 140–141.

5. Indiana Code 36-1-3-2, 36-1-3-3, 36-1-3-4, 36-1-3-5.

6. The Local Government Study Commission, which recommended the Home Rule Act, acknowledged the following in its 1981 report to the General

Assembly, titled "Understanding the New Local Government Law": "Like traditional local government powers, Home Rule powers are delegated powers; they have been freely given and may be freely limited or taken away by the General Assembly."

7. Indiana Code 36-1-3-8.

8. Bender, "Home Rule, Revisited," 240.

9. Indiana Constitution, Article 4, sections 22 and 23.

10. Also in 1993 the legislature altered the annexation requirements within Lake County in northwest Indiana. Towns with populations greater than 27,000 (that is, Merrillville) would no longer be required to obtain consent from the legislative body of a second- or third-class city (that is, Gary, Hammond, or Hobart) when annexing territory within three miles of their corporate boundaries.

11. Indiana Code 5-1.4. State Treasurer Joyce Brinkman's challenge to the constitutionality of this bill was dismissed in October 1997.

12. U.S. Advisory Commission on Intergovernmental Relations (ACIR), *State Laws Governing Local Government Structure and Administration,* report no. M-186 (Washington, D.C.: ACIR, 1993), 59.

13. If the population of a second-class city falls below 35,000, the city can choose to remain a second-class city or convert to a third-class city.

14. Third-class cities may choose to employ a city manager in addition to a mayor. See Indiana Code 36-4-12.

15. The elected assessor, auditor, and treasurer serve ex officio as the board of county commissioners, even though the Unigov mayor (elected countywide) actually functions as the county's chief executive officer.

16. There are exceptions to these general rules: the three-mile perimeter restriction does not apply in Lake County (northwest Indiana), and towns may incorporate in Hancock County (east of Indianapolis) within four miles of Indianapolis.

17. Kerry Thompson and Timothy McCaulay, "Municipal Annexation," *Municipal Law IX* (Indianapolis: Indiana Continuing Legal Education Foundation, 1992), 2.

18. Indiana Code 36-1-3-9; see also 36-1-4-18, which extends the territorial reach of powers granted under 36-1-4-5 and 36-1-4-6.

19. For example, according to a 1985 attorney general's opinion, cities and towns in Indiana are not mandated by state law to provide law enforcement services. The county sheriff is responsible for responding to calls from the public within incorporated municipalities (except for those concerning the violation of city or town ordinances). Opinion 85-9, 44.

20. Indiana Code 36-1-7; also 36-10-3-29 (authorizes units to create joint parks and recreation departments). However, note that 36-1-7-3 specifies the form and contents of interlocal agreements, and 36-1-7-4 and 36-1-7-5 indicate when interlocal agreements require state approval.

21. Indiana Code 36-4-5-6, 36-4-5-5.

22. See, for example, Indiana Code 5-22, 36-1-9, 36-1-9.1, 36-1-9.5, 36-1-10, 36-1-10.5, 36-1-11, 36-1-12, 36-1-12.5, and 36-1-13; 5-22.

23. Indiana Code 36-1-4-15, for example, authorizes cities, towns, and counties to "fix the level of compensation of [their] officers and employees." But see Indiana Code 36-4-7-1 et seq. specifying the procedures and deadlines to be followed by second- and third-class cities in setting the compensation of elected and appointed officials and of employees.

24. Indiana Code 5-10.3.

25. The state Board of Accounts offers training to local officials and staff on fiscal management. The Indiana Commission on Public Records advises local governments on the improvement of records systems. The Division of Rehabilitation Services of the Indiana Family and Social Services Administration provides technical assistance on federal compliance. The Indiana Department of Natural Resources provides technical assistance on local flood and erosion control programs, historic preservation, and parks and recreation planning.

26. Indiana Code 36-7-14, 36-7-7.

27. David J. Bennett and Stephanie E. Stullich, *Financing Local Government in Indiana* (Fort Wayne: Lincoln Printing Corp., 1992), 23.

28. Sandra K. Bickel, "State Board of Tax Commissioners," *Municipal Law IX* (Indianapolis: Indiana Continuing Legal Education Foundation, 1992), 6.

29. Since 1973, the state has authorized, and the Indiana Department of Revenue has collected, two other forms of local option income taxes. In 1983 the state authorized a different county-option income tax, revenues from which were not restricted to property tax relief. Counties may adopt either type of income tax but not both. In 1987 a county economic development income tax was authorized for capital needs associated with economic development projects. Counties may adopt this economic development income tax in addition to either of the other two county-option income taxes. Lake County is separately authorized to impose an "employment tax."

30. The innkeeper's tax is authorized for Allen, Brown, Clark, Elhart, Floyd, Howard, Jefferson, Knox, Lake, Laporte, Marion, Monroe, St. Joseph, Tippecanoe, Vanderburgh, Vigo, Wayne, and White Counties. Hendricks and Marion Counties impose the admissions tax. The food and beverage tax is authorized for Allen, Delaware, Henry, Madison, Marion, and Vanderburgh Counties.

31. According to the Indiana Fiscal Policy Institute, local property taxes amounted to $33 per $1,000 of personal income in 1993, compared with a Midwest average of $37 and a national average of $35. Total local taxes per $1,000 of personal income were just $37 in Indiana, compared with $44 in the Midwest and $45 nationwide.

32. Bickel, "State Board of Tax Commissioners," 18.

33. Indiana Code 36-4-7-6 et seq.

34. Bickel, "State Board of Tax Commissioners," 15.

35. Indiana Code 5-11; see also 5-13, which establishes methods to be used by local officials in receiving, recording, investing, and making payments from public funds; 5-24.

36. Indiana Code 3-5-3-1.

37. Indiana Code 3-10-1-4 (the nominees in the smaller towns may be chosen in town party conventions), 3-8-2.

38. Indiana Code 3-9-2, 3-9-4.

39. Indiana Code 5-14-1.5, 5-14-3.

40. See, for example, Indiana Code 5-6-11-2, 5-6-11-5.5, 5-6-11-6 et seq., 35-44-1-1 et seq., 36-4-8-13, 36-7-4-223, 36-7-4-909, 36-7-12-16, and 36-7-18-11; 5-8-1.

41. Thomson Consumer Electronics, which manufactures the small dishes, used to have manufacturing facilities in the state. The company is headquartered in Carmel, Indiana, a suburb just north of Indianapolis.

42. Bender, "Home Rule, Revisited," 238–239, 243.

IOWA

Paul Coates, Jack Whitmer, and Tom Bredeweg

Constitutional amendments in 1968 and 1978 granted home rule to Iowa cities and counties, respectively. For cities, the promise of home rule has been disappointing because it has not resulted in any significant independence from state interference. Following the 1968 amendments, sweeping legislation consolidated the city code and further restricted cities, particularly with regard to budgetary and financial matters. Home rule has been more positive for counties, however, because counties can create local laws on issues not covered under state statutes. Historically considered extensions of state government, counties regard the power to address local issues as a significant improvement.

The state has retained a stranglehold on revenues for both cities and counties. Both units are restricted to the property tax and a small portion of the sales tax as the major sources of tax revenue. To access the sales tax requires passage of a referendum. Both units have limits on the tax rate and the percentage of the residential value that can be accessed. In recent years and at various times, they have been subjected to growth limits. The state has not been reluctant to impose mandates on cities and counties or to limit local authority. Examples include restricting the ability of cities to pass gun controls and mandating that counties pay increased costs for mental retardation services. As a result of state action, home rule has not been enhanced since the passage of the amendments. In some cases, there has been a return to pre–home rule conditions.

Governmental Setting

Iowa has a population of about 2.5 million; the state consists of 950 incorporated cities and 99 counties. As in other midwestern states, Iowa's history as a farming center has resulted in a dispersed population.[1] Iowa did not evolve one or more very large metropolitan centers—a characteristic that separates Iowa from its neighboring states of Minnesota, Illinois, Wisconsin, Missouri, and Nebraska. As a result, about 40 percent of the population still resides in rural areas and cities of less than 2,500 population.

Iowa has eight metropolitan areas as defined by the U.S. Bureau of the Census. Because of the lack of a dominant center, the state has remained rural. All incorporated units in Iowa are called cities, and with few exceptions they all have the same legal powers. Not only the powers but also the structures of elected offices are comparable among counties as well.

Iowa has experienced a steady decline in population for most of the past hundred years.[2] Agriculture, the traditional economic base for rural Iowa, no longer needs a large labor pool; that, plus the decline in the number of individuals who earn their livelihood directly from farming, has left most rural cities and counties reeling. Basic services such as law enforcement and water and road maintenance are difficult for many rural cities to maintain. The single biggest problem for rural cities, and for the state as a whole, is the inability to retain young people. Iowa ranks in the top five states in percentage of older people. Unlike the Sun Belt states, Iowa achieves that status by loss of young people rather than through influx of the elderly.

Beginning in the 1980s, the state and the local governments became much more aggressive in trying to diversify the economy beyond production agriculture by providing various tax incentives, loans, and grants directly to businesses. These efforts met with some success, resulting in a stabilized population in some parts of the state. However, the growth has been unequal; urbanized areas are experiencing growth, whereas most rural areas continue to decline. This pattern might not be significant in many states, but in Iowa (where the population has been traditionally dispersed), it is having a major effect on the state's character. Today, Iowa is increasingly being divided into two worlds—fast-growing suburban areas and declining rural areas. As a result, local governments use their home rule powers to promote varying agendas as they forge their relationship with the state.

At the state government level, the executive branch comprises seven elected offices: attorney general, secretary of agriculture, state auditor, secretary of state, state treasurer, governor, and lieutenant governor. The governor has administrative authority over state agencies, even if they have appointed boards, such as the Department of Transportation. Together with the item veto, the governor's control over administrative agencies gives the office considerable power.

Like many states in the Midwest, Iowa is often thought of as a Republican state. That perception was accurate until the 1960s, when the Democrats captured the governor's office. They relinquished control to the Republicans from 1968 until 1998, when a Democrat was elected. Control of the legislature has alternated between parties. The Democrats held both houses from the mid-1980s until 1992. They held the senate until 1996, when for the first time in fourteen years a single party held the governor's office and both houses of the legislature. At the presidential level, Iowa was considered a Republican state until 1988, when the state's seven electoral votes went to the Democrats, a trend that continued through 1996.

The party system exists at the county level but not at the city level. As at the state level, both parties are competitive, and each holds about half of the county elected offices. In recent years, the administrative offices at the county level have been slightly more Republican, whereas the supervisors have been slightly more Democratic. Regardless of party affiliation, the philosophical leanings of county officials tend to be conservative in terms of the role of government in providing programs.[3]

Home Rule in Iowa

Historical Development

Iowa municipalities first gained home rule in 1851, before the present constitution was adopted in 1857. The first home rule statute was enacted to provide an alternative to "special charters"; for each city charter, legislative approval was required. This practice was carried over from the territorial system in which all powers were vested in the territorial legislature, which then granted charter status to incorporated cities. The 1851 home rule statute offered great opportunities, but the cities that stood to gain the most did not choose to utilize the power. Between 1838 and 1857, the forty settlements interested in local self-government had obtained special charters from the territorial legislature and the early state legislature.

The Iowa Constitution prohibited the legislature from issuing special charters, requiring instead that it pass only general laws that were uniform throughout the state. In 1858 a general incorporating act established the basis for all future municipal incorporation. Municipalities were classified as towns (less than 2,000 population), second-class cities (2,000–15,000), or first-class cities (over 15,000). In addition, there were forty special-charter cities that were allowed to retain their original charters until 1951. During the 1857–1868 period, the courts increasingly restricted city powers. The courts tended to perceive cities as having no inher-

ent power beyond that granted and prescribed by the legislature. This tendency culminated in 1868 with Dillon's Rule.

In 1868 Judge John Dillon of the Iowa Supreme Court encumbered not only Iowa municipalities but also municipalities throughout the United States. Dillon's Rule states that municipalities have only those powers expressly granted by the legislature, which can be modified only by implied powers.[4] Implied powers flow out of the express powers that are deemed essential for the accomplishment of the purpose and objectives of the municipalities. Implied powers can be invoked only when they are absolutely indispensable. An example of implied powers can be found in zoning laws; state law provides express powers to create certain types of zones but does not specify the restrictions that local governments put in the zones.

These tenets and strict interpretations of the legislature's statutes have crippled both Iowa cities and the Iowa General Assembly. By 1950 there were 2,700 sections in the Iowa Code pertaining to municipalities. The legislature demonstrated session after session that it had neither the time, the knowledge, nor the will to interpret local concerns and formulate effective statutes. Local governance and public management became more complex; problems that required immediate resolution were invariably and indefinitely postponed.

The home rule reform effort in Iowa began slowly with a 1949 "study committee," but little was accomplished until the 1960s. Although legislative home rule was attempted in 1963, by 1965 it had been challenged so often that many public policy makers, as well as the courts, were convinced of its ineffectiveness. A final push ended with the passage of the 1968 constitutional amendment granting home rule authority to all Iowa cities. The actual implementation of home rule for cities came in 1972 with the passage of the unified code that changed the financial structure of cities.

The final action on home rule in Iowa occurred in 1978 with the passage of a constitutional amendment granting home rule to counties. Having observed the aftermath of the constitutional amendment that granted home rule to cities, county leaders sought to avoid the creation of a unified code section for counties.[5] Although home rule granted counties the power to pass ordinances, county leaders suspected that the legislature might limit the areas in which counties could use their new powers. Moreover, county structure was diffuse, and the power and independence of different offices was jealously guarded. Counties, therefore, wanted to determine for themselves how they would carry out their new powers, without interference from the legislature.[6]

Definition of Home Rule

The 1968 constitutional amendment stipulates three limitations to Iowa cities' control over local affairs. First, home rule power cannot be inconsistent with the laws of the General Assembly. Second, home rule power must be exercised only with regard to local affairs and government. Third, home rule power does not include the power to levy taxes.

Under a 1971 revision to the Iowa Code (Title XV), cities gained an additional form of local government known as the home rule charter form. The revision also resulted in the creation of a statewide City Development Board, with the power to rule on annexation and similar boundary issues, and a statewide City Finance Committee, which would set accounting and budgeting standards. Cities were given the majority of the members on the City Finance Committee; this was important because it allowed cities to influence the financial structure under which they operate.

For Iowa counties, the passage of the constitutional amendment in 1978 meant that they could pass ordinances—something that previously had been possible only on a case-by-case basis. Although historically cities had the power to create local laws, counties had no such power. Because counties were extensions of the state, it seemed unnecessary that they should have local authority. The constitutional amendment for counties also contained the three limitations that applied to cities.

Structural Features

The Home Rule Amendment of 1968 granted Iowa cities home rule, but it was a legislative action following the amendment that created the structural options for cities. Under the code revisions of 1971, cities have a choice of six different forms of organizational structure: mayor-council, council-manager at large, council-manager with wards, commission, special district, and home rule charter. For home rule charter cities, an odd number of council members are elected on a nonpartisan basis. A city form can be changed if a petition with a sufficient number of signatures is presented to the city council. The council must appoint a charter commission to study the issue, and the commission may recommend a new charter. A proposed charter is presented to the voters for their approval at the next general election. If a new form is adopted by majority vote, it cannot replace the existing form for six years; however, the existing form can be challenged at any time by a different proposal.

By the late 1960s, unwarranted annexation by cities for defensive rather than development purposes was rife. The City Development Board was created by a 1971 initiating act to oversee city annexation, incorporation, and dissolution. The board determines if a city is capable of providing services to the annexed area within a set number of years. Some extraterritorial authority is permitted to cities, which can control zoning within a two-mile radius of their corporate boundaries if the county that contains the city is not zoned. If the county is zoned, the city has subdivision power within the two-mile limit. In addition, cities are allowed to own facilities such as airports, water wells, and landfills outside their legal jurisdiction.

The code revisions of 1971 also created a City Finance Committee, which for the first time developed a uniform chart of accounts for cities. Although uniformity was a mandate on cities, the creation of the committee was generally seen as positive, because cities not only had majority representation but also achieved some fiscal control not granted as part of home rule.

Although it did not result in a unified code, the implementation of home rule for counties did unleash forces of change that eventually altered county government. Those changes were first codified in 1983 with the passage of county finance legislation, which consolidated more than thirty levying funds into two operating levies and a debt levy. This legislation severely strained internal relationships within the county courthouses because it gave county supervisors additional powers to allocate financial resources.[7] As a result, functions such as roads, conservation, welfare, and many others had to compete for funds rather than having a designated levy restricted by function. Instead of making judgments on each levy, the board of supervisors considers the overall levies and appropriates according to its priorities.

A second major initiative, county charter legislation, occurred in 1988. Traditionally, counties in Iowa have six elected offices, of which five are essentially administrative and one (the supervisor) is both legislative and administrative. The charter legislation allows for four different forms of county government structure: board-elected executive, board-manager, charter, or the current form (with six elected offices). Regardless of the form, county elections are partisan.[8] Under the charter legislation, county offices can be combined and elected offices eliminated.[9]

In addition to the forms for individual cities or counties, Iowa law allows for a consolidated city-county form, a consolidated county-county form, and a "community commonwealth." The community commonwealth is a county and one or more cities or townships in the county or in another county. This form allows for one county to be part of a unit outside its existing boundaries. To date, the one effort to utilize this form was overwhelmingly defeated at the polls.[10]

Functions of Local Government

Functional Responsibilities

The functions of cities in Iowa have evolved in virtually identical patterns to those in other midwestern states. As the frontier matured into an agrarian economy, communities sprang up to provide the goods and services required to support the countryside. As people began living closer together, the need for typical city services developed. Heavier traffic required better streets than country lanes; commercial centers and the concentration of people required more extensive law enforcement; and the proximity of dwellings magnified the need for fire protection.

Unlike counties, cities were never thought of as administrative units of the state. Cities were established to provide services that were in addition to the base level of service provided by the county and state governments. Virtually every municipal function today can be traced to that historical approach—an approach that is also instructive regarding the type of services performed by cities.

Traditional functions of cities in Iowa can be categorized into three groups: public safety, public works, and code enforcement. Police and fire protection have been nearly universal services since the earliest cities took shape. Today, emergency medical and rescue teams have become a part of public safety. Streets, water, sewers, sidewalks, and the collection and disposal of waste have dominated public works activities. Code enforcement in a very broad sense implies the establishment of regulations, whether for protection, sanitation, or tranquility.

Iowa cities perform some special functions, often as adjuncts to more traditional services. Parks and recreation, libraries, and other public amenities were provided as citizens looked to the city to offer leisure activities unavailable through other means. More recent functions include economic development and the provision of cable television and emerging communications technologies.

As in many states, county government in Iowa performs a dual role as an extension of the state and as a unit of local government. As an arm of the state, counties perform functions in lieu of having locally based state operations. The reason for this system is to provide locally based services that are administered uniformly throughout the state; examples include elections, vehicle registration, land and real estate record maintenance, mental retardation services, and criminal prosecution.

Some services are neither completely mandated nor entirely optional. Examples include roads, conservation, public health, law enforcement, and services for the mentally ill and the developmentally disabled. Counties must provide services but may decide the level to which the service is funded.[11] Although the county has some discretion, each service is operated according to state rules. In some cases, failure to adequately support the service with local funds can jeopardize the county's share of tax revenue; for example, inadequate road service may result in less funding from the state road use tax.

Counties may choose to provide services related to economic development, culture, or recreation. They can also create ordinances to control some activities, such as animal control. If counties opt to exercise zoning authority, they must follow statutory guidelines.[12]

In addition to exercising their powers as individual units, cities and counties may informally make financial contributions for small projects or activities, share equipment, or maintain roads interlocally. Other cooperative activities are more formalized. Contracts may be developed between local units for specific services or activities, such as law enforcement, libraries, eco-

nomic development, juvenile detention facilities, mental health facilities, and purchasing. In most cases, these arrangements are ongoing, although there are examples of one-time services or purchases. In addition to contracting with cities, many counties contract with each other. In county-to-county contracts, the most common areas covered are detention and mental health services.

A more flexible approach to interlocal cooperation is a 28E agreement. Named after the code section that created them, 28E agreements allow local governments to exercise any authority jointly that they can exercise independently. Generally, the 28E agreement results in the creation of a new entity with the responsibility to administer programs or provide services.

The organizations that are formed under the 28E agreement derive their authority from the member governments and receive much of their funding from those members. The 28E organizations can do only those things specifically designated in the agreement, and they have no taxing authority. Besides the funds received from the member governments, many of the 28E organizations obtain fees for services and secure grants for various activities and service.[13]

Both cities and counties can create special districts and public authorities. Examples of special districts are water, sewer, and drainage districts. Districts can be administered by a governmental unit or, in some cases, by an appointed board that is responsible for policy and administration. These authorities are limited to the specific function and normally raise funds through the authority of the local unit of government. Cities and counties can create public authorities that provide specific services, but on a jurisdiction-wide basis rather than in a limited area, like the special district. Examples of public authorities are public housing authorities, parks and recreation boards, and transit authorities. Such authorities usually have a board, the members of which are appointed by the jurisdiction that administers the authority. The board's funding can come from the jurisdiction or from fees and grants.

In addition to the public bodies that can be created by the local units, there are statutory bodies that administer some local services. Examples are library boards, hospital boards, conservation boards, and public health boards. The members of these boards often are appointed by the jurisdiction, but in some cases (such as hospitals), they are elected. Most receive all or part of their funding from the local units of government or from fees for service.

Administrative Discretion

Local governments in Iowa have authority to administer services within the dictates of state performance standards. Both cities and counties can develop their own personnel policies, except in the cases of retirement and collective bargaining. Iowa local governments are part of the state retirement system and are obliged to contribute employers' share. Even cities that have separate law enforcement retirement programs have little discretion because the programs are administered at the state level. Iowa has a public-sector collective bargaining law that requires local governments to negotiate if a bargaining unit is formed and votes for union representation. Iowa is a right-to-work state, so membership in the union is not compulsory for employees.

Both cities and counties are required to bid public improvements that are over $50,000, excluding supplies. The units are not required to accept the low bid if the jurisdiction has documented performance concerns. However, if there are no performance issues, the unit is expected to accept the lowest bid.

Cities and counties that choose to zone may do so according to specific legislation that guides the process. They must appoint both a zoning commission and a board of adjustment. The zoning commission is an advisory body to the city council or board of supervisors. The decisions of the board of adjustment are final but can be appealed to the state courts. Both cities and counties can utilize a variety of regulations inside a zone, except within agricultural zones. These zones have had to accommodate agricultural changes affecting the size and nature of animal operations, particularly in the area of swine operations, which require large-scale facilities. Cities can zone only within their jurisdictional boundaries, unless the county does not have zoning. In that case, the city is allowed to zone in a two-mile radius beyond its corporate boundaries.

Both cities and counties can adopt subdivision regulations. For cities, the two-mile radius applies regardless of whether or not the county implements zoning or subdivision regulation. Both units are allowed to control animals and activities such as open burning of yard waste. Except for procedural matters and the rights of appeal to the courts, the state does not have any veto authority over zoning and subdivision regulation.

Economic Development

Today, both cities and counties are actively involved in economic development. Changes in the traditional agricultural economy and concerns over population loss have spurred both cities and counties to become active participants in economic development activities designed to broaden the economic base and provide employment opportunities for young people. Cities have been involved in these efforts since the 1970s; counties became active in the 1990s. Both units of local government may use zoning authority, tax abatements, and tax increment financing. Local units can also provide loans and grants for development. Most areas of the state are served by economic development organizations that receive a majority of their funding from cities and counties. Many of these organizations are multijurisdictional, transcending city boundaries and in some cases county boundaries.

Tools such as tax abatements and tax increment financing are controlled to some extent by state law. There is a ten-year limit on tax abatements, but they can be renewed. Abatements have become very popular for attracting both industry and housing. Tax increment financing (TIF) requires the city or county to designate an urban renewal district. Once the district is established, the government normally issues bonds for improvements and then uses the growth in valuation to pay off the debt. These districts can be established for up to twenty-five years, although most do not last that long.

One major drawback to using TIF is the requirement that the debt be counted toward the 5 percent of assessed valuation limit for city or county debt. The debt limit issue has become a problem in cities, which tend to be the major users of TIF. Moreover, the use of TIF has become a divisive issue: once a city declares a TIF district, all increased tax revenue goes toward servicing the debt. This has the effect of denying counties and other taxing jurisdictions the new revenue that may accrue to the designated district.

Fiscal Autonomy of Local Government

Local government in Iowa has never had a great deal of authority in fiscal matters, and the passage of home rule did little to change that situation. Before and after the amendments to the constitution in 1968 for cities and 1978 for counties, the state exercised detailed control of local governments' budgets, tax rates, debt limits, bonding procedures, and expenditure classifications. The passage of the constitutional amendments did prompt reorganization of the financial structure in cities and counties. These state-mandated changes resulted in a reduced number of expenditure categories; for counties, centralized budgetary authority was assigned to the board of supervisors.

Before these amendments were enacted, cities budgeted and appropriated from seven functional funds. Each fund had a tax rate ceiling and specific allowable disbursements; movement of resources between funds was prohibited. The rewrite of the city code following the passage of the home rule amendment created four program areas but allowed discretion with regard to shifting funds between programs. Before the county finance system was rewritten in 1980, counties had thirty-six funds, each with its own levy. After the new system was adopted, there were three levying funds and a smaller number of expenditure categories.

Local Revenues

The general fund is used by cities for public safety, administration, and many of the traditional services provided by the city. Iowa law sets a maximum tax rate of $8.10 per $1,000 of taxable valuation. Two-thirds of all cities in Iowa levy at the maximum rate. Two other funds are designed to alleviate budget hardships on the general fund. First, a trust and agency fund can be established to pay for specific employee benefits. Although not stipulated, the levy rate is limited to the amount sufficient to raise funds to pay the expenses allowed by statute. Second, there is an emergency fund that, when triggered, allows the city to impose an additional twenty-seven cents per $1,000 taxable valuation for general purposes. Other funds with limited purposes and functions can be created. Among nearly two dozen funds that can be established with a respective tax levy are those for emergency medical services, civic facilities, levee maintenance, and transit. State law specifies how funds may be established and revenues used.

Cities, more so than counties, have traditionally utilized debt financing. Public works projects such as water plants, wastewater plants, streets, sewers, and public buildings are examples of the areas in which debt is incurred by cities. In recent years, cities have used debt through tax increment financing as a tool for economic development. They have also begun to use revenue bonds for improvements in fee-based services to preserve the debt limit for general-obligation bonds and tax increment financing. Although city debt has grown, it has yet to approach the debt limit of 5 percent of assessed valuation.

Another source of city revenue is enterprise revenue such as utility fees for water, electricity, gas, and wastewater treatment. These sources can account for as much as 50 percent of total revenues, depending on the number of utilities offered by the city. Until recently, utilities that had a surplus of revenue could use it for other than operational purposes. Today, there are legal and financial constraints that prevent significant transfer of utility revenues.

A relatively new source of revenue to cities is the local-option sales tax. Since the revenue source became available in 1985, nearly 400 cities have opted for the sales tax, generating an amount equal to 13 percent of city property taxes collected statewide.

Although cities in Iowa are fortunate in having a diverse revenue stream, they are dependent on the property tax to fund many critical local services. The property tax accounts for about 20 percent of the total revenue to cities, but it remains virtually the sole source for public safety and other essential local programs.

For counties, the property tax is the single largest source of funds. Counties have three basic operating levies, each with a maximum limit. Two of the funds—the general levy and the rural services levy—have specific limits. For the general levy, this is $3.50 per $1,000 of taxable valuation; for the rural services levy, it is $3.95 per $1,000 of taxable valuation. Thus, for a resident in the unincorporated area, a total of $7.45 per $1,000 could be levied under the basic levies.

The general fund and the rural services fund also have supplemental levies to help relieve the burden of basic levies. Sup-

plemental levies proved useful in the late 1980s, when costs for mental health services increased rapidly. There are no legal limits on the supplemental levies if demand for services continues and, therefore, costs increase.

The third fund (created in 1996) covers costs associated with provision of mental health care. This fund was created to replace the use of supplemental levies, which had rapidly increased in the early 1990s. The mental health fund is limited by a formula that includes an average of past expenditures on mental health and the level of reimbursement from the state.

Because their major areas of responsibility are roads and human services, counties (unlike cities) do not realize revenue from user fees but instead receive funding through a combination of state-shared revenues and local property taxes. Counties receive the most state-shared revenue from their portion of the state road use tax fund. Counties receive 29 percent of the statewide funds that are collected through gas taxes, vehicle registrations, and driver's license fees. Counties also receive state funds for human services costs, primarily in the area of mental health care. The state also offsets some property tax credits. In recent years the replacement of tax credits has failed to keep pace with the lost revenue because the state has capped its contributions.[14]

Monies from the levying funds are deposited into the operating funds that bear the same titles as the levies. Thus, counties have a general services fund, a rural services fund, and a debt fund. In addition, counties have a secondary road fund, which is not a levying fund but is used to combine all funds that go to secondary roads, including those from the state road use tax fund. Based on the amount decided by the board of supervisors, money from the general and the rural services fund for roads is transferred to the secondary road fund. Once in the road fund, monies cannot be withdrawn, thereby providing built-in protection against transfers for unauthorized uses. A similar protection exists for funds that are allocated to purchase land for county conservation purposes.

Counties can create other funds if they wish, provided they conform with accepted accounting principles.

Counties traditionally have not used debt financing to support major capital projects. Because they can borrow against state road funds and because funds allocated to secondary roads are protected, counties can fund projects and purchase equipment without resorting to debt financing. This situation is beginning to change as counties take on additional services that require physical facilities and as property tax growth becomes more limited. Counties and cities in Iowa both have a debt limit of 5 percent of assessed valuation within the jurisdiction. Currently, no counties approach this limit. Despite the array of other revenues and protests from the agricultural and business community, the property tax still funds critical local services. Through legislative action, the taxable portion of property value continues to shrink. In particular, the legislature has imposed a formula that prevents cities from benefiting from the growth of residential valuation resulting from either new construction or increased value.[15]

The largest users of local property taxes are the school systems, which take about half of the total tax. Of the remaining tax, cities and counties are the next major users, followed by special-purpose units. Both the assessment of the value of property and the collection of the tax are county functions. The property tax is levied against agricultural, commercial, industrial, and residential property; utilities; and until recently, machinery and equipment. Except for agricultural property, all property is taxed on market value as determined by the assessor. Agricultural land is assessed on a productivity basis.

Local Expenditures

Cities in Iowa have numerous expenditure funds, each of which is subject to restrictions. Funds are either limited by a rate ceiling (such as the general fund) or by function (such as the fund for employee benefits). In some cases, funds are limited by both. In addition, enterprise funds are restricted to supporting the expenditures needed to operate utilities and provide for needed reinvestment.

Major expenditures in cities are for maintaining the physical infrastructure of water, sewer, and streets. In the service area, public safety is the major expenditure, followed by recreational and cultural programs. In recent years, efforts in economic development have become more important. This is reflected in targeted expenditures on industrial parks and housing development. In addition, cities use tax incentives such as tax increment financing and abatements. Although technically not expenditures, they are seen as supplements to expenditures for economic development.

Counties have four expenditure funds: the general services fund, the rural services fund, the mental health fund, and the secondary road fund. The primary operating fund is the general services fund; it is from this fund that a county supports most administrative offices and departments, except the office of the county engineer. The rural services fund supports activities such as weed eradication, sanitary disposal projects, county libraries, and airport authorities. The mental health fund, created in 1996, is designed to relieve pressure on the general supplemental fund by allowing a direct levy that is tied to past expenditures and the amount of state support, which has been increasing. The secondary road fund supports the county engineer's office and road department activities. This fund is also used to support conservation activities related to road maintenance in county parks.

Expenditures for mental health care have increased so rapidly that they now surpass spending on roads in more than half of the counties. Another fast-growing area of expenditures for counties is new requirements for managing women and juveniles in detention facilities. Because of these costs and the need for additional jail space, law enforcement is now a major competitor for county dollars.

State Government Grants-in-Aid to Localities

The state shares some revenues with local government, the largest of which is a share of the state road tax fund. Counties and cities receive 29 percent and 20 percent, respectively, of the state fund. The road funds are distributed to cities on a population basis and to counties based on a formula that includes population and a factor of need. The other major state revenue is reimbursements for property tax credits. In recent years the state has used property tax incentives to assist homeowners, businesses, agriculture, and the elderly. Reimbursement of the various credits by the state has been a long-standing point of contention between local governments and the state. Because of budgetary problems in the 1980s, the state fell short of fully reimbursing local governments for property tax credits. Today the state has adopted timetables to move gradually to fully funding credits.

Unfunded Mandates

Although many local officials concede that home rule exists, mandates undermine the capacity of local units to exercise authority. Federal and state initiatives such as the Americans with Disabilities Act, environmental legislation related to landfills, road construction specifications, and jail standards directly affect autonomy. Underfunding of mandated services and state-generated property tax credits are more insidious forms of assault. Increases in compulsory spending as a proportion of local budgets reduce the ability of officials to exercise true decision making.[16] For cities, this is exemplified in state-mandated environmental regulation for water and sewer; for counties, in the requirements to pay for certain mental health services and jail standards.

Funding for the mandated services that counties perform in their role as arms of the state are sometimes shared with the state. However, in recent years the state has been increasingly reluctant to keep pace with costs, thus jeopardizing counties' discretionary programs. In some cases, such as vehicle registration, counties can retain some administrative fees to cover costs. Even for functions for which there is a fee and/or administrative allotment, counties often subsidize the function through the general property tax.

Access to Local Government

Local Elections

Local election rules make running for elected office easy and usually inexpensive. When more than two candidates seek the same elected position, the local unit of government can decide whether to have a primary election to reduce the number of candidates to two or wait until after the regular election and have a runoff if there is not a qualified winner. In cities (except one, Davenport, which has an original charter), elected positions are nonpartisan. All county elected positions are partisan. All elections are administered through the county auditor. Cities and schools reimburse the auditor for the costs incurred in managing their elections.

Citizen Controls over Actions of Local Officials

In Iowa, access to public meetings and public records are built on a foundation of openness. Budgets, bond issues, and approval of plans and specifications for major expenditures all require specific public hearings. Public records, with the exception of certain personal and medical care information, are available for inspection. They can be obtained by anyone willing to pay the cost of providing the records.

Initiative, referendum, and recall can be written into a home rule charter for cities or counties but otherwise do not exist as an option in Iowa state or local governments. Because the courts have not been clear on the status of these provisions, only a few special charters include them. Elected officials can be removed from office for specific causes such as malfeasance in office or criminal conduct.

State-Local Relations

The relationship between state and local government in Iowa is on shaky ground, primarily because the state is unwilling to give localities any independence on fiscal matters; state mandates and preemption also inhibit local control.[17] State government officials in both the executive and legislative branches extol the virtues of local control, but their actions are often to the contrary. Moreover, the courts tend to side with state control rather than deferring to home rule. For their part, local officials often focus much of their energies on complaining about the state and rarely test the limits of home rule authority.

The lack of local control over finance has reduced the significance of home rule authority. The state legislature has virtually eliminated the ability of city and county governments to capture an increased tax base from residential growth or inflation. Compensating rate hikes are often counterproductive to economic development efforts; state contributions are either capped at certain rates or restricted to narrow uses. A series of property tax limitations, which began in 1991, further proscribed local decision making.[18] Such recent actions seem to violate the spirit of home rule, a promise that is yet to be fulfilled.

Notes

1. Des Moines is the largest city, with a population just under 200,00 and a metropolitan population of about 350,000.

2. Iowa experienced steady losses in population from the late 1800s until 1990, when the census numbers leveled off.

3. See Michael Manno, "The Political Ideology of County Supervisors in Iowa" (M.A. thesis, Iowa State University, 1997). Manno surveyed the political ideology of county supervisors.

4. "Municipal Home Rule in Iowa: House File 380," *Iowa Law Review* 49 (1972): 826–862.

5. See Donald Cleveland, "Home Rule: What the H— Is It?" *The County* (September 1997): 8–11. Cleveland, then executive of the Iowa State Association of Counties, discusses counties' approaches toward implementation of home rule.

6. Elected administrative offices include county attorney, auditor, recorder, sheriff, and treasurer. Except for Woodbury County, which eliminated the recorder position, all counties have all five positions.

7. Before the finance law was enacted, each function in the county had its own levy. Today the county supervisors determine the amount each function will receive based on three levying funds.

8. This marks a difference between cities and counties in Iowa, because cities are not allowed to elect on a partisan basis. The exception is Davenport, which operates under a special charter.

9. Although Iowa law allows for some offices to be combined, the charter legislation is more flexible because it does not prescribe the distribution of functions that existed in the earlier law.

10. In 1994 Polk County—which contains Des Moines and is the largest county in Iowa—overwhelmingly rejected a commonwealth charter that would have moved some services to the county level and reconfigured the county structure.

11. For example, counties can determine the extent to which they maintain roads, where to locate roads, and when to vacate a road.

12. In a designated agricultural zone, for example, the county cannot restrict any use that is related to agriculture.

13. For example, councils of government provide planning services and administer some programs such as rural transit.

14. The biggest gap in funding occurs with the homestead credit for homeowners. The 1997 session of the legislature addressed this problem, but it will take years for the provisions to be phased in to fully fund the credits.

15. Concerned about the rapid rise in property taxes, the legislature instituted a rollback provision on residential property in the 1970s that limited growth to less than that of inflation. This provision exists today and allows local units of government to capture less than 60 percent of the market value for tax purposes.

16. State-mandated provision of mental retardation services has fiscally distressed counties.

17. Moreover, the state restricts cities and counties from regulating gun-control measures, tobacco use in public buildings, and pesticides.

18. Property tax limitations on cities were removed in 1994 but were extended for counties until 1997. There is an effort in the current legislative to reimpose these limitations.

KANSAS

H. Edward Flentje

State-local relations in Kansas operate along a continuum between home rule and state paternalism. An underlying cultural preference for local self-government makes Kansas a strong home rule state, a situation that is reflected in an effective constitutional provision for city home rule and less effectual statutory home rule for counties. Substantial local discretion in carrying out a wide range of public functions combined with considerable local autonomy in finance further enhances the practice of local self-government. Historically, compelling state purpose on occasion has transcended home rule, and the exercise of state authority has rendered local self-government temporarily impotent. In more recent times, issues of economy, equity, efficiency, and effectiveness have prompted state prescription; state lawmakers rationalize the state-local division of labor, construct state-local partnerships in the delivery and financing of services, and seek order in state-local finance. Although contentious state limits on local revenue-raising capacity historically have affected the balance between state paternalism and home rule, state lawmakers in 1999 erased a century-old practice of state limits on local property taxes. In Kansas, then, the balance tends toward home rule.

Governmental Setting

Crusading abolitionists, fervent Prohibitionists, insurgent populists, and Progressive reformers loom large in the state's history. In abolishing slavery, securing national Prohibition, realigning political parties in 1896, and embracing the Progressive Party in 1912, Kansas has been at the forefront of national political change. Kansas newspaper editor, author, and political commentator William Allen White wrote in 1922, "When anything is going to happen in this country, it happens first in Kansas . . . these things come popping out of Kansas like bats out of hell."[1]

Strains of these political upheavals continue in Kansas politics, but more pervasive to the practice of government in Kansas was and is an underlying cultural preference for self-government. Kansas governments took initial shape in the latter half of the nineteenth century, when competitive individualism, laissez-faire economics, and a political penchant for self-rule permeated the nation. New Englanders brought the skills of local government to the Kansas Territory, and after statehood, in 1861, Kansas boomed economically. The state's population surged from 107,000 in 1860 to 1,477,000 in 1890. State lawmakers immediately made generous provision for local government, and residents readily took advantage of this delegated authority to organize counties, townships, cities, and schools. From the beginning of statehood to the mid-1890s, communities of neighbors formed 105 counties, 1,509 townships, 329 cities, and 9,284 school

districts—one government on average for every 130 people.[2] Kansans had embraced local self-government with a vengeance.

The passion of Kansans for local self-government has cooled over the past century, but it remains a political instinct. Kansas continues to diffuse governmental authority, with 105 counties, 1,353 townships, 627 cities, 1,482 special districts, and 324 school districts—more local governments than in any other state except for the larger and more populous states of California, Illinois, Pennsylvania, and Texas.[3] However, this natural inclination toward self-government should not be interpreted to mean that home rule is alive and well in each of the state's 4,000 local jurisdictions. Many have suffered long-term declines in population, traceable to the turn of the nineteenth century, mostly as a consequence of agricultural economics but more often as a result of impotence in local governance. Today, more than half of the townships serve fewer than 200 residents; more than half of the cities have populations under 500; and one-third of the counties serve populations of fewer than 5,000 people.

More critical than size to the quality of home rule in Kansas cities and counties is a long-standing commitment to professional management—which has fortified home rule and found fertile ground in Kansas politics.[4] Fifty-six Kansas cities, inhabited by two-thirds of the state's total city population, have adopted the manager form of city government; another fifty-two cities have established the position of city administrator by ordinance; and thirteen of the larger counties have established the position of county administrator. Further, when faced with a choice, Kansas voters opt for professional management. City voters thus far have approved the city manager plan in fifty-seven of eighty elections, or 71 percent of the time. City voters have chosen to abandon the manager plan only once in thirty-four abandonment elections.

On occasion, compelling state purpose has caused Kansans to transcend their propensity toward local self-government and exercise paternal state rule. Vivid examples of state paternalism occurred during the state's engagement with national political movements, particularly Prohibition and Progressivism. Kansas, for example, became in 1880 the first state in the union to adopt a constitutional prohibition on the manufacture or sale of intoxicating liquors. In deference to local rule, state lawmakers charged localities with enforcement, which proved ineffective. State lawmakers responded to violations of law with the Police Government Act, which allowed city residents to create by petition a state board of police commissioners with authority to override local attempts at enforcement. State control of local police was implemented in a half-dozen Kansas cities, including Wichita, and continued for twelve more years but to little avail.

Antiliquor forces demanded more aggressive action, and state lawmakers armed law enforcement officials with extraordinary powers to search and seize, institute grand juries, enjoin and abate alleged nuisances, and oust officials for lax enforcement of prohibitory laws. The state's attorney general was given full authority of enforcement if local jurisdictions failed. Another law authorized ousting from office any public official who failed to enforce prohibitory laws or who appeared in public while intoxicated; another made city government liable for any property damage or personal injury resulting from intoxication within the jurisdiction. Thus, home rule was effectively eclipsed.

In the first two decades of the twentieth century, Progressive reformers began to redress perceived imbalances in state-local relations. State agencies were established to supervise local officials in the delivery of services, for example, in the areas of tax administration, fire safety, and road improvements. State lawmakers prescribed duties and began mandating levels of compensation and benefits for local officials, such as police and firemen. Public services formerly delegated to local jurisdictions were reassigned to newly created state agencies or officials. In the name of efficiency, economy, equity, and effectiveness, Progressives broadened the practice of state paternalism at the expense of home rule—a trend that continues today.

Home Rule in Kansas

Historical Development

For the first hundred years of statehood, home rule endured in a legal maze. Drafters of the state constitution had written provisions intended to "prevent the lumbering up of the statutes with local laws."[5] However, in an environment permeated by Dillon's Rule—a legal interpretation that cities and counties, as instruments of the state, have only that authority explicitly granted by the state—state lawmakers began almost immediately littering state statute books with local laws.[6] Special legislation, though adopted most often in response to local officials seeking clarification in local authority, was occasionally enacted with punitive intent. State courts largely ignored the constitutional limitations on special legislation and condoned state legislative action. A 1906 amendment to the constitutional limitation on local legislation specifically assigned state courts responsibility for enforcing the special-legislation ban. This caused a slight deviation in state legislative practice: rather than naming a single city or county in state law, state lawmakers began designing local laws with reference to population, assessed valuation, and other categories. Again, state courts sanctioned the legislature's creativity, and the lumbering of state statutes continued.

The state's cultural preference for local self-government and the century-long practice of special legislation were reconciled with the adoption of a constitutional amendment granting home rule to cities. Urban legislators decried the absurdities, inconsistencies, and confusion cause by myriad local laws, and the League of Kansas Municipalities proposed a home rule amendment. In the late 1950s, a state legislative committee and a state commission on constitutional revision worked independently but similarly recommended constitutional language drawn from the American Municipal Association's *Model Constitutional Provisions* and the constitution and statutes of Wisconsin. A reworked amendment was adopted by Kansas voters in November 1960 by a 55–45 margin.

Definition of Home Rule

The 1960 home rule amendment to the Kansas Constitution gives cities the power to initiate local legislation and a degree of immunity from state control.[7] The amendment begins, "Cities are hereby empowered to determine their local affairs and government including the levying of taxes, excises, fees, charges and other extractions."[8] In general, under home rule, cities may enact legislation on any subject not covered by state law; exempt themselves from state legislation that does not apply uniformly to all cities; and supplement uniform state laws with local provisions. In general, state lawmakers may exercise control over cities only through uniformly applicable laws. The language of the amendment ends with a clear statement of intent: "Powers and authority granted to cities pursuant to this section shall be liberally construed for the purpose of giving cities the largest measure of self-government."

The home rule amendment applies to all cities and is self-executing—that is, no state legislative action is required for a city to exercise home rule powers. Cities may exercise home rule powers through an "ordinary" ordinance or through a "charter" ordinance. A city may enact legislation by ordinary ordinance when no state law exists or when a city wishes to supplement a uniform state law. By charter ordinance, a city may exempt itself from the application of a state law not uniformly applicable to all cities. Enactment of a charter ordinance requires a two-thirds majority vote of the city governing body; publication of the ordinance for two consecutive weeks in the official city newspaper; and a sixty-day waiting period, during which citizens may initiate a protest petition to force a referendum on the ordinance. If a petition signed by at least 10 percent of the number voting in the last regular city election is filed, the ordinance must either be withdrawn or submitted to a referendum. If submitted to a referendum, the ordinance must be approved by a majority of those voting. A city governing body may also submit a proposed charter ordinance directly to referendum. More than 3,000 charter ordinances have been adopted by Kansas cities since the adoption of constitutional home rule.[9]

Three important limitations on city home rule are written into the constitutional amendment. First, the legislature is specifically empowered to enact "general law, applicable to all cities, for the incorporation of cities and the methods by which city boundaries may be altered, cities may be merged or consolidated and cities may be dissolved."[10] Second, cities are empowered to levy taxes, excises, fees, charges, and other extractions except when such action is "limited or prohibited by enactment of the legislature applicable uniformly to all cities of the same class." Moreover, the legislature may not establish more than "four classes of cities for the purpose of imposing all such limitations or prohibitions." Third, cities are subject to state legislative enactments "prescribing limits of indebtedness" regardless of whether such enactments are uniform or nonuniform. In sum, these provisions clearly give state lawmakers authority to prescribe city boundaries, incorporation and dissolution, debt limits, and taxes. Except for debt limits, however, cities are immune from special legislation. In the case of boundaries, incorporation, and dissolution, state lawmakers may act only through "general law, applicable to all cities" and in the case of taxes, only through uniform limitations on no more than four classes of cities. Any city ordinance on these three matters would be subject to state law.

Structural Features

Constitutional home rule powers have largely rendered special legislation and state laws concerning classes of cities meaningless. Under current law, for example, each city is classified as a city of the first, second, or third class.[11] Furthermore, hundreds of additional statutory provisions apply to a single city or to narrow classes of cities defined by population, assessed valuation, or other such schemes. Because such laws are by definition not uniformly applicable to all cities, a city may exempt itself from such laws through charter ordinance—except for those

laws concerning debt and possibly those concerning taxes.

State statutes make three basic forms of government (mayor-council, commission, and manager forms) available to cities, but ultimate authority on governmental form is decided by city governing bodies and city electors. Through home rule, cities may determine the nature of local governance virtually without state interference. Cities may decide, for example, whether to hold partisan or nonpartisan elections and how to elect officials (that is, in by-district, at-large, or a mix of district and at-large elections). Cities may also determine governing body size, mayoral powers, terms of office, compensation of governing body members, powers and compensation of appointed officials, and rules for the conduct of business. As a result of these choices, nearly half of the 627 Kansas cities operate under a form of government unique to that city.

The constitutional language providing for city home rule specifically assigns the power for determining "the methods by which city boundaries may be altered" to the state legislature, and state lawmakers have enacted general annexation laws applicable to all cities.[12] Cities may annex land through limited powers of unilateral annexation, by petition of landowners, or by approval of the board of county commissioners acting as a boundary commission. Within certain statutory limitations, a city may unilaterally annex city-owned land, platted land adjoining the city, land lying mainly within the perimeter of the city, land that will make city boundaries straight and harmonious, and certain tracts of land adjoining the city. The city must prepare a plan for extending services to the area proposed for annexation, give notice to property owners, and hold a public hearing on or near the property proposed for annexation. Agricultural lands of twenty-one acres or more cannot be annexed without the consent of the owner. Moreover, cities may also annex adjoining lands with the consent of landowners and may annex land by order of the board of county commissioners, which acts as a quasi-judicial boundary commission and follows statutory procedures in making such an order. Aggrieved parties in annexation proceedings, including cities, may appeal to the state district court.

Kansas counties achieved home rule in 1974 by statutory enactment rather than by constitutional amendment. Consequently, state lawmakers may at any time add limitations, restrictions, or prohibitions to county home rule, and they have frequently done so. Eight such limitations were written into the original home rule statute, and that number had grown to thirty-one by 1999. Although most of the exemptions written into county home rule have a rational basis (for example, with respect to changing county boundaries or legislating on state-assumed services), more recent exclusions appear contrary to the intent of home rule. For example, a number of exemptions preclude the exercise of home rule on state laws that are clearly nonuniform, such as laws concerning hospitals, civic centers, community college tuition, library boards, sale of property, community mental health and retardation, zoning, and domestic violence. As a result, state lawmakers may more easily intrude into county home rule than city home rule.

County home rule is intended to work similarly to city home rule. County home rule applies to all counties and is self-executing. Counties may exercise home rule through ordinary resolutions or charter resolutions, although a protest petition signed by at least 2 percent of those voting in the most recent November election is sufficient to force a referendum on a charter resolution. The state legislature may limit county home rule by enacting laws uniformly applicable to all counties or by writing statutory exemptions into the county home rule statute.

There are differences, however, between city and county home rule. Cities in Kansas have extraterritorial powers not available to counties. For example, a city may purchase land beyond city boundaries to serve a public purpose. The exercise of such powers is not uncommon in securing city water supply, wastewater treatment, solid waste disposal, recreational facilities, and flood control, among other city purposes. Under state law, cities may also exercise planning and zoning controls within three miles of city borders—as long as the affected territory is afforded representation on the city planning commission. Cities may also issue industrial revenue bonds to companies operating outside city limits. Both cities and counties may contract with other jurisdictions to deliver public services beyond official borders.

Functions of Local Government

Functional Responsibilities

A century ago, services offered by state government consisted of little more than a university, an agricultural college, a normal school, schools for the blind and deaf, hospitals for the mentally handicapped, a reformatory, and two reform schools. Essential public services—such as law enforcement, fire protection, public education, roads, assistance to the poor, public health, administration of justice, tax administration, and election administration—were carried out at the local level. With reluctance, state government has since taken over local services or formed partnerships with local units to deliver and finance services. State highways and highway finance were inaugurated in 1928; state government assumed county responsibility for financing and administering public welfare in 1974; and in the mid-1970s, courts were unified under the administration of the Kansas Supreme Court.

County governments were originally created to administer basic state-prescribed services such as law enforcement, administration of justice, tax administration, election administration, and property records. In time, counties established services primarily in response to an agricultural constituency (for example,

county roads, county fairs, agricultural extension, and eradication of noxious weeds). More recently, larger counties have responded to urban demands and assumed the administration and financing of a broader array of public services. These services include public and mental health and hospitals; parks and recreation; libraries, museums, and zoos; cemeteries; community colleges; emergency medical services; solid waste disposal; planning, zoning, and code enforcement; economic development; fire protection; juvenile detention and community corrections; and port authorities and airport operations.

Services offered by Kansas cities vary as widely as their populations (from 9 to 330,000). Kansas cities may offer most urban services. Among them are police and fire protection, streets and highways, water supply and water quality, public health, parks and recreation, municipal courts, libraries, cemeteries, housing, public transportation, hospitals, emergency medical services, solid waste disposal, planning (including zoning and code enforcement), environmental regulation, economic development, airport operations, public buildings, museums, zoos, sports and convention facilities, port authorities, and parking facilities. Cities may operate a wide range of utility functions, including airports, convention facilities, electric, gas, public parking, water supply, and processing of solid waste, storm water, and wastewater. Cities may create within their boundaries benefit districts or special-assessment districts to finance various public improvements. They also may establish central business districts, business improvement districts, and self-supported municipal improvement districts to finance various improvements in designated areas.

Cities may offer most services that counties offer. However, cities do not initiate services traditionally assigned to county government (such as election administration, property records management, or agriculturally related services); nor do they offer those services organized solely on a countywide basis (such as mental health and corrections facilities and community colleges). In some cases, a city may administer countywide services, such as public health or planning, through an interlocal agreement with county government. State limitations on city finances restrict which services may be offered, but the electorate may override most such limitations. State law does preempt cities, as well as counties, from regulating pesticides—one of the few state preemptions of city functions.

Most of the nearly 1,500 special districts in Kansas have been initiated through petitions by citizen. These districts have some form of independent finance authority and serve more than twenty special-purpose functions, including airports, cemeteries, community buildings, conservation, drainage, fire protection, flood control, groundwater management, hospitals, housing, industrial development, irrigation, libraries, lighting, municipal energy, parks and recreation, ports, public utilities, rural roads, sewers, special improvements, transportation, and water supply.[13] (Education functions are excluded.) The more numerous special districts include 728 cemetery districts, 323 fire districts, 105 conservation districts, 95 watershed districts, 77 drainage districts, and 74 sewer districts. County government participates in the formation of most of these districts, either as sponsor or originator. In addition to independent special districts, cities and counties have established numerous subordinate districts, similar in form to special districts but dependent on city or county finance authority.

The existence of 4,000 local jurisdictions in Kansas has spawned interlocal cooperation in delivery of services and consolidation of functions.[14] Kansas statutes, combined with respective home rule powers, make virtually any form of interlocal cooperation between or among cities and counties possible. Local jurisdictions have opted for interlocal agreements that preserve the authority of cooperating parties rather than functional consolidations that may require giving up authority to another entity. Although no agency keeps track of the exact number and status of interlocal agreements in Kansas, informal surveys suggest that a few thousand such agreements are now in operation statewide.

Administrative Discretion

Cities and counties exercise substantial administrative discretion with respect to personnel, administrative procedures, contracting and purchasing, and other aspects of local management.[15] A few state laws establish minimal standards for local personnel. For example, sheriffs are required to complete law enforcement training; county appraisers are required to be certified; and county engineers must be licensed professional engineers. Cities and counties may elect to have employer-employee relations regulated by the Kansas Public Employer-Employee Relations Board. Essentially, the jurisdiction is required to recognize bargaining units and to meet and confer with bargaining units on conditions of employment. State laws forbidding discrimination based on race, gender, age, or disability apply to cities and counties as well as to most other employers.

Planning and zoning are performed locally by cities and counties under a uniform state statute revamped in 1991.[16] Cities and counties may create local planning commissions and establish procedures for the adoption and annual review of comprehensive plans, adoption of subdivision regulations, and general business conduct of such planning commissions. Public hearings are required, and jurisdictions and property owners affected by local planning and zoning must be notified. Once a commission has been established and has adopted a comprehensive plan, local governing bodies may not act independently of the planning commission. Local governing bodies must adhere to an adopted plan in making public improvements and must consult with the commission in amending the plan or zoning regulations. Generally, the governing body may override recommendations of the planning commission through a two-thirds majority vote; however, if property owners representing 20 percent of the property in the area protest the rezoning, a three-fourths majority of the governing body is required for the rezoning. The statute also provides for coordination of planning between and among affected cities and counties and authorizes local governing bodies to create joint planning commissions through interlocal agreement.

Economic Development

Cities may undertake almost any development function, limited only by the will of the city governing body and, ultimately, by the consent of the governed. City governing bodies with home rule powers may establish community development organizations, enterprise zones, and economic development banks. County governments also have broad development functions but, in practice, would rarely undertake urban development projects within city boundaries without the consent of an affected city.

Fiscal Autonomy of Local Governments

Local Revenues

On the revenue side of local finance, cities in Kansas are specifically preempted from levying taxes on incomes, gasoline and other fuels, and alcoholic beverages. They may levy the following:

- property taxes within a framework of state law;
- sales taxes in 0.25 percent increments up to 2 percent, subject to several exceptions;
- franchise taxes on gross receipts of utilities operating with city franchise (for example, natural gas and electricity, telephone, and cable television) at locally determined rates;
- transient guest taxes at rates that are determined locally;
- a tax on earnings from intangible property in 0.125 percent increments up to 2.25 percent;
- occupation taxes at locally determined rates;
- a wheel tax of $5 or $10 per vehicle; and
- an emergency telephone tax not to exceed $0.75 per access line.

Although the property tax base is prescribed in state law, property assessment and valuation are generally conducted by locally appointed county appraisers in accordance with state regulations and with state assistance and oversight to ensure consistency among local appraisals throughout the state. The property of railroads and private utilities is appraised solely by the state. The tax base for the other local revenue sources, except for franchise and occupation taxes, is prescribed in state law and cannot be altered at the local level. The tax base for franchise and occupation taxes may be determined locally through home rule. Cities may

Table 1. Summary of City and County Tax Revenues in Kansas, FY 1998

Revenue source	Revenues[a]					
	County		City		Total	
Property tax	$618,163	79%	$389,503	52%	$1,007,666	66%
Sales and use tax	128,300	16	309,500	41	437,800	29
Franchise tax	0		35,000	5	35,000	2
Mortgage registration	25,021	3	0		25,021	2
Vehicle registration	12,117	2	0		12,117	1
Transient guest tax	960	—	13,105	2	14,065	1
Intangible property	2,022	—	1,554	—	3,576	—
Total	$786,583		$748,662		$1,535,245	

Source: Kansas Legislative Research Department, *Kansas Tax Facts, 1998 Supplement to the Sixth Edition* (December 1998), 45 (table VI). The distribution of local sales tax revenues between counties and cities was estimated from information from the Kansas Department of Revenue. Annual data are not compiled for franchise, occupation, or telephone taxes. An estimate of franchise taxes for fiscal 1998 is based on an earlier estimate made by McFadden Consulting Group, "An Analysis of the Impacts of Retail Wheeling on the State of Kansas" (report prepared for the Kansas Legislature's Task Force on Retail Wheeling, 18 August 1997).

    a. Revenues are in thousands of dollars. A dash (—) indicates that the percentage is negligible.

also sell city services, such as water and wastewater treatment, to other jurisdictions.

Since the early days of statehood, state lawmakers have put legal limits on the levying of property taxes by cities and counties. The issue became highly contentious in 1970, with the adoption of the aggregate levy limit, essentially a state tax lid on local property taxes. Robert Docking (governor, 1967–1975) made the tax lid the political equivalent of a loyalty oath for state office and a "battleground" between home rule and state rule on local taxes.[17] Hardly a campaign for any state office occurred without candidates pledging homage to the tax lid. During this same period, however, state lawmakers quietly riddled the tax lid with exemptions and made the lid subject to exemption by local action through home rule powers. By 1988, 289 cities had exempted themselves from the tax lid by charter ordinance.[18] In the 1999 legislative session, state lawmakers gave home rule a dramatic boost by suspending "all existing statutory fund mill levy rate and aggregate levy rate limitations on all political subdivisions"[19] and freeing local units from state oversight of local property tax levies. Nevertheless, some state lawmakers warned that local abuse of property taxes would lead to a speedy reinstatement of the tax lid.

Counties generally have access to, and similar limitations on, the same revenue sources as cities, including the same preemptions. Counties may not levy franchise taxes, occupation taxes, or a wheel tax, but they may levy a mortgage registration tax. The rate (26 cents per $100) and base of the mortgage registration tax is set in state statute. Table 1 summarizes city and county tax revenues for 1998.

Both counties and cities rely on the property tax for more than half of their revenue, although counties depend on the tax to a greater extent than do cities. Local sales, franchise, and transient guest taxes bolster city revenues. Other sources provide less than 1 percent of total city and county tax revenues. The tax on earnings from intangible property, which was abandoned by most jurisdictions because of its unpopularity, generated less than $4 million in fiscal 1998—a negligible amount. No jurisdiction levies a wheel tax.

Kansas has a long history of giving cities and counties generous authority to issue debt, which has resulted in local defaults during difficult economic times.[20] Although a number of state statutes prescribe limitations on the issuance of debt by cities and counties, current state law authorizes cities and counties to issue:

a variety of both long and short term bonds and similar debt instruments including general obligation bonds, revenue bonds, industrial revenue bonds, local residential housing bonds, temporary notes, no fund warrants and revenue anticipation notes. Further, cities and counties . . . may enter into long term lease-purchase agreements and installment contract agreements as long as the agreements are made subject to annual appropriations by the governing body.[21]

State law does prescribe procedures for the issuance of debt, such as public notice, registration, annual reporting, and election procedures (if elections are required). Before general-obligation bonds may be issued, competitive public sale usually is required. Bonded debt limits are set in state law at 30 percent of assessed valuation for cities and 3 percent for counties, but numerous exceptions for particular jurisdictions and specific purposes have been written into the law.

Local Expenditures

Historically, cities and counties have had wide latitude in local spending. Indeed, before the 1930s, city and county governing bodies generally were free to spend with minimal state oversight. As a result, poor spending practices emerged in some jurisdictions. Money was borrowed to pay operating expenses. Money was shifted from fund to fund. Financial records were not well kept.[22] In 1933 Gov. Alf Landon called for state action to rectify local abuse, and state lawmakers prescribed procedures for local spending through the enactment of the cash basis law and the budget law. However, spending priorities continue to be determined by city and county governing bodies.

Although they may have been viewed as onerous when adopted, the cash basis law and the budget law are well accepted today. The cash basis law requires cities and counties to operate on a cash basis, that is, to spend no more than available revenues and to incur no debt except under lawful procedures for the issuance of debt.[23] The budget law prescribes procedures for local budgeting: annual budgets must be prepared on state forms, with estimates of revenue and expenditures; public notice and public hearings on the budget must be held; calendar deadlines for budget submission and adoption must be met; limitations on "miscellaneous" funds must be followed; and local budgetary information must be submitted to the state.[24]

Once a local budget is adopted, the law limits transfers between funds and requires public notice and hearings for any amendment to the adopted budget. No state law addresses bankruptcy proceedings. Although a city or county theoretically could exercise home rule powers and declare bankruptcy, there is no record of a jurisdiction doing so. Such an occurrence would likely indicate that a jurisdiction had violated the cash basis law.

State Government Grants-in-Aid to Localities

Inequities in the property tax base coupled with the unpopularity of property taxes have led to two basic forms of state assistance to local governments in Kansas: (1) shared revenues that allow cities and counties to share major revenue sources with the state and (2) state grants to local units. Both forms tend to equalize the financial base across jurisdictions and generally reduce local reliance on the property tax.

Three major programs in which the state shares revenues with cities and counties are shared highway-user taxes, the local ad valorem tax-reduction fund, and city-county revenue sharing. In fiscal 1999, $155.1 million in state highway taxes were shared with cities, counties, and townships for road maintenance and improvement. Roughly 3.4 percent of state sales tax revenues (or $55.1 million in fiscal 1999) was allocated to local jurisdictions levying property taxes for the purpose of reducing property taxes. Another 2.3 percent of state sales tax revenues (or $36.6 million in fiscal 1999) was shared solely with cities and counties for locally determined priorities.

Local discretion varies with each of these shared revenue programs. Highway-user taxes must be spent on road maintenance and improvement, but priorities are locally determined. Funds for ad valorem reduction must be applied directly to reducing the local mill levy. City-county revenue sharing allows complete local discretion. Another nine programs provide cities and counties with minor, earmarked assistance from designated state revenues.[25] This assistance is prescribed by state statute for certain jurisdictions or for narrowly defined purposes (for example, enforcement of bingo laws in certain jurisdictions, firefighters' relief, alcohol treatment, and waste tire management).

A number of state grant-in-aid programs provide financial assistance from state general funds for services administered by cities and counties, such as libraries, community corrections, soil conservation, public health, emergency medical services, community mental health, community mental retardation, economic development, community arts, juvenile detention, and services for the aging.[26] The purposes of this aid are prescribed by statutes that stipulate the assistance, annual appropriations, and priorities of state agencies administering the assistance.

These various forms of state assistance to local governments in Kansas have contributed a degree of order and equity in state and local finance at a modest cost to local autonomy. Although the distribution formulas for allocating state revenues to cities and counties are always subject to debate, existing allocations are unquestionably more equitable than disparities in the property tax base among cities and counties.

Unfunded Mandates

The underlying cultural preference of Kansans for local self-government, coupled with the capacity of cities and counties to generate local revenues and obtain state financial assistance, has made the issue of unfunded mandates less contentious in Kansas than in other states. Although the issue surfaces continually in state legislative discussions, the state budget office consults with local officials to identify the costs that proposed legislative actions would likely impose on cities and counties. This procedure, along with effective lobbying by associations of city and county officials, derails most ill-conceived proposals.

More than 900 specific constitutional or statutory provisions that mandate some form of city or county action have been identified.[27] These mandates are categorized according to area of involvement (governance, finance, state supervision or preemption, organization, or citizen preemption) and generally apply to county more so than to city governments. Nearly half originated in 1960–1990, after the adoption of city home rule. Governance mandates, which compose one-fourth of the total, often allow initial local decision making but then prescribe what to do once a decision is made (if the governing body does act).

Another category of mandates either subjects local officials to some form of supervision by state officials or preempts local action on certain subjects. Finance mandates (one-fifth of the total) either require or restrict local action with respect to taxing, spending, borrowing, or investing. Organization mandates constrain local organization by requiring the employment of certain local officials or specifying the duties of local officials.

More than 150 state mandates authorize citizens to preempt certain actions taken by city and county governing bodies through the use of protest petitions. That is, a local governing body is authorized by the state to act on a particular subject, but that action may be preempted by citizens opposing such action. Citizens may protest the action by petitioning the governing body and forcing either rescindment or a referendum. If submitted to a referendum, the action does not become effective until a majority of those voting in the referendum support the measure.

These mandates reflect the state's paternalism with respect to cities and counties in Kansas. In practice, however, city and county governing bodies may exempt themselves from a significant number of state mandates through the exercise of home rule powers. Many mandates have accumulated in state statute books since statehood and are archaic, obsolete, and irrelevant. Many others lack enforcement. Larger, more sophisticated jurisdictions maneuver around them, and smaller jurisdictions ignore them.

Access to Local Government

Local Elections

State statutes provide a specific framework for conducting city and county elections, but the extent to which local governing bodies may alter prescribed election procedures is open to question.[28] City governing bodies and city electors may determine election issues related to the form of government, such as type of election (by district or at large, partisan or nonpartisan) and what the terms of office and term limits will be. However, most cities and counties comply with election procedures prescribed in state statutes.

State laws also limit local campaign finance and prescribe rules concerning conflicts of interest that apply to all state and local governmental officials and employees. Campaign finance laws are nonuniform; therefore, a city or county governing body may use home rule powers to exempt itself from the laws or write its own prescriptions for the jurisdiction. The city of Wichita, for example, has enacted its own campaign finance ordinance.[29] The conflict-of-interest law, which does apply uniformly, requires public officials and employees to disclose substantial business interests and prohibits them from making contracts affecting those interests.[30]

Citizen Controls over Actions of Local Officials

All elected public officials, except judicial officers, are subject to recall, a requirement originally written into the Kansas Constitution in 1914 and last revised in 1974.[31] Grounds for recall are conviction of a felony, misconduct in office, and incompetence or failure to perform duties prescribed by law. To force a recall vote, a sufficient number of registered voters from the election district of the official being recalled must sign an appropriate petition with the local election officer. Petitions must secure within ninety days at least 40 percent of the number voting in the last general election for the office of the official being recalled. Once a petition is determined to be sufficient, the election officer calls a special recall election to be held within sixty to ninety days. No more than a majority of the members of a local governing body less one may be recalled at the same time.

Citizens may also initiate ouster proceedings against any person holding a city or county office, either elective or appointive. State statutes provide that any officeholders who willfully misconduct themselves in office, willfully neglect to perform any duty enjoined upon them by law, or commit any act constituting a violation of any penal statute involving moral turpitude will forfeit the office or be subject to ouster. After receiving written complaint of violations, the attorney general or county attorney investigates the complaint and if reasonable cause is found initiates court proceedings to oust the officer. Ouster proceedings are quite rare in Kansas.

Initiative and referendum apply to city government in Kansas but not to county government. A proposed ordinance (which may be initiated by citizens) that is accompanied by a valid petition is either adopted by the governing body or submitted to a referendum. A valid petition must be signed in cities of the first class by at least 25 percent of the number voting in the last regular city election; in cities of the second and third class, by 40 percent of the number voting in the last regular city election. The ordinance becomes effective once a majority of the voters in a referendum vote in favor of the proposal. Initiative and referendum do not apply to administrative ordinances, ordinances providing for public improvements paid for by the levy of special assessments, or ordinances subject to referendum or election under another state statute.[32] Any ordinance adopted through the initiative procedure may be amended or repealed upon voter approval at any succeeding regular election but not by action of the city governing body for a period of ten years.

Citizens have substantial access to city and county government through state laws providing for open meetings and records.[33] Any prearranged meeting in which a majority of a quorum of the members of a governing body are present and discuss business of the body must be open to members of the public. A local governing body may go into executive session (that is, they may close a meeting to the public) only for purposes specified in statute, including matters related to discussion of nonelected personnel, attorney-client privilege, employer-employee negotiations, acquisition of real property, and confidential data concerning the financial affairs of a business.

All legislative and administrative bodies (but not judicial agencies) fall within the scope of the open meetings law. The open records law allows citizen access to "any recorded information . . . in the possession of a public agency," although many exceptions are written into the law. Most exceptions to open records are designed to protect the privacy of individuals, such as an individual's criminal history, medical or psychological treatment, or personnel records.[34]

State-Local Relations

Historical precedent, legal precedent, and political culture underpin home rule in Kansas and sustain local self-government in the state. Although the vitality of home rule varies in relation to population, economics, and, significantly, the quality of professional management, the potential for home rule is available to each city and county in the state.

Since the early 1900s, state government has moved to shape state-local relations on a more rational basis. The division of labor between state and local jurisdictions has been refined. State-local partnerships in financing and delivering services have been forged. State-local finance has been given a degree of order. These changes have steadily increased state prescription but at the same time permit substantial discretion at the local level.

Numerous state policy issues are resolved without consideration of the effect on state-local relations. However, when the proper balance of state prescription and local autonomy is at stake, Kansans instinctively err on the side of home rule.

Notes

1. William Allen White, quoted in Kenneth S. Davis, *Kansas* (New York: W. W. Norton, 1976), 170–171.

2. James W. Drury, *The Government of Kansas*, 4th ed. (Topeka: KU Capitol Center, University of Kansas, 1993), 215, 228, and 278; "Incorporation of Cities in Kansas," *Kansas Government Journal* (October 1991): 278; Adel F. Throckmorton, *Kansas Educational Progress, 1858–1967* (Topeka: State Department of Public Instruction, June 1967), 11.

3. U.S. Bureau of the Census, Department of Commerce, "Government Organization," *1992 Census of Governments* 1 (March 1994): 3.

4. H. Edward Flentje, ed., *Selected Solely upon the Basis of Administrative Ability* (Wichita: Wichita State University, 1993).

5. James W. Drury, *Home Rule in Kansas* (Lawrence: Governmental Research Center, University of Kansas, 1965), 15. Original constitutional language called for "general laws" in the organization and financing of cities and in the conferring of corporate powers. Special legislation was specifically prohibited in Article 2, section 17, as follows: "All laws of a general nature shall have a uniform operation throughout the state; and in all cases where a general law can be made applicable, no special law shall be enacted." These provisions were designed to limit the state legislature's powers with respect to interfering in the governance of a particular local government, but in practice they were to little avail.

6. For an examination of state actions that were designed to control cities, see Barkley Clark, "State Control of Local Government in Kansas: Special Legislation and Home Rule," *Kansas Law Review* 20 (1972): 631–683.

7. For elaboration on initiative and immunity as two dimensions of autonomy, see Gordon L. Clark, *Judges and the Cities* (Chicago: University of Chicago Press, 1985), 60–81. This discussion of home rule draws heavily from "Local Government Powers—Home Rule" in Michael R. Heim, *Kansas Local Government Law* (Topeka: Kansas Bar Association, 1991).

8. Kansas Constitution, Article 12, section 5.

9. Don Moler, ed., *Constitutional Home Rule in Kansas*, 8th ed. (Topeka: League of Kansas Municipalities, September 1994), 75.

10. State lawmakers have established the ground rules for incorporation and dissolution of cities and for changing city boundaries through annexation in state laws uniformly applicable to all cities. Kansas Statutes Annotated, 15-115 et seq. generally provides for a territory with a population of at least 300 or more to be incorporated as a city upon presentation of a petition signed by fifty electors to the board of county commissioners. After complying with requirements for public notice, public hearing, and consideration of statutory criteria, the board may deny or order the incorporation. If the territory is within five miles of an existing city, a unanimous vote of the board is required to order incorporation. Kansas Statutes Annotated, 15-111 provides for the dissolution of a city by only a two-thirds majority vote of city electors in an election, which is called upon presentation of a petition by a majority of city voters to the city governing body. For more detail, see Heim, *Kansas Local Government Law*, 2-5–2-17.

11. Chapters 13, 14, and 15 of Kansas Statutes Annotated, which comprise more than 300 pages and 1,000 statutory provisions, apply to first-, second-, and third-class cities, respectively. See Kansas Statutes Annotated 15-124, 14-101, and 13-101. Although exceptions exist as a result of prior laws, city classification is generally as follows: a city becomes a city of the third class upon incorporation. A city of the third class may become a city of the second class upon reaching a population of 2,000 but may remain a city of the third class until reaching a population of 5,000. A city of the second class may become a city of the first class upon reaching a population of 15,000 but may remain a city of the second class until reaching a population of 25,000. Currently, a gubernatorial proclamation is required for a city to move from one class to the next.

12. Kansas Statutes Annotated, 12-519 et seq.

13. For more elaboration and statutory citations on special districts, see "Special Districts, Other Limited Purpose Entities and Regional Bodies" (chap. 13) in Heim, *Kansas Local Government Law;* and *Local Governments of Kansas—An Inventory of Governmental Taxing Units, 1991* (Topeka: League of Kansas Municipalities, September 1991).

14. See H. Edward Flentje and Michael R. Heim, *City and County Authority for Consolidation and Cooperation in Kansas* (Wichita: Hugo Wall Center for Urban Studies, June 1992).

15. Unless state funds are involved, no state agency or official is charged with enforcing state laws concerned with local administration. As a consequence, larger, more sophisticated jurisdictions maneuver around state statutes that constrain local administration; smaller jurisdictions simply ignore such laws. State limitations on local administrative discretion may be enforced through active public scrutiny or legal challenge, which are infrequent.

16. Kansas Statutes Annotated, 12-741 et seq.

17. Glenn W. Fisher, *The Worst Tax? A History of the Property Tax in America* (Lawrence: University Press of Kansas, 1996), 23.

18. Heim, *Kansas Local Government Law*, 9-4.

19. Session Laws of Kansas, volume 2, chapter 154, section 72, 1350.

20. See James E. Boyle, *The Financial History of Kansas* (Madison: Bulletin of the University of Wisconsin, August 1908).

21. Heim, *Kansas Local Government Law*, 8–10.

22. Clarence J. Hein, *State Supervision of County and City Expenditures in Kansas* (Lawrence: Governmental Research Center, University of Kansas, 1957), 4.

23. Kansas Statutes Annotated, 10-1101 et seq.

24. Kansas Statutes Annotated, 79-2925 et seq. Because no state agency or official is charged to perform such duties, local budgetary information that is submitted to the state is neither reviewed nor even compiled.

25. For a general description of these state revenues and their disposition, see Kansas Legislative Research Department, *Kansas Tax Facts*, 34–49, table IX.

26. See Kansas Legislative Research Department, *Overview of the FY 1997 Governor's Budget Report* (Topeka: Kansas Legislative Research Department, 1996), 18.

27. For more information, see H. Edward Flentje, "State Mandates on Cities

and Counties in Kansas: An Overview," in *An Inventory of State Mandates on Cities and Counties in Kansas,* ed. H. Edward Flentje, Darron Leiker, and Mark Detter (Wichita: Hugo Wall School of Urban and Public Affairs, Wichita State University, 1994). This study did not identify state mandates as unfunded mandates.

28. For example, state law provides that general city elections shall be held on the first Tuesday in April. Legal opinions differ on whether this statute is nonuniform and therefore subject to city home rule powers. No city has attempted to alter the timing of its elections through the exercise of home rule, and therefore no court has resolved the issue. See "Local Election Laws, Public Officers and Ethics" (chap. 6) in Heim, *Kansas Local Government Law.*

29. See Code of the City of Wichita, 2.56.070.

30. See Kansas Statutes Annotated, 75-4301 et seq.

31. Kansas Constitution, Article 4, section 3. For details of statutory requirements for recall (that is, form, substance, sponsorship, timing, filing, and petition sufficiency), see Kansas Statutes Annotated, 25-4318 et seq.; see also 60-1205 et seq., for details on ouster proceedings.

32. See Kansas Statutes Annotated, 12-3013.

33. See Kansas Statutes Annotated, 75-4317 et seq., 45-215 et seq.

34. For details on these exceptions, see Heim, *Kansas Local Government Law,* 5-18–5-22.

KENTUCKY

Janet W. Patton

Kentucky's constitution reflects the principle of Dillon's Rule that local governments are legal subdivisions of the state, deriving their powers from the state and doing only those things permitted by the constitution and the General Assembly. In the spirit of Dillon's Rule, the General Assembly plays an active role in local government. An extensive array of state statutes governing local activities reinforced by a centralized state tax system create rules that authorize but also constrain and constrict local government.

In 1980 the General Assembly enacted a law granting cities home rule, and in 1994 voters ratified a constitutional amendment authorizing the legislature to grant cities any power or function that furthers a public purpose and does not conflict with any constitutional or statutory provision. A power or function is in conflict if it is expressly prohibited by the state or if the law comprehensively addresses the subject. State-local relations in Kentucky are an intricate mixture of constitutional, statutory, administrative, and political features.

Governmental Setting

As a border state, Kentucky's development has been subjected to a wide range of crosscurrents. Its basic political institutions reflect its origins as part of Virginia, and its political culture reflects the fierce individualism of the frontier Scots-Irish who wanted land of their own and distance from their neighbor. Its regional diversity reflects its varied geography and its settlement patterns. It has been said that "there are few other places in the nation where there have been stronger emotional attachments to place than Kentucky." Strong regional identity overlays generally weak local governmental institutions. The values of the political culture reflect the existing social order, protecting the status quo and resisting change. Kentucky has a "highly personalistic, rather than ideological, brand of politics."[1]

Local political systems have great diversity and fragmentation. In 1996 the state had 120 counties, 435 cities, 15 area development districts, 1,300 special districts, and 176 school districts. The county government is important both politically and for personal identity. Municipal government is becoming more significant as the state becomes more urban.

Historically, coal, tobacco, bourbon, and horses have been considered the mainstays of Kentucky politics, and to varying degrees these interests have shaped the values and habits of governance in each of the 120 counties. This agrarian tradition, however, has been overlaid by a growing industrial urban economy anchored by the United Parcel Service, Ford Trucks, and health maintenance organizations in Louisville; a Toyota plant in central Kentucky; and the Cincinnati International Airport in

northern Kentucky. Although this "golden triangle" is prospering, rural Kentucky—especially the isolated areas of Appalachia—continues to languish with high unemployment and low educational attainment. Even though the power structure is more variegated than formerly, economic interests continue to dominate politics and government, and the passion for statewide politics can match that of any state in the country.[2]

The 1891 constitution is a long, detailed document in which term limitation was embraced, taxes and salaries were capped, and, generally, as little as possible was left to uncertainty.[3] The governor dominates Kentucky government. Even before governors were able to seek reelection, the office had significant powers. Formal powers were augmented through an extensive political patronage system covering contracts and jobs, even at the county level.[4] In the 1970s the legislative body, the General Assembly, began a slow but steady process of asserting its independence from the governor and increasing its role in setting policy.

Home Rule in Kentucky

Historical Development

Before 1980, powers were granted to cities in very specific, narrowly focused statutes. It was difficult to determine the precise powers and responsibilities of cities. In response to local government pressure for more autonomy and flexibility, the 1980 General Assembly replaced hundreds of statutes with a single law granting cities a qualified version of home rule. Although the state courts have upheld this general grant of authority, the state continues to determine the scope of local government. Uncertainty about the General Assembly's authority to grant home rule ended in 1994, when voters ratified a constitutional amendment permitting the legislature to grant home rule to cities.

Definition of Home Rule

On the basis of the 1980 statute and the 1994 constitutional amendment, local government in Kentucky has statutory home rule. The law specifies that "a city may exercise any power and perform any function within its boundaries, including the power of eminent domain in accordance with the provisions of the Eminent Domain Act of Kentucky, that is a furtherance of a public purpose of the city and not in conflict with a constitutional provision or statute."

The statutory definition of conflict is that a "[a] power or function is in conflict with a statute if it is expressly prohibited by statute or there is a comprehensive scheme of legislation on the same general subject."[5] Court cases have interpreted a comprehensive scheme as an area "where the state has occupied the field." In a series of cases, the state supreme court reasoned that "if state legislation is determined to be comprehensive, local governments have no power to enact any legislation on that subject, even if there are gaps or vague areas in the state law." More recently the court has provided more latitude to local governments by ruling that "municipal regulation is not always precluded simply because the legislature has taken some action in regard to the same subject. The true test of concurrent authority is the absence of conflict."[6]

Although the courts have upheld the statutory grant of home rule, the Kentucky Supreme Court has also affirmed the general principles of Dillon's Rule. Specifically, the court continues to hold that as a "general rule . . . a city possesses only those powers expressly granted by the constitution and statutes plus such powers as are necessarily implied or incident to the expressly granted powers and which are indispensable to enable it to carry out declared objects, purposes and expressed powers."[7]

Structural Features

Kentucky's constitution prohibits local privilege and special legislation. However, the General Assembly has devised creative strategies to circumvent such prohibition by passing legislation that applies only to certain localities. This is particularly true for Louisville, which is the only first-class city, and Lexington–Fayette Urban County Government, which is the only urban county government.

The 1891 constitution replaced the existing system of special charters with a classification system for cities. A 1994 amendment permits the General Assembly to classify cities on the basis of factors in addition to population, such as tax bases, forms of government, geography, or other reasonable characteristics.

Table 1. City Classification System in Kentucky

Type of city	Population	Number of cities
First class	100,000 or more	1
Second class	20,000–99,999	11
Third class	8,000–19,999	19
Fourth class	3,000–7,999	95
Fifth class	1,000–2,999	123
Sixth class	under 1,000	185
Urban county government	no size limit	1

Source: Kentucky League of Cities, *Funding Our Future: A Report on Kentucky City Tax Structure* (Lexington: Kentucky League of Cities, 1996), 7.

The current city classification system and all state statutes relating to cities remain in effect until changed by the General Assembly. The pre-amendment and still-current system provides for six classifications based on population (see Table 1).

Reclassification has not happened routinely when city size changes. Cities may request reclassification from the General Assembly, which must concur by statute. Although all cities in a classification must be subject to the same requirements, many of the applicable state statutes provide for a variety of options within a classification.[8]

Kentucky statutes currently provide for four forms of city government: mayor-council, mayor-aldermen, commission, and city manager. In each plan, there is an elected mayor and an elected legislative body. Any city may create a nonelective position of city administrative officer, who is directly responsible to the mayor or board of commissioners.

The mayor-council and the mayor-aldermen plans are examples of "strong" mayor forms of government. The mayor-aldermanic form applies only to the first-class city of Louisville; power is separated between the mayor (who exercises executive power) and the aldermanic council (which exercises legislative power). There is no separation of power in the commission plan in which a board of commissioners, comprising the mayor and four commissioners, wield executive, legislative, and administrative powers. In the city-manager form, the city manager is appointed by the board of commissioners and charged with administering the city. The manager is chief administrative officer of the city but does not possess the autonomy and internal administrative authority that city managers have in most states. The city manager supervises all employees but does not have authority to hire and fire. The board of commissioners retains legislative and executive authority. Only by popular vote can a plan of government be changed. Any approved change must stay in effect at least five years from the effective date of the change.[9]

The General Assembly cannot by legislation incorporate a city, but it does set the conditions and procedures for incorporation. A minimum population of 300 is required, but there is no minimum area, distance, tax base, or density. A petition, which includes the reasons for incorporation, the services to be provided, and the plan of government, must be signed by two-thirds of the voters residing in the proposed city. Alternatively, it may be approved by a number of real-property owners equal to the number of owners of at least two-thirds of the assessed value of the real property in the proposed city. A court hearing must be held within twenty days of submitting the petition. The court effectuates the incorporation if the area meets all standards, is able "to provide necessary city services to residents within a reasonable period," and demonstrates that "the interests of adjacent areas and local governments will not be unduly prejudiced."[10]

State law provides two methods for dissolution of a city. If a city fails for at least one year to operate government by the election or appointment of officers and the levying and collection of taxes, it may be dissolved by a circuit court judgment in response to a petition filed by one or more residents of the city. If a petition signed by a number of registered voters of the city equal to 20 percent of those voting in the last presidential election and a majority of those voting on the issue support dissolution, the city is dissolved within thirty days.[11]

State statute provides that a city council may annex adjacent unincorporated land by ordinance. No county or state agency approval is needed. A referendum is not required in the annexing city but may be required in second- through sixth-class cities if 50 percent of the voters in the proposed annex area so petition. First-class cities (that is, Louisville) are required to extend services to the annexed areas and limit the tax rate to one commensurate with the services provided. In addition, first-class cities are subject to differing procedural requirements, depending on whether a cooperative compact with the county is in effect. Second- through sixth-class cities can annex unincorporated land by vote of the city council, unless 50 percent of the voters or landowners in the area sign a petition and force a referendum, or unless the courts find that the city did not act fairly or consistently with the requirements of the law. If a petition drive results in a referendum, 55 percent of those voting must vote against the annexation to block the proposed annexation.[12] In general, Kentucky's process makes annexation difficult,[13] unless there is voluntary agreement of the parties involved.

Counties are an important unit of local government, functioning as political and administrative subdivisions of the state. The basic structure of county government is set in the constitution, and—despite the vast difference between the smallest county (with less than 3,000 people) and the largest (with approximately 650,000)—all counties (except Fayette) are governed under a uniform organizational structure. The constitution specifies a long list of elected county officials, but discretion is given to the General Assembly to prescribe the powers, functions, duties, and compensation of those county officials.[14]

Kentucky's enabling legislation allows governments to be consolidated as either an urban county or a county charter government. Under the Peake-McCain Act, if a petition is signed by 5 percent of those voting in the last election in the county and in each city, a commission must be formed; a comprehensive plan for an urban county government must then be submitted and voted on by the citizens in a referendum. If a simple majority votes to adopt the charter, a consolidated urban county government is created.[15] In 1972 voters in Lexington–Fayette County approved a merged urban county government charter.

The legislature in 1990 enacted procedures for forming a charter county government or for partially (not totally) consolidating services. Initiation of the charter county process requires a petition signed by 20 percent of county residents voting in the preceding regular election. Upon certification, a study commission is appointed, the membership of which comprises 55 percent county and 45 percent city representation. The county judge-executive chairs the commission, which must develop a comprehensive plan for consolidation of services, functions, or governments to be submitted for a countywide referendum.[16]

Cities sharing a common boundary are permitted by state law to transfer incorporated territory by adopting identical ordinances in each city and by submitting a petition of support signed by voters in the area.[17] There is provision for state takeover of school districts and counties in certain circumstances, but there is no provision for state takeover of cities.

Home rule in Kentucky is limited to powers within the corporate boundaries. Specific statutory authorization is needed by cities to exercise extraterritoriality. Currently, there are extraterritorial grants of authority to some or all cities for functions such as flood control, river ports, mass transit systems, and utility service.[18] Cities have the power to enact subdivision regulations within five miles of the city with approval of the county fiscal court.

Functions of Local Government

Functional Responsibilities

Since 1980 cities have been granted discretion by the General Assembly to exercise any power and perform any function that furthers a public purpose and does not conflict with the constitution or state statute. In practice, most of the cities confine their activities to traditional municipal services such as public works, streets, fire and emergency services, police, solid waste disposal, parks and recreation, planning and zoning, and housing and community development.

Reflecting its origin as part of Virginia—from which it derived its political institutions when it became a separate state in 1792—Kentucky assigns to counties the responsibilities of tax assessment and collection, law enforcement, and many other functions of local government. Kentucky counties are responsible for record keeping, automobile registration and licensing, voter registration and elections, jails, and roads. They also undertake services such as parks, solid waste disposal, public works, fire fighting, and emergency services.

Cities and counties have statutory power to create individually or jointly special districts to carry out particular public purposes. More than 1,300 special districts have been formed in Kentucky as a way of "getting anything done in the complex maze of Kentucky government with its statutory limits and mandates."[19] State statutes permit more than thirty different types of special districts, providing considerable opportunity to skirt constitutional bonding limitations and taxation constraints. Among the vast array of local services provided by special districts are education, water service, sewer service, fire protection, libraries, flood control, airport facilities, ambulance service, hospitals, solid waste disposal, housing, and public transit.

The statutory authority for cooperation is found in the Interlocal Cooperation Act of 1962 and in the statutory authority to create joint special districts. Basically, local governments can sign a joint agreement to perform any function that they each have the power to do separately, including the ability to enter into a revenue-sharing agreement. All agreements are to be approved by the attorney general, except those that provide for the construction or repair of municipal roads or bridges.

Fifteen area development districts were created by state statute in 1971 in response to federal requirements for substate districts to plan and implement federal grant-in-aid programs. The districts function as links between state and local governments and are the institutional mechanism for intrastate regional activity.[20]

Administrative Discretion

State statutes and court cases stipulate local government administrative actions, which vary by class of city. On the one hand, the state tends to be very prescriptive; on the other, local elected officials tend to assume that they have considerable discretion in interpreting and conforming with state requirements.

Political patronage traditionally has been a hallmark of local government employment. In recent years, however, the General Assembly has enacted a wide range of laws governing local personnel issues. All cities are required to have a personnel classification plan and a personnel pay plan adopted by ordinance. Civil service systems are optional for all cities except first-class cities. Those cities without a civil service system are covered by a number of other state statutes governing personnel decisions.[21]

There is one civil service system for first-class cities and another for second- and third-class cities, which may be adopted by fourth- and fifth-class cities. The mandated first-class city system, called "classified service," covers all employees except specified administrators. A six-member civil service board administers the classified service.

Civil service is optional for second- through fifth-class cities, which may adopt civil service for all employees, for some departments and employees, or for none at all. For those cities choosing to enact a municipal civil service system by ordinance, state statutes outline the process and define the legislative functions associated with adopting a classification plan, providing adequate compensation, and establishing by ordinance personnel policy as deemed necessary and proper. Locally the civil service system is administered by a three-member civil service board appointed by the mayor and approved by the legislative body.[22]

In 1994 the General Assembly mandated that every city adopt a code of ethics. Although the law provides local communities with considerable discretion in writing their own code, it does require that certain issues be addressed, such as nepotism and conflict of interest.

State statutes give local government the power to acquire goods and services. However, in providing cities with at least four different methods of acquisition, the law has created a "nightmarish web of technicality." Procurement is "an extremely confusing process."[23] Unless a municipality has established other procedures, it is legally obliged to advertise for bids for any contract or purchase that exceeds $10,000.

Cities can also choose to adopt the model procurement code. Designed to alleviate potential problems in the procurement process, the code gives cities considerable flexibility to determine the qualifications of bidders, to modify contracts once they are issued, to purchase perishables, to implement emergency procedures, to supervise acquired property, and to report activities.[24]

Countywide land-use planning is required in counties with populations of 300,000 or more. In all other cities and counties, it is permissible. For those local governments that choose to implement comprehensive land-use planning, state law covers designating a planning unit, organizing a planning commission, developing and updating a comprehensive plan, and adopting and implementing a zoning ordinance. A city or county may establish an independent planning unit only if a joint city-county planning unit cannot be established.[25]

Economic Development

Cities and counties in Kentucky consider economic development to be among their highest priorities. Local governments have considerable authority to promote economic development by developing industrial parks and undertaking infrastructure improvements. In doing so, localities hope to attract new or expanding business, establish and maintain enterprise zones, grant tax credits and issue industrial bonds, and create revolving loan funds.

Localities can create an industrial development authority to promote economic development. As extensions of local government, authorities can utilize government office space and clerical support, issue revenue bonds, and acquire land through condemnation. Property taxes are not assessed on industrial sites owned by authorities.

Industrial foundations are privately and publicly funded mechanisms used by communities to acquire and develop industrial sites. Industrial development corporations or foundations are usually nonprofit, receive funds from both city and county government, and have both private- and public-sector representatives on their boards.

The state has a number of incentives, loans, grants, and tax breaks that it uses to encourage economic growth. One of the largest state aid programs to localities is the Local Government Economic Development Fund. Also, a part of the coal severance tax is returned to coal-impacted counties for development projects.[26]

Local governments can use their own funds to renew and revitalize blighted areas. Many small and medium-sized cities have sponsored "main street programs" to renovate their Victorian-era store fronts. The larger cities use local funds to match community development grants from the federal Department of Housing and Urban Development. Local governments are able to use their own funds for economic and community development without voter approval.

Fiscal Autonomy of Local Governments

Local Revenues

Kentucky cities receive revenue from a variety of sources. User fees and service charges produce 44 percent of city revenue; taxes constitute 39 percent; intergovernmental transfers total 11 percent; and the remainder comes from regulatory fees, franchise fees, parking violations, sale of property, and investment interest. User fees and service charges can be levied only to cover the cost of providing the service. The revenue is "dedicated," must be separately accounted for, and can be spent only on providing the charged service. Thus, user fees and service charges cannot produce general-purpose revenue for the city. Funds to provide for traditional city services must come from taxation or intergovernmental transfer.

Kentucky has a highly centralized tax system. More than 77 percent of all state and local taxes are collected by the state, and state statutes substantially limit and restrict local taxing authority. City tax revenue comes from two main sources: real estate ad valorem taxes and occupational and business license taxes.[27]

Real estate ad valorem taxes are required to be levied in proportion to the assessed value of property. Even though the Kentucky Constitution requires assessments to be 100 percent of market value, only recently have they begun to approach full assessment statewide. As assessments have gone up, the rate of taxation has remained low. Kentucky is forty-seventh among the states in local revenue from the property tax.[28] HB 44, passed by

a special session of the legislature in 1979, provides that if growth in revenues from the property tax from the previous year is greater that 4 percent, then voters may petition for a referendum on the proposed increased taxes.

Local governments are forbidden by the state constitution from levying either an income tax or a sales tax. However, local taxes—such as an occupational license fee, net profits tax, tourism and recreation tax, and insurance premium tax—can be collected at the local level. These taxes are the largest source of tax income for most medium-sized and large cities. An occupational license tax requires an employee to pay a flat percentage (usually 1 or 2 percent) on the income earned within the jurisdiction; businesses pay a percentage fee on their net profits for the "privilege" of working and doing business in the community. License fees are considered levies for the privilege of carrying out a certain activity.

Cities can levy earmarked taxes such as motel and restaurant taxes, the proceeds of which must be used to promote tourism and recreation. In addition, statutes permit funding for improvements to facilities (such as sewers) by assessments and user fees. Detailed state statutes regulate the process cities must follow in levying assessments.

Before 1994, Kentucky's constitution required two-thirds of the local voters to approve a general-obligation bond. Furthermore, statutes required cities to levy an adequate tax to pay the interest on the bond and to create a sinking fund to repay the bond. Few local governments used general-obligation bonds to fund debt. Instead, they turned to special districts and public corporations to finance capital projects. For example, a not-for-profit holding company issued lease revenue bonds to finance a public project and then leased the project to the local government for an annual rental payment on a year-to-year renewable lease.

A 1994 constitutional amendment permits local governments to issue general-obligation bonds for more than one year without voter approval. The amendment retains a debt limit of 10 percent of the assessed taxable property value for cities with populations of 15,000 or more; 5 percent for cities with 3,000–15,000 population; 3 percent for cities with less than 3,000 population; and 2 percent for counties and taxing districts. The 1996 Local Government Debt Act specifies the conditions and limitations local governments must meet to incur debt beyond a year.

State law permits local governments to use revenue bonds to finance a number of projects, such as utilities, airports, and hospitals. Industrial revenue bonds can be used to construct industrial buildings and pollution control facilities but may not be used for sales activities, commercial or medical office buildings, or commercial enterprises that provide financial services. Certain specified projects (such as hotels and motels and mass communication facilities) must gain the approval of the state Private Activity Bond Allocation Committee before issuing revenue bonds.[29] Revenue bonds do not require a referendum vote. User fees, special assessment taxes, or rents may be utilized to repay revenue bonds.

Local Expenditures

Local governments have broad authority to spend funds on governmental services. The major items of expenditure by first- and second-class cities in 1995 were, in order, public works and utilities, police, capital projects, fire and emergency services, debt services, community development and social services, central government, streets, parks and recreation, and solid waste disposal. For third- through sixth-class cities, a much higher proportion of expenditures went to public works and utilities and to debt service.[30]

All cities are required to maintain an accounting system on a fund basis and in accordance with generally accepted principles of governmental accounting. Moreover, they are required by state law to submit financial records for audit. The results of the audit are published locally.[31] Sources of repaying municipal debt must be described in the budget.

Although it changed the process by which long-term debt is incurred, the 1994 constitutional amendment made clear that local governments must have an annual budget that delineates expected revenues and expenditures. The constitution prohibits governments from spending any funds in excess of expected revenues in a fiscal year.[32] There are no expenditure limits on specific budget items other than that implicit in expected revenues.

There is no statutory provision for a city or county to declare bankruptcy or go into receivership. The state may require local governments to raise funds necessary to meet legal obligations. A city is prohibited from dissolving if it has outstanding debt.

State Government Grants-in-Aid to Localities

The Commonwealth of Kentucky provides a vast array of financial assistance to local government. Programs are administered by many agencies, and the definition of state aid to local governments varies considerably. Those that have received the most funding have been programs supporting rural, county, and municipal roads; local government economic assistance and development; law enforcement and fire fighting; and jails and courts.

In most of these programs, the aid goes to the local government for expenditure. The funds are earmarked by subject matter, and the recipient government has some discretion in approving specific activities or projects to be funded. However, in the largest program, Rural Secondary Road Aid (which provides funds for road repair at the local level), the state decides which roads will be repaired and makes the repairs. A number of low-interest state loan programs, such as the infrastructure loan program, also are available to local governments.[33]

Unfunded Mandates

Because more responsibility has been shifted to the local level, cities are increasingly facing fiscal problems caused by unfunded or partially funded mandates. The mandates that have provoked the most concern by local officials in recent years include solid waste collection and disposal, application of state-prevailing wage laws to local government public works construction projects, state (and federal) standards for jails and law enforcement, and state requirements for record keeping and personnel classification and pay.[34]

The General Assembly is required to prepare a fiscal note for all proposed legislation that might have a fiscal effect on local governments. It is not uncommon, however, for the fiscal note to conclude that the impact could not be accurately calculated. The degree to which local governments comply with state mandates varies by program and locality. The trend is toward a stronger effort by state government to enforce its mandates.

Access to Local Government

Local Elections

The state board of elections sets the rules and regulations for elections and voting in Kentucky. These procedures are administered at the local level by the county clerk, who is responsible for organizing and running all local elections. A county board of elections oversees the electoral process, which includes determining precinct boundaries for the county, securing polling places for each precinct, and selecting precinct election officers. The county board comprises the county clerk, the county sheriff, and two other board members appointed by the state Board of Elections. Although voting registration and record keeping are a local process, since 1972 the state has had a uniform automatic process for creating and maintaining voting lists.[35]

Citizen Controls over Actions of Local Officials

Kentucky lacks the formal participatory features of the initiative, referendum, and recall but does provide many opportunities for citizen involvement. Citizens can and do petition government, but these petitions have no legal standing, except in those areas specified by state law such as incorporation, annexation, merger, or a proposed increase of more than 4 percent in property tax revenue. The Kentucky Constitution provides for the impeachment of locally elected officials by the local legislative body.

Kentucky's Open Records Law requires that "all public records shall be open for inspection by any person . . . except as otherwise provided." Among the exceptions provided in the law are "public records containing information of a personal nature where the public disclosure thereof would constitute a clearly unwarranted invasion of personal privacy." Preliminary drafts, recommendations, and memorandums are also excluded.[36]

State-Local Relations

Although local governments in Kentucky are becoming more involved in ever-widening programmatic areas, the General Assembly keeps pace by amending and fine-tuning basic enabling legislation. Some of this legislation seems trivial. In 1992, for example, the General Assembly decided that cities may not prohibit trains from sounding their whistles within city limits. Other measures, such as recent legislation requiring localities to pay the prevailing wage, however, are far reaching and have major impact.

Within the constitutional and legally prescribed state-local structure, personality, patronage, and politics dominate Kentucky's political system. The state sets goals and legitimizes actions for local governments. Local officials, however, retain a high degree of independence in both action and enforcement. Politics tends to be traditional and resistant to change, yet at times the political system is dynamic, initiating legislation such as the Kentucky Education Reform Act. The pressures for change coming from local government are spurred mostly by activists at the community level. There is, however, no formal, widespread citizens' movement demanding more responsive government. In some communities, citizens and officials are propelling changes at the local level and are calling for broader discretion and more local control. Although they may agree rhetorically with such sentiments, in practice state officials tend to continue to micromanage local government from the state level.

Notes

1. Penny Miller, *Kentucky Politics and Government* (Lincoln: University of Nebraska Press, 1994), 3.

2. Neal R. Peirce and Jerry Hagstrom, *The Book of America* (New York: W. W. Norton, 1983), 387; Miller, *Kentucky Politics and Government*, 3–11.

3. Legislative Research Commission, *Kentucky Government,* informational bulletin 137 (Frankfort, Ky.: Legislative Research Commission, 1994), 31.

4. Miller, *Kentucky Politics and Government*, 7.

5. Legislative Research Commission, *Kentucky Municipal Statutory Law,* informational bulletin 145 (Frankfort, Ky.: Legislative Research Commission, 1997), 35–36.

6. Rita Ferguson and Kenneth Witt, "Home Rule in Kentucky Cities," *Municipal Law News* 7, no. 3 (October 1993): 1.

7. Legislative Research Commission, *Kentucky Government*, 151.

8. Miller, *Kentucky Politics and Government*, 270.

9. Legislative Research Commission, *Kentucky Municipal Statutory Law*, 46–57.

10. Ibid., 13–14.

11. Ibid., 15.

12. Ibid., 15–18.

13. Sheryl G. Snyder and Frank F. Chuppe, "Kentucky's New Anti-Annexation Statute," *Municipal Law News* 2, no. 3 (October 1988): 6.

14. Legislative Research Commission, *Kentucky Government*, 137.

15. Robert Kline and Janet Patton, "Can Local Government Be Restructured?" *Kentucky Journal* (November 1989): 4.

16. Legislative Research Commission, *Kentucky Government*, 155.

17. Legislative Research Commission, *Kentucky Municipal Statutory Law*, 19–20.

18. Ibid., 105–106.

19. Miller, *Kentucky Politics and Government*, 290.

20. Legislative Research Commission, *Kentucky Government*, 131–132.

21. David C. Fowler, "Civil Service," *Municipal Law News* 10, no. 1 (February 1996): 7–8.

22. Legislative Research Commission, *Kentucky Municipal Statutory Law*, 95–96.

23. William Reynolds and Rita Ferguson, "Municipal Contracts in Kentucky," *Municipal Law News* 6, no. 1 (February 1992): 7.

24. Reynolds and Ferguson, "Municipal Contracts in Kentucky," 7.

25. Legislative Research Commission, *Kentucky Municipal Statutory Law*, 125–130.

26. Kentucky Economic Development Cabinet, "New Tools to Create Jobs in Your Community" (report to the Seminar on Economic Development, Lexington, 5 May 1992). Coal-impacted counties are those counties that produce or mine coal and through which the coal travels to market. As part of economic development, severance tax money can be used to fund repairs to roads damaged by coal trucks.

27. Kentucky League of Cities, *Funding Our Future*, 29–30.

28. Ibid., 22–23.

29. Legislative Research Commission, *Kentucky Municipal Statutory Law*, 74–76.

30. Kentucky League of Cities, *Funding Our Future*, 73–74.

31. Legislative Research Commission, *Kentucky Government*, 151.

32. Legislative Research Commission, *Kentucky Municipal Statutory Law*, 6.

33. Kentucky League of Cities, *Funding Our Future*, 29–30.

34. Ibid., 21.

35. Legislative Research Commission, *Kentucky Government*, 43–46.

36. "Open Records," *Municipal Law News* 10, no. 3 (October 1996): 18.

LOUISIANA

Richard Engstrom and Robert K. Whelan

"Home rule" is a concept that is often said to exist more in name than in practice. Although most state constitutions provide for some form of home rule, legislative and judicial interpretations of these provisions have minimized their impact on local governments. Louisiana, however, is a clear exception to this pattern. If states could be ranked according to the degree to which home rule is actually provided to local governments, Louisiana would no doubt be among the leaders, regardless of the measure employed. Provisions of the state constitution adopted in 1974 were intended to end a period of de facto state legislative supremacy over local government. This intention has been recognized and respected by the state's supreme court, resulting in an environment very favorable to the exercise of authority by local governments.

Governmental Setting

Several factors distinguish Louisiana from other states. First, the state's governmental history is somewhat different. During its colonial era, Louisiana was governed by the French and the Spanish. Local government institutions with unique names, such as parishes and police juries, are part of that legacy. The state's political traditions are also somewhat unique.

Second, the state has a different economic base than other states. Cotton and sugar were the main bases of the plantation economy before the Civil War, along with commerce in the port city of New Orleans. Louisiana never developed a solid base of high-productivity manufacturing employment; the percentages of workers employed in manufacturing industries were historically low and remain so today (about 13 percent of nonfarm employment in 1997). Oil was discovered early in the twentieth century, and oil, gas, and petrochemical industries developed after World War II. Given a somewhat "populist" bent in Louisiana politics, the government's financial situation became tied to revenue from these industries. When oil and gas prices were high, the revenue picture was bright; when prices were low, state revenues declined. This greatly affected local governments, which were dependent on state government revenues. State administrations in the 1980s and 1990s have succeeded in making the state less dependent on oil revenues, which have been declining, and local governments have benefited from the state's improved fiscal health.

Third, the state's population characteristics differ somewhat from those of other states in the South. The percentage of African Americans in the state (32 percent according to 1996 census bureau figures) is among the highest in the South. However, it is the presence of large numbers of "Cajuns" in the Roman Catholic French parishes in the southern part of the state that creates an ambience different from that found in most of the Protestant South. Cajun voters, among other things, are more tolerant of alcoholic beverages and gambling.

Fourth, Louisiana's recent political history is somewhat unique. In his classic study of Louisiana politics up to the mid-1950s, Allan Sindler concluded that "compared to the factional chaos of some other Southern states, recent Louisiana politics has been distinguished by a cohesive bifactionalism and by the dominance of the governor in state politics."[1] Factions in the Democratic Party between 1920 and 1952 were identified as pro-Long and anti-Long, in reference to the state's charismatic politician, Huey P. Long. The Long faction was known for its governmental programs, including highways, hospitals, and homestead tax exemptions—and also for its venality. In contrast, the anti-Long reformers believed in a limited role for state government and ran relatively "clean" governments while in office.

The tradition of bifactionalism is gone, and the Republican Party has become a more important force in state politics during the last two decades. Since 1971 the governor has either been a particular Democrat (Edwin W. Edwards [1972–1980, 1984–1988, 1992–1996]) or a Republican (David Treen [1980–1984], Buddy Roemer [1988–1992], or Mike Foster [1996–present]). Broadly speaking, Edwards pursued a populist agenda, with strong political support from the French-speaking parishes in South Louisiana and African American voters throughout the state. The Republican governors have emphasized efficiency and governmental reform; they have had strong political support from the rural areas of North Louisiana and the suburban parishes around New Orleans.

The election of Republican governors is widely believed to be facilitated by the state's open primary system.[2] All of the gubernatorial candidates appear on the same ballot in the primary election. There are no partisan primaries in state elections. If no candidate receives a majority of the votes cast, the top two vote recipients compete in a runoff election. A Republican candidate has entered a runoff in every gubernatorial election since this system has been in place, sometimes against Democratic candidates, who would not have been selected under the old system in which the Democratic nominee was selected by a majority vote within a closed Democratic primary.

Although the tradition of bifactionalism is gone, Louisiana politics still revolve around a dominant governor. Louisiana's governors have the powers of "strong" governors. They propose the budget and generally set the legislative agenda. Almost everyone in Louisiana politics looks to the governor's office as the center of the state political and policy process.[3]

Home Rule in Louisiana

Historical Development

Before the 1974 constitution was adopted, local governments in Louisiana were seriously constrained in their exercise of authority. The Louisiana Supreme Court has long held (as have courts in other states) that "parishes and municipal corporations of this state are vested with no powers, and possess no authority, except as conferred upon, or delegated to, them by the Constitution and statutes."[4]

The previous state constitution, adopted in 1921, was a heavily amended, detailed, three-volume document filled with material that was more appropriately contained in statutes than in a constitution. This was particularly true of the article on local and parochial affairs, which constituted over 36 percent of the entire document[5] and was said to be filled with "statutory trivia."[6]

The Local and Parochial Affairs Article contained seven amendments that allegedly provided local governments with home rule. Specific home rule provisions were added for the cities of Shreveport and New Orleans in 1948 and 1950, respectively; a general provision for all municipalities was added in 1952. The parishes of East Baton Rouge and Jefferson were also the subjects of specific home rule amendments in 1946 and 1956, respectively; two general provisions were added for parishes, one in 1960 and another in 1968.[7] Despite the numerous provisions, however, the quality of home rule afforded to local governments was not impressive, and their authority remained constrained.

All of the municipal home rule amendments in the previous constitution were autonomy-type provisions in which there was assumed to be a dichotomy between statewide and local concerns. Under these provisions, the state was to have exclusive jurisdiction over statewide matters, and local governments would have exclusive jurisdiction over purely local matters. The general home rule provision explicitly authorized municipalities (whether or not they had adopted home rule charters) to exercise authority over their "local affairs, property and government." This appeared to be a broad grant of power. It was preceded, however, by a declaration of state supremacy.[8] Adjudicators focused on the declaration of supremacy, not on the powers reserved for the municipalities; consequently, interpretations of this home rule provision more often limited than authorized municipal actions. The constitutional provisions effectively constrained rather than delegated authority to municipalities.[9]

The only area that was unambiguously covered by the "local affairs, property and government" clause was the structure of local government. State statutes specified the governance arrangements for municipalities, at the time, usually a version of the "weak" mayor–council format.[10] Local executive and legislative institutions could be arranged differently, however, through a home rule charter. A governance arrangement specified in a home rule charter, which had to be approved by the voters, was deemed a matter of local concern protected by the home rule provision. Municipal home rule in Louisiana was therefore, in application, little more than the authority to structure government in a manner thought most appropriate for a particular municipality; only 12 of the roughly 300 municipalities in the state had taken advantage of this option. Home rule did not grant municipalities an unambiguous authority to act on matters of particular concern to a municipality. Indeed, it did not even preclude the state from mandating (through general legislation) minimum salaries and other working conditions for municipal policemen and firefighters, a practice widely viewed as a state intrusion on a strictly local concern.

The first two amendments to the 1921 constitution concerning home rule for parishes applied to specific parishes only. A partial consolidation of the City of Baton Rouge and the Parish of East Baton Rouge was authorized by a 1946 amendment,[11] and Jefferson Parish was authorized to adopt a home rule charter by a 1956 amendment. Neither of these amendments affected the powers originally allocated to these parish governments in the state's constitution and statutes.

However, two general home rule authorizations for parishes, added by amendments in 1960 and 1968, contained initiative-type home rule provisions that gave parish governments with voter-approved home rule charters "full power and authority to conduct and operate the parish government . . . in any and all matters not *prohibited* by State law" (emphasis added). This language reflected a shift in the thinking of many home rule advocates around the country and altered the method by which powers were allocated. Rather than dichotomizing authority along state and local lines, as the 1952 autonomy-type provision for municipalities did, this method enhanced local authority by not prohibiting—rather than specifically authorizing—local government action. This measure was intended to avoid restrictive judicial attitudes, which had largely obliterated the state-local distinction.

The basic governance arrangement for parishes in Louisiana has been a police jury, an elected body with both legislative and administrative responsibilities. "Police jury" is misleading, in that members of this body do not function as police officers or jurors in the traditional sense. A police jury both enacts ordinances and functions as the county executive. Membership on a police jury ranges from five to fifteen, and election is through single-member districts. Forty-seven of the state's sixty-four parishes are governed through this arrangement.[12]

The general home rule provisions for parishes allowed other structural arrangements to be adopted. The 1961 amendment limited the options to either the commission form of government or a council-manager arrangement. The amendment adopted in 1968 contained no structural limitations.

Only one parish, Plaquemines, adopted a home rule charter under a general provision. Plaquemines adopted a commission form of government in 1961, under the first of the general provisions. The commission's exercise of power through the initiative was reviewed only once by an appellate court, with a result favorable to the parish. The commission's practice of transferring large sums of money from the parish treasury to the parish school board, which is a separate jurisdictional entity, was upheld because no state law prohibited the parish government from doing so.[13]

The amendments authorizing home rule for East Baton Rouge and Jefferson parishes—although not providing for any expansion in the powers of these parish governments—did contain an important protection that enhanced their autonomy when it came to internal matters. The amendments specified that the "structure [and] organization" of the home rule "plan of government" adopted by the voters in these parishes were under the control of the parish, not statutes. The courts have found that this protection exempts these parishes from state-mandated minimum wages and other prerequisites for local government employees—something the autonomy provision had failed to do for municipalities.[14]

Definition of Home Rule

The meaning of home rule in Louisiana was changed significantly when a new state constitution was adopted in 1974. The home rule provisions were designed to provide municipal and parish governments with much greater authority to act on local matters. The constitution contains a self-executing initiative provision that is applicable to all localities, regardless of whether or not they have a home rule charter. A simple majority vote in a referendum may grant local authorities that do not have home rule charters the right to "exercise any power and perform any function necessary, requisite or proper for the management for its affairs, not denied by its charter or by general law." Localities similarly may adopt a home rule charter to enable them to exercise powers "not denied by general law or inconsistent with this constitution."[15]

These provisions were intended to free local governing authorities to respond to matters of local concern without first securing authorization from the state. State law, henceforth, would prohibit local governments from doing certain things, rather than provide authorization for them. Some limitations on local governments are expressed in the constitution itself. For example, parishes and municipalities are precluded (not surprisingly) from defining and specifying the punishment for felonies, from enacting ordinances governing private and civil relationships (such as marriage and divorce), and from abridging the general "police power" of the state.[16] Other limitations have been imposed by statute through what have been called "no, no" laws.[17] For example, one statute adopted in 1980 explicitly precluded parishes and municipalities from regulating hazardous wastes.[18]

Local governments also have been prohibited from licensing, regulating, and taxing the operators of casinos and enacting minimum wage requirements that exceed those established by the federal government. The legislature, however, has not been exceedingly restrictive. Indeed, in 1985 a statute granted municipalities the same initiative powers that are authorized in the constitution, the exercise of which is no longer contingent on a majority vote in a municipal referendum, as originally required by the constitutional provision.[19]

The courts have not been entirely excluded from determining whether or not local governments are authorized to do particular things under the initiative provisions, however. Whether a local action has been precluded is not always clear. For example, it is sometimes argued that a state preemption is implied by a statute rather than made explicit. Whether or not a particular action by a local government falls within an excluded category of activity may also be the subject of debate.

The state's judiciary has been much more receptive to the exercise of power by local governments since the adoption of the initiative provisions. The Louisiana Supreme Court recognized that these constitutional changes constituted a grant of "broad residual powers" to the local units[20] and acknowledged that this necessitated "a corresponding adjustment in the judicial attitude toward home rule prerogatives." Consequently, the court defers less to the state level on issues concerning local government authority. The court has stated that, "Home rule abilities and immunities are bestowed by the constitution in terms too full and general to warrant narrow construction of them by the courts," and that any exemptions to them therefore "should be given careful scrutiny by the courts."[21]

Although this new approach toward home rule by no means guarantees that courts will rule in favor of the local exercise of authority (especially with regard to taxation powers), it does create a much more favorable judicial climate for local governments. The supreme court held in 1994 that powers that had been authorized through home rule charters adopted before the 1974 constitution can only be denied through a constitutional provision, not by a statute, because the constitutional provision recognizing these charters does not contain the expression "not denied by general law," as do the initiative provisions.[22] A power not currently denied within that document, therefore, can only be withdrawn by constitutional amendment.

Structural Features

Each governing authority must prepare a general code of ordinances and make it available for public distribution. Municipalities are divided into three classes: cities (populations greater than 5,000), towns (populations of 1,000–5,000), and villages (populations less than 1,000).[23] Unless prohibited by the constitution, the legislature may, within its discretion, create new corporations, reincorporate existing municipalities, and revise, amend, or repeal any existing charters or impose new ones.[24]

The provision of the 1974 constitution authorizing parishes and municipalities to adopt home rule charters does not limit the legislative and executive arrangements that may be adopted through such charters. A parish or municipal governing body may either appoint or call for the election of a commission to draft a home rule charter; an election must be called for this purpose if at least 10 percent of the registered voters, or 10,000 registered voters (whichever is fewer) endorse a petition requesting such an election. The size of these commissions may range from seven to eleven members.[25] The adoption of a home rule charter is contingent on a majority vote among those voting on the issue in a referendum. A majority vote is likewise required to amend or repeal such charters.[26] The constitution also authorizes home rule charters that consolidate local governmental units. Charter commissions that are considering consolidation must have at least one representative from each of the affected units, and the adoption of a consolidated arrangement is contingent on a majority vote within each of those units.

The number of local jurisdictions with home rule charters has increased to over forty under these provisions. A total of twenty-eight municipalities had home rule charters as of 1997, as did fourteen parishes and three consolidated governments (the latter being Baton Rouge–East Baton Rouge Parish, Lafayette–Lafayette Parish, and Houma–Terrebonne Parish). Almost all of the remaining municipalities are now governed by a "strong" mayor–council arrangement, as specified in the Lawrason Act, the state's basic statute concerning non–home rule municipalities.[27] All of the non–home rule parishes continue to operate under the police jury system.[28]

The governance arrangements specified in all of the home rule charters adopted pursuant to the 1974 constitution are subject to the "structure and organization" protection that had been provided in the earlier plans for Jefferson Parish and Baton Rouge–East Baton Rouge Parish.[29] Thus, the state is virtually precluded from altering these arrangements. This protection has been employed to invalidate state efforts to alter the composition of local boards and commissions established within home rule charters.[30]

Residents of any unincorporated area with a population greater than 300 may propose the incorporation of an area. Upon presentation of a certified petition signed by 25 percent of the electors, the governor calls a special election to determine if the unincorporated area will become a municipality. Any legal opposition to the incorporation must be filed in the district court for that area within thirty days. If the municipality is incorporated, the governor appoints officers who hold office until the next general municipal election.[31]

A parish is a political corporation created by the legislature for the purpose of aiding in the administration of government.[32] As such, citizens have no vested right in a particular plan of the parish, because it is subject to the regulation of legislatures.[33] Parishes possess the same privileges that a corporation possesses, such as acquiring or holding property.[34] Parishes operate with police juries or commissions or under home rule charters.[35]

Extraterritoriality exists in several respects. Municipalities often extend services to areas outside city limits, for water and sewer lines, for example. Municipalities sometimes own property outside city limits, particularly industrial parks, but a city's police authority over these areas remains ambiguous. Extraterritoriality may also exist in some cooperative endeavors; for example, city and parish services in the area of law enforcement may overlap.[36]

One unusual situation is found in the composition of the New Orleans Aviation Board, which manages the New Orleans International Airport. The airport belongs to the City of New Orleans; however, it is located in the City of Kenner in Jefferson Parish and has a runway that extends into St. Charles Parish. The aviation board has members from both the City of Kenner and St. Charles Parish. The mayor of New Orleans appoints these "outside" members, with the approval of the New Orleans City Council. In reality, Kenner and St. Charles recommend their choices, and these are ratified by New Orleans officials. Another example of extraterritoriality in the New Orleans area is the Sewerage and Water Board, which provides some drainage for Jefferson Parish. Capital costs are shared by the two parishes.[37]

Functions of Local Government
Functional Responsibilities

Municipalities now have initiative-type powers that allow them broad discretion to act on matters not preempted by the state. Actual practice does not vary from the legal description of functional responsibilities. State preemption has not been a major problem for local governments.

Parish governmental authority is shared by the police jury (or a governing board established through a home rule charter) and a number of other elected officials, including the school board, law enforcement officials, and assessors. Traditionally, parishes are responsible for the operation and management of public facilities, including the courthouse and jail, libraries, and parish roads. Roads have been a major police jury function, and police jurors often are viewed as the "roads commissioners" for their districts. Education, which is supervised by the school board, usually is the most costly parish function. Law enforcement is a vital parish function, and elected officials such as the sheriff, district attorney, coroner, clerk of court, and district court judges are important political and governmental actors. The assessor, an elected official, sets property tax rates and collects property taxes. Parish responsibilities may expand through the adoption of home rule powers. Initiative-type powers are available to parishes, with or without home rule charters, upon approval of the voters.

The legislature is authorized to create special districts, boards, agencies, and commissions and to grant them rights and powers, including the power of taxation and the power to incur debt and issue bonds. A local government subdivision may consolidate and merge into itself any special district or local public agency having jurisdiction within its boundaries (except school districts). This provision is only effective if approved by a majority of electors voting in the local subdivision and in the affected special district. Such a consolidation occurs only if the indebtedness of the local public agency is assumed by the governing authority.[38]

Intergovernmental agreements are commonly used by local governments in Louisiana.[39] Any parish, municipality, or political subdivision of the state may enter into agreements between or among themselves to engage jointly in the construction, acquisition, or improvement of any public project; the promotion and maintenance of any undertaking; or the exercise of any power, provided that at least one of the participants to the agreement can lawfully exercise such power.[40]

Administrative Discretion

A comprehensive statutory civil service system is in effect for cities with populations over 100,000 and municipal fire and police departments in cities with a minimum population of 7,000. The civil service is divided into unclassified and classified services. Persons in the unclassified service include elected officials, heads of executive departments, and city attorneys.[41]

The Louisiana Administrative Procedures Act (APA) governs any state agency that makes rules, regulations, or policy or that formulates or issues decisions implementing federal or state laws. In Louisiana, the APA does not apply to parishes or municipalities, school boards, or other units of local government that perform governmental functions.[42] Thus, local governments have the discretion, in general, to set administrative procedures.

All public works contracts worth more than $30,000 (including labor, material, and purchases or supplies) must be advertised. Contracts must be let to the lowest responsible bidder. However, there has been wide variation in the implementation of this law. Political subdivisions are authorized to adopt the Louisiana Procurement Code, which governs state contracts for services and supplies.[43]

Although every parish and municipality may create a planning commission,[44] many have not done so. Such commissions adopt master plans for the physical development of a territory, including the general location and extent of streets, levees, schools, and public utilities and a zoning plan. The existing enabling legislation for planning in the state was adopted in 1946. Most professional planners would agree that this legislation is deficient in its ability to promote sound planning. The current legislation does not identify what a comprehensive plan entails and addresses only physical development issues. Implementation tools, such as zoning and capital budgeting, do not even have to conform to such a plan.

Economic Development

Louisiana provides a number of tax exemptions to attract new businesses and to promote economic development in the state. These include exemptions from the sales tax, corporate income tax, natural resources severance tax, and petroleum products tax.

New manufacturing establishments receive a five-year exemption from property taxes under the Louisiana Constitution. Since 1992 an inventory tax credit has been allowed against corporate and individual income taxes for property taxes that are paid to political subdivisions on inventory held by manufacturers, distributors, and retailers.

The state constitution permits the state to extend tax abatement against locally taxed property. Affected local jurisdictions have no say nor any appeal against such decisions. The state can abate taxes up to the full value of a new manufacturing establishment or in addition to an existing one. Abatements last for five years, with renewal possible for a second five-year period. In Louisiana, abatements are granted by the state Board of Commerce and Industry. Since the state does not lose any money, there is an incentive to continue the program, although substantial amounts of money are lost by local governments because of the contraction of the tax base.[45]

The Louisiana Enterprise Zone Program was enacted in 1981 for the purpose of stimulating business and industrial growth in the depressed areas of the state. Its incentives include rebates of some sales and use taxes and tax credits for new jobs. The state Department of Economic Development (DED) instituted a Regional Economic Development Alliances (REDA) program to build "lasting, productive, results-focused partnerships" between the DED and local communities. In FY 1992 the program received a budget of $1.5 million from the state.[46] The heart of the enterprise zone program is a package of tax credits and other incentives to businesses locating within designated urban and rural enterprise zones. These incentives are in addition to other state-sponsored incentives, which include a property tax exemption on manufacturing facilities and equipment.

The most distressed 25 percent of census bureau tracts qualify for enterprise zone incentives. Enterprise zones require both state designation and designation by a parish or municipality. Enterprise zone incentives in Louisiana come mostly from the state, with some incentives provided by local government. The five main tax incentives for enterprise zones are (1) one-time tax credits of $2,500 for new employees, (2) exemption from state taxes on building or building improvements materials, (3) exemption from state taxes on machinery, (4) exemption from local taxes on construction or building improvements, and (5) exemption from local taxes on machinery and equipment.[47]

Fiscal Autonomy of Local Governments

Local Revenues

The state constitution authorizes parishes and municipalities to impose property, sales, and occupational license taxes. Property is to be assessed at a percentage of its fair market value or in the case of agricultural, marsh, and timber lands, at its "use value." These assessments, however, are made by elected assessors, many of whom arguably have a vested interest in maintaining low assessments of their constituents' property. Basic limits of 4 mills and 7 mills of assessed valuation are imposed on parishes and municipalities, respectively. In addition, a homestead exemption of up to $75,000 may be claimed on parish property taxes if a residential unit is owned by the person or persons occupying it. Both parish and municipal millage rates may be increased if a majority of the voters in a referendum approve the increase.[48]

Sales taxes of up to 3 percent are also authorized by the constitution, and the state can authorize an increase in the sales tax through either a general or special law. However, the basic sales tax (and any increases in it) must be approved by the voters in a respective parish or municipality.[49] The state may also exempt items from these sales taxes; almost 30 percent of the local sales tax base purportedly has now been exempted. Items exempted by the state in 1996, for example, include the purchase of automobiles that were to be subsequently leased and the purchase of trucks and trailers to be used in interstate commerce. Only a simple majority vote in the legislature is required to provide exemptions (whereas the repeal of an exemption requires a two-thirds vote).

Local governments have had to lobby intensely to protect this tax base. The Louisiana Municipal Association estimated that 75 percent of its lobbying effort during the 1996 fiscal session of the legislature consisted of "defensive lobbying" in response to what it described as the "tax exemption insanity" that inflicted the legislature.[50] In 1986 the state repealed its occupational license taxes but authorized parishes and municipalities to impose them, up to specified maximum amounts.[51]

The constitution also specifically forbids parishes and municipalities from imposing certain taxes, including an income tax, severance tax, and a tax on motor fuels. Moreover, local governments may not raise revenues by imposing a license fee on vehicles or by conducting a lottery.[52] State statutes likewise both authorize and prohibit certain forms of taxation. Local taxes on alcoholic beverages and chain stores are authorized, for example, whereas taxes on video poker and riverboat gambling are prohibited.

Whether or not a local government has the power to impose a specific tax is, not surprisingly, sometimes a question for the courts to decide. Some of the taxes adopted by the City of New Orleans, for example, have been challenged, and not all have survived judicial scrutiny. Under its home rule charter, New Orleans has the authority to impose "all kinds and classes of taxes or license fees," provided that they are "not expressly prohibited by the [state] Constitution." Some taxes adopted by the city have been upheld because there were no prohibitions. A surcharge of $100 that had been imposed on the owners of every parcel of land separately listed or assessed on the tax rolls, for example, was upheld when the supreme court ruled that it was not a form of property taxation and therefore did not conflict with the property tax system authorized in the constitution.[53] An inheritance tax was also approved because no provision of the constitution was found to prohibit it.[54]

Other taxes adopted by New Orleans, however, have been found to violate constitutional provisions. The city's effort to label as an "earnings tax" a 1.5 percent levy on the annual gross earnings above $5,000 of everyone working in the city (including those who did not live in the city) was rejected by the supreme court, which found it to be an income tax and therefore prohibited by the constitution.[55] Two efforts by the city to tax tobacco products have been unsuccessful. A "tobacco consumption privilege tax" of 10 percent (temporarily increased to 20 percent) was found by the court to be a sales tax exceeding 3 percent that had been neither authorized by the state nor approved by voters.[56] A subsequent "ownership tax" that was levied on the tobacco products stocked by retailers was likewise struck down.[57] A 4 percent levy on the gross receipts of companies that provided telecommunications services was found not to be a "privilege tax" as the city claimed but rather an occupational license tax in conflict with the constitutional provision.[58]

The question of "who pays" permeates all issues in state-local relations in Louisiana. The $75,000 homestead exemption presents a particular problem for local government revenue raising. A major effort to reform state finances by Gov. Buddy Roemer failed in the late 1980s. At this writing, there are no reform efforts under way to change the financial system. Financial issues will remain a major source of state-local conflict.

Louisiana local governments must follow a three-step statutory process before they can issue debt. First, a statutory debt ceiling is set at a percentage of the assessed valuation of taxable property. In general, all bond issues must not exceed 35 percent of the assessed value, and no single issue may exceed 10 percent. Second, voters must approve each general-obligation bond issue. Third, the state Bond Commission must validate local action and then must approve the issuance of the debt and the acceptance of the bid.[59]

Local Expenditures

A primary difference between city and parish expenditures is that in cities, more money tends to be spent on basic services. In parishes, by contrast, more is spent on specialized areas, such as transportation, culture and recreation, and health and welfare. In 1995, 63 percent of the City of Shreveport's general-fund budget of $117 million was spent on basic services: 22 percent went to public works (including sanitation, streets, and drainage), 21 percent to police, and 20 percent to fire. Sixteen percent of the budget went to general government expenditures, including insurance, transit, and economic development; 6 percent went to parks; 5 percent went to finance. The remainder was allocated to other expenses (for example, building maintenance).[60]

By contrast, East Baton Rouge Parish (which is consolidated with the City of Baton Rouge) spent 28.2 percent of a $322 million budget on public safety in 1997. General government expenditures composed 14.57 percent of the budget. Transportation made up 13.85 percent of the total. Other uses constituted 11.73 percent of the budget. Capital outlay was 8.4 percent; conservation and development, 6.7 percent; sanitation, 6 percent; debt service, 5.6 percent; culture and recreation, 3.25 percent; and health and welfare, 1.7 percent.[61] Consolidation also affects allocation of expenditures. In a $271 million budget for 1994–1995, Lafayette spent 19.3 percent on capital outlay, 15.3 percent on debt services, 16.2 percent on administration, 14.7 percent on recreation, and 2.4 percent on general accounts.[62] After the city's consolidation with Lafayette Parish, somewhat different patterns emerged. More than 11 percent of the $382 million total was allocated to the parish obligation in juvenile justice and detention.[63]

New Orleans reflects more of a big-city pattern. In a $376 million budget for 1994, the police department received $91 million dollars—almost 25 percent of the total. The fire department represented 14 percent of the total, or $53 million. Other major expenditures included community development (housing), with $25.2 million (6.7 percent); judicial and other parish agencies,

with $24.4 million (6.5 percent); and the health department, with $21.4 million (5.7 percent). Receiving less than 5 percent of the budget were sanitation, the chief administrator's office, the finance department, lights and gas, and property management.[64] The 1997 budget report shows that 42 percent of a $334 million budget was allocated for public safety; 30 percent, for general government expense; and 16 percent, for public works.[65]

Cities and parishes are required by state statute to have a balanced budget. It is possible but not likely that a city or parish will become bankrupt. For one thing, a city's assets cannot be seized by creditors. When Tangipahoa Parish faced serious financial difficulties in the early 1990s, the courts appointed an overseer for the parish budget, but the parish did not enter bankruptcy. The overseer discovered that the parish's taxes had not been raised for many years. The low tax rate was not sufficient to pay increases in state-mandated costs, particularly in the district attorney's office. The tax base in the parish was enhanced by economic growth. Tangipahoa regained fiscal stability.[66]

State Government Grants-in-Aid to Localities

State aid to major units of local governments (parishes, municipalities, school districts, and sheriffs) can be divided into three types of assistance: (1) categorical aid targeted for specific purposes, (2) shared aid related to the jurisdiction of origin, and (3) general aid distributed by formula.

The lion's share of state aid (90 percent in FY 1995–1996) comprises categorical aid to local governments. However, about 86 percent of this goes to local school districts to support elementary and secondary education, primarily through a constitutionally mandated minimum foundation program (MFP), which was approximately $1.8 billion in 1996. Spending for elementary and secondary education accounted for 22.6 percent of the total state budget in 1996. MFP funding is based on a complicated formula that considers the number of pupils and special costs for programs in certain weighted categories, for example, students requiring extended instructional time and remediation.[67]

Another example of categorical aid is state supplemental pay for policemen and firemen. This has amounted to about $45 million in a typical fiscal year since 1990. This money is not a bonus but serves as a base for employee benefits. The transportation trust fund is another form of categorical aid which supports highway and road improvements.[68] The state budget for FY 1996–1997 provided local governments with almost $150 million in supplemental pay to police and firemen, for mass transit and parish transportation, and for rural and urban development funds.[69]

Shared aid comes from severance taxes, royalty funds, video poker revenues, and state sales tax dedications to local entities. For example, 25 percent of the fees and fines from video poker are returned to local law enforcement officials. Shared aid constitutes 5 percent of total state aid.

General aid is almost entirely financed from dedicated funds and makes up 5 percent of total aid. The largest amount is revenue sharing; $90 million from the general fund is allocated annually to parishes. This money is distributed on the basis of population (80 percent) and number of homesteads (20 percent) in each parish.

Unfunded Mandates

Although the state pays for many costly programs, it also imposes many expensive mandates on local government. For example, the state mandates how and where local governments invest their funds, what they charge for certain services, and what staffing patterns will be followed. In one recent legislative session, laws were passed that mandated a pay increase for some local law enforcement and judicial officials and stipulated the level of fees for some local functions. In addition, a state law mandated around-the-clock, two-person staffing of a fire department's fire fighting apparatus.

Mandates create serious problems for parish governments, particularly in regard to the judicial system. In Louisiana, parish governments are required to pay the general operating expenses for state district courts, district attorneys, and coroners. Salaries of court reporters, for example, are set and raised by the district judges without the approval of the parish governing body that pays them. In addition, parishes must not only supplement funding for the sheriffs and clerks of court but also pay the salaries and expenses of assessors and elections administrators.[70]

Access to Local Government

Local Elections

Louisiana, like the other Deep South states, has a history of racial discrimination that included denying the right to vote to African Americans. Not until the implementation of the federal Voting Rights Act (VRA) of 1965 were racially discriminatory voter registration practices discontinued. The VRA has also been critical in protecting the state's African Americans from having their subsequent voting strength diluted by discriminatory electoral systems. Provisions of that act were employed to prevent the state's parishes from switching from single-member districts, as had been required by state law, to at-large elections following the growth in the African American vote. Since the adoption of the VRA, many of the state's municipalities have abandoned at-large elections in favor of either districted systems or mixed electoral arrangements that include districts. A 1989 survey found that in about one-third of municipalities in the state with populations of 2,500 or more (of which at least 10 percent were African American), all of the council members were elected from districts; in another third, most of the members were elected from districts. The election of African Americans

to municipal councils was found to occur almost exclusively in majority African American districts.[71]

Under the Louisiana Constitution, the electors of each local government subdivision have the exclusive right to choose their governing authority.[72] Under Louisiana's version of the open primary, which has been used since 1975, all candidates run in the same primary, regardless of party affiliation. If no candidate receives a majority of the votes in that primary, then the top two finishers compete in a runoff election, again, regardless of party affiliation.

Louisiana has an election campaign finance disclosure act that requires each candidate for public office to have a campaign treasurer manage his or her funds. Each campaign treasurer must file detailed, certified reports of contributions and expenditures for specified reporting periods. It is unlawful for candidates to pay money for endorsements or for contributors to give money in exchange for favors from any candidate. Because of the history of election problems in Louisiana, the legislature has enacted a 600-foot campaign-free zone around polling places. In addition, the law requires that voters be informed of who is responsible for publications regarding candidates and prohibits persons from making and or distributing knowingly false statements about candidates.

Citizen Controls over Actions of Local Officials

A state or local official, whether appointed or elected, will be removed from office for conviction of a felony and may be impeached and removed for malfeasance or gross misconduct. Impeachment is by the state house and trial by the state senate. Once convicted, the public officer is automatically removed from office without pay. If convicted of a felony, the public officer is removed by a district court following a suit instituted by the district attorney within ten days after the conviction is final and appeals are exhausted.[73]

A candidate can contest an election on the grounds of substantial error, fraud, or other unlawful activities. Moreover, elections may be contested based on allegations that the result would have been different if not for irregularities or fraud in the conduct of the election.

Public officials, except judges, may be recalled unless they have less than six months to serve in office. To seek the recall of any public official, a petition signed by at least 33⅓ percent of the number of registered voters in the affected voting area (with exceptions for smaller areas) must be submitted to the governor. If the petition is sufficient, the governor then orders a recall election. The majority of the votes cast determines the result.[74]

Public meetings are conducted pursuant to Robert's Rules of Order, procedures first published in 1876 by General Henry M. Robert. Louisiana has both open-meeting and public records laws. Unless they are specifically designated as executive sessions, most meetings of public bodies are open to the public.[75]

State-Local Relations

Although parishes and municipalities are authorized to adopt home rule charters under the state constitution, fewer than fifty units of local government operate under such charters. This understates the amount of home rule available to local governments in Louisiana, however, because home rule powers of the initiative type are available with voter approval to parishes without charters and are granted to the state's municipalities by statute. Powers assumed under these initiative provisions are subject to preemption by the state, but this has not been a major problem for local governments. The state legislature has not been particularly restrictive, and the state supreme court has tended not to proscribe local exercise of powers. The philosophy embraced in the 1974 constitution has caused the courts to be more permissive of local governments, at least when taxes, fees, or other efforts to raise revenue are not involved.

The number of local jurisdictions with home rule charters has increased slowly. Most recently, St. Tammany Parish adopted a home rule charter in 1998 and abandoned the police jury system for a parish president–council form of government in 2000. Although the state grants significant home rule powers, it lags behind other states in the region in areas such as comprehensive planning and growth management legislation.

It is difficult to discern clear trends in state-local relations in Louisiana, in part because policymakers tend to think in terms of particular problems (for example, passing the annual budget) rather than in terms of questions of state-local relationships.

The most contentious issues are financial ones. The policy of unfunded fiscal mandates continues to irritate local governments. The state-imposed $75,000 homestead exemption on property taxes presents a particular problem for local governments' ability to generate revenue. A major effort by Gov. Buddy Roemer to reform state finances failed in the late 1980s; currently, there are no efforts to change the financial system. Thus, the question of "who pays?" continues to permeate state-local relations in Louisiana.

Notes

1. Allan P. Sindler, *Huey Long's Louisiana: State Politics, 1920–1952* (Baltimore: Johns Hopkins Press, 1956), 248.

2. Wayne Parent, "The Rise and Stall of Republican Ascendancy in Louisiana Politics," in *The South's New Politics: Realignment and Dealignment,* ed. Robert H. Swansbrough and David M. Brodsky (Columbia: University of South Carolina Press, 1988), 214–216.

3. See Ed Renwick, "The Governor," in *Louisiana Politics: Festival in a Labyrinth,* ed. James Bolner (Baton Rouge: Louisiana State University Press, 1982), 75–88.

4. *State v. Jordan,* 20 So. 2d 543, 545 (1945).

5. Louis Newman, "Local Government in the Constitution," in *Focus on CC-73,* ed. Louis E. Newman (Baton Rouge: Institute of Governmental Research, Louisiana State University, 1973), 26.

6. Mark T. Carleton, "Elitism Sustained: The Louisiana Constitution of 1974," *Tulane Law Review* 54 (April 1986): 575.

7. Louisiana Constitution (1921), Article XIV, sections 22, 37, 40; 3(a), 3(c); 3(d), 3(g).

8. Louisiana Constitution (1921), section 40(g).

9. Richard L. Engstrom, "Home Rule in Louisiana: Could This Be the Promised Land?" *Louisiana History* 17 (Fall 1976): 438–444; Gordon Kean, "Local Government and Home Rule," *Loyola Law Review* 21, no. 1 (1975): 64–66.

10. Richard L. Engstrom, "Municipal Government" in *Louisiana Politics: Festival in a Labyrinth,* ed. James Bolner (Baton Rouge: Louisiana State University Press, 1982), 185–199.

11. Engstrom, "Home Rule in Louisiana," 443–444. See William C. Havard and Floyd L. Corty, *Rural-Urban Consolidation: The Merger of Government in the Baton Rouge Area* (Baton Rouge: Louisiana State University Press, 1964).

12. See, generally, Ann Doherty, "The Police Jury: Its Origins and Evolution," *Louisiana Parish Government* (April 1973): 39–40; Marvin Lyons, "A Study of Parish Governing Authorities in Louisiana" (M.A. thesis, University of Alabama, 1968); June Savoy Rowell, "Parish Government," in *Louisiana Politics: Festival in a Labyrinth,* ed. James Bolner (Baton Rouge: Louisiana State University Press, 1982), 143–179.

13. *Vinson v. Plaquemines Parish Commission Council,* 199 So 2d. (1967), 1, 3.

14. Engstrom, "Home Rule in Louisiana," 446–447.

15. Louisiana Constitution (1974), Article VI, sections 7, 5(e).

16. Louisiana Constitution (1974), Article VI, sections 7, 5(e); *City of Shreveport v. Curry* 357 So. 2d (1980), 1078, 1081.

17. John Parkhurst, "Article VII—Local Government," *Chicago Bar Record* 52, no. 1 (1970): 100.

18. Louisiana Statutes Annotated, R.S. 30:1136(c).

19. Louisiana Statutes Annotated, R.S. 4:627(a); 23:651; 33:361. See also James C. Percy, "A Question and Answer Review of Act 908 of 1985: The New Lawrason Act," *Louisiana Municipal Review* (November–December 1985): 10–11.

20. *City of Shreveport v. Kaufman,* 353 So. 2d (1977), 995, 997.

21. *Francis v. Morial,* 455 So. 2d (1984), 1168–1173. See also *City of New Orleans v. Board of Commissioners of the Orleans Levee District,* 640 So. 2d (1994), 252; *Lafourche Parish Council v. Autin,* 648 So. 2d (1994), 356.

22. Louisiana Constitution (1974), Article VI, section 4. See also G. Roth Kehoe, "*City of New Orleans v. Board of Commissioners:* The Louisiana Supreme Court Frees New Orleans from the Shackles of Dillon's Rule," *Tulane Law Review* 69 (1995): 809–822.

23. Louisiana Constitution (1974), Article VI, section 10; section 3; Louisiana Statutes Annotated, R.S. 33:341.

24. *City of New Orleans v. Board of Supervisors,* 43 So. 2d (1949), 237; *Bardford v. City of Shreveport,* 428 So. 2d (1983), 401.

25. Louisiana Statutes Annotated, R.S. 33:1395.

26. Louisiana Constitution (1974), Article VI, sections 5(a)–5 (c).

27. Louisiana Statutes Annotated, R.S. 33:321–463.

28. *Louisiana Roster of Officials* (Baton Rouge: Secretary of State, 1997).

29. Louisiana Constitution (1974), Article VI, section 6.

30. *Lafourche Parish Council v. Autin,* 648 So. 2d (1994), 356; *Francis v. Morial,* 455 So. 2d (1984) 950.

31. Louisiana Statutes Annotated, R.S. 33:3.

32. Louisiana Constitution (1921), Article XIV, section 3(a); Louisiana Constitution (1974), Article VI, section 1(b); *State ex rel. Brady v. Marrero,* 13 Orleans App. (1915) 98; *Meyer v. Parish of Plaquemines,* 11 So. 2d. (1942) 291.

33. *Quartemont v. Avoyelles Parish Police Jury,* 229 So. 2d (1969) 199, writ denied 230 So. 92.

34. Louisiana Statutes Annotated, R.S. 33:1329, 1330.

35. Louisiana Statutes Annotated, R.S. 33:1276.

36. Dan Garrett, attorney for Louisiana Municipal Authority (telephone interview, 14 July 1999).

37. Anthony J. Mumphrey (telephone interview, 11 July 1999).

38. Louisiana Constitution (1974), Article VI, sections 19, 16.

39. Louisiana Constitution (1974), Article VI, sections 19.

40. Louisiana Statutes Annotated, R.S. 33:1323.

41. Louisiana Constitution (1974), Article X, sections 1, 2; Louisiana Statutes Annotated, R.S. 33:2391, 33:2471, 33:2522.

42. Louisiana Statutes Annotated, R.S. 49:950.

43. Louisiana Statutes Annotated, R.S. 38:2212, 39:1554.

44. Louisiana Statutes Annotated, R.S. 33:101.

45. W. Bartley Hildreth, *State-Local Fiscal Relations in Louisiana* (Baton Rouge: Public Administration Institute, Louisiana State University, 1986), 20–22.

46. Select Council on Revenues and Expenditures in Louisiana's Future (SECURE), *Yes, We Can!* (Baton Rouge, April 1994).

47. Arthur C. Nelson and Robert K. Whelan, "Rural Enterprise Zones," *Economic Development Commentary* 13, no. 3 (Fall 1989): 27–35.

48. Louisiana Constitution (1974), Article VI, sections 26, 27; Article VII, section 18–25.

49. Louisiana Constitution (1974), Article VI, section 29.

50. Louisiana Municipal Association, "Louisiana Municipal Association Progress Report," *Louisiana Municipal Review* 61 (August 1996): 6.

51. Louisiana Statutes Annotated, R.S. 47; 341; 26:491, 492; 47:10; 27:312; 27:93.

52. Louisiana Constitution (1974), Article VII, sections 4(c), 5; Article XII, section 6.

53. *ACORN v. City of New Orleans*, 377 So. 2d (1979), 1206, 1212.

54. *Hildebrand v. City of New Orleans*, 549 So. 2d (1989), 1218.

55. *City of New Orleans v. Scramuzza*, 507 So. 2d (1987), 215.

56. *Reed v. City of New Orleans*, 593, So. 2d (1992), 368.

57. *Circle Food Stores Inc. v. City of New Orleans*, 630 So. 2d (1993), 281.

58. *Radiofone Inc. v. City of New Orleans*, 630 So. 2d (1994), 694.

59. Hildreth, *State-Local Fiscal Relations in Louisiana*, 54–55.

60. City of Shreveport, "1995 Annual Operating Budget," 36.

61. Consolidated Government of Baton Rouge, "1997 Comprehensive Financial Report," xvii.

62. City of Lafayette, "Budget Document 1994–1995," 24.

63. Lafayette Consolidated Government, "Budget Document 1998–1999," 14.

64. Bureau of Governmental Research, "1994 Budget, Overview and Commentary" (New Orleans), table B.

65. Department of Finance for City of New Orleans, "Progress Through Perseverance" (1997), xvii.

66. Dan Garrett, attorney for Louisiana Municipal Association (telephone interview, 14 July 1999); Timothy E. Joder, director, Louisiana Urban Technical Assistance Center (LUTAC) (personal interview, 15 July 1999).

67. Louisiana House of Representatives, House Legislative Services, *State and Local Government in Louisiana: An Overview* (Baton Rouge, December 1995), 123–127.

68. W. Bartley Hildreth, "State and Local Fiscal Relations in Louisiana," in *Louisiana's Fiscal Alternatives: Finding Permanent Solutions to Recurring Budget Crises,* ed. James A. Richardson (Baton Rouge: Louisiana State University Press, 1988), 95.

69. Louisiana Municipal Association, "Progress Report" (Baton Rouge), 3–6.

70. Louisiana House of Representatives, *State and Local Government in Louisiana*, 243–247.

71. Richard L. Engstrom, et al., "Louisiana," in *The Quiet Revolution: Minority Voting Rights and Representation in the South*, ed. Chandler Davidson and Bernard Grofman (Princeton, N.J.: Princeton University Press, 1994), 112, 112–116, 125–135.

72. Louisiana Constitution (1974), Article VI, section 11.

73. Louisiana Constitution (1974), Article X, sections 24, 26; Louisiana Statutes Annotated, R.S. 42:1411, 1412.

74. Louisiana Statutes Annotated, R.S. 18:1299–1300 et seq.

75. Louisiana Statutes Annotated, R.S. 42:873.

MAINE

G. Thomas Taylor and Kenneth T. Palmer

The authors wish to acknowledge the assistance of William W. Livengood, director of legal services, Maine Municipal Association; Grant Pennoyer and Shirrin Blaisdell, Maine State Legislature, Office of Fiscal and Program Review; David Elliot, principal analyst, State of Maine, Office of Policy and Legal Analysis; Robert S. Howe, executive director, Maine County Commissioners Association; Robert E. Miller, Esq., former city solicitor, City of Bangor; and Mary Casciotti, assistant manager, Town of Orono.

Between 1820, when Maine joined the Union, and 1969, when voters approved a home rule amendment to the state constitution, Maine's nearly 500 towns and cities were closely regulated by the state legislature. Moreover, the state courts narrowly interpreted municipal powers according to Dillon's Rule, under which they denied a locality any power not explicitly provided in its charter. Maine courts did not significantly modify that stance until 1987, when the legislature revised the 1970 legislation enabling home rule to encourage greater latitude for local governments. In the past decade, Maine communities appear finally to be enjoying an increased level of home rule authority.

Governmental Setting

Although Maine's political life traditionally has centered in its small towns, the state has strictly regulated localities. Maine communities tend to be closely knit, a characteristic enhanced by the state's rugged terrain and harsh climate and the scattered, often isolated locations of the communities, some of which exist on islands off the state's coastline. The town meeting tradition inherited from Massachusetts (from which Maine separated in 1820) remains strong in parts of the state.[1] Many members of the state's large legislature (151 representatives, 35 senators) begin their careers in local politics, serving on town councils and boards of selectmen, and some maintain these ties while serving in the state capital. It is not uncommon for a legislator to serve also as a local official. The small size of most Maine communities (and their small professional staffs) has further inclined the legislature to act in proprietary fashion toward localities. Moreover, there is no large urban center that might provide a political base for demands for local autonomy. In 1997 the state's three largest communities (Portland, Lewiston, and Bangor) together accounted for about 10 percent of the state's 1.24 million people.

Maine's participatory political culture has helped shape its governmental structure: the prevailing view is that citizens should not only participate in the political process (the state has one of the highest rates of voter turnout in the country) but also hold governmental positions. The consequence has been a large number of elected and appointed offices and the wide use of boards and commissions. From 1820 to the 1970s, the legislature was almost entirely a citizen body, and state executive officers were mostly selected by the legislature or by citizen boards. More recently, the legislature has added staff, and most executive officers are appointed by and serve at the pleasure of the governor. At the local level, localities cling to the town meeting form, even as they elect boards of selectmen and appoint other officials. To provide some direction to localities, the Maine Municipal Association, an organization of municipal governments, provides key services (such as legal, insurance, and lobbying) that many communities and counties cannot afford on their own.

The property tax is a major impetus for rationalizing state-local relations in Maine. Towns and cites are heavily dependent on the tax, which dominates the state tax structure. Another concern is the functional weakness of county governments, whose tasks are mostly limited to law enforcement and road maintenance. County governments share the "middle place" in the state-local structure with regional planning commissions, councils of governments, and economic development districts. The abundance of organizations at this level has prompted a major gubernatorial task force to study the possibilities of restructuring and enhancing county government. Moreover, towns need to coordinate services. For the idea of home rule to expand operationally in Maine—a concept that is now legally endorsed by the courts—these issues must be addressed.

Home Rule in Maine

Historical Development

Until 1969, Maine communities had little authority not specifically granted by the state legislature. In interpreting municipal powers, state courts held closely to Dillon's Rule. As the Maine Supreme Judicial Court stated in an 1837 case, towns "have been denominated quasi-corporations, and their whole capacities, powers, and duties are derived from legislative enactments."[2]

Definition of Home Rule

In 1969 Maine voters amended the state constitution to provide for home rule. The amendment (section VII-A) states that "the inhabitants of any municipality shall have the power to alter and amend their charters on all matters not prohibited by Constitution or general law, which are local and municipal in character, [and] the legislature shall prescribe the procedure by which the municipality may so act." The first enabling act, passed in 1970, created an ambiguity that caused courts not to modify their earlier stance. The legislation provided that a municipality might exercise any power that the legislature had the power to confer upon it, "which is not denied either expressly or by clear implication." The language seemed to impel judges to deny a power to a community unless authority could be found under various state enabling acts.[3]

In 1987 the legislature made an explicit revision: the enabling law "should be liberally construed to effect its purposes." The most important change was the addition of a standard of preemption, under which the legislature would not implicitly deny a power claimed by a municipality unless the ordinance in question "would frustrate the purposes of any state law." The case of *School Committee v. Town of York* (1993) suggests a more generous regard for home rule by Maine's high court. The Supreme Judicial Court rejected a claim by the York School Committee that a provision in the new town charter which granted financial powers violated Maine school law. The court found that "municipal legislation will be voided only where the legislature has expressly prohibited local regulation, or where . . . legislation would frustrate the purpose of a state law."[4]

Structural Features

Maine has fairly elaborate procedures for preparing and adopting (or revising) a municipal charter. A number of voters equal to at least 20 percent of the votes cast in the municipality in the last gubernatorial election must, within 120 days, sign a written petition to that end. Within 30 days, a municipal election shall be scheduled (to take place within 90 days) to form a charter commission. The commission consists of six voter members (elected in the same manner as municipal officers) and three members who are appointed by the municipal officers. The commission submits its final report within twelve months, after

which an election takes place in which at least 30 percent of the electorate must participate.[5]

Maine law includes a brief section on consolidation, secession, and annexation, but rarely has it been invoked. These processes must be accomplished through a private or special act of the legislature.[6] For example, in 1922 the towns of Dover and Foxcroft merged through consolidation to become Dover–Foxcroft.

Municipalities own facilities beyond their boundaries (for example, airports, gravel pits, and dams). However, municipalities do not control or regulate activities beyond the city limits. Facilities and activities are subject to zoning and other ordinances of the community in which they are located.

Some seventy-five Maine towns and cities currently have charters. Another hundred or so communities operate under the Town Manager Enabling Act of 1939, which permits a community to transform its town meeting–selectmen form of government into a town meeting–selectmen–manager form. The state has been one of the strongest adherents of the town manager plan in the country. About forty communities currently use the "pure" council-manager plan (mostly those with 5,000–20,000 populations). Generally, a community that wants a specialized or hybrid type of local government structure will prepare a charter; other localities use the enabling statute.

Many small towns employ a manager. The most popular version is the town meeting–selectmen–manager form, which is used in about 130 communities with 500–3,000 people. The town meeting determines general policy and approves expenditures, and the board of selectmen enacts a limited number of ordinances, such as regulating traffic on public ways. The board hires the manager. In the town meeting–council–manager form, the council has more legislative power than a board of selectmen, but less authority than the council in the pure council-manager arrangement. A handful of communities (with populations of about 5,000) use this form. A fourth version is the town meeting–selectmen–administrative assistant form, found mainly in communities with fewer than 2,000 people, which resembles the town meeting–selectmen–manager structure. The main difference is that the administrative assistant has less authority than the manager, and the office is usually not in the charter. Finally, a few larger cities use the mayor–council–administrator form, under which an elected mayor is the chief executive officer, aided by a full-time administrator who reports to the mayor. These cities exhibit more traditional forms of urban politics because a substantial proportion of their population is of French Canadian ancestry.[7]

Town meeting municipalities write ordinances that designate the powers, duties, and procedures of town government, but many residents do not recognize the value of a formal charter. One study reported that only 75 Maine towns and cities have adopted a charter; 381 have not done so. Only 16 additional charters have been framed since the advent of home rule. However, more than half of all charter cities and towns have revised their documents significantly since the early 1990s.[8]

By 1970, one-quarter of town meeting municipalities had added town managers, although they still retained a "peoples' assembly." Most towns with over 2,000 population have adopted the town meeting–selectmen–manager form; towns with less than 1,000 population remain under a pure town meeting–selectmen form.

In practice, small-town managers undertake a number of different roles, which vary from one community to another. They may serve as clerk, purchasing agent, treasurer, tax collector, road commissioner, welfare director, and building inspector. In general, the manager is responsible for the administration of all of the municipality's operations except the schools. Managers are prohibited from assuming the office of tax assessor.

Since the passage of Maine's home rule statute in 1970, towns and cities have had the authority to adopt, under a local charter, nearly any form of government that employs a town or city manager. Thus, a town or city may select the statutory town manager plan or it may choose a governmental structure outlined within its own home rule charter and develop its own list of duties and responsibilities for the manager.[9]

Counties in Maine, as in other New England states, traditionally have been very "weak" compared with towns and cities. In 1988 counties received slightly under $30 million in property tax revenues, whereas municipalities collected over $700 million. Counties are primarily concerned with law enforcement; most operate a county jail; and all have a sheriff's department, which provides police services for communities that are too small to have their own department. Counties obtain about 30 percent of their funds from fees and charges. In Maine, all persons convicted of class D and E crimes (mostly misdemeanors) and all persons sentenced to prison for nine months or less must be housed in county jails. The state reimburses the counties for these costs. Counties also share in the state tax on the transfer of real estate; these funds support the office of recorder of deeds.

The legislature occasionally has considered abolishing county governments. However, county officials such as sheriffs, deputy sheriffs, and judges of probates (probate judges are the only judges elected in Maine) have always managed to ward off these moves. In 1985 the legislature began to give the counties a more autonomous budget process. After the 1996 legislative session, all but two counties were empowered to enact their own budgets. In some cases, the commissioners enact a budget; in others, the task is assigned to a special budget committee, which usually includes municipal officials. Only one county (Aroostook) has a county charter. Four counties have county managers or administrators, who operate with limited executive authority, primarily with regard to budgetary matters. The new managers have not replaced existing elected county officials. An exception

is in Cumberland County (Portland area), where the county manager has replaced the county clerk and has also become the state's "strongest" county manager.

Functions of Local Government

Functional Responsibilities

Maine has been described as a union of towns. Its 434 towns and 22 cities are the major service providers at the local level. Cities and towns have broad authority to develop and implement ordinances and to undertake economic and community development activities. However, municipal revenue sources are tightly controlled by the state. Under Maine's home rule–enabling act of 1970, municipalities may exercise any power or function that the legislature has authority to confer on them. Municipalities provide most basic services such as public works, police and fire, planning and community development, code enforcement, and recreation. Variation in both the quality and quantity of services is related to population size, among other variables. Municipalities with over 5,000 population provide a wider array of services, whereas the smallest towns offer few services and rely more on volunteerism.

Counties' authority to issue ordinances is very restricted, as is their role in economic and community development. Indeed, a parallel substate regional system comprising economic development districts, regional planning commissions, and councils of government was established in the 1970s and effectively foreclosed most county initiatives. Administrative operations of Maine county government are closely delimited by statute.

There is little duplication in service delivery between municipalities and counties. Municipalities are Maine's general-purpose governments. In contrast, counties are restricted by law and tradition to a narrow range of functions (for example, roads, courts, and corrections).

Although duplication of efforts is rare, it can occur in the area of public safety. Counties may offer some municipalities (especially the smaller towns) the option of contracting out for patrol coverage from the sheriff's department when there is no local police department. The state police and the sixteen county sheriffs' offices collectively provide coverage to all geographic areas within the state. In the smallest towns, the problem is a lack of police service, not duplication. The larger towns and cities generally have professional police departments and have little need for the sheriff's office.

Maine has relatively few special districts or single-purpose governments when compared with the large number (456) of municipalities. In 1987 a total of 198 special-purpose governments existed in Maine, including 73 water districts, 43 sewer districts, and 25 housing and community development districts. During the past ten years, a number of new solid waste–disposal districts have been created.

In addition, Maine has 159 school districts comprising 73 school administrative districts (SADs), 13 community school districts, 34 unions, and 39 cities or towns with their own individual systems. SADs began under the leadership of Gov. Edmund S. Muskie during the 1950s and involve numerous cooperating communities. Unions involve two communities. School districts represent one of Maine's few substate regional experiments.

Local government contracting with other towns, counties, or the private sector is a voluntary, cooperative option that may increase in the future. Under Maine's Intergovernmental Cooperation Act of 1963, municipalities were allowed to contract for the joint provision of services, but little activity occurred until the mid-1980s.[10] In some instances these arrangements had evolved from an informal mutual-aid pact (especially for police and fire) to a formal contract between two or more local governments. To gain economies of scale, small towns may elect to cooperate with larger units (such as cities, councils of government, and county governments) for certain services. Surveys of local officials reveal that one-third of the approximately 200 manager communities use joint service or purchasing agreements as a major strategy.[11]

Administrative Discretion

Charters usually designate, respectively, the municipal offices that will be filled by council appointment and the chief executive. The council (or board of selectmen) appoints the manager. When a mayor is elected, the council's role is to confirm the nomination of the mayor. Councils usually appoint the city attorney, treasurer, clerk, and assessor. In addition, councils appoint members (or confirm the mayor's nominations) to all municipal boards, with the exception of the elected school board.[12]

Managers are usually granted the authority to appoint the tax collector and the heads of departments of police, fire, public works, parks and recreation, and welfare. Under some charters, managers appoint nearly all offices, except the members of the municipal board and the municipal attorney, who are named by the council. In other communities, the manager's appointment powers are quite limited. Within Maine, managers span a continuum between "weak" and "strong."

Except in a few large communities, cities and towns did not begin to draft personnel procedures until the 1970s. Encouraged by the rapid spread of organized labor in Maine's municipalities and school districts, communities enacted various personnel and administrative ordinances (especially those with an appointed professional administrator). There was much less change in localities with part-time selectmen and the town meeting form.

Personnel management regulations provide the manager with the right to one public hearing during any removal proceeding, before the council or board of selectmen takes action.[13] Under Maine's Freedom of Information Act, the board has a right to deliberate in executive session on employee performance evaluations.

Until recently, many small communities did not have written policies for purchasing, contracting, hiring consultants, and bidding. Instead, these issues were handled on an ad hoc basis by the elected officials, sometimes resulting in charges of favoritism. By contrast, larger cities such as Bangor and Portland adopted detailed policies that supplemented various sections of their city charters. Many smaller and medium-sized communities have followed suit since the early 1990s. The Maine Municipal Association publishes widely used handbooks for moderators of town meetings, municipal officials, and tax collectors and treasurers.

Until growth management legislation was passed in 1988, local planning throughout the state was uneven. Larger towns and cities usually hired professional planners who drafted comprehensive plans and zoning ordinances, subject to approval by their respective legislative bodies. Some smaller communities hired planners from regional planning commissions. Only about 20 percent of Maine's municipalities engaged in planning-implementation activities such as zoning.

Under the growth management law, municipalities had to conduct a structured, professionally designed planning process that included deadlines, guidelines for the comprehensive plan, land-use ordinances, and capital improvement plans. The initial phase targeted "top tier" communities, defined as the fastest growing municipalities from 1980 to 1987. By law, a community's land-use plan and zoning ordinance had to conform to its adopted comprehensive plan. A key state requirement forced localities to designate both areas of growth and rural areas of lower density as part of land-use plans. The legislation set forth broad goals in areas such as job development, protection of natural and historic resources, preservation of marine-related activities along coastal areas, and access to recreation lands.

Because of major budgetary problems, the legislature in 1992 made the planning process less mandatory. Some communities that had initiated a citizen-oriented, bottom-up participation process continued their work, producing impressive results that blended professional planning with citizen involvement. Many communities, however, slowed down or simply returned to their earlier habits of no planning.

Economic Development

Municipalities may engage in economic and community development activities and use own-source revenues for projects that benefit private entities, as long as a public purpose is served. Although cities and towns cannot use such funds to grant tax credits, they may use them for developing industrial parks, establishing and maintaining enterprise zones, renewing or revitalizing blighted areas, creating revolving loan banks or funds, and improving infrastructure related to specific economic or community development projects. Funds can also be used to develop municipal districts.[14] Counties, however, may not use own-source funds for any of these projects.

Cities and towns are permitted to use own-source revenue for development projects subject to voter approval (by a simple majority). Such decisions are made mainly in town meetings, which still play a prominent role in setting financial policy in most of Maine's small towns. For municipalities without the town meeting, the charter specifies the voting procedure. Counties have no provision for a vote of their citizens and, in general, have very restricted authority on matters of community and economic development.

Fiscal Autonomy of Local Governments

Local Revenues

Other than the property tax, municipalities lack the option of creating sources of revenue such as a local sales tax or local income tax. Real and personal property taxes, motor vehicle (excise) taxes, and sewer-use fees may be levied by towns and cities. Municipalities may raise taxes, but they cannot alter the tax base without a change in the state statutes. Taxable property is set by state law. Cities and towns do not have the authority to exempt property or assess at less than fair market value. Over time, the state has expanded its list of exemptions, especially in the non-profit area (that is, houses of worship, institutions of higher education, and health facilities). These exemptions translate into billions of dollars of uncollected revenue that potentially could benefit certain municipalities (especially large communities) and those with major educational and health facilities.

Moreover, although full value assessment is the state law, enforcement is uneven because state agencies (such as the Bureau of Taxation, Property Tax Division) are underfunded. Only a small number of Maine's 1,500 assessors are professionally trained and certified. The larger cities (Portland, Lewiston, Auburn, and Bangor) have joined with the Maine Municipal Association in proposing alternative local tax options such as local sales taxes, accommodations (entertainment and tourism) taxes, and mandatory fees in lieu of taxing hospitals and other exempt institutions. However, interest groups and small towns have resisted these initiatives.

The property tax has been criticized since the 1970s because of municipalities' heavy reliance on it. (In fiscal 1995 the property tax constituted about 86 percent of municipal revenue; the remainder comprised excise taxes, licenses, fines, and invested income.) A modest circuit-breaker provision eases the tax burden on households with the lowest incomes. Municipalities can utilize user fees, including cable television franchises, garbage collection fees, park fees, and numerous others, but relatively few do so. Through citizen initiatives and referendums, a few towns and cities have started tax caps.

The revenue-raising capacity of counties is restricted; exact authority depends on the specific county. Maine counties can

Fig. 1 County Revenues in Maine, 1992

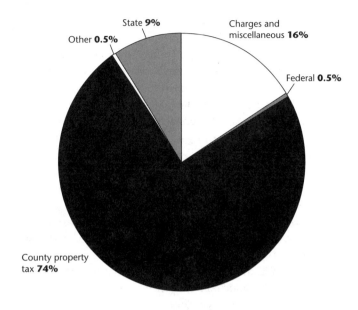

Source: 1992 Census of Governments, vol. 4, Government Finances, no. 3, Finances of County Governments (January 1997), 62–63.

Fig. 2 Municipal General Fund Revenues in Maine, 1995

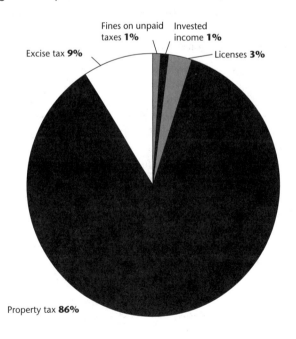

Source: Maine Municipal Association (MMA), *Local Government Fiscal Survey 1995* (Augusta: Local Government Resource Center, MMA, March 1996).

levy property taxes (collected as part of municipal taxes) and have limited powers to levy miscellaneous fees (for example, for registry of deeds and mapping services). As general-purpose governments, counties have few revenue sources. However, they can sell some county services (such as expanded law enforcement coverage) to municipalities, particularly smaller towns. Counties cannot alter the tax base without first obtaining a change in state law. Thus, the budget process determines the county tax, which is collected by the municipalities. Town officials often decry having to pay county taxes that produce few services for their communities. Counties have no caps on the amount of money they can raise. See Figures 1 and 2 for percentage breakdowns of revenues for counties and municipalities, respectively.

Cities have some authority to incur debt. The maximum allowed is 7.5 percent of state evaluation for general purposes, and the total must never exceed 15 percent when schools and sewers are included. Cities can use revenue bonds for specific reasons and general-obligation bonds, which guarantee the full faith and credit of the municipality.[15] Counties may not incur debt except by legislative approval.

The principal state restriction on municipal and county spending is a debt limitation. The state requires cities, towns, and counties to audit their financial activities, either by a chartered public accountant or the state auditor. Copies of town and city audits must be filed with the state auditor (counties are not required to file). Both municipalities and counties are required by law to maintain a balanced budget. Both may invest their funds and have a choice of investments specified under state laws.

Local Expenditures

Because of the diversity of budget formats and accounting categories (especially in smaller towns of fewer than 2,000 people), expenditure data reports are uneven and comparisons are problematic. Manager communities have experimented with performance, program, and zero-based budgeting. However, the line-item format remains popular with most town meetings and councils and is practiced by most communities. It is easily made operational through the warrant document, whereby citizens vote on each expenditure item on town meeting day. Elected members of councils also seem to relish the tight control afforded by the line-item format. Balanced budgets are required by local charters and the state constitution. See Figures 3 and 4 for percentage breakdowns of expenditures for counties and municipalities, respectively.

Bankruptcy of Maine municipalities is very rare. In 1939 the state used a special procedure (Title 30-A 61-01X) for the municipal insolvency of Eastport, which established a board to take over the local government. Through state intervention, an insolvent municipality may return to better financial health.

Fig. 3 County Expenditures in Maine, 1992

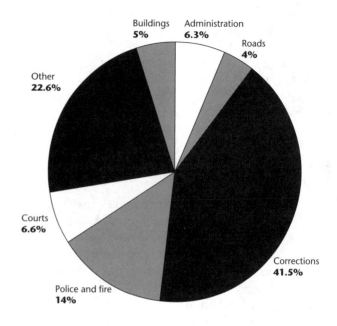

Source: 1992 Census of Governments, vol. 4, Government Finances, no. 3, Finances of County Governments (January 1997), 62–63.

Fig. 4 Municipal Expenditures in Maine, 1995

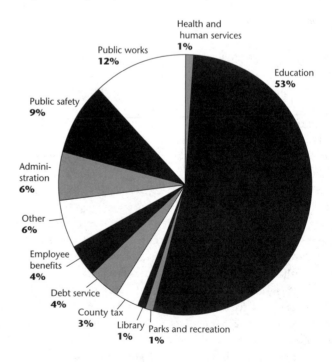

Source: Maine Municipal Association (MMA), Local Government Fiscal Survey 1995 (Augusta: Local Government Resource Center, MMA, March 1996).

State Government Grants-in-Aid to Localities

In fiscal 1996–1997 Maine state government gave 38 percent of its general-fund budget ($824 million) to localities; municipalities received more than 95 percent of that amount. If the state municipal revenue-sharing program is included, the state figure rises to 40 percent. The revenue-sharing program commits slightly more than 5 percent of revenues from state sales and income taxes to general-purpose assistance for communities (counties are not included), which amounted to $77.7 million in fiscal 1996–1997.[16]

The largest state-aided programs are in education. In 1996–1997 the state devoted $688 million to K–12 education; about five-sixths of that amount was committed to the operation of Maine's 160 school districts and one-sixth to the state's teacher retirement fund. The education subsidy is, by statute, intended to meet about 55 percent of local school costs. Generally, as Maine's state share has increased in recent decades, so too have state mandates.[17] For example, in 1957 the state contribution was only 22 percent, but this virtually amounted to a "blank check" for local schools.

Other programs include support for highways and roads ($23 million, through the Department of Transportation) and clean-up of solid waste and other natural resource projects ($20 million, through the Department of Environmental Protection). Reimbursement for municipal general assistance ($6 million) is administered by the Department of Human Services. Together with education and revenue sharing, these programs made up nearly 99 percent of state financial assistance to localities in 1997. Municipalities also enjoy exemptions from state sales and gas taxes (valued in 1997 at $43 million).

Since 1983, funds for road improvement have been disbursed to communities as block grants. About 95 percent of all Department of Transportation municipal assistance is administered as block grants (town way bridges are the only major program not included in the block grant). Towns and cities also have limited discretion over how to spend their natural resource and general assistance funds. General assistance housing subsidies vary according to local economic conditions.

Unfunded Mandates

Mandates are not unusual. Maine has, for decades, assigned new responsibilities to communities without compensatory funding. For example, the Municipal Collective Bargaining Law of 1969 significantly increased costs for localities. However, unfunded mandates became an important issue in Maine in the late 1980s, at a time when the state undertook several new policy initiatives. The most troublesome mandates dealt with solid waste disposal, economic development, and the expansion of state standards regarding the recruitment and employment of municipal personnel in areas such as fire protection, code en-

forcement, and animal control. In the late 1980s the state's economy turned sharply downward, and communities pressed for relief. Voters approved by referendum a constitutional amendment in 1991 (Article 9, section 21) stipulating that the state may not require a local unit of government to expand or modify its activities that would in turn require additional spending of local funds, unless the state provides 90 percent of the funding. The legislature may by a two-thirds vote create an exemption to the requirement.

Although the costs of mandates have decelerated, their number has not waned. In the 116th session (1992–1994), the legislature utilized the exemption provision to enact twenty-one new mandates without the required funding. However, these involved very small sums of money and were mostly local and special bills (for example, "an act to increase the debt limit for the Richmond Utilities District").

In other cases, the impact of mandates has been buffered. Some token funds have been appropriated to accompany mandates. In one instance, the state moved quickly to reduce a town's property tax valuation after the sudden departure of a large business; as a result, the community gained additional state school funding. Moreover, the attorney general has determined that the mandate provision does not apply to the state's municipal revenue-sharing program. The provision has not yet been tested in the state courts.

Access to Local Government

Local Elections

Few municipalities include nomination and election procedures in their charters, although they are permitted to so formalize them. Instead, most charters reference the statutory election procedures in Title 30-A (for municipal elections) and Title 21-A (for state elections).[18] Only three municipal charters establish a partisan contest for elected officials. Maine's sixteen counties, however, maintain on the ballot each elected official's respective party label.

Citizen Controls over Actions of Local Officials

Perhaps because of Maine's "direct democracy" tradition of the town meeting, home rule and the initiative, referendum, and recall provisions to protect citizens from their elected representatives did not become issues until the 1970s, paralleling increased use of the initiative and referendum at the state level.[19] Unless a charter provision states otherwise, citizens may, by state statute, either petition to have the legislative body of a municipality consider a proposed action (initiative) or review an action of the legislative body by direct vote of the electorate (referendum).[20] A provision for recall is permitted if a charter so specifies; such a provision appears in the charters of thirty-five towns and cities in Maine. Because most town meetings elect town officials for only one year, recall is often redundant. Nevertheless, some larger towns and cities have added recall provisions since the 1980s. Counties have no recall arrangements.

Right-to-know legislation, enacted in 1988, covers all state and local governments and public educational institutions. All meetings must be open to the public, and adequate provisions must be made for posting the time, agenda, and place of the meetings. Nearly all charters clearly establish open meeting, notice of meeting, and executive session arrangements either by referencing Maine's freedom of information law or by including in the charter similar "right to know" requirements.[21]

State-Local Relations

State government in Maine has recently recognized the growing responsibilities of local governments. The legislature has altered its home rule legislation to encourage the courts to provide more flexibility to municipalities, and the Maine Supreme Judicial Court appears to be supportive.

The legislature has also broadened certain financial grants to localities, especially for road maintenance, to permit them more discretion. Significantly, counties for the first time can enact their own budgets. Additionally, four counties employ newly created administrators. Further, the state has limited unfunded mandates. By the mid-1990s, communities were less beholden to the financial obligations that the state had imposed on them in the 1980s, especially in the area of solid waste management.

The background for these home rule tendencies is the financial tension between state and local governments. The expenditures of localities nearly doubled in 1982–1988, setting the sixth-fastest growth rate in the country. However, because the state government experienced financial distress in the 1990s, state contributions to municipalities and counties grew by only 2 percent per year between fiscal 1989–1990 and fiscal 1998–1999, slightly below the rate of inflation. The reduction has burdened communities. Additionally, the state continues to regulate tightly some local government processes, especially charter creation and the appointment of municipal personnel.

Angus King, the state's popular Independent governor, has raised public awareness of local management inefficiencies, such as too many school superintendents and not enough intergovernmental cooperation. He has established a task force to make recommendations on expanding the role of county government. Maine's need to reconfigure its local government revenue stream—which is dominated by the property tax—and to develop a consensus on state funding for education are the current "hot button" issues.

Notes

1. For more on the history of Maine, see Richard W. Judd, Edwin A. Churchill, and Joel W. Eastman, eds., *Maine: The Pine Tree State from Prehistory to Present* (Orono: University of Maine Press, 1995).

2. See John Dillon, *A Treatise on the Law of Municipal Corporations*, 5th ed. (Boston: J. Cockroft, 1911); Anwar Syed, *The Political Theory of American Local Government* (New York: Random House, 1966); Michael L. Starn, "Municipal Home Rule: Grassroots Democracy or a Symbolic Gesture," *Maine Townsman* 45 (January 1983): 5–11.

3. Robert W. Bower Jr., "Home Rule and the Pre-emption Doctrine: The Relationship Between State and Local Government in Maine," *Maine Law Review* 37 (1985): 335.

4. See *School Committee v. Town of York*, 626 A. 2d 935 (ME 1993), 239.

5. See Orren C. Hormell, *Maine Towns* (Brunswick, Maine: Bowdoin College, 1932); James J. Haag, *Introduction to the Charter Drafting Process* (Orono: Bureau of Public Administration, University of Maine, 1970).

6. See Maine Revised Statutes Annotated, Title 30-A, section 215, on consolidation; section 2171, on secession and annexation.

7. James J. Hagg, Charles Morris, Richard Michaud, and G. Thomas Taylor, *The Manager Plan in Maine*, 2d ed. (Orono, Maine: Margaret Chase Smith Center for Public Policy, 1993).

8. Geoffrey Herman, "Municipal Charters: A Comparative Analysis of 75 Maine Charters," *Maine Townsman* 54 (August 1992): 8–9.

9. Kenneth T. Palmer, G. Thomas Taylor, and Marcus A. LiBrizzi, *Maine Politics and Government* (Lincoln: University of Nebraska Press, 1992), 161–166.

10. See Maine Revised Statutes Annotated, Title 30-A, section 2201, chapter 115, on interlocal cooperation.

11. Palmer, Taylor, and LiBrizzi, *Maine Politics and Government*, 187. See also "1996 Summer of Intergovernmental Agreements. Report of Findings" (Maine Development Foundation, Augusta, May 1997). Among fifty-eight respondents, 349 agreements were found (only three respondents reported having no agreements).

12. In a few cases, a council member sits on an otherwise elected school board. Under Biddeford's unusual city charter, the mayor serves as ex officio chair of the school board.

13. See Maine Revised Statutes Annotated, Title 30-A, section 2633.

14. For economic development regulations, see Maine Revised Statutes Annotated, Title 30-A, sections 5251 and 701-900. See Title 30-A, section 5251, on the tax incremental finance district.

15. Maine Revised Statutes Annotated, Title 30-A, section 5401, on the Revenue Producing Facilities Act.

16. Maine State Legislature, Office of Fiscal and Program Review, *Summary of Major State Funding Disbursed to Municipalities and Counties, January 1998* (Augusta, 1998).

17. State regulations have greatly increased and intensified. For example, the Education Reform Act of 1984 requires statewide assessments of pupil achievement in the fourth, eighth, and eleventh grades and sets elaborate high school graduation requirements, among other provisions. The intrusiveness of these requirements was eased in the 1990s because of funding issues and because of the extensive use of waivers by the state Department of Education, especially for schools in smaller communities.

18. See Maine Revised Statutes Annotated, Title 30-A, for municipal elections; Title 21-A, for state elections.

19. Palmer, Taylor, and LiBrizzi, *Maine Politics and Government*, 49–50.

20. Maine Revised Statutes Annotated, Title 30-1A; Herman, "Municipal Charters," 11–13.

21. Maine's Freedom of Information Law, Maine Revised Statutes Annotated, subsection 401 et seq.

MARYLAND

Andrée Reeves and Patricia S. Florestano

Since local governments were first created in Maryland more than 350 years ago, the state has developed one of the least complex local government structures in the nation. Its most prominent governmental features are the relatively small number of governmental units, the emphasis on counties instead of municipalities as the primary service providers, and the unique status of the City of Baltimore. Maryland's counties and municipalities enjoy major elements of home rule, but their discretion is limited. The General Assembly still maintains important controls. The constitution extends home rule to counties and cities through several processes, although it does not convey complete authority over local affairs to either. Charter home rule grants the greatest local autonomy; it is reserved for counties, which, along with Baltimore city, are the primary service providers in the state. Counties also may adopt code home rule, which is easier to achieve than charter home rule but conveys fewer powers. Municipalities may elect to draft and enact their own charters, and the legislature is prohibited from passing special legislation relating to them. The City of Baltimore generally is treated as a charter county, and the provisions governing it are set out in the state constitution.

Governmental Setting

From the Atlantic Ocean to the Appalachian Mountains, Maryland encompasses varied topographical, economic, and political characteristics. Small geographically (9,838 square miles), its population of slightly more than 5 million places it nineteenth among states but fifth in terms of population density. Largely suburban dwellers, Marylanders seem drawn to the metropolitan area west of the Chesapeake Bay. Two-thirds of all the state's residents live in the Baltimore city and in the counties of Anne Arundel, Montgomery, Prince George's, and Baltimore.

Maryland's first European settlers, under William Claiborne, arrived from Virginia and settled on Kent Island in 1631. The king of England chartered Maryland to Cecil Calvert, second baron of Baltimore, in 1632, and colonists from England arrived in 1634. Settled by the Roman Catholic Calvert family, Maryland was known for its religious tolerance, which attracted Quakers, Anabaptists, Presbyterians, and others so that Catholic dominance eventually dissipated.[1] Trade in tobacco, the primary crop, impelled the state's slave-based economy.

The uniformity and simplicity of Maryland's local government structure are apparent in the small number and limited variety of local governments in the state. Maryland ranks forty-fourth among states in the number of local governmental units (401).[2] It has no townships or independent school districts. The counties and Baltimore city serve as school districts. The state

has created only 223 special districts. The 23 counties and 155 incorporated municipalities are its primary units of local government. The paucity of municipalities results from the authority bestowed on counties to approve municipal incorporation within their boundaries.[3]

From the start, Maryland seemed to be torn between conflicting viewpoints. The Calvert and Claiborne forces fought for control of the initial colonial settlements.[4] As a state, Maryland remained loyal to the Union during the Civil War, but its citizens were far from unified. Racial desegregation, gambling, and sales of alcohol have been divisive issues over the years.

Because of the state's topographical diversity, watermen on the Eastern Shore have little in common with western Maryland's mountain people or with Baltimore's suburbanites. Although the census bureau considered Washington, D.C., and Baltimore to be one metropolitan area in 1992, the economy of the former rests heavily on governmental activities, whereas the latter is an industrial port city. Occasionally, one hears Washington, D.C., referred to as "white collar" and Baltimore as "blue collar."

Maryland's economy is diversified. The Chesapeake Bay's fishing industry and the Port of Baltimore provide employment and revenues for the state. Fishing rights and pollution in the bay and the lower Potomac River are sources of contention with other states. Baltimore's spice industry, machine tool operations, banks, and location as headquarters of the Social Security Ad-

Table 1. Maryland Counties

County	Population	Per capita income	Taxable base (in $1,000s)	Budget (in $1,000s)
Allegany	74,100	$12,980	$1,167,759	$85,709
Anne Arundel	460,480	18,695	11,346,254	662,812
Baltimore City	736,014	11,994	8,309,372	1,589,956
Baltimore County	713,600	20,405	15,206,711	1,196,032
Calvert	63,920	17,032	1,882,308	84,138
Caroline	28,900	11,812	382,340	19,696
Carroll	139,300	17,421	2,607,446	130,246
Cecil	78,010	14,471	1403,477	60,459
Charles	111,050	16,690	2,309,786	101,000
Dorchester	30,000	13,500	563,486	21,888
Frederick	175,350	16,905	3,394,437	160,404
Garrett	29,450	11,329	614,938	24,264
Hartford	209,100	15,972	3,479,290	188,592
Howard	281,030	22,439	5,907,383	289,115
Kent	18,770	16,108	434,206	17,784
Montgomery	805,930	27,471	28,433,423	1,692,675
Prince George's	769,000	17,392	15,079,660	1,081,334
Queen Anne's	37,450	17,100	883,179	34,380
St. Mary's	112,400	14,270	1,390,998	70,341
Somerset	24,280	11,120	257,623	12,743
Talbot	32,330	22,163	1,137,465	28,595
Washington	126,950	13,520	1,915,956	80,021
Wicomico	78,950	14,618	1,328,895	62,195
Worcester	39,830	16,681	2,111,090	55,592

Sources: Populations and per capita income for 1995 are from *Maryland Statistical Abstract* (Annapolis: Maryland Office of Planning, Planning Data Services). Local government taxable base and local government budget are from *Maryland Manual, 1994–1995* (Annapolis: State Archives of the State of Maryland).

ministration and the nearby National Security Agency are a few of the state's economic assets. The Inner Harbor development and aquarium, plus the U.S.S. *Constellation,* Fort McHenry, Pimlico Racetrack, and Camden Yards, bolster Baltimore's tourist appeal. Johns Hopkins University, the University of Maryland's professional schools, the Baltimore Museum of Art, and the Walters Art Gallery are important both economically and culturally.

Although Maryland's economy is diversified, its economic resources are unevenly distributed. Baltimore city and the Appalachian areas in the west are economically distressed, whereas suburban areas of Baltimore and Washington, D.C. (such as Montgomery County, which is among the highest-income counties in the country, and Prince George's County) prosper (see Table 1).

The most important characteristic of Maryland's local government is the critical role played by counties as the major service providers. As such, counties often have what usually are considered municipal powers. They run (and partially finance) the state's public school systems, including its community colleges.

Except for Baltimore city and its population of 736,014, municipalities range in size from Port Tobacco's 36 to Rockville's approximately 45,000.[5] Baltimore has unique status as an independent city exercising both municipal and county powers; Baltimore County nearly surrounds it but has no jurisdiction within the city limits. The city is treated by the state as the equivalent of a county, thus enhancing its authority.

Home Rule in Maryland

Historical Development

Counties were established long before municipalities in Maryland. The original counties performed few governmental functions, usually those pertaining to the judiciary and record keeping. St. Mary's County was the first in 1637. As the population grew and gradually moved inland, additional counties were created. By 1776, eighteen counties had been established. Twenty-three counties had been formed by 1872 and exist today much as they did then.

Almost fifty years after the establishment of the first county, the formal process of creating municipal governments began. The 1683 "town act" systematized the organization of cities and towns in Maryland, authorizing the colonial government to select land sites and establish communities and to provide for their governance. The now defunct St. Mary's was the first incorporated city in Maryland. Annapolis, the oldest existing municipality, was incorporated in 1708. Town government in the early Maryland colony was simple; five to seven commissioners held office during good behavior.[6]

Baltimore city has been a legal governmental entity since the General Assembly created it through Chapter 12 of the Acts of 1789. The Maryland Constitution of 1851 permitted the community to separate from Baltimore County and incorporate as a municipality. The General Assembly granted the city broad powers of self-government as early as 1898, and Article XI-A of the constitution gave it home rule authority in 1915.

The same 1915 home rule amendment, supplemented by statutes, enabled counties to adopt home rule.[7] A 1966 constitutional amendment allowed a simpler county home rule procedure.[8]

Years after Baltimore city and the counties first received home rule authority, the electorate ratified a 1954 constitutional amendment providing basic municipal home rule.[9] Under it, cities and towns may enact, revise, and amend their own charters. The legislature is prohibited from incorporating municipalities and from adopting special legislation relating to them.

Definition of Home Rule

Maryland constitutional provisions grant home rule but do not define it. Although it enumerates areas in which local governments may operate, Maryland law nevertheless allows the legislature substantial power to intervene when two or more local jurisdictions are involved. Local government organization and authority are detailed in the state constitution. A separate article (XI) for Baltimore city establishes and provides for the election of a mayor and city council.

Home rule ordinarily is associated with local governmental authority to draft and adopt charters, and charter counties follow this procedure. Code home rule, which requires no charter drafting, accomplishes a similar result for some counties and spells out lawmaking procedures that normally would be included in a charter. A code county is defined in the constitution and in statutes as "a county which is not a charter county under Article 11A of this Constitution and has adopted the optional powers of home rule provided."[10] In the governing statutes, code home rule status refers to counties "under and having the authority of Article XI-F of the Constitution and this article."[11] Any county that has not adopted a charter may opt to become a code county by satisfying the requirements set out in Article XI-F of the constitution.

In Maryland, most counties (and sometimes, special districts) operate as municipal corporations with ordinance-making authority rather than as quasi-municipal corporations serving simply as agents of the state.[12] Maryland counties exercise governmental powers (for example, police and fire protection) and proprietary functions (for example, maintaining markets). These dual roles are especially evident in the large, urban counties. These and other counties not only enact local ordinances but provide services such as garbage collection, planning and zoning, street and sidewalk maintenance, and operation of recreational facilities (for example, golf courses), for which they charge fees.

Structural Features

Home rule is available to counties and municipalities, although municipalities have less extensive home rule authority than do counties. Baltimore city enjoys privileged status and is addressed in legal provisions much like the state's counties are in terms of home rule and functions.[13] Maryland counties subscribe to one of three basic forms of local autonomy: charter, code, or commissioner. These classifications range from substantial authority to no home rule authority. Powers bestowed on charter counties and Baltimore city are substantial, and their ordinance-making authority covers most local matters. Code counties have less authority, but they also may opt for charter status. Commissioner counties enjoy no home rule, but they can elect to upgrade their status.

A county becomes a charter county and acquires home rule when a charter board drafts a charter and voters approve it in a referendum.[14] The constitution provides that the General Assembly shall, by public general law, grant express powers to charter counties. The Assembly has granted thirty-two such powers through the Express Powers Act.[15] Under the constitution, charter counties must create elected legislative bodies (county councils) in which lawmaking powers are vested,[16] and they have clear authority to enact, amend, or repeal all local laws relating to matters listed in the Express Powers Act, including local laws passed by the General Assembly.

The General Assembly is restricted from enacting public local laws that apply only to one charter county, while denying coverage to others, on any subject contained in the express powers. It retains full authority to enact both general legislation and general local bills (that is, bills applying to two or more local governments) and to prescribe areas of local activity. In effect, the efficacy of home rule depends on the legislature's willingness to abstain from interfering in local affairs.

Since 1948, eight counties have adopted charter forms of government.[17] (See Box 1.) Voters in three counties (Cecil, Dorchester, and St. Mary's) rejected charter home rule. Six of the charter counties have forms of government similar to the municipal mayor-council type, dividing executive and legislative powers between an elected executive and an elected council. The other two charter counties (Talbot and Wicomico) chose council-manager plans, with the council retaining both executive and legislative powers. The council elects a chairperson and appoints an administrator or manager.

A 1966 constitutional amendment enabled counties to adopt home rule more easily.[18] This mechanism, code home rule, is an inferior form of home rule authority, allowing fewer local powers than charter home rule. A county becomes a code county when two-thirds of its commissioners vote to put on the ballot a resolution to make the county a code county, and the county voters approve that resolution. Five counties have elected the code form of home rule.

As with charter counties, the legislature extends powers granted under the Express Powers Act to code counties, but with important exceptions. The procedure for enacting local laws differs, as does that for incurring debt, for example.[19] Code home rule counties still exercise greater authority than do the non–home rule commission counties.

Not only do constitutional and statutory provisions allow local citizens to determine their local government structures and policies, but the legislature rarely interferes with local actions. Thus, charter and code counties are subject to far less legislative control over their internal activities than are non–home rule counties. Once a county has adopted a charter, the legislature may not enact a law on any subject affecting only that jurisdiction if the subject is covered by any power granted by the Express Powers Act. Legislation must apply to two or more counties to avoid being designated local law and thereby prohibited.

Nonetheless, because the General Assembly can legislate for two or more units selectively, it has a pronounced effect on local affairs. In some instances, it has adopted essentially local legisla-

BOX 1. MARYLAND LOCAL GOVERNANCE

Charter counties	Code counties	Commissioner counties
Anne Arundel	Allegany	Calvert
Baltimore[a]	Caroline	Carroll
Hartford	Kent	Cecil
Howard	Queen Anne's	Charles
Montgomery	Worcester	Dorchester
Prince George's		Frederick
Talbot		Garrett
Wicomico		Somerset
		St. Mary's
		Washington

a. The City of Baltimore functions as both a municipality and a charter home rule county.

tion. Local governments must rely on their legislative delegations to restrain or motivate legislative action. When the delegation disagrees with local officials over a local proposal, little is likely to change; thus, the delegation becomes more important than the local officials in determining local policy. Legislation directed toward code counties must be general and applicable to all.

Ten counties have no home rule.[20] They operate under a constitutional provision for county commissioners, which all counties had before 1948.[21] Commissioners are elected countywide, by district, or through a combination of both; their number, pay, powers, and duties are prescribed by the legislature. A considerable body of law has developed pertaining to this form of government.[22] Commissioners may not legislate on local matters without the prior consent of the legislature. Although in a strict sense these counties are merely administrative subunits of the state, they do exercise a significant number of governmental powers. The state reserves the right to rescind those powers at any time. The General Assembly may enact public general laws applying to all the commissioner counties equally, or it may adopt public local laws pertaining to a specific subject in a particular commissioner county.

The current constitution also allows the General Assembly to create additional counties.[23] To qualify, an area must have at least 400 square miles, a population of more than 10,000, and approval of the affected voters. State law also permits the consolidation of cities but does not permit cities and counties to be consolidated. It does, however, authorize interlocal service agreements.

The 1954 constitutional amendment that granted home rule

to cities and towns requires the General Assembly to classify municipalities into not more than four classes based on population. So far, only one class has been established, and it includes all municipalities, regardless of size.[24] Article XI-E of the constitution also preserved existing charters and revenue sources available to municipalities at the same time that it permitted them to adopt new charters or amend old ones. Article 23A of the Annotated Code is the basic general law now pertaining to municipalities that provides for their creation, annexation, and express (and other) powers. No municipality exercises all the powers granted under this article.

Most municipalities have mayor-council forms of government. The mayor usually is popularly elected independent of the council and has executive responsibilities. About one-third of Maryland municipalities (51 of 157) employ the commission form, characterized by a unity of executive and legislative functions. Because of initial charter differences and subsequent amendments, however, some of these governments more nearly resemble council-manager forms. In municipalities with the commission form, commissioners (who are elected either at large or by district) serve as both the executive and legislative branches of government. A few municipalities opt for a council-manager form consisting of a popularly elected council responsible for both legislative and executive functions. The council hires a professional full-time manager to administer municipal affairs. The manager reports to the council and serves at its pleasure. According to the Maryland Municipal League, the state's municipal governments have been hybridized to some degree.[25]

Baltimore, which functions both as a municipality and a county, has a municipal form of government, but the Express Powers Act for municipalities specifically excludes the City of Baltimore.[26] The constitutional home rule powers applicable to it are those that provide the basis for charter county home rule. Unlike charter counties, the city derives its express powers from public local laws enacted piecemeal by the General Assembly and included collectively as Article II in the 1964 Baltimore home rule charter, the current governing document. Baltimore may not change this article; nor may the state legislature make public local laws applying only to the city. Nevertheless, the Assembly may modify the city's powers through state public general law.

Baltimore's mayor-council government is unique in Maryland. Three officials are elected citywide: the mayor, the comptroller, and the president of the city council. Together with the solicitor and director of public works, who are appointed by the mayor, these officials function as the board of estimates, which develops the budget, awards contracts, and supervises city purchases. Legislative authority rests with a nineteen-member city council elected from six districts. The council's authority is limited, however, because it may only reduce the budget. The ordinances that the council passes are subject to a mayoral veto, which takes a three-fourths vote to override.

For more than 300 years, the state legislature retained strong control over the incorporation and management of the cities and towns by enacting local legislation. Hence, except for Baltimore city, until 1955 each municipality in the state had its own individual act of incorporation and a charter enacted as a public local law of the General Assembly. Any local charter amendment necessitated a state legislative act. The charters under this arrangement spelled out the boundaries, governmental organization, voter qualifications, revenue-raising authority, and functional powers of specific municipalities. Minimal standards for incorporation were established because close legislative supervision was ensured. Requirements that are still in effect include a minimum population of 300 but no specifications as to land area or distance from another municipality. Such provisions might encourage numerous new cities and towns, but since the General Assembly delegated authority for the process to the counties, political (rather than legal) barriers have made incorporation difficult.[27]

Incorporation of a new municipality now takes place entirely at the local level. Incorporation requires a minimum population, local initiative, local petitions, and the approval of the governing body of the affected county. Counties have been niggardly in granting approval. Only four municipalities have incorporated since 1970.[28] Municipalities are found in twenty-one of the state's twenty-three counties and include approximately 15 percent of the state's population. Several communities, such as Bethesda and Silver Spring (which many people believe to be cities), are not incorporated, even though their respective populations are larger than those of any municipality in the state except Baltimore.[29] Their local services are furnished by their respective counties. The "new town" of Columbia that was developed through private investment also is not incorporated.

Municipalities may annex unincorporated territory contiguous to and adjoining their borders. Successful annexation necessitates a referendum and approval by a majority of those voting within both the city and the area to be annexed. Consent to the proposal by 25 percent of the registered voters and 25 percent of the property owners in the area to be annexed is required. Constituent petitions for annexation must include the signatures of 20 percent of the registered voters in the area for the municipal government to call a referendum on the issue. Public notice and hearing are required. The county also may authorize a referendum by a two-thirds vote of its legislative body. There were 104 annexations between 1990 and 1995 involving 2,000 people and 8.8 square miles of territory. No single annexation involved 1,000 or more persons during this period.[30]

Municipalities may acquire or sell real or leasehold property for any public purpose and may erect buildings on that property.[31] The constitution and statutes do not mention if municipalities may own or operate property outside their corporate limits. The state courts, however, have ruled that municipalities have an implied power to purchase property outside their corporate limits.[32] A statute explicitly prohibits municipal corporations from establishing or locating any type of penal institution outside their corporate limits, unless the governing board of the county in which the institution is located has granted approval.[33]

Municipalities have no general authority to regulate activities beyond their corporate limits, except in maintaining order. They can "enforce all ordinances relating to disorderly conduct and the suppression of nuisances equally within the limits of the municipality and beyond those limits for one half mile, or for so much of this distance as does not conflict with the powers of another municipal corporation."[34]

Functions of Local Government

Functional Responsibilities

Although Maryland counties provide more local services than do municipalities, municipalities are authorized to perform a wide range of functions. Except for Baltimore, however, no municipality exercises all of the powers allowed. Most provide adoption and enforcement of building and housing codes, planning and zoning, police and fire protection, refuse collection, street lighting, water and sewerage, and park and recreation facilities. Only eight have social service programs. Health, hospitals, education, and welfare generally are not municipal concerns.

Regardless of their form of government, all Maryland counties (including Baltimore city) not only are administrative units for state programs but also provide general government functions, including programs for public safety, public works, health, social services, libraries, culture and recreation, economic development, and capital facilities. Counties also operate and partially finance the public school systems, including the sixteen county and regional college systems. County boards of education, elected in ten counties and appointed by the governor in others, administer the public schools.

In practice, counties and Baltimore city are the primary providers of most of the local services. Because large areas of Maryland are not incorporated, many receive municipal-type services from their county governments. These practices are especially prevalent in the metropolitan areas around Baltimore city and Washington, D.C. In both municipalities and counties, the types and extent of local government activities vary.

Maryland statutes provide for the establishment of a variety of public authorities and special districts to furnish specified services within defined boundaries. Relatively few (223) have been created to date. Most have been set up by the General Assembly or by counties; few municipalities have exercised their option to establish such districts. Special districts (such as the Washington Suburban Sanitary Commission) are of vital importance, whereas others have minimal impact.

Depending on its orientation, a special district may be involved in drainage or the provision of levees, the administration of public housing programs, airport control, waste disposal, sanitation concerns, soil conservation, water pollution control, or transit. Other functions may include erosion control, marinas, parking, parks, pedestrian malls, pest control, recreation, road maintenance, special police, fire protection, and street lighting.

Special taxing districts have the authority to levy property taxes, impose fees, and incur debt, and they may be created by the state or by counties and municipalities.[35] Their services include storm drainage, street and area lighting, public parking facilities, pedestrian malls, ride sharing, bus systems, and commercial district management, among other purposes. Special tax districts have discretionary authority over their spending, as long as the monies are directed toward performing the specified service. They may not spend funds outside their boundaries without special permission. Some of these districts, particularly those in Montgomery County, are called villages and for census purposes are considered municipalities.

Municipal corporations have specific statutory authorization to create two kinds of public authorities to exercise jurisdiction within their geographic limits. They may set up a board of port wardens to regulate municipal waterways and establish commercial district management authorities for any commercial area within their geographical limits. Such commercial districts may levy fees on the businesses within the authority's jurisdiction. Whether municipalities may establish additional public authorities under their home rule power currently is under debate

Maryland statutes allow counties and municipalities to engage in a variety of formal and informal cooperative ventures. Entities that transcend county boundaries include regional planning and development agencies, such as the Baltimore Metropolitan Council, the Metropolitan Washington Council of Governments, and the Maryland–National Capital Park and Planning Commission, among others. There are also commissions to deal with waste disposal matters.

Maryland local governments also participate in several interstate compacts. For example, Allegany County and the City of Cumberland cooperate with local governments in West Virginia to manage the area's air traffic. Montgomery and Prince George's counties, along with the District of Columbia and Virginia, are heavily involved in the Washington Metropolitan Area Transit Authority, which manages transit facilities in the metropolitan Washington area.

By statute, counties and municipalities also have general authority to cooperate with other governments. For example, they can lend property, services, and other assistance to other political subdivisions for public purposes. County commissioners in two counties may cooperate with other local governments to perform government functions.[36] Counties are permitted to establish soil conservation districts that include more than one county, watershed associations, and shore erosion control districts. They may also establish and maintain local detention centers jointly.[37]

Administrative Discretion

Although Maryland is among those states that waive sovereign immunity of local governments, its local governments enjoy substantial freedom from procedural requirements relating to their administration of local affairs. A 1985 study by the U.S. Advisory Commission on Intergovernmental Relations (ACIR) ranked Maryland sixth among the states in terms of local discretionary authority. Nevertheless, procedural specifications are inconsistent. The state details procedures for adoption of local ordinances in counties but not in municipalities. Conversely, state laws mandate codification of municipal ordinances but not those of counties. Moreover, elected county office vacancies are to be filled by appointment, but vacancies in municipal offices are not addressed.[38]

In personnel practices, Maryland authorizes its cities to adopt merit systems[39] and mandates coverage for specified county employees. Affirmative action, comparable worth, or equal-pay-for-equal-work plans are not required for either type of jurisdiction; nor is residency a qualification for municipal or county employment. State law does specify personnel training for police employees in both cities and counties. A general state prohibition against political activity applies to all local employees. Employees are not permitted to engage in collective bargaining, and public safety officers specifically are prohibited from striking.[40]

Employee benefits in both types of localities include workers' compensation coverage, but neither cities nor counties are required to establish local retirement systems or to participate in the state system. State law makes no provision for health insurance, family leave, day care, or other benefits for local employees.[41]

To some degree, Maryland coordinates and supervises local administration of state functions, by hosting informal conferences, providing advice and technical assistance, requiring reports, and reviewing local action, for example. Nevertheless, Maryland does not substitute state control for local administration.

The extent to which local governments have discretionary power to contract and bid depends on the type of local government. Charter and code counties have broader discretion than do commissioner counties. Charter counties have authority to set up competitive bidding for any county work and to make and award the requisite contracts. They also have broad discretion to participate in procurement contracts for materials, supplies, and equipment with the state Department of General Services. Most commissioner counties have express power to arrange competitive bidding procedures for any county work and to award contracts to purchase materials and supplies for amounts greater than $15,000. They also may require that contractors post bonds for county work or contracts. When the General Assembly has not granted explicit authority to contract, a commissioner county must request the Assembly's approval. Under the municipal Express Powers Act, municipalities have the authority to enter procurement contracts for materials, supplies, and equipment.[42]

The state establishes bidding procedures for local governments and requires competitive bidding for certain types of contracts. Public bodies (that is, the state or any of its local governments) are required to include the prevailing wage rate in requests for contract bids or proposals, in the specifications for public works contracts, and in the contracts themselves.[43] Local governments also must request a specified amount of security for construction contracts.

State law grants specific planning and zoning authority and control of land use to municipalities (including the City of Baltimore) and to noncharter counties. Municipalities and noncharter counties must create planning and zoning commissions charged with preparing comprehensive zoning plans that must be submitted to the local legislative bodies for approval. State law prescribes the form of such commissions and the content of the local plans. Charter counties are exempt from many of those provisions,[44] but they may have additional specifications in their charters. The statutes specify additional requirements that must be included in county plans. All local governments may enact laws for landmark and historic preservation.

Economic Development

Maryland grants local governments authority to engage in economic or community development activities. Twenty-one counties have established economic development agencies.[45] Counties may grant tax credits, develop industrial parks, establish and maintain enterprise zones, revitalize blighted areas, and make infrastructure improvements targeted to specific economic or community development projects. Municipal authority is somewhat more limited. Cities and towns may establish enterprise zones, renew blighted areas, and make infrastructure improvements to aid in economic or community development. They also may set up commercial district management authorities to promote business within the corporate limits.[46]

Local governments may use locally generated own-source revenues for economic or community projects that benefit private entities, and they may do this without a local referendum on the issue. For example, Howard County's "new town" of Columbia was instigated by private investors; the county approved the development and adopted other measures to facilitate its establishment. The constitution authorizes the City of Baltimore to provide loans for redevelopment or improvement structures within the city that are to be used for residential or commercial purposes.[47]

State statutes also allow the creation of enterprise zones to generate development in areas where unemployment is high, income is low relative to the median family income of the host jurisdiction, and the population has decreased substantially.[48] Baltimore has been particularly active in establishing enterprise zones, creating the Charles Center (a business, hotel, and cultural complex), revitalizing the wharf area, and encouraging home ownership with "sweat equity" programs.[49] Economic incentives offered by local governments, such as exemptions or tax credits for development purposes, are limited and must be approved by the General Assembly.

Fiscal Autonomy of Local Governments

Local Revenues

Maryland exercises a high degree of control over local budgeting, taxing, and borrowing authority; thus, local governments have little revenue-raising authority. Cities and counties impose property taxes based on state-controlled assessments; these taxes constitute the most important source of funding, somewhat less than one-third of their total income (see Table 2).[50] Although local governments have discretion over property tax rates, the state centralizes the assessment process. The Real Property Valuation Division of the state Department of Assessments and Taxation is responsible for administering all real property tax laws. The state also requires uniform rates on all similar taxable property within a jurisdiction.

State fiscal aid is the second largest source of money for counties, whereas for municipalities other than Baltimore, it is relatively unimportant. Another major source of local funds is the local income tax authorized by the General Assembly in 1967 that piggybacks onto the state income tax (that is, local income tax is collected through the state collection process and is then returned to the local governments). Before 1967, local governments received a portion of the state income tax. In that year, the General Assembly authorized them to piggyback the state tax on incomes at 20–60 percent of the state rate. Currently, all counties and Baltimore city levy income taxes. Other municipalities may not tax incomes; however, some may receive a portion of the revenues from this source raised by their respective counties. Additional important resources derive from user fees and charges based directly on provision of a service.[51] Both municipalities and counties may tax business, tourism, and entertainment; these taxes are relatively unimportant in the total local revenue picture.

Municipalities and counties may not levy taxes on retail sales or uses without state permission, and none do. They are, however, authorized to tax the sale or use of fuels, utilities, space rentals, or controlled dangerous substances.[52] Code counties may also levy local property transfer taxes; other jurisdictions must obtain legislative approval. Eleven counties are authorized

Table 2. Maryland County and Municipal Revenues, FY 1995 (in percent)

Source of revenue	Charter county	Code county	Commissioner county	Baltimore city	All counties	Municipal
Property taxes	31%	28%	27%	23%	29%	32%
Income taxes	18	11	14	6	15	7
Other local taxes[a]	6	4	2	3	5	2
Licenses and permits	1	1	0	1	1	2
Federal grants	5	8	6	14	7	4
State grants[b]	18	32	32	31	23	7
Other intergovernmental source	0	0	0	1	0	4
Fines and forfeitures	0	0	0	0	0	1
Service charges	12	10	9	10	11	30
Miscellaneous	5	4	4	4	4	6
Debt proceeds	4	1	6	7	5	4
Total	100	99	100	100	100	99
Total local taxes	55	44	44	31	49	40
Total intergovernmental	23	40	37	46	30	16

Source: Compiled from tables prepared by the Maryland Department of Legislative Services.

Note: Revenues collected by the Washington Suburban Sanitary Commission are apportioned to Montgomery and Prince George's counties on a fifty-fifty basis. They include other local taxes, service charges, and miscellaneous.

a. Other local taxes include revenue from sales and service taxes; admission and amusement taxes; "front foot" assessments (that is, tax valuations on property fronts, either street fronts or waterfronts); public utility taxes; recordation taxes; and other local taxes not elsewhere classified.

b. State grants do not include state contributions to social services boards.

to impose impact fees on new development to fund capital programs and services; to date, nine are exercising that option.

The state government imposes some limits on municipal and county taxes. For example, in addition to setting the range of rates on the state income tax, it caps amusement and admissions tax rates. The state also limits the 911 emergency telephone system tax that local jurisdictions may levy. Local units have more discretion on property taxes and may set their own property tax rates. The constitution allows the legislature to limit property tax rates, but the General Assembly has never exercised that option. The General Assembly also may set maximum limits on property tax rates levied by municipal corporations; this option is subject to approval by a majority of the voters in a municipal corporation voting on the issue.[53] Such tax limits are found in individual charters. The state requires that certain statewide tax credits be applied to property tax revenues.

The state constitution authorizes the legislature to limit counties' debt, but it does not specify the purposes for which local debt is allowed.[54] Charter, commissioner, and code counties have different restrictions. For charter counties, the aggregate amount of bonds and other outstanding indebtedness may not exceed 15 percent of the assessable base.[55] Debt based on revenue or enterprise bonds is limited only to the amount generated from the pertinent project. Charter counties also can establish special taxing districts and authorize debt of up to 15 percent of the assessable base within the special district. Short-term debt

and state or federal loans are not considered part of the debt and thus do not count against such limitations. The General Assembly can limit the maximum amount of bonded indebtedness for code counties when their rates are deemed excessive, but the legislature has never exercised that option.[56] State law imposes no limitations on debts in commissioner counties, although their debt creation is limited insofar as they are required to secure prior authorization from the General Assembly.

Baltimore city has no limitations on general-obligation debts. The General Assembly may impose a limit on the amount of outstanding debt the city has at any one time only insofar as the charter counties are limited.[57] Again, the General Assembly has not exercised such an option.

The General Assembly can limit the maximum amount of debt that other municipal corporations can create, although voters in the affected municipality must ratify any such law. A municipal corporation may also impose debt limitations on itself through its legislative powers, again subject to voter approval.[58] Of the 155 municipalities, 42 include debt limitations in their charters, either in dollar amounts or in terms of the percentages of assessable base.

Municipalities may issue both general-obligation bonds and revenue bonds. Unless the municipal corporation's charter requires a referendum on the issue of bonds, municipal legislative bodies may authorize bonds by resolution or ordinance.[59] A maximum bond life for local bonds is imposed, but there is no ceiling on the interest rate that a municipality may pay. A local referendum is not required for local bond issues, unless the resolution or ordinance or the municipal corporation requires it. State law provides for, but does not require, the maintenance of a sinking fund for local debt service. Because the state does not prescribe the investment of idle funds by cities and counties, localities may decide how to invest. Short-term debt is permitted.

Local Expenditures

Local governments spend more for education than for any other function. Because they serve as school districts, counties spend the lion's share—more than 88 percent of all education expenditures. The counties and Baltimore city spend much of their budgets on education, including a small portion for higher education. Public works, public safety, interest on general debt, parks and recreation, highways, sewerage and sanitation, and housing and community development make up most of the remaining outlays. Municipalities other than Baltimore spend the most on general government, public safety, transportation, sewer and water, parks and recreation, and debt service (see Table 3).

The state has tightened its control of local financial management. All local governments must adhere to uniform accounting procedures and observe a common fiscal year. Cities, but not counties, are required to adopt annual operating budgets and to hold at least one public hearing before budget adoption. Maryland law mandates an independent postaudit for all local governments; the audit content is specified by the state, and the audits must be filed with the state. Moreover, the state may audit accounts of any county unit that collects taxes.[60]

In some ways, Maryland restricts its local units less than some other states do. It does not impose general expenditure limits, specify a balanced budget for either municipalities or counties, or make any provision for state assumption of the fiscal management of a locality in the event of default on obligations or bankruptcy.

State Government Grants-in-Aid to Localities

About 25 percent of Maryland's general expenditures go to local governments. This percentage is among the lowest of all the states if the rankings are calculated on a per capita expenditure basis. As might be expected, local government aid back to the state is a mere fraction of state revenues.[61]

Most state grant money is allocated for education, and funds go to community colleges as well as to elementary and secondary education. Counties and Baltimore city may also receive state monies for school construction. After education, police and local highways are the two most important functional areas for state grants; both receive about one-sixth as much money

Table 3. Maryland County and Municipal Expenditures, FY 1995 (in percent)

Expenditure	Charter county	Code county	Commissioner county	Baltimore city	All counties	Municipal
General government	6	6	5	6	7	11
Total public safety	10	10	7	10	16	19
Police protection						14
Fire protection						3
Other public safety						2
Total public works	14	14	10	14	18	44
Transportation						14
Sewer and water						23
Other public work						6
Parks and recreation	3	3	1	3	2	9
Community development	2	2	1	2	2	3
Economic development	0	0	1	1	7	2
Debt service	8	8	4	7	5	8
Miscellaneous	3	3	1	2	2	4
Health	3	3	4	4	8	—
Social services	1	2	2	1	1	—
Primary and secondary education	44	44	56	44	32	—
Community colleges	5	5	7	4	0	—
Libraries	1	1	1	1	1	—
Natural resources	0	0	0	0	0	—

Source: Compiled from tables prepared by the Maryland Department of Legislative Services.

from the state as does education. Health and hospitals get about half that allocated to public higher education—much less than designated for elementary and secondary schools. Some funding goes to general government support, but public welfare transfers are minimal.[62]

State rules and controls vary with the grant and sometimes with the type of local units involved, but accounting and auditing requirements apply to all. Similarly, local governments exercise more discretion on some spending decisions than on others. Generally, the funds must be spent for a specified purpose; however, local officials may determine what aspect of a program is to be funded.

Functional interest groups, such as the Maryland Education Association (MEA) and various police organizations, may have as much (or more) leverage on state grants-in-aid legislation as do local entities. In the 1970s MEA organized schoolteachers to petition against referendum-enacted legislation extending state aid to parochial schools. The measure was defeated in the election. Because of its media and the size of its legislative delegation, Baltimore city's requests have always commanded attention. Other jurisdictions, such as the counties of Montgomery (now the most populous local unit in the state), Prince George's, Anne Arundel, Howard, and Baltimore, have developed considerable clout on local grant issues. The most important influences have come from citizen demands for better schools, roads, and public safety.

Unfunded Mandates

Like local governments elsewhere, Maryland counties and municipalities bristle at state requirements to undertake activities at their own expense. Nevertheless, Maryland imposes fewer such requirements on local government than do other states. A 1990 study by the U.S. Advisory Commission on Intergovernmental Relations found that only eight states had fewer laws pertaining to local governments.[63]

Although the law does not specify uniform oversight mechanisms for state grants, provisions for individual grants may include control by a designated state agency. The prospect of losing state grant money compels local governments to comply with grant conditions, albeit reluctantly. Local units may seek adjudication to test the validity of conditions or fund distribution.

Fiscal notes must be attached to any proposed legislation that involves expenditures, and they must be made available to the public. Fiscal notes outline the cost involved, the projected future cost, the proposed source of revenue for financing the requirement, and the fiscal impact on local governments.

Access to Local Government

Local Elections

Marylanders elect a total of 1,766 local government officials. Of these, 323 are county officials, 868 are municipal officers, and 575 serve in special districts.[64] County elections in Maryland are conducted on a partisan basis, whereas municipal elections may or may not be, depending on the charters.

For all local elections, the state sets voter qualifications and establishes voter registration procedures; one registration suffices for state and local elections. Statutes direct local governments to allow absentee and write-in votes in local elections. The constitution sets quadrennial election dates for county (but not municipal) officials on the Tuesday following the first Monday in November. Statutes establish dates for municipal primaries and general elections.[65]

Maryland does not specify candidate qualifications for local elections; however, members of an organization that advocates the overthrow of the federal or state government through force or violence are ineligible to hold any office, elective or appointive.[66] No expenditure limits apply to candidates for local office, but disclosure of campaign finances is required.

Each county has a gubernatorially appointed board of supervisors of elections.[67] Accountable to the state Board of Elections, local boards are responsible for implementing state and applicable federal election laws, establishing and changing precinct boundaries, providing suitable polling places, and assigning voters to precincts. Candidates for local office file with the county boards.

Citizen Controls over Actions of Local Officials

Although Marylanders have considerable leeway in the selection of local officials, removing them is another matter. State law neither subjects local officials to impeachment nor provides for their recall. Local officials convicted of crimes forfeit their offices, and state law establishes procedures for filling vacancies at the county level and in Baltimore city (procedures are not specified for other municipal offices).[68] The constitution stipulates that upon conviction of willful neglect of duty or misbehavior in office, the mayor of the City of Baltimore shall be removed by the governor and a successor elected.[69] The state imposes no ethics law.

Citizens must influence local ordinances through the election of local officials and other political activity because the state makes no provision for citizen initiation of legislation at either the state or local level. There is no requirement that locally enacted legislation be submitted to referendum upon citizen petition.

State law stipulates that all local government meetings in which official business is conducted shall be open to the public. All government records must be open to public scrutiny as well.

State-Local Relations

Maryland's state and local governments experience some of the push-pull relationship that characterizes other states. At the state level, interest groups pressure the governor and the General Assembly to exert more control at the same time that local officials are seeking more autonomy and, particularly, increased financial resources. Conflicts that are not resolved in court may be mitigated by local legislative delegations that secure state action. Or, problems—such as unanswered local demands for authority to levy a sales tax—are simply allowed to fester.

Conversely, state and local governments often cooperate to solve local problems, particularly when state-directed resources are at stake, as in times of natural disaster. For less dramatic concerns, advice and assistance are sought or offered. For example, the state may use local school buildings for meetings, and localities often call on state colleges and universities for information and guidance. In recent years, there have been more interactions among state and local officials to discuss common problems. The election of two county executives and one metropolitan mayor to the gubernatorial seat probably contributed to this development.[70]

The Maryland Municipal League and the Maryland Association of Counties, along with specialized interest groups such as the Maryland Education Association, play a part in bringing issues important to local governments to the attention of the state. Local issues, particularly educational or financial needs or actions, in turn may become important election issues.

The Achilles' heel of state-local relations in Maryland is the confusion caused by the General Assembly's ability to enact general local laws, which preempt local authority. These laws, which are actually special local legislation, are allowed by the constitution as long as they apply to at least two units. Attempts to broaden local powers constitutionally suffered a blow with the defeat at the polls of a 1968 proposed constitution that would have strengthened local governmental home rule authority. More than a quarter of a century later, there is little change in state-local relations.

Notes

1. Aubrey C. Land, "Provincial Maryland," in *Maryland: A History,* ed. Richard Walsh and William Lloyd Fox (Annapolis: Archives Division, Hall of Records, Department of General Services, 1983), 12.

2. U.S. Bureau of the Census, *1992 Census of Governments,* http://www.census.gov/govs/www/govstruc.html.

3. Annotated Code of Maryland, Article 23A.

4. Robert J. Brugger, *Maryland: A Middle Temperament, 1934–1980* (Baltimore: Johns Hopkins University Press, 1988), 12–13.

5. *1995–1996 Maryland Statistical Abstract* (Regional Economic Studies Institute and the Maryland Department of Business and Economic Development), 15–18.

6. Chapter 7 of *The Acts of 1708.* Patricia S. Florestano and Herbert C. Smith,

"Maryland 1994: Democratic Dominance in Decline" (paper presented at the annual meeting of the American Political Science Association, Chicago, 1997).

7. Annotated Code of Maryland, Article 25A and others.

8. Maryland Constitution, Article XI-F.

9. Maryland Constitution, Article XI-E.

10. Maryland Constitution, Article XI-F; Annotated Code of Maryland, Article 25B, section 1.

11. Annotated Code of Maryland, Article 25B, section 1.

12. Municipal corporations are voluntary creations that have the authority to enact local ordinances and usually enjoy some immunity from suit in the performance of their governmental functions. Cities and towns are municipal corporations, and counties may be. Usually, however, counties are quasi-municipal corporations having some, but not all, of the powers of municipal corporations. They ordinarily have no ordinance-making power, and they perform governmental functions as agents of the state.

13. For example, see Annotated Code of Maryland, Political Subdivisions—Miscellaneous Provisions Article, section 1-101. Tax—Property Article, section 1-101 says "'County' means a county of the State and, unless expressly provided otherwise, Baltimore City," as does the Tax—General Article. Real Property Article, section 1-101 states "'County' includes Baltimore City."

14. The charter board is appointed by the county commission, acting either on its own accord or as a result of a petition by 5 percent of the registered voters or 10,000 voters, whichever is less (Maryland Constitution, Article XI-A, section 1A).

15. Annotated Code of Maryland, Article 25A.

16. Maryland Constitution, Article XI-A, section 3.

17. The following counties have adopted charter forms since 1948: Montgomery (1948), Baltimore (1956), Anne Arundel (1964), Wicomico (1964), Howard (1968), Prince George's (1970), Hartford (1972), and Talbot (1973).

18. Maryland Constitution, Article XI-F.

19. The procedure for adopting legislation is set out in the statutes governing home rule for code counties. See Annotated Code of Maryland, Article 25, section10(b).

20. The following ten counties do not have home rule: Calvert, Carroll, Cecil, Charles, Dorchester, Frederick, Garrett, Somerset, St. Mary's, and Washington.

21. Maryland Constitution, Article VII.

22. Most of this body of law is contained in Annotated Code of Maryland, Article 25.

23. Maryland Constitution, Article XIII.

24. Annotated Code of Maryland, Article 23A, section 2(b)(10) states that "the General Assembly hereby declares that there is one class of such municipal corporations. Every municipal corporation in this State . . . shall be taken and considered as a member of that class, and as subject to the constitutional and statutory laws applicable thereto."

25. Kevin Best, manager of research and information management at the Maryland Municipal League, said, "We have some municipalities with governing bodies called commissions and chief appointed officials called 'managers' exercising powers more characteristic of the council-manager form of municipal government. Also, many Maryland towns with commissioners do not divide functional responsibilities, as is done in the more traditional municipal commissions." E-mailed message to authors, 7 June 1999.

26. Annotated Code of Maryland, Article 23A, section 2(a) states, "The legislative body of every incorporated municipality in this State, *except Baltimore City,* by whatever name known, shall have general power to pass such ordinances not contrary to the Constitution" (emphasis added).

27. Annotated Code of Maryland, Article 23A, section 20.

28. *Municipal Year Book 1997* (Washington, D.C.: International City Management Association, 1997), 37.

29. For example, according to the 1990 census, Silver Spring has 76,200 residents; Dundalk, 65,800; and Bethesda, 62,936.

30. *Municipal Year Book 1997,* 36–37.

31. Annotated Code of Maryland, Article 23A, section 2(b)(24).

32. *Birge v. Town of Easton,* 274 Md. 635, 337 A.2d 435 (1975). In a previous ruling, the Maryland Court of Appeals, the state's highest court, noted that since state statutes impose no "geographical limitations" on the location of municipal projects, the court in effect had "applied the principle that a municipality if not prohibited by law may acquire property outside its corporate limits where such an acquisition is reasonably necessary to the exercise of powers expressly granted." *Grinnell Co. v. City of Crisfield,* 264 Md. 552, 287 A.2d 486 (1972), as cited in *Birge v. Town of Easton* 274 Md. 635, 337 A.2d 435 (1975).

33. Annotated Code of Maryland, Article 23A, section 8A.

34. Annotated Code of Maryland, Article 23A, section 2(b)(23).

35. Annotated Code of Maryland, Article 23A, sections 44 and 44a.

36. Annotated Code of Maryland, Article 23A, section 8C; Article 25, section 3(y).

37. Annotated Code of Maryland, Article 25, various sections.

38. U.S. Advisory Commission on Intergovernmental Relations (ACIR), *The Question of State Government Capability* (A-98) (Washington, D.C.: ACIR, 1985), 288; ACIR, *State Laws Governing Local Government Structure and Administration* (M-186) (Washington, D.C.: ACIR, 1993), 34.

39. Annotated Code of Maryland, Article 23A, section 2(b)(19).

40. ACIR, *State Laws Governing Local Government Structure and Administration,* 48.

41. Ibid., 54.

42. Annotated Code of Maryland, Article 25A, section 5(F); Article 25, section 3 (l); Article 23A, section 2(b)(24A).

43. Annotated Code of Maryland, State Finance and Procurement Article, section 17-110 et seq., section 17-210.

44. Annotated Code of Maryland, Article 66B (for municipalities and non-charter counties); Article 25A (for charter counties); Article 66B, sections 3-05, 3-06, 4-09. This article does not apply to the chartered counties of Maryland, except as provided in Article 66B, sections 3.05(a)(1)(iii), (v), (vi), and (viii); 3.05(a)(4) and (b); 3.06(b) and (c); 4.01(a)(2); 4.09; 5.03(d); 7.01(c); 10.01; 11.01; 12.01; and 13.01, subject to subsection (b) of section 7-03.

45. The counties that have established economic development agencies are Allegany, Anne Arundel, Calvert, Caroline, Carroll, Cecil, Charles, Dorchester, Frederick, Garrett, Harford, Howard, Montgomery, Prince George's, Queen Anne's, St. Mary's, Somerset, Talbot, Washington, Wicomico, and Worcester.

46. Annotated Code of Maryland, Article 23A, section 2 (for municipalities); Article 25, section 3 (for commissioner counties); Article 25A, section 5 (for charter counties); Article 25B, section 13A (for code counties); Article 23A, section 2(b)(35).

47. Maryland Constitution, Article XI-G.

48. Annotated Code of Maryland, Article 83A, section 5-403.

49. Elizabeth Lyons-Rexford, "Privatized Economic Development: A Case Study of Baltimore, Maryland" (Ph.D. diss., University of Maryland, College Park, 1994).

50. The yield is minimally affected by state-adopted circuit breaker programs on property taxes for homeowners and renters whose net worth does not exceed $200,000; it is also affected by homestead exemptions for the blind and for veterans with 100 percent permanent disabilities. ACIR, *Significant Features of Fiscal Federalism 1994,* vol. 2 (Washington, D.C.: ACIR, 1995), 132, 139.

51. For example, utilities, cable television, garbage collection, and parks and recreation. ACIR, *Significant Features of Fiscal Federalism 1994,* 131, 139, 220.

52. Annotated Code of Maryland, Tax-General Article, section 11-102.

53. Maryland Constitution, Article XI-F, section 8; Article XI-E, section 5.

54. Maryland Constitution, Article XI-E, section 5.

55. Annotated Code of Maryland, Article 25A, section 5 (P). An exception is made for consolidated public improvement bonds, which must be authorized by the General Assembly.

56. Maryland Constitution, Article XI-F, section 8; Annotated Code of Maryland, Article 25B, section 22.

57. Maryland Constitution, Article XI, section 7.

58. Maryland Constitution, Article XI-E, section 5; Article 23A, section 40.

59. Annotated Code of Maryland, Article 23A, sections 31, 37(a), 38, 34(3), 32(a).

60. ACIR, *State Laws Governing Local Government Structure and Administration.*

61. U.S. Bureau of the Census, *Statistical Abstract of the United States 1997* (Washington, D.C.: U.S. Bureau of the Census, 1997), 312, table 494.

62. Council of State Governments, *Book of the States 1996–1997* (Lexington, Ky.: Council of State Governments, 1992), 411.

63. ACIR, *Mandates: Cases in State-Local Relations* (M-173) (Washington, D.C.: ACIR, 1990).

64. U.S. Bureau of the Census, *Popularly Elected Officials in 1992* (preliminary report, October 1994), 6.

65. Annotated Code of Maryland, Article 33.

66. Maryland Constitution, Article XVII; Article XV, section 3.

67. Annotated Code of Maryland, Article 33, section 2-201 et seq.

68. Annotated Code of Maryland, Article 23A, section 2(b)(25) allows municipalities "to remove or temporarily suspend from office any person who has been appointed to any municipal office and who after due notice and hearing is adjudged to have been guilty of inefficiency, malfeasance, nonfeasance, misconduct in office, or insubordination; and to fill the vacancy caused by such removal or suspension."

69. Maryland Constitution, Article XI, section 6.

70. Spiro T. Agnew (1967–1969) and Parris N. Glendening (1995–2003) were county executives. William Donald Schaefer (1987–1995) was mayor of Baltimore.

MASSACHUSETTS

Meredith Ramsay

The author thanks the following: for their contributions of knowledge and expertise during the early stages of research, James M. McKenna, general partner of Municipal Management Systems in Dover, Mass., and Kevin Paicos, town administrator of Easton, Mass.; for comments and suggestions on an earlier draft of the chapter, Marilyn Contreas of the Massachusetts Department of Housing and Community Affairs, Deborah Eagan of the Massachusetts Municipal Association, and Michael P. Curran, town counsel of Canton, Mass. Timothy Dwinal at the University of Massachusetts, Boston, provided research assistance.

Local self-government is a venerated tradition in the Commonwealth of Massachusetts, and municipalities still cling to the special status they have enjoyed since colonial times. Cities and towns are the preeminent units of local democracy, since counties are being abolished and no unincorporated land mass remains. However, intergovernmental relations are inherently unstable, there are tendencies toward centralization, and the taxing and spending capacity of Massachusetts's localities is restricted by a property tax limit and unfunded mandates. During economic recessions, the state's older and poorer communities are especially affected by these limits to local autonomy. The Home Rule Amendment, which passed in 1966, is a reasonably expansive grant of home rule authority to localities, but it is grafted onto a large body of regulation and highly restrictive state law, resulting in mixed messages for political subdivisions.

Governmental Setting

The Commonwealth of Massachusetts, in the heart of New England, has an area of just over 8,000 square miles. Its 351 cities and towns range in size from 98 people in the small town of Gosnold to almost 600,000 in Boston, the capital. More than 100 towns have fewer than 5,000 residents. Total population now exceeds 6 million people, with an average population density of 768 persons per square mile. More than half the state's population resides in the Boston metropolitan area. Current state law makes no provision for extraterritorial jurisdiction, annexation, or other boundary changes because there are no unincorporated areas remaining. All of the land is located within one of the cities or towns.[1]

Over the centuries, immigration has transformed the Native American and English population of colonial times into an amalgam of national groups. According to the 1990 U.S. Bureau of the Census figures, the largest single ancestry group is Irish (21 percent), followed by English (14.5 percent), Italian (13.6 percent), French (9.9 percent), Portugese (6 percent), and Polish (5.1 percent). In 1990 African Americans, Hispanics, Native Americans, and Asians constituted more than 12 percent of the state's population.

Since its founding, Massachusetts has led the rest of the nation in significant ways. The first battle of the American Revolution was fought and won in Lexington. The Constitution of the Commonwealth, ratified in 1780, is the oldest written constitution in the world that is still in effect. It was the first to establish a separation of powers. Harvard, founded in 1638, was the first university in America. Today, Massachusetts boasts 121 institutions of higher learning, and the state is renowned for its universities, research facilities, and hospitals. The nation's first public parks, public schools, and public libraries were founded in Boston. The Bay State claims the first newspaper, telephone, railway, and subway. More recently, the first automatic digital computer was developed at the Massachusetts Institute of Technology.

In addition to the traditional farming, textile, and tourist industries, the state's economy is sustained by a wide range of manufacturing and commercial enterprises. Industrial diversification and a large pool of skilled workers have allowed Massachusetts to maintain strength in manufacturing, ranking sixth among the fifty states by value. Financial and telecommunications industries are growing rapidly, as are other high-tech industries such as biotechnology, biomedicine, artificial intelligence, marine sciences, and polymer technology. The Port of Boston and Logan International Airport make Boston one of America's busiest transport centers.

In contrast with New Hampshire, its conservative neighbor, Massachusetts has embraced progressive social policies throughout most of its history. It was the birthplace of the movements for universal education and the abolition of slavery. It was the first state to protect the rights and welfare of women, children, and the mentally retarded. Traditionally, the Democratic Party has been dominant in Massachusetts, and the state has sent a long line of prominent Democrats to Washington, including President John F. Kennedy and Speakers of the House John W. McCormack and Thomas P. "Tip" O'Neill. The past two governors, William Weld and Paul Cellucci, have both been Republicans, however, in keeping with a national trend. Organized labor is strong and limits local discretion in significant ways, particularly with reference to public-sector wages, benefits, and other personnel matters, such as discrimination laws and fair labor standards.

Home Rule in Massachusetts

Historical Development

In 1648 the Laws and Liberties of the Massachusetts Bay Colony explicitly recognized the tradition of local self-government. The Puritans were the largest of the sects escaping persecution for their religious beliefs through immigration. They organized their new towns around church congregations and secured a large measure of independence from external authority. In the Massachusetts Bay Colony, the church was the polity, and governing decisions were made by local Congregational (Puritan) leaders, known as "selectmen." Their meetings developed into a formal legislative body known as the "town meeting," a format also used in other parts of New England.

Throughout most of the seventeenth century, only members of the Congregational Church were permitted to vote. In 1691 the Crown gave the Massachusetts Bay Colony a new charter that centralized power in the Great and General Court and thus limited local autonomy.[2] The new charter replaced religious qualifications with property qualifications for voting, and Congregationalist hegemony gave way to political and religious pluralism. Puritanism, which viewed all man-made institutions (the state in particular) as inherently prone to corruption, had nevertheless laid the moral foundations for local autonomy and resistance to tyranny, which are still prominent features of American local and national political culture.[3]

When the Massachusetts Constitution was adopted in 1780, it consolidated the General Court's power over localities. Cities and towns operated under a series of general laws, acceptance statutes, bylaws, and special acts of the legislature. As the state's population increased, this arrangement became cumbersome for the larger communities. In 1821 the constitution was amended to allow the legislature to institute city forms of government (mayor and council) in any community with more than 12,000

inhabitants, if desired by the majority of the community's voters.[4] This amendment was adopted as an administrative convenience and was never intended to establish home rule.

Throughout the nineteenth century, local governments in Massachusetts were increasingly subjugated to the authority of the "parent state," and the Massachusetts Supreme Judicial Court consistently upheld this redistribution of power.[5] In 1868 Dillon's Rule further established the principle that local governments in the United States are fully subject to state legislative authority and dependent upon the states for whatever degree of autonomy the states choose to grant them. But as local government responsibilities enlarged around the turn of the century, this dependency became an insupportable burden for both state and local officials, who increasingly called for a sharing of legislative power in order to retain responsive government in the Commonwealth.

In the pre–home rule period, any city or town in Massachusetts could petition the legislature for a special-act charter. In response to the home rule movement in the early twentieth century, the General Court enacted the Model Charter Law in 1915. With subsequent amendments, the law allowed communities with 12,000 or more residents to adopt charters, without individual legislative sanction, from one of the following variations or plans: mayor-council, council–town manager, representative town meeting–board of selectmen, open town meeting–board of selectmen, city manager–council (with the council elected by proportional representational voting), and "strong" mayor–council.

This law allowed communities to change their form of government without involving the state legislature, but it did little to encourage innovation or allow for extensive problem solving at the local level. Regardless of the form of local government that any community might adopt, Dillon's Rule had created a dependency by local officials on the General Court to enact special and general enabling acts to address local issues.

In 1917 the Massachusetts Constitutional Convention rejected eight petitions for a municipal home rule amendment. The issue resurfaced and was defeated, regularly, for fifty years afterward. Ultimate ratification could be attributed to the massive suburbanization that occurred after World War II, which created a new political force and a new national home rule movement outside the old cities.

In November 1966 the voters amended the state constitution to institute authentic home rule. The Home Rule Amendment provides local governments with the power to design a form of structural governance that best suits the community's needs.[6] Unlike the earlier Model Charter Law, it authorizes municipalities to exercise genuine local control, within specified limits. Of the state's 304 towns, 34 have special-act charters, 63 have adopted home rule charters, and the rest continue to operate under a series of general laws, acceptance statutes, bylaws, and special acts, as they have done since colonial times. Of the 47 cities in Massachusetts, 22 have special-act charters, 14 operate under one of the standard options made available by state law,[7] and 11 have home rule charters.[8]

For ten years after the enactment of the amendment, a strong economy allowed the state to provide generous levels of aid to localities, and there were few restrictions on the new charters. However, the 1980–1993 period was sobering for cities and towns, which had grown accustomed to substantial fiscal autonomy and a high degree of state and federal largesse. First came a prolonged recession, double-digit inflation, and unfunded federal mandates, which diminished the state's capacity to provide grants-in-aid. Then the property tax limit, known as Proposition 2½, was introduced in 1980. General revenue sharing was reduced in the mid-1980s, costing Massachusetts approximately $140 million.[9] In the wake of devolution and another recession (1989–1993), Massachusetts's political subdivisions were burdened with increased responsibilities for service provision and reduced state financial support. Although the economy has since brightened, the lesson learned was that regardless of formal decision-making structures, political and economic forces in the larger environment strongly affect home rule powers.

Legal scholars believe that the Great and General Court never intended to relinquish wholesale control over the most significant legislative powers and duties. Rather, the objective of the Home Rule Amendment was to improve the efficiency of government at all levels by loosening the reins of authority. Thus, the Home Rule Amendment provided cities and towns with a limited form of self-executing constitutional home rule, but final oversight of municipal functions was retained in the General Court.[10]

Definition of Home Rule

The Home Rule Amendment reaffirms the principle of local self-government in matters of purely local concern. Through a wholly local process with no involvement by the state legislature, cities and towns are authorized to design, enact, and amend their own charters. The legislature is prevented from enacting a special law affecting a single municipality, unless it does so on the prior petition of the municipality itself, except in extraordinary cases. A municipal government may exercise any power or function consistent with the constitution or with laws enacted by the general court in accordance with powers specified by its charter. Municipalities usually exercise this devolved authority through the adoption of ordinances or bylaws.

When compared with other states, the regulatory authority retained by Massachusetts's General Court seems considerable, but the state's authority has typically been exercised in ways that honor the principle and tradition of local self-government. To maintain the integrity of the relationship between the state and its subdivisions, the House of Representatives prohibits the Local Affairs Committee from adopting special legislation submitted by special interests without evidence of clear support by the local legislative body (for example, the town council or town meeting). Thus, many communities believe they can continue to manage their business without a formally adopted home rule charter.

The Local Affairs Committee in particular, and the state house and senate generally, have been exceedingly generous in adopting as "home rule" bills virtually any piece of legislation that is filed by a municipality, either authorizing it to do something or providing it with an exemption from some otherwise "general law." Much of this legislation is unnecessary because of the devolution-of-powers provision in the Home Rule Amendment.

Structural Features

The Home Rule Amendment and the Home Rule Procedures Act allow communities to create, adopt, or amend a local municipal charter without state legislative approval. Under the Home Rule Amendment, the legislature has the power to regulate elections, levy taxes, borrow money or pledge the credit of cities and towns, dispose of park land, enact civil law, and punish felonies and impose imprisonment for any violations of law. The General Court has "preemptive" power to regulate in all other areas of law, through the passage of general and special laws. For example, when real estate interests mounted a successful statewide referendum in 1994, the state abolished (by preemption) locally enacted rent-control ordinances in Boston, Brookline, and Cambridge.

Two restrictions from amendments to the state constitution are carried over into the Home Rule Amendment. Article II (1821) provides that no town of fewer than 12,000 inhabitants may be classified as a city and thus qualify for a mayor-council form of government. Article LXX (1926) provides that no town of fewer than 6,000 inhabitants may adopt a representative town-meeting structure (in which the right to participate in lawmaking is restricted to elected town-meeting members). Only seventy-four communities have adopted home rule charters so far; six have adopted the mayor-council form; five have adopted the council-manager form; eighteen have adopted the representative town meeting; and forty-five have formally adopted the open town meeting, which allows all registered voters in the community to take part in the lawmaking process.

Functions of Local Government

Functional Responsibilities

Each municipality's legislative body must raise and appropriate funds, approve the operating and capital budgets, enact local bylaws, and vote to accept or reject the state's local option statutes at its annual town meeting.[11] Municipalities must also assess and collect taxes and maintain financial records, which must be audited annually by an independent auditor. Cities and towns must regulate local land use, building construction as determined by the state building code, and local traffic and parking. State law further requires that municipalities provide for the public health by regulating the preparation and sale of food.

Local government services include road maintenance, trash collection, water and sewer, emergency medical services, libraries, cemeteries, and the care of public shade trees. Municipalities must preserve the peace and public safety, which is the responsibility of local police and fire departments, building inspectors, health departments, and civil defense personnel. Comprehensive recreational and social services are often provided as well.[12]

Unlike that of other New England states, the Massachusetts Constitution does not specifically mention county governments. Their functions are limited to managing jails, houses of correction, and courthouses on a regional basis. A few provide minor services, such as spraying for insects. Like municipalities, they are political subdivisions of the state and have no independence to act, except as provided by the General Court, through legislation. They are not units of government in the strict sense, since, with one exception, they are without representative bodies.[13] Because their powers and duties are so limited, the state recently abolished seven of fourteen counties on the ground of inefficiency and transferred their functions to the Commonwealth.[14] It is only a matter of time before the remaining counties are abolished and their boundaries dissolved.[15]

Among the state's public authorities are the Massachusetts Turnpike Authority, the Massachusetts Water Resources Authority, the Massachusetts Bay Transportation Authority, and the Massachusetts Port Authority. Regional schools, ambulatory care, and regional development and planning agencies are commonplace. No legislation is needed to enable municipal governments to exercise jointly powers that they can exercise alone.[16]

Pressures for regionalism have been growing, and there are a number of innovative regional initiatives in progress, without state involvement. For example, two towns are jointly constructing a new library, and seventeen towns have constituted a Southeastern Regional Council of Governments, which specializes in highway and public works cooperation and coordination, including purchasing. Other regional councils of governments are being planned. Municipalities still tend to control local service provision.

Special-purpose districts, also called "improvement districts," are an old phenomenon in Massachusetts. Under state law, municipal governments may form such districts, and they may require those who would benefit from the amenity to pay for it. Water and sewer districts are found all over the Commonwealth, but there is a superabundance of them on Cape Cod. In the town of Barnstable, for example, there are half a dozen or so water departments and fire chiefs but no town water department or fire department.

School districts generally are town agencies coterminous with other municipal boundaries. School department employees are employees of the city or town. There are, however, a sizable number of regional districts, both for regular schools and for vocational school districts. The schools are generally controlled by separately elected school committees and are administered not by the city or town officers per se but by superintendents appointed by school committees.

Administrative Discretion

Many statutes that predate home rule initially controlled local personnel practices. Organized labor is a powerful force that has shaped this area of the law. The Civil Service Law governs all aspects of personnel matters for communities that adopt its provisions and options, including adoption of civil service for a single department or all municipal employees, except teachers.[17] Other statutes cover employee relations in specific departments. Recruitment, retention, and benefits of selected employees are primarily state controlled. The law also provides for multiple appointing authorities, which has led to conflicting requirements.

The Home Rule Amendment allowed cities and towns to centralize all practices and appointive-removal authority into one office (for example, city or town manager, selectmen, or mayor). Although this is an improvement, many towns and cities still do not have centralized personnel practices, and many that have home rule charters have chosen to retain certain earlier provisions. Moreover, even if a charter is adopted, certain state provisions that disrupt complete local control still apply. In 1980, as part of Proposition 2½, many municipal governments were given the option but decided by local vote not to abolish the civil service system either in their town or in selected departments.

The Collective Bargaining Statute,[18] civil rights laws, and workers' compensation statutes limit local autonomy in personnel matters. The state can require affirmative action in these circumstances:

• a city or town has been subjected to a Massachusetts Commission Against Discrimination (MCAD) consent decree to hire minorities and women in nontraditional jobs (usually ordered by MCAD pursuant to complaints by protected classes);
• a city or town has a filed an approved affirmative action plan with MCAD, establishing certain hiring goals that must be met to qualify for state grants; or
• a city or town is under an affirmative action court order establishing strict quotas (usually because of an egregious pattern of discrimination in hiring).

Medical technicians and municipal assessors are regulated and must be certified by the state. However, training requirements for other classes of public employees are largely absent.

Some state-provided licenses, such as the commercial driver's license and the pesticide applicator's license, relate to specific duties. Many professional associations offer certification programs, which occasionally are financially supported by the state. Fee-based in-service training programs are offered to cities and towns. All of these provisions increase the professionalism of municipal workers and ordinarily are not considered invasive.

Any city or town with a population exceeding 10,000 may establish its own pension system, which must be governed by an independent retirement board.[19] Municipalities are otherwise required to participate in a regional pension system. Currently, there are more than 100 such municipal retirement systems in the Commonwealth. In 1996 the state created the Public Employee Retirement Administration Commission to oversee and regulate pension boards and encourage their administrative reform. A weekly employee withholding, plus an assessment paid by the city or town, funds the retirement systems. State law establishes employee contributory rates and standardized retirement benefits schedules.

With certain exceptions, municipalities may contract for services on terms authorized by their legislative assemblies. The state regulates most municipal service, commodities, and construction contracts. The Uniform Procurement Act stipulates procedures for purchase of supplies and services, for the disposal of surplus supplies, and for the acquisition and disposal of interest in real property.[20]

All municipalities with populations of more than 10,000 must establish a planning board to administer the Subdivision Control Law (which generally governs new developments)[21] and zoning bylaws; there must also be a zoning board of appeals. Smaller communities depend on the thirteen regional planning agencies. Local planning boards have the authority to adopt regulations governing the design and construction of roads, drainage systems, and utilities that service subdivisions. Planning board decisions are based on regulations that are already in place before a developer submits a subdivision plan.

Communities have traditionally relied on their zoning powers to control development. The State Zoning Act specifies the procedures, format, rights, and duties that must be followed.[22] Local permit-granting authorities may grant zoning variances in accordance with the strict standards established in state law. Zoning moratoriums, which allow communities to adjust their land-use policies over one or two years to improve growth management, must also conform to the requirements of the State Zoning Act.

Economic Development

To foster and oversee economic development, state law authorizes any city or town to create an industrial development finance authority, an economic and industrial development corporation, a redevelopment authority, or a development and industrial commission.[23] Two or more municipalities may jointly create such development agencies, which must be approved by voters. Economic opportunity areas may negotiate a tax abatement for a specified time period. All economic development activities are stringently regulated.

Fiscal Autonomy of Local Governments

Local Revenues

Cities and towns raise their revenues from property taxes, state aid, local receipts, and other available funds. Property taxes, although limited by Proposition 2½, still account for the largest share of municipal revenues. The percentage of revenue from this source varies widely among municipalities, but it averages about 50 percent. State aid averages about 25 percent, except in the Commonwealth's poorest cities, where these proportions are often reversed. User fees and charges for services now average about 20 percent of local revenues. Municipalities decide which programs and services will be supported by user fees and charges, within the provisions of state statutes. Typically, they include but are not limited to motor vehicle excise, water and sewer charges, penalties and interest, charges for services, licenses and permits, fines and forfeits, investment income, and a hotel-motel tax. The largest receipts are produced by the hotel-motel tax and motor vehicle excise taxes, followed by user fees, licenses, and permits. The Commonwealth reserves to itself the right to levy income taxes and sales taxes; no local sales tax or income tax is permitted.

In the 1970s, when aid from the state was declining and unfunded federal and state mandates were rising, cities and towns resorted to increasing property taxes, as often as needed, to balance their budgets. By 1980, the property tax burden ranked fourth highest in the United States, when measured as a portion of individual income.[24] This ranking earned the state the epithet "Taxachusetts." The stage was thus set for voters to join in the nationwide "tax revolt," which had begun in 1978 in California with the passage of Proposition 13.

Until 1980, the property tax rate was established each year by the mayor or by the city or town council. The tax-limiting statute known as Proposition 2½, which was passed by referendum, removed that discretion.[25] By the mid-1980s, cities and towns had cut their tax rates by 15 percent annually until they had attained the required reduction of 2½ percent of the community's assessed valuation (the levy limit). The law also limits the amount the property tax can be raised from year to year to 2½ percent, and it sets the maximum property tax rate at 2½ percent. The law later was amended to provide an automatic override of the levy limit, based on the value of a community's new growth. Additional overrides to tax above the 2½ percent-plus-growth limit are allowed when approved by a majority of voters.

Proposition 2½ revolutionized the municipal budgeting process in Massachusetts and altered local governance in numerous though uneven ways. The levy limit tends to be so restrictive that exclusion referendums are required to raise additional taxes to fund most large-scale capital projects (for example, new buildings). These project-specific votes tend to be difficult to achieve because rarely is there unanimous agreement among large, heterogeneous electorates, especially in older cities with expanding concentrations of retired voters on fixed incomes and shrinking constituencies for public schools. Many exclusions and overrides have passed in the newer, smaller, more homogenous and affluent communities.

After twenty years, Proposition 2½ is still overwhelmingly popular with voters, but its effects are irregular and many local government administrators view it as a major setback for home rule.[26] Municipalities that are experiencing significant growth are spared the worst ramifications. But declining older urban areas with low tax bases now depend on state aid for more than 40 percent of their revenue; eight cities depend on the state for at least half of their funds. Economic expansion since 1994 has enabled such generosity, but if there is another recession, the state will again be forced to reduce local aid, as it has in the past. The poorest cities will again be in danger of financial insolvency, as they were during the recession in 1989–1993. If they should default on the repayment of bonds, they would come under state supervision or even receivership.

Massachusetts tightly regulates local government borrowing.[27] State law establishes debt limits and procedures for the issuance of short- and long-term municipal debt. With certain exceptions, a city's debt may not exceed 2½ percent, and a town's debt may not exceed 5 percent of the equalized valuation of said city or town. The purpose of municipal borrowing and length to maturity are also regulated by the state. Debt limits are so high that they pose no practical barrier to a well-strategized capital-spending plan supported, in part, by debt issuance. Debt referendums are not required for general-obligation debts within the Proposition 2½ tax-levy limits.

The Massachusetts Municipal Association has recently tried to create opportunities for municipal government to aggregate its debt issuance in "bond banks," to assist marginal credit communities and very small bond issues. Although the state's banking interests were aggressive opponents, the bond bank project eventually foundered because wealthier communities lacked sufficient incentive to participate.

Local Expenditures

Public education typically claims most of municipalities' resources. There are no state laws requiring local appropriating bodies to adopt an annual expenditure within a specified revenue figure, but since the passage of the 1993 Education Reform Law, municipalities have had to meet mandatory school spending requirements. Most municipalities have been required to in-

crease their spending on education in conjunction with increases in state education aid.[28] However, communities with a limited ability to support their public school systems are allowed to reduce their allocation of local revenue for education; the state provides enough education aid to make up the difference. These "Chapter 70" funds bring the community closer to a foundational level of school spending. State and federal education mandates place a floor under school budgets; Proposition 2½ sets the ceiling.[29]

Towns with a property valuation of $1 million or more must create an elected or appointed finance committee to exercise fiscal oversight. The committee's main statutory responsibility is to review the budget prepared by the executive body and make recommendations to the town meeting regarding the budget and other areas of finance. A balanced budget is required by the state.[30] State law sets forth a mandatory budget format for cities but not for towns. All municipalities must employ a professional accountant, whose authority, together with that of town treasurers and tax collectors, is strictly governed by state law.[31]

Massachusetts is one of only four states authorized to take over the financial administration of local governments, in certain conditions.[32] Takeover is authorized when municipalities are unable to pay interest or principal on bonds.[33] During the 1989–1993 recession in Massachusetts, the city of Chelsea went into state receivership, and five other cities came under the supervision of state finance control boards.[34] In 1997 the state abolished Middlesex, Hampden, and Worcester Counties, when they defaulted on bonds.

State Government Grants-in-Aid to Localities

The Department of Revenue annually notifies every city, town, and regional school district of the state aid they will receive for the coming year and the assessments that will be deducted. These notices were originally printed on cherry-colored paper and thus came to be called "cherry sheets." The largest categories of state aid are Chapter 70 education aid and the lottery. Education aid is distributed according to a complex formula based on a foundation budget. The foundation budget is recalculated annually for every locality, taking into account the economic and demographic profile of the locality's school district relative to the rest of the state. The discrepancy between the foundation budget and the community's ability to pay generally determines the amount of education aid the community receives from the state. The Education Reform Law aimed to reduce inequalities across school districts and to bring all districts up to a reasonable standard of foundational spending by fiscal 2000. Since the law was passed in 1993, the state increased its annual level of spending on K–12 education by $1.6 billion to meet this goal.

Aid from the State Lottery Commission proceeds are distributed to municipalities according to a formula that takes into account population and equalized valuation. Cities and towns with relatively lower property values receive proportionally more lottery aid than those with greater property values.[35] (See Table 1.) Lottery aid has grown from $306 million to $670 million since fiscal 1992 because the lottery cap has been phased out. All revenues generated by the lottery are returned to cities and towns.

Cherry sheet appropriations to cities and towns will total $4.8 billion in 2001, which is an increase of 4 percent over fiscal 2000 levels and the eighth consecutive annual aid increase. The state reimburses cities and towns for tax exemptions granted to qualifying veterans, blind persons, surviving spouses, and elderly persons, as well as reimbursements for tax abatements. Competitive grants are sometimes difficult to obtain because most programs are in high demand and cannot respond to all requests.

Table 1. Revenues and Expenditures for Two Massachusetts Municipalities of Comparable Size, One Poor and One Rich

	Chelsea	Wellesley
Population (1996)	27,608	26,809
Per capita income (1989)	$11,559	$32,253
General revenue sources, FY 1999		
Total general revenues	86,241,340	60,646,281
Tax levy	19,332,172	44,026,162
	(22%)	(73%)
State aid	52,001,295	5,660,170
	(60%)	(9%)
Local receipts	14,867,873	8,464,238
	(17%)	(14%)
Other	40,000	2,495,711
	(<1%)	(4%)
Cherry sheets, FY 1999		
Total estimated receipts	52,000,563	5,655,701
Education	43,000,924	3,488,280
General government	8,999,639	1,811,421
Total estimated assessments	1,712,642	959,670
Net estimated state aid	50,287,921	4,696,031
Revenues and expenditures, FY 1998		
Revenues (total of all funds)	98,516,888	94,429,304
General revenue	76,036,820	54,858,125
Special revenue	13,125,556	4,704,426
Capital projects	89,125	36,765
Enterprise fund	7,951,311	33,867,054
Trust revenue	1,314,076	962,934
Expenditures (total)	94,177,255	92,649,489
Education	39,782,493	31,725,492
Public works	11,441,903	28,490,137
Police	4,771,739	3,655,981
Fire	4,731,113	2,953,905
All other	33,450,007	25,823,974

Source: Massachusetts Department of Revenue, Division of Local Services (30 June 1999). See Web site http://www.state.ma.us/dls/.

Table 2. Massachusetts Governor's Recommendation for Distribution of Direct Local Aid, FY 2001

"Cherry sheet" aid	Estimated spending, FY 2000	Recommended spending, FY 2001
Treasurer	$1,249,170,978	$1,266,170,978
Municipal services and abatements	26,642,550	24,124,000
Veterans' services	7,706,310	8,388,590
Libraries	26,745,181	26,745,181
Education	3,226,329,119	3,407,383,755
Public safety	23,737,040	28,208,284
Transportation and construction	43,472,110	43,472,110
Total	$4,601,803,288	$4,804,492,898

Source: "The Governor's Budget Recommendations for FY 2001" (Commonwealth of Massachusetts, Fiscal Affairs Division, 26 January 2000). See Web site: http://www.state.ma.us/fin.htm.

Some of the more complex programs require the services of professional consultants, especially in smaller towns with fewer staff.

In 1981 there was a general consensus that annual increases in local aid were essential to make the newly enacted Proposition 2½ viable. During the 1980s, local reliance on state aid grew by 50 percent. When the state was hit with a severe recession in 1989, precipitating a budget crisis, local aid programs were sharply reduced.[36] Local aid has once again attained the same level it reached in the mid-1980s, but its primary purpose now is to fund education reform (see Table 2). The former president of the Association of Town Finance Committees commented, "the consensus that state aid is critical to the success of Proposition 2½ was lost in the economic recession and the implementation of education reform."[37] School enrollments have been rising since 1990, and economic forecasters expect public education to claim an increasing proportion of local and state revenue.

During the most recent recession, Massachusetts passed several laws that purportedly assisted local governments financially but actually were cost-deferral strategies. For example, there was legislation to allow deferral of teacher's summer payroll until a subsequent fiscal year. In essence, that cost would continually be transferred to each subsequent year, with actual funding to take place in some unspecified future year. Another example of the deferral strategy was the state's proposal to bundle delinquent taxes and sell them as assets to speculators. Affluent, well-managed local communities rejected both plans, but many local governments that were hard-pressed by impossible service demands, declining revenues, and interest groups adopted these plans.

Unfunded Mandates

Proposition 2½ discourages unfunded state mandates by requiring a two-thirds vote of both houses for legislative enactment. But unfunded mandates that were in effect before 1981 remain in effect. Antimandate laws have been moderately successful. However, some observers propose that they should be strengthened because new legislation (both state and federal) continues to impose new obligations and limit choices.[38]

Local officials sometimes refer to the 1993 Education Reform Law as an unfunded mandate, even though it technically is "self-funding." Notwithstanding the actual state takeover of school administrations in Chelsea, in 1989, and Lawrence, in 1997, because of gross fiscal mismanagement, education has been largely independent in Massachusetts and continues to be so.[39] Under the Education Reform Law, however, city and town governments assume greater fiscal and funding responsibility. "Super-committees"—comprising members of the local school committee, the superintendent, a local finance committee representative, and a member of the board of selectmen or town manager—are intended to bring a sense of balance to the funding and budgeting process in local government.

The Education Reform Law, although not technically an unfunded mandate, has radically altered local spending and local autonomy. This effect was fully intended and, in the view of many local officials, was a necessary and appropriate remedy for the substantial variation in municipal educational spending that prevailed before the law's passage. It is not known if state funding will stay at promised levels during periods of economic recession or if local governments will be expected to assume the burden.

Access to Local Government

Local Elections

Local elections are governed by municipal charters or bylaws and are strictly regulated by state law. The state does not set dates for local elections, but it does require that town elections be held in March, April, or May, unless other arrangements are stipulated by town charter. City elections are held in November of odd years. The state establishes voter qualifications but not candidate qualifications. It sets voter registration procedures and mandates that one registration will suffice for all elections. State law also requires cities and towns to allow write-in votes and to provide absentee ballots. The state imposes financial disclosure requirements but does not limit campaign expenditures of candidates for local office. State law strictly regulates the selection of election officers and requires that both major political parties be represented equally. The state requires cities and towns of more than 6,000 residents to create new voting precincts every ten years. Each precinct must contain approximately the same number of inhabitants but no more than 4,000 people.[40]

Citizen Controls over Actions of Local Officials

Those local communities that have adopted recall procedures usually require the signatures of 20 percent of registered voters, but this limitation is not imposed by the state. Although often invoked as a political threat, recalls are rarely resorted to, and even more rarely are they successful. There is no impeachment in cities and towns.

A resident of a city that has been duly organized pursuant to one of the optional city charters can petition the city council or school committee to adopt, amend, or rescind a local law, regulation, vote, or resolution by means of an initiative petition.[41] Town council governments also have this feature. In cities that have not adopted formal charters under the Home Rule Amendment, similar options may be available within the special legislative acts that organized the city.

In towns, the local initiative process is simple. To bring a matter before the annual town meeting, a resident need only acquire the signatures of at least ten registered voters and submit the petition to the board of selectmen. Petitions submitted for a special town meeting must have 100 signatures.

In a city operating under one of the optional city charter plans, and in cities with home rule charters, a referendum procedure is available.[42] Again, similar provisions may be set forth in the charters of those cities that were organized under special acts of the legislature. Referendums are allowed in both a binding and an advisory capacity.

The Open Meeting Law, the Public Records Law, the Conflict of Interest Law, and the Standards of Conduct for Public Officials are designed to ensure the openness of proceedings and the integrity and professionalism of local officials.[43] Additionally, the state office of inspector general has been established to prevent and detect fraud, waste, and abuse in the expenditure of public funds, including those from federal, state, or local sources and in programs involving procurement of services and supplies. The inspector general may also receive and investigate any allegations of fraud, waste, or abuse.

State-Local Relations

Although home rule exists in Massachusetts in a meaningful way, the degree of autonomy that local governments enjoy is highly contingent upon political and economic conditions and trends in the larger environment. Before the passage of the Home Rule Amendment, municipal government was considered a "creature of the state"; home rule was dispersed, erratic, and embodied in chaotic statutes, bylaws, special acts subject to the caprices of local practice. The 1966–1980 idyll in which home rule was enjoyed was cut short by economic recession, Proposition 2½, and former president Ronald Reagan's New Federalism, which constrained local governments to abandon social policy priorities and focus instead on public management skills; localities were required to do more with less.[44]

In the 1990s the state's economy rebounded, and in 1994 the elimination (by preemption) of rent control in Boston, Brookline, and Cambridge contributed to a prolonged statewide real estate boom. The resulting increase in municipal planning and spending capacity has meant that cities and towns are once again enjoying a good measure of home rule.[45] Nevertheless, the Commonwealth's strong economy may be masking the real limits of local autonomy, which undoubtedly will become manifest during economic recessions, regardless of the formal decision-making powers that the state grants to localities.

Notes

1. The terms *city* and *town* are ambiguous. Their definitions are not formalized in law, and they are often used interchangeably. A "city form of government" refers to the mayor-council or mayor-council–town manager form. Since only communities of 12,000 or more inhabitants are authorized to adopt a city form of government, communities of that size are often referred to as cities, even though they may not have adopted a mayor-council form. On the other hand, some communities of 12,000 or more residents, regardless of their form of government, still call themselves towns. Municipalities are legally defined as either cities or towns.

2. Edwin Andrus Gere and Michael P. Curran, eds., *Modernizing Local Governments in Massachusetts: Home Rule* (Bureau of Public Affairs, Boston College; Bureau of Government Research, University of Massachusetts Amherst, 1968).

3. A. James Reichley, *Religion in American Public Life* (Washington, D.C.: Brookings Institution, 1985).

4. Boston received its first charter that same year (1821). In 1914 Norwood was one of the first municipalities in the world to adopt a manager form of government by special act of the legislature (Gere and Curran, *Modernizing Local Governments in Massachusetts*, 23).

5. Gere and Curran, *Modernizing Local Governments in Massachusetts*, 21.

6. Massachusetts Constitution, Article II, as amended by Article LXXXIX (89).

7. General Laws of the Commonwealth of Massachusetts, Chapter 43.

8. The General Court can tailor a municipal charter by stipulating that certain provisions of the general laws remain in effect for a community that still desires to operate under requirements specific to towns. Thus, in the case of Southbridge, a sort of hybrid city-town was created.

9. Allan Tosti, "After 15 Years, Has Proposition 2½ Reached Its Limit?" *Municipal Advocate* 15, no. 2 (Boston: Massachusetts Municipal Association, 1996), 18–21.

10. James M. McKenna, "Municipal Home Rule in Massachusetts" (University School of Law, Suffolk, Mass., 1990). See also Massachusetts Constitution, Article LXXXIX, 6, 8.

11. State law requires that annual town meetings be called in March, April, or May and be completed by June 30 of each year. Towns may also hold special meetings as needed.

12. *Finance Committee Handbook* (Boston: Association of Town Finance Committees).

13. Barnstable County has a legislative body called the Assembly of Delegates (under a 1988 home rule charter) and is the exception. Councils of government have replaced Franklin and Hampshire Counties (which were recently abolished) and operate within their old boundaries.

14. Seven of the fourteen county governments have been abolished. They are Berkshire, Essex, Franklin, Hampden, Hampshire, Middlesex, and Worcester. General Laws of the Commonwealth of Massachusetts, chapter 48, section 5 of the Acts of 1997; General Laws of the Commonwealth of Massachusetts, chapter 300 of the Acts of 1998. See David Baier, "Elimination of Counties Gains Momentum," *The Beacon* 23, no. 2 (February 1997).

15. Governor Cellucci has targeted Plymouth and Bristol Counties for elimination.

16. Interlocal agreements are authorized by General Laws of the Commonwealth of Massachusetts, Chapter 40, section 4.

17. The major provisions are General Laws of the Commonwealth of Mass-

achusetts, Chapter 32B (which provides guidelines regarding group insurance benefits) and Chapter 30 (which is the Civil Service Law). General Laws of the Commonwealth of Massachusetts, Chapters 30, 31.

18. General Laws of the Commonwealth of Massachusetts, Chapter 150E.

19. General Laws of the Commonwealth of Massachusetts, Chapter 32.

20. General Laws of the Commonwealth of Massachusetts, Chapter 40, section 4; Chapter 30; Chapter 40, section 22D; Chapter 45, section 5A; Chapter 30B, section 1–19.

21. General Laws of the Commonwealth of Massachusetts, Chapter 41, sections 81K–GG.

22. General Laws of the Commonwealth of Massachusetts, Chapter 40A.

23. General Laws of the Commonwealth of Massachusetts, Chapters 40D; 121C; 21B; 40, section 8a.

24. John Robertson, "Municipal Finance Trends in the Proposition 2½ Era," *Municipal Advocate* 15, no. 2 (Boston: Massachusetts Municipal Association, 1996), 22–25.

25. General Laws of the Commonwealth of Massachusetts, Chapter 59, section 21C.

26. Tosti, "After 15 Years," 18–21. See also Lawrence Susskind and Jane Fountain Serio, eds., *Proposition 2½: Its Impact on Massachusetts* (Cambridge: Oelgeschlager, Gunn, and Hain, 1983).

27. General Laws of the Commonwealth of Massachusetts, Chapter 44.

28. General Laws of the Commonwealth of Massachusetts, Chapter 70.

29. *Finance Committee Handbook*.

30. U.S. Advisory Commission on Intergovernmental Relations (ACIR), *State Laws Governing Local Government Structure and Administration* (Washington, D.C.: ACIR, 1993), 46.

31. General Laws of the Commonwealth of Massachusetts, Chapter 39, section 16; Chapter 44, section 32; Chapter 43C, section 11.

32. ACIR, *State Laws Governing Local Government Structure and Administration*, 36.

33. Massachusetts Constitution, Article XXXXIV (44), section 19A.

34. See David R. Berman's discussion of the state takeover of the city of Chelsea in "Takeovers of Local Governments: An Overview and Evaluation of State Policies," *Publius* 25 (1995): 55–70.

35. In 1997 the economically distressed city of Chelsea received about $3.5 million in lottery, Beano, and charity game funds, whereas Wellesley—a far wealthier community of approximately the same size—received less than $1 million.

36. Robertson, "Municipal Finance Trends in the Proposition 2½ Era," 22–25.

37. Tosti, "After 15 Years, 20.

38. Ibid., 18–21.

39. Berman, "Takeovers of Local Governments." Massachusetts is one of twenty or more states that have adopted laws to enable the takeover of "academically bankrupt" school districts in the last decade.

40. General Laws of the Commonwealth of Massachusetts, Chapters 51, 54.

41. Unless otherwise specified in the city's charter, a local initiative petition requires that at least 20 percent of the voters sign the petition. The city council or school committee must pass the measure within twenty days from the date of filing, or the measure must be submitted to a vote at a special city election within forty-five days.

42. When a petition is signed by at least 12 percent of the registered voters and filed with the city clerk within twenty days of passage of a measure, it serves to "suspend" the implementation of such measure. It also requires that the appropriate body reconsider such action. If the measure is not rescinded, it must be submitted to the voters in a referendum.

43. General Laws of the Commonwealth of Massachusetts, chapter 39, section 23; Chapter 66, section 1; Chapter 268A, sections 1, 23. See also Chapter 55, section 13.

44. For further analysis of this widespread phenomenon, see Peter Eisinger, "City Politics in an Era of Federal Devolution," *Urban Affairs Review* 33 (1998): 308–325.

45. The increase in municipal planning and spending capacity has also resulted in a shortage of affordable housing.

MICHIGAN

Kenneth VerBurg

Michigan's system of local government is complex, based as it is on the New England town model construed by the Continental Congress. The Northwest Ordinance (1787) directed that Michigan and the other states of the Northwest Territory were to be surveyed into areas of thirty-six square miles that were later organized into township governments. These, together with counties, were to be the state's emissaries, extending government to all regions of the state. Cities and villages, by contrast, were given authority to govern and serve populated settlements. With the Progressive movement, cities and villages gained home rule status in 1909, whereas townships and counties looked to the state for specific authority and responsibility. Only in the mid-1960s did townships and counties gain a degree of discretionary authority to tailor the state-prescribed form and set of duties to better fit localized needs, values, and circumstances. Organizational distinctions—and to a degree, functional distinctions—remain among the state's 1,242 townships, 565 cities and villages, 83 counties, and numerous special districts.

Governmental Setting

The governmental setting of Michigan is not easily characterized. Slogans such as the "Great Lakes State," "A Peninsula State," or the "Automotive Capital" describe only a limited aspect of the state and its politics. But such slogans conjure a singular image that is misleading:

On the surface, Michigan's politics seem to be those of a typical northern industrial state. Actually, the Wolverine State has passed through several stages in a political history that remains as unique as that of any state. Its Yankee origins made it part of greater New England and gave it an appropriate political personality to match. The Yankee influence predominated through the Progressive era at the end of the nineteenth and beginning of the twentieth centuries and gave the state its progressive foundations and heritage.[1]

From those New England roots Michigan developed a resolute moralistic political culture, a political perspective that holds that all of the people have an undivided interest—a commonwealth—in the government that exists to implement certain shared moral values. The body politic is not quite so easily categorized today, however. Those stages of history to which Elazar referred have left their marks in terms of what the state's residents perceive as appropriate public policies. Thus, although the southwest quadrant of the state continues its moralistic bent, the larger southeast portion has taken on an individualistic (or marketplace) quality, where bargaining in pursuit of self-inter-

ested public policy prevails. Other segments of the state include the wilderness-rich upper peninsula, the agricultural "thumb" area, and the resource-rich northern lower peninsula.

State officials practice a "politics of balance," because among the delegates representing various interests at the state capitol in Lansing, seldom does one coalition take control. Gov. James Blanchard (1983–1991), for example, found this to be the case in 1984, when Democrats controlled state government. The party passed a "temporary" increase in the state personal income tax, which spawned a recall that removed two Democratic senators. Republicans took their place and control of the state senate.

Well-organized interest groups engender a politics of balance; large industry and small companies are represented, as are otherwise competitive groups of labor unions, environmentalists, governmental watchdog groups, welfare organizations, and public and mental health advocates. Among the cadre of interest groups seeking to influence policy are representatives of local government. Advocating the concerns and interests of their respective constituents are the Michigan Municipal League, the Michigan Townships Association, and the Michigan Association of Counties. The Michigan Education Association is the teachers' organization, and the Michigan Association of School Boards represents the educational management interests in Lansing.

County sheriffs, chiefs of police, county deputies and municipal police, state police, county prosecutors, and judges have associations to speak for their particular segment of the law enforcement community. County road commissioners have an organization to protect counties' share of the state gasoline and vehicle license taxes, as do librarians to protect their penal fine revenues. Competition exists between and among members of these groups and associations, and policy makers mediate the differences in search of balance.

Home Rule in Michigan

Historical Development

As one of the earliest states to respond to the overtures of the Progressive reform movement, Michigan has nearly a century of experience with municipal home rule. Two sections of the 1908 Michigan Constitution introduced the concept and practice of home rule for the state's cities and villages. Article 8, section 20 directed the state legislature accordingly:

The legislature shall provide by a general law for the incorporation of cities and by a general law for the incorporation of villages; such general laws shall limit their rate of taxation for municipal purposes, and restrict the powers of borrowing money and contracting debts.[2]

The new language meant that the legislature could no longer continue the practice of writing and amending the charters of individual cities and villages. Nor could legislators manipulate local officials by threatening to change a municipal charter. Previously (in 1895), the legislature had begun a new practice by enacting two general statutes—the General Law Village Act and the Fourth Class City Act—that were designed as general-purpose charters for all municipalities that incorporated under them. (A number of villages and a few cities continue to operate under these laws, even though after 1908 all cities and villages could organize as home rule governments.)

Article 8, section 21 of the 1908 constitution, though, directed the legislature to lessen its control over cities and villages by allowing them to write and amend their own charters. The 1963 constitution, under which the state operates today, expanded the right of home rule: "No enumeration of powers granted to cities and villages in this constitution shall limit or restrict the general grant of authority conferred by this section."[3] Moreover, the spirit of what the delegates to the 1963 constitutional convention intended is captured in the following statement: "The provisions of this constitution and law concerning . . . cities and villages shall be liberally construed in their favor."[4] The general statute for cities is the Home Rule City (HRC) Act; for villages, the Home Rule Village (HRV) Act.[5]

Definition of Home Rule

The concept of municipal home rule is complicated in part by nomenclature. What exists, in fact, is a limited degree of self-rule. Unlike states, municipalities do not derive their authority directly from the people. Thus, a local municipality is not "a state within a state." Rather, governing authority is granted or withheld by the state. "Home rule" suggests that the people within a local municipality may adopt a local charter permitting officials to do whatever they find to be in the interests of residents—or denying officials the exercise of certain powers. The reality is that home rule is still a grant of power directing a local polity to command, permit, or deny certain things, usually by local choice.

Nonetheless, the manner in which home rule is granted can have a chilling or stimulating effect on the relationship between a state and its municipalities. The exclusionary approach spawned by Dillon's Rule—that is, the doctrine that a grant of power to a municipality not listed is denied—results in uncertainty and doubt about the exercise of local authority. When the state maintains a close rein on its progeny, uncertainty may exist about what may be done and how a given authority may be exercised. An alternative approach is the devolution of powers.[6] With this underlying philosophy, grants of home rule are broad and sweeping, and the constitution and the legislature list only those powers that are denied a local municipality. If a function or responsibility is not on the list, a city or village may safely presume that it does indeed possess the power.

The legislative expression of the 1908 Michigan grant of home rule was more akin to the notion of devolution of powers (Article 7, section 22). The legislature implemented these constitutional provisions by adopting the home rule cities and villages acts in 1909.[7] At the outset, two statutes were rather faithful expressions of the directives of the constitutional convention delegates. Over the decades the legislature amended them a number of times. Sometimes the changes came in response to a court decision; at other times, in response to new technological and social conditions.

Michigan courts, by and large, have ruled in favor of cities and villages on home rule issues. A 1994 state supreme court opinion, for example, said, "Accordingly, it is clear that home rule cities enjoy not only those powers specifically granted, but they may also exercise all powers not expressly denied."[8] Such an affirmation of self-governance would seemingly be sufficient to dissuade state legislators from infringing on local autonomy. Yet lobbyists of the Michigan Municipal League report that they must remind state lawmakers about the constitutional restrictions on their power when it comes to home rule units. However, local officials frequently request changes in the law and conditions that they cannot achieve locally.

Structural Features

The opportunity (or lack of it) to pass legislation applying to a particular jurisdiction affects very directly the character and quality of home rule and local autonomy in a state. At one extreme, the nineteenth-century legislature created municipal charters or amended them by special legislation or local acts, a practice that exposed local units to outside political interference. This was the case in Michigan, until the state adopted general acts that served as charters, and later adopted the home rule provisions that made the writing of charters a local responsibility. The 1963 constitutional convention strengthened the earlier prohibition forbidding the enactment of any special act, unless it is approved by a vote of two-thirds in both houses of the legislature and by a referendum in the community to which the local act is directed.[9] Thus, it is difficult to enact special legislation that controls and influences home rule units.

As with most formal rules, however, other practices were devised to evade such directives, such as using a population or property tax base "boundary" on legislation so that it qualifies as a general law and applies only to a particular city or small groups of them. For example, one statute, which has since been repealed, set the salaries for police judge, clerk, bailiff, and stenographer in cities with a population of "not less than 125,000 and not more than 200,000." Usually such "class" legislation has been easy to identify as "all cities having a population of cities greater than 1,000,000." It is through this mechanism, for example, that the state authorizes Detroit to levy a city income tax higher than in any other city.[10] At the other end of the continuum, state law exempts jurisdictions with populations of 25,000 or less from certain provisions relating to incompatible office holding. Another law excuses jurisdictions with under 4,000 population from a general requirement for annual financial audits. (Biennial audits for such units meet the state requirement.)

In resolving the differences between big city problems and those of smaller municipalities, representatives of the state municipal league find it difficult to satisfy respective wants and needs without employing the "class" approach. Provisions pertinent to "cities of a class" are usually enabling in nature rather than mandatory, and cities often request them. For example, the legislature inserted a provision into the HRC Act to permit by ordinance cities of more than 150,000 population to override charter provisions and establish four-year terms for officials who previously served for less than four years. A local populace, of course, could have changed the charter by initiative or referendum. As such, the legislative amendment was an intrusion into local affairs.

The home rule grant is vulnerable to state intrusion by general statute as well. Despite protests by city and village lobbyists, the legislature may adopt a general statute. To illustrate, the legislature amended the city and village planning statute by stating that in their zoning ordinances, units "shall provide for the use of single family residence by an occupant of that residence for a home occupation."[11] Although local zoning ordinances may regulate traffic and hours of operation at such locations, the statutory change appears to have been a legislative response to demand by persons who were unable to obtain relief at the community level.

BOX 1. FORM OF ORGANIZATION, MICHIGAN CITIES AND VILLAGES

Form	Number
Mayor-council	93
Council-manager	195
President-council (villages)	34
General law village, with manager	33
General law village	278

Perhaps the most vigorous local response to a state legislative action began in 1999. The legislature passed a law denying local units the right to require their employees to live in the jurisdiction employing them. Municipal union officials and municipal employees were pleased. The Michigan Municipal League, however, responded by circulating a petition to be voted on in November 2000. The ballot question, if approved by voters, would require the legislature to obtain approval of two-thirds of the members in each house to restrict further any action limiting local powers.

Michigan law does not limit the type of city government a city or village may have, although the statutes impose some minimal requirements. The HRC Act, for example, directs each city in its charter to provide for the election of a mayor as chief executive officer, a legislative body, and the election or appointment of a clerk, treasurer, and other "necessary" officers. Beyond those limited instructions, the statutes are silent with respect to the form of government; that is, council-manager, "strong" mayor, or commission form (see Box 1). The statutes are also silent with respect to whether elections will be partisan or nonpartisan. (The Michigan Municipal League reports that more than 90 percent of the cities and villages have nonpartisan elections.[12]) The state attorney general reviews local charters before gubernatorial approval, but such review is based on statutory compliance.

In times past, the matter of forming new cities or villages and expanding their boundaries was largely a matter in which state government played no role. The HRC Act's principal provision required that an area proposed for incorporation have a population of at least 2,000 and at least 500 persons per square mile.[13] (Standards for villages are much lower.) Annexation was a matter of strictly local concern. A city and adjacent township could agree by mutual resolution to change the boundaries. Most annexations, though, were controversial and contentious. Cities held an advantage over the township in the way that vote-counts were structured. Legislators with growing township and city constituencies found it difficult to satisfy demands because compromise was so elusive.

In 1968 the legislature created a state boundary commission to oversee the processes. The law permits annexation to be initiated in several ways. The most common method, though, is by petition of landowners (often developers) who wish to have their land annexed to the city. City and village councils may also initiate the action, but few do so, even though they commonly support annexation proposals that others initiate. Township residents, too, may initiate annexation but rarely do unless they badly need public water or sanitary sewer services. (Cities typically provide such utility services but usually do not extend such services beyond the municipal boundary.)

Consequently, the state boundary commission makes decisions on contentious issues. The commission order is final if the area has fewer than 100 residents; other situations are subject to referendum upon citizen petition. State law requires approval by the state boundary commission to incorporate cities before local residents vote on the issue.[14]

Functions of Local Government

From an operational perspective, the allocation of functional powers is a "contest" between the state and local units over which is going to do the people's business. In general, the assignment of functions has been rather stable over time but is subject to change.

Functional Responsibilities

The dynamics of shifting functions are highlighted by the 1963 constitution, which replaced justices-of-the-peace with a district court system. Cities that had municipal courts could continue to operate their courts or, depending on the size of the city, serve as the administrative host for a district court. Cities no longer have the option of establishing a municipal court, and now—some twenty-five years after these rules took effect—only five small suburbs adjacent to Detroit maintain a municipal court apart from the district court system.

Nevertheless, Michigan cities and villages are only minimally prohibited from deciding which public services to provide. The Michigan Municipal League board of directors does not regularly direct its lobbyists to seek authority to take on new functions. Michigan cities, for example, do not lobby to build and operate public hospitals, solid waste landfills, or jails and prisons that are now county and state responsibilities. More commonly, the municipal lobbyists assume defensive postures, fighting the legislature on matters that interfere with or limit the latitude of cities and villages.

Counties and townships in Michigan face a somewhat similar situation. They cannot, of course, invoke the "home rule" argument in their debates, because (except for Wayne County) they operate entirely under general statutes. Counties carry out many functions in collaboration with either the state or townships and cities and in some instances, on a district basis with other counties. Counties administer public health and mental health services as agents for corresponding state departments. They house the general trial courts and some courts of limited jurisdiction, fund county police services, and operate county jails and, occasionally, juvenile homes.

County agencies also operate as outreach arms of state government in administration of elections, prosecution of criminals, registration of property, and maintenance of vital records. Counties assume a "supervisory" role over local property tax assessment and collection. With respect to some other functions such as building construction permits and inspection, sanitary sewers, and planning and zoning, counties often collaborate but have "secondary" standing; that is, they may exercise the powers only if the townships and cities do not. In other instances such as surface water management, road maintenance (outside cities and villages), dog licensing, and others, counties are largely sole providers.

The other local units—cities, villages, and townships—have their own repertoire of services and regulations. Cities and villages own and operate most of the public water supply and wastewater treatment facilities, have their own fire and police protection services, maintain the local street systems, provide park and recreation programs, and administer the local property tax system, elections, waste collection, and recycling. Many are also involved in economic development projects, including downtown development, industrial recruitment, and housing. A few sponsor major facilities for the arts and sports.

Townships are empowered to provide all of these services except road and highway maintenance. However, because their populations are generally more scattered, they are less involved in service provision. Similarly, although they possess the authority to exercise various regulatory powers—such as zoning, subdivision regulation, billboard and sign control, parking restrictions, housing occupancy, sidewalk maintenance, and numerous other areas of activity—townships and most villages are not highly active regulators. Regulatory powers are exercised most vigorously in larger settlements, usually cities.

Another form of local government is the special district and authority. Michigan law permits a variety of these special-purpose units, and the state has created a few of them. The single most important units are educational districts—some 580 public school districts and 29 community college districts. Other forms include the Huron–Clinton Metropolitan Authority[15] in southeast Michigan, which operates a major park system in five counties. Another operates the airport in Lansing, the state capital. They undertake numerous other functions in multijurisdictional settings; among them are public water and wastewater treatment facilities, watershed management, storm drains, public transportation, public health and mental health (as divisions of county governments), public buildings, libraries, and virtually any function that a local government itself can provide.

Although state statutes often spell out organizational and financing details for these units, many others are formed with a great deal of flexibility by the intergovernmental agreements that constitute the units' charters. Typically, these units have low public visibility or scrutiny and are principally responsible for local oversight. Occasionally, however, the media want to know how districts and authorities are spending public dollars or providing public services.

Administrative Discretion

In terms of administrative arrangements, Michigan home rule units have a good deal of discretionary authority. Cities and villages that are organized under the home rule statutes can decide how to structure their governments, which duties and responsibilities to assign, and what the administrative dynamics among officials will be. Such is not the case, of course, with general-law village, township, and county governments that operate under general statutes, which impose a great deal of direction on such matters. However, the several types of governments—whether organized on the basis of home rule charter or general statute—must deal with some provisions imposed by state government, such as those to do with personnel management.

The presence of organized labor in the automotive industry has given Michigan a reputation of being a strong union state. Collective bargaining was not widespread in the public sector, however, until Michigan adopted the Public Employee Relations Act (PERA) in 1969. It made collective bargaining a way of life in virtually all cities and large villages. Public employers must now bargain with their employee organizations. Municipal unions do not have the right to strike or withhold services, although they do so on occasion, usually without penalty.

In 1972 the legislature made binding arbitration mandatory for public safety officers. If the involved parties are unable to reach an agreement (and under certain other conditions), either side may request the state agency to appoint an arbitrator to review the facts and to select the last offer from either side on a particular disputed issue. This provision applies only to police officers and fire fighters, but the policy represents a significant state-level intrusion into local affairs.

The state constitution and statutes also permit cities and villages to establish civil service systems for their employees. The statutory provisions prescribe the manner in which the civil service provisions are to be implemented, including an appointed civil service board. Most if not all of the cities that employ one of these civil service options have done so before adopting the collective bargaining legislation.

Regarding most other administrative matters, the state has been more helpful than intrusive. For example, the state has established defined-benefit personnel retirement accounts that are especially beneficial to smaller jurisdictions that find it difficult to operate independently. At the same time, larger jurisdictions may choose to participate in state programs or establish their own.

State government does not set standards for competitive bidding that localities must follow, nor must a position be created to administer purchases and contracts. State law, as well as local charters and ordinances, establish disclosure and voting standards to preclude conflicts of interest. At the same time, the state purchasing agency offers assistance to local units to make purchases under established state contracts. Such a service may not be especially beneficial to larger units or those linked to a purchasing cooperative, but for small units needing to buy a new police car, for example, the state contract can be very helpful.

Many limits on local discretion are those that have grown out of federal legislation. Federal statutes such as the Civil Rights Act, the Family and Medical Leave Act, the National Voter Registration Act, and more recent statutes dealing with health insurance and environmental matters impose significant constraints on the municipalities but especially on small units that have limited professional staffs.

Land-use regulation in Michigan is highly decentralized. All local units may establish planning commissions and adopt zoning ordinances, and many cities, villages, and townships have done so. A few counties have planning commissions and zoning ordinances, but the county's regulatory authority is restricted to those townships that do not have their own zoning. For the most part, the state does not regulate land use except from the perspective of natural resource development and environmental management. The state owns expansive areas of forestland that it manages. In addition to wildlife, state law protects wetlands over five acres as well as lakes and streams.

However, the state does not regulate land use in the general sense; neither does it develop comprehensive areawide plans for the use of land. These matters tend to be viewed as local responsibilities, and local units make many of the decisions. For example, the state gives local units discretion to apply the state's Farmland and Open Space Preservation Act. Local units also may make basic subdivision decisions, although this control recently has been reduced.

Economic Development

State government and local units are primarily partners rather than competitors for new development or redevelopment. The Michigan Jobs Commission (the state department dealing with business and economic development) directs the state's economic development promotion, assists in recruiting prospective developers, and often assists with grants for infrastructure and worker training for new developments.

In 1997 a major redevelopment cooperative program eliminated all taxes, except sales taxes, from certain "brownfield" areas (that is, contaminated sites lying idle) for a period of twelve years. Local units proposed "renaissance" zones to a state committee that made the final selections. The committee chose several urban and rural sites, and the state promotional efforts began. State and local officials hope that the tax incentives as well as the liability associated with contaminated sites will lead not only to remediation but to new productive use and eventual growth in the tax base.

Although some local jurisdictions are large enough to recruit development or redevelopment entrepreneurs and to finance certain public improvements, many do not have this capacity. Many local units have focused their development activities through downtown development authorities (DDAs). Such authorities sometimes receive outright grants from their local jurisdictions but mostly rely on tax increment financing, a mechanism that permits existing taxing jurisdictions to receive their usual tax revenue but not to benefit from the growth in the tax base in the DDA territory. The revenue growth is used to finance DDA projects.

Fiscal Autonomy of Local Governments

Grants of authority to local units are important if these governments are to be effective in meeting the needs of their residents and providing for the health and safety of visitors. Financial resources are also essential. The two major revenue sources are property taxes and intergovernmental revenue, or state aid. The cities' "other" category is also substantial and reflects, in part, the revenue that the largest cities generate from the personal income tax.

Local Revenues

Michigan cities and villages have a variety of financial resources, the principal one being the general property tax. Cities have authority to levy a personal income tax, and both units can not only assess fees and charges for services but also make special assessments for public improvements. In addition, the state shares revenue from several state taxes, and cities have capacity to incur debt. Counties and townships, in contrast, have little taxing discretion. They rely mainly on property taxes for about 60 percent of their revenue, about 5 mills (that is, $5 per $1,000 of property valuation) for counties and 1 mill for townships. Other revenues derive from service fees and special assessments. Figures 1–4 show revenues for a representative city, village, county, and township.

Home rule cities and villages depend significantly on local property taxes. The general authorizations in both the HRC and HRV Acts permit a levy to $20 per $1,000 of assessed valuation (or 20 mills), with the assessments set at 50 percent of market value. The 20 mill limit applies in each city, unless the local charter sets a lower limit. Many city and village charters do not authorize the full amount.

The HRC Act contains another provision that permits cities to levy an additional 3 mills for garbage and refuse collection. This represents a state intrusion into local responsibility, because

Fig. 1 City Revenues by Source, 1996

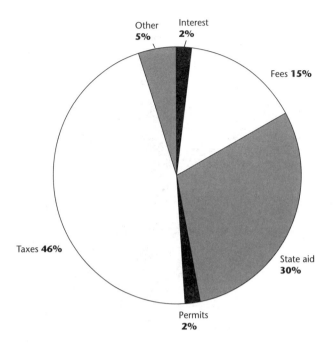

Source: Compiled by the Michigan Municipal League from F-65 Local Unit Fiscal Reports, Michigan Dept.

Fig. 2 Village Revenues by Source, 1996

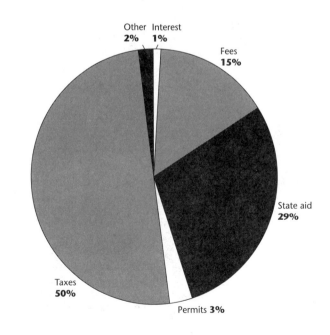

Source: Compiled by the Michigan Municipal League from F-65 Local Unit Fiscal Reports, Michigan Dept.

Fig. 3 County Revenues by Source, 1996

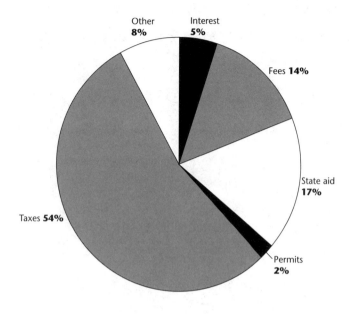

Source: Compiled by the Michigan Municipal League from F-65 Local Unit Fiscal Reports, Michigan Dept.

Fig. 4 Township Revenues by Source, 1996

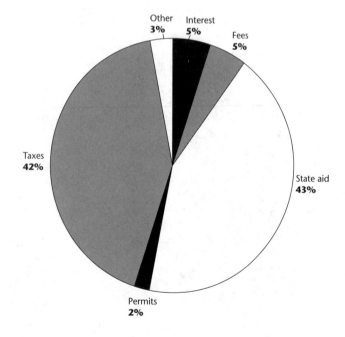

Source: Compiled by the Michigan Municipal League from F-65 Local Unit Fiscal Reports, Michigan Dept.

the act permits the levy even if a local charter is silent on the question. Many cities do not exercise this grant of authority. Most now charge user fees to pay for this service.

The property tax authorization is indirectly limited by at least two other constitutional provisions. A 1978 citizen-initiated constitutional amendment requires cities and other taxing units to reduce their maximum millage authorizations by a factor equal to the extent that property assessment increases exceed the consumer price index (CPI). Initially, this was not a difficulty for cities that levied a tax lower than their authorized rates. Over the years, however, the accumulated reduction, or "rollback," has had an effect. Rollbacks may be restored with voter approval.

A second constitutional change restricts the maximum increase in assessments to the annual CPI or 5 percent, whichever is less. This restriction was part of Michigan's 1994 school finance package that resulted in the greatest tax shift in the state's history. Schools now depend almost entirely on state grants for operating funds. The reform is slowing the overall rate of growth in municipal property tax bases. The assessed valuations are uncapped when property ownership changes.

Michigan cities, with voter approval, may also levy a personal income tax. About 20 do so. The general provision is that the city income tax is 1 percent on residents' income and 0.5 percent on that of nonresidents who work in the city. Special personal income tax rates of 3 percent (for city residents) and 1.5 percent (for nonresidents employed in the city) had been established for Detroit. Now, though, the legislature has directed the city to reduce these rates over a ten-year period to bring them in line with statewide city rates. This state policy gives home rule cities a degree of freedom and, at the same time, withholds it. City officials and voters decide whether to levy the tax—and indeed, whether to offset the income taxes by property tax decreases—but they may not choose the amount they wish to levy. The requirement for voter approval diminishes the authority of local officials.

County and township treasuries depend on the property tax as the main source of local revenues. General-law townships have authority to levy 1 mill without voter approval; charter townships can levy up to 5 mills. Counties have general authority to impose a general tax of 5 mills without voter approval. Most counties also depend on a series of voted millages for "popular" services such as senior citizen programs, libraries, police patrol, and jail operations. The generally low township tax and township entitlement to a per capita share in the state sales tax receipts results in a substantial reliance on state aid for general funds. Counties also receive a good deal of state assistance for human health, police, road services, and some general-purpose revenue. The HRC and HRV Acts permit cities, villages, counties, and charter townships to incur general-obligation debt to a maximum of 10 percent of the property tax base of a jurisdiction. (General-law townships have no overall debt limit.) Incurring debt that is supported by the authority to tax without limit as to rate or amount, however, requires voter approval. Another statute permits a municipality to incur, without a referendum, a limited obligation commitment, namely as a first obligation of the municipal treasury. Debt of this type is exempt from the 10 percent ceiling. Also exempt are revenue bonds or notes used to finance revenue-generating improvements. Generated revenues secure these debt instruments. A fourth type of debt instrument is a bond or note to make public improvements that directly benefit private property. The respective property owners (and the property itself) secure this form of debt.

For some time, the state has closely supervised the issuance of any debt. The current policy is to leave such scrutiny to lawyers, financial advisers, and investors. This not to say that the state is not concerned about the financial health of the municipalities. Although the state has established a number of rules, ultimately compliance is left to those who bear the risk of the debt instruments. In addition, the state operates a debt pool whereby smaller cities and villages can issue debt at a lower administrative cost.

Local Expenditures

Michigan law requires all local jurisdictions to adopt an annual balanced budget and to maintain the financial records in accordance with a state uniform chart of accounts that complies with standards of generally accepted accounting principles (GAAP). The budgeting provisions of this statute are limited and do not require the methods and procedures that fiscally sound governments otherwise follow. However, all local jurisdictions with their own budgets are required to hold public hearings on the proposed budget. The accounting side of this law, however, is much more prescriptive. Jurisdictions must employ the uniform chart of accounts and employ auditing firms to audit the records and prepare a report. Local units must file the audit reports with the state treasury department which monitors deficits.[16]

The state budgeting statute and audit requirements, as well as the state oversight of local finances, apply also to counties and townships. Michigan counties expend a good deal of their resources on courts, because the state's general trial courts (and many with limited jurisdiction) are associated with county government. Also noteworthy are the large proportions of both county and township expenditures on general government and public safety. The expenditures reflect the functions for which these governments are responsible. Figures 5–8 show expenditures for a representative city, village, county, and township.

Only rarely have Michigan local governments been in financial receivership. However, during the 1980s, three cities experienced major changes in their industrial tax bases and found themselves bankrupt or nearly so. A court-appointed financial

Fig. 5 City Expenditures by Source, 1996

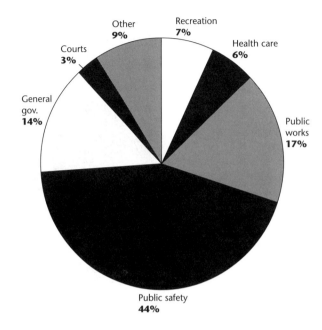

Source: Compiled by the Michigan Municipal League from F-65 Local Unit Fiscal Reports, Michigan Dept.

Fig. 6 Village Expenditures by Source, 1996

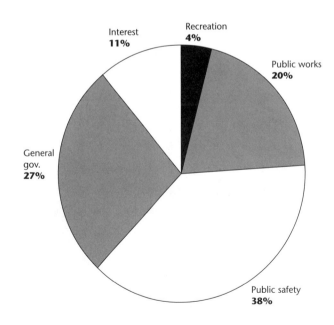

Source: Compiled by the Michigan Municipal League from F-65 Local Unit Fiscal Reports, Michigan Dept.
Note: Spending on health care and courts was 0%.

Fig. 7 County Expenditures by Source, 1996

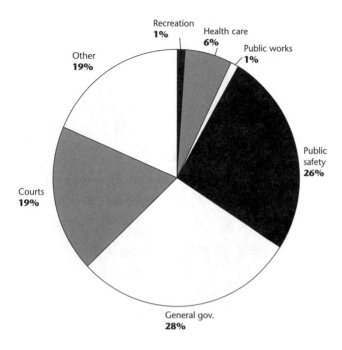

Source: Compiled by the Michigan Municipal League from F-65 Local Unit Fiscal Reports, Michigan Dept.

Fig. 8 Township Expenditures by Source, 1996

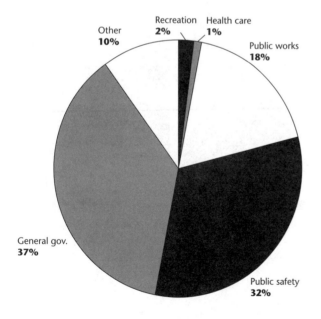

Source: Compiled by the Michigan Municipal League from F-65 Local Unit Fiscal Reports, Michigan Dept.
Note: Spending or Courts was 0%

receiver managed two of the cities; the third survived with the assistance of the state treasury department and generous state loans. Since then, the legislature established processes for state review of local financial conditions and for state takeover of municipal units in times of crisis. In general, the audit reports form the basis for state review. In jurisdictions where problems exist, local officials and the state can enter into an agreement outlining the steps to be taken. Alternatively, state officials can ask the governor to appoint a financial "receiver" who assumes the role of financial director for the crisis period.

State law requires each fund of a jurisdiction to be fiscally solvent. The oversight is evidenced largely in correspondence between state and local officials regarding certain accounts or funds that are in deficit. The usual letter from the state indicates that a deficit exists and asks officials to file a plan to eradicate the deficit within a three-year period.

State Government Grants-in-Aid to Localities

Several reasons explain the appropriateness of a larger unit, such as the state, to levy a tax and then share some of the proceeds with member units. Some taxes, such as the sales tax, are more efficiently collected by the larger unit, and the tax is also somewhat more difficult to avoid. Moreover, a state levy enables a degree of reallocation of fiscal resources from wealthier to poorer districts.

One of the long-standing state-collected, locally shared taxes is the general sales tax. By constitutional provision, the state shares with cities, villages, and townships approximately 1.3 cents from each 6-cent general sales tax collection. The amount is distributed on a per capita basis. The state also shares an additional portion of the state sales tax collections with these municipalities on a population and "tax effort" formula. These state-shared revenues are general revenues and not restricted as to use.

The third major state-shared tax is the gasoline and vehicle license tax. The first 10 percent of these revenues is designated for public transportation systems, most of which are now operated by special districts or authorities. Cities and villages share 21.8 percent of the remaining gasoline and vehicle tax collections on the basis of population and primary and secondary street mileage. Municipalities decide where and how to use these funds (for example, for routine maintenance, major repairs, or new construction). County road commissions and the state highway department each receive 39.1 percent of the total available for distribution.

In 1997 local units demonstrated their political strength in determining how revenues from a contentious gasoline tax increase were to be distributed. Gov. John Engler and his state transportation department asserted that as a condition of the tax increase, the state agency should take responsibility and money for some 9,000 miles of major intergovernmental roadways. With vigorous lobbying and public relations efforts, the local unit associations were successful in getting a tax increase passed without relinquishing control of roads.

Unfunded Mandates

A citizen-initiated constitutional amendment in 1978 directed the state, henceforth, to require no new services or activities or an increase in levels of services of local units without appropriating the associated cost—otherwise known as unfunded mandates.[17] Because of this provision, both the state and localities are on their guard. At the state level, legislators and other officials exercise care in the way they word new mandates. For example, the legislature does not mandate counties to create new judgeships where they are needed; instead, new legislation authorizes the particular board of commissioners to establish a new judgeship if they so wish. Even though the state now pays judges' salaries, the strategy protects the state from having to pay the cost of office space, courtroom, staff, and other related expenses. Another legislative strategy is to assign a new function to a state agency and in a few instances, actually to agree to pay the cost of new mandates. In the area of elections administration, for example, the state reimburses local expenses incurred in conducting a presidential primary election every four years. The state also has paid the cost of new equipment needed by county and municipal clerks to access a new state-level qualified voter file.

Local officials have asked the state attorney general and the courts to overturn numerous unfunded mandates. In a 1980 lawsuit, a school board (and later, some eighty other districts) successfully argued that the state was obligated to pay the costs of special education and transportation programs that the state had ordered local school districts to provide. (School boards in Michigan are independent of municipalities.) The state supreme court ordered the state to pay the plaintiff school districts some $200 million. But to keep other districts also from suing for reimbursement, the state legislature devised a plan to compensate the others as well. The total cost to the state has exceeded $800 million![18]

Access to Local Government

Local Elections

Cities and townships constitute the basic voter registration districts in Michigan. The clerks of the jurisdictions bear the administrative burden for nearly all elections in the state. Because these officers maintain the voter registration files and conduct both state and local elections, all voters must meet a common standard to register to vote. In cooperation with local clerks, the state established a qualified voter file (QVF) in 1998. Municipal clerks continue to administer registered voter files, but the burden is less onerous because most voter registration is incidental to driver's license and personal ID card applications. Local clerks derive their polling lists from the QVF network. The Michigan Elections Bureau oversees the administration of elections and voter administration.

In a related issue, state legislators and local clerks have tried to reach consensus on procedures to conduct elections by mail. Even though many voters cast absentee ballots by mail, municipal clerks protest that converting an entire election to a mail system will require changing some of the fundamental rules for processing election paperwork. This debate is likely to continue, because it has political implications. Republicans fear that Democratic candidates may be advantaged by larger turnouts in the large cities if they make it easier for residents to vote than it is now.

At the urging of county and municipal clerks, the state has tentatively limited the number of elections and permitted the exercise of local discretion. To reduce the frequency of elections, the state legislature established "standard" election dates for cities: an August primary and November general elections to be held in odd-numbered years. Most cities have adjusted to this schedule.

Two other provisions also limit the number of elections. Election scheduling commissions in each county schedule special elections for the purpose of filling vacancies or handling other issues. Taxing jurisdictions may now hold only two elections a year for the purpose of increasing taxes.

State statutes are silent on the matter of partisan or nonpartisan elections for cities and villages. The Michigan Municipal League reports that more than 90 percent of the cities have nonpartisan elections.[19] On the other hand, township and county officials (by state law) are elected on a partisan basis.

Cities and villages have no discretion to regulate campaign finances. State law, through the provision of the elections code, regulates this matter. The amount a person may contribute to a local political campaign is based on the population of the district and is limited to $500 (in a district of 85,000) and $3,400 (in a district of 250,000).[20]

Citizen Controls over Actions of Local Officials

The Progressive reforms of initiative and referendum are alive and well in Michigan. The HRC and HRV Acts require local charters to provide for initiative and referendum, for waiting periods to allow for petition filings, and for modest signature thresholds. The right of recall is highly regulated by state law and is less readily available because local officials seek to limit its use. Uniform procedures apply to all elected officials; for example, officials must obtain signatures equal to a certain percentage of votes cast in prior elections, and they must comply with deadlines. These are not matters left to home rule preferences; neither do local officials protest that the state legislature should leave these requirements to local discretion, even though most recall actions occur at the municipal and township level.

Recall petitions must contain signatures equal to 25 percent of votes cast for the office of governor in the jurisdiction during the previous election. The county election commission may deny petitions for lack of clarity or because of allegations of wrongdoing pertaining to actions in a previous term. However, any "clear and timely" allegation may be stated on the petition, and voters decide the veracity of allegations. Other restrictions stipulate that recall petitions may not be filed until the person has been in office for at least six months, and no recall election may be held during the six-month period preceding a regular election. These recall rules circumscribe Michigan court decisions, which generally have favored residents over officials. The higher signature requirement, along with numerous procedural hurdles and limitations, have somewhat reined in the use of the recall.

In terms of citizen responsiveness, the result of these rule changes is equivocal. On the one hand, the rules have made it more difficult to employ recall privileges and to use the process to harass public officials. On the other, the rules have come about, at least in part, because of irresponsible use of the privilege in some cases. Examples are losers filing for recall immediately after an election, small antagonistic groups carrying out a vendetta against one or two public officials, or filing just before an election to "stain" a candidacy.

In the wake of Watergate, the Michigan legislature enacted rules requiring open public meetings and public access to documents held by the jurisdiction. The Open Meetings Act (OMA) certainly changed the way some city councils conduct business. With a few exceptions, current rules require open meetings and advance notice of meetings. Citizens have a right to attend all such meetings and to address the council. Citizen plaintiffs in court actions are entitled to public representation or to recovery of legal fees if they prevail.

Despite numerous exceptions, the Freedom of Information Act (FOIA) permits a person to obtain a copy of any nonexempt document from the appropriate official within five days. Depending on the scope of the document, the cost of such retrieval is modest and limited by case law.

State-Local Relations

Michigan has almost a century of experience with municipal home rule. The philosophical goal at the time it was enacted into law (as it is today) is to give cities and villages a broad range of local discretion to act and adopt policies with minimal direction, influence, and interference from officials at the state capital. It was hoped that home rule would encourage local officials to be not only responsible but also responsive to the needs and wants of local residents. Moreover, home rule provisions would serve to restrain state legislators and other officials from using their powers to compel local officials to take certain actions. These aspirations largely have been realized.

Township officials and their state association, however, demonstrate little interest in formalizing a home rule relationship. Their lobbyists are active at the state capitol, and the legislature is sufficiently responsive to their demands. Rather than considering a major restructuring, township officials are content to battle over narrower issues.

County officials are also ambivalent about home rule. Although charter county government is available to all eighty-three counties, only Wayne County (Detroit) operates under its own home rule charter. The county home rule statute permits little flexibility, partly because local county officials argued that their positions should remain elected rather than appointed (a county home rule charter would put their elective independence at risk). Several counties have had elections to establish charter county government, but voters have not endorsed such a measure, except in Wayne County.

As state-local relations evolve, local governments likely will have more autonomy in some areas and less in others. Local discretion will thrive in terms of the form and structure of organizations. There are few indications that the state will interfere with those issues. Local autonomy, however, will decrease with respect to how local units perform their functions. If state government regulations continue to expand to govern the increasingly interdependent relationships among people and local units, the future likely does not bode well for more local autonomy. If, for example, the mobility of people or technological changes continue to increase, human interaction as well as intergovernmental activities will continue to increase; it seems likely, therefore, that state officials will increasingly call for statewide standards. Many distinctions based on local values will be sacrificed.

It appears, then, that state-local relations will become increasingly contentious. State officials currently find themselves in competition with localities on numerous issues, as evidenced by an ongoing battle between the state Department of Transportation and county and city road groups. In the area of educational performance, some state officials advocate state takeover of local schools whose students do not meet minimal scores on standardized state tests. Preserving farmland and open space is another potential area of conflict. The state does not have an overall plan for land use or even for regions of the state. Cities, villages, and townships administer land-control devices and usually do not exercise these powers collaboratively.

Local officials, especially those enjoying the support of their state associations, are not intimidated by the legal authority and political power of officials at the state level, especially that of state legislators. Rather, officials and lobbyists aggressively offer explanations, make demands, generate public support, and negotiate deals. Now that legislators are "term-limited" (six years in the state house and eight in the state senate), municipal representatives may become even more confident about their relative standing.

Home rule policy requires a knowledgeable and informed constituency, a constituency at both state and local levels that values highly the right of home rule. From the perspective of state officials, many issues have statewide significance requiring statewide uniformity. For example, because state and local governments rely increasingly on electronic technology to communicate and do their work, in a collaborative system, consistency and compatibility will be paramount, and officials at both levels will be held to stringent standards.

A further deterrent to expanded home rule is the fact that many decisions of the state legislature are initiated not by legislators but by outsiders. As the special interest groups make their claims, principles of home rule are accorded only secondary status rather than respected as consistent criteria for public policy making. The municipal home rule principle appears to serve as an effective barrier against state interference on matters of structure and organization and some administrative questions. But it is also clear that the municipalities have no guarantees that legislators will give priority to home rule principles when addressing the demands of other groups. If their standing and authority is not to wane, home rule units and other local governments will need to be ever vigilant.

Notes

1. Daniel J. Elazar, quoted in *Michigan Government and Politics,* ed. William P. Browne and Kenneth VerBurg (Lincoln: University of Nebraska Press, 1995), xxviii.

2. Michigan Constitution (1908), Article 8, section 20.

3. Michigan Constitution (1963), Article 7, section 22.

4. Michigan Constitution (1963), Article 8, section 2.

5. Michigan Public Acts 279, 1909; Michigan Compiled Laws Annotated, 117.1–117.38; Michigan Public Acts 278, 1909; Michigan Compiled Laws Annotated, 78.1–78.28.

6. Jefferson B. Fordham, *Model Constitutional Provisions for Municipal Home Rule* (Chicago: American Municipal Association, 1953).

7. For cities, Michigan Public Acts 279, 1909; Michigan Compiled Laws Annotated, 117.1–117.38. For home rule villages, Michigan Public Acts 278, 1909; Michigan Compiled Laws Annotated, 78.1–78.28.

8. *City of Detroit v. Walker,* 520 N.W.2d 133 (Mich.1994).

9. Michigan Constitution (1963), Article 4, section 29.

10. Michigan Compiled Laws Annotated, 729.101–729.106 (Repealed by PA 87, 1983); Michigan Compiled Laws Annotated, 141.503(2).

11. Michigan Public Acts 377, 1994; Michigan Compiled Laws Annotated, 125.271a.

12. Michigan Municipal League, *Michigan Municipal Review* (Ann Arbor: Michigan Municipal League, May 1997).

13. Michigan Compiled Laws Annotated, 117.7. The section establishes lower thresholds for cities that are seats of county government or villages that seek to become home rule cities.

14. Michigan Public Acts 278, 1909; Michigan Compiled Laws Annotated, 78.1–78.28. The author of this chapter serves as the chairperson of the state boundary commission.

15. Michigan Compiled Laws Annotated, 119.51.

16. The Michigan Municipal League compiles the financial data from reports filed with the state treasury department.

17. Michigan Constitution, Article IX, section 29.

18. *Durant v. Department of Education,* 557 N.W.2d 309 (Mich. 1980).

19. Michigan Municipal League, *Michigan Municipal Review.*

20. Michigan Public Acts 590, 1996; Michigan Compiled Laws Annotated, 169.252.

MINNESOTA

Philip H. Wichern

This project began during the author's sabbatical leave financed by the Department of Political Studies and the University of Manitoba. Work space and editorial comments were provided by Professor Thomas Scott, director of the Center for Urban and Regional Affairs, University of Minnesota, Minneapolis, where the author was visiting scholar (1995–1996). Special thanks for research assistance to Stan Peskar, League of Minnesota Cities attorney; the staff at the State of Minnesota Legislative Library; and the anonymous state and local officials who provided insights as well as information. Gerry Currie, state house committee researcher, provided information on the history of special legislation.

In 1894 and 1895 officials from Minneapolis and St. Paul petitioned the state legislature for special laws authorizing them to adopt and govern under home rule charters. Instead, in 1896 the legislature passed and voters approved a constitutional amendment guaranteeing that "any local government when authorized by law may adopt a home rule charter for its government. For almost a century, however, state law authorized only cities. By the 1920s most larger cities had adopted home rule charters, but home rule faded in significance for most local governments. Even when all municipalities were reclassified as cities in the 1970s, the number of home rule cities did not increase significantly. In the late 1980s, when several cities abandoned home rule, the question was asked, "Is home rule still alive?"[1] Home rule governance continued in 108 cities (including the state's most populated), and Ramsey County, which became the state's first home rule county in 1992. No further expansion of home rule is likely and in the broader contexts of state and local governing reviewed here, home rule has declined in significance.

Governmental Setting

In the late 1990s Minnesota governments benefited from robust state and national economies which, along with stringent fiscal restraints, produced state revenue surpluses and reduced pressures on local governments. Some of the state's surplus funded property tax rebates as well as increases in state transfers, such as the first increase in ten years for school districts and K–12 schools. Issues included property tax reform and how the projected state surpluses should be spent. Except for local control of schools and community-based planning and policing, issues of local autonomy (including home rule) were not on the state policy agenda. Instead, the policy trend was intergovernmental cooperation and public-private partnerships, especially in dealing with inner city crime and affordable housing, as well as in delivery of the state's highly regarded health care and social services programs.

Another prominent feature of Minnesota's governmental setting is the distinctions and tensions between the "Twin Cities" (that is, Minneapolis–St. Paul) and the "out-state" in terms of patterns of population concentration, economic development, and policy priorities. Of the 4.6 million residents in Minnesota in the mid-1990s, more than 2.8 million (61 percent) lived in the seven-county Twin Cities metropolitan area.[2] At the same time, there was significant development and population growth in six second-tier commuter counties (four in Minnesota and two in Wisconsin, across the St. Croix River to the east of the Twin Cities). In that larger metropolitan region, the population of residents and commuters approached 4 million and 83 percent of Minnesota's total population. The inner cities and poorer suburbs in that region elected a vocal and powerful group of Democratic-Farmer-Labor (DFL) state legislators who championed progressive legislation and programs that mandated additional responsibilities for all local governments without regard to home rule status.

In the 1990s the 17 percent of the state's population resided in out-state Minnesota, in smaller urban centers and in more rural and northern remote areas. They lived on the remaining farms and smaller cities in the state's south, central, and west (Red River valley) regions. Residents also clustered in or around the Lake Superior port of Duluth (the state's third largest city), on the state's "Iron Range," and around thousands of lakes in the state's central and northern areas. Residents of these areas and their elected representatives not only promoted out-state priorities and challenged "metro" dominance but also elected legislators who helped to fashion the state's progressive social, economic, and environmental programs which improved their regions. Home rule was not considered, but local rather than state policy making was a frequent out-state issue.

Home Rule in Minnesota

Historical Development

Minnesota's local governments were created when Minnesota was officially designated a separate territory in 1849. The first Territorial Assembly created counties, townships, and school districts by specific or "special" legislation.[3] Later that year, several hundred residents in the growing urban settlement on the Mississippi called St. Paul requested and were given separate status as "a town corporate." In 1854 St. Paul became the territory's first incorporated city with its own charter. By 1858, when Minnesota became a state, Minneapolis and six other cities obtained incorporation with their own charters, along with 106 towns. For the next forty years, efforts were made to curb the growing numbers of special laws, but the practice continued despite adoption of general "statutory" law which applied to all local governments or municipalities.

Nevertheless, officials from Minneapolis and St. Paul petitioned the legislature in 1894 and 1895 for special legislation that would allow their residents to write, adopt, and govern under home rule charters espoused by the national Home Rule Movement. After extensive hearings and debate, the state legislators rejected special legislation that would authorize home rule in three cities. Instead, in 1896 the legislators passed and voters approved constitutional amendments further limiting special legislation and allowing any local government authorized by state law to adopt a home rule charter by following the prescribed process of charter commission selection and referendum approval. Those amendments later became sections 3 and 4 of Minnesota's current constitution.

In 1896 the legislature passed the first enabling legislation authorizing Minnesota cities to adopt home rule charters. However, that privilege was not then or subsequently extended to other municipalities such as towns and villages or to any other local governments until 1987. Over the next quarter-century, sixty-five of Minnesota's ninety-two cities adopted home rule charters, including twenty-two of twenty-five cities with more than 5,000 residents. A prominent political scientist characterized the home rule amendment as "one of the most beneficial amendments ever added to the constitution."[4] A decade later the same expert concluded that home rule had "on the whole been successful," but it also "had fallen considerably short of perfection." Assenting to the expert's recommendations, the legislature rejected extending home rule to other local governments.[5]

Home rule faded as an issue as Depression problems became the focus of local, state, and federal actions. New state and federal mandates were applied to home rule cities as well as other local governments. After 1973, when all of Minnesota's munici-palities were reclassified as cities, most did not exercise their new option to become home rule cities. In the late 1980s two cities abandoned home rule, reducing the number to 108 (or 13 percent) of Minnesota cities. In 1987 Ramsey County, which includes St. Paul and the state capital, successfully lobbied for legislation authorizing it to create a charter commission that would draft a home rule charter. After voter approval in November 1992, Ramsey County officially became Minnesota's first home rule county.[6] However, separate legislation allowing other counties to follow Ramsey was "put on the shelf": it was not introduced in the following years, and other counties did not receive similar special legislation. There have been few other efforts to extend the home rule option to other local governments or to regional agencies such as the Metropolitan Council.

Definition of Home Rule

Section 4, Article 12 of the Minnesota Constitution begins with the guarantee that "any local government when authorized by law may adopt a home rule charter for its government." It then mandates that "a charter shall become effective if approved by such a majority of voters of the local government as the legislature prescribes by general law." The following section (section 5) provides that charter commissions will be prescribed by the legislature, along with general procedures for amending and repealing home rule charters. The laws that more fully define home rule were brought together to form Chapter 410 of the Minnesota Statutes. Section .015 defines a home rule charter city as "any city which has adopted . . . a (home rule) charter" by the procedures specified in the state's constitution and other provisions in that chapter. After 1987 those same procedures were applied to Ramsey County through an amendment specific to counties that was added to the chapter.

When the Minnesota Statutes were revised in 1973, all municipalities (cities, towns, villages, and one borough) were renamed and classified as either home rule or statutory "cities" (officially after July 1, 1976). A home rule charter city operates under chapter 410 of the Minnesota Statutes, whereas a "statutory city" is governed under Chapter 412. In 1995, 108 of Minnesota's cities (13 percent) were governed under home rule charters; 746 (87 percent) were "statutory" cities.[7]

Despite the legal distinctions, the operational differences between home rule and statutory cities are not always evident in their powers and functions. Home rule charters may authorize "any municipal powers which the Legislature could have delegated to the city as long as they are consistent with state statutes."[8] However, state statutes have mandated and limited local governments' activities, and charters can only authorize what is not in conflict with or superseded by state law. Also, only the powers designated in the home rule charter can be exercised. Most recent charters substitute for older listings of powers a general authorization allowing the city to exercise all the powers that state laws allow.

Home rule charters may also legally mandate organizational and electoral arrangements not prescribed for statutory cities in state laws. However, most home rule charters prescribe the same forms of local government organization as those forms prescribed by state law for statutory cities. Chapter 412 of the Minnesota Statutes limits the choice to one of three forms: the standard plan, Plan A, or Plan B. The standard plan provides for an elected mayor and small council, along with an elected city clerk. Plan A specifies a clerk appointed by the mayor and council, whereas Plan B allows the elected mayor and council to appoint a city manager. Most home rule cities (68 percent) operate under the standard plan or Plan A, as do an even higher percentage of statutory cities (80 percent). Only four home rule charters prescribe institutional arrangements not prescribed for statutory cities, and virtually all of those are "strong" mayor systems in which the mayor appoints key administrators with council approval.[9] In other words, in practice, the powers and form of governing in most home rule cities are similar to those found in statutory cities.

Structural Features

Although Minnesota's constitution bans special legislation for "any special or exclusive privilege, immunity or franchise," specific laws are allowed for local governments, as long as the local governing body or voters approve the special legislation before it becomes law (Article XII, sections 1 and 2). In each legislative session, special legislation requested by local officials is passed, such as the 1987 law allowing Ramsey County to write and adopt a home rule charter.

In matters of annexation, incorporation, merger, and boundary setting, Chapter 414 of Minnesota Statutes applies to both home rule and statutory cities without significant differences. In 1959 that legislation set statewide criteria and procedures for annexations, incorporations, and boundary changes and created the Minnesota Municipal Board, to which all applications for incorporation, annexation, merger, and detachment were required to be submitted for approval. The members of the board were directed to hold local hearings when parties contested applications and make decisions based on applying Chapter 414 criteria. The resulting decisions were made binding on the applicants, subject to judicial appeals (which were mostly unsuccessful). Chapter 414 and the Municipal Board dramatically reduced incorporations and increased the number of annexations, larger incorporations, and consensual boundary adjustments for forty years (only 12 of more than 1,000 cases were taken to court in 1992–1995). A 1997 law mandated a 1999 "sunset" of the board and other additions to Chapter 414, but the basic statutes still apply to home rule and statutory cities.[10]

Minnesota's 87 counties are mandated by state laws to provide a broad range of regional functions. Within those counties (and the cities located within those counties), 1,800 townships operated in the 1990s (1,000 less than in 1942). More than 1,500 were classified as rural townships, whose annual meetings and three elected supervisors administered a very limited range of rural services such as township roads and organization of volunteer fire fighting. The other 300 townships were classified as urban townships, which provided more extensive and urban functions in areas contiguous to or near cities. Although having some of the powers and responsibilities of cities, urban townships have not been granted the home rule charter option or access to all of the state funds available to cities and counties. The result is many conflicts between township residents who want more city services (and state funds available after annexation or incorporation) and other residents who want less services and oppose urban development, city services, and increases in property taxes.

Cities have extraterritorial powers, including the right to own and use property outside the city limits for city purposes, such as garbage dumps or city golf courses. In addition, a city may service and initiate annexation proceedings for areas outside its boundaries, if residents request urban services or the area demonstrably needs city services and lies within city planning areas specified for development and servicing.

Functions of Local Government

Functional Responsibilities

Minnesota state laws mandate and allow a wide range of functions for both cities and counties. These jurisdictions also are authorized to cooperate through joint powers agreements to undertake functions for the local good. Home rule charters may add requirements that are not prescribed by state laws to cities. For example, for localities to undertake new functions, some charters require referendums on new capital expenditures or a charter amendment for specific functions, since home rule jurisdictions must be empowered by their respective charters to act.

However, general patterns apply equally to home rule and non–home rule governments. Both cities and counties have been allocated broad authority to issue ordinances, to budget and finance (through taxes and borrowing), to administer and operate local facilities and a variety of public service systems (including public safety, courts, and corrections), and to plan and regulate land use. Cities retain primary jurisdiction for sanitation and for housing and urban renewal. Moreover, they may operate income-producing enterprises, such as municipal liquor stores, which are not authorized for counties or townships. However, counties are responsible for providing services for the state that are not provided even by larger cities. Perhaps the most important services are processing drivers' and vehicle licenses, recording motor vehicle ownership changes, and providing assessment and tax information to property owners. Important shared responsibilities include the supervision of elections, the collection and dissemination of electoral data, and the recording of property assessment and tax data.

In addition, many counties have sought and receive special legislation to expand their functions. For example, the state's most populous county (Hennepin, which includes Minneapolis) administers its own medical center, Level 1 Trauma Center and Teaching Hospital (in downtown Minneapolis), in addition to its own Health Plan, a solid waste incinerator, regional parks, and trails for light rapid transit, walking, and biking. Some counties operate housing and redevelopment authorities and economic development authorities, though those functions are more common to cities or special districts. In actual practice, then, counties provide many functions and facilities in the largest cities as well as state services to a much broader geographical area and larger population.

Primary and secondary education are the core functions of Minnesota's 458 school districts, and the schools that the districts administer (in addition to dozens of independent private schools statewide) are regional and local service providers for health and recreational services. School districts absorb an average of 47.7 percent of local property tax revenues throughout the state. Increasingly, school districts work with cities and counties in planning and facilities development.

In addition, more than 375 other local and regional districts perform important functions, including economic development, housing, soil and water conservation (along with watershed regulation), regional hospitals, mosquito and pollution control, regional parks and recreation management, and waste management.[11] Two-thirds of these special-purpose districts are authorized to finance themselves from property taxes directly, whereas the other districts finance themselves through revenues from their operations or grants from participating local governments and the state.

Several of Minnesota's efforts to develop regional cooperation are noteworthy. Of the twelve regional development commissions authorized by Chapter 462.473 of Minnesota Statutes, three dissolved in the early 1980s. However, in the 1990s, nine continued to plan and promote economic development in their multicounty regions. One of the most studied is the Metropolitan Council, which was created in 1968 to gather data on, plan for, and address problems of land-use development in the seven-county Twin Cities (Minneapolis–St. Paul) metropolitan area. During its first thirty years, members of the council were appointed by the governor: sixteen were appointed from districts in which the area was divided, and a chair was appointed at large. (All also served at the pleasure of the governor.) In 1994 the council's responsibilities were expanded to include administration of the metropolitan transit bus service, regional housing, and regional wastewater treatment.[12]

Given all of these local and regional governments (as well as state departments and agencies)—and the fragmented distribution of functions among them—cooperation (and conflict) is a critical factor in the delivery of local government services in Minnesota. The Minnesota Statutes have been amended to provide for many forms of local cooperation, including joint powers agreements and regional commissions and districts. A 1992 survey estimated an average of 8.5 agreements for each Minnesota city, a total of more than 7,000 for all cities in the state.[13] There were more agreements for public safety services, public works, and general government functions than for environmental services, parks and recreation facilities, community development, and various other functions. Extensive cooperative agreements exist for emergency and disaster responses, as was demonstrated by the response to the 1997 floods that ravaged areas along the Red and Minnesota Rivers. To encourage further development of cooperative arrangements, 1993 legislation created a state Board of Government Innovation and Cooperation that selects and funds pilot projects by local governments that demonstrate local and regional cooperation.

Administrative Discretion

Minnesota Statutes specify local government structures and legal and management standards but leave most of the actual operations to local governments, subject to state auditing and review. Until recently, local governments had discretion over administrative procedures, rules, and systems; however, "micromanagement" and "performance measurement" legislation was introduced in the mid-1990s. Contracting, purchasing, and bidding procedures are primarily within the powers of local governments but are subject to audit by the state auditor and investigation by the state attorney general's department. Land-use planning, zoning, and various types of land-use and building controls are in the administrative discretion of counties and cities.

Within the Twin Cities metropolitan area, the Metropolitan Council has additional review authority of comprehensive land use, transportation plans, and waste treatment administration powers. This authority constrains local development decisions and planning, which continue to be the ultimate responsibility of the local governments within the council's area of jurisdiction (7 counties, 140 cities, 50 townships, and 48 school and other special districts).

Throughout the state, local governments' discretion is limited by state requirements as well as by federal programs' mandates and incentives. The result is extensive paperwork that must be completed and bureaucratic rules that must be followed to provide local affordable housing, improved education, public safety, recreation, redevelopment, social services, and public transportation.

Economic Development

State statutes and executive policies (as well as sections in home rule charters) authorize cities to organize and fund a variety of economic development activities through either departments or separate economic development agencies. These latter agencies often combine commercial and physical land-use development under housing and redevelopment authorities (HRAs), economic redevelopment agencies (ERAs), or port authorities. Counties, cities, and urban townships cooperate in economic development through regional development commissions (RDCs) authorized by the Regional Development Act. In the 1990s there were nine RDCs that were jointly financed by the state and by local governments.[14]

Probably the most important policy tool for local economic development in the 1980s and 1990s was tax increment financing (TIF). TIF allows the increased increment of tax capacity attributable to new development to be dedicated to the repayment of bonds borrowed to facilitate the development. Initially intended to benefit inner cities' urban renewal, TIF quickly became a means for cities to attract industries and land development by guaranteeing the repayment of bonds used to buy, clear, service, and improve development sites (both in inner cities and in suburbs). However, the school districts and counties in which city TIF was created soon discovered that their revenues were also being limited. As a result, in the 1990s, the use of TIF by cities was increasingly challenged and limited by state laws.

Fiscal Autonomy of Local Governments

Local Revenues

Minnesota laws and regulations limit revenue sources for local governments. The local property tax remains a primary source of funding for all types of local governments. Cities are allowed to operate revenue-producing enterprises, and other local governments may charge for the use of facilities or services. A 1995 state law provided for creation of toll roads, but the only one initiated (in 1996) failed to win the approval of all the cities through which the toll road would have been built. Table 1 provides a breakdown of revenue sources for Minnesota cities and counties in the mid-1990s.

The ad valorem local property tax includes assessment and rate-setting functions, the administration of which is assigned by state law to employees of counties and larger cities. The nation's most complex system of statewide property tax classifications and formulas—which are used to calculate local taxes, property tax credits, and local government aid that must be included in budgets—is administered by state finance department employees. The foundation of the system is ad valorem market value evaluations by county and city assessors. State law established class rates; that is, the percentage of each property's market value subject to tax. As well as tax rates, each year state finance department employees also calculate and distribute to local governments an amount of homestead and agriculture credit aid (HACA), which is deducted from each local jurisdiction's tax levy and forwarded to local governments from state funds in addition to other state grants, thereby reducing property owners' actual levies. In 1995 the amount forwarded to local governments was over $595 million.[15]

Table 1. Revenue Sources of Minnesota Cities and Counties, 1995 (in percent)

Revenue sources	Counties	Cities (more than 2,500)	Cities (less than 2,500)
State grants	28.2%	27.3%	34.0%
Federal grants	12.4	4.3	6.5
County and local grants	–	1.2	1.9
Property taxes	39.9	36.2	26.0
Service charges	7.7	6.9	7.9
Other sources	11.8	24.1	23.7
Total revenues	$3.1 billion	$2.5 billion	$290 million

Source: Online reports from the Office of the State Auditor, State of Minnesota (http://www.osa.state.mn.us).

State laws allow larger cities to levy hotel and sales taxes, but local governments are not authorized to add their own local income taxes to the state and federal income taxes or to operate lotteries or casinos. Local governments can charge fees and make charges for particular services taxes. Cities are allowed to operate and earn revenues from enterprises such as municipal liquor stores, golf courses, ice arenas, swimming pools and beaches, airports, convention centers, and other revenue-producing enterprises. In addition to receiving revenues from funds that they have invested, cities and counties may realize revenues from increased taxes related to redevelopment projects, after the loans required to finance such development have been repaid and the taxes designated for loan retirement through tax increments have expired.

In the 1990s Minnesota local governments received less federally derived revenue (including grants-in-lieu of taxes for local federal properties and institutions). Federal aid was increasingly combined with additional state aid and mandates into shared costs programs which also required local expenditures. Minnesota local governments were required to fund increasing proportions of the shared cost programs that they provided to their residents.

Local Expenditures

In the 1990s the largest percentage of expenditures in many counties comprised the budgets for county health and social services, averaging 34 percent, except in the most populous county, where budgets accounted for 62 percent of expenditures. Most cities spent less than 15 percent on such expenditures but much more on police and fire services (over 30 percent). Counties averaged 16 percent for both public safety and general government operations, and 17 percent of their expenditures were allocated for highway maintenance. Cities spent significant percentages of their budgets on public works (including streets and roads), through direct expenditures and through capital debt payments. Expenditures for parks and recreation facilities, libraries, and other government activities were less than 5 percent on average.

Minnesota law and the state finance department prescribe budgeting procedures, reporting requirements, accounting and auditing arrangements, as well as the "truth in taxation" process, which replaced limits on current expenditures. Many other aspects of local governments' financial operations are limited, including their capacity to borrow and form tax increment financing contracts. Local governments are required to maintain balanced current budgets; budget shortfalls (or surpluses) are carried over into the next year. Auditing and state involvement is swift when local governments are reported to be in financial trouble, to protect against bankruptcy or receivership.

State Government Grants-in-Aid to Localities

As with property tax assessment and levies, Minnesota has developed an extensive and complex web of shared-cost programs and funding for particular local government activities. However, in the 1990s two state aid programs provided large amounts of general-purpose funds (the use of which was determined by the local governments receiving them): homestead and agriculture credit aid (HACA) and local government aid (LGA). Although $262 million less than the amount of HACA credits, $337 million in LGA funds were distributed to cities (as well as $3 million to townships) in 1995.[16] Distribution to individual cities and townships was based on ensuring past levels of aid and applying measures of local government need. Local governments that had received high levels of aid in the past, such as inner cities, received more aid because they had decreased populations (but an increased need for housing for the elderly) and declining commercial and industrial property values. Faster growing suburban cities and eligible urban townships with growing residential, commercial, and industrial property values received less aid. In addition, a tax-sharing plan provided for 40 percent of the increase in commercial and industrial property values for needy jurisdictions in the Twin Cities metropolitan area. These funds were to be pooled and redistributed based on the formula used by the state finance department.

Unfunded Mandates

Unfunded (and partially funded) mandates were major components of local government expenditures in Minnesota during the 1990s. Not only was there an accumulation of federal and state mandates for general services and programs, but also there were numerous specific requirements included in state laws regarding employees, facilities, citizens' and animal rights, and many other aspects of local governing. In the 1990s new laws produced additional mandates. State oversight increased the reporting requirements of local governments to state agencies whose role it was to investigate and take action when previously legislated mandates were not being followed. Home rule did not appear to make a significant difference in terms of either number or type of mandates or responses to them by local governments, but much more study of this feature is needed to make reliable conclusions.

Access to Local Government

Local Elections

Minnesota Statutes prescribe many details and features of local elections. Cities and counties are responsible for administering voter registration and elections. Statutory cities' election dates are set by statute, but home rule charters may provide for other dates and time periods. However, home rule charters must conform to state laws and relevant court cases. For example, although some home rule charters authorize recall and impeachment elections which are not allowed in statutory cities, court cases have established that home rule officials (like other local government officials) can only be removed by recall for malfeasance or nonfeasance, which most often includes proven financial mismanagement and stealing or other criminal actions.

The general trend in Minnesota is toward more flexible and easier voter registration for local as well as general elections. Again, home rule charters are not as significant as state laws in determining which procedures and rules are enforced. State investigation of complaints and irregularities is extensive for both home rule and non–home rule local government elections. Despite efforts to make voting easier, voting levels are not necessarily higher in home rule cities (or in Ramsey County) than in other local jurisdictions. Citizen participation was lower in local elections that were held separately from state elections in all jurisdictions, except in those jurisdictions in which high-profile local campaigns were waged by candidates or issue-advocacy groups.

Citizen Controls over Actions of Local Officials

Home rule charters can authorize citizen controls not prohibited or authorized in general legislation. For example, home rule charters can and do provide for initiative and referendums on matters such as property acquisition. Charters can mandate proportional representation or representation by wards or at large. However, most of these citizen controls are not mandated by charters, and the home rule charters that authorize them usually limit their use, as do state laws.

In setting local budgets, local governments are required to follow procedures mandated by the 1988 reform known as "truth in taxation," which requires every local government and taxing jurisdiction to disclose proposed local levies and to allow public feedback. By the middle of September each year, a tentative budget must be completed, and the resulting proposed property tax levy must be certified to the county auditor. The budget and tax levy must also be publicized in local papers, and property owners must be informed by mailed notices. In the two months following the announcement of the proposed levy, each local government must hold at least two well-publicized public meetings at which the budget and levies are presented and taxpayers' comments heard. Only after those requirements are completed can local governments' budgets be finalized.

State laws require referendum approval for the borrowing of funds for schools and cities. Some home rule charters prescribe even more stringent requirements for borrowing for large expenditures than state laws prescribe (especially in election years) for taxpayers to exercise control over local budget decisions. However, few (if any) members of the public attend the required meetings, other than the local public officials who must hold the meetings.

Public access to local government meetings and information is mandated by a state open meeting law that also covers records. The minutes of meetings and other relevant information of virtually all local governments must be available upon request, within reasonable terms of confidentiality and costs. However, although metropolitan counties and cities cooperate with cable television companies to broadcast coverage of county board and city council meetings (which they are not required to do), relatively few citizens view the televised meetings or access the information available at local libraries and government offices. Therefore, official openness and provisions for citizen participation do not necessarily translate into local control by citizens over local officials' actions.

With regard to the impacts of home rule, there is no evidence that citizen involvement or control is significantly higher in home rule than in statutory cities. Neither is there evidence that after initially high levels of involvement in charter writing and adoption, home rule governing makes a significant long-term difference in voter turnout. Voters and local officials may have more control over local spending and recall of local officials in home rule cities (depending on how the charter is written), but the degree of control has increasingly been limited by the expansion of state (and federal) laws and funding regulations.

State-Local Relations

In Minnesota, home rule does not differentiate a local government's functions, funding, or levels of citizen participation. Home rule is limited to larger cities and Ramsey County. Other than Ramsey County's adoption of a home rule charter in the early 1990s, there has been little recent development or even interest in home rule. Statutory cities and other local governments' powers have been expanded by general and special legislation; home rule, therefore, is a local option more useful to res-

idents who want to require particular processes such as referendums on ordinances and borrowing. Nevertheless, home rule charter provisions must conform to state laws and changing state mandates (for example, "truth in taxation" requirements for local budgeting). Home rule charters will continue to be used in the cities and counties in which they now exist, but home rule is not likely to become the major trend or issue it was a century ago.

Notes

1. Stan Peskar, "City Home Rule: Is It Still Alive in Minnesota?" *Minnesota Cities* 74, no. 12 (December 1989): 8–10.

2. In 1995 Minneapolis's estimated population was 365,889, and St. Paul's was 271,120. The seven counties included Ramsey (the state's smallest), Hennepin (the most populated, with more than 1 million residents in and around Minneapolis), and "first-ring" counties, including Anoka, Washington, Dakota, Scott, and Carver. The total 1995 population was estimated to be 2,448,770 (Metropolitan Council Forecasts, *Blueprint Supplement*, 10 October 1996).

3. See William Anderson, *City Charter Making in Minnesota* (Minneapolis: Bureau for Research in Government, University of Minnesota, 1922), 3.

4. Ibid., 19.

5. William Anderson, *Local Government in Minnesota* (Minneapolis: University of Minnesota Press, 1935), 69, 71.

6. Michele Timmons, Judy Grant, Teri Popp, and Heidi Westry, "County Home Rule Comes to Minnesota," *William Mitchell Law Review* 19 (1993): 811–870.

7. *The Minnesota Legislative Manual 1995–1996* (St. Paul: Election Division, Secretary of State, 1996).

8. Joel Jemnik, *Handbook For Minnesota Cities*, 6th ed. (St. Paul: League of Minnesota Cities, 1993), 51.

9. *Minnesota Legislative Manual 1993–1994* (St. Paul: Election Division, Secretary of State, 1994), 286–298. The charters of Minneapolis and St. Paul create "strong" mayor systems. The Ramsey County charter specifies a county board of commissioners–county administrator system similar to the form of government that existed before the home rule charter and that exists in surrounding counties.

10. The 1997 amendment transferred the Minnesota Municipal Board's functions to the Office of Strategic and Long Range Planning in the state planning agency, Plan Minnesota. Another amendment created a process for alternative dispute and arbitration processes. See Minnesota Statutes, Chapters 414.11 and 572A.015.

11. *1992 Census of Governments*, vol. 1 (Washington, D.C.: U.S. Department of Commerce, Bureau of the Census, 1994), 3 (table 3).

12. For more information on the Metropolitan Council and related politics, see Myron Orfield, *Metropolitics* (Washington, D.C.: Brookings Institution; Cambridge, Mass.: Lincoln Institute of Land Policy, 1997).

13. Beth W. Honadle and Patricia Weir, *Choices for Change: Local Government Cooperation and Restructuring in Minnesota* (St. Paul: University of Minnesota Extension Service Distribution Center, 1995).

14. *Minnesota Legislative Manual 1993–1994*, 240.

15. See "State Spending for Local Government Aid," available from the State of Minnesota Web site: http://www.mnplan.state.mn.us/reports/cashflow/govaid.html.

16. "State Spending for Local Government Aid," State of Minnesota. For more information, see John Tomlinson, "The History of Local Government Aid to Cities," *Minnesota Cities* 77, no. 1 (January 1992): 10–12.

MISSISSIPPI

Annie Johnson Benifield

Thanks are expressed to W. Martin Wiseman, Director, John C. Stennis Institute of Government, Mississippi State University, for his review and comments.

Mississippi is the least populous, urbanized, and economically developed state in the Deep South. Almost 50 percent of its people live in rural areas, and a quarter live below the federal poverty line.[1] The Mississippi constitution and statutes centralize power in the state legislature, and that has proven to be a formidable obstacle to local governance. The state continues to function with a political culture that originated in an exclusively rural and agrarian past; its political apparatus still struggles to meet the needs of a mostly rural, poor, and an uneducated populace while parts of the state are rapidly undergoing urbanization. In an effort to address the changing needs of its citizenry, the state of Mississippi granted some autonomy to counties and municipalities in the 1980s.

Governmental Setting

Located within Mississippi's 82 counties are 297 cities (28 of them with a population of 10,000 or greater), 159 school districts, and 345 special districts.[2] The special districts are single-purpose governmental entities created by constitutional amendments and state statutes to carry out state functions. A total of 883 governing bodies currently operate within the state, and there are 1,400 geographical taxing districts. Counties perform a variety of important functions for the state and are also the most important units of local government, due to the rural nature of the state.

Jackson, the state capital, is located in Hinds County. Hinds, Rankin, and Madison Counties constitute one of the three metropolitan statistical areas in the state. The Jackson metro area has more than 100,000 inhabitants. Of the two other statistical areas, one extends into Tennessee and encompasses only one county in Mississippi: Desoto. The other is located on the Gulf Coast, in Hancock, Harrison, and Jackson counties. This area is the mostly rapidly growing part of the state and is home to a number of recently constructed gambling casinos. Owing to the presence of these casinos, Mississippi has done well in economic performance, despite the fact that much of the state is extremely rural and poverty-stricken.

Hinds County is the most populous county in the state, with 254,000 residents, whereas Issaquena has fewer than 2,000, which would not qualify that area as a city, according to the state's classification of municipalities. For the most part, Mississippi is still a rural state, since the majority of its population lives in areas having fewer than 2,500 residents, which is the U.S. Census definition of urban.

The Mississippi state constitution sets up a governing structure in which the primary source of power is the state legislature. Although there is some evidence of two-party politics occurring in the state, the legislature is dominated by Democrats, who control 69 percent of the 174 seats. However, the reverse is true in the congressional delegation; Republicans control four of seven seats in the U.S. Congress, including both Senate seats. Evidence of a two-party system is strongest in the executive branch. In 1991, voters elected the first Republican governor since the 1870s, and they reelected him in 1995. The state apparatus contains a plural executive, in which the governor is the weakest link. All executive officials are elected statewide and exercise power separate and distinct from the governor. Democrats control most of the statewide elected positions. The governor exercises no independent control over these elected officials.

Home Rule in Mississippi

Historical Development

The state of Mississippi functions under a constitution written in 1890, when the southern planter class took power back from the carpetbaggers and African Americans following Reconstruction. This is the fourth such document written since Mississippi became a state in 1817. The existing constitution establishes the fundamental structure and government of Mississippi. Few changes have been instituted to alter the structure that protects the southern way of life, which includes powerful, aristocratic, agrarian planters and landowner interests. Low property taxes and the consolidation of power in the state legislature, rather than in local government, is reflective of these interests. The current constitution has been amended approximately 119 times in a little more than a hundred years. Mississippi's constitution is accused of hobbling gubernatorial authority, sustaining an unwieldy state bureaucracy, and restricting local governments.[3] In order to alter their structure or institute fundamental changes, local governments frequently go to the legislature to get local or private legislation passed or to amend the constitution.

Definition of Home Rule

Home rule is the power granted to local units of government to exercise some autonomy in deciding the form of political structure and to exercise some local fiscal control. The Municipal Home Rule Act, passed by the state legislature in 1985, states:

The governing authorities of every municipality of this state shall have the care, management and control of the municipal affairs and its property and finances. In addition to those powers granted by specific provisions of general law, the governing authorities of municipalities shall have the power to adopt any order, resolutions or ordinances with respect to municipal affairs, property and finances which are not inconsistent with the Mississippi Constitution of 1890, the Mississippi Code of 1972, or other laws of the State of Mississippi.[4]

This grant of power by general law allows local governments to act if no state statute or constitutional provision explicitly deals with a particular matter. The constitution grants the legislature exclusive jurisdiction over local government affairs.[5] The Mississippi Supreme Court affirmed that cities owe their existence to the state legislature, which has absolute powers over them.[6] The legislature, in granting home rule authority to municipalities, specifically excluded the authority to levy taxes of any kind or increase the levy of any authorized tax; issue bonds of any kind; change the requirement, practice, or procedures for municipal elections or establish any new elective offices; change the structure or form of municipal government; permit the sale, manufacture, distribution, possession, or transportation of alcoholic beverages; grant any donations;[7] or regulate, directly or indirectly, the amount of rent charged for leasing private residential property in which the municipality does not have a property interest, unless such actions are specifically authorized by another statute or law of the state of Mississippi.[8] State law must be followed in all of the above instances.

The power of municipalities to assess property, levy taxes, borrow money, and contract debts is still controlled by the legislature. Municipalities have the power to amend their special charter only by following the manner and method specified by state statute.

The legislature has made other efforts to increase local autonomy in Mississippi as well. A home rule provision for counties went into effect on October 1, 1989. The County Government Reorganization Act 1988 requires each county in the state to construct and maintain roads and bridges on a countywide basis unless exempted by a majority of the qualified voters of the county.[9] The statute grants counties the authority to make and execute policies in property and finances that are not forbidden by the constitution or by state statutes. Limitations similar to those in the home rule statute for cities are mentioned in the county statute. However, Mississippi seems inclined to grant more autonomy to municipalities than to counties, since counties are appendages of the state and are directly responsible for carrying out state functions.

Structural Features

The primary source of municipal powers is the legislature, whereas county powers come primarily from the state constitution and state statutes. Periodically, municipalities seek local and private acts from the state legislature even though the legislature has granted limited home rule authority. A municipality often seeks such acts when it wishes to address a problem germane only to that locality and the authority has not been provided by general law. Theoretically, under home rule, municipalities would be free to act without requesting such a provision; however, it is still unclear to the municipalities, especially those in areas where urbanization is rapid, how much latitude they have or specifically which powers they may exercise.

Optional forms of government set forth by statutory law fall into four categories: weak mayor–board of aldermen, strong mayor–council, council-manager, and commission. Until 1892 all municipalities received special charters from the state legislature. These charters gave a city its name, established its boundaries, designated its form of government, and provided specific political and corporate powers. The legislature enacted more than 802 separate statutes for the creation of 295 municipalities. In 1892 the legislature drafted a general law charter for all municipalities, which initially specified a mayor–board of aldermen form of government (the other forms were added as options later). Those municipalities already in existence in 1892 were given the option of retaining their special charter or conforming to the new provision.[10] Approximately twenty-three municipalities continue to use the original private charter granted by the state.

All municipalities with more than 2,000 residents are classified as cities. Cities may adopt the commission form of government whether they function under the general law or special charters. Cities with a population less than 10,000 tend to retain the mayor–board of alderman form of government. Seventy percent of the 297 cities have failed to change from that form of government, as allowed by state statute. The city of Columbus, the eighth-largest city, still operates under its original private charter even though its population exceeds 20,000.[11] The private charter restricts the city's ability to address the changing needs of an ever increasing urban population.

The power of the mayor in the mayor–board of aldermen form of government (also known as the charter form of government, since it was the only permissible form in 1892) is weak, and the board of aldermen dominates policy making. Statutory law provides that cities of less than ten thousand people elect five members to the board of alderman, and cities of ten thousand or more elect seven. Power is jointly shared by the mayor and the board of aldermen, with each exercising some power independent of the other. Mayors are simply figureheads and can vote only to break a tie.

Municipalities with populations of 300 to 1,999 are designated as towns by the constitution. When less than 300 residents live in an area, it qualifies as a village. Villages and towns must adopt weak mayor–strong council form of government. Mississippi has 167 towns and 24 villages.[12] If the population of a village drops below 92 according to the last census count, state statute provides for automatic dissolution, and the county assumes control of the unincorporated area.

In 1976 the state legislature added the "strong" mayor–council structure as an acceptable form of government for municipalities.[13] Under this form, power is consolidated in the hands of a single individual—the mayor. The mayor exercises almost complete autonomy regarding hiring, firing, and budget planning and holds veto power; however, the appointment of department heads requires a majority vote by the city council for approval. Council approval is also required for the city budget. The size of the elected council—five, seven, or nine members—is dependent on the population of the city. In 1976 Bay St. Louis was the first city in Mississippi to adopt this form of government. By 1996 seven of the twenty-eight cities in Mississippi with a population great than 10,0000 had a mayor-council form of government. Ten of the largest municipalities adopted the strong mayor–council form: Jackson, Biloxi, Gulfport, Bay St. Louis, Greenwood, Hattiesburg, Laurel, Tupelo, and Meridian. The last five converted from the commission to the strong mayor–council form. The primary reason for making these structural changes is to meet the changing needs of the citizenry as a result of urbanization.

The procedure for changing the form of municipal government varies. Any municipality may adopt the mayor-aldermen (code charter) form by a majority vote of electors; if the question is voted down at a special or general election, it may not be revisited for four years. The procedure for adopting the mayor-council form is more complicated and requires a petition signed by 10 percent of the qualified voters within the city's jurisdiction (20 percent of qualified voters if the population is less than forty thousand). Within ten days of receiving the petition, the municipal clerk must determine that the signatures are in order and, if so, certify the petition. An election is required, and a majority of the voters must approve the ballot measure. If the question is voted down, it may not be revisited for two years.

Under the council-manager form, a municipality has a mayor and five council members.[14] Any city can select the council-manager plan, but so far only three have done so: Pascagoula, Gautier, and Picayune. (Moorehead and Grenada are special charter cities on council-manager plans.) Under state law, this plan requires the city council to hire a professional manager with a four-year college degree to operate the city on a day-to-day basis. The council exercises exclusive power concerning the hiring and firing of the manager. When a mayor exists under this structure, he or she performs primarily ceremonial duties but may also exercise formal legislative power by voting.

Until the 1980s the largest cities in Mississippi used the commission form of government.[15] Three commissioners are elected, with each having equivalent power in the decision-making process. Now only Vicksburg implements it. That city has a two-to-one black majority in its mayor and two commissioners. They are resisting inquiries from suburban white groups about change in form.

Clarksdale claims to have a commission form but through the years has expanded its council to five or six members and now more closely resembles the mayor-alderman (or code charter) form. In Clarksdale, the executive and administrative functions are not assigned to specific commissioners. The mayor votes only when there is a tie. Commissioners serve as department heads and implement the policies that they made in their capacity as policy makers. This structure fragments the power of government among the three individuals who perform both legislative and executive responsibilities. In spite of the city's overall needs, each commissioner focuses on his or her departments' needs. This is conceivably the least effective form of local governance, since the entire city's needs are not addressed systematically. Equal disbursement is one method used to eliminate acrimony among commissioners, and that, too, tends to undermine good governing. Eventually, legal challenges by citizens may result in the discontinuation of this structural form of city governance in Mississippi because commissioners are elected at-large instead of by wards or districts, as increasingly is the case in Mississippi and other states.

Through general law, the state authorizes cities to annex property in unincorporated areas.[16] Annexation can be initiated by city ordinances or resolution or by petition by residents. An area can be taken into a municipality if its residents petition to become part of a specific community. Any area in a county that is not part of an existing municipality and is located adjacent to a municipality can be annexed.[17] According to state statute, a municipality must demonstrate its ability to provide services to any area it wishes to annex. The annexed area is still responsible for any indebtedness incurred by the county, school district, or special district of which it was a part. Municipalities are required by statute to submit an improvement plan for the area and a schedule for accomplishing such improvements. State statute states that annexation can take place with a majority vote by the city council without a referendum being required. Once notice is posted and a hearing is held, the city council adopts a resolution effectively annexing the affected area. Deannexation can be achieved by using the same procedures specified for citizen-initiated annexation.

Only municipalities with a population of 100,000 or more can incorporate into their boundaries properties constituting an airport or air navigational facility. So far, only Jackson, the state capital, is able to take advantage of this provision. As the population increases along the Mississippi Gulf Coast, the cities of Biloxi and Gulfport may soon be able to take advantage of this statute and annex the Harrison County Airport.

Counties in Mississippi were originally prohibited from exercising any autonomy in deciding their structure. The state constitution and statutes set forth the framework for county officials and their duties.[18] Neither the constitution nor statutory law provides any discretion to counties in the selection of officials. Although counties, like cities, are general-purpose governments, counties and cities are very dissimilar in the powers the state allocates to them.

The counties in Mississippi differ not only in geographical size but also population. The population of four counties in Mississippi exceeds 100,000, whereas ten have less than 10,000 inhabitants. Only twelve counties in Mississippi have a population over 50,000. The majority of counties are predominantly rural, and therefore county government is essential in providing services to residents. The constitution establishes the governing structure for counties.

County officials serve as extensions of the state's bureaucratic structure by carrying out its mandated functions. The constitution states that all counties must have the following four positions, which are elected at-large: county clerk, circuit clerk, treasurer, and sheriff. The commission form of government preserves existing political practices and maintains the status quo, so there has been little change in the power structure of rural communities in Mississippi.[19]

The board of supervisors is the legislative body directly responsible for policy making in a county.[20] Supervisors perform both legislative and executive functions. They not only head departments but also prepare and adopt the annual budget for the county. Power is further fragmented into different departments, which include county road maintenance, bridges, ferries, courthouses, jails, hospitals, health departments, libraries, and garbage disposal. Since Mississippi is predominantly rural, maintenance of local roads often dominates the policy agenda in many communities that are not part of an incorporated area.[21]

Most governing provisions for local units of government come from statutory law rather than from the state constitution.

The state constitution, however, sets the term and often the salary of elected officials at the county level. The county sheriff is one of the most powerful individuals in rural communities in Mississippi. The state constitution bases the sheriff's salary on the population of the county. For the sole purpose of determining other salaries, the legislature divides counties into eight classes based on assessed valuation of real, personal, and public service corporation property.[22] In order to abolish a county position that is specified by statute or the constitution, the county must obtain from the legislature private legislation or an amendment to the constitution. This is just one illustration of how the state limits the autonomy of county governments. The constitution gives the legislature the power to determine the mode for filling vacancies at the county level, which further limits the counties' control over local matters.

Until 1988 all counties were subdivided into five units called beats. Under this governing system, each beat has approximately the same population and elects a single representative to the board of supervisors. The five members of the board have equal power in the decision-making process. One member is chosen to serve as president and is responsible for presiding over meetings, although no additional grant of power results from serving in this position.[23] Each supervisor is an executive in his or her own jurisdiction. The county budget is divided equally among members to spend in their respective areas. The state allows a minimum salary of $20,000 for this part-time position, a figure that increases depending on the valuation of property in each county.

In 1988 the state legislature approved the County Government Reorganization Act, which allowed counties to change from the beat system to the unit system. Forty-four of the eighty-two counties have done so. Whereas the beat system fragmented power, since each commissioner zealously guarded his or her turf irrespective of the county's needs, the unit system facilitates more systematic countywide planning, if only in a single policy area. Community-wide needs are assessed and revenue is distributed according to these needs, instead of evenly among the commissioners as under the beat system.

Functions of Local Government

Functional Responsibilities

The state legislature grants general powers to municipalities in certain policy areas. Municipalities are required to address a variety of public issues. They can levy and collect taxes and appropriate municipal funds to address public health, safety, and welfare concerns. They can create hospitals, parks, schools, waterworks, electric utilities, houses of correction, cemeteries, and sewers. Additional state statutes grant municipalities the power to change by ordinance the meeting dates of the governing authority; sue and be sued; purchase and hold real and personal property for municipal purposes; sell and convey such property; acquire equipment and machinery by lease-purchase; donate surplus goods to certain public schools and nonprofitable charitable corporations; loan certain funds received under the Federal Housing and Community Development Act of 1974; contract with private persons or entities for the collection of delinquent payments owed to the municipality; make contracts; perform all acts regarding the property and affairs of the municipality necessary to the exercise of its governmental, corporate, and administrative powers; and exercise such powers as conferred by law.[24] Certain restrictions are still applicable to municipalities, as provided under the Municipal Home Rule Statute. The autonomy of a municipality is also limited by certain statutes that existed prior to home rule.

Counties are primarily appendages of the state. Counties are responsible for providing state services to residents, including services in the areas of public health, safety, and welfare. Counties perform many of the functions that municipalities do, such as waterworks, sewers, waste disposal, fire protection, schools, jails, roads, and hospitals.

Some cooperation exists between counties and cities. In 1974 the state legislature, through the Interlocal Cooperation Act and Cooperative Service District Act, gave municipalities, counties, and school districts the power to contract with each other and with state and federal agencies. Prior to passage of these acts, cities occasionally permitted their police or fire personnel to assist counties on an emergency basis. These two acts facilitated a more cooperative relationship between cities and counties. An interlocal agreement between Lowndes County and the city of Columbus addresses the parks, library, emergency management, and airport authority.[25] Agreements between other jurisdictions provide for joint city and county jails and fire protection in unincorporated areas.

Some cities and counties in Mississippi are consolidating their economic development activities, because they see their futures invariably linked. The Columbus-Lowndes Economic Development Association, for example, was set up to address the economic development of both the county and the city. The state allows local governments to use revenue collected from property taxes to fund these quasi-governmental structures. Other quasi-governmental corporations have been set up to meet the changing needs of communities that are experiencing growth.

The state is divided into eight planning and development districts, quasi-governmental bodies that encompass all eighty-two counties. These entities were set up to secure grants from various sources, provide services, and assess areas where cooperation can be achieved in local communities. Administrative fees are paid with grant money, when it is available, although each government must commit revenue to the continuing operation of such a district even when it opts out. Cities are reluctant to support the total consolidation of governmental services with counties or special districts because they would lose their autonomy. In part their reluctance stems from the wariness of citizens, who are concerned that higher property taxes and a reduction in services might result from such an arrangement.

In spite of the lack of governmental consolidation, regional cooperation does take place, especially when county and city officials consider airports, hospitals, jails, prisons, and solid waste disposal. Although consolidation is viewed as a means of increasing efficiency, eliminating duplication of services, and reducing costs, all of which benefit the citizens, it is also viewed as threatening the loss of local jobs in a community. Because consolidation invariably involves winners and loser, both city and county officials are reluctant to risk losing power or influence through governmental consolidation.

Both the state constitution and general law authorize interlocal service agreements between communities. Although interlocal agreements exist, only a few communities have considered the total merger of county and city services: Adams County and the city of Natchez; Jackson County on the Gulf Coast and several of its cities (Pascagoula, Moss Point, and Escatawpa); Desoto County and the numerous rapidly growing small towns and special districts near Memphis; and Harrison County and Biloxi and Gulfport.[26] No total mergers have taken place, but in some cases certain functions have been consolidated. For example, on July 1, 1987, the Warren County School System and the Vicksburg Public School System voluntarily consolidated to form the Vicksburg-Warren School District. As urbanization occurs, primarily as a result of casino gambling on the Gulf Coast, more communities may see the benefits of consolidating services, and more regional agreements may be formulated to enhance the overall economic development of an area.

Administrative Discretion

Local governments in Mississippi have been granted some mandatory as well as administrative powers. The Mississippi Constitution and state statutes provide the parameters for the powers of municipalities and counties. Municipalities can sue and be sued; purchase and hold property; sell and convey property; make contracts; loan certain funds; contract with private individuals and entities; donate surplus land; levy taxes; appropriate municipal funds for expenses; and change ordinances.[27] However, other statutes may prohibit, preempt, or regulate the use of these powers.

Limited functional home rule authority characterizes Mississippi cities and counties, which means they may choose from a narrow set of structural options set forth by the constitution and by state statutes. Cities have broader discretionary authority in their choice of structure than counties. There are at least four forms of governing available for cities to choose from, whereas counties are limited to the beat or unit system, depending on voter approval.

Counties and municipalities exercise power as a result of their authority to address safety, public health, and welfare concerns. The discretionary authority of a municipality extends only within its boundaries.

In personnel matters, Mississippi is an "at will" employment state. An individual works solely at the discretion of the employer. Termination can take place at any time for any reason or no reason at all. Statutory law allows counties to exercise some limited autonomy. If a county chooses the unit system, it is required to hire a county administrator to handle personnel matters, such as hiring and firing. A written personnel manual is required under this system.[28] Under the beat system, each county supervisor or sheriff is responsible for hiring his or her personnel, and no written formal procedures are required. Counties operating under this system may opt to hire a county administrator, but they are not required to do so by state law. Counties with a population of more than 100,000 are allowed to hire recreational supervisors for public parks and playgrounds.[29] Only four counties in Mississippi fall into this category: Hinds, Harrison, Jackson, and Rankin. It is in a county's best interest to have a written personnel manual, to ensure compliance with federal and state laws on personnel-related matters.

Cities have far less discretion than counties on personnel issues. They must comply with all related federal and state statutes regarding employment. Mississippi statutes prevent teachers and other public employees from striking.[30] State and federal statutes take precedent over county and municipal personnel policies.

Public bidding rules mandated by state statute govern the procurement of materials and services by counties and municipalities. The state requires that each county set up a central purchasing system. The minimum amount of flexibility that a county has depends on whether it operates as a unit or beat system. A board of supervisors under the unit system cannot make any purchases, whereas one under the beat system has the authority to do so. The state Office of Purchasing and Travel in Jackson is responsible for obtaining contracts for the purchase of many commodities for state agencies, including counties. A county purchasing clerk can procure any item from a state-authorized vendor without competitive bids when the amount is less than $500. However, when an item exceeds that amount, the competitive bid process is required. Advertisements must be placed in a local paper that has countywide distribution or fliers must be posted in the county courthouse and other public places. A county may opt not to post notice or advertise if the purchase is over $500.00 but less than $5,000.00 and if two competitive bids have been obtained from vendors. State statute gives preference to resident contractors in the state, county, city, or political subdivision over nonresidents and also allows counties to set aside for minority businesses no more than 20 percent of all annual purchases in the community.[31]

By statute the state governs the procurement and contracting of municipalities in the same way as it does that of counties.[32] Municipalities are allowed to develop their own purchasing system as long as they comply with state law. The same open-bid rules apply regarding purchases over $500.00, and the minority set-aside program is applicable to municipalities. Municipalities are required to go through the state Office of Purchasing and Travel for the procurement of many of their supplies from state-authorized vendors.

Although the state legislature has granted limited home rule authority to municipalities, it still micromanages local governments. The Mississippi Code, Title 17, Chapter 1, sets forth guidelines for the adoption of zoning ordinances by municipalities. A notice of public hearings is required when the zoning board adopts a comprehensive plan for the municipality. State statute sets the method and procedure for changing zoning ordinances. Many Mississippi cities and towns have adopted the Standard Codes of the Southern Standard Building Code Congress of Birmingham, Alabama, which set parameters regarding land use and zoning.[33]

Economic Development

In order to encourage economic development, the state permits municipalities to offer businesses some waivers with regard to property taxes; however, the state allows local government to grant only a ten-year exemption to business enterprises.[34] The state prohibits local governments from granting industry an exemption on the school district tax.

Fiscal Autonomy of Local Governments

Local Revenues

Taxing authority can come only from the state legislature. The state provides a variety of sources of revenue for cities and counties. It allow municipalities to collect revenue from municipal-owned utilities, city utility tax, ad valorem tax, personal property tax, special assessments, street and cemetery taxes, privilege tax, and aid from other governments. Municipalities may offer homestead exemptions and industrial tax exemptions. Mississippi was the first state to levy a retail sales tax, in 1932, and it followed that two years later with general sales and amusement taxes. In 1950, the state allowed cities to impose a city sales tax, which the state administered. Municipalities were allowed a choice of no sales tax, 0.5 percent tax on retail sales or gross income, or 1 percent on retail sales or gross income.[35] Eighteen years later the state abolished this provision and began to provide a share of state sales tax only to incorporated municipalities.[36]

The state levies a 7 percent general sales tax, which it shares sparingly with its subdivisions. This is one of the primary sources of revenue for all municipalities in Mississippi. Sales tax is rebated to each municipality on a monthly basis.

Municipalities can also levy a 2 percent tax on the gross revenue that utility companies make from customers located within their jurisdiction. The State Tax Commission collects this revenue and returns it to the municipality after withholding a 5 percent administrative fee.[37] At least a third of local government revenue originates from municipal-owned utilities, such as water, electric power, gas, and transit.

Another source of revenue that the state allows municipalities is called the "privilege tax," which is a license fee imposed on all business activity. The charge for the license is dependent on the size of the municipality or the volume of business or both.[38]

The legislature has granted additional authority to some cities to levy and collect a hotel or restaurant tax. The amount may vary from 0.5 to 6 percent, depending on the municipality. For instance, the city of Columbus levies a 2 percent tax on motel rooms and a 2 percent tax on restaurant and lounge bills. Fifty percent of the restaurant and lounge revenue is then allocated to Mississippi University for Women (MUW) and 50 percent to the Tourism Board. The 2 percent motel tax is specifically earmarked for bond payment for the Trotter Convention Center, located in the city. Jackson, Oxford, Starkville, and Tupelo are allowed by state statute to levy a special tax on hotels, motels, prepared food, beer, and alcoholic beverages. The state also permits the city of Natchez to levy a 3 percent lodging tax and 1.5 percent restaurant tax for tourism promotion. Not all cities have sought and received legislative authority to collect revenue from these sources.

Counties are allowed to levy taxes on real and personal property to raise revenue. Property tax is the primary source of revenue for county governments in Mississippi. The State Tax Commission collects 1 to 2.5 percent on hotels and motels, which is called an occupancy tax. Prepared food and beer or alcoholic beverage sales taxes represent a special tax source for counties. Six counties in Mississippi are allowed by the state to collect this special tax: Adams, Alcorn, Harrison, Lauderdale, Lowndes-Columbus, and Warren. The state does not share sales tax revenue with counties.

Property tax increases can be imposed by both municipalities and counties. Local governments have unlimited authority to increase property tax assessments up to 10 percent annually without voter approval; when the millage rate is more than 10 percent higher than the previous year's assessment, voter approval is required. However, when debt service is the reason for increasing property tax in excess of 10 percent annually, voter approval is not required. (This figure is based on the previous year's assessments and collections.) Exceptions are also granted to fund school districts, county roads, bridge levies, payment of principal and interest on bonds, and new programs mandated by the state. Municipalities can make increases in excess of 10 percent for up to five years as long as an election is held and voter approval is obtained each time. There is also a homestead exemption reimbursement that the state provides to cities. Any governing body can levy a special tax that does not exceed one-quarter mill on all taxable property located within its jurisdiction.[39]

Personal property tax can be levied by municipalities. This assessment is levied primarily on automobiles. Although this tax is collected by the county when a license is issued, the county retains only a collection fee. Revenue from this source goes primarily to the school district and to the municipality. Any personal item that requires a license, such as a trailer home or a boat, is covered under this provision.

Special assessments can be made when a municipality engages in work that may benefit property owners. These activities include, but are not limited to, construction or repair of streets, highways, alleys, parks, sidewalks, water mains, water connections, sanitary disposal systems, and storm covers and other surfaces. Improvements cannot be made unless property owners agree to make payment. Municipalities with fewer than 1,000 persons may assess a two mills tax for street improvements and a two mills tax for cemetery improvement and upkeep, with majority vote approval.

Local Expenditures

The constitution and statutes dictate budget structure and format as well as taxing authority, debt limits, and balanced budget restrictions for any governmental unit within the state. Constitutional provisions and statutory laws control short-term and long-term debt.[40] State law specifies the conditions under which local governments can incur debt, including the types of bonds, their maximum life span, the interest to be paid, and the ceiling for issuance.[41] State statutes allow counties and municipalities jointly to issue bonds on behalf of a specific local project, such as a convention center.

All units of government are required to adopt an annual operating budget that is balanced. Both counties and cities must approve a budget where the expenditures do not exceed the estimated revenue. Technically, local governments cannot engage in deficit spending; however, they are allowed to borrow money in anticipation of grant funds from the federal or state government.

State Government Grants-in-Aid to Localities

State aid to municipalities comes in the form of general assistance. Assistance is provided to county and city governments as well as to school districts by the state. The largest sources of this revenue are the cities' share of sales tax revenue and homestead exemption reimbursements. Cities also receive from the state revenues that result from a privilege tax levied by the state on passenger vehicles with a seating capacity that exceeds seven. Municipalities that have gas-producing properties located within their jurisdiction share in the county portion of the gas- and oil-severance tax. According to state statute, the amount cannot exceed one-third of the tax revenue produced within that locality and returned to that county. Counties also derive a portion of their revenue from gas-producing properties located within municipalities.

In 1984, the state legislature created the Municipal Revolving Fund, which distributes surpluses from the general fund to municipalities based on population. The state imposes no restrictions on how municipalities spend these funds. In the 1990s, the popularity of the gaming industry in Mississippi resulted in budget surpluses in the general fund, which produced unexpected windfalls for many municipalities, especially the most populous. However, a downturn in the gaming industry or the overall state economy could change the picture.

In 1989, the state legislature passed an equity funding measure that eliminated some of the fiscal distress felt by local communities. This legislation reduced the gap between rich and poor school districts by requiring an equal level of spending per student, with the state helping those districts that cannot come up with enough money.[42] Ad valorem taxes for schools, however, cannot be increased by more than 10 percent from one year to the next without voter approval. A school tax is assessed on license plates, and a great deal of variation occurs from school district to school district. The county or the city raises the millage on real property to generate the revenue that school districts require. The infusion of capital from casino gambling has further lessened the financial pressures on local government because the state distributes these funds back to the local communities. The State Tax Commission collects the revenue from the gaming industry based on net earnings after payout. By law the state receives 8.8 percent, and the county and city where the casino is located divide 3.2 percent. Proration between the county and the city is based on which has the larger population and the location of the casino. Both cities and counties may levy a license fee or tax. Biloxi, D'Iberville, and Vicksburg levy an annual license tax of $150.00 per gaming device. Counties, such as Warren, Harrison, Hancock, Tunica, Washington, Adams, and Coahoma, have also levied an annual license fee or tax on gaming equipment (card games, slot machines, table games, or other gaming devices) located within their jurisdictions.

Counties are allotted gasoline tax revenue by the state based on the tags sold and the miles of road within their jurisdiction, which amounts to two or three cents per gallon. Counties may share up to $40,000 of the state excise tax on gasoline and oil with the municipalities located inside their boundaries.[43] Although counties collect three separate charges on motor vehicles, they keep only the privilege tax: $15.00 for cars and $8.75 for trucks. The registration fee is submitted to the state, and the ad valorem tax, based on the assessed value of the vehicle, goes to schools and the city. All values are established by the State Tax Commission for uniformity.

The state of Mississippi shares with its counties the revenue from the gasoline tax; truck and privilege tax; oil-, gas-, and timber-severance tax; liquor privilege tax, Grand Gulf distribution; insurance rebates; payments in lieu of taxes; and gambling contract fees.

Unfunded Mandates

A 1996 legislative study of federal mandates found that state agencies estimated that they spent approximately $90 million, of which $28 million were state treasury funds, to implement the eighteen most burdensome mandates. A follow-up study in 1999 found similar results, the only differences being a slight increase in total cost and a few additional mandates deemed as burdensome by state agency heads.[44] However, these two analyses did not examine the impact of state government–imposed mandates on local governments. This question, according to officials in the governor's office, has not been an issue in the state.

Access to Local Government

Local Elections

Municipalities hold elections as specified by the state constitution and state statute. The Mississippi Constitution states that all general elections for state and county officers shall be held every four years on the first Tuesday after the first Monday in November.[45] Elections are held every four years on the first Tuesday after the first Monday in June, as prescribed by statute, for mayors, council members, and boards of aldermen.[46] If vacancies occur at the county level, the governor may appoint individuals to fill them until a regularly scheduled or special election can be held. State statute specifies whether or not office space shall be provided for city council members. Only in cities with a population over 190,000 shall members of the council be provided with individual office space in city hall. So far, only one municipality—Jackson, the state capital—meets that qualification.

Citizen Controls over Actions of Local Officials

There are no provisions in the state constitution or statutes for the recall of local officials. Voting in elections is the means by which citizens exercise control over local officials in the cities and counties. Citizens can circulate a petition in an effort to be annexed, but no referendum or initiative process is available to them with regard to elected officials.

State-Local Relations

Although Mississippi is granting municipalities more autonomy, only a few substantive changes have occurred in state-county relationships. Cities have benefited from the general provisions of statutes primarily by changing their form of government. Devolution of power is increasingly in vogue, so the state legislature may grant additional powers to both municipalities and counties in the future. Amending the constitution seems to be the most feasible means of bringing about more dramatic changes in local government autonomy, since statutory law involves challenges and opinions by the state attorney general. Moving the decision-making process closer to the community might actually facilitate a continuation of the status quo in many communities, as Dale Krane and Stephen Shaffer found in *Mississippi Government and Politics*. However, with economic development increasingly an issue, change may be more forthcoming than one might imagine for a primarily rural state. As Mississippi continues to transform itself from a rural agrarian state to a more urbanized state with varied employment opportunities, change is inevitable. In the future, local communities may demand more authority to meet the changing needs of their constituents.

The dynamics of economic development, especially the gaming industry, have already brought phenomenal change to Mississippi, especially on the Gulf Coast. Change may be viewed negatively by both citizens and officials in many rural communities; however, the realities of welfare reform and the need for economic development are likely to facilitate rapid changes in entire communities. As competition increases for economic development, greater demands for change may be forthcoming, especially since casino gambling has provided some surplus capital for a very poor state and many local communities.

Theoretically, home rule provisions as adopted by the state legislature in Mississippi should provide more autonomy for municipalities and counties than they actually do. However, it is difficult to ascertain the implications of these provisions, since the constitution and statutes micromanage or mandate so many policies. All powers dealing with the financial affairs of local governing bodies are still controlled by the state legislature. Powers to make assessments, borrow money, and contract debt are specifically controlled under section 80, Chapter VIII, of the state code. Although the state has granted limited home rule authority to local governments, it has not included the authority to levy taxes, increase authorized taxes, or issue bonds.[47] It is difficult for local governments to find areas where the state legislature has not already legislated or set specific parameters that limit the options for local governments to be innovative or creative.

Notes

1. United States Bureau of the Census. *State and Metropolitan Area Data Book 1997–98* (Washington, D.C.: Government Printing Office, 1999), A-1.

2. U.S. Bureau of the Census. *1992 Census of Governments, Government Organization* (Washington, D.C.: Government Printing Office, 1993), 297.

3. Ann O'M. Bowman, and Richard Kearney, *State and Local Government*. 3d ed. (Boston: Houghton Mifflin, 1996). Amending the constitution is a three-step process: an amendment must be proposed by the state legislature; ratified by the voters; and inserted by the legislature.

4. Mississippi Code of 1972, section 21-17-5; and P. C. McLaurin Jr. and Michael T. Allen, *Municipal Government in Mississippi: A Handbook for City Officials* (Mississippi State: Mississippi State University, Center for Governmental Technology, 1997), 4.

5. Mississippi Constitution, Article IV, section 88.

6. *Adams v. Kuykendall*, 35 So. 830, 83 Mississippi 571 (1904).

7. Article IV, section 66, of the state constitution forbids the grant of donation or gratuity in favor of any person except by concurrence of two-thirds of the state legislature.

8. Mississippi Code, section 21-17-5.

9. Mississippi Code, section 19-3-40.

10. Robert B. Highsaw and Charles N. Fortenberry, *The Government and Administration of Mississippi* (New York: Crowell, 1954).

11. "Columbus' Government Structure a Liability," *The Commercial Dispatch*, May 29, 1998, 4A.

12. 1996 Census of Population, State Data Center of Mississippi.

13. Mississippi Constitution, Article IV, section 88, and Mississippi Code 21-8-1 through 21-8-47.

14. Mississippi Code, sections 21-9-1 through 21-9-83; 21-17-1 though 21-17-19.

15. Mississippi Code, sections 21-5-1 through 21-5-23.

16. *State Laws Governing Local Government Structure and Administration* (Washington, D.C.: Advisory Commission on Intergovernmental Relations, 1993).

17. Mississippi Code, section 19-5-201.

18. Mississippi Constitution, Article IV, sections 91, 102, 103, 135, 138, 139, and 170.

19. Dale Krane and Stephen D. Shaffer, *Mississippi Government and Politics: Modernizers versus Traditionalists* (Lincoln: University of Nebraska Press, 1992).

20. Mississippi Constitution, Article VI, section 170.

21. Interview with Lowndes County Supervisor Leroy Brooks, May 29, 1998, Columbus, Mississippi.

22. The Mississippi Code 1942, 1952 Supplement, section 4159 specifies the classification scheme for counties: class one, $25,000,000; class two, $20,000,000 to $25,000,000; class three, $15,000,000 to $20,000,000; class four, $10,000,000 to $15,000,000; class five, $8,000,000 to $10,000,000; class six, $6,000,000 to $8,000,000; class seven, $3,000,000 to $6,000,000; and class eight, less than $3,000,000.

23. Mississippi Code, section 19-3-41.

24. Mississippi Code, sections 11-45-25, 21-17-1, 21-33-45, 21-33-87, 27-39-307, 17-9-1, 21-17-3.

25. Interview with Lew Cornelius, Lowndes county administrator, May 29, 1998.

26. Krane and Shaffer, *Mississippi Government and Politics*.

27. Mississippi Code, sections 11-45-25; 21-17-1; 17-9-1; 21-33-45; 21-33-87, and 27-39-307.

28. Mississippi Code, section 19-2-9.

29. Mississippi Code, section 55-9-51.

30. Mississippi Code, sections 37-9-75 and 25-1-105.

31. Mississippi Code, Title 31, covers county purchasing and contracting.

32. Mississippi Code, sections 31-7-49 and 31-7-12.

33. McLaurin and Allen, *Municipal Government in Mississippi: A Handbook for City Officials*. 198.

34. Mississippi Constitution, Article VII, sections 182 and 192, and Mississippi Code, section 21-19-43.

35. Mississippi Code, section 27-65-73.

36. The state remits to each municipality 18.5 percent of the sales taxes collected within it. County governments do not receive any revenue from this source.

37. Mississippi Code, sections 21-33-201 and 21-33-207.

38. Dana B. Brammer and John W. Winkle III, ed., *Mississippi Municipal Government Book* (University: Public Policy Research Center, University of Mississippi Press, 1987), 67.

39. Mississippi Code, section 17-3-31.

40. Mississippi Code, section 21-33-301.

41. Mississippi Code, section 21-33-301.

42. Krane and Shaffer, *Mississippi Government and Politics.*

43. Mississippi Code, section 27-5-103.

44. *Federal Mandates and Mississippi's State Government: Cost and Implementation, Joint Committee on Performance Evaluation and Expenditure Review,* Mississippi Legislature, Report #349. Nov. 12, 1996.

45. Mississippi Constitution, Article IV, section 102.

46. Mississippi Code, section, 21-11-7.

47. Mississippi Code, section 21-17-5; Brammer and Winkle, *Mississippi Municipal Government,* 8.

MISSOURI

E. Terrence Jones and Don Phares

The authors thank Claude Louishomme, a Ph.D. candidate in the Department of Political Science at the University of Missouri–St. Louis, and Dr. Andrew Theising of Focus St. Louis for collecting much of the basic information.

Missouri is a conservative state, both fiscally and politically. In this context, however, it has provided considerable autonomy to local jurisdictions, especially cities and counties, to engage in diverse activities as long as they can obtain voter approval for funding. Both the state and localities are constrained by a constitutional amendment; localities must get voter approval for any revenue increase. The state allows local governments to derive revenue—with voter approval—not only from the property tax but also by taxing general sales, utility usage, and earnings. This local autonomy has produced problems such as extreme political fragmentation, especially in the St. Louis area, and a lack of regional solutions to regional issues. State control is far less pronounced than elsewhere, but this puts the burden on localities. Currently, there is little to suggest change in this status, but advancing federal devolution may well alter this.

Governmental Setting

Missouri is a relatively populous state (ranked fifteenth nationally), with about 5.5 million people. Its economy is sound, with personal income in the mid range of states and a state gross product ranking of seventeenth. Despite this comfortable economic setting, the state and most local units spend frugally. In terms of total tax burden, Missouri ranks forty-ninth; in spending, it is forty-eighth. Its fiscal capacity is far above fiscal effort.[1] This fiscal conservatism permeates tax and spending policies for all governmental units and provides the context for much of local fiscal operations.

The state's conservative environment has led to underfunded programs, perhaps most notably in K–12 education. A court decision has mandated greater state involvement to produce more equity and adequacy in school funding.[2] However, the controversy surrounding K–12 education continues and has resulted in a second constitutional limitation on state revenue-raising capacity.[3]

Missouri is also characterized by a proliferation of local governments, especially in the state's largest urban area, St. Louis. St. Louis County contains ninety-two municipalities serving about 60 percent of the population. The county serves the remaining unincorporated area and is the state's second largest provider of municipal-type services. This fragmentation has produced a "grab the wealth" mentality in unincorporated areas. Since taxation of both sales and utilities (called gross receipts) is permitted through enabling legislation, any unincorporated pockets of such taxable wealth (especially gross receipts) are pursued by existing cities through annexation or by new incorporation.

Missouri also is unique in other, nonfiscal ways. In 1876 the City of St. Louis withdrew from St. Louis County. Because most of the wealth, business, and population was in the city, the city became a city and a county (and is a coterminous school district). However, despite six attempts to reorganize the city and county between 1926 and 1990, only the St. Louis Metropolitan Sewer District (MSD) was created (in 1954). Moreover, the St. Louis and Kansas City Boards of Police Commissioners are appointed by the governor and largely are state controlled—a vestige of the Civil War.

Home Rule in Missouri

Historical Development

Home rule in Missouri emerged from a decades-long struggle in the mid–nineteenth century between the City of St. Louis and the state. Frustrated by what it perceived as incessant meddling by the legislature, the city's political forces urged home rule for cities with greater than 100,000 population to be included in the new 1875 constitution. Also at the city's behest, the 1875 constitution included a procedure whereby the city could separate itself from St. Louis County, which it did.[4] By 1880 both St. Louis and Kansas City, the only eligible jurisdictions, had adopted home rule charters. Although the state allowed these two cities extensive autonomy (for example, types of political offices and their terms and allocation of power between the executive and legislature), the state continues to control both police departments and limit taxation authority.

The 1945 constitution lowered the population barrier for home rule to 5,000 and extended the option to counties with populations of 85,000 or assessed property valuation of $450,000,000. The constitution does not use the term "home rule" but instead authorizes jurisdictions to adopt their own charters.[5] As of 1997, Missouri had thirty-two charter cities, which collectively contained about one-third of the state's residents. Excluding the City of St. Louis, which is a city and a county, there are three other charter counties. Together, they include about 40 percent of Missouri's inhabitants.

During the past fifty years, municipal charters have been added at a steady rate of five to seven a decade; nevertheless, more than seventy eligible cities have not opted for home rule. The City of St. Louis charter was explicitly recognized in the 1945 constitution;[6] St. Louis, Jackson, and St. Charles Counties adopted charters in 1950, 1970, and 1992, respectively. Five of the remaining eight charter-eligible counties have established charter commissions, but the recommendations were rejected by the voters.[7]

Definition of Home Rule

Missouri has a schizophrenic approach to local home rule. It has a well above-average number of municipalities (almost 900) and counties (over 100) rooted in its "keep government close to the people" political culture. At the same time, the legislature and, to a lesser extent, the constitution have imposed both generic and specific limitations on local jurisdictions, reflecting a Madisonian checks-and-balances philosophy. The most recent significant and major manifestation of constitutional control over local governments was the 1980 passage of the so-called Hancock Amendment, which essentially mandates a public vote on each and every proposed local tax, license, or fee increase.[8]

Local governments, as a group, have rarely lobbied for more autonomy and instead have been coconspirators with state legislators to maintain the status quo. Rather than seeking the authority to chart their own destiny, localities have made changes by having their local legislators modify statutes. The major exception to this generalization was the successful 1971 effort to amend the constitution so that home rule cities were not limited by specific authorization of powers but instead were granted "all powers which the General Assembly . . . has the authority to confer upon any city, provided such powers are consistent with the Constitution of this State and are not limited or denied by the charter so adopted or by statute"; moreover, "such a city shall, in addition to its home rule powers, have all powers conferred by law."[9] Noncharter cities, on the other hand, can do only what the statutes permit.

Structural Features

In addition to seemingly universal language, the General Assembly often uses geographic and size descriptors to limit the applicability of certain statutes. Gambling, for example, is only allowed in jurisdictions that border the Missouri or Mississippi Rivers, and many other laws are worded so that only one county or municipality qualifies. In addition, the City of St. Louis traditionally has been considered unique and is the leading recipient of special legislation.

Had it survived, a 1994 Missouri Supreme Court ruling would have invalidated some 500 laws that were written explicitly for a single jurisdiction (in this instance, St. Louis County). This judicial interpretation would have not only affected the ability of localities to raise adequate revenues but also undone many past negotiated agreements. In 1995 a statewide vote changed the constitution to accommodate this special legislation for St. Louis County. As a result, even though Missouri nominally has only villages (less than 500 population) and Class IV (500–2,999 population), Class III (3,000 and over), and home rule cities, special legislation has generated a confusing array of alternatives. Occasional attempts to codify and simplify state legislation covering municipalities generally have not been successful. One exception was a 1975 statute eliminating Class I and II categories, since no cities qualified as such.

Cities can choose from four structural forms. Most cities (80 percent) have the "weak" mayor–council form; about 10 percent of cities select the city administrator form (in which a professional administrator is appointed by the mayor and the council but reports to the mayor); and less than 5 percent use the council-manager form. The commission form, although authorized, now only exists in two cities. Villages and towns must use an elected board of trustees. The Missouri Constitution establishes a four-year maximum for any single term.[10]

A city charter can be initiated either by ordinance to establish a charter commission, which is passed by a city's legislature, or by petition (at least 10 percent of the number voting in the last general city election must sign the petition). The electorate votes simultaneously on whether or not to establish a charter commission and on the thirteen individuals who will serve on the charter commission. The commission then has one year to write and submit a proposed charter to the electorate; if a simple majority approves, it is adopted.[11]

Counties have four classifications based on assessed valuation; charter counties are a subset of the largest, Class I counties. It is more challenging for a county to adopt a charter than it is for a municipality.[12] The petition needs 10 percent of the vote in the preceding gubernatorial election; because there is always a much higher voter turnout than in a municipal contest, more signatures are needed. Municipal elections are held in April, whereas the gubernatorial race is coterminous with presidential elections. The existing three elected county commissioners, who typically have a stake in the current structure, select the fourteen charter commission members. As with municipalities, the charter group must submit its proposal within a year, and a simple majority is required for approval. There are also explicit limitations on taxation authority; counties may not decide on matters to do with public education; and if the proposal fails, two years must pass before voters may vote on another proposal.

State law favors incorporation over annexation. The former requires a modest number of petition signatures and a simple majority in the area to be incorporated. The latter needs concurrent majorities in the annexing and the annexed area(s) and, in St. Louis County, the approval of a boundary commission. Counties are allowed to consolidate, dissolve, or annex. The constitution also has a special section allowing the City of St. Louis and St. Louis County to enter into a wide range of agreements, including complete merger or city reentry.[13]

Cities and counties may own property outside their own boundaries; the most notable example is the City of St. Louis's Lambert International Airport, located entirely within St. Louis County, more than five miles from city limits. For the most part, cities can use their zoning powers to regulate land use for up to two miles outside their boundaries when that area is unincorporated.[14]

Functions of Local Government

Functional Responsibilities

The state expects counties to administer much of government's daily business and to provide administrative and prosecutorial services for the courts.[15] It both specifies functions and, for noncharter counties, dictates which appointed or elected officials will execute functions. Principal functions of counties include property assessment, law enforcement, law prosecution, court record keeping, collection of selected local taxes, estate administration, auditing, record keeping, and maintenance and disbursement of county funds.

In most counties, almost all of these functions are administered by officials who are elected countywide and therefore not under the direct control of county commissioners. This is also the case in the City of St. Louis, where officials who conduct county-type functions are elected separately and therefore are not subject to mayoral authority. The other three charter counties have transformed most of these offices into appointed positions, and incumbents report to either the executive or the legislative body.

Although the state limits how cities, towns, and villages operate by mandating balanced budgets and detailing the possible structural forms, for example, it does not tell jurisdictions what to do, except in the area of K–12 education.[16] As a result, Missouri's municipalities can decide what level of service and which activities to provide; they may also have part-time or even volunteer employees. Cities can also choose to assume the county's law enforcement role by establishing their own police departments, and many have. Most local amenities, such as swimming pools, are almost always municipal.

There are almost 1,000 special districts and public authorities and more than 500 school districts in Missouri. According to a 1997 tally,[17] the most common functions provided by these special-purpose governments are roads, fire protection, and ambulance. Others purposes include water, libraries, public housing, drainage, and soil and water conservation. State legislation makes establishing special districts and public authorities a relatively straightforward matter. The state legislature almost always allows localities to create "newly minted" governments to address problems; moreover, the state is relatively generous in providing taxing and bonding authority. There is no single pattern for the governance of these entities. Most have separately elected boards and are independent political subdivisions, but in some situations (for example, drainage districts, housing authorities) counties and municipalities appoint the boards.

With this plethora of governments, there is no shortage of opportunities for interlocal cooperation. The constitution broadly interprets and encourages such activity:

Any municipality or political subdivision of this state may contract and cooperate with other municipalities or political subdivisions thereof, or with other states or their municipalities or political subdivisions, or with the U.S., for the planning, development, construction, acquisition or operation of any public improvement or facility, or for a common service, in the manner provided by law.[18]

There is no definitive audit of the number and type of interlocal agreements, but one analysis of St. Louis County uncovered hundreds of such agreements.[19]

Administrative Discretion

Missouri municipalities and counties have wide discretion on personnel matters, and there are few limitations. These include mandated leaves of absence for reserve and guard duty and required leaves of absence for adoption of children. There are also standard prohibitions on conflicts of interest and, since the 1980s, requirements for written financial disclosures for officials. Missouri's labor movement has been successful in gaining collective bargaining rights for all public employees except police officers and teachers.

There are few prior restrictions on local jurisdictions' contract and procurement activities. Instead, after-the-fact auditing by the state auditor is used to maintain control. The auditor is elected in off-year elections (for example, 1994, 1998), whereas the other statewide officials are chosen in presidential years (for example, 1996, 2000). The practice of alternating elections is intended to keep the auditing function somewhat separate from other political forces.

Planning and zoning runs contrary to Missourians' individualistic political culture, and many a battle has been waged over whether or not a county should adopt land-use controls. The largest (that is, Class I) counties can adopt planning and zoning by legislative action, but all others require a majority vote. Less than one-third of Missouri's counties have planning and zoning, although planning and zoning do exist in all the highly urbanized areas. Municipalities are authorized but not required to have planning and zoning.

Economic Development

Much of the direct financial support for economic development is provided by the Missouri Department of Economic Development through grants and tax concessions. There are, however, provisions enabling localities to act. Most of these were in place before 1985, but a few have been modified since. The Urban Redevelopment Corporations Law, which is the most widely used (especially in St. Louis), allows a city to declare an area "blighted" and then to assemble an economic redevelopment plan.[20]

All real property taxes on improvements are exempt for the first ten years. For the next fifteen years, they are taxed at 50 percent of assessed value. Only after twenty-five years does the property achieve full value. This provision has been used extensively, especially by the City of St. Louis. Many jurisdictions have questioned the efficacy of this provision, most notably the city school district, which loses most of the property tax revenue (its major tax source) because of exemptions.

Tax increment financing is also available to any city, village, incorporated town, or county. A development area is defined, "blighting" is declared, and a redevelopment project is then undertaken. Included in project costs are professional services, land assembly, and public works or infrastructure. Tax increment financing has become particularly contentious in St. Louis County, where cities compete for projects using tax increment financing as a lure.

Legislation also permits the establishment of economic development districts and industrial development boards, which have the power to issue revenue bonds and receive funds. Cities have the authority to establish special business districts. Locally generated revenues may be used by both cities and counties for a variety of economic or community development purposes (such as tax credits) and projects (such as industrial parks, enterprise zones, and other infrastructure improvement). Voter approval rarely is required.[21]

Fiscal Autonomy of Local Governments

Local Revenues

Although fiscally conservative, Missouri has provided rather liberal enabling legislation to allow localities to raise revenues with voter approval. Thus, whereas the property tax is the local fiscal mainstay in most states, Missouri localities (especially cities and counties) are allowed to tax general sales, utility usage, and earnings. At present, the maximum levels allowed are 4 percent for sales, 11 percent for utilities, and 1 percent for earnings. The Missouri revenue pattern compared with that of the United States is shown in Table 1.

The Missouri Constitution stringently limits the revenues of both state and local jurisdictions. Passed in 1980, the so-called Hancock Amendment[22] mandates voter approval for virtually any increase in local revenue. The severe financial implications for some political entities has prompted legal challenges, but to no avail. For example, the St. Louis Metropolitan Sewer District (MSD), which serves St. Louis City and County, needs millions of dollars to comply with federal and state environmental provisions. However, voters will not pass a tax increase. Under the constraints of the Hancock Amendment, unless the MSD could obtain the needed resources, it would remain in violation of the provisions. Some recent decisions by the Missouri Supreme Court have allowed local fees-for-service to be exempted if the fees meet strict criteria set forth by the court. The MSD has benefited from this exemption, and other localities may as well.[23]

That localities in Missouri have more fiscal leeway than in most states[24] is demonstrated by the 1 percent earnings tax in St. Louis and Kansas City—their largest revenue source. Localities may also use a "piggyback" on the state general sales tax; the most pronounced example is a 4 percent local add-on to the total 4.225 percent state rate. Currently, more than 500 cities and 100 counties use the sales tax, often for multiple purposes. Taxation of utility gross receipts—including gas, electricity, and water—has become the dominant revenue source for many municipalities.

As depicted in Table 1, the share of revenue coming from in-

Table 1. Local Government Revenues for Missouri and Total United States, FY 1995

| Source of revenue | Missouri | | Total United States | |
	Dollars (in millions)	Percent	Dollars (in millions)	Percent
Intergovernmental	$2,945	26.8%	$259,093	34.2%
Property tax	2,916	26.5	193,933	25.6
General sales tax	941	8.6	27,930	3.7
Public utility taxes	280	2.5	6,928	0.9
Individual and corporate income	244	2.2	14,651	1.9
Current charges	1,577	14.3	107,280	14.2
Utility revenue	933	8.5	64,789	8.6
Insurance trust revenues	184	1.7	15,687	2.1
Other[a]	974	8.9	67,109	8.8
Total revenues	$10,994	100.0%	$757,400	100.0%

Source: For Missouri data, see http://www.census.gov/govs/estimate/95stlmo.txt. For U.S. data, see http://www.census.gov/govs/estimate/95stlus.txt.
  a. Not elsewhere classified.

tergovernmental sources is distinctly less for Missouri than for the United States. Much of this difference can be explained by the lesser role of the state in providing assistance to localities, including local schools. Property taxes represent about the same relative amount, which is accounted for primarily by school and special districts. However, if data on municipal use of nonproperty taxes could be extracted (none are available), one would see that there is a greater local reliance on general sales and gross receipts taxes. This reliance is expressed obliquely in Table 1 by utility taxes (which are almost three times the U.S. average) and sales taxes (which are more than twice that amount). The use of an earnings tax in St. Louis and Kansas City results in a higher figure for income taxes.

Limitations on local revenues are strictly defined by the Hancock Amendment, which requires voter approval for virtually any change;[25] limits have shifted to a more powerful constitutional basis. One peculiar twist is a minimum levy required for school districts. As one facet of a major school finance reform in 1993, school districts were required to levy a minimum of $2.75, well above the prevailing rate in many districts. That this was not voter approved is largely a function of a court decision that found Missouri school financing to be inadequate and inequitable.

Local indebtedness is limited constitutionally. Cities and counties are capped at 5 percent of the value of taxable tangible property. School districts increase up to 10 percent; counties and cities may incur an additional 5 percent; and cities may become indebted by an additional 10 percent for public improvements and may levy any associated costs to geographically defined "benefit districts" where the improvements are made.[26] Anything above the 5 percent cap requires approval by four out of seven voters at general municipal, general, or primary elections; two-thirds voter approval is required at all other elections. Bankruptcy is handled under federal law and may lead to disincorporation under state law.

Local Expenditures

Table 2 shows the pattern of local expenditures for Missouri and the United States. Education leads and is almost 10 percent above the national average. This reflects less state involvement in K–12 funding, a ramification of school finance reform.[27] Social services expenditures are also substantially below the national average. The remaining categories are not dramatically different, except interest on debt, which is well below the U.S. average and reflects Missouri's fiscal conservatism.

Local governments in Missouri provide much the same array of services found elsewhere, with some variation in emphasis. There are no expenditure limits per se; available revenues limit expenditures. Many growing areas have quite robust budgets and provide diverse services. This is particularly true where, for example, tax increment financing has resulted in a large commercial development or a locality has realized increased revenue

Table 2. Local Government Expenditures for Missouri and Total United States, FY 1995

Expenditure	Missouri Dollars (in millions)	Missouri Percent	Total United States Dollars (in millions)	Total United States Percent
Education	$5,137	46.2%	$276,763	36.4%
Social services[a]	703	6.3	89,163	11.7
Transportation[b]	749	6.7	40,558	5.3
Public safety[c]	1,050	9.5	66,567	8.8
Environment and housing[d]	930	8.4	73,071	9.6
Administration[e]	486	4.4	35,327	4.6
Interest on general debt	335	3.0	32,485	4.3
Other (not elsewhere classified)	1,719	15.5	145,434	19.3
Total expenditures	$11,109	100.0%	$759,368	100.0%

Source: For Missouri data, see www.census.gov/govs/estimate/95stlmo.txt. For U.S. data, see www.census.gov/govs/estimate/95stlus.txt.
a. Welfare, hospitals, health, and social insurance administration.
b. Highways, air transportation, parking facilities, sea and inland port facilities, and transit subsidies.
c. Police and fire protection, corrections, and protective inspection.
d. Natural resources, parks and recreation, housing and community development, sewage disposal, and solid waste management.
e. Financial administration, judicial and legal, general public building, and other governmental administration.

by becoming a venue for gambling boats. However, localities tend to struggle with higher taxation and/or lower service levels. Except for mandating a balanced operating budget and requiring all cities to submit an annual budget to the state auditor, the state is not involved. Many localities ignore budgetary requirements, and there is virtually no enforcement. The state does not explicitly mention what functions cities may undertake; it only stipulates that they cannot be involved with school districts.

State Government Grants-in-Aid to Localities

Unlike many other states, Missouri does not have a tradition of sharing revenues with its local jurisdictions. For a long time, motor fuels taxes provided the most state-shared revenue: 15 percent to counties for roads and bridges and 15 percent to incorporated cities, towns, and villages of more than 100 population. The cigarette tax is also shared with localities.[28]

Recently, however, a type of sharing has been introduced through the taxation of excursion gambling boats. The two forms of gaming revenues for localities—$1 for admission and 2 percent of net winnings—go only to those units that are home docks for riverboat gaming, presently only nine out of almost 1,000 municipalities and counties in the state. This has produced a fiscal windfall but only for very few cities. Other localities have pursued state legislation to put all gaming revenues into a pool for redistribution.

The only other type of state sharing is represented by the earmarking of certain funds for K–12 education. This includes all state gaming revenues (for lottery, bingo, and the state portion of riverboat excursion gaming, which is 18 percent of net win and $1 for admission), 1 percent of the state's 4.225 percent general sales tax, and portions of the cigarette and insurance company taxes.[29] Although substantial, the dollar amounts for education are in fact just another way for the state to pay its share for local education. Riverboat gaming revenues are significant for most of the home dock localities, motor fuels are much less so, and all other revenues are minor. Thus, Missouri does not have a true revenue-sharing plan for its localities. Rather, in the spirit of fiscal conservatism, the state provides enabling legislation for localities to enact or increase other taxes but always with voter approval.

Unfunded Mandates

Before the passage of the Hancock Amendment in 1980, the state was able to impose additional costs on localities in two ways. It could mandate new programs or increases in existing activities (for example, by insisting on twenty-four-hour police protection or compliance with environmental standards). Alternatively, the state could unilaterally eliminate taxes or components of a tax base used by localities; for example, the intangible personal property tax (a source of local revenue) was eliminated by state action. Portions of the general sales tax have been exempted over the years, thereby causing revenue losses for localities that "piggyback" on the state tax. Although legally the state "may" provide reimbursement for lost local revenues, it does not. This changed in 1980 with the Hancock Amendment, which stated, "state support to local governments [is] not to be reduced, additional activities and services [are] not be imposed without full state funding."[30] This clause has provided considerable financial protection to localities and has been supported by court decisions relating to, for example, salary increases for county officials and operations of the City of St. Louis Police Board.

Access to Local Government

Local Elections

The General Assembly assumed nearly complete control of state and local elections when it passed the Comprehensive Election Act of 1977.[31] The statute vests electoral administration in the county clerk or, for those few larger jurisdictions that qualify (including the three largest counties of Jackson, St. Louis City, and St. Louis County), a board of election commissioners. A board of election commissioners represents even more state control, because its four members (two from each major political party) are appointed by the governor with the advice and consent of the senate.

The statutes dictate the date of elections for municipalities and counties and myriad other details, including ballot printing. With the exception of the City of St. Louis, all municipal elections are nonpartisan, whereas all county contests are partisan.

State statutes also provide the conditions under which any political party qualifies for official status. Local jurisdictions retain some modest flexibility on filing procedures and media access, but state campaign finance laws govern both contributions and reporting.[32]

Citizen Controls over Actions of Local Officials

State statutes provide a uniform process for removing either municipal or county officials who neglect their official duties,[33] but citizens must initially lodge a notarized complaint with the county prosecuting attorney. The prosecuting attorney can then decide whether or not to proceed and can initiate charges. The governor has the authority to involve the attorney general in the proceedings and if the prosecuting attorney decides not to act, the attorney general can proceed with the case. Citizens reenter the process when a jury trial is held. Because such proceedings are a civil action, a three-quarters majority is required to uphold the charge.

Recall provisions apply only in Class III cities (that is, those with at least 3,000 population) and in cities whose charters specify recall provisions. A recall petition must be signed by at least 25 percent of the registered voters in the appropriate district (ward for a council member, entire city for a mayor). Moreover, a petition can only apply to someone who has been in office at least six months and must state succinctly the alleged rationale for recall.[34] If an elected official is recalled (a simple majority is required), he or she cannot be a candidate in the next election for that office. In Class IV cities (those with 500–2,999 population), the mayor (with the consent of a majority of the legislative body) may remove any elected or appointed official; the legislative body may unilaterally remove by a two-thirds vote any elected or appointed official. Charter counties and cities typically have recall provisions, but they vary. Noncharter counties, by default, must rely on the same process for cities.

Although, in the tradition of midwestern progressivism, the constitution authorizes both initiatives and referendums for statewide legislation, it and the statutes are silent about such provisions for local ordinances. Initiatives are used to form municipalities and, in most instances, special districts; voter signatures totaling at least 15 percent of the turnout in the proceeding gubernatorial election are required for municipalities, whereas the number for special districts varies by type.[35] Most city and county charters contain provisions for both initiatives and referendums.[36]

Perhaps the only time the word "liberal" is found in the Missouri statutes is with regard to citizen access to public meetings and records. In 1987 the General Assembly forthrightly stated that "it is the public policy of this state that meetings, records, votes, actions, and deliberations of public governmental bodies be open to the public unless provided by law" and that this statement "shall be liberally construed and their exceptions strictly construed to promote this public policy."[37] This intention was expanded in the 1997 legislative session. Typical exceptions include legal actions, property negotiations, and meetings in which private concerns are discussed .

State-Local Relations

Local governments in Missouri, especially cities, have considerable autonomy concerning their functional responsibilities. The state is relatively quiet about what they should do; thus, service levels vary widely in small incorporated areas with volunteer governments and in jurisdictions that are larger and more programmatically diverse. Because localities tend to ask the state for permission to do what they wish, the state does not need to enact broad-scope legislation. Thus, Missouri statutes are riddled with special legislation that often applies to a single government, the City of St. Louis being a prime example.

Constraints on local fiscal activity are embodied in the 1980 Hancock Amendment, which requires voter approval for any tax, license, or fee increase. In the absence of some natural growth in the tax base, getting new revenues or increasing existing ones is difficult. Voter approval can be a major obstacle. Without state legislative involvement, localities are fiscally constrained and so are their activities.

It is difficult to discern any clear trend toward more or less autonomy for Missouri localities. (The exception is in the area of K–12 education, where a new state funding formula and rules and regulations are more significant than in the past.) There has been a tendency toward slightly more autonomy, for example, in terms of zoning control of billboards along state highways or use of earmarked taxes for health and youth services. However, there has been a virtual absence of broad regional solutions, especially in the St. Louis area.

The capacity of local governments to obtain additional resources—especially crucial in an age of federal devolution—is likely to be contentious. Federal government cutbacks adversely affect the state and localities even more so. But how will cuts be met or new programs put in place without voter approval of revenue increases? Utility deregulation is another emerging factor of particular import to municipalities. Deregulation could also have significant adverse revenue implications for the gross receipts tax, which is a major source of funds for cities. There is also likely to be continued litigation over the Hancock Amendment and variable interpretation of what is "fee for service" (which is exempt) and what fee or charge is covered. This takes on even more importance in light of the shift toward fees and charges and away from taxes.

A second issue pertains to the extreme governmental fragmentation in St. Louis County and the relation of the county to St. Louis City. With ninety-two cities (plus other jurisdictions), a land-grab mentality prevails: anything that will generate revenue is seized upon, including sales, gross receipts, and gaming taxes. Moreover, there is an ongoing push for more incorporations and annexations. Exacerbating matters is St. Louis City's deteriorating financial status and the fact that there are not broad-scope approaches to regional problems. How can the city and county work more in concert with each other? What will the state do to encourage this, and does the state even want to? These questions remain open.

Notes

1. Donald Phares, "Financing Local Governments," in *St. Louis Currents: A Guide to the Region and its Resources*, ed. James E. O'Donnell (St. Louis: Missouri Historical Society, 1997), 55–64.

2. *Committee for Educational Quality and Lee's Summit School District v. State of Missouri*, 878 S.W.2d 446 (1994). Senate Bill No. 380, 87th General Assembly, State of Missouri (1993).

3. Missouri Constitution, Article X, section 18(e).

4. James Neal Primm, *Lion of the Valley: St. Louis, Missouri*, 2d ed. (Boulder: Pruett, 1990), 321–326.

5. Missouri Constitution, Article VI, sections 18 (a) and 19.

6. Missouri Constitution, Article VI, section 31.

7. John Ballard, "County Government in Missouri," in *Missouri Government and Politics*, ed. Richard J. Hardy, Richard R. Dohm, and David A. Leuthold (Columbia: University of Missouri Press, 1995), 306.

8. Missouri Constitution, Article X, section 22.

9. Missouri Constitution, Article VI, section 19(a).

10. Missouri Constitution, Article VI, section 10.

11. Missouri Constitution, Article VI, section 19.

12. Missouri Constitution, Article VI, section 18.

13. Missouri Constitution, Article VI, sections 30(a), 3, and 5.

14. Missouri Revised Statutes, Chap. 89.

15. Missouri Revised Statutes, Title VI.

16. Missouri Revised Statutes, Title VII.

17. State Auditor of Missouri, "Review of 1997 Property Tax Rates," report no. 98-07 (Jefferson City: Office of the State Auditor of Missouri, 9 February 1998).

18. Missouri Constitution, Article VI, section 16.

19. U.S. Advisory Commission on Intergovernmental Relations (ACIR), *Metropolitan Organization: The St. Louis Case* (Washington, D.C.: ACIR, 1988).

20. Missouri Revised Statutes, Chap. 353.

21. Missouri Revised Statutes, Chaps. 99.800–99.856, 251.500, 100.250–100.297.

22. Missouri Constitution, Article X, sections 16–24.

23. *Keller v. Marion County Ambulance District*, 820 S.W.2d 301 (1991).

24. Donald Phares, "State and Local Revenue and Expenditure Policies," in *Missouri Government and Politics*, ed. Hardy, Dohm, and Leuthold, 205–221.

25. Phares, "State and Local Revenue and Expenditure Policies," note 24.

26. Missouri Constitution, Article VI, section 26 (a–d).

27. Phares, "State and Local Revenue and Expenditure Policies," note 2.

28. Taxpayers Research Institute of Missouri (TRIM), in cooperation with the Public Policy Research Centers, University of Missouri–St. Louis, *Handbook of Missouri Taxes* (Jefferson City: TRIM, 1998), 40.

29. TRIM, *Handbook of Missouri Taxes*, 43–44, 49, 65–67.

30. See Missouri Constitution, Article X, section 21.

31. Missouri Revised Statutes, Title IX, Chap. 115.

32. Missouri Revised Statutes, Title IX, Chap. 130.

33. Missouri Revised Statutes, Title VIII, Chap. 106.

34. Missouri Revised Statutes, Title VII, Chap. 71.

35. Missouri Revised Statutes, Title VII, Chap. 72.

36. For example, see St. Louis County Charter, Article IX of the Missouri Constitution.

37. Missouri Revised Statutes, Title XXXIX, Chap. 610.

MONTANA

Kenneth L. Weaver

Montana's version of home rule, termed "self-government powers," is based on a 1972 constitutional grant of all powers not prohibited to those units of local government that adopt a charter or amend their existing plan of government. At present, one county, both consolidated city-county governments, and thirty of Montana's municipalities have adopted self-government powers. However, most have not explored the opportunity to apply their augmented local governing authority. Those jurisdictions that have done so have fared well when their self-government powers have been tested in the courts. The phrase "home rule" does not appear in the 1972 constitution nor in the implementing statutes.

Montana's unique local government review process is also mandated by the 1972 constitution. The local government article requires that, every ten years, voters in every local jurisdiction must be asked by ballot whether or not they wish to elect a study commission of citizens to undertake a two-year review of their unit of local government. The elected study commissions are empowered to ballot for voters' consideration recommendations concerning the adoption of self-government powers as well as the form and structures of their local government.

Governmental Setting

One of the striking characteristics of Montana's governmental structures is the substantial degree to which the state relies on elected citizen volunteers to represent citizen needs, expectations, and demands at both the state and local level. For example, the state's term-limited legislature comprises a house (with 100 members elected to two-year terms from single-member districts) and a senate (with 50 members serving four-year overlapping terms who are elected from senate districts, each of which comprises two adjacent house districts). Montana's preference for ample elected representation is also demonstrated in an executive branch that includes not only an elected governor and lieutenant governor but also a separately elected attorney general, secretary of state, auditor, and superintendent of public instruction. Similarly, the seven members of the state supreme court, which serves as the state's single appellate jurisdiction, are also directly elected.

Elected representation is also found at the local level in the traditional three-member boards of county commissioners, which are augmented by as many as ten additional elected county officers, including the county attorney, sheriff, clerk and recorder, clerk of district court, county superintendent of schools, and treasurer. There are some 635 elected county officers, in addition to the 35 locally elected district court judges and 56 elected justices of the peace. The state's 129 incorporated cities and towns elect an additional 731 mayors and council members.

In total (and not including elected school boards or special-district boards), Montanans elect at least 1,612 officials to "represent" less than 900,000 citizens who are spread sparsely and unevenly across the nation's fourth largest state. In short, Montana has at least one elected official for every 550 citizens.

Arguably, it is the Big Sky state's huge size, remarkable physiography, and socioeconomic diversity that best explains its complex political culture, including its penchant for rampant representation. The self-perceived interests of that 50 percent of the state's population living outside incorporated city or town limits are not the same as those of the 275,000 residents of the six largest cities (with populations greater than 25,000) nor of the remaining 275,00 citizens scattered among the smaller and widely dispersed incorporated cities and towns. The mountain valleys of western Montana are experiencing tremendous population growth rates, with corresponding advances in apparent middle-class affluence imperfectly mirrored in escalating property tax values. On the other hand, predominantly agricultural eastern Montana is experiencing sustained population decline matched by declining property tax values. The state's historic and continuing economic dependence on the exploitation of natural resources (such as fossil fuels, forest products, metals mining, and agriculture) and tourism fractionates the polity into both commodity-based interest groups and more broadly based factions that generally favor or oppose historic natural resource production practices. Thus, although the population of the state is small, the competing political interests are as energetic as they are diverse.[1]

Partisan politics, however, is much less evident in local government structures than in state and national office. County officials nominally are elected on a partisan ballot but typically disclaim partisan influence on their decision making. The overwhelming preponderance of municipal officials are elected on a non-partisan ballot.

Although Montana's huge size, varied physiography, and socioeconomic diversity may help explain the state's preference for an abundance of representation and for a more or less balanced two-party political system, the continuing dependence of localities on state government is somewhat more difficult to understand. Certainly the progressive 1972 state constitution contemplated a much more robust autonomy for the state's 56 counties and 129 incorporated municipalities than has been realized in the ensuing twenty-five years since its ratification. For example, Montana's 1972 constitution mandates that every ten years, all units of local government elect a panel of citizen volunteers to study their unit of government and to ballot any recommendation for changes in structures, powers, and service delivery, including locally devised charters providing for self-government powers. This local government review process is unique to Montana and has resulted in sixty-nine voter-approved changes in local government structures and powers, including the adoption of twenty-two self-governing charters.

Despite the local government review process, Montana local governments are relatively dependent on the state, because most units of county and municipal government are organized as "general powers" governments. In Montana, local governments with general powers have traditionally relied on legislative delegation of authority to perform any governmental function, provide any governmental service, or alter their governmental structures and organization. One Montana scholar[2] has argued that this narrow Dillon's Rule tradition has been liberalized somewhat by the Montana Supreme Court since the adoption of the 1972 constitution. However, a great deal of local government "housekeeping" legislation is still required each biennial ninety-day session of the state legislature, just to enable Montana's local governments to respond to local needs. This pattern continues despite the opportunity inherent in the 1972 constitution for local governments and their citizens to adopt self-governing powers and to reduce their day-to-day operational and fiscal dependency on state government.

The pace of local government reform in Montana has been modest but not because of constitutional or legislative barriers impeding the development of more self-reliant local government. Rather, needed reforms have come slowly because local leaders apparently are reluctant to recognize and respond appro-priately to the dramatic changes confronting so many Montana counties and communities. Impressive, even explosive population growth in western Montana (which is paralleled in much of eastern Montana by population decline) imposes unprecedented demands not only on the local property tax base but also on local infrastructure, service delivery, land-use planning, and other health, safety, and welfare responsibilities of local government. Complicating the governing tasks of local officials has been a property tax freeze imposed by voter initiative (I-105) on local government in 1986 and by an even more restrictive property tax limitation imposed by the 1997 and 1999 legislative sessions.[3] Moreover, the devolution of the American federal system, combined with the accelerating pace of demographically driven social change in Montana, will make even greater demands on county and municipal governments.

Home Rule in Montana

Historical Development

Even before Montana became a state, Dillon's Rule limited the governing powers of the territory's few and scattered municipalities. As early as 1887 the Supreme Court of the Montana Territory held that municipal corporations have no inherent right of local self-government. Sixty-three years later, in 1950, the Montana Supreme Court reiterated its Dillon's Rule interpretation of municipal powers under the state's first constitution (adopted at statehood in 1889).[4] However, the court did acknowledge in a number of ambiguous decisions that cities, when acting in a *proprietary* capacity, probably were entitled to the protection of the due process clause of the state constitution. Thus, in *Milligan v. Miles City,* the court held that "a city operating a municipal light plant under legislative authority acts in a proprietary capacity and stands on the same footing as a private individual or business corporation similarly situated."[5]

By 1957 the Montana Municipal League advocated the adoption of a constitutional amendment enabling the local governing body or a local charter commission to propose a home rule charter for voter consideration. Although the proposal was passed by the state house during the 1957 legislative assembly, it failed to achieve the constitutionally required two-thirds majority to amend the constitution.[6]

During the ensuing fifteen years of continuing local dependency on the state's biennial legislature, "counties and municipal corporations labored under the heavy weight of a judicially imposed Dillon's Rule, and the pinch-penny control of a rurally dominated legislature that showed little sympathy for the needs of cities and towns."[7] As a result, local officials would become a significant voice in the call for a constitutional convention.

Following (and in part enabled by) the painful process of reapportioning, and in the wake of the U.S. Supreme Court's "one person, one vote" decisions, a more "citified" legislature called for a constitutional convention in 1969. The measure passed with a 65 percent majority and was, in turn, followed by the election of 100 delegates to Montana's 1972 constitutional convention.

Champions of effective local self-government reasoned that home rule was the key to stronger and more responsive local government in Montana. The 1972 constitutional convention was viewed as the only possible way to achieve a redistribution of governing powers. Proponents argued that Montana needed a new constitutional foundation from which local government could proceed.[8] Self-government powers would allow localities to deal effectively with local problems. Moreover, greater flexibility in fashioning local government structures would enable and encourage local responsiveness and intergovernmental cooperation. These outcomes were achieved in what would be hailed as one of America's most progressive state constitutions.[9]

Definition of Home Rule

The 1972 Montana Constitution made it possible for both counties and municipalities to acquire broad self-governing powers by including language that was not based on the traditional "home rule" formulation but instead was based on a theory of "residual powers," sometimes referred to as "derivative powers."[10] Rather than granting specifically enumerated powers to local governments, or restraining legislative interference in local affairs, the 1972 constitution mandates that "a local government unit adopting a self-government charter may exercise any power not prohibited by this constitution, law or charter."[11]

In fact, the term "home rule" does not appear in the 1972 Montana Constitution nor in the implementing statutes, thereby avoiding any confusion with a narrower theory of home rule adopted in other states. Rather, the term "self-government powers" is widely and commonly used by Montana courts, local officials, and others to differentiate municipalities and counties with self-governing charters from local governments that possess more limited "general powers." The implementing statutes define self-governing powers to include the specific authority to "provide any services or perform any functions not expressly prohibited by the Montana Constitution, state law or its charter"; furthermore, the courts are required to liberally construe the self-governing powers of local units.[12]

Having established that local governments with self-governing powers are to have all powers not prohibited, the implementing statutes then enumerate the specific powers that are legislatively prohibited or that require legislative delegation or consistency with state regulation.[13] As one experienced county attorney has noted, "While this approach leaves local government subject to legislative control, it has the advantage of providing the broadest possible potential range of local power and of reducing judicial intervention to determining whether or not a power has been denied."[14]

This approach to local self-governing powers does not shield any area of local policy from legislative purpose. Indeed, the absence of constitutional protection of local affairs is a marked departure from home rule as practiced in some states. In operational terms, 30 of Montana's 129 incorporated cities and 3 counties (including the two consolidated city-county governments) have self-government powers.

With respect to the thirty municipalities that have taken on self-governing powers, most have not explored the opportunity to expand their governing authority. Those that have done so have fared well when the application of their expanded governing powers was tested in state courts.[15] In general, the Montana Supreme Court has recognized and applied the local self-governing principle of shared powers.[16]

Examples of how municipalities have applied their self-governing powers include successful efforts to impose local development fees, extend municipal service, and provide additional services not previously authorized by the legislature. However, an effort by one municipality to use its charter-based self-governing powers to impose what was held by the court to be a legislatively prohibited local sales tax was unsuccessful.[17]

Structural Features

As in the 1889 constitution, the 1972 state constitution precludes the legislature from passing any "special or local act when a general act is or can be made applicable."[18] As a result, there is little special-privilege legislation impacting local governments. The only legislation that significantly and differentially effects the several classes of municipalities provides somewhat greater flexibility to the smaller jurisdictions, particularly with respect to the election versus appointment of certain municipal officials, the staffing requirements for police and fire protection, and the hours the city or town hall must be open for business. The legislature has adopted a municipal classification structure that provides for the following classes of cities:

• cities of the first class, with populations of 10,000 or more, the largest of which is Billings, with a 1994 estimated population of 86,578;

• cities of the second class, with populations of less than 10,000 but more than 5,000, the largest of which is Miles City, with a 1994 estimated population of 8,745;

• cities of the third class, with populations of less than 5,000 but more than 1,000, the largest of which is Sidney, with a 1998 estimated population of 4,865; and

• towns with populations of less than 1,000, the smallest of which is Ismay, with a 1994 estimated population of 20.

There are no other general-purpose municipal entities such as villages or townships in Montana.[19]

A 1972 constitutional provision stipulated that each unit of local government may by local vote adopt, amend, or abandon an optional or alternative form of government.[20] In response to this mandate, the legislature required in 1975 that each local government unit adopt one of five generic models set forth in statute. These forms include commission, commission-chairman, commission-executive (for example, mayor-council), commission-manager, and the town meeting form.

At present, there are no examples of the commission form of municipal government, even though all but 3 of Montana's 56 counties have adopted this model. There are only 11 commission-manager forms of municipal government (7 with self-governing charters), which are typically but not exclusively found in the larger cities. There are 112 commission-executive (mayor-council) forms of municipal government, 11 of which are embedded within self-government charters. Two small municipalities adopted the commission-chairman (parliamentary) form in 1976 as a result of Montana's first local government review process. Pinesdale is the only municipality to have the town meeting form, even though at least 75 towns that have populations of less than 1,000 might be expected to favor this low-cost form of municipal government.

In addition to these five generic models of local government structure, the 1972 constitution provides for the adoption by local voters of a self-governing charter, which may be applicable to virtually any structure and automatically attributes self-governing powers to the local government.[21] At present, one county, two city-county consolidated governments, and an additional nineteen municipal governments have adopted self-governing charters. Thirteen of these local government charters provide for a separately elected chief executive; seven provide for an appointed manager as chief executive. The town meeting charter provides for a "town chairman." One county government charter provides that the entire commission shall perform the executive functions.

For a community to incorporate as a municipality, the statutes require that two-thirds of the registered electors residing within the proposed limits of the municipality petition the county to call an election; not more than 300 registered electors are required to sign the petition. The proposed boundaries must include at least 300 inhabitants and must be more than three miles from any presently incorporated city or town. A simple majority of those voting is required to decide the question which, if in the affirmative, will lead to the election of the officers of the new government.[22]

The statutory provisions enabling annexation of land into an incorporated municipality are in some respects much more complex than incorporation law and have undergone extensive review by the courts. The following standards must be met before a municipality may extend its boundaries through annexation: (1) the area must be contiguous to the municipality's boundaries; (2) no part of the area may be included within the boundary of another municipality; (3) the proposed annexation must conform to a comprehensive plan; and (4) no part of the area to be annexed may be included within a rural fire district.[23]

Fifty-three of Montana's fifty-six county governments are facsimiles of midwestern prototypes at the time of the closure of the western frontier[24]—attesting to the durability of the original structures. Montana's first constitution, adopted in 1889 upon admission to the Union, provided for three-member boards of county commissioners and specified the election of the usual slate of county officers (that is, the county attorney, sheriff, treasurer, clerk and recorder, clerk of district court, assessor, surveyor, coroner, public administrator, and superintendent of schools). The state's sixteen original counties were subsequently cloned during a frenzy of "county-splitting" in the first two decades of the twentieth century[25] to produce the present fifty-six county governments.

The exercise of municipal extraterritorial jurisdiction for subdivision review, zoning, and building inspection is limited by law to between one and four and one-half miles beyond the city limits, depending on the nature of the specific function being performed and the size of the municipality. Even this limited extraterritorial jurisdiction is coming under increasing legislative scrutiny, because rural developers have sought to pursue their interests solely under the less restrictive regulatory environment of county government.

The framers of the 1972 constitution mandated that each unit of Montana local government "review its structure and submit one alternative form of government to the qualified electors at the next general or special election."[26] To conduct the decennial review, local study commissions are elected to a two-year term of uncompensated office and are provided with a local property tax–supported budget to carry out their work. The elected study commissions may propose virtually any form of government and respective governing powers that do not violate the constitution or state law.

In short, the 1972 constitution inhibited local government powers by requiring voter approval of any actions. After three complete cycles (1974–1976, 1984–1986, and 1994–1996), the local government review process has resulted in the local election or appointment of 1,433 citizen study commissioners who review the structures and powers of their respective units of city and county government. The reviews have resulted in sixty-nine voter-approved changes in local government structures and powers, including the adoption of two city-county consolidation charters, one county charter, and sixteen municipal charters (six of which provide for the city manager plan of government).[27] Perhaps of greater significance in an era of intensified citizen distrust of government, however, is simply the opportunity for the voters to assert the right of review and to participate directly in fashioning the instruments of their own governance.

Functions of Local Government

Functional Responsibilities

Most Montana municipalities provide the usual array of police, fire, and emergency services, as well as recreation, cultural, and specialized services for youth and senior citizens. Each municipality also operates a city court of limited jurisdiction. Water, wastewater, and garbage services are typically but not exclusively provided by the municipality as a proprietary (enterprise) activity funded by fees-for-service. Most larger municipalities have also assumed responsibility under enabling state law for land-use planning and zoning within the city limits. Environmental regulation, notably air quality monitoring and enforcement of state and local standards, is performed in several of the largest cities. Few Montana municipalities conduct public assistance or welfare programs of any kind; these functions are the exclusive domain of county government.

In general, county government in Montana enforces state law and collects the property taxes for redistribution to the state and to all other local government entities in the county. Counties generally conduct the delivery of human services and public assistance which is, at this writing, undergoing a massive reorganization and reform under state direction. Counties conduct elections (other than for the K–12 system) and operate the state's district courts of original jurisdiction and the county's justice courts of limited jurisdiction. The locally elected county attorney serves as the state's attorney in the prosecution of state law violations. The elected county sheriff provides rural law enforcement, operates jails (usually for both the municipal and county jurisdictions), and serves subpoenas and other legal notices.

Counties are responsible for maintaining roads beyond municipal jurisdictions—an especially costly program in a state noted for severe winter conditions and with a scattered population (nearly half of whom live miles beyond city limits). Land-use planning responsibilities and even zoning authority have been assumed by counties that are experiencing rapid growth. These counties have adopted a comprehensive master plan seeking to curb the worst environmental and cost consequences of rural sprawl and poorly conceived twenty-acre "ranchette" development.[28]

With or without self-governing powers, Montana's municipalities and counties have substantial authority by law to create special districts and public authorities for the purposes of providing a higher level of service and assessing or taxing property owners within the district to recover the costs of doing so.[29] Municipalities often use special districts as assessment mechanisms to fund facility capital improvements through the sale of bonds. Special districts are also often employed simply to recover operations and maintenance costs for services such as neighborhood street lighting, citywide street maintenance, fire hydrant maintenance, and (in at least one case) citywide tree maintenance.

Since the imposition of a freeze on Montana property taxes in 1986,[30] municipalities increasingly have relied on the creation of special districts as a means to shift the cost burden of certain services out of the property tax–supported general fund and to an assessment-supported special district. This tendency is most evident in Montana's larger municipalities, which typically have the benefit of trained and experienced city managers who likely are more innovative than elected executives in coping with a frozen tax base.

In addition to enabling municipal and county governments to create a wide array of service districts, state law also provides for the creation of semiautonomous "authorities," notably port authorities, airport authorities, and parking commissions. These local entities are governed by boards of commissioners who are typically appointed by the local governing body for an uncompensated term of office.

The Interlocal Cooperation Act implements a broad grant of constitutional authority to local governments, enabling them to cooperate in the delivery of public services.[31] Since 1985 hundreds of interlocal agreements have been negotiated by Montana local government units under this authority. More than half of the interlocal agreements are for public safety, including law enforcement, dispatch, confinement facilities, and fire protection. Other functions include land-use planning, refuse disposal, financial accounting, recreation facilities, and disposal of junk vehicles. However, few of these agreements address cooperative purchasing, and few have been negotiated between local governments and either public schools or state agencies. There appears to be far greater potential under existing statutes for mutually advantageous use of interlocal agreements by cooperating local governments than heretofore realized. Impediments to expanded local application of cooperative service agreements do not appear to be inherent in existing law.[32]

Administrative Discretion

In general, state law establishing employee classification, compensation, and benefit rights and procedures do not extend to municipal employees. However, a number of state laws establishing antidiscrimination and fair labor practices do extend to the local government workplace and to the employment relationship. Notable among these are the "wrongful discharge" statute, collective bargaining laws, minimum wage and overtime compensation requirements, and the various employment equity provisions applying to protected-class persons such as women, minorities, veterans, and disabled persons. Most municipal employees are eligible for participation in the state retirement program, the Public Employee Retirement System (PERS). All employees are covered either by the state's workers' compensation program or by a less costly risk management and insurance program provided by the Montana Municipal Insurance Authority under the aegis of the Montana League of Cities and Towns. Municipal governments, unlike county governments, are empowered by statute to set the compensation of their employees and their elected officials.

Also set by statute during the 1995 legislative session was a tough new ethics law with new and broadened limitations for local officials and employees.[33] Included are prohibitions related to employment activities, post–public service employment, use of public resources (including the elected official's time), nepotism, conflict of interest, and campaign practices.

There is little in the way of professional personnel management assistance available to local government officials. Only three or four of the largest municipal jurisdictions have a human resources manager on staff; the League of Cities has no professional human resources person available for consultation; and the state Department of Administration is simply not staffed or funded to provide direct personnel management assistance to local governments. The Local Government Center at Montana State University provides regular training for municipal officials on various human resource management topics; assists in the development of position descriptions, performance appraisal procedures, and compensation plans; and provides model personnel policies.

The Montana Administrative Procedures Act and the Administrative Rules of Montana do not apply to local government. Rather, municipal and county governments are obliged to conform to an antiquated body of statutes titled "General Operation and Conduct of Business."[34] Many of these statutes are ambiguous and contradicted by more recent statutes providing specific administrative procedures and rules to accomplish particular purposes. Few municipal governments have adopted their own local administrative code and therefore depend heavily on the general statutes for day-to-day procedural guidelines.

Municipal governments have broad authority to buy, sell, mortgage, lease, hold, manage, or dispose of any interest in real or personal property and to contract with individuals, corporations, or other governmental entities. Contracts for the purchase of certain types of equipment (such as motor vehicles) and certain services costing in excess of $25,000 must by law be let to the lowest responsible bidder after bids have been advertised.[35]

Under Montana law,[36] a municipal governing body may create an advisory planning board to recommend and review land-use policies, plans, and improvements. To create a planning board, the county commission must concur. The commission may opt instead to create a combined city-county planning board to exercise advisory jurisdiction throughout the county.

State law establishes the composition and qualifications of the uncompensated members of both the planning board and the zoning board. In general, a municipal government has the authority to divide the city or town into zoning districts to regulate the construction or use of structures therein.[37] The governing body itself may grant variances to established zoning ordinances, or it may create and appoint a board of adjustment to hear, review, and decide on land owner petitions for variance. The decisions of the board of adjustment may be appealed only to a court of record, which in Montana is the district court.

Economic Development

The Montana Development Corporation Act[38] enables the creation of development corporations, which may in turn receive public monies, borrow from public entities, and make loans to private firms, corporations, and companies for the purpose of promoting business and general economic development. The local development corporations often serve as the lead agency in coordinating the Montana Certified Cities Program. The program includes some forty-seven municipalities and is organized to attract business and tourism.

The state Department of Commerce operates two major programs which provide infrastructure renewal and economic development resources on a competitive and shared-participation basis to qualified local entities, most frequently municipalities. The Community Development Block Grant Program ($7.4 million in 2000) is funded by federal pass-through dollars (that is, intergovernmental transfer payments from the federal government to state governments that are, by law, reallocated by state governments to fund local programs). By contrast, the Treasure State Endowment Program ($12 million in 2000–2001) is funded by earmarked interest earnings on the state's coal severance tax fund. In addition, there are a number of smaller-scale grant and revolving loan funds available from various state agencies. Notable among these are tourism promotion resources generated by a statewide 4 percent lodging (hotel-motel) tax, of which $1.9 million of the approximately $8.7 million annual yield is allocated back to local and regional tourism promotion agencies.

Montana law permits the creation of industrial parks by private, nonprofit organizations and provides significant property tax advantages to the local economic development organization or port authority owning and operating the industrial park. If approved by resolution of the governing body of the local taxing jurisdiction, the industrial park may be exempted from the annual property tax levy of the jurisdiction approving the exemption.[39]

Municipal governments are empowered by law to adopt urban renewal plans and projects for the prevention and elimination of blighted areas within their jurisdictions.[40] To accomplish this purpose, they may create a "tax increment financing district," thereby enabling the city government to fund the project by dedicating the "incremental taxable value" of any taxable property within the district to fund renewal projects within the district. Tax increment resources may be used, for example, to retire debt incurred for capital improvements within the district.

Fiscal Autonomy of Local Governments

Local Revenues

Because there is no general sales tax in Montana—and because municipalities have no local option taxing authority—the municipal tax base is limited to the value of taxable property. At present, there are twelve distinct classes of taxable property in Montana, and the tax rate of each class is set by state law.[41] The most important class of taxable property for municipal governments is typically residential and commercial real property and improvements (Class IV), with a tax rate of 3.86 percent of the assessed (market) value of the property.[42] The summation of the taxable value of all taxable property within a local jurisdiction is its property tax base, which when divided by 1,000 equals the value of 1 property tax mill. As of 1999, the average property tax mill value for incorporated municipalities in Montana was $4,470.[43] The range extends from a mill value of $226,015 in Billings (1998 population of 91,750) to $48 in Bear Creek (1998 population of 42).

A few resort communities are also empowered to levy a "resort tax," which essentially is a general sales tax of as much as 3 percent targeting the goods and services associated with resort economies such as motels, hotels, restaurants, bars, and luxury goods.[44] Only four municipalities currently impose a resort tax. The Town of West Yellowstone, for example, has a resident population of only 1,000 yet serves as the western gateway for one million annual visitors to Yellowstone National Park. In 1999 the town's 2.5 percent resort tax on a limited range of goods and services generated $1.5 million in revenue, for a 1999 general-fund budget of $1.9 million.

Because tax rates are set by state law—and because the county assessor or appraiser who calculates the taxable valuation (mill value) for each jurisdiction within the county is typically a state employee—local governments have no responsibility or authority to set either taxable valuations or tax rates for their respective jurisdictions. What they can set is the mill levy, which is capped by state law and frozen at 1996 levels. The 1998 average general-fund mill levy of Montana municipalities was 78.88; when all additional special mill levies are included, the municipal average is 93.39. This average has increased by only 2 percent in the past five years, generally reflecting the effectiveness of the property tax freeze.

The property tax freeze has since been extended and made even more restrictive by the 1997 legislature. County and municipal officials are increasingly hard pressed to maintain expected levels of service delivery because of the fiscal constraints imposed by a frozen property tax base. Since the imposition of a property tax freeze in 1986, the purchasing power of the average Montana county government has declined by 21 percent and that of city government by 9 percent.[45] Because Montana does not have a general sales tax that might be relied on to offset the erosion of annual inflation, municipalities have come to depend on transfer revenues derived from state taxes that are imposed on the growing number of electronic gambling machines in Montana. Nearly $24 million in gambling machine revenue was returned to the county and municipal jurisdictions of origin in 1998. In some municipalities, gambling revenue constituted as much as 15 percent of annual general-fund resources.

The only other locally generated revenues are limited by state law to a narrow range of specified fees, such as the fines and forfeitures generated by the city court or by subdivision review and building inspection fees, animal control, and business license fees. The revenues from all of these sources are deposited in the general-fund accounts of the city. Fees for water, wastewater, and garbage and landfill services must by law be accounted for within the enterprise (proprietary) fund group and are not transferable to fund the general operations of municipal government.

Montana municipalities are limited in the amount of public debt they can incur. A municipality may not incur more debt or sell more bonds than the equivalent of approximately 28 percent of the taxable value of the property within the jurisdiction of the city or town. An additional increment of debt ceiling is permitted for the purpose of funding the construction of municipal water or sewer systems.

In general, municipalities may issue two types of debt instruments. General-obligation bonds may be used to fund all manner of general-fund or enterprise fund capital equipment or capital improvements. These bonds are backed by the municipality's full faith and credit and require voter approval. Revenue bonds are used primarily for fee-for-service undertakings (such as a water system or parking facility) or for some other predictable revenue stream (such as an assessment for services provided by a special district). Revenue bonds do not require voter approval for repayment of the debt.[46]

Local Expenditures

Montana's Municipal Budgeting Law[47] requires that all appropriations and expenditures be classified as salaries and wages; maintenance and operations; capital outlay; interest, and debt redemption; or miscellaneous. A typical general-fund budget for a Montana municipality would allocate the largest share (often more than 50 percent of its annual appropriation) to meeting public safety requirements. In the larger cities, staffing costs of the police and fire departments result in public safety expenditures that often exceed 60 percent of the municipality's total general-fund expenditures. In the smaller cities and towns, the budgeted costs of the volunteer fire departments and the thinly staffed police departments are usually quite modest, typically less than 35 percent of a municipality's general-fund expenditures.

For most cities and towns, the balance of the general-fund budget is dedicated largely to the operations and maintenance costs associated with public works, notably street maintenance, which would be expected to consume as much as 20 percent of the total general-fund budget. Cultural services and facilities such as parks, recreation, and libraries might receive, in aggregate, 10–12 percent of the municipality's total general-fund appropriation.

The average general-fund appropriation for Montana's 129 incorporated cities and towns in fiscal 1999 was approximately $1,112,000, ranging from an average of $12.6 million for the seven Class I cities to a modest $147,000 for the 78 incorporated towns. The average annual general-fund expenditure per capita is a rather meager $287, varying between a high of $308 for Class I cities and a low of $283 for towns.[48]

Most municipalities provide utility services (such as water, wastewater, and garbage) as proprietary activities funded by fees-for-service rather than property taxes. The rate structure, which all too often is flat rated and not metered in many of the smaller jurisdictions, seldom provides a revenue stream adequate to fund capital replacement. As a result, too many of the state's 180 public water systems, 191 public wastewater facilities, and 105 sanitary landfills are in urgent need of major repairs or replacement, recently estimated to be $350 million.[49]

The Montana Budgeting, Accounting and Reporting System[50] specifies both the format of budgets and the financial reporting requirements for local governments. Local governments' final budgets must balance proposed expenditures and available resources. Additionally, the state has adopted the Montana Single Audit Act. Under the act, the governing body of a municipality receiving more than $200,000 in revenue (or $25,000 in federal revenues) can mandate that an audit be conducted every two years by a qualified independent auditor.

A municipality may declare bankruptcy if its governing body adopts a resolution declaring that it is insolvent and unable to meet its debts. The resolution must also state that the municipality wishes to adjust its obligations under the provisions of the federal municipal bankruptcy laws.

State Government Grants-in-Aid to Localities

Welfare services in Montana are delivered primarily through county government. The recently reformed welfare delivery system known as Families Achieving Independence in Montana has now been implemented throughout the state by the Montana Department of Public Health and Human Services.

Grants-in-aid from the state to local school districts include both unrestricted and restricted grants. In fiscal 1997, localities received approximately $392 million in direct, unrestricted state aid for the primary purpose of equalizing K–12 education funding across the state. Restricted grants such as special-education programs for school districts and cooperatives totaled $28 million and $4 million, respectively.

Unfunded Mandates

Under a long-established statute, the legislature cannot require local governments to perform an activity or provide a service or facility without first providing the local government the specific means to finance the activity, service, or facility. The significance of this so-called Drake Amendment[51] has increased during recent legislative sessions as the legislature has sought to balance its own budget amid self-imposed revenue reductions. As a result, the issue of state-imposed unfunded mandates on local governments has not been significant in the past ten years, whereas legislative restriction of local government revenues has been, especially during the 1997 and 1999 legislative sessions.

Access to Local Government

Local Elections

With the exception of K–12 elections, which are conducted by school district administrators, all other local elections are conducted by the county election administrator. Municipal governments have no role in the conduct of elections for municipal office. The county election administrator prepares the ballots, trains the election judges, oversees the elections, and counts and canvasses the vote. Because state election law is quite detailed, the county election administrator has little discretionary judgment. Moreover, local governments (with or without self-governing powers) may not deviate or alter election procedures by ordinance or by charter.

Citizen Controls over Actions of Local Officials

The Montana Recall Act[52] provides that any local elected or appointed official may be recalled from office by petition of the qualified electors. In the case of municipal officials, the petition must contain the signatures of 20 percent of the number of persons registered to vote at the preceding municipal election. Reasons for recall include physical or mental lack of fitness, incompetence, violation of the oath of office, official misconduct, or conviction of a felony offense.

Both statewide and local lawmaking powers are extended to the people by the constitution and implementing statute.[53] By petition of 25 percent of the registered voters at the last general municipal election, municipal electors may initiate and amend ordinances or require a vote on existing ordinances. However, the powers of initiative and referendum do not extend to ordinances dealing with the annual budget, bond proceedings (other than ordinances authorizing bonds), or the establishment or levy of assessments pledged to the payment of bond principle or interest.

Montana's 1972 constitution makes explicit the public's right to examine public documents and to observe the deliberation of all public agencies, except when an individual's right of privacy clearly exceeds the merits of public disclosure.[54] Moreover, meetings are subject to the open-meeting law when a quorum of a public agency (including a city council or county commission) is convened—whether in person or by electronic means—to hear, discuss, or act on a matter within its jurisdiction. Such meetings must be open to the general public, unless the presiding office finds that the right of individual privacy clearly exceeds the merits of public disclosure. Violations of the statute will flaw the resulting decision of the governing body and could result in criminal prosecution.

State-Local Relations

Montana's elected mayors and council members are becoming increasingly aware of a widening gap between the essential and pressing needs of their communities, on the one hand, and the constraints of limited fiscal and human resources to meet those needs, on the other. That the turnover rate among these officials will probably continue to exceed 30 percent every two years, however, may well deplete innovation capacity in those municipal governments most needful of knowledgeable leadership.

In some cities and towns, the available revenues from a frozen property tax base will prove insufficient to fund the infrastructure replacement and enlargement essential to sustain a burgeoning population growth that exceeds 5 percent per year in some western communities. In far too many other communities, especially in eastern Montana, the loss of population combined with continuing erosion of the property tax base threaten the delivery of even the most basic services expected of a municipal government. Transfer revenues from state-collected taxes on gambling machines, however, may offset inflation in many cities and towns, even at the risk of increasing dependency on this inherently precarious source of revenue.

The ability of state agencies to intervene constructively to assist local officials or to help narrow the widening gap between local needs and local resources is limited to the existing and insufficiently funded infrastructure renewal programs such as the Community Development Block Grant Program and the Treasure State Endowment Program.[55] Tax reform, as championed by the Montana Association of Counties and by the Montana League of Cities and Towns, would provide flexible, local option taxing authority and stable local revenue streams. But the likelihood of such reform seems remote.

To what extent will local officials use the governing tools extended to them by the 1972 constitution? Self-governing powers will not necessarily solve local problems. However, the larger and professionally managed municipal governments in Montana that have adopted self-governing charters have also demonstrated considerable management innovation. These governments have used their augmented powers to achieve fiscal stability as well as efficient and responsive service delivery, despite frozen property tax bases and relatively little assistance from the state.

Notes

1. See Michael P. Malone and Richard B. Roeder, *Montana: A History of Two Centuries* (Seattle: University of Washington Press, 1976), 288–289.

2. See James J. Lopach, "Local Government under the 1972 Montana Constitution," *Montana Law Review* 51, no. 2 (summer 1990).

3. SB 195 (1997 legislative session) extends the property tax freeze at 1996 values and requires voter approval of any increased property tax mill levy with at least 40 percent voter turnout required. SB 184 (1999 legislative session) froze property tax values.

4. David R. Mason, "Home Rule in Montana—Present and Proposed," *Montana Law Review* 19, no. 2 (spring 1958): 82 (citing *Davenport v. Kleinschmidt*, 6 Mont. 502, 527 13 Pac. 249, 253 [1887]), 83 (citing *Dietrich v. Deer Lodge*, 124 Mont. 8, 13, P.2d 708,711 [1950]).

5. Mason, "Home Rule in Montana," 96. For a differentiation between governmental and proprietary powers, see Eugene McQuillin, *The Law of Municipal Corporations*, 3d ed., vol. 2a (Chicago: Callaghan, Callaghan, 1996), 378.

6. Mason, "Home Rule in Montana," 82.

7. Richard Roeder, "The 1972 Constitution in Historical Perspective," *Montana Law Review* 51, no. 2 (summer 1990): 268.

8. Paraphrased from James D. Moore, "Local Government: Old Problems and a New Constitution," *Montana Law Review* 33, no. 1 (winter 1972): 157.

9. For comment on the 1972 constitution and the adoption process, see Daniel J. Elazar, "Principles and Traditions Underlying American State Constitutions," *Publius* 12, no. 1 (winter 1982): 22.

10. At the time, this approach was advocated by the American Municipal Association, the ACIR, and the Municipal League. Moore, "Local Government," 168. See also McQuillin, *Law of Municipal Corporations*, 349; Albert L. Strum, "Development of American State Constitutions," *Publius* 12, no. 1 (winter 1982): 94.

11. Constitution of the State of Montana, Article XI, section 6. The reference to the extension of self-government powers to other local governments with "optional forms" of government means that a unit of local government may, with local voter approval, acquire self-government powers without adopting a charter. See Montana Code Annotated, 7-3-103.

12. Montana Code Annotated, 7-1-106.

13. Montana Code Annotated, 7-1-111–114.

14. Michael W. Sehested, "Self-Government Powers in Montana," MSU Extension Publication 303 (Bozeman: Montana State University, August 1975). For an excellent analysis of the evolution of judicial interpretation of self-governing powers since the 1972 constitution, see Moore, "Local Government," 168; Lopach, "Local Government under the 1972 Montana Constitution," 478–485.

15. Lopach, "Local Government under the 1972 Montana Constitution," 478.

16. See *D & F Sanitation Service v. City of Billings*, 219 M 437, 713 P.2d 977, 43 St. Rep. 74 (1986).

17. *Montana Innkeepers Association v. City of Billings*, 206 Mont. 425, 671 P.2d 21, St. Rep. 1753 (1983).

18. Constitution of the State of Montana (1972), Article V, section 12. See also Article V, section 26 of the 1889 constitution.

19. See Montana Code Annotated, 7-1-4111 for the statutes establishing the municipal classification system and the procedures to alter classification. Montana counties are not classified based on population but on taxable valuation.

20. Constitution of the State of Montana, Article XI, section 3.

21. Constitution of the State of Montana, Article XI, section 5; Montana Code Annotated, 7-3-702.

22. Montana Code Annotated, 7-2-4401 et seq.

23. Montana Code Annotated, 7-2-4701 et seq.

24. The three exceptional counties include the two consolidated city-coun-

ties of Anaconda–Deer Lodge and Butte–Silver Bow, both of which employ self-governing charters with a commission-executive plan of government. Also included is tiny Petroleum County, with a 1994 population of 534 and a commission-manager plan of government dating from 1942.

25. For an account of the "county splitting" movement, see Malone and Roeder, *Montana: A History of Two Centuries,* 190–191.

26. Constitution of the State of Montana, Article XI, section 9.

27. Two additional charters were adopted and subsequently abandoned by the voters in Madison County and the City of Poplar.

28. Montana Code Annotated, 76-2-201. Only Gallatin County has adopted development impact fees to help mitigate the disproportionately high service costs of rural residential development.

29. See generally Montana Code Annotated, Title 7, Chapter 12.

30. Initiative I-105 adopted by the voters in November 1985 froze property tax mill levies for all local government entities effective July 1, 1986.

31. Constitution of the State of Montana, Article XI, section 7.

32. At the municipal level of government, most mayors and council members are indeed elected "citizen volunteers" who experience a 30–40 percent turnover rate in local office every two years and who preside over a small staff of employees, few of whom are prepared professionally for public service. Similarly, only a few of Montana's counties employ professional administrators to oversee the day-to-day operations and finances of county government. In short, the greatest impediment to local governments that use interlocal agreements may simply be limited "management innovation" capacity.

33. Montana Code Annotated, 2-2-101.

34. Montana Code Annotated, 2-4-102, Title 7, Chapter 5.

35. Montana Code Annotated, 7-1-4124, 7-5-4301.

36. Montana Code Annotated, 76-1-105.

37. Montana Code Annotated, 76-2-302.

38. Montana Code Annotated, 32-4-201.

39. Montana Code Annotated, 90-5-112, 15-24-1902.

40. Montana Code Annotated, 7-15-4209.

41. Montana Code Annotated, 15-6-101.

42. As a result of SB 195, the present Class IV tax rate will be lowered in successive years to 0.022 percent to offset any increase in statewide taxable valuation.

43. "Montana Municipal Profiles" (Bozeman: Local Government Center, Montana State University, 1996).

44. Montana Code Annotated, 7-6-4461.

45. Douglas J. Young, "Local Government Finance Since I-105," *Montana Policy Review* 4, no. 2 (fall 1994): 1–7.

46. Montana Code Annotated, 7-7-4423.

47. Montana Code Annotated, 7-6-4225.

48. "Montana Municipal Profiles" (Bozeman: Local Government Center, Montana State University, 1999).

49. "Survey of Montana Local Government Infrastructure Needs" (Helena: Montana Department of Commerce, January 1997).

50. Montana Code Annotated, 7-6-4224, 2-7-503.

51. Montana Code Annotated, 1-2-112.

52. Montana Code Annotated, 2-16-601.

53. Constitution of the State of Montana, Article III, sections 4 and 5; Article XI, section 8; Montana Code Annotated, 7-5-131.

54. Constitution of the State of Montana, Article II, sections 8–10; Montana Code Annotated, 2-3-201.

55. For an assessment of program performance, see Richard L. Haines, "Does Treasure State Endowment Work?" *Montana Policy Review* 4, no. 6 (fall 1994): 29–34.

NEBRASKA

Dale Krane

The author thanks Tim Kelso, Michael Nolan, the late Frank Koehler, and Professors B. J. Reed and Robert Blair for their valuable comments.

Nebraska ranks third in the nation in the number of local units of government per capita.[1] The state constitution grants cities with a population greater than 5,000 residents the authority to write their own city charter. Only Omaha (the largest city in the state) and Lincoln (the state capital) have adopted a city charter, and thus each city may enact almost any ordinance consistent with state statutes and the city charter. Nevertheless, it is prudent for these two cities to seek legislative approval either to engage in new activities or to defend a new proposal. A legislative decision granting new authority to any of the state's municipalities, however, is not the definitive word. The state supreme court has ruled that its decisions are the ultimate declaration of what is to be considered "statewide versus local affairs." Because state supreme court decisions over time have shifted traditionally municipal functions away from home rule charter authority to state authority, many observers believe that "for all practical purposes, home rule in Nebraska does not really exist."[2]

Governmental Setting

It is possible to fit all of New England plus more than half of New York state into Nebraska. The Platte River—"the Nile of Nebraska"—transverses the state from west to east. Unique to the Great Plains, the river creates a natural thoroughfare that was used by the pioneers moving west along the Oregon Trail. As telegraph and railroad lines were built from the Missouri River to the Rockies, the Platte valley became home to most of the state's citizens. There are about 1.7 million "Cornhuskers" in Nebraska, making it thirty-seventh in population and fifteenth in territorial size; most live in localities strung along Interstate 80, which for much of its route through Nebraska parallels the Platte River. Half of the state's population lives within fifty miles of downtown Omaha. The state's counties typically are large in territory and thinly populated. Of the ninety-three counties, thirty-four have less than 5,000 residents, and ten have fewer than 1,000 residents; yet several are larger in territory than some east coast states.

The settlement of the Great Plains was extremely rapid, in Nebraska even more so than in other states. The railroads lured settlers from Europe; the railroad land companies named and platted the towns according to plans that located these rail stops with a specified number of miles between stops as required to maintain profits. This rapid population boom driven by the railroads explains why "it is no wonder that all the towns looked alike!"[3]

Agribusiness dominates the state's economy and utilizes 96 percent of the state's land. Multinational food companies have located numerous facilities in Nebraska to process the state's vast production of corn, soybeans, wheat, and cattle. Industrial activity grew slowly, but with World War II and the post-war arrival in Omaha of the Strategic Air Command, the economy began to diversify. Nebraska, especially the Omaha metropolitan area, is home to a surprisingly extensive and varied list of industries. Lincoln and smaller cities in the northeastern quarter of the state also support a number of manufacturing plants.

Nebraska escaped the bloody wars over slavery that ravaged its southern neighbor Kansas, and that violence "deflected to Nebraska more numerous immigrants who preferred a place where there was less interference with European traditions, customs, and manners."[4] These newly arrived pioneers saw little need for anything other than a "simple government with little expense."[5] Daily life in the tiny villages fostered a spirit of egalitarianism coupled with the attributes of farmer frugality and self-reliance. Nebraska political culture emphasizes an individual's choices over those of the body politic; for example, Nebraska was the last of the Plains states to prohibit alcohol, the last to adopt seat belt laws, and next to the last state in the nation to use state money to fund local schools.

The main institutional features of Nebraska state government include a relatively "strong" governor, a non-partisan unicameral legislature, a state administrative structure that is only partially responsible to the governor, and an archly independent state supreme court. Though the state constitution confers several important powers on the governor, historically Nebraska governors have underplayed their authority and have acted as administrators first and legislative leaders second.[6] Part of the reason for this gubernatorial behavior can be found in the legislature. Governors encounter difficulty in trying to influence the state legislature because its members are elected on a nonpartisan basis; instead of the typical two-party division, this situation results in forty-nine parties, one for each state senator. As a consequence, majorities are extremely fluid, change from vote to vote, and are not easily organized by the chief executive or by political party. Unfortunately, this non-partisanship leaves legislators more vulnerable to interest groups.[7]

The state administrative structure is divided between those agencies that are under the direct control of the governor ("code agencies") and those that are not under the control of the governor ("non-code agencies"). Nebraska does not suffer from extreme fragmentation of executive officials, because (except for the governor and lieutenant governor) only the secretary of state, attorney general, treasurer, and auditor are elected independently. However, over forty agencies, boards, commissions, councils, and departments are not subject to direct control by the governor, including administration at all levels of education. Conversely, the departments that are subject to the governor account for the bulk of the money spent by state government. The supreme court administers the unified state judicial system. County courts and district courts carry the burden of court work. In 1991, in an effort of cope with growing case loads, a court of appeals was established, as was an office of dispute resolution.

With a numerically small and highly homogeneous population, politics in Nebraska is very intimate; most of the political activists know each other. This intimacy, however, has not stood in the way of a long history of political opportunism; popular (and brazen) political figures have been known to switch political party affiliation to pursue another office. Consequently, although the Republican Party has been the dominant party in Nebraska, the Democrats have had their share of successes over the years. The governorship in particular has changed political hands with regularity.

Home Rule in Nebraska

Historical Development

The first wave of home rule legislation in the United States began in Missouri in 1875 and ended in 1912 in Nebraska and Texas. During this period, twelve states adopted similar constitutional home rule provisions: "all established home rule through the use of a specific charter document, and all provided for voter approval of the charter."[8] Although Texas gave its cities broad powers to annex, tax, and select a form of government, Nebraska granted cities with a population of 5,000 or more only the authority to write their own charters.[9]

The passage of the Nebraska constitutional amendment on home rule came toward the end of the Populist-Progressive reform period. No particular event appears to be associated with the establishment of home rule in Nebraska.[10] Most likely, support for home rule rested on the belief that "the larger cities in the state would be free of excessive control by a rural-dominated legislature. Local citizens would build features of 'good government' into their charters."[11]

Although twenty-nine cities meet the minimum population requirement for home rule status, home rule in Nebraska has not been popular. Only Lincoln, Omaha, and Grand Island adopted home rule charters, in 1917, 1922, and 1928, respectively. No other cities have enacted charters, and in 1963 Grand Island abandoned home rule to reorganize city government under a city manager plan.

Definition of Home Rule

According to the Nebraska Constitution, "any city having a population of more than five thousand (5,000) inhabitants may frame a charter for its own government, consistent with and subject to the constitution and laws of the state."[12] The bulk of Article XI describes the procedures for the self-execution of home rule.

The Nebraska Supreme Court in 1901 declared that the power to create a municipality rests with the state legislature. By implication, "there can be no such thing as an inherent right of local self-government. . . . A city is a creature of the legislature. It can have no rights save those bestowed upon it by its creator."[13] This 1901 decision relied heavily on the precedents set out in 1868 by Judge Dillon in Iowa. Dillon had ruled that municipalities may only exercise those powers expressly granted to them by the state legislature. The passage of a constitutional amendment creating the option of home rule in Nebraska did little to alter the 1901 position of the state supreme court. In 1922 the court expressed its discontent with the doctrine of municipal affairs that had emerged in many of the original home rule states by stating that a clear demarcation is impossible to make between what is a matter of statewide concerns and what is a matter for municipal affairs; therefore, the only available course of action is case-by-case analysis.[14] The ultimate effect of this 1922 decision "which has no basis in the constitutional language of the home rule amendment, has been to amend the amendment in such a way as to undermine its basic purpose."[15]

For three decades following the 1922 decision, cities won several "municipal affairs" decisions. In the mid-1950s, the state supreme court reversed course and began to hold that more and more local activities were matters of statewide concern.[16] This "judicial determinism" extended even to local activities such as street administration.[17] By 1980 Professor A. B. Winter, the state's foremost authority on home rule, declared,

Nothing in the current Nebraska statutes gives firm recognition to the fact that the cities of Omaha and Lincoln operate under home rule charters. . . . [T]he record does not reveal any advantages to this system, with the possible exception of some intangible prestige stemming from the possession of the home rule label. . . . [T]here is, today, no area which has been designated a matter of strictly or purely local concern which has not been shifted to the statewide classification.[18]

The state supreme court reaffirmed in 1982 that it is not bound by legislative findings that a matter is of statewide concern; moreover, the court asserted that it would continue to make determinations on a case-by-case basis. A concurring opinion in this case concluded that the home rule provisions of the state constitution "have slowly been dying as the judicial hatchet has chopped away the life support system."[19] No court case since 1982 has altered Professor Winter's assessment.

Structural Features

Nebraskans exhibit a strong attachment to "local control" through their support of a large number and variety of units of government. In addition to 93 counties, there are 544 municipalities (more than in California), 452 townships, 668 school districts, 23 natural resource districts, 19 educational service units, 4 public power districts, 31 rural electric districts, and an unknown number of other single-purpose districts.

Table 1 demonstrates that, although village government and politics may have disappeared in most other states, the "real heart of local government in Nebraska is in its villages and cities."[20] Four-fifths of the state's communities contain fewer than 2,500 residents, and the modal city is a village with less than 500 persons. Thirty-four municipalities have populations of 2,500–10,000; only thirteen cities possess more than 10,000 residents and account for fully two-thirds of the state's population. Omaha (with about 360,000 residents) and Lincoln (with about 200,000 residents) account for one-third of Nebraskans.

These sharp differences in scale directly influence the passage of legislation related to municipal affairs. The power to create a municipal corporation rests solely with the state legislature.[21]

Table 1. Classes of Municipal Corporations

Municipal class	Population range	Number of municipalities	Percent of municipalities	Percent of state population
Metropolitan	300,000 or more	1	0.0025%	22.0%
Primary	100,000–299,999	1	0.0025	12.5
First class	5,000–99,999	29	5.3	23.4
Second class	800–4,999	113	20.7	11.5
Village	100–799	400	73.5	30.6

The constitution prohibits the passage of "local or special laws" related to twenty-one specific topics, six of which apply to local government affairs. However, the state legislature routinely passes laws affecting the conduct of local government by targeting legislation to one or more of the five population-based classes of municipal corporations. The state's codes organize the forms and powers of municipalities by class, and there are distinctive differences of discretionary authority by class. For example, villages use a trustee form of government, second-class cities operate with a "strong" mayor–council form, and first-class cities have a "weak" mayor–council form. Omaha and Lincoln each constitute their own municipal class; as such, the state legislature commonly writes laws that apply to only one of these two cities.[22] The state code contains separate chapters for "cities, counties, and political subdivisions," for "county government," for "cities and villages; laws applicable to all," and for each of the municipal classes. Put another way, there is no one convenient list of the laws pertaining to Nebraska local governments; instead, one must search through fifty-nine of the state code's eighty-six chapters to assemble a complete list of statutes that govern any particular city. Discussions in this chapter are based primarily on those statutes that are generally applicable to all municipal corporations and all political subdivisions, unless specifically noted.

The state legislature's use of municipal classes forces local officials, the League of Nebraska Municipalities, and local groups to band together to influence "local affairs" legislation. However, because they are each in a class by themselves and because they are home rule charter cities, Omaha and Lincoln must also pressure the legislature for any needed changes (or to prevent objectionable changes) in the laws related to their respective municipal classes. "The net result of home rule status, therefore, is to increase the lobbying workload and expense of Lincoln and Omaha as compared with other state municipalities."[23] Of course, the size and economic importance of these two cities also contribute to the amount of local legislation they generate.

Not only do Nebraskans have a penchant for numerous, small-scale jurisdictions, they also prefer part-time, amateur, "grassroots" administration. Villages function with a board of trustees, with the clerk serving as the only full-time municipal officer; some villages also have a full-time police officer. Cities typically operate with the mayor-council form. One city (Nebraska City) operates with a commission form. Although the Progressive movement left many marks on Nebraska government, only nine cities use the city manager form (eight of the nine are first-class cities), and thirty-five cities have hired city administrators to assist the mayor and council.

Municipal incorporation typically begins when a village first appears; then, over time, it gains enough population to become a city. Villages may be incorporated by a county board without a hearing upon petition of a majority of taxable inhabitants of an area. As the population of a locality grows, the local officials may opt to move to the next municipal class. To do so, local officials must file with the secretary of state a certification that the municipality has the requisite number of residents and must also issue a proclamation declaring the city's new status.[24] Other than population minimums, there are no apparent limits or requirements related to area.

Cities may annex by municipal ordinance only contiguous or adjacent territory. A detailed plan must be available for inspection and a public hearing held, but the city does not have to hold a referendum or obtain the approval of a majority of the residents in the area(s) to be annexed.[25] The guidelines that must be followed are (1) the land must be of "urban" or "suburban character" (but agricultural use is not by definition "rural"); (2) the city must provide services to the annexed area within one year of annexation; (3) the city may not annex property for revenue purposes only; and (3) the city must assume net bonded indebtedness on a pro rata basis. Property owners opposed to annexation may appeal to district court, but the burden of proof that the area was annexed for impermissible purposes rests on those opposed.[26]

Municipalities exercise extraterritorial jurisdiction in matters of land use. A city's zoning authority extends for one, two, or three miles beyond the municipal boundaries (second, first, and primary and metropolitan classes, respectively), and property owners within this area may not plat or subdivide property without the city's permission.[27] Likewise, municipalities may own facilities and property beyond their boundaries, primarily in support of basic utilities, aviation fields, and industrial development.

Counties, first, are an arm of state government and, second, provide basic government services to the state's rural population. With ninety-three counties Nebraska ranks tenth in the nation. Eighty percent of the counties possess fewer residents today than sixty years ago. The structure and functions of county government are set by the state legislature, except for some minor constitutional provisions related to area, organization, elected officers, and revenues. The authority of county governments is exercised either by a board of commissioners (comprising three to five members) or a board of supervisors (seven members), as well as by a long list of other elected officials, including an assessor, a clerk, a register of deeds, a sheriff, a clerk of county or district court, a county attorney, a public defender, a school superintendent, and a surveyor.[28] Home rule charters are not available for counties. "Structurally, county government in Nebraska has seen few changes since World War I";[29] "Buffalo Bill or Old Jules could probably still find their way around most of the state's courthouses."[30]

Functions of Local Government

Functional Responsibilities

Municipalities possess a fairly broad range of discretion in their actions, primarily related to the usual tasks of general administration, public safety, public works, quality of life, social services, transportation, and utilities. They also have some regulatory authority over local commercial enterprises, local markets, and personal property. Functional responsibilities of counties pertain either to service delivery to rural populations (law enforcement, health and hospitals, and public welfare) or to their role as agents of the state government (revenue collection, corrections, election administration, highways and roads, record keeping, and licenses). State law specifies that counties provide "protective services" for dependent, aged, blind, disabled, ill, infirm, mentally disordered, or mentally retarded persons.[31] Counties provide proportionally more correctional and human service activities than do cities; conversely, cities provide proportionally more services pertaining to quality of life (for example, libraries and recreational facilities) and public safety than do counties.[32]

Nebraskans' attachment to small local government manifests itself in the sheer number of special districts and governing bodies. Although the U.S. Bureau of the Census counts 1,047 special districts (including 23 natural resource districts, 418 fire protection districts, and 133 housing and community development districts), the secretary of state has been unable to obtain an accurate count. A unknown number of other single-purpose districts and public authorities exist to provide services as diverse as cemeteries, drainage, hospital, industrial or residential development, irrigation, mosquito abatement, power generation, reclamation, weather control, and weed control.[33] Typically, special districts are governed by a board elected either by the qualified voters or by the property owners in the district.

A common view among Nebraskans is "any government larger than a single farmer and a couple of neighbors is a tyranny worse than anything ever contemplated by King George III."[34] This fierce attachment to "local control" manifests itself most strongly in the 668 school districts, which puts Nebraska in fifth place nationally. Nebraska has twice as many school districts as Kansas (324) and Iowa (379) primarily because there are 378 "elementary-only" districts, 76 percent of which have 30 or fewer students.[35]

Municipalities may establish several types of special districts and independent corporations, but once created, "they stand on their own legal feet as separate entities and are governed exclusively by their own boards or commissions. The parent city council no longer has control."[36] For example, cities and villages may create an airport authority, which can be financed by a tax levy, by revenues collected from use of the facilities, and by bonds. Similarly, cities of any class may create a public housing authority. Sanitary and improvement districts (SIDs) may be created by local developers to fund industrial or residential development. SIDs possess the power to tax property holders, issue bonds, and establish land-use rules.[37]

The 1963 Interlocal Cooperation Act authorizes local units of governments "to make the most efficient use of their taxing authority and other powers by enabling them to cooperate with other localities on a basis of mutual advantage"; moreover, "two or more public agencies may enter into agreements with one another for joint cooperative action."[38] Cooperation among Nebraska local governments is common but varies by region.[39] The northeast corner of the state—where Nebraska, Iowa, and South Dakota share boundaries—is the home of one of the nation's ten oldest regional councils of government.[40] Lancaster County and the City of Lincoln also cooperate extensively, as evidenced by a county-city building, numerous consolidated departments and commissions, and joint budgets and planning.[41] The mechanisms of cooperation range from informal memoranda of understanding to formal contracts for service provision; from shared equipment, facilities, and personnel to mutual aid in an emergency and interconnected utility systems as part of joint power agreements.

In other areas of the state, hostility and resistance to interlocal cooperation are more the norm, and interlocal cooperation is rare enough to make headlines.[42] In recent years the state legislature has passed several pieces of legislation designed to induce more cooperation and even consolidation of governments and public functions. Legislative Bill 1114 offers an incentive for counties and municipalities by allowing an additional levy of up to 5 mills per $100 in support of cooperative activities.[43] Constitutional amendments passed in the November 1998 election granted the authority to legislate the merger and consolidation of local governments, to allow a merged city and county to have different tax rates outside the city limits, and to repeal and eliminate constitutional provisions for townships.[44]

Administrative Discretion

The "general powers" accorded to Nebraska counties and municipalities are quite extensive. Cities of all classes and counties may (1) sue and be sued; (2) purchase, lease, or otherwise acquire real estate and personal property; (3) sell, convey, or exchange real or personal property; and (4) make or enter into contracts "and do all other acts necessary or incident or appropriate to the exercise of its corporate powers."[45] Counties may also enter into compacts with other counties. In the exercise of its police power (as delegated by the state legislature to cities), the municipal legislative body "is the sole judge as to what laws should be enacted and as to when such police powers should be exercised"; courts are enjoined not to "interfere with ordinary business affairs of municipalities except in a clear case of mismanagement and fraud."[46] One of the most important legal differences between counties and municipalities is "a county does not possess the double governmental and private or proprietary character that a city does, as a municipal corporation authorized to own and operate a utility, treated as a private corporation engaged in a purely private business enterprise, separate and distinct from its governmental functions."[47]

Administrative boards and utility agencies are commonly created by municipalities to acquire and provide a variety of services. In the small localities across Nebraska, boards for health, housing, libraries, public works, and parks and recreation are traditional administrative organizations that offer more "community" participation than the more conventional city departments headed by a single person.[48] Municipalities have considerable discretion to establish electric power and other utility agencies.[49]

Nebraska's laws on personnel management establish a civil service system for county government employees and for the employees of all cities with 5,000 or more population that have full-time police officers or full-time firefighters. Any city or village with less than 5,000 residents may adopt a civil service act and may create a civil service commission; the two home rule charter cities both include a civil service system in their charter powers. Although Nebraska is an "employment at will" state, the civil service system statute applicable to counties specifically declares "members of the personnel policy board shall be persons *in sympathy with the application of merit principles to public employment*" [italics added].[50]

The state legislature has established pension plans for police officers and for firefighters. Cities and counties are also authorized to establish retirement plans and other fringe benefit plans for employees, and their employees are covered by the state workers' compensation program.

Public employees in Nebraska (including local government workers) have the right to be represented by employee organizations of their own choosing and to negotiate collectively with employers over the terms and conditions of employment. When disputes arise, the employees, the employer, or the attorney general may petition the state Commission of Industrial Relations to mediate the dispute and issue a final order.[51]

All governmental entities in Nebraska are covered by public bidding statutes designed "to invite competition, guard against favoritism, improvidence, extravagance, fraud, and corruption, and to secure the best work or supplies at the lowest possible price."[52] State laws give preference to residents, mandate adherence to fair labor standards by contractors bidding for public works projects, and set values below which bids are not required.[53]

All counties, cities, and villages are authorized to establish a planning commission and to adopt zoning regulations for "the purpose of promoting health, safety, morals, and the general welfare of the community." To exercise regulatory power over land and structures, the local government must create the planning commission and must receive and adopt a comprehensive development plan that meets the specifications established by state law. A board of adjustment may be established by the city council; in villages, the board of trustees may act as the board of adjustment. A city council may not take final action on matters related to comprehensive plans, capital improvements, building codes, development of subdivisions, annexation of territory, or zoning until it has received the recommendation of the planning commission, if such commission has been created; however, the city council may decide not to accept the commission's recommendations.[54] Matters relating to a municipality's jurisdiction beyond its corporate boundaries will be assumed by the municipality's interjurisdictional planning commission, some members of which are chosen by the county board.[55]

Economic Development

In response to the 1980s farm crisis, the state legislature in 1987 launched a series of economic development initiatives, including the Employment Expansion and Investment Act, the Employment and Investment Act, the Quality Jobs Act, the ethanol production credit, the Enterprise Zone Act, and the Microenterprise Development Act.[56] Common to all of these measures is the use of state income tax credits; the amount of the credit varies based on factors such as how many jobs a business creates, the amount and duration of new investment made in the business, and the location of new jobs or investment. In the case of enterprise zones, the state Department of Economic Development accepts formal applications from counties, cities, villages, or tribal governments. The proposed area is designated as an enterprise zone if it meets two of three criteria: high unemployment, high poverty, or significant population loss.[57]

The Nebraska legislature also equipped municipalities with financial tools capable of enhancing economic growth and coping with contemporary urban problems. For example, the 1989 municipal infrastructure redevelopment fund dedicated $4.5 million from the cigarette tax to local infrastructure projects.[58] The 1991 local option municipal economic development program permits municipal property or sales taxes to be spent on direct grants or loans, public works improvements, land purchases, job training, and the salaries of city employees working on the program.[59] City or village councils must prepare a written plan, submit it by resolution to a public hearing, and obtain approval by a public vote. Monies from the property tax may not exceed four-tenths of 1 percent of taxable valuation; the local option sales tax may range from one-half cent to one and one-half cents.

The 1978 Nebraska Community Development Act, designed to eliminate and prevent blight and to upgrade substandard areas within corporate limits, has been very successful. Municipalities are permitted to create a community redevelopment authority to formulate a "workable program" for utilizing appropriate public and private resources.[60] The authority may issue bonds for up to fifteen years' duration; the bonds are secured by pledging part of the property tax revenue attributable to the increased value due to the redevelopment of the facility or location. In other words, the act permits Nebraska localities to use "tax increment financing" (TIF).[61] TIF has been used since 1980, first by Omaha and Lincoln and now by about sixty Nebraska cities. The state revenue department estimated that in 1995, about $10.4 million in property taxes had been diverted from local governments to retire TIF loans. Local school officials (who have no say in the award of TIF) are concerned about the effect that the popularity of TIF might have on school property taxes.

Fiscal Autonomy of Local Governments

Local Revenues

Nebraska for most of its history has functioned with a minimal state government. Most public services, other than state highways and higher education, were provided and paid for by local governments. In the century since statehood in 1867 to 1967, Nebraska state and local governments relied on a single source of revenue: the property tax, both real and personal.[62] The state managed to survive on such a narrow fiscal base because the state legislature opposed state aid to local schools. During the 1960s, however, many Nebraskans came to believe that their state had been "left behind, old, outmoded, a place to come from or a place to die."[63] In 1965 the legislature enacted an income tax, but this provoked a two-pronged reaction. In 1966 voters not only approved a referendum to prohibit the state from levying a property tax but also elected a new governor who pledged to broaden the tax base. Gov. Norbert Tiemann "pulled Nebraska kicking and screaming into the twentieth century"[64] by his vigorous support for the Revenue Act of 1967; the resulting tax system was based on an income tax and a state sales tax. Since 1967 the proportion of state and local revenues from each of the three sources—property tax, income tax, and sales tax—has shifted significantly. By 1998 property taxes constituted slightly less than 43 percent of the state and local revenue mix.[65]

Since 1967, the revenue sources for Nebraska local governments have been expanded. Municipalities are permitted to raise revenue from a surprisingly lengthy list of possible sources, including bonds and notes, business and occupation taxes, cost recoveries, franchises, gaming, "in lieu of" taxes, interest income, licenses and permits, motor vehicles, municipal enterprises, rents and royalties, service charges, and utility funds. Cities rely on four main sources of funds: property taxes, sales tax, licenses and permits, and franchise fees (see Table 2). By comparison, counties still draw about half their funds from property taxes and are supplemented by state aid and licenses and permits.

Municipalities, after a local election, may impose a sales tax of between one-half and one and one-half cents on top of the

Table 2. Percentage Distribution of Total Revenues, by Source and Type of Local Government, 1992–1993

Source	Omaha	Lincoln	First class	Second class	Villages	Counties
Property	26.9%	33.1%	21.9%	36.0%	29.0%	49.9%
Sales tax	23.4	25.6	21.7	3.2	1.4	0.0
Franchise fees	15.3	11.3	6.7	6.6	8.6	7.4
Licenses and permits	22.5	15.1	19.9	16.4	17.7	18.4
Utility surplus	0.6	0.0	2.2	8.6	14.1	0.9
State funds	8.4	12.6	16.9	21.1	22.9	19.2
Local transfers	0.2	2.5	7.5	6.1	4.4	1.7
Reduction in reserves	0.0	0.0	3.2	2.1	2.0	1.1
Federal and other	2.7	0.0	0.1	0.0	0.0	1.5

Source: Committee on Revenue, Nebraska State Legislature, *A Comprehensive Guide to the Nebraska State and Local Tax System* (Lincoln, Neb.: Committee on Revenue, 1996).

state sales tax (food is exempted). As of 1997, seventy-four cities and towns levied a local sales tax. The trend among the larger cities in the 1990s showed increased reliance on sales taxes.[66] For example, in 1996 the proportion of sales tax and property tax to total revenues for Omaha was 45.2 percent and 25.4 percent, respectively. For Lincoln, the state capital, this distribution in 1997 was 41 percent and 30 percent. Gaming and occupation taxes are also becoming increasingly popular revenue sources.

Although the property tax has decreased somewhat in importance for municipalities, the tax continues to be the monetary mainstay for school districts and county government. Almost two-thirds of the total statewide property tax levy goes to K–12 education; by contrast, county government receives about 15 percent of the total levy, and cities garner about 12 percent.[67] The base for the property tax is assessed value of the property.[68] Elected county assessors oversee property valuations and assessment and are required to keep valuations within 92–100 percent of fair market value.[69] However, nearly 3,000 separate political subdivisions, which possess the authority to tax property, determine the tax rate itself. This fragmented situation requires the multiple tax rates that are applied to each parcel of property to be merged into a single statement. A property owner may challenge an assessment first at the county level; the owner may then appeal to the Tax Equalization and Review Commission (TERC) at the state level.[70] Appeals may continue to the state Board of Equalization and Assessment, which supervises property tax administration; ultimately an appeal may go to the state supreme court.[71] Homestead exemptions are available for low-income elderly, the disabled, and other specified persons.

Several factors converged by the late 1980s to create a crisis in Nebraska's system of property taxation. The result led to (1) a significant increase in state aid to local schools, (2) equalization of assessments statewide, and (3) a lid on property taxes. A lid was first imposed on school districts in a 1989 statute that also increased school aid, but this attempt did little to quell what has become Nebraska's version of California's Proposition 13 tax re-

volt. After a few additional but abortive attempts, the state legislature in 1996 imposed a dramatically more restrictive lid. Effective July 1, 1998, the tax rate per $100 valuation is limited to forty-five cents for municipalities, forty-five cents for counties, $1.10 for school districts (drops to $1.00 in 2002), and other specific limits for various types of special districts and public authorities. The 1996 legislation permits cities and counties to levy an additional five cents to encourage interjurisdictional cooperation to gain cost savings. It also allows counties to allocate up to fifteen cents to miscellaneous districts, public authorities, and various agricultural and historical societies. The grand total property tax rate (of all jurisdictions) on a single property may not exceed $2.24; this ceiling lowers to $2.10 in 2002. A public body may exceed the mandated rate limit by gaining approval through an override election.[72]

Counties, cities, and villages may issue a mix of bonds, coupons, and warrants.[73] Public bodies, other than sanitary and improvement districts (SIDs), may issue bond anticipation notes. Any city or village may issue revenue bonds. Any county or city is permitted to issue bonds for internal improvements or to aid railroad construction. Most municipal debt is approved by the council and mayor rather than by a public vote. SIDs may borrow money or issue bonds for corporate purposes, but the value may not exceed 1.4 percent of the taxable valuation in the district.[74]

Because the state government constitutionally may not go into debt, the state has developed the practice of using the bonding authority of local governments to raise revenues for road construction. This unusual situation contributes to the lack of a local debt limit. The absence of a debt limit does not necessarily result in profligate practice, as evidenced by Omaha, which has operated with a debt ratio under 1.5 percent through the 1990s.

Local Expenditures

The relatively distinct functions performed by counties and municipalities are reflected in their expenditures (see Table 3). Along with the levy limits that went into effect in 1998, the state legislature imposed a restricted fund expenditure limit, stating that local governments may not increase their budget by more than 2.5 percent per year beyond any annual valuation growth.[75] An additional 1 percent is permitted if the local governing body approves it by a three-fourths vote. Exemptions include capital improvements, bond indebtedness, jointly financed service (first two years only), repair of damage caused by natural disaster, and court judgments. Affected governments may maintain service levels by increasing productivity, consolidating with other governments, or entering into interlocal cooperative agreements.[76] In 1998 the legislature tightened the tax limits even more by including sales tax revenues under the restricted funds category which is used to constrain expenditure growth; that is, even if the local sales tax brings in more funds, the total monies the locality may spend is still restricted to the lid limit.[77]

Table 3. Percentage Distribution of Total Expenditures, by Function and Type of Local Government, 1992–1993

Function	Omaha	Lincoln	First class	Second class	Villages	Counties
Human services	0.1%	2.4%	0.2%	1.1%	1.8%	7.4%
Transportation	19.0	22.5	21.8	27.8	32.8	22.1
Public safety	32.1	35.1	31.2	21.9	12.2	19.3
Quality of life	22.7	21.1	24.3	22.7	24.7	6.0
Corrections	0.9	0.0	0.0	0.0	0.0	8.3
Governmental administration (debt service)	24.2	7.1	16.7	20.3	17.7	31.0
Increase in reserves	0.4	11.9	1.5	4.2	4.4	4.9
Unclassified	0.6	0.0	4.3	2.0	6.5	2.0

Source: Committee on Revenue, Nebraska State Legislature, *A Comprehensive Guide to the Nebraska State and Local Tax System* (Lincoln, Neb.: Committee on Revenue, 1996).

Governing bodies must adhere to the Nebraska Budget Act, which prescribes budget practices and requires that pertinent information be made available to the public. Although the state constitution requires the state government to maintain a balanced budget, it is not entirely clear that local governments must do so. The act states that "the amount to be raised from taxation . . . plus the estimated revenue from sources other than taxation and the unencumbered balances shall equal the estimated expenditures, plus the necessary required cash reserve, for the ensuing year."[78] However, the act also allows political subdivisions to propose a supplemental budget, if additional expenses will be necessarily incurred or if reasonable circumstances lead to insufficient funds. Bonds, coupons, and warrants may be issued in anticipation of revenues. Nebraska municipalities may file for Chapter 13 bankruptcy, but there is no procedure for receivership, and there is no statute assigning the state responsibility for a bankrupt jurisdiction.

State Government Grants-in-Aid to Localities

Tax and expenditure limitations are not the only mechanisms by which the legislature has sought to relieve the local property tax burden. Since 1967 the state has acted to assume or subsidize local activities. Initially, the state tried to exempt various categories of property from the tax levy, but this eventually led to court action. State assumption of local functions such as county Medicaid, municipal courts, and larger proportions of local education have had more impact. In 1988–1998, state aid to local government grew an average of 9.9 percent per year; aid to individuals (for example, Medicaid and other services that previously were administered locally) has grown by 10.1 percent a year. By 1996 state government had increased its share of school costs to 41 percent; nevertheless, Nebraska still was among the bottom ten states for state aid to local education.[79]

State aid to local governments ($653.5 million) accounts for the single largest slice (36 percent) of 1995–1996 general-fund ap-

propriations in Nebraska; 22.6 percent of the general fund is allocated for aid to individuals ($411 million). The combined budgets for the five largest state agencies absorb only 14 percent of general-fund appropriations ($252.3 million). State aid to local governments can be subdivided into aid to education (83.55 percent), homestead exemption (5.4 percent), aid to cities (2.7 percent), aid to counties (2.0 percent), and other (6.35 percent). The highway user revenue distribution fund is the second largest source of state aid and is divided 23.3 percent each to counties and municipalities; the remainder goes to the state Department of Roads. Motor vehicle taxes are returned to counties and the different classes of cities through separate formulas. In 1983 the state took over the responsibility for funding social services (especially Medicaid) and public assistance from county governments as part of a major effort to reduce local property tax burdens. Together, Medicaid and public assistance now constitute 84 percent of state aid to individuals.[80]

Unfunded Mandates

A 1993 report from the Nebraska Rural Development Commission's Mandate Project lists six state-initiated mandates among a long list of federal mandates with which local governments must comply. These state mandates include inspections of food processing facilities and eating establishments; inspections of program service centers for women, infants, and children; health inspections for well drillers and pump installers; and management of solid waste. Another mandate requires K–12 school curricula to incorporate cultural diversity education.[81]

According to the League of Nebraska Municipalities, "it is important to emphasize that the largest unfunded mandate on municipalities and other public employers is the state law requiring public employers to pay employees 'comparability.'" The comparability-of-pay mandate is enforced by the Commission of Industrial Relations (CIR). The CIR has the authority to order a rate of pay based on a group of comparable governments or locations. Local government officials complain (1) that the CIR's wage determinations do not follow any "clearly articulated standards that are uniformly applied" and (2) that comparability is difficult to calculate, and for Omaha and Lincoln comparability often involves locations in states far removed from Nebraska.[82] Most small cities and villages as well as rural counties have few organized employees, and so comparability is seldom an issue.

Access to Local Government

Local Elections

Cities and villages may hold local elections following procedures set in the state code or in the charter, code, or bylaws of the political subdivision. Variation in representation exists among localities; for example, Lincoln's city council has four members elected by district and four elected at large, whereas Omaha's city council is completely district based. Local elections are set for the first Tuesday in April in even-numbered years. Special elections may be called at other times. If a local election (for example, for a bond issue) is set by the municipality to coincide with a state election, then the general election laws of the state apply.[83] Municipal clerks oversee local elections, but state elections are the responsibility of the county clerk; in counties with a more than 100,000 population, the county election commissioner is responsible.

The Nebraska Political Accountability and Disclosure Act covers campaign practices; imposes campaign finance limitations; defines permissible expenditures, loans, and transfer funds; and requires campaign committees to file statements of receipts and expenditures.[84] The act applies to political parties, to business and business associations, and to any person, business, or organization that gives a candidate more than $100. Anonymous contributions are prohibited, as is the use of public funds for any political materials, newsletters, or mailings. Lobbyists are required to register with the clerk of the legislature, to complete a detailed application form, and to later make detailed reports about their activities and expenses.

The Nebraska Political Accountability and Disclosure Act also specifies what constitutes a conflict of interest by a public official or what would constitute improper use of the official's position. Similarly, the act contains an extensive list of prohibited actions that an individual may not take to influence a public official. All state and local officials must file statements of financial information before assuming office, annually while in office, and within thirty days of leaving office.[85]

The Nebraska Accountability and Disclosure Commission oversees the act's enforcement. The commission's nine members include the secretary of state, four members who are appointed by the governor from lists submitted by the state legislature, and four who are appointed by the secretary of state.[86]

Citizen Controls over Actions of Local Officials

In 1897 the Nebraska legislature provided for use of the initiative and referendum—the first state in the nation to do so—and in 1912 a constitutional amendment authorizing their use was adopted.[87] Initiative and referendum were designed originally to allow ordinary citizens to propose legislation without going through the formal legislative process. However, the use of these instruments has been altered by the recent adoption of a law permitting commercial petition circulators. That is, any individual or group desirous of challenging existing policy can now hire persons to obtain the signatures of registered voters on an initiative or referendum petition. What once was a vehicle for the expression of local public sentiment now has become a tool of well-financed interests, including some from outside the state.[88]

Elected officials of all local governments—counties, cities, villages, and special districts—may be removed from office in a recall election that has been obtained through petition by registered voters whose number is at least 35 percent of the total number of votes cast for that office in the last election.[89] If a majority votes for recall, the office is declared vacant and then is filled according to state statute. If the recall fails (or is a tie), the official may be subject to a recall election after twelve months have passed, provided another petition is filed. Recall is no idle threat in Nebraska; in any year, one can usually find a recall petition drive or election underway somewhere in the state.

Citizen control is enhanced by the state's open meeting and open records laws which ensure "that the formation of public policy is public business and may not be conducted in secret." Meetings include all regular, special, or called meetings (formal or informal) of any public body in which policy is discussed, formed, passed, or any other action is taken. Closed sessions for specific situations may be held after an open vote.[90] Closed sessions are not permitted for the discussion of the appointment or election of a new member to the public body. Public records are liberally construed to include not just the minutes, motions, and budgets of public bodies but also the correspondence, memoranda, and phone records of all public officials.[91]

State-Local Relations

Frank Koehler, longtime dean of city managers in Nebraska, was once asked to describe home rule in Nebraska. His terse answer was, "Home Rule! What home rule?" Local government autonomy is narrowly construed in constitutional language permitting municipalities with more than 5,000 residents the option to frame a charter and the state supreme court's 1901 decision based on Dillon's Rule. The discretionary authority of all local governments is further constrained by the state legislature, which in many ways acts as a "super city council" for municipalities and villages. The state legislature annually enacts dozens of bills pertaining to minute changes in the laws for one or more classes of municipalities. It is estimated that 20–25 percent of all bills in the state legislature concern "local affairs."

The causes of this extreme local focus are threefold. First, given the strict interpretation of Dillon's Rule in Nebraska, cities and villages as a practical matter must seek state legislative authorization for new actions. Second, although citizens want local control, they do not hesitate to lobby the legislature to overturn local decisions that they oppose. Third, because state legislators willingly listen to and act on these demands, the legislature becomes the de facto city council for the state's communities.

The absence of home rule in Nebraska is further compounded by the state supreme court's stance on the doctrine of local affairs. The court declared that it alone—not the state legislature—has the power to determine which governmental activities are of municipal versus statewide concern. By this logic, the

Nebraska Supreme Court has effectively abandoned the original position set out by Judge Dillon; that is, whether a matter is of statewide or local concern is a decision to be made by the elected representatives of the people and the state legislature, not by the state courts. Despite the state's history of reform, Nebraska local government officials find themselves at the end of the twentieth century in a legal straightjacket fashioned in the nineteenth century.

Notes

1. Steve Molnar, *Reorganizing Nebraska's Local Government Structure* (Lincoln: Nebraska Tax Research Council, 1996), 8.

2. Arthur B. Winter, "Nebraska Home Rule: The Record and Some Recommendations," *Nebraska Law Review* 59 (1980): 626.

3. Dorothy W. Creigh, *Nebraska: A Bicentennial History* (New York: Norton, 1977), 105.

4. Frederick C. Luebke, "Time, Place, and Culture in Nebraska History," *Nebraska History* 64 (1988): 154.

5. Addison E. Sheldon, *Nebraska Civil Government* (Lincoln, Neb.: University Publishing, 1924), 42.

6. Susan Welch, "The Governor and Other Elected Executives," in *Nebraska Government and Politics*, ed. Robert D. Miewald (Lincoln: University of Nebraska Press, 1984), 37.

7. Members of the state's unicameral legislature are referred to as "state senators." The power of interest groups in Nebraska's unicameral legislature is well documented; for example, see Jack Rodgers, Robert Sittig, and Susan Welch, "The Legislature," in *Nebraska Government and Politics*, 78–86. See also Clive S. Thomas, "Interest Groups Grow but Their Power Wanes in State Government: Is the West Different?" *Points West Chronicle* (Autumn 1994): 6–7.

8. James C. Olson and Ronald C. Naugle, *History of Nebraska*, 3d ed. (Lincoln: University of Nebraska Press, 1997). See especially Chapters 17, 18, and 21.

9. Robert D. Miewald and Peter J. Longo, *The Nebraska State Constitution: A Reference Guide* (Westport, Conn.: Greenwood Press, 1993), 155.

10. Winter, "Nebraska Home Rule," 602.

11. James E. Anderson, Richard W. Murray, and Edward F. Farley, *Texas Politics: An Introduction*, 2d ed. (New York: Harper & Row, 1975), 267.

12. Article XI, sections 2–4 of the Constitution of the State of Nebraska of 1875 (as amended through 8 November 1994), *Nebraska Blue Book, 1994–95* (Lincoln, Neb.: Clerk of the Legislature), 196–197. There are three relatively simple procedures for the adoption of a home rule: (1) a convention of fifteen freeholders elected by city voters writes the charter, (2) the proposed governing document is filed with the city clerk and published for review by local residents, and (3) the document is approved by a majority of qualified voters.

13. *Redell v. Moores*, 63 Neb. 219, 88 N.W. 243 (1901).

14. *Consumers Coal Co. v. City of Lincoln*, 109 Neb. 51, 189 N.W. 643, 646 (1922).

15. Winter, "Nebraska Home Rule," 616.

16. Winter, "Nebraska Home Rule," 619–622.

17. *Omaha Parking Authority v. City of Omaha*, 163 Neb. 97, 77 N.W. 2d 862 (1956).

18. Winter, "Nebraska Home Rule," 610, 614, 626.

19. *Jacobberger v. Terry*, 211 Neb. 878, 320 N.W. 2d 903, modified on other grounds, 212 Neb. 145, 322 N.W. 2d 620 (1982), as cited in Richard E. Shugrue, "Home Rule in Nebraska: Problems and Opportunities" (a report for the Nebraska Commission on Local Government Innovation and Restructuring, Lincoln, 11 September 1997).

20. Robert D. Miewald, "Local Government," in *Nebraska Government and Politics*, 169.

21. The power to create a municipal corporation rests solely with the state legislature. By definition, a municipal corporation is a "political subdivision, created as a convenient agency for exercise of such governmental powers of the state as may be entrusted to it by constitutional or legislative act." *Schlientz v. City of North Platte*, 172 Neb. 477 (1961).

22. League of Nebraska Municipalities, *1997 Newly Elected and Appointed Officials Handbook* (Lincoln: League of Nebraska Municipalities, February 1997), 18.

23. Winter, "Nebraska Home Rule," 614.

24. Laws of Nebraska, 16-102, 17-220, 17-311. The source used for this all other references to Nebraska state statutes is the *Municipal Statutes of Nebraska—1995 Update*, as complied by the League of Nebraska Municipalities (Lincoln).

25. For a detailed description of annexation procedures, see Laws of Nebraska, 16-117.

26. *West's Nebraska's Digest 2D*, vol. 22 (St. Paul, Minn.: West's, 1996), Municipal Corporations, Articles 1.29 (1–4), 1.33(9), 1.36(1), 1.36(3). There are restrictions on the annexation of villages or second-class cities by a city of the first class (see Laws of Nebraska, 16-122).

27. Laws of Nebraska, 16-901, 16-902. Extraterritorial zoning authority covers property use and includes building codes for businesses, farms, and industry as well as residences.

28. Every Nebraska county has a clerk, treasurer, sheriff, and attorney. Other officials are found based on the county's population. For example, counties with over 3,000 residents must elect an assessor; with over 7,000, a clerk of the court; with over 16,000, a register of deeds; with 50,000–150,000, a county surveyor or county engineer; with over 150,000, an elected county engineer; and with 200,000, an elected comptroller. *County Government in Nebraska*, publication #2 (Lincoln: League of Women Voters of Nebraska Education Fund, October 1990), 6–7.

29. *County Government in Nebraska*, 9.

30. Miewald, "Local Government," 169.

31. Laws of Nebraska, 24-104.03.

32. *A Comprehensive Guide to the Nebraska State and Local Tax System* (Lincoln: Committee on Revenue, Nebraska Legislature, 1996), 233.

33. *Nebraska Blue Book, 1994–95*, 915.

34. Miewald, "Local Government," 184.

35. *Omaha World-Herald*, 13 January 1997, 1–2.

36. Arthur B. Winter, *Understanding Nebraska Municipal Government* (Lincoln: Nebraska Department of Economic Development, June 1975), 59.

37. *Unicameral Update* (Lincoln: Nebraska State Legislature, Unicameral Information Office, 9 February 1996), 6.

38. Laws of Nebraska, 13-802.

39. *Nebraska Municipal Review* (Lincoln: League of Nebraska Municipalities, 1996), 12–13.

40. During the past twenty years, these area governments have cooperated to develop arboretums and "eco-paths," centers for law enforcement and technology, roads and transit systems, and facilities for solid waste, water, recycling, and composting. Other activities include purchasing and complying with Aid to Disabled Americans requirements.

41. *Nebraska Municipal Review* (Lincoln: League of Nebraska Municipalities, 1997), 5, 8.

42. *Omaha World-Herald*, 15 June 1996, 16.

43. LB 1114 (1996), Nebraska Legislature.

44. Whether or not the state legislature's new authority to mandate the merger of local units will prompt more interlocal cooperation remains to be seen, but at least now the legislature has the authority to act.

45. *1997 Newly Elected and Appointed Officials Handbook*, 18–21.

46. Laws of Nebraska, 23-104, 63.15(5). Despite this statutory language, the state supreme court has overturned the efforts by the state legislature to give municipalities the authority to make binding decisions about liquor licenses. The court, relying on a "free market" clause in the state constitution, has greatly restricted the grounds on which licenses may be denied and has weakened localities' ability to influence the final decisions of the state Liquor Control Commission. See *Nebraska Municipal Review* (Lincoln: League of Nebraska Municipalities, September 1993), 10–11.

47. *State ex rel. Johnson v. Gage Co.*, 154 Neb. 822, 49 N.W. 2d 672 (1951). Counties may provide a public telephone system, but none do so. See Laws of Nebraska, 86-401–86-412.

48. Winter, *Understanding Nebraska Municipal Government*, 57.

49. Laws of Nebraska, 18-2401–18-2485. Nebraska is the only state in which all electric power is supplied by public entities; that is, no private firm sells electricity in the state.

50. Laws of Nebraska, 23-2521(1).

51. *Nebraska Blue Book 1994–95*, 682.

52. *Anderson v. Peterson*, 221 Neb. 149, 375 N.W. 2d 901 (1985).

53. Laws of Nebraska, 73-101–73-106.

54. *1997 Newly Elected and Appointed Officials Handbook*, 37.

55. Laws of Nebraska, 19-901. Local governments may adopt uniform or standard codes for buildings, mechanical systems, fire protection, and construction or repair of structures. They also may levy fees or fines related to planning and zoning (19-922); 19-901, 19-903, 19-907–19-912,19-930, 19-931.

56. *Comprehensive Guide to the Nebraska State and Local Tax System*, 239–265; for the Microenterprise Act, see *Nebraska Municipal Review* (Lincoln: League of Nebraska Municipalities, 1998), 8.

57. *Nebraska Municipal Review* (Lincoln: League of Nebraska Municipalities, 1993), 5–7.

58. Laws of Nebraska, 18-2601–18-2608.

59. The 1991 act was made possible by the passage of a constitutional amendment in 1990.

60. Community redevelopment authorities in Nebraska may be a private enterprise.

61. Laws of Nebraska, 18-2101–18-2144.

62. *Omaha World-Herald*, 11 October 1998, 1A–2A.

63. Neal R. Peirce and Jerry Hagstrom, *The Book of America: Inside 50 States Today* (New York: Warner Books, 1984), 580.

64. Luebke, "Time, Place, and Culture in Nebraska History," 166. Governor Tiemann, it should be noted, was defeated in his bid for reelection.

65. *Omaha World-Herald*, 11 October 1998, 1A–2A.

66. Counties may levy a sales tax up to one and one-half cents for the joint operation of public safety services, unless a city in the county already has a sales tax.

67. *Comprehensive Guide to the Nebraska State and Local Tax System*, 54.

68. The distribution of the total statewide property tax assessment among classes of property is approximately 40 percent residential, 30 percent agricultural, 21 percent commercial, and the remainder primarily motor vehicle.

69. Counties with a population of at least 3,000 residents must elect the county assessor. In counties with fewer residents, the county is not required to elect the assessor; the county board would make an appointment.

70. TERC is composed of three members appointed by the governor and confirmed by the state legislature.

71. The state Board of Equalization and Assessment consists of the governor, the secretary of state, the state treasurer, the state auditor, and the state tax commissioner.

72. *Comprehensive Guide to the Nebraska State and Local Tax System*, 73–76.

73. Political subdivisions may issue short-term bonds, coupons, and warrants, as long these notes are charged against the proper fund of the issuing jurisdiction. Laws of Nebraska, 10-102.

74. Laws of Nebraska, 10-137, 10-201.01, 31-510.

75. To prevent jurisdictions from building up large budget balances before the levy limits went into effect, the state legislature passed a companion bill along with LB 1114. This bill (LB 299) restricted budget growth to 2 percent over the prior year and adjusted for population growth (or student enrollment). Also, the legislature sought to protect low-taxing districts from having their per pupil expenditure drop below the state average of $4,600 by legislation designed to funnel state aid toward these districts and away from high-levy districts (LB 806). *Omaha World-Herald*, 22 April 1997, 1A–2A.

76. Carol Ebdon and John Bartle, "Budget Responses to Local Government: Tax Limits in Nebraska: Who Decides?" (paper presented at the annual conference of the Association for Budgeting and Financial Management, Washington, D.C., 1998).

77. *Nebraska Municipal Review* (Lincoln: League of Nebraska Municipalities, 1998), 7.

78. Laws of Nebraska, 13-5. The Nebraska Budget Act does not apply to public power districts; a separate section of state code applies to their fiscal practices; 13-505.

79. *Omaha World-Herald*, 11 October 1998, 2A.

80. "State of Nebraska Biennial Budget, FY 1995–96 and FY 1996–97" (report of the Appropriations Committee to the Nebraska Unicameral, Ninety-fourth Legislature, First Session).

81. *Nebraska Mandate Project Report* (Lincoln: Nebraska Rural Development Commission, 1993), 1–6.

82. *Nebraska Municipal Review* (Lincoln: League of Nebraska Municipalities, February 1997), 4. The mandate on comparability recently resulted in a four-year struggle among the City of Lincoln, its firefighters, and the CIR.

83. Laws of Nebraska, 19-3002–19-3052, 32-404.

84. Laws of Nebraska, 49-14.

85. Laws of Nebraska, 14-1493.

86. The governor and the secretary of state each appoint two citizens (who are selected at large) to the Accountability and Disclosure Commission. Each of the secretary's appointees must be drawn from the two political parties. See Laws of Nebraska, 49-14.105.

87. LB 807 (1982) states, "the power of the initiative allows citizens the right to enact measures affecting the governance of each municipal subdivision of the state," and "the power of the referendum allows citizens the right to repeal or amend existing measures, or portions thereof, affecting the governance of each municipal subdivision in the state." Also see Laws of Nebraska, 18-2501–18-2538.

88. *Omaha World-Herald*, 9 June 1996, 10B.

89. Laws of Nebraska, 32-13.

90. Closed public meetings may be held for matters primarily related to collective bargaining, investigations of criminal misconduct, deployment of security, or where unnecessary personal injury may result during a performance evaluation.

91. Laws of Nebraska, 84-14, 84-7, 84-1408, 84-712.03.

NEVADA

Robert P. Morin and Eric B. Herzik

An image of Nevada conjures up notions of individualism, neon lights, gambling, entertainment, mining, ranching, desert, and sagebrush. Nevada is individualistic and highly urbanized, but urban and rural parts of the state represent quite divergent policy and fiscal interests, which results in local government dichotomy. Governmental authority is centralized, and local governments are afforded little autonomy. Nevada possesses one of the most centralized fiscal systems in the nation, with the state controlling approximately 80 percent of the total revenue of counties and cities. Home rule exists in name only.

Governmental Setting

Nevada became a state in 1864. Old Nevada (1864–1960) was essentially a small-population, slow-growth, homogeneous, rural state with undifferentiated economies.[1] Rapid growth began in the 1960s. Nevada has been the fastest growing state in the nation since 1970. It is projected that Nevada's population will more than double to 3.47 million by 2016. Rapid growth has transformed Nevada into the thirty-ninth most populated state in the nation, with 88 percent of the population located in metropolitan areas.[2]

New Nevada (1960–present) is dependent upon Clark County. In 1980–1990, the population of Clark County grew by 278,372, a growth rate of 60 percent. It is estimated that the Clark County area, with a 1996 population of 1.08 million, will have a population of 2.62 million by 2016. A solid and growing economy is a necessity because new Nevada's revenues are driven by Clark County's economy and growth.[3]

Geography and a dominant single-industry economy have traditionally characterized Nevada, directly molding the structure and operation of state and local government. Approximately 85 percent of all lands located in Nevada are owned by the federal government. Nevada has a mostly desert terrain, and less than 1.5 percent of its approximately 71 million acres of land has been cultivated.[4] From 1864 to 1931, mining for silver, gold, and copper was the dominant industry. Since 1931, gaming tourism has been the dominant industry. Growth in Nevada's population has not been evenly distributed throughout the state because of geographic limitations and the explosive growth of the gaming-tourism industry in Clark County.[5]

Nevada's political culture is individualistic and emphasizes limited government, fiscal conservatism, fragmentation of state governmental power, and citizen control over government at the ballot box.[6] Nevada is becoming more Republican than Democrat. Nevada's party competition classification in the 1970s was two-party, Democratic dominant; however, in the 1980s this classification changed to two-party, Republican leaning. Southern Nevada tends to be Democrat, whereas northern and rural Nevada tend to be Republican. Whether Republican or Democrat, Nevadans are politically conservative. State and local government in Nevada is driven by the basic fiscal conservatism of the state's politics. Nevada historically has provided a relatively low level of state services, resulting in a low tax burden.[7]

Nevada's constitution structures state government by apportioning power among the legislative, executive, and judicial branches. The constitution provides for a weak, fragmented, and decentralized executive branch. The governor, who possesses package veto power (that is, the formal power to veto a bill in its entirety), shares executive power and authority with other elected officials, boards, commissions, and councils.[8] The bicameral legislature is a citizen legislature and employs a biennial budget system.[9] Because of the legislature's part-time status, low levels of staff support, and crowded agenda during a 120-day biennial session, long-term budgeting and policy issues rarely are addressed in any significant manner.

Nonetheless, the legislature is the dominant branch of state government. The judicial branch consists of a seven-member supreme court and district, family, justice, and municipal courts. The constitution, which provides for the various types of courts, grants considerable authority to the legislature to determine the structure and operation of the judicial system. Legislative and executive branch officials are elected on a partisan ballot; state judges are elected on a nonpartisan ballot.[10]

Home Rule in Nevada

Historical Development

In 1854 the Utah Territorial Legislature created Carson City, the first organized unit of local government in Nevada. Nevada became a separate territory in 1861, and statehood was secured on October 31, 1864.[11] Nevada structures and operates state and local government under the original 1864 constitution, which is often amended by the voters and is firmly based on Populist and Progressive philosophies.[12] The legislature was required by the constitution to establish a system of uniform county and township governments. The constitution prohibits local or special laws that would single out a specific county, except where classifications are reasonable and are generally applicable.[13] The territorial legislature established eleven counties, and the legislature established six counties after statehood. A 1940 constitutional amendment prohibited the legislature from abolishing a county unless approved by the majority of the county's voters at a general or special election.[14] The legislature was authorized to enact special acts for municipal corporation purposes. The constitution required the legislature to provide for the organization of cities and towns through general laws; moreover, it mandated that the legislature restrict cities' and towns' power to tax, assess, borrow money, contract debts, and loan credit.[15]

In 1907 the legislature enacted Chapter 266 of the Nevada Revised Statutes, authorizing the creation of city governments by general charter. In 1915 the legislature enacted Chapter 267, a second statutory provision for general-charter authority which specifically authorized a commission form of city government. The constitution was amended in 1968 to allow the legislature to consolidate Ormsby County and Carson City, with Carson City performing the functions of city and county governments.[16] The constitution required the legislature to create one type of special district, the school district.[17]

Definition of Home Rule

Nevada historically has been, and continues to be, a classic Dillon's Rule state. County and city government derive all authority from the state; no authority is directly conferred by the constitution.[18] The judiciary has exercised judicial restraint and consistently adhered to the Dillon's Rule philosophy embodied in the constitution. In 1919 the Nevada Supreme Court held that counties were creatures of the legislature, subject to constitutional limitation. The court determined that a county derived its name, mode and manner of government, and rights and powers from the legislature.[19]

In 1989 the legislature created Bullfrog County, a 144-square-mile area carved out of Nye County. The purpose of Bullfrog County was to enhance Nevada's ability to receive federal funds under the Nuclear Waste Policy Act. Nye County sued the state, successfully contending that the Bullfrog County legislation violated Nevada's constitutional prohibition against legislation applicable to only one county. In 1989 the legislature repealed the enactment creating Bullfrog County.[20] In 1876 the court held that a municipal corporation was a creature of the legislature and that it derived all of its powers, rights, and franchises from legislative enactment or statutory implication.[21] In 1908 the court upheld the constitutionality of Chapter 266, the general-charter enactment.[22] In 1924 the constitution was amended to permit the legislature to grant home rule to cities; however, the legislature never enacted the requisite implementation legislation. The legislature also has historically and consistently adhered to the Dillon's Rule philosophy. Currently, home rule exists in name only, not in terms of legal authority or actual practice.[23]

Structural Features

Nevada has only 240 units of local government; special districts are the most prevalent form of local government. The manager-council form of government is found in approximately 80 percent of Nevada municipalities. County governments are created directly by the legislature; the boundaries and the county seat are specified by law.[24] Moving the county seat (which has occurred sixteen times) is accomplished by state legislative enactment or special election held at the county level.[25]

All seventeen counties are governed by similar multimember organizational structures that combine executive and legislative functions and are given the discretion to employ a professional manager. Town governments are closely tied to county governments. Towns are governed by a town board consisting of three elected residents and two county commissioners. Alternatively, the elected county commissioners act as the town governing body with the assistance of a citizen's advisory council, five members of which are appointed by the board of county commissioners.[26]

City governments are created by general or special charter. Generally, cities are granted broader powers than are counties; legislative grants of power allow some autonomy and discretion within municipal jurisdictional boundaries. Cities established under special charter remain directly under legislative control; specific legislative approval for that city (and that city only) must be obtained for any change in its governmental structure or service activities.[27] Although Chapter 266 is labeled a grant of home rule, home rule exists in name only. The legislature is specifically granted the authority to create or alter the form of city organization by special act or charter. A mayor-council form of government is required. General charters treat all similarly situated cities the same; however, the legislature still may enact legislation that will impact all general-charter cities.[28]

Chapter 267 not only authorizes a commission form of city government but also establishes a method for general incorporation that allows local autonomy in selecting a particular form of city government. Chapter 267 incorporation is rarely used, because special charters historically have been used by the legislature; moreover, Chapter 267 imposes additional procedures for incorporation. Two elections are required: the first election is to select electors to draft a charter, and the second election is to approve the draft charter. Chapters 266 and 267 allow for incorporation by citizen petition; the signatures of one-third of the qualified electors within the boundaries of the proposed city are required. The board of county commissioners holds hearings on the proposal, issues a written opinion, and calls an election. A majority vote of those voting in the election is required for successful incorporation.[29]

To incorporate by special charter, local residents draft a charter and present the proposed charter to the legislature. Subject to legislative amendments, the proposed charter is then enacted through the normal legislative process. Chapter 268 allows a majority of a city's governing body or citizens to propose charter amendments by petition, which must be signed by at least 15 percent of those registered voters who voted in the preceding general city election. Proposed charter amendments must be submitted to city voters for approval at the next primary or general city election or primary or general state election. Chapter 268 also authorizes the legislature to amend city charters.[30]

Chapter 265 provides two methods for "disincorporation." First, a city is automatically disincorporated if less than 150 electors residing within the limits of any incorporated city cast ballots at any general election. Second, a board of county commissioners possesses the authority to disincorporate a city upon petition of a majority of the legal voters residing within the limits of the affected city.[31] Chapter 268 allows city government expansion of boundaries through annexation. An area of proposed annexation must be contiguous to the city.

Annexation may be achieved through two methods. First, the city governing board may pass a resolution of annexation, publish a notice, and set a public hearing. Annexation is accomplished only if a majority of the property owners in the affected area do not protest the annexation. Second, annexation is accomplished if all of the property owners in the affected area sign a petition requesting the governing body of the city to annex the area.[32]

Each special district is the result of a specific enactment of the legislature. Special districts possess only those powers given to them by the legislature.[33] Some special districts are countywide; others are established to coincide with the area of the problem to be addressed or the service to be provided. Nevada's seventeen school districts have coterminous boundaries with the counties; however, school districts are governed separately by school boards. Each school board appoints a professional manager, the superintendent of instruction, who administers the schools in the district.[34]

Cities can own and operate facilities outside city limits; several have airports and water treatment plants or wells. Some areas that are scheduled for annexation are part of county plans and probably already receive some city services. The two urban

counties of Washoe and Clark have encountered this type of overlap.

Functions of Local Government

Functional Responsibilities

The functional responsibilities of Nevada local government are specifically set forth and controlled by the legislature. Local governments possess little functional autonomy. A county has the authority to create an office of the public defender, to establish a law library, and to appoint a road supervisor and manager. Counties may, with specific legislative approval, combine offices such as district attorney and public administrator. The functional responsibilities of counties include government administration, public safety, public works, judicial administration, health, sanitation, welfare, libraries, culture, recreation, administration of elections, administration of records and information, land-use control, building codes, finances, and ordinance-resolution formulation. Counties also possess authority over property assessment, tax collection, and licensing.[35]

The functional responsibilities of city government are specifically set forth and controlled by the legislature through special charters, general charters, and legislative enactments. Depending on the nature of the charter, cities are governed by a mayor-council or commission form of government and may employ a professional manager. The state mandates a clerk, treasurer, attorney, and a municipal court. The functional responsibilities of cities include government administration, public safety, public works, judicial administration, public health, libraries, recreation, land-use control, provision of utilities, granting of franchises, licensing and regulation of businesses, and formulation of ordinances.[36]

Subject to county approval, unincorporated towns can assume authority similar to that of cities. Land use and tax rates remain county functions and are not assumed by unincorporated towns. Special districts are specifically created by, and their functional responsibilities are set forth in, legislative enactments. The types and responsibilities of special districts include fire protection, libraries, water, sewer, flood control, hospitals, airports, convention centers, redevelopment, fair and recreation, housing, and local general improvement. Local general improvement districts possess the most autonomy by providing up to seventeen specific services. The only significant powers not provided to general improvement districts are police protection services, planning, and zoning.[37]

Interlocal cooperation is achieved through mechanisms established by legislative enactment. Special districts have been established to serve as regional entities (in which counties and cities are represented) to facilitate interlocal cooperation and policy goals. The Interlocal Cooperation Act allows for interlocal contracts, joint exercise of power, and the consolidation of governmental services.[38]

Administrative Discretion

Local governments in Nevada are afforded little discretion concerning administrative rules and procedures. Statutes delineate administrative procedures for county governments. General charters, special charters, and statutes delineate administrative procedures for city governments. Local government financial administration is uniform by virtue of various statutes, including the Local Government Budget Act, as is public personnel administration. Local governments employ a merit system, and personnel administration is legislatively determined under the Local Government Employee-Management Relations Act. Local governments may establish employee-management relations boards, and public employees may form employee organizations and engage in collective bargaining, but strikes are illegal. The Public Employees Retirement Act regulates the administration of public employee retirement benefits. The legislature has also provided for group insurance and medical and hospital services for employees of local government.[39]

The Administrative Procedure Act applies to local government in the areas of fiscal administration, public personnel administration, planning, and zoning. Also limited is local governments' discretion concerning contracting and purchasing authority. The Local Government Purchasing Act imposes competitive bidding requirements and allows local governments to purchase supplies, materials, and equipment through the state Department of Administration.[40]

The legislature has authorized counties and cities to establish planning commissions and to enact ordinances regarding land use, planning, and zoning. Chapter 278A establishes standards, conditions, and procedures for the authorization of planned developments.[41] In 1989 impact-fee legislation was enacted by the legislature as a way for local governments to require builders to pay for some of the roads, sewers, drainage projects, and water lines necessary for new development.[42] The legislature has afforded local government little functional autonomy concerning planning and zoning matters; however, the lack of a state plan for guidance in orderly growth and the existence of diverse economies across Nevada has resulted in "fend for yourself planning" among local governments.[43] The state's statutory control over local planning and zoning matters is so detailed as to specify the time limits for submission of final subdivision maps to a planning commission and to limit the ability of local governments to deny certain kinds of land divisions.

Specific legislative enactments have mandated interlocal cooperation for planning. The Tahoe Regional Planning Agency (TRPA) is a multistate planning agency established pursuant to an interstate compact. The authority of local government concerning the location and construction of all public works, planning, subdivision regulation, and zoning is subordinated to the powers of the TRPA. In 1989 the legislature mandated local governments in Washoe County to cooperate and develop a regional plan; if local governments in Washoe County were unable to cooperate, the legislature itself would have developed a land-use plan.[44]

Economic Development

Local governments in Nevada lack the authority to engage in development activities in the absence of specific enabling legislation enacted by the legislature. The legislature allows local governments to engage in urban renewal, to establish an urban renewal agency, and to issue bonds. Local governments may designate redevelopment areas and formulate redevelopment plans. Local governments have been given the authority to establish historic districts and issue revenue bonds for industrial development.[45]

Fiscal Autonomy of Local Governments

Local Revenues

Beginning in the late 1970s, Nevada moved from being more decentralized to more centralized than the average state and local revenue system in the United States.[46] In 1979 the legislature enacted a tax relief package; in response, voters defeated a constitutional initiative to limit local property taxes similar to California's Proposition 13. As a result, control of local revenues has been shifted from local elected officials to the legislature, its Interim Finance Committee, and the Nevada Tax Commission. Nevada currently possesses one of the most centralized fiscal systems in the United States. The state controls, in one way or another, approximately 80 percent of the total revenues of local governments.[47] Local governments are subject to an extensive scheme of state revenue controls. The state, the legislature, and the Nevada Tax Commission control every significant source of local government revenue by determining (1) the rate that may be levied, (2) the base on which the rate may be levied, (3) the total amount of revenue that can be raised, and (4) how revenue will be used or distributed.[48] The strictest state controls have been applied to sales and property taxes, the two most significant sources of local government revenue.[49]

Before the reduction in local property taxes in 1979 and a tax shift in 1981, only school district revenue was highly centralized. Local governments primarily survived on their own tax base. State-mandated property tax reduction was compensated for by increased reliance on sales tax revenue, to the detriment of rural units of local government without commercial centers. In 1981 the legislature enacted a tax shift program to jointly limit property tax revenue and to redistribute sales tax revenue to make up for lost property tax revenues. In 1989 the legislature uncoupled the limits on property tax revenue growth from the sales tax distribution. "Fair share" legislation enacted in 1991 designated counties with a significant local retail sales tax base as exporting counties that depended on their own sales tax–generated revenues. Smaller counties were designated as importing counties, and those that were unable to generate their own sufficient sales tax revenues were supplemented by sales tax revenues transferred from exporting counties.[50] The net effect of the state's action to uncouple property and sales taxes has been an improved intercounty revenue distribution system.[51]

State control over the sales tax is extensive. The state determines what is taxable and the rate and distribution of revenue. Sales tax revenues are collected by the state and distributed to local government, first among counties and then within counties (revenue is distributed to the county and each incorporated city within the county). Intracounty distribution is fairly straightforward. If there are no incorporated cities, the county receives all of the revenue. If incorporated cities exist within the county, revenues are apportioned to the county and each incorporated city on the basis of their respective populations.[52]

The property tax is subject to the centralized and comprehensive control of the state. The state determines (1) the definition of taxable property, (2) assessment practices, (3) the ratio of assessed-to-market value, (4) the maximum tax rate, and (5) the rate of revenue growth. The constitution limits the total property tax level to $5.00 per $100 of assessed value. The legislature has further restricted the total property tax level to $3.64 per $100 of assessed value.[53] A local property tax rate is the composite of many overlapping tax entities, including the county, cities, and special districts. The maximum tax rate local governments may impose is figured by dividing the previous year's allowable revenues (plus 6 percent) by the current year's value of property on the preceding year's tax roll. This tax rate is then applied to all property, including new property. The tax rate may be increased beyond this limit only by a local election or appeal to the Nevada Tax Commission.[54]

The state has also imposed a centralized and comprehensive fiscal scheme for less important local governmental revenue sources resulting from taxes. The state establishes by formula the rate, use, and distribution of revenues derived from cigarette, liquor, real property transfer, basic motor vehicle privilege, supplemental motor vehicle privilege, and motor vehicle fuel taxes.[55] Specific legislative enactments allow certain local governments to impose a lodging room tax and to impose an additional motor vehicle fuel tax for road infrastructure purposes. State law provides counties and cities the fiscal autonomy to impose various fines and fees for permits and licenses.[56]

The state has imposed on independent school districts a centralized and comprehensive fiscal scheme. The state distributes revenues to the school districts based on formulas that take into account each county's sales tax revenues, motor vehicle privilege tax, assessed property values, number of special education units, and weighted enrollment. Many special districts generate revenue from fee-for-service charges.[57]

Although the constitution previously limited the level of state general-obligation debt to 1 percent of the state's assessed property value, voters approved a ballot question in 1990 that increased the limit to 2 percent. Debt issued for the purpose of protecting or preserving the state's property or natural resources is excepted from the 2 percent constitutional debt limit. The state limits local government issuance of general-obligation debt by requiring voter approval in a referendum.[58] The state also limits local government issuance of general-obligation debt by establishing caps that are tied to total assessed property value.

Counties can issue general-obligation debt up to a limit of 10 percent of the county's assessed value. The general state limit on outstanding general-obligation debt for cities is 30 percent; however, city charters set limits of 10–40 percent. Cities are subject to an additional limit of 20 percent of assessed value on the value of outstanding warrants, certificates, and other nonbond general-obligation debt. The general-obligation debt limit for towns is 25 percent; for school districts, it is 15 percent. The general-obligation debt limit for special districts varies from none for the Washoe County Airport Authority, up to 50 percent for general improvement districts, to 3 percent for fair and recreation boards in counties with populations of less than 250,000.[59]

Nevada has established an allocation system based on relative population for allowable private activity debt for counties and cities. In 1981 the legislature enacted a state bond bank to assist local governments in undertaking natural resource projects.[60]

Local Expenditures

Local governments possess little autonomy in terms of local expenditures because of the centralized fiscal and functional status of state and local intergovernmental relations. Much of local government spending is prescribed by federal- and state-mandated functions and procedures.[61] The major categories of county and city expenditures are general government, public safety, judiciary, public works, culture and recreation, community support, health and sanitation, welfare, debt service, and depreciation and amortization. The major categories of school district expenditures are instruction, administration, building operation, student and staff support, and central office. Special-district expenditures consist of current operations (for example, general government, public safety, public works, intergovernmental services, sewers, and miscellaneous services), debt service (that is, principal interest expense), and depreciation and amortization.[62]

A series of statutes and the Local Government Budget Act set forth the requirements and control the form and substance of local government budgets. The state imposes budgeting requirements on both tentative and final budgets, public inspection, quarterly reports, financial accounts, types of funds, adjustment of expenses and revenues, accounting, audits, and review of annual audits by the state Department of Taxation.[63] The state and local governments are required to have balanced budgets. Statutes set forth the conditions constituting a severe financial emergency. After a hearing, the Nevada Tax Commission is authorized to enter an order requiring the state Department of Taxation to take over the management of local governments.[64]

State Government Grants-in-Aid to Localities

State grants-in-aid have little significance, because the state's centralized fiscal system effectively transfers money from the state to local governments, and revenue is distributed on an intercounty and intracounty basis.

Unfunded Mandates

Local government operates within the structure of a highly centralized fiscal system and has lacked the fiscal capacity to raise independently own-source revenues to fund state mandates. Nevada has responded to various federal unfunded mandates by passing them to local governments without the requisite revenues to comply with such mandates. To further exacerbate the problem, Nevada has imposed its own unfunded mandates on local government. In 1992 the Nevada Association of Counties balloted a referendum question against unfunded state mandates. In a general election, 82 percent of the voters said "no" to unfunded state mandates. A 1993 legislative enactment ended unfunded state mandates and required the legislature to identify a specific funding source for any new or expanded program.[65]

Access to Local Government

Local Elections

Nevada employs a direct, closed primary election system and requires voter party registration. Primary elections are held in September, and general elections are held in November of even-numbered years for state and county officials. The state mandates the election of commissioners, clerk, treasurer, recorder, auditor, assessor, district attorney, and sheriff at the county level. The legislature is authorized to increase, diminish, consolidate, abolish, and establish the election, duties, and compensation of elected county officials.[66]

Elected county officials run on a partisan ballot and serve four-year terms.[67] The legislature has mandated a seven-member board of commissioners in heavily populated counties and a five-member board of commissioners in moderately populated counties, with elections held on a district basis.[68] Lightly populated counties have the discretion to establish a three- or five-member member board of commissioners upon passage of a county ordinance and voter approval in a primary or general election. Elections for three- and five-member boards are held on an at-large basis; however, district elections may be adopted upon board action or citizen petition and voter approval in a general election.[69]

Elected city and school board officials run on a nonpartisan ballot and serve four-year terms. Primary elections are held in May, and general elections are held in June of odd-numbered years for city and school board officials. The electoral structure of special-charter cities varies according to the legislative authorization contained in each charter. All special-charter cities elect the city council, which consists of three to six members, on an at large or district basis. Many cities elect a mayor, attorney, municipal judge, and clerk. All Chapter 266 cities elect a mayor and the city council. In first-class cities, the council must consist of nine members, with one elected from each of the city's eight districts and one elected at large. In second- and third-class cities, the council must consist of three or five members as established by city ordinance, with one elected from each of the city's three or five districts. In second- and third-class cities, the council may establish at-large elections by city ordinance; however, members must reside in the district they represent. The electoral structure of Chapter 267 commission cities varies according to the provisions of each charter as proposed by citizen petition. The conduct of local government campaigns are subject to the state's Campaign Practices Act.[70]

Citizen Controls over Actions of Local Officials

Nevadans have a long tradition of taking matters into their own hands at the polls and have shaped the structure, operation, and direction of state and local government. The original constitution provides for impeachment of all state officers (except justices of the peace) for misdemeanor offenses or malfeasance in office.[71] The legislature is authorized to provide for the removal from office of other civil officers for malfeasance or nonfeasance; city councils are allowed to expel members for similar reasons.[72] Constitutional amendments established recall in 1912, initiative in 1912, and referendum in 1904, allowing citizens control over the actions of all state and local government officials.

To effectuate a state or local recall election, a recall petition must be signed by at least 25 percent of those registered voters who voted in the preceding general election in which the official was elected. At the county and city levels, initiative petitions must contain the signatures of at least 15 percent of those registered voters who voted at the last preceding general county or city election. At the county and city levels, referendum petitions must contain the signatures of at least 10 percent of those registered voters who voted at the last preceding general county or city election.[73] The legislature has enacted "sunshine" legislation applicable to state and local governments that provides for open meetings and open records.

State-Local Relations

Local governments exist and operate in accordance with the philosophy of Dillon's Rule; for any authority not directly conferred by the constitution, localities depend entirely on the legislature. Local governments possess little autonomy in terms of local revenues and expenditures because of Nevada's centralized fiscal system. The constitution and legislature have provided local government home rule in name only.

The legislature historically has resisted expanding local governments' scope of authority through legislatively enacted home rule. The recent trend has been in the direction of less local autonomy. The 1979 and 1981 tax relief enactments resulted in control of local revenues being shifted from local elected officials to the state. State fiscal centralization resulted in less local autonomy.

Nevada's adherence to the philosophy of Dillon's Rule has recently been criticized as outdated and inappropriate in contemporary Nevada.[74] Home rule and local government autonomy is an emerging issue because of recent social, demographic, and economic changes. State-level centralization and control regarding local government was perhaps an appropriate response for the state up until the 1960s, because Nevada was essentially a rural state with undifferentiated economies. Nevada is no longer a homogeneous state and probably never will be again. Changing demographics mean that the state must confront the dichotomous needs of urban and rural Nevada. Intergovernmental fiscal relations have emerged as possibly the most important fiscal issue facing governments in Nevada. The state legislature may well be moving in the direction of granting autonomy to local governments as evidenced by the enactment of a 1997 statute that allowed all counties the option of increasing the sales tax by one-eighth of a cent.[75] A movement in the direction of local government home rule and autonomy may well be the solution to adequately addressing Nevada's diverse needs and demands.

Notes

1. State of Nevada, Department of Administration, *Perspectives: A Biennial Report of Nevada State Agencies* (Carson City, Nev.: Department of Administration, 1992); Glen Atkinson and Ted Oleson, "Nevada Local Government: Coping with Diversity under Centralization," in *Legislative Issues: 1993, Nevada Public Affairs Review,* ed. Jill M. Winter and Glen Atkinson (Reno: Senator Alan Bible Center for Applied Research, University of Nevada, 1993).

2. Nevada's population grew from 494,900 in 1970, to 800,508 in 1980, to 1,201,833 in 1990. Nevada remains one of the least densely populated states, with 11 people per square mile, and is the tenth most urbanized state in the nation. Nevada is composed of seventeen counties. Clark County (the Las Vegas area) and Washoe County (the Reno area) are urban, whereas the other fifteen counties are rural. Robert P. Morin, "Nevada," in *Proceedings Roundtable: State Budgeting in the 13 Western States,* ed. Robert Huefner, F. Ted Hebert, and Carl Mott (Salt Lake City: Center for Public Policy and Administration, University of Utah, 1996), 80; State of Nevada, Department of Human Resources, *State Health Programs, Health Facilities and Services, and Demographic Information Nevada Health Catalog* (Carson City, Nev.: Department of Human Resources, 1993), 45.

3. Eric B. Herzik and Robert P. Morin, "Nevada," in *Proceedings Roundtable: State/Local Budgeting Issues in the Thirteen Western States,* ed. Carl Mott, Daniel Sloan, and Robert Huefner (Salt Lake City: Center for Public Policy and Administration, University of Utah, 1995).

4. Russell R. Elliott, with William D. Rowley, *History of Nevada,* 2d ed. (Lincoln: University of Nebraska Press, 1987), 14.

5. Nevada legalized casino gambling in 1931. The service industries, led by gaming tourism, are the dominant force in Nevada's economy. The mining industry is significant in five rural counties: Eureka, Nye, Elko, Humboldt, and Lander Counties account for 80 percent of the gross yield from mining. Agriculture, manufacturing, and wholesale trade constitute small sources of employment and sectors of the Nevada economy. Robert D. Ebel, *A Fiscal Agenda for Nevada: Revenue Options for State and Local Government in the 1990s,* ed. Robert D. Ebel (Reno: University of Nevada Press, 1990), 31–62.

6. An individualistic political culture is characterized by a political environment in which politics is practiced as an open marketplace and in which individuals and interest groups pursue social and economic goals. Daniel L. Elazar, *American Federalism: A View from the States,* 3d ed. (New York: Harper & Row, 1984); Thomas R. Dye, *Politics in States and Communities,* 8th ed. (Englewood Cliffs, N.J.: Prentice Hall, 1994); Ann O. Bowman and Richard C. Kearney, *State and Local Government,* 3d ed. (Boston: Houghton Mifflin, 1996).

7. M. Kimberly Beal, Lindsay Fairhurst, and Judy Calder, *Public Opinion in Nevada: Selected Legislative Issues,* November–December 1996, ed. M. Kimberly Beal, Lindsay Fairhurst, and Judy Calder (Reno: Senator Alan Bible Center for Applied Research, University of Nevada, 1997), 13. Nevadans are not necessarily opposed to spending on state programs; however, they want others (such as visitors, tourists, gamblers, and corporations) to bear much of the tax burden. Jill Winter, Judy Calder, and Donald Carns, "Public Opinion on Selected Legislative Issues: November 1992," in *Legislative Issues,* ed. Winter and Atkinson.

8. Robert P. Morin, "The Fragmented Executive Branch," in *Towards 2000: Public Policy in Nevada,* ed. Dennis L. Soden and Eric Herzik (Dubuque, Iowa: Kendall/Hunt, 1997).

9. The state constitution provides for a bicameral legislature. The state senate is composed of twenty members serving four-year terms. The Nevada Assembly is composed of forty-two members serving two-year terms. A. Constandina Titus, "The Legislature," in *Towards 2000,* ed. Soden and Herzik.

10. The Supreme Court expanded from five to seven members beginning with the 1998–1999 term. Nevada voters have repeatedly rejected proposed constitutional amendments to create an intermediate appellate court. Dennis Neilander, "The Judicial Branch," in *Towards 2000,* ed. Soden and Herzik.

11. Poor relations between the Utah Territory and federal government in the 1850s and an unsuccessful petition submitted to the California Legislature for annexation in 1853 led to Nevada becoming a separate territory in 1861. The California gold rush, poor Utah Territory–federal government relations, the discovery of silver in the Comstock Lode, and President Lincoln's desire to strengthen the Union position by securing additional antislavery congressmen during the Civil War and Reconstruction resulted in Nevada securing statehood. Eleanor Bushnell and Don W. Driggs, *The Nevada Constitution: Origin and Growth,* 6th ed. (Reno: University of Nevada Press, 1984), 1–18.

12. The Nevada Constitution has been amended almost 120 times. Don W. Driggs and Leonard E. Goodall, *Nevada Politics and Government: Conservatism in an Open Society* (Lincoln: University of Nebraska Press, 1996), 67.

13. Donald L. Shalmy and Elizabeth N. Fretwell, "Home Rule: History, Types and Benefits," in *Legislative Issues: 1995, Nevada Public Affairs Review,* ed. Jill M. Winter (Reno: Senator Alan Bible Center for Applied Research, University of Nevada, 1995).

14. The Nevada Territorial Legislature established nine counties on November 25, 1861, and two additional counties were subsequently established when Nevada was a territory. The state legislature established three counties in the 1800s and three counties in the 1900s. State of Nevada, Secretary of State, *Political History of Nevada,* 9th ed. (Carson City, Nev.: Secretary of State, 1990).

15. Nevada Constitution, Article VIII.

16. The Carson City–Ormsby County consolidation has been the only city-county consolidation in Nevada. State of Nevada, *Political History of Nevada.*

17. Nevada Constitution, Article XI.

18. Bushnell and Driggs, *The Nevada Constitution.*

19. *County of Pershing v. Sixth Judicial District Court,* 43 Nev. 78, 181 Pac. 960, 183 Pac. 314 (1919); *State ex rel. Wichman v. Gerbig,* 55 Nev. 46, 24 P. Jd. 313 (1933); AGO 91-3 (4-9-91); AGO 92-1 (2-3-92).

20. Bullfrog County contained the proposed nuclear waste storage site at Yucca Mountain and had zero population and a corresponding lack of need for public funds and services. The Bullfrog County legislature created a three-member board, appointed by the governor, to govern the county and to apportion the federal funds to other Nevada counties on a formula basis. State of Nevada, *Political History of Nevada;* Driggs and Goodall, *Nevada Politics and Government.*

21. *Rosenstock v. Swift,* 11 Nev. 128 (1876).

22. *State ex rel. Williams v. Second Judicial District Court,* 30 Nev. 25, 94 Pac. 70 (1908).

23. Nevada Constitution, Article VIII.

24. Nevada ranks forty-seventh out of the fifty states in smallest number of units of local government. Nevada has seventeen counties, seventeen independent school districts, seventeen unincorporated cities, and forty-four towns; the remainder are special districts. Ebel, *A Fiscal Agenda for Nevada*.

25. State of Nevada, *Political History of Nevada*.

26. Ebel, *A Fiscal Agenda for Nevada*.

27. Eleven of Nevada's seventeen incorporated cities are governed under special charters established by the legislature. Special charters are specifically drawn for the city named in the charter. Ebel, *A Fiscal Agenda for Nevada*.

28. Five cities are incorporated under the provisions of Chapter 266. Ebel, *A Fiscal Agenda for Nevada*.

29. One city is incorporated under the provisions of Chapter 267. Nevada Revised Statutes (1995), Chapters 266, 267.

30. Nevada Revised Statutes (1995), section 268.010.

31. Nevada Revised Statutes (1995), Chapter 265.

32. Ebel, *A Fiscal Agenda for Nevada*.

33. Approximately fifteen chapters of the Nevada revised statutes cover different types of special districts. Ebel, *A Fiscal Agenda for Nevada*.

34. Nevada Constitution, Article XI. James W. Guthrie, Gerald C. Hayward, Michael W. Kirst, Julia E. Koppich, Mary Lee McCune, and James R. Smith, *Nevada School District Organization and Control: Meeting the Challenges of Growth and Diversity* (Berkeley, Calif.: Management Analyses and Planning Associates, 1996).

35. Deloitte and Touche LLP, *Lake Tahoe, Nevada* (Reno: Deloitte and Touche, 1997).

36. Driggs and Goodall, *Nevada Politics and Government*.

37. Ebel, *A Fiscal Agenda for Nevada*.

38. Airport and housing authorities, the Las Vegas Convention Authority, and the Reno Sparks Convention and Visitors Authority are examples. Nevada Revised Statutes (1995), Chapter 277.

39. Nevada Revised Statutes (1995), Chapters 244, 268, 354, 288, 286, 287.

40. Nevada Revised Statutes (1995), Chapters 233B, 332.

41. Nevada Revised Statutes (1995), Chapter 278, sections 268.110–268.300, 278A.010–278A.590.

42. Reno is the only city that uses impact fees as a significant part of a local growth management strategy. Robert E. Parker, "Urban Growth Management in Southern Nevada," in *Towards 2000*, ed. Soden and Herzik.

43. Connie Anderson, Glen Atkinson, and Theodore Oleson, "Fiscal Interdependence and the Need for Regional Cooperation," in *Legislative Issues*, ed. Winter, 69.

44. Anderson, Atkinson, and Oleson, "Fiscal Interdependence and the Need for Regional Cooperation," in *Legislative Issues*, ed. Winter, 69.

45. Nevada Revised Statutes (1995), Chapter 279, sections 384.005, 349.400–349.670.

46. Ebel, *A Fiscal Agenda for Nevada*, 368.

47. Fiscal centralization refers to the degree to which the state restricts local government autonomy to determine the level and mix of revenues and expenditures. Atkinson and Oleson, "Nevada Local Governments," in *Legislative Issues*, ed. Winter and Atkinson; Steven D. Gold, *Reforming State-Local Relations: A Practical Guide* (Denver: National Conference of State Legislators, 1989).

48. Atkinson and Oleson, "Nevada Local Governments," in *Legislative Issues*, ed. Winter and Atkinson.

49. Ebel, *A Fiscal Agenda for Nevada*.

50. Nevada exporting counties include Clark, Churchill, Carson City, Elko, Washoe, Eureka, and Humboldt. Nevada importing counties include Douglas, Esmeralda, Lander, Lincoln, Lyon, Mineral, Nye, Pershing, Storey, and White Pine.

51. Atkinson and Oleson, "Nevada Local Governments," in *Legislative Issues*, ed. Winter and Atkinson.

52. Ibid.

53. Ebel, *A Fiscal Agenda for Nevada*.

54. Atkinson and Oleson, "Nevada Local Governments," in *Legislative Issues*, ed. Winter and Atkinson.

55. State of Nevada, Legislative Commission of the Legislative Counsel Bureau, *Laws Relating to the Distribution among Local Governments of Revenue from State and Local Taxes*, Bulletin No. 97-5 (Carson City, Nev.: Legislative Commission of the Legislative Counsel Bureau, 1997).

56. Lionel Sawyer and Collins, *The Feasibility of Forming a Separate Political Subdivision at Lake Tahoe* (Reno: Lionel Sawyer and Collins, 1997).

57. Deloitte and Touche LLP, *Lake Tahoe, Nevada*.

58. Nevada Constitution, Article IX. In addition to Nevada, forty-one other states impose the requirement of voter referendum approval of government general-obligation debt. Ebel, *A Fiscal Agenda for Nevada*, 678–703.

59. Ebel, *A Fiscal Agenda for Nevada*.

60. Local government natural resource projects, financed through the state bond bank, are exempt from the constitutional limit on state debt. Ebel, *A Fiscal Agenda for Nevada*.

61. Atkinson and Oleson, "Nevada Local Governments," in *Legislative Issues*, ed. Winter and Atkinson; Ebel, *A Fiscal Agenda for Nevada*.

62. Deloitte and Touche LLP, *Lake Tahoe, Nevada*.

63. Nevada Revised Statutes (1995), Chapter 354.

64. Nevada Constitution, Article IX; Ebel, *A Fiscal Agenda for Nevada*.

65. For example, Nevada has imposed an unfunded collective bargaining mandate on local governments, which has removed local governments' flexibility in their budgets and made it more difficult to finance capital facilities. Atkinson and Oleson, "Nevada Local Governments," in *Legislative Issues*, ed. Winter and Atkinson; David R. Berman, "State-Local Relations: Patterns, Politics and Problems," in the *Municipal Year Book 1994* (Washington, D.C.: International City/County Management Association, 1994). The advisory referendum question against unfunded state mandates was unanimously endorsed by all seventeen member counties of the Nevada Association of Counties. Bjorn P. Selinder, "Unfunded Mandates: An Unfair Solution to Government Budgetary Woes," in *Legislative Issues*, ed. Winter and Atkinson.

66. Nevada Constitution, Article IV.

67. Nevada Constitution, Article XV.

68. Heavily populated counties are those with 400,000 or more population; moderately populated counties are those with 100,000 or more but less than 400,000 population. Nevada Revised Statutes (1995), sections 244.016, 244.014.

69. Nevada Revised Statutes (1995), sections 244.011, 244.025, 244.027, 244.050; *State ex rel. Fall v. Kelso*, 46 Nev. 128, 208 Pac. 424 (1922); *Hanson v. Board of County Commissioners*, 75 Nev. 27, 333 P.2d 994 (1959); *Acree v. Valley*, 78 Nev. 444, 375 P.2d 545 (1962).

70. Nevada Constitution, Article XV; Nevada Revised Statutes (1995), Chapters 31, 213, 265, 266, 275, 276, 294A, 344, 465, 470, 517, 573, 662. Cities with populations of 20,000 or more are classified as first-class cities; with more than 5,000 and less than 20,000, as second-class cities; with 5,000 or less, as third-class cities. Nevada Revised Statutes (1995), sections 266.055, 266.095, 255.220.

71. The impeachment procedure involves a two-step process. First, impeachment charges must be brought by a majority of the elected members of the Nevada Assembly. Second, conviction requires the concurrence of two-thirds of the elected members of the state senate. An impeachment conviction does not extend further than removal from office and disqualification to hold any office of honor, profit, or trust under the state. Nevada Constitution, Article VII.

72. City councils possess the authority to punish council members for disorderly conduct and may expel a member for cause with the concurrence of two-third of the council members. Nevada Constitution, Article VII; Nevada Revised Statutes (1995), section 266.240.

73. Nevada Constitution, Articles II, XIX.

74. Shalmy and Fretwell, "Home Rule," in *Legislative Issues*, ed. Winter.

75. Bill O'Driscoll, "Nevada's longest, costliest session ends," *Reno Gazette-Journal*, 8 July 1997, 1A.

NEW HAMPSHIRE

John F. Camobreco and Mark V. Ebert

The authors thank Andrea Reid of the New Hampshire Department of Revenue Administration and H. Bernard Waugh of the New Hampshire Municipal Association for their help.

The paradox that characterizes New Hampshire's state-local relations is that although this state still clings fervently to "direct democracy" at the local level, its cities, towns, and counties are allowed very little independent governance. Not only is there no legal provision for home rule in New Hampshire, but the state's supreme court has historically favored the supremacy of the state legislature's power in disputes between the state and its localities. The localities of greatest importance are towns and cities; counties play a very limited role in local governance, and most of the governing functions that might be performed by them in other states are performed by towns in New Hampshire. Although cities and towns recently gained the power to change their governmental forms independent of state legislative approval, New Hampshire remains a state in which local "direct democracy" is tempered by localities' limited powers.

Governmental Setting

New Hampshire is one of the oldest settled areas in America. Immigrants arrived in 1623 near what is now Portsmouth, on the Atlantic coast. The body of municipal law in New Hampshire has been evolving since 1639, and by the time of the Revolutionary War, most municipalities that are present today existed in one form or another.[1] Adopted in 1784, the New Hampshire Constitution is one of the oldest in the nation, and little of it has changed since that time. Consequently, the laws regarding local government are deeply rooted in the state's history and culture and are not easily modified.

Economically, New Hampshire has always been a state friendly to business and the free enterprise system. During the industrial revolution of the 1800s, New Hampshire became one of the world's leading producers of textiles. The mills along the rivers in the southern region of the state attracted many French Canadian immigrants, who sought steady employment and a change from the harsh farming life. Today, the descendants of these immigrants make up almost a third of the state's population. Descendants of the original English Protestant settlers and a minority of other ethnic groups complete the ethnic composition of the state.

New Hampshire is no longer a major textile producer, but its low taxes and attractive business climate have lured many modern manufacturers of high-technology products. It is the only state besides Alaska without a broad-based income or sales tax.

Despite New Hampshire's small population of roughly 1.2 million, it has been the fastest growing state on the East Coast since the mid-1960s.[2] This growth is expected to continue well into the twenty-first century, particularly in the state's southernmost counties.[3] The New Hampshire of today is a mix of economic prosperity based on information-age products and traditional forms of local government that continue to endure.

New Hampshire has been characterized as having a moralistic-individualistic political culture,[4] which is manifested in a desire to preserve traditional New England small-town life and an individualistic streak that deplores excessive governmental activity, particularly taxation. Examples of this individualism and independence include the New Hampshire Constitution, which still includes a right of revolution,[5] and the state motto, "Live Free or Die." Although there are pockets of social conservatism in New Hampshire, the state is perhaps best described as libertarian; minimal governmental involvement in all areas of life is the general preference.

Politically, New Hampshire is one of the few states dominated by the Republican Party, although this may be beginning to change. The Republicans continue to hold a solid majority in the state house of representatives, but the Democrats gained a slim majority in the state senate after the 1998 election. The state also elected its first Democratic governor in sixteen years in 1996 (Jeanne Shaheen), and she was reelected in 1998. Shaheen is also the first woman to be elected governor; she gained office in part by pledging to veto any broad-based tax. Despite Shaheen's success, registered Republicans in the state still far outnumber registered Democrats, and Republicans currently hold the state's two U.S. House seats and the two U.S. Senate seats.

New Hampshire's long history of distaste for strong government is reflected in the state's governing structure. The emphasis on citizen control is apparent in the New Hampshire House of Representatives, with its 400 members. The state house and the 24-member state senate make for a state legislative body of 424, which is the third largest governing body in the English-speaking world and by far the biggest state legislature.[6] These citizen-legislators are paid only $100 a year.

New Hampshire is also only one of two states to have retained a two-year governor's term. The governor is further weakened by the presence of the Executive Council, a body of five separately elected members that must approve all gubernatorial appointments. The Executive Council is yet another vestige from the early days of independence from Britain, when checking the power of the executive was foremost in the minds of the newly free citizens. Although the governor has the power to appoint the commissioners of executive branch agencies, these commissioners all serve four- or five-year terms. These term lengths, combined with the governor's two-year term, dilute gubernatorial control of the executive branch.

Perhaps the most distinctive feature of New Hampshire government is at the local level, where the town meeting is still the primary method of local governance. Of the 235 incorporated municipalities in New Hampshire, 222 are towns. All but a handful of these still operate under the town meeting form of government, despite a 1979 change in state law that allows towns to adopt some representative forms of government. The majority of the state's population live in towns, as reflected by the fact that about two-thirds of the representatives in the state house are elected from towns.[7] The remaining 13 municipalities are cities, only one of which has a population of more than 50,000 (Manchester). The 10 counties in the state are not nearly as important as the cities and towns as units of local government.

Home Rule in New Hampshire

Historical Development

One of the paradoxes about New Hampshire—a state that seemingly believes in a large degree of local governmental control—is that the state legislature historically has had absolute power over municipalities. This power has been continually reaffirmed by the New Hampshire Supreme Court, which in a number of court cases has made it clear that the governing powers of municipalities are strictly limited to those explicitly granted to them by the state legislature.[8] In fact, the New Hampshire Municipal Association cautions local officials to find the specific state statute authorizing a local action before taking it rather than assume that the municipality has the power to take the ac-

tion.[9] Therefore, towns, cities, and village districts have limited and restricted powers. New Hampshire is not legally a home rule state; although the tradition of home rule has generally been recognized by the legislature, in reality municipalities have little leeway to perform functions not specified by the state legislature.[10]

During the early part of New Hampshire's existence, towns in effect were the sole form of local government. It was not until 1846 that the first of New Hampshire's thirteen cities, Manchester, was incorporated. By this time, the New Hampshire Supreme Court had conceded that when the population of a place began to exceed 10,000 or 12,000 some form of representative government became necessary. However, population seems historically not to have been a large factor in determining which areas incorporated themselves as cities. In 1867 general legislation was passed to provide uniform regulations for cities.[11]

Definition of Home Rule

The state constitution was amended in 1966 to allow cities and towns to change or amend their charters—provided that the change was approved by local referendum and that the change did not conflict with general law on forms of government allowed for these municipalities.[12] Before this amendment, only the state legislature had the power to change the form of government used by a municipality; now, all changes must be approved by local referendum. This constitutional amendment was codified into more specific law in 1979, with the passage of legislation known generally as home rule–municipal charters.[13] Despite its name, a home rule–municipal charter is not a legal provision for home rule but rather allows municipalities only to change their form of government and does not confer any additional power on them. Any confusion stemming from the original legislation was clarified by a revision to it passed in 1988, which specified that municipalities could exercise powers only specifically granted to them.[14] However, the state supreme court had already made it quite clear that the 1979 statute referred only to a municipality's ability to change its form of government and did not imply additional powers for local governments.[15]

Despite the tradition of strict limitations on local governmental authority, the state has begun to loosen the reins in the past decade. The state legislature has made increased use of specific enabling legislation that has allowed municipalities additional freedom. For example, in the past there existed a very specific list of areas on which localities could spend money. This lengthy list has now been replaced by a general statement allowing localities to spend money on anything that is not specifically prohibited.[16]

The state may still exercise preemption, however. The premise of the preemption doctrine is that a local regulation that expressly contradicts state law (or even state legislative intent) is invalid. Preemption most overtly manifests itself in conflicts between local governments and the state regarding state agency regulations. These conflicts have been on the rise since the late 1970s and, in many instances, have been adjudicated. In keeping with its decisions about limited home rule, the state supreme court has mostly sided with the state in these matters.[17] For example, it has preempted localities from additional regulation of chemical defoliants and hazardous waste sites, ruling that these areas are already regulated by the state.[18] With regard to local zoning regulations, the court has also upheld the sole authority of the state.[19]

Structural Features

The two major forms of local government in New Hampshire are towns and cities. Village districts and counties also exist but do not play as large a role in local governance. The 1979 home rule–municipal charters legislation set forth new guidelines for the forms of government that municipalities could employ. Because of revisions to this legislation in 1988, 1991, and 1995, towns now have two major options, with some variations.

The town meeting–board of selectmen format is the primary option and is currently used by all but six of the state's 222 towns. However, since 1995, towns using this form of government have had the choice of using a ballot procedure, rather than the traditional town meeting, to decide town issues. A representative town meeting—wherein a group of individuals are elected to represent separate districts of the town at the town meeting—is also allowed, but no towns use this system. The remaining six towns use the second major form of government allowed, the town council–town manager format. This is a representative form of government but may include a budgetary town meeting, as it does in four of the towns.[20]

Those towns using the town meeting–board of selectmen format are constrained by general state legislation that guides the operation of these local governments. The board of selectmen act merely as the *governing* body of the town, whereas the town meeting itself is the real *legislative* body. What this means, in general, is that most town decisions—large or small—must be made at the annual town meeting. The selectmen then act as an executive and administrative branch, carrying out those decisions and performing daily administrative tasks as necessary. The state municipal association advises selectmen that if they have doubts about their power to perform a specific function, they should put the matter to a vote at the town meeting.[21]

The annual town meeting itself must be held on the second Tuesday of March or May and usually includes two separate sessions: the meeting itself (to discuss and decide all town business) and the voting for town officers and ballot articles. The subjects to be discussed at the meeting must be made known in advance, and citizens have the right to petition the selectmen to put specific items on the meeting agenda. The meeting is overseen by a moderator, who is elected every two years.[22]

As a result of legislation passed in 1995, towns using the town meeting–board of selectmen format may now use the ballot box rather than the town meeting to vote on town business. Under the traditional system, the voting booth is used only to elect town officials and to vote on zoning ordinances. Under the new "official ballot" system, the town meeting is used to debate and amend agenda items, but no final vote is taken. The voting on these agenda items is done at a later date, in the privacy of the voting booth, at which point no changes to the proposed legislation can be made. Towns that wish to use this procedure must have it approved by a three-fifths majority. In 1999 about forty-five towns employed the official ballot system, with more scheduled to vote on whether to use the procedure in future elections.[23]

Because cities are governed more by their own specific charters than by general legislation, it is difficult to make generalizations. However, under the home rule–municipal charters legislation and its revisions, all cities must choose either a mayor–board of aldermen (or mayor–city council) format or a city manager–city council format. Representation ranges from all ward (Manchester) to completely at large (Portsmouth), and elections can be either partisan or nonpartisan.[24] Eight of the thirteen cities in New Hampshire currently operate under the city manager–city council format. A general meeting can be held in a city if enough petition signatures are gathered. However, the court has ruled that votes taken at these meetings cannot override the actions of the city's representative body.[25]

Village districts were first permitted by the state legislature in 1849 for the purpose of fire protection. Their operations have expanded since then, but the main objective is to provide services in a more efficient manner. Village districts must be created upon petition of ten or more legal voters in the area affected. A village district must hold its annual meeting between January and the end of April. Its governing board of village commissioners has duties and powers similar to those of selectmen in towns (village districts are governed like towns). Residents of village districts vote and pay taxes in both the village district and towns in which they live.[26]

There are ten counties in New Hampshire, but their governing role is dwarfed by the towns and cities, which provide most local services. Counties have an executive branch of three county commissioners who prepare the budget and are responsible for certain administrative duties. The county delegation is the legislative branch of each county. The delegation is unusual in that its membership consists of each state representative from that county. Thus, county delegations range from 13 to 121. Their primary duty is to approve the budget prepared by the county commissioners.[27]

The boundaries of all municipalities are determined by the state legislature; the municipalities themselves have no direct control over these boundaries. Since 1903, however, there has been a state law requiring a local referendum for any proposed boundary change, and such a change is not valid unless approved by two-thirds of the voters in each municipality affected. Annexation is also controlled by the state legislature and requires a similar local referendum. In addition, the state legislature has sole control over the creation of new municipalities; in this case, a local referendum is not required but may be held if the legislature so desires.

The boundaries of most municipalities in New Hampshire have remained unchanged for the past 150 years, and annexation has been rare for the past century. The superior court of a county decides any boundary disputes between municipalities. Towns can control land use or own facilities (for example, landfills) outside their boundaries only through intergovernmental agreements with other municipalities, which require state approval.[28] There are currently twenty-four unincorporated places in New Hampshire, which must follow the laws applicable to towns.[29]

Functions of Local Government

Functional Responsibilities

Specific enabling legislation from the state must be granted to municipalities for all their activities. Even then, the state may still preempt local ordinances. Towns are specifically allowed to enact ordinances on general police powers, public facilities and institutions, animal control, fire control, garbage and snow removal, auto regulation, regulation of noise, and restaurant health and licensing. Towns are allowed to have boards of health with wide regulatory powers. Towns are also required to serve as the welfare providers of last resort; that is, towns must adopt realistic welfare guidelines and provide welfare to those who meet these guidelines. Welfare subsidies may be provided to those who do and those who do not meet the state or federal standards for welfare. In addition to these powers, cities may regulate liquor sales and taxi services.[30] Counties have very limited functions but do provide services such as nursing homes and correctional facilities.[31]

Village districts are the most common type of special district in New Hampshire. State law provides authorization for two or more governmental units to form special districts, which may exercise any powers that each municipality could exercise individually. This means that municipalities can form special districts for purposes such as fire protection, highways, and refuse disposal. Intergovernmental agreements regarding the disposal of solid waste are fairly common; currently, there are twenty-nine in force in the state.[32]

Administrative Discretion

Local governments do have a large degree of control over their personnel management decisions and their administrative procedures. For the most part, municipalities can hire and dismiss employees at will, unless a collective bargaining agreement is in place. However, because state law requires that at least ten employees must have a common interest in order to unionize, many of the smaller towns do not have unions. Employment procedures covering police officials are more regulated by the state. For example, should a municipality wish to dismiss them, elected police chiefs are entitled to a pretermination hearing, and appointed police chiefs have a right to a superior court hearing.[33]

Municipalities also have fairly broad powers to make contracts and are limited only by a general "necessary and convenient" clause.[34] There is no general legislation requiring this contracting to be done through the competitive bid process, but state law does stipulate that counties must use this process, and many city charters contain competitive bid requirements. In addition, cities that opt to create a purchasing department must institute competitive bidding for all purchases over $100. Towns have the authority to establish purchasing departments, but they are not required to follow competitive bidding procedures. State law requires competitive bidding on state-guaranteed bonds for flood-control projects.[35]

Local governments have been given broad discretion over planning, zoning, and land use by a standard state zoning-enabling act. Under the act, municipalities may adopt zoning ordinances that regulate and restrict the size, location, and use of buildings. Lot sizes and population density are also subject to similar local regulation. The state zoning act stipulates that local zoning ordinances must cover districts rather than individual land parcels; moreover, ordinances must be consistent with a "comprehensive plan," but this plan need not be a separate document or even a written document.

The New Hampshire Supreme Court often upholds local zoning ordinances that are challenged (because these ordinances are presumed to be legal), and the burden of proof is on the challenger to demonstrate that an ordinance is invalid. However, the state may override local land-use controls through preemption (that is, it can build regardless of local zoning ordinances). In addition, state approval is required for certain types of terrain alteration, such as the construction and expansion of shoreline buildings, filling and dredging of wetlands, and installation of private sewage systems.[36]

Economic Development

State law allows both cities and towns to create industrial development authorities. However, state law prohibits the use of public funds to help private businesses, unless there is a public benefit involved. This means that municipalities are not allowed to establish enterprise zones, which provide tax breaks for specific areas. Industrial development authorities must be able to justify their existence based on the public benefits they will provide. These authorities typically establish revolving loan funds and act as developers of particular areas. They also are involved in marketing and liaison between the state and local governments and local businesses. Although no enterprise zones are allowed, cities may establish central business service districts. Moreover, towns may establish tax increment districts, which often are instituted in dilapidated areas of the municipality. Tax revenues are then used to refurbish deteriorating buildings.[37]

Fiscal Autonomy of Local Governments

Local Revenues

Revenue for the operation of municipal government, county government, and public schools is derived primarily from the local property tax. Cities and towns adopt budgets and appraise property within their borders at full and true market value. The state Department of Revenue Administration then sets the tax rate. After receiving reports of appropriations made by each municipality and computing local assessed property values and other sources of municipal revenue, the department sets the tax rate so that revenues will equal expenditures. Therefore, the state does require municipal budgets to be balanced; technically, however, there is no state-imposed limit on the amount of money that may be raised or spent. Property is appraised as of April 1, the beginning of the tax year. The fiscal year begins on January 1, unless a municipality has adopted the "optional fiscal year," which begins on July 1. Towns and cities may levy only property taxes, motor vehicle taxes, and certain business license taxes. Counties may levy only property taxes, but instead of a countywide rate, each municipality in the county pays a portion of the tax based on an equalized valuation of that municipality's property. Department of Revenue Administration figures for fiscal 1994 indicate that the average municipality raised approximately 47 percent of its revenue through the property tax; motor vehicle fees provided nearly 10 percent. The remainder was primarily derived from interfund operating transfers (12.5 percent), state funds (8 percent), user charges (5.7 percent), and proceeds from long-term bonds and notes (5 percent).[38]

City budgets are adopted according to procedures in the city charters. Town budgets are adopted at the annual town meeting. Items to be voted on at the town meeting are listed in a warrant, which is posted in advance of the meeting. "Petitioned articles" are items (including budget items) that citizens have requested be included in the warrant. At the town meeting, the town appropriates funds for the fiscal year, which for most towns will have begun two months before the meeting. Appropriation is accomplished through the adoption of a town budget. The tax rate (expressed as dollars of taxes per $1,000 of tax valuation) is calculated by dividing the total appropriations minus estimated nontax revenue by the total taxable valuation. The Department of Revenue Administration has the authority to delete appropriations not made in conformance with state statutes.

Granting of tax exemptions is a function of the state legislature, which requires municipalities to grant certain tax exemptions and gives them the option to grant others. Real estate that is owned by the state or used for schools or for religious or charitable purposes is exempt from taxation. Mandatory "personal" tax exemptions are available to disabled servicemen, persons with disabilities, and persons who are sixty-eight years or older. The legislature has given towns the option to grant exemptions for blind persons, aviation facilities, and solar energy systems. Size of exemptions vary greatly across municipalities.

Because property taxes are due on December 1 or thirty days after bills are sent (whichever is later), a town's current maintenance and operating expenses may not be met by the cash flow resulting from payment of property taxes. To meet this need, towns may issue tax anticipation notes if authorized by majority vote at a town meeting. The notes may not exceed the total tax levy of the prior fiscal year. This limit is applied to the total tax levy of the current fiscal year once that amount is known. To meet expenses between January 1 and the March town meeting, the town treasurer may, without a town meeting vote (but with the approval of the selectmen), issue tax anticipation notes in a total principal amount not greater than 30 percent of the total tax receipts during the previous fiscal year. These notes must be repaid within a year. Towns may also elect to bill taxes twice a year, with payment due dates in June and December.

Borrowing and selling a municipality's bonds or notes (other than tax anticipation notes) require a two-thirds vote at a town meeting or a two-thirds vote of the governing board of a city, county, or town council. Bonds or notes may be issued only for purposes specified by statute, such as acquisition of land, construction or alteration of public buildings, purchase of equipment of a lasting character, and payment of judgments. A municipality's total amount of debt is limited to a percentage of the municipality's total equalized assessed valuation (that is, 1.75 percent for towns and 7 percent for school districts). Municipalities must include the repayment of debt in their yearly appropriations. If they do not, the Department of Revenue Administration may add it into estimations when calculating a property tax rate. This is the only instance in which this state agency may unilaterally increase a municipality's appropriations.[39]

Local Expenditures

Proportionally large budget items for most cities are police and fire protection; the average city spends over 20 percent of its budget on these areas. Water and sewer utilities are also large budget items for some cities, but the amount spent varies drastically from city to city. Large budget items for towns also vary greatly because some towns have no common water supply and some rely on the state police in lieu of establishing a local force.

On average, the top three expenditure categories for towns in terms of budget percentages in fiscal 1994 were bridges (13.1 percent), ambulance service (12.6 percent), and building inspection (8.6 percent).[40]

Tax billing, collection of taxes, and expenditure of properly appropriated funds is a function of municipal officials. Generally, town officials may not spend money for any purpose unless that amount was specifically appropriated by the town meeting. Appropriated amounts that are not spent or committed to be spent by the end of the fiscal year lapse into the general fund. Lapsed amounts must be appropriated again the following year or used to reduce the following year's tax rate. Since the state Department of Revenue Administration sets the tax rate to cover appropriations, municipal bankruptcy is highly unlikely, and there are no statutes that directly address it. However, there is a statute that allows municipalities to raise additional funds in the case of a deficit caused by a bookkeeping error.[41]

Most towns have adopted the Municipal Budget Law, which provides for a committee to oversee and analyze town expenditures. The budget committee is responsible for proposing a budget for adoption at the annual town meeting and must hold a hearing on the proposed budget before the meeting. The total amount appropriated may not exceed the total amount recommended by the budget committee by more than 10 percent. However, individual budget line items may be increased by the town by more than 10 percent, provided that the total appropriation does not exceed the total recommended by the budget committee.

In towns that have adopted the Municipal Budget Law, town selectmen may transfer an unexpended balance from one budget line item to another if the full amount appropriated in the line to be reduced is not needed. The budget committee's proposed budget is posted with the warrant in advance of the annual meeting. For an appropriation to be valid, its subject matter must have appeared in the warrant. New budget line items may not be added during a town meeting.

State Government Grants-in-Aid to Localities

Although New Hampshire has no state sales or income tax, it does impose a tax on hotel and motel rooms, restaurant meals, interest and dividends, and the net profits of business operations in the state. The revenue generated from these sources is part of the state general fund and is distributed to municipalities according to the state-municipal revenue-sharing formula. The formula's elements are population (to measure demand for local services), equalized valuation (to measure a community's ability to pay for local services), and tax commitment, which is the amount of property taxes appropriated and committed for collection (to measure a community's willingness to tax itself for local services). The Department of Revenue Administration annually allocates revenue-sharing aid to reduce a municipality's tax rate.

The state also taxes railroad property and distributes the revenue to communities based on the proportion of the value of the railroad in each community. Other sources of state aid to municipalities are derived from water pollution–control project bonds and national forestland. State aid is also available for highways, bridges, and education and may require a partial contribution from the municipality.[42] The amount sent to each municipality varies; in fiscal 1995 the top five state grants to local governments were for shared revenues distribution ($45.5 million), highways ($19.5 million), water pollution control ($12.3 million), meals and rooms tax distribution ($9.2 million), and municipal bridges ($6.8 million).[43]

Unfunded Mandates

Concern about unfunded state mandates on localities resulted in a 1984 amendment to the New Hampshire Constitution, which prohibits such mandates. The amendment says that the state will not mandate or assign any new or expanded programs that require local expenditures unless such programs are fully funded by the state or approved by a vote of the local legislative body.[44] It is permissible for the state to pass on federally mandated costs to localities, but the state must justify the costs by identifying the specific federal statute or regulation. In 1990 the New Hampshire Supreme Court decided that a 1989 amendment to the municipal trust workers law was unconstitutional because it could result in additional municipal expenses that were unfunded by the state.[45]

Access to Local Government

Local Elections

The laws regarding local elections in New Hampshire reflect a high degree of state government control. All procedures for town and village district elections (including the dates of these elections) are specifically set out in general state statutes. (Elections take place during town and village meetings, whose dates are set by the state.) Polling hours are virtually the only aspect of the town and village district election process not specified by state law. Although most of these general election statutes apply to cities as well, certain procedures for city elections may be set by specific city charter (in particular, the dates of elections and the polling hours).[46]

Citizen Controls over Actions of Local Officials

Towns operating under the town meeting–board of selectmen format may recall selectmen for overspending appropriations, but selectmen cannot be impeached. Cities and towns with town councils may include provisions for the impeachment or recall of officials in their specific charters.[47]

The existence of "direct democracy" in the form of the town meeting makes tools such as the initiative and referendum practically moot in towns with this form of government. Issues of particular concern to the town's citizens that are not already on the agenda can be added to the town meeting warrant through a petition process.[48] The New Hampshire Supreme Court has interpreted the home rule–municipal charter legislation to mean that cities and town-council towns may include initiative and referendum provisions in their charters; specific state authorization was granted in 1991.[49] Specific laws usually allow for the indirect initiative, which means that proposed citizen legislation is submitted to the voters only if it is not first adopted by the legislative body. The referendum allows citizens to negate legislation already passed by the legislative body.[50]

In New Hampshire, where most local political decisions are made at town meetings, meetings and public records are quite open. The state has had a public records and meetings access law since 1967, which was repeatedly strengthened and subsequently made a constitutional amendment in 1976.[51] Even mere advisory committees are covered by this law. Public records are open unless statutorily exempt or unless it is determined that the benefits of disclosure are outweighed by the benefits of nondisclosure. Exempted are personal school records, internal personnel documents, and commercial or financial information deemed to be confidential. The burden of proof is on the public body to show that a record is not public; merely labeling a document "confidential" usually is not enough to prevent disclosure. The New Hampshire Supreme Court has consistently upheld the right-to-know law and has ruled that this right does not depend on a demonstration of "need" to see the records in question.[52] Court records are also presumed to be open and public; the burden of proof rests on those seeking nondisclosure.[53]

State-Local Relations

Despite New Hampshire's long tradition of "direct democracy" at the local level, home rule simply does not exist. The philosophy behind this condition presumably is that a large state legislature filled with ordinary citizens is the best representative of the public interest. Thus, it is the state legislature that historically has held supreme governing power in New Hampshire (and continues to do so). The New Hampshire Supreme Court has consistently ruled that state legislation supersedes most types of local autonomy. Conflicts between the state government and its localities generally have been decided in favor of the state.

In the past twenty years the state has deferred somewhat to local governments. By constitutional amendment, localities have restricted unfunded state mandates. The New Hampshire Supreme Court has already decided one case on this subject in favor of municipalities, basing its decision on this amendment. In addition, although the court historically has ruled in favor of the state in contests between the state government and its municipalities, municipalities recently have prevailed. The state leg-

islature also seems more willing to grant municipalities the power to carry out certain tasks through specific enabling legislation.

Any notion that local governments are gaining more autonomy must be balanced by the fact that they do not have home rule. Recently, the New Hampshire Municipal Association tried to push a home rule constitutional amendment through the state legislature. To be ratified as an amendment, it had to be passed by both houses of the legislature and then approved by two-thirds of the state's voters. The legislation was approved by the state house but defeated by the senate. Nevertheless, this was probably the proper course of action for proponents of home rule. If municipalities in New Hampshire wish to gain additional autonomy or approximate home rule authority, they will have to do so legislatively—either through further amendments to the state constitution or by convincing the state legislature to grant them more powers.

Notes

1. Peter Loughlin, *Local Government Law*, vol. 13 of *New Hampshire Practice* (Charlottesville, Va.: Michie, 1995).

2. Michael Barone and Grant Ujifusa, *The Almanac of American Politics, 1996* (Washington, D.C.: National Journal, 1995).

3. Mark Hayward, "Rockingham County Is Hot; Coos Is Not," *Union Leader*, 8 May 1997, A1.

4. Daniel Elazar, *American Federalism* (New York: Harper & Row, 1984).

5. New Hampshire Constitution, Part one, Article 10.

6. Evan Hill, *The Primary State: An Historical Guide to New Hampshire* (Taftsville, Vt.: Countryman Press, 1976), 4.

7. Loughlin, *Local Government Law*, section 191.

8. *Seabrook Citizens for the Defense of Home Rule v. Yankee Greyhound Racing, Inc.*, 123 N.H. 103, 456 A.2d 973 (1983); *Region 10 Client Management v. Town of Hampstead*, 120 N.H. 885, 424 A.2d 207 (1980); *Amyot v. Caron*, 88 N.H. 394, 190 A. 134 (1937); *Berlin v. Gorham*, 34 N.H. 266 (1856).

9. New Hampshire Municipal Association, *Knowing the Territory: An Introduction to Local Government Law for Town Officials* (Concord: New Hampshire Municipal Association, 1995), 6.

10. Loughlin, *Local Government Law*, section 61.

11. Loughlin, *Local Government Law*, sections 112 and 13.

12. New Hampshire Constitution, Part one, Article 39.

13. New Hampshire Revised Statutes Annotated, 49-B.

14. New Hampshire Municipal Association, *The Town Official's Handbook* (Concord: New Hampshire Municipal Association, 1992), 5.

15. *Girard v. Town of Allenstown*, 121 N.H. 268, 428 A.2d 488 (1981).

16. Andrea Reid, New Hampshire Department of Revenue Administration, personal communication, April 1997.

17. Loughlin, *Local Government Law*, section 66.

18. *Stablex Corporation v. Town of Hooksett*, 122 N.H. 1091, 456 A.2d 94 (1982); *Town of Salisbury v. New England Power Co.*, 121 N.H. 983, 437 A.2d 281 (1981).

19. *Region 10 Client Management v. Town of Hampstead*, 120 N.H. 885, 424 A.2d 207 (1980).

20. Loughlin, *Local Government Law*, sections 193–201; John Andrews, executive director, New Hampshire Municipal Association, interview, February 1998.

21. New Hampshire Municipal Association, *The Town Official's Handbook*.

22. Loughlin, *Local Government Law*, sections 211, 213, and 232.

23. Office of the New Hampshire Secretary of State, personal communication, March 2000.

24. Loughlin, *Local Government Law,* sections 140 and 135.

25. *Kelley v. Kennard,* 60 N.H. 1 (1880).

26. Loughlin, *Local Government Law,* sections 15 and 321–327.

27. Toni M. Addario, New Hampshire Association of Counties, personal communication, July 1996.

28. New Hampshire Revised Statutes Annotated, 53-A:5.

29. Loughlin, *Local Government Law,* sections 16–19.

30. Ibid., sections 744–745, 893–894.

31. Toni M. Addario, personal communication, July 1996.

32. Loughlin, *Local Government Law,* section 81; New Hampshire Department of Environmental Services, personal communication, 1997.

33. Bernard Waugh, chief legal counsel, New Hampshire Municipal Association, interviews, July 1996 and April 1997.

34. New Hampshire Revised Statutes Annotated, 31:3.

35. Loughlin, *Local Government Law,* section 776.

36. Peter Loughlin, *Land Use Planning and Zoning,* 2d ed., vol. 15 of *New Hampshire Practice* (Charlottesville, Va.: Michie, 1995), sections 2, 12, and 39.

37. Bernard Waugh, New Hampshire Municipal Association; Dennis McCann, Office of State Planning; and Andrea Reid, Department of Revenue Administration, interviews, July 1996.

38. Andrea Reid, interview, April 1997, and personal communication, August 1997.

39. Andrea Reid, interview, April 1997.

40. Andrea Reid, personal communication, August 1997.

41. New Hampshire Revised Statutes Annotated, 41:9.

42. New Hampshire Municipal Association, *The Town Official's Handbook* and *Knowing the Territory;* Andrea Reid, interview, September 1996.

43. Andrea Reid, interview, April 1997.

44. New Hampshire Constitution, Part one, Article 28-a.

45. *New Hampshire Municipal Trust Workers' Compensation Fund v. Flynn,* 133 N.H. 17, 573 A.2d 439 (1990).

46. Loughlin, *Local Government Law,* sections 1182, 1185, 1312, 1315, and 1326; Bernard Waugh, interview, July 1996.

47. Bernard Waugh, interview, July 1996; New Hampshire Revised Statutes Annotated, 49-c:13.

48. New Hampshire Revised Statutes Annotated, 39:3.

49. *Harriman v. City of Lebanon,* 122 N.H. 477, 446 A.2d 1158 (1982).

50. Loughlin, *Local Government Law,* section 909.

51. New Hampshire Constitution, Part one, Article 8; Loughlin, *Local Government Law,* sections 652, 653, and 655.

52. Petition of Keene Sentinel, 136 N.H. 121, 612 A.2d 911 (1992); *Mans v. Lebanon School Board,* 112 N.H. 160, 290 A.2d 866 (1972).

53. Loughlin, *Local Government Law,* sections 701, 715, 718, 714.

NEW JERSEY

Ernest C. Reock Jr., Alma Joseph, and Michele Collins

New Jersey is the ultimate suburb-state. Located between two major out-of-state cities, New Jersey's 566 municipalities cover the entire area of the state; the largest, Newark, includes only about 3 percent of the total population. Limited constitutional home rule provisions leave local control dependent on legislative deference. But that deference is forthcoming, since present and former local government officials comprise a substantial part of the legislature's membership. State legislation and rule making lean toward procedural uniformity, rather than policy control, and the state makes numerous options available to local communities. Recent trends in home rule have been mixed, but there is a clear movement toward a larger role for state government and a smaller one for local government. The movement is an almost inevitable outcome of the fragmentation of the state into so many small local units.

Governmental Setting

Benjamin Franklin is reported to have likened New Jersey to a keg tapped at both ends. The history of New Jersey, located between the Delaware and Hudson Rivers, with a major port city at each end of the state, can been seen as a process of filling up the empty space between Philadelphia and New York City. But that open space has been dwindling in recent decades. Whereas in 1900 the New Jersey population was only 40 percent that of New York City and Philadelphia combined, by 1996 it was up to 92 percent.[1]

The New Jersey population has always grown more from in-migration than from natural increase, and the in-migration has come from very diverse sources. In the earliest years, Dutch settlers moved to northeastern New Jersey from New Amsterdam and from Long Island. The English who founded Newark came to establish a theocratic colony because seventeenth-century Connecticut was too liberal for them. English Quakers settled in the lower Delaware Valley, as did Swedes, and the Scottish proprietors who controlled much of the land in the colony imported countrymen to settle their estates.[2]

In the mid-nineteenth century the state hosted waves of Irish and German immigrants, followed by newcomers from eastern and southern Europe at the end of the century, from the American South following World War II, and from Central and South America and Asia in the latest decades.

Within the last thirty years New Jersey has become the most heavily populated state in the country, with a density of more than one thousand persons per square mile. In the older sections of the northeast, municipal populations exceed forty thousand persons per square mile. The highest concentrations are found in the corridor extending southwest from New York toward Philadelphia, and the central part of the state has truly become the place where those cities meet. Data from recent censuses show the center of population moving steadily toward the southwest, a shift with potentially painful political consequences for the older communities of the northeast. Although the state's total population continues to grow, it does so at less than the national rate, which led to the loss of two seats in the U.S. House of Representatives between 1970 and 1996.

An important factor in understanding government in New Jersey is its geographic location between New York and Philadelphia. Extensive streams of New Jersey residents commute daily to the cities, and there is a smaller but still significant counter-flow, mostly of lower-paid workers. Many, possibly most, New Jersey residents give their primary attention to these cities, rather than to New Jersey affairs. New York and Philadelphia newspapers circulate throughout the state. All of the large network television channels originate in the cities, a fact that makes political campaigning for statewide offices unusually expensive.

New Jersey is a state of small towns, and their residents treasure them. The largest city, Newark, makes up only 3.3 percent of the state's population, and it is declining in size. In contrast, the population continues to expand into the countryside, moving outward from the central corridor. Although reformers frequently inveigh against the multitude of small municipalities,[3] most voters consider consolidation to be best for someone else, not for themselves.

New Jersey state government once was characterized by one of the weakest offices of governor in the country. However, with the "new" constitution of 1947, this changed, and New Jersey's governor now is probably one of the strongest in the country. The governor is the only officer elected statewide and has extensive powers to appoint and remove the cabinet officers who head up the twenty departments into which all state functions must be grouped. The governor has both a conditional veto to propose changes in enacted bills and a line-item veto to eliminate specific provisions in the annual appropriations act.[4] Gubernatorial elections are held in odd-numbered years to separate them from national elections.

The bicameral legislature also has undergone substantial revision in recent decades. Under judicial mandate, the legislature's electoral system was changed in 1966 such that its members now are elected from forty legislative districts rather than from counties, with the voters of each district choosing one senator for a four-year term and two assembly members for two-year terms. It was expected that this change would expand the influence of the urban areas at the expense of rural areas. In practice, the changes led to only a few gains for the cities, considerable loss of influence for rural areas, and greatly enhanced power for the suburbs.

The state constitution of 1947 created a unified court system headed by a supreme court, which makes rules governing all of the courts in the state and has jurisdiction over admissions to the bar and discipline of attorneys. All state court judges are appointed by the governor with the advice and consent of the Senate, and they are precluded from political activity and outside employment by strict rules. The supreme court is considered highly activist, having made landmark decisions on legislative apportionment, the obligation of municipalities to provide affordable housing, and issues of equity in public school finance.

Home Rule in New Jersey

Historical Development

New Jersey's first constitution, adopted hurriedly in July 1776, paid little attention to local government. It acknowledged counties as the basis for representation in the legislature but mentioned townships only as electoral districts for constables and tax appeal commissioners, who were to be selected by the annual town meetings. When a new constitution was written in 1844, the framers directed little attention toward state-local relationships. They mentioned townships as the electoral jurisdiction for justices of the peace and made provisions for ascertaining their populations for this purpose. Otherwise, the constitution ignored local government, and the general statement that "the legislative power shall be vested in a senate and general assembly"[5] precluded any claims for constitutional home rule in New Jersey.

Definition of Home Rule

In 1947, when the current constitution was drafted, the delegates and staff included persons who were well aware of arguments for local home rule. Although they avoided including an explicit grant of home rule, they did address the issue:

The provisions of this Constitution and of any law concerning municipal corporations formed for local government, or concerning counties, shall be liberally construed in their favor. The powers of counties and such municipal corporations shall include not only those granted in express terms but also those of necessary or fair implication, or incident to the powers expressly conferred, or essential thereto, and not inconsistent with or prohibited by this Constitution or by law.[6]

Some writers emphasize the sweeping nature of this provision;[7] however, judicial decisions since 1947 have been mixed. Although some courts have taken a strict constructionist approach to local powers, most have honored the spirit of the constitutional provision while supporting the state's right to preempt activity in any given field.

The New Jersey Supreme Court has not always been deferential to local governments when individual rights have been involved. Landmark decisions in 1975, 1983, and 1986 ruled that all municipalities have a constitutional obligation through their land-use decisions to provide a realistic opportunity for meeting the region's need for housing for moderate and low-income families.[8] The legislative response has provided municipalities with multiple ways of meeting this obligation under the supervision of a state Council on Affordable Housing, and housing opportunities have broadened, but not to the extent that low-income housing advocates had envisioned.[9]

Structural Features

Many of New Jersey's governmental institutions originated in the colonial period. A handful of cities acquired charters from the colonial legislature, but other units of local government grew haphazardly as settlements arose from various directions. The first systematic approach to local government came in 1798 when the legislature enacted a law that divided the entire area of the state into 104 townships, established them as a "body politic and corporate in law," and granted them specific, but limited, powers to raise money for poor relief, road construction and maintenance, and other purposes.[10]

The law provided for an annual town meeting at which officers were elected and taxes authorized. The town meeting selected five freeholders to serve as a township committee to supervise expenditures during the year. Use of the annual town meeting persisted until 1899.[11]

The original 104 townships proliferated through legislative action during the early nineteenth century. Territory for each new township had to be taken from an existing township.[12] Although townships gradually acquired additional authority during the nineteenth century, they were generally regarded as a limited form of local government with few powers. As population centers began to develop, those who controlled township governments either could not or would not provide the additional services that a more urbanized population desired. When this happened, the legislature typically enacted a special law creating a new municipality within a township and giving it a charter specifying its officers and powers. The terms borough, town, and city were used interchangeably.[13]

Following the Civil War, state legislators realized the political benefit of enacting special local laws, and state involvement in local affairs reached new extremes. The backlash that developed resulted in the adoption in 1875 of a constitutional amendment stating:

The Legislature shall not pass private, local or special laws . . . regulating the internal affairs of towns and counties; appointing local offices or commissions to regulate municipal affairs. . . . The Legislature shall pass general laws providing for the cases enumerated in this paragraph.[14]

After state legislators found treating all municipalities by uniform laws to be unwieldy, they resorted to classification of municipalities. This classification led to definitions of the five types of municipalities now recognized in New Jersey: cities, towns, boroughs, townships, and villages.

Increasing demand for expanded local government powers caused the legislature in 1878 to authorize the creation of new boroughs from part of a township if the residents so wished; the number of boroughs grew dramatically.[15] Similar legislation was enacted for cities and villages. All of these grants of local authority have now been rescinded, and the legislature has reclaimed its power to create new municipalities. The last new municipality established was the Village of Loch Arbour, where about three hundred residents in 1956 used a forgotten statute to create a village from part of Ocean Township, and the total number now stands at 566.

Whereas in earlier years some of the non-township local governments resembled special districts, exercising extraordinary powers within a portion of a township, by the beginning of the twentieth century they were recognized as separate and distinct geographic and governmental units without overlapping jurisdictions.[16] Moreover, in the Home Rule Act of 1917 the legislature formally acknowledged townships as full-fledged municipalities and granted a long list of specific powers to municipalities of all five types. Today, the governmental authority of New Jersey municipalities rarely varies from place to place or type to type.

Where the municipalities do vary is in the organization of their government. Each type of municipality—city, town, borough, township, and village—has a governmental structure outlined in law unless a community has taken advantage of one of the optional form-of-government laws. The borough, town, and city laws provide for a weak mayor and council form of government. The township and village laws provide for government by committee.

Three optional charter laws are available to the residents of any municipality in the state. The commission form of government, made available by a law of 1911, is today used in thirty-two municipalities, and the Municipal Manager Act of 1923, never very popular, is in use in seven places. The third law, the Optional Municipal Charter Law, was passed in 1950 and has seen considerable use. It provides four different forms of government: the "strong" mayor-council option is used in sixty-five places, covering 36 percent of the state's population; the council-manager plan is used in forty-one places, with about 12 percent of the population; and the other two forms, which offer not-quite-so-strong mayor-council plans, are used in twenty-one relatively small places. With minor restrictions, any of these forms can be adopted in any municipality. Use of the optional charter plans confers no additional municipal powers and does not change the type name of the municipality.

When the state constitution was rewritten in 1947, the 1875 constitutional amendment language quoted above was essentially carried over. However, a new section was added:

Upon petition by the governing body of any municipal corporation formed for local government, or of any county, and by vote of two-thirds of all members of each house, the Legislature may pass private, special or local laws regulating the internal affairs of the municipality or county. . . . Such law shall become operative only if it is adopted by ordinance of the governing body of the municipality or county or by vote of the legally qualified voters thereof.[17]

This paragraph has served as the basis for legislation authorizing special charters for municipalities and counties, and a handful of municipalities have made use of the law.

Action to use any of the optional charter laws or the special charter provision may be initiated either by the voters through a petition process or, in some cases, by an ordinance of the municipal governing body. However, no change in form of government may go into effect without a referendum of the voters.

Historically, counties in New Jersey have been governed under a committee system, with the governing body called a board of chosen freeholders. For many years a board consisted of persons representing individual townships or wards of cities, sometimes numbering as many as thirty-five members.[18] Since the 1960s representation has generally been through small boards in at-large elections. While the board functions as the governing body, individual members, usually called "freeholders," generally take responsibility for supervising specific departments of the county government.

In 1972 the legislature enacted an optional county charter law, like the optional municipal charter law, authorizing a variety of different governmental structures.[19] Six of the twenty-one counties have made use of this law, five of them choosing a county executive option similar to the strong mayor-council form. The other county chose a county manager form of government. In addition to changing the top legislative and executive organization of the county government, the optional county law grants extensive powers for reorganizing the administrative structure, much of which otherwise is controlled by general state laws. In practice, the county executive option has been described as creating five of the most powerful county executives in the nation.[20]

Annexation of territory and consolidation of municipalities are authorized by state law;[21] however, since the entire area of the state is covered by incorporated municipalities, the agreement of both jurisdictions is required. Except for minor boundary revisions, agreement is seldom reached.

The legislature has delegated its constitutional responsibility to "provide for the maintenance and support of a thorough and efficient system of free public schools" to about six hundred local school districts. Generally, the school districts are coterminous with municipalities, but there are about seventy regional districts that cover more than one municipality. Most boards of education are elected, and the tax levies included in their budgets are subject to approval by the voters. In a few cases the boards are appointed by the mayor and the budget is subject to approval by a board of school estimate dominated by municipal officials.

Functions of Local Government

Functional Responsibilities

Legal statutes authorize municipalities to undertake a wide range of activities but rarely mandate any. The largest single activity is providing for public safety and, within that category, police protection. Most municipalities have their own police department, although a considerable number of the smaller, rural communities still rely on the state police for this function. Fire protection runs a distant second to police protection. There are few fully paid fire departments in the state, with municipalities historically relying on volunteers.

The second largest area of municipal activity is public works, with the function evenly divided among streets and drainage, garbage and trash disposal, and sewers and sewage processing. The mix in any given municipality varies, and some municipalities contract out a substantial portion of their public works responsibility.

Third in magnitude after public safety and public works is the conduct of general municipal government—the activities necessary to keep everything else running. These include tax assessment, tax collection, planning, record keeping, and such human resource activities as those for youth, senior citizens, child care centers, and anti-poverty programs.

Counties frequently serve as the jurisdictional units within which a state function is carried out. In many cases, operational control and supervision rests with state agencies, while the county is responsible for the facilities used and for substantial portions of the cost. This division of responsibilities has been particularly true with regard to the court system and welfare functions.

Historically, the court system and public welfare have been the primary county government functions in New Jersey, and this probably continues to be true today. However, their impact on county finances has been reduced in recent years through the transfer of many court costs to the state and a general de-emphasis of the welfare system. Counties play a substantial role in staffing the prosecutors office, providing security for the courts, and running correctional and penal institutions. County public health activities have grown in recent years as the function has dwindled at the municipal level. A number of counties support significant library systems to supplement municipal libraries. The counties for many years have operated county vocational school districts, and recently they have added a system of county colleges, which provide a two-year curriculum.

The state has passed laws permitting municipalities to subdivide themselves into special districts for certain purposes. A municipality that creates a district can authorize a special property tax in that area for support. Not incidentally, creation of a special district enables the municipal governing body to place the cost outside of its budget and general tax levy. By 1999 municipalities had established 156 fire districts, 13 garbage disposal districts, and 2 water districts.[22] School districts are the most prevalent form of special district.

Legislation has been in effect for several decades authorizing and encouraging local government units to share services,[23] and municipalities have taken considerable action along these lines, though no one has tabulated it in any comprehensive way. In 1998 complaints about steadily increasing property taxes led the governor to appoint a Property Tax Commission to investigate ways of mitigating the burden. A major recommendation of the commission was for the state to encourage the sharing of services among units of local government.[24] The state established two new programs: the Regional Efficiency Development Incentive Program, which will provide grants and loans to support studies of interlocal service agreements, and the Regional Efficiency Aid Program, which will subsidize actual agreements for such shared services.[25]

Administrative Discretion

Although some of the optional charter laws mandate the presence of an appointed chief administrative officer—either a manager or a business administrator—the majority of local government units, which are not under these laws, are not required to have such an office. However, state legislation authorizes the governing body of noncharter municipalities and counties to create the office by ordinance or resolution and to delegate to the administrator all or any portion of the executive responsibilities of the governing body.[26] About 60 percent of the noncharter municipalities and most of the fifteen noncharter counties have done so.

Certain boards and commissions (such as a board of health and a local assistance board) and certain local offices (such as the municipal clerk, tax assessor, tax collector, and chief financial officer) are required at the local level by general state law. Otherwise, the administrative organization of local governments is relatively unhindered by state requirements.

Any local government unit may join the state personnel system through referendum, and it then is bound by the rules of that program. Once a member of the system, it may not withdraw. Roughly half of the municipalities and almost all of the counties have come under the state system, with most adoptions occurring many years ago.

Over the past thirty-five years many local offices formerly filled by election, such as municipal clerk, tax assessor, and tax collector, have been changed to appointive positions. Eligibility to serve in such capacities now is dependent upon the satisfactory completion of a state test and often on the completion of a designated series of training programs.[27] The same approach has been extended to local positions that have always been appointive, such as finance officers and public works directors. Professional organizations of local officials have been eager to agree to the training and testing requirements in return for enhanced job security, but elected officials and top management have not always been as enthusiastic, since enhanced job security restricts their powers of appointment and removal.

Collective bargaining by public employees has been a fixture in New Jersey since the 1960s, and unionization is widespread at all levels of local government. State regulations are enforced by the Public Employment Relations Commission.[28] Labor disputes involving police and fire departments, where strikes are forbidden, are subject to compulsory arbitration.

Local governments have conducted purchasing and contracting for many years under the detailed state restrictions contained in the Local Public Contracts Law. With certain exceptions, the law requires that purchases exceeding $17,500 be made only through competitive processes and after advertisement. However, this limit may be revised by the governor every five years, using an index based on market conditions. The law encourages cooperative purchasing among local governmental units, and a recent study found that most of the municipalities, school districts, and counties were involved in some form of cooperative purchasing agreements.[29]

Land-use planning and control are areas where there is a con-stitutional basis for municipal home rule. A 1927 amendment to the state constitution then in effect authorized the legislature to enact general laws under which municipalities, other than counties, could adopt zoning ordinances, and identical language was carried over to the current constitution.[30] Almost every municipality in the state has adopted a zoning ordinance and has both a planning board and a zoning board of adjustment. The procedures to be followed are prescribed in detail by the Municipal Land Use Law, and both the legislation and the litigation are voluminous.

Whereas school districts in the past enjoyed considerable leeway in curricular matters, the state's adoption of core curriculum standards in 1996, enforced through required high school completion tests, has imposed significantly more restrictive state controls.[31]

Economic Development

As the older communities of the state deteriorated over the years, New Jersey struggled to find governmental mechanisms to help in their economic development and redevelopment. Early programs, which still exist, include property tax abatements, state aid, and the delegation of special local taxing powers in a few places.

Currently, the Local Development and Housing Law, enacted in 1992, authorizes any municipality to create a redevelopment authority for any area that the municipality designates as "in need of rehabilitation."[32] In the New Jersey Redevelopment Act of 1996 the state created an office to coordinate many of its efforts to assist the poorest urban municipalities The New Jersey Redevelopment Authority may make low- or no-interest loans, provide equity investments, issue local guarantees, and extend technical assistance. At present, 67 communities are involved in projects with the authority.[33]

A somewhat older program to assist in the economic development of local areas is the urban enterprise zone law, enacted in 1983. Benefits to businesses in a zone originally included tax credits for new hires, unemployment insurance rebates, and sales tax exemptions for corporate purchases of equipment and materials used on site. In 1992 the impact of the law was significantly increased when the state cut in half the state sales tax on retail transactions within a zone.[34] Authorization of special improvement districts constitutes another attempt by the state to provide tools to municipalities for economic development. Any municipality may create such a district and may levy a special assessment on real property within the area, to be collected by the municipal tax collector along with regular property taxes. The funds are turned over to a district management corporation for use in providing services that will promote economic growth and employment within the district.[35] The New Jersey Supreme Court has ruled that the special district charges are an assessment and not a tax and, therefore, are not subject to the "uniformity" clause in the state constitution.[36] Currently, there are forty-seven such districts in New Jersey.[37]

Fiscal Autonomy of Local Governments

Local Revenues

The state has not levied a property tax since 1946, but the property tax is the dominant feature of local government finance, serving as the major support of county governments, municipal governments, and local school districts. According to the state constitution:

Property shall be assessed for taxation under general laws and by uniform rules. All real property assessed and taxed locally or by the State for allotment and payment to taxing districts shall be assessed according to the same standard of value, and such real property shall be taxed at the general tax rate of the taxing district in which the property is situated, for the use of such taxing district.[38]

Municipalities serve as the taxing districts for the property tax. The tax is a residual tax. Each local government unit prepares its own budget, determines the non–property tax revenue it may anticipate, and deducts this amount from its total revenue needs. The balance is certified to the county board of taxation as the tax levy required. The county board determines the tax levy for each municipality and calculates the general tax rate. This rate is certified to the municipal tax collector, who bills each property owner for the taxes due for county, municipal, and school purposes through a single, consolidated tax bill. There are no statutory tax rates or tax-rate limits, except for very special and limited purposes. In 1999 the total property tax came to $13.5 billion, of which 54 percent went for the use of the schools, 26 percent for municipal governments, and 20 percent for counties.

Although assessments are supposed to be made at 100 percent of market value, they vary from municipality to municipality. Statewide, the average assessment rate is about 85 percent of market value, but some municipalities, which have not revalued their property in years, may have assessment-sales ratios as low as 15 percent.[39]

The statewide equalized property tax rate hit a peak of $3.71 per hundred dollars of true property value in 1971. Over the next seventeen years it declined steadily to $1.70 in 1988 as school enrollments dropped while state aid for schools increased and the tax base grew steadily. Between 1988 and 1998 the statewide tax rate rose to $2.46, with attendant political criticism.

At different times over the past decades the legislature has redefined the taxable property tax base. In two major instances the state exempted a type of property from municipal property taxes—public utility property and personal property used in business—then made a commitment to replace the lost property tax revenue with direct payments to the municipalities. The result

Table 1. Principal Sources of New Jersey Municipal Revenue, 1994

Revenue source	Counties	Municipalities
Property taxes	50%	44%
Property tax replacement revenues	–	14
Payments in lieu of property taxes	–	2
State aid	21	15
Other local revenue	24	17
Surplus reappropriated	5	9

Source: Fifty-seventh Annual Report of the Division of Local Government Services, 1994, Statements of Financial Condition of Counties and Municipalities, State of New Jersey, December 1995, p. 50.

has been two fairly substantial revenue streams from the state to the municipalities, which the state calls aid and the municipalities regard as their just reimbursement for giving up property taxes they formerly levied.

The principal sources of municipal revenue are shown in Table 1. The largest single source is the property tax, making up almost half of the total. Other property-tax-related revenues—state payments to replace lost tax base and payments in lieu of property taxes—added another 16 percent. Other local revenues—licenses, fees, and permits, fines from municipal courts, and parking meter collections—amounted to 17 percent of the total.[40] State aid, other than replacement revenues, totaled about 15 percent of all municipal revenue, and 9 percent of the revenue in the municipal budgets came from surplus.

County government revenues also are shown in Table 1. Here, again, the property tax is the dominant source, providing half of the total, with state aid representing another one-fifth. Own-source miscellaneous revenues, including fees charged by county officers, such as the county clerk, the surrogate, and the sheriff, and charges for the use of county institutions brought in about one-quarter of the total. Surplus funds reappropriated were fairly minor, covering only 5 percent of the budget. County revenues are a little more than half of those in the 566 municipalities.

School districts have only two significant sources of revenue: state aid, which makes up 38 percent of the total, and property taxes, which contribute about 59 percent. Federal aid, miscellaneous local revenues, and surplus are minimal.[41]

State law imposes limits on the debt that local governments may issue. For municipalities the limit is 3.5 percent of the average of the prior three years' valuation. Counties may borrow up to 2 percent, and school districts 4 percent, of the same base.[42] However, there are a number of exceptions that allow borrowing beyond these limits.

Local Expenditures

Local government financial affairs are regulated in considerable detail by the state. A Local Finance Board, appointed by the governor with the advice and consent of the State Senate, has the power to issue rules and regulations binding on all counties and municipalities.

The board has the authority to assume supervision of the financial affairs of local government units that fall into fiscal difficulty under specified conditions, such as defaulting on bond payments. The board also approves extensions of credit beyond the normal debt limits and proposals for the creation of local authorities.[43]

Balanced county and municipal budgets must be prepared in formats specified by the state Division of Local Government Services, and they must be approved by that agency before final local adoption. The division aims to ensure that required procedures have been followed and that all necessary items have been included in the budget, rather than to enforce policy decisions concerning the amount or purpose of appropriations:

The Local Budget Law specifically precludes the director [of the division] from substituting his or her judgment as to the level of appropriation when reviewing local budgets. As long as the proper appropriations are made for debt service, deferred charges, statutory expenditures, cash deficit of preceding year, and reserve for uncollected taxes, the director's judgment cannot be substituted for that of local officials.[44]

Table 2. Principal Expenses of New Jersey Counties and Municipalities, 1994

Expenditures	Counties	Municipalities
Public safety	18%	32%
Police	*2*	*23*
Fire	*–*	*8*
Other	*16*	*2*
Public works	7	24
Roads	*3*	*7*
Sewers and sewage processing	*–*	*6*
Garbage and trash disposal	*–*	*6*
Public buildings and grounds	*3*	*2*
Other public works	*1*	*2*
Health and welfare	32	3
Health	*21*	*2*
Welfare	*11*	*1*
Education	9	3
Recreation	3	3
Judiciary	6	2
General government	14	20
Statutory expenses (pensions, benefits)	11	13

Source: Fifty-seventh Annual Report of the Division of Local Government Services, 1994, Statements of Financial Condition of Counties and Municipalities, State of New Jersey, December 1995, p. 51.

The reserve for uncollected taxes is one of the items that is checked thoroughly. In the 1930s a number of New Jersey municipalities defaulted on their obligations due to low tax collections. As a result, state law now requires a "cash basis budget," in which the tax levy must be increased by a reserve to allow for less-than-full tax collection.

In 1975, when the state was considering a large increase in state aid for schools, there was concern that the additional state funding would produce no impact on total property taxes because municipalities would raise their tax levies proportionately. The original "solution" was to place a one-year cap on municipal budget increases. As the legislation progressed, the one-year cap became a permanent "budget cap," which survives today.[45] Most municipalities may increase their total annual appropriations by no more than the lower of 5 percent or a price deflator calculated by the U.S. Department of Commerce. This rather restrictive law is ameliorated by the inclusion of a long list of exceptions to the limitations, by the provision for "cap banking" if the full permissible increase is not used in any one year, and by authority to exceed the cap if that is approved by the voters in a referendum. Widely resented when first implemented, the "budget cap" law now is generally accepted, although designing a budget with some costs under the cap and others outside of the cap remains a local art form. The state has imposed similar budget caps on county and school district budgets. An annual audit of each county and municipal budget must be made by a state-certified auditor and copies filed with municipal and county governing bodies and with the state.[46] The state commissioner of education administers similar fiscal controls for school districts.

In the last decade, the commissioner of education has taken over administration of the three largest school districts in the state: Newark, Jersey City, and Paterson. Although fiscal considerations were a factor in these actions, all three districts were regarded as failing educationally. Upon takeover, the local board of education and superintendent are dismissed and the commissioner appoints a new superintendent to run the district, with broad powers to replace personnel and implement new programs.

State Government Grants-in-Aid to Localities

The combination of heavy local reliance on the property tax and fragmentation of the state into almost six hundred local taxing districts leads to wide variations in the amount of taxable property in each community. In this context, state aid to localities is essential to level the playing field and has become one of the largest items in the state budget.

By far the largest state aid program is state aid to schools. School aid had been in existence for many years, but it received a major boost after 1973, when the state courts declared the state aid program constitutionally deficient.[47] The program implemented in 1976 increased state aid to about 40 percent of local school costs and teacher pensions, based on a formula that provided aid in inverse ratio to the property wealth of each school district. The new aid program was possible only through the enactment of the state's first personal income tax, with the revenue dedicated by constitutional amendment to property tax relief.

The 1976 law, in turn, was declared unconstitutional in 1990, with the court now stipulating that the state must ensure that expenditures per pupil in twenty-eight of the poorest urban districts be raised to the level in the wealthiest suburban schools.[48] Over the next six years the state resisted full implementation of the court decision through multiple appeals and decisions.

In 1996 the state passed the Comprehensive Educational Improvement and Financing Act. This law, still in effect, includes sixteen different formulas, providing in 1998–1999 $4.8 billion in aid to districts. In addition, the state government supported almost $1 billion in contributions to pension funds and social security for local school personnel. Despite all of the statutory changes, state aid still covers about 40 percent of all educational costs, including pensions. It is a dynamic aid program, with annual amounts depending on the wealth of the community, school enrollments, the number of children with specific handicaps or coming from families below a specified income level, and various other factors.

State aid to municipalities is much smaller. In 1999 property tax replacement payments totaled $750 million, and other aid about $977 million. The latter figure is made up mostly of funds appropriated as Consolidated Municipal Property Tax Relief Aid. This program consolidates a number of earlier appropriations; it has been a static program that merely carries forward for each municipality the appropriations made in prior years under a multitude of smaller aid formulas. In 1999 new legislation provided for adjusting these amounts annually by a cost index.

State aid for counties, about $750 million in 1994, includes aid for county roads, a share of the operational costs for county colleges, and the state's share of the cost of county hospitals and other health programs.

Unfunded Mandates

Local government officials in New Jersey long resented what they considered to be an unacceptable number of state mandates that contributed to the high level of the property tax.[49] A strong lobbying effort, particularly by the New Jersey State League of Municipalities, culminated in a constitutional amendment approved by the voters in November 1995 stating that:

any . . . law, . . . or rule or regulation, . . . which is . . . an unfunded mandate upon boards of education, counties, or municipalities . . . shall cease to be mandatory in its effect and expire.[50]

The amendment also creates a Council on Local Mandates, appointed by the governor, legislative leaders, and the chief justice to enforce the ban on unfunded mandates. It includes the interesting statement: "The decisions of the Council shall be political and not judicial determinations."[51] The legislature, in enacting a statute to implement the amendment, expanded on this language by stating:

Pursuant to Article VIII, Section II, paragraph 5(b) of the New Jersey Constitution, rulings of the council shall be political determinations and shall not be subject to judicial review.[52]

New Jersey apparently now has a fourth branch of government, with a narrow but final jurisdiction. Thus far, the council has received few appeals and has issued only procedural decisions, but some potentially landmark cases are pending. Although no laws or regulations have been invalidated yet, the presence of the amendment and the law are said to have had a "chilling effect" on some proposed legislation.

Access to Local Government

Local Elections

Elections in New Jersey are frequent. Fire districts vote in February, school boards in April, and nonpartisan municipalities in May, the primary is in June, and the general election is in November. In addition, referenda on various public questions may pop up at almost any time.

Elections are conducted under statutory rules, which are highly detailed and are supplemented by many court decisions. The principal election supervisors are the county boards of election, the superintendent of elections in those counties that have one, and the municipal clerk in each municipality.[53] Very little discretion is permitted at the local level.

The Election Law Enforcement Commission has monitored, regulated, and reported campaign contributions and expenditures since 1973. The state has broadened the scope of the law on several occasions since that time, and it now covers a wide range of electoral activities at all levels of government.[54]

Citizen Controls over Actions of Local Officials

Until recently, the power to recall local officials was granted only under the optional county and municipal charter laws enacted in the twentieth century. However, in 1993 the voters approved a constitutional amendment extending the power of recall to all elected officials in the state.[55] Enabling legislation superseded the power of recall contained in the optional local government laws,[56] and the procedures required have been described as so difficult that the law will seldom be used successfully.[57]

Although New Jersey does not have the initiative or referendum at the state level, the legislature has included these powers with regard to local ordinances in the optional county and municipal charter laws. In addition, there are a number of specific instances, such as the school tax levy and local bonding ordinances, where referenda are authorized or required.

The Open Public Meetings Act, also known as the "Sunshine Law," has been in place since 1975. It requires that due notice be given for the meetings of all public bodies and that all official actions be taken in a public meeting. Certain subjects, such as pending personnel actions, may be discussed in executive session, but minutes must be kept and made available promptly.[58] A law approved in 1963 provides, with specific exceptions, that all records made and maintained by any agency of the state or any political subdivision thereof shall be public.[59]

The law specifies that any citizen of the state may inspect any public record during regular business hours and make or purchase copies. Again, considerable litigation has accumulated, with representatives of the media frequently in court and frequently criticizing the law as too weak.

State-Local Relations

The status of home rule in New Jersey is mixed. While few provisions of the state constitution serve as guarantees, legislative deference to local interests is common.

The year 1947 is something of a watershed in New Jersey, since it marks the writing of the state's present constitution. However, some aspects of state control over local governments antedate that year. The power to create new local government units had been reclaimed by the legislature by 1947, after a fling in the nineteenth century at delegating this power to citizens throughout the state. State control over local finances predates 1947, including budget review, auditing requirements, limits on purchasing and the issuance of debt, and the right to take over the financial affairs of failing municipalities. Perhaps the most onerous aspect of state control was the state's limiting of local revenue sources largely to the property tax, a policy that was rooted in the state's past.

On the other hand, some home rule powers were in place in 1947. The constitutional prohibition against special local laws dates to 1875, a statutory grant of authority for municipalities to engage in a wide variety of functions was included in the Home Rule Act of 1917, and the zoning power was guaranteed to municipalities by constitutional amendment in 1927.

In some areas, state control has increased since 1947. The state has co-opted parts of the local property tax base and imposed limits on increases in local budgets. The state has designated a core curriculum for the schools and has taken over the administration of three large school districts. It has mandated collective bargaining and, in some cases, compulsory arbitration for public-sector employees. State tests have replaced election for a number of local officials. New campaign finance rules limit the completely free hand of local citizens and officials. Judicial directives have required municipalities to provide for low- and moderate-income housing.

A number of actions taken since 1947 can be construed as increasing local home rule, starting with the 1947 constitutional language urging on the courts a liberal construction of laws dealing with local government. Optional local charter laws and the authority to adopt special charters and appoint municipal and county administrators have broadened the powers of citizens and public officials at the local level. The measures providing for recall, local initiative and referendum, and open public meetings and public records have increased the power of the voters. Laws enacted by the state to provide more tools for local governments should be considered as increases in home rule. These laws provide authority for redevelopment, for urban enterprise zones, for shared local services, and for special improvement districts.

Although local officials almost universally complain about state infringement on their prerogatives, there still is a substantial area for local initiative in New Jersey. State control of local governments generally extends to procedures rather than to policies. Although the state may tell the municipalities how to do something, it rarely tells them what to do. Local government officials still have a great deal of latitude in deciding which functions they should perform and how much they should spend on them. This latitude is not the result of very explicit constitutional home rule provisions. Instead, it is more a matter of legislative deference to local concerns. This deference is not too surprising given the composition of the legislature. In 1999 its 120 members included 7 incumbent mayors, 22 former mayors, another 27 persons who had served on municipal governing bodies, and 19 persons who had at one time been on a county governing body.[60]

The impact of the state mandate–state pay amendment to the constitution is still to be determined. While the prohibition on unfunded mandates appears to be a significant step toward strengthened home rule, it may hold the potential for state assumption of governmental functions formerly considered strictly local responsibilities. If so, it would merely accelerate a trend that has been under way for some years. While New Jersey's state government has historically been among the smallest in the country in proportion to population, and its local governments in the aggregate have been among the largest, this is changing. Between 1987 and 1997 New Jersey state government employment per 10,000 residents grew by 19 percent, while local government employment dropped by 2 percent.[61] It may be that governing only 7,400 square miles through 566 municipalities, 21 counties, and about 600 school districts is becoming less viable.

Notes

1. *Statistical Abstract of the United States* (Washington, D.C.: Bureau of the Census, 1999), Tables 26 and 48.

2. John E. Bebout and Ronald J Grele, *Where Cities Meet: The Urbanization of New Jersey* (Princeton: D. Van Nostrand, 1964), 10–15.

3. Alan J. Karcher, *New Jersey's Multiple Municipal Madness* (New Brunswick: Rutgers University Press, 1998).

4. Constitution of New Jersey, 1947, Article V.

5. Constitution of New Jersey, 1844, Article IV, section I, paragraph 1.

6. Constitution of New Jersey, 1947, Article IV, section VII, paragraph 11.

7. Michael A. Pane, *New Jersey Practice.* Vol. 34: *Local Government Law* (St. Paul: West Publishing, 1987), 23–24.

8. *Southern Burlington County N.A.A.C.P. v. Mount Laurel Township,* 67 N.J. 151, 336 A.2d 713 (1975); *Southern Burlington County N.A.A.C.P. v. Mount Laurel Township,* 92 N.J. 158, 456 A.2d 390 (1983); *Hills Development Corporation v. Bernards Township,* 103 N.J. 1, 510 A.2d 621 (1986).

9. New Jersey Statutes Annotated 52:27D-302 et seq.

10. New Jersey Laws, 1798, Chapter DCXCVI, 289.

11. Albert J. Wolfe, *A History of Municipal Government in New Jersey since 1798* (Trenton: New Jersey State League of Municipalities, 1990), 5.

12. Karcher, *New Jersey's Multiple Municipal Madness.*

13. Ernest C. Reock Jr. and Raymond D. Bodnar, *The Changing Structure of New Jersey Municipal Government* (Trenton: County and Municipal Government Study Commission, State of New Jersey, 1985), 3–5.

14. Constitution of 1844, Article IV, section 11, as amended September 7, 1875.

15. Wolfe, *A History of Municipal Government in New Jersey since 1798,* 10–12.

16. Ibid., 10–15.

17. Constitution of New Jersey, 1947, Article IV, section VII, paragraph 10.

18. Harris I. Effross, *County Governing Bodies in New Jersey* (New Brunswick: Rutgers University Press, 1975), 236.

19. New Jersey Statutes Annotated 40:41A et seq.

20. Mark J. Magyar, "The Mini-Governors: County Executives Wield CEO Clout," *New Jersey Reporter* (August 1999), 8ff.

21. Annexation: New Jersey Statutes Annotated 40A:7-12 et seq.; consolidation: New Jersey Statutes Annotated 40:43-66.35 et seq.

22. Compiled from twenty-one county abstracts of ratables for 1999.

23. New Jersey Statutes Annotated 40:48B-1 et seq.

24. *Property Tax Commission: Report of Recommendations to Governor Christine Todd Whitman* (Trenton: State of New Jersey, September 1998).

25. Christine Todd Whitman and Jane M. Kenny, "State Incentives for Shared Services," *New Jersey Municipalities* (May 1999), 24 ff.

26. Municipalities: New Jersey Statutes Annotated 40A:9-136; counties: New Jersey Statutes Annotated 40A:9-42.

27. *A Summary of Training-Based Certification of Local Public Officials in New Jersey* (New Brunswick: Center for Government Services, Rutgers University, 1992).

28. Pane, *New Jersey Practice,* 335ff.

29. Frank Haines and David Mattek, *Cooperative Purchasing in New Jersey,* paper in process for Center for Government Services, Rutgers University.

30. Constitution of New Jersey, 1844, Article IV, section VI, paragraph 5, as amended September 20, 1927. Constitution of New Jersey, 1947, Article IV, section VI, paragraph 5.

31. *Comprehensive Plan for Educational Improvement and Financing* (Trenton: New Jersey Department of Education, 1996); Margaret E. Goertz and Malek Edwards, "In Search of Excellence for All: The Courts and New Jersey School Finance Reform," *Journal of Education Finance,* 25 (summer 1999), 5ff.

32. New Jersey Statutes Annotated 40A:12A-1 et seq.; David G. Roberts, "Redevelopment: Not So Urban Anymore," *New Jersey Municipalities* (February 1999), 8ff.

33. New Jersey Redevelopment Authority Web site, at *http://www. state. NJ.US/njra/index.html.*

34. J. Christian Bollwage, "Elizabeth's Urban Enterprise Zone: Building Bridges Between Government and Business," *New Jersey Municipalities* (June 1997), 12 ff.

35. New Jersey Statutes Annotated 40:56-65 et seq.; Brian Hak and John E. McCormac, "Special Improvement Districts—Effective and Fair," *New Jersey Municipalities* (May 1997), 12ff.

36. *2nd ROC-Jersey Associates v. Town of Morristown,* 158 N.J. 581, 731 A.2d (1999).

37. Information provided by Beth Peterson, executive director, Downtown New Jersey, Inc., March 2, 2000.

38. Constitution of New Jersey, 1947, Article VIII, section I, paragraph 1(a).

39. *The Potential Impacts of Revaluation on Property Tax Burdens in Newark: A Final Report* (New Brunswick: Center for Government Services, Rutgers University, 1999), 9A, Table 1.

40. Robert Benecke, *The Municipal Budget Process* (New Brunswick: Center for Government Services, Rutgers University, 1997), VI-4

41. Philip E. Mackey, *The Condition of Education in New Jersey: 2000 Edition* (New Brunswick: Public Education Institute, Center for Government Services, Rutgers University, forthcoming), Figure 4.5.

42. Robert Benecke, *Municipal Finance Administration in New Jersey* (New Brunswick: Center for Government Services, Rutgers University, 1998), IV-3.

43. Ibid., II-3-5.

44. Ibid., I-6.

45. New Jersey Statutes Annotated 40A:4-45.1 et seq.

46. Benecke, *Municipal Finance,* VII-11 ff.

47. *Robinson v. Cahill,* 62 NJ 473, 355 A.2d 129 (1973).

48. *Abbott v. Burke,* 119 NJ 287, 575 A.2d (1990).

49. "State Payment for Mandated Municipal Programs: Better Late Than Never," *New Jersey Municipalities* (April 1988), 4; "Municipal Leaders Speak on 'State Pay for Mandates,'" ibid., 14ff; "League Supports Ban on Federal and State Mandates at Trenton Press Conference," *New Jersey Municipalities* (March 1994), 12ff.

50. Constitution of New Jersey, 1947, Article VIII, section II, paragraph 5(a), as amended effective December 7, 1995.

51. Ibid., paragraph 5(b).

52. New Jersey Statutes Annotated 52:13H-18.

53. *A Study Guide for NJ Municipal Clerks* (New Brunswick: Municipal Clerks Association of New Jersey in Cooperation with the Center for Government Services, Rutgers University, 1997), 5-1ff.

54. New Jersey Statutes Annotated 19:44A-1 et seq.; *1997 Annual Report* (Trenton: New Jersey Election Law Enforcement Commission, State of New Jersey, 1997).

55. Constitution of New Jersey, 1947, Article I, paragraph 2b as amended effective January 1, 1994.

56. New Jersey Statutes Annotated 19:27A-1 et seq.

57. Michael A. Pane, "New Recall Law Raises Serious Questions," *New Jersey Law Journal,* 141 (August 7, 1995), 1776.

58. Eric Martin Bernstein, "Open Public Meetings Act ("Sunshine Law"): A Primer for Elected Officials." In *Powers & Duties of the Municipal Governing Body* (New Brunswick: Center for Government Services, Rutgers University, 1997), 44ff.

59. New Jersey Statutes Annotated 47:1A-1 et seq.

60. Count based on biographies of legislators in *Manual of the Legislature of New Jersey, 1999* (Newark: Skinder-Strauss Associates, 1999), 217–292.

61. Bureau of the Census, *Census of Governments.* Vol. 3, no. 2, Compendium of Public Employment (Washington, D.C.: Government Printing Office, 1987, 1997), Table 9.

NEW MEXICO

John G. Bretting

New Mexico is not very different from the other forty-nine states when it comes to home rule provisions. Although home rule is supposed to facilitate autonomy and freedom from state government encroachment, it does not create "free and autonomous" municipal governments. Rather, home rule in New Mexico might best be conceived in terms of specific units or degrees of freedom from state governmental control.[1] Although there are ninety-nine cities with municipal charters in New Mexico, only nine municipalities[2] enjoy the status of home rule municipalities.

Governmental Setting

The state's uniquely rich and diverse history, politics, cultures, and economics influence the context of municipal and state government. In 1998 New Mexico commemorated three historical events that framed the development of the state. The arrival of the first Spanish settlers in Nuevo Mexico 400 years ago coincided with the establishment of El Camino Real, which translates into "The True Road" and refers to the travel route (primarily for trade) that extended from New Mexico to "Old Mexico." The year 1998 also commemorated the 150th anniversary of the signing of the treaty by which New Mexico became a territory of the United States.

The land mass we currently call the State of New Mexico was inhabited before the arrival of the Spanish settlers. Twelve thousand years ago, the state was home to Clovis man,[3] and various Native American civilizations thrived there (including the Anasazi and Hohokum) before the arrival of the conquistadors. Consequently, New Mexico is unique in that it features some of the oldest continuously inhabited settlements in North America. The indigenous peoples of New Mexico, for the most part, were not relocated by the federal government. Most of today's descendants reside on the land of their ancestors and are members of one of the nineteen self-governing pueblos found within the state's borders.[4]

In terms of land mass, New Mexico ranks fifth and is equal to the combined area of Maine, New Hampshire, Massachusetts, Rhode Island, Connecticut, New York, New Jersey, and Delaware. The varied cultures and the political economy of the state are heavily influenced by the patterns of landownership. The U.S. federal government owns 33 percent of the state's land; the state owns 12 percent; and 10 percent has been allotted to Native Americans, leaving only 45 percent of the state's total land mass in the hands of private owners.[5] These patterns of ownership contribute to the state's relatively low population density, excluding the four metropolitan areas of Albuquerque (which includes the City of Rio Rancho), Las Cruces, Santa Fe, and Farmington.

Primarily a rural state, more than one-half of New Mexico's population lives along the Rio Grande corridor. Another one-third is concentrated in the Albuquerque metropolitan area. These population concentrations shape the behavior of the state legislature, as exemplified by the influence of representatives from the most populous county, Bernalillo County .

The population of New Mexico is best described as tricultural, consisting of "Anglo" whites, Hispanics, and Native Americans (49 percent, 39 percent, and 9 percent, respectively). The remainder constitutes a mixture of African Americans and Asian Americans. This pluralistic population mix contributes to the long-term inclusion of Hispanics in territorial, state, and local politics. In fact, New Mexico is the only state that conducts legislative sessions in both Spanish and English.

In terms of per capita income, New Mexico is in the bottom 10 percent of American states. Because it is one of the poorest states in the nation, New Mexico has continuously received more direct payments from the federal government than it has contributed.[6] Moreover, the poor economic condition prevents the state and local governments from extracting more revenues from their citizenry. New Mexico citizens continue to be taxed at a fairly high rate. State and local tax effort, per capita, reflects New Mexico's inability to produce enough locally generated revenue to make federal assistance unnecessary.

Public-sector employment (26 percent), wholesale and retail trade (24 percent), and service-related jobs (25 percent) are the dominant sectors of the state's economy. The state does not have a significant manufacturing sector. Many of the career opportunities are in low-paying service or sales jobs. With continued downsizing of the federal government's presence in New Mexico's economy (including military base closures and reductions at the federally funded major scientific laboratories of Los Alamos and Sandia Labs), state economic development officials have aggressively courted outside firms and industries. Like most other states, New Mexico has experienced some—but rather limited—success in doing so.

New Mexico became the forty-seventh state in January 1912. Until World War II, however, with the development of atomic and defense-related industries, the state's population did not grow. The subsequent influx of people changed the political culture of the state. Los Alamos (a combined city-county government created by the federal government for atomic research, which became part of New Mexico in 1948, when it was incorporated) possesses a scientific political culture. By contrast, the surrounding areas of north-central New Mexico maintain traditional Mexican-Spanish political cultures and have remained the same for more than 300 years.[7] The southeastern portion of the state is often referred to as "Little Texas" because of its conservative ideologies and economic connections to Texas. The Albuquerque region reflects not only the political cultures within the state but also those of recent migrants from other states.

Even with its unique characteristics, New Mexico has on numerous occasions paralleled national trends. Before the advent of the New Deal in the 1930s, the Republican Party controlled the state. During the New Deal era, political party competition grew. The Democratic Party built a strong power base during the 1940s, 1950s, and 1960s, resulting in one-party domination at state and local levels. This has shifted in recent decades to competitive two-party systems; today, state and local positions vary from party to party, but national-level posts tend to be captured predominantly by Republicans.

Home Rule in New Mexico

Historical Development

The evolution of New Mexico's municipal code and the ultimate approval of a home rule amendment to the New Mexico Constitution has been a long and arduous process. Before 1884, municipalities in New Mexico were chartered by a special act of the Territorial Legislature. After 1884, New Mexico permitted the chartering of municipal governments by general act of the Territorial Legislature. Soon after statehood, changes in the general municipal charter laws enabled two forms of government for incorporated municipalities: the commission-manager form and the mayor-council form.[8]

Definition of Home Rule

The New Mexico Constitution provides local governments a reasonable degree of autonomy in determining their government structure. Furthermore, local governments have been given a great deal of autonomy in carrying out local government functions. On the surface, they enjoy "broad functional home rule."[9] The New Mexico Constitution declares, "A municipality which adopts a charter may exercise all legislative powers and perform all functions not expressly denied by general law or charter."[10] In 1917 the New Mexico Legislature passed legislation authorizing municipalities to adopt a charter of their own.

Finally, after more than a decade of lobbying by home rule advocates, the voters of New Mexico approved a home rule amendment in November 1970. Article 10, section 6, subsection E of the 1991 constitution (also referred to as the Home Rule Act) states, "The purpose of this section is to provide for maximum local self-government. A liberal construction shall be given to the powers of municipalities." Consequently, any incorporated city in New Mexico can adopt a new charter and change its form of government under the home rule provision. Such cities are allowed to adopt any form of government they desire. The incorporated "home rule" municipal government is not subject to the specific provisions found in the general charter act.[11] Although the full extent of this amendment remains to be seen, it is reasonable to assume that a home rule charter gives municipal officials greater leeway. With regard to fiscal matters, however—especially those relating to the levying of taxes—power is still centralized within the state legislature.[12]

Structural Features

New Mexico has the traditional substate units of government: counties, municipalities, school districts, special districts, and public authorities. The state grants them the authority to levy and collect taxes. However, New Mexico—with its unique heritage—has two additional extra-local governmental units that predated statehood: Native American pueblos and Acequias.[13] Through tribal law, pueblos can exercise numerous local government powers. Acequias are grassroots community water associations that are remnants of the Spanish colonization of New Mexico.

In the past, New Mexico laws classified municipal corporations into three classes: cities with populations over 3,000; towns with populations of 1,500–3,000; and villages with populations under 1,500 but greater than 150 people.[14] These distinctions have been eliminated from the statutes.[15] However, many municipal governments still adhere to these labels until they reach the next population threshold and call an election to decide whether or not to change their name (for example, from village to city).

Before 1989, any municipality with 3,000 or more persons (according to the last federal census) could be organized and governed as a commission-manager[16] municipality if approved by the electorate. If the qualified electors of the municipality did not elect to be governed under the commission-manager form, the municipality would be governed under the form of government in existence on the day of the election in which the commission-manager form was rejected.

The New Mexico Municipal Code provides for three types of municipal charters, two of which prescribe a specific form of government, and the other is open ended. The mayor-council and the commissioner-manager forms are specific, whereas home rule charters are open. In New Mexico, the mayor-council form of government is most popular. Eighty-nine of the ninety-nine incorporated municipal governments in New Mexico are mayor-council governments. The majority of the cities operate under the general charter specifications of New Mexico law. The notable exception is the City of Albuquerque, which operates under a home rule charter approved in April 1974.[17] The commission-manager form exists in the cities of Alamogordo, Aztec, Clovis, Hobbs, Las Cruces, Lovington, Raton, Rio Rancho, Truth or Consequences, and Tucumcari.

New Mexico's most populous county (Bernalillo) and largest city (Albuquerque) attempted consolidation in 1972. Bernalillo County voters defeated the proposal in the same year. There have been unsuccessful attempts to resurrect the consolidation effort, most recently in 1980 by the Bernalillo County Commission's consolidation task force.[18] At present, Los Alamos is New Mexico's only combined city-county government.

To petition for incorporation as a New Mexico municipality, an area must have a population density of at least one person per acre, and it should not exist within the boundaries of an already existing municipality. A petition containing a name for the new municipality and the legal description of the property to be incorporated must be signed by 200 qualified electors or by the owners of no less than 60 percent of the land. This petition must be accompanied by adequate funding for a census and a map or plat of the proposed municipality's boundaries. In the second stage of incorporation, the county government investigates and determines if all the conditions have been met; a census is then conducted. Within forty-five days of a positive assessment by the county, an election is held for the petitioning area to become a municipality. If the majority of voters support the measure, the area becomes a municipality, and an election for municipal officers may follow within two weeks.

The ease with which a municipality in New Mexico may be incorporated contributes to the notion of "cities without suburbs," a term coined by David Rusk, former mayor of Albuquerque. "Cities without suburbs" conjures the image of poorer inner cities circled by separately incorporated suburban cities. This phenomena creates problems for the older "core" cities because they cannot annex additional territory to enhance their tax base and remain a competitive substate unit of government.

Municipalities in New Mexico enjoy considerable latitude when it comes to the annexation of territory. Three methods for annexing territory to a municipality are provided for in section 3-7-1 of the New Mexico Statutes Annotated (1978): (1) the arbitration method, (2) the boundary commission method, and (3) the petition method (also referred to as "voluntary annexation"). The arbitration method is initiated by a city that desires to annex contiguous territory. The governing body may, by resolution, declare that the benefits of municipal government are or can be made available within a reasonable time to the territory that the city proposes to annex. A copy of the resolution with a copy of a plat of the territory that the city proposes to annex must be filed with the county clerk. After a resolution is filed, a board of arbitration comprising seven members is established. Three members represent the city; three members represent the residents of the territory that the city desires to annex; and both "sides" choose the final member. Determination by a majority of the seven members of the board of arbitration is considered final.

A three-member independent commission, known as the municipal boundary commission, is established to determine the annexation of territory to a municipality when a municipality petitions the commission to annex territory to the municipality or a majority of landowners in an area petition the municipal boundary commission to annex the territory to the municipality. Members of the commission are appointed by the governor. One of the members must be an attorney who is licensed to practice in New Mexico, and no more than two members are members of the same political party. At a public hearing held to determine whether annexation will take place, the commission determines if the territory is contiguous to the municipality and if the municipality to which the property is proposed to be annexed will provide services. If the municipal boundary commission determines that the conditions are met, the commission orders annexation of the property to the municipality.

Petition is the most frequently used method of annexation by municipalities in New Mexico. For a territory contiguous to a municipality to be annexed, a petition to that effect must be (1) signed by the owners of a majority of the number of acres in the contiguous territory; (2) accompanied by a map showing the boundaries of the territory proposed to be annexed and the relationship of the territory to the existing boundary of the municipality; and (3) presented to the governing body, which by ordinance either accepts or rejects annexation. If the governing body approves the annexation, a copy of the ordinance, along with a copy of the plat of the property to be annexed, is filed with the county clerk. After the official filing, the contiguous property becomes part of the municipality.

Voluntary annexation is driven by the rate of growth in the extraterritorial jurisdictions of the more populous cities in New Mexico. When the advantages of annexation seem obvious to a

Table 1. Classification of New Mexico Counties

Class	Criteria	
	Population	Assessed property value
A	More than 100,000	More than $75 million
B (over)	Less than 100,000	More than $300 million
B (under)	Less than 100,000	$75–$300 million
C	Less than 100,000	$45–$75 million
1st over		$27–$45 million
1st under		$14–$27 million
H[a]	—	—

a. "H" class counties are defined as having land area not more than 144 square miles.

majority of landowners, they initiate the petition method. New Mexico municipalities seldom use arbitration for annexation. The City of Albuquerque is controlled by the Metropolitan Boundary Act for Class A Counties,[19] which states that annexation can occur only by petition of property owners.

New Mexico municipalities enjoy extraterritorial powers (formally referred to as extraterritorial planning authority) in matters of land-use regulation. Zoning authority extends for five miles beyond the municipality's limits into the surrounding county. The authority does not extend into a contiguous municipality. Municipalities can own land and make improvements to the land outside their boundaries when these improvements provide public infrastructure such as sanitary landfills, treatment plants, and water wells.

Counties have played a central role in New Mexico's political history. They can be traced to the Spanish colonial era and a later Mexican policy that provided for *partidos,* or "parcels," which are comparable to the geographic subdivision and governmental jurisdiction of the American county.[20] They were governed by a centralized appointed official, the prefect. Throughout the territorial period, the boundaries of counties were changed by the legislature regularly to accommodate various constituencies. When New Mexico became a state in 1912, this flexibility ended. New Mexico consists of thirty-three counties. The division of Valencia County in 1981 created the most recent county, Cibola.

New Mexico's counties are classified by the state legislature on the basis of population and assessed property value. The county classification scheme exists to establish an equitable salary schedule for county officials.[21] The classifications are also used to determine county budget parameters. Table 1 outlines the New Mexico county classification system.

Initially counties in New Mexico were created to assist the state in the administration of policies. However, when New Mexico counties were granted incorporation authority in 1876, demands for local services subsequently increased, and county governments took on a new appearance. Officials such as the county clerk, assessor, and treasurer serve in the "traditional"

manner, as administrative arms of the state. County government, especially in the rural part of New Mexico, provides basic local government services, including law enforcement (by the county sheriff's department), construction and maintenance of roads and bridges, and coordination of emergency medical services, including 911 networks. Moreover, counties provide and promote innovative leadership in areas such as economic development, land-use planning, and development regulations. Some county commissions construct and operate regional facilities, including libraries, hospitals, and airports.

Functions of Local Government

Functional Responsibilities

Cities in New Mexico perform public services similar to those in other states, including police, fire, public works, sewer and sanitation, public transportation, aviation, planning, public housing, economic development, environmental health, human services, public library, and recreation and culture such as leisure services and public museums. Problems of cities include financial difficulties, boom and bust cycles, high rates of unemployment, and racial differences unique to their respective city. The City of Rio Rancho, a bedroom community of Albuquerque, has become one of the fastest-growing cities in America because a microchip manufacturing plant has relocated there. Negative side effects include suburban sprawl and traffic congestion. Simultaneously, Rio Rancho's growth is responsible for the dislocation of traditional small ranches *(ranchitos)*. The intensive extraction of groundwater by manufacturing processes additionally threatens the future water supply, growth, and development of the greater Albuquerque–Bernalillo County region.

There are more than 100 special districts in New Mexico. The unique character of the state's political jurisdictions is carried over to special districts. The most distinctive and prominent special districts are land grants stemming from the Spanish colonial land-tenure system.[22] Nineteen community land grants have been recognized as legitimate since the 1848 Treaty of Guadalupe Hidalgo. Resources are pooled under community land grants; the land is *ejido* (held in common) by heirs of the original grant. Elected boards maintain legal responsibility and authority and administer the land grants.

The State of New Mexico provides several incentives to promote intergovernmental (interlocal) cooperation. One example, the Solid Waste Act, promotes regional management of solid waste dumps.[23] Approved in the 1993 legislative session, the act encourages regional solid waste retention facilities. This legislation takes advantage of the Joint Powers Act, which permits the cooperative delivery of any municipal or county function. Through the powers vested in the Joint Powers Act, the Lincoln County Regional Solid Waste Authority was established.[24]

Administrative Discretion

The types of administrative discretion exercised by local governments foster mixed opportunities. State law imposes training requirements for law enforcement officers in cities and counties. Likewise state law mandates workers' compensation coverage for county and city employees. Cities and counties may establish their own merit systems for recruitment and promotion of personnel. The Administrative Operations and Procedures Act mandates that all local government meetings and records be open to the public.

The governing body of a municipality or county may contract for the management of programs and activities. However, when occupancy tax revenues fund the contract, the types of activities and expenditures are regulated by state statute.[25] Authority to purchase is established by municipal charter or county legislation. Although broad based in scope, purchasing authority is subject to limitations such as those associated with the "Buy New Mexico" program, whereby preference is given to individuals and firms who contribute to the economy of New Mexico. Municipalities exercise planning, zoning, and land-use controls within their boundaries. Additionally, they control land use within their extraterritoral jurisdictions. Until 1999, when their authority was revoked by executive order of Gov. Gary Johnson, municipalities enjoyed extensive discretion in the area of collective bargaining.[26]

Two areas in which municipalities do not enjoy discretion are fireworks and liquor licenses. The Fireworks Licensing and Safety Act expressly removed municipalities' general authority to regulate fireworks and replaced it with limited authority to regulate only certain specified devices.[27] The state legislature also controls the authority to issue liquor licenses. No municipality (including home rule cities) can issue permits that allow for the sale and consumption of distilled alcoholic beverages. With local approval (option by referendum), municipalities may issue limited-service beer and wine licenses. The passage of an additional referendum permits home rule municipalities to levy and collect a beer and wine license tax.

Economic Development

The State of New Mexico cooperates with local governments to promote economic development. Under the Local Economic Development Act and the provisions of the 1994 constitutional amendment removing the state's antidonation clause, cities and counties are empowered to use public resources to encourage local and regional opportunities. Further, the act promotes joint powers agreements to plan and support regional economic development projects.

Local and regional economic development departments enjoy the authority to provide land, buildings, and infrastructure as tools to encourage business growth and to attract new business ventures. Direct or indirect assistance can include public works improvements, payments for professional service contracts enabling local or regional governments to implement or plan projects, direct loans or grants, loan guarantees, and grants for public works infrastructure improvements essential to the location or expansion of a qualifying business.

The 1993 Enterprise Zone Act allows for the establishment of enterprise zones in a wide variety of geographic areas (for example, municipalities, counties, and Native America nations, tribes, or pueblos) in New Mexico.[28] The act provides tax relief at the state and local levels and zoning relief at the local level; it improves the local services and economic status of enterprise zone residents through cooperative projects, including private and local neighborhood organizations. State agencies cooperate with enterprise zones by administering state-funded grant and loan programs, coordinating on-site educational training programs funded by the federal Job Training Partnership Act, and matching community development block grants. Local governments may elect, by resolution, to use tax increment procedures for financing enterprise zone projects (as provided in the 1993 Enterprise Zone Act).

Fiscal Autonomy of Local Governments

Local Revenues

The New Mexico Constitution enables the state legislature to control local fiscal matters, especially those relating to the imposition of taxes.[29] Furthermore, Article 9, section 12 provides a millage cap for local governments.[30] County governments are responsible for assessing property valuations, hearing property tax appeals, and enforcing the constitutionally mandated millage cap.

The property tax in New Mexico is not the primary "fiscal work horse" for municipalities as it is for municipalities in many states. Extensive in scope, the gross receipts tax (both the redistributions from the state and the local option gross receipts tax) provides the lion's share of revenues. New Mexico taxes both goods and services and is among only nineteen other states that tax the sales of food. The gross receipts tax is perceived as a regressive tax; as such, the state provides an end-of-year income tax credit for low-income families to lessen the burden of this tax.[31]

In addition to the gross receipts tax and the property tax, municipalities generate revenues from franchise taxes, lodgers' taxes, licenses and permits, state-shared taxes, charges for services, fines and forfeits, and other miscellaneous revenue streams. State-shared taxes include the gasoline tax, local-option gasoline tax, automobile license distribution, cigarette tax rebate, and state gross receipts tax rebate (above and beyond the local gross receipts tax option).[32] Property tax revenues are the major source of funding for the thirty-three counties in New Mexico. Table 2 compares the principal sources of revenues for Albu-

Table 2. Primary Revenue Streams for New Mexico's Largest City and County, 1996 (in percent)

Source of revenue	Albuquerque	Bernalillo County
Taxes	41.5%	82%
Property	36	54
Gross receipts	49	28
Selective sales taxes	12	<1
Charges	31.5	3
Miscellaneous	27	15

Source: "City and County Government Finances" (Washington, D.C.: U.S. Bureau of the Census, 1996).

querque and Bernalillo County (the state's largest city and county, respectively) to illustrate the differences between local government and county government revenue streams.

The state constitution specifies the terms of indebtedness and the purposes for which general-obligation bonds can be secured by local governments.[33] A vote of qualified electors is required before the governing municipality issues bonds. Local governments may issue a variety of revenue bonds specified by constitutional home rule powers and state statutes.[34] Types of revenue bonds include (but are not limited to) gross receipts tax revenue bonds, gasoline tax revenue bonds, project revenue bonds, fire district revenue bonds, and economic development–gross receipts tax revenue bonds. The issuance must be authorized by an affirmative vote of three-fourths of all members of the governing body. If a majority of the governing body but less than three-fourths of all members vote in favor of adopting the ordinance, it does not become effective until the qualified electorate approves it at regular or special election.

Local Expenditures

Like most American cities, New Mexico municipalities expend revenues on services such as police and fire protection,

Table 3. Primary Expenditures for New Mexico's Largest City and County, 1996 (in percent)

Expenditure	Albuquerque	Bernalillo County
Law enforcement	15%	14%
Fire	8	3
Parks and recreation	10	4
Airport	6	0
Solid waste	12	0
Roads and bridges	4	7
Sewerage	4	0
Housing and economic development	5	0
Corrections	4	12
Hospital	0	23
General administration	7	18
Other	25	19

Source: "City and County Government Finances" (Washington, D.C.: U.S. Bureau of the Census, 1996).

roadways, and sewer and sanitation. Table 3 depicts the difference in expenditure priorities between cities and counties in New Mexico, as illustrated by Albuquerque and Bernalillo County.

Except for the nine cities that have local home rule authority—which must comply with the state-imposed balanced budget requirement but enjoy greater flexibility in terms of reporting—New Mexico cities (and counties) must submit their entire annual budgets to the state Department of Finance and Administration for review and approval. This mandate ensures local government compliance with state regulations, including a balanced budget provision. To prevent default on any local revenue bonds, interest, or principal payments, local governments in New Mexico may receive authorization from the state's distribution intercept fund.[35]

State Government Grants-in-Aid to Localities

The state government provides substantial grants-in-aid (in addition to the gross receipts tax rebates) to municipalities in New Mexico. The smaller cities and more rural areas of this poor state do not enjoy the fiscal capacity to deliver important public goods and services. The most significant portion of state aid for schools (approximately two-thirds) is directed to local school systems to compensate for statewide variances in property values. The remainder of state aid for education goes to higher education. The second largest state aid expenditure is highway spending, closely followed by public welfare and public health and hospital expenditures.

Direct federal expenditures have a major impact on the political economy of many New Mexico local governments. Various reports estimate that, in 1995, these direct expenditures (for research laboratories, military installations, defense contractors, and service organizations) contributed about 15–28 percent of the jobs in the state.

Unfunded Mandates

As in many states, the issue of unfunded mandates has attracted much attention in New Mexico. Most local governments complain that they are unduly burdened by these mandates to the extent that they cannot generate adequate own-source revenues for the provision of basic services and therefore are unable to comply with legislative requests. The Legislative Finance Committee has studied and continues to assess the impact of unfunded mandates. Additionally, since the mid-1980s, all new legislation has been reviewed by the committee to determine the fiscal effect on local governments. The extensive system of state grants-in-aid lessens the fiscal impact of unfunded mandates. Furthermore, for small cities in New Mexico, a fund is available to offset unfunded mandates.

Access to Local Government

Local Elections

Local elections in New Mexico are carefully controlled by the state. Earlier in the state's history, elections were fraught with inconsistencies, graft, and corruption. A favorite fable tells of the time when the burro carrying the ballot box got swept away by the raging Rio Grande—nevertheless, the local precinct boss already "knew" that the box contained votes for the Democratic candidate! Despite this lore, the state legislature has developed numerous controls and regulations to prevent fraud and abuse in elections. A 1991 amendment to the New Mexico Constitution stipulated that "a municipal clerk shall not amend, add or delete any information from the registered voter list."[36]

A 1991 state law "empowers the Secretary of State to investigate complaints concerning conduct of elections held pursuant to the Municipal Election Code and issue the findings to the appropriate enforcement authority."[37] Additionally, the secretary of the state regulates the write-in ballot qualifications and absentee ballots. Potential write-in candidates must comply with state law and reside in the municipality in which they seek election.

Citizen Controls over Actions of Local Officials

Home rule municipalities and counties enjoy the powers of referendum, initiative, and recall if their charters so specify. These powers cannot be exercised, however, until the charter (or amendment to the charter) has been approved by the voters. An example of excessive use of these tools of "direct democracy" is found in Alamogordo—dubbed the Recall Capital of New Mexico. Over the past fifteen years, factional local politics have spawned more than a dozen referendums or recall elections. On three occasions, public officials have been recalled, and referendums have been passed six times to limit water and sewer rates. Open meetings and open records are required of all localities by the state.[38]

State-Local Relations

State laws governing local government structure and administration in New Mexico are onerous, numbering close to 100. Constitutional provisions and state statutes—combined with court decisions and opinions of the New Mexico attorney general—result in a complex, confusing, and frequently contradictory body of rules governing the behavior of local governments. The notion that broad functional home rule exists is an exaggeration. Municipalities can exercise many legislative powers and perform numerous functions; indeed, the state actively promotes intergovernmental cooperation between municipal and county governments, for example. Nevertheless, municipalities are severely constrained (especially in financial matters) by the state constitution, the behavior of the state legislature, and the decisions of the courts.

New Mexico's population is heavily urbanized. More than 70 percent of the state's approximately 1.5 million citizens live in one of the state's five largest cities (that is, Albuquerque, Rio Rancho, Las Cruces, Santa Fe, and Farmington) or in the respective metropolitan areas of those cities. More and more New Mexicans depend on municipal governments for basic public goods and services. It is reasonable to conclude, then, that as New Mexico becomes more urbanized and as demands on local governments increase, state laws regulating the structure and administration of local governments will also increase—thus further limiting the authority of municipalities in New Mexico.

Notes

1. Maurilio Vigil, " Local Governments," in *New Mexico Government*, 3d ed., ed. Paul Hain, F. Chris Garcia, and Gilbert K. St. Clair (Albuquerque: University of New Mexico Press, 1994), 181.

2. The municipalities include Albuquerque, Alamogordo, Clovis, Grants, Gallup, Las Cruces, Los Alamos, Rio Rancho, and Silver City.

3. Clovis man was a mammoth hunter succeeded by Folsom man.

4. F. Chris Garcia, "New Mexico: The Setting," in *New Mexico Government*, ed. Hain, Garcia, and St. Clair, 12.

5. Ibid., 1.

6. Ibid., 6.

7. Ibid., 15–16.

8. Maurilio Vigil, Michael Olsen, and Roy Lujan, *New Mexico Government and Politics* (Lanham, Md.: University Press of America, 1990), 169.

9. United States Advisory Commission on Intergovernmental Relations, *State Laws Governing Local Government Structure and Administration* (Washington, D.C.: U.S. Government Printing Office, 1993), 181.

10. New Mexico Constitution (1991), Article 10, section 6, subsection D.

11. New Mexico Statutes Annotated (1978), 3-11-1–13-4.

12. Vigil, "Local Governments," 181.

13. For the most comprehensive documentation of these governments, see Jose Rivera, *Acequia Culture: Water, Land, and Community in the Southwest* (Albuquerque: University of New Mexico Press, 1998).

14. Vigil, "Local Governments," 167.

15. The director of the New Mexico Department of Finance and Administration now determines the distinctions, which were eliminated from the statutes in 1981.

16. New Mexico's commissioner-manager form is more commonly referred to as the council-manager form elsewhere.

17. Albuquerque–Bernalillo County League of Women Voters, *Know Your Local Governments* (Albuquerque: City of Albuquerque, 1975), 175.

18. F. Chris Garcia and Paul L. Hain, *New Mexico Government*, revised ed. (Albuquerque: University of New Mexico Press, 1981), 170; Vigil, Olsen, and Lujan, *New Mexico Government and Politics*.

19. New Mexico Statutes Annotated (1978), 3-57-1.

20. Vigil, "Local Governments," 157–160.

21. Ibid., 160–167.

22. Ibid., 180–184.

23. The unavailability of dumpsites in areas immediately surrounding larger metropolitan areas is an acute issue in the state. In New Mexico, federal agencies, Native American tribes, and pueblos hold more than 40 percent of all land. In most instances, the metropolitan areas are adjacent to federally controlled properties and/or properties controlled by Native Americans. These landowners prohibit the establishment of solid waste dumps.

24. The Lincoln County Regional Solid Waste Authority encompasses the territory of Lincoln County, a portion of neighboring Eddy County, and includes the municipalities of Roswell, Ruidoso, and Alamogordo.

25. New Mexico Statutes Annotated (1978), 3-38-21 (enacted by Laws 1996, Chapter 58, 8) requires the maintenance of complete and accurate financial records. Moreover, funds must be maintained in a separate account, and they shall not be commingled with any other money.

26. New Mexico Senate Bill 99, the Public Employee Collective Bargaining Act, provided for a three-member Public Employee Labor Relations Board. The board was responsible for holding collective bargaining hearings, certifying and decertifying representatives, appointing mediators, and fact finding in the event of an impasse.

27. New Mexico Statutes Annotated (1978), 60-2C-1 et seq.

28. New Mexico Statutes Annotated (1978), 5-9-1–15 (enacted by Laws 1993, Chapter 33, 2) is designed to stimulate the creation of new jobs, particularly for economically disadvantaged workers and long-term unemployed individuals, and to promote revitalization of economically distressed areas.

29. Under New Mexico Statutes Annotated (1992 Supplement), section 3-18-2, home rule municipalities do not have the power through initiative to alter the taxing scheme mandated by the state constitution and statutes. Garcia and Hain, *New Mexico Government,* 181; Vigil, Olsen, and Lujan, *New Mexico Government and Politics.*

30. The precise language of Article 9, section 12 is that "No city shall contract any debt except by an ordinance, which shall be irrepealable until the indebtedness therein provided for shall have been fully paid or discharged, and shall specify for the purposes to which the funds to be raised shall be applied, and which shall provide for the levy of a tax, *not exceeding twelve mills on the dollar* upon all taxable property within such city, sufficient to pay the interest on, and to extinguish the principal of, such debt within fifty years" (emphasis added).

31. Garcia and Hain, *New Mexico Government;* Vigil, Olsen, and Lujan, *New Mexico Government and Politics,* 107.

32. "Annual Financial Report, 1989–1990" (Santa Fe: New Mexico Department of Finance Administration, 1992), 113.

33. New Mexico Constitution, Article 9.

34. New Mexico Statutes Annotated (1978), Chapter 3, Article 31.

35. New Mexico Statutes Annotated (1978), 6-22-1–3.

36. Additionally, the registered voter list constitutes the registration list for the municipal election. The registered voter list does not have to be returned to the county clerk. The municipality bears the reasonable cost of preparation of the voter lists and signature rosters.

37. New Mexico Statutes Annotated (1992 Supplement), Chapter 3, Articles 8 and 9.

38. New Mexico Statutes Annotated (1978), sections 10-15-1–4, 14-2-1–3.

NEW YORK

Jeffrey M. Stonecash

New York state government is heavily involved in local governments. Sixty percent of the state budget goes to local aid. The state also mandates local activities in a wide array of areas. The involvement of state government is extensive because the population is relatively liberal and predisposed to having an active state government that shapes local practices. Interest groups, such as teachers' unions, also continually seek state mandates to achieve policies they want. Although local governments have some autonomy, they find many of their actions significantly affected by reliance on state funding and state-mandated policies.

Governmental Setting

The state constitution grants local governments considerable autonomy but with a significant limit. Local governments cannot use this autonomy to adopt powers that conflict with state laws. State government retains the right to pass laws that specify state interests and limit the autonomy of local governments. State officials (both elected and unelected) have been inclined to constrain the options of local governments, particularly by enacting mandates. The courts have upheld the right of state government to enact mandates.[1]

There are several reasons why the state has been involved in local affairs. New York has a relatively liberal population,[2] which has resulted in an active state government, and its state and local taxes are among the highest in the country. For most of the last fifty years, the state has played a significant role in shaping public policy. This liberal tendency has been propelled by the significance of New York City in electoral politics. The population of New York City is heavily liberal and Democratic, and because it has constituted 40–58 percent of the state's total population over most of the century, "the City" has played a significant role in the political process.

Governors in particular have been affected by New York City. Given the city's electoral weight, Democratic governors have had to focus on mobilizing voters in New York City to provide a large enough margin of votes to overcome the Republican advantage in the rest of the state. For many decades, this led to an emphasis on state aid for local (New York City) problems. Providing aid to the City prompted other areas of the state to demand state aid. Republican candidates, who might be less sympathetic to New York City, also have had to take into account the needs of the City to avoid being beaten too badly. This political

need for both parties to respond to the problems of New York City and other localities has led to a tradition of activist governors willing to provide state aid and become involved in local affairs.[3]

Moreover, New York has strong unions, which often seek state-mandated work rules and benefits from local governments, such as pension arrangements. In 1994 New York led the states in percentage of unionized labor force (private and public) at 28.9 percent; the national average was 15.5 percent. Among public employees, 72.9 percent were unionized in New York compared with the national average of 38.7 percent.[4]

Teachers' unions seek required courses, required expenditures on specific activities (such as counseling and art programs), and limitations on what voters may affect in school budget referendums. For example, almost all school budgets are submitted to public referendums. If the school budget is voted down, however, state law requires that a local "austerity budget" must go into effect, even without voter approval. The austerity budget includes almost all school expenses, except transportation and sports. Teacher salaries and negotiated raises are defined as part of the austerity budget. Although strongly supported by teachers' unions, the requirement of an austerity budget limits the ability of local residents to affect school budgets. The conditions of a liberal population, the relative size of New York City, and unions have produced extensive state activity regarding local affairs and state involvement in local government.

Home Rule in New York

Historical Development

The state was not always involved in local affairs, and constitutional provisions addressing home rule were not always present. State government became involved because local governments encountered fiscal difficulties, which led to state regulatory intrusion and in turn prompted arguments for some local government autonomy.

In the early 1800s local governments had considerable autonomy, and the state had an equivocal record of involvement.[5] Local governments used this autonomy to borrow extensively and acquire heavy debts, which they could not pay off during the economic crisis of 1837. Critics argued that the state should impose limits on borrowing by local governments. During the latter part of the 1800s, local governments again encountered debt problems as they borrowed funds to support the development of railroads. Debt problems spurred further efforts to constrain the level of local borrowing and led to prohibitions of municipal borrowing to support private pursuits of individuals or corporations. Fiscal problems during the Great Depression resulted in further efforts to constrain local borrowing and financial practices.[6]

The gradual accumulation of state regulations was accompanied by local efforts to define limits on state intrusions. Periodic constitutional conventions have provided opportunities to include language granting local governments more autonomy. Although this language was gradually inserted during the twentieth century, the practice of the courts (when presented with state mandates) has been to rule that the state can intrude when state interests are involved. State interests have been defined broadly such that a wide range of intrusions by the courts have been approved.

Definition of Home Rule

The New York Constitution of 1938 outlines the broad rights of local governments. It grants and comments upon local governments' autonomy in two sections. Article IX first defines a "bill of rights for local governments." Local governments are given the right to have an elected legislative body, to adopt local laws, to agree with other local governments to provide services cooperatively, to use eminent domain to acquire land, and to apportion the costs of governmental services. No local government can be annexed by other local governments without the permission of the people within the area to be annexed.

The powers of local governments are then elaborated upon in a section titled "Powers and duties of legislature; home rule powers of local governments; statute of local governments." This section of the constitution, although purporting to define home rule, begins with a discussion of what the *state legislature* shall do. The language is positive about home rule but also includes statements about the rights of the legislature.[7]

In this section, local governments are granted powers—but the legislature is the institution given the power to enact statutes to "secure" rights. The rights of local governments exist, but their specification and protection are assigned to the legislature,

which can enact general laws about local governments. Local governments, in turn, can enact local laws, as long as they do not conflict with general laws enacted by the legislature. The legislature not only secures rights but also can enact general laws which local governments cannot override. Local governments have autonomy, but their enactments cannot be inconsistent with general laws passed by the legislature.

This constraint on local governments has lead to numerous conflicts, which have reached the courts. In several cases over the years, the Court of Appeals (the highest court in the state) has consistently rendered decisions "protecting the Legislature's power to act by ordinary legislation if a 'matter of state concern' is involved." The courts "have found state concerns even in seemingly local matters."[8] Although local governments in New York would seem to have considerable autonomy, the state retains the right to enact general laws that serve state concerns.

Structural Features

New York has a wide array of local governments, including counties, cities, towns, villages, school districts, and special districts. The state comprises fifty-seven counties and New York City. Within each county there are cities, towns (which cover areas outside of cities), and villages (which can extend inside the boundaries of two or more towns). There are also numerous special-purpose and special-district governments. New York City, which is a product of a consolidation of five counties during the 1890s, has a unified government, with many subdivisions. The number of local governments in New York is shown in Table 1.

The role of the state in creating these local governments varies. Counties and towns often are regarded as involuntary forms of government. They were created by the state to serve state purposes. Counties were intended to be general-purpose governments. Towns also were created by the state and given taxing authority so they could support local town courts. Counties have been given more flexibility as to their form of govern-

Table 1. Local Governments in New York, 1993

Type of government	Number	Percentage of total
County	57	0.5%
City	62	0.6
Town	932	8.4
Village	557	5.0
School districts	717	6.4
Special purpose	1,292	11.6
Special district	7,535	67.6
Total	11,152	100.0

Source: Appendix B, "Local Government Entities, Component Units, and Special Purpose Units, 1993," in New York State Office of the State Comptroller, Special Report on Municipal Affairs (Albany: New York State Office of the State Comptroller, December 1994), 628–629.

ment. A constitutional amendment adopted in 1959 allowed counties to adopt home rule charters and to choose different forms of government (for example, county executive–county legislature form or manager form). Nineteen counties have adopted a home rule charter, which is done through a local referendum. For a chartered form of county government to be adopted, there must be a double majority, that is, a majority in any city within the county and a majority within the area outside the city. The other counties have retained the approach of a board of supervisors. School districts are also creations of the state legislature, and education is defined as a responsibility of the state.

Cities and villages are more voluntary entities. They were created by the state legislature based on petitions to incorporate. Cities have the option to choose among a council-manager, "strong" mayor-council, "weak" mayor-council, or commission form of government. All villages have a mayor and two or four trustees.

All local governments can be changed, essentially by two ways. Completely new governments can be created or existing ones can be divided or consolidated. Change can also occur in a more piecemeal fashion. Other forms of local government can be changed at the local level. For towns, villages, and special districts, there are provisions for changes, including creating and dividing governments and consolidating, dissolving, and annexing territory. All changes require specific and elaborate procedures. The general rule is that local governments cannot be changed without the consent of the local government involved and its population.[9]

Although the legislature retains the power to create towns, alterations can be made at the local level. Existing towns may be divided or two towns may be consolidated. For a division, a petition signed by 5 percent of the voters in the last gubernatorial election must be filed. A two-thirds majority of the town board of supervisors must vote in favor of the division, and then there must be a public hearing. A public referendum must then take place, and a majority within each separate area must approve the motion. To consolidate towns, a proposition must be submitted to the voters, followed by a public hearing. A majority in each town must approve.

Villages can be created at the local level if the area has at least 500 residents and is no more than five square miles. Again, there must be a petition, a proposal submitted to voters, a public hearing, and a vote by the public. If the proposal involves creating a village in one town, only a majority of voters within the area seeking to become a village must approve the motion. If an area involving two towns is involved, there must be majorities within each area.

Annexation efforts face similar requirements. A petition must be submitted by those wishing to be annexed. The request must be reviewed, and a resolution must be adopted by a majority of the governing boards of the annexing government and the area to be annexed. A referendum must take place, and a majority of voters within the area to be annexed must approve.

Change can also occur without fundamentally altering existing governments. Specific functions might be shifted among governments; responsibilities may be reassigned, and the relative roles of local governments may change, albeit incrementally.[10] To formally move a service from one government to another or to consolidate services, a referendum must be submitted to voters. For such a transfer to occur, a double majority (in both jurisdictions) must be attained. In some cases, there must be a majority in every jurisdiction involved.

As a result of such restrictions, there has been little change in the number of counties, cities, towns, and villages in recent decades. On the other hand, creating special districts is not difficult, and their number has increased significantly. Although there has not been a reduction in the number of local governments, there has been considerable change in local governments' responsibilities.

Counties, in particular, have assumed responsibility for many activities that once were handled by cities and towns, such as welfare and public health. Individual counties have taken over airports, baseball stadiums, and zoos, among many other specific activities.[11] Counties have also undertaken new activities, such as emergency 911 services. The role of counties has evolved gradually, because cities can no longer afford to pay for zoos or stadiums, for example. Moreover, for counties to receive state aid, state law encourages transfer of responsibility to the county, with the state agreeing to pick up the cost if the county assumes responsibility. Although complete consolidations of local governments are infrequent, it is significant that transfer of functions among local governments is occurring.

Although responsibilities often are reshuffled, the state still allows local governments (particularly cities) to own facilities beyond their borders. Municipalities—which were the first significant, general-purpose local governments—often were the initiators of airports and water systems (pumping plants and pipeline systems), and they still may retain control over facilities originally developed by them. They may not, however, control zoning activities beyond their borders.

Functions of Local Government

Functional Responsibilities

State government in New York generally does not specify what each local government must do. The general approach is permissive: most local governments may engage in activities and provide functions, if they so desire.[12] All local governments provide policing, traffic control, zoning, road maintenance, and parks and recreation.

Counties are the primary agents of the state. When a local

Table 2. Local Government Activities, as Specified in the New York State Constitution

Counties are required to

provide for office of sheriff;

provide probation agency, jail, detention facilities, civil defense plan, and board of health;

provide medical care for cases of polio and tuberculosis;

provide for office of superintendent of roads, who must prepare county road map, inspect bridges, and maintain all roads within county;

maintain road machinery fund;

serve as social service district and provide for care of residents; and

provide veteran's service agency.

Cities/towns/villages are required to

appoint dog control officers and maintain pounds; and

appoint local historian to collect, preserve, and file historical material.

Towns are required to

provide for office of superintendent of roads, who is required to keep a record of exact location, character, and the condition of certain highways in town clerk's office;

maintain bridges less than twenty-five feet in length that have been determined to be safe by the county superintendent; and inspect bridges.

---

government responsibility is required, a requirement usually is imposed on county government. In a few cases, requirements for an activity have been imposed on cities, towns, and villages (see Table 2). Counties are responsible for basic services such as public health and transportation.

Despite this permissiveness, the state has not been passive in trying to shape which governments assume various responsibilities. Over time the state has provided inducements in the form of state aid to encourage specific local governments to cease to engage in an activity and transfer responsibility to another government. Transfers usually involve shifting a responsibility to the county. Statewide functions transferred to counties include public welfare in the 1930s, public health in the 1950s, and public libraries in the 1960s and 1970s.[13]

Special districts are designed to provide specific services and to confine the taxation to pay for the services to the area receiving the service. Special districts are created to match the distribution of costs with the distribution of benefits. Only counties and towns may create special districts. There are separate, specific rules for the creation of county and town special districts, and a general pattern is followed. A local government or a minimum number of taxpayers may initiate special-district formation. The request is then reviewed by the body (county or town), which will then either approve or reject the motion. Residents can request a permissive referendum (one granting authority for the district) by filing a petition with a minimum number of signatures. If the authorizing local government will be using its bonding authority to issue bonds to support district activities, the issuance must be approved by the state comptroller. Creating special districts is much easier than making other governmental changes (such as consolidation or annexation), which explains why there have been so many special districts in New York.

Special districts covering more than one county must be created by the state legislature. Other special districts that serve as public authorities also are created by the state. Urban renewal agencies, industrial development agencies, and public benefit authorities, for example, have specific functions and operate within limited areas.[14]

Local governments have the authority to engage in cooperative efforts with other local governments. It is easier for governments to cooperate on service delivery than it is for them to merge functions. Cooperative efforts can be pursued without a public referendum. Police may share a crime lab or equipment, or a city and county may share purchasing activities. There is a wide array of cooperative agreements among local governments.[15] On the other hand, merging departments or eliminating a department in a local government entity is much more difficult because of the referendum requirement.

Administrative Discretion

Local governments have discretion in deciding whether they will assume a function, but once they decide to do so, the state becomes involved. There are numerous state regulations that take effect if a local government performs a function.[16] Indeed, the decision by a local government even to exist activates many state mandates. Local governments can decide the overall size of their labor force, but there are significant constraints on classification and negotiation with the labor force. If a civil service position is created or altered, the change must be filed with the county arm of the state Civil Service Commission, which approves the grade and job definition.

The most significant constraint on cities involves labor negotiations with fire and police unions. These two departments constitute almost one-half of personnel in many cities. The state has legislated compulsory arbitration if local negotiations among police and firefighters break down. As a consequence, it is unusual for disputes to be resolved in local negotiations. This process has constrained local efforts to contain labor costs, especially because police and fire personnel are among the highest paid local employees and receive the most generous benefits.[17] Police, for example, work twenty years and can retire with half pay and full insurance benefits immediately upon retirement. Moreover, the state exempts police and firefighters from making any contribution to their respective retirement systems, despite state legislation allowing such contributions.

There are other state requirements that constrain local governments. Scandals with contractors in the early 1900s resulted in Wick's Law, which requires that any construction project be bid as four separate contracts, the assumption being that having multiple contracts avoids concentrating power with one contractor. There must be a general contractor and subcontractors for HVAC (heating, ventilation, and air conditioning), plumbing, and electricity. It is widely argued, however, that this requirement increases the cost of local government construction projects. Although these aspects of bidding and contracting are regulated, local governments in general can determine who does work, at what price, and under what conditions.

All local governments are allowed to engage in planning activities, and all form long-range plans. Zoning, however, is a power granted only to cities, towns, and villages.[18] The real control over the location of activities is with governments other than at the county level. Much as elsewhere in the country, however, plans and zoning decisions as mechanisms to control development are relevant primarily for areas experiencing growth.

Economic Development

Perhaps the most important local option available to local governments is the ability to create industrial development authorities. These authorities allow local governments to pursue economic development projects. Once authority is approved by the state comptroller, local governments may acquire land for projects through eminent domain, offer incentives for projects, issue bonds to support projects, and set up variable repayment schedules. Moreover, bonds can be backed by revenue generated from the project rather than from property values. This allows the bonds not to be counted against the assessed value of the local government.

Fiscal Autonomy of Local Governments

Local Revenues

The power to tax is derived from the state, and the state has used that power to impose limits on local taxation powers. The state specifies what taxes can be used, what can be taxed, what limits there are on taxes, how money can be borrowed, and how much debt a city can carry.[19] The state also requires that all local governments have balanced budgets, but there are always disputes about what funds and reserves should be counted in what ways in assessing whether or not a budget is balanced.

For many years, the only tax available to local governments was the property tax. Following the adoption of the state sales tax in 1966, the state allowed local county governments to add a local option. The state sales tax is now 4 percent, and local governments can add 3–5 percent to that amount. Funds are available to be distributed as county governments wish. They often are shared with cities, towns, villages, and school districts, although the percentages shared with other local governments vary considerably from county to county. New York City is the only city authorized to impose a local income tax, which it does.

The state allows local governments to conduct their own as-

sessments of local property. Local governments have moved very slowly to the required full value assessment of property, and most do not yet assess at full value. That the state has designated some properties as tax exempt is the most significant state impact on the local property tax for many local governments. The state has defined colleges and universities, museums, YMCAs, churches, historical societies, and many other nonprofit organizations as exempt from local property taxes. Nevertheless, local governments are expected to provide police and fire protection to all local organizations, to maintain relevant roads, and to remove snow from their frontages, but these organizations cannot be forced to contribute to these costs. The effect of these limitations is severe in some cities, where at least 50 percent of local property is tax exempt.

In response to this constraint on revenues, cities have sought to impose a gross utilities tax on tax-exempt organizations or to impose charges for services. The state must authorize these means of generating revenue—a difficult feat, because the nonprofit organizations argue that these costs will harm organizations performing valuable services in communities. The effect of these state limitations has been to restrain the ability of local governments to raise revenue to respond to problems they face.

The state also constrains local governments by generally limiting the extent of taxation and borrowing. Counties, cities, and villages cannot impose a tax rate beyond 2 percent of the full value of local property. New York City can tax up to 2.5 percent of the full value of property. Towns and school districts face no limits. There also are limits on the amount of debt as a percentage of the full value of property. Counties, small cities, and villages cannot have debt that exceeds 7 percent of property values. Large cities can incur 9 percent, whereas New York can have 10 percent. In the area of real property rates, local governments are free to set their rates, as long as they do not exceed state-defined tax rates. Local governments are free to pursue projects such as the development of zoos, baseball stadiums, and other local projects.

Although taxation limits are important, few local governments approach their tax limit.[20] The real limitation many local governments face is public hostility to high taxes, which is exacerbated by two specific tax situations in New York. State-imposed local government Medicaid contributions and school district financing practices probably increase informal pressures for local governments to hold down taxes.

When the state adopted Medicaid, it adopted one of the most generous packages of benefits in the country.[21] Originally the federal government paid 50 percent, and the state and local governments each contributed 25 percent. The local portion was raised through the county property tax. As Medicaid costs rose, hostility to the local contribution increased, and eventually the state picked up an additional 15 percent, leaving local governments to contribute 10 percent. This mandatory local contribution to Medicaid increases local property taxes, and county executives regularly plead for the state to assume the remaining 10 percent. The requirement has also reduced the ability of local governments to raise more revenue for other local purposes.

The other crucial practice that has affected the general tax climate involves schools. Schools face no tax limitations, and like other local governments in New York, there are no expenditure limitations or caps imposed on them. State laws about how school budgets and taxes are set, however, have had a significant effect on the overall level of local taxes and the general hostility to taxes. State-mandated implementation of austerity budgets for schools (when the public votes down school budgets) is important. If a school negotiates contracts that bind it to pay raises of 9 percent for five years (which happened during the late 1980s and early 1990s), this contractual agreement becomes part of the obligation of the district and is included in its austerity budget. Any tax increases necessary to pay for the austerity budget automatically go into effect. Voters often find this confusing and strongly resent the subsequent tax increase that occurs despite voter rejection of the school budget. This creates significant hostility to tax increases and constrains the extent to which elected officials of other local governments are willing to raise taxes. Although this situation does not involve a formal state limit on counties, cities, towns, and villages, the fiscal independence of schools has affected the overall tax climate.

Local Expenditures

Because local governments in New York are allowed to function in a broad array of policy areas, they are also allowed to expend funds in many areas. There are no expenditure limitations on local governments, nor are there required budgeting formats. However, each local government must annually report to the state comptroller its revenues and expenditures, using uniform categories designated by the state. Local governments must have balanced budgets, but there are numerous examples of local governments compensating for revenue shortfalls in current operating budgets by shifting categories of current expenditure obligations to the capital budget and borrowing money to pay these costs.[22] These practices usually are criticized when state audits are conducted, but many local government practices are not caught by audits until several years afterwards. Even then, the state often only suggests that the practice not continue. Local governments can go into bankruptcy, as almost occurred with New York City in the 1970s and Troy in the 1990s. In these cases, the state created a supervisory board to control local finances until the local fiscal problems were eliminated.

The relative magnitudes of local government sources of revenues and expenditures are shown in Table 3. New York City's expenditures are so enormous that they dwarf other local governments, so its figures are presented separately. New York City, counties, and cities derive large portions of their revenue from property and sales tax revenues, with another substantial portion coming from state aid. They also derive approximately 30 percent from other sources, including fees and fines. Towns, villages, and schools differ in that their major source of revenue is the local property tax. Towns and villages receive little state aid, whereas schools receive almost 40 percent of their revenue from state aid. All local governments have some responsibility for public safety, sanitation, highways, and culture-recreation activities. General-purpose governments, New York City, counties, and cities assume the primary responsibility for social programs such as social services and health.

Table 3. Revenue Sources and Expenditures of New York Local Governments, 1995

	New York City	Counties	Cities	Towns	Villages	Schools
Revenues (% from each source)						
Property taxes	18.8%	25.5%	28.3%	56.1%	47.8%	52.2%
Other taxes	24.0	21.9	21.4	9.3	7.5	1.2
State aid	18.4	15.5	12.6	7.6	4.5	38.2
Federal aid	10.6	12.4	6.0	3.0	4.3	3.5
Other	28.3	24.7	31.2	24.0	35.9	4.9
Total revenue ($ millions)	$40,711	$13,329	$2,753	$4,066	$1,486	$17,834
Expenditures ($ millions)						
General	$1,334	$1,234	$309	$486	$191	
Public safety	3,640	1,299	675	402	251	
Health	5,928	1,939	38	60	3	
Sanitation	600	399	185	539	151	
Highways	361	353	116	594	115	
Social services	7,778	3,921	0	2	67	
Culture and recreation	407	158	134	250	157	

Source: New York State Office of the Comptroller, *Special Report on Municipal Affairs, 1995* (Albany: New York State Office of the Comptroller, 1996), 23–75.

State Government Grants-in-Aid to Localities

New York began as a decentralized state, with local governments responsible for most services. Although the state has taken on responsibility for the direct delivery of some services, the primary route of state involvement has been through state aid and mandates. Assistance to local governments constitutes almost 60 percent of the state budget, and the level and distribution of state aid is a primary focus of budget battles each year.

Over the last several decades, the state has increased its tax effort, surpassing local tax effort, so the state can provide more aid to local governments.[23] Like other states in the Northeast, the state has gradually taken on a greater fiscal role.[24] The state now provides extensive aid to local governments, but much of that is for local education and not general-purpose governments. Figure 1 presents the trends for three indicators of fiscal centralization, or the relative state role in fiscal affairs. The three indicators are the proportion of all state and local tax revenue raised by the state, the proportion of all direct general expenditure handled by the state, and the proportion of local general revenue that comes from the state.[25]

Despite this greater state role in recent decades, New York is still a relatively decentralized state fiscally. Local governments provide the bulk of direct delivery of services. State government provides considerable aid, but services are delivered primarily through local governments. Local governments provide a fairly high level of services and have one of the highest tax efforts in the country.

The state provides aid through a multitude of grants. The number of aid programs has grown so much that there is now an annual, one-inch-thick *Catalog of State and Federal Programs Aiding New York's Local Governments*,[26] which details for each program the nature of the aid, the amount funded under each program, and contact information. This aid has come with numerous mandates, and many local officials regard these as unfunded mandates.[27] State officials counter that although each mandate does not have funding attached to it, the state provides considerable aid which does enable localities to meet many obligations.

There was a major effort to increase state aid to cities during the 1960s and 1970s, but that effort slowed after the state overextended its debt obligations during the 1970s. Since then there has been a gradual but steady increase in state aid.[28] In real dollars, in the last fifteen years state aid increases to most local governments have been small. Schools have received most of the aid (roughly an $11 billion increase), leaving other local governments with essentially no increases.[29] State aid in general is so contentious that the issue of whether state government aid should be increased and mandates reduced consumes much of the state budget debate.

Unfunded Mandates

Although the state has been reluctant to take on more direct delivery, it has not been hesitant to intrude and impose mandates on local governments. In a comparative state study during the 1970s, New York imposed more mandates than almost any other state.[30] The state has traditionally relied on local delivery but has consistently sought to shape how local governments perform their duties. Local officials continue to plea for the extent of mandates to be reduced.[31] Some of these mandates (such as the local education "austerity budget" rule and the fire and police personnel rules) cost local governments a great deal of money. State legislators are aware of these costs and regularly introduce bills to require reimbursement for mandates or fiscal impact statements any time a state mandate is adopted. These bills regularly fail because most legislators do not want to constrain

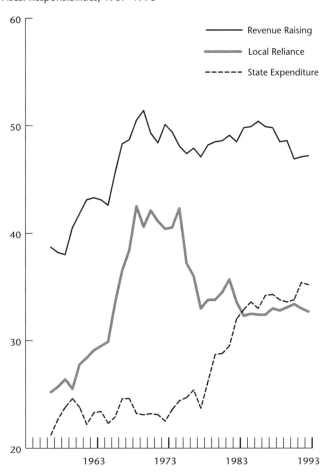

Fig. 1 The Increasing Role of the State of New York in State-Local Fiscal Responsibilities, 1957–1993

Source: "Government Finances," GP-5 Series (Washington, D.C.: U.S. Bureau of the Census, various years.)

Note: Revenue raising is the proportion of all state and local tax revenue raised by the state. State expenditure is the proportion of all state and local direct general expenditure handled by the state. Local reliance is the proportion of all local general revenue derived from state aid.

the state's option to intervene in local affairs. Nonetheless, the problem of costly state mandates is widely recognized.

Access to Local Government

Local Elections

Local elections are the means by which citizens seek to affect policy choices. In New York the procedures surrounding elections are determined by the state. The two-party system is strongly entrenched, and the parties have used the state legislative process to define the rules for getting on the ballot.[32] There are very specific provisions for the number of signatures candidates must gather and the way in which these signatures must be presented. The specificity of these conditions allows numerous challenges to petition filing, with some candidates being denied access to the ballot. There are also strict procedures by which parties nominate candidates.

Local governments have little control over the conduct of elections. All local elections are held in November. The board of elections in each county, acting as agents of the state, maintains all registration files and arranges for the handling of election-day activities (including setting up polling sites, bringing registration lists, and arranging for poll watchers). The only exception to these practices is school elections. Local school districts maintain their own voter registration lists of eligible voters, and they schedule the election of school board officials and votes on school budgets, generally in the months of March, April, and May.

Citizen Controls over Actions of Local Officials

Local governments are granted the power to adopt and amend laws (Article IX, section 2c)—as long as they are not inconsistent with the state constitution—relating to the "powers, duties, qualifications, number, mode of selection and removal . . . of [their] officers."[33] The courts have ruled that the use of powers such as the recall (and initiative) must be granted in home rule charters. Although there are no systematic inventories of the provisions of local charters, many local charters contain language allowing for these actions. The courts have also ruled that these procedures cannot be added to charters through local statutory changes, which has made their adoption difficult. Thus, although the state legislature could grant the use of the recall and initiative to local governments, it has not done so, and local constituencies have not pressured the state to revise local charters to add these provisions.

Local officials may submit questions about local government structure or debt for citizen consideration through the referendum, but citizens cannot initiate these referendums. Most government records are legally open, but citizens may have to submit requests to obtain some of them. Open meetings were not required until the late 1980s, when, following numerous complaints about closed meetings, the state legislature passed a law requiring that all meetings in which official business is discussed must be open. That has not prevented closed party caucus meetings to be held before official public meetings convene.

State-Local Relations

State government in New York is heavily involved in local governments. There is a long history of such involvement, and despite a continual focus on the importance of reducing mandates, there has been little change. There are strong lobbying efforts to maintain state mandates and an activist political culture that supports intrusion by the state.

The immediate future of autonomy for local governments is mixed and difficult to predict. In 1994 Republican George Pataki was elected governor. He is the first governor in decades with a largely conservative agenda. Governor Pataki has indicated that he wants to reduce state mandates, but he faces powerful interest groups which oppose such efforts. Fire and police personnel do not want any reductions in state benefits. Teachers do not want any program requirements repealed. Governor Pataki has sought and achieved a significant state tax cut, which will mean less state aid in the future unless there is significant economic growth.

The combination of strong efforts to maintain mandates and reduced state revenues does not create an optimistic fiscal future for local governments (except for, perhaps, school districts). The reduction in state revenues will also decrease the likelihood of the state assuming the remaining local obligation for Medicaid. The immediate future suggests that local governments will continue to face numerous state mandates but with no significant increases in state aid.

Notes

1. James D. Cole, "The Ghost of Home Rule," *St. John's Law Review* 59 (1985): 713; Joseph F. Zimmerman, "The Development of Local Discretionary Authority in New York," *Rockefeller Institute Reprint Series* 11 (1984).

2. Robert S. Erikson, Gerald C. Wright, and John P. McIver, *Statehouse Democracy* (New York: Cambridge University Press, 1993), 16.

3. Jeffrey M. Stonecash, "'Split' Constituencies and the Impact of Party Control," *Social Science History* 16, no. 3 (Fall 1992): 455–477.

4. Steven Greenhouse, "New York Again the Most Unionized State: Nearly Double the U.S. Average, Due to Rise in Government Unions," *New York Times*, 22 October 1995, 38.

5. Ray L. Gunn, *The Decline of Authority* (Ithaca, N.Y.: Cornell University Press, 1988).

6. Richard Briffault, "Intergovernmental Relations," in *The New York State Constitution: A Briefing Book*, ed. Gerald Benjamin (Albany, N.Y.: Temporary State Commission on Constitutional Revision, 1994).

7. "The Constitution," in *The Legislative Manual* (Albany, N.Y.: Department of State, 1988–1989), 77.

8. New York State-Local Legislative Commission, *New York's Local Government Structure: The Division of Responsibilities* (Albany: New York State Legislative Commission on State-Local Relations, April 1983), 14.

9. New York State-Local Legislative Commission, *New York's Local Government Structure*, 108–133.

10. U.S. Advisory Commission on Intergovernmental Relations (ACIR), *Pragmatic Federalism: The Reassignment of Functional Responsibility* (Washington, D.C.: ACIR, 1976).

11. New York Legislative Commission on State-Local Relations, *New York's State-Local Service Delivery System*, 314–315, 319–323; Jeffrey M. Stonecash, "The Shifting Resources and Responsibilities of Governments in Onondaga County, 1991" (report prepared for the Onondaga County Legislature, October 1991), 48–91.

12. Local governments can own land outside their jurisdictions, and some cities own airports and water-processing facilities built outside the local jurisdiction.

13. New York Legislative Commission on State-Local Relations, *New York's State-Local Service Delivery System: Legal Framework and Services Provided* (Albany: New York Legislative Commission on State-Local Relations, April 1987), 319–323.

14. Ibid.

15. New York Blue Ribbon Commission on Consolidation of Local Governments, *Interim Report of the Governor's Blue Ribbon Commission on Consolidation of Local Governments* (Albany: The Commission, November 1991), 63–91.

16. Ibid., 41–58.

17. These generalizations are based on interviews with local officials in the Syracuse area.

18. New York State-Local Legislative Commission, *New York's Local Government Structure*, 89–92.

19. U.S. Advisory Commission on Intergovernmental Relations (ACIR), *State Limitations on Local Taxes and Expenditures* (Washington, D.C.: ACIR, 1977); ACIR, *Measuring Local Discretionary Authority*, M-131 (Washington, D.C.: ACIR, 1981); Jeffrey M. Stonecash, "State Policies Regarding Local Resource Acquisition," *American Politics Quarterly* 9, no. 4 (October 1981): 401–425; New York State Legislative Commission on State-Local Relations, *New York's Limits on Local Taxing and Borrowing Powers: A Time for Change?* (Albany: New York State Legislative Commission on State-Local Relations, December 1983); Jeffrey M. Stonecash, "The Politics of State-Local Fiscal Relations," in *Governing Partners*, ed. Russell L. Hanson (Boulder, Colo.: Westview Press, 1998).

20. New York State Office of the Comptroller, *Upstate and Suburban New York State, 1994 Profile* (Albany: New York State Office of the Comptroller, 1994), 88.

21. Steven D. Gold and Sarah Ritchie, "The Role of the State in the Finances of Cities and Counties in New York," in *Governing New York State*, ed. Jeffrey M. Stonecash, John Kenneth White, and Peter W. Colby (Albany: SUNY Press, 1994), 63–81.

22. Martin Shefter, *Political Crisis/Fiscal Crisis* (New York: Basic Books, 1985); Charles Brecher and Raymond D. Horton, *Power Failure* (New York: Oxford University Press, 1993), 143–155.

23. Jeffrey M. Stonecash, "Taxes and Policy Debates in New York State," in *Governing New York State*, ed. Jeffrey M. Stonecash, John Kenneth White, and Peter W. Colby (Albany: SUNY Press, 1994), 235–241.

24. Jeffrey M. Stonecash, "Fiscal Centralization in the American States: Increasing Similarity and Persisting Diversity," *Publius* 13, no. 4 (Fall 1983): 123–137; Jeffrey M. Stonecash, "Fiscal Centralization in the American States: Findings from Another Perspective," *Public Budgeting and Finance* 8, no. 4 (Winter 1988): 81–89.

25. Jeffrey M. Stonecash, "Centralization in State-Local Fiscal Relationships," *Western Political Quarterly* 34, no. 2 (June 1981): 301–309.

26. New York State Legislative Commission on State-Local Relations, *Catalog of State and Federal Programs Aiding New York's Local Governments* (Albany: New York State Legislative Commission on State-Local Relations, 1993).

27. New York State Legislative Commission on State-Local Relations, *New York's System of State Aid: Perspectives on the Issues* (Albany: New York State Legislative Commission on State-Local Relations, December 1984), 95–124.

28. David S. Liebschutz and Sarah F. Liebschutz, "Political Conflict and Intergovernmental Relations," in *Governing New York State*, ed. Jeffrey M. Stonecash (Albany: SUNY Press, 2000).

29. New York State Office of the Comptroller, *Upstate and Suburban New York State*, 9.

30. U.S. Advisory Commission on Intergovernmental Relations (ACIR), *State Mandating of Local Expenditures* (Washington, D.C.: ACIR, 1978).

31. Betty Flood, "Mulling Mandate Relief," *Empire State Report* (February 1994): 39–43.

32. Jeffrey M. Stonecash, "Political Parties and Conflict," in *New York Politics and Government*, ed. Sarah F. Liebschutz (Lincoln: University of Nebraska Press, 1998), 63–79.

33. "The Constitution," *The Legislative Manual*, 76.

NORTH CAROLINA

James H. Svara

On the surface, North Carolina appears to be in want of local autonomy, but a complex mix of provisions and practices enhances the position and integrity of local governments. Several characteristics contribute to state control of local government affairs. First, the state is responsible for rural roads. Second, the state covers basic educational expenses. Third, all local government bonds or notes must be approved and sold by the Local Government Commission, an agency of state government. Finally, North Carolina continues to be a Dillon's Rule state (that is, localities depend on the legislature for any authority not conferred by the state constitution) and uses special legislation extensively.

The prevailing opinion among public officials in the state, however, is that these characteristics benefit local governments. State involvement in roads and education has relieved the fiscal burden on local governments. Bonding restrictions have reduced the cost of borrowing, helped to protect governments from excessive debt, and encouraged higher bond ratings by national investor rating services. North Carolina has one-third of all triple-A bonds and more than any other state. Local legislation promotes flexibility and experimentation.

Generally, state policies enhance the position of general-purpose local governments. Municipalities may expand through unilateral annexation, and existing cities are protected from new incorporations close to their borders. Policy and common practices limit the role of special districts. Counties have fiscal responsibility for schools and provide for the construction of school facilities; they also have broad authority to provide urban-type services. Cities and counties are permitted to share in the provision of services and to transfer functions.

Government Setting

North Carolina is a state with a shifting demographic, economic, and political character and several personalities. A relatively small and predominantly rural state in 1900—when less than 10 percent of its 1.89 million residents lived in urban areas—North Carolina had achieved the position of tenth largest state in the 1990 census, with a population of 6.63 million people.

Almost half the population lives within municipal boundaries, and the census classifies 57 percent of the state population as metropolitan. An agricultural economy based primarily on tobacco has given way to a mix of diversified agriculture, with pigs and poultry joining tobacco as major products and a manufacturing sector that ranges from a shrinking low-skill textile industry to high-tech firms and research institutes. Universities and industry are closely linked in the Research Triangle and Charlotte regions.

The governor has extensive executive powers over the departments that report to him but only limited control over the eight departments with directly elected heads. The governor did not acquire the veto until 1997. Politics is now two-party competitive, with the state's Progressive (but not liberal) and conservative traditions epitomized by its two leading elected officials, Gov. Jim Hunt and Sen. Jesse Helms.

The state's distinct mountain, Piedmont, and Coastal Plain regions are still identifiable, but growing urban centers in the mountains and along the coast share characteristics with the substantially urbanized Piedmont. North Carolina does not have a single dominant city, although Charlotte (with approximately 500,000 population) is distancing itself from the other large cities. Rather, the state has five cities with populations in excess of 100,000, seventeen with 25,000–99,999 population, and twenty-eight with 10,000–24,999 population. Overall, there are 516 municipalities and 100 counties. There are also 321 special districts (a low number relative to other states) and no independent school districts.[1]

The state has a Progressive tradition reflected in the assumption of responsibility for basic needs by state government and in the organization of local government. Since the early 1800s North Carolina has stressed centralized authority and responsibility. When people have sought improvements in governmental services, "they tended to look to the state rather than to local governments."[2]

Home Rule in North Carolina

Historical Development

The major historical trends pertain to the development of local governments and their services and shifts in intergovernmental responsibility for financing and providing services. The changes in home rule per se have been modest and indirect. Extensive state control has persisted with little change. North Carolina was slow to develop cities with extensive service needs. From 1850 until the start of the Great Depression, the scope and quality of public services expanded, accompanied by high rates of bonded indebtedness in the 1920s. Local governments had exercised complete freedom in borrowing money and issuing bonds, but local governments' credit problems led to the creation in 1927 of the County Government Advisory Commission to supervise borrowing. Its successor, the Local Government Commission, with jurisdiction over all local governments, continues to play a major role in local government affairs.

The depression ended expansion and produced a fundamental reordering of responsibility for services in the state. The state took over funding of rural highways, the minimum costs of education, and county prisons. It abolished independent school districts (putting the schools under county control) and tightened the fiscal controls of local governments. Because federal assistance was available, counties were given responsibility for public welfare and had an incentive to establish health departments. In the 1960s the state took over responsibility for all courts and covered operating expenses of the court system, although counties retained responsibility for constructing and maintaining court facilities.

Other major changes since the 1930s have been to broaden the annexation authority of cities and to expand state-shared revenues. In 1959 and 1967, changes in state law not only broadened the powers of cities and counties to plan, zone, and regulate land development but also promoted greater cooperation between cities and counties. Constitutional amendments in the 1970s limited new municipal incorporations and provided greater flexibility in local government financing.

Definition of Home Rule

Local governments in North Carolina operate under state control, although the state has given extensive power to cities to control their own expansion and development, and counties are authorized to provide a wide range of services. The General Assembly virtually has complete power to create or abolish municipal corporations; it can alter their boundaries, change their structures, and grant or take away their legal powers. There are no charters for counties.

Structural Features

North Carolina is a "modified" Dillon's Rule state in that legislation provides for "broad construction" of powers granted to local governments and a "narrow reading" of statutes that limit the powers of local government. The test for determining a local government power is whether it is "reasonably expedient" to the exercise of an express power.[3] There is extensive, although not unlimited,[4] use of local bills in North Carolina. The state legislature uses special acts to create municipalities and to give powers to selected local governments that are not available generally. Local legislation is generally viewed as a flexible, responsive tool to meet local needs. If the legislative delegation from the county supports the proposed local bill, usually it will be approved as a courtesy by the entire General Assembly. Exceptions would apply to controversial local changes or ones that are viewed as having important statewide consequences.

Local laws initially approved as experiments may be converted to general legislation.[5] For example, Raleigh received permission to carry out satellite annexation in 1967. Other cities received similar authority in the next two legislative sessions in 1969 and 1971. In 1974 an act was passed to permit such annexations statewide. General laws apply to all cities statewide or to cities of a particular "class" (that is, all cities above a certain size). North Carolina does not, however, have a general classification system under which cities of different sizes have different powers.

A city may be created only by an act of the legislature. The General Assembly may incorporate an area with or without a local referendum. In creating a new municipality, two approaches are used. The more common approach has been for a legislator to introduce a bill accomplishing the purpose and seek to get it passed. In the 1999 session of the legislature, however, state house and senate rules were adopted requiring use of the alternative approach: review and approval by the Joint Legislative Commission on Municipal Incorporation, a legislative agency.[6] Legislation also increased the standards for approval by the commission.[7] Once approved, the incorporation may be either immediate or subject to approval by residents of the area to be incorporated. Thus, the approval of residents is possible but not required. In the 1981–1994 legislative sessions, the legislature approved incorporation for forty-nine communities; residents in ten of these voted against incorporation.[8]

Only the legislature may abolish a municipality. It does so by repealing the charter. The legislature has exercised this power only at the request of residents of an area, normally because a city government has become inactive.[9]

The legislature also creates the framework within which consolidation of municipalities, counties, or city-counties would occur.[10] The governments interested in consolidation create a charter or governmental study commission. The commission may call for a referendum on its proposed plan of governmental consolidation. If passed by a majority of voters, the consolidation becomes effective when enacted by the General Assembly. Since 1933 there have been eight referendums on consolidating the primary city and county governments in four counties.[11] None has been successful, although the highest pro-consolidation vote of 42 percent occurred in the Wilmington–New Hanover referendum of 1995 (where there had been referendums in 1933, 1973, and 1987). Two counties that have also rejected the idea previously—Durham (county and city) and Mecklenburg (City of Charlotte)—have commissions that are considering consolidation.

There is limited home rule for charter revisions that pertain to form of government and the structure of the governing board. Cities may adopt the council-manager or mayor-council form of government (or add an administrator to the mayor-council form). They may alter the size of the council, terms of office, and the nature of members' constituency (that is, at large, by district, or a combination) and determine the use of partisan ballots and the method by which the mayor is selected (at large, by district, or a combination). Following a public hearing, the city council may change the charter by ordinance without a referendum. It may propose a change and allow the voters to determine if it will be accepted. City voters can also force a referendum by petition of 10 percent of the city's voters or 5,000 voters, whichever is less.

There is also provision for citizen initiation of a ballot measure, which is decided in a referendum. For an initiative, the same number of signatures is required as that for a petition to hold a referendum on a council action. Or the General Assembly may alter the city's charter. Other types of changes in the charter must be approved by the legislature.

Counties may adopt the county-manager form of government by resolution. They may alter the board of commissioners with respect to number of members, terms of office, mode of election (that is, at large; nominated and elected by district; nominated by district and elected at large; or residing in districts but nominated and elected at large). Counties may also determine how the chairperson will be selected (selected among the members or by direct election for a two- or four-year term).[12] A resolution approved by the county commissioners is subject to referendum.

The council-manager form of government is strongly established in the state. All cities with more than 25,000 population use the form, as do 93 percent of cities with 5,000–25,000 population and 65 percent of cities with 2,500–5,000 population.[13] Among the 100 counties, 91 have managers, 3 have appointed the chairperson of the commission as manager, and 5 have administrators who, though lacking all the formal powers of the manager, essentially are managers.[14]

A constitutional amendment passed in 1972 indicated the state's preference for annexation of newly developing areas outside cities over incorporation of new municipalities.[15] New municipalities may not be incorporated within prescribed distances from an existing municipality with more than 5,000 population. The limits are one mile for a city of 5,000–10,000, three miles for a city of 10,000–25,000, four miles for a city of 25,000–50,000, and five miles for a city of 50,000 or more. The General Assembly may override these restrictions only by a three-fifths vote of the members of each house; such overrides have been rare.

State policy favors the expansion of existing municipalities and grants them unilateral authority to annex urbanized areas at their borders. This approach—annexation at the city's initiative of contiguous areas that are developed for urban purposes—has been available to cities since 1959. As long as the required conditions are met in the area to be annexed, prescribed procedures are followed, and services are made available to the annexed areas, cities are free to annex without approval by the residents of the area to be appropriated. Annexation can occur across county lines without the approval of the affected county.

There are three other methods by which annexation may occur: annexation by legislative act, voluntary annexation of areas contiguous to a city, and voluntary annexation of areas not contiguous to a city. The legislative method is normally used only at the request of a city to meet circumstances that are not accommodated by the standard method (for example, annexation of land for public facilities surrounded by areas of limited development or annexation involving rivers and lakes). Voluntary annexation of contiguous areas can be approved by the city council after receiving a petition from all the owners of real property within the area to be annexed. Satellite areas may be annexed upon the petition of property owners.[16]

State statute permits nearby cities to enter into an agreement whereby they divide the territory that each will eventually annex.[17] The agreements, which may endure for up to twenty years, encourage orderly planning for the extension of boundaries and facilities; such agreements also serve to alert residents in areas adjacent to such cities of likely changes in boundaries.[18] In the absence of an agreement, a dispute between cities that wish to annex the same area is resolved in favor of the one that first adopted a resolution of intent under the nonvoluntary approach or that which first received petitions under the voluntary approach.[19]

The largest number of annexations results from one of the voluntary methods, but more people and property are annexed under the nonvoluntary method.[20] In 1980–1990 North Carolina had 4,577 annexation actions, the fifth most numerous in the country; the state ranked second with 2,142 actions in 1990–1995.[21] The population annexed in the earlier period was 313,000, almost 5 percent of the 1990 state population—a number exceeded only by Texas. In 1990–1995 the state ranked first with the annexation of 157,100 persons, almost 14 percent of the total population annexed nationally during this period. Ten cities have added more than 10,000 persons through annexation between 1980 and 1995. Thus, annexation continues to be an important tool used by cities to bring newly developing areas within their boundaries.

The county is a "body politic and corporate," a civil subdivision of the state and a legal entity that can buy and hold property, sue and be sued, and enter into contracts.[22] Although created to perform functions for the state, counties can exercise any powers assigned by the legislature not prohibited by the constitution. A board of county commissioners may alter its structure (subject to voter approval) and set its own rules of procedure with few limitations. The board is allowed to adopt the county manager form of government.

The law, however, dictates many features of county government. The sheriff and register of deeds are elected, and each county has boards of education, social services, and elections. Each county is covered by boards of health and mental health, although some of these boards serve more than one county. The commissioners appoint at least some members of these boards, with the exception of the board of education (members of which are elected) and the board of elections (members of which are appointed by the state board). Boards must appoint a clerk and an attorney. County commissioners take formal action through orders, resolutions, and ordinances.

Municipalities may exercise planning controls in areas outside their boundaries.[23] In general, a city of any size may establish planning jurisdiction for one mile outside its boundaries. This authority may not be exercised, however, if the county already is enforcing zoning, subdivision regulations, and the state building code in the prospective extraterritorial jurisdiction zone. With cooperation between the city and county, a variety of other approaches can be arranged. With the approval of the board of county commissioners, a city may extend its jurisdiction to two miles (cities of 10,000–25,000) or three miles (cities over 25,000) outside its city limits.

Another option is for the city to request that the county exercise any of the land-use regulatory powers within the city's extraterritorial jurisdiction or within the city limits. Finally, a city may come to an agreement with the county about which areas each will control. Municipalities may also own facilities beyond their city limits and have the power to condemn land for facilities, although some counties can block condemnation.

Functions of Local Government

Functional Responsibilities

Cities and counties generally have complementary functions. Cities are responsible for public safety, public works, community development, recreation, and human relations functions, whereas counties are responsible for social services, schools, and traditional county functions. Counties serve all residents whether or not they live in incorporated areas.

Despite this common division of labor, counties are authorized to engage in most of the functions that cities can provide, and vice versa. The major exceptions to dual authority are human services provided by counties and the street and sidewalk

network that only cities can provide.[24] The latter makes it advantageous for developing areas to be annexed by municipalities because they could not obtain a full range of municipal-type services from counties. On the other hand, the ability of counties (or, under agreement, municipalities) to provide other services in unincorporated areas helps to reduce the need for the creation of special districts.

Special districts are utilized to meet certain needs. Ninety percent of the 321 special-purpose governmental units in 1992 were in three areas. Drainage and soil and water conservation accounted for 46 percent of the districts; housing and community development authorities accounted for 31 percent; and water and sewer districts accounted for 14 percent. The latter allowed some communities to have water and sewer services without incorporation.[25]

Various forms of intergovernmental cooperation are authorized. It is possible for governments to contract with other governments for virtually all functions. Counties contract with cities for extension of city infrastructure, and cities contract with counties for services. It has also been common for certain functions to be transferred to the county after the function has been developed within municipalities.[26] Library systems, hospitals, and solid waste disposal are now largely county functions. Functional consolidation of city and county services has also occurred, particularly in the area of planning.

Highways are the shared responsibility of cities and the state. Public roads and streets outside cities and those that accommodate travel into and through cities are the responsibility of the state. Other streets and roads within cities are the responsibility of city governments. All streets and highways are financed primarily from state and municipal shares of vehicle-related revenues. Planning for thoroughfares in cities is also a shared responsibility, and the city's thoroughfare plan must be approved by the state after being adopted by the city. In addition, the state Board of Transportation also is required to consult with county commissioners annually about secondary road needs.[27]

Administrative Discretion

The General Assembly has delegated broad authority for personnel administration to cities and counties. Cities are authorized to create, change, abolish, and consolidate city offices and departments and to determine how to organize the city government. The only restrictions pertain to altering offices that are defined by law.[28] In counties, there is the same grant of authority to the board of county commissioners as found in cities, but appointments are determined by state law.[29]

Cities have flexibility in classification of positions and compensation but must have classification and pay plans. They have some discretion in determining what type of benefits to offer to employees. Cities also can choose to participate in the Local Government Employees' Retirement System. The state deter mines retirement ages. Cities are also required to make certain retirement benefits available to law enforcement officers that are not available to other retirees.[30] Workers' compensation for medical or rehabilitation treatment and time lost because of injury is required by the state, with local choice as to whether the program will be fully insured or self-insured. An employer-financed program of unemployment compensation is also required. State law bans collective bargaining by public employees and prohibits strikes by public employees.[31]

Cities and counties may adopt zoning ordinances and control the conversion of undeveloped land through subdivision regulations. Agricultural or farming operations are excluded from these regulations. County governments can exercise planning jurisdiction over any part of the county that is outside the jurisdiction of a municipality. Although counties may control land use, many had not exercised this authority until a state watershed protection requirement based on 1989 legislation forced counties "to implement what amounted to state-mandated zoning in parts of North Carolina where the Z-word is hardly uttered in public."[32]

The power of local governments to make purchases and enter into contracts is derived from the legislature and is subject to limitations and restrictions imposed by the legislature.[33] Both formal and informal bidding processes are used. Local governments are required to adopt verifiable percentage goals for minority business participation in building projects that exceed $100,000 in value. The state prohibits city officials from choosing a contractor in which officials have a conflict of interest.[34] The state also has a statute covering gifts and favors that is designed to restrict the use of such inducements to influence who receives public contracts.[35]

Cities and counties may acquire property through eminent domain for a variety of purposes.[36] Condemnation does not have to be preceded by efforts to acquire the property by gift or purchase, and initiation of a condemnation proceeding does not preclude negotiating the purchase of the property. The government must give at least thirty days' notice of its intent to initiate condemnation, along with an estimate of the amount of "just compensation" for taking the property. If the owner of the property questions the appropriateness of the action or objects to the amount offered, the court oversees the determination of just compensation that reflects the property's fair market value.

Economic Development

Cities and counties have broad authority to engage in activities related to community and economic development, industrial promotion, and urban renewal. Counties may also create special authorities that issue industrial revenue bonds, subject to the approval of the state Department of Commerce and the Local Government Commission. Local governments may provide public services and facilities to attract new development, such as extending water and sewer lines, expanding water supply and sewage treatment facilities, and improving streets and roads (cities only). In addition, local governments may acquire property and build public facilities to support private development, such as off-street parking. The state has provided broad authority for cities and counties to build industrial parks, assemble other potential industrial sites, construct and lease or sell vacated buildings, and prepare sites for industrial properties or facilities.[37]

Local governments are permitted to convey real property to a private company, in return accepting over a ten-year period the increased property and sales tax revenues that will result from the improvements made by the company to the property. There is also a long-standing provision that permits appropriations "for the purposes of aiding and encouraging the location of manufacturing enterprises," although the total investment in economic development programs cannot exceed 0.5 percent of a government's tax base. Under the redevelopment statute,[38] local governments may make property available to private developers either directly or after improvements have been made, as long as redevelopment procedures have been followed. It is also possible under this statute to condemn property for specified activities that will support development.

General-obligation bonds may be used to support development activities if approved in a referendum. Revenue bonds may be used without voter approval to finance a public service enterprise improvement if sufficient revenue will be generated to retire the debt. The state constitution does not, however, permit local governments to offer property tax exemptions or special classifications. A local government may not offer a special classification to a property owner if it is not available statewide. No such special classifications have been enacted, so local economic development officials may not offer them to developers.[39]

Fiscal Autonomy of Local Governments

After the widespread fiscal distress of the Great Depression, North Carolina established tight financial controls over local governments. One author notes that "state oversight of local government finance is more centralized in North Carolina than in any other state, both through the financial laws under which local governments operate and through the activities of the L[ocal] G[overnment] C[ommission]."[40] The LGC approves financing and sales of debt, authorizes general-obligation bonds, establishes policies, and arbitrates in situations (for example, by determining the amount municipalities must pay when portions of fire districts are annexed). The LGC has substantial regulatory power based on the Local Government Budget and Fiscal Control Act and the Local Government Bond Act, which were enacted in 1971 but originated with legislation in the late 1920s. The LGC oversees local government fiscal management, including the annual audit process, accounting systems, cash and investments, and debt repayment.[41] The LGC has the ultimate power to take action in the event of actual or likely default on debt service payments.[42]

The LGC prefers to act as adviser, but its regulatory powers are substantial. When governments consider debt financing, commission staff members review local conditions and consult with local officials. Staff members also negotiate the arrangements and terms of non-general–obligation bonds, thereby influencing local government financial and debt management. Formal approval of the LGC is necessary before any debt is issued.

Local Revenues

The property tax is the largest unrestricted local government revenue source and the one that can be altered with greatest flexibility.[43] (Table 1 summarizes major city and county revenue sources.) Although the property tax is a local governmental tax, the state can affect this revenue source by granting exemptions of certain types of property or by reducing the value of property or the tax rate, as long as it does so uniformly on a statewide basis.[44] The state excludes the first $20,000 in the property value for low-income residents, the elderly, or totally and permanently disabled homeowners. In 1994 and 1995 the state exempted business inventories from the tax base and eliminated an intangibles tax that had been collected by the state and largely returned to local governments. The state reimburses local governments for these lost revenues, but there is a perennial concern that state legislators will conclude that the state cannot afford these payments to cities and counties.

North Carolina has a broad constitutional limitation that prevents local governments from levying property taxes "except for purposes authorized by general law . . . unless the tax is approved by a majority of the qualified voters" of the jurisdic-

tion.[45] To implement this provision, the legislature has identified three sets of functions with differing restrictions regarding the use of property taxes. Group I is essentially for debt service in cities and for courts, elections, jails, schools, and social services in counties, and it consists of functions for which taxes may be levied without limit or voter approval. Group II functions include most basic municipal and county functions and are those for which property taxes may be levied without a vote within a $1.50 rate limitation. (City or county voters can agree to raise the limit above $1.50 through referendum.) Group III functions include community action and manpower programs in both cities and counties, mental health and sedimentation control programs in cities, or bus lines and public housing in counties; they cannot be financed by property taxes unless approved by the voters.

Local-option sales taxes of 2 percent are collected by the state and distributed to the counties.[46] Half is returned to the county from which it was originally collected. The other half—the result of two separate 0.5 percent local options—are pooled statewide and allocated among the counties on a per capita basis. Thus, this portion operates as a state revenue-sharing program, with some equalization of resources on the basis of population. When the General Assembly alters the overall state sales tax, it jeopardizes this local revenue source. In its 1995 session the legislature reduced the sales tax on food from 4 percent to 3 percent but left the local 2 percent share unchanged. If the move to eliminate the food tax is successful in the future, the local share also may be cut.

Local governments may choose to use other revenue sources, for example, by imposing taxes on privilege licenses for cable television, animals, and motor vehicles and on 911 services. Local governments in about seventy counties are permitted by local act to levy occupancy taxes on hotel and motel rooms.[47] They can use a variety of user charges for services such as water and sewerage. A range of fees must or can be imposed. Among the latter are development impact fees and charges for regulatory services. Cities and counties share in the net profits of alcoholic beverage control stores operated by the state.

State statutes limit the amount of outstanding debt as a percentage of the appraised value of taxable property.[48] The net debt may not exceed 8 percent of the city or county's valuation. This is not a great imposition, however, because debt usually does not approach this limit; in 1994 the percentage of general-obligation bonded debt for cities was below 1 percent excluding enterprise debt and under 2 percent including it.[49]

Local Expenditures

Cities and counties are differentiated by their expenditures (see Table 2). Cities emphasize utilities, public safety, and transportation; counties emphasize education and human services. The Local Budget Fiscal and Fiscal Control Act creates the

Table 1. Revenues of North Carolina Cities and Counties, 1995–1996

Municipalities revenue	Per capita	Percent	Counties revenue	Per capita	Percent
Property tax	$248	18%	Property tax	$334	37%
Sales tax	97	7	Sales tax	123	14
Intergovernmental sources	171	13	Intergovernmental sources	171	19
Governmental sales and services	82	6	Sales and service	78	9
Utility	518	39	Other tax	27	3
Miscellaneous	228	17	Miscellaneous	161	18
Total	$1,343	100%	Total	$894	100%

Source: *Fiscal Summary of North Carolina Municipalities, 1996* (Raleigh: North Carolina League of Municipalities, 1997); and *Fiscal Summary of North Carolina Counties, 1996* (Raleigh: North Carolina Association of County Commissioners, 1997).

Table 2. Expenditures of North Carolina Cities and Counties, 1995–1996

Municipalities expenditure	Per capita	Percent	Counties expenditure	Per capita	Percent
Utility	$510	39%	Education	$244	30%
Debt service	114	9	Debt service	63	8
Public safety	226	18	Human services	234	28
General government	93	7	General government	74	9
Transportation	127	10	Public safety	109	13
Other	216	17	Other	100	12
Total	$1,285	100%	Total	$824	100%

Source: Fiscal Summary of North Carolina Municipalities, 1996 (Raleigh: North Carolina League of Municipalities, 1997); and *Fiscal Summary of North Carolina Counties, 1996* (Raleigh: North Carolina Association of County Commissioners, 1997).

framework for controlling expenditures. This law requires that budgets be balanced (overall and within each major fund) and that funds be budgeted before they can be spent. Local governments must maintain accounting systems consistent with generally accepted accounting principles as well as the rules and regulations of the Local Government Commission. Local governments' financial accounts are audited annually by an independent public auditor. The act mandates fund accounting and requires a general fund, enterprise funds, and capital project funds. Budgetary accounting (with appropriations and estimated revenues recorded in the accounting system) is also required, except for the financial plans of internal service funds. The LGC recommends that local governments end the year with a legally available fund balance of at least 8 percent and preferably a larger proportion.[50] Bankruptcy—a problem that gave rise to the creation of the LGC—is unlikely as long as local finances continue to be monitored. Local governments may choose the type of budgeting system, for example, line-item or performance budgeting.

The Local Budget Fiscal and Fiscal Control Act restricts expenditures from any source of revenues to spending for "public purposes." The courts have interpreted this to mean that governments should not undertake functions traditionally provided by the private sector.[51]

State Government Grants-in-Aid to Localities

In the early twentieth century the state relied on local governments to pay for as well as to administer most public services. Over time, state government has progressively increased its share of total state and local revenues. Whereas in 1900 local governments levied over three-quarters of taxes to support state and local functions, in 1992 they levied only 21 percent. The state share increased from 23 percent to 55 percent. (The federal share also expanded from less than 1 percent to 24 percent.)[52]

The state provides three-quarters of total state-local expenditures on higher education, public welfare, and highways. Two-thirds of the total funding (including federal) for public education comes from state sources.[53] The next largest state contribution is 32 percent for health and hospitals.

State taxes that are shared with local governments are the beer and wine taxes (cities and counties); state franchise tax and gasoline tax (cities only); and real-estate transfer tax (counties). The major state reimbursements are the equivalent of the amount formerly raised through the intangible and business inventories taxes, which were eliminated in 1994 and 1995.

Unfunded Mandates

Given the nature of the relationship between state and local governments in North Carolina, the concept of unfunded mandates is not particularly meaningful as a discrete set of controls. The state sets the terms for a wide range of local governmental activities, most of which have financial implications for local governments. It rarely provides full funding to offset the costs of compliance or service provision, although none of its mandates are entirely unfunded. The most expensive state mandates for cities and counties are adequate facilities for public schools; local shares of Medicaid costs; local shares of Aid to Families with Dependent Children costs; various water-testing requirements; wastewater monitoring; solid waste recycling, landfill construction regulations, and increased tipping fees; pension benefits for law enforcement officers; compliance costs associated with implementing the federal Occupational Safety and Health Act (state administered); fire inspections; and watershed protection. There are more than eighty state mandates specifying standards, procedures, and/or services.[54]

Access to Local Government

Local Elections

Cities and counties may fashion their governing boards by choosing among certain features. The number of members, partisanship, type of constituency, and method of choosing the mayor or commission chairperson are local choices.

Elections are administered under state law, usually by county officials.[55] If city elections are partisan, they must be conducted by the county board of elections. The state Board of Elections oversees the process and has the authority to overturn the results of local elections when necessary and order new elections. Based on interpretations of state law, the board determines registration guidelines and voter eligibility, counts votes, decides outcomes, and handles protests.

Citizen Controls over Actions of Local Officials

Recall of council members is permitted for some cities.[56] Citizens may initiate and vote on charter amendments in cities. The number of signatures needed to call a referendum is 10 percent of the voters or 5,000 signatures, whichever is less. Other referendum purposes include approving the sale of alcohol in various forms; issuing bonds and levying taxes to supplement the revenue of a revenue bond project; and approving property tax expenditures above permitted limits or for certain restricted functions. County officials may not hold a special referendum unless it has been specifically authorized by state law or a special act of the legislature.[57] There is no provision for statewide initiative to put questions on the ballot.

The North Carolina open meetings law covers all "public bodies,"[58] including the governing board, committees of the board, and each board or commission created by the governing board (for example, a planning commission). All official meetings of public bodies must be open to the public. An official meeting is one in which a majority of the members gather to take action, hold a hearing, or deliberate.

The law permits closed sessions for three major reasons: (1) when public sessions could give an unfair advantage to a party with which the government has a potentially adversarial relationship (for example, when real property is to be acquired, there is litigation, or investigations of illegal criminal conduct are being considered); (2) when public sessions could invade personal privacy (for example, when an employee's performance—including that of the city or county manager—is being assessed or when information from confidential records is being considered); and (3) when other situations specified in the law occur (for example, when the location or expansion of an industry is being discussed or attorney-client privilege is invoked). The public body must first meet in open session and then vote to go into closed session. The motion must state the general purpose of the closed session. Grievances against closed sessions may be adjudicated. Records (both traditional and electronic documents) must be open, unless the law or a regulation specifies that they be closed.[59]

State-Local Relations

In terms of local autonomy, North Carolina is characterized by apparent contradictions. The legal framework for intergovernmental relations is heavily tilted toward the state. The state occupies a very large fiscal role and controls many aspects of local finance. It provides and/or pays for a wide range of governmental functions. Despite this high level of state activity, city and county officials are generally positive about the state's approach for several reasons.

First, general-purpose governments are strongly supported. They control their own destiny in the sense that they do not face competition from special districts. For the most part, municipalities do not have to contend with governmental fragmentation on their borders and are able to develop orderly approaches to absorbing newly developing areas. Second, there is considerable flexibility. Local bills permit local governments to craft special arrangements. Cities and counties have considerable freedom in developing cooperative approaches to service provision and delivery.

Third, there is fiscal stability. Although local governments are dependent on state government for revenues and are vulnerable to changes in state policy on reimbursements and shared taxes, they have some measure of "freedom" from taxpayer revolts because local property tax rates are relatively low. Furthermore, state controls have contributed to lower bond ratings.

The trend in North Carolina is toward more local autonomy, although the basic state-dominated relationship remains intact. Local units are receiving more freedom to deal with issues such as school performance and alternatives to welfare, but they are also expected to be more accountable for results. Selected local governments have been given some new revenue options, although the proposal from city and county government associations for a tax menu from which local governments could choose has not been accepted.[60] A state version of mandate reform passed in 1995 requires notice and a fiscal note when new mandates are imposed on local government. It also gives cities and counties more input into administrative rulemaking by the state.[61] A tension between state and local officials continues, but it is a "creative tension."[62] The major issue that will affect trends in the future is the continuing commitment by the state to fund shared revenues. For cities, the biggest issue is preservation of unilateral annexation; for counties, how devolution of human services will affect state-local relations.

The tradition of government in North Carolina does not square well with traditional definitions of "local autonomy," nor are national-level issues framed in the same way in this state compared with other states. Provision of public services in North Carolina is a joint endeavor that includes state and local governments. Responsibilities are intermixed. The terms of the relationship are established by the state, but general-purpose local governments are accepted and protected as major actors in these joint undertakings. The notion that there are separate spheres of state and local action and that local governments have identifiable prerogatives that amount to a measurable level of autonomy over their sphere is largely absent. What might be viewed as intrusiveness, interference, or restriction elsewhere is generally accepted in North Carolina as part of the way that the state and local governments go about meeting the needs of citizens of the state.

Notes

1. U.S. Bureau of the Census, *1992 Census of Governments* (Washington, D.C.: U.S. Government Printing Office, 1994), table 3.

2. Charles D. Liner, ed., *State and Local Government Relations in North Carolina: Their Evolution and Current Status*, 2d ed. (Chapel Hill: Institute of Government, University of North Carolina, 1995), 12.

3. General Statutes of North Carolina, 153A-4 (for cities) and 160A-4 (for counties).

4. North Carolina Constitution, Article II, section 24 does impose some lim-

itations on local bills. They cannot be used, for example, in matters pertaining to health, sanitation, and the abatement of nuisances; changing the names of cities; authorizing the laying out of highways; and regulating labor, trades, mining, or manufacturing.

5. David M. Lawrence and Warren Jake Wicker, eds., *Municipal Government in North Carolina*, 2d ed. (Chapel Hill: Institute of Government, University of North Carolina, 1995), 34.

6. See General Statutes of North Carolina, 120-158–120-174. The review can also be initiated by petition of 15 percent of the population in the areas proposed for incorporation (General Statutes of North Carolina, 120-163.)

7. House Bill 964 added requirements for minimum population density and reasonable level of services before a positive recommendation for incorporation can be made.

8. Lawrence and Wicker, eds., *Municipal Government in North Carolina*, 48, 49.

9. Ibid., 49.

10. General Statutes of North Carolina, 153A-401–153A-405.

11. Lawrence and Wicker, eds., *Municipal Government in North Carolina*, 205.

12. General Statutes of North Carolina, 158A-81, 158A-58–158A-60.

13. David M. Lawrence, comp., *Forms of Government of North Carolina Cities* (Chapel Hill: Institute of Government, University of North Carolina, 1994), 40. Among smaller towns, the proportion using the council-manager form drops off substantially to 30 percent among those with 1,000–2,499 population and 8 percent for those with fewer than 1,000 population.

14. North Carolina Association of County Commissioners, *1995 Directory of North Carolina County Officials* (Raleigh: North Carolina Association of County Commissioners, 1995).

15. North Carolina Constitution, Article VII, section 1.

16. There are five conditions to be met: (1) the area is no more than three miles from the city limits, (2) none of the area is closer to another city than to the annexing city, (3) entire subdivisions are included in the annexation, (4) the total area does not exceed 10 percent of the existing city area, and (5) the city is able to provide full services to the satellite area. See General Statutes of North Carolina, 160a-58.1.

17. General Statutes of North Carolina, 160A-58.21–160A-58.28.

18. Liner, ed., *State and Local Government Relations in North Carolina*, 47.

19. Lawrence and Wicker, eds., *Municipal Government in North Carolina*, 57.

20. Ibid.

21. The total area annexed in the 1980s was 460 square miles; that annexed in the 1990s was 287 square miles. Figures in this paragraph are from Joel Miller, "Annexations and Boundary Changes in the 1980s and 1990–1991," *The Municipal Year Book, 1993* (Washington, D.C.: International City Management Association, 1994), 100–109; and "Boundary Changes, 1990–95," *The Municipal Year Book, 1997* (Washington, D.C.: International City Management Association, 1997), 35–37. *The News & Observer*, 1 July 1997, 7A, reviewed Durham's growth in land area from 12.8 square miles in 1925; 36.7, in 1966; 67.7, in 1987; and 91.1, in 1997.

22. Fleming Bell, ed., *County Government in North Carolina* (Chapel Hill: Institute of Government, University of North Carolina, 1989), 6.

23. General Statutes of North Carolina, 160A-360. When the city enforces zoning or subdivision regulations, it must make some provision for citizens in the outlying area so that they may have a voice in the decision making of the planning agency and the zoning board of adjustment. The city must ask the county commissioners to appoint outside members to these two bodies. The number of persons appointed and their voting power are determined by the city.

24. Liner, ed., *State and Local Government Relations in North Carolina*, 37.

25. Ibid., 23.

26. Lawrence and Wicker, eds., *Municipal Government in North Carolina*, 16–17.

27. General Statutes of North Carolina, 136-66.1, 136-44.8. The recommendations should be followed "insofar as they are compatible with its [the board's] general plans, standards, criteria, and available funds."

28. Under General Statutes of North Carolina, 160A-146, the city cannot abolish a position required by law (for example, the city attorney), combine offices when forbidden by law, or discontinue or reassign functions assigned by law to a particular office.

29. The sheriff and register of deeds are elected and have authority over appointing and removing their staff. Appointments in the health and social services departments, in area mental health authorities, and in local emergency management agencies must be made in accordance with the provisions of the State Personnel Act. Cooperative extension employees are appointed jointly by the board of commission and the state Cooperative Extension Service. The boards of elections and education also control their own staff. Bell, ed., *County Government in North Carolina*, 227.

30. Lawrence and Wicker, eds., *Municipal Government in North Carolina*, 130.

31. General Statutes of North Carolina, 128-27(a)(1–5); 95, Article 12. One provision (General Statutes of North Carolina, 95-97) that prohibits public employees from becoming members of unions has been found to be unconstitutional.

32. Mike McLaughlin and Jennifer Lehman, "Mandates to Local Government: How Big a Problem?" *North Carolina Insight* 16 (May 1996): 71.

33. Local governments are required to use a formal bidding process for construction or repair work estimated to cost $100,000 or more (with additional requirements covering projects that exceed $500,000) and for the purchase of materials or equipment in excess of $20,000. Contracts for professional services or acquisition of real property are exempted. Local governments may collect informal bids (such as telephone or written quotes or catalog prices with no bid deposit) for expenditures over $5,000 but less than the amount necessitating use of formal contracts. For contracts with a value of less than $5,000, the city may use any procedure it considers appropriate. Normally, at least three competitive bids must be received for projects that exceed $100,000. For other purchases, no minimum number is required. The statute requires that contracts must be awarded to "the lowest responsible bidder, taking into consideration quality, performance and the time specified in the proposals for the performance of the contract." The same standards apply to informal contracts. General Statutes of North Carolina, 160A-11.

34. Lawrence and Wicker, eds., *Municipal Government in North Carolina*, 504. The current provision regarding conflict of interest is found in General Statutes of North Carolina, 14-234. The restriction applies to a person who owns more than 10 percent of the stock in a company. In cities with less than 7,500 population, it is possible for an official to contract with the town government if certain requirements are met.

35. General Statutes of North Carolina, 133-32.

36. General Statutes of North Carolina, 40A-3(b).

37. General Statutes of North Carolina, 158-7.1.

38. General Statutes of North Carolina, 160A-512.

39. Lawrence and Wicker, eds., *Municipal Government in North Carolina*, 607.

40. K. Lee Carter, "State Oversight of Local Government Finance," in Liner, ed., *State and Local Government Relations in North Carolina*, 80.

41. General Statutes of North Carolina, 159. The staff of the Local Government Commission regularly monitors local government financial conditions, looking for problems such as low levels of available reserves and poor tax collection rates. The commission also monitors deposits and investments by local governments based on semiannual reports filed by local governments.

42. In the case of general-obligation bonds, the powers are the broadest. The Local Government Commission is authorized to order a governing board to raise a sufficient amount of taxes or other revenues to meet its debt obligation and adequately maintain its sinking funds. Local officials who refuse to implement an order of the commission forfeit their office or position. General Statutes of North Carolina, 159-36.

43. Utility revenue is a larger source for cities but is tied closely to the service provided; that is, it is not a general revenue.

44. General Statutes of North Carolina, 105-275–105-278.9.

45. General Statutes of North Carolina, Article V, section 2(5).

46. General Statutes of North Carolina, 105, Article 39 (one-cent local option sales tax passed in 1971), Article 40 (half-cent option passed in 1983), and Article 42 (half-cent option passed in 1985 [Reg. Sess., 1986]).

47. Lawrence and Wicker, eds., *Municipal Government in North Carolina*, 224.

48. General Statutes of North Carolina, 159-55(c).

49. Lawrence and Wicker, eds., *Municipal Government in North Carolina*, 396–397. Debt issued for utility facilities is not included in the calculation of net debt.

50. General Statutes of North Carolina, 159, Article 3; 314.

51. Lawrence and Wicker, eds., *Municipal Government in North Carolina*, 293.

52. Liner, Ed., *State and Local Government Relations in North Carolina*, 38 (table 3-3).

53. U.S. Advisory Commission on Intergovernmental Relations (ACIR), *Significant Features of Fiscal Federalism*, vol. 2 (Washington, D.C.: ACIR, 1992), 323, 265.

54. McLaughlin and Lehman, "Mandates to Local Government," 48. A study committee of the North Carolina Association of County Commissioners in 1993 could find only one totally unfunded mandate: the requirement that counties cover the energy costs for public schools (for which the state eliminated its partial contribution in 1993). See also McLaughlin and Lehman, "Mandates to Local Government," 71, 58–68. Not included in the number of mandates discussed here are requirements regarding structures (for example, requiring the creation of a city council or board of social services).

55. General Statutes of North Carolina, 163, subchapter IX.

56. According to the North Carolina League of Municipalities, fifteen cities are authorized to recall (memorandum to author from Kim Smith, assistant general counsel, 28 October 1996).

57. Bell, ed., *County Government in North Carolina*, 339–340.

58. General Statutes of North Carolina, 143-318.9–143-318.18.

59. General Statutes of North Carolina, 132.

60. Mike McLaughlin, "A Tax Menu for Local Government: Yes or No?" *North Carolina Insight* 16 (May 1996): 99–101. New options include hotel-motel tax in sixty-six counties and thirty-three municipalities, prepared food and beverage tax in nine local governments, local land transfer tax in seven counties, and amusement tax in two units.

61. McLaughlin and Lehman, "Mandates to Local Government," 43.

62. James Blackburn, quoted in McLaughlin and Lehman, "Mandates to Local Government," 50.

NORTH DAKOTA

Mary Grisez Kweit and Robert W. Kweit

The authors wish to thank Chet Nelson, legislative budget analyst and auditor, North Dakota Legislative Council; Connie Sprynczynatyk, executive director, North Dakota League of Cities; and Doris Bring, auditor, Grand Forks County, for their assistance on this project. They also wish to thank the following people from the city of Grand Forks: John O'Leary, director, Department of Community Development; Charles Durrenberger, senior planner; John Schmisek, auditor; and Ken Vein, director, Public Works Department.

North Dakota is a large but sparsely populated state with more local governments per capita than any state in the union. The state maintains elaborate statutory restrictions on local government autonomy but allows numerous exceptions. Moreover, a vote of local citizens can in many instances override state restrictions. Home rule and a 1993 state law that encourages experimentation with forms of government, government powers, and intergovernmental agreements give local governments substantial freedom to seek local solutions to problems, but the state's conservative culture and local governments' limited resources have restricted their use of the flexibility provided by the state. In the 1990s an increasing number of municipalities adopted home rule to obtain the authority to impose sales taxes, which were needed to replace declining federal dollars and to provide funds to foster economic development.

Governmental Setting

The years of major settlement in North Dakota were between 1878 and 1915, when railroad companies—promising cheap land and a mild climate—lured immigrants from abroad and from the eastern United States to settle along the newly built lines stretching west. Many towns began as railroad construction camps, evenly spaced along the tracks. Settlements mushroomed, and in the expectation that rapid growth would continue, communities built churches, banks, schools, opera houses, and anything else local residents thought they would need. But the settlers had overestimated what the arid and harsh environment could sustain. Summer droughts and winter blizzards soon convinced many that their hopes could not be achieved in North Dakota, and the population began to decline, leaving behind a thinly populated state with too many communities, too many governments, and too many public institutions for the population to support.

North Dakota's 70,665 square miles are inhabited by 638,800 people. In addition to being one of the most rural states in the union, it has the highest number of local governments per capita: one for every 231 people.[1] North Dakota has 1,343 townships, 361 municipalities, 53 counties, and 236 school districts; in addition, it has assorted other special districts—rural ambulance service districts, health districts, irrigation districts, park districts, public library districts, fire districts, soil conservation districts, water management districts, and regional planning districts.[2] Of the 361 municipalities, only 9 have populations larger than 10,000; these account for 43.8 percent of the total state population. Three hundred and thirteen municipalities have populations of less than 1,000.

For the most part, North Dakotans cling to their communities and tend to be suspicious of outsiders who might meddle in their affairs or attempt to change their way of life. Their attachment to local governments that are made up of friends and neighbors is probably related to a historical belief that the state was being controlled by outsiders—a belief that, in many cases, was correct. Until the early years of the twentieth century, the railroad companies that had helped to populate the state played a significant role in state politics. In one classic example, Alex McKenzie, an employee of the Northern Pacific railroad, from his base in St. Paul, "issued orders to his minions in the legislative and executive departments at Bismarck."[3] When McKenzie went to jail in 1900, the stage was set for the "Revolution of 1906"—that is, the election of the first Democratic governor—which ushered in the Progressive Era; in North Dakota, the Progressives' banner was not only "good government" but also "North Dakota for North Dakotans."[4] The insurgents battled big business and the eastern capitalists, and it was during this period that initiative, referendum, and recall became state law.

North Dakota politics shifted even further to the left with the emergence of the Non-Partisan League—which dominated state politics from 1915 to 1921—and of William Langer, an alumnus of the league who personally dominated North Dakota politics through the 1930s. Successfully employing classic populist rhetoric in an otherwise solidly conservative, Republican state, Langer and the Non-Partisan League left behind a long list of reform legislation that included the creation of a state-owned bank, grain mill, and grain elevator. State residents continue to blend conservative political values with a populist streak.

Like those of many other states, the state laws of North Dakota—known as the Century Code—tend to soporific and absurd specificity.[5] Section 40-05-01, for example, which describes the "powers of all municipalities," includes seventy-seven subsections. Since the seventy-seven subsections were apparently not adequate, section 40-05-02 adds an additional twenty-nine. But because there are few restrictions that cannot be overcome by a creative community, North Dakota actually gives its local governments remarkably free rein. The Tool Chest Bill, passed in 1993, clarified and expanded local government discretion to reorganize and cooperate in order to provide services more efficiently and effectively. Under this legislation, municipalities and counties are required either to establish an advisory committee to study the existing form and powers of the local government or to place on the ballot, every five years, the issue of whether to establish such a committee.[6]

The impetus behind the Tool Chest Bill was the recognition, on the part of state government, that North Dakota had too many governments for too few people. Developed by a state-appointed study commission, the legislation was supported by a number of North Dakota public interest groups, including the League of Cities, the Township Officers Association, and the Parks and Recreation Association. Some state and local officials may have supported the bill because they perceived legislation that merely encouraged consolidation and cooperation as more palatable than an alternative bill—which would have required, by state mandate, the consolidation of North Dakota's fifty-three counties into fifteen. (Many wags claimed that the sheer length of the Tool Chest Bill aided its passage, as few legislators were willing to wade through all of its eighty pages.)

Although North Dakota local governments are remarkably free to seek solutions to their problems, they do not necessarily do so. There are three reasons that this is the case. First, no matter how much flexibility the state gives to communities like Ayr (population 19) or Grano (population 9), they will never be able to solve their most obvious problem: their existence. With the consolidation of farms and the ease of access to larger communities, most of the 361 municipalities in the state have little reason for being. Second, local governments do not necessarily have the management skills and expertise that are required to take advantage of the opportunity to solve problems. Third, the state's culture does not encourage innovation. North Dakota is antigovernment, antitax, and antichange. In addition, the suspicions that in the early years of the state's existence were focused on outside interests are now focused increasingly on state government—and, in the larger communities, even on local government. A strong tradition of individualism leads North Dakotans to reject government—even local government—as a potential source for the solution of problems.

North Dakota governors drive themselves around the state, and many state legislators return to their districts every other weekend to meet with constituents and to "visit" about the legislative session. Such extraordinary ease of access to state officials means that the values held by citizens—resistance to innovation and a tendency toward individualism, for example—have effects that reach well beyond the local level. And the initiative and referendum, legacies of North Dakota's populist past, are used so liberally that the state government finds it virtually impossible to take unpopular action, such as raising taxes.

Home Rule in North Dakota

Historical Development

Home rule is authorized in Article VII, section 1, of the state constitution, which was ratified in a special election held October 1, 1889. The purpose of the section is "to provide for maximum local self-government by all political subdivisions with a minimum of duplication of functions." Section 6 includes the following language: "No home rule charter shall become operative in any county or city until submitted to the electors thereof and approved by a majority of those voting thereon. In granting home rule powers to cities, the legislative assembly shall not be restricted by city debt limitations contained in this constitution."

Finally, in 1969, the state legislature passed enabling legislation to permit municipalities with populations greater than 100 to implement home rule. This legislation provided the means for carrying out the constitutional provision. The two largest cities in the state—Fargo and Grand Forks—adopted home rule charters in 1970, and Minot followed in 1972. Currently there are thirty-five municipalities with home rule.

The legislature authorized home rule for counties in 1985, but only three counties have adopted it: Cass, Walsh, and Richland. In 1993, Grand Forks County submitted a home rule charter to the voters, but it was soundly defeated. County residents' suspicion of the city and fears of increased taxes contributed to its defeat.

As noted earlier, the Tool Chest Bill enables and encourages all local governments in North Dakota to exercise powers that are similar to those granted under home rule. Under the bill, local governments may create advisory committees to study their form of government; among other actions, these committees may recommend joint powers agreements with other units of local government—even those in other states or in Canadian provinces. The bill also provides statutory procedures for local governments to transfer responsibilities to county government.

Definition of Home Rule

Home rule is available to any North Dakota municipality with a population over 100. The Century Code grants sixteen powers to home rule municipalities, many of which differ little from those granted to municipalities that do not have home rule.[7] The additional powers afford greater flexibility and control in the following areas: the imposition of taxes; the list of required public offices; the definition of police powers; the development and enforcement of ordinances; and the structure and conduct of elections (home rule municipalities are free to establish local initiative and referendum regardless of the government structure). In sum, the ordinance states:

It is the intention of this chapter to grant and confirm to the people of all cities coming within its provisions the full right of self-government in both local and city matters within the powers enumerated herein. The statutes of the state of North Dakota, so far as applicable, shall continue to apply to home rule cities, except insofar as superseded by the charters of such cities or by ordinance passed pursuant to such charters.[8]

In several municipalities with home rule, the municipal auditors describe increased flexibility as the greatest advantage of home rule. Many home rule municipalities have used their expanded authority to impose new taxes.

One city manager gave the following endorsement of home rule:

Prior to the adoption of home rule, I knew Title 40 of the Century Code like the palm of my hand. This was necessary because of the daily decisions that needed to be based upon what was permitted by the legislature. Over the past few years, I've paid less and less attention to the state legislature (a happy thought) because I no longer need to know what's in State law. Under home rule, I only need to know what the problem is and whether we have the right, and the capacity, to solve the problem. It's a nice change, and it works![9]

Structural Features

Although neither the constitution nor state law formally designates classes of municipalities, both contain references to specific communities and make distinctions that have the effect of singling out particular communities or groups of communities. For instance, the constitution specifically identifies the locations of eight schools of higher education.[10] State law exempts certain municipalities from mill levy requirements; it also prohibits school districts from raising the levy more than 18 percent in any given year but specifically exempts Fargo from that restriction. But the law also specifies ways in which communities can circumvent the limitation: for example, if a majority of voters approve, or if property tax valuation has increased by 20 percent or more and other conditions hold.[11] Distinctions are also made on the basis of the size of the jurisdiction: different population thresholds are set for different purposes, such as property tax

limitations or (until the passage of the Tool Chest Bill) the size of the governing body.

The mayor-council and council-manager forms of government have always been available to all municipalities, and since passage of the Tool Chest Bill, all communities can opt for the commission form, as twenty-seven have done. (Before the passage of the Tool Chest Bill, only communities whose populations were over 500 could establish a commission government.) Municipalities also have the option of changing from the mayor-council system to the "modern council" form.[12] Under this system, the council is composed of not less than four members, one of whom is the mayor; council representation may be at large or by ward. Over 90 percent of cities in North Dakota employ some version of the mayor-council system, including the modern council form.[13] Only one city—Minot—uses the council-manager form of government.

Although the Century Code originally specified the number of council members on the basis of population and required council members to be elected by ward if the population was greater than 600, the Tool Chest Bill allows all municipalities to determine the size of their councils and to choose between at-large and ward representation. Home rule cities may use a combination of at-large and ward representation.

State law gives counties a great deal of discretion over municipal incorporation. Any contiguous territory not exceeding four square miles can be considered for incorporation. A population census and a land survey are required. To initiate the incorporation process, citizens must present the county commission with a petition for incorporation, along with a detailed plan for service delivery and financing. If the commission approves the petition, an election is called; a majority vote of those in the territory to be incorporated is required for approval of the incorporation.[14]

Annexation can occur in one of three ways. First, in a territory that is adjacent to an incorporated municipality, annexation can occur if three-quarters of the qualified electors (or owners of property valued at three-quarters of the total value of the property in question) sign a petition. Second, the governing body may adopt a resolution describing the property to be annexed. If no more than one-quarter of the owners of real property protest, the property will be annexed. Finally, a municipal corporation may petition the state for annexation. The attorney general then establishes an annexation review commission to consider the petition and to decide whether it should be completed and under what terms.[15] Annexation is usually accomplished relatively easily, normally through adoption of a resolution.

Given the small size of cities and the absence of townships in much of the western part of the state, counties provide important services to citizens and to other levels of government. Counties are organized under the commission form of government, with between three and five commissioners who must meet at least four times per year. Four forms of county-manager government may be established by petition of 10 percent of the electorate or by a resolution of the county commission and majority approval at the next primary election. The manager may be elected or appointed, and the government itself may take a "short form" (a smaller number of required offices) or the standard form.[16] However, no counties have taken advantage of these options.

Regardless of governmental structure, county responsibilities and processes are specified in detail by state law. For example, the Century Code requires certain offices: a county auditor, a county treasurer, a register of deeds, a clerk of the district court, a sheriff, and a state's attorney. (A county superintendent of schools is optional.) Most offices are elective, and salaries are set by the state on the basis of county population.[17] The county is also required by state law to appoint people to seventeen other positions—from the coroner to the vector control district board (which deals with disease-carrying insects). State law specifies procedures for combining positions. It also covers matters such as the procedures for stating mileage claims, the bonding of county officers, and restrictions on the powers of the state's attorney.[18]

As noted earlier, home rule is available to counties.[19] Upon its own initiative or in response to a petition by 2 percent of the electorate, the county commission may appoint a charter commission of at least five people to draft a home rule charter, which must be ratified by a majority vote.

The Century Code also provides for the establishment of township government.[20] The first step is a petition to the county commission, which may originate from a single congressional township or from two or more neighboring congressional townships; in either case, the area must have a minimum property valuation of $20,000 and at least 25 electors. (Congressional townships are those areas, usually six miles by six miles, that were established when the federal government sent out surveys during the years that the territory was first laid out.) The petition must be signed by 25 percent of those who cast votes in the last election for governor. In the next step, an election is set to determine whether a township should be organized. The establishment of a township requires a majority vote at an annual meeting. State law specifies the procedures for the meeting in detail and requires that it be held on the third Tuesday of March.[21]

An incorporated municipality has zoning authority in surrounding unincorporated areas of the county.[22] The area of jurisdiction depends on the size of the municipality. For municipalities with populations under 5,000, zoning authority extends for one-half mile. For those with populations above 5,000 but below 25,000, extraterritorial jurisdiction extends for one mile. The jurisdictions of larger communities extend for two miles, and they have the option of expanding the jurisdiction to four miles. In addition to the members of the municipal zoning commission who are appointed by the municipality, the county appoints members: one member in the smallest communities (under 5,000 pop-

ulation), two members in the medium-size communities (5,000 to 25,000), and three members in the largest communities.

Functions of Local Government

Functional Responsibilities

Municipalities provide a wide variety of services not offered by the state: among other activities, they establish departments, levy taxes, approve budgets, and deal with infrastructure and land-use issues. They are free to create a broad spectrum of businesses, with the exception of liquor stores. (Former professor and lieutenant governor Lloyd Omdahl has observed that "some North Dakota cities get around this restriction by organizing private associations to run local liquor stores to use the money for city services and projects. These are often believed to be municipal liquor stores but they are not and cannot be under the state constitution.")[23]

Many county functions are specified by state law. Among the required tasks are building and maintaining a county highway system, administering social services, conducting elections, protecting citizens and their property through law enforcement, collecting and distributing taxes for other local government entities, maintaining property records, and undertaking land-use planning. Counties are also "providing an ever-increasing variety of other services, such as ambulance services, cemeteries, parks, programs for the elderly, job development, war memorials, weather modification, historical centers, veterans programs, and the list goes on."[24]

Townships are limited to twenty-one enumerated powers in addition to zoning.[25] In practice, the most common township functions are weed control and road construction and repair.

Special districts are permitted in a number of functional areas under conditions and according to procedures that are specified in the Century Code. Municipalities may undertake park functions themselves, but any incorporated municipality may establish a park district by a two-thirds vote, as most of the larger cities have done.[26] A variety of other special districts may be established under various procedures—irrigation districts, soil conservation districts, and rural ambulance districts, for example. (There is one hospital district in North Dakota.) Municipalities may also establish authorities specified in the Century Code; these include municipal power agencies (which may be established jointly by more than one municipality), steam heating authorities, and parking authorities.[27] Special districts and authorities are permitted to levy taxes.

The most commonly used procedures for interlocal cooperation are the establishment of city-county departments and the execution of joint powers agreements. For instance, Grand Forks maintains a city-county health department. Joint powers agreements enable local governments to cooperate in administering local functions. An example is the agreement between Stutsman County, the city of Jamestown, and the Jamestown school board to conduct joint elections. The Tool Chest Bill encourages interlocal cooperation.

Administrative Discretion

North Dakota local governments are given substantial administrative freedom. The only limits in the area of personnel are guidelines on conflict of interest and nepotism. Any municipality with a population over 4,000 may establish a civil service system. The system may be established by the municipal government, or the citizens may request the creation of such a system—a process that requires a petition of 20 percent of electors and approval by a 60 percent vote. The civil service system is permitted to specify minimum employment qualifications for fire, police, or other departments and may include provisions for protection against suspension, removal, or discharge except for adequate reason.[28]

The Century Code specifies procedures for the adoption of municipal ordinances and requires that they be codified in a list of ordinances. State law requires county commissions to keep a record of their proceedings, which must also be published in an official newspaper. (Citizens are required by state law to designate an "official newspaper" in which all government announcements are published.) The law establishes an agenda for county commission meetings but not for municipal council meetings. It also specifies procedures for filling vacancies in elected offices at both the municipal and county levels.[29]

State law requires that any project costing more than $100,000 be advertised for competitive bids.[30] The request for bids must be advertised for three consecutive weeks in the official newspaper and in a widely circulated trade publication. Bidders must post bonds. State law also specifies the content of the advertisements, the place where plans must be filed, and the procedure for the opening of bids.

Both municipalities and counties are given expansive powers over planning and zoning. To exercise their powers, they must establish a zoning commission. State law describes the means of appointing the members of the commission, their terms of office, and procedures that the commission must follow.[31]

Economic Development

The state provides municipalities—and, to a lesser extent, counties—a great deal of authority with respect to taxing, borrowing, and lending for economic development. Municipalities can establish economic development organizations, industrial parks, enterprise zones, loan or grant pools, and job training projects. Both cities and counties are empowered to acquire property; issue revenue bonds; and lease properties to industrial, commercial, or nonprofit organizations, health institutions, or school districts (for vocational education).[32] The process for issuing the bonds is detailed but not limiting.

North Dakota allows municipalities to establish job development authorities either independently or in cooperation with other political subdivisions. The authorities are established by the local governing body, which appoints a board of directors for three-year terms. Four mills may be levied to support the actions of the authority or to contract with an outside industrial development organization. The authority may loan or grant funds or property, provide loan guarantees, or invest its resources.[33]

The state allows municipalities and counties to grant partial or complete tax exemptions for ad valorem increases in the value of tangible property for up to five years. Agricultural processing plants may be given an extra five-year exemption. A municipality may, in addition, negotiate payments in lieu of taxes for up to twenty years; such arrangements are subject to the approval of the state board of tax equalization, which may also grant state income tax relief to projects granted exemption.[34]

Municipalities and counties are authorized to provide a variety of services to promote development, such as evaluating proposed sites, undertaking marketing efforts, and conducting labor supply availability studies. The governing body may also propose up to 1 mill to finance vocational or on-the-job training; a 60 percent majority is needed to pass.[35] Under urban renewal laws, a municipal governing body may declare any area to be a slum or blighted, which allows the municipality to take a range of actions: it can exercise eminent domain to acquire the property; it can improve, develop, or sell the property; or it can issue bonds for redevelopment, at up to 12 percent interest for private sale and at not less than par for public sale. Tax increment financing may be used to develop a blighted area, provided that a public hearing is held.[36]

Fiscal Autonomy of Local Governments

Local Revenues

Local governments in North Dakota are guaranteed the right to levy and collect property tax, which is the major form of local taxation. Under conditions specified in their charters, home rule municipalities are permitted to levy other taxes, and most levy a sales tax.[37] Municipalities are also permitted to license and tax a number of specific activities such as transient businesses, taxi services, bowling alleys, public dance halls, auction houses, and resale shops.

In 1981 the state legislature set the assessed value of property at 50 percent of market value. The taxable value of the property of utilities, businesses, and railroads is 10 percent of assessed value, and residential property is taxed at 9 percent of assessed value. Municipal assessments are reviewed by the county, with the county commission acting as a board of equalization. The numbers are then sent to the state tax commissioner and are reviewed by the state board of equalization.[38]

For municipalities with populations of less than 5,000, the property tax limit is 38 mills. Municipalities with populations over 5,000 may levy an additional 0.5 mill for each 1,000 in popu-

Fig. 1 North Dakota City Revenues, 1984–1993

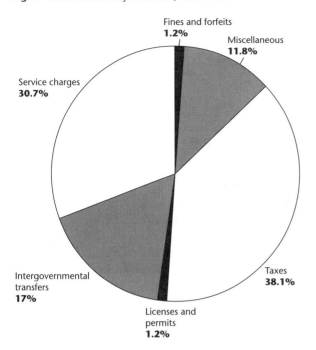

Fines and forfeits
1.2%

Miscellaneous
11.8%

Service charges
30.7%

Intergovernmental
transfers
17%

Licenses and
permits
1.2%

Taxes
38.1%

Source: "Revenue and Expenditure Assessment of Fifty-three North Dakota Cities," compiled for the North Dakota League of Cities by August Ternes, Office of the State Auditor, 1993.

lation, up to 40 mills. Municipalities may also pass a resolution to raise the mill levy by 10 mills, subject to approval by the electorate. The mill levy is designed to cover general government activities, but local governments may impose additional levies for twenty-nine other purposes. Taxes levied to pay interest on bonded debt or on debt principal at maturity, for example, are not subject to the overall mill limit. Municipalities may impose additional mill levies for the arts (up to 5 mills), the planning commission (up to 1 mill), animal shelters (up to 0.5 mill), libraries (up to 4 mills), and many other purposes.[39]

Counties are limited to 23 mills for the general fund, but again there are many loopholes; the thirty-five exceptions to the limits include airports (up to 4 mills); farm-to-market roads (up to 15 mills); roads built and maintained with federal aid (up to 15 mills); and gopher, rabbit, or crow destruction (0.5 mill).[40] There are mill levy limits for school districts, park and recreation districts, and townships, but in each case there is a laundry list of exemptions for monies used for specific purposes. Special credits apply to people who are 65 or older or who are permanently and totally disabled and earn less than $10,000 per year.

No local government may incur indebtedness exceeding 5 percent of the assessed value of its taxable property, but again there are exceptions: for example, a community can exceed state limits on debt through a two-thirds vote; and, if a majority of the voters approve, it may exceed the limits to issue bonds to purchase a utility or undertake water or sewer projects.[41]

Bond issues must be approved by a 60 percent vote, but again there are exceptions—such as an emergency, a shortfall in the fund of a special improvement district, or the need to raise matching funds for a federal-aid highway project.

A two-thirds vote is needed to issue bonds for the following purposes: (1) street improvements, bridges, or urban renewal; (2) regional or county correction centers or park and recreation facilities; (3) public school buildings.

In a fiscal study of fifty-three municipalities for the years 1984–1993, the North Dakota League of Cities found that the largest source of municipal revenue was local taxes (38.1 percent), followed by service charges (30.7 percent).[42] The full revenue picture is shown in Figure 1.

Local Expenditures

The form of both municipal and county budgets is set by the state tax commissioner and the state auditor, although home rule municipalities and counties are given greater flexibility in budget form. The major categories of municipal expenditure are police, fire, engineering, water and sewer service, transportation, health, recreation, highways and streets, and general administration. Expenditures must be grouped into three categories: (1) maintenance and operating expenses, (2) capital and betterment expenses, and (3) debt retirement requirements.

Municipal auditors are required to publish a notice of a public hearing, to occur not later than October 1, to enable citizens to discuss the proposed budget and the tax levy necessary to fund the expenditures. The final budget must be completed by October 1; by October 10, two copies must be sent to the county auditor, who will calculate the final tax rates and send the final budget to the state auditor by January 1. Municipalities are required to have a balanced budget.[43]

The major categories of county expenditure are roads, health care, and sheriffs. County auditors prepare the county budgets and are required to include a "detailed breakdown" of revenues and expenditures; transfers in and out of each fund; and beginning and ending balances for the preceding year, the current year, and the ensuing year—as well as a tax levy request for the ensuing year. Public notice must be given of a hearing at which citizens may comment on the budget, and the county commission must determine by October 1 the tax levy that is necessary to balance the budget. The budget must be forwarded to the state auditor by January 1.[44]

State law includes neither expenditure limits nor provisions for bankruptcy or receivership of local governments. There is a provision, however, that requires municipalities that are dissolving to pay their debts. If there is not adequate money, the county commission will levy a tax on all taxable property within the boundaries of the dissolving jurisdiction.[45]

Figure 2 shows the expenditure patterns for fifty-three North Dakota municipalities between 1984 and 1993.

Fig. 2 North Dakota City Expenditures, 1984–1993

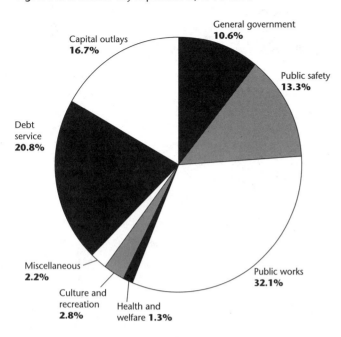

- General government **10.6%**
- Capital outlays **16.7%**
- Public safety **13.3%**
- Debt service **20.8%**
- Miscellaneous **2.2%**
- Culture and recreation **2.8%**
- Health and welfare **1.3%**
- Public works **32.1%**

Source: "Revenue and Expenditure Assessment of Fifty-three North Dakota Cities," compiled for the North Dakota League of Cities by August Ternes, Office of the State Auditor, 1993.

State Government Grants-in-Aid to Localities

Local governments in North Dakota receive between one-third and two-thirds of their budgets from the state. Apart from state aid to local schools, the major sources of state transfers are the state aid distribution fund, which combines monies from various sources: taxes on tobacco products, oil taxes, and other tax income.[46] Thirty-seven percent of the money raised from the highway tax is distributed to counties on the basis of the number of vehicles registered in the county. Of that amount, 27 percent is distributed to incorporated municipalities on the basis of a population formula.[47] By constitutional requirement, the highway money must be used for highway construction and maintenance.[48]

When the state legislature banned localities from imposing personal property taxes, it began providing state money to help replace those funds; the replacement funds are roughly equivalent to the amount that would have been raised in 1970, augmented by a growth factor. The replacement funds and state revenue-sharing funds are disbursed to counties, municipalities, and townships: half on the basis of population and half on the basis of the dollar amount of tax levies on real property in the jurisdiction. All money from a levy of 1.5 mills on tobacco products is distributed twice a year to municipalities on the basis of population. There are no limits on how any of this money should be spent, but the state may require reports on the local disbursement of the funds.[49]

Unfunded Mandates

Most unfunded mandates are federal requirements administered by the state, and the majority affect service areas, such as health care and water and sewer services. Compliance appears to be high. Localities are required to file a financial report with the state auditor's office.[50]

Access to Local Government

Local Elections

As noted earlier, North Dakota government is very accessible to its citizens. Because of the small number of people in the state, citizens are often personally acquainted with their government officials. This is certainly the case in most municipalities, where the government is run by friends and neighbors who can be reached at the local cafe if there are complaints.

Although municipalities are permitted to require voter registration for local elections, North Dakota is the only state in the union that requires no registration for any state election. Any citizen who meets the minimum requirements set by federal law may vote in North Dakota, except for convicted felons and those judged mentally incompetent. State law specifies in detail the procedures for both municipal and county elections, including the dates, the location and staffing of polling places, and the order of the names on the ballot; state law also prohibits the use of party identification on the ballots. To be nominated for municipal office, a candidate must submit a petition signed by at least 10 percent of the vote last cast for that office, with the total not to exceed 300 signatures.

Citizen Controls over Actions of Local Officials

In 1989, the North Dakota legislature extended recall to local officials. Within a local jurisdiction, a petition signed by 25 percent of the vote last cast for governor will force a special election within forty to forty-five days. Initiatives and referendums are permitted in municipalities that have the commission or the modern council form of government, and in municipalities with five- to seven-member councils. They are also permitted in home rule municipalities that operate under other forms of council government. Home rule counties may permit initiative and referendum. All meetings of local officials must be open to the public, and only some personnel records may be closed.

State-Local Relations

North Dakota's local governments have substantial freedom to seek local solutions for local problems. Although the state has elaborate statutory restrictions on local government autonomy, state law specifies many exceptions. Often, state restrictions can be overridden by a majority vote of local citizens. In addition, home rule is available to both municipalities and counties.

Most important, statutory restrictions were loosened substantially in 1993, with the passage of the Tool Chest Bill. Financial controls on political subdivisions remained unchanged, but the Tool Chest Bill provided local governments with many options for modifying government size and structure and vast opportunities for intergovernmental cooperation, even across state and national borders. In North Dakota, the level of local government autonomy is determined less by state control than by local government capacity and initiative. The limitations are obvious for the 309 of the 361 municipalities with populations of less than 1,000.

Both the history and culture of the state and the small size of its local jurisdictions encourage responsiveness to the people, most of whom have traditionally preferred a caretaker government with minimal responsibilities. Few of the many local governments have taken advantage of home rule, but some have made extensive use of the provisions of the Tool Chest Bill. Nevertheless, it is likely that many political subdivisions are unaware of the flexibility afforded by that legislation.

More than one observer has wondered whether there is any reason for the continued existence of the state of North Dakota.[51] Nevertheless, local communities are attempting to reverse the state's pattern of population decline, and economic development is probably essential to such efforts. Indeed, in recent years, the major change in local government has been an increase in the number of special districts established to encourage economic development. Home rule also plays a role in economic development efforts: the number of home rule municipalities expanded rapidly in the 1990s, and much of the incentive was the ability to impose a sales tax, some part of which is usually dedicated to economic development. The head of the state economic development and finance department points to home rule as a factor in the success of economic development initiatives.[52]

Despite their increasing importance, economic development efforts have the potential to lead to conflict, as residents who are opposed to change square off against those who argue that North Dakota's communities must change to survive. And because of the importance of home rule to economic development, there may be more conflict over proposed home rule charters in the future.

Notes

1. Lloyd B. Omdahl, *Governing North Dakota 1999–2001* (Grand Forks, N.D.: Bureau of Governmental Affairs, 1999), 71.

2. Lloyd B. Omdahl, *Governing North Dakota 1997–1999* (Grand Forks, N.D.: Bureau of Governmental Affairs, 1997), 81.

3. Robert P. Wilkins and Wynona H. Wilkins, *North Dakota* (New York: Norton, 1977), 110.

4. Wilkins and Wilkins, *North Dakota,* 113.

5. The North Dakota Century Code is the name given to the compilation of state laws as amended through the last legislative session.

6. Once the committee is created, it is required only to "consider" certain changes, such as the creation of joint powers agreements between municipalities, counties, tribal governments, school boards, and park boards within the state and in other states and provinces. Under the terms of the Tool Chest Bill, local governments can change their form or size, shift their responsibilities to other governments, change or share elected or appointed offices, and change elective offices to appointive ones. Other political subdivisions—such as townships, park districts, and school districts—are not required to consider changes in their structures or responsibilities but are allowed to make many of the same changes or agreements if they so desire.

7. North Dakota Century Code, 40-05.1-06.

8. Ibid., 40-05.1-06.

9. R. A. Schempp, city manager, Minot, North Dakota, letter to Lloyd Omdahl, July 15, 1991.

10. North Dakota Constitution, Article VIII, section 6.1.

11. North Dakota Century Code, 57-15-14.

12. Ibid., 40-04.1.

13. Omdahl, *Governing North Dakota 1999–2001,* 94.

14. North Dakota Century Code, 40-02.

15. Ibid., 40-51.2.

16. Ibid., 11-11-01, 11-09.1.

17. Unless the county has home rule or exercises the right to make the determination under the powers of the Tool Chest Bill, the state determines whether an office is elective or appointive.

18. North Dakota Century Code, Title 11; Omdahl, *Governing North Dakota 1999–2001,* 76–77.

19. North Dakota Century Code, 11-09.

20. Ibid., 58-02-01.

21. Ibid., 58-04-01.

22. Ibid., 40-47-01.1.

23. Omdahl, *Governing North Dakota 1999–2001,* 81.

24. Ibid., 74.

25. North Dakota Century Code, 58-03.

26. Ibid., 40-49-02.

27. Ibid., 40-33.2, 40-33.1, 40-61.

28. Ibid., 40-44.

29. Ibid., 40-11, 11-11, 40-08, 44-02.

30. Ibid., 48-01.1-03; Ken Vein, director, Public Works Department, city of Grand Forks, interview with authors, January 31, 1996.

31. North Dakota Century Code, 40-47, 11-33.

32. Ibid., 40-57.

33. Ibid., 40-57.4, 40-57.4-03.

34. Ibid., 40-57.1-03, 40-57.1-04.

35. Ibid., 40-57.2, 40-57.2-04.

36. Ibid., 40-58-10, 40-58-20, 40-58-20.1.

37. During its 1995 session, the state legislature defeated a proposal to limit the local sales tax to no more than 1 percent.

38. Omdahl, *Governing North Dakota 1999–2001,* 102; North Dakota Century Code, 57-11-03, 15-12-01, 15-13-04.

39. North Dakota Century Code, 57-15-08, 57-15-10.

40. Ibid., 57-15-06, 57-15-06.7.

41. Ibid., 21-03.

42. "Revenue and Expenditure Assessment of Fifty-three Selected North Dakota Cities," compiled for the North Dakota League of Cities by August Ternes, Office of the State Auditor, 1993.

43. North Dakota Century Code, 40-40.

44. North Dakota Century Code, 11-23.

45. North Dakota Century Code, 40-53.1.

46. Omdahl, *Governing North Dakota 1999–2001,* 102.

47. North Dakota Century Code, 40-21.

48. North Dakota Constitution, Article X, section 11.

49. North Dakota Century Code, 54-27, 57-36-31, 54-27-20.1, 54-27-20.2.

50. John Schmisek, auditor, city of Grand Forks, interview with authors, January, 29, 1996; and Vein, interview.

51. See, for instance, Jon Margolis, "The Reopening of the Frontier," *New York Times Magazine,* 15 October 1995, pp. 51–57.

52. *Grand Forks Herald,* 21 January 1996, p. F8.

OHIO

Jack L. Dustin

The author acknowledges the assistance of John E. Gotherman, Ohio Municipal League; Robin DeBell, law director, city of Springfield; A. J. Wagner, auditor, Montgomery County; Stephen Metzger, treasurer, Clark County; Larry Hussman; and Jesse Lightle, research assistant, Center for Urban and Public Affairs.

The Ohio Constitution gives all municipalities, small or large, home rule powers to exercise local self-government, enact regulations, and provide utilities. Counties and townships also may adopt a form of home rule under the general laws of Ohio. Home rule played an important role in the development of inventive, industrious, and prosperous communities throughout the state. It is also fair to claim that home rule authority in Ohio influenced the development of local self-government throughout the United States. Passage of Ohio's home rule amendment in 1912 permitted the city of Dayton to install a city-manager form of government one year later. The "Dayton Plan" became a model for governance across the nation.[1] Cincinnati expanded local self-government to include land-use development when it introduced a municipal master plan and zoning a few years later. Cincinnati's actions inspired the U.S. Department of Commerce to establish a national standard for city planning in 1928.[2] For these reasons and others, Ohio is frequently called the "home rule state."

Governmental Setting

After Ohio became a state in 1803, its policy makers and administrators almost single-mindedly concentrated on internal improvements—canals, railroads, and highways—to create wealth for the state's citizens. They implemented their growth policies through local initiatives.[3] The state's policy of giving municipal governments great freedom to decide issues affecting their development complemented their diverse geography, populations, resources, and industries.

State development incentives and home rule reinforced extensive industrialization and urbanization. Seven major cities had emerged in Ohio by 1900, and until 1960 they developed at amazing rates. Industries in Akron, Cincinnati, Cleveland, Columbus, Dayton, Toledo, and Youngstown ranked among the nation's most important through much of the twentieth century.[4]

In 1990 Ohio's population of 10,847,000 made Ohio the seventh largest state. Eighty percent of the state population resided in sixteen metropolitan areas. State policies and local self-government at first favored the development of central cities, but new technology and growth politics shifted the advantages to the suburbs. By the 1970s growth in Ohio's major central cities had all but stopped. More than 725,000 people migrated from five of the seven central cities between 1960 and 1990.[5] Only Columbus and Toledo did not lose population after 1960, primarily because they annexed open land ahead of the migration. Extensive migration and suburban growth in the 1990s led to the development of twenty-three cities on the "edge" of these urban centers.[6] Ohio today comprises 88 counties, 942 municipalities, 1,314 townships, 666 school districts, and 513 special districts, of which 267 possess taxing powers.[7]

Within the last two decades, communities outside of Ohio's central cities and older suburbs increased their political influence as people and businesses migrated there. The migration of households and industry outward, often encouraged by tax abatements, road construction, and state development incentive programs, has been associated with social and economic problems in central cities, the decline of older suburbs, and the loss of family farms. In the mid-1990s interest groups representing central cities, mature suburbs, and family farms joined together to challenge Ohio's development policies.[8] Should their political coalition survive, they will likely also challenge home rule authority over growth and development.[9]

Home Rule in Ohio

Historical Development

In 1803 Ohio became the seventeenth state of the Union and the first state to be organized out of the Northwest Territory. As provided in the Articles of Confederation of 1785, surveyors laid out the territory in townships of six-mile squares. Two years later the Northwest Ordinance of 1787 provided for the creation of ten counties in Ohio.[10]

The Ohio Constitution provided for township government and established its form and powers through general laws. Townships are unincorporated areas and divisions of counties. Three elected trustees govern each township. Counties encompass townships and are political divisions of the state. They enforce state laws and implement state policy. General laws prescribe for county government a commission of three elected officials and eight additional elected offices.[11] In 1961, and again in 1967, the General Assembly amended the general laws to allow counties to appoint a chief executive, to vary the size of commissions, and to adopt various methods of electing commissioners and county officers. Both counties and townships may exercise home rule powers if electors of the jurisdictions approve charters.[12]

The 1803 constitution did not provide for municipal government. Without standing under the law, municipalities required individual chartering and special acts by the General Assembly in order to exercise any authority. The state addressed municipal powers in its 1851 constitutional convention. Voters approved amendments that provided for the organization of cities and villages and uniform general laws pertaining to municipalities throughout the state. When the General Assembly carried out this charge in 1852, Ohio became the first state to have a municipal incorporation law. State statutes abolished the practice of chartering municipalities individually and designated municipalities as first or second class. The General Assembly also set restrictions on local government structure, taxation, and authority to incur debt.[13]

Although Ohio established a model municipal law, the state legislature continued its practice of adopting special legislation. The General Assembly in 1869 rewrote the state statutes to correct this problem. Legislators repealed 185 special acts and adopted a municipal code containing 61 chapters and 732 sections. However, the statutes did not completely eliminate special legislation for another thirty years.[14]

In 1902 the Ohio Supreme Court voided the state's municipal code in *State ex rel. Attorney Gen. v. Beacom*. The General Assembly again turned to the issue of how to authorize municipal governance. The drafters of the code adopted limited self-government based on the legal precedents established in Ohio cases, such as *Bloom v. City of Xenia* (1877), *Ravenna v. Pennsylvania* (1887), and *Markley v. Mineral City* (1898). The courts in these rulings followed Dillon's Rule, contending that municipal powers should always be denied unless expressly granted in state law. However, arguments for greater powers of self-government over local matters continued to mount. In 1910 Ohioans overwhelmingly voted to hold a state convention to consider home rule and other amendments to the constitution. The constitutional convention put forty-one amendments before voters, and they approved thirty-three; one, Article XVIII, became known as the "home rule amendment."[15]

Definition of Home Rule

Delegates to the 1912 constitutional convention had three purposes in mind when they drafted the home rule amendment: to liberate municipalities from the control of the state such that municipal home rule powers would prevail over state laws in local affairs; to allow municipalities to own and operate utilities; and to grant charter municipalities the right to exercise self-determination over their form of government.[16]

Convention debates centered on terminology and how to distinguish "local affairs" from "the welfare of the state as a whole." Ultimately, the drafters of the home rule amendment left many details out and the language ambiguous. This decision meant state courts would play a significant role in defining home rule in Ohio. Yet, protected by the state constitution, municipal self-government has remained strong since 1912.[17]

Section 3 of Article XVIII defines the principle of home rule in Ohio:

Municipalities shall have authority to exercise all powers of local self-government and to adopt and enforce within their limits such local police, sanitary and other similar regulations, as are not in conflict with general laws.

The vagueness of section 3 soon led to court rulings. For example, municipalities did not know when home rule powers became effective. In *Village of Perrysburg v. Ridgeway* (1923) the courts found that home rule powers were self-executing. This interpretation meant municipalities could exercise home rule powers without adopting a charter or receiving authority through a statute.[18] Another important point of contention involved the powers of local self-government. The courts ruled these powers were confined to affairs that were purely local, that is, without extraterritorial effect.[19] Over the decades, the courts have articulated more clearly the limitations of home rule powers. The limitations include taxing, fixing and regulating hours of labor, creating courts and appointing judges, eliminating merit civil service, denying citizens rights to exercise initiative and referendum legislation, assuming debt or carrying deficits, and utilizing public resources and exercising powers for purposes not "public" in nature.

Structural Features

Section 1 of Article XVIII states that every municipal corporation shall be either a city or a village and that all municipalities having a population of 5,000 or more shall be cities. As required by section 2 of Article XVIII, general laws provide for the incorporation and the government of municipalities. New villages may be created by petition signed by a majority of landowners. The petition is presented to the county commissioners, who verify that the proposed village incorporates an area of at least two square miles and has a population density of at least 600 persons per square mile. The proposed village must also be at least three miles from an existing municipality. This provision may be ignored if the existing municipality approves the incorporation or does not have an interest in annexing the territory. The Ohio Revised Code, or state statutes, also allows a township to incorporate as a city within three miles of a municipality if its population is 25,000 thousand or greater.[20]

Ohio courts have ruled that the reclassification of a village as a city is not self-executing. The Ohio Revised Code specifies three methods by which a village may verify that it has become a city: the decennial U.S. Census; a special federal census; and if 5,000 residents register or vote in a general election.[21]

In *Morris v. Roseman* (1954) the courts found that Article XVIII section 2, of the state constitution gives the General Assembly the authority to set the procedures and organization of noncharter municipalities. For example, the Ohio Revised Code details how noncharter municipalities, by a vote of the electorate, may adopt or repeal one of three forms of government: the city-manager plan, commissioner plan, or federal plan. Noncharter governments may not modify their structure without statutory authorization, including a vote to repeal the optional forms of government. In the case of charter municipalities, the charter prevails over the procedures and the organization of local government detailed in general laws.[22]

Today, 228 of the state's 942 municipalities have home rule charters. Of the 228, 91 chartered a manager-council form of government. Separating city from village charter municipalities, 72 cities in Ohio govern through the manager-council form of government, 97 govern through the mayor-council form, and the remaining 6 employ an administrator to support their council.[23]

Section 7 of Article XVIII authorizes a municipality to adopt a charter, and the charter will prevail unless the power of self-government concerns matters not purely local (as noted above). Charter and noncharter municipalities exercise substantive municipal powers, incurring debt, levying taxes (subject to limitations), imposing eminent domain, and so forth. In the case of charter municipalities, substantive and procedural powers of local self-government will prevail over state laws. Noncharter municipalities also may exercise substantive powers of local self-government, but with respect to procedure and form and structure, the statutes prevail. However, police powers are a different matter altogether. Charter and noncharter municipalities may not exercise police powers in conflict with state law. If local police powers conflict with the general laws of Ohio, the state laws prevail, regardless of whether a charter exists. A conflict exists when the local exercise of police power permits or licenses activities prohibited by the Ohio Revised Code or when the code permits or licenses activities prohibited by the municipal charter.[24]

The idea of conflict between the state and a municipality is important. The constitutional framers and courts did not want municipalities to be autonomous.[25] They sought to establish a complementary relationship between the state and the municipalities. Section 3 of Article XVIII granted powers "as are not in conflict with general laws." State courts have ruled that this phrase applies only to police powers. As might be suspected, differentiating between a local matter and a state concern, or determining if a conflict exists between the municipal and state exercise of a police power leads to frequent tests in Ohio courts.

Home rule gives all municipalities in Ohio equal standing when dealing with one another. Nonetheless, intermunicipal disputes do occur and bring into focus questions of extraterritorial powers. Home rule does not give municipalities extraterritorial powers. The courts have consistently upheld the principle of "no outside effect" to define the scope of municipal powers. The modern approach is that if there is extraterritorial effect, then the courts balance the interests of the municipality and the state. Given this principle, Ohio law considers boundary changes to be matters for the General Assembly to determine. Boundary changes involve annexations of land from townships (unincorporated areas) to municipalities; mergers of unincorporated and municipal governments; consolidations of municipalities; annexations of land that involve municipalities and unincorporated governments from more than one county; and annexation and detachment of land between municipalities.[26] The fact that municipal boundaries may extend into neighboring counties illustrates the territorial scope of home rule.

State law establishes three methods for making boundary changes. The first method allows a majority of adult freeholders from a territory contiguous to a municipality to petition the board of county commissioners for annexation. The second, or municipal petition method, requires the annexing municipality to file a petition with the board of county commissioners and requires that electors in the area to be annexed vote in a referendum. A majority vote of the electors is needed, and if rejected, no other efforts to annex the territory can be taken for five years. However, this does not preclude a different annexation or a petition from resident freeholders. The third method concerns two adjoining municipalities and territory inhabited by no more than five voters. This method allows municipalities to change their boundaries by ordinance.[27]

Although municipalities may not exercise powers of local self-government beyond their boundaries, they do have standing in extraterritorial matters. Municipalities may carry out municipal public purposes outside of their boundaries. In *McDonald v. City of Columbus* the courts gave Columbus immunity from county zoning laws even though the land in question (a city park) was located outside of its boundaries. The courts have also recognized municipal interests in protecting water lines, property acquisition, and platting territory outside municipal boundaries.[28] Until 1997 state statutes granted extraterritorial preemption to cities in platting property three miles from their boundaries and to villages in platting one and one-half miles from their boundaries.

The Ohio Constitution, as rewritten in 1851 and amended in 1933, grants the legislature the power to enact laws to guide the organization and the government of counties as "creatures of the state." The constitution does not preclude the state from increasing or decreasing the number of counties. State law limits the legislative authority of counties; ordinances passed by counties may not conflict with the legislative powers of townships and municipalities.[29]

In 1933 the state amended its constitution to grant counties home rule powers. County home rule may be achieved in two ways. The first method requires that 8 percent of the county electorate sign a petition to place the question of home rule on the ballot or that county commissioners place the question on the ballot. If the vote is in favor of home rule, then voters elect a charter commission to formulate the charter, which goes before the electorate of the county. The second method permits citizens to draft a home rule charter, and after 10 percent of the electorate has signed a petition calling for a vote, the charter is put to a vote.[30]

There are two types of county home rule powers. Home rule grants counties some or all powers given to municipalities or it preserves the county role and reorganizes the structure. Counties that adopt home rule with municipal powers become a "hybrid" city-county. This city-county may exercise municipal powers as permitted in the Ohio Revised Code either concurrent with or exclusive of other municipalities. Concurrent powers do not supersede those of municipalities and townships. Approving a concurrent county charter requires a majority vote in the entire county. Exclusive powers means the authority of the county supersedes that of municipalities and townships in areas where the county exercises its powers. Exclusive county home rule requires a majority vote in (1) the county; (2) the largest municipality; (3) the county outside of the largest municipality; and (4) the majority of the county's municipalities and townships. These conditions apply to counties with populations less than 500,000. Counties with populations greater than 500,000 must meet majorities only under the first, second, and third provisions. So far, only one county in Ohio has adopted concurrent home rule authority.[31]

The General Assembly provides for the election of township trustees and defines their powers. The Ohio Revised Code was amended in 1991 to grant townships limited home rule powers. Home rule townships may pass ordinances that do not conflict with general laws, are purely local in nature, and impose civil fines for violations. Townships may establish, revise, or impose building codes as long as the changes do not conflict with county codes. Generally, townships may exercise powers necessary to ensure the safety, health, and welfare of the community, although township actions may not contradict general laws or municipal or county regulations, resolutions, and ordinances.[32]

If they adopt home rule, townships lose important services provided by counties. Planning, engineering, legal counsel, and police are four governmental services that counties typically provide for townships. However, townships without home rule may choose to provide for their own police, and they often do.[33] Since home rule became permissible in 1991, eight townships have voted for home rule, one of which subsequently repealed home rule because it was too great of a fiscal burden.[34]

Functions of Local Government

Functional Responsibilities

Home rule prevents the state legislature from becoming involved in everyday local affairs. Chartered home rule municipalities are free from state statutes in two areas: form of government and governing procedures. Charters allow municipalities, for example, to establish and organize departments, commissions, boards, and other divisions as they wish. Municipalities may regulate their communities provided the regulations are not in conflict with state police powers or other constitutional rights and due process guarantees. In general, charters do not increase the magnitude of local powers; rather, they give local officials and citizens the ability to decide for themselves the organization and processes and to address matters that either are not mentioned in the Ohio Revised Code or are treated differently in the charter.

Municipalities may levy taxes and incur debt, subject to limitations, as permitted by state law; arrest and jail individuals under their own ordinances; and provide fire protection, utilities, libraries, hospitals, corrections, and docks, wharves, and piers. They also have the authority to construct and maintain streets. However, the courts have reserved a public interest in access to municipal streets for utilities and control over streets in times of emergency. Municipalities may construct public buildings, airports, industrial parks, parking lots, and access ramps to state and federal highways. They plan, zone, and regulate land uses and may redevelop blighted areas and provide incentives for economic development.[35]

One of the key powers extended to municipalities by the constitutional framers was that of providing utilities. Municipalities may individually or jointly own, lease, and operate utilities. They may exercise extraterritorial powers to acquire land, condemn property for right-of-way, and protect their utilities. Municipalities may fix reasonable rates, although the courts have decided the reasonableness of rates as "the point where they [utility rates] have become taxes."[36]

Home rule allows municipalities to offer or refuse utility services outside of their boundaries. The state constitution does not identify or restrict who may receive municipally owned or operated utilities. The constitution limits the disposal of surplus services to 50 percent of the total capacity of the utility, but the 50-percent standard does not apply to water or sewer services. In

State ex rel. McCann v. City of Defiance the courts upheld the principle that the state may not legislate limits or place restrictions on the municipalities that own or operate public utilities beyond those specified in the constitution. Despite confusion about how to measure 50 percent of a service, and despite complaints from neighboring governments who want utility service or lower rates, this basic home rule power has not been amended.[37]

Counties, too, may provide utilities such as solid waste disposal and sewerage. In the 1950s state legislation gave counties the authority to enter into service partnerships with municipalities, special districts, townships, or other taxing authorities. Concerned about economic growth and solid waste problems in 1989, the state once again expanded the scope of county affairs. The General Assembly called upon counties to organize solid waste management districts and to develop solid waste management plans in collaboration with municipalities and townships. At about the same time, the state gave counties the authority to create economic development programs.[38]

The county carries out state policy and administers state funding programs for local governments through its offices. The county comprises eleven elected offices: three commissioners, clerk of courts, treasurer, recorder, prosecutor, sheriff, engineer, auditor, and coroner. Although these county officials are fundamentally equal in political terms, their administrative duties, salaries, and terms of office vary. For example, the county commissioners adopt the budget for the other offices, decide tax levy and bond questions for county purposes, and administer state road, health, solid waste, and sewer policies. Commissioners also may exercise administrative authority over some portion of federal Community Development Block Grant funds.[39]

The state retains authority over all courts. In addition to the state supreme court, appeals court, common pleas court (civil, criminal, probate, domestic relations, and juvenile divisions) and court of claims, there are municipal, county, and mayor courts. Neither municipalities nor counties have the authority to create courts or appoint judges. Counties keep court records and provide for the maintenance of courts. Only the General Assembly has the constitutional authority to create courts, appoint judges, and define jurisdictions.[40]

The state also provides for special districts. By state statute, twenty types of special purpose districts may be created. General laws provide for the establishment, governing body, and financing (for example, taxing authority) of the special districts. Each type of special district must be specified in the Ohio Revised Code and verified by a court, county, township, or municipal authority. Municipalities may create or participate in twelve different types of special districts: arts and culture (the newest type), conservancy, ambulance, park, fire, solid waste, transit, port authority, joint economic development zones, community development, water, and sanitary districts.[41]

Special districts provide the clearest example of interlocal cooperation. For example, the state requires the creation of a city health district and a general health district comprising the townships and villages in a county. However, cities may elect to combine the city district with the general health district. The state constitution permits municipalities to transfer their powers to a consenting county, given voter approval. Less controversial, the state authorized in 1975 the creation of councils of government. One year later, the General Assembly amended the Ohio Revised Code to allow municipal and county authorities to create "commissions" to plan transportation development. Local governments may also lend their credit to one another.[42]

Ad hoc cooperation occurs regularly among local governments. Dozens of interlocal, public-private, and multicounty organizations exist in Ohio. The newest forms of interlocal cooperation include tax sharing and public safety.[43] There is also some evidence that local governments have begun to act more regionally in planning. Over the last few years, several countywide comprehensive plans have been completed, and numerous multigovernmental economic development organizations have been created.[44]

Administrative Discretion

Charter municipalities may simplify or change procedural matters to achieve more effective governance. Procedures for elections, at-large or ward representation, the number of council or commission members, ordinances, and referendum votes are among the areas in which municipalities gain options through chartering. Furthermore, charters may easily be repealed or amended.

The constitution grants charter and noncharter municipalities the authority to fix and regulate hours of work as well as establish minimum wage and welfare benefits, but since these are police powers, the local exercise is invalid if it conflicts with state law. State statutes provide procedures for administering civil service provisions in noncharter cities and in those cities that are silent on the civil service or merit system. The constitution requires that the appointment and promotion of state, city, county, and school employees be based on merit and fitness. Villages are exempt from this law. Charter cities may simplify the administration of this civil service requirement, although they may not abolish it.[45]

The courts have specifically limited home rule powers in two areas of administration. In *Board of Trustees of Pension Fund v. Board of Trustees of Relief Fund* the courts ruled that the General Assembly could create a police and fire pension fund. The courts reasoned that this issue fell under the "statewide effect" principle.[46] A second limitation of home rule in personnel matters came in a 1989 case before the Ohio Supreme Court. The court said municipalities had to abide by state laws requiring binding arbitration in municipal police and fire labor disputes (*Rocky River v. State Employment Relations Board*).[47]

Charter municipalities may adopt specific contracting and purchasing procedures. Noncharter municipalities follow state statutes. Regardless of whether they have a charter, municipalities may not delegate legislative or governmental power through a contract. Also, all public officials and employees must abide by conflict-of-interest and other ethical behavior standards established in the Ohio Revised Code (Chapters 102 and 2921) and the Ohio Ethics Law of 1973. For noncharter municipalities, state statutes require bidding procedures on contracts exceeding $10,000 and identify authority and administration responsibilities. Other provisions address intergovernmental contracts, delay costs, cost overruns, payment details, prevailing wage requirements, bonding, evidence of nondiscrimination, competitive bidding, certification of fiscal officers, separate bids by trade, and emergency purchases.[48]

Home rule permits municipalities to plan and zone property. Charter and noncharter municipalities plan and control land use without state approval. The state legislature by statute set forth the procedures for preparing a master plan in 1915, for zoning properties in 1920, and for subdivision and regional planning in 1923. In 1926 the U.S. Supreme Court upheld Ohio's grant of authority to municipalities and established a precedent for the nation (*Village of Euclid v. Amber Realty Co.*). In later years Ohio extended planning powers to regional commissions (1935) and to counties and townships (1947).[49]

Economic Development

In the second half of the twentieth century, Ohio state courts and public officials began to take a broader view of development. Federal programs to address blight and disinvestment in central cities led to the creation of community development organizations. In 1975 Dayton commissioners divided the city into six "priority boards" to increase citizen participation in setting priorities for services and capital improvements and to respond to neighborhood needs. These "mini-city halls" institutionalized the citizen participation mandated in federal Model Cities programs.[50]

Ohio also tackled other development problems in the 1970s, such as environmental protection and rural poverty. The state amended its statutes requiring environmental impact statements; pollution falls under the police power and "statewide concern" doctrine. For example, state officials regulate environmental compliance at municipal, county, and district wastewater treatment plants. Furthermore, in *State v. City of Bowling Green* (1974) the Ohio Supreme Court rejected the argument that municipalities were independent from the state in regard to environmental matters. The court found that home rule did not preclude the state's sovereign authority over extraterritorial matters. In this case, the city of Bowling Green was liable for damages related to the pollution of a stream.[51]

Ohio is agricultural as well as industrial, and state economic development programs have broadly distributed development authority among local governments. Typically, the state legislature has expanded urban programs over time to suburban and rural communities. For example, Ohio amended legislation enabling cities to abate property and other taxes so that any locality could promote development through tax abatement.[52] Enterprise zones also illustrate this point. There are now at least 247 enterprise zones in Ohio. The zones may be as small as a single firm or as large as an entire political jurisdiction.[53] In effect, any community in the state, rich or poor, may establish an enterprise zone.

The General Assembly has created twelve major economic development programs. Of the twelve, seven come under the direct authority of local governments. In addition to enterprise zones, the state allows municipalities, counties, and townships to create "community reinvestment areas." These areas differ from enterprise zones in that they must include residential properties. Again, tax exemptions are the primary incentive for development.[54]

One other development program should be mentioned. Voters in 1990 amended the Ohio Constitution to make housing clearly a public purpose. The General Assembly then introduced programs to finance and plan affordable housing. These programs fill part of the gap left by federal programs and support the principle that all communities must provide their fair share of affordable housing.[55] This example as well as the others above illustrate the expanding application of the principle of "statewide effect" to limit home rule authority.

Fiscal Autonomy of Local Governments

Local Revenues

Municipal revenues come from locally levied taxes and fees, state taxes and fees shared with municipalities, special local assessments, bonds, federal aid, and special state grants and financing. Article XVIII, sections 6 and 13, of the constitution give the General Assembly the authority to regulate and restrict municipal powers to tax and incur debt. Municipal authority to tax property is further limited to 1 percent of true value unless a higher rate is approved by voters. Local governments may ask voters to approve a levy that exceeds this limitation if the levy meets provisions required by law or if the levy satisfies provisions required by a municipal charter.

The Ohio Constitution does not enumerate substantive powers to tax. However, the courts have held that the power to tax is a valid exercise of local self-government under Article XVIII, section 3, of the Ohio Constitution. The constitution also allows the state, by general laws, to regulate powers of taxation and debt. Not surprisingly, municipal taxing authority frequently has been challenged in the courts. The Ohio Supreme Court dealt with this issue soon after voters adopted the home rule amendment. The court wrote: "There can be no doubt that the grant of authority to exercise all powers of local government includes the power to tax."[56]

Municipalities may not tax state properties; yet, state em-

Table 1. Municipal Revenue Sources in Ohio, 1999

Revenue source	Percentage of total revenues
Federal government	27%
Income tax	23
Sales tax	19
Charges for services	18
Licenses, fees, and permits	4
Other[a]	9

Source: Ohio Budgetary Financial Report for the fiscal year ending June 30, 1999.

a. Other revenue includes interest revenue, gains on the sale of investments, sale of assets, rents and royalties, escheats, contributions and donations from private sources, and other financing sources.

ployees must pay local income taxes, and the state must pay for municipal utilities consumed on its properties (*McConnell v. City of Columbus*, 1961). The General Assembly reserves the right of budgetary oversight and limits what municipalities may tax. On the other hand, the constitution does not limit the state's authority to influence municipal taxes. For example, the state may decide to exempt low-rent properties from municipal property taxes; in *Chase v. Board of Tax Appeals* the court allowed the state to exempt metropolitan housing authority properties.

Municipal-levied taxes include property, income, lodging, and motor vehicle license taxes (see Table 1). Municipal fees are for such things as utilities, parking, licenses, and building permits and inspections. The property tax, which has historical precedent and is mentioned in the constitution, has become a secondary source of municipal revenues since the 1960s. The constitutional convention of 1851 required uniform rules for property taxation and established the principle of exemption for churches and schools. In 1902, when the state legislature wrote a new municipal code, it terminated the state's use of property tax. Thus, property became a "local" source of revenue. Property tax in Ohio is levied on public utility property (real and personal), tangible personal property, and real property. In 1910 the state established separate laws for utility properties and created a Tax Commission that would assess these properties. The Tax Commission was replaced by the Department of Taxation and a Board of Tax Appeals in 1939, which supervise all local property taxation and resolve tax disputes.[57]

In 1929 a constitutional amendment separated tangible property from real property and limited tangible property to business. Tangible property includes machinery, equipment, and inventories. Therefore, it is primarily a tax on business operations. Tax reductions on real property (land and buildings) do not apply to tangible property. Since the late 1960s the General Assembly has gradually lowered taxable value and increased credit. Tangible property tax exemptions are in place for energy conservation equipment, property used in agriculture and in enterprise and foreign trade zones, and property shipped to Ohio for storage.[58]

The basic characteristics of real-property taxation were re-

vised by constitutional and statute amendments in 1972. The General Assembly set the tax value at 35 percent of true value, established a ten mill limit without voter approval, and required the county auditor to make annual property value adjustments and reappraise all properties every six years. Other historical changes illustrate the state's ability to influence local property tax revenues. Concern for poverty in the 1960s led to homestead exemptions in 1971 and to eight additional refinements. A 1973 constitutional amendment required valuation of agricultural land according to "current use." Tax revolts and inflation caused the General Assembly to roll back residential property taxes in 1979 and 1980. In 1982 legislators authorized property tax exemptions in enterprise zones.[59]

The state's decentralized governmental organization and broad authorization to tax make the system very complex. State and local units of government share revenues from some taxes, such as income, gasoline, and motor vehicle taxes. Taxing authority even overlaps political boundaries. In some cases, six governmental entities tax property within a single municipality (for example, two school districts, community college, township, county, and municipality).

Amendments to the state constitution passed in 1912 opened the door for taxing income. The state began to tax wages in 1933. Toledo became the first municipality to levy a personal income tax, in 1946. In 1957 the General Assembly adopted a uniform code for the municipal income tax. Currently, the state permits municipalities to tax incomes up to 1 percent without voter approval. The state has adopted two major revisions since 1957: in 1992 it allowed income tax credits for job creation; and in 1993 it allowed municipalities to share income tax revenues with school districts. Ohio also permits school districts to levy an income tax (passed in 1981). Currently, 120 school districts tax incomes at rates ranging from 0.25 percent to 1.50 percent.[60]

More than five hundred municipalities tax income. The income tax rate ranges from 0.25 percent to 2.5 percent.[61] On average, income taxes account for 33 percent of city revenues; only user fees generate more, at 34 percent (see Table 1). In contrast, property tax produces only about 9 percent of total city revenues. The state grants four major income tax exemptions: military pay; income from religious and educational institutions; profits of public utilities except long distance telephone companies; and interest on dividends.[62]

The state shares with municipalities revenues from its income tax and from taxes on sales, corporate franchises, and public utilities. It also shares revenues from fees and licenses charged on motor vehicles, gasoline, estates, house trailers, grain, liquor, and pawnbrokers. Part of the state's portion of sales tax (the other part is levied by counties) is transferred to two local government revenue funds that are distributed by formula to local governments. Finally, municipalities are also permitted to assess properties for public improvements such as sidewalks and road repair. State statutes specify the maximum assessment.[63]

Ohio limits municipal borrowing and debt as well as the power to tax. Section 13 of the home rule amendment (Article XVIII) gives the General Assembly the authority to limit municipal debt. State laws detail the procedure municipalities must follow to borrow money.[64] Charter municipalities may further limit debt by establishing tax rate ceilings and dedicating tax revenues to specific expenditures. Municipalities may borrow money by issuing general obligation bonds, self-supporting general obligation bonds, mortgage revenue bonds, revenue bonds, and short-term financing notes. State statutes dictate the manner in which both bonds and tax levies will be put before the electors. Charter municipalities may impose additional restrictions on property tax millage, percent of tax on income, and the duration of the taxes. Finally, the state constitution prohibits cities from using their assets to support a loan to private corporations and prohibits the state from assuming the debts of cities.[65]

Local Expenditures

Tax revenues are deposited in fund accounts, and expenditures are made from the designated accounts. State statutes, charters, and ordinances and resolutions establish the fund accounting system. The fund accounts generally include a general fund, sinking fund, bond retirement fund, special funds created by bond issues and tax levies, a special fund for each revenue source other than property tax, a trust fund, and a public utility fund. State law prohibits comingling or transferring certain funds, for example, funds created by a special purpose tax levy. Other funds may be transferred by ordinance.[66]

Municipalities are required to file budgets with the county budget commission. In practice, this process is only a formality; counties, as local governments, do not have authority over municipal budgets. The municipal fiscal year runs from January 1 to December 31, whereas the state fiscal year begins on July 1 and ends June 30. Councils and commissions must pass an appropriation measure based on an official certificate approved by the county budget commission. The certificate verifies that expenditures do not exceed revenues. No ordinance may be approved until the county auditor certifies that tax revenues will be great enough to pay for anticipated expenses. Municipalities decide their internal budgeting procedures, but they generally follow state budget schedules. Public safety, utilities, capital outlays, and debt service use up almost 75 percent of a typical municipal budget (see Table 2). Unencumbered appropriated funds may be carried over and appropriated the following year. Encumbered funds not spent need not be reappropriated, but the funds cannot be included in the following year's balance. Contingency funds may be created as long as they do not exceed 3 percent of the total appropriations.[67]

Expenditures related to contract purchases are controlled by state statutes or by municipal charter. State statutes limit contracts to $10,000 without an ordinance. Charters may set a lower or higher limit. In general, state statutes and charter provisions describe how contracts must be executed, and they establish fair competition among bidders. The statutes and charters include provisions requiring that contracts be enforced during terms of office, bid requirements, and emergency purchase and prevailing wage standards.[68]

Following the default on outstanding notes by the city of Cleveland in 1979, the General Assembly passed the Fiscal Emergency Act. This act provided that a municipality may be declared in "fiscal emergency" if any one of six conditions existed, among them, defaulting on a general obligation for more than thirty days or failing to meet its payroll for thirty days. In a fiscal emergency the state may create a Financial Planning and Supervision Commission with powers to assist a fiscally distressed municipality to develop a financial accounting and reporting system, to approve budget appropriations in total but not in detail, and to issue local government fund notes.[69]

State Government Grants-in-Aid to Localities

As mentioned above, the state shares tax revenues with local governments through two major programs, the Local Government Fund and the Local Government Revenue Assistance Fund. The state distributes these funds to counties using a formula based on population and property values. County budget commissions then decide how the funds will be distributed to local governments. State revenue transfer payments go into municipal general fund accounts, and the funds may be used as determined by local officials.

The state also provides municipalities with infrastructure development funds through three major programs. The Ohio Public Works Commission Infrastructure Program was approved in 1987. The program funds 90 percent of project costs for the repair and replacement of local roads, bridges, water lines, wastewater facilities, and solid waste disposal plants. The state may grant up to $120 million each year. Nineteen districts implement the program through public works integrating committees. Representatives from municipalities and townships sit on the committees according to locally determined selection formulas.

Table 2. Municipal Expenses in Ohio, 1999

Expenditure category	Percentage of total expenditures
Public assistance and Medicaid	29%
Education	26
Local government support/other	10
Health and human services	9
Debt service/proprietary	8
Justice/public protection	6
Transportation	5
Capital outlay	4
General government	2
Community and economic development	1
Environment	1

Source: Ohio Budgetary Financial Report for the fiscal year ending June 30, 1999.

Local governments submit project proposals to the committee, and it reviews and recommends projects to the state Public Works Commission up to its allocation of state funds. The committees also review and recommend projects seeking money from the state's Local Transportation Improvement Fund (which accumulates gasoline tax revenues).[70]

The third major infrastructure development fund provides aid to municipalities through the Ohio Water Development Authority and the Department of Development. For example, Water Development Authority provided credit and loans to the city of Akron when it built a solid waste incinerator. The state Department of Development assisted Cleveland and Columbus in developing sports stadiums. Overall, growth politics and extensive suburban development result in the wide dispersal of state funds.[71]

Unfunded Mandates

State mandates affect municipal governments in two major areas: the environment and criminal justice.

Two environmental mandates affect municipalities in urban areas. The state requires automobile emission inspections in urban counties but not in rural counties, and it ordered counties to organize solid waste management districts in 1989. These districts have the authority to plan for disposal and waste reduction. Municipalities and townships participate through the district planning committee. Typically, municipalities manage collection and recycling programs independently, although the state may require that the solid waste management district meet certain recycling and reduction objectives.[72]

In the criminal justice area, the state adopted two laws impacting local jurisdictions. New statutes require local law enforcement agencies to establish specific procedures for notifying the public about individuals classified as sexual predators and for handling domestic violence incidents. These mandates will increase costs significantly for local law enforcement agencies.[73] Overall, these mandates fall most heavily on older, urbanized areas.

Access to Local Government

Local Elections

Soon after Ohio voters adopted the home rule amendment, the Ohio Supreme Court heard arguments concerning a municipality's authority to control local election processes. In *Fitzgerald v. City of Cleveland* the court found that control over local elections was "a matter peculiarly belonging to the municipality" and that it represented the "very idea of local self-government." The courts also noted the difference between the exercise of political power, meaning local self-government, and the exercise of police power, meaning actions to safeguard an election.[74] As with municipal control over other features of home rule, that over political processes must pass the tests of reasonableness

and constitutionality. For instance, qualifications required of council members or procedures for enacting ordinances must pass these tests.

The state decides these issues when a municipality does not have a charter or when the charter is silent. Municipalities may, through a clause in their charter, adopt state election statutes and thus give the statutes the force of a charter provision, but in cases of conflict between municipal and state procedures controlling elections, charter provisions prevail. Article V, section 7, of the Ohio Constitution states that "all nominations for elective state, district, county and municipal offices shall be made at direct primary election or by petition." The courts found this provision did not apply to charter municipalities. In *State ex rel. Taylor v. French* the courts found that a charter gave municipalities the authority to expand the range of electors (municipalities permitted women to vote in local elections before they received the franchise from the state) and adopt proportional representation.[75] Noncharter municipalities follow state statutes in regard to calling and holding elections and defining the number of elected offices.

Citizen Controls over Actions of Local Officials

Article II, section 1, of the Ohio Constitution allows citizens of all municipalities—chartered as well as unchartered—to initiate legislation and to repeal legislation adopted by councils and commissions through a referendum. In effect, the initiative and referendum make citizens residing in municipalities coequal with the municipal legislature. Charter municipalities may adopt their own procedures for exercising their initiative and referendum powers, but if a charter is silent on these powers, state statutes will control the manner in which they will be exercised.[76]

Noncharter municipalities may avoid a referendum vote by adopting two consecutive emergency ordinances. The first ordinance repeals the ordinance contested by a referendum petition, and the second emergency ordinance re-enacts the ordinance. Councils and commissions may also repeal or amend ordinances adopted through an initiative legislative process. Charter governments may exercise this authority as well, unless it is expressly denied in the charter.[77]

Citizens may amend or abolish municipal home rule charters but not home rule powers provided through state statutes. Electors may initiate the drafting of a charter by a petition signed by 10 percent of the registered voters. They may also amend it in the same fashion. A majority vote for a charter or an amendment carries the motion. Citizens may also initiate or repeal the ownership or lease of a public utility.[78] Even public employees may initiate charter amendments. In the city of Springfield, firefighters initiated an amendment requiring the city to maintain a minimum staffing level in their department.

The state constitution permits the General Assembly to adopt procedures for recalling public officials. Noncharter municipalities follow state procedures last amended in 1995. Citizens may remove an elected official from office through a recall vote. Putting a recall issue before the voters requires a petition signed by at least 15 percent of the electors who voted in the last election. Candidates to replace the removed officials may be submitted for a vote on the same ballot. Charter municipalities may adopt recall provisions or ignore them. The "if silent" condition for initiative and referendum does not apply to recall.[79]

Open meetings and records are another means of providing citizen access to government. Ohio requires charter and noncharter municipalities to make public meetings open at all times. However, municipalities may provide for executive sessions closed to the public under certain circumstances. These sessions must be approved by a quorum and roll-call vote of the municipal council or commission for the purpose of discussing personnel matters; the purchase of property in a competitive bidding process; legal matters pertaining to a court action; negotiation in a collective bargaining process; matters that the state or federal government requires to be confidential; and security issues.[80]

No legislation or resolution may be adopted in an executive, or private, session. Minutes from regular meetings and special meetings must be recorded and open to the public. Minutes from executive sessions may reveal only the purpose of the session. Notice requirements pertain to all meetings. There are some differences, however, between noncharter and charter municipalities. For example, if a charter states that all meetings shall be public, the council or commission may not hold an executive session, as permitted under state statutes.[81]

State-Local Relations in Ohio

Home rule represents a means for advancing local development as well as good governance. Moreover, home rule supports Ohio's growth politics. It establishes a rough economic and political equality among communities, enabling growth coalitions within these communities to target, utilize, and develop public resources. Home rule has reduced but not eliminated state interference in local affairs. Special acts and logrolling still occur when local governments want to exercise authority not explicitly granted in the Ohio Revised Code.

Home rule in Ohio produces and sustains social, political, and economic tension between local governments. Home rule legitimizes and perpetuates individualistic behavior. While theoretically attractive, individualistic behavior causes each municipality to compete with all others for enterprise, state funds, and whatever else may benefit them. They also compete to exclude whatever is unwanted, for example, special needs housing or waste facilities. Municipal competition has contributed to poor and decaying central cities, and the decay is spreading to older suburbs due to legislative action or action on matters of statewide concern such as annexation, incorporation, and merger as well as poor decision making by some central cities.[82] As communities fashion policies to enhance their wealth, they lose sight of their economic dependence on others, their need to collaborate with others to achieve the greatest good for residents, and their civic obligations to people and institutions outside of their boundaries. Ohio's fiercely independent, inventive, and competitive communities made Ohio a leader through most of the twentieth century, but holding on to this old formula seems necessary to prevent pre-1912 politics from once again favoring (on whatever bases) private and state interests and thereby weakens the state's ability to sustain growth and progress. In the future, state leaders need to look for partnering with their viable general-purpose subdivisions—municipalities.

Notes

1. Dennis R. Judd, *The Politics of American Cities: Private Power and Public Policy*, 3d ed. (Glenview: Scott, Foresman, 1988), 105–106. For the development of city-manager government in Dayton see Landrum R. Boning, *City Manager Government in Dayton* (Chicago: Public Administration Service for the Committee on Public Administration of the Social Science Research Council, 1940); and Judith Sealander, *Grand Plans: Business Progressivism and Social Change in Ohio's Miami Valley, 1890–1929* (Lexington: University of Kentucky Press, 1988), 85–128.

2. Stuart Meck with Jason Wittenberg, "A Smart Growth Agenda for Ohio: A Working Paper" (Chicago: American Planning Association, Research Department, Smart Growth Project, July 17, 1998, draft), 6.

3. See Harry N. Scheiber, *Ohio Canal Era: A Case Study of Government and the Economy, 1820–1861* (Athens: Ohio University Press, 1969); and John P. Blair and Keith Ewald, *Manufacturing Development Policy: Economic Restructuring in Ohio* (Dayton: Wright State University Press, 1991), 19–35.

4. Blair and Ewald, *Manufacturing Development Policy.*

5. "Population of Ohio and Ohio's Top Ten Cities, 1800–1990," available at www.odod.ohio.gov/osr/srpopu.htm.

6. Richard D. Bingham et al., *Beyond Edge Cities* (New York: Garland Publishing, 1997), 3–44.

7. Information available at http://winslo.state.oh.us.

8. Farm interests mobilized quite strongly. See "Ohio Farmland Preservation Task Force: Findings and Recommendations," report to Gov. George V. Voinovich, June 1997, available at www.state.oh.us/agr/FINALRpt2.html#anchor345186; and Robert Gurwitt, "The Quest for Common Ground," *Governing*, June 1998, 16–22.

9. Under pressure from the coalition, the state legislature created the Office of Farmland Preservation and Gov. Robert Taft organized the Urban Revitalization Task Force (1999). The legislature also debated laws in 1997 and 1998 that would require the counties to develop geographic data for assessing the effects of growth and require counties to develop countywide plans, integrate transportation and land-use planning, and provide fiscal incentives to property owners and developers. See Ohio House bills 117 and 670 and Senate bills 99, 162, and 285, 1998.

10. George W. Knepper, *Ohio and Its People* (Kent: Kent State University Press, 1989), 47–69.

11. Stephen Cianca, "Home Rule in Ohio Counties: Legal and Constitutional Perspectives," *University of Dayton Law Review* 19 (winter 1994): 536.

12. *Know Your Ohio Government* (Columbus: League of Women Voters Education Fund, 1987), 89–93.

13. Delos F. Wilcox, *Municipal Government in Michigan and Ohio: A Study in the Relations of City and Commonwealth* (New York: Columbia University, 1896), 63–74.

14. Ibid., 72.

15. Isador Grossman et al., "Report on the Scope and Limitation of Home Rule Powers of Municipalities under the Ohio Constitution," report to the Research Committee of the Fact Finding and Policy Committee of the Regional

Committee, Columbus, Ohio, April 21, 1928. Norman Blume, "Municipal Home Rule in Ohio," Ph.D. diss., Ohio State University, 1956, 30–34.

16. *Constitutional Home Rule for Ohio Cities,* report of the Municipal Home Rule Committee of the Municipal Association of Cleveland, 1913, 13–20.

17. John E. Gotherman, "Municipal Home Rule," *Ohio Municipal* 2 (March–April 1990): 25; and George D. Vaubel, *Municipal Home Rule in Ohio* (Buffalo: William S. Hein, 1978), 363.

18. Grossman, "Scope and Limitation of Home Rule Powers," 5.

19. For example, see John E. Gotherman, "Municipal Home Rule in Ohio," *Capital University Law Review* 8 (1978): 247–248.

20. Vaubel, *Municipal Home Rule in Ohio,* 31–42; and Ohio Municipal League, *Municipal Government in Ohio* (Columbus: Ohio Municipal League, 1996), sections 10.03–10.04.

21. Ohio Municipal League, *Municipal Government in Ohio,* section 10.03.

22. Vaubel, *Municipal Home Rule in Ohio,* 35–39.

23. Ohio Municipal League, *Municipal Government in Ohio,* appendix to ch. 12.

24. See Gotherman, "Municipal Home Rule," 248–249.

25. Blume, "Municipal Home Rule in Ohio," 31–34.

26. Ibid., 1519–1521 and 1550–1551.

27. Arlene L. Polster, "The Issue of Annexation," graduate research project, Wright State University, 1994, 9–12.

28. Vaubel, *Municipal Home Rule in Ohio,* 421–422.

29. Ibid., 1516–1517.

30. Cianca, "Home Rule in Ohio Counties," 535–536.

31. Ibid., 548–551.

32. Ibid., 551–553.

33. Ibid., 551–553.

34. Information provided by the Ohio Township Association, Columbus, Ohio, February 1999.

35. Article XVIII, Ohio Constitution, sections 2, 3, and 7.

36. Vaubel, *Municipal Home Rule in Ohio,* 1453.

37. Ibid., 1462–1463.

38. Jack L. Dustin, "Interlocal Government Cooperation in Cuyahoga and Montgomery Counties," report to the State and Local Government Commission of Ohio, Columbus, Ohio, May 1993, 29–32.

39. *Know Your Ohio Government,* 89–93.

40. Vaubel, *Municipal Home Rule in Ohio,* 23–26.

41. Ibid., 26–29 and 1514–1519.

42. Ibid., 1540–1548; and *Know Your Ohio Government,* 92–95.

43. Dustin, "Interlocal Government Cooperation," 32–35.

44. For example, Medina and Clark Counties have developed countywide comprehensive plans. An example of interlocal economic development cooperation is the I-70/I-75 Development Association. This organization lists as members more than thirty-five local governments and many more quasi-governmental organizations.

45. Article XV, section 10, of the Ohio Constitution establishes civil service requirements. See also Vaubel, *Municipal Home Rule in Ohio,* 436–443.

46. Ohio Municipal League, *Municipal Government in Ohio,* section 11.11. Vaubel also identified other "statewide effect" cases regarding police and fire departments, for example, *City of Cincinnati v. Gamble* (1941) and *State ex rel. Arey v. Sherrill* (1944), in *Municipal Home Rule in Ohio,* 445–450.

47. Ohio Municipal League, *Municipal Government in Ohio,* section 11.11.

48. Ibid., sections 20.01, 20.04, and 20.10–20.26.

49. Meck and Wittenberg, "A Smart Growth Agenda for Ohio," 6–7.

50. Jack Dustin, "Decentralization in an Interdependent World," conference paper, annual meeting of the Urban Affairs Association, 1995, 7–9.

51. Vaubel, *Municipal Home Rule in Ohio,* 1507.

52. Farris Lyn Conley-Welsh, "An Evaluation of Tax Abatement in the Miami Valley and the State of Ohio," graduate research project, Wright State University, 1993, 2–6.

53. Michael Wasylenko, *Taxation and Economic Development: A Blueprint for Tax Reform in Ohio,* ed. Roy Bahl (Columbus: Battelle Press, 1996), 496; and The Urban Center, Cleveland State University, "Ohio's Enterprise Zone Program:

An Analysis of Existing Program Performance and a Future Program Vision," report summary prepared for the Ohio Economic Development Study Advisory Committee to the Ohio Senate, April 22, 1998.

54. Wasylenko, *Taxation and Economic Development,* 497; and The Urban Center, "Ohio's Enterprise Zone Program," 7.

55. Ohio Revised Code, Chapter 51.

56. The municipal power to tax was challenged and upheld in *State ex rel. City of Toledo v. Cooper* (1917) and *Zielonka v. Carrel* (1919).

57. *Ohio's Taxes: A Brief Summary of Major State and Local Taxes in Ohio* (Columbus: Department of Taxation, State of Ohio, 1998), 79–131.

58. Ibid., 119–120.

59. Ibid., 119–120.

60. Ibid., 88–94.

61. Ohio Municipal League, *Municipal Government in Ohio,* section 40.18.

62. *Ohio's Taxes,* 86.

63. Ohio Municipal League, *Municipal Government in Ohio,* sections 40.03–40.20; and *Ohio's Taxes,* 178.

64. There are three basic limitations on municipal borrowing. The first is that net debt, with or without voter approval, may not exceed 10.5 percent of taxation value. The second is that a municipality may not incur net debt greater than 5.5 percent of taxation value without a vote of electors. Net debt does not include twenty important types of securities, such as self-supporting securities (for example, user fee services), securities backed by collection of special assessments, and securities issued to back up loans from the state. The third debt limitation prohibits municipalities from taxing property in excess of ten mills without voter approval. This limitation comes into effect when municipalities propose to issue unvoted bonds. From Ohio Municipal League, *Municipal Government in Ohio,* section 42.06.

65. Gotherman, "Municipal Home Rule," 41; and Ohio Municipal League, *Municipal Government in Ohio,* chs. 40 and 42.

66. Ohio Municipal League, *Municipal Government in Ohio,* sections 36.27–36.29.

67. Ibid., sections 36.30–36.34 and 36.36–36.38.

68. Ibid., sections 20.01–20.05.

69. Ibid., section 36.40.

70. "Ohio Public Works Commission," at www.pwc.state.oh.us/mission. htm; and Ohio Municipal League, *Municipal Government in Ohio,* section 40.23.

71. Steve Bennish, "Dayton's Turn for Funds?" *Dayton Daily News,* February 7, 1999, sec. A.

72. Home rule does not preclude the state from exercising its own powers. For example, in *State ex rel. Southard v. City of Columbus* (1934) the courts upheld the state's authority to require municipal compliance in areas of sewer, water supply, and other services necessary for preserving peace and protecting health and property.

73. Montgomery County Sheriff Gary Haines and County Commissioner Charles Curran, pursuant to discussions of the Montgomery Jail Advisory Board.

74. Vaubel, *Municipal Home Rule in Ohio,* 388–389.

75. Ibid., 392, footnote 10, and 395–397.

76. Gotherman, "Municipal Home Rule," 250–251; and Ohio Municipal League, *Municipal Government in Ohio,* section 11.14.

77. Ohio Municipal League, *Municipal Government in Ohio,* sections 32.42 and 32.57.

78. Ibid., section 32.55; and Gotherman, "Municipal Home Rule in Ohio," 258–260.

79. Vaubel, *Municipal Home Rule,* 397–408.

80. Ohio Municipal League, *Municipal Government in Ohio,* sections 33.01–33.08.

81. Ibid., sections 33.05–33.07.

82. Jack L. Dustin, "Cooperative Communities—Competitive Communities: The Role of interlocal Tax Revenue Sharing," Urban Policy Monograph Series on Regional Competitiveness and Cooperation, Ohio Board of Regents Urban University Program, 1994.

OKLAHOMA

David R. Morgan, Robert E. England, Michael W. Hirlinger, and James T. Laplant

Comparatively speaking, Oklahoma is a young state; in 1907 it became the forty-sixth state to join the Union. Its rural, frontier, preindustrial character is still very evident. The landscape is dotted with small family-owned farms centered on "towns" that are heavily reliant on agribusiness. The state contains only two large cities: Oklahoma City, with about 450,000 people, and Tulsa, with about 375,000. Of the remaining approximately 600 cities and towns, only about a dozen have 25,000 or more residents. In fact, more than 430 municipalities are governed under the statutory "town" form of government, and most of these are under 1,500 in population.[1] Only about 15 percent of cities in the state operate under a home rule charter.[2] Although charter cities enjoy a degree of independence from state control, the overwhelming majority of incorporated areas in Oklahoma operate without a charter, under state constitutionally defined forms of government.

Governmental Setting

Oklahoma means "land of the red people" in the Choctaw language.[3] Modern Oklahoma was part of the Louisiana Purchase of 1803. Although many people thought the state might be the first to be carved out of the vast territory secured from France, it was the last. In many respects Oklahoma's early history was affected by President Andrew Jackson's Indian policy. By 1830, the U.S. Congress had approved the forced migration of the five so-called civilized tribes (Cherokees, Choctaws, Seminoles, Chickasaws, and Creeks) from Mississippi, Alabama, and Georgia to Indian Territory—present-day eastern Oklahoma. The period from 1840 to 1865 is known as the "Golden Years of the Indian Republics." Any uninvited white interlopers in Indian Territory were escorted out by the military.

During Reconstruction after the Civil War, the federal government required the five tribes, in retribution for their alliance with the Confederacy, to surrender a large portion of Indian Territory to Plains Indian tribes. Eventually, Native Americans in the state were allotted parcels of land for private ownership, in contrast with the traditional Indian system of communal land ownership.

At noon on April 22, 1889, the Great Land Rush officially opened western Oklahoma, known then as Oklahoma Territory, to non-Indians. In a series of other land runs and assignments, most of what had been Indian Territory was opened for settlement. In 1907 Oklahoma Territory (modern-day western Oklahoma) and Indian Territory (modern-day eastern Oklahoma) were united to form the forty-sixth state.

Oklahoma's history helps explain the nature of local government in several ways. First, city, county, and state government officials must be concerned not only with intergovernmental relations among themselves and with the federal government but also with numerous sovereign Indian nations. American Indian taxing, gaming, and service delivery issues have become prominent in recent years and are largely being worked out in the courts.

Second, after non-Indians were allowed into Oklahoma in the late 1880s, migrants streamed largely from the South into eastern Oklahoma and from the agrarian Midwest into western Oklahoma. Both early migration streams resulted in deep social, economic, and political conservatism; a poor state; and a state dependent on agribusiness and natural resources (coal, natural gas, timber, and oil).

Finally, the state's admittance to the Union coincided with the Progressive and Populist movements. The Progressive movement in the state encouraged the adoption of various "direct democracy" mechanisms, such as the initiative and referendum (and recall for charter cities), and the adoption of the council-manager form of government for charter cities. The state constitution manifests the Populist influence in Oklahoma politics. It is a lengthy document replete with restrictions on railroads and large corporations, whose avaricious practices were thought to be a threat to the well-being of the common folks. Frequently, changes in local policies require a change of the state constitution, not statutes. This political culture—"the collective orientation of people toward the basic elements in their political system"[4]—plays a vital role in explaining the structure and functioning of government institutions, the orientations and behavior of political leaders, and public policies made in the name of the people.

Home Rule in Oklahoma

Historical Development

Oklahoma has 588 municipalities, 77 counties, 581 school districts, and 498 special districts.[5] Since only municipalities in Oklahoma are granted home rule, our primary focus is on this unit of local government.

Oklahomans have adopted only one state constitution. This constitution has always provided for municipal home rule. A 1995 survey of charter cities conducted by the Oklahoma Municipal League found, for example, that Enid, Oklahoma, was granted home rule in 1907, the year of statehood.[6]

Definition of Home Rule

In Oklahoma, "home rule" is referred to as "charter city." For our purposes, the two terms are synonymous. Provisions outlining home rule status are found in the Oklahoma Constitution (Article XVIII, municipal corporations) and Oklahoma Statutes (Title 11). Any city with 2,000 or more residents may adopt a home rule charter.

The first step toward becoming a charter city is electing a "board of freeholders," consisting of two representatives from each ward in the town. The board drafts a charter. If approved by a vote of the citizens of the community and then by the governor, the charter becomes the law of the city. Unless provisions to the contrary are in the charter, it may be repealed by a majority of voters in an election requested by the city council or through the initiative petition process. Any town with more than 1,000 people may choose to become a "city" and change from the "town" form of government to one of three statutory forms of government—aldermanic, council-manager, or "strong" mayor.[7]

For each of the three forms of government, the statutes define clearly who will be elected, in what numbers, and what their powers will be. Similarly, administrative procedures and provisions are also outlined with specificity for officials in towns and cities operating under statutory forms of government.[8]

The only explicit restriction that the state constitution places on home rule grants of authority is that a charter must be "consistent with and subject to the Constitution and laws of this state."[9] The Oklahoma courts have held that this charter provision is self-executing. The courts have also ruled that city charters supersede state laws if the subject is strictly local or municipal in character. Otherwise, state law is supreme. In Oklahoma, court decisions almost always uphold city charters in regard to local elections, for example. On the other hand, such matters as

control of alcoholic beverage sales and employee unionization are considered within the province of the state. One other limitation is noteworthy: home rule cities cannot levy any tax that the Oklahoma legislature has not authorized.

Counties in Oklahoma do not have home rule. In 1992 the state legislature attempted to change the law by passing HB 2257, the County Home Rule Charter Act. This legislation allowed any county with a population of less than 550,000 and with a metropolitan area of 250,000 or more to adopt a county charter. Tulsa County was the only jurisdiction in the state that met the criteria. State courts declared the law unconstitutional. It would seem that legislative attempts to change Oklahoma's antiquated county commissioner system must be systematic and not particularistic, if they are to pass judicial muster.

Despite the appearance of a fairly broad grant of power to Oklahoma charter cities, a 1993 Advisory Committee on Intergovernmental Relations (ACIR) study classifies Oklahoma as having only "structural" home rule as opposed to a "broad functional" home rule.[10] The ACIR applies the term *structural* to those states that allow local governments to determine their own form of government. A reading of the ACIR document does not reveal the basis for Oklahoma's classification. Other than restrictions on taxation, the Oklahoma home rule provision seems reasonably liberal. In fact, a staff attorney for the Oklahoma Municipal League stated that she thought the state's home rule provisions are fairly broad.[11]

Structural Features

Table 1 shows municipalities in Oklahoma by form of government and home rule status. Most cities in Oklahoma (73 percent) operate under the town form of government. Only 15 percent (86 of 588) of all cities have "home rule." Of the 86 home rule cities in the state, fully 87 percent prefer the council-manager form of government. This finding is not surprising given the impact of the Progressive movement on Oklahoma politics.

Occasionally, state lawmakers in Oklahoma resort to the use of "local legislation" to affect cities and counties. For the most part, though, this device is used to single out the state's two

Table 1. Municipalities in Oklahoma by Form of Government and Home Rule Status, 1996

Form of government	No charter	Charter	Total	Total as percentage of all municipalities
Aldermanic	39	4	43	7%
"Strong" mayor	4	7	11	2
Council-manager	28	75	103	18
Town	431	0	431	73
Total	502	86	588	100%

Source: Oklahoma Municipal League, *OML Handbook for City and Town Officials* (Oklahoma City: Oklahoma Municipal League, 1996), 17–20.

largest cities or counties—Oklahoma City (Oklahoma County) and Tulsa (Tulsa County)—for special treatment. These two cities are much larger than any other in the state, and the two counties contain about 35 percent of the total state population. The two cities and counties often see their needs as differing significantly from those of other communities in the state. Thus, officials from those two areas sometimes ask their legislators to support measures that treat the two largest communities as special cases. One example was the unsuccessful attempt to give special consideration to Tulsa County for home rule. The legislation was written in such a way that not even the state's largest county could qualify. In this case, for various reasons, Oklahoma County officials and legislators from that area did not want the capital county even to be able to consider a home rule charter. Another example of local legislation was the provision by which the two largest counties (defined in this case as those above 300,000 population) could levy a sales tax of not more than one cent, with voter approval, to be used solely for the purpose of constructing buildings and facilities for lease to the federal government. The hope was that Oklahoma or Tulsa County would prove attractive as a site for one of the Department of Defense's new accounting and record-keeping centers.

Oklahoma is one of forty-one states that authorize municipal annexation by general law.[12] Most authorities consider Oklahoma's annexation laws are extremely liberal in application. Property owners can petition to have their land annexed (so-called voluntary annexation), but this simple provision is misleading. In actuality, the courts have allowed cities to take in vast amounts of territory under this seemingly benign provision. Judges have also held that the annexed property can be of any shape, which allows for extensive gerrymandering. If the city wants to annex a piece of property and can get the owner's consent, it then becomes possible for local decision makers to attach without consent another, perhaps sizable piece of property to the original tract. The only limitation is that the property for which consent has been given must make up a majority of the total area in question. In the early 1960s Oklahoma City annexed so much territory that it temporarily (until the creation of Jacksonville–Duvall County, Florida, in 1967) became the largest city in size in the United States. There is no statutory requirement that annexation be subject to a referendum.

Oklahoma is one of thirty-four states that require a referendum, and majority approval of each affected city in that referendum, for consolidation of cities.[13] No such consolidation of separately incorporated municipalities has occurred in recent times. Only fourteen states allow for consolidation of counties; Oklahoma is not one of them.

Functions of Local Government

Functional Responsibilities

Local governments perform two basic functions for citizens: they manage political conflict and they deliver services. Although service delivery can take on political overtones, it usually is more administrative than political in nature and constitutes the essential character of local government. Or, as the old saying goes, "local government is where the rubber meets the road."

Cities provide a number of essential services, such as police protection, fire services, refuse collection, storm alert, water, parks, libraries, civic centers, housing authorities, and so forth. Counties in Oklahoma provide health care, farm-to-market roads, county court services, property tax assessment and collection, restaurant inspections, juvenile services, and many other basic services.

Governmental functions performed by cities and counties overlap very little. Property tax assessment, for example, is performed solely by the county. Each jurisdiction may operate its own jail, but some cooperation does exist. For instance, in largely rural territory annexed by a city (such as Oklahoma City or Norman), the county may agree to continue road maintenance. The two entities may work together in such areas as road and bridge projects. Cities often contract with the county to house and feed city prisoners in the county jail.

For the most part, the 581 school districts in Oklahoma are independent, and public schools are funded by local property taxes (about 30 percent of funds), state appropriations (about 65 percent), and federal funds (about 5 percent).[14] The number of school districts has been reduced by about one-half since 1962. In recent years, the state legislature has passed legislation fostering further school consolidation.

Most of Oklahoma's 498 special districts serve only one function, and only about 15 percent have taxing authority. The three most common functions performed by special districts are water supply to rural or fringe areas (about 225 districts), soil conservation (about 100), and housing and community development (about 120). These special districts are governed by boards appointed by mayors.[15]

Title 60 of the Oklahoma Statutes provides municipalities with the ability to create public trusts. Unlike cities, a public trust in Oklahoma is not subject to the constitutional debt limitation and therefore may issue revenue bonds. Trusts must be operated as a legal entity separate from the municipality, rather than as a department of the city. State laws on tort liability, purchasing and competitive bidding, and open meetings and open records that apply to cities also apply to public trusts.[16]

Landmark legislation allowing intergovernmental cooperation in the Sooner State passed in 1965. This general statute authorizes local governments to cooperate to provide a range of services and facilities, none of which are specified in the law itself. The councils of government in the state rely on this legislation to sanction the cooperation that localities within their jurisdictions undertake for various purposes. The Oklahoma Municipal Assurance Group was also established under the act. This agency allows cities and towns to pool their insurance needs. Without this broad legal authority, localities presumably could enter into formal interlocal agreements only by specific act of the legislature.

State law authorizes certain cooperative arrangements among local governments in Oklahoma and mandates others. In 1963 the legislature mandated the establishment of city-county boards of health for all counties of 225,000 people and above (Oklahoma and Tulsa Counties only). Later, with the approval of the state commissioner of health, boards of health in any county were authorized to form multicounty health districts. In 1982 the state permitted the creation of regional solid waste districts. These bodies can be created by agreement between cities or counties for the purpose of sharing the costs of construction, operation, and maintenance of solid waste disposal sites. Finally, counties or parts of counties may join together to establish emergency medical districts to finance and operate emergency medical services.

Administrative Discretion

Since local governments are the legal offspring of the state government, it should come as no surprise that state laws affect local policies and procedures. The ACIR report cited above provides considerable detail on state policies that help shape and restrict local government structure. It reveals that Oklahoma has been one of the most active states in altering state laws governing local government structure and administration. The ACIR notes that between 1978 and 1990 Oklahoma enacted twenty-five laws affecting local government structure and administration.[17] Many changes were in the areas of financial management and personnel management.

The changes made in financial management reflect the attempt of the Oklahoma legislature to professionalize local governments. Since 1978 the state has mandated the use of uniform accounting procedures by local governments and also has established local government purchasing standards.[18]

In the area of personnel management, Oklahoma state law requires that cities engage in collective bargaining with police and fire employees; it permits cities to do so with other employee groups. Although the ACIR report states that Oklahoma has joined thirteen other states in mandating binding arbitration between cities and their employees, this provision applies only to police and fire. Finally, Oklahoma is one of twenty-four states that "require cities and counties to establish public employee retirement systems or participate in the state system."[19]

Title 11 of the Oklahoma Statutes provides cities with the ability to enter into contracts with private firms or other political subdivisions. Title 62 outlines purchase-order law in great detail. In 1991 the legislature passed House Bill 1549, which provides municipalities with an alternative purchasing and payment process. The intent of the legislation was to expedite payment for city purchases.[20] Competitive bidding law is found in Title 61 of the Oklahoma Statutes. With exceptions, bids are generally required for any contract in excess of $7,500.[21]

According to state statutes (Title 11, section 43-101), cities in Oklahoma have the ability to regulate land use through planning and zoning activities in order to promote the health, safety, morals, and general welfare of the community. Land management techniques include city adoption of building regulations, codes, and permits. Cities may also adopt and administer a comprehensive city plan. State statutes require that the regulation of land and building use be uniform for each class or kind of building throughout each zone or district. However, cities can grant variances, or exceptions, if they follow state statutory limitations of this discretionary power (Title 11, section 44-107). State statutes provide for city planning commissions to oversee the development and administration of the comprehensive plan and local boards of adjustment to hear appeals concerning variances.

One of the most significant statutes enacted by the Oklahoma legislature has been the Governmental Tort Claims Act of 1978. In the act, the state of Oklahoma waives its sovereign immunity and that of its political subdivisions. The Governmental Tort Claims Act declares that "the state or a political subdivision shall be liable for loss resulting from its torts or the torts of its employees acting within the scope of their employment subject to the limitations and exceptions specified in this act." The Governmental Tort Claims Act "supersedes all home rule charter provisions and special laws on the same subject heretofore."[22]

Economic Development

Since the great crash of the state's economy in the early 1980s, the state legislature has offered a plethora of bills fostering local economic development efforts. The Local Development Act of 1992, for example, allows cities to use incentives and exemptions from local taxation, tax increment financing, and tax apportionment bonds and notes as economic development strategies. Other significant economic development legislation includes the Oklahoma Agricultural Linked Deposit Program of 1987, the Municipal and County Development Bonds Act of 1991, and the Oklahoma Quality Jobs Program Act of 1993. Cities, without a vote of the people, can grant tax credits; create industrial parks; establish and maintain enterprise zones; create revolving loan banks and funds; undertake housing weatherization, relocation, and revitalization projects; and undertake infrastructure improvements targeted to specific or community development projects. For the most part, counties can undertake similar activities.

Oklahoma law, unlike Texas law, does not provide cities with extraterritoriality powers. In other words, cities cannot own or operate facilities beyond their boundaries. This limitation also applies to counties in the state.[23]

Fiscal Autonomy of Local Governments

Local Revenues

Historically, cities in Oklahoma have been underfunded compared with cities in other states.[24] The state constitution prohibits municipalities from directly levying a property tax for current operations. However, property taxes can be used to retire city debt.

Assessing, levying, and collecting taxes is strictly a county function. The elected county assessor sets the value of all taxable property except railroads and public utilities; the state retains authority over those forms of property. The state constitution limits taxable property values to no more than 35 percent of fair market value. In 1992 the voters of the state approved a proposition to allow each county, by popular vote, to abolish the tax on personal property.

The constitution also creates a county excise board of three local citizens—one appointed by the district judge, one by the county commissioners, and one by the state tax commission. The principal duty of the board is to apportion the taxes raised within the county. With few exceptions, the constitution imposes a limit of 15 mills ($15 per $1,000 of value) for operating costs of all governments. Five mills go to local schools. The board allocates the remaining 10 mills among other local jurisdictions. In practice, counties receive the full amount. Local school districts, again with constitutionally imposed limits, may vote additional taxes to support local public education. In April of each year, the county excise board becomes the board of equalization. It hears and adjudicates complaints from property owners about the assessed value of their property. Since 1937 the Oklahoma Constitution has provided for a $1,000 homestead exemption.

In Oklahoma, cities rely heavily on the municipal sales tax and user fees. Virtually all cities have voted a sales tax of at least one cent, more than two-thirds of cities levy two cents or more, and a majority of cities levy a three-cent sales tax.

Most city revenue in Oklahoma comes from taxes—about 47 percent from the sales tax—26 percent from charges and fees, and the balance primarily from intergovernmental transfers and revenues. That revenue stream is atypical of other U.S. cities. The typical U.S. city receives 35 percent of its funds from intergovernmental sources (with 35 percent of that amount coming from the federal government). For all U.S. cities, 41 percent of revenue comes from taxes, and 53 percent of that amount from the property tax. Nationwide, user fees and charges constitute about 14 percent of municipal revenues. Once again, Oklahoma is different because its cities do not have access to the property tax for current operations.

Counties receive most of their revenue from three sources:

40 percent from intergovernmental transfers, of which about 85 percent is from the state; about 30 percent from property taxes; and 20 percent from charges for services. Remaining funds come from a variety of other taxes and miscellaneous revenue. About one-third of all expenditures by counties is for roads, highways, and bridges. Other costly functions are hospitals (about 17 percent) and law enforcement (about 5 percent).

To finance capital improvements, local officials can sell general obligation bonds upon approval by the voters. The issue of revenue bonds does not require a vote of the people. Special districts with taxing and borrowing authority can be created and can issue revenue bonds.

Total city and county indebtedness is limited by Article 10, section 26, of the Oklahoma Constitution and is calculated as a percentage of assessed property value in the jurisdiction. As of 1996 the limit was set at 10 percent.[25] Such indebtedness can be incurred only with the approval of three-fifths of qualified voters. Debt restrictions do not apply to revenue bonds issued by local utility authorities or public trusts.

Local Expenditures

Where does local money go? Hospitals top the list at 14.5 percent of general expenditures. The next highest areas of spending among cities in the state include police (12.5 percent), streets and highways (11.1 percent), fire (8.9 percent), and parks and recreation (6.3 percent).

State law requires local governments to balance their budgets. Municipal officials have two options for budgeting public funds. They can budget under the terms of the Municipal Budget Act of 1979, which "provides what many believe is a very modernistic approach to governmental budgeting."[26] Alternatively, they can use the traditional budgeting method, referred to as Title 68, which is not as flexible. To change from Title 68 to the 1979 budgeting law, the governing body of the city must adopt a resolution.

Major differences between the two procedures include more flexibility with the newer budgeting procedure in scheduling budget preparation and public hearings. Under the Municipal Budget Act, cities may calculate and appropriate 100 percent of estimated revenues. Under Title 68, city officials can appropriate no more than 90 percent of the previous fiscal year's actual revenues. Furthermore, under the new law the governing body can authorize an appropriate representative (city manager or town administrator) to approve transfers within funds, whereas under Title 68 only the governing body can approve such transfers.[27]

Technically, the Oklahoma Constitution prohibits cities from going bankrupt. State law mandates a balanced budget, and, debt limits are determined by the assessed valuation of property within the jurisdiction. Local budgets must be certified by state officials each year, and state law requires independent audits of expenditures.[28]

State Government Grants-in-Aid to Localities

According to Donald A. Murry and his colleagues, "Oklahoma is a fiscally centralized state—one in which state government provides a relatively high degree of financial support to local units of government."[29] For example, in fiscal 1992 Oklahoma state government's share of state and local general revenues was 63 percent, the seventh highest in the nation. But, as Murry et al. also note, "Municipalities in Oklahoma are relatively self-sufficient and do not rely on intergovernmental revenues."[30] In fiscal 1992, for instance, state government payments of $1.869 billion represented 34 percent of local government receipts. School districts received the lion's share of the state largess, $1.633 billion, or 71 percent of school district revenues. County governments received about $173 million, or about 25 percent of county government revenues. Municipalities received $63 million in state aid, representing only about 3 percent of the total $2.257 billion in city revenues.[31] Cities in Oklahoma receive state grants-in-aid to build roads, and the state also supports other city activities. In addition to state aid, federal programs are essential to the economic development efforts of Oklahoma cities. Of the various federal programs, perhaps the two most salient are the Community Development Block Grant (CDBG) and the Home Investment Partnership Program (HIPP), both administered by the Oklahoma Department of Commerce. In 1995 the CDBG program provided cities in the state with about $21.5 million, and the HIPP program added another $9 million to city coffers.[32] Both of these programs allow city officials significant discretionary power in the selection of activities and projects.

Three other popular federal community development programs also provided Oklahoma cities with significant funds in 1995: Community Services Block Grant, $2.6 million; Weatherization Assistance Program, $1.3 million; and Emergency Shelter Grants, $900,000.

Unfunded Mandates

The State of Oklahoma imposes mandates on local governments, many of which are not popular with administrators. Most notable are mandates in the area of environmental quality. These regulations and restrictions may be issued by federal agencies or the Oklahoma Department of Environmental Quality. Environmental mandates in the areas of safe water, landfills, and sewer testing seem to be the most burdensome. Also, city officials often complain about state collective bargaining mandates. Collective bargaining with police and fire employees is mandatory if desired by the groups. Moreover, new state laws on binding arbitration may give citizens the opportunity to vote for the action proposed by the arbitration.

Access to Local Government

Local Elections

Cities operating under statutory forms of city government have very little flexibility in organizing local elections and defining other attributes of the governmental setting. Almost all significant aspects of city government are defined by law. For example, in a statutory aldermanic form of government, the mayor must be elected at large, but citizens can decide whether one or two council members will be elected from each ward.

In contrast with the statutory forms of government, officials and citizens in charter cities largely define the nature of their city government. City charter provisions can supersede state law with respect to the conduct of elections, terms of office for the governing body, compensation, initiative and referendum, recall, and appointment and removal of officers. In addition, an opinion by the state attorney general recognized that municipal charters can provide for lobbying.[33]

Citizen Controls over Actions of Local Officials

The Oklahoma Constitution provides for initiative and referendum petitions for both cities and counties.[34] According to the constitution, every petition must be signed by a number of registered voters equal to or greater than 25 percent of the total number of votes cast at the preceding general election. Most charter cities retain this requirement. Municipalities use this power periodically; counties use it much less often. Oklahoma is not among the twenty-three states that provide for the recall of local elected officials. However, recall can be added as a direct democracy mechanism in charter cities.

Title 25 of the Oklahoma Statutes, sections 301–314, sets forth the rules and procedures concerning open meetings and open records. The Oklahoma Open Meeting Act requires that all meetings of public bodies be held at specified times and places that are convenient to the public and that they shall be open to the public. All public meetings must be preceded by advanced public notice of the meeting time, place, and agenda. In all meetings of public bodies, the vote of each member must be publicly cast and recorded. Issues and topics that can be addressed in executive session are very limited in the state and are usually related to employment, negotiations concerning employee groups, and confidentiality issues. Minutes of all public bodies are open to the public. A person attending a public meeting may record the proceedings by videotape or audiotape. Willful violation of open-meeting and open-record provisions is a misdemeanor, punishable by a fine of up to $500 and/or one year in the county jail.

State-Local Relations

Although only about 15 percent of all municipalities in the state operate under charters, those that do have taken full advantage of home rule. Most of these cities chose the council-manager plan, reflecting the impact of the Progressive movement. The constitutional provision for home rule established at statehood has encouraged more experimentation with municipal forms and structures than would have occurred otherwise. Counties are another matter; Oklahoma lags behind most other states in providing for either home rule or optional forms of county government.

The anomalous treatment of cities and counties in Oklahoma is difficult to comprehend. Perhaps more than anything else, this situation is a testimony to the continued political power of county officials, particularly the commissioners, who strongly oppose any significant change in the status quo. Over a number of years, various lawmakers have introduced bills calling for alternative forms of county government, to no avail. Reform opponents usually charge that such legislation is the first step toward county consolidation, which rural politicians and residents strongly resist.

In other areas of state-local relations, Oklahoma continues to modernize. The ACIR reports that the state was among a small group that made a large number of legislative changes affecting local financial and personnel management. Systematic comparisons of interlocal cooperation among the states are rare, but clearly Oklahoma has begun to take steps to allow and encourage local jurisdictions to work together in addressing concerns of an areawide nature.

Related to home rule is the question of how "Dillon's Rule" applies in Oklahoma. This doctrine, which limits municipal governments to exercising only those powers delegated by the state, has not been overturned explicitly by constitution or statute. Counties in Oklahoma are severely constrained, functioning almost solely as administrative extensions of state government. The status of cities in the state is less clear cut. In general, though, there is no indication of any overt rejection of Dillon's Rule in Oklahoma.

Notes

1. Oklahoma Municipal League, *OML Handbook for City and Town Officials* (Oklahoma City: Oklahoma Municipal League, 1996), 15.

2. Calculated from information presented in Oklahoma Municipal League, *OML Handbook,* 17–20.

3. Much of the information in this section is taken from David R. Morgan, Robert E. England, and George G. Humphreys, *Oklahoma Politics and Policies: Governing the Sooner State* (Lincoln: University of Nebraska Press, 1991), chaps. 1, 3, and 4.

4. Walter A. Rosenbaum, *Political Culture* (New York: Praeger, 1975), 4.

5. The information on cities comes from Oklahoma Municipal League, *OML Handbook,* 17–20, whereas that for other units of local government comes from Morgan et al., *Oklahoma Politics and Policies,* chap. 12.

6. Oklahoma Municipal League, *1995 Oklahoma Municipal Charter Survey* (Oklahoma City: Oklahoma Municipal League, 1995), 5.

7. Oklahoma Municipal League, *OML Handbook,* 13.

8. For a discussion of the town form of government, see Oklahoma Statutes, Title 11, section 12-101–12-114; for the aldermanic form of government, see Title 11, section 9-101–9-118; for the council-manager form, see Title 11, section 10-101–10-121; and for the "strong"-mayor form of government, see Title 11, section 11-101–11-1125.

9. *Oklahoma Constitution 1991*, Article XVIII, section 3.

10. Advisory Commission on Intergovernmental Relations, *State Laws Governing Local Government Structure and Administration* (Washington, D.C.: ACIR, March 1993).

11. Sue Ann Nicely, staff attorney, Oklahoma Municipal League, telephone conversation, August 19, 1993.

12. ACIR, *State Laws Governing Local Government Structure and Administration,* 25.

13. Ibid.

14. Morgan et al., *Oklahoma Politics and Policies,* 200–202.

15. Ibid., 202–203.

16. Oklahoma Municipal League, *OML Handbook,* 297–301.

17. ACIR, *State Laws Governing Local Government Structure and Administration,* 7.

18. Ibid., 10.

19. Ibid.

20. Oklahoma Municipal League, *OML Handbook,* 78.

21. Ibid., 82.

22. Oklahoma Statutes 1991, Title 51, sections 153, 170.

23. Rodney Ray, city manager, City of Owasso, Oklahoma, telephone conversation, January 8, 1998.

24. Information and data reported in this section come from Morgan et al., *Oklahoma Politics and Policies,* 193–195.

25. Oklahoma Municipal League, *OML Handbook,* 71.

26. Ibid., 69.

27. Ibid., 70.

28. Information in this paragraph comes from Rodney Ray, city manager, City of Owasso, Oklahoma, telephone conversation, January 8, 1998.

29. Donald A. Murry et al., *In Search of Smaller Government: The Case of State Finance in Oklahoma.* (Oklahoma City: Oklahoma 2000, 1996), 47.

30. Ibid., 50–51.

31. Ibid.

32. We thank Cecil Carter and Byron DeBruler, Oklahoma Department of Commerce, for providing this data.

33. Oklahoma Municipal League, *OML Handbook,* 14.

34. Oklahoma Constitution, Article 18, section 4(a).

OREGON

Carolyn N. Long

Oregon local governments are among the most autonomous jurisdictions in the union and have vast discretionary authority. The state has a history of citizen involvement, progressive politics, and a willingness on the part of state officials to maximize government discretion at every level. All municipalities in the state have home rule charters, and counties—whether home rule or general law—have broad discretion and authority over local concerns. Oregon has the nation's only elected regional government, which was organized in 1992 under a home rule charter approved by voters.

Despite their extensive authority to use local discretion to meet local needs, Oregon local governments are not without problems and policy constraints. The fiscal health of the state has been in dire jeopardy since successful citizen tax revolts in 1990 and 1997 limited property tax revenues; and since 1991, when the spotted owl was declared an endangered species, the state has faced declining timber revenues from federal lands. Local discretionary authority and the willingness to adopt innovative policies will be put to the test as many counties and municipalities strive to balance citizens' demands with declining revenues.

Governmental Setting

Rich in natural resources, Oregon has historically attracted people for employment, recreation, and quality of life. Although it is the tenth-largest state in terms of area, its population is relatively small: approximately three million. Partly because of its size, Oregon has tremendous variety in terms of geography, economy, natural resources, culture, and politics. The northwest sector of the state has a diversified economy and is experiencing high population growth, while the territory to the south and east of the Cascades is very rural, with slow population growth and an economy that depends on agriculture and wood products.

Differences in local government functions and structure have more to do with local socioeconomic characteristics and culture than with home rule status. Oregon has been described as having a "moralistic political culture," which means that political participation is encouraged, government is viewed as a positive force in society, and political conflict is issue oriented.[1] Although this description may fit the western part of the state, some qualification is in order. The eastern and western parts of the state differ geographically, climatically, economically, and politically. Eastern Oregonians tend to be conservative and individualistic, to have little confidence or trust in national or state government, and to hold more traditional social values (concerning lifestyle issues, for example) than their neighbors in western Oregon.[2] Although they are suspicious of all levels of government, east-

ern Oregonians have significantly more confidence in their local governments and less confidence in state government than western Oregonians.[3]

In its structure and role, state government in Oregon is similar to that of other states in the union. It has a bicameral state legislature: the senate consists of thirty members elected for four-year terms, and the house consists of sixty members elected for two-year terms.[4] As a result of a ballot initiative passed in 1992, senators are limited to eight years of service and representatives are limited to six years.[5] In addition to providing a forum for the discussion of issues facing Oregonians, the primary functions of the legislature are to review and revise the governor's budget and to pass laws to generate revenue, although the legislature is prohibited from spending revenue in excess of monies generated.[6]

The executive branch in Oregon is composed of the governor and five other state elected officials: the secretary of state, the treasurer, the attorney general, the commissioner of labor and industries, and the superintendent of public instruction. All state elected officials are limited to serving two four-year terms. The governor must submit a budget to the legislature every two years, has veto power over legislative bills, and is responsible for coordinating with federal and local governments.[7] A number of the state executive agencies work in close contact with county and municipal government.

The judicial branch includes the state supreme court, the court of appeals, the tax court, and circuit courts. The supreme court consists of six associate justices and a chief justice, selected by the court. The justices are elected for six-year terms. There are no term limits for judicial offices.

The judicial branch interacts with local governments in many areas. The supreme court interprets constitutional provisions, charters, and ordinances and determines what local governments may or may not do under existing statutes. In addition, the judicial branch is involved in awarding damages or penalties in cases where a local government is a party.

In the 1970s, the state was divided into fourteen regional governments. Each region is either mostly urban or mostly rural, and the regions cross traditional county and municipal lines. Each region's powers are limited to those expressly granted by the legislature. In 1984 the regional governments formed a voluntary association, the Oregon Regional Councils Association, to promote greater cooperation between all levels of government. The association provides a forum for discussion and for the exchange of information on issues of concern. One of the regions in the northwestern sector of the state—Metro—covers approximately 460 square miles, includes the urban portions of three counties and twenty-four cities, and has a population of over 1.2 million. The nation's only elected regional government, Metro is responsible for a number of regional services.[8]

Oregon has 240 incorporated municipalities, 36 counties, and 950 special districts. Oregon's local governments derive their powers from the state constitution and various state statutes—and, where relevant, from a home rule charter.

Home Rule in Oregon

Historical Development

There are three types of general-purpose local governments in Oregon: municipalities, counties, and regional governments. The state constitution and various state statutes provide voters with the opportunity to obtain home rule status at each level. The constitution was first amended in 1906 to give citizens of cities and towns exclusive power to enact and amend their charters to allow for home rule status. Later amendments specifically proscribed the state from interfering with municipal home rule charters.[9]

In 1958 the constitution was amended to authorize counties to adopt home rule charters.[10] Oregon state law stipulates the procedures that counties must follow to obtain a home rule charter. The state legislature has provided two avenues through which a county can secure a home rule charter: through an officially appointed committee or an initiative petition.[11] In 1990 the state constitution was amended to allow voters in the Metro service district the option of adopting a home rule charter.[12]

Despite their popularity in the state, home rule charters are not necessary for autonomous local government. Oregon has historically provided local governments with a large degree of discretionary authority. In the past two decades the state legislature has relaxed most of its restrictions on local governments and passed a number of statutes that legally provide local governments with practically the same level of autonomy that can be achieved with home rule.

Definition of Home Rule

The purpose of home rule in Oregon is to permit and encourage local solutions of problems and to authorize policy innovation without state authorization. Home rule counties and municipalities have the authority to determine their governmental organization and structure. In jurisdictions without home rule, state law controls the form, organization, functions, finances, and powers of local government.

Home rule charters also empower local governments to enact legislation on matters of municipal, county, and regional concern and afford them the discretion to provide services and improvements that benefit local areas. Unlike general-law counties, which are restricted by the state legislature from taking similar action, home rule counties can increase or impose new taxes without voter approval.[13]

Structural Features

All of Oregon's 240 incorporated municipalities have adopted home rule charters that provide them with the freedom to tailor the structure and organization of government to meet local needs.

Four basic forms of local government can be found in Oregon: "weak" mayor, mayor, commission, and council manager. Most small municipalities in Oregon—those with populations under 2,500—have "weak" mayor systems, whereas all but five of those with populations over 2,500 have council-manager governments.

Oregon's largest city, Portland, has a commission form of government, in which the city's major department heads are elected directly by the voters and function collectively as the city council. Apart from the fact that the mayor has the authority to assign and reassign department heads, the mayoral role is mostly ceremonial.

Oregon does not have classes of municipalities, and there is no local or special-privilege legislation in the state. With respect to incorporation, any area that is not included in another municipality and that has at least 150 residents may be incorporated as a municipality. Incorporation requires a petition signed by 20 percent of the voters in the proposed municipality and a hearing by the county governing body to determine whether the proposed boundaries would be beneficial to the populace. Upon a finding of benefit, the county must call an election in the proposed municipality. If a majority of those voting approve the proposal, then the area is incorporated.

Municipalities can own and control the development of facilities beyond their jurisdictional boundaries; however, unless a municipality owns the land, it cannot control development or regulate behavior in unincorporated areas that are contiguous to the jurisdiction.

The two basic forms of county government in Oregon are general law and home rule. The twenty-seven general-law counties in the state are established (and ultimately governed) by the state constitution and the state legislature. Thirteen of the general-law counties employ the county court system of government, while the remaining fourteen use a board of commissioners.

One example of how the distinct political cultures in Oregon's two principal regions affect local government structure is the fact that the county court system of government is found only in the eastern part of the state. This more traditional form of county government consists of two commissioners and a county judge, who serves as the presiding executive officer. In addition to probate duties and juvenile court responsibilities, the county judge has full-time administrative supervision of county business. General-law counties are allowed by law to appoint (rather than elect) county administrators, and five counties have chosen to do so. However, general-law counties are bound by the state constitution to elect sheriffs, treasurers, clerks, and municipal assessors.

Currently, nine counties operate under home rule charters. The most significant difference between home rule counties and general-law counties is that home rule counties have complete discretion over the organization of county offices: that is, they can create, abolish, or consolidate offices and departments as they see fit. Eight of Oregon's nine home rule counties have made such changes in county organizational structure. Washington County, for instance, is managed by an appointed administrator; an elected, full-time commission chairman; and four part-time commissioners. Multnomah County has a board chairman who is responsible for administration and four additional board members elected by district. Both Josephine and Benton Counties are managed by three full-time commissioners, plus a number of administrative assistants. Umatilla County is also governed by three full-time commissioners, as is Jackson County, which added an appointed administrator. Lane County is administered by a board of five full-time members and an appointed administrator. And, in an interesting experiment, Clatsop County is managed by five part-time volunteers and a full-time manager.[14]

Whether it has home rule will not necessarily make a significant difference in the number or variety of services that a county offers—primarily because, over the years, the Oregon state legislature has enacted a number of statutes that grant municipalities and counties a great deal of discretion in local governance. An example of the broad discretion granted to Oregon local governments is the 1941 Incorporation Act, which allows a municipality to "take all action necessary or convenient for the government of its local affairs," and states that any county "may by ordinance exercise authority within the county over matters of county concern."[15]

Substantively, the largest grant of general, ordinance-making authority was provided to counties in 1973, when the state legislature delegated to counties the power to legislate on matters of county concern, either through the county governing body or through citizen initiative and referendum.[16] Before 1973, counties had to lobby the state each time a new service was needed at the county level. Of course, the state legislature could always revoke these broad grants of discretionary power, but this seems unlikely, given the state's political culture and long history of citizen-based politics.[17]

Interestingly, the 1973 legislation does not seem to have discouraged counties from seeking home rule status. Five of the nine home rule counties received their charters after 1973, and charter commissions frequently refer home rule options to the ballot box, although three attempts during the 1996 election were unsuccessful.

In 1992 Metro became the nation's only elected regional government to be organized under a home rule charter. The charter created a seven-member council and the new position of auditor, and expanded the council's authority and taxing powers. Metro generates revenue from fees for services, government grants, and voluntary dues paid by local governments. The council can raise up to $12.5 million a year in taxes on goods and services without a popular vote and can create broad-based taxes with voter approval. The home rule charter broadly empowered the council with the authority to address issues of "metropolitan concern"; as a result, Metro has become increasingly important in regional land-use planning and growth management.[18]

The broad statutory powers given to municipalities, counties, and regions in Oregon and the powers reserved under home rule charters have given Oregon local governments an enormous amount of administrative discretion. Historically, the national Advisory Commission on Intergovernmental Relations ranked Oregon local governments as having the highest degree of local discretionary authority when compared to local governments in the other forty-nine states.[19]

Functions of Local Government

Functional Responsibilities

Since World War II incorporated municipalities in Oregon have grown in number and increased their scope of authority. Almost all municipalities are involved in general, legal, and fiscal administration; community development; building maintenance; and law enforcement. Over half of Oregon municipalities are also involved in record keeping, parks and recreation, human resources, courts, and elections. An increasing number of municipalities offer fire service, libraries, emergency service, street maintenance, and recycling.[20]

The number and variety of functions provided by municipal governments in Oregon is strongly linked to their size and to their proximity to other urban areas. Almost 45 percent of municipalities with populations under 1,000 have a narrow scope of functions (between one and five); in contrast, 80 percent of medium-size municipalities (those with populations between 2,500 and 19,999) and 80 percent of larger cities (those with populations of 20,000 or more) have a moderate (between six and nine) to broad (between ten and sixteen) scope of functions. Eighty percent of Oregon municipalities that are adjacent to other urban areas are more likely to have a moderate to broad scope of functions than those that are more isolated. Conversely, 80 percent of Oregon municipalities that are not adjacent to urban areas offer a narrow to moderate scope of functions.[21]

At the county level, the number of functions expands every year. The 1994 Survey of Oregon Counties revealed that all of the thirty-three counties surveyed provided administration and central services, assessment and taxation, county surveying and school funds, district attorney's office, economic development, elections and recording, health services, juvenile services, land-use planning, mental health, roads, and sheriff and jail services.[22]

County functions have also extended into such areas as animal control, community corrections, community development, county fairgrounds, court support, emergency management, parks and recreation, senior citizens' services, libraries, and solid waste management. Some functions, such as mental health and other social services, are contracted out by counties to nonprofit providers. The less densely populated counties in eastern Oregon are least likely to provide services that are not essential, such as libraries, streetlights, and water or sewer services.[23] Some services, such as solid waste management and senior citizens' services, are provided at a multicounty or regional level. There are few, if any, differences in the number of functions provided in home rule and general-law counties, after controlling for urban versus rural status (five of Oregon's home rule counties are rural, and four are urban).[24]

Oregon's 950 special districts—separate, independent government organizations with their own governance structures—provide a number of services, such as water services, rural hospitals, and fire protection. Special districts are most prevalent in the rural areas of the state and are funded primarily by property tax revenues.

The Oregon constitution and state statutes give municipalities, counties, and special districts the power to create and oversee local improvement districts.[25] Common improvements include street paving and the addition of curbs, sidewalks, storm and sanitary sewers, streetlights, and off-street parking.

Recognizing that the diversity of functions provided at the municipal, county, and special-district levels created a need for interlocal cooperation, in 1967 the state enacted several laws to encourage such cooperation and to increase local government efficiency. Under this legislation, Oregon local governments may enter into written agreements with other local government units to perform government functions.[26] Such agreements allow local governments to consolidate departments; share administrative officers; and jointly construct, own, operate, or lease facilities and equipment. If necessary, intergovernmental entities may even be created to act on behalf of the local units that have entered into such agreements. These entities have the power to issue revenue bonds according to the procedures specified in state law but are prohibited from levying taxes or issuing general-obligation bonds. Informal interlocal cooperation is encouraged through the Oregon Regional Councils Association, an organization created in 1984 that promotes communication between all levels of government.

Administrative Discretion

As noted earlier, legislation and the state constitution provide Oregon local governments with a great deal of autonomy. However, this does not mean that local governments are completely isolated from the state. In a number of areas, the state establishes goals or standards to guide local government operations and provides essential training to local government officials.[27]

Under state law, all local governments must prepare comprehensive plans that meet state standards concerning land use, development, housing, and conservation. State interference with local government is greatest with respect to land-use planning and the creation of urban growth boundaries.

The state created the Regional Problem Solving program, a pilot initiative administered by the Metro regional government. Under this program, Metro supervises the collection of land-use data from municipalities and counties and uses the information to forecast regional transportation and land-use needs. Metro then creates a comprehensive land-use plan and is empowered to compel local governments to prepare comprehensive plans that fit the regional one.[28]

The Oregon Department of Land Conservation and Development oversees the state's land-use planning program. The department's main role is to review municipal and county land-use plans to ensure that local governments are complying with state programs and to coordinate state and federal land-use programs. The state agency also administers grants to municipalities and counties and provides them with essential technical assistance. Although their land-use plans must comply with the state's goals, once local governments receive their planning grants they have significant discretion in the implementation of local land-use plans.

Economic Development

The state assists local governments with economic development through a number of means. The state sponsors meetings, workshops, newsletters, and on-site visits to help local leaders develop economic strategies. Through the Oregon Economic Development Department, municipalities, counties, and other governmental entities can obtain loans and grants for public works, safe drinking water, and housing rehabilitation projects, as well as funding for community facilities such as emergency shelters, day care centers, senior citizens' centers, and family counseling centers. The department also helps local residents find state and federal funding for rehabilitation or development projects and assists local governments in arranging financing to meet basic infrastructure and community development needs. Enterprise zones and job training are provided through the state's Strategic Investment Program; under this program, the state assists local governments to obtain financing—and training, if necessary—for development plans, then gives local governments broad authority to implement the plans. The types of economic development projects undertaken by a county or municipality will depend on its particular characteristics and needs.

Oregon local governments have broad administrative discretion with respect to economic development and have been very innovative. Oregon was one of the first states to use tax increment financing. Beginning in the late 1950s, municipalities and counties began setting up urban renewal agencies; the first was in Portland. Special commissions drew lines around urban renewal districts, froze the assessed property values, and issued bonds to finance improvements within the districts. As rehabilitation efforts led to increases in property values, the revenues generated from property taxes increased as well, and that money was then invested and used to pay off the bonds.

Fiscal Autonomy of Local Governments

Local Revenues

Any discussion of fiscal autonomy in Oregon would have to begin with a brief review of state and federal legislation that affects local governments' ability to raise revenue. Two measures enacted in the 1990s have had a significant impact in this area.

Ballot Measure 5, passed in 1990, amended the state constitution to significantly reduce property tax revenues for municipalities, counties, and other nonschool local governments. The measure phased in a property tax limit over a five-year period, ultimately reducing property taxes by 45 percent and limiting these taxes to 1.5 percent of market value. Local governments are not allowed to exceed the restrictions, even by direct vote of the people. Measure 5 did not provide for replacement revenues, and it has had a serious impact on local revenues for approximately half of Oregon's municipalities and counties; the most disastrous effects have been felt in rural eastern Oregon.[29]

Ballot Measure 50, passed in 1997, was the second successful effort by voters to limit state and local government reliance on the property tax as a revenue source. The measure rolled back

assessed property values to 90 percent of their 1995–1996 levels and capped growth in assessed value at 3 percent a year, resulting in a significant decline in property tax revenues. In addition, the measure required an average statewide cut of 17 percent in the tax levies that are used to support general operating expenses (these levies are separate and distinct from the property tax). The measure also required voter approval of any increase in fees that was designed to replace revenue generated from property taxes and added a "double-majority" requirement to the approval of any new taxes: any additional levies against real property must be approved by at least 50 percent of the voters in a general election in which at least 50 percent of eligible voters cast a ballot. Although Measure 50 allows local governments to ask voters to consider temporary levies that would override the 17 percent cut and the 3 percent limit, the vote on such a request must meet the double-majority requirement.

Even with ballot measures 5 and 50 and several other restrictions on raising revenues, taxes on residential, rental, and business properties remain the largest single source of local government revenue—accounting, in 1995, for 42.5 percent of all general, own-source revenue. The rest of the money used by local governments comes from fees and charges, which are often used to fund specific services. For counties, the largest other own-source revenues are derived from interest earnings and sewer, public housing, and solid waste charges. For municipalities, the largest other own-source revenues are derived from sewer charges, interest earnings, franchise fees, land development permits, licenses, and service charges and user fees.[30] The only taxes not typically used by Oregon state and local governments are sales taxes, which have been defeated by voters at the ballot box at least eight times.

Although local revenue sources are the primary source of funding for the vast majority of local services, particularly at the county level, local governments also receive revenue from nonlocal sources, such as federal and state timber receipts, state grants-in-aid, and state revenue sharing (for example, cigarette, liquor, and gas taxes).[31] Frequently, state revenue transfers are earmarked for specific services.

Declining revenue from property taxes and timber receipts has placed significant fiscal constraints on Oregon local governments. In response, municipalities and counties are assigning priorities to expenditures, putting off capital projects, and choosing not to provide some services. During the 1990s, in order to make up for lost revenues, Oregon local governments began to rely more on user fees and to impose them on an increasingly broad range of services.[32] In 1994, for example, every county reported an increase in revenue from user fees, ranging from 4 percent to 253 percent, or an average of 42 percent (the median was 30 percent).

All Oregon counties, and some larger Oregon cities, are permitted to use general-obligation bonds for development projects. Counties may issue and sell general-obligation bonds if the action is approved by a majority of the voters in a general or special election. However, state law prohibits aggregate indebtedness from exceeding 2 percent of the real market value of all taxable property in the county.[33] Unless proscribed by state law or the city charter, cities with populations of 85,000 or more may issue general-obligation bonds upon approval of a majority of voters. With some exceptions, cities are restricted from issuing bonds that are in excess of 3 percent of the real market value of the taxable property within city boundaries.[34] All local governments, municipalities and counties alike, are authorized to issue revenue bonds for facilities that will later generate revenues, such as water lines and sewer systems. Regardless of the revenue source, local government, or a combination of the state and local government, retains a great deal of discretion in the operation of most services at the municipal and county levels.

Local Expenditures

Aside from schools, which are funded at the state level through local property taxes, the largest portion of a local government's budget goes to public safety, followed by sewer services, roads, social services, interest on the general debt, parks, libraries, and planning.[35] Some expenditures, such as water, sewer, and solid waste services, are fully funded by fees. Revenue generated from gas taxes and monies from federal grants may be earmarked for particular services. Comparatively speaking, municipal and county expenditures for general administrative functions have been growing more slowly than other categories of expenditure and represent a smaller proportion of total expenditures than they did in previous years.

The Oregon constitution and state law define restrictions on local government expenditures and on the state's obligation to local government debt. All levels of government are bound by a balanced budget requirement: budget deficits are forbidden. The state is prohibited from assuming the debts of municipalities and counties except under exceptional circumstances, such as war.[36] Counties are restricted from having debts or liabilities that exceed $5,000, and a county that declares bankruptcy will be incorporated into adjacent counties. Oregon local governments are required by law to submit an annual audit to the state, and to submit periodic reports of their fiscal condition if requested to do so by the secretary of state. Municipalities and counties can contract out for the audits, but all audits and reviews must be made in accordance with standards prescribed by the State Audits Division. The division also evaluates the audits or reviews to ensure compliance with these standards.

State Government Grants-in-Aid to Localities

State and federal aid to Oregon's general-purpose local governments dropped dramatically during the 1980s and 1990s. Except for a small upward movement in 1984, municipalities have experienced an uninterrupted decline since 1978 and a 54 percent reduction between 1984 and 1999. Counties had to withstand a sharper reduction in aid, but the loss was temporarily offset by increases in revenue from federal timber sales. However, this revenue source has plummeted since the spotted owl habitat came under federal protection in the 1990s. State payments to counties during 1995–1996 amounted to over $300 million, of which almost half were for health and social services (for example, mental health, maternal and child health, and juvenile, elderly, and veterans' programs). These payments account for approximately 25 percent of total county revenues.[37]

Unfunded Mandates

In the past, state mandates that have been particularly onerous for Oregon municipalities and counties were in the areas of public safety, personnel benefits, planning and community development, and public contracting. Surveys conducted in 1992 and 1994 revealed that an overwhelming number of municipal and county officials, representing approximately 83 percent of the municipalities and 95 percent of the counties, were concerned that increases in unfunded mandates and decreases in grants-in-aid would have an adverse affect on local fiscal health.[38]

In 1996 voters approved a ballot measure amending the state constitution so that the state legislature is now required to reimburse local governments for the costs of unfunded state mandates for new state programs. Exceptions to this requirement include laws involving crimes, judicial decisions, voter-approved initiatives, federally mandated programs, and programs that inform citizens about government activities. In addition, the state legislature can bypass the legislation and enact an unfunded mandate with a three-fifths vote of both houses.[39]

Access to Local Government

Oregon has always been recognized for its progressive politics and high levels of citizen involvement. The state capital in Salem is small, quaint, and very much open to the public; it is not uncommon for citizens to have relatively easy access to all state elected officials. The initiative, referendum, and recall; public hearings and advisory committees; and, most recently, the mail ballot are all features of what has become known as the "Oregon System" of participatory processes.

Local Elections

County governments play a central role in voter registration, the distribution of absentee ballots, and the administration of elections (distributing ballot boxes, selecting polling places, and so forth). The mail ballot—approved by the legislature for testing in 1981 and made permanent in 1987—is generally used for all state and local elections and was used for the first time in the primary and general national elections in 1995–1996. Innovations such as the mail ballot account for Oregon's well-deserved reputation for forward-thinking, citizen-based politics.

Following the practice in most western states, many municipal elections in Oregon are nonpartisan. For those primary elections in which partisanship is a factor, Oregon has a closed primary system that requires citizens to register their political affiliation.

Citizen Controls over Actions of Local Officials

Oregon has quite liberal provisions for referendum, initiative, and recall. Citizens may directly enact charter provisions and ordinances, amend or repeal actions taken by elective bodies, and end the terms of elected officials. Oregon has had these provisions at the state level since 1902, when the state constitution was amended to allow citizens to take these actions.[40] In 1906, citizens were empowered to enact charter provisions and ordinances and to amend or repeal actions by local government units. The power to recall local public officials was added to the constitution in 1908.[41]

As is evident from the wealth of ballot measures offered in each election, the initiative process is very popular among Oregonians. In the 1994 general election, for example, citizens considered eighteen ballot measures, ranging from a ban on the use of dogs for cougar and bear hunting to initiatives dealing with physician-assisted suicide and campaign finance reform. In the 1996 general election, Oregonians considered twenty-three ballot measures—the highest number since 1914. Eleven of these measures would have had some effect on state or local government expenses or revenues. Between 1902 and 1996, Oregonians passed 99 out of 288 initiative measures and 25 out of 61 referendum measures. During the same time period, the legislature referred 363 measures to the people, of which 206 passed. In a statewide public opinion survey conducted by Oregon State University in 1994, 69 percent of respondents indicated that the presence on the ballot of so many measures would not decrease the likelihood that they would vote, and 28 percent said that it would actually increase the likelihood that they would vote.[42]

The state has a tradition of innovative policies, such as the "Bottle Bill," mail ballots, state health care programs, physician-assisted suicide, campaign finance reform, and regional land-use policies. The state has a history of grassroots politics, with widespread and frequent use of direct initiatives. Oregonians can even amend the state constitution through the ballot box.

State-Local Relations

The state of Oregon is well known for its citizen involvement and progressive, innovative politics. Part of this innovation is found in the state's commitment to and confidence in local government. Since the turn of the century, several amendments to the state constitution and a number of state laws have increased the autonomy of municipal and county governments. Despite variation between the urban and rural areas of the state, there are few actual differences between the types of counties and municipalities in Oregon, and municipalities and counties of varying size and population share similar discretionary authority.

Interestingly, at the county level, the innovation for which Oregon is known makes home rule status somewhat meaningless. Of course, since every Oregon city enjoys home rule authority, there is no difference in governmental autonomy among cities.

However, regardless of the level of autonomy that Oregon municipalities and counties enjoy, fiscal restraints and citizens' increasing demands for services will cause local governments to face new obstacles in the future. Oregonians should be comforted with the knowledge that local government in the state is armed with a great deal of autonomy to meet these growing demands. In the state of Oregon, at least, it looks as if the municipal and county governments will become the new "laboratories of democracy" as they use their broad discretionary authority to meet these challenges.

Notes

1. Daniel Elazar used the early migration and settlement patterns of different religious and ethnic groups to develop classifications of three primary subcultures, which he labeled "moralistic," "individualistic," and "traditionalistic." Recent research by M. M. Reeves, which examined Oregon's progressive social policies, supports this characterization. See Daniel Elazar, *American Federalism: A View from the States*, 3d ed. (New York: Crowell, 1984); and M. M. Reeves, "The States as Polities: Reformed, Reinvigorated, Resourceful," *The Annals of the American Academy of Political and Social Science* 509 (1990): 83–93.

2. Mark Brunson and Brent Steel, "Sources of Variation in Attitudes and Beliefs about Federal Rangeland Management," *Journal of Range Management* 49 (January 1996): 69–75; Courtland Smith and Brent Steel, "Core-Periphery Relationships of Resource-Based Communities," *Journal of the Community Development Society* 26, no. 1 (1995): 52–70.

3. Brent Steel and Nicholas Lovrich, *Survey of State and Local Government Issues in Oregon and Washington* (Corvallis, Ore.: Program for Governmental Research and Education, Oregon State University, 1992).

4. Unless an election is held to fill a vacancy, legislators are elected in even-numbered years from single-member districts.

5. There is a twelve-year limit on the total number of years served in the state assembly. *Oregon Blue Book, 1997–98* (Salem, Ore.: Secretary of State, 1997), 150.

6. *Oregon Blue Book*, 151. All legislative deliberations are open to the public, including committee hearings. Because the state constitution prohibits amendments to be introduced during floor debate, most of the work of the state legislature takes place in committees, where legislators craft legislation, amend bills, table bills, and so forth.

7. The governor also chairs the State Land Board (created under Article VIII, section 5, of the state constitution), which is responsible for managing state lands and waterways. The proceeds from these lands are contributed to the common school fund, and the board distributes this money to counties for school support on a semiannual basis. The governor also chairs the Progress Board, which sets strategic goals for the state. *Oregon Blue Book*, 112.

8. Examples include regional transportation planning, land-use planning, solid waste disposal, regional landfill and transfer stations, and a number of performing arts and sports centers. *Oregon Blue Book*, 333.

9. For example, a constitutional amendment enacted in 1910 reads as follows: "The Legislative Assembly shall not enact, amend or repeal any charter or act of incorporation for any municipality, city or town. The legal voters of every city and town are hereby granted power to enact and amend their municipal charter, subject to the constitution and criminal laws of the State of Oregon." Oregon State Constitution, Article XI, section 2.

10. Ibid., Article VI, section 10.

11. Ibid. The procedures are codified in the Oregon Revised Statutes, 203.710–203.810.

12. Oregon State Constitution, Article XI, section 14(1).

13. Several state laws restrict the imposition of taxes or any increase in tax levies without voter approval. These laws do not affect counties with home rule charters, and some counties have levied taxes on gasoline, rental cars, hotels, and motels without voter approval.

14. Richard Cockle, "Home Rule Vexes Umatilla County," *The Oregonian,* January 23, 1996, p. B3.

15. Bureau of Governmental Research and Service, *Handbook of City Councilors* (Eugene, Ore.: Bureau of Governmental Research and Service, 1980), 36.

16. Oregon Revised Statutes, 203.030–203.065. These county legislative powers apply only outside of incorporated cities, unless city councils agree to abide by the laws. The only restriction on this general ordinance-making authority is that the counties cannot do anything to contradict state or federal laws or the state or federal constitution.

17. Bill Penhollow, assistant executive director, Association of Oregon Counties, telephone interview, March 1, 1996.

18. James Mayer, "Metro Questions and Answers," *The Oregonian,* April 20, 1994, p. C4.

19. U.S. Advisory Commission on Intergovernmental Relations, *Measuring Local Discretionary Authority* (Washington, D.C.: Government Printing Office, 1981), 59. However, when there is conflict between local enactment and state law, there is still some uncertainty as to which will prevail. Judicial activity in this area dates back to 1914. In *Branch v. Albee,* the Oregon Supreme Court ruled that local enactments would prevail if the subject matter was predominantly of "local concern." In *Heinig v. Milwaukee* (1962), the court held that a state law that conflicted with a municipal rule was inapplicable to the city. In *LaGrande/Astoria v. PERB* (1978), the court amended *Heinig* with the following principle: home rule amendments prevent the state legislature from enacting and amending charters but do not prevent it from enacting substantive laws applicable to cities.

20. Bruce Weber, Karen Seidel, and Brent Steel, *Oregon's Cities and Counties in Transition: Fiscal Condition, Fiscal Decisions, Fiscal Prospects* (Corvallis, Ore.: Program for Governmental Research and Education, Oregon State University), 26.

21. Ibid., 27.

22. Martha J. Bianco, *County Services and Revenues in Oregon FY 94–95* (Portland: Center for Urban Studies, Portland State University, 1995), 14–15.

23. Local factors significantly influence the nature and extent of services provided by each county. In the 1994 Survey of Oregon Counties, county officials identified a larger number of local factors affecting service levels than they had in previous years. Over 50 percent of respondents indicated that population growth was the biggest factor; other factors included increases in criminal activity, demands for health and mental health services, mill closures, declines in timber harvests, an aging population, economic growth, and environmental and fishing regulations. Over 60 percent of respondents noted that residents were demanding more services, particularly in the area of administration of justice, followed by social services, land-use planning, the development of roads, and solid waste.

State factors, such as legislative mandates affecting service levels, also affect the number and variety of functions offered by county governments. Yet another factor is the primary revenue source for the county. For instance, because their principal revenue source has experienced declines in recent years, counties that are more dependent on property taxes tend to contract out services or to turn to multicounty agencies. Of course, fiscal constraints also influence the nature and variety of services offered by counties. Bianco, *County Services and Revenues,* 26, 28, 50.

24. Ibid., xix.

25. For cities, see Oregon Revised Statutes, 223.387–399; for counties, see 203.030–203.065.

26. Ibid., 190.010.

27. For instance, in regard to personnel management, local governments have a large amount of discretion in hiring and firing and are not bound by state civil service requirements, yet they must meet statewide standards for affirmative action. The state also has a strong public employees union, governed by the State Employee Relation Board; the union oversees all employment issues at the state level—including collective bargaining arrangements, which currently take place behind closed doors. The workshops provided by the Oregon Department of Revenue, which offer continuing education to municipal assessors, tax collectors, treasurers, and budget officials, offer an example of the state's role in training local officials.

28. Senate Bill 100 requires local governments to prepare land-use plans.

29. Bruce Weber, Brent Steel, and Robert Mason, "Measure 5: What Did Voters Really Want?" 1991 Legislative Discussion Paper (Salem, Ore.: Oregon Economic Development Department, 1991), 2; Brent Steel, Bruce Weber, and Karen Seidel, "The Impact of Ballot Measure 5 on County and City Government Finances," Legislative Discussion Paper (Salem, Ore.: Oregon Economic Development Department, 1991), 5; Weber, Seidel, and Steel, *Oregon's Cities and Counties,* 34.

30. Bianco, *County Services and Revenues,* xxvi. In 1994 these local revenue sources made up the majority of each county's total revenue (mean equals 51 percent).

31. Another element affecting local government fiscal autonomy is the federal Endangered Species Act. For a number of years, Oregon has relied on revenue generated from timber sales to help fund county projects, and the act places this revenue source in jeopardy. Federal forest receipts are derived from thirty-one of Oregon's thirty-six counties; eighteen of Oregon's western counties, which contain Oregon and California railroad grant lands managed by the federal Bureau of Land Management, also generate revenue from the sale of timber, and fifteen counties sell timber directly from state-owned forests. Overall, county timber revenues have declined anywhere from 3.5 percent in the Portland, Oregon, region to over 24 percent in Linn and Lane Counties. Weber, Seidel, and Steel, *Oregon's Cities and Counties,* 58–63. The loss in statewide revenue caused by declining timber sales has had more of an effect on functions provided at the county level than the cutbacks that resulted from Measure 5.

32. Weber, Seidel, and Steel, *Oregon's Cities and Counties,* 15.

33. Oregon Revised Statutes, 287.054.

34. Ibid., 287.004. Bonds for local improvement districts, bonds issued for water systems, sanitary or storm sewers, sewage disposal plants, hospitals, gas power or lighting facilities, and bonds for the acquisition or construction of off-street parking facilities are not included in this restriction.

35. Bianco, *County Services and Revenues,* xxv.

36. Oregon State Constitution, Article XI, sections 8, 9, and 10.

37. Weber, Seidel, and Steel, *Oregon's Cities and Counties,* 9–10.

38. Ibid., 5, 53.

39. Oregon State Constitution, Article X, section 15. The measure requires a retention vote four years after passage.

40. As practiced in Oregon's local jurisdictions, the initiative gives citizens the power to propose and enact or repeal laws independent of the elected body. To place a statutory initiative measure on the ballot, 6 percent of the voters who participated in the previous election must sign a petition; initiatives on constitutional amendments require a petition signed by 8 percent of registered voters. Under a referendum, measures already enacted by the legislature are submitted to a vote of the people. For a referendum to be placed on the ballot, 4 percent of registered voters at the preceding election must sign a petition.

41. Oregon State Constitution, Article II, section 18.

42. Brent Steel, Nicholas Lovrich, and Bruce Weber, *1995 Pacific Northwest Survey of State Government Issues* (Corvallis, Ore.: Program for Governmental Research and Education, Oregon State University, 1995).

PENNSYLVANIA

Beverly A. Cigler, with the assistance of Richard D. White Jr.

Pennsylvania's 2,568 municipalities, 67 counties, and 1,505 active and 693 inactive authorities comprise a complicated, diverse, and fragmented governmental system. In this Dillon's Rule state, only 71 local governments have adopted home rule charters since 1972, when the home rule charter law passed.[1] Special legislation enacted in 1997 allowed Allegheny County, which includes Pittsburgh, to use a simplified home rule charter process. County residents subsequently voted by referendum for a modern county government with an elected executive, appointed professional manager, and elected council.

In mid-2000, Pennsylvania became the twelfth state since 1992 to take over a school districts because of academic failure. Eleven districts are receiving varying amounts of grant money and have the power to reorganize, privatize, or change their schools, extend the school year, and change teachers' duties that are not mandated by contract. The state has taken direct control of one district and given the other ten a three-year deadline to improve scores or face state takeover. The state's attempt to place the Harrisburg School District under the control of the mayor of the capital city was stopped by a state supreme court injunction in July 2000.[2]

Governmental Setting

Pennsylvania is a state of contrasts.[3] Ranked fifth among states in population (with nearly 12 million residents in 1990), it is an urban state with large metropolitan areas surrounding Philadelphia in the east and Pittsburgh in the west. It also has the largest rural population of any state, with 31 percent of its residents living in the sparsely populated countryside and mountainous regions. Nearly one of every five residents lives outside of a metropolitan area, and nearly a fourth live in small urban places vastly different from the large metropolitan areas. Political consultant James Carville refers to Pennsylvania as "Pittsburgh, Philadelphia, and Alabama in between." Daniel Elazar classifies the state's political culture as individualistic.[4]

Pennsylvania's history is characterized by moderation in politics, (but that is changing),[5] fierce localism, regional conflict, and partisanship—tax collectors and judges, for example, still run on party labels. Unique among the states, Pennsylvania counties must have at least one commissioner from the minority party in the county.

Home Rule in Pennsylvania

Historical Development

Pennsylvania's governmental design owes much to the state's history and tradition.[6] Its basic structure can be traced to 1681, when King Charles II of England granted a charter to William Penn to establish a proprietary colony in the New World. Penn created county governments, making each county responsible primarily for the local court system, law enforcement, and elections. As the population spread westward and northward, more counties were created, with the last established in 1878. As settlements developed around trading centers, transportation routes, and county seats, residents required services that county governments could not or would not provide. Townships largely filled the service void. Penn's original charter authorized the subdivision of counties into townships for the administration of local government functions. The first townships were formed in 1682 in the areas around Philadelphia, in the southeastern part of the state. As settlers moved westward, they formed townships in frontier areas, often before the population was large enough to justify a separate county. Thus, in most areas of the state the oldest subdivisions are townships.

Borough government, also authorized in Penn's charter, developed later. Two-thirds of the current boroughs were incorporated between 1850 and 1910, when the state industrialized and urbanized and put an extensive railroad network in place. Most of Pennsylvania's present cities were boroughs first and did not become cities until their population increased. As the Industrial Revolution brought more development to the state, the fiscal viability of many townships was jeopardized, since the cities and boroughs annexed their developed portions. In 1899 the legislature tried to remedy the problem by providing for two categories of townships—first class and second class—based on population density. The legislature designated as first class those townships with a population density greater than 300 people per square mile and permitted them to preserve their character through the use of different revenue powers. In the 1930s and 1940s the legislature granted second-class townships the same powers. To become a township of the first class, second-class townships must have a population density of 300 people per square mile and voters must approve the change of classification in a referendum. Despite the law, many townships meeting the density requirement remain second class. First-class townships are uncommon and have large, dense populations exceeding ten thousand. Most are located in suburban Philadelphia and Pittsburgh.

Owing to rapid urbanization between the end of the Civil War and World War I, economic and political activity became more concentrated in rapidly growing cities and boroughs. In 1937 first-class townships received important protection against annexation of territory by adjoining municipalities through the requirement of approval of any annexation by a referendum vote of the entire township. The law helped prevent their legal "disappearance." Second-class townships long sought similar protection but did not gain it until passage of the 1968 amendments to the state constitution.

Beginning after 1920 and accelerating after the end of World War II in 1945, first-class townships located on the fringe of metropolitan areas grew rapidly. Township government emerged as an equal to other municipal classifications, and the legislature expanded the powers of townships to equal those of other classifications. In the last two decades, the population of older, more central townships peaked as they became mature, fully developed municipalities. Many townships of the second class are experiencing a growth boom currently.

Pennsylvania was not significantly influenced by the Progressive Movement's efforts to reform municipal governments at the beginning of the twentieth century. The home rule law of 1972 came almost a century after Missouri became the first state to grant constitutional home rule in 1875. Home rule has helped the few local governments that use it to increase citizen participation and has enabled a modest local initiative in procedural and substantive matters. It has not, however, revolutionized local government operation, nor has it entangled municipalities in legal difficulties.

Pennsylvania uses Dillon's Rule, the well-accepted principle of municipal law that a local government, as a municipal corporation, is an instrumentality of the state deriving its powers and very existence from the state, and that a local government may exercise only such powers as are expressed or derived from acts of the legislature. Home rule must be weighed in the light of the 1968 Pennsylvania Constitution, which in Article IX deals with the power of the legislature to create, regulate, control, and merge local governments. The article directs the General Assembly to provide certain laws and limits its power over local governments in certain respects. The home rule charter and optional plans provisions (sections 2 and 3 of Article IX) give constitutional rights to municipalities as well as directives to the legislature concerning these rights.[7]

Acting under that authority, the legislature passed the Home Rule Charter and Optional Plans Law of April 13, 1972.[8] Upon adoption of a home rule charter, a governmental entity essentially discards the municipal code under which it had been functioning. All municipalities have the right to adopt optional plans of government, which alter the municipality's structural form and administrative organization. However, the municipality continues to be subject to its particular municipal code regarding municipal powers.

Definition of Home Rule

Home rule communities can determine for themselves what structure their government takes and what services it performs. Municipalities can draft and amend their own charters and exercise any power or perform any function not denied by the state constitution, the legislature, or their home rule charters. Counties, townships, boroughs, and cities may choose among such alternative plans as an executive or mayor-council form of government, a council-manager plan, or a small municipality plan for communities with fewer than 7,500 in population. Municipalities and counties without home rule can act only where specifically authorized by state law; home rule jurisdictions can act anywhere except where they are specifically limited by state law.

Municipalities that are considering adopting home rule create study commissions to recommend a governmental form, and the recommended form must be voted on at a popular election. The home rule provision does not reverse Dillon's Rule, since local units are not given complete independence, but relaxes it. The last sentence of Article IX, section 2, of the Pennsylvania Constitution states: "A . . . municipality which has a home rule charter may exercise any power or perform any function not denied by this Constitution, by its home rule charter or by the General Assembly at any time." Article III of the Home Rule Charter and Optional Plans Law lists ten areas in which self-government is limited:

1. The filing and collection of municipal tax claims or liens and the sale of real or personal property in satisfaction thereof

2. The procedures in the exercise of the powers of eminent domain, and the assessment of damages and benefits for property taken or injured or destroyed

3. Boundary changes of municipalities

4. Regulation of public schools

5. The registration of electors and the conduct of elections

6. The fixing of subjects of taxation

7. The fixing of the rates of nonproperty or personal taxes levied upon nonresidents

8. The assessment of real or personal property and persons for taxation purposes

9. Defining or providing for the punishment of any felony or misdemeanor

10. Municipal planning under the provisions of the Pennsylvania Municipalities Planning Code

Article III of the Home Rule Charter and Optional Plans Law also prohibits certain powers. No municipality can:

1. Enact an ordinance or take any other action dealing with the regulation of the transfer, ownership, transportation, or possession of firearms

2. Retroactively increase any fee or charge for any municipal service that has been provided

3. Determine duties, responsibilities, or requirements placed upon any business, occupations, and employers including the duty to withhold, remit, or report taxes or penalties levied upon them or upon persons in their employment, except as expressly provided by the legislature

A fourth prohibition applies to counties; they cannot exercise within any municipality in the county a power or function being exercised by the municipality, except under certain conditions, which are listed under the authority of the municipality or by an ordinance initiated in a variety of ways.

Structural Features

Special legislation aimed at a particular unit is prohibited. However, counties, municipalities, and school districts are classified by population, and the legislature may pass separate legislation for each class even if there is only one unit in a particular class.[9] Home rule gives a municipality unlimited power over the structure and organization of its own government but limits its powers over municipal boundary change, school districts, and municipal authorities. The state has passed uniform legislation for consolidation, merger, and boundary change procedures for municipalities. The closest municipal involvement with schools is through the sponsorship of a community college. Most municipal authorities are organized under the Municipality Authorities Act of 1945,[10] and attempts by local governments to exercise home rule powers over authorities failed.

With just seventy-one governments adopting home rule charters in the state, structural home rule is not high on the public agenda, nor is there significant interest in hiring professional managers. Only eleven municipalities have adopted optional plans of government: three cities, two boroughs, and six townships. Contemporary municipal reform centers on tax reform and planning and zoning issues. Local governments want more flexibility from the state, and the state is attempting to find ways to encourage local action. County governments advocate tax reform that better integrates county and school tax systems, since both rely on the property tax.

Five counties have home rule charters and one has special and limited home rule (Allegheny County).[11] Philadelphia is a city-county consolidation that has eliminated county offices. Philadelphia's strong mayor charter dates to 1952; Pittsburgh adopted the equivalent of home rule in 1974, as did Scranton. Home rule charters in five of the seventeen home rule cities provide for recall of elected officials. The legality of recall provisions in home rule charters became doubtful when in September 1993 the Pennsylvania Supreme Court declared the recall provisions in the Philadelphia Home Rule Charter unconstitutional.[12]

If a government study commission recommends home rule, it drafts a charter, and approval of a majority voting in a referendum leads to adoption of the charter. A 1974 amendment to the home rule law placed home rule municipalities under the provisions of the Pennsylvania Municipalities Planning Code. Municipalities may also use the government study commission process to adopt an optional plan, with the commission selecting from among a council-manager plan, an executive council plan (with three variations), or a plan for small municipalities in which the elected executive doubles as president of a council.

Municipalities adopting optional plans gain no home rule powers and remain subject to the provisions of their municipal code (except where it is superseded by the structural provisions of the optional plan). Optional plans are not popular with Pennsylvania municipalities. Only twelve optional plans have been adopted, and one of those was repealed in 1981.

Government study commissions are elected by popular vote. Since 1972 more than 200 government study commission questions have appeared on the ballot in nearly 200 different jurisdictions in 41 counties. Most appeared immediately after the passage of the home rule law. The study commissions issued reports in 163 cases. The election of one commission was voided by a court, and one commission's term expired before it filed a report. Eighteen commissions recommended no change. Twenty-two proposed optional plans; the voters approved twelve and defeated ten. One optional plan was later repealed and replaced by a home rule charter. One optional plan that was defeated proposed the repeal of an existing home rule charter and its replacement by an optional plan. More than 120 commissions wrote home rule charters, and voters defeated half of them. One defeated charter proposal tried to repeal and replace an existing charter. One commission recommended amendments to an existing charter. Five government study commissions were active in July 2000.

In Pennsylvania, all land is located within municipal boundaries, which is to say, all land is incorporated and is served by a municipal government with powers to provide needed services. As a result, annexation is not widely employed to extend municipal services. Only eighteen annexations occurred in the state between 1980 and 1990, for example, and that they involved less than one square mile and fewer than 500 persons. As townships became equal in powers and services to cities and boroughs, the utility of annexation declined, given that expansive township governments could provide needed services.

Due to the legislature's failure to enact uniform boundary change legislation, the courts in 1974 invalidated all preexisting annexation provisions still found in the municipal codes. The landmark decision, *Middle Paxton Township v. Borough of Dauphin* (326 A.2d 343, 458 Pa. 396, at 400, 1974), brought annexation actions to a standstill in the state. The initiative and referendum procedure established in the constitution (Article IX, section 8) remains the sole method of effecting annexations The procedure does not require approval of any governing body and is operative even without the passage of implementing legislation. The initiative and referendum procedures can be used to change the boundaries of any county, municipality, or similar future general-purpose unit of local government. It does not apply to school districts, municipal authorities, or other special-purpose units. The major key to successful boundary change appears to be obtaining the support, or at least the acquiescence, of officials of the municipality losing territory in advance of a change effort. In sum, the court decision gave the townships protection from annexation through requiring a referendum in the entire township.

More important than annexation are the procedures for municipal mergers, which have changed dramatically in recent years, reflecting changing popular views of the local government system. The Municipal Consolidation or Merger Act of 1994 (53 Pa C.S. 731 et seq.) provided for the merger or consolidation of municipalities and also replaced previous legislation providing merger or consolidation procedures for financially distressed municipalities (Municipalities Financial Recovery Act of 1987). The 1994 legislation provided the first uniform statutory process for combining municipalities, and several of them have consolidated since.

Pennsylvania's local governments and municipalities can own property or facilities beyond their boundaries. An example is the purchase of a golf course. Municipal authorities tend to use this option more than municipal governments.

Functions of Local Government

Functional Responsibilities

General-purpose governments include 67 counties, 1,548 townships, 1 town, 56 cities, and 963 boroughs. Special-purpose governments include 501 school districts and 2,198 authorities—a third of all authorities in the United States—that provide specific services such as sewer, water, recreation, airports, financing, and parking. These public corporations are created by general-purpose governments or school districts without a voter referendum, but once formed, their decisions are not subject to approval or veto by the governments or school districts. Only 64 Pennsylvania municipalities serve populations of 20,000 or above; 80 percent are under 5,000 population. Forty-two of the

67 counties are over 50 percent rural, and seven are 100 percent rural, although just 8 counties serve populations of less than 25,000.[13]

The number of local governments has been stable for the past few decades, with two major exceptions. Small school districts, those enrolling under 5,000 students, were consolidated in 1963, decreasing the number of districts from 2,056 to 501 today. A trend within the educational system is the creation of charter schools. Authorities, first established during the Depression, have proliferated at a rapid pace, largely due to their use as financing mechanisms.

Cities are classified by population, with Philadelphia, Pittsburgh, and Scranton alone in their respective population categories. These three elect strong mayors with broad administrative, appointive, and removal powers. Other cities operate under a weaker commission form, with mayors and four other council members elected for four-year, overlapping terms. The mayor serves as commission chairperson and has a ceremonial function as well as powers equal to those of council members; the chairperson has no veto power. Each of the other commissioners heads a department: accounts and finance, streets and public improvement, public safety, and parks and public property. A controller and treasurer are elected at-large for four-year terms, with other appointments made by the council. Between 1957 and 1972, small cities could adopt the mayor-council plan or the council-manager plan by referendum. Twenty-two of the fifty-one small cities use the commission form; eleven use the mayor-council form; and four use a council-manager form.

Boroughs are the second most common form of municipal government and are not classified by population. However, when a borough reaches ten thousand in population, it may become a city by state law. Boroughs are generally small units and are almost evenly divided between those urban and rural in character. Less than a fifth have populations exceeding five thousand. Borough government uses the weak-mayor system, with a mayor who is elected to a four-year term and who cannot hire employees or direct programs. Borough mayors execute and enforce ordinances and regulations and represent the borough at community events.

The dominant body in borough government is the elected council, which usually has seven members with four-year overlapping terms. Tax collectors, tax assessors, and auditors are elected and independent of the council, although the council may appoint other officials. Boroughs with populations greater than one thousand may choose to elect only five members. In boroughs that are divided into wards, one or two council members are elected from each ward, and the council elects one member to serve as council president and preside at meetings. Approximately a fifth of Pennsylvania's boroughs have a manager appointed by the council, and a borough secretary is often the key link for information in the overall organization.

Early in Pennsylvania's history, the primary duty of most township officers was road maintenance. The governing bodies of townships, cities, and boroughs now make policy decisions, levy taxes, borrow money, authorize expenditures, and direct the administration of their governments. Municipal responsibilities are broad, yet the powers conferred upon local governments by home rule are often not exercised. Some powers are shared with the state, the national government, other communities, or the private sector. Today, Pennsylvania's municipalities have similar statutory powers, for the most part, and the same basic responsibilities for the provision of public services. This homogenization has taken many years to achieve, due to historical precedents and resistance to change. Common local services include police and fire protection, emergency management, maintenance of local roads and streets, water supply, sewage and refuse collection and treatment, parking and traffic control, local planning and zoning, parks and recreation, health and safety regulations, libraries, museums, concerts and other community activities, licensing of businesses, and building code enforcement.

Most local governments have specialized bureaucratic units to deliver services, many of which are powerful and independent entities in their own right. These entities include nearly 2,400 volunteer fire departments (the most of any state) and about 100 paid or combination paid/volunteer fire departments. It also includes more than 2,500 police departments, most of them with full-time officers but about 250 with part-time personnel. State police alone cover the needs of nearly 1,400 communities, which is a controversial use of state funds. Contracted police are used in about a hundred communities, and there are also about two dozen regional police departments. The state's local governments employ nearly 145,000 individuals full-time. Collectively, the municipalities have more than 1,600 planning commissions and several thousand police, fire, and nonuniform pension funds.

Pennsylvania has a county-township form of government.[14] Counties, and to a lesser extent townships, were originally created to service scattered populations. Boroughs and cities were established to service population concentrations or urban settlements, both large and small. Counties are empowered by the state to serve largely as administrative agents for the delivery of human services and have limited responsibilities. Citizens are more likely to turn to their smaller hometowns for leadership—municipalities with few personnel and heavy reliance on volunteerism. Most elected and appointed officials work part-time. Larger governments have professional management and planning staffs, but there are only about four hundred municipal managers.

Most counties vest daily administration in an appointed chief clerk. Counties fall into nine population classes, and most counties have a three-member board of county commissioners as their chief governing body. Numerous other elected, independent officials, or "row officers," include a treasurer, coroner, recorder of deeds, prothonotary, clerk of courts, register of wills, sheriff, district attorney, jury commissioners, auditor, and controller.

Townships, cities, and boroughs make policy decisions, levy taxes, borrow money, authorize expenditures, and direct the administration of their government. Depending on the type of municipal government, the number and titles of officials and governing boards vary. Many municipal governments have mixed electoral systems that include at-large and ward elections. Second-class townships, the most common form of government in the state, generally have three supervisors who hold six-year terms.

Counties are agents of the state for law enforcement, judicial administration, and the conduct of elections. They perform property assessments, and some are involved in regional planning, solid waste disposal, and public health, including drug and alcohol abuse. Counties are key providers of welfare services, including mental health. Many counties establish housing and redevelopment authorities; conduct community development programs; maintain homes for the indigent, aged, and handicapped; and support local libraries and community colleges. Because of their geographic size, counties have increased responsibilities for mass transportation and environmental protection, with a few becoming more active in economic development and growth management.

Sewer and water authorities are the most common of the public authorities; multipurpose authorities are least common.[15] Authorities cannot levy taxes and are required to finance their operations, services, and facilities through revenues produced from service charges or lease rentals. They can acquire, construct, improve, maintain, and operate projects and borrow money and issue bonds to finance them, as well as exercise the power of eminent domain. Municipalities and authorities have considerable effect on each other in the area of financing and a largely neglected need for coordination. General-purpose governments in the state have comprehensive borrowing powers, so they no longer need to create authorities to avoid restrictive limitations on municipal power to incur debt. Authorities persist and proliferate because they are perceived as effective ways of coping with spill-overs and intergovernmental issues, although there is growing interest in making public authorities more accountable to the governments that created them.

School districts are administered by nine-member school boards elected by voters for four-year overlapping terms, except in Philadelphia. School district taxation, assessment, and borrowing influence general-purpose governments, and the trend is toward increased cooperation (for example, shared recreational facilities). In mid-2000, the state gave the popular and successful mayor of Harrisburg control of the 8,760 Harrisburg school district, in the capital region. The state gave him sweeping authority to oversee the district. However, the Harrisburg School Board sued the state, arguing that the district, which has a lower failure rate than others covered by the Education Empowerment Act of 2000, was treated differently than other districts. The state constitution bars the legislature from enacting special or local laws that could be covered by general laws. The Harrisburg takeover occurred without input from the district, another issue with constitutional implications, since special or local bills must be advertised in the locality affected at least thirty days before introduction in the General Assembly. In July 2000, the state supreme court blocked the mayor from exercising the sweeping powers given to him by the state. Harrisburg is being treated like the other school districts, which were given three years to improve scores or face state takeover.

The state has more than seventy-one councils of government, which are voluntary organizations of two or more local governments.[16] These councils engage in joint purchasing of materials, shared administration, and joint planning, among other activities. Rural governments participate less in councils of government than their urban counterparts, and the rural councils generally provide a limited range of services. Nine regional planning agencies across the state offer advisory planning, gather data, perform analyses, and provide technical assistance to counties and municipalities in economic development, transportation, and other planning areas.

Administrative Discretion

County commissions are the legislative and executive branches of the county, responsible for passing ordinances, assessing all real and personal property for tax purposes, registering voters, and maintaining county buildings. Even home rule counties must organize and operate under a modified commission form in which legislative powers are vested in the board of county commissioners, while executive and administrative authority is dispersed among a variety of popularly elected administrative officers (county row officers), the courts, and the board of commissioners itself.

State law places no limitation on the form of government that home rule counties can adopt, but some accommodation must be made for the popular election of at least some county officials. For example, three counties feature a single-executive type of government, as does Allegheny County. One uses a five-member council, and another uses a three-member board of commissioners. Some have an appointed county administrator to assist in an administrative capacity, whereas others vest daily administration in the appointed chief clerk, who may have expanded responsibilities.

General-purpose governments vary in their organization and activities because they serve diverse communities, but most small governments provide the same basic services as large ones. Service delivery in the smaller communities is constrained by low population density, greater reliance on volunteerism, limited revenue sources, limited staff, and few or no professional administrators. Elected officials are the central actors in this pattern of governing, serving as both program managers and policy makers. Some municipalities have given over the administration of health to the state Department of Health. Solid waste collection is often contracted out to the private sector, as are other services, such as police. Some functional consolidations in which two or more communities agree to deliver a service jointly have occurred, most notably with community police forces and solid waste collection.

There are few requirements in the government codes related to personnel. Most municipalities do not have personnel manuals and rely instead on their solicitors to deal with issues. Many counties have personnel departments and manuals, but the responsibilities often fall to the chief clerk. Municipal positions generally do not fall under civil service, but county programs, which generally receive state or federal funds, are required to follow state salary guidelines and to use selection procedures administered by the State Civil Service Commission.

A 1999 court decision expanded the scope of the state's whistleblower law to apply to all agencies that receive public monies from the state, including appropriated and pass-through funds.[17] The impact is likely to be that the law will apply to for-profit and not-for-profit service providers working in the areas of drugs and alcohol, mentally handicapped, the aged, detained juveniles, work-release prisoners, and nursing homes.

There is no uniform procurement code that applies to all municipalities, but enabling legislation sets forth the authority of local entities to purchase goods and services, as well as the methods required for particular types of purchases.[18] The legislation also details the advertising and financial security requirements for competitive bidding and the procedures for soliciting competitive bids. The allowable methods of procurement are competitive sealed bids, competitive price quotations, sole-source acquisition, and competitive negotiations. Legislation also covers anti–bid rigging provisions and joint purchasing.[19] A particular type of sole-source acquisition known as piggyback purchasing is permitted; municipalities can purchase materials, supplies, and equipment through contracts entered into by the Commonwealth. A number of municipalities have begun to buy through cooperative purchasing. Pennsylvania courts are known for strictly construing the legislation governing procurement, so the seemingly simple process of purchasing goods and services is cumbersome.

The Pennsylvania Municipalities Planning Code permits municipalities to create a planning agency (usually a planning commission) and a comprehensive plan and to enact zoning ordinances.[20] All counties have planning commissions, with varying degrees of capability. Because growth management is a key concern of citizens, the governor, and the legislature, numerous legislative bills have been intensely debated over the last three years. In June 2000 the state revised the code to rationalize the zoning process, to permit joint planning among municipalities, and to provide new financial and technical assistance incentives to spur local action. The most problematic part of the planning code before these revisions was the requirement that local governments provide for every zoning use within their municipality. Now they will be able to provide for every use within their collective borders if they choose to do intermunicipal planning. This incentive to cooperate is untested across the fifty states.[21]

Economic Development

Pennsylvania communities have wide authority in the area of community development. The most significant recent legislation, passed in October 1998, created 12 "Keystone Opportunity Zones" that include 54 counties, 185 local governments, and 133 school districts.[22] Tax abatement through credits, exemptions, waivers, and deductions for taxable economic activity is expected to reduce taxable economic activity to zero within a zone. The program fosters community and economic development to address business attraction and retention, educational improvement, housing reinvestment, and quality of life issues. Several municipalities have also created neighborhood investment districts to foster the rebirth of their downtowns.

Pennsylvania also has the usual array of economic development agencies common in large urban states across the nation. What is new is that some counties are taking increased interest in economic development, creating new entities and funding mechanisms as well as industrial parks. State funding for stadium development has been controversial in several cities.

Fiscal Autonomy of Local Governments

Local Revenues

The legislature has clearly defined the narrow range of municipal discretion as to tax matters.[23] Real estate taxes are the leading local revenue producer, accounting for more than 68 percent of taxes collected. They are the only taxes authorized by law to be levied by all classes of local government. These taxes account for more than 80 percent of the total tax revenues of school districts, 39 percent of those for municipalities, and 94 percent of the total tax revenues of counties.

Pennsylvania is unusual among the states in enabling its local governments, except counties and school districts, to levy a broad range of non–real estate taxes. Non–real estate taxes account for 32 percent of all tax revenues and 15 percent of all local revenues, ranging from 2 percent for counties to almost 31 percent for second-class townships. The earned income tax is the second highest revenue generator, with occupation and personal property taxes minor in comparison. Types of non–real estate taxes include earned income or wage, per capita, occupation,

occupational privilege, intangible personal property, real estate transfer, amusement, and mercantile and business privileges taxes. Nontax revenues come from public service enterprises, water supply and sewer charges, state and federal grants, licenses, permits, and fines.

Municipal borrowing is subject to limits set by the state legislature under the authority of Article IX, section 10 of the constitution. Debt limits are set for all units, except Philadelphia, by the Local Government Unit Debt Act. Debt limits are placed on local governments based on their municipal revenues. In 1968 Pennsylvania became one of the more liberal states regarding borrowing by all classes of local government. The amount of debt that a local government may incur without a voter referendum was liberalized by the use of a formula based on the average income of the municipality or other unit during a specified period of years.

Cities and counties may incur particular forms of debt, including lease-rental debt, tax and revenue anticipation bonds, general obligation bonds, and revenue bonds. Excluding authority debt incurred on behalf of nonprofit hospitals, roughly twice as much debt exists for county or municipal purposes under authority obligations than under direct obligations of counties and municipalities. Recent years have seen a marked shift from authority financing to direct debt for school purposes.

The debt limits of municipalities, counties, and school districts are based on their annual revenues. The borrowing base of a municipality is computed by arithmetic average of the total revenues for the preceding three full fiscal years. By the nonelectoral process, a county may borrow 300 percent of its borrowing base, and any other local government units may borrow 250 percent of their borrowing base. There is no limit on electoral debt, which is debt approved by the electors of a municipality, nor on self-liquidating debt, which is debt repaid solely from rents or user charges. The limit for lease-rental debt—that debt incurred by an authority and repaid through lease-rental payments by the municipality—and other nonelectoral debt combined is 400 percent for counties and 350 percent for municipalities and school districts. The combination of nonelectoral debt and lease-rental debt cannot exceed the lease-rental limitations.

All borrowing, including the issuance of tax anticipation notes, is governed by the terms of the Local Government Unit Debt Act. Due to unwise local investments around the nation in recent years, many observers to Pennsylvania state government expect the state to propose broad reform legislation soon.

Overall, state authority greatly reduces local governments' fiscal flexibility. Their flexibility is further influenced by the appropriateness, variety, and productivity of their revenue sources and whether their sources of significant revenue potential can be varied over the years in response to changing demands for services and new circumstances. Flexibility is diminished when local governments must rely extensively on earmarked sources, whether taxes, charges, or special assessments and tightly drawn tax bases. Pennsylvania continues to specify which of its jurisdictions can levy taxes, what the taxes can be used for, and how the levies must occur.[24]

The "millage cap" on real estate taxes illustrates the differences in taxing power between home rule communities and other communities, with the former not subject to the cap limits established in the various local government codes. That is, home rule communities may establish their own real estate tax rate limits. Nor are home rule municipalities and counties subject to the limit on local income taxes imposed on local government by the Local Tax Enabling Act of 1965.

Local Expenditures

The differences among classes of local government are significant for understanding expenditures. Per capita expenditures are highest in Philadelphia, Pittsburgh, and Scranton; other cities also have high per capita expenditures, whereas the lowest expenditures are in boroughs and in townships. The major areas of expenditures for all cities, boroughs and townships are police, fire, inspections, streets and highways, health services, libraries, parks and recreation, water supply and other municipal utilities, interest, general government, sewers, solid waste, and miscellaneous. Half of capital outlays are for streets and highways and public service enterprises.

County expenditures are primarily for general government, judicial expenses, highways, health, corrections, human services, interest, and miscellaneous.

Counties are the major human service providers in Pennsylvania. The total available funds for county human services exceeds $1 billion per year, 85 percent of which are federal and state funds and the rest of which are county general funds.[25] The primary programs include mental health and mental retardation, child welfare and juvenile justice, aging, nursing homes, drug and alcohol, and adult services. Funding is used for prevention and education, crisis intervention and protection, assistance and income transfers, treatment, in-home services, residential and institutional care, and for integrating services. Another major area of county spending is corrections. Unlike human services, the full cost of operating jails and prisons rests with the counties. Counties handle elections and tax assessment and may have responsibility for some public works projects; transportation; public safety, especially emergency management and communications; land-use planning and zoning; and solid waste management.

Municipalities, quasi-public agencies, private utilities, and private firms provide most public works services. In contrast to their lack of discretion in fiscal matters, Pennsylvania's local governments have very broad discretionary powers in the area of land use, although most of the state's municipalities still do not have comprehensive plans or utilize their zoning authority.

Townships are increasingly adopting building codes (which are voluntary in the state), and zoning, housing, and parking regulations. They are empowered to construct and maintain sewage systems; provide and operate parks, playgrounds, and other recreational facilities; establish a police force; and provide for street lighting and other services.

Most counties use modern accounting and auditing practices, meaning records are made on a double entry basis and transactions are automatically reported against the established budget. Separate funds are created where required or when they pertain to specific areas of concern, such as projects funded by the proceeds from debt. Most municipalities are small and unsophisticated but follow state law and use line-item budgets.

The various government codes set forth statutory requirements for auditors and controllers and govern their duties.[26] The state has established extensive reporting requirements and has passed legislation dealing with distressed municipalities and school districts. Recently, there has been a pronounced increase in bankruptcy filings by entities served by municipalities, which then must collect their claims in bankruptcy proceedings. As a result, the state has been proactive in providing assistance to local governments on ways to interact with other providers of municipal services.

State Government Grants-in-Aid to Localities

State and national government financial assistance to Pennsylvania local governments is significant. The state provides many grants and subsidies from its general fund, especially for local education. Other major grants include those for mental health and mental retardation, urban mass transit, child welfare, police and fire pensions, firefighters' relief funds, local health programs, community colleges, public utility tax rebates, county courts, aging programs, sewage treatment plants, and libraries. Many federal funds go first to the state and then to local units for highways, welfare, health, education, and housing and community development. Local governments often contribute a share of financial and administrative support to a program before other funding is forthcoming.

Approximately 38 percent of the state's general fund budget goes to local government grants and subsidies. The major program is for local education. Other major grants are for mental health and mental retardation programs, urban mass transit, local road and bridges, child welfare programs, police and fire pensions and firemen's relief funds, local health programs, aging programs, sewage treatment plant operations, libraries, drug and alcohol abuse programs, and housing and redevelopment. The major increases in state funding in recent years have been for environmental programs, growth management, and assistance to volunteer fire departments.

Information is not sorted by the number, types, or amounts of state grants per community. It is significant, however, that the funds for intermunicipal cooperation, shared administrative services, and core planning functions have tripled in the last few years, to about $3.5 million in 2000. Another large source of local funds is returns from the state's liquid fuels tax.[27]

Upon taking office in 1995, Gov. Tom Ridge worked to eliminate the "walking around money" that legislators used for special projects for their home districts. On the other hand, the governor has been widely criticized for replacing the walking around money with community revitalization program funds, which have very poorly defined selection criteria and are now characterized as the governor's walking around money.

Additional state funding to municipal governments is the more than $600,000 provided for periodic training of municipal officials. These funds are distributed to the various municipal associations that organize the training.

Unfunded Mandates

As a Dillon's Rule state, neither the legislature's Local Government Commission nor the Governor's Center for Local Government Services keeps records on the number and types of mandates. Nearly everything affecting local government could be construed as a mandate.[28]

Access to Local Government

Local Elections

The Pennsylvania Constitution states that elections are to be free and equal and that no power, civil or military, can interfere with the free exercise of the right of suffrage. Citizens eighteen years of age or older are eligible to vote if they hold U.S. citizenship for at least one month and if they reside in the state thirty days immediately preceding the election. Other constitutional provisions concern election days, offices to be filled by election, rights of electors, bribery of electors, election and registration laws, voting machines, violation of election laws, election districts, election officers, contested elections, and absentee voting.

The legislature may enact legislation on voting and elections, and the majority of such legislation is contained in the Registration and Election Codes of the Commonwealth. The courts further clarify election law. The secretary of state is the chief election officer, and the Bureau of Elections, which is supervised by the commissioner of elections, performs the administrative elective functions. These functions relate to campaign expense reporting, voter registration, absentee balloting, candidate requirements, and election legislation.

Citizen Controls over Actions of Local Officials

Most Progressive Movement reform bypassed Pennsylvania. Provisions for the impeachment and recall of local officials and for initiatives and referenda are few and weak. The state's Sunshine Law, passed in 1986 and amended periodically, defines a meeting as any prearranged gathering of an agency attended by a quorum of members held for the purpose of deliberating agency business or taking official action.[29] All public agencies are required to take all official actions and conduct all deliberation leading up to official action at public meetings. The phrase "deliberation leading up to official action" leads to a gray area; for example, if the three county commissioners should talk together about county business, would that constitute an official meeting?

The Open Records Law, known as Right to Know, requires that minutes be taken of all public meetings and that they be promptly recorded and open to public inspection. Citizens denied access to public records have limited recourse through the county court of common pleas. The legislature is considering designating an administrative agency as the enforcement agency, as is the case in some other states. Local officials are governed by the state public officials and employee ethics law, which is administered by the State Ethics Commission.[30]

State-Local Relations

The broad flexibility that the state grants to localities for land-use planning is underutilized, and the state is struggling to devise incentives that would motivate local action to manage growth wisely.

Two or more local governments can cooperate jointly in the exercise of any governmental function, and municipalities can delegate powers to other local units.[31] The Intergovernmental Cooperation Law was enacted in 1972 to implement the provision of Article IX, section 5 of the new constitution. This intergovernmental cooperation provision, commonly referred to as Act 180, is very broad: "A municipality . . . may . . . cooperate or agree in the exercise of any function, power or responsibility with . . . one or more . . . municipalities . . . (Act 180, section 4). This broad legislation enables communities to have contract programs, joint programs, councils of government, joint authorities, as well as a myriad of other types of partnerships. Joint purchasing is a common practice, and equipment sharing, joint police forces, contract police services, shared recreation facilities, circuit-riding managers or finance officers, and joint code enforcement programs are becoming more common.

Although the authority for intermunicipal cooperation is broad, cooperation is just beginning to occur. Municipal-county cooperation is hampered by the different responsibilities of each government type.

The key trend in state-local relations is increased state interest in providing financial and technical assistance to local governments, especially for land-use planning, intermunicipal cooperation, regional policing, job training partnerships between governments and the private sector, and the conservation of natural and recreational resources. There is some increase in the tension among local governments, however. Many older boroughs, surrounded by sprawling townships, are revenue-poor, but their wealthy neighbors oppose consolidation. Several efforts to increase regional cooperation have fallen short of expectations.

Notes

1. This chapter revises and expands on Beverly A. Cigler's "Home Rule in Pennsylvania," a paper presented to the American Political Science Association annual conference, Washington, D.C., September 25, 1993. Numerical data on municipalities and employees are updated from the "1999 Pennsylvania Fact Sheet" of the Pennsylvania Department of Community and Economic Development. Short titles or common descriptions of laws are used when appropriate. If the law is codified within a specific title of the Pennsylvania Consolidated Statutes (Pa.C.S.), the volume number of the consolidated statute title and the section number of the first provision of the cited law are provided. When reference is made to a noncodified, freestanding law, two citations are provided. The official citation is provided first, followed by the citation in Purdon's Statutes (P.S.), an unofficial annotated compilation of Pennsylvania laws produced by the West Group. The official citation includes the act number and year, with special session number, when applicable, along with the pamphlet law (P.L.) designation, which is the page designation of the law in the applicable year's sessions' laws. When only a portion of the act is cited, the relevant sections of the law are provided. The second citation references the law as placed, by volume and section, in Purdon's Statutes. The format used here is consistent with that of the legislature's Local Government Commission and practice in the state.

2. Education Empowerment Act of 2000.

3. The data in this section are drawn from a database maintained by the Center for Rural Pennsylvania, a legislative agency, as well as reports from the Governor's Center for Local Government Services of the Pennsylvania Department of Community and Economic Development. The center publishes more than forty official handbooks geared to local officials from each type of government and each population class, including specialized manuals on land use and zoning, fiscal management, home rule, insurance, budgeting, civil service, open meetings and records, purchasing, and taxation. Specific examples are: *Elective Office in Local Government*, 7th ed., November 1993; *Township Commissioners Handbook*, 6th ed., June 1990; *Township Supervisor's Handbook*, 9th ed., March 1997; *Borough Mayors Manual*, 9th ed., September 1993; *Citizen's Guide to Pennsylvania Local Government*, 5th ed., November 1991; *Borough Council Handbook*, 8th ed., May 1995; *Manual for Chief Clerks/Administrators*, 2d ed., 1997; *City Government in Pennsylvania*, September 1993; and *Solicitor's Handbook*, 2d ed., 1999.

4. On political culture, see Daniel Elazar, *American Federalism: A View from the States*, 2d ed. (New York: Harper and Row, 1984). Much of this section is taken from an unpublished manuscript by the author, "Pennsylvania: Fragmentation at the Grass Roots," 1998. The author also obtained very helpful information from numerous informal discussions with staff members of the Local Government Commission, the Governor's Center for Local Government Services, and the various local government associations, which separately represent boroughs, townships, counties, cities and municipalities, school districts, and authorities.

5. Pennsylvania ranks sixth among the fifty states in the number of hate groups, although hate crimes have dropped steadily since 1993. The state has nineteen active hate groups, according to the Southern Poverty Law Center. *Philadelphia Inquirer*, June 27, 2000, and *Region of Diversity: Respecting Differences and Finding Common Ground*, Susquehanna Conference, Harrisburg, October 1999.

6. This section draws on the Department of Community and Economic Development's *Home Rule in Pennsylvania*, 1992 and reports written by the Local Government Commission of the Pennsylvania General Assembly, including "The Home Rule Charter: An Examination of Article IX of the Constitution of Pennsylvania," *Pennsylvania County News*, March–April 2000, 20–25 and 38–39.

7. In this chapter, all parts of the Pennsylvania Constitution regarding home rule and municipal codes are utilized, including the home rule law and the following codes: Home Rule Charter and Optional Plans Law 53 Pa.C.S. 2901; Optional Third Class City Charter Law Act 399 of 1957, P.L. 901; 53 P.S. 41101; Second Class County Code Act 230 of 1953, P.L. 723; 16 P.S. 3101; Borough Code Act 581 of 1965, P.L. 1656; 53 P.S. 45101; County Code Act 130 of 1955, P.L. 323; 16 P.S. 101; First Class Township Code Act 331 of 1931, P.L. 1206; 53 P.S. 55101; Second Class Township Code Act 69 of 1933, P.L. 103; 53 P.S. 65101; Third Class City Code Act 317 of 1931, P.L. 932; 53 P.S. 35101. For how Dillon's Rule is established in law, see *City of Clinton v. Cedar Rapids and Missouri River Railroad Company*, 24 Iowa 455, 475 (1868); 1 Dillon, Law of Municipal Corporations, 448–449 (5th ed. 1911); and *City of Philadelphia v. Fox*, 64 Pa. 169 (1870). Article IX, section 2 of the Pennsylvania Constitution reads:

Municipalities shall have the right and power to frame and adopt home rule charters. Adoption, amendment or repeal of a home rule charter shall be by referendum. The General Assembly shall provide the procedure by which a home rule charter may be framed and its adoption, amendment or repeal presented to the electors. If the General Assembly does not so provide, a home rule charter or a procedure for framing and presenting a home rule charter may be presented to the electors by initiative or by the governing body of the municipality. A municipality which has a home rule charter may exercise any power or perform any function not denied by this Constitution, by its home rule charter or by the General Assembly at any time.

8. P.L. 184, No. 62; 53 P.S. 1-101 et seq. The state legislature chose to treat home rule and option plans in the same legislation. This decision makes it very difficult for nonlawyers to separate the results of home rule from the many types and options available to the state's municipalities. See Home Rule Charter and Optional Plans Law 53 Pa.C.S. 2901; Optional Third Class City Charter Law Act 399 of 1957, P.L. 901; 53 P.S. 41101; Second Class County Code Act 230 of 1953, P.L. 723; 16 P.S. 3101; Borough Code Act 581 of 1965, P.L. 1656; 53 P.S. 45101; County Code Act 130 of 1955, P.L. 323; 16 P.S. 101; First Class Township Code Act 331 of 1931, P.L. 1206; 53 P.S. 55101; Second Class Township Code Act 69 of 1933, P.L. 103; 53 P.S. 65101; Third Class City Code Act 317 of 1931, P.L. 932; 53 P.S. 35101. Other general legislation of significance for general-purpose governments and school districts includes the following: Eminent Domain Code Act 6 of 1964(1), P.L. 84; 26 P.S. 1-101 General Local Government Code 53 Pa.C.S. 101; Pennsylvania Election Code Act 320 of 1937, P.L. 1333; 25 P.S. 2601; Public School Code of 1949 Act 14 of 1949, P.L. 30; 24 P.S. 1-1-1; Library Code Act 188 of 1961, P.L. 324; 24 P.S. 4101; Administrative Code of 1929 Act 175 of 1929, P.L. 177; 71 P.S. 51; Vehicle Code 75 p.c. 101.

9. When examining state-local relations in Pennsylvania it is important to recognize that many population classifications include just one unit. As such, legislation might apply to only one jurisdiction. For this reason, scholars view Pennsylvania as the "textbook" example of a state that circumvents its own constitution, which does not permit enactment of special legislation targeted to a specific unit.

10. Municipality Authorities Act of 1945, Act 164 of 1945, P.L. 382; 53 P.S. 301.

11. This section draws on the Department of Community and Economic Development's *Home Rule in Pennsylvania*, 1992 and reports written by the Local Government Commission of the Pennsylvania General Assembly, including "The Home Rule Charter: An Examination of Article IX of the Constitution of Pennsylvania," *Pennsylvania County News*, March–April 2000, 20–25 and 38–39.

12. See *Reese*, 665 A. 2nd 1162 (PA 1995).

13. Data are drawn from the "1999 Pennsylvania Fact Sheet" of the Pennsylvania Department of Community and Economic Development.

14. This section draws on many of the more than forty local government handbooks published by the state Department of Community and Economic Development, all of which are updated approximately every two years.

15. This section draws on Beverly A. Cigler, "Municipal Authorities in Pennsylvania," consultant's report for the Coalition to Improve State and Local Government," Carnegie Mellon University, Pittsburgh, Penn., 1993.

16. This section draws on Beverly A. Cigler, *Intermunicipal Cooperation in Pennsylvania,"* Center for Rural Pennsylvania, Harrisburg, Penn., 1990, which provided baseline data on councils of government and the extent of their services.

17. See Whistleblower Law Act 169 of 1986, P.L. 1559; 43 P.S. 1421, and *Denton v. Silver Stream Nursing and Rehabilitation Center,* 739 A.2d 571 (Superior Court, 1999).

18. Purchasing procedures are defined in the various county and municipal codes. For example, see Second Class County Code Act 230 of 1953, P.L. 723; 16 P.S. 3101; Borough Code Act 581 of 1965, P.L. 1656; 53 P.S. 45101; County Code Act 130 of 1955, P.L. 323; 16 P.S. 101; First Class Township Code Act 331 of 1931, P.L. 1206; 53 P.S. 55101; Second Class Township Code Act 69 of 1933, P.L. 103; 53 P.S. 65101; Third Class City Code Act 317 of 1931, P.L. 932; 53 P.S. 35101. There is also a special Steel Products Procurement Act 3 of 1978, P.L. 6; 73 P.S. 1881. Municipalities that purchase motor vehicles must abide by the provisions of the Motor Vehicle Procurement Act 62 Pa.C.S. 3731.

19. Cooperative Purchasing (Piggyback) (in The Administrative Code of 1929) Act 175 of 1929, P.L. 177, section 2403; 71 P.S. 633; Anti-Bid-Rigging Act 62 p.c. 450

20. Pennsylvania Municipalities Planning Code (M.P.C. or PA M.P.C.) Act 247 of 1968, P.L. 805; 53 P.S. 10101. Also important to planning, however, are the Pennsylvania Sewage Facilities Act (Act 537) of 1965, P.L. 1535; 35 P.S. 750.1 and the Municipal Waste Planning, Recycling and Waste Reduction Act (Act 101) of 1988, P.L. 556; 53 P.S. 4000.101; The Clean Streams Law Act 394 of 1937, P.L. 1987; 35 P.S. 691.1. The governor signed the most sweeping amendments to the code in thirty years in June 2000.

21. Other important revisions to the planning code include provisions for: updating county comprehensive plans at least every ten years and reviewing municipal comprehensive plans every ten years; incorporating input from municipalities and school districts in county planning; allowing municipalities to impose impact fees if they implement a joint municipal comprehensive plan through a joint municipal authority; granting priority in state grants for those municipalities that engage in intermunicipal planning; defining forestry activities permitted in all zoning districts; permitting the sharing of tax revenues under joint zoning; transferring development rights among municipalities under a joint municipal agreement; allowing traditional neighborhood development.

22. It is widely argued that this program is a form of "walking around money," since zones were created in every part of the state despite a published selection process.

23. On assessment, see (1) Second Class County Assessment Law Act 294 of 1939, P.L. 626, 72 P.S. 54521; (2) General County Assessment Law Act 155 of 1933, P.L. 853; 72 P.S. 5020-101; (3) Third Class County Assessment Board law Act 348 of 1931, P.L. 1379; 72 P.S. 5342; (4) Fourth to Eighth Class County Assessment Law Act 254 of 1943, P.L. 571; 72 P.S. 5453.101; Clean and Green Act Pennsylvania Farmland and Forest Land Assessment Act of 1974 Act 319 of 1974, P.L. 973; 72 P.S. 5490.1. On tax revenue, see the various codes and the Local Tax Collection Law Act 394 of 1945, P.L. 1050; 72 P.S. 5511.1.

24. This section is adapted from Beverly A. Cigler, "Adjusting to Changing Expectations at the Local Level," in *Handbook of Public Administration,* 2d ed., ed. James L. Perry (San Francisco: Jossey Bass Publishers, 1996), 60–76, and Beverly A. Cigler, "Revenue Diversification Among American Counties," *The American County: Frontiers of Knowledge,* ed. Donald C. Menzel (Tuscaloosa: University of Alabama Press, 1996), 166–183. See also Local Government Unit Debt Act 53 Pa.C.S. 8001.

25. The County Commissioners Association tracks funds received from the state.

26. The principal legislation is Municipalities Financial Recovery Act (Distressed Municipalities) Act 47 of 1987, P.L. 246; 53 P.S. 11701.101.

27. The $3.5 million figure was provided by staff at the Governor's Center for Local Government Services. See the Liquid Fuels Tax Municipal Allocation Law Act 655 of 1955, P.L. 1944; 72 P.S. 2615.1.

28. This is the conclusion of staff at the legislature's Local Government Commission.

29. Sunshine Act (Open Meetings) 65 Pa.C.S. 701.

30. Open Records Law (Right-To-Know) Act 212 of 1957, P.L. 390; Municipal Records Act 53 Pa.C.S. 1381; and Public Official and Employee Ethics Act 65 Pa.C.S. 1101. There is also a Local Taxpayers Bill of Rights Act 53 Pa.C.S. 8421.

31. The 1968 amendments to the Pennsylvania constitution added the sections "Intergovernmental Cooperation" and "Area Government and Area-Wide Powers." The most important law for implementing the sections is the Intergovernmental Cooperation Act of July 12, 1972, P.L. 762, which is now codified. 53 Pa.C.S. authorizes two or more units to cooperate jointly on anything they can do alone by entering into joint agreements. Of growing interest in the state is a reform of 2301 Municipal Consolidation or Merger Act 53 Pa.C.S. 731.

RHODE ISLAND

Elmer E. Cornwell

The thirty-nine cities and towns of Rhode Island collectively encompass all of the territory of this smallest of states. There are five counties, but they have no governing role; their only function is to serve as districts for court administration.

Despite the autonomy of the earliest Rhode Island settlements, the cities and towns have long been considered creatures of a powerful state government, from which they must derive all of their powers. From the home rule amendment to the state constitution, passed in 1951, they gained control of the structures of their governments but little new governing authority. Most have adopted home rule charters. In a recent trend, the state has been preempting, through legislation applying to all local units, key policy areas once handled locally.

Governmental Setting

The central concern for local autonomy in Rhode Island gradually gave way as the state government became dominant. A movement to recapture local autonomy ensued, leading to passage of the home rule amendment to the state constitution. In a powerful counterpoint to the home rule movement, the state began to impose mandates in areas like education, and it began to take over land use, environmental, and other concerns, in the name of promoting higher standards and statewide uniformity. Thus, as the cities and towns gained control over their forms of government in recent decades, they lost more and more control over a growing list of critical policy areas.

The broader governmental setting in which local government in the state developed and functioned has been an unusual one. The political forces and alignments found in other industrial states were present and important in Rhode Island, but the thoroughness of the control that first one coalition and then another was able to exercise at the expense of their opponents was extraordinary. From the early days of industrialization of the state economy (the 1790s) until the Great Depression, control of the state came to rest in the hands of the mercantile class and, in time, the factory owners and industrial entrepreneurs.[1]

Their control, which during the latter part of the nineteenth century took the form of a powerful statewide Republican machine, was based on legislative malapportionment and a property-holding franchise. Immigrants, first Irish and then French Canadians, Italians, Portuguese, and others, flooded into the state and provided the labor force for the burgeoning textile and other manufacturing enterprises. The legislative apportionment system heavily favored the small towns, whose old-stock Anglo-Saxon Protestant inhabitants were willing, especially for a price, to send machine-sponsored Republican legislators to Providence. These legislators formed dependable majorities in both chambers of the General Assembly, which did the bidding of the machine leaders. The leaders made sure that no legislation passed inimical to the interests of the economic elite.[2]

Until 1888 naturalized citizens could not vote unless they owned property. That year, the constitution was amended to allow all citizens to vote, with the exception that a citizen still had to own property to vote in city council elections.[3] Since cities then had the traditional weak-mayor, strong-council form of government, the GOP was able to retain control of the councils and thus control of municipal governments. At the state level, the governorship was also weak, to the point of near powerlessness, and the General Assembly was endowed constitutionally with almost all government power.

By dint of waging a long rearguard action to stave off reforms of either franchise or legislative apportionment, the dominant economic interests in the state were able, through the Republican Party, to maintain their control of the General Assembly until 1932 and the governorship until 1934, when they gave way to the Democratic tide of Franklin D. Roosevelt. In 1935, with its newly won control of the General Assembly and the governorship, the Democratic Party finally got its turn at the helm. With occasional setbacks, the party retained control of state politics and government thereafter, riding the tide of the blue-collar electorate, which had finally been released and energized. This power shift made the urban voters the basis of a new governing coalition of labor, immigrants, and the two-thirds of the population that was Catholic. The role of the small towns and their voters shrank, along with the Republican Party, to minority status.[4]

The local units, the cities and towns of Rhode Island, played important roles in the political and economic development of the state at the same time that they were being fundamentally changed in the process. The industrial revolution transformed certain towns into bustling and rapidly growing manufacturing centers. Other towns declined as their populations were siphoned off to the mills. Notwithstanding these changes, the cities and towns continued to be building blocks in the construction and maintenance of governing majorities at the state level. They also continued to play their role as local governments.

Home Rule in Rhode Island

Historical Development

It would be hard to overestimate the importance of the towns as foundations of government in Rhode Island. The four earliest settlements were Providence (1636), Portsmouth (1638), Newport (1639), and Warwick (1642). Each was a separate town with distinct leaders and motivations, in some cases religious. For example, Roger Williams founded Providence to escape the strict religious orthodoxy of the Massachusetts Bay Colony.

Given this beginning, the assertiveness of the towns down through the history of the state is not surprising.[5] The towns (some of which eventually acquired city stature) have remained to the present the only significant local government units. There are special districts (for example, fire districts) within towns, and some towns have combined to form larger school districts. There are also entities like the Narragansett Bay Water Quality Management District Commission and Water Supply Boards, but they are functional rather than territorial.

Legally, the constitutional principle that the towns were the creatures of the state and could exercise only those powers explicitly granted to them triumphed.[6] Legal theory notwithstanding, the uniqueness and local patriotism of the towns supported the notion that each be left, as much as possible, to run its affairs as it chose. The town meeting tradition, which was nearly universal until the advent of constitutional home rule, fostered these local feelings and assertions of autonomy.

Following the adoption of the home rule amendment to the constitution in 1951, the trends in the development of local government became more complex. The most compelling grievances behind the home rule movement were unwanted state interference and corruption in local government. In an example of the former, the General Assembly had forced upon city government public safety commissions with state-appointed members.[7] Machine politics in several Rhode Island cities became one of the first targets of local reform groups using the new amendment.[8]

During the first decade following adoption of the constitutional amendment, ten of the thirty-nine cities and towns used the home rule option: including five of the eight cities and three of the largest towns, which had outgrown the traditional town form of government.[9] Modernizing and professionalizing government were also motives for adopting home rule charters.

A three-day constitutional convention was convened on June 1, 1951, for the limited purpose of considering amendment of the constitution to provide for home rule for cities and towns and other specified matters. Its handiwork was put before the voters on June 28 at a special election and passed overwhelmingly. Section 1 of the amendment reads: "It is the intention of this Article to grant and confirm to the people of every city and town in this state the right of self-government in all local matters."[10] This language was considerably more sweeping than the reality turned out to be.

The mechanism to be used by a town in claiming this right was a special election to approve the question, "Shall a commission be appointed to frame a charter?" and to choose nine nonpartisan commissioners. They would have a year to frame a charter, which would then need voter approval at a general election.[11] The charter could later be amended if voters approved changes offered to them by the town or city council.[12]

Neither the state legislature nor the constitution prescribed models, so the commissioners were free to prepare a draft charter according to their beliefs as to what would benefit the community and gain acceptance at the polls.[13] In practice, the key decisions were the kind of executive (elected or appointed manager), whether or not towns would retain the town meeting, and what municipal departments would be set up.[14]

Four of the eight cities in the state were so anxious to seize home rule that they had charters ready for voter approval at the November 1952 general election.[15] All had had problems with local machine politics and saw home rule as an engine for basic reform. Accordingly, they wrote provisions into their charters for nonpartisan elections in odd-numbered years. These innovative arrangements were challenged and held unconstitutional.[16]

The constitutionality problem was solved, as others would be in the future, by legislative enactment of specific validation acts. This encounter with the courts, however, foreshadowed a series of decisions that struck down municipal efforts to use charter language to secure substantive authority; the courts held that education, the establishment of crimes and penalties, various licensing initiatives, and other matters all remained exclusively state prerogatives.[17] Ultimately, the constitutional phrase "in all local matters" came to mean the structural aspects of local government and little more.

Definition of Home Rule

There really is no formal and succinct definition of home rule in Rhode Island. The pertinent amendment to the constitution, quoted earlier, purports to grant the "right of self government in all local matters." Court decisions, as already noted, whittled this formula down to the point that it applies only to local jurisdiction over governmental structures, and Dillon's Rule—the notion that state government is supreme—still governs in almost all questions of governmental power.

Structural Features

Neither before nor after the adoption of home rule did the

state offer local government models to follow. City home rule charters tended to follow, structurally, the general outlines of pre-existing legislative charters, although they incorporated popular reforms, such as "strong" mayors, unicameral councils, and executive budgets. Town home rule charters varied widely. When the smaller towns wrote charters, they tended to stick with traditional arrangements but could use the amending process to upgrade the system later. Both before and after the adoption of home rule, the General Assembly frequently passed special acts for individual cities and towns. Local governments still had to seek from the legislature the power to do things not already specifically permitted.

There never was an unincorporated area in Rhode Island. Gradually, the outlying parts of the original territory of Providence were set off and incorporated as separate towns by the General Assembly. All such decisions were made individually, as the issues arose. A similar process continued throughout the state during the eighteenth and nineteenth centuries. The last two of the present towns were established in the early twentieth century.[18] During the eighteenth century the state created the five counties by combining clusters of towns, but they never have had any role in government save as judicial districts.

There is no formal classification of towns and cities. Before home rule, the legislature, when it saw fit, granted city charters to towns that had seemed to outgrow traditional town government.[19] Today, some towns have larger populations than the smallest cities, some of which have adopted charters with mayor-council systems but are still referred to as towns. Cities and towns can enter into cooperative arrangements with one another, but their territorial jurisdiction is limited to their boundaries. There are few cooperative arrangements. Cities and towns monitor and answer each other's fire alarms and police calls, where appropriate. A reservoir for one community may be located in another. The Providence Water Supply Board services a number of towns, as does the Narragansett Bay Commission's sewage treatment system. School districts combining two or three small towns have been set up under state auspices.

Functions of Local Government

Functional Responsibilities

Rhode Island cities and towns have the functions and powers that local governments in other states generally exercise. These include appropriating town funds to defray all community expenses; levying property taxes to cover budget appropriations; maintaining roads and streets; providing recreation facilities and programs; providing police and fire protection; and issuing licenses for liquor establishments, restaurants, pawn brokers, and other retail businesses. The school committee proposes a school budget, which the town government must approve and fund out of the property tax. Actually, cities and towns have little real control over school spending since the school committee can

Table 1. Average Allocation of Property Tax Revenue, by Municipal Population Category, 1997

Population	Number of municipalities	Percent spent on education	Percent spent on other services
Under 10,000	11	69%	31%
10,000–20,000	12	62	38
20,000–40,000	10	60	40
40,000 and up	6	43	57

Source: From data compiled by the state Office of Municipal Affairs.

call on the education commissioner and the courts to force the city or town to supply adequate funds.

The cities and towns also manage harbors and beaches and related facilities, if there are any. Through the office of the city or town clerk they are responsible for recording deeds, births, deaths, and marriages; issuing marriage licenses and dog licenses; and other similar duties.[20]

Many special authorities, commissions, special districts, and the like have been created by acts of the General Assembly to assume certain local services and responsibilities. Many have taxing power, and they can serve parts of towns (for example, fire districts), or whole communities, or combinations of adjacent towns. There is no general legislation authorizing formats for these entities; each was set up ad hoc at local initiative.[21]

Data are available on the functional distribution of expenditures for local communities, but generalizing from them is difficult. The size of the local unit—city or town—is an important variable affecting the allocation of funds among the various programs and responsibilities. Table 1 categorizes communities by population to illustrate expenditure patterns.

In every city and town, education is by far the largest single budget item. The percentage allocated to schools declines as the size of the community increases due to the fact that the smaller the town, the fewer services are provided to residents. By the same token, the complexities of city administration and city life demand more expensive services.

Table 2 provides more detailed data on the distribution of local expenditures among various government services. To avoid excessive detail, the table highlights only one community from each of the four population categories used in Table 1, usually the median one by population, with Providence also included.

In Table 2, zeroes for sewerage expenditures indicate that property owners make payments directly to the state Narragansett Bay Commission, which is responsible for sewage treatment for much of the Providence metropolitan area. A zero for fire protection indicates a volunteer department. The high education costs for Cranston and Providence reflect receipt of extra state and federal money for special education and bilingual education and similar programs characteristic of urban areas. Table 3 provides data on the revenue sources available to the five communities profiled in Table 2.

Local governing units have a number of powers and respon-

Table 2. Budget Expenditures of Select Municipalities, 1997

	Richmond	Barrington	Newport	Cranston	Providence
1990 population	5,351	15,849	28,277	76,060	160,728
Total expenditures[a]	$11,548,000	$32,818,000	$66,857,000	$134,209,000	$321,645,000
Percent spent on					
Education	81%	62%	40%	54%	49%
General financial admin.[b]	0.5	7	2	4	14
Public works	3	5	4	7	3
Police	3	4	9	11	8
Fire protection	0	4	9	13	8
Sewerage/sanitation	0	3	11	0	0
Parks and recreation	0.4	0.4	2	1	2
Debt service	0.2	9	1	6	8
Other	12	5	23	5	7

Source: Percentages are based on data supplied to the state by cities and towns.
   Notes: Richmond, Barrington, Newport, and Cranston are the median communities in the four population categories listed in Table 1. Providence was added to the table as the largest city and capital.
   a. Totals local, state, and federal funds.
   b. Expenditures of treasurer, tax collector, and assessors.

Table 3. Total Revenues Received by Select Municipalities, by Source, 1997

Revenue source	Richmond	Barrington	Newport	Cranston	Providence
Property tax	$6,298,000	$27,215,000	$39,036,000	$99,491,000	$175,580,000
Other local[a]	320,000	2,798,000	6,320,000	4,426,000	25,379,000
Federal	0	0	540,000[b]	0	0
State[c]	4,533,000	1,843,000	7,975,000	27,565,000	113,440,000
Other	397,000	962,000	12,986,000	2,727,000	7,246,000
Total	$11,548,000	$32,818,000	$66,857,000	$134,209,000	$321,645,000

Notes: Richmond, Barrington, Newport, and Cranston are the median communities in the four population categories listed in Table 1. Providence was added to the table as the largest city and capital.
   a. Licenses and fees.
   b. Newport receives federal money because of its naval installations.
   c. Most of the state money is for school support.

sibilities that are shared with the state or are exercised under specific legislation that either requires or permits them. For example, local governments can borrow on their own authority up to a prescribed debt limit, beyond which they must seek legislative authorization in each instance. Each city and town must maintain a probate court and have a board of canvassers to perform voter registration and other election duties set by state law. The state mandates the adoption of planning and zoning policies and codes and allows each community to establish a housing authority and a redevelopment authority. Individual septic systems are controlled largely by the state, but towns can, with state approval, develop sewer systems.

There is no difference between those functions carried on by local units that still bear the title of "town" and those carried on by "cities." The law makes no systematic distinction between the two categories.[22] Cities came into being via shift of title from "town" for the most part because they needed more appropriate governmental structures: for example, a mayor (or manager) and a council that combine the powers of the town meeting and the town council. However, the freedom allowed to communities under the home rule option led many of the larger towns to do

away with the town meeting and concentrate its powers in the council, while retaining the title of "town." Most of the larger towns also created a manager executive position, but some have gone so far as to provide for a chief who is popularly elected and called "mayor." They are still labeled a town. None of these changes caused significant confusion because state law does not differentiate between the two categories in any significant respect. All have the same powers and limitations, absent special acts applicable to individual communities.

Administrative Discretion

In the twentieth century, local governments lost many of their traditional responsibilities to the state or the federal government. The federal government largely took over poor relief. By the mid-1930s the federal "safety net," centering on the Social Security system, was well advanced.

The Rhode Island state government also has moved to take over or closely regulate the delivery of a number of the important services that had long been identified with local government. In 1964 there was a major and quite abrupt shift of responsibilities from the local governments to the state in the area of health administration. Legislation abolished the roles of the local health authorities in the cities and towns and conferred their duties and responsibilities on the State Department of Health.[23]

Personnel management rules and practices are not prescribed by the state government. Local governments can and do make such rules and other provisions as they see fit. The state did not have a civil service system for its employees until the 1940s, thus there was a long-standing patronage tradition. The same seems to have been the case with most local governments as well. With the advent of home rule, many of the charters that were written and adopted contained civil service merit system provisions—some quite detailed, and others mandating that such a system be set up by ordinance. The follow-up on these civil service provisions varied from none at all to more complete and conscientious. Some charters contained detailed merit system rules; however, courts have ruled that the terms of a labor contract with a town take precedence over the town's charter when the two conflict.[24] In other words, even though the state as such may not have prescribed personnel policies, state labor law and the courts have in effect done so.

One of the most profound changes in local government and its operation, and in the burdens borne by local officials, came about with the enactment between 1961 and 1967 of state legislation guaranteeing the right to organize and specifying arbitration procedures for local police, fire fighters, teachers, and other municipal employees.[25] Since government is highly labor intensive, union contracts invariably have a major impact on local budgets. They also limit management prerogatives in each of the departments and divisions of local government. One of the reasons prompting adoption of home rule charters unquestionably has been the desire to have full-time professional administrators on board to handle labor negotiations. The state-imposed arbitration laws have substantially reduced the control that councils, mayors, managers, or town meetings have over local budgets, and thus they have substantially weakened home rule.

The state never attempted to mandate a comprehensive administrative code, but it did enact prescriptions piecemeal. State law governs to a considerable degree what city and town treasurers, clerks, and tax collectors can and should do and how they should do it.[26] The law also has things to say about accounting procedures, and it mandates in explicit terms that there be an annual audit and the format to be used.[27]

In 1992 the state subjected municipal purchasing practices to new regulatory legislation pertaining to the award of municipal contracts, including the maximum dollar amount for purchases that could be made without competitive bidding. Many local governments, particularly those with home rule charters, had similar rules in place but had to conform to state rules, which took precedence.[28]

The state passed its first land-use legislation in 1921; it allowed and empowered cities and towns to adopt zoning ordinances. In 1972 legislation *requiring* that local communities provide for a planning commission or planning board went onto the statute books. Then, starting with legislation passed in 1988, the legislature put in place requirements for the preparation of city and town comprehensive plans and mandating state approval before they could take effect. In 1991 the state enacted equally detailed legislation requiring all local governments to revise their zoning legislation in specified ways. In short, virtually all local control over land use has been subject since 1991 to strict and detailed state supervision.[29]

Another traditional area of local concern and regulation is the building code. In 1970 the General Assembly enacted the Rhode Island Maintenance and Occupancy Code to ensure that structures used as dwelling units met minimum standards of public health.[30] The local government units were to enforce this elaborate code of standards. In 1981 the state passed further legislation adopting a state building code that would supersede all existing local codes.[31] Local building inspectors now enforce that state code. Here, too, the state assumed a formerly local government responsibility.

Constitutional language explicitly permits the General Assembly to pass general laws "which shall apply alike to all cities and towns, but which shall not affect the form of government of any city or town."[32] Collectively, the enactments cited above wrought massive shifts of local government responsibility, some in politically sensitive areas, to the state government.

Economic Development

In at least one case a town sought and received special state legislation to set up and operate an economic development commission. Towns can engage in some limited activities of this sort on their own initiative. There are some general provisions of state law that allow cities and towns to exempt property from taxes in order to encourage business to move into or remain in the community. The state enacted legislation entitled Exemption or Stabilization of Taxes on Qualifying Property in the early 1990s. Other legislation allows cities and towns to exempt from property taxes the inventories of wholesale and retail establishments and to exempt business office equipment, computers, and so forth.[33]

Enterprise zone legislation was first passed in 1982, which set up a state council to designate such zones, presumably at the request of a community.[34] In general, with regard to enterprise zones and the other options open to local governments to foster economic development, communities can take initiatives pursuant only to state legislation passed to permit very specific efforts. Within limits, communities can use local revenues in aid of economic development, such as to pay for sewer line expansion or for the laying out of access roads; however, either the council (in cities and towns without town meetings) or the town meeting would have to approve. If a bond issue is involved, a popular referendum usually would be required for approval.

Fiscal Autonomy of Local Governments

Local Revenues

In general, the fiscal affairs of local governments in Rhode Island are under the increasingly tighter control of the state. Aside from small sums raised from license and other fees, the only significant sources of local revenue are the local property tax and the automobile excise tax. The latter is really a property tax on registered automobiles, and the state passed legislation in 1998 to phase it out gradually. The state makes a payment to each city and town equal to the lost revenue. With insignificant exceptions, cities and towns cannot levy any other taxes. The income tax and the sales tax are strictly state levies, which go to support the state budget.

The total valuation of property in the community represents the tax base, adjusted by exemptions for church and certain other nonprofit institutions' property (colleges, hospitals, and so forth). There are certain other exemptions, or partial exemptions, for veterans, the elderly, the disabled, and the like. Each city and town is required by law to revaluate property at specified intervals. On the basis of the results, all property must then be assessed at its full and fair cash value or a uniform percentage thereof, but no more than 100 percent.[35]

In levying the tax on real estate, the financial town meeting or the council, as the case may be, fixes the amount of revenue that must be raised and then calculates the tax rate per thousand dollars of valuation that will raise that amount.[36] By state legislation passed in the mid-1980s, no community may set its tax levy more than 5.5 percent in excess of the levy of the previous year. If a city or town feels that it must raise more revenue to support the upcoming budget, it must secure permission from the Office of Municipal Affairs of the State Department of Administration.[37]

The state enacted further requirements pertaining to local budgeting in 1979 as the Property Tax and Fiscal Disclosure Municipal Budgets Act. Section 2 of the act reads:

The purpose of this chapter is to establish a procedure under which towns and cities may levy property taxes; to provide for full disclosure of the effect of rate and base changes on property tax revenues; to establish a procedure for public hearings on proposed budgets; to require municipalities to adopt a balanced budget; and to provide for fiscal oversight of municipalities incurring an operating deficit or an accumulated deficit in the preceding fiscal year.[38]

Each of these objectives is implemented with detailed language. The law mandates balanced budgets for communities and specifies the manner and time frames for paying off any deficits.

Cities and towns may borrow on their own authority up to a total indebtedness equivalent to 3 percent of the total property valuation of the community. Any borrowing beyond that limit must be authorized by state legislation in each instance, and such legislation usually provides for a popular referendum in the community to approve the bond issue. A general exception to this limit is borrowing in anticipation of taxes or of state or federal grants.[39]

Local Expenditures

The forms and types of expenditures typical of local government budgets are listed in section 7 of the Tax and Fiscal Disclosure Act: education, general financial administration, public works, police, fire, sewerage, other sanitation, parks and recreation, debt service, and "other." Cities and towns are not required to follow this list in their budget documents but do so in a general way. The 5.5 percent tax levy cap and balanced budget requirement are the operational limits on local government expenditures in a given year.

The bankruptcy issue has not arisen in relation to any Rhode Island community per se, although there have been some close calls. In three recent instances, bankruptcy would have been the outcome had the state not stepped in. The city of Central Falls reached a point at which it was in debt and could not fund services, including education. To deal with that situation, the state, by legislation, took over the city's school system.[40]

The city of Providence and the town of West Warwick also encountered severe budget and deficit problems. In each case, the state began to monitor the finances of the community to ensure that it overcame its problems. In short, the issue of bankruptcy is not likely to arise. Past experience suggests that the state will step in with appropriate monitoring or remedial efforts. It is quite possible, however, that one or more of the older cities of the state, with their limited tax bases, will face the same kind of problem that Central Falls faced.

State Government Grants-in-Aid to Localities

The number and type of grants-in-aid to local communities have changed considerably in recent years. There are five principal grant-in-aid programs, the oldest and by far the largest of which is aid to education. The total state grant for education in fiscal 1999 was $518,025,812.[41] The next largest program was general revenue sharing at $19,726,331, followed by the Payment in Lieu of Taxes program, which assists communities with large amounts of tax exempt property, at $15,852,246; aid to distressed communities, for those cities and towns that have the highest tax burdens relative to taxpayer wealth, at $6,162,500; and reimbursement for town payments of tuition for higher education courses taken by police officers, at $550,065.[42]

Save for the last of these, the moneys are apportioned according to a set formula. The education funds must be spent for the designated purpose, but the communities are free to spend the other moneys as they see fit. There is a general proviso in the law according to which the state can withhold funds if a city or town fails to comply with certain statutes.[43]

The cities and towns have considerable political leverage in relation to these state funds and in other matters as well. Many legislators represent districts that are entirely or largely in a single community. They, in particular, but all legislators to a degree, must be attentive and sympathetic to the impact of state decisions, especially budgetary ones, on their constituents. Local officials see any threat to the funding of these grant-in-aid programs as a threat of a property tax increase or service cut.

Unfunded Mandates

In 1979 the state legislature passed the first in a series of acts in response to complaints from city and town officials that they were constantly being mandated to do things that they had to fund themselves. The legislation recited a number of "mandates" that would not be reimbursable, such as the conduct of elections, and other things that are part and parcel of the governing process. Mandates in other areas would be reimbursable. The Department of Administration is to identify and publish a list of reimbursable mandates and keep the list up to date. The list dated 1995 contained no less than forty-two items. The communities are to submit requests for reimbursement in the manner prescribed.[44]

The mandates that have caused the loudest complaints include numerous ones relating to education (many of them predating 1979, the year in which the reimbursement system would go into effect) and mandates to provide fire departments with minimum equipment and to make public buildings handicapped accessible. One can probably assume that compliance with the law is variable. The cities and towns are probably assiduous in filing formal requests to be reimbursed for larger costs but not smaller ones.

Access to Local Government

Local Elections

As noted earlier, a number of Rhode Island communities have opted for nonpartisan elections in odd-numbered years. In such instances, they must go to the legislature for authorization, which tends to grant approval quite readily in most cases. In practice these locally tailored systems follow all state election law provisions other than the particular innovations that the community specifically requests. The local board of canvassers is responsible for conducting all elections, state and local, and is answerable to the state in the discharge of those responsibilities.

In nonpartisan communities, the party committees remain in place and are not barred from informal participation in local elections, but their names do not appear on the ballot. They continue to support and solicit local votes for state candidates. The state has enacted an elaborate system for regulating campaign contributions. The system applies to all candidates for public office at all levels. It requires a series of reports of receipts and expenditures.[45]

Citizen Controls over Actions of Local Officials

Other means by which the public influences local officials and local policy making include impeachment or recall procedures and initiative and referenda procedures. Impeachment does not apply to local officials. Some communities have written recall provisions into their home rule charters, but there is no general state legislation that applies to local governments.[46]

Rhode Island has not been very hospitable to any of the forms of direct democracy. A long struggle to provide for the initiative at the state level has yet to bear fruit. However, a number of cities and towns have written that mechanism into their charters along with the option of challenging existing laws via petition and referendum. Use of these devices has been very limited. In this area, too, there is no state authorizing legislation for local communities to use.

State legislation guarantees citizens' access to the meetings of all public bodies, state as well as local.[47] State law also establishes open records—public access to all official public documents—with a few exceptions, such as to protect individual privacy and shield internal working papers and the like.[48] Ethics legislation falls into the category of public access in that such legislation is often drafted (as in Rhode Island) to encourage citizens to file complaints against officials for violating the ethics code.[49] The state constitution incorporates a provision setting up an Ethics Commission with extraordinarily broad powers.[50]

In these three areas—open meetings, open records, and ethics—the centralizing tendencies noted earlier in substantive policy areas have also manifested themselves. Local communities have shown no great resistance to these moves, although some may feel that the state-level regulations are not as well suited to local situations as they might be.

State-Local Relations

Home rule was introduced in Rhode Island to deal with real problems but gained much of its support from people who felt nostalgia for an earlier era when local governments were truly autonomous and masters of their own houses. The Rhode Island version of home rule enables it to exist as harmoniously as possible with the state's tradition of a strong legislative institution exercising almost unlimited power. The language reserves to the General Assembly the authority to legislate as it always had, while effectively limiting home rule to the crafting and altering of governmental structures. This balance has minimized the clash that might otherwise have developed between home rule and legislative sovereignty.

So, what has home rule contributed in Rhode Island? Its major contribution seems clearly to have been (and will be for the few remaining non–home rule towns) that it facilitated the modernization and professionalization of traditional local governments. Today, it borders on the impossible for towns, even the very small ones, to conduct their business with part-time amateurs. Local affairs have become too complex and too demanding. More important, the ever growing web of relationships between the local governments and the state has grown beyond the capacity of traditional local officeholders to handle.

Without the ability to write home rule charters, it is difficult to see how the towns could have coped with the mounting demands on their governments or how the state could have relied on the towns to carry out new state policies. If towns had had to go to the General Assembly for each incremental change they required, modernization and professionalization would have progressed far more slowly, painfully, and chaotically. Home rule provided cities and towns with the mechanism for change, the incentive to plan carefully and comprehensively, and the popular education and participation without which change is difficult to accept.

Notes

1. See Peter J. Coleman, *The Transformation of Rhode Island, 1790–1860* (Providence: Brown University Press, 1969), ch. 6.

2. See Lincoln Steffens, "Rhode Island, A State for Sale," *McClure's Magazine* 24 (February 1905).

3. Amendment VII.

4. See Erwin L. Levine, *Theodore Francis Green: The Rhode Island Years, 1906–1936* (Providence: Brown University Press, 1963), ch. 8; and William G. McLoughlin, *Rhode Island: A History* (New York: Norton, 1978), 201–208.

5. Sidney V. James has written of the early years: "At every occasion the towns kept asserting their importance. Localism, protean and puissant, steadily subverted the intent of the patent and charter" (that is, the governing documents granted by the Crown). *Colonial Rhode Island: A History* (New York: Scribner's Sons, 1975), 56. At various points James discusses local government.

6. The constitutional principle called Dillon's Rule, enunciated by Iowa state supreme court justice R. Dillon in *Merriman v. Moody's Executors*, 25 Iowa 163, at 170, 1868, accurately characterizes the relationship between state and local government in Rhode Island.

7. See Matthew J. Smith, "The Real McCoy," *Rhode Island History* 32 (August 1973), 67–86.

8. Levine, *Theodore Francis Green,* 181 and McLoughlin, *Rhode Island: A History,* 202.

9. The cities of Pawtucket, Central Falls, Woonsocket, and Newport, plus East Providence, which became a city when it adopted its charter, and the towns of Barrington, Lincoln, and North Kingstown.

10. The Home Rule Amendment was adopted as No. XXVIII; in the reenacted and edited constitution of 1986, it became Article 13.

11. Rhode Island Constitution (1986), Article 13, section 6.

12. Ibid., Article 13, section 8.

13. However, each city and town had to have a council. See Rhode Island Constitution (1986), Article 13, section 3; see also Rhode Island General Laws, Title 45, Chapter 5, section 1.

14. The Model City Charter, published in many editions by the National Municipal League, left the devising of administrative structures up to the council (see 1964 edition, New York, p. 26).

15. See note 9.

16. See *Flynn v. McCaughey,* 81 R.I. 143 (1953).

17. See, for example, *State v. Krzak,* 97 R.I. 156 (1964) and *Hurd v. City of East Providence,* 103 R.I. 518 (1968).

18. Territory was taken from South Kingstown in 1901 to form Narragansett, and territory from Warwick in 1913 to form West Warwick.

19. The present eight cities and their dates of incorporationare: Providence, 1831; Newport, 1853; Pawtucket, 1885; Woonsocket, 1888; Central Falls, 1895; Cranston, 1910; Warwick, 1931; and East Providence, 1957.

20. For the powers of cities and towns see Rhode Island General Laws, Title 45, towns and cities, especially Chapters 2 (general powers), 7 (town clerk), and 8 (town treasurer).

21. The most common bodies of this kind are regional school districts, water districts/commissions, fire districts, land trusts, sewer authorities, refuse disposal authorities, and waterfront authorities.

22. See Rhode Island General Laws, Title 43, Chapter 3, section 9: "The word 'town' may be construed to include 'city' . . ."

23. Rhode Island General Laws, Title 23 (health and safety) contains Chapter 1 (Department of Health) and Chapter 2 (local health officers) among others. In the latter, one finds that all but one of the sections have been repealed. Section 16 reads in part: "Whenever in the general laws . . . the words 'local health officer' [are] . . . used appropriate wording shall be substituted so as to vest such power and authority in the state department of health." These changes were enacted in 1964.

24. See, for example, *City of East Providence v. Local 850, International Association of Firefighters,* 117 R.I. 329 (1976).

25. The respective chapters in the Rhode Island General Laws, Title 28 (labor and labor relations), are 9.1 for fire fighters, 9.2 for police officers, 9.3 for teachers, and 9.4 for other municipal employees.

26. For clerks see Title 45, Chapter 7, and for assessors, Title 44, Chapter 5.

27. Rhode Island General Laws, Title 45, Chapter 10.

28. See ibid., Title 45, Chapter 55, entitled "Award of Municipal Contracts."

29. See ibid., Title 45, Chapter 22.2, Rhode Island Comprehensive Planning and Land Use Act, and related chapters. See also Peter Lord, "R.I. builds model for planned development," *Providence Journal,* January 21, 1990.

30. Rhode Island General Laws, Title 45, Chapter 24.3.

31. See ibid., Title 23, Chapter 27.3, section 100.1.1 and subsequent sections. Section 100.1.2 reads in part: "The general assembly hereby finds and declares that a state building code for Rhode Island is necessary to establish adequate and uniform regulations governing the construction and alteration of buildings and structures within the state."

32. Rhode Island Constitution (1986), Article 13, section 4.

33. See Rhode Island General Laws, Title 44, Chapter 3, sections 9 through 9.3, 29, 40, and 3.1.

34. Ibid., Title 42, Chapter 64.3.

35. Ibid., Title 44, Chapter 5, sections 5, 11, and 12.

36. Ibid., Title 44, Chapter 5, section 1.

37. Ibid., Title 44, Chapter 5, section 2.

38. Ibid., Title 44, Chapter 35.

39. Ibid., Title 45, Chapter 12.

40. Ibid., Title 45, Chapter 52.1.

41. Ibid., Title 16, Chapter 7, deals with state school support.

42. See ibid., Title 45, Chapter 13; and Title 42, Chapter 28.1.

43. Ibid., Title 45, Chapter 13, sections 1.1 and 2.

44. Ibid., Title 45, Chapter 13, sections 6 through 10.

45. Ibid., Title 17, Chapter 25, especially section 2.

46. In 1992 four-year terms were introduced for the governor and the other state officers along with a limited recall provision for just those offices. Rhode Island Constitution (1986), Article 4, section 1.

47. Rhode Island General Laws, Title 42, Chapter 46.

48. Ibid., Title 38, Chapter 2.

49. Ibid., Title 36, Chapter 14.

50. Rhode Island Constitution (1986) Article 3, section 8. For powers of the commission, see *In re Advisory to the Governor (Ethics Commission),* 612 A2d.1 (1992).

SOUTH CAROLINA

Cole Blease Graham Jr.

Pressures stemming from urban growth, national civil rights policy, and the global economy have encouraged local self-governance in South Carolina. Compared with South Carolina's restrictive past, the state constitution today allows general power to cities and counties for local spending, administrative management, and provision of services.

Governmental Setting

A governmental setting may be defined as "the particular pattern of orientation to political action in which each political system is embedded."[1] For its first two centuries, South Carolina had a very traditionalistic setting, with a planter elite at the top of the social hierarchy; poor whites and a few African American artisans, tenants, or small landholders in the middle; and enslaved African Americans at the bottom. After the planters' decline, varying economic, social, and political elites continued the status quo and limited popular government.

At mid-twentieth century, county legislative delegations,[2] comprising one senator and an apportioned number of members of the state house,[3] dominated local governments, especially counties. The entire legislature annually passed a "supply bill," or budget, for each county as special or "local" legislation. An unwritten rule required majority delegation support, but ultimately the county senator could veto "automatic enactment" of the supply bill in the senate.[4]

Typically, even after the supply bill was passed, a delegation governed the county in minute detail. A board of county commissioners could be created, changed, or abolished by special act—in other words, by the county senator. New board members or specific salaries were often named in the supply bill.

After South Carolina's post–World War II economic development, political power began to be distributed more widely, creating the foundations for change. The first break came in 1948, when the Charleston County delegation permitted the establishment of a local county council.[5] Next came *Reynolds v. Sims* and related court decisions that based state legislature representation on population.[6] Smaller counties did not have enough population for an individual senator, and more populated counties required several. One senator had trouble representing two or more small counties; several senators in one county could lead

to disagreements. Focus moved to county modernization and home rule.

Home Rule in South Carolina
Historical Development

Before the Civil War, local governments in South Carolina had no regular structure, and services varied widely. Judicial districts administered courts and elected legislators. Cities were independently chartered and counties did not exist.[7] In 1868 a new state constitution designated judicial districts as counties.[8] Elected boards of county commissioners governed the new counties. As legal creatures of the state, counties were limited constitutionally to "county purposes," such as oversight of roads, prisons, and court support.[9]

A new constitution in 1895 required counties to provide for the poor and to levy a school tax. New counties could be formed or old county boundaries changed, but there were no provisions for a county governing body. The county purpose[10] restriction continued, allowing counties to provide "statewide" services or facilities only with legislative permission. Framers of these restrictions did not envision suburban developments and demands outside city limits for services such as recreation, water, or fire fighting.

Cities were empowered to deliver general municipal services within corporate boundaries. Although restricted to the property tax, cities were able to share state revenue and to generate fees from municipal enterprises. Some were enabled by special legislation to sell selected municipal services, such as water or fire protection, beyond corporate boundaries.[11]

In 1966 the General Assembly created a committee of legislators and citizens to study the 1895 constitution. The committee recommended a new article for local government,[12] which was ratified as Article VIII on March 7, 1973, after a successful referendum in the 1972 general election. School districts were excluded. Article VIII prohibits new special-purpose districts but did not abolish existing ones.

Definition of Home Rule

There is no straightforward definition of home rule in South Carolina, but Article VIII instructs that the state constitution and state statutes be "liberally construed" in favor of local government subdivisions to include powers fairly implied and not prohibited.[13] The legislature is limited to general laws "for the structure, organization, powers, duties, functions, and the responsibilities of counties"[14] and cannot pass special laws for counties or cities.

Structural Features

As many as five forms of city and county governments may be developed. Major code provisions describe structures or forms of government and how they are changed, once adopted; activities or functions of municipalities and counties; their fiscal authority; and the autonomy of their personnel or human resource systems.

Cities may choose one of three forms: a "strong" mayor or mayor-council form, a council or "weak" mayor form, or a council-manager form. Counties have four options: council, council-supervisor, council-administrator, or council-manager. The statutes define each form in detail, including the size of council and the specific duties of the executive. In the county council-manager form, the treasurer and the auditor may be appointed by council rather than popularly elected as they are in the other forms. The county manager's powers are more expansive than those of a county administrator, whose authority over elected officials is limited. A fifth option, a board of commissioners,[15] became unconstitutional in 1976, because it required special implementation legislation.[16]

Each jurisdiction had to choose a form by July 1, 1976, and if decided by referendum, keep it until July 1, 1978. Subsequent change could be made every four years by a statutorily prescribed process.[17] For the most part, jurisdictions continued with their original choice. Among cities, Charleston has a "strong" mayor form, and Columbia, Greenville, and Florence have the council-manager form. Most counties use a council-administrator form, although two counties, York and Greenwood, have a county council and manager.

Article VIII defines essential features of counties and incorporation of new cities. A county must have at least 500 square miles, assessed taxable property worth $2 million, and 15,000 inhabitants. There can be no more than forty-six counties.[18] The essential requirements for municipal incorporation are minimum population density, adequate distance from an existing municipality, service feasibility, and a successful election.[19] A

minimum area, initial population size, or minimum ad valorem tax base are not required. More than half the approximately 270 municipal governments have fewer than 1,000 residents.

Minimum population density means at least 300 persons per square mile, except for the sea islands and coastal areas within two miles of the Atlantic Ocean. The exempted areas must have a total of 150 dwelling units or one dwelling per three acres of land. The boundaries of an existing municipality must be at least five miles away, unless the area to be incorporated has been refused annexation, has 15,000 residents, or is in a county with fewer than 15,000 residents. A service feasibility study must justify the new municipal government and demonstrate a plan to provide services.

An election determines the certification of incorporation to the South Carolina secretary of state and the form of government. Incorporations are infrequent in South Carolina. An incorporated city can lose its charter if it ceases to function or if it falls below a population of fifty.[20]

Compared with states like neighboring North Carolina, where cities may initiate annexation based on statutory standards of contiguity or density of residents or structures, South Carolina has restrictive annexation laws. There is essentially one annexation process in which at least 75 percent of the freeholders[21] owning 75 percent of the assessed valuation of the real property in the area to be annexed petition the council.[22] The municipal council acts to accept by ordinance; no election is required. A proposed annexation may be challenged in state court. The process works best when all real estate owners in the area to be annexed sign the petition.

For distribution of electricity, South Carolina was basically carved into four utility franchise areas by the Territories Act of 1968.[23] Duke Energy, Carolina Power and Light, South Carolina Electric and Gas, and the state's electric cooperatives each have specific geographic service areas. Policy makers regard them as a stable, statewide base for economic development.

It is arguable that the state's electric suppliers do not want annexation reform. Fewer than two dozen South Carolina cities still own an electricity distribution grid, but the utilities and cooperatives fear the loss of "retail" business to them. One obstacle is how to calculate the "buyout" value of infrastructure financed and installed by a utility, or a special service district, in an annexed area. Also, utilities and special districts argue that their customer base shrinks when a city expands and takes over, thus requiring higher rates for a smaller share of retail customers. These issues will become more complicated as electric utilities are deregulated, as they did with long-distance telephone companies.

In 1992, almost two decades after the local government amendment, the legislature passed consolidation legislation.[24] Actual consolidation under the statute may be quite difficult. Individual utilities retain existing franchises. Special-purpose districts and cities may opt out of a consolidated government if voters within their boundaries reject a consolidation proposal.

Consolidation is initiated by a county council or by petition of 10 percent of the county's registered voters. A charter commission plans the new government. The commission's eighteen members must be evenly divided among relevant county councils, city councils, and special-purpose districts. The commission has one year to complete a plan for voters in the county to approve or reject.

The 1973 local government article did not eliminate special laws empowering many municipal governments to supply water and electricity beyond corporate limits. General authorization limits extraterritorial provision of water and electricity to contiguous municipal boundaries and requires contract renewal every two years. Cities with populations over 70,000 in the 1940 census and of 50,000–60,000 in the 1950 census are exempt from the contiguity requirement.[25]

Functions of Local Government

Functional Responsibilities

Cities and counties are general-purpose local governments that exercise authority under broad constitutional or legislative definition. Municipal corporations are empowered to "enact regulations, resolutions, and ordinances"[26] consistent with the state constitution and state statutes. These powers enable cities to provide "roads, streets, markets, law enforcement, health, and order" to promote security and the general welfare. Cities may levy a property tax, a business license tax, and a parking surtax on business licenses in specific areas. Cities provide recreation services and code enforcement, such as building codes. Cities may also provide police protection outside city limits and send police officers to aid other cities in emergencies.

Similar to cities, counties have the power to enact "regulations, resolutions, and ordinances" consistent with the state constitution and statutes. In accordance with the 1973 home rule amendment, the mention of specific powers in statutes does not limit the general power of counties. Among eighteen functions, the county provides general public works, water and sewer, criminal justice, public health and social services, transportation, planning, economic development, recreation, public safety, elections, and libraries.[27] Counties may also create special tax districts to provide varying service levels and to minimize dual taxation challenges.

The state has 91 school districts and 297 special-purpose districts. Ten multicounty councils of government (COGs) coordinate intergovernmental planning for land use, infrastructure, and transportation development among cities, counties, other local governments, and public service providers. The special-purpose districts deliver a specific service or a small number of related services, such as water or water and sewer.[28] They are often fiscally independent of municipalities and counties, and their boundaries follow no specific pattern.[29] Under the "county purpose" doctrine, status as a special-purpose district was often the only way that citizens in densely settled areas could obtain needed services. The legislature did not violate the constitution if it created a special district before 1973 to provide a municipal-type service in the county—just so long as the special district did not cover the total county territory.

South Carolina special districts have a vocal and powerful lobby to protect their interests. Because the legislature and many counties have single-member representation districts that overlap special-district service areas, special districts may have a strong voice in the election of a specific state legislator or county council member.

Cities maintained extraterritorial powers granted before 1973. For example, the city of Columbia has developed a large-scale water system, including fire protection and wastewater collection, in a fast-growing metropolitan area. By comparison, the cities of Greenville and Charleston cover relatively small territories, and county governments have become relatively more prominent there. There are also many special-purpose districts in the Greenville area.

Cities and counties have few restrictions on services offered by contract to individuals or corporations. Cities may contract to provide services outside city limits but not within service areas allocated by the Public Service Commission for utilities. The State Law Enforcement Division must be notified if outside areas are added by contract to police jurisdiction. One municipality may contract to provide services within another municipality, if permitted. Counties may administer functions jointly and share costs with the state, a municipal corporation, a public service district, or other public subdivision.[30] Counties are empowered to make and execute contracts with other jurisdictions and within municipalities, including those related to planning, zoning, and land-use controls.[31]

The constitution permits the General Assembly to authorize regional councils of government.[32] The ten regional councils in South Carolina study common problems of local government, such as planning, transportation, recreation, public works, human services, and economic or industrial development. Many intergovernmental cooperative agreements are based on recommendations from these studies.[33] State-local concerns are studied by an advisory commission on intergovernmental relations coordinated by the Regional Development Office of the State Budget and Control Board.

Administrative Discretion

South Carolina statutes require a county to adopt a personnel system, though not specifically a merit system, to regulate all appointed employees. State employees working within a county are covered by the state merit system. Regulated county em-

ployees may be protected from arbitrary discharge by a grievance procedure. If none is in place, a hearing process is described in the statute,[34] subject to final review by the county
council.

Although cities are not required to adopt a job classification
or pay plan or to provide for an annual evaluation of employee
job performance, many voluntarily have a merit system. Civil
service commissions may be created in cities with the commission form and in cities with populations of 5,500–65,000 in the
1970 census.[35]

City and county employees are not required to live within
the jurisdiction in which they work, and there are no restrictions
on the political activities of employees. South Carolina is a right-
to-work state, and local government employees are not authorized to engage in collective bargaining or to strike. State law requires training for law enforcement officers. Auditors, assessors,
and appraisers must also be trained in property tax assessment.
Affirmative action programs are required for schoolteachers and
administrators. The broad affirmative action requirements for
state agencies provide the background framework for local
units.[36]

State law makes cities and counties participants in the state
retirement system and does not authorize the establishment of a
separate city or county retirement plan. City and county workers are covered by the state workers' compensation system.[37]

Counties must have an accounting and reporting system for
managing funds as well as procedures for issuing revenue and
general obligation bonds. A land-use system and a system of
business license taxes must also be in place. Counties may create
franchises, except for telephone and telegraph services and gas
and electric utilities suppliers. A county may create special tax
districts within its boundaries to provide different service levels,
but this measure is controversial.[38]

By ordinance, cities must provide administrative codes or
agencies. Ordinances must also be the basis for systems of city
fines, budgets, and procedures for granting, renewing, or extending franchises. Systematic procedures for borrowing money
and making contracts must also be specified. State statutes also
describe in more detail procedures for general finance administration, taxation, paving bonds, planning and zoning, and administration of other public works. Counties, but not cities, are
required to provide a centralized, competitive purchasing system.[39] In practice, many cities have well-developed systems.
Both have an established tradition of coordinating purchasing
decisions with state government for increased economies of
scale.

Economic Development

South Carolina has a comprehensive community development law for municipal governments. It defines the conditions
of blight and identifies a conservation area in which blight may
be imminent. The municipal council is authorized to create a re-

development commission. State law defines the powers of the
commission and requires a redevelopment plan based on public
hearings and municipal council approval. The redevelopment
commission may contract with businesses and other public entities and issue bonds to finance specific projects. Municipalities
also may form joint redevelopment commissions. A 1994 act authorizes municipalities to create a redevelopment authority to
deal with the closing of federal military facilities.[40]

The Enterprise Zone Act of 1995 (EZA-95) gives counties and
businesses additional incentives and responsibilities for new investments. New businesses may claim larger tax credits for creating new jobs and may use the state individual income tax withholding of employees to finance training and new infrastructure. New investment must be located in a specified enterprise
zone and must be approved by the state Coordinating Council
for Economic Development (CCED) based on a positive cost-
benefit ratio. The methodology for calculating the ratio is promulgated as a state regulation.

EZA-95 amends the Industrial Revenue Act to allow a county
to substitute a fee in lieu of taxes for new investment of as little
as $5 million. In addition to a positive cost-benefit ratio, the Bu-
reau of Economic Advisors (BEA), which is a section of the
State Budget and Control Board, must recommend the project
as one of paramount importance. Both the BEA and the county
council must find that the project serves proper governmental
purposes.

In 1988 the state began a large-scale, statewide geographical
information system (GIS), to map county and local community
infrastructure needs, especially the details of the more than 350
public water and wastewater systems, as a basis for cooperative
development. Each of the ten regional councils has developed a
GIS center. Studies in 1999 estimated infrastructure funding
needs of $57 billion by 2015, more than half of which is directly
related to transportation. Currently truck fees are the main
source of revenue for transportation projects.[41]

Municipal governments participate in industrial parks as defined by limits of incorporation or through municipal contracting in interlocal agreements. Counties, individually or jointly,
may develop an industrial or business project involving land,
buildings, and improvements, such as pollution-control facilities
for manufacturing or commercial activity. The State Budget and
Control Board must approve revenue bonds issued by county
boards. Legislation in 1996 updated the provisions for payment
of a fee in lieu of taxes for qualified properties in an industrial
development park. A county board may mandate that a county
or municipality acquire a developed project.[42]

Fiscal Autonomy of Local Governments
Local Revenues

South Carolina cities and counties have limited revenue
home rule, even though about 75 percent of their revenue origi-

nates locally. Article X, section 1 of the state constitution provides for an ad valorem tax on all real and personal property.[43] A two-thirds vote by the General Assembly is required for any changes in assessment ratios. The State Tax Commission assesses key industrial property, such as manufacturing and distribution facilities. Local governments assess all other property, updating the appraisal every five years.

Article VIII, section 7 empowers counties to tax different areas at different rates, depending on services provided. State law restricts the property tax and stipulates how local governments may spend property tax revenue. About half of all locally generated revenue comes from the property tax, and about one-quarter comes from licenses and permits. The remainder comes from service and revenue charges, which may be adjusted locally, or from the local-option sales tax.[44]

The local-option sales tax (LOST) rolls back property taxes, except for public education, up to 63 percent in the first year after a majority of county voters approves the 1 percent increase. The rollback feature increases by 2 percent to a cap of 71 percent after five years. Cities and counties share the revenue. Counties approving the LOST but generating less than $2 million share revenue from "donor" counties that produce more than $5 million. No county redistributes more than 5 percent of its total collections.

Six counties first approved the LOST in the November 1990 general election. Counties in which the measure failed were able to vote again one year later. To date, twenty-six counties, mostly in rural areas or the coastal plains rather than in metropolitan areas or the Piedmont, have approved the measure.

Local revenue is an ongoing legislative concern. In 1996 the legislature tried unsuccessfully to restrict local taxing powers by requiring a two-thirds vote of a county or municipal council to increase a local tax rate. The General Assembly invited reform proposals from a study panel of state chamber of commerce and city, county, and school district leaders. The Speaker of the house did not favor the reforms, and they stalled. He said they were "too liberal" and "not as tight on taxing authority" as he would have liked them to be.[45]

Nevertheless, changes were passed to allow local governments more flexibility in levying new taxes and fees to respond to increased service demands.[46] Local governments were able to add a 1 percent capital projects sales tax for up to seven years, if it were approved by local referendum.[47] In addition, a county or municipality may now impose an accommodations tax and a hospitality tax on food businesses by action of the positive majority of its governing body.[48] As a trade-off, no county or municipality was allowed to impose a new tax after December 31, 1996, without legislative authorization. Counties, municipalities, and school districts may not increase property tax rates by more than the increase in the consumer price index (CPI). Exceptions are made if the increase is needed to provide disaster relief (which must be approved by majority council vote), to offset a prior year's deficit, or to comply with a judicial decision. The act also allows local governments to collect service charges and user fees.

Additional sources of revenue for political subdivisions include state funding of the homestead exemption for local property taxes and portions of the inventory tax, aid to fire districts, and categorical grants. State categorical grants are mainly pools of federal money that individual state agencies control administratively. They have increased significantly in number and amount since 1990. Recreation grants have grown at the highest rate. All counties and about one-third of cities report state grants, but only a handful of local jurisdictions receive more than $100 per capita in state grant funds.

Bond issues by political subdivisions must pursue public rather than private interests. Public purpose requires that a higher standard be met for direct public benefit than would be required of private individuals or organizations. Public interests must also fall within local government functions identified in the state constitution or general law. City and county general obligation debt is limited constitutionally to 8 percent of assessed property value.[49] A referendum is required for general obligation bonds issued by cities,[50] and the bonds must mature within forty years. For counties, a referendum is required for debt exceeding the 8 percent limit. No interest ceiling is set, and short-term borrowing, though permitted, is rarely used.

When referendums fail, which has most often been the case recently, jurisdictions seek alternatives. General-purpose units have used revenue bonds when the new spending may be linked to an adequate fee. Some jurisdictions, especially public school districts, have negotiated lease-purchase agreements since lease-purchase agreements do not count toward the total debt limit.

Local Expenditures

In 1993–1994 South Carolina local governments spent more than $1.6 billion; counties spent approximately two-thirds ($1.024 billion).[51] Municipal general funds went to public safety (40 percent) and administration (20 percent). Public safety and administration in counties received almost 30 percent each.

Additional types of expenditure for cities were environment and housing (14 percent), recreation and culture (9 percent), transportation (7 percent), and other categories (10 percent). Environment and housing (11 percent), health and human services (10 percent), transportation (7 percent), recreation and culture (5 percent), and other categories (8 percent) were among county expenditures. Salaries and wages were 57 percent of municipal expenditures and 47 percent of city outlay. Expenditures for operations were about even—33.4 percent for cities and 35.4 percent for counties. Cities spent 9.1 percent overall for capital, equipment, land, and construction. Counties spent 16.9 percent.

The fiscal or budget year for county governments is July 1–June 30. Each county department or administrative unit makes a detailed report at fiscal year's end. The county council adopts an operating and capital budget at the start of the fiscal year and identifies all sources of anticipated revenues, including taxes. Supplemental appropriations must specify the sources of the funds. By law, counties are required to develop and create an accounting and reporting system by which to take in, keep, allocate, and spend all funds. County councils may require "reports, estimates, and statistics" in budget preparation.[52]

Cities independently determine their fiscal year dates. Municipal councils adopt a budget by ordinance, regardless of the form of government. Preparation and submission of a proposed budget and the preparation of the annual financial report are the responsibility of the mayor in the mayor-council form and the manager in the council-manager form.[53]

Article X, section 7(b) requires a balanced budget for each political subdivision. Any overruns must be completely financed in the next fiscal year. County councils balance budgets annually by levying the property tax as a "balancing tax." Special-district boards enact a budget to levy taxes when enterprise revenue is not enough to meet operational and maintenance expenses, sinking funds, and interest charges to carry forward any surplus or deficit.[54]

There are no clear processes by which a county, a city, or a special district may declare bankruptcy. A municipal government with a population of less than fifty automatically loses corporate status. The secretary of state determines whether incorporation should be revoked if a municipal government has not provided any services, collected any revenue, or held an election in the past four years.[55]

State Government Grants-in-Aid to Localities

Excluding K–12 education and welfare expenditures, South Carolina ranks thirty-second among states in per capita state aid to general-purpose local governments.[56] Local governments argue that they provide many services, but the state government neither allocates enough resources for them to do the job nor allows them adequate "revenue home rule" to raise revenues locally. In the 1980s and 1990s state-shared revenue allocated by formula through the local government fund decreased in constant dollars.[57]

Unfunded Mandates

In 1986 a study cataloged 683 federal and state mandates on local government in South Carolina.[58] Although a specific mandate may affect several types of local government, counties appeared to bear the brunt; 93 percent of existing mandates affected counties. There is some consolation for counties because they also were the biggest recipients of state-shared revenue. Federal and state mandates affected 39 percent of municipalities and 17 percent of special-purpose districts.

The basis for a state mandate may be a constitutional provision, a statutory provision, an administrative regulation, or other legal requirement. State mandates put fiscal stress on local government budgets. For example, state employees deliver health and social services in local areas, but these employees must have office space and support services, such as personnel and finance, to do their jobs. The county has to provide offices and support because the state does not spend adequately. Local operations or expenditures mandated by the state compete with local demands for increased services and activities.

Generally, there are four types of state mandates: (1) active (a legal requirement for a specific activity or a service meeting state standards); (2) restrictive (for example, annexation rules that prevent rapid expansion of municipal tax and service bases); (3) traditional (activities that local governments believe are expected of them by the state); and (4) federal pass-through or federal grant requirements, which are enforced by the state as grants administrator.

To help identify mandated costs, the General Assembly passed a fiscal note bill in 1983 that has since been revised.[59] Today, any state tax bill must have a fiscal impact statement attested to by the state Department of Revenue. Bills and resolutions requiring state expenditures must have a fiscal impact and cost statement attested to by the director of the State Budget and Control Board. A bill that requires counties or municipalities to spend money allocated under the State Aid to Subdivisions Act or the use of county funds or other resources must be supported by appropriate estimates of fiscal impact by the state Department of Revenue or the State Budget and Control Board.[60]

The State Aid to Subdivisions Act requires county councils to appropriate reasonable funds for county offices of state agencies established by state law.[61] When disputes arise, state agency officials negotiate agreements with individual councils. On rare occasions, the State Budget and Control Board may intervene to assist local provision of services.

Access to Local Government

Local Elections

In South Carolina registering to vote in a state election also qualifies voters to participate in local elections. Registration is open and maintained by a board of registration in each county. A voter may participate in the nominating primary of only one party but may vote without regard for party in the general election.[62]

State law sets the date for local government elections. County and school board officers typically are elected in the general elections; municipal officers are often elected on a special date in an odd-numbered year to minimize influences from other elections. Local governments must provide for absentee voting in local elections and allow write-in votes. South Carolina municipalities have authority to operate nonpartisan elections, but counties do not. State law stipulates the general methods for election to municipal council, qualifications for candidates, and terms. Municipal governments define ward lines and supervise their elections. Cities have the discretion to allow a county election commission to conduct elections in lieu of a separate municipal commission.[63]

Counties must elect council members by single-member districts, unless an approved at-large system is in place. There is no provision for the popular election of the chair of a county council; elected members choose a chair.[64]

All candidates for local offices are required to disclose economic interests, although campaign expenditures are not limited. Political parties are certified and decertified by state law.[65]

Citizen Control over Actions of Local Officials

Citizens have only indirect control over local officials. County officials who do not have the capacity to discharge their duties may have their office declared vacant by grand jury indictment and subsequent trial. County and city councils are empowered to remove a manager or administrator. Public officers and employees may also be removed from office for a variety of specific illegal actions. A new, comprehensive state ethics law also restricts the conduct of legislators, public employees, and lobbyists with respect to the public interest.[66]

Direct public participation through the initiative and referendum for local ordinances was originally provided in the 1976 local government law, but these provisions have been repealed by the state legislature.

South Carolina has enacted "sunshine" provisions and an open records law.[67] State law requires that all meetings of local government units be announced and open to the public when official actions are made. Public records must be made available for inspection during reasonable hours.

State-Local Relations

This brief review of South Carolina local government leaves many issues for study and debate. For example, constitutional change brought home rule in 1973, but cities and counties express frustration that it is only "expenditure" home rule. Local fiscal autonomy, annexation, consolidation, and state and federal local government mandates continue to be debated.

In 1994, for the first time in over a century, the South Carolina House of Representatives became a Republican majority. South Carolina Republicans generally endorse less government and lower taxes than do Democrats. More fiscal home rule is doubtful, especially if there is a concomitant tax increase. It is unclear whether recent reforms give local units the capacity to raise enough revenue to meet important service priorities.

Among ongoing questions, what is the best structural relationship among counties, cities, and special districts? Counties now discharge functions for which special districts were created.

School districts were excluded from the 1973 revisions. Should the relationships among local governments become more centralized or more market oriented? Should a citizen "shop" for public services from various public or private providers or receive most essential services from one major provider?

As counties continue to expand services, how are they going to manage increased administrative activity? Will the old forms be sufficient? Will the call of some citizens for a stronger executive function in county government relate successfully to elected council members and department heads and the variety of appointed commissions in the county?

If structural changes are needed in local government, how are they to be implemented? Confounding the issue further are the following circumstances: (1) most special-purpose districts created by the legislature before the 1973 constitutional revision still exist; (2) city annexation policies and actions depend on unique political influences in neighboring cities and the surrounding county more than on consensus-based plans; (3) despite the recent adoption of procedures to consolidate city-county and special-purpose districts, many jurisdictions may opt out for practical reasons; and (4) planning and zoning commissions may not be able to coordinate economic growth with general city and county governments.

South Carolinians continue to pursue the ideal of home rule as a way for citizens to govern through local bodies to provide governmental services unique to each jurisdiction. No two communities express the same needs for services or level of services; nor do they endorse identical means to pay for services. The search will continue for fairness and balance between state and local interests and among the many competing jurisdictions.

Notes

1. Daniel J. Elazar, *American Federalism: A View from the States,* 3d ed. (New York: Harper & Row, 1984), 109. Elazar identifies three major culture types: moralistic, individualistic, and traditionalistic.

2. George R. Sherrill, "South Carolina," in *County Government Across the Nation,* ed. Paul W. Wager (Chapel Hill: University of North Carolina Press, 1945).

3. Each county was apportioned one seat in the 124-member state House of Representatives. The rest were apportioned by population.

4. The senator had leverage because no other senator would challenge a supply bill. To interfere in another county's matters was simply to ask for trouble for one's own county. See Ralph Eisenberg, "The Logroll, South Carolina Style," in *Cases in State and Local Government,* ed. Richard T. Frost (Englewood Cliffs, N.J.: Prentice-Hall, 1961), 155–163.

5. Robert H. Stoudemire, "Charleston County Governmental Organization," *University of South Carolina Governmental Review* 6, no. 4 (1959): 1–4. Significant local growth associated with World War II military operations was more than the Charleston County senator wanted to control.

6. 377 U.S. 533 (1964). At the low end of the spectrum in 1970 was McCormick County, with about 8,000 people, and the counties of Allendale and Calhoun, with about 10,000 each. Under the delegation system, each county had one state senator, regardless of population size.

7. Modern-day Charleston was the first incorporated city (June 23, 1722). Its original charter was modeled after that of New York City. The General Assembly chartered additional cities, for example, Camden in 1791, Beaufort in 1803,

and Columbia and Georgetown in 1805. After 1896, municipalities were incorporated under general statutes.

8. South Carolina Constitution of 1868, Article IV, section 19.

9. William J. Blough, "Local Government in South Carolina," in *Government in the Palmetto State,* ed. L. F. Carter and David S. Mann (Columbia: University of South Carolina Bureau of Governmental Research and Service, 1984), 168.

10. South Carolina Constitution, Article 10, section 6.

11. Two competing views are generally referred to as the Cooley Doctrine and Dillon's Rule. See Thomas Cooley, *A Treatise on the Constitutional Limitations Which Rest upon the Legislative Power of the States of the American Union* (Boston: Little, Brown, 1868); and John F. Dillon, *Commentaries on the Law of Municipal Corporations,* 5th ed. (Boston: Little, Brown, 1911). Under the Cooley Doctrine, local units govern as a matter of constitutional right and thus are shielded from restrictions imposed by the state government. Dillon's Rule limits local government powers to the express provisions of state statutes. The county purpose doctrine in South Carolina is an example of Dillon's Rule.

12. South Carolina Committee to Make a Study of the South Carolina Constitution of 1895, *Final Report* (Columbia: The Committee, 1969).

13. South Carolina Constitution, Article VIII, section 17. See also South Carolina Code of Laws, *Case Notes* 21 (1976), 299.

14. South Carolina Constitution, Article VIII, section 7.

15. South Carolina Code of Laws 5-5-10–13-100; 4-9-10–1230; act 283 of 1975; 4-9-20.

16. *Duncan v. County of York* (1976) 267 SC 327; 228 SE2d 92.

17. South Carolina Code of Laws, 5-5-30.

18. South Carolina Constitution, Article VII, section 4, section 3.

19. South Carolina Code of Laws, 5-1-30, 5-1-50, 5-1-60, 5-1-70.

20. South Carolina Code of Laws, 5-1-100. James Island, South Carolina's most recently incorporated municipality gained chartership in 1993 but lost it in 1996.

21. Generally, a freeholder is a person eighteen years of age or older or a corporation with legal title to real estate and ownership of at least one-tenth undivided interest in a single property and whose name is on county tax rolls (South Carolina Code of Laws, 5-3-240). An earlier provision allowing a 25 percent freeholder petition with majority referendum became unconstitutional because it omitted nonproperty owners. The state association of municipalities advocates restoring this provision and changing the petition to 25 percent of electors.

22. South Carolina Code of Laws, 5-3-150.

23. The 1978 act (Act 473, South Carolina Code of Laws, 6-23-10 ff.) provides that "municipalities may jointly purchase, construct, own and operate electric distribution facilities." See also South Carolina Code of Laws, 58-27-620, 58-27-640.

24. South Carolina Code of Laws, 4-7-10 et seq. and 48-10 et seq.

25. South Carolina Code of Laws, 5-31-1910, 5-31-1920, 5-31-1930.

26. South Carolina Code of Laws, 5-7-30.

27. South Carolina Code of Laws, 4-9-30(5).

28. Charlie B. Tyer, "The Special Purpose District in South Carolina," in *The Local Government Landscape,* vol. 1 of *Local Government in South Carolina,* ed. Charlie B. Tyer and Cole Blease Graham Jr. (Columbia: Bureau of Governmental Research and Service, 1984), 75–89.

29. Special districts are often criticized for contributing to inefficient and poorly coordinated local government services and for adding to the strain on city and county finances by skimming lucrative revenue bases.

30. South Carolina Constitution, Article VIII, section 13.

31. South Carolina Code of Laws, 5-7-60, 4-9-30(3), 4-9-40.

32. South Carolina Constitution, Article VIII, section 15.

33. For an overview of the regional approach in South Carolina, see Jan Tuten, "Collaborative Planning in SC: Balancing Growth and Quality of Life," *South Carolina Public Policy Forum* 7, no. 2 (spring 1996): 4–11.

34. South Carolina Code of Laws, 4-9-30(7).

35. South Carolina Code of Laws, 5-19-10 et seq.

36. South Carolina Code of Laws, 23-23-10 et seq.; 12-37-110, 59-1-510, 59-1-520, 1-13-110.

37. South Carolina Code of Laws, 42-1-10.

38. South Carolina Code of Laws, 4-9-30(5).

39. South Carolina Code of Laws, 5-7-260, 5-21-10, 5-23-10, 4-9-160, 11-35-50.

40. South Carolina Code of Laws, 31-10-10 et seq., 31-12-10 et seq.

41. South Carolina House of Representatives, *Legislative Update* 16, no. 1 (12 January 1999): 8.

42. South Carolina Code of Laws, 4-1-170, 4-29-10 et seq., 4-29-80.

43. Taxation of property has to be equal and uniform within a series of specified classes: (1) manufacturing, utilities, and mining at 10 percent of fair market value; (2) transport companies at 9 percent; (3) legal residences and up to five contiguous acres at 4 percent; (4) agricultural properties at 4 percent for individuals or partnerships and 6 percent for corporations; (5) other real properties or business inventory at 6 percent; (6) farm machinery at 5 percent; and (7) all other personal property at 10.5 percent.

44. South Carolina Code of Laws, 4-10-10 et seq.

45. House Speaker David Wilkins, R-Greenville, quoted in Michael Sponhour, "House GOP Questions Tax Plan," *The State,* 5 February 1997, B1, B4.

46. Senate Bill 409, the Local Government Fiscal Authority Act, amends South Carolina Code of Laws 4-9-55.

47. York County, which is part of the Charlotte, North Carolina, metropolitan statistical area, enacted a capital projects sales tax effective May 1, 1998.

48. The cumulative rates of the local accommodations tax and hospitality taxes are limited, and municipal councils must agree if a county should impose either tax within its boundaries at rates beyond specified thresholds. Proceeds must be used for tourism-related projects. For counties with more than $900,000 in state accommodations tax collections, the local money may be used for operating or maintaining tourism facilities.

49. South Carolina Constitution, Article X, section 14. The South Carolina Association of Counties favors raising the limit to 12 percent.

50. South Carolina Code of Laws, 5-21-250.

51. Holley H. Ulbrich and Ellen W. Saltzman, "City/County Money Book," *South Carolina Policy Forum* 7, no. 3 (summer 1996): 17–33.

52. South Carolina Code of Laws, 4-9-39(8), 4-9-140.

53. South Carolina Code of Laws, 5-7-260, 5-9-30(5,6), 5-13-90(3,4).

54. South Carolina Code of Laws, 4-9-140, 6-11-260.

55. South Carolina Code of Laws, 5-1-100.

56. Jonathan Walters, "Cities Have a Simple Message for States This Year: Set Us Free," *Governing* (January 1992): 40–43.

57. Marion W. Middleton, "Why South Carolina Local Governments Need a Local Option Sales Tax," *South Carolina Forum* (April–June 1990): 47.

58. Janet M. Kelly, "State Mandated Local Government Expenditures and Revenue Limitations in South Carolina. Executive Summary" (Columbia: Advisory Commission on Intergovernmental Relations, June 1988).

59. A fiscal note estimates the fiscal impact of a state mandate on local government and is attached to proposed legislation requiring local expenditure. A fiscal note presumably slows down the number of state mandates, but local government officials generally argue that the General Assembly continued to pass mandated expenditures at about the same rate before and after the fiscal note requirement. State mandates continue to be a source of some friction between state and local leaders.

60. South Carolina Code of Laws, 2-7-71, 2-7-72, 2-7-76.

61. South Carolina Code of Laws, 6-27-55.

62. South Carolina Code of Laws, 7-7-620, 7-13-1040. Except for municipal and presidential primaries, primaries are conducted by the county election commission (South Carolina *Code of Laws,* 7-13-15). County election commissioners are appointed by the senatorial delegation and at least half of a county's house members.

63. South Carolina Code of Laws, 7-15-365, 7-15-410, 7-13-1380, 7-13-1850, 5-15-20, 5-15-40, 5-15-145.

64. South Carolina Code of Laws, 4-9-90, 4-9-110.

65. South Carolina Code of Laws, 8-13-1120, 7-9-10.

66. South Carolina Code of Laws, 4-11-40, 8-1-10 et seq. (8-13-100 et seq.)

67. South Carolina Code of Laws, 30-4-70 et seq.

SOUTH DAKOTA

Tim Schorn, Dave Aronson, Buffie K. Main, and Kenneth J. Tauke

Home rule, a relatively recent innovation in South Dakota, is available to counties and municipalities across the state. Despite the fact that home rule can bring more governmental decisions closer to the people, it has been adopted by fewer than a dozen municipalities and counties. Cautious by nature, South Dakotans are reluctant to accept innovation in government unless they are solidly convinced of its advantages.

Governmental Setting

Though the state retains a rural character, South Dakota's population is relatively evenly split between urban and rural residents. The state covers 77,615 square miles and has a population of over 730,000—fewer than 10 people per square mile. South Dakota encompasses 64 organized counties, 2 unorganized counties, 9 Native American reservations, more than 300 towns and cities, and nearly 1,000 townships.[1] Only five communities in South Dakota have more than 15,000 residents. Some jurisdictions near growing urban areas have required an increase in governmental responsibilities and services; however, the populations of most municipalities and counties are decreasing, requiring consolidation of services. For example, of the 3,288 school districts that existed in 1957, consolidation and elimination have left only about 170.

South Dakota's political culture tends to be conservative, and its residents generally favor easy access to elected officials. Historically dominated by Republicans, the state has had twenty-three Republican governors, five Democrats, and one Populist. Of its U.S. senators, seventeen have been Republican and eight have been Democrats. Twenty-three U.S. representatives have been Republican and ten have been Democrats. The last time South Dakotans voted Democratic in a presidential election was in 1964, when they chose Lyndon Johnson over Barry Goldwater. They voted against their favorite son, George McGovern, in favor of Richard Nixon in 1972. But South Dakota's "prairie populist" spirit is also evident in the fact that George McGovern, Tom Daschle, and Tim Johnson—all Democrats—were elected to the U.S. Senate by a rather conservative electorate.

Despite their independent, individualistic, and conservative nature, South Dakotans have occasionally exhibited a progressive streak. Under Governor Peter Norbeck (who held that post from 1917 to 1921), South Dakota established a number of state-owned entities, including a cement plant—still in operation—and a state coal mine. In addition, under the Rural Credits Act, the state government established a program during the 1920s and 1930s that allowed farmers to borrow money against state revenues (because more loans were issued than the state could afford, the program failed).

The structure of South Dakota's state government is like that of most states: it has a governor as chief executive, a bicameral legislature, and a supreme court. Most of the constitutionally required offices are filled through statewide elections: this list includes the attorney general, the secretary of state, the treasurer, the auditor, the commissioner of school and public lands, and the three members of the public utilities commission. The lieutenant governor runs on a joint ticket with the gubernatorial candidate. Thirty-five senators are elected from equally apportioned districts, and two representatives are elected from each district. Supreme court justices are appointed by the governor and serve for three years; after that time, the justices must be approved in a general election in order to retain their seats.

South Dakota was admitted to the union on November 2, 1889, following the division of the Dakota Territory. Statehood appealed to all Dakotans because it would allow them to elect their officials rather than have them appointed by the president; residents of the region had begun in 1882 to hold meetings concerning eventual state government. At the most important of the early meetings—the "Philadelphia Convention of South Dakota," held in Sioux Falls in September 1883—a document was drafted that served as the basis of the South Dakota Constitution. It was ratified on October 1, 1889, and still serves as the constitution today.

Home Rule in South Dakota

Historical Development

A relatively recent innovation, home rule was approved by the voters in 1962, after a failed attempt the previous decade. As a topic of discussion, however, it had been around since the 1930s. At the 1934 organizational meeting of the South Dakota Municipal League, Herman James, president of the University of South Dakota, spoke to the league about the advantages of home rule. Twenty-one years later, on June 24, 1955, the league passed a resolution calling for the establishment of "a committee to formulate the principles and concepts of Home Rule to control the program of pressing for legislation allowing the establishment of Home Rule; and . . . [for] the Municipal League [to] press for legislation in these terms."[2]

Meetings between this committee and the home rule subcommittee of the South Dakota Legislative Research Council led eventually to legislative approval of a constitutional amendment in 1957. However, the amendment was defeated in the 1958 general election, 104,138 to 94,599: in that first effort, voting on the amendment "was light and it was clear there was little public understanding of what was involved."[3] The amendment was reintroduced in 1961 and approved in 1962 by a vote of 95,737 to 87,888. Home rule in South Dakota follows the "Fordham Approach"—which, rather than spell out all the powers that exist under home rule, explains its limitations instead. Those limitations tend to be few.

Rapid City was the first city in the state to attempt—albeit without success—to take advantage of the new home rule provisions. The first failed effort occurred in 1965, the second in 1976. One student of the election came up with a number of reasons for voters' failure to approve home rule: among them were the skill and prestige of the opposition, the perception that home rule was a partisan issue, and the fact that voters may not have known exactly what they were voting on (perhaps because the proponents of home rule had failed to draft a charter).[4]

The first municipality to adopt home rule was the city of Springfield. On July 24, 1984, by a vote of 190 to 27, voters adopted a charter that had as its primary purpose the acquisition and operation of the University of South Dakota at Springfield, which had been marked for closure by Governor William Janklow. However, the city was unable to acquire the university and the state chose to shut down the school and turn it into a prison.

In Brookings, home rule was adopted to provide the city with the freedom it needed to manage Brookings Municipal Utilities, Brookings Hospital, and Brookview Manor (a long-term care facility). To be effective and efficient in their operations, to take advantage of new technologies, and to compete successfully with the private sector, these city-owned entities require the same flexibility that private businesses enjoy. Without home rule, they would be much more restricted. Among other advantages, home rule allows them to do business outside of the city.

Along with Springfield, Sioux Falls, and Brookings, three other South Dakota towns have opted for home rule: Elk Point, Beresford, and Fort Pierre. Elk Point, the latest addition to the list, approved home rule on September 14, 1999. Like Beresford and Brookings before it, Elk Point chose home rule for the purpose of managing its own utilities—cable television, Internet, and telephone service.

Definition of Home Rule

In 1969, the Constitutional Revision Commission recommended changes in the amendment that allowed home rule, including a change that would allow counties as well as municipalities to have home rule. The change was accepted by the voters in 1972 by a vote of 152,474 to 107,296. Article IX, section 2, now allows any county or municipal government to adopt a home rule charter. In addition, "a chartered governmental unit may exercise any legislative power or perform any function not denied by its charter, the Constitution or the general laws of the state."[5]

Because their powers are still restricted by both constitutional provision and statute, even home rule local governments are not sovereign. Nevertheless, they still have greater authority and discretion than non–home rule units of government, which may exercise only those powers that are specifically granted to them by the state legislature in its statutes or incorporated into the state constitution.

South Dakota's home rule amendment was created to be self-executing, meaning that failure on the part of the state legislature to implement the amendment would not prevent home rule from going into effect.[6] Under the home rule amendment, local governing units have inherent rights and the prerogative to exercise vast local powers, entirely apart from any action by the state legislature. If the legislature believes the exercise of any home rule powers to be contrary to the general laws of the state or believes that those powers have been exceeded, and if a home rule jurisdiction challenges the state's assertion, the matter will be determined by the courts.

Local governments' resources are dwindling, and citizens are more and more resistant to tax increases; at the same time, citizens' demands for service quantity and quality are growing. Effective and efficient administrative structures and procedures are highly important in this environment—as is apparent if one examines the reasons that South Dakota local governments are choosing home rule. Home rule allows municipalities and counties to address directly—without interference from state government—the issues that are of greatest concern to them, from consolidation of county services to control over utilities.

An important factor to consider when examining home rule

in South Dakota are the limitations placed on local governments. Under Article IX of the state constitution, the state legislature has the power to prohibit local governments from exercising power in seven areas.

First, home rule jurisdictions are not allowed to "enact private or civil law governing civil relationships except as incident to the exercise of an independent county or municipal power."[7] Second, they may not define or provide for punishment of crimes except for violations of ordinances or charter provisions. There are also limits on how serious a penalty may be prescribed. Third, home rule units may not change laws that relate to elementary or secondary education. Fourth, they may not change property tax assessment practices. Fifth, a home rule jurisdiction may not "exempt itself from providing the necessary personnel and facilities to perform services required by general law."[8] Sixth, home rule jurisdictions may not deny referendum on ordinances. Seventh, they may not regulate utility rates or conditions that are already regulated by the South Dakota Public Utilities Commission.[9] It should also be noted that home rule jurisdictions may not set standards, whether by ordinance or charter, that are less stringent than those set by the South Dakota Codified Law.[10]

Since the inception of home rule government in Sioux Falls, taxation issues have set the city at odds with the state. The first of these conflicts involved a state law passed in 1995 that denied the city the right to impose permit and inspection fees in excess of the actual cost thereof. The state's position was that the imposition of permit and inspection fees was a matter of statewide concern, but the circuit court disagreed, declaring the law unconstitutional because it was directed at the city of Sioux Falls and not all municipalities within the state. Moreover, the court judged the imposition of permit and inspection fees to be a matter of purely local concern.

Structural Features

South Dakota municipalities are provided for in the state constitution and are legal creations of the state legislature; as such, they generally have only those powers that are granted by the constitution or the legislature. In order to incorporate, a community must have at least 100 residents, including at least thirty electors. The first step in the process of incorporation is a petition signed by not less than 25 percent of the registered voters.[11] The application for incorporation must identify the type of government to be formed; the number of trustees, commissioners, or wards; the boundaries and area, according to the required survey; and the resident population, according to the most recent federal census. No territory can be incorporated if it lies within three miles of the corporate limits of any existing incorporated municipality unless the territory has applied to be annexed by the incorporated municipality and the municipality has refused or failed to do so. However, a territory that is within three miles of an incorporated municipality may incorporate if it is in a different county and has a post office prior to incorporation.[12]

South Dakota has four classes of incorporated municipalities. First-class municipalities, or cities of the first class, of which there are 13, are those with populations of 5,000 or more. Second-class municipalities, or cities of the second class, of which there are 105, have populations of more than 500 but less than 5,000. Third-class municipalities, or towns, of which there are 190, have populations of less than 500. The fourth class is made up of the special charter (home rule) municipalities.

Since municipalities are creations of the legislature, they may be the focus of special legislation that awards different rights on the basis of the class to which they belong. For example, first-class municipalities are exempt from the legislation that sets standards for the connection of plumbing fixtures to public water systems.[13]

South Dakota has an eclectic array of local forms of government. First- and second-class municipalities (cities) may select one of three organizational forms, each of which allows for some discretion and variation, depending on the needs of the community: the mayor-council (aldermanic) form, the commission form, or the council-manager form. Until 1907, all first- and second-class municipalities were required to use the mayor-council form of government; many continue to use it today. Town government (third-class municipalities) is similar to the mayor-council (aldermanic) form of government except that the council is known as a board of trustees and is made up of three to five members, one of whom is chosen by the board to serve as president.

The commission form was first allowed in 1907, and ten municipalities now operate under this form. The state allows two forms of commission government, consisting of a mayor and either a two- or four-member commission. Under the commission form, legislative and executive functions are combined, and the commissioners are the directors of various service areas. The council-manager form of government has been authorized since 1918. Nine cities in South Dakota had operated under this model of government, but for various reasons all but two—Vermillion and Yankton—abandoned the council-manager form.

South Dakota's largest city, Sioux Falls, has a new home rule charter that provides for a "strong" mayor–council form of government. The charter requires eight part-time council members: five representing various districts within the city and three representing the community at large.

South Dakota has sixty-six counties—which, even in a relatively rural and agricultural state, show a good deal of diversity. Some are very rural, others urban. Some have an extensive tax base; others do not (those in the latter category struggle to provide basic services). Minnehaha County, the largest, is home to over 124,000 people, and its county seat—Sioux Falls—is the financial, cultural, and industrial capital of the state (as well as its largest city, with over 120,000 people). Jones County, the least populated, is an agricultural county of only 1,300 people. County boundaries were for the most part drawn in the nineteenth century, though some were not solidified until the twentieth century.

Some counties have consolidated services in order to be more efficient and cost-effective. The latest consolidation occurred in 1978, with the joining of Washabaugh and Jackson Counties. In the past few years, two factors have caused renewed interest in county consolidation: the desire to reduce the cost of government and the need to adjust to the state's slow growth rate.

Counties are considered agents of the state, but the state legislature is generally prohibited from enacting any private or special laws that regulate county affairs. As noted earlier, South Dakota's county governments may be either organized or unorganized bodies. County government structure is based on a board of county commissioners, which is made up of three or five members elected on a partisan ballot. The commissioners, who handle the legislative function, act as a group and do not exercise individual powers. They have the power to set salaries, establish the positions of deputies and clerks, and hire and fire at will—though the last power is limited by the right of the public employees to join labor and employee organizations.[14] The executive functions of the county are divided into six offices: sheriff, auditor, register of deeds, treasurer, state's attorney, and coroner.[15]

The auditor serves as the clerk for the board of commissioners and authorizes payment from county funds; he or she also serves as the local election administrator. The treasurer collects taxes and fees and may make payments from county funds only when the auditor has issued a warrant for payment to be made. The state's attorney prosecutes crimes committed in the county and provides legal counsel to the board of commissioners and to other public officials. He or she also heads the county health board. Part-time state's attorneys (those in less populated counties) may maintain a private practice.

Although home rule in counties allows for the council-manager form of government, no South Dakota county has adopted this form of government. However, two counties—Shannon and Todd—have opted for home rule.[16]

Functions of Local Government

Functional Responsibilities

Municipalities are responsible for a number of services, including police and fire protection, sewer and water services, streets, and parks. Municipalities cooperate with counties in areas such as fire protection, parks and recreation, libraries, airports, and fairs.[17] (Cooperation between local governmental units is permitted under the South Dakota Constitution.)[18]

Counties were created to be the administrative and judicial arms of the state, but their responsibilities have grown to include, among other things, property assessment, public record keeping, road and highway maintenance, law enforcement, the provision of public health and welfare services, and the administration of elections.[19] In addition, counties are responsible for maintaining abandoned cemeteries, disposing of solid waste and contaminated material, providing burial for indigent residents, arranging and implementing disaster relief and protective measures, undertaking flood control, protecting groundwater from pollution, and providing assistance to developmentally disabled residents. Counties also have optional powers to offer other services: for example, they may provide ambulance services, a county nurse, drainage and irrigation systems, drug education programs, and historic preservation. They may own and operate libraries, airports, and parks; promote industrial, tourist, and recreational activities; control predators, weeds, and pests; establish veterans' memorials, museums, and fairs; and maintain a public defender's office.[20]

Special districts, headed by an elected board of directors or trustees, may be created to provide various services and facilities: for example, road maintenance and repair; ambulance services; rural fire protection; and sanitary, irrigation, watershed, and water projects.[21] South Dakota currently has more than 200 special districts.

Administrative Discretion

Municipal governments in South Dakota have a number of general corporate powers, such as to sue or be sued, to acquire or dispose of real and personal property, to construct municipal buildings, and to provide the necessary supplies for the use of the municipality. Municipalities have all of the necessary general police powers as well, such as prohibiting disorders, disturbances, and "houses of ill repute." They may also prohibit all gambling except that owned and operated by the state. South Dakota municipalities have the power to engage in the retail alcohol business, and a number of cities and towns have a municipal liquor store and bar.[22]

As it is their responsibility to protect the health and welfare of citizens, zoning remains within the purview of municipalities and counties. Municipal governments may exercise jurisdiction over any territory up to one mile beyond their corporate limits. In addition, jurisdiction may be exercised over any "public ground or park" that belongs to the municipality, whether that land is inside or outside the corporate limits. Municipalities and counties in South Dakota generally perform contracting, purchasing, and bidding procedures through a competitive process.[23]

Economic Development

Municipal governments in South Dakota have the authority to take part in economic development projects and to create business improvement districts (BIDs) within the boundaries of an established business area. Within a BID, a municipality may use funds for a range of purposes, including off-street parking, landscaping, malls, bus shelters, plazas, sidewalks, and sculptures, as well as to sponsor activities and promote events. Municipalities also have the power to foster economic development by encouraging and assisting the creation of new industry and business.[24] For example, they may issue bonds; acquire or construct projects; enter into revenue agreements with individuals, private corporations, or governmental bodies; or offer property tax abatements.

Like municipalities, counties can issue bonds and offer tax incentives to encourage growth and development. In addition, counties have the authority to use monies from their general fund to assist nonprofit corporations and associations in the promotion of industrial, tourist, and recreational activities. Enterprise zones are state-designated, economically disadvantaged areas for which special loans can be made available.[25] Tax-free zones and free ports are not yet an option in South Dakota.

Fiscal Autonomy of Local Governments

As noted earlier, home rule does not allow complete freedom from state control: the state's interest is paramount. However, the line between matters of state and local concern is often blurry. For example, because of restrictions in state law, local governments cannot make changes in the taxation of personal or real property. But this restriction does not prohibit a local government from raising new revenues by imposing new and different types of taxation not disallowed by its charter, the state constitution, or the general laws of the state. When home rule is proposed, citizens' fears often center on local power to impose or increase taxes and fees.

Local Revenues

In South Dakota, property taxes are one of the major revenue sources for municipalities and counties alike, but they are by far the leading source for counties. Among municipalities, the percentage of revenue that comes from the property tax varies from town to town. Some earn part of their revenue from municipal liquor stores or municipally owned utilities. Also, except on fuel, municipalities may levy a 1 percent sales tax on top of the state's 4 percent. A municipality may increase its sales tax rate above 1 percent, but the revenue generated from the tax increase may be used only for capital improvements. An additional 1 percent is also allowed for certain goods and services—namely, lodging, alcoholic beverages, prepared food, and admissions.[26]

County assessors undertake the valuation of property, and state law requires tax levies to be based on full and true valuation. Within the limits set by the state, local governments control the rates. For property taxes, "the levy may not exceed twenty-seven dollars per thousand dollars of taxable valuation."[27]

Sioux Falls, the largest city in the state, receives its revenues from a number of sources, but those vary widely in level of importance; the sales tax is the leading provider of revenue. The city of Vermillion (pop. 11,000) receives revenue from four primary sources; all of the sources are relatively equal in importance, but since 1996, property tax has been Vermillion's primary or secondary source of revenue.

Effective January 1, 1996, the city of Sioux Falls imposed an additional tax of 1 percent on hotel and motel rooms; revenues were to be used by the Sioux Falls Convention and Visitors Bureau. However, because state law restricts municipalities to a 3 percent sales tax, the state legislature responded by passing a bill limiting the taxation power of home rule municipalities.[28] On July 2 of that year, the city of Sioux Falls sued the state, arguing that the new legislation was intended to limit the city's taxing authority under home rule.

The state contended that home rule cities should adhere to state limits on taxes and fees. In particular, the state feared that the city of Sioux Falls might initiate an income tax or increase its general sales tax. The state held that city residents should be protected from taxation without representation. (Under the home rule charter, any new form of taxation has to be approved by the citizens, but neither increases in existing taxes nor new or increased fees require their approval.) In addition, the state argued that because the imposition of a city sales tax might make the state reluctant to increase its own sales tax (out of fear of imposing an excessive burden on citizens), a city sales tax could effectively preempt the state's ability to increase the sales tax.

The city countered the claim of taxation without representation by arguing that visitors and residents alike who pay the accommodation tax benefit from city services while using facilities located within the city. With respect to the state's claim that a city sales tax would limit the state's own taxing authority, the city held that the state's right to levy additional taxes is not undermined by a local unit's right to do so. The revenue generated from the accommodation tax, assessed and used locally in Sioux Falls, was asserted to be a matter of purely local concern and not a matter that affected statewide interests.

On March 19, 1997, the governor signed new legislation prohibiting county, municipal, and other local governmental entities from enacting or increasing, unless permitted by statute,

in any form a tax, fee, or charge that is: related to the state lottery; similar to a tax which provides revenues to the state; or similar to state licensing or regulatory fees enacted by statute or adopted by rule. The provisions of this section do not prohibit any tax or fee enacted and imposed on or before March 1, 1996.[29]

Because this act repealed the earlier legislation, the suit brought in July of 1996 was dismissed.

Local Expenditures

South Dakota state law limits appropriations to costs for materials and expenses that arise in the exercise of municipal powers. Local budgets must "conform to the uniform classification in the municipal accounting manual published in accordance with" the state accounting manual for municipalities and other agencies. Each municipality's clerk must report to the county auditor the total amount of indebtedness and the purpose for which it was issued, along with the liabilities, assets, resources, expenditures, and the total receipts and disbursements as of the closing date of each fiscal year.[30]

Expenditures are limited to the appropriated amounts, but they do not have to be limited to the amount of revenue raised: there is no requirement, as such, for a balanced budget at the local level. There is, however, a limit on general-obligation debt.[31] Theoretically, a local government may go bankrupt, but it would simply default on the amounts owed: the bondholders would bear the burden.

In accordance with the recommendations of the state Department of Legislative Audit, each municipality must appoint a financial officer to oversee its accounting systems. Each year, a municipality's auditor or clerk provides the governing body with an estimate of the expenses to be incurred and the amount of revenue that must be raised for the annual budget.[32] Typically, general government and administration, public safety, and maintenance and transportation rank at the top of municipalities' budgets.

Every two years, all municipalities and counties are subject to a financial and compliance audit overseen by the state auditor general. Municipalities with less than $600,000 in annual revenue may, in lieu of a formal audit, submit an annual report to the auditor general on forms prescribed by the Department of Legislative Audit. Those municipalities that receive federal funding may be required by federal regulations to have a formal annual audit. The auditor general may audit the books and records of any office or officer of any political subdivision (1) at the request of the governing body or (2) if the auditor general finds that special reasons exist to do so.[33]

Roads and bridges are the primary expenditure for counties, with law enforcement a distant second. With respect to bankruptcy, counties are in the same situation as municipalities: if a county goes bankrupt, bondholders bear the burden.

State Government Grants-in-Aid to Localities

The South Dakota state government offers little in the form of grants-in-aid to localities. Monies that come from the federal government, such as block grants, are given to various local governments at the discretion of the governor. One type of grant from the state government comes in the form of state property tax relief to counties and their subdivisions: no money actually changes hands, but the citizens of a subdivision may be granted a reduction in their property tax bill.

Unfunded Mandates

South Dakota prohibits unfunded mandates. Thus, the state government may not require any county, municipality, or school district to perform a new service unless the state provides sufficient funding.[34]

Access to Local Government

Local Elections

In South Dakota, the State Board of Elections and the secretary of state establish and monitor the rules for local elections; among other things, these entities specify the required forms and procedures for petitions, ballots, and public notices. How municipalities elect their officers depends on their form of government, but municipal elections must be in conformance with state guidelines.

The county auditor is in complete charge of the registration of all electors in the county, and the finance officer of each municipality is the county auditor's deputy for the purpose of assisting in such registration.[35] Each voting precinct must be presided over by an election board consisting of at least two precinct deputies and one precinct superintendent; the superintendent is in charge of conducting the election in that precinct.

Annual elections for municipal officers are traditionally held on the second Tuesday of April, but the municipal governing body may choose to hold a general municipal election in conjunction with a school district election on a date agreed upon by the governing bodies of the municipality and the school district. In every respect except date, special elections must be conducted according to the same procedures that apply to annual municipal elections. State law also requires that the notice of the special election state any question or questions to be voted upon.

Under state law, only candidates for commissioner, council member, or mayor in first-class municipalities are required to file a statement of financial interest with the county auditor (if elected, candidates are required to file any corrections or additions to that statement within fifteen days of assuming office). However, any municipality, regardless of size, may adopt an ordinance that requires candidates to report campaign contributions and expenditures.

The state constitution provides that any resident or registered voter of a municipality may circulate an initiative or referendum petition. The Republican and Democratic Parties are recognized political parties in South Dakota. New political parties may form by filing petitions signed by 6,505 registered South Dakota voters.

Citizen Controls over Actions of Local Officials

In 1889, South Dakota became the first state in the country to add the initiative and referendum process to its constitution. This provision allows voters, through a petition process, to directly propose a new law or constitutional amendment, then vote it into existence without legislative approval. Referendum requires a new law passed by the legislature to be subject to voter approval before it can go into effect. These two forms of direct legislation, first used in 1908, rest on the presumption that the legislature may not always adequately represent the people; thus, citizens themselves should be able to pass laws they desire and nullify laws they oppose. In 1972, the state constitution was amended to allow constitutional amendments by initiative; and in 1988, a statewide vote eliminated the requirement that an initiative receive legislative approval before being placed on the ballot.

South Dakota ballot initiatives have a 40 percent success rate, and referendums have an 83 percent success rate; of the 206 constitutional amendments that have been on the ballot, 105 have been adopted—a 51 percent success rate. Of the eight amendments initiated by South Dakota citizens, four passed; the other 198 amendments were proposed by the legislature.[36]

Individual municipalities determine the rules and regulations that govern the jurisdiction; these are set forth in the articles and bylaws of the corporation through which the municipality was established. Included in these rules and regulations are impeachment and recall procedures. In all first- and second-class municipalities, voters may remove the mayor, commissioners, or aldermen from office at any time.[37]

Notice of meetings to be held by the municipal governing body must be published in the official newspaper designated by the governing body. Within thirty days after each meeting, the proceedings must be published in the same newspaper. Official meetings must be open to the public; however, subject to the approval of a majority of the governing body, municipalities are authorized to hold executive or closed meetings for specific purposes. State law requires that meeting records be available and open to inspection by any person during normal business hours. Records that are secret or confidential cannot, by law, be subject to public inspection.[38]

State-Local Relations

Home rule in South Dakota remains somewhat underused. As a means of enabling municipal and county governments to exercise more power—thus bringing power closer to the people—home rule is an idea that might be expected to appeal to the populist streak in South Dakotans' natures. But because the notion that municipal and county government could exercise more authority causes consternation among some state residents, home rule has not been enthusiastically embraced by more than a few counties and towns.

In 1986, one noted student of South Dakota politics concluded that even after only fourteen years of experience with home rule in South Dakota, a number of conclusions could be drawn.

Home rule has proved a viable, readily available, and worthwhile option when only through home rule could a specific objective or objectives be attained. . . . In short, what home rule makes possible is the "tailoring" of government to meet a special situation without the necessity of seeking state legislative help or interference.[39]

As the economy of South Dakota becomes more diverse, especially through the growth of the technology sector, more local governments will take advantage of the opportunity to acquire control over the local technological and information infrastructure. Moreover, as rural counties see a continued decrease in population and a possible erosion of their tax base, the necessity for cuts in county budgets and services may make consolidation of services more appealing. Finally, as more municipalities and counties seize the opportunities presented by home rule, momentum—and possibly pressure—will build in other jurisdictions, resulting in a "snowball" effect. The likely trend, therefore, is one of growth in the "home rule industry."

Conflict is most likely in those counties—such as Pennington (Rapid City), Minnehaha (Sioux Falls), and Brown (Aberdeen)—that encompass the largest metropolitan areas. There, the remaining rural residents will be wary of losing influence to a county government dominated by city dwellers and city governments. The rural residents may feel that they have more in common with rural residents of other counties than with urban county residents, and may therefore want the power of urban voters to be diluted through the greater exercise of authority by state government. Nevertheless, rural residents will be in the minority, and the vote will be stacked against them.

As the number of home rule jurisdictions increases, the state's authority over money and services will decrease. The governor and the legislature in Pierre may find themselves more and more superfluous as the decisions that are most important to the people are being made in Sioux Falls, Brookings, Elk Point, and so on. By bringing government closer to home, this shift would seem to suit the independent, individualistic natures of South Dakotans. The conservatism of state residents will not necessarily prevent change and innovation; instead, it may encourage local government to attempt to gain power at the expense of the higher—and more distant—level of government.

Notes

1. Unorganized counties contract with another county for county services.

2. Quoted in W. O. Farber, "Home Rule in South Dakota: Prescription for Tailor-Made Government," in *Local Government at a Crossroads: Choices for South*

Dakota, ed. Russell L. Smith (Vermillion: Governmental Research Bureau, University of South Dakota, 1986), 176.

3. W. H. Cape, *Toward Home Rule in South Dakota,* quoted in Farber, "Home Rule in South Dakota."

4. David M. Gugin, "An Inquiry into Rapid City's Rejection of Home Rule," *Public Affairs* 23 (November 1965), quoted in Farber, "Home Rule in South Dakota," 178.

5. See South Dakota Constitution, Article IX, sections 1, 2, and 3.

6. Farber, "Home Rule in South Dakota," 179.

7. Ibid., 180.

8. Ibid.

9. Ibid., 181.

10. Ibid.; South Dakota Codified Law, 6-12-5.

11. South Dakota Codified Law, 9-3-5; see also the minimum population requirements in 9-3-1.

12. Ibid., 9-3-2, 9-3-3, 9-3-1.1.

13. Ibid., 9-47-28.

14. See South Dakota Codified Law, Title VII; *A White Paper Report: County Consolidation in South Dakota* (Vermillion: Governmental Research Bureau, University of South Dakota, September 1, 1997), app. 3, pp. 54–58; see also *Lindsey v. Minnehaha Co.,* 281 N.W.2d 808 (S.D. 1979) and *General Drivers and Helpers Union v. Brown Co.,* 269 N.W.2d 795 (S.D. 1978).

15. W. O. Farber and Loren Carlson, "Government of South Dakota," unpublished draft, 1990, 137.

16. Ibid., 139.

17. Farber and Carlson, "Government of South Dakota," 137, 141.

18. South Dakota Constitution, Article IX, section 3, states in part that "every local government may exercise, perform, or transfer any of its powers or functions, including financing the same, jointly or in cooperation with any other governmental entities.

19. Farber and Carlson, "Government of South Dakota," 137. See also the South Dakota Association of County Officials' Web site at www.sdcounties.org.

20. See South Dakota Codified Law, Title VII, Chapters 7, 8, 14, 18, 24, 26–28, 33, 34, 38, 40, 41, and 50.

21. South Dakota Codified Law, 6-16-1.

22. Ibid., Title IX, Chapter 12.

23. Ibid., 9-29-1, 5-18-1.

24. Ibid., Title IX, Chapters 54–55; 9-55-4, 9-55-3, 9-54-1, 9-54-2, 10-18-6.

25. Ibid., 7-18-16, 7-18-12, 1-16G-9.

26. Ibid., 10-52-2, 10-52-8.

27. Ibid., 10-12-34.1, 10-12-32.

28. Ibid., 6-12-13.

29. Session Laws 1997, Chapter 42, section 2.

30. South Dakota Codified Law, 9-21-3, 9-21-6, 6-9-1.

31. Ibid., 9-21-9, South Dakota Constitution, Article XIII, section 4.

32. South Dakota Codified Law, 9-22-23.

33. Ibid., 4-11-4.

34. Ibid., 6-15-1.

35. Ibid., 12-4-2.

36. The secretary of state's Web site is www.state.sd.us/state/executive/sos/initiati.htm.

37. South Dakota Codified Law, 9-13-29.

38. Ibid., 1-25-1, 1-25-2, 1-25-3, 1-25-4.

39. Farber, "Home Rule in South Dakota," 187.

TENNESSEE

Lon S. Felker, Michael P. Marchioni, and Platon N. Rigos

The history of state-local relations in Tennessee is a checkered one. Until the 1950s, the general assembly had considerable power over local governments: it was not unknown, for example, for municipalities to lose their charters and to be forced to beg them back from the state. In the 1950s, municipalities managed to take a measure of control away from counties and the legislature. Among the many changes that made this possible was the creation of home rule provisions for municipalities and the relaxation of requirements for the annexation of adjacent lands.

East Tennessee, the region in which municipal home rule has been most popular, is home to all but one of the thirteen municipalities that adopted home rule between 1955 and 1972. Although Tennessee allows home rule for counties (and is known for one of the oldest post–World War II consolidations, that of the city of Nashville and Davidson County), most counties have not availed themselves of the option. Paradoxically, full home rule in Tennessee weakens local governments' revenue-raising ability, which may explain its lack of popularity.

Governmental Setting

Tennessee gained statehood in 1796 with the passage of its first constitution. Subsequent constitutions passed between 1835 and 1870 created a form of government closely mirroring that of other states: among the similarities are a bicameral legislature and a governor who is empowered to veto individual items in a bill.

The state has historically been divided into three major parts, called grand divisions: East, Middle, and West Tennessee. These regions differ in terms of culture, topography, and economy. The Civil War exacerbated the already serious sectional conflict between the grand divisions. In an effort to prevent it from seceding from the state, Confederate forces occupied East Tennessee, which was strongly pro-Union. During Reconstruction, previously suppressed Republican elements from East Tennessee dominated state politics, playing a major role in the election of a series of pro-Union governors. The sectional and partisan rivalries that had begun before the War between the States continued to shape Tennessee politics well into the twentieth century.[1] The wounds inflicted by the Civil War never properly healed, and left a legacy of intersectional bitterness.

In Daniel Elazar's typology of political culture, southern and western Tennessee would be described as adhering to a traditionalistic culture, while residents of the northern and eastern parts of the state would be described as holding moralistic beliefs.

From Reconstruction until the 1920s, rural forces dominated Tennessee politics. Agriculture was the primary economic activity, and urban industries received little encouragement. In the next phase of its political history—from the 1920s until the end of the 1940s, Tennessee state politics were dominated by what was known as the Crump machine—the instrument of E. H. Crump, of the city of Memphis and Shelby County. Through a coalition of West Tennessee Democrats and East Tennessee Republicans, the machine managed to stymie efforts on the part of Middle Tennessee forces to gain control of the general assembly. With his eastern Republican allies, Crump was able to dictate public policies that were favorable to the western region and to deny resources to Nashville and Middle Tennessee. Only with the rise of a new politics in the post–World War II era—and the increasing success of politicians such as Estes Kefauver and Al Gore Sr.—did the Crump machine and its legacy of corruption fade into obscurity.

Long a rural and agrarian state, Tennessee began to develop an urban and industrial economy in the 1940s and 1950s. The New Deal of the 1930s and the creation of the Tennessee Valley Authority contributed to this development—in particular by making available the hydroelectric power needed to support new industry.

Even as recently as 1998, the division between urban and rural Tennessee remained the state's major political cleavage. Fueling much of the legislative agenda, this conflict periodically erupts into heated exchanges and sometimes yields controversial legislation. It was this rural-urban split that led, in the 1950s, to the first effort to authorize home rule.

Home Rule in Tennessee

Historical Development

From Reconstruction until the mid-twentieth century, Tennessee local politics were shaped by the frequent use of special legislation (known in the state as private bills). In 1953 a state constitutional convention was held to examine a number of questions, including the nature of home rule.

With the backing of the Tennessee Municipal League, the convention adopted a stronger and more detailed home rule clause, which provided that any municipality could, by ordinance, submit the home rule issue to the electorate. Following such a referendum, the municipality could continue to operate under its existing charter, amend it, or adopt a new charter. However, the taxation powers of home rule municipalities could not be enlarged (through the raising of a new tax) except by general act of the legislature. General act legislation was also required for any measures that created, merged, consolidated, or dissolved municipalities. Finally, the general assembly was prohibited from authorizing municipalities to tax incomes, estates, or inheritances.[2]

The home rule amendment also included a "sleeper" provision for annexations by general law—which, as will be seen later, turned out to be beneficial to municipalities. Until passage of this amendment, annexations could be contested only in the courts, which had for many years refused to interfere, on the grounds that any differences should be resolved by legislative action.

By 1965, twelve municipalities, all of them in East Tennessee, had adopted home rule. Memphis is the only home rule municipality outside of the eastern division of the state.

Amendment Six, one of the changes made at the convention, limited special legislation by providing that no private bill concerning a municipality or county could be passed without the approval of a two-thirds majority of the local governing body or a simple majority in a local referendum.[3] The amendment also prohibited the state legislature from passing special acts to remove local incumbents from office, abridge the terms of local officials, or alter the salaries of local officials.

Another amendment empowered the general assembly to authorize the consolidation of any or all municipal functions with county functions; in a consolidated government, service systems are merged and under the control of one unified government. While the Tennessee Municipal League "vigorously supported" this amendment, its adoption seems to have forestalled rather than encouraged consolidation efforts throughout Tennessee.[4]

Definition of Home Rule

Municipalities that wish to adopt home rule write their own charters, then adopt them in a referendum.[5] Once a home rule charter is adopted, it is also amended through local referendum. Local government reorganization can be accomplished entirely through locally approved charter changes.

A municipality that chooses home rule gives up the advantages of having the legislature pass private acts for it. Thus, residents must approve, through a local referendum, any tax increases or changes in the home rule charter. This requirement has effectively weakened the taxation power of home rule local governments, and may account for the fact that since 1972, not a single municipality has voted to adopt home rule. In fact, several municipalities have been tempted to rescind their home rule status in order to be able to initiate new taxes by special act.

Structural Features

As noted earlier, special legislation was the dominant means of handling local affairs until 1953, when it was severely restricted by the requirement for approval by the local governing body or through a local referendum. Nevertheless, since private acts may be used by non–home rule (general law) municipalities to impose new taxes, such legislative devices are far from extinct. The required two-thirds approval of the local governing body is not difficult to obtain when increased revenues will result.

Of the 923 local governments in Tennessee, 93 are counties, 339 are municipal governments, and 140 are independent public school systems. In addition, there are 477 metropolitan, regional, municipal, or airport special districts.

Tennessee is one of the few states in which the education function is carried out by municipalities and counties as well as by independent school boards. Dependent school districts (93 county and 33 municipal), which are administered in various ways by municipalities and counties, number 126.[6] Some have school boards that are appointed by the municipal governing body; others have boards that are elected by the residents or appointed by the mayor; still others have school boards that are made up of municipal officials who serve in an ex officio capacity.

Incorporation is relatively easy, requiring a minimum population of 200 and an assessed valuation of $5,000 per person. The major restriction is that an incorporation cannot take place within two miles of an existing municipality. A special act and a local referendum approving the charter give life to the new unit of local government.

Tennessee allows extraterritorial jurisdiction.[7] When a municipal planning commission is designated as the regional planning commission, the municipality may exercise zoning power beyond its boundaries and within the planning region if the county is not exercising such zoning power.[8] Zoning power may extend up to ten miles beyond jurisdictional boundaries, depending on the municipality's population. Most municipalities with populations of more than 10,000 are entitled to the five-mile zone.

The rules for annexation changed in the 1950s. Originally, annexation could occur only through a popular vote by the residents of the area proposed for annexation or the residents of the annexing jurisdiction. Under the new rules, municipal governing bodies were empowered to annex territory by ordinance, through a simple majority vote of the legislative body. Only an aggrieved party having standing in a quo warranto proceeding can challenge an annexation in court. Usually such a suit is filed by a property owner whose property borders on or lies within the territory that is subject to the annexation ordinance, although the county can choose to join such a suit.[9] The property owner must challenge the annexation on the grounds that it "reasonably may not be deemed necessary for the welfare of the residents and property owners of the affected territory and the municipality as a whole."[10]

Should the municipality fail to prove the reasonableness of the annexation, then the municipality is barred for two years from enacting another annexation ordinance on the same territory or parts of it. Voluntary annexation is possible by referendum, and approval by a simple majority of the residents of a particular area suffices. However, the governing body of the municipality considering the annexation may hold a parallel annexation referendum for its own residents. Should that occur, both groups must give majority consent for the annexation to take effect.[11]

Through legislation passed in 1998, the Tennessee General Assembly provided structures and processes to enable local governments to manage growth cooperatively within each of the state's ninety-five counties.[12] The law requires each municipality to identify an urban growth boundary (UGB) and to develop a plan for it. The area encompassed by the UGB must include the corporate limits of the municipality as well as contiguous, unincorporated areas where growth is permitted to occur. The territorial control of the municipal regional planning commission extends only as far as the UGB. The county must develop a plan for all portions of the county that lie beyond the UGBs of the municipalities and classify those areas as either planned growth areas or rural areas. All Tennessee counties are expected to have approved growth plans in place by the end of 2000.

Historically, three principal charter forms have existed in Tennessee: private act charters, home rule charters, and general law charters. Private act charters are those adopted before 1953. After that year, no further incorporation by private act was allowed. If a private act municipality wishes to amend its charter, the legislative delegation introduces the amendment in the general assembly. Once it is approved by that body, the municipal electorate must ratify the new private act. Home rule charters are those crafted by citizens in the thirteen home rule municipali-

ties. General law charters are "form charters" written into the state code, which municipalities may choose to adopt. Recent amendments to the state code have added provisions to enable a community to customize a general law charter to meet its needs.[13] (A fourth kind of charter, known as a metropolitan government charter, features a "strong" mayor system and district elections, and can be found among home rule counties and in the Nashville city-county consolidation.)

Aside from these general provisions, there are two types of structural options available under the Tennessee Code Annotated: mayor-aldermanic charters (which are similar to "weak" mayor systems) and commission- or council-manager charters. Under a mayor-aldermanic charter, the mayor lacks the power of appointment (appointment is by majority vote of the board), and the number of alderpersons varies from two to eight. Most elections are by district (called wards, as in most "weak" mayor systems throughout the nation).

Commission- and council-manager charters are patterned after the council-manager form of government as defined by the International City/County Management Association. Commission government in Tennessee dates back to the 1920s—when, like many other states, Tennessee was swept by the commission craze. The form's popularity derived largely from its perceived flexibility and administrative accountability. Small municipalities (those with populations between 1,500 and 5,000) may have three to five commissioners. Municipalities with populations over 5,000 elect five commissioners for staggered, four-year terms. Elections may be at large or from single-member districts. The commissioners may appoint one of their members as mayor, or local residents may elect the mayor to a four-year term. The manager serves at the pleasure of the commission and appoints all other administrative posts.[14] To incorporate under a commission charter, a community must have at least 1,500 residents and at least $5,000 in real property.

Counties in Tennessee used to be run by "quarterly county courts" of between nine and twenty-five members who were equivalent to justices of the peace in other states. Eventually, county governing bodies came to be called boards of commissioners and were elected from between nine and twenty-five districts. No more than three members may be from one district. A county executive—a nonvoting member of the board who is elected by popular vote—has veto power over legislative actions and appoints department heads with the approval of the commission.

Other county executive officers are the assessor of property, the county clerk, the register of deeds, the sheriff, and the county trustee; some counties also elect clerks of the chancery, circuit courts, general sessions courts, and constables.[15] Constables are elected from districts; the number of constables that may be elected can be no more than half the number of county commissioners. In some counties, local statutes require additional offices; examples are county coroner and chief administrative officer for highways and roads. If necessary, county legislative bodies may create judicial commissioners, who have the power to issue arrest warrants. County boards of commissioners may also elect a county surveyor every four years. As noted earlier, most counties in Tennessee (with the exception of Knox and Shelby) have not adopted home rule and continue the older system of county governance.

Functions of Local Government

Functional Responsibilities

Tennessee municipalities provide a wide range of services, including public safety (police and fire), road and street construction and maintenance, parks and recreation, waste collection and disposal, sanitation, health, emergency services, and planning and zoning. Some municipalities operate their own utilities, although utilities are more often operated by other agencies, either private or public. Most medium-size municipalities operate housing programs through housing departments or housing authorities. Finally, many Tennessee municipalities administer school systems, a characteristic that sets them apart from municipalities in most states in the South.

As administrative arms of the state, counties help provide state services—such as education and health care—at the local level. Counties are also charged with responsibility for highways, public safety, the court system, licensing, the settlement of estates, and the preservation of legal papers. As general-purpose governments, counties duplicate many of the services provided by municipalities—in particular, education, public safety, road construction and maintenance, solid waste collection and disposal, and parks and recreation. Local schools account for a large part of the budget in most Tennessee counties. A few counties, such as Knox County, in which Knoxville is located, have instituted consolidated school systems.

Consolidated metropolitan governments (Nashville only, so far) are required to extend their general services district to the total area of the former county, including both the municipalities that approved the consolidation and those that elected to remain independent. The urban services district, however, includes only the major city in the county and the municipalities that elected to be included in the consolidation. The governing body of the Nashville/Davidson metro government, the metropolitan council, determines which services are to be provided to residents of the general service district and which are to be provided to the urban service district only.[16]

The services that Nashville/Davidson classifies as urban are public safety, solid waste collection, and recreation. Services provided by the metro government are financed from the common revenue pool of the unified city-county government. The urban service district's budget can be financed through a mandatory additional property tax as well as through other revenues that the metropolitan council may decide to allocate.[17]

Apart from consolidation, special districts are the most widely used method of addressing municipal problems. Compared with other states, however, Tennessee has made surprisingly little use of special districts, except for schools and utilities (typically, water or electricity). Lack of revenue-raising authority is a major drawback for special districts in Tennessee. Moreover, experts have observed that "the districts have been run by self-perpetuating boards not responsible to ratepayers or subject to regulation by the state's Public Service Commission."[18] To address the highly independent conditions under which special districts operate, a 1973 statute set up some limited controls by county judges and the Public Service Commission.[19]

Utility districts have served another, albeit unintended purpose: they have provided ambitious municipalities with leverage to enlarge their territory. In the 1970s, Johnson City, a home rule jurisdiction in northeastern Tennessee, managed to acquire a number of bankrupt utility districts outside its corporate limits. It later used its role as service provider to persuade residents of the utility district of the advantages of annexation by the city.

Tennessee grants broad statutory authority for municipalities and counties to exercise joint powers and enter into contractual agreements. State statutes further specify that municipal or county agencies whose governing boards are separate from the municipal or county governing body—municipal utility boards, for example—may enter into interlocal agreements for joint or cooperative action with other public agencies. However, the governing body of the political subdivision with which the agency is affiliated must approve any such agreements.[20]

In the late 1930s, some municipalities in East Tennessee jointly purchased land and constructed Tri-City Airport, a new municipal airport. All the major municipalities in the region that provide financial support to Tri-City Airport have representatives on the airport commission (the airport's governing body).

Some municipalities have entered into agreements with the surrounding county to establish industrial parks; the city of Bristol and Sullivan County are one example. On the other hand, some municipalities see themselves locked in a zero-sum game for economic development that precludes extensive cooperation with their neighbors. Although councils of government were established in the past, their current function seems to be largely symbolic.

Administrative Discretion

The staffing of boards and commissions at the municipal level has been a particularly complex issue in Tennessee. First, municipal boards and commissions do not necessarily follow the standards for personnel qualification and merit selection that are followed by state agencies. Second, the lengths of terms and methods of appointment vary widely from one municipality to another. Finally, little or no compensation is offered for service. Because of these three factors, the individuals most likely to be appointed to boards and commissions are socially prominent or politically well connected individuals. Some slots on boards or commissions are filled by popular election; others are filled through appointment by the city council, the chief executive, or both. As noted earlier, some boards, such as those that serve utility districts, are self-perpetuating.

In the case of some municipal administrative appointments, the state civil service commission establishes certain policies and guidelines and sometimes sits in on selection and promotion boards for public safety officers and other administrative personnel. However, the civil service commission is frequently conspicuous in its absence from these proceedings. Administrative discretion on the part of department heads and elected public officers is often the decisive influence in such appointments.

Tennessee's Uniform Procedures Act regulates the administrative procedures and activities of all state agencies.[21] Municipal administrative structures and procedures are guided by charter provisions and by the Tennessee Code Annotated. For some municipal agencies, compliance is routine. Water and sewer services, for example, must file periodic reports with the Division of Water Pollution Control of the Tennessee Department of Environment and Conservation. Separate boards and commissions within municipalities are free to develop their own administrative procedures.

Where suspected malfeasance, misfeasance, or misappropriation of funds has taken place, the matter is normally turned over to the Tennessee Bureau of Investigations. Crimes and misdemeanors committed within local government are prosecuted through the state attorney general's office.

The Municipal Purchasing Act, enacted by the Tennessee General Assembly in 1983, establishes no specific procedures for the implementation of the provisions contained therein: municipalities are supposed to devise methods of compliance. The act affects only those municipalities whose charters or private acts have no specific requirements relating to public advertisement and competitive bidding; the act also exempts some specific purchases.[22]

Every municipal council and county commission is empowered to adopt and amend a zoning ordinance. A general law authorizes municipal and county governing bodies to appoint a planning commission of between five and ten members; the statute also requires the mayor or county commission to strive for racial proportionality on the planning commission.[23] The planning commission is responsible for certifying to the municipal or county governing body a zoning plan, the text of a zoning ordinance, and zoning maps. Any rezoning must be referred to the planning commission for approval, but the municipal or county governing body can override its disapproval. Municipal

or county legislative bodies may also create a three- to five-member board of zoning appeals to interpret and grant exceptions to the zoning ordinances.[24] For municipalities, substantial extraterritoriality prevails in planning and zoning.

The Tennessee Department of Economic and Community Development, with the approval of the Local Government Planning Advisory Committee, creates and defines the boundaries of planning regions. The regional planning commission must include between five and fifteen members, nominated by the chief elected officials of the counties and municipalities in the region.[25] A prime mission of the regional planning commission is to prepare and maintain a regional plan. Any parts of such a plan that are approved by a municipal council have the same force and effect as a plan prepared by the municipal planning commission. State law also includes a provision for the creation of community planning commissions for unincorporated communities.[26]

Economic Development

Economic development in Tennessee has been somewhat hampered by state constitutional provisions. For example, Article II, section 31, reads:

The credit of this State shall not be hereafter loaned or given to or in aid of any person, association, company or municipality, nor shall the State become the owner in whole or in part of any bank or a stockbroker with others in any association, company, corporation, or municipality.[27]

This provision and a general prohibition against the commingling of public and private funds have prevented many municipalities and counties from gaining state support for industrial parks and other economic development projects.

However, some statutes passed since 1988 have permitted local governments to foster economic growth: these laws support a range of economic development initiatives, including industrial parks, enterprise zones, and community-based development organizations.[28]

Some municipalities and counties have created their own private industrial development boards, through which they can finance projects by obtaining private funding from lending institutions.[29] Local governments may give their industrial development boards powers to buy property, construct buildings, and accept payment in lieu of taxes.

As long as a municipality or county is using current funds for a project, it may do so with no more authorization than a majority vote of the council or county commission. However, if borrowing is required, the municipality (home rule or otherwise) must first obtain a Certificate of Public Purpose and Necessity from the state Department of Economic and Community Development. The municipality is then required to hold a referendum or a public meeting and place the matter before the public for a decision. (A referendum is not required for the issuance of revenue bonds.)[30]

In short, state law requires municipalities to be creative in funding economic development. While legal hurdles are significant, they are not insurmountable.

Fiscal Autonomy of Local Governments

Home rule has minimal impact on the fiscal status of Tennessee municipalities and counties: there is little difference between the revenue-raising capabilities of a home rule and non–home rule municipality, and no form of state aid is affected by home rule status. Home rule jurisdictions do, however, enjoy an additional degree of autonomy with respect to governmental organization, including the freedom to relocate the budget office within the executive branch. (In many non–home rule municipalities, the finance officer or municipal recorder is not under the supervision of the local government manager or chief administrative officer but instead answers to the board of aldermen, council, or commission.)

Local Revenues

The cardinal fact about the state's revenue system is the absence of a state income tax: all Tennessee revenues are raised from state and local sales taxes, property taxes, user fees, alcohol and beer taxes, bank excise taxes, and license fees. Until 1953, municipalities relied only on the property tax. Any municipal council has the power to enact a sales tax as long as the authority and the level of taxation (1.0 or 0.5 percent) have been previously specified by the state legislature. Within the limits imposed by the state general assembly, the shared sales tax is a major source of municipal revenue.

As shown in Table 1, the property tax constitutes the largest source of locally raised revenue for both municipalities and counties. All other tax rates are more or less set by the state, and the property tax is one of the few taxes wholly controlled by local governments.

Real property is assigned to one of four classifications and assessed at the following percentages: (1) public utility property, 55 percent of value; (2) industrial and commercial property, 40 percent of value; (3) residential property, 25 percent of value (unless it contains two or more rental units, in which case it is defined as industrial and commercial property); and (4) farm property, 25 percent of value. The state mandates that the ratio of assessment to value of property in each class be equal and uniform throughout Tennessee. Counties are responsible for all assessments within their jurisdiction.

Indebtedness can provide additional funds to Tennessee municipalities. General-obligation bonds can be issued if the municipality (home rule or otherwise) first holds a public meeting in an advertised place and then obtains approval through a referendum.[31] As noted earlier, revenue bonds—often the favorites of

Table 1. Tennessee Local Government Operating Revenues for FY 1996–1997 (Estimate)

Source	Amount	Percent of total
State government	$574,180,473	6.8%
State-shared taxes	2,089,626,200	25.0
State funding for primary and secondary education		
Federal government	454,817,104	5.4
Local property taxes	2,290,599,283	27.4
Local sales and service taxes	1,149,948,309	13.7
Other local revenue	1,811,374,566	21.6
Total	$8,370,545,935	100.0

Source: Tennessee Advisory Commission on Intergovernmental Relations (TACIR).

local officials who do not wish to take a chance with taxpayers—do not require a referendum. Of course, revenue bonds depend on the market's evaluation of the revenue base that will be used to repay the bonds.

Local Expenditures

There are no expenditure limitations on local government in Tennessee, but local governments can spend only for purposes authorized by state law, and municipalities are required to maintain a balanced budget. As counties are legally considered state agencies, the same balanced budget mandate applies to them. Bankruptcy is not mentioned in most documents pertaining to municipal or county finances, including the Web site of the Municipal Tennessee Advisory System of the University of Tennessee at Knoxville.[32] It is unclear whether bankruptcy is not mentioned because there are no codified rules that apply to it or because the state treats it as a unique event in which it might intervene.

State Government Grants-in-Aid to Localities

State-shared taxes are an important source of revenue not only for municipalities but for county and other local governments as well. The state-determined formula for sharing sales tax revenues is based on population and applies to all municipalities, regardless of charter status, and to city-county consolidated government. Roughly four-fifths of sales tax revenues are earmarked for municipalities.[33] The state also shares portions of the revenues raised from a number of other taxes, including those on gasoline and motor fuels, crude oil and coal, and beer and other alcoholic beverages.[34]

Unfunded Mandates

The Tennessee Constitution gives some protection against mandates by requiring that "no law of general application shall impose increased expenditure requirements on cities or counties unless the General Assembly shall provide that the state share in the cost."[35] Unfortunately, nothing specifies how much of the cost the state has to share, and local officials often find themselves frustrated when the state mandates an action or service for which their localities lack funds.[36]

Unfunded state mandates imposed on municipalities and counties in recent years have been most visible in the area of waste management: the state has imposed regulations concerning waste treatment and disposal, mandated procedures and regulations for the management of landfills, banned certain activities (tire burning, for example), and set limits on tipping fees.[37] Where violations have occurred, the state has imposed penalties and fines. Not even home rule cities can escape such state regulation—as Johnson City discovered when it continued to use its landfill beyond the state-mandated closing date.

Access to Local Government

Local Elections

State laws dictate many aspects of citizen participation, from voting to electoral activities and public meetings. A comprehensive law to regulate all elections, enacted by the general assembly in 1972, superseded provisions in private act charters and other conflicting general laws relating to the conduct of municipal elections.[38]

The municipal attorney generally writes the text of an initiative, but the state board of elections controls almost all other matters, including the timing of elections. There are virtually no state rules governing local candidates, parties, or media, other than those that stipulate either partisan or nonpartisan elections, according to the local charter.

Citizen Controls over Actions of Local Officials

Some Tennessee municipal charters provide for the ouster of elected public officials. Municipalities may use these provisions or proceed under state law, which allows only judicial ouster under procedures outlined in general law. Procedures for a judicial ouster apply to all municipal officers, including persons holding any "office of trust or profit." Under the statute any officer is liable for such removal

who knowingly or willfully neglects to perform any duty enjoined upon such officer by any of the laws of the state, or who shall in any public place be in a state of intoxication produced by strong drink voluntarily taken, or who shall engage in any form of gambling, or who shall commit any act constituting a violation of any penal statute involving moral turpitude.[39]

This judicial ouster provision does not apply to public employees who are not officers in a specific public office.

State laws, especially those pertaining to bond issues, regulate initiatives and referendums, which often appear on municipal ballots.

Open meetings and open records are both very much a part of the Tennessee way of doing public business. Tennessee's very strong sunshine law mandates that all meetings involving two or more state or local legislative officials be conducted with prior notice and open to the public. The only exclusion allowed under the open public records law requires that candidates and officials sign a form before their campaign finance or personal financial statements can be released to the public.[40]

State-Local Relations

Has home rule made a difference? For the average citizen, no. Even otherwise well-informed citizens may be unaware that they live in a home rule municipality. For most, home rule is just a concept, and one of limited importance in the realm of state-local relations.

To local government managers, council members, municipal attorneys, judges, and state legislators, home rule may have greater saliency. But, with few exceptions, it is difficult to argue that home rule municipalities have fared better fiscally or politically than their general law or private act counterparts. True, some home rule municipalities have aggressively pursued annexations, but so have some non–home rule municipalities.

Victor Hobday, in surveying changes to private act charters submitted to the general assembly, reports that in the overwhelming majority of cases (81 to 94 percent in some years), such changes were routinely approved by the state legislature once they had obtained the support of two-thirds of the city council. Thus, the advantages of home rule for a municipality wishing to alter its charter were apparently minimal.[41]

At least among municipalities, the heyday of home rule is past; the last municipality to adopt home rule did so in the early 1970s. Home rule for counties followed a slightly different trajectory. After observing the trend among municipalities, counties had begun, by the mid-1970s, to lobby the general assembly for home rule powers of their own. Municipalities, however, were concerned about the threat of double taxation: as Herbert J. Bingham noted, the Tennessee Municipal League opposed "county home rule powers to duplicate city services without prohibiting county-wide taxes for rural-only services."[42]

Although the state legislature did grant counties the option of adopting home rule charters, only two counties, Knox and Shelby (the counties in which Knoxville and Memphis are located), have opted for county home rule.[43] The chief fruit of county home rule has been consolidated school districts.

As a strategy, home rule has proved too weak and limited to alter the balance of power between state and local government. Most significantly, it did not provide the municipalities with fiscal independence from the state. Tennessee's municipalities have yet to attain the degree of legal and fiscal autonomy that home rule once appeared to offer.

Notes

1. V. O. Key Jr., *Southern Politics in State and Nation* (Knoxville: University of Tennessee Press, 1984), 59.

2. Such actions would be allowed as long as the new charter's provisions or its amendments were not inconsistent with any general act of the general assembly. Lee Seifert Greene, David J. Grubbs, and Victor Hobday, *Government in Tennessee*, 4th ed. (Knoxville: University of Tennessee Press, 1982), 114–115.

3. See Greene, Grubbs, and Hobday, *Government in Tennessee*.

4. Ibid., 272.

5. Tennessee Constitution, Article XI, section 9; see also Tennessee Code Annotated, Chapter 6, section 122 (1995).

6. Each of the ninety-three county school systems is administered by a board of education. Under general law in effect as of January 1992, the county board of education is appointed, but special legislation permits the election of board members in nearly half of the counties. Since the fiscal requirements of the county school systems are reviewed and provided for by the county legislative body, county school systems are not counted as separate governments.

7. See Tennessee Code Annotated, 13-3-102.

8. Ibid., 13-7-302–306.

9. H. J. Bingham, *Municipal Politics and Power: The Tennessee Municipal League in Action* (Nashville: Municipal Press, 1986), 33–34; Tennessee Code Annotated, 6-51-101–114, 6-51-103.

10. Leslie Schechter, *Tennessee Municipal Handbook* (Knoxville: Municipal Technical Advisory Service, University of Tennessee, 1994), 134.

11. Tennessee Code Annotated, 5-51-103(a), 6-51-105.

12. Public Chapter 1101.

13. Sidney Hemsley, *Getting to Know and Love your Municipal Charter* (Knoxville: University of Tennessee Press, December 1992); Schecter, *Tennessee Municipal Handbook*, 10.

14. In some municipalities the commissioners have administrative titles and responsibilities, such as commissioner of fire protection and law enforcement.

15. Constables' responsibilities may be limited to acting as process servers or undertaking some peacekeeping duties.

16. W. J. Finane, *Financing a Metropolitan Government in Tennessee* (Knoxville: Institute for Public Service and the Appalachian Regional Commission, 1988), 2.

17. Ibid., 3.

18. See Greene, Grubbs, and Hobday, *Government in Tennessee*, 275.

19. Ibid., 276.

20. Tennessee Code Annotated, 12-9-104(a).

21. Ibid., Title 4, Chapter 5.

22. Public Chapter 451, codified as Tennessee Code Annotated, 6-56-306. See William R. Bailey and James H. Leuty, *Purchasing Guide for Municipalities* (Knoxville: Municipal Technical Advisory Service, University of Tennessee, July 1984), 1, 2.

23. Tennessee Code Annotated, 13-4-101.

24. Ibid., 13-7-201 et seq.

25. Ibid., 13-3-101, 4-3-727.

26. Ibid., 12-3-101–105, 12-3-201–203, 13-4-101–105.

27. Finane, *Financing a Metropolitan Government*, 7.

28. Tennessee Code Annotated, Title 13, Chapter 16, part 2; Title 13, Chapter 28; Title 13; Title 14, part 2; Title 13, Chapter 13, part 1.

29. Ibid., 4-31-101.

30. Ibid., 9-21-206–208, 9-21-302–303.

31. Ibid., 9-21-206–208.

32. The authors have thoroughly investigated all sources of information, including the Municipal Technical Advisory Service Web site, which is very comprehensive. See *http://mtas.ips.utk.edu.mtastable.html*.

33. See Tennessee Code Annotated, 67-6-103.

34. See Tennessee Code Annotated, 54-4-203–204, 60-4-101, 67-3-67, 67-3-603–604; 54-4-103, 54-4-204, 67-3-803, 67-3-812; 60-1-301; 67-7-104, 67-7-110; 57-3-202–203, 57-3-302, 57-4-301, 57-4-306, 57-5-102, 57-5-201, 57-5-205, 57-6-103, 57-9-115, 57-9-201, 57-9-205.

35. Tennessee Constitution, Article II, section 24.

36. "State Constitutional Provisions," in *MTAS Municipal Handbook* (Knoxville: University of Tennessee, September 16, 1999).

37. Tennessee Code Annotated, 68-212-202, 68-212-108, 68-211-866(b).

38. Ibid., Title 2, Chapter 740, Public Acts of 1972.

39. Tennessee Code Annotated, 8-47-101.

40. Tennessee Code Annotated Citations, 08-44-101–106, 08-44-201.

41. Victor C. Hobday, *An Analysis of the 1953 Tennessee Home Rule Amendments*, 2nd ed. (Knoxville: Bureau of Public Administration, University of Tennessee, May 1976), 73–74.

42. Bingham, *Municipal Politics and Power*, 116.

43. The tax provisions within the metro government in no way tie the hands of the metro council in levying other "citywide" taxes and applying those revenues to the general service funds. In fact, Nashville/Davidson metro collects all local wholesale beer taxes levied by the city and the county and applies these toward the general services budget, as beer regulation and licensing requirements are uniform throughout the county.

TEXAS

Charldean Newell and Victor S. DeSantis

Three distinctive features characterize the governmental setting in Texas. First, for a state with a basic distrust of and dislike for govern-
ment, Texas has a lot of governments. Second, inconsistency predominates in the way that local governments are created, in their authorized
functions, and in their practical operations. Nowhere is such inconsistency more evident than in the fact that home rule is available to mu-
nicipalities but not to counties. Third, many provisions of the state constitution erect barricades that prevent governmental innovation.

Although Texas ranks very high among the fifty states in the degree of discretionary authority offered to municipalities, the state falls to
the bottom in the ranking for counties.[1] Because of the many legal constraints placed upon them, counties have particular difficulty develop-
ing innovative solutions to governmental problems.

Governmental Setting

Since local governments are creations of state governments, local political structures and operations are heavily influenced by both the state's prevailing political culture and economic history. In Texas, two of the political cultures described by Daniel Elazar predominate: the traditionalistic culture, which is based on paternalism and elitism (the "ins" strive to main the existing social order) and the individualistic culture, in which people approach government as if it were a business ("let's make a deal").[2]

The prevailing political attitudes in the state can be attributed to its unique history. Six flags have flown over Texas: those of Spain, France, Mexico, the Republic of Texas, the southern Confederacy, and the United States, with the most unusual being that of the independent republic. Texas can claim a patrón system, slavery, and rebellion as part of its history.

Government and the economy are intertwined visibly in Texas. The state's economic history has been dominated by water (or the lack of it), oil, and—in the modern era—information technology. Water determined whether cattle (in the dry west) or cotton (in the rainy east) would control the economy—and hence state politics. Oil became king in 1901, when the Spindle-top gusher was brought in. In the 1980s and 1990s, Texas began to look much more like other states, with a heavy reliance on information-based industries such as computer manufacturing, financial services, and retailing headquarters. The result was a series of tax skirmishes between traditional and information-based industries. As a consequence of long-standing cultural and economic ties to Mexico and a very long common border, Texas has been a strong supporter of the North American Free Trade Agreement (NAFTA). NAFTA, in turn, is both an economic en-gine for much of the state and a source of demand on transportation resources.

The state's population characteristics are another important factor in the Texas governmental setting. The 1999 intercensal population estimate was 20 million, of whom 55 percent were non-Hispanic whites; 32 percent were Hispanic; 11 percent were African American; and 3 percent were Asian, Pacific Islanders, or American Indians. By 2030, groups that now constitute minorities are predicted to make up 63 percent of the total population, with Hispanics accounting for most of the growth. This dynamic racial and ethnic mix makes for volatile politics, especially in the large cities, such as Houston and Dallas, where African Americans and Hispanics—who together constitute over two-fifths of the population—often have different viewpoints on public policy issues.

In contrast to its reputation, the population of Texas is heavily urban. The state has twenty-eight metropolitan areas, and 84 percent of the population lives in cities.

Until the 1980s, Texas had historically been a one-party, Democratic state; in the 1980s and early 1990s, it became a two-party state; and by the late 1990s Texas was well on its way to becoming a one-party, Republican state. By 1998 all six elected state executives were Republicans. The Republicans hold the elective Railroad Commission, the State Board of Education, and most judgeships. The legislature is split, as is the U.S. congressional delegation.

The rapid emergence of the Republican Party reflects the historic conservatism of the state, its disenchantment with the liberalism of the national Democratic Party, and the in-migration of Republicans from the Midwest and North. Regional differences do exist, however: Republicans are strongest in the major metropolitan areas, especially the suburbs; conservative Democrats dominate west Texas, the Panhandle, small cities, and rural areas; liberal Democrats are strongest in urban areas, in south Texas, and in areas—such as the Gulf Coast—where labor unions are influential.

Texas is currently governed by a state constitution that is well over a century old. Because it was written in reaction to the strong executive government that characterized Radical Reconstruction, the constitution was designed to limit government rather than to provide it with authority. Because of its age and rigidity, the Texas Constitution has been amended repeatedly and is currently in need of substantial revision.[3]

One important feature of the Texas Constitution is that it grants the second-most-populous state in the nation only a short biennial legislative session (140 days). The constitution also places Texas legislators decidedly at the bottom of the pay scales for the fifteen most populous states (legislative—but not executive or judicial—salaries are determined by the constitution). Because of the brevity of the legislative session, legislators rely heavily on extremely powerful presiding officers: the lieutenant governor in the senate and the speaker of the house of representatives, who not only appoint committees and their chairs but also essentially control the calendars. The other major result is that legislators rely on influential lobbyists—representing interests such as oil and gas, insurance, banking, and trial lawyers—to help furnish "information" during the short session. The governor is constitutionally weak and must rely on persuasive powers rather than legal authority. An interesting peculiarity of Texas politics is that, through 1997, it was the only state that had had two women governors.

Like those of other states, local governments in Texas fall into three general categories: counties, municipalities (cities, towns, and villages), and special districts. County and municipal governments are general-purpose governments that provide a wide array of services; special districts are generally single-purpose governmental units. Special authorities, essentially a variation of special districts, are used primarily for matters relating to transportation and public housing. School districts fall under the category of special districts.

As of the 1997 Census of Governments, Texas—with 4,700—ranked third among the fifty states in the total number of local governments.[4] With 254, Texas has the largest number of county governments in the nation (Georgia is next, with 157 counties). In 1997, there were 1,171 municipalities, which had grown in number by only fifteen since 1987. As of that same year, Texas had 1,087 independent school districts and 2,182 special districts. Because of consolidations, the number of school district governments dropped by 2.2 percent between 1987 and 1997. Over the same period, however, the number of nonschool special districts increased by 15.4 percent.

Home Rule in Texas

At the time that the state constitution was written, the state was largely rural and devoted mostly to farming and ranching; only 8 percent of the population lived in urban areas. Taking on their traditional role as extensions of state government, counties carried out limited state responsibilities in rural areas. As the governments that were closest to the people, cities and towns benefited from Texans' lack of trust in government: they were created to be more responsive to the local citizenry and granted a greater degree of responsibility and flexibility than counties. Counties, for example, lack even the basic power to enact ordinances and must operate through resolutions.

Historical Development

The sixth constitution of Texas, ratified in 1876, delineates the powers of local governments in various sections of eight different articles. As is to be expected from a document written at that time, the constitution generally favors farming and ranching interests and inadequately addresses urban concerns.

Municipal and county home rule developed along different tracks in Texas.[5] The Texas constitution provided in 1876 that municipalities with populations under 10,000 would be governed by general laws, while those with populations of 10,000 and over would be governed by special laws (the population break was lowered to 5,000 in 1909). The details of local government structure and procedures were decided by the legislature, and the larger cities became increasingly unhappy with such a cumbersome arrangement. Finally, in 1912, Texas voters approved a constitutional amendment, effective in 1913, to allow home rule for municipalities with populations of 5,000 or more. Adopted at the height of the Progressive Era, the municipal home rule legislation reflected the principles and beliefs of Progressive reformers.[6]

The restrictive form of county government in Texas, which required all counties to have the same governance structure, came under fire in the late 1920s. In 1933 the legislature proposed, and the citizens ratified, a constitutional amendment establishing home rule for Texas counties with a population of 62,000 or more. In contrast to the succinct, 250-word statement authorizing municipal home rule, the county amendment and its enabling legislation ran to more than 10,000 words: the effect was to create a procedure that was totally unworkable. During the thirty-six years that this provision was in effect, thirteen eligible counties attempted unsuccessfully to achieve home rule status. The electorate chose to eliminate the county home rule amendment from the constitution in 1969. Ironically, the passage of the Texas county home rule provision preceded the publication (in 1956) of the first Model County Charter by over two decades. Thus, although Texas was at the forefront of the county government home rule movement, it remains the only state to have both passed and revoked a constitutional provision for county home rule.

Definition of Home Rule

The legal definition of home rule in Texas is very simple. "A municipality is a home-rule municipality if it operates under a municipal charter that has been adopted or amended as authorized by Article XI, section 5, of the Texas Constitution."[7] Operationally, home rule is considered to have three advantages for a municipality: (1) greater flexibility in form of government and financial affairs, (2) improved ability to meet service demands, and (3) avoidance of legislative interference in local matters. Home rule does not preclude the legislature from occasionally passing local bills, nor does it allow a municipality to skirt state law. Nevertheless, municipalities with home rule charters essentially operate on the premise that state law tells them only what they cannot do (for example, exceed a stipulated property tax rate), not what they can do.[8]

Home rule in Texas is not significantly different from home rule as practiced in other states. Home rule allows a municipality to

• Determine its own form of government and methods of conducting elections.
• Amend the municipal charter.
• Exercise legislative power (this authority includes the right to annex territory, set tax rates, exercise wide-ranging regulatory power, and control planning and development).
• Exercise police powers.
• Provide for direct democracy in the municipal charter in the form of the initiative, referendum, and recall.

With respect to these powers, the state maintains some control: for example, it sets ceilings on tax rates and determines the frequency of elections.

Structural Features

Although Article III of the Texas Constitution prohibits the legislature from interfering with municipal affairs, the legislature periodically passes "population bracket" bills that are, in effect, local laws. One such law limited the regulatory powers of environmentally conscious Austin, the state capital, to allow for "dirty" development within the city. In another example, the legislature created a new section of the Local Government Code to regulate property development in any "unzoned municipality with a population of more than 1.5 million" if the governing body of that municipality chose to be covered by the new regulations (Houston is the only city with a population of 1.5 million).[9] The courts have tended to adopt a hands-off posture when municipalities challenge such legislation.

Five classes of municipality are recognized in Texas. Types A, B, and C operate under the general laws of the state and are distinguished mainly by population size and the amount of incorporated territory that they encompass. Special law municipalities are those created during the years that Texas was an independent republic or by any subsequent state legislation; any special law municipality that has amended its charter in any way is now considered a home rule municipality. Home rule municipalities are those that operate explicitly under a home rule charter.[10]

Texas's long history of relying on reform structures in the operation of municipal government dates back to the Galveston hurricane and flood of 1900, which led to the creation of the commission form of government. Although the 304 home rule municipalities (as of 1999) are granted the authority to adopt any form of government, most function under the council-manager plan (271); far fewer have chosen the mayor-council (19) or mayor-manager (14) forms. Although the designations vary—some municipalities, for example, refer to the local governing body as a mission or a board of aldermen—the legislative body is, in effect, a city council.

In the absence of home rule, all 254 Texas counties are constitutionally mandated to operate under the commission form. The commissioners court, which is made up of the county judge (elected at large) and four commissioners (elected by district), exercises both legislative and executive authority but must share some degree of executive authority with a number of elected executive officials, such as the county clerk, coroner, sheriff, treasurer, attorney or solicitor, and tax assessor. The idea of directly electing executive department heads can be traced to the principles of nineteenth-century Jacksonian democracy, which called for maximum citizen involvement in government and supported a number of practices—such as long ballots and frequent turnover of elected officials—to achieve that end.

Home rule municipalities can set their own boundaries and, subject to provisions for notice, fair hearing, and (if the charter so specifies) election, annex and exchange territory. To help control development on the outskirts of municipalities, Texas law grants municipalities extraterritorial jurisdiction: limited authority over unincorporated areas that are contiguous to their corporate boundaries. The amount of territory depends on population size, and ranges from one-half mile for municipalities whose populations are under 5,000 to five miles for municipalities with 100,000 or more inhabitants. While municipalities have considerable flexibility to establish development policies and create land-use and zoning regulations, county authority is limited to the regulation of subdivisions and does not include general authority to regulate land use. State law provides for the creation of new counties, but such an event is unlikely since any new county would have to be created out of an existing county or counties, and voters in all affected counties would have to consent to the procedure.[11]

Functions of Local Government

Functional Responsibilities

Texas citizens look to local government to provide basic services such as law enforcement, fire protection, streets and roads, solid waste collection, water and sewer services, parks and recreation, and general administration of programs for the common good. Because they are not constrained by the lack of home rule and the lack of ordinance power (as counties are) or by limited jurisdiction (as special-purpose governments are), municipalities have the greatest latitude in providing these services.

All municipalities have broad authority to pass any ordinance, rule, or police regulation that "(1) is for the good government, peace, or order of the municipality or for the trade and commerce of the municipality; and (2) is necessary or proper for carrying out a power granted by law to the municipality or to an office or department of the municipality."[12] Home rule municipalities are further stipulated as having "full power of local self-government." In practice, Texas home rule municipalities engage not only in traditional municipal functions but also own and operate sports arenas and ballparks, airports, radio stations, and amusement parks. They routinely form partnerships, both with other governments and with the private sector—the former to achieve cost savings in service provision and the latter most often for economic development.

Because they lack ordinance power, counties carry out their business through notices, citations, writs, resolutions, and similar processes. The commissioners court is empowered specifically to (1) establish public ferries; (2) develop and maintain roads; (3) build and repair bridges; (4) "appoint road overseers and apportion hands" (that is, allocate labor to work crews); (5) exercise control over ferries, highways, roads, and bridges; (6) provide for the needy—and, within the limits of the Health and Safety Code, public health; and (7) establish a cost review process for public improvements costing more than $100,000.[13] The Texas Local Government Code spells out the duties of other elected county officials. In practice, counties focus their attention on roads and bridges, and on administering welfare, public health programs, and law enforcement—including the construction and operation of jails. In some urbanized areas, the county serves as a catalyst for economic development.

The creation and operation of counties and municipalities are spelled out in the Texas Local Government Code, which provides a consistent set of procedures for all general-purpose governments. However, the rules and regulations that govern special-purpose governments are not as clear—both because these districts are created in various ways and because their governing bodies often develop additional rules that help to structure their procedures and operations. Although some early special districts were created by constitutional amendment, Texas statutes now authorize the creation of special districts either through special acts of the legislature or under general laws. Those statutes further authorize general-purpose governments to create some types of special districts (especially for the provision of utilities, basic services, and economic development); state agencies can create other types (especially those involving natural resources); and the legislature itself creates still others.

Texas statutes include authorization for about two dozen types of nonschool special districts, the largest number of which are in housing and community development (395), soil and water conservation (211), and water supply (202). Of the 840 multiple-function special districts, more than 69 percent provide a combination of water and sewer services.[14]

The continued rapid growth of nonschool special districts has presented Texans with an interesting dilemma. Because special districts can be created easily and have independent taxing and borrowing authority, they have become an increasingly popular means of providing limited services to wider geographic areas. However, they only add to the difficulty of coordinating many local governments in a given area and make it difficult for counties and municipalities to raise taxes. Moreover, they are often less accountable to the public than general-purpose local governments.

State law permits two standard forms of interlocal cooperation: the agreement and the contract. For example, a school district and a city may agree to trade parcels of land to facilitate development of both a junior high school and a new park. Several farsighted municipalities own extensive water rights—a very important asset in a state with only one natural lake and a history of drought—and contract to sell water to other municipalities.

Administrative Discretion

Under the Texas Local Government Code, general-purpose municipalities with populations of 10,000 or more may adopt either the state civil service system for firefighters and police officers or create their own system.[15] The seventy-three municipalities that have adopted Chapter 143 (shorthand for the state system) have found themselves administering what amounts to a union contract written into statute.[16] In addition, these localities must cope with two different sets of personnel requirements: one for police and fire and another for all other municipal employees. Counties, on the other hand, have few restrictions on personnel actions other than those imposed by federal law.

Texas municipalities have considerable autonomy to establish administrative procedures, promulgate rules, and develop internal management practices and systems. State law requires municipalities to use competitive bidding on purchases of $15,000 or more; and, in the cases of municipalities whose populations are under 100,000, on purchases of $5,000 or more for insurance. In addition, if such businesses exist within the county in which the municipality is located, notification of purchases between $3,000 and $15,000 must be given to at least two historically underutilized businesses drawn from a list prepared by the state. Counties must arrange competitive bidding for purchases in excess of $15,000.[17]

Through the related powers of extraterritorial jurisdiction (ETJ) and annexation, municipalities have limited control over growth and development in the areas outside their corporate limits. The particulars are complex, but ETJ essentially allows municipalities to regulate development by applying municipal regulations regarding construction, sanitation, utilities, and related matters.[18] As noted previously, the size of the ETJ depends on the population of the municipality.

Annexation power allows municipalities to bring adjacent unincorporated areas into the municipal boundaries as long as the amount of land annexed in any given year does not exceed a specified amount: 10 percent of existing land area for a home rule municipality, one mile for Class A general law municipalities, and one-half mile for Class B general law municipalities. To avoid disannexation proceedings, the municipality must extend basic services within sixty days and full services within four-and-one-half years (beginning in 2002, full services must be provided within two-and-one-half years). State law also includes provisions for municipal annexation of water and sewer special districts.

Within their corporate limits, municipalities have considerable authority to regulate growth and development through policy guidelines and ordinances covering a range of issues—from landscaping to parking spaces to building materials to noise buffers. One of the most curious situations in Texas is that giant Houston (over 1.7 million population) continues to rely only on building covenants and to exist without zoning.

County commissions can pass resolutions in the name of public health and safety, but they do not have any general authority over zoning or land use. They can, however, regulate subdivisions in unincorporated areas. When a subdivision is to be built in a municipality's ETJ, whichever set of subdivision regulations is more stringent—the municipality's or the county's—prevails.[19]

Economic Development

Texas municipalities—and, to a lesser extent, counties—are provided wide latitude in the economic development arena. Permissible organizational arrangements include public-private partnerships, quasi-governmental economic development corporations, and purely public economic development programs. For many economic development efforts, municipalities provide direct financial assistance to fully or partially private agencies (such as chambers of commerce).

Local development can be financed through local general revenues, local hotel occupancy taxes, local option sales taxes, federal or state grants-in-aid, municipal general-obligation or revenue bonds, and tax increment financing.[20] The local option sales tax is limited by state-mandated ceilings on the combined sales tax rate, and the use of general-obligation and revenue bonds was limited by a series of tax law changes enacted in the 1980s. Tax increment financing was authorized by state legislation in 1981 and approved by voters in a 1982 constitutional amendment.

Texas municipalities, counties, and school districts have the authority to abate certain taxes in eligible areas for up to fifteen years. Although tax abatements have been very popular in recent years, many municipalities and school districts have begun to take a more cautious approach, adding specific performance clauses to tax abatements. State rules mandate how fees can be charged and the uses to which they may be put, but Texas municipalities do use development impact fees to help meet capital needs.

Texas law also allows municipalities to create special business zones to encourage economic development. To foster export development, both state and federal law allows municipalities to establish foreign trade zones, within which many customs clearances and duties may be relaxed or removed. In 1983 Texas passed legislation allowing municipalities and counties to apply to have depressed areas designed as enterprise zones; within such zones, local governments may offer various financial incentives and limited regulatory relief. State enabling legislation for the creation of public improvement districts was enacted in 1987 and amended in 1993. To finance improvements of public services and other amenities, the local government imposes a tax increase on businesses within such districts. Texas municipalities have historically been involved in establishing industrial or commerce parks to attract and retain business.

Fiscal Autonomy of Local Governments

Local governments in Texas are constrained by limitations on tax rates and tax increases, and by prohibitions against certain kinds of taxes, such as income and payroll. They are less encumbered in their spending. The state has an extensive reporting system that requires localities to report their financial transactions and, in some cases, follow state-mandated procedures.

Local Revenues

The only minimum tax base in Texas pertains to the property tax. The state has a uniform tax appraisal system administered through appraisal districts in each county that perform the property assessments for all taxing entities in the county. This system ensures that the tax valuation of real property remains consistent with market value in the community. The law permits, but does not mandate, exemptions that have the effect of lowering the value of the base. The most common exemptions are for homestead status, ownership by someone sixty-five or older, and personal automobiles. Exemptions are also granted for solar or wind-powered energy devices. Disabled persons are granted exemptions, and disabled veterans are granted partial exemptions.

The most universal local tax is the ad valorem property tax, which is collected by municipalities, counties, and several types of special districts, including school and hospital districts. Maximum rates are set by state law. Municipalities can collect a general retail sales tax of up to 1 percent—1.5 percent if the municipality is outside a metropolitan transit district and 2 percent if a corresponding decrease in the property tax occurs. Counties and hospital districts also have limited authority to collect a general sales tax;[21] counties have sought, unsuccessfully, legislation to allow them the same flexibility as municipalities to adopt a local option general sales tax. Most localities also receive revenues from bonded indebtedness, and many, from fines. Municipalities may assess a hotel and motel occupancy tax as well as other selective sales and gross receipts taxes, such as those on liquor store sales. Municipalities may also levy special assessments—for installing a sidewalk in front of a citizen's home, for example.[22] Virtually all local governments receive some funds from intergovernmental transfers and user fees. Utility franchise fees are an important source of revenue for municipalities.

Up to ceilings established by state law, local governments have great discretion in determining their rates of taxation. As of 2000, the county property tax rate ceiling was $.80 per $100 assessed valuation, with a possible add-on for specific farm-to-market road projects. Per $100 of assessed valuation, municipalities with populations under 5,000 can levy up to $1.50; municipalities with populations of 5,000 and over (basically, home rule municipalities) can levy up to $2.50. Type B general law municipalities (generally under 1,000 population) can levy only $.25. School districts may levy up to $1.50 per $100 of assessed valuation for operations, plus an additional $.50 for debt repayment. Most jurisdictions provide a homestead tax exemption—a reduction in the property tax base for a principal residence—that was $15,000 as of 1998.

Although very stringent with regard to state debt, Texas permits local governments to accrue considerable debt; in fact, the combined interest payments on local government debt account for about 87 percent of the state's annual debt service of $4.75 billion.[23] Local governments may issue both general-obligation and revenue bonds, though the specific authority to incur debt and requirements for public approval vary with the type of government and the method of financing. The amount of debt for localities is limited by what the citizens are willing to vote for and the bond underwriters are willing to accept. Localities must be able to cover debt service in their operating budgets.

Local Expenditures

For municipalities, the largest categories of expenditure are for public safety (fire and police); environmental quality, parks and housing; utilities; streets and transportation; and debt service. Because municipalities do not bear significant responsibility for public health, education, or welfare, expenditures in these areas are negligible. Counties' major expenditures are for health and welfare, public safety (principally, law enforcement and jails), transportation and roads, general government (including the court system), and debt service. School districts spend 89 percent of their funds on educational programs, with most of the rest allocated to capital outlay. Special districts vary according to the type of district and the purpose for which the district was created. The state sets no legal limits on expenditures.

Local governments in Texas use the full spectrum of budget formats—line-item, program, performance, and zero-based. However, general-purpose governments are required, regardless of what other budget format may be used, to (1) balance their budgets and (2) present to the public—via the municipal clerk or county clerk—a detailed, itemized budget that compares previous expenditures with expected revenues.[24] All local governments are required to have public hearings on the budget to receive citizen comments, and to have an annual external audit of expenditures. Bond investors and state and federal oversight agencies require a full financial and compliance audit. To ensure uniform accounting practices, all local governments are required to follow the Governmental Accounting Standards Board recommendations. Any political subdivision with independent taxing authority (that is, municipalities, counties, and special districts) can declare bankruptcy and proceed to receivership under procedures established by federal law.[25]

State Government Grants-in-Aid to Localities

Much of the "state" aid to localities is in the form of federal pass-through funds—to which Texas adds little or no state funding—for purposes such as public health or poverty relief. However, the state provides some help to local governments. Some of the most valued state dollars are those that support the maintenance and construction of state highways, farm-to-market roads, and bridges; also highly valued are the state funds that provide a 10 percent match to gain federal funds for the maintenance of interstate highways. Although the Texas Department of Transportation (Tex-DOT) spends almost $3.5 billion every two years, it can fund less than one-third of the projects it deems worthy: population growth, combined with a state ceiling on highway and road expenditures, has created a huge backlog of demand. Tex-DOT does not fund local streets at all; however, counties can add $10 to the motor vehicle registration fee to help pay for county roads and bridges.

Other state-funded programs support economic development efforts, including the construction and renovation of buildings, and programs to revitalize downtown areas. Direct assistance from the Texas Department of Housing and Community Affairs helps local governments provide essential public services and resolve financial, social, and environmental problems. The Texas Natural Resource Conservation Commission sends localities almost $500 million each year to support environmental cleanups, to assist small or rural communities to comply with municipal waste regulations, and to subsidize the disposal of low-level radioactive wastes and the recycling of materials (such as tires) that are hard to dispose of.

According to the Texas Legislative Budget Board, Texas spent $13.02 billion on aid to localities for fiscal year 1997. The state also received $12.13 billion in federal funds during this period, most of which was parceled out to the localities.[26]

By far the largest expenditure of state dollars to aid local governments goes to fund public education, grades kindergarten through twelve. Since the 1960s, Texas has typically paid for between 47 and 49 percent of the cost of public education, with local property taxes and some federal funds making up the rest. The state's share for fiscal years 2000–2001 was budgeted at $28.6 billion. Huge disparities in funding between one school district and the next have been a source of controversy in Texas, but the state has failed to solve the problem. The extensive network of community colleges in Texas received $1.5 billion for 2000–2001 from the higher education appropriation but are largely funded by local property taxes imposed by the fifty special districts that govern them.

Unfunded Mandates

Texas is no exception to the nationwide shift of service burdens from states to localities. These shifts involve many basic but costly services. One example concerns major, court-mandated changes in public education funding: instead of providing adequate support for public schools, the state created a "Robin Hood" system that forced wealthy local school districts to give money to poorer districts. The state tempered the mandate—providing an additional $1 billion in school funding—only after loud public outcry against the Robin Hood scheme, which remains in place. Other examples include the Tex-DOT's decision to assign to municipalities whose populations are 50,000 or more the burden of maintaining highway rights-of-way, and a general lack of state support for federal mandates to clean up the air and water. Environmental cleanup is a considerable burden in Texas, which has for many years ranked either first or second in pollution measures.[27] Clean air remains a goal but not a reality: most of the larger metropolitan areas in the state have not even come close to meeting cleanup mandates.

Calculating the fiscal impact of mandates on localities is not feasible for two reasons: first, the state has not passed a mandate reimbursement measure, which would facilitate uniform calculations; second, localities have responded with differing intensities to the mandates.[28]

Access to Local Government

Since Texas denies initiative and recall at the state and county levels, citizen access to government would seem to be mainly through municipal governments. However, some observers argue that because of the predominance of elected over appointed officials, counties may afford a higher degree of political access than municipalities—even in the absence of two elements of direct democracy.

Local Elections

State law gives home rule municipalities the authority to "(1) create offices; (2) determine the method for selecting officers; and (3) prescribe the qualifications, duties, and tenure of office for officers."[29] However, state law requires that charter and charter amendment elections be confined to the date of the municipal general election—or, when such a date is not feasible, to one of the four dates specified in the state's uniform election code.[30]

Counties are the arm of the state for the conduct of general elections, and county primary and general elections concur with state elections. Counties have no authority beyond what is granted them in the Texas Election Code.[31] As a result of Progressive Era reforms, Texas municipalities rely on nonpartisan election procedures for municipal offices, while "unreformed" counties rely on partisan procedures.

Although home rule municipalities can determine the size of their legislative bodies and select the method of council election (at large, district, or some mix), a number of high-profile court challenges—including one to the city of Dallas—have tossed both issues into the state and federal courts. Special district elections are conducted similarly to municipal elections, but state law applies somewhat more restraint to the conduct of judicial elections.

Texas elections are known to be rather freewheeling; spending at any level is more a function of how much money the candidate can raise than any limitation set by state law. Candidates for office in the state must file periodic reports with the Texas secretary of state on their fund-raising and expenditures.

Citizen Controls over the Actions of Local Officials

One of the cornerstones of Progressive Era reform was the idea that citizens should have a more direct role in local governance. Reformers embraced the initiative, referendum, and recall as a means of holding elected officials accountable and ensuring their responsiveness. At the turn of the nineteenth century, when it was still issuing special charters to the larger cities in the state, the Texas legislature began placing initiative, referendum, and recall provisions into new special charters.

Upon the implementation of the home rule provision in 1913, home rule municipalities had the option of dropping these direct democracy provisions; however, the overwhelming number did not. Such provisions remain very popular in most Texas home rule municipalities: 85 percent have initiative and referendum, and 91 percent have recall provisions.[32]

For state and county governments, Texas law allows referendums but neither initiative nor recall. County officials are not even subject to impeachment, but members of the county legal system are subject to removal by the district court; district court judges are subject to removal by higher judges; and any public official is subject to a quo warranto suit if he or she is occupying a public office illegally.[33]

The state Open Meetings Act and Public Information Act, together with media watchdogs, help to maintain access to government. The Open Meetings Act mandates a published agenda, a quorum of the governing body to convene, voting in open session, and penalties for violation. It allows for closed meetings on legal and personnel matters and on real estate and electric utilities transactions. It does not guarantee a citizen the right to determine the agenda or to speak to items on the agenda.

The Public Information Act permits anyone to submit a request for information to the custodian of public records of a governmental agency; requires a reasonable response time; allows the governmental unit to make a reasonable charge for copying material; establishes the state attorney general as the arbiter of disputes; and sets up misdemeanor punishments for failure to comply with the act. In 1990 the state legislature established a process for creating, maintaining, and disposing of local government records and set out the conditions for complying with these new regulations.

State-Local Relations

Local government home rule in Texas is characterized by several important patterns and trends. While municipalities continue to be in a strong position to chart their destiny in the new century, the prospects for county governments are more limited, particularly outside a handful of heavily urban counties. Increasing concern about the proliferation—and growing influence of—special districts is also an important aspect of the Texas local government landscape.

As we move into the twenty-first century, municipalities, with expansive grants of home rule authority from the state, continue to be innovative and responsive in meeting citizens' demands. Texas municipal governments are highly professionalized and at the forefront of modern management techniques and service delivery methods. As the state population continues to grow, pressures created by increasing urbanization will bring new challenges to local governments and their leaders.

Texas counties continue to provide the traditional, state-oriented services that have long been in their domain. Particularly in urban parts of the state, however, counties are taking increasing responsibility for service delivery in areas that are best approached from a regional perspective, such as environmental

protection and land-use planning. Thus, despite their structural limitations, counties have grown in importance. But they remain ill equipped to deal with the demands that citizens and other levels of government place on them. Continued reform and innovation in county government are essential to keeping organization and management capacities in line with the demands of the new century; yet in Texas, the lack of home rule authority forces county government to move forward slowly, and in a piecemeal fashion. While many other states have granted their counties greater degrees of discretionary authority, the state of Texas seems reluctant to do so in any systematic, comprehensive way. In 1952, Clyde Snider maintained that county dependence on state institutions was a "major obstacle in the path of county progress."[34] Certainly, there is no place where this observation is more accurate than in Texas.

Despite the fact that many of their services are provided by special districts, the public (except in the case of school districts) has little understanding of the roles and authority of these government units.[35] Yet the continued growth of special districts, as both service providers and taxing agents, will be a significant challenge to coordination and control at the local level. Unfortunately, as the national and state governments push more power and responsibility onto local governments—often without additional funding—the problems associated with special districts are less and less likely to be addressed. Because special districts provide a simple and flexible means of addressing local problems, their disadvantages tend to be overlooked.

Texas has a strong tradition of local municipal government; its home rule municipalities not only enjoy a large measure of independence but have also been remarkably innovative—to the point of having had a national influence on management practices. Members of the urban county coalition have worked together to find creative ways to address new demands on Texas counties, but counties remain hamstrung by structure, and the rural counties continue to have considerable influence on the state legislature. The flexibility of special-purpose governments is also a problem; these governments can often do as they please and are subject to little control by general-purpose governments. Until the state finds some way to address the problems associated with counties and special districts, it will be unable to meet some of the demands of the twenty-first century.

Notes

1. U.S. Advisory Commission on Intergovernmental Relations, *Measuring Local Discretionary Authority* (Washington, D.C.: U.S. Government Printing Office, 1981), table 20, p. 59.

2. Richard H. Kraemer, Charldean Newell, and David F. Prindle, *Texas Politics*, 6th ed. (St. Paul: West Publishing Company, 1996), ch. 1; based on Daniel J. Elazar, *American Federalism: A View from the States*, 2d ed. (New York: Crowell, 1972), 89.

3. See Senator John Montford, "Comparison of Current and Proposed Constitutions," prepared by the senator's office, January 1992.

4. Bureau of the Census, U.S. Department of Commerce, 1997 Census of Governments, vol. 1, *Government Organization* (Washington, D.C.: Government Printing Office, 1998), table 3, p. 3; Bureau of the Census, U.S. Department of Commerce, *Statistical Abstract of the United States,* 108th ed. (Washington, D.C.: U.S. Government Printing Office, 1988), table 452, p. 74.

5. Excellent sources on the history of home rule in Texas include John P. Keith, *City and County Home Rule in Texas* (Austin: Institute of Public Affairs, University of Texas, 1951); Roscoe C. Martin, "The County Home Rule Movement in Texas," *Southwestern Social Science Quarterly* 15, no. 4 (March 1935): 1–11; and Terrell Blodgett, "Municipal Home Rule Charters," *Public Affairs Comment* 41, no. 2 (1996): 1–7.

6. A 1991 amendment allowed home rule cities that had dropped below 5,000 in population to continue to have the authority to amend their charters.

7. Texas Local Government Code, 1998, 5.004.

8. Blodgett, "Municipal Home Rule Charters," 2–3.

9. Texas Local Government Code, 212.041–212.050.

10. Ibid., 5.001–5.005.

11. Ibid., 42.021 and 43.001–43.002.

12. Ibid., 51.001, 51.072.

13. Ibid., 81.022, 81.028.

14. Bureau of the Census, 1997 Census of Governments, table 9, pp. 13–14.

15. Texas Local Government Code, Chapter 143.

16. Seventy-two are active; one held a subsequent election to withdraw from the system.

17. Texas Local Government Code, 252.021, 252.0215, 262.023.

18. Ibid., Chapters 42 and 43. These chapters are thirty-eight pages long and spell out a number of special circumstances, exceptions, and special conditions.

19. See Texas Local Government Code, Chapter 232.

20. Robert R. Weaver, *Local Economic Development in Texas* (Arlington: Institute for Urban Studies, University of Texas at Arlington, 1986), 25–27.

21. Texas Tax Code, Chapters 321 and 323; Texas Health and Safety Code, Chapter 285.

22. Robert L. Bland, *Financing City Government in Texas: A Revenue Manual for City Officials* (Austin: Texas Municipal League, 1986), passim; supplemented by an interview with the author on November 21, 1995.

23. Bureau of the Census, U.S. Department of Commerce, *State and Local Finances in 1991–92* (Washington, D.C.: Economics and Statistics Administration, 1994), 89.

24. Texas Local Government Code, 102.003, 111.004.

25. Ibid., 140.001.

26. *Fiscal Size-Up: 2000–01 Biennium, Texas State Services* (Austin: Texas Legislative Budget Board, 2000), 18, 33, 43.

27. See, for example, Todd Sloane, "Environmental Survey of the States: Survey Finds States Still Going Green," *City and State,* July 5, 1993, 5.

28. See Janet M. Kelly, "Mandate Reimbursement in the States," *American Review of Public Administration* 24, no. 4 (December 1994): 351–373.

29. Texas Local Government Code, 26.041.

30. Ibid., 9.002.

31. Texas Election Code, Chapters 251–257.

32. Blodgett, "Municipal Home Rule Charters," 6.

33. Texas Election Code, 7.21–7.22.

34. Clyde Snider, "American County Government: A Midcentury Review," *American Political Science Review* 46 (March 1952): 74.

35. In 1995, the Texas legislature passed a type of home rule provision for school districts, but, as of early 2000, no school district had elected home rule, and no one was certain how it might work.

UTAH

F. Ted Hebert and Mark G. Bedel

Utah adopted constitutional home rule for municipalities by amending its constitution in 1932, but since that amendment became effective, only five cities have attempted to adopt charters. Only one home rule charter is in place today. Much more important for the state's local governments was the decision of the Utah Supreme Court in State v. Hutchinson in 1980.[1] By broadly construing the legislature's grant of general welfare power to local governments, the court essentially established "statutory home rule" for local governments. Although the court's interpretation does not extend to taxing authority, it has increased sharply the discretionary authority of local governments. In many details of their activities, however, local entities are controlled by the legislature through unfunded mandates, which today number in the hundreds.

Governmental Setting

Utah is similar to other western mountain states in important respects: it is sparsely populated, with just over 2 million people spread over almost 85,000 square miles; it has rapidly growing urban concentrations (1.7 million people in the five Wasatch Front counties); it is a mostly arid, desert basin with some plateau regions and high mountain ranges; and it is politically conservative. But in other respects, Utah is different. Euro-American settlement of Utah began in 1847 with the arrival of Mormon pioneers, members of the Church of Jesus Christ of Latter-day Saints (LDS Church). They established a theocracy and set about founding communities throughout the region that would become the Utah Territory in 1850. In addition to the present-day state of Utah, this territory included most of Arizona and Nevada and parts of Oregon, Idaho, Wyoming, Colorado, New Mexico, and California.[2]

Many Utah communities were established by families directed to settle the region by early Mormon Church leaders. In the earliest period, church institutions provided local government. Grievances were settled by bishops' courts or other church institutions.[3] Even after the territorial government had been established, theocratic structures were largely retained.[4] The deliberate maintenance of a theocracy caused considerable tension between Mormon settlers and the federal government. Together with polygamy, theocracy long prevented Utah from becoming a state. To meet one condition for admission to the Union, Utah framed its constitution so as to strictly prohibit the interference of any church with state functions.[5]

Like the politics of many states of the mountain west, the politics of Utah is quite conservative today. The Republican Party dominates statewide elective offices; only one office—that of attorney general—is filled by a Democrat. The Republican Party holds 72 percent of the seats in the state house and 62 percent of those in the state senate. Although persons moving in from other locations have influenced the state to some extent, 65 percent of the state's adult population indicate the LDS Church as their religious preference. The power of the church and its members is significant in Utah politics, and its influence is especially felt when "moral" issues arise, for example, issues concerning the family or gambling or alcohol regulation.[6]

Local government in Utah is provided through 29 counties, 40 school districts, and 236 cities and towns. Several state agencies provide services, particularly welfare services, from their own offices located throughout the state. The most rapidly expanding form of government is the special district, which counties, cities, and towns have authority to establish for a variety of purposes (including water, sewer, flood control, garbage, transportation, recreation, health care, and fire protection). There are 343 special districts as well as 58 redevelopment agencies, 17 housing authorities, 13 health divisions, and 11 mental health districts.[7]

Home Rule in Utah

Historical Development

The 1932 amendment to the state constitution allowed incorporated cities and towns to adopt a charter (that is, home rule) by election. Counties were not included in this grant of constitutional home rule authority.

The Utah Supreme Court defined constitutional home rule in 1933 as follows:

The power granted by the constitutional provision to chartered cities is no greater than that possessed by the Legislature and which it may, if it sees fit, confer on unchartered municipalities by general law. The difference is that, when a city adopts its charter pursuant to the amendment, then the powers which it may exercise are directly conferred by the Constitution, and may not be controlled by the Legislature except as to those matters and things reserved to the Legislature by the Constitution.[8]

Of the five cities that have attempted to adopt municipal charters, only three actually adopted them. Two of the three have since repealed their charters, leaving only one charter municipality today.

Several factors limited the implementation of the charter provision. Probably the most significant was the widespread perception that adopting a charter was largely a means to change structure and would not lead to greater functional autonomy. Most efforts to pass charters were motivated by the desire to adopt the council-manager form of government.[9] Council-manager charters were passed in Ogden in 1951 and Provo in 1955.[10] However, Tooele adopted a charter in 1963 specifically to establish a "strong" mayor form of government.[11] The necessity of adopting a charter to achieve structural reform was obviated in 1977 when the state legislature authorized two alternative forms of municipal government.[12] Ogden and Provo repealed their charters in order to adopt the statutory "strong" mayor form. Tooele remains the only charter city today.

Another factor inhibiting the adoption of municipal charters is the complexity of the constitutionally prescribed process. The electorate must first vote to establish a "commission" to "frame a charter." The constitution sets no time limit for the commission to complete its work and submit a proposed charter. If the commission does propose a charter, a second election must be held to adopt it. This two-election process is lengthy and costly.

Finally, there has been confusion regarding the powers that are available to chartered cities. The constitutional grant of authority to chartered cities states that the grant shall not "be deemed to limit or restrict the power of the legislature in matters relating to State affairs, to enact general laws applicable alike to all cities of the State." City leaders could never be certain that proposed city actions, except those specifically authorized by the legislature, would not conflict with the legislature's authority to pass "general laws" relating to "State affairs." For several years after adoption of the 1932 amendment, the prevailing view was that the charter provision was a hollow grant of authority.[13]

Definition of Home Rule

Throughout much of the state's history, local government authority has been entirely subject to state law. Dillon's Rule was the standard for construing local government authority until the Utah Supreme Court abandoned it in 1980. In *State v. Hutchinson* the court stated that Dillon's Rule "is archaic, unrealistic, and unresponsive to the current needs of both state and local governments and effectively nullifies the legislative grant of general police power to the counties."[14] At issue was a Salt Lake County ordinance that required the filing of disclosure statements by any candidate for the office of commissioner. Although no statute specifically authorized the county to impose campaign disclosure requirements on candidates, the court adopted a new construction, stating that:

When the State has granted general welfare power to local governments, those governments have independent authority apart from, and in addition to, specific grants of authority to pass ordinances which are reasonably and appropriately related to the objectives of that power, i.e., providing for the public safety, morals, and welfare.[15]

Thus, "statutory home rule," based on the grant of general welfare power and court interpretation, exists for counties and municipalities. Although today they can rely on *Hutchinson* in adopting ordinances, they are likely to look for specific statutory authorization. The legislature could repeal the general welfare authority of local governments or enact a statutory rule of strict construction, but it has not attempted to do so. It does, however, regulate specific local government powers through statutory enactment, repeal, amendment, or preemption. Also, the Utah Supreme Court has held that the *Hutchinson* rule of broad construction is not a source of local taxing power.[16]

Structural Features

The Utah State Constitution prohibits the legislature from making special laws where a general law can be applicable.[17] However, the legislature has enacted laws that affect only one county or city by making the laws apply to a class that has only one county or city.

Classification of counties and municipalities is based on population.[18] There are six classes of counties and four of cities (see Table 1).

The state constitution originally required the legislature to prescribe a uniform system of county government. The basic form of county government specified by the Utah Code is a three-member county commission, elected at large, in which the commissioners serve as both legislators and executives. In addition to the commission, each county elects a treasurer, sheriff, auditor, recorder, clerk, attorney, surveyor, assessor, and—if the county is part of a state prosecution district—a district attorney. County commissions may combine some of these positions, and they have done so in the state's less populous counties.

In 1971 the constitution was amended to require the Utah legislature to authorize optional forms of county government, sub-

Table 1. Classifications of Utah Local Governments

Counties class	Population	Number of counties
First	700,000 or more	1
Second	125,000–699,999	3
Third	18,000–124,999	10
Fourth	10,000–17,999	4
Fifth	3,500–9,999	7
Sixth	less than 3,500	4

Municipalities class	Population	Number of cities
First-class cities	100,000 or more	2
Second-class cities	60,000–99,999	5
Third-class cities	800–59,999	130
Towns	less than 800	99

ject to referenda. The statute currently in effect allows for alternative structures and management arrangements. There are four optional "structural forms": general county (modified), urban county, community council, and consolidated city and county.[19] They provide different ways of structuring representation in the county legislative body. Under all of them, the county legislature may be chosen by district and may be restricted to legislative activities—a substantial departure from the at-large, commission system of the traditional county in Utah. The forms differ from each other in how cities, towns, and urbanized unincorporated areas are treated. Most important, under both the community council form and consolidated city and county form, there are provisions that would allow city-county consolidation.

Any one of these structural forms may be combined with any one of five management types, including expanded county commission, elected county executive-council, elected county executive and chief administrative officer-council, council-manager, or council-county administrative officer.[20] The distinction between the last two choices is that the statute prescribes the manager's principal duties, whereas the county administrative officer's duties are set by the plan adopted.

Although the optional forms may change the composition of the county legislative body and establish an elected executive, none of the other elected officials—for example, sheriff, treasurer, or auditor—are affected. However, it may be possible to alter them by consolidating several of these positions.

Five counties have adopted optional forms, all choosing the general county (modified) structural form. Cache County (in 1986) and Salt Lake County (in 1998) both adopted council plans with elected county executives. Grand County adopted an optional plan in 1992 with a council and a county administrative officer. San Juan County, which contains a significant portion of the Navajo Indian Reservation, was ordered by a federal court in 1984 to elect its three county commissioners by district. Morgan County adopted the expanded commission form in 1997.

Governmental structures of Utah cities and towns vary by classification.[21] Cities of the first and second classes traditionally had five- or three-member commissions, but none do so today. Towns and cities of the third class are placed under council-mayor ("weak" mayor) forms, but it is not uncommon for members of the council to assume responsibility for aspects of municipal administration—in effect borrowing from the commission form.

Two alternative forms are available to Utah cities and towns by popular vote: the council-mayor ("strong" mayor) form and the council-manager form. All first- and second-class cities have abandoned the commission form. Salt Lake City has adopted the council-mayor form, as have five second-class cities and three third-class cities. Only three cities have adopted the council-manager form. Few have chosen the council-manager form because a manager, if one is desired, can be authorized by local ordinance.[22] A local council can create a manager position without a referendum, and twenty-six third-class cities, generally the larger ones located in the urban regions of the state, have done so. In addition, state law permits cities and towns to create administrative positions to head one or more departments.[23] These positions are often titled as city/town administrator or manager, or even administrative assistant to the mayor/council. These "unofficial" managers number around forty throughout the state. Thus, most third-class cities and all towns have maintained their traditional council-mayor forms while gaining the ability to appoint an administrator or manager. Since the decision to create the position is made by the council (rather than by referendum), the council is free, at a later time, to abolish the manager position.

Incorporation and dissolution of municipalities are provided for by statute.[24] The minimum population for incorporation is one hundred, but some towns remain incorporated even though their population has dropped below that figure. The town of Ophir had a population of only twenty-five in 1990.

No minimum geographic area is required for an incorporation or annexation, but determining boundaries has become very contentious in recent years due to unprecedented growth in the state's urban area. Disputes between municipalities attempting to annex the same desirable unincorporated areas led to passage of the Boundary Commission Act in 1979.[25] The law establishes a state policy on annexation that favors sound urban development, sets standards for annexation, requires municipalities to make annexation policy declarations for each area over five acres, and establishes boundary commissions in each county. The law has helped resolve some, but not all, boundary issues. The boundary commission does not deal with proposals to incorporate new municipalities in areas previously designated for annexation by existing municipalities. Such conflicts can be resolved only by the county legislative body and, when a petition to incorporate meets the statutory requirements, an incorporation election.

Some highly urbanized areas of Utah consist of many small- or moderate-sized municipalities combined with large areas of densely populated but unincorporated communities served by the counties. The state constitution grants municipalities authority to provide local public services and "to acquire by condemnation, or otherwise, within or without the corporate limits, property necessary for such purposes, subject to restrictions imposed by general law for the protection of other communities."[26] Municipalities may also acquire and own water rights for supplying water to their inhabitants. Due to the extreme importance of water to inhabitants of the arid west, the state constitution prohibits municipalities from alienating water rights. They may only exchange water rights or sources of water supply for others of equal value.[27]

Functions of Local Government

Functional Responsibilities

Both municipalities and counties provide important local government services to Utah residents, with counties also serving as extensions of state government in such areas as voter registration, property tax assessment and collection, recording of deeds, and law enforcement. The incorporated cities and towns typically provide fire protection, planning and zoning, water services (sometimes separate potable and irrigation systems), sewer services, parks and recreation services, and local streets.

Urban counties are permitted to create municipal service districts. These are special districts with taxing authority that provide municipal-type services in unincorporated but densely populated county areas. This capacity is especially important for Salt Lake County and for other counties in densely populated northern Utah.

Neither counties nor cities in the state have responsibility for educational functions. There are independent school districts. Most welfare services are provided directly by the state through Department of Human Services offices located throughout the state. Counties have primary responsibility for local health services and services for the aging.

The state constitution was amended in 1974 to provide the legislature with power to authorize local governments to establish special districts that can incur debt to be paid from tax revenues.[28] State laws covering special districts provide that counties and municipalities may create special districts or authorities by ordinance.[29] Through this device, counties and municipalities may exceed tax revenue and bond limits by which they are otherwise bound. Special districts may be governed by separate boards—either elected or appointed—or the county/city governing body may serve as the board. The governing arrangement depends on the specific statutory authorization for the type of special district created.

The utility of special districts is enhanced by the Interlocal Cooperation Act, which authorizes all agencies and political subdivisions of the state to enter into agreements with each other and with Native American tribes for the joint exercise of governmental powers.[30] Under the provisions of the act, a local government may also contract with another public agency to provide a service directly, even if it is outside the public agency's normal geographic jurisdiction. Many such agreements have been entered into, including agreements for multicounty associations of government to provide planning services and to administer some common programs, such as aging, housing, and job training services. Virtually every county and municipality is a member of one of the seven associations covering the entire state.

Administrative Discretion

Although many aspects of local government administration come under state oversight and must fit within a statutory framework, local officials have some areas of broad discretion. They are free to work out the details of policy implementation. For example, although statutes require budgeting and accounting oversight by the state auditor, no specific budget format is required. Similarly, local officials may choose to adopt the state procurement code or establish their own procurement procedures; they are encouraged to invest idle funds through the state treasurer's investment pool but may choose not to do so. Thus, while they must adhere to minimum standards for accounting, preparing budgets, and filing annual financial reports, local officials have considerable discretionary authority in making operational and spending decisions.

Local administrators, with the cooperation of funding authorities, have discretion in determining the extent to which they will provide staff training and development activities. Whereas some training is mandated by state statutes (for example, for law enforcement personnel), most training is discretionary. Some local governments choose to invest in technical and managerial training for their employees; others find such investments difficult to justify.

Planning and zoning authority have been specifically granted to county and municipal governments through state enabling legislation.[31] These functions are carried out by planning commissions established by ordinance and appointed by the local government's legislative body or executive. Some counties have established county service areas (districts or townships), pursuant to state law, for the purposes of planning and zoning in urbanized but unincorporated areas. Communities vary greatly in their staffing of the planning and zoning function; the more urban ones—or those facing more growth pressure—generally give planning and zoning more attention.

Economic Development

Utah's urban counties and larger municipalities have made considerable use of neighborhood redevelopment agencies to stimulate local development.[32] These agencies may exercise the power of eminent domain upon a formal finding of blight. They then employ "tax increment financing" for development of the property. A prerequisite is the adoption of a community general plan.

Another development tool is the Enterprise Zone Act,[33] which particularly benefits Utah's rural counties. Counties with high unemployment rates, low per capita income, and net out-migration may apply for enterprise zone status. Within these zones, a manufacturing firm that creates new jobs or invests in new facilities or equipment is eligible for state corporate franchise tax or personal income tax credits. Today there are fifteen enterprise zone counties—all rural.

Although it is a source of revenue rather than a development tool, the Utah Permanent Community Impact Fund provides development resources to local governments.[34] The fund, consisting of federal mineral lease revenues from the huge tracts of nontaxable federal land within every rural county, is administered by a board that is part of the state Department of Community and Economic Development. The board makes low-interest loans and grants to local governments in areas affected by natural resource production, often to finance local development activities such as planning, infrastructure, and revolving business loan funds.

Fiscal Autonomy of Local Governments

Local Revenues

The fiscal practices of Utah counties, municipalities, and special districts are governed by the Uniform Fiscal Procedure Acts.[35] Among the standard procedures required is the use of uniform fiscal years for counties (the calendar year) and municipalities (a year beginning on July 1). All local governments must have balanced budgets (except in certain emergencies), and any deficits must be paid with revenues from the next fiscal year. Carryover funds are allowed, and certain reserve funds can be created to plan for capital improvements or to provide for future contingencies—all within limits based on annual revenues. Retained earnings from enterprise funds can be transferred to other funds with certain restrictions.

Local accounting and auditing procedures must conform with the *State of Utah Uniform Accounting Manual,* and annual independent audits are required; however, small towns and special districts may submit unaudited financial statements. The statutes establish procurement procedures for counties and cities and give the state auditor power to evaluate the practices of towns and special districts.

Debt limits are set by the constitution for counties, municipalities, and school districts. Generally, they may not incur debt in excess of taxes for the current year. Specifically, counties are limited to 2 percent of taxable property; school districts, 4 per-

Table 2. Revenue of Utah Counties and Cities (in percent)

Source of revenue	County FY 1997	City FY 1998
Property tax	35.31%	18.40%
Fee in lieu of taxes	2.04	1.56
General and use sales tax	8.53	25.20
Utility franchise tax	–	6.99
Transient room or hotel/motel tax	2.15	0.57
Federal aid	6.22	3.57
State aid	11.97	6.51
From other local government	2.77	2.52
Licenses, permits, and fees	3.94	5.02
Charges and miscellaneous	27.07	29.67

Source: Based on individual county and city data from the Office of Utah State Auditor; www.sao.state.ut.us/html/survey.htm.

Note: County fiscal year ended December 31, 1997; city fiscal year ended June 30, 1998.

cent; and municipalities, 4 percent (with an additional 4 percent for water, lights, and sewer for first- and second-class cities and 8 percent for third-class cities and towns). The constitution also prohibits the state from assuming the debt of any county or municipality. Special districts of various types are subject to statutory debt limits.

The property tax is an important source of revenue for both counties and cities (see Table 2). Counties depend on it for more than one-third of their revenue. Unlike a number of other states, Utah has no overall property tax rate limit; instead, the various types of local government are individually limited. Counties with less than $100 million of taxable property value can impose tax up to 0.36 percent of taxable value; those with $100 million or more, up to 0.32 percent. These limits may be exceeded, however, under the Truth-in-Taxation law, which gives counties (especially those where the base of taxable value is shrinking) authority to impose a "certified tax rate" (described below) even if that rate exceeds the standard limits. In addition, counties may levy property taxes for many specific purposes, such as special improvement districts, libraries, emergency services, disaster recovery, local health departments, municipal-type services in unincorporated areas, and paying judgments. Many of these purposes have their own statutory limitations.

The property tax limit imposed on municipalities of all sizes is set at 0.7 percent of taxable value. Municipalities can exceed this limit only by creating special districts, under their control.

Procedurally, elected county assessors place valuations on real and nonexempt personal property. The legal standard is "fair market value," with a 45 percent reduction for primary residences.[36] The State Tax Commission assesses mining property, public utilities, railroad property, airlines, and other transportation properties, all commonly referred to as "centrally assessed" properties. The commission also oversees the practices of county assessors and conducts sales-ratio studies within counties. On the basis of these studies, it issues factoring orders requiring assessors to raise or lower assessments to ensure that assessments approximate fair market value.[37]

The state's Truth-in-Taxation law was adopted in 1985 and is designed to ensure that reassessments do not automatically yield property tax windfalls to local governments.[38] It requires that the county auditor annually calculate for each taxing entity in the county a "certified tax rate." This is the rate that will produce the same amount of property tax revenue as was collected by the entity in the prior year. "New growth" is excluded from the taxable value base, so that the certified tax rate is not depressed by true new growth but *is* depressed by reappraisals, factoring adjustments, or other changes in assessments not associated with "new growth." If a taxing entity intends to adopt a tax rate above the certified tax rate, it or the county must publish a quarter-page newspaper notice, mail a notice to all property owners indicating the effect of the proposed tax rate, and hold a public hearing before voting to increase the levy. "New growth" is taxed at the certified tax rate or the rate the county finally adopts. Thus, it may generate additional revenue.

The effect of the Truth-in-Taxation law is to compel all local governments to treat almost any *revenue* increase from the property tax (beyond that produced by new growth) as if it were the result of a decision by the governing body to increase *tax rates,* thereby limiting property tax increases. The law seems to have done this. Between 1981 and 1985 the property tax on a typical residence increased 28 percent. Between 1985 and 1990 the increase was only 4 percent.[39]

In addition to property taxes, municipalities and counties have available the option of imposing a sales and use tax (collected by the state).[40] As Table 2 shows, this tax is the source of more than one-fourth of city revenue.[41] Prior to 1981, sales and use tax revenue was allocated to local governments entirely on a point-of-sale basis. Today, 50 percent of revenue is distributed according to point-of-sale and 50 percent by population. Hence, there is an advantage to levying the tax even if there are no major tax-generating retail outlets within the jurisdiction. Presently, municipalities and counties are authorized to impose a 1 percent rate. An important addition for some communities is the "resort tax," a special 1 percent tax that municipalities may impose if their transient room capacity is equal to or larger than 66 percent of the permanent population. Counties may levy a tax of up to 3 percent of room rent for transient rooms (plus 0.5 percent for Salt Lake County only), 7 percent for auto rentals, and 1 percent for restaurant meals. The revenue from most of these levies can be used only to promote tourism and to provide convention and cultural facilities. Four increments to the general sales tax are available with voter approval: 0.1 percent for botanical, cultural, and zoological organizations; 0.25 percent for public transit; 0.25 percent for "light rail"; and 1 percent for

rural county or city hospitals (in small population counties only).

The utility franchise tax is especially important for municipalities. It is imposed on the utility bills of individuals and organizations, including nonprofit organizations, and is an especially important consideration for Salt Lake City, which, like many capital cities, has extensive property not subject to property tax. The maximum rate allowed is 6 percent. Counties in Utah are not permitted to levy the utility franchise tax.

Federal and state aid are important revenue sources to both cities and counties, but especially to the latter. Much of the state aid is derived from the tax on motor fuels and is targeted to the maintenance of streets and roads.

Both counties and municipalities generate substantial amounts of revenue from licenses and fees as well as from charges and miscellaneous sources (including impact fees on new development, library fines, parks and recreation fees, and charges for other services). These fees, charges, and miscellaneous sources generate more than one-fourth of total revenue in both cases.

Local Expenditures

One function dominates county general expenditures: law enforcement, including corrections (see Table 3). The next major function, judged by spending, is health and hospitals. All other spending categories, with the possible exception of parks, recreation, and natural resources, are of lesser importance.

City expenditures show a somewhat different pattern, reflecting variation in the responsibilities assigned to cities. As was true for counties, law enforcement stands out, but not corrections, since in Utah that is a county responsibility at the local level. Cities spend little on health, but they spend a substantially higher percentage than counties on streets and roads. Fire protection consumes over 9 percent of city budgets but less than 3 percent of county budgets. Similarly, planning and zoning receive greater city attention. Cities typically use enterprise funds to operate their water and sewer systems and some electric distribution systems.

Comparing county and municipal spending patterns, it is clear that counties attend to activities related to legal and financial matters, responsibilities they are specifically assigned. They substantially surpass cities in percent spent on corrections, judicial and legal services, and financial administration.

From a process perspective, both counties and cities must follow the Utah Fiscal Procedures Acts. They must prepare tentative annual budgets and hold public hearings before approving their final budgets. These approved budgets, filed with the state auditor, then guide their spending.

There are no statutes specifically allowing Utah local governments to go into receivership or bankruptcy, nor are they specifically prohibited from filing for bankruptcy. Utah has no legal

Table 3. Direct, General Expenditures of Utah Counties and Cities (in percent)

Function	County FY 1997	City FY 1998
Welfare	5.63%	—
Health and hospitals	12.86	0.52%
Libraries	3.09	2.37
Streets and roads	7.89	18.64
Police protection	11.70	20.01
Corrections	13.38	—
Fire protection	2.44	9.18
Parks, recreation, and natural resources	9.32	11.68
Planning and zoning	1.07	2.15
Economic development and redevelopment	3.69	4.20
Housing and community development	—	2.59
Judicial and legal	5.23	1.65
Financial administration	7.25	3.84
General administration	2.27	7.04
General public buildings	5.50	3.31
Interest	1.91	2.66
Other	6.78	10.16

Source: Based on individual county and city data from the Office of Utah State Auditor; www.sao.state.ut.us/html/survey.htm.

Note: County fiscal year ended December 31, 1997; city fiscal year ended June 30, 1998.

precedent of any local government attempting to file for bankruptcy. Issues that would surround such an event thus remain unsettled.

State Government Grants-in-Aid to Localities

One type of state intergovernmental aid far exceeds all others: aid to Utah's forty local school districts for public education purposes under the state's Minimum School Program. (School districts in Utah are independent of other local units of government.) The largest aid program to counties and municipalities is distribution of a portion of the state gasoline tax for local road purposes. Revenue from motor fuels taxes, license taxes, and registration fees is designated for purposes relating to roads, highways, and travel. A portion of these moneys (25 percent after certain deductions) is distributed to municipalities and counties according to a formula that is based on population and road miles. The effect of these dedicated revenues from the state is seen in the large portion of county and municipal expenditures devoted to roads.

Although principal social service programs are provided directly by state agencies, there is significant sharing with counties. The state provides formula grants to counties for services to the aging and for mental health, substance abuse, and general health services, with expectations that counties will secure federal funds and payments from individuals as well.

Unfunded Mandates

In 1991 the Utah Advisory Council on Intergovernmental Relations investigated the extent of state imposed mandates affecting local governments.[42] The Utah Constitution, code, and administrative code were searched, and hundreds of state mandates were identified (see Table 4).

The council found that the mandates affecting municipalities and counties were quite similar to each other (see Table 5). Finance practices (taxation, budgeting, money management, and treasury procedures) are heavily mandated, as are human resource management practices. Counties and larger cities are required to have merit systems, with special provisions for law enforcement and fire personnel. All local government employees are part of the State Public Employees Retirement System. Public safety mandates include many provisions concerning the conditions of jails, animal care, fire protection, and juvenile detention facilities.

Although the Utah League of Cities and Towns and Utah Association of Counties have long protested the large number and expense of state mandates, each legislative session brings passage of additional mandates. The state has not adopted effective mandate-limitation legislation. In 1992 the legislature added a requirement that its legislative fiscal analyst evaluate bills under consideration for their fiscal effect on local government,[43] but this requirement has not significantly restrained the adoption of new mandates.

Access to Local Government

Local Elections

Local government elections and qualifications for candidacy are extensively controlled by state statutes, with conduct of elections the responsibility of the county clerk, city recorder, or town clerk.[44] About the only flexibility counties and municipalities have is to establish, change, or combine voting precincts. They may also choose to use automated voting machines.

Most municipal elections are conducted on a nonpartisan basis. Candidates are nominated at a primary election held in October, separate from the state, county, and school board primaries held in June. However, if there is no more than twice the

Table 4. Utah State Mandates, by Affected Local Government

Local government type	Number of mandates
Counties	157
Cities and towns	146
School districts	104
Special districts	63
Redevelopment agencies	37

Source: Steve Taggart, State Mandates Study (Salt Lake City: State of Utah Office of Planning and Budget, 1991).

Table 5. Functional Uses of State Mandates in Utah

Mandate type	Mandate type as percentage of all mandates	
	Cities and towns	Counties
Procedural	10.2%	11.5%
Personnel	11.6	10.2
Services	8.9	12.7
Finances	28.8	25.5
Business regulation	1.4	1.3
Environment/health	7.5	8.3
Public safety	13.7	14.6
Infrastructure	8.2	3.9
Land use	5.5	9.6
Other	4.1	2.5

Source: Steve Taggart, *State Mandates Study* (Salt Lake City: State of Utah Office of Planning and Budget, 1991).

number of candidates needed to fill an office, a primary need not be held. Any third-class city or town may exempt itself from the primary election requirement by adopting an ordinance providing for either a party convention or a partisan primary method of nominating candidates. County elections (like state elections) are partisan.

The state has mandated that counties and cities with populations of ten thousand and above adopt ordinances establishing campaign finance disclosure requirements.[45] These statutes were enacted after the *Hutchinson* case and set detailed minimum requirements for the local ordinances. Local governments may impose additional requirements or penalties.

Citizen Controls over Actions of Local Officials

Utah law does not provide for removal of elected officials by recall, and local government officials are not subject to impeachment. They can be removed for "high crimes, misdemeanors, or malfeasance in office," under a judicial proceeding similar to a civil trial.[46] The proceeding may be initiated by "any taxpayer, grand jury, county attorney, or district attorney for the county in which the officer was elected or appointed, or by the attorney general."

The state constitution vests the power of initiative and referendum for both state and local laws in the people.[47] The legislature has enacted procedures for handling petitions and elections on local initiatives and referenda.[48] Local government budgets are specifically exempt from these procedures.

Utah has an Open and Public Meetings Act that applies to every "public body," including county commissions, city councils, planning commissions, and administrative commissions and boards.[49] Meetings may be closed for certain specified reasons, such as the discussion of the character, professional competence, or health of an individual; strategy sessions regarding collective bargaining, litigation, or real property transactions; or discussion of security devices or investigative proceedings. An open meeting must first be called in which the public body votes to close a meeting. Minutes or a recording must be kept of all closed meetings, except for those regarding an individual's health or deployment of security devices. These records become public after a reasonable time. Suits may be filed to compel compliance or to enjoin violations of the act. Any action taken by a public body in violation of the act is voidable. Attorney fees and court costs may be awarded to a successful plaintiff.

Local governments are also covered by Utah's Government Records Access and Management Act.[50] The purposes of the act are to standardize records management and to make records available to the public, as much as possible, while protecting the privacy rights of individuals. It is applicable to all local governments and requires that all records be classified as public, private, controlled, protected, or exempt. Most records are considered public, and every person has the right to inspect them free of charge or to take a copy subject to reasonable fees to cover costs. Records may be obtained from any storage medium as long as the records are reproducible. If anyone is denied access to a record, the denial may be appealed administratively and to the courts.

The Utah Public Officers' and Employees' Ethics Act is intended "to set forth standards of conduct for officers and employees of the state and its political subdivisions in areas where there are actual or potential conflicts of interest between their public duties and their private interests."[51] It requires disclosure statements, prohibits acceptance of certain gifts over $50, prohibits use of government information and assets for personal gain, and restricts personal investments that would create a substantial conflict of interest. Violation of the act can result in removal from office or dismissal from employment and can lead to a misdemeanor or felony conviction. A transaction entered into in violation of the act can also be rescinded. Additionally, Utah has an antinepotism law applicable to all local governments.[52]

State-Local Relations

Local governments in Utah began their history under centralized control. In many respects, control remains centralized today. Although the availability of statutory home rule provides counties and municipalities an opportunity to enter important areas of activity from which they formerly might have been barred, such opportunities can always be withdrawn by the Utah legislature. Constitutional home rule for municipalities, although a part of the document, has been of little effect. Only one city uses it. With the exception of the larger cities that otherwise would have commission governments, few municipalities or counties have used the alternative forms of government available. Home rule and the alternative forms are principally directed to structural innovations, offering no opportunities for programmatic innovations or freedom from legislative restrictions.

State government assumes strong policy responsibility in Utah, especially in the area of social service policy. Major responsibilities of counties and cities (as judged by spending) are roads and streets, law enforcement, parks and recreation, health, and fire services. Mandates imposed by the state are common, and efforts to limit them have not been effective. The legislature, then, generally keeps a tight rein on local governments.

Although Utah remains conservative, principally Mormon, heavily Republican, and state-centered, several forces are at work that may test the state's restrictions of local autonomy. Two of these forces are Utah's rapid population growth and its changing demographics. The state is among the fastest growing in the nation, because of in-migration and a high natural rate of increase. Demographically, the population becomes ever more concentrated in the three metropolitan areas. This concentration results in expanded urban problems that fall heavily on local governments. Simultaneously, many smaller Utah communities that once depended on mining and agriculture for economic sustenance are losing their abilities to support full services. Although some areas of the state have tourism potential, conflicts surrounding land use complicate full development. With these present and continuing changes, there is a greater demand from local officials to recognize the diverse local government needs, to reduce state restraints, and to enhance local autonomy.

Notes

1. *State v. Hutchinson*, 624 P.2d 1116 (1980).

2. Leonard J. Arrington, "Colonization of Utah," *Utah History Encyclopedia* (Salt Lake City: University of Utah Press, 1994), 106–108; Andrew Love Neff, *History of Utah, 1847–1869* (Salt Lake City: Deseret News Press, 1942), 216ff.

3. Michael D. Stewart, "The Legal History of Utah," *Utah History Encyclopedia* (Salt Lake City: University of Utah Press, 1994), 323.

4. Alvin Charles Koritz, *The Development of Municipal Government in the Territory of Utah* (M.A. thesis, Brigham Young University, 1972).

5. Utah State Constitution, Article I, section 4.

6. Q. Michael Croft, *Influence of the LDS Church on Utah Politics, 1945–1985* (Ph.D. diss., University of Utah, 1985).

7. Information provided by the Office of the Utah State Auditor.

8. *Wadsworth v. Santaquin City*, 28 P.2d 161, at 168 (1933).

9. The council-manager movement came to Utah slowly. Most cities that adopted manager plans (and most that have one today) did so by council ordinance. See Thomas W. Thorsen, *City Manager Experience in Utah* (M.A. thesis, University of Utah, 1948); B. H. Stringham and Dale W. James, *Utah Experiences with the City Manager Idea* (Salt Lake City: Institute of Government, University of Utah, 1948).

10. J. D. Williams, *The Defeat of Home Rule in Salt Lake City* (New York: Holt, Rinehart and Winston, 1960), 3.

11. Brian Hall, *Home Rule Governance and Utah Municipalities: A Brief Analysis of Home Rule in the United States and Utah* (Salt Lake City: Utah League of Cities and Towns, 1995), 5.

12. Utah Code, sections 10-3-1201 et seq.

13. F. Robert Paulsen, *Utah Experience with Constitutional Home Rule* (Salt Lake City: Institute of Government, University of Utah, 1948).

14. *State v. Hutchinson*, 624 P.2d 1116, at 1118 (1980).

15. *State v. Hutchinson*, 624 P.2d 1116, at 1126 (1980).

16. *Mountain States Telephone and Telegraph Company v. Salt Lake County*, 702 P.2d 113 (1985).

17. Utah State Constitution, Article VI, section 26.

18. Utah Code, section 17-16-13 and section 10-2-301, respectively.

19. Utah Code, sections 17-35b-301 et seq.

20. Utah Code, section 17-35a-501 et seq.

21. Utah Code, sections 10-3-101 et seq. and sections 10-3-1201 et seq. See also David R. Colvin and F. Ted Hebert, "Cities and Towns: Choosing a Form of Government." In *Public Policy Perspective* (Salt Lake City: Center for Public Policy and Administration, University of Utah, 1990).

22. Utah Code, section 10-3-924.

23. Utah Code, section 10-3-901.

24. Utah Code, sections 10-2-101 et seq. for incorporation and sections 10-2-701 et seq. for dissolution.

25. Utah Code, sections 10-2-401 et seq.

26. Utah State Constitution, Article XI, section 5.

27. Utah State Constitution, Article XI, section 6.

28. Utah State Constitution, Article XIV, section 8.

29. Utah Code, Titles 17A and 17B.

30. Utah Code, sections 11-13-1 et seq.

31. Utah Code, sections 10-9-101 et seq. for municipalities and sections 17-27-101 et seq. for counties.

32. Utah Code, sections 17A-2-1201 et seq.

33. Utah Code, sections 9-2-401 et seq.

34. Utah Code, sections 9-4-301 et seq.

35. Utah Code, sections 17-36-1 et seq. for counties; sections 10-5-101 et seq. for towns; sections 10-6-101 et seq. for cities; and sections 17A-1-401 et seq. for special districts.

36. Utah Code, section 59-2-103.

37. Utah Code, section 59-2-704.

38. Utah Code, section 59-2-901 et seq.

39. Utah Foundation, *State and Local Government in Utah* (Salt Lake City: Utah Foundation, 1992), 94.

40. Utah Code, sections 59-12-101 et seq.

41. Detailed revenue and expenditure data for local governments are available from the Office of Utah State Auditor: www.sao.state.ut.us/html/survey.htm.

42. Steve Taggart, *State Mandates Study* (Salt Lake City: State of Utah Office of Planning and Budget, 1991), 1. The council adopted a definition based on that used by the National League of Cities, stating that a mandate is a legal requirement—constitutional, statutory, or administrative—that local units provide a specified service, meet state standards, engage in a particular activity . . . or that establishes certain terms and conditions of local public employment.

43. Utah Code, section 36-12-13(2)(c).

44. Utah Code, Title 20A; specifically for municipalities, sections 10-3-201 et seq.; and for counties, sections 17-16-1 et seq.

45. Utah Code, sections 17-16-6.5 and 10-3-208.

46. Utah Code, sections 77-6-1 et seq.

47. Utah State Constitution, Article VI, section 1.

48. Utah Code, sections 20A-7-501 et seq. and 601 et seq.

49. Utah Code, sections 52-4-1 et seq.

50. Utah Code, sections 63-2-101 et seq.

51. Utah Code, sections 67-16-1 et seq.; also, for counties, sections 17-16a-1 et seq., and for municipalities, sections 10-3-1301 et seq.

52. Utah Code, sections 53-3-1 et seq., made applicable to special districts by section 17A-1-201.

VERMONT

Paul S. Gillies

Home rule in Vermont, like moonlight, is a reflection of a stronger light. That light is the state—which, within constitutional limits, has exclusive power to control towns and people.[1] The legislature wants to be generous with the towns, but it is a strict parent, and it can take away local control—as it did in 1997, when a statewide property tax was reinstated after a sixty-year hiatus—as well as bestow it.[2] The 1998 state election campaign became a referendum on the property tax issue, revealing deep differences among Vermonters on the essential question of the relationship between the state and the towns.

Equally important is the relationship between the state and the voters. Vermonters are bred to believe in local control. At town meeting, Vermonters exercise more authority than residents of most states. At the beginning of the new millennium, the tension between representative power and direct democracy defines local government in Vermont.

Governmental Setting

To understand Vermont, you first need to think about life on a small scale. About 600,000 people, give or take a few tourists, live in Vermont. The largest city (Burlington) has only about 40,000 people—and, like most of Vermont's cities, has seen its population decline during the past twenty years.[3] Although in many parts of Vermont there is growing fear of suburban sprawl, many Vermonters still live in small towns and villages, which are run principally by volunteer officials.

Geography also helps define Vermont. The Green Mountains split the state down the middle, and east-west travel is limited to mountain passes, many of which are closed in winter. For many years, the "mountain rule" required governors to alternate from the east and west sides of those mountains. In towns split evenly by the mountain range, the rule extended to state representatives as well: a representative elected from the west side of town would not run for reelection the following year, even if no candidate from the east side came forward. Some towns even chose to remain unrepresented rather than to violate the mountain rule.

Many of the earliest towns were on high ground, but after the first generation or two of settlers—when better roads and bridges had been built and spring runoff was more under control—towns sprang up on the valley floor. Most early farms were hill farms, but many were abandoned by the beginning of the twentieth century because of the difficulties of getting milk to market. Eventually, many former hill farms became second homes for well-to-do nonresidents.

Vermont contains 246 towns, 9 cities, 45 villages, and a host of other political subdivisions, including solid waste districts, fire districts, and regional planning commissions. Each of the fourteen counties has its own shire town and courthouse, but the town is the basic unit of government and cultural identity in Vermont.[4]

The strength of the town as a political subdivision cannot be overestimated. From the beginning, the state was ruled by the towns: each town had one vote in the various revolutionary councils that led to independence, and one vote in the Vermont General Assembly (which at first consisted only of a house of representatives). Representatives were elected at town meetings. The one-town, one-vote rule continued until a federal court insisted on reapportionment in 1966.[5]

What the legislature does is of interest to every Vermonter, but what people see of government in Vermont is local government. The snowplow goes by early in the morning, run by the town. The police department answers to the local governing body, the select board. Fire and rescue are usually local, and often volunteer. Elections are conducted at the town hall by the town clerk. Towns are responsible for highways, sewer and water service, zoning and planning, and just about everything that the state does not provide. Things get done at the town level.

State government, by contrast, is something to read about in the local paper. When Vermonters pay for groceries at the local store, the clerk may well refer to the sales tax as "something for the governor," using his or her first name familiarly, with just a touch of irreverence. The state seems far away, and hard to reach. If you want something done—like building an ice rink or adding on to the town library—you do it yourself, or you talk your community into doing it. Although towns sometimes look to Montpelier for more authority and more financial assistance, Vermonters—with their historic ideological investment in local control—remain suspicious of shared power, and the state often plays little more than an educational or advisory role when it comes to implementing state programs at the local level.

On one day of the year—town meeting day, in March—voters control Vermont. They elect local officers, set the town and school budgets, and vote on all manner of public questions, from zoning bylaw amendments to matters of fiscal policy. Voters at town meeting engage in direct democracy: for that one day, the voters run the government. Nevertheless, the limits of voter authority are more narrowly drawn than they were in the past. For example, voters' more extensive powers once included the right to undo or reverse anything that their local elected or appointed representatives did.[6] The legislature has become wary of delegating power to municipal government; as a consequence of this change in the state's view of the towns, representative government has replaced direct democracy in important ways.

During every town meeting, there comes a time when the state representatives and senators have a chance to speak and answer questions. (The legislature closes down during town meeting week.) The process is politely brief. After the legislators are done, residents return to the articles and the business of deciding how the town will be run. Nothing so appropriately demonstrates the delicate balance of state and local interests in Vermont as that encounter. What the senators and representatives do at the statehouse affects everyone, but what the voters do at a town meeting is to decide for themselves, by majority voice vote or written ballot, the important questions, such as who should hold office and how much the town will spend in the coming year.

State issues do not escape town meeting debate. The notice and warning for annual meeting often includes an article supporting or opposing a legislative proposal. In earlier years, the legislature was not reluctant to place difficult questions as referenda at town meetings; in 1854, for example, residents were asked whether a law should be enacted to establish prohibition; in 1910, whether a new state library and courthouse should be built in Montpelier; and in the 1970s, whether Vermont should create a state lottery. And the opinions of voters—as expressed through town meeting—carry weight in the statehouse. Constitutional amendments require votes in the senate and house for two successive legislative sessions, followed by popular ratification.[7]

State government has about 6,000 employees—a relatively small number when compared with the over 10,000 (largely volunteer) officials who work in local government. The executive branch of state government consist of four agencies—transportation, human services, natural resources, and administra-tion—as well as a number of other departments and boards. The legislature has 180 members: 30 senators and 150 representatives.[8]

The two-year term for legislators, the governor, and other constitutional officers is celebrated in Vermont as a means of ensuring that government remains close to the voters. The judiciary consists of a five-member supreme court, and subordinate superior, district, family, probate, and environmental courts. Members of the judiciary serve six-year terms and are generally appointed. The governor makes the initial appointment, which is confirmed by the senate. At the expiration of the first term, the general assembly votes on whether individual judges or justices will continue in office.[9] This rule applies to all supreme, superior, district, and family court judges. Probate court judges are elected by probate district, for four-year terms. Each superior court consists of one appointive judge and two assistant judges, usually lay persons, elected for four-year terms. The probate judge is also an elective position.[10] Judicial home rule is manifested in an elective judiciary.

Politics play an important role in the election of state officials, but election to local offices is determined on a decidedly nonpartisan basis. People run on their reputations and experience, not political affiliation, and any display of party ideology at the local level is generally ignored by everyone.

Home Rule in Vermont

Historical Development

Vermont considers itself the last outpost of direct democracy in the world: Vermonters hold the belief—which is not always completely valid—that the voters can control every decision at any level of government. Vermont has always gone its own way, and has a tradition of tolerance and independence. Its 1777 constitution was the first in the United States to guarantee universal manhood suffrage, regardless of property, and the first written constitution anywhere to forbid slavery.[11] Before joining the union in 1791, Vermont enjoyed fourteen years as an independent state. Vermont is offended when the federal government tells it what to do; Vermont towns are equally offended when the state attempts the same thing; and voters regard all levels and forms of government with similar suspicion.

The first laws governing Vermonters were town charters issued by Benning Wentworth, an early New Hampshire governor. First to be chartered was Bennington, in 1749; Bennington is in the southwest corner of Vermont, next to New York, and it was a fitting place for Wentworth to begin establishing his authority in the area then known as the New Hampshire Grants.

New York disputed that authority, and used legal, political, and military means to prevent settlers with New Hampshire charters from creating a separate government in the Grants. For their part, the settlers used the conflict between New Hampshire and New York to their own advantage, eventually declaring themselves independent of British rule and New York authority in 1777.[12] New York did not give up its claims willingly, and not until 1789—in return for $30,000 in settlement of New York claims to Vermont land—would it agree to support Vermont's admission to the union.

Definition of Home Rule

The Vermont Constitution establishes the legislature's authority to "grant charters of incorporation, ... constitute towns, boroughs, cities and counties."[13] Local legislation is enabled by state law, and general municipal laws in state statutes define the duties and powers of local officials and the authority of the electorate.[14] To Vermonters, "home rule" means the decisions that they make locally, from enlarging the powers of the constable to enacting zoning bylaws, from changing the compensation awarded to the collector of delinquent taxes to holding up a state highway project until the legislature can take another look at it.[15] Formal home rule, in the sense that local government has some independent right to enact law without underlying legal authority from the state, does not exist in Vermont.

Vermonters are free to make a rich variety of choices, most of which involve how local government will work and how it will affect their lives at home. Exercising the power to choose, after an opportunity to debate the issue, is the heart of the Vermont experience.

The relationship between the state and its residents is more likely to be the subject of legislative action than the relationship between the state and the towns: in effect, most state legislation regulates the actions of individuals instead of authorizing the town to regulate such actions. Instead of 246 different versions of a rule, Vermont has one rule that applies to all—a situation that allows for greater fairness (or at least consistency) in administration.

Whether the state created the towns or the towns created the state is a subject occasionally debated in Vermont. The answer is not important, but the question illustrates the complexity of the relationship. When state government enacts a law mandating action by local government, local government obliges. Sometimes there is resentment, but the grumbling is as traditional as complaining about taxes.

Structural Features

General law encourages local option: the best state laws affecting municipalities in Vermont recognize the advantage of adapting to local needs and the fact that there is often more than one way to do something. (When Vermonters complain about federal law, the lack of flexibility is often the chief focus of complaint.)

There are no formal classes of cities or towns in Vermont.

Each is defined by the laws that govern it—whether charter, general law, or a mixture of both. Vermonters may adopt the town manager form of government (often known outside Vermont as the council-manager form). They may enlarge or diminish the size of the select board, set the due date for taxes, and allow taxes to be collected with a discount or by installment. They may set the hours the polls open on election days and (by petition) increase the percentage of votes needed to enact a zoning amendment. They may set the opening hour and even move the date of town meeting.[16]

The greatest level of flexibility, however, comes through enactment of a charter. Many Vermont towns look only to the general law for direction, but some communities have special governance charters, proposed and voted on at town meeting and then ratified by the legislature. These charters provide a host of ways of conducting business that differ from those of the traditional town system; often, a town that adopts such a charter serves as an incubator for ideas that the legislature eventually incorporates into general town law.

Through a petition signed by 5 percent of the voters, residents of a Vermont town can organize themselves to support and draft a charter that will remove the town from the authority of general law and specify something different.[17] Legislative oversight of municipal charters sometimes results in a decision to rewrite or refuse to ratify a particular provision, but the legislature is for the most part willing to allow towns the opportunity to experiment with new approaches to governance. In fact, voters' freedom to create a town government to their liking is almost unlimited, as long as the legislature approves. Only when the core functions of state government are involved—in the case of taxation, for example—or when a proposal contradicts the constitution has the legislature chosen to reject a charter or provision. Comity between the legislature and the towns is largely a reflection of the state's historic respect for independence and experimentation.

Charters are better than general law at defining the authority of voters. Some charters, for example, establish clear authority for public recall, initiative, and referendum. General law includes no provision for such actions, so a town that does not have a special charter cannot, for example, recall a public official. Whereas general law authorizes only the right to petition for disapproval of an ordinance within forty-five days of its adoption by the select board, charters may authorize petitioners to call for the enactment of ordinances.[18] Charters sometimes allow voters to petition to overturn discretionary decisions of the board itself.

A charter is the only way a village or settled area of a town can become a city; thus, all cities have charters. Some cities are really towns by another name, where voters approve the budget at a city meeting and enjoy all the powers of voters in towns.

The town of Brattleboro is the only municipality in Vermont

that uses a representative town meeting: small districts in the town elect representatives to make many of the decisions that, in a more traditional town, would be made at town meeting, with all voters having a say.

Brattleboro and many Vermont cities share the view that representative government is simply more manageable and efficient than gathering voters in a single room to make decisions that are vital to the community. Some even argue that representative government is more democratic than the town meeting system because, except in the smallest towns, the number of voters who attend town meeting are often a minority of the total checklist. Because Vermonters believe (with Emerson) that everybody is always wiser than anybody, the standard for action at town meeting is a majority of those present and voting, no matter how few turn up.

The relations between towns make for interesting conflicts and opportunities. A town's water supply may be on land that it owns in a neighboring municipality; the neighboring town can tax the land, although it would not be subject to tax if it were located in the town that owns it. A road running from one town into another cannot be discontinued without the approval of the select boards of both towns. Town plans must be approved by the regional planning commission.[19]

The towns have integrity. Boundary lines seldom change, and never without the full support of both municipalities. In the nineteenth century, a few towns split into two or three, usually over factional differences created by geography, but merger or annexation of towns has never occurred. The identity and independence of a town is too strong. Several years ago, for example, the city of Rutland wanted to merge with the town of Rutland, but the town was opposed to the proposal. City representatives took the argument to the state legislature, which debated whether to repeal the city charter and make the town absorb the city. If this had happened, the city, with its larger population, would inevitably have ruled the town, enjoying all the additional tax base and development opportunities. Town taxes would have increased accordingly, to pay for services that would have been delivered principally to city residents and that may not have been available to townspeople. To many legislators, the idea seemed imperialistic, and the proposal never made it to the floor.

With the exception of boundary line adjustments to correct inadequate surveys and the incorporation of some towns as cities, the map of political divisions in Vermont has remained virtually the same for two centuries. What has changed is the use of the land, which has often made commercial and residential boundaries more important than town lines.

County lines are important principally for legislative districting and the jurisdiction of courts. Town life has so absorbed Vermonters' attention there has never been much interest in regionalizing services at the county level. Vermonters are townspeople. Everything else is an afterthought.

Functions of Local Government

Functional Responsibilities

Despite centralizing tendencies in the state legislature, topography that defies town boundaries, and a perpetual concern about high taxes, Vermonters still look to the towns to solve local problems. Vermont cities and towns are responsible for local highways, water and sewer systems, public safety, zoning and planning, and the administration of the local property tax. Solid waste collection and disposal and public transportation systems have been regionalized, as have the districts formed by towns to deliver these services. Counties' duties are limited to maintaining courthouses for civil proceedings and the offices of state's attorney and sheriff. Apart from whatever is required to fulfill these responsibilities, there is virtually no county or regional government in Vermont. In every aspect of municipal, regionalized, and county functions, however, the state plays an increasingly dominant role through funding and the provision of basic legal standards.

Highways are divided into classes.[20] The state builds and maintains the interstate and major thoroughfares, while the towns are responsible for local roads and trails. Bridges are funded principally with state funds, which gives the state an oversight role in the bridges' placement and design. Many towns maintain thirty or more miles of unpaved roads, and most own trucks and graders.

Sewer and water systems are managed by a variety of entities in Vermont, depending on the history of the area. Towns manage some; in other cases, villages or fire districts run the systems. In rare cases, such systems cross town boundaries and are shared by special districts created by the legislature for that purpose.

Police services are provided by the state, the county, and the town or city. State police sometimes provide coverage to towns without local departments. In other cases the county sheriff provides services by contract with the town. Cities and larger towns maintain their own police services.

The volunteer fire department is the mainstay of most communities. Funded by appropriations at town meeting, these nonprofit corporations are otherwise independent of the town. They elect their own officers and make their own decisions on purchasing equipment and providing training to their volunteer forces. A few cities and larger towns have paid municipal fire departments that answer to the select board or to an appointed city or town manager.

No state law mandates interlocal cooperation, and it is rare in Vermont. Firefighters and police officers assist each other when needed, but regionalization of municipal services is seldom discussed. Under a state program, towns that are willing to share the vehicles are eligible for low-interest loans for the purchase of highway equipment. The program has had no takers. Regional

BERLIN, VERMONT: A TRADITIONAL TOWN

How does the Vermont system work in practice? Berlin, a town of about 2,700, borders the state capital, Montpelier. Covering about thirty-five square miles, Berlin is home to the region's only hospital, only airport, and only shopping mall. Aside from a few miles of commercial sprawl, the town is mostly rural. And apart from a few struggling dairy farms, most residents are home owners who work in other towns.

The town gets the road plowed to allow its residents to get to work. Berlin has its own grader, plow trucks, and garage. If there is a problem with the roads, the town road crew fixes it. The town provides police protection through a municipal department. Fire services come from a volunteer department. Berlin operates the system of sewers and pumps that serves the commercial section of town; Montpelier, at the end of the pipeline, runs and operates the treatment facility. Montpelier draws water from Berlin Pond, then sells some of it back to Berliners. Most residents have their own septic tanks and artesian wells.

Students from Berlin attend the local elementary school but travel across the valley to U-32, in East Montpelier, for high school. U-32 is operated as a union school district serving the towns that surround Montpelier. Back in the 1960s, Montpelier was one of a group of towns considering regionalization of education services; at the last minute, however, Montpelier refused to join the union. The other towns formed a union despite Montpelier's withdrawal. For those towns, the regional high school was an economic necessity, but it was also a reaction to the lack of control that the towns had felt before the union was formed. Berlin students, for example, had attended high school in other towns, and Berlin voters had nothing to say about the budget or the administration. Although Berlin is only one of six towns in the union, it has a voice in the administration of the high school through an elected board member and through its right to participate in direct votes on issues such as the budget and the use of construction bonds.

Ambulance service used to come from Montpelier, but outlying towns are trying to create their own regional service. Berlin has joined the effort, in part because of the promise of lower costs, but also because of the need for a feeling of ownership and control. Berlin changed its allegiance on ambulance services to express its independence from Montpelier. However, because of lack of agreement among the participating towns, the regional service has yet to be established.

---

planning commissions and solid waste districts are entities that allow town representatives to talk with each other on a regular basis, but their authority is narrow and they often fail to function as governmental units because citizens never stop thinking of themselves as townspeople first.

Ambulance service and sewage disposal are examples of "government by contract" in Vermont: towns pay private firms to undertake these functions. Such arrangements are more common than special districts, in part because of the strong sentiment favoring towns as administrative units. Local control is lost at the town border, and citizens are easily frustrated by the sense of having little voice in how rates are determined or how funds are spent.

Perhaps the best example of this relationship between the taxpayers and the towns is the county budget, which, as provided by statute, is adopted by agreement of the two assistant judges for the county, after a public hearing to which all county residents are invited.[21] Although these meetings are rarely well attended, and residents may have great trust in the judges, many townspeople nevertheless resent the county's authority to impose a tax without greater public involvement.

Administrative Discretion

The town hires the people it needs to work on the roads, maintain the water and sewer systems, and ensure public safety. Less than one-fourth of all Vermont towns have a formally designated manager, but many have some form of administrator to keep the business of local government running efficiently.

Where no town manager system has been adopted, the select board remains the operational as well as the policy-making body.

Although there is some union activity in larger departments, most municipal employees are not organized. They are paid wages set by the select board, and they usually serve at the board's pleasure. In towns with a manager, the department heads report to that official.

Boards meet two or three times a month. Between meetings, it is common practice to rely on a single member of the select board to make decisions and to have the board ratify his or her work later if it involves commitment of funding. This arrangement underscores a central principle of town government: only the select board can expend money. The state does not intrude in such matters.

Without a town manager, each town function may be delegated to a different board member, who agrees to be available when emergency work needs to be done—for example, to evacuate a neighborhood before a bridge floods out or to order repairs on the sewer pumping station.

No state law requires towns to engage in public bidding practices, although most do so for common-sense reasons. Some towns are regularly criticized for favoring local officials when awarding contracts for supplies or equipment, but most have a keen sense of conflicts of interest.

Zoning and planning are handled by a zoning administrator, zoning board, and planning commission; the administrator and the board and commission members are all appointed by the select board. The enabling state law provides a foundation on which the town builds a municipal plan, bylaws, and subdivision regulations. The state Act 250 process regulates larger developments; in addition to zoning, there are a host of other permit programs regulating land use in Vermont.[22] Regional planning commissions provide assistance to towns in implementing local zoning.

Economic Development

Few Vermont towns have any formal program for economic development. Many have industrial parks, and regional and state economic development programs are available for assistance with grant applications and funding.

Before 1997, when the state adopted its new education funding law, neighboring towns often competed for new business. The imposition of a statewide tax on nonresidential property, however, is expected to reduce the zeal of some towns to encourage new business growth: more development means greater demand for local services, and the cost of providing those services will no longer be largely offset by the amount of value new businesses add to the local grand list. The state does its best to encourage economic development in areas of need, but location still rules the choices of most new business.

One of Vermont's most serious problems is the changing character of its larger communities. Suburban sprawl has occurred where the market justified its development, sometimes in spite of the towns' best efforts at zoning. In the late summer of 1997, the Vermont Supreme Court recognized a new tool for guiding land-use decisions through the Act 250 process: the secondary impact of growth is now an established criterion by which to judge the suitability of new projects.[23] Such secondary impacts may include effects on the economies of other towns or, when a project is slated for the edge of a town, the impact on established downtowns.

Growth, whether commercial or residential, is not immediately embraced as a public good in Vermont. The charm of the small, rural state is being challenged, particularly by large retail outlets, and many Vermonters would be willing to forgo development rather than have to pay the high costs that come with increased service demands.

Fiscal Autonomy of Local Governments

Fiscal autonomy in Vermont is a function of the source of funds. Since most revenues are raised locally (with the exception of those used for education), decisions about raising and spending money are principally local ones.

Local Revenues

Vermont towns receive many forms of state assistance, but the major part of any town budget comes from local property taxes (see Table 1). Although limited experimentation with local

Table 1. Berlin, Vermont: 1997 Revenues

Property taxes	$849,562
State payments	117,132
Fees	58,003
Interest and penalties	63,721
Other	18,564
Total	$1,106,982

Source: Berlin Town Report (1997), 22–23.

rooms and meals taxes is a feature of the new education funding law, neither local sales and use taxes nor local income taxes are generally available to alleviate some of the burden on property taxpayers.

The budget is adopted by a majority of the voters at the annual town meeting. In many towns, this is a floor meeting, where line items are changed and amendments are offered and voted on—a little more for the town clerk this year, a little less for the constable, for example. No law limits the amount of money a town may appropriate at town meeting. The natural conservatism of taxpayers takes care of that.

The select board sets the local tax rate annually, on the basis of the amount of revenues approved at town meeting. Some city charters allow the city council to set a tax rate at any level as long as it remains below a certain percentage of the grand list. (The voters must approve budget amounts beyond that limit.)

The process of setting the tax rate is simple math—a matter of dividing the grand list by the amount of taxes to be raised locally. The grand list is created by the local board of listers, who appraise real and personal property according to recommended state standards, usually using the cost method of appraisal. Appraisal of property for tax purposes is primarily a local function, although some larger communities have turned over the work of the listers to professional assessors, an action that may be authorized by charter or by special act of the legislature. Listers receive assistance from district advisors appointed by the state. The state also estimates the quality of local grand lists and penalizes communities that fail to achieve listings that are comparable with fair market value.[24] State law governs how appraisals are conducted, but state officials are minimally involved in how the list is prepared, beyond offering a little advice.

Towns may borrow funds for capital expenditures by voting to issue municipal bonds to pay for long-term projects. The limit on debt is ten times the amount of the grand list. Only the voters may approve bonding, even in cities where some of the powers otherwise reserved to voters are assumed by the city council.[25]

Local Expenditures

Each town function—highways, police, sewer and water, and other services—has a budget to which the money raised through taxes, user fees, and borrowing is allocated (see Table

Table 2. Berlin, Vermont: 1997 Expenditures

Highways and bridges	$487,167
General government	455,861
Debt service	103,361
Engineering fees	67,913
Public safety	296,431
Water pollution operations	120,056
Total[a]	$1,555,000

Source: Berlin Town Report (1977), 16.
   a. Includes additional miscellaneous expenditures.

2). Spending decisions are made by the select board or school board. Few other town offices have the authority to expend public funds (the exceptions include the elected board of library trustees). Expenditures are limited to the amount of revenue generated through the property tax and from outside sources, including state aid for highways and other grants.

There is no penalty for deficit spending, but the prospect of facing angry taxpayers at next year's town meeting is sufficiently intimidating to keep budgets under control. If unanticipated expenditures come up during the year, the select board will usually make drastic cuts in other areas of expenditure to avoid a deficit if possible.

Every officer who handles money is audited by elected town auditors annually, in time for a report to be prepared for town meeting. Most towns also hire professional auditors to check the work of the town treasurer and others who collect funds and deposit them into the town's various accounts. School districts are required to use professional auditors at least once every three years.[26]

Fiscal conservatism is a feature of local government in Vermont. Taxpayers have a direct say in what the budget will be, and carefully scrutinize the figures at town meeting to ensure that there is no waste. The occasional surplus is at times more offensive to taxpayers than a deficit, and usually results in the following year's budget being cut back accordingly. To date, no Vermont municipality has been declared bankrupt, although there are some communities with high debt burdens.

State Government Grants-in-Aid to Localities

State government contributes funds to local treasuries annually, principally for highways and schools. The legislature distributes highway funds proportionally, in accordance with the number of road-miles in the town relative to the state as a whole. School aid is now distributed according to a formula that includes resident income, the value of property in the town, and the needs of school districts.[27] Limited state funds are also available to municipalities for training, equipment, and loans. Towns with state facilities such as prisons, highway garages, and office buildings also benefit from state payments in lieu of taxes.

Money from the state always has strings attached. In the case of education funding, for example, the town is required to fund

its schools adequately and to maintain them according to minimum state standards.[28]

Because of these requirements, towns have had to "retire" many of their smaller schools and to centralize others, in order to ensure adequate funding for school libraries, guidance counselors, and teachers' salaries.

As noted earlier, in 1997 the state legislature enacted a dramatic change in the way schools are funded. Under Act 60, towns with large grand lists and relatively low tax rates are required to send revenues to the state for distribution to relatively poorer towns, in order to guarantee each student the same basic educational opportunity. School districts may still negotiate teachers' contracts at the local level and set basic policies on student life, but tax increases and the new redistribution formula represent efforts on the part of the state to ensure educational quality and outcome, regardless of the student's town of residence. The system has its outspoken opponents, many of whom complain that the new formula, along with the continuing pressure of minimum school standards, threatens local control of education.

Local officials have broader authority in the case of state highway money. The funds must be spent on maintenance, but precisely how that will be done is left to the discretion of town officials. Discretion in the design and construction of paved highways and bridges, however—when the state pays 80 to 90 percent of the total cost—is narrower.

Recently, the Vermont Agency of Transportation has become more willing to listen to local officials who are intent on preserving a particular landmark bridge or ensuring that highway improvements will not necessarily result in higher speeds. As a result the Intermodal Surface Transportation Efficiency Act (ISTEA), the regional planning commission—which is made up of members from every community within the region—now establishes priorities for the use of federal highway capital construction funds. This approach helps target funds to projects of regional significance.

Unfunded Mandates

Determining how many unfunded mandates are now imposed on local government depends on where you start counting. From the time state government was formed, the legislature has told local officials—in ever-increasing detail—what to do and how to do it. Fix the roads according to state specifications, make up the grand list and include the details specified by state law, conduct elections according to the code: each of these is essentially an unfunded mandate, but at the time these duties were first imposed there was no state government other than the governor and the legislature. If the state wished to act, it had to do so through the towns.

For their part, the towns have always resisted the idea—put forth by state courts more than once—that they are mere creatures of the legislature, created to perform administrative functions for the state.[29] The towns have too much self-respect and independence to accept the view that a town is nothing more than a local state agency. In their relations with the state, towns are always wary of the cost—in money and energy—of implementing and administering new programs. The loud objections of municipal officials are not lost on legislators, many of whom began their political lives in local office. When some new program needs to be administered, legislators think twice before assigning the responsibility to local government; in fact, in many cases, state government absorbs the impact.

Vermont is not as big in population or fiscal capacity as many counties—or even cities—in other states. With the arrival of good roads and modern communication facilities, the practical impediments to centralization have disappeared. Where something must be done, state government is the first choice among many legislators, in part because they know that the towns will resist the imposition of new responsibilities. While towns may be engines of creativity for solving their own problems, the state is looking elsewhere to find a good and faithful servant to perform its assigned tasks.

This shift is most clearly illustrated by Act 60: by enacting this legislation, the state put itself back in the business of administering the property tax—a job that it abandoned in 1931, when the income tax first was adopted in Vermont. To give local officials a means of learning about the new law—and to ensure compliance—every town is now connected to the state by a computer. (The computers are paid for by the state, and state officials visited town offices to set up the software that will support the connection.) In addition, Act 60 provides local officials with detailed instructions on how to ensure uniformity in tax assessment. Even the residents' traditional power to exempt certain buildings from the property tax (by means of a vote at town meeting) has been removed and given to the legislature.

Although the state does not have the same degree of oversight for any other program, Act 60 is not the only example of the shifting of local authority to the state. Liquor licenses are now issued by the state liquor control agency and the town, but if there is a problem it is the state, not the town, that acts to suspend or revoke the license. Local zoning decisions are appealable to the Vermont Environmental Court, where the hearings are principally *de novo:* that is, the court starts over again, as though nothing had previously occurred.[30] Finally, whether the sagging bridge in the center of town will be repaired this year depends on the availability of state money.

By attempting to protect themselves from unfunded mandates, towns have inadvertently discouraged the state from making laws that respect the ability of local government to function according to professional standards. In seeking to preserve their identities, towns have consigned themselves to a perpetual childhood—a role that is unjustified by the record. Over the years, Vermont towns have generally performed their duty to the law and the state with competence, despite wide diversity in popula-

tions and financial conditions. When a job needs to be done, someone will do it. It's just that the work never seems to end, and many local officials are bone tired from picking up the gauntlet.

Access to Local Government

Local Elections

The authority of Vermont voters extends far beyond the election of officers to represent them at the federal, state, and local levels. Vermonters have the right to adopt local budgets, enact zoning bylaws and other ordinances (or at least, in communities with populations of at least 5,000, to petition to disapprove of these local laws), and petition for a host of changes to the way that local government is run.

Vermont has never enacted statutes or constitutional amendments authorizing initiative or referendum at the state level, but both options are well established for local government. Take the sale of town-owned land, for example. If the select board votes to sell such land, it must give the public special notice; on the date of the board vote, a sixty-day period begins during which 5 percent of the total voting population may petition the select board to put the question to a public vote.[31] The voters' decision to approve or disapprove of the sale of the land is final.

Longevity in local public office is a tradition in Vermont. Many town clerks receive awards for fifty years of continuous service, and a select board member who has served twenty or thirty years is not unusual. Sometimes this is because no one else wants the job, but in many instances the official chooses to stay because the local office helps define his or her role in the community.

State law governs the voting process, from the number of ballots printed to the way in which the results are certified after the counting is done. Elections, whether for petitioned articles or the selection of officials, are run by local officials: the town clerk is the presiding officer, and the local board of civil authority is responsible for maintaining the voter checklist and ensuring that the polls are adequately staffed. Voters may determine the number and location of polling places by petition and vote.[32] Some towns use computer scanning devices to count the ballots, but in most rural towns the hand count is still the rule.

Except during the primary and general elections for federal and state candidates, political parties play virtually no role in Vermont's elections. Local candidates are nominated by petition, and party names do not appear on the ballot.

Citizen Controls over Actions of Local Officials

The Vermont Constitution and state statutes mandate the openness of government at all levels. With the rare exception of an executive session, every meeting is open. Every document touched by the hands of a public official is public and available for copying, with the exception of several categories of records—such as personnel records—whose confidentiality no one would challenge.[33]

At every board meeting, the public must have an opportunity to have its say. No binding decision can be made outside a public meeting, and decisions must be made by open vote and then written into the minutes of the meeting. The minutes must be available within five days of the adjournment of the meeting. Citizens have a right to take the town to court to retrieve a public document that has been refused to them, and the town is required pay their legal expenses for the effort.

These laws are sometimes annoying to local officials, but they are the foundation of Vermonters' relationship with government, particularly at the local level. There is a sense of ownership of the public trust. This is our town; this is our select board; those are our records and our money: every voter, every member of the community has a right to observe and inquire, in order to understand the conduct of public affairs and to ensure the dedication of every public official.

Impeachment and public recall are rare in Vermont at the local level, even though there are notorious examples of officials who should have quit but insisted on remaining in office—despite having been charged with (or convicted of) a felony for taking town money. Officers are allowed to serve out their terms unless they are judged mentally incompetent or move out of town before their years are up. This standard is based on the idea that the job is tough enough: incumbents in most local offices are required to make unpopular decisions, at least occasionally, and should not be punished for what the job requires.

State-Local Relations

The T-shirt slogan says, "Vermont Is What America Used to Be." Whether true or not, Vermonters act that way: resisting change, insisting on local control to the extent that it is feasible, requiring public officials—particularly those whom they can reach and touch—to be accessible and responsive to their needs.

Vermonters also worry a great deal about the direction of things. They worry that as towns grow there is less community, less identity, less definition of what makes their town special. They worry that tradition is passing away too rapidly.

Town government has changed little since it first started in the eighteenth century. Deeds are typewritten now and photocopies are recorded in the latest deed book, but that book is then placed on a shelf next to the volumes with handwritten deeds from the early years of the town. Select boards still meet and conduct the business of the town, and townspeople still break in on meetings to tell off the members of the select board when they do something objectionable. The roads are still plowed, taxes collected, elections held.

There are changes, of course. Smaller percentages of residents involve themselves in town affairs—but then, if every voter on the checklist showed up at the annual meeting, most towns would not have enough chairs to seat everybody. Computers are more common in town offices now. Every town is linked to the state capital, and nothing better illustrates the direction in which Vermont is heading than that simple modem connection.

It would not be easy to prove that towns have more or less autonomy than they did twenty years ago. More laws have been enacted that allow towns the option of choosing between different alternatives—setting the terms of officers, deciding whether to give the constable criminal arrest powers, choosing the date and time of the annual meeting—but there is nevertheless a feeling of loss of local control.

Independence is a way of town life. State government does not appear on any regular basis to tell local officials how to do their jobs, and if it tried it would find itself not very welcome. Listers list, select boards select, clerks clerk, seeing their duty directly in the law rather than having to learn it from some state official. That is the way it has always been and how it is always likely to be. Vermont is too wedded to the idea of localism to accept anything less.

The discussion is far from over. In coming years, it is likely that towns will continue to ask the legislature for more independence—not constitutional home rule, but the ability to make choices and fashion a government to their own liking. It is likely that the legislature will continue to resist, but eventually it may indulge its towns in experiments with special powers. Such actions will be received with unconditional goodwill by Vermont towns.

In a book that includes a chapter on every state in the union, Vermont is likely to seem a little different to the reader. That is intentional. The fear that this state is becoming like everywhere else is pervasive, and the people of Vermont go out of their way to repudiate or reject the style and the pace of life of the city and the suburb, even though Vermont has cities and suburbs of its own, which often look like those everywhere else.

What keeps Vermont unique is its government—annual town meeting, the select board meeting held on alternate Monday nights, the town clerk whose grace and wisdom have come to symbolize the town itself. As long as the town lasts, so will Vermont.

Above all else, Vermont is best known by its traditions—town meeting, a citizen legislature, loyalty to incumbency, small-town life, fiscal conservatism, and social progressivism. History surrounds Vermonters, and they are never allowed to forget how things used to be or how they used to be done. New ideas arrive every day. The global economy dictates what Vermonters do for work. National policies drive the state budget. The snow that falls on Vermont is usually part of a weather pattern originating in Canada and the West, but to many Vermonters it is still a Vermont snowstorm in the Vermont winter. No one ever succeeded in Vermont thinking any differently.

Notes

1. A good general reference on Vermont and its government is Michael Sherman, ed., *Vermont State Government Since 1965* (Burlington: University of Vermont, 1999).

2. Laws of Vermont, no. 60 (1996, Adj. Sess.).

3. See http://www.state.vt.us/health/vs97.

4. See http://www.state.vt.us/vtmap.

5. *Buckley v. Hoff,* 234 F.Supp. 191, 198 (D.Vt.1964), aff'd and modified sub nom. *Parsons v. Buckley,* 379 U.S. 359, 364, 85 S.Ct. 503, 506, 13 L.Ed.2d 352 (1965).

6. *Cabot v. Britt,* 36 Vt. 369 (1863).

7. Vermont Constitution, Chapter 2, sections 72–73.

8. Vermont Statutes Annotated, Title 3, 2202-3102; Vermont Constitution, Chapter 2, sections 13, 18.

9. Ibid., section 43; sections 29, 30, 31; Chapter 2, sections 32–34.

10. Vermont Constitution, Chapter 2, sections 50–51.

11. Ibid., Chapter 1, Article 1.

12. See, generally, Michael Bellisles, *Revolutionary Outlaws: Ethan Allen and the Struggle for Independence on the Early American Frontier* (Charlottesville: University Press of Virginia, 1992).

13. Vermont Constitution, Chapter 2, section 6.

14. Vermont Statutes Annotated, Title 24, 2291.

15. Ibid., Title 19, 1511.

16. Ibid., Title 24, 1231; Title 17, 2650; Title 32, 4872, 2655; Title 24, 4404; Title 17, 2640.

17. Ibid., Title 17, 2645.

18. Ibid., Title 24, 1972.

19. Ibid., Title 19, 790; Title 24, 4350.

20. Ibid., Title 19, 302.

21. Ibid., Title 24, 133.

22. Ibid., Title 10, 6001.

23. *In re WalMart Stores, Inc.,* 709 A.2d 397 (1997).

24. Vermont Statutes Annotated, Title 24, 1521; Title 32, 5405(g).

25. Ibid., Title 24, 1761, 1758.

26. Ibid., 1681, 563.

27. Ibid., Title 19, 306; Title 16, 4002.

28. Ibid., 164.

29. *Burlington v. C. V. Ry. Co.,* 82 Vt. 5, 71 Atl. 826 (1909); *Sargent v. Clark,* 83 Vt. 523, 77 Atl. 337 (1910).

30. Vermont Statutes Annotated, Title 7, 223; Title 24, 4470.

31. Ibid., Title 24, 1061.

32. Ibid., Title 17, 2452–2455; 2502.

33. Ibid., Title 1, 313, 317.

VIRGINIA

Keeok Park

Virginia is a tradition-bound state grappling with changes in state-local relations. In reflection of its conservative political culture, virtually all aspects of state-local relations are dominated by "Dillon's Rule" and the practice of city-county separation. Dillon's Rule, named for Iowa supreme court justice John Dillon, holds that local governments can exercise only those powers that are expressly granted to them by the state.[1] The practice of city-county separation creates a political dichotomy in which cities operate independently of their surrounding counties. Many local government officials, local government associations, and scholars note that these two rules often constrain the discretion of local governments or discourage interlocal cooperation. Despite challenges to the validity of these rules, both Dillon's Rule and the practice of city-county separation will probably continue to dominate state-local relations.

Governmental Setting

Virginia is rich in heritage, with its origin going back to 1609 when Capt. Christopher Newport of the London Company established Jamestown with 114 men. Through the early colonial, revolutionary, civil war, and world war years and beyond, it has been home to so many historical actors, events, and sites that it may be called the greatest museum of the Republic. The marks and traces of Patrick Henry, Thomas Jefferson, and Robert E. Lee and historical sites such as Jamestown and Williamsburg are only a few of the display items in this museum.

However, as is true of other states, history alone cannot describe the nature of Virginia, because it is full of modern structures and activities. Stretching from the Atlantic Ocean to the Blue Ridge Mountains, Virginia contains numerous semiconductor manufacturing plants, sports stadiums, state-of-the-art military installations, and modern cities and suburbs. Partly because of its proximity to the capital of the United States, it also hosts government workers, lobbyists, interns, professional conference attendees, and tourists. Visitors to Virginia are likely to encounter such future-oriented activities as computer shows, air shows, and massive construction works as well as such tradition-bound activities as horse riding, county fair going, tobacco farming, and moonlighting. In essence, Virginia is a state of the past and the future, where traditional and modern life styles exist side by side.

Demographically, Virginia is an urban state. More than 78 percent of its close to 7 million residents (it is the twelfth most populous in the United States) reside in metropolitan areas. In the 1980s Virginia's average annual population growth rate was

about 1.6 percent. In the 1990s its population continued to grow, albeit at a slower rate; the annual growth rate was about 1.1 percent between 1990 and 1999.[2] Population growth in the past two decades or so was greatest in suburban areas, whereas rural and central city areas lost and continue to lose residents. In addition, the population growth was most prominent in the urban and suburban counties in Northern Virginia. One population estimate indicates that more than 50 percent of state residents reside in the three largest metropolitan areas—Northern Virginia, Richmond, and Hampton Roads.[3]

Reflecting its rich heritage and tradition, Virginia politics is still strongly influenced, if not dominated, by rural conservatives. In the General Assembly, representatives from rural areas still control many important committee chairmanships, and important Assembly decisions are frequently negotiated and determined behind the scenes. Conservative religious groups and rural politicians commonly promote political actions based on such principles as "saving unborn children" and "preserving tobacco farms," often generating contentious debates with and election campaigns against their liberal opponents, who are mostly from urban areas. This conservative political culture has been chipping away at the more than one-hundred-year-old Democratic dynasty in the General Assembly, as Virginians increasingly perceive the Republican Party as the new conservative party of the South. The General Assembly election in 1999 manifested the shift in party preferences as the Republican Party gained control of both houses of the Virginia legislature for the first time in history. The conservative culture is also reflected in the outcomes of state and national elections. In 1996, for example, the Republican presidential nominee captured Virginia's electoral votes for the eight straight time.[4] In 1997 Virginians confirmed this conservative trend by electing a Republican governor who promised to cut the local motor vehicle taxes and advocated the rights of unborn children. More recently, Texas governor George W. Bush easily beat a more moderate candidate, Arizona senator John McCain, in the 2000 Republican primary, reflecting, once again, the conservatism of Virginia voters.

Home Rule in Virginia

Historical Development

Local government in the Commonwealth of Virginia began in 1634, when the General Assembly established eight shires to function as rural and administrative arms of the state. Beginning with the city of Williamsburg in 1722, the General Assembly also created many cities and towns to provide services in densely populated areas. When the first constitution was drafted in 1776, Virginians were so preoccupied with independence from Great Britain that they did not even mention, except by implication, local government. However, as they went through five more constitutions, local government became one of the most important components of the basic law of the commonwealth.[5] Although numerous changes were made in the nature and role of local government through the five constitutions, the one thing that remained consistent was the state's iron grip on local government. The constitution of 1971, currently governing and believed to be the most generous in granting discretionary authority to localities, reaffirms this tradition by giving the General Assembly wide latitude to control local government behavior. Local governments can exercise only those powers that are specifically granted to them by the General Assembly.

The Constitution of Virginia establishes four types of local government: city, town, county, and regional.[6] Cities are incorporated municipalities with charters and are completely independent of their surrounding counties. Towns are also incorporated municipalities with charters but remain part of their counties. Counties are administrative arms of the state and provide services to residents in unincorporated areas and incorporated towns. Regional governments are units of general government organized within defined boundaries, as determined by the General Assembly. As of 1999, 40 cities, 190 towns, 95 counties, and 156 special districts served about 7 million Virginia residents. There were no regional governments.

A unique feature of local government in Virginia is the statewide practice of city-county separation. All cities are completely independent from their surrounding counties in terms of territory, population, tax base, and service authority. This feature was developed in an incremental fashion from the state's early days. The earliest hint of city-county separation can be found in a 1645 statute that treated James City (now Jamestown)

and James City County separately in representation in the General Assembly. Whereas each county was represented by four burgesses in the General Assembly, James City and James City County were represented by six (five for James City County and one for James City).[7] This practice of separate representation continued to the next centuries, accompanied by a logic that the service needs of cities and counties were different. City residents were urban, and they desired and were willing to support high levels of municipal services, such as water supply and fire protection, whereas county residents were mostly rural and shunned those services. In part because of this distinction between urban and rural needs, city-county separation was codified after the constitution of 1869 and has since remained a major feature of Virginia local government.[8]

Definition of Home Rule

All local governments in Virginia are the "creatures" of the state, and their powers and actions are constrained accordingly. Unlike most states, which moved toward home rule in the early twentieth century, Virginia still remains legally committed to Dillon's Rule. Local governments can exercise only those powers that are expressly granted to them by the state through the constitution, general laws, special legislative acts, or charters.[9] This strict application of Dillon's Rule is codified neither in the constitution nor in the statutes but is acknowledged by the courts through statutory interpretation and by the customary usage of state and local officials.[10]

Throughout Virginia's history, the state gave local governments the power to experiment and search for new forms of government. In 1908, for example, the city of Staunton was allowed to appoint a city manager, becoming the first city in the United States with a reformed government. After the turn of the century, cities and counties were given the power to create special districts for specific purposes, and in 1971 they were given the power to create regional governments to provide metropolitan-wide services. However, the state has never given local governments the constitutional right to rule themselves. When the current constitution was being adopted in 1971, the constitutional revision commission recommended that cities and counties be allowed to exercise any power or perform any function that is not explicitly denied to them. The General Assembly, however, declined to accept this commission proposal and continues to reject similar constitutional amendment proposals.

Since the constitution does not give home rule to local governments, the phrase "home rule" is found neither in the constitution nor in the state statutes. The closest the Code of Virginia comes to providing discretionary powers to a chartered locality is in the police power section:

A municipal corporation shall have and may exercise all powers it now has or which may hereafter be conferred upon or delegated to it under the Constitution and laws of the Commonwealth and all other powers pertinent to the conduct of the affairs and functions of the municipal government, the exercise of which is not expressly prohibited by the Constitution and the general laws of the Commonwealth, and which are necessary or desirable to secure and promote the general welfare of the inhabitants of the municipality.[11]

Given that Virginia still practices Dillon's Rule, the courts and government officials interpret these police powers as being limited in scope, and the spirit behind the police power section certainly does not extend to other areas, such as land use and taxation.

Structural Features

All cities and towns in Virginia operate with a charter. The charter is a special act of the General Assembly that applies to a particular city or town. It serves as a "little constitution" for the locality involved, setting forth its physical boundaries, form of government, and allowable powers and the limitations on those powers. Although initiated, developed, and adopted at the local level, the charter must pass the General Assembly. Because a charter cannot foresee all the powers that a locality may need to govern effectively as circumstances change, the General Assembly must regularly deal with a large number of charter revisions and other special legislative acts for specific localities. As a result, special legislative acts are widely used by the General Assembly to address specific local needs.[12]

Once a community becomes a city with a charter, it operates independently of the county and can perform all functions listed in its charter. A town, once incorporated, receives a similar municipal charter but remains a subdivision of the county in which it is located. The town therefore receives from the county major public services, such as education, health, and welfare. For these and other services, the town residents must pay taxes to both the county and the town governments. Because they serve as administrative arms of the state and as units of local government, counties generally operate without a charter (therefore referred to as quasi-public corporations) and have more difficulty than municipalities in securing their independence from the state. Although counties may elect to apply for a charter and function as municipalities, they will still be obligated to perform such state functions as welfare and education. As of 1998, only three counties (Chesterfield, Roanoke, and James City) had adopted charters.

Neither the constitution nor the code classifies cities today. However, the code did classify them into first and second classes until 1997, and that tradition continues informally. First-class cities have populations greater than 10,000, and second-class cities have populations between 5,000 and 10,000. Second-class cities share their court clerks, sheriffs, and commonwealth's attorneys with the county in which they are located. In other words, second-class cities share the court system with counties, whereas first-class cities do not.

All cities, counties, and towns are required to meet a few structural conditions. All cities and counties, unless exempted by relevant laws, are required to elect five state constitutional officers: a circuit court clerk, a commissioner of the revenue, a commonwealth's attorney, a sheriff, and a treasurer. These constitutional officers act as both local and state officials, and their salaries are paid by the state. Cities and towns are required to elect a mayor and a council. The council members appoint officers, hold investigative hearings, and appoint professional managers for administration. The mayor supervises employees, exercises general veto powers that can be overridden by a two-thirds vote of the council, and exercises a line-item veto power over appropriation ordinances or resolutions.

The code does not specify any specific forms of government for cities and towns. However, because of the restrictions imposed on the forms of government before 1997, cities and towns have adopted one of the three following forms: the general councilmanic plan, the modified commission plan, and the city or town manager plan. Under the general councilmanic plan, the voters of a city or town elect a mayor to exercise administrative powers and three to eleven council members to exercise legislative powers. Under the modified commission plan, the voters of a city elect council members at large, and the council members exercise the legislative, executive, and administrative powers of the city. Under the city or town manager plan, council members are elected at large to exercise all legislative powers. The council appoints a manager who exercises administrative powers, including the appointment of officers, at the council's pleasure.

The code specifies six different forms of government for counties, four of which are available to all counties.[13] Under the traditional form (known as the commission form in other states), a board of three to eleven supervisors is elected by districts and exercises both legislative and administrative powers. Alternatives to the traditional form are the county board, the county executive, the county manager, the county manager for Arlington County, and the urban county executive. Under the county board form, a chief administrator without appointment powers is employed by the board to facilitate county administration. Under the county executive, county manager, and county manager for Arlington County forms, an executive or manager with appointment powers is employed by the county board. Under the urban county executive form, an executive is elected at large to act as the chief administrator.[14]

The state laws concerning incorporation and annexation are numerous and detailed. To be incorporated as a town, a community must have at least 1,000 inhabitants; to be incorporated as a city, it must have at least 5,000 inhabitants. Any incorporation plan must be approved by a majority of the qualified voters in the area and also by the General Assembly in the case of cities and by the circuit court in the case of towns.[15] In practice, incorporation of cities or towns is a rare phenomenon. Most counties vehemently oppose any attempt by a community to become a city because its residents will stop paying taxes to them after successful incorporation.[16] Town incorporation is somewhat easier because the incorporated community still remains part of the county in which it is located. After town incorporation, the residents of the community pay personal property, utility, and motor vehicle license taxes only to the town, but they continue to pay other taxes, including property taxes and sales taxes, to the county.

Because of the practice of city-county separation, annexation is as controversial as incorporation, if not more so. If part of a county is annexed to a town, the county shares the population, territory, and tax base of the annexed area with the town. If part of a county is annexed to a city, however, the county loses this territory, population, and tax base to the city at once and, most likely, forever. Because of the contentious nature of annexation, state laws governing it are numerous and complex.[17] Annexation can be initiated by a city or a town council, by 51 percent of the qualified voters of the area that is proposed to be annexed, or by 51 percent of the real estate owners, in number and in land area, of the proposed area. The initiator must first notify the Commission on Local Government of its intention to annex. The commission then holds a hearing, researches the case, and makes its nonbinding recommendation as to whether or not the annexation should take place. After the petition is filed, a special three-person annexation court is formed to decide the case. The court considers a variety of factors, including the service needs of the area proposed to be annexed; the municipality's need of land for development; and the county's ability to provide services to the people remaining in the county.

The General Assembly has devised various methods of moderating the contentious process of annexation.[18] The annexation court can reduce or enlarge the area under petition, require the city to assume a portion of existing county debt, require the city to pay the county for the value of public improvements made to the annexed area before the annexation, and require the city to pay the county for lost net revenues for a five-year period after the annexation. Regardless of whether a city or town accepts the annexation decision of the court, it cannot file a new annexation petition until ten years have elapsed since the effective date of the annexation or the date of the final order denying the annexation. The General Assembly also grants to urban counties with high population densities a full or partial immunity from city-initiated annexation and frequently imposes a moratorium on city-initiated annexation.[19]

Cities and towns (but not counties) in Virginia may seek to exercise their powers outside their boundaries, subject to the zoning regulations of the locality in which the power is sought to be exercised. In addition, they may purchase and own pieces of land outside their jurisdiction for specific purposes, such as

solid waste disposal and housing of prison inmates. However, most of the facilities outside their jurisdictions are owned and operated by special districts that are formed jointly with other jurisdictions.

Functions of Local Government

Functional Responsibilities

Adherence to Dillon's Rule does not mean that local governments lack significant functional authority. Because of city-county separation, both cities and counties are responsible for providing education, health, and welfare services to their residents. They may also perform a variety of other functions, including zoning, public safety, community and economic development, parks and recreation, and housing.[20] A 1981 study of local discretionary authority by the U.S. Advisory Commission on Intergovernmental Relations (ACIR) reported that only seven states grant their localities more discretion than Virginia. The only major differences between the city and county service functions are that all cities build and maintain their roads, most cities operate public utilities, and many cities provide additional urban services such as solid waste disposal, whereas all counties rely on the state for road building and maintenance, most counties do not operate public utilities, and some counties provide rural services, such as irrigation and land preservation.[21]

Cities and counties can also create single or multijurisdictional special districts, such as park, water and sewer, and hospital authorities.[22] However, the types of special districts that are allowed and their functions and responsibilities are limited by state statutes. As a result, Virginia has only 156 special districts, which is fewer than most other states in absolute terms and relative to state population.

Administrative Discretion

Virginia has not delegated any significant discretion to local governments on personnel matters. State personnel laws are numerous and cover a broad range of local employment practices.[23] Local governments must follow state minimum wage requirements, establish a grievance procedure to afford an immediate and fair method for resolving employee-employer disputes, provide equal pay irrespective of the sex of their employees, and compensate employees with disabilities for the loss of their opportunity to work. They are prohibited from recognizing any labor organization as the sole bargaining agent of a group of employees and from negotiating any collective bargaining agreement with any labor organization. No state law requires local governments to have affirmative action plans and residency requirements for public employees.

State law allows local governments to issue ordinances to exercise their powers, but it also imposes numerous limitations on the kinds of ordinances that can be passed and the procedures that must be followed in passing them.[24] For example, in order to pass any ordinance imposing taxes or authorizing the borrowing of money, the locality must publish descriptive notice of its intention to propose the ordinance and must record an affirmative vote of the majority of the entire governing body. State law also allows local governments to issue resolutions to deal with administrative matters. Resolutions are not required to meet any strict standards as to their form, but they should be clear enough to establish the intent of the governing body. Other requirements on administrative procedures include those on the frequency of council meetings, quorum and the method of voting, and conflicts of interest.

All purchasing and procurement by local governments must be in accordance with the provisions of state public procurement law unless alternative policies and procedures are adopted.[25] Competitive bidding or competitive negotiation is required in the procurement of goods, services, insurance, or construction unless exempt by law. Contractors must not discriminate in employment because of race, religion, color, sex, or national origin except where religion, sex, or national origin is a bona fide occupational qualification reasonably necessary to the normal operation of the contractor. In addition, conflict of interest laws require members of local governing bodies to refrain from contracting for business with their local governments and to abstain from voting on items of personal interest.

Zoning is one of the services that local governments are permitted to perform at their option. Most local governments that adopt a zoning ordinance divide their land area into residential, business, manufacturing, conservation, and (in the case of counties) agricultural zones. They also use such techniques as rezoning, variances, and special-use permits to overcome the inflexibility of their zoning ordinances. All jurisdictions that engage in zoning are required to appoint a planning commission, issue a subdivision ordinance, and prepare a comprehensive plan to manage and control community planning and development activities.

Economic Development

Cities, towns, and counties have the legal authority to conduct various economic and community development activities.[26] They can acquire, lease, or sell land for development of business and industry, regulate sewage disposal and water service, manage development in historic areas, prepare capital improvement programs, and issue bonds to finance these developmental activities. With the approval of the General Assembly, they can also create community development authorities to improve infrastructure, adopt "main street" programs to revitalize downtown areas, form nonprofit industrial development authorities to promote industry, and establish enterprise zones to renew urban economies. These special entities or programs do not usually come with the power to impose a property tax or the power of eminent domain, but they are widely used by local governments to promote development of the local economy. Local governments, directly or through these entities, may provide low-interest loans to private businesses, give a partial exemption from real estate taxes to selected types of business, and issue industrial development revenue bonds for nonprofit corporations.

Fiscal Autonomy of Local Governments

Local Revenues

State laws grant local governments various taxing powers.[27] Cities and counties are allowed to impose real property taxes on land and building structures; personal property taxes on motor vehicles and household goods; local sales taxes on merchandise sold; business, professional, and occupational license (BPOL) taxes; consumer utility taxes on the use of telephone, water, or power services; restaurant meals taxes; transient occupancy taxes on lodging in hotels, motels, and campgrounds; tobacco taxes on cigarettes; severance taxes on the extraction of coal, oil, and natural gas; admissions taxes on tickets to sporting events; local income taxes; and other taxes, including those on bank stocks and franchise licenses. In addition, they can impose a variety of service, permit, and license charges. Property taxes are the largest source of local revenue for most cities and counties (see Table 1).

These taxing powers come with restrictions. State statutes set maximum rates on local sales, local income, BPOL, motor vehicle license, and other taxes. Efforts by local governments to increase the rates of these taxes have been largely unsuccessful. The local sales tax rate, for example, has been capped at 1 percent since it was enacted in 1966, despite numerous attempts by

Table 1. Revenue Sources of Virginia Cities and Counties, 1996–1997

Source of revenue	Cities	Counties
Local revenues		
Property taxes	32.96%	42.74%
Sales taxes	5.07	4.33
Other taxes	12.79	7.39
Service charges	5.84	5.84
Other	4.28	4.38
Total, local revenues	60.94	64.68
State aid	31.98	29.70
Federal aid	7.08	5.62
Total	100.00%	100.00%

Source: Percentages calculated by the author from numbers obtained from Virginia Auditor of Public Accounts, *Comparative Report of Local Government Revenues and Expenditures: Year Ended June 30, 1997* (Richmond: Commonwealth of Virginia, 1998), Exhibits A, B, C, E, and F.

Note: Total expenditures do not include debt service and transfers to other local governments.

localities to increase it. Restrictions on property taxes are relatively minor. There are no caps on real and property tax rates, and the rates can be increased by simple ordinances. Real property, however, must be assessed at least every two years in cities, and at least every six years in counties, at 100 percent of the fair market value. The assessment of real property is done by city or county assessors, and the equalization of assessment is done by the equalization board appointed by the circuit court. Restrictions on local income tax are more severe. This tax, authorized only for Northern Virginia cities and counties, is capped at 1 percent, must be approved in a local referendum, must be used only for transportation needs, and automatically expires five years after enactment.

The amount of state control over borrowing by local government is onerous.[28] Local governments are authorized to incur debts only for specific purposes outlined by the General Assembly. Resolutions authorizing the borrowing of money must be passed by a recorded affirmative vote of a majority of all members of the local governing body, and a public hearing must be held prior to adopting any resolution authorizing the issuance of bonds. The issuance of short-term revenue anticipation notes and revenue bonds does not require a referendum. The issuance of long-term general obligation bonds is more difficult. Although counties are not limited in the amount of general obligation debt that they can incur, their debt proposals must be supported by a majority of the qualified county voters. Cities do not have to hold a referendum but may not incur debt in excess of 10 percent of the assessed value of real estate subject to taxation in the city.[29] The code also establishes a maximum bond life of forty years from the date of issue and prohibits any additional referendum on a bond proposal within one year of its defeat.

Local Expenditures

Given that cities and counties perform similar functions, city and county expenditure categories are similar. Since all school boards are their subordinate agencies, most cities and counties spend a large portion of their budget on public education. Other major expenditure categories for both cities and counties include public safety, public works, health and welfare, parks and recreation, general administration, and debt service. Most cities tend to incur higher public works costs than counties because cities have to maintain their roads (the state maintains major county roads) and many of them operate public utilities. The expenditure data for cities and counties presented in Table 2 reflect this difference and other differences between cities and counties.

Some expenditures are required by the state. For example, cities and counties are required to pay a portion of the salaries of their constitutional officers, such as treasurer and commissioner of the revenue, make timely debt payments, and share the costs of certain state-mandated programs such as social services, building-code enforcement, and public health. There are no ex-

Table 1. Expenditures of Virginia Cities and Counties, 1996–1997

Expenditure	Cities	Counties
Education	48.66%	60.03%
Public safety	17.07	11.79
Health and welfare	11.30	10.86
Public works	9.64	5.32
Administration	4.42	4.21
Parks and recreation	4.22	3.30
Other	4.69	4.49
Total	100.00%	100.00%

Source: Percentages calculated by the author from numbers obtained from Virginia Auditor of Public Accounts, *Comparative Report of Local Government Revenues and Expenditures: Year Ended June 30, 1997* (Richmond: Commonwealth of Virginia, 1998), Exhibits A, B, C, E, and F.
   Note: Total expenditures do not include debt service and transfers to other local governments.

penditure limits or provisions for a balanced budget, bankruptcy, or receivership.

The state imposes a considerable amount of control over other local financial matters.[30] State laws require that all local governments follow the statewide uniform accounting procedures; utilize a uniform fiscal year, from July 1 through June 30, for their mandatory operating budget; and show previous and proposed expenditures for each item in the budget (essentially line-item budgeting). State laws also require that local governments hold at least one hearing before adopting the budget, arrange for a post–fiscal-year audit by an independent public accountant, and file an annual statement of receipts and disbursements with the state auditor of public sccounts.

State Government Grants-in-Aid to Localities

As aid from the federal government continues to decline, the importance of state aid grows. State aid already makes up, on average, about 30 percent of total local revenues. Each year the state dispenses close to 30 percent of its revenues as financial aid to local governments. Categorical and competitive grants are given to localities for specific uses (for example, public education and public assistance), revenue sharing funds (such as lottery profits and Alcohol, Beverage, and Control profits) are given to localities, and capital assistance is provided to a selected number of localities to help meet their capital costs. Since most of the state aid is given in the form of categorical grants, local governments do not have much discretion over the administration and spending of the money. In allocating revenue sharing funds, the state relies on formulas that do not consider need. In the 1996–1997 fiscal year, the state dispensed $1.754 billion of intergovernmental aid to local governments. Of this amount, 53 percent was for public education, 17 percent for revenue sharing, 12 percent for social services, 8 percent for criminal justice, 5 percent for transportation, and 5 percent for other uses.[31]

Unfunded Mandates

Local governments are subject to a variety of state mandates. They must provide child and mental health services, enforce the Uniform Statewide Building Code, process state income tax returns and forward them to the Department of Taxation, and, if sponsoring airports, secure a license or permit from the state's Department of Aviation, among other things. These state mandates take one of three forms: compulsory orders, conditions of financial aid, and regulation of optional activities. Compulsory orders are requirements with which localities must comply, regardless of financial aid. Conditions of financial aid are requirements that arise as a condition of receiving financial aid. Regulation of optional activities includes activities that are not mandated but are subject to state regulations if performed.

When the Joint Legislative Audit and Review Commission compiled data on all types of mandates in 1993, it identified 220 compulsory, 90 condition of aid, and 81 regulation of optional activity mandates in the areas of health and human services, education, public works, administration, public safety, and others. Among these, 290 were state mandates, 56 were joint federal and state mandates, and 45 were federal mandates. By 1999 the number of mandates had increased to 519: 274 compulsory order, 136 condition of financial aid, and 109 regulation of optional activity mandates.[32]

Access to Local Government

Local Elections

State laws regulate local elections in detail. Election regulations cover such matters as uniform election dates in all cities, towns, and counties; registration requirements of voters; voter qualifications; nonpartisan nature of nominations; and the allowance of absentee voting. In addition, all candidates, except those who run for office in towns of fewer than 2,500 people, are required to reveal all receipts and disbursements that occur during their campaign processes in a financial disclosure report filed with the State Board of Election.

Citizen Controls over Actions of Local Officials

Initiatives and referendums on local ordinances or resolutions are not authorized (however, referendums are used for other purposes, including bond issuance, charter revision, and city-county consolidation). Recall elections are also not authorized, but elected officials may be removed from office by a judicial procedure. Local voters may file a petition with the circuit court for removal of any locally elected officer or officer appointed to fill an elective office. The petition must be signed by at least 10 percent of the qualified voters of the local jurisdiction in which the official is elected. Upon receiving the petition, the circuit court may remove the official for neglect of duty, misuse of office, or incompetence in the performance of duties; upon conviction for limited types of misdemeanors; or upon conviction for the manufacture, sale, gift, distribution, or possession, with intent to distribute, of an illegal substance. All public meetings must be conducted openly. All minutes must be recorded, and the books, records, and accounts of cities and counties must be open to the examination of all persons without charge.

State-Local Relations

Dillon's Rule and the practice of city-county separation affect almost every aspect of state-local relations in Virginia. Because of these two long-held rules, local governments in Virginia cannot exercise any powers that are not in their charter or not given to them through special legislative acts. Dillon's Rule restricts the autonomy of local governments, and the practice of city-county separation hinders intergovernmental cooperation between cities and counties. Therefore, both cities and counties would prefer to do away with Dillon's Rule, and many cities would prefer to end the practice of city-county separation.

The adherence to Dillon's Rule has its merits, however. The state can engender order and certainty in the local service functions, maintain uniform policies throughout the state, and check excessive local discretionary authority. Moreover, the abolition of Dillon's Rule would not be the panacea to many problems of state-local relations. Given that local governments perform a wide range of functions already, abolishing Dillon's Rule might not increase the degree of local autonomy dramatically. It may not solve the fiscal problems of many urban cities and counties that seek greater taxing authority to address their specific needs. The number of state mandates would continue to increase even in the absence of Dillon's Rule. However, abolition advocates claim that it could at least relieve the burden on local governments to get General Assembly approval for numerous trivial matters, such as changing city council meeting dates. In the current system, the only way for local governments to obtain the additional powers they need to meet changing local needs is either to obtain a special legislative act that is written specifically for them or to have their charter change approved. Therefore, it is not surprising that many city and county officials, the Virginia Municipal League, and the Virginia Association of Counties endorse the abolition of Dillon's Rule and the establishment of home rule.

City-county separation is more harmful to cities than to counties because cities are financially disadvantaged under the current structure. As a result of higher numbers of elderly and poverty-stricken people within their population, cities must collect more taxes per capita than counties to support their dependent populations. In contrast to counties, cities receive less state aid per capita primarily because they have to construct and maintain their own roads, whereas roads in the counties are built and maintained by the state. Because of the city-county separation, cities cannot access the resources of their surrounding counties, which are often richer and have smaller dependent populations. Territorial growth is very difficult for cities because of the opposition their annexation attempts would face from counties.[33] Cities that cannot grow through annexation deteriorate much faster than cities that can.[34]

Dillon's Rule and city-county separation have been in existence for more than a century. Many scholars, local government officials, and state legislators challenge the applicability of these doctrines to local governments that are entering the twenty-first century. In fact, proposing various constitutional and legislative changes to reverse these rules has become a perennial ritual in the General Assembly. For example, a group of twenty-four high-growth communities from the Northern Virginia, Tidewater, and Blue Ridge areas petitioned the General Assembly to grant them the power to control development by limiting home construction and by charging fees to finance the infrastructure needed by growing populations. The bills that reflect their home rule wishes regarding growth control were rejected by house and senate committees in February 2000. Part of the reason for their defeat is that the General Assembly is dominated by rural interests, and Northern Virginia, where local governments seek greater discretionary authority, is under-represented in many important committees in the General Assembly. Unless the balance of power in state politics shifts dramatically, local governments in Virginia are likely to continue to operate under the two rules that were devised more than a century ago.

Notes

1. See John Dillon, *A Treatise on the Law of Municipal Corporations*, 5th ed. (Boston: J. Cockroft, 1911).

2. Julia H. Martin and Donna J. Tolson, "1999 Virginia Population Estimates," *Spotlight on Virginia* 4 (January 2000), 1–8.

3. Julia H. Martin and Donna J. Tolson, "Virginia's Population: Changing Patterns of Growth," *University of Virginia News Letter* 72 (May–June 1996), 1–8.

4. Larry J. Sabato, "The 1996 Presidential Election and Congressional Contests in Virginia: A Status Quo Election with Spice," *University of Virginia News Letter* 73 (February 1997), 1–8.

5. Virginians revised their constitution in 1830, 1851, 1869, 1902, and 1971 by constitutional conventions. They made numerous amendments between these revisions, and, since 1971, they have amended the constitution almost every year.

6. Commonwealth of Virginia, Constitution of Virginia, effective July 1, 1971, with amendments to January 1, 2000 (Richmond: Office of the Clerk of the House of Delegates, 2000), Article VII, section 1.

7. The 1776 constitution also gave Williamsburg and Norfolk representation in the House of Delegates apart from their counties, even though their colonial charters did not indicate any intention of conferring on them a position of independence from their surrounding counties. For more on the early history of Virginia local governments in general and city-county separation in particular, see Jack D. Edwards, *Neighbors and Sometimes Friends: Municipal Annexation in Modern Virginia* (Charlottesville: Center for Public Service, 1992), and Chester W. Bain, *A Body Incorporate* (Charlottesville: University Press of Virginia, 1967).

8. However, the state constitution did not officially recognize city-county separation until 1971.

9. A simple example can illustrate the constraining effects of Dillon's Rule on a local government. In 1990 the city council of Charlottesville considered passing an ordinance to ban the use of Styrofoam food packaging within the city territory because the production, consumption, and disposal of Styrofoam were believed to be hazardous to human health and because nondegradable plastic products were inundating the city's landfill. By then, similar bans had been enacted by several cities outside of Virginia, including Newark, New Jersey (1989), and Berkeley, California (1990), on the use of plastic grocery bags. The Charlottesville city council decided not to pass any prohibition ordinance, however, because neither the city charter nor the Code of Virginia provided the power to ban Styrofoam products. See Avi S. Garbow, *Policy Analysis of Proposal to Ban Styrofoam Food Packaging in the City of Charlottesville* (Charlottesville: Unpublished manuscript, 1990), 1–11.

10. Robert M. De Voursney, "Powers and Responsibilities of Municipal Government." In *Handbook of Virginia Mayors and Council Members,* ed. Sandra H. Wiley and Mary Jo Fields (Charlottesville: Center for Public Service, 1993), 11–19. An example of a court case where Dillon's Rule was applied is *County Board of Arlington v. Brown* (1985). In that case, the Virginia Supreme Court ruled that the county did not have the authority to lease some county-owned land to a developer. The decision of the court was based on the statute that lists the means to dispose of property by a county; leasing is not among the means listed.

11. Virginia Code Commission, Code of Virginia (Richmond: Commonwealth of Virginia, 2000), 15.2-1102.

12. The constitution gives the General Assembly broad power to use special, as well as general, legislation in providing for city and county organization, government, and powers, except for twenty different items, including assessing and collecting taxes, exempting property from taxation, and changing or locating county seats.

13. Virginia Code, 15.2-300–15.2-858.

14. Of the ninety-four cities and towns with a population of more than 2,500, only thirteen operate under the mayor-council form (known in Virginia as the general councilmanic form). This trend toward alternative forms of municipal government is not paralleled by counties; eighty-five of ninety-five counties operate under the traditional form.

15. Virginia Code, 15.2-3600–15.2-3605.

16. The sensitivity of counties toward the incorporation issue is widely known in Virginia. When the Disney company was considering building a historical theme park in Prince William County, county officials asked the company to forever renounce its right to incorporate the future theme park area into a municipality or to promise not to secede from the county in order to join an independent city. With expenditures for roads and other infrastructure improvements for the theme park projected to reach more than $100 million, county officials did not want to lose the future revenues from the theme park to other jurisdictions. The company rejected the request, and it became one of the most contentious issues facing the two parties. See Spencer S. Hsu, "Five County Planners Threaten to Oppose Park Unless Disney Vows Not to Secede," *Washington Post*, August 28, 1994, B3.

17. Virginia Code, 15.2-3100–15.2-3244.

18. An example of a contentious annexation battle between a county and its cities is the case of Petersburg, Hopewell, and Prince George County. These three jurisdictions engaged in a series of annexation battles between 1985 and 1990. When it was over, more than $6 million had been spent on legal fees alone, yet nothing had been accomplished. See Edwards, *Neighbors and Sometimes Friends*, 140–149.

19. The first statutory moratorium on city-initiated annexation was imposed in 1971 and lasted until 1979. The second moratorium was imposed in 1987 and was expected to last until 2000.

20. Local governments may and do exercise their service authority alone or jointly. One study found that 438 written interlocal service agreements existed between local governments in 1989 (see Paul Fisher and Mary Jo Fields, "Intergovernmental Relations," 56–66). However, about 90 percent of these agreements involved counties and towns, whereas only about 10 percent involved cities. These figures reflect the practice of city-county separation in that cities and counties, without overlapping jurisdictional powers, have few incentives to cooperate.

21. The functions of towns are very different from those of cities and coun-

ties in that they do not provide education and health and welfare services.

22. Virginia Code, 15.2-4300–15.2-6416.

23. Virginia Code, 15.2-1500–15.2-1543.

24. Virginia Code, 15.2-1426–15.2-1433.

25. Virginia Code, 11-35–11-80.

26. Virginia Code, 15.2-1800–15.2-1906.

27. Virginia Code, 58.1-3000–58.1-3993.

28. Virginia Code, 15.2-2607–15.2-2663.

29. The Virginia Constitution, Title VII, Article 10. A county may be treated as a city for the purpose of incurring bonded indebtedness if a majority of the qualified county voters support it in a referendum. Once adopted, the city status is irrevocable and statutory provisions on city borrowing apply.

30. Virginia Code, 15.2-2500–15.2-2513.

31. Virginia Department of Accounts, *State Aid to Localities* (Richmond: Commonwealth of Virginia, 1998), 1–22.

32. Commission on Local Government, *1999 Catalog of State and Federal Mandates on Local Government* (Richmond: Commonwealth of Virginia), Appendix D.

33. Another problem is that city-county separation discourages cooperation between cities and counties. Because the jurisdictional powers of cities and counties do not overlap, competition for economic development is fierce and cooperation in providing services through joint governmental structures, such as special districts, is hampered. In this vein, the town reversion option granted to cities in 1988 and the regional cooperation act, passed in 1995 to give preferential treatment in state aid allocation to projects that benefit more than two jurisdictions, are conducive to cooperation among local governments. For example, after reverting to town status in 1994, South Boston was able to end decades-old territorial and taxing conflicts with its surrounding county.

34. David Rusk, *Cities without Suburbs* (Washington, D.C.: Woodrow Wilson Center Press, 1993), 9–20.

WASHINGTON

Meredith A. Newman and Nicholas P. Lovrich

This essay draws, with permission, from the course work of graduate students enrolled in a seminar in intergovernmental relations at Washington State University, Vancouver, in the spring of 1996. The authors gratefully acknowledge the outstanding work of Don Benton, Kirsten Birkeland, James Bryant, Maureen Chan-Hefflin, Dianna Cruz, Michael Digiustino, John Fromdahl, Sue Groth, Roxanne Jones, Donna Loper, Cassie McVeety, and Lori Reeves, as well as the earlier research assistance of Michael Ditty, Henry Saylor-Scheetz, and Craig Pridemore. The authors would also like to thank Gary Lowe, former executive director, Washington State Association of Counties; Stan Finkelstein, executive director, Association of Washington Cities; and Richard Yukubousky, executive director, Municipal Research and Services Center of Washington, for their invaluable assistance. An earlier version of this paper was delivered at the annual meeting of the Western Political Science Association, San Francisco, California, March 14–16, 1996.

During the past three decades, Washington has moved away from an economic base founded on agriculture and natural resources and toward a more knowledge-based, high-tech economy. This shift has been accompanied by dramatic social and cultural changes, including increasing urbanization. Despite these changes, the frontier tradition that saw the Washington territory to statehood remains a pronounced political undercurrent. Adherents to this tradition—proponents of self-reliance and rugged individualism—often feel threatened by the characteristics of the "new" Washington: a rapidly expanding population, growing ethnic diversity, and a government that must expand to keep pace with public service demands.

The general disaffection of citizens toward government that characterizes contemporary American politics and the significant policy differences between rural and urban residents of Washington make governance options difficult to propose and often generate significant debate in public affairs circles.

As one such option, home rule constitutes a limited and strictly regulated opportunity for municipalities and counties to adopt a charter of their own design. In most circumstances, the permitted changes affect only the structure of local government; fiscal discretion rests firmly with the state.

Governmental Setting

Formerly a relatively sparsely settled area dominated by timber harvesting, farming, and fisheries, the Evergreen State now serves as a primary trade route to the Pacific Rim and is the headquarters for some of the world's largest companies, including Boeing, Weyerhauser, and Microsoft. Dramatic changes in the state's economy occurred less as a result of calculated planning than as the natural consequences of regional economic growth and technological progress. The growth of government in Washington evolved similarly, with only limited planning for the future.

Early municipalities and counties provided the most basic functions of local government—namely, law enforcement and records management—largely in accordance with models common to midwestern states. As the population grew, development of public roadways became a primary concern, and as small municipalities grew into more complex urban settlements, social welfare programs became increasingly important. Eventually, substantial population densities brought the need for large-scale public water and public power networks, sewer systems, and other public services and infrastructure. Most recently, environmental programs and plans to manage urban growth have become central concerns of governance.

The provision of adequate infrastructure and public services, environmental management, and growth management are the central issues facing Washington today, and proposals for governance options must be designed to help address those concerns. With growing public concern about the expanding role of state government, and with the increasing need for state and local government to accomplish more with less (in accord with "reinventing government" efforts), addressing these issues will create a major challenge for Washingtonians in the coming years.

State government in Washington is quite similar in structure to the majority of state governments in the United States: a governor, a bicameral legislature, and an independent judiciary. Other elected officials include the lieutenant governor, secretary of state, treasurer, auditor, attorney general, superintendent of public instruction, commissioner of public lands, and insurance commissioner.

The strong commitment to populist forms of civic engagement that characterizes Washington's "moralistic" political culture is much in evidence at the local government level.[1] A legacy of grassroots activism also figures prominently in local politics in the Evergreen State.

Home Rule in Washington

Historical Development

The provision for home rule status included in Washington's original constitution applied only to first-class municipalities—those with populations of 20,000 or more (at the time of statehood, in 1889, only Seattle and Tacoma were this large).[2] Despite the increase in the number of municipalities that met the population requirement—and despite the fact that, in 1964, Amendment 40 lowered the requirement to 10,000—the home rule option was not widely exercised during the eighty years that followed statehood. There are two likely reasons for this lack of enthusiasm: first, in most municipalities, existing revenues were generally sufficient to meet service demands; second, even municipalities without home rule charters had relatively flexible governance structures available to them. The rather cumbersome legal requirements for securing a home rule charter were a further disincentive.

The desire for home rule grew significantly, however, as local governments came to regard federal and state controls over their activities as unduly restrictive. Municipal home rule initiatives generally floundered, however, until the enactment of the Optional Municipal Code, in 1967, which allowed for substantially increased political independence from state dictates. Under the Optional Municipal Code, the municipalities that chose to become reclassified as "code cities"—also known as "statutory home rule cities"—enjoy virtually all the attributes of home rule with respect to structure (e.g., choice of mayor-council, council-manager, or commission format), but still have strict limitations on their ability to create additional revenue sources.[3] To date, only 10 municipalities have home rule charters, but 165 of Washington's 275 municipalities are code cities.[4]

The state legislature did not grant counties the authority to seek home rule until 1948. Apart from King County (greater Seattle area), whose voters adopted their charter soon after authority was granted, no other counties adopted home rule until 1978. Since then, Clallam (Port Angeles area), Pierce (Tacoma area), Snohomish (Everett area), and Whatcom (Bellingham area) Counties have adopted home rule charters.

Definition of Home Rule

Home rule in Washington is rather loosely defined by state legislation as a uniform system of municipal and county government, separate from the state-specified model for local government entities, whereby limited authority is granted under the state constitution for the adoption of alternative methods of organization, assessment, collection of revenues, and the promotion of business within a municipality or county; this authority is governed by municipal and county charters and the general law of the state.[5] Given this framework, it is fair to say that home rule exists in Washington only in modified form and is strictly subject to constitutional provisions and general law. In most other states in which it is permitted, home rule allows considerable flexibility in governmental structures, business practices, and taxing mechanisms; in Washington, however, the parameters within which local governments can exercise home rule powers are quite limited.

The logical antithesis of home rule is, of course, Dillon's Rule.[6] Under this legal doctrine, to which the state of Washington subscribes, municipal and county corporations, as creatures of the state, have only those powers that are expressly granted to them by the state legislature. While a home rule charter in Washington allows local voters to determine how best to structure their government and gives them the discretion to set their own standards for government functions, these structures and standards must in all cases be consistent with state law and are subject to legislative veto.[7] A 1990 study conducted by the Municipal Research and Services Center of Washington confirmed the relative lack of authority granted to home rule jurisdictions in the state: the study concluded that because constitutional home rule for Washington's first-class and other chartered municipalities was never definitively specified in the state constitution, these jurisdictions are left "subject to total control by the legislature."[8]

Judicial rulings have tended to reinforce the state's preeminence in intergovernmental relationships; in numerous cases, the courts have applied Dillon's Rule to various classes of municipal corporations, including cities, towns, port districts, and—most recently—chartered first-class cities.[9] These several judicial precedents have reflected the view that local governments derive all of their powers and legal rights from the state.

Thus, home rule in Washington constitutes a rather limited and highly regulated opportunity for municipalities and counties to adopt a charter of their own design. In most circumstances, the permitted changes affect only the structure of the government (for example, which officials are elected and which are appointed). The charter may also prescribe the creation of citizens' boards, define officials' specific responsibilities, and describe how those officials are to be elected. In some rare circumstances, additional authority for raising revenues may be granted via a home rule charter, but such changes are strictly limited by state guidelines and require approval by the state legislature and governor, in the form of a state statute.

It is important to note that Washington is one of the few states that lacks an income tax, and the state legislature is, accordingly, highly protective of its taxing authority; to ensure adequate resources for state government, the legislature keeps very tight control over the property tax, sales taxes, excise fees, and revenues from licenses. Consistent with such efforts, the state remains determined to limit, within fairly strict parameters, local fiscal discretion. For their part, Washington's municipalities and counties and their associations—the Washington State Association of Counties, the Washington Association of County Officers, and the Association of Washington Cities—are engaged in a constant battle to expand their range of revenue sources.

Structural Features

Washington relies on the "general and uniform" laws of the state and on the judicial interpretation of those laws to control the authority and operation of local governments. Constitutionally, the intent of the state legislature must govern all official governmental actions, and conflicting charter provisions and locally enacted ordinances must yield to that intent. In effect, a local government charter is not only the operative law of a municipality or county; it is also a law of the state of Washington.

Municipalities are assigned one of four classifications on the basis of population. First-class municipalities are incorporated jurisdictions with populations above 20,000. Second-class municipalities are incorporated jurisdictions whose populations are between 10,000 and 20,000. Third-class municipalities are those whose populations are greater than 1,500 but less than 20,000. (Because no municipalities in the second-class population range currently exist, the population range for the third-class category currently encompasses that of the second-class category.) Incorporated settlements whose populations are between 300 and 1,500 are classified as fourth-class municipalities. Fourth-class municipalities are alternatively referred to as towns, and all other municipalities are called cities.[10]

According to state law, any municipality with a population of more than 10,000 may frame a charter for its own government. As a first step, the legislative authority of the municipality must provide the electorate with the names of at least fifteen candidates—all of whom must have resided within the jurisdiction for at least two years—to be constituted as a charter commission to frame a charter. Within forty days of election, the charter commission must make a charter available for public view for a peri-

od of four weeks. Once the charter is adopted by majority vote, it is authenticated and must be placed into law by official proclamation of the mayor.[11]

Municipal charters generally bring fewer dramatic structural changes than do county charters. Whether a municipality is a home rule or code city, its citizens have only three options for structuring their government: mayor-council, council-manager, and mayor-commission. Municipalities that are neither home rule jurisdictions nor code cities must operate under the mayor-council form.

Under the mayor-council form, which has been adopted by 227 of Washington's 275 cities, an elected mayor exercises executive power, and independently elected council members exercise legislative authority.[12] Council members are generally elected from geographic districts within the municipality, although at-large elections are allowed and are commonplace. In larger cities, both the mayor and council members generally serve full-time, and the mayor often exercises considerable executive authority. In smaller jurisdictions, the posts tend to be part-time, and the mayor's scope of authority is generally narrower.[13]

Under the council-manager form, an elected council appoints a manager who is responsible for day-to-day operations and who serves at the direction of the council. There may be an elected mayor, but his or her powers are generally no greater than those of other council members.[14] Forty-five Washington cities use the council-manager form of government.

Under the mayor-commission form, currently the least popular form of government in Washington, the mayor and commission members are elected at large, and each commission member focuses on a specific functional area; one commissioner may be responsible for public works, for example, while another may be responsible for law enforcement and criminal justice. Like the mayor-council form, the mayor-commission form is a "weak" mayor system. In jurisdictions that have implemented this form of government, the structure has generally given rise to competition between the mayor and the commissioners responsible for various functional areas, leading voters to reject the mayor-commission form in favor of another model.[15] As of 2000, only three Washington code cities operated under this structure.

Washington counties are recognized as legal subdivisions of the state.[16] Both executive and legislative authority in county government are predominantly under the control of a three-member elected commission; each commissioner represents a particular district, but all three commissioners are elected countywide.

Under a home rule charter, voters can significantly alter the traditional form of county government. With the exception of the prosecuting attorney and district and superior court judges, voters may eliminate all the prescribed elected officials and create a governmental structure of their own choosing. County home rule has a much briefer history than municipal home rule and, to date, has been adopted by only five of the state's thirty-nine counties. These five, however, have implemented a range of governmental structures: King County, for example, operates under a mayor-council form, whereas Clallam County's model closely resembles the state-mandated form that is used by non–home rule counties. While there are several fundamental differences between charter (home rule) counties and those operating under the traditional structure, the one area where there is little, if any, difference is fiscal policy.

One option available under a home rule charter that has never been adopted by any county is consolidation with constituent cities or special districts. Voters in Clark County and the city of Vancouver (1982), Thurston County and the city of Olympia (1990), and Spokane County and the city of Spokane (1995) have all considered and rejected such consolidations. In Thurston and Spokane Counties, boards of "freeholders" (the term applied to citizens serving on county charter commissions) were elected, but their charter proposals were rejected; in Clark County, the effort to promote the election of freeholders to draft a charter was unsuccessful, and when the county commission placed a proposition on the ballot that would have created a board of freeholders, voters rejected it.

The rules in Washington governing local jurisdiction are quite similar to those in other states. Policies on municipal annexations, incorporations, and boundary determinations are structured primarily to protect the interests of existing county governments. Each county maintains an independent boundary review board that is empowered to consider proposals for incorporation; the board's chief consideration is the county government's ability to maintain countywide services with the remaining tax base.

Under the state's annexation policies, municipalities may annex territory by several means: they may (1) extend utility services to an area on condition of voter support for future annexation, (2) gain the agreement of a majority of property holders in the area proposed for annexation, or (3) gain approval for annexation through a public vote within the annexing jurisdiction. Since passage of the Growth Management Act (GMA), in 1990, municipal and county governments in areas that are experiencing substantial growth (or that wish to plan under GMA rules) are required to agree to urban growth boundaries (UGBs). Once these boundaries have been designated, it is relatively easy for municipalities to annex territory within the UGB.

The legislature has, on numerous occasions—usually associated with watershed management and the provision of utilities—allowed municipalities or counties extraterritorial jurisdiction. Washington municipalities and counties are allowed to own facilities (for example, water wells, radio towers) outside of their corporate limits, but only where statutory law permits such ownership in connection with an approved municipal or county government activity.

While the state constitution formally forbids special-privilege legislation for local governments, the legislature has frequently enacted statutes that apply only to a single county or municipal government. The language typically refers, for example, to "all counties of a particular size and containing a particular feature," but the legislature knows full well that only one county or municipality fits the description.

Functions of Local Government

Functional Responsibilities

Perhaps the most problematic aspect of local government in Washington is the overlap in services provided by municipalities and counties. Both types of jurisdiction, for example, may provide services in the following categories: fire, water, sewer, solid waste, libraries, parks and recreation, public transit, roads, land use, public health, economic development, law enforcement, and social welfare. In more rural areas, the county government tends to predominate in a wide range of service areas, but as the level of urbanization increases, so does the likelihood that services will be delivered by both county and municipal government. In 1967, to promote greater interjurisdictional cooperation under such circumstances, the state legislature passed the Interlocal Cooperation Act, a statute authorizing cities, counties, towns, and some special districts to contract with one another to provide services jointly (through consolidation and shared funding) or to provide them individually on a regional basis.[17] This statute was amended in 1979 to include all forms and entities of local government.

The tradition of local governance in Washington is somewhat unusual in one important respect: the range and number of special districts.[18] The widespread use of special districts reflects the importance of public policy making at the local level in the state. In fact, according to a report by the Washington Local Governance Study Commission, "Washington is not only eighth in the country in total number of special purpose districts, . . . but competes for first place in the number of such districts per capita."[19]

Administrative Discretion

Washington local governments have the power to devise their own administrative rules and regulations as long as they do not contradict those contained in the constitution, the Washington Administrative Code, or the Revised Code of Washington. Local governments are authorized to carry out all personnel management activities, such as hiring, training, making appointments, assigning transfers, and setting policies on sick leave and probationary periods.[20] In the areas of law enforcement, corrections, and fire protection, the state requires academy certification of personnel who are awarded long-term appointments in salaried municipal or county positions. All counties are required to maintain a civil service commission to oversee the hiring of staff for the sheriff's department.

Local governments may freely choose health insurance carriers and approved day care facilities, and they may designate other specific types of employee benefits.[21] Of course, local governments fall under federal and state employment laws pertaining to equal employment opportunity, workers' compensation, workplace safety, family leave, collective bargaining, and veterans' preference, and they must also comply with the requirements of the Americans with Disabilities Act. Washington is known as a strong union state, in good part because the state's civil service law was enacted through a citizen initiative process orchestrated by organized labor. Given this unique history, the fundamental structure of labor law in Washington is highly protective of employees generally, and of public employees in particular. Most employees in municipal and county government are represented by unions and enjoy strong collective bargaining rights.

Washington's local governments have only modest discretion in the areas of bidding, contracting, and purchasing; their fiscal and legal procedures have to comply with the guidelines prescribed in the Budgeting, Accounting, and Reporting System (BARS) maintained by the state auditor. Moreover, every contract (even a minor one) in which a municipality or county is a party must be officially ratified by council or board action. Washington has one of the nation's most demanding public meetings laws and also maintains strict requirements for campaign finance reporting. As a consequence, all municipal and county business is conducted in a "fishbowl."

In the late 1980s, the rapid growth of the Puget Sound area and the Interstate 5 corridor (which runs from the Oregon border to the Canadian border and goes through Tacoma and Seattle) propelled urban growth planning to the political forefront. With passage of the Growth Management Act, in 1990, the state moved aggressively into policy areas that had previously been primarily under local government control. Under the GMA, all counties experiencing rapid growth (originally, thirteen western Washington counties) are required to work with their municipalities to develop and agree upon a single comprehensive plan delineating how growth will be accommodated for the next twenty years. Such plans must provide for the protection of environmentally sensitive areas, wildlife habitat, and farmland; make provision for low- and moderate-cost housing; and limit concentrated urban service infrastructures to areas within designated urban growth boundaries. Counties beyond the original thirteen that elect to operate under the GMA are entitled to state support for their planning efforts. Where municipalities and counties are unable to agree on a comprehensive plan or fail to adopt the requisite zoning ordinances, state regional hearing boards have the authority to hear and mediate disputes and to order compliance if mediation fails.

Economic Development

Over four decades ago the state legislature began to involve local governments directly in preserving, if not promoting, the economic climate of Washington's cities. Under provisions of the Urban Renewal Law—enacted in 1957 and revised in 1965—municipalities were authorized to develop specific plans for the renovation of the built environment, which would entitle the local jurisdiction to some urban renewal funds available from the state. Subsequent legislation enacted in 1977 permitted local governments to establish foreign trade zones to support local economic development efforts. The early 1980s saw the passage of two major pieces of economic development legislation: the Industrial Development Revenue Bonds Act (1981) and the Community Redevelopment Financing Act (1982).[22] Under these two pieces of legislation, local governments, working in conjunction with the state, had the authority to provide limited state financing for efforts to attract private industry and support other forms of local economic development.

Nevertheless, until 1985, local governments' authority to engage directly in economic development was limited to a narrow range of activities undertaken in the major metropolitan areas in the Puget Sound region. In 1985, however, the state legislature made a dramatic shift away from its historical reluctance to grant local governments economic development authority independent of state-directed priorities. Of the several bills passed concerning local government involvement in economic development, the most significant was also the simplest and shortest: "It shall be in the public purpose for all cities to engage in economic development programs. In addition, cities may contract with nonprofit corporations in furtherance of this and other acts relating to economic development." Such authority was also extended to counties and port districts. More recent legislation, which allows local governments to partner with private sector entities, has further expanded local government's role in economic development.[23]

Fiscal Autonomy of Local Governments

Local Revenues

The state's fiscal practices underscore the limited and limiting nature of financial discretion available at the local government level. Local governments' authority to raise revenue is vested with the state. Taxing authority must be granted expressly to local governments by the state, either in statute or in the state constitution. The state has authorized very specific taxing options for counties. Additional revenues are generally available to municipalities through license fees and fees for service.

For Washington municipalities, the principal sources of revenue are charges for utility services (almost 40 percent of revenue); local taxes on property, retail sales, and business operations (about 10 percent of revenue each); state and federal transfers (about 10 percent of revenue); and whatever user fees, property sales, and other sources of supplemental income are allowable by law (about 20 percent of revenue).

Close to half of all county revenue comes from a general tax on all property located within the county, including incorporated areas. (The county share of the property tax is the largest portion, with minor shares going to the city of origin and the state.) The county has an additional property tax that is levied only in unincorporated areas; these revenues are dedicated predominantly to road maintenance and improvement. The other primary sources of revenue for county governments are state and federal transfers (about 30 percent of revenue), charges for services (about 20 percent), and user fees (about 10 percent).

There is a single property tax in the state, of which state, county, and municipal governments each receive a share. Property taxes currently raise more than $2.5 billion statewide annually. Property is generally assessed at 100 percent of "true and fair" value.[24] The general property tax has a limit of $1.65 per $1,000 of assessed value, and the overall levy may not increase in any one year by more than 6 percent, after allowances for growth. The property tax limit may be raised beyond 6 percent only by a vote of the people on a ballot proposition submitted by county commissioners.

Counties and municipalities also rely heavily on both a portion of the state sales tax and on state-authorized sales taxes. The state-imposed cap on the county sales tax is 1 percent, although an additional 0.1 percent is authorized for criminal justice programs and another 0.1 percent for jail construction. A state-run sales tax equalization program is intended to ensure that smaller municipalities and sparsely populated counties receive a larger share of statewide sales taxes than they would receive solely on the basis of population: under this program, municipalities and counties that collect more than 120 percent of the state average provide a portion of their excess to municipalities and counties that collect less than 80 percent of the state average.

Several state revenue-sharing plans also provide significant revenues to local governments. After allocations for state uses and administrative costs, a portion of the state's fuel tax is distributed to municipalities and counties on the basis of population and road-miles. Similar state revenue-sharing arrangements exist for capital improvements, library services, emergency telephone services, transportation planning, street and road maintenance, environmental preservation, and numerous other programs. Until 1999, gasoline taxes and the state's motor vehicle excise tax were the two major sources of shared revenue in the Evergreen State; in that year, Initiative 695 reduced the latter tax to a uniform $80 for all vehicles, creating a major challenge for the governor and the state legislature that remains unmet at this writing.

Not surprisingly, form of governance—home rule status—is unrelated to a local government's authority to incur and repay debt. Factors that do influence local government debt include state constitutional constraints, federal and state land-use laws, the jurisdiction's ability to repay, the nature of the local tax base, the assessed value of taxable property, the jurisdiction's proximity to expanding urban centers, the purposes of the financing and the conditions under which it is sought, environmental concerns, and residents' increasing demands for services.[25] In the Evergreen State, "creative financing" is the local approach to fiscal affairs. Typical forms of debt at the local level include low-interest state loans, local revenue bonds, limited or unlimited general-obligation bonds, vouchers, special restricted bonds, and lines of credit.[26]

Local Expenditures

Local expenditures are heavily controlled by state-mandated services and state and federal grant requirements. These requirements, as a percentage of all expenditures, are greatest at the county level and somewhat lower at the municipal level.

County government expenditures are heavily weighted toward criminal justice services: approximately half go to law enforcement, corrections, and juvenile services. The next major category of expenditure is courts and judges, followed closely by financial and records services (assessor, auditor, election services, and so forth).

Municipal expenditures are more broad ranging and differ substantially from one jurisdiction to another. As is the case at the county level, criminal justice services take up a substantial chunk of municipal budgets: law enforcement alone takes up one-third of municipal expenditures. Where a fire department is maintained, fire services (including emergency medical services) require close to one-quarter of the typical municipal budget. The next major category of expenditure, financial and records services, is followed by numerous other competitors for limited municipal dollars.

Local governments are not required to maintain a balanced budget. Liabilities incurred by an officer or employee of a county, city, or town in excess of any budget appropriation is not the liability of the local government; the liability is incurred by the officer or employee in question. Also, except upon court order or in the case of emergencies, the local legislative body may not approve any claims for expenditures in excess of the total amount appropriated for any individual fund.[27] Federal bankruptcy laws apply to Washington municipalities. While it is theoretically possible for a municipality to go bankrupt, it is not likely, since municipalities do not have the freedom to incur debt to the point of jeopardy.

The state requires audits of all local governmental entities—including municipalities of all sizes, counties, school districts, public commissions, the liquor control board, the state lottery commission, and port and sewer districts—at least once every three years.[28] In practice, however, counties are audited annually.

All local government audits are performed by the state, and the cost of the state examiner's audit is charged back to each audited entity.

Although municipalities and counties may elect or appoint auditors, local auditors are ex officio deputies of the state auditor and act under his or her direction. As such, their duties are necessarily circumscribed and consist of submitting financial reports to the state auditor's office, overseeing the budgeting process, and maintaining their jurisdiction's financial records under the Budgeting, Accounting, and Reporting System (BARS) administered by the state auditor.[29] BARS details the manner in which funds are collected, received, and expended for any purpose whatever by all public officers, employees, and other persons exercising public authority.

State Government Grants-in-Aid to Localities

State grants-in-aid make up a significant share of local government budgets and are critical to many local government functions, particularly in the area of capital investments. The five areas most dependent on state grant-in-aid funding are capital improvements, rural fire protection, emergency services, law enforcement training, road construction and engineering, and libraries.

Competition among local governments for state grants-in-aid is keen, and most major cities and all counties actively lobby the state legislature and state agencies on behalf of their jurisdictions. Not surprisingly, the state prefers to administer grants to localities where need is greatest. In many cases regional boards are appointed by state agencies to award and monitor such grants in accordance with state eligibility guidelines.

The state constitution regards public education as a primary state responsibility. State funding for primary and secondary education as well as community colleges bypasses local government and goes directly to school districts and community college boards. The state superintendent of public instruction, an independently elected executive official, serves as a powerful force in advocating for the needs of public education in the Evergreen State.

Unfunded Mandates

The federal government has imposed significant and costly requirements upon Washington's local governments, particularly with respect to the environment and worker safety. Generally, the state does not impose more stringent requirements in these areas than the federal government dictates.

At the state level, the Washington Administrative Code explicitly stipulates that "the state does not impose responsibility on local governments for new programs or increased levels of service under existing programs, unless costs thereof are paid by the state." Moreover, effective July 1, 1995, programs without full reimbursement were prohibited by action of an initiative passed by a strong majority.[30] Nonetheless, despite these strong prohibi-

tions, there is often a pronounced difference between the law and actual practice; in many instances, the level of state support provided does not fully compensate local governments for the costs that they incur by complying with legislation. Examples include state-required improvements to 911 services; the planning provisions of the Growth Management Act; state-mandated increases in sentencing for drunk driving and drug offenses; and the Becca Bill, which requires protective custody, treatment, or both for chronic runaways. As devolution continues and responsibilities for programs and services are shifted increasingly to the subnational level, unfunded mandates are likely to gain further significance.[31]

Access to Local Government

Local Elections

Local governments are mandated by state law to conduct and oversee balloting for any and all elections of federal, state, legislative, judicial, county, city, town, special district, and precinct officials.[32] State law also sets most rules and regulations pertaining to elections. Upon the request of the local governing body, local governments may, however, hold special elections. To exercise this option, the governing body must present a resolution to the county auditor at least forty-five days before the proposed election date. At that time, the county auditor will determine whether or not such an election is to be held and will choose one of six dates as recommended by the state. The county auditor also has the power to call a special election at any time to raise an excess levy or bond issue to cope with a natural disaster.

State rules regarding both candidacy and party affiliation generally apply to candidates running for local office. Home rule local governments are permitted to formulate their own rules on these subjects, but such rules generally replicate those of the state. Candidates running for state office are required to file for candidacy starting the fourth Monday in July, and record their filing no later than Friday of the same week.[33] Candidates for local office usually file for candidacy at the county auditor's office.

Washington and Oregon were among the first states to adopt vote-by-mail provisions on a test basis; Washington made its first attempt in a 1995 general election. This change in voting methods significantly increased voter participation in the several counties where it was tried, but the innovation remains controversial, and its impact on electoral outcomes, if any, has yet to be determined.

Citizen Controls over Actions of Local Officials

The power of impeachment is among the reserved prerogatives of the citizens that serve to define Washington's grassroots orientation (others being referendum and initiative rights). To initiate an impeachment of a local official, voters must prepare a petition stating both the reasons and the matters of complaint.[34]

The petition must be signed by at least 25 percent of the votes cast for all candidates in the election in which the accused local official was elected. The document is then reviewed by the office of the secretary of state; if sufficient evidence is found, it is passed on to the house of representatives, where a two-thirds majority is required to remove the official. An official who is found guilty is subject to trial, judgment, prosecution, and punishment in accordance with the laws of the state. Given the onerous requirements, it is no wonder that impeachment attempts are extremely rare and that examples of successful removal are nonexistent.

The power to undertake impeachment and removal is granted to code cities only, and counties do not provide for initiative and referendum authority (unless they are home rule counties whose charters specifically provide for these forms of direct democracy). Nonetheless, and in contrast to those of many states, Washington's policies on initiative and referendum are quite progressive. Through exercise of these powers, citizens can render any ordinance or policy established by local governments subject to the majority approval of the local electorate. The use of the initiative and the referendum at the municipal level thus represents a beachhead from which local autonomy can be advanced.

According to the state constitution, "the first power by the people is the initiative."[35] In order to pursue an initiative, the citizens of a municipality must present to the municipal clerk a petition signed by at least 25 percent of the total votes cast for mayor in the last municipal election. Once the clerk has determined that the number of signatures is sufficient, the council can either pass the proposed ordinance without alteration or call for a special election in which the issue will be voted upon by the citizens (the first option must be exercised within twenty days, and the second within thirty to sixty days). Court review of the proposed ordinance is required if the first option is exercised.[36]

Requirements for undertaking a referendum at the local level are the same as those for undertaking an initiative: the petition requires at least 25 percent of the total votes cast in the last election for the office of mayor. The filing of a qualified petition bearing sufficient signatures for a referendum suspends the ordinance in question until it is either found legally insufficient by some court proceeding or is defeated by a majority vote of the jurisdiction's registered voters.

Under Washington's Open Public Meetings Act, which was passed in 1971, all citizens have equal and unrestricted rights to observe the government conduct business. All local government meetings—those of public commissions, boards, councils, committees, subcommittees, departments, divisions, offices, and any other public agencies—are open to the public, and no member of the public is required to fulfill any conditions in order to attend.[37] Furthermore, twenty-four hours in advance of any special meeting called by a local public agency, local newspapers must be informed of the time and place of the meeting and the business to be discussed. If a meeting must be adjourned and continued at another time, local authorities are required to make public the time, place, and subject matter to be covered in any continuations.

Citizens also have the right of access to all information regarding public business and decisions, including local government budgets, tax records, ordinances, administrative policies, and program provisions. Local governments are under state mandate to provide the public with access to such information and to permit and facilitate the copying of government information. Moreover, in 1994, the state legislature created a task force on public information access to "identify specific means of encouraging and establishing widespread, public, electronic access to the public records held by state and local governments."[38]

State-Local Relations

Washington has changed considerably since its frontier beginnings. Over the past century, economic vitality and sustained population growth have reshaped its culture, its economy, and its very way of life. Despite those changes, however, governance is still largely dependent upon nineteenth-century models and practices.

The concept of home rule in Washington has been a limited one from the beginning. Given that it exists "at the whim of the legislature," home rule is vulnerable.[39] Moreover, without significant fiscal autonomy at the local level, any discourse on home rule rings somewhat hollow. The lack of fiscal autonomy is especially significant in the context of increasing devolution of federal programs to state and local government.

The changes in local governance that have occurred over the decades tend to be scattered and ad hoc: various levels of government, acting independently, have made incremental adjustments to address specific problems. The results—duplication and lack of coordination in service delivery—have fed the public perception that government is inefficient and unresponsive.

Through the limited provisions of the state's home rule statutes, some opportunity to experiment with public policy issues is available to public-spirited citizens of Washington. In collaboration with local government officials and state legislators who have some background in local government, Washingtonians continue to refine their structures of governance and to reexamine the relationship between state and local government.

If home rule is to be given a greater role in reinventing government, a tightening of the legislative definition of home rule may be a necessary first step to the strengthening of municipal authority. The legislature could provide some relief simply by amending and recodifying the statutes governing the powers of chartered jurisdictions.[40]

Three bills recently passed by the house, but subsequently rejected by the senate, would have offered substantial support to local government reform at the county level: under this legislation, counties with fewer than 75,000 would have been permitted to opt out of growth management planning requirements; county electorates would have been permitted to vote on increasing the number of commissioners, establishing the initiative, and adopting the power of referendum; and counties would have been permitted to replace elected county coroners with professional medical examiners.[41] Of course, what the legislature enacts it is also free to amend and repeal, unless restricted by the constitution. Thus, the problem of home rule may be less one of proper definition and more one of locus of control, especially fiscal control. After all, like all other municipal powers in Washington, home rule still exists "at the whim of the legislature," instead of reflecting a privileged position in the state constitution.

Notes

1. Daniel Elazar's well-known classification of political subcultures in the United States places Washington in the "moralistic" category, which means that the political arena is viewed as a special realm of collective action in which the public interest or the common good should be pursued by all participants. The other categories are "individualistic" (where self-interest dominates) and "traditionalistic" (where preservation of the status quo dominates).

2. Revised Code of Washington, 35.01.010.

3. Ibid., 35A.

4. Stan Finkelstein, Association of Washington Cities, personal communication, July 26, 1996.

5. See Constitution of the State of Washington, Article XI, sections 10 and 11.

6. Henry Campbell Black, *Black's Law Dictionary*, 6th ed. (St. Paul, Minn.: West Publishing Company, 1990), 458.

7. David C. Nice, John C. Pierce, and Charles H. Sheldon, eds., *Government and Politics in the Evergreen State* (Pullman: Washington State University Press, 1992).

8. Municipal Research and Services Center of Washington, *The Erosion of Home Rule—The Need to Strengthen Powers of Municipal Self Government in Washington* (Olympia: Association of Washington Cities, December 1990), 20.

9. See *Tacoma v. Taxpayers*, 108 Wn.2d 679, 743 p.2d 793 (1987). See also *Massie*

v. Brown, 84 Wn.2d 490, 527 P.2d 476 (1974), and *Chemical Bank v. WPSSS*, 99 Wn.2d 772, 666 p.2d 329, 372-293 (1983).

10. Revised Code of Washington, 35.01.010, 35.22.280, 35.23.440, 35.23.370.

11. Ibid., 35.22.030, 35.22.050, 35.22.080.

12. Finkelstein, personal communication.

13. Nice, Pierce, and Sheldon, *Government and Politics.*

14. Ibid.

15. Ibid.

16. Constitution of the State of Washington, Article XI, section 1.

17. Revised Code of Washington, 39.34.

18. Ibid., 85.38.

19. State of Washington Local Governance Study Commission, *Final Report of the Local Governance Study Commission* (Olympia: State of Washington, 1988), 44.

20. Revised Code of Washington, 41.06.150.

21. Ibid., 41.04.205

22. Ibid., 36.01.125, 35.21.800, 39.84, 39.898.

23. Ibid., 35.21.703, 36.01.085, 53.08.245; Chapter 43, section 63A.

24. Between 1944 and 1972, assessments were limited to 50 percent of true and fair value; before 1944, they were limited to 20 percent.

25. Revised Code of Washington, 39.36.020–900; Constitution of the State of Washington, Article VIII, section 6.

26. Revised Code of Washington, 39, 46, 020-[1].

27. Revised Code of Washington, 35.33.125, 35.33.081, 35.33.091.

28. Ibid., 43.02.260.

29. Ibid., 43.09.200; for school districts, see 28A.505.120.

30. Ibid., 43.135.010.4.c., 43.135.060.1.

31. Jonathan Walters, "The Black Hole of Block Grants," *Governing: The Magazine of States and Localities* 1996, p. 11.

32. Revised Code of Washington, 29.

33. Ibid., 29.15.010.

34. Constitution of the State of Washington, Article V, section 1; Article I, section 33.

35. Ibid., Article II, section 1a.

36. Revised Code of Washington, 35.17.260, 35.17.290.

37. Ibid., 42.30.

38. Ibid., 42.17.261.

39. Brachtenback, 1954, in Municipal Research and Services Center of Washington, *Erosion of Home Rule.*

40. See Revised Code of Washington, Chapter 35.22.

41. House Bill Report HB 2370, February 12, 1996; House Bill Report HB 2145, February 6, 1996; House Bill Report HB 2398, February 7, 1996.

WEST VIRGINIA

Kenneth A. Klase

West Virginia is a small state geographically and one of the most rural, with only 41 percent of its 1.8 million people living in standard metropolitan statistical areas. Local governments are subject to the state constitution, which severely limits their autonomy, determines their institutional rules and organizational structures, and imposes strong fiscal restraints. Every aspect of local government activity is closely regulated by state government through constitutional or statutory requirements. These circumstances create a classic unitary relationship between West Virginia's local governments and their state government in spite of home rule provisions that have been in place since 1936 for municipalities with populations of 2,000 or more.[1] Local governments have begun to press for changes in state-local relationships, but there are few indications that they will change any time soon.

Governmental Setting

West Virginia's political institutions originated in the political environment of antebellum Virginia. The Civil War precipitated the separation of some of the western counties of Virginia to form the state of West Virginia. Its original constitution and subsequent replacements have emphasized the popular election of officials and restrictions on state and local powers. West Virginia's penchant for minimal government from the end of the Civil War through the New Deal permitted economic interests from outside the state to dominate the state economy and exploit its natural resources. There is also a legacy of oppression and hostility between corporate and labor interests, which affects state politics. The historical dominance of industrial interests has left the state poor and economically dependent on a few industries.[2] Since the end of World War II in 1945, the state economy has been in serious trouble due to persistent unemployment and population loss. The state's employment growth rate continues to lag behind the national average.

West Virginia's political culture has been traditionalistic, emphasizing custodial government and the preeminence of political elites, with strong undertones of individualism. Traditionalistic political culture is oriented toward preserving the existing political order and governing elites, thus sustaining the status quo and minimizing government activity. Most West Virginians lack trust in their state and local government officials, but they still want government to address certain kinds of problems. The state's economic plight means relatively low incomes, which restricts government revenue generation. Consequently, government is limited in its ability to respond to citizen demands.[3]

Moreover, the state constitution is derived from Virginia's traditionalistic political culture and still contains provisions that severely limit the capacity of local governments to act in spite of amendments that have removed some of these restraints.[4]

Home Rule in West Virginia

Historical Development

The state-local government relationship in West Virginia is highly centralized. In fact, West Virginia has centralized some functions to a greater degree than most other states, especially with respect to highways, education, and welfare. The Tax Limitation Amendment to the state constitution passed in 1932 and the financial deficiencies of local governments in the Depression era left local governments unable to fund these activities, and the state has since consolidated its control over them.[5] Centralized state control persists despite explicit home rule provisions for municipalities with populations of more than 2,000. The Home Rule Amendment to the state constitution was passed in 1936 in part to eliminate the need for special legislation to amend existing municipal charters.

West Virginia local governments have developed what has been characterized as a classic unitary relationship with their state government. In a unitary system, all power is vested in the central government, which may delegate specific powers and responsibilities but retains authority to alter them at its discretion. The state government determines the functions, finances, and organizational structures of local governments.[6] The state legislature has significant plenary power over the activities and affairs of local governments in the state and has exercised it over time in a manner consistent with Dillon's Rule, which holds that all power resides with the state.[7]

Definition of Home Rule

The state determines to a significant extent what powers the local units may exercise. The power of the state government is not mitigated by the Home Rule Amendment to the state constitution. The amendment grants to municipalities with populations of at least 2,000 the power and authority to "pass all laws and ordinances relating to municipal affairs." Nevertheless, in reality home rule is virtually meaningless because municipalities cannot enact ordinances or laws inconsistent or in conflict with the state constitution or with the general laws of the state. The real meaning of home rule in West Virginia is a limited grant of structural autonomy, and even that is circumscribed by enabling statutes that prescribe the forms of municipal charters and other statutes that detail municipal powers. County government is not afforded even this token home rule. State statutes determine local government functions and operational procedures, and constitutional provisions limit property taxes and grant the state control over other taxing powers.[8]

Structural Features

There are 707 local governments in West Virginia, including 55 counties, 55 school districts, 231 municipalities, and 366 special districts. There are no large cities, and of the 231 municipalities, only 15 have a population over 10,000.[9] Each of these local governments is subject to the state constitution, which limits their autonomy, determines their institutional rules and organizational structures, and imposes severe fiscal restraints.

Prior to adoption of the Home Rule Amendment, municipalities with populations of less than 2,000 were granted charters under provisions of general state statute (that is, all municipalities in this class operated under a common general charter), whereas cities with a population of 2,000 or more were granted a charter or amendments to their charter by special legislation. The Home Rule Amendment revised this procedure for municipalities with populations of 2,000 or more; they are now allowed to create, revise, or amend their charter without state government approval.[10]

In order to incorporate as a municipality, residents submit to the county commission a petition, signed by 30 percent of the residents of the area to be incorporated, which requests a special election on incorporation. If a majority of those voting on the issue vote in favor of incorporation, the county commission issues a certificate of incorporation. Newly incorporated municipalities are classified as follows: Class I, population exceeding 50,000; Class II, population of 10,000 to 50,000; Class III, population of 2,000 to 10,000; Class IV, town or village, population less than 2,000.[11]

During the special election on incorporation, voters elect members of a charter board to draft the charter, and that charter will specify election procedures and establish the structure of the municipal government. The structures available to choose from are mayor-council, "strong" mayor, commission, city manager, and city manager-mayor. Most municipalities in West Virginia (209 of 231) use the mayor-council plan of government, with the balance using the city manager or strong mayor plans. (Class IV towns and villages, which operate under state general law without individual charters, must use the mayor-council form of government.) After the draft charter is approved by the attorney general, a public hearing is held and revisions are made. Then the charter must be approved by a majority vote of qualified voters in a special election. Any revisions and amendments subsequently made to the charter follow a similar procedure.[12]

The state constitution contains the only restrictions on the authority of the state. The legislature is prohibited from enacting special legislation changing county seats; regulating county affairs; incorporating cities, towns, and villages; or amending their charters. It is also prohibited from enacting special legislation where general legislation might be used and from changing the prescribed structure of county government. In general, the state constitution prohibits the use of special legislation. Except for these constitutional restrictions on its powers, the state legislature may expand or contract the powers of local units as it deems appropriate, and it retains the right to legislate on any matter relating to local units.[13] Thus, West Virginia municipalities can exercise only those powers conferred on them by the legislature, and Dillon's Rule has not been mitigated by the provisions of the Home Rule Amendment.

The powers exercised by municipalities are enumerated in state statutes or derived from constitutional charter provisions, which are quite limited.[14] The major effect of the Home Rule Amendment is to permit municipalities with populations over 2,000 to choose their form of government.[15]

Municipal boundaries can be changed through annexation processes (election, petition, and minor boundary adjustment) stemming from authority vested in the legislature and outlined in statute. In annexation by election, a petition for a special election on the annexation must be filed by at least 5 percent of the municipality's residents, and the territories annexed must meet statutory requirements for population and area. A majority of qualified voters within both the city and the territory proposed for annexation must vote in favor for the annexation to take place. Guidelines for the election process are detailed in state statute.[16] The governing body of a municipality may annex territory without election if two petitions are filed and verified by the county commission, one with the signatures of a majority of the qualified voters of the territory requesting annexation, and the other containing the signatures of a majority of the property owners of the territory requesting annexation. Territories annexed under this method must also meet the statutory requirements for population and area. A city may also apply to the county commission for a minor boundary adjustment. Upon receipt of an application, the county commission holds a hearing on the proposed annexation. If the proposed change is substantially opposed at the hearing by any landowner within the territory to be annexed, the commission will dismiss the application.[17]

In addition to the annexation powers noted above, municipalities have a limited power of extraterritoriality. Municipalities may extend their authority beyond their boundaries in certain instances, for example, to provide fire protection service on a contract basis up to three miles beyond their corporate limits.[18] They also may own property and sometimes do operate facilities beyond their boundaries.

West Virginia counties took on the basic structure they have today when the state constitution of 1872 was amended in 1880. The amendments of 1880 require counties to adopt a plural form of governance that divides the county's governmental powers among seven independently elected offices: county commissioners, county clerk, circuit clerk, county sheriff (also county treasurer), county assessor, county prosecuting attorney, and county surveyor of lands. Although this division might have made sense in creating checks and balances, it makes it more difficult to coordinate dispersed functions and to respond to public service needs.[19]

The amendments established that counties are primarily administrative arms of the state government. Although counties were initially viewed as primarily administrative, they have gained some additional authority and responsibilities as well as lost some major functional responsibilities. However, the state constitution continues to deny them home rule. Furthermore, the courts have continued to support the view that counties may exercise only those powers expressly granted to them by the state constitution and statutes. Those powers can be expanded or contracted at the will of the state. Currently, counties in West Virginia are able to exercise little initiative when confronting a problem or a demand for additional services, since they often lack the authority or financial resources to respond. Thus, the institutional capacity to govern West Virginia counties is severely restrained by state government.[20]

Functions of Local Government

Functional Responsibilities

The power of municipalities to perform various functions is directly derived from state statutes.[21] Municipalities in West Virginia provide a wide range of services, and the state has granted them additional responsibilities and powers over the years. They enforce city laws; maintain domestic order; provide fire protec-

tion; build, repair, and clean city roads; supply and purify water; provide park and recreation services; perform building inspections; and operate libraries. The extent of services offered varies widely depending on the class of the municipality.[22]

Counties in West Virginia provide traditional services: law enforcement; public welfare; health and hospitals, including physical and mental health services; recording and licensing; and judicial administration, in the form of local circuit and magistrate courts. Construction and maintenance of buildings (courthouses and jails), election administration, libraries, airports, recreation, and promotion of agriculture are also important county functions. Counties also may provide fire protection, water, sewerage, or garbage disposal services and establish flood control projects. In addition, some counties fund ambulance services, industrial parks, and visitor bureaus. However, a few functions that are traditionally assigned to counties in other states have been substantially (education and welfare) or entirely (highways) assumed by the state in West Virginia.[23]

The extent of county services varies depending on population and whether the county has a major municipality within its borders. The state's larger counties offer a broader range of services than its smaller ones, but compared with counties in other states, West Virginia's counties do not provide a particularly wide range of services due to the rural nature of the state; the cumbersome, plural government structure imposed by the state, which inhibits their ability to respond to service demands; and lack of home rule authority, particularly with respect to revenue choices and service options.[24]

Special districts are independent, special-purpose governments established to perform a specific service or several related services, such as water services, wastewater collection and treatment services, or both. By taking advantage of economies of scale, they are often able to provide services that might not otherwise be affordable. As has occurred elsewhere in the nation, the number of such special districts has grown rapidly in West Virginia, from 290 in 1987 to 366 in 1994. Most of the special districts in West Virginia are public service districts, which are created, enlarged, and dissolved by county commissions, subject to the approval of the state Public Service Commission. The powers, responsibilities, and decision-making procedures of these public service districts are dictated in detail by state statute.[25]

Counties and municipalities in West Virginia have no legal relationship, and their cooperation is neither explicitly authorized nor mandated in statute. However, the state has established regional planning and development councils to promote greater communication and cooperation among local governments. The state has also mandated cooperation and interaction in a few specific areas, for example, regional jails and regional solid waste disposal. More commonly, cooperation occurs where officials choose to cooperate in order to achieve a joint objective. By statute, municipalities may enter into formal intergovernmental agreements with other local governments in their area and coordinate activities within the framework of areawide councils of government. Despite the potential for intergovernmental cooperation, West Virginia's local governments do not interact with one another on a regular basis.[26]

Administrative Discretion

Despite home rule provisions for municipalities over 2,000 in population, municipalities have relatively little discretion except with respect to structural organization. Even the structure is prescribed by state enabling legislation. Counties have even less discretion in aspects of structure and administration. Both counties and municipalities have the authority to adopt local ordinances; however, they must be consistent with the state constitution and statutes. The procedures for their enactment and codification are prescribed in state statute.[27]

West Virginia counties and municipalities are not required by statute to adopt a merit system for personnel administration except for state-mandated merit selection of municipal police and fire personnel. Municipalities that have paid fire or police departments are required to have separate civil service systems for each, with individual civil service commissions whose composition and functions are stipulated by statute. In addition, all municipalities whose police or fire departments are supported in whole or in part at public expense are required by statute to establish a separate pension or relief fund for each department, to be administered by separate boards of trustees.[28]

State statutes require municipalities and counties to use competitive bidding for purchases and contracts. Municipalities are authorized to provide by ordinance for the types of purchases for which competitive bidding is required and the method and manner of bidding. Counties must have competitive bidding for purchases and contracts over $5,000; like municipalities, they are authorized to make rules and regulations governing competitive bid procedures.[29]

Despite the existence of regional planning councils, county and municipal governments in West Virginia generally have been adverse to long-range planning. Whereas most counties do not have active planning commissions, most municipalities have planning commissions that function under statutory authority.[30] City councils in West Virginia have the power to enact and amend land-use and zoning ordinances, which are administered by planning commissions and boards of zoning appeals. Although counties are also authorized to enact zoning and land-use regulations, they generally do not utilize this authority.

Economic Development

State statutes authorize municipalities and counties to perform economic development activities. Municipalities are authorized to create integrated departments of development, and municipalities and counties are authorized to participate in county and municipal development authorities and area development corporations. State statute authorizes counties and municipalities to acquire, lease, loan, purchase, and sell industrial and commercial projects and to finance these activities through loans and the issuance of revenue bonds. The state has also created authorities to oversee community infrastructure and enterprise zones. The Community Infrastructure Authority finances infrastructure projects by issuing loans or community infrastructure revenue bonds of the state. The Enterprise Zone Authority provides information and assistance to businesses in enterprise zones and has the authority to create enterprise zones. Municipalities and counties must designate the enterprise area as economically depressed, under state-prescribed definitions, and then ask the state authority to declare it an enterprise zone. Such designation may entitle the area to certain tax exemptions or tax credits. State statute dictates the requirements for creating and designating zones as well as selecting candidates for preference.[31]

In specified circumstances, the 1990 Local Powers Act provides counties with the authority to impose fees and make expenditures for county development. Counties are authorized to collect fees for the costs associated with capital improvements or provision of other services attributable to new development projects. Counties can levy impact fees related to population growth and public service needs if they can demonstrate that they meet a prescribed population growth rate, adopt a countywide comprehensive plan, adopt zoning and subdivision ordinances, adopt formal building permit and review systems, and provide for capital improvement programming. If they comply with these provisions, counties are authorized to assess, levy, collect, and administer any tax or fee that municipalities are authorized to impose. There are provisions that require a referendum if county actions are protested through citizen petition.[32] The growth criteria of the general legislation were stipulated in such a manner as to apply only to several counties in the eastern panhandle of the state, to enable these counties in the rapidly growing region near Washington, D.C., to be granted additional sources of revenue. Counties that meet the growth criteria have been unable to secure citizen support for the other required provisions.

Fiscal Autonomy of Local Governments

West Virginia state government places relatively severe restrictions on the fiscal autonomy of local governments. The state exercises control over property tax assessments and collections, limits tax rates, controls budgets and tax levies, and limits the amount of and the procedures for incurring debt as well as sets the provisions for its retirement. The state exercises this control through constitutional limits, legislative statute, and administrative oversight.[33]

Local Revenues

The principal limitation on the fiscal capacity of local governments in West Virginia results from the 1932 Tax Limitation Amendment to the state constitution, which stemmed from Depression era concerns for property tax relief. It limits the ability of local governments to raise revenue through property taxes. As indicated in Table 1, the amendment divides real and personal property into four classes and establishes the maximum allowable levy rates for each class. The maximum allowable levy rates are significantly below national averages and are responsible for relatively low property-tax revenue.

Tax revenue for local governments is further limited by the provisions of the Property Tax and Homestead Exemption Amendment of 1982, which exempts the first $20,000 of assessed valuation of any residence owned by a citizen who is more than sixty-five years of age or is permanently and totally disabled.[34]

The maximum property tax levy rates specified in the Tax Limitation Amendment can be augmented by additional levies approved by referendum. These "excess" levies can increase the maximum property tax rates by up to 50 percent for a period of up to three years in counties and municipalities if approved by 60 percent of the jurisdiction's voters. Excess levies can increase the maximum property tax levy rates for school districts (defined by county) by up to 100 percent for a period of up to five years if approved by a majority of the school district's voters. Seventy-six percent of school districts, 38 percent of counties, and 23 percent of municipalities have excess levies in place.[35]

The reappraisal by county assessors of all property in the state to 60 percent of fair market value as mandated by the Appraisal Act of 1990 provides additional property tax revenue, but increases are limited to a maximum of 10 percent annually. The potential for windfalls from reappraisal has made the passage of excess levies more difficult in the last several years in spite of the fact that they are essential to the support of local government services, given the tax limitations imposed.

The state has allowed counties to impose various fees and other taxes over the years, but counties are still significantly con-

Table 1. Maximum Property Tax Rates, by Government Type (Cents per $100 of Assessed Value)

Government	Class I	Class II	Class III	Class IV
County	14.30	28.60	57.20	57.20
School district	22.95	45.90	91.80	91.80
Municipality	12.50	25.00	0.00	50.00
State	0.25	0.50	1.00	1.00
Total maximum rate	50.00	100.00	150.00	200.00

Source: West Virginia State Constitution.
Notes: Class I, personal property used in farming; Class II, farm real estate and owner-occupied homes; Class III, property not in Class I or II and located outside a municipality (primarily automobiles and commercial properties); Class IV, property not in Class I or II and located inside a municipality (primarily automobiles and commercial properties).

Table 2. Distribution of City and County Revenues, by Source, 1991

City source	Percent of city total	County source	Percent of county total
Business and occupation tax	41.8%	Property tax	55.5%
Fees	17.6	Coal severance tax	11.9
Property taxes	13.9	Excess levy	7.8
Miscellaneous	13.4	Fees	6.1
Utilities tax	5.6	Federal payments	1.6
Bond levy	2.3	Property stamps	1.3
Hotel occupancy	1.1	Hotel occupancy	1.0
Wine and liquor	1.1	Investment income	0.8
Federal payments	0.9	State grants	0.7
Coal severance tax	0.9	Wine and liquor	0.1
Investment interest	0.7	Miscellaneous	13.0
State grants	0.6		
Excess levy	0.2		

Source: West Virginia Tax Department data as reported in William S. Reece, "Local Government Finance and Its Implications for Economic Development." In West Virginia in the 1990s: Opportunities for Economic Progress, ed. Robert Jay Dilger and Tom S. Witt (Morgantown: West Virginia University Press, 1994), 290, 295.

strained in their ability to respond to any demands for additional services. Municipalities in West Virginia have the added advantage of being able to impose a business and occupation tax on the gross income of businesses operating within the city limits. Although municipalities are restricted by statute from exceeding the state's business and occupation tax rate, the tax has become the largest source of municipal revenue (42 percent). Fees (totaling 18 percent) on refuse collection, fire protection, parks, and other municipal services are the second largest source of revenue, followed by property taxes (14 percent).[36] Table 2 provides the distribution of city and county revenues by source. By almost any standard, the revenues of West Virginia's local governments are insufficient to support adequate levels of public services. Furthermore, they are inadequate to meet citizen demands for additional local spending, particularly for public education.[37]

Constitutional and statutory limitations on debt apply to the amount, time, and method of repayment; a vote is required for authority to incur debt. Proposals to issue bonded indebtedness must win 60 percent approval in the vote before the debt can be incurred. Bonded indebtedness is limited by statute to 2.5 percent of assessed value, but that cap may be exceeded, to the constitutional maximum of 5 percent, for a few purposes. Bonds must be approved by the state attorney general, and repayments must be made through the state Sinking Fund Commission. These restrictions apply only to general obligation indebtedness backed by the full faith and credit of the government. Few West Virginia local governments incur such indebtedness anywhere near their bonding capacity, presumably to avoid repayment from property tax revenues needed for current expenses. Most resort to issuance of revenue bonds when borrowing is necessary.[38]

Table 3. Distribution of City and County Expenditures, by Function, 1991

City	Percent of city total	County	Percent of county total
Law	23.1%	Administration	40.99%
Administration	19.9	Courts and sheriff	36.43
Fire	18.0	Miscellaneous	4.62
Streets	14.5	Health	3.13
Sanitation	7.5	Water and sewer	2.60
Parks and recreation	6.6	Parks and recreation	2.42
Miscellaneous	2.9	Library	1.69
Transportation	2.6	Fire	1.50
Health	1.4	Elections	1.48
Library	1.3	Planning and development	1.42
Housing	1.0	Emergency	1.07
Planning and development	0.6	Transportation	1.00
Elections	0.2	Human resources	0.61
Human resources	0.2	Sanitation	0.60
Water and sewer	0.2	Housing	0.36
Arts	0.1	Arts	0.07
Emergency	0.1		

Source: West Virginia Tax Department data for 1991, as reported in William S. Reece, "Local Government Finance and Its Implications for Economic Development." In *West Virginia in the 1990s: Opportunities for Economic Progress,* ed. Robert Jay Dilger and Tom S. Witt (Morgantown: West Virginia University Press, 1994), 289, 294.

Local Expenditures

Table 3 contains data on the distribution of city and county expenditures by function. The major categories of municipal expenditures (administration, law, streets, and fire protection) account for over 75 percent of municipal expenditures. Sanitation and parks and recreation also account for large portions of municipal expenditures, with the remainder spread over a wide variety of services, including transportation, water and sewer, health, libraries, and housing. The major categories of county expenditures—general administration, including county commissions and county assessors, county courts and sheriff's offices—account for over 77 percent of all county expenditures. A wide variety of other services are provided, including water and sewer, health services, and parks and recreation.

State restrictions on municipal budgets in West Virginia are typical of restrictions in many other states. West Virginia requires local governments to have balanced operating budgets. Deficits not exceeding 3 percent of levy estimates are allowed but must be satisfied in the succeeding year.[39] There are no provisions for bankruptcy or receivership. Dissolution and forfeiture of charter are possible for municipalities that vote for those options and settle their debts beforehand.

State Government Grants-in-Aid to Localities

The state encourages local governments to undertake certain activities and to provide certain types of services by offering intergovernmental grants-in-aid, which are distributed as follows:

education, 95.7 percent of all grants; general local government support, 1.5 percent; health and hospital, 1.4 percent; highways, 0.3 percent; and other, 1.1 percent.[40] State government in West Virginia provides local governments with over $1.3 billion in grants. This amount represents almost one-half of all local government expenditures, with most of the assistance ($1.2 billion) going to school districts. Obviously, the state exercises considerable influence and control over school districts as well as other local governments.

Unfunded Mandates

The state has preempted local government authority in several areas by issuing mandates. The state established the Regional Jail and Prison Authority in 1985, which preempted local control over correctional facilities, to oversee the operation, maintenance, and construction of regional jails. Local government officials serve on the regional jail commissions, but their control over the operation and maintenance of existing jails and the location and financing of new ones is preempted. Solid waste disposal is another area where the state has imposed mandates. In this case, the state acted to prevent groundwater contamination by requiring landfill location plans and specifying capacity limits and other specific criteria.[41]

Access to Local Government

Local Elections

Election procedures are fully covered by state law, and local officials have little discretion over them.[42] Although general elections are regulated by the state, their administration falls largely to the counties, which in turn depend on local government for actual administration. Various duties are assigned to county officials—the county commission, clerk of the circuit court, county clerk, board of ballot commissioners, and election commissioners and clerks—related to establishing precincts, printing and distributing ballots, preparing and delivering voting machines, and ascertaining the election results.[43]

Citizen Controls over Actions of Local Officials

Citizens of municipalities with appropriate charter provisions can undertake initiatives and referenda upon petition by at least 10 percent of qualified voters, and recall upon petition of at least 20 percent. Although initiative, referendum, and recall authority may be included in home rule charters, only a small percentage of West Virginia municipalities have chosen to provide for their use, and they are rarely used even in those cities that have provided for them. The state constitution requires that municipalities utilize the referendum for approving general obligation bond issues, debt levies, and "excess" property tax levies. State statute requires the referendum for some service fees under specified circumstances.

State law requires that the proceedings of all governing bodies, including those of local governments, be open to the public. There must be public notice of meetings, and the minutes of governing bodies must be made available to the public.[44]

State-Local Relations

The functional and fiscal autonomy of local governments in West Virginia are constrained by constitutional and statutory provisions. The structural autonomy that the state constitution grants to municipalities may be the only benefit accruing to them from supposed home rule provisions.

Although municipalities in West Virginia have been viewed in some studies as having broad functional home rule,[45] in a practical sense municipal functional autonomy is anything but broad. Every aspect of local government activity is closely regulated by state government through constitutional or statutory requirements. The structural and functional autonomy of municipalities is greater than that of counties, which have none. West Virginia local governments suffer severe restrictions in fiscal autonomy and revenue inadequacies derived from the Tax Limitation Amendment to the state constitution and lack of revenue options. Particularly in the area of fiscal autonomy, West Virginia local governments are still feeling the repercussions of events that occurred during the Depression. Not only were the tax limitations imposed by the state in that era never lessened, but functional arrangements that resulted from the financial insolvency of local governments in that era remain in place to this day. The state government retains centralized control over many functions for which local governments in other states have at least some responsibility. There is also a strong preference among state government leaders in West Virginia to retain state-local relationships as they are, with highly centralized controls over virtually all responsibilities and activities of local governments. Thus, West Virginia local governments have developed a classic unitary relationship with their state government. It is a relationship characterized by diminished local government autonomy in spite of limited structural home rule provisions in the state constitution and enabling statutes.

There is little indication that state government is going to lessen its restrictions on local government autonomy. To the contrary, state government seems inclined to retain control over local government responsibilities and activities. Local governments appear to be circumventing their fiscal constraints by creating more and more special districts to jointly provide capital-intensive public services.[46] The only deviation from strictly imposed fiscal and structural constraints has been the 1990 Local Powers Act, passed in response to growth and development in the eastern panhandle of the state; but even there, the restrictions on eligibility are such that no local governments have taken advantage of the act. They have not taken advantage of it for

the same reason that they have not taken advantage of the change relating to the Local Powers Act.

As a result of the constraints on their structural, functional, and fiscal autonomy, local governments in West Virginia face significant difficulties in governing. Although most local governments are not in fiscal stress, most are experiencing chronic scarcity of resources. Counties and municipalities are reexamining their own resources and taking whatever actions they can to ensure their financial solvency.[47]

Their diminished capacity for home rule makes West Virginia local governments subject to significant internal conflict (among constitutional officers of the county) and intergovernmental conflict (between cities and counties, and between local governments and the state), much of which goes unresolved over time. Many of these conflicts are the result of centralized state control and lack of local revenue options. Most local officials are convinced that local governments in West Virginia would be better able to deal with conflict if the state granted them substantial home rule authority, even if that raised the potential for conflict.[48]

The status of local autonomy has significant implications for local governments in West Virginia. The most adverse effects are in the area of fiscal autonomy. Without additional fiscal resources, local governments are unable to provide adequate levels of local service and are not able to respond to citizen demands. This situation will likely continue unless fiscal and organizational restrictions imposed by state government on local governments are eased.

Local governments are seeking expanded powers, especially with regard to new revenue sources.[49] The statewide property tax reappraisal completed in 1996 has improved the fiscal resources of local governments to some extent, but the limitations on the generation of revenues from the property tax are constraining. Local governments in West Virginia need additional autonomy, especially fiscal autonomy in the form of revenue options, to have the flexibility to respond to changing circumstances.

Notes

1. Richard A. Brisbin, et al., *West Virginia Politics and Government* (Lincoln: University of Nebraska Press, 1996), 142.

2. Ibid., 18–22.

3. Ibid., 22–25.

4. Daniel J. Elazar, *American Federalism: A View from the States*, 3d ed. (New York: Harper and Row, 1984), 114–137.

5. Claude J. Davis, et al., *West Virginia State and Local Government* (Morgantown: Bureau for Government Research, West Virginia University, 1963), 26–27.

6. Brisbin, et al., *West Virginia Politics and Government*, 62.

7. Advisory Commission on Intergovernmental Relations, *Local Government Autonomy: Needs for State Constitutional, Statutory, and Judicial Clarification* (Washington, D.C.: ACIR, 1993), 15–18.

8. Brisbin, et al., *West Virginia Politics and Government*, 62–63.

9. Ibid, 155.

10. Mavis A. Mann, *The Structure of City Government in West Virginia* (Morgantown: Bureau for Government Research, West Virginia University, 1953), 2.

11. Brisbin, et al., *West Virginia Politics and Government,* 156.

12. Eugene R. Elkins, *Municipal Home Rule in West Virginia* (Morgantown: Bureau for Government Research, West Virginia University, 1965), 23–26.

13. Davis, et al., *West Virginia State and Local Government,* 26–27.

14. Ibid., 430.

15. Eugene R. Elkins and Todd H. Bullard, *Manual of West Virginia Municipal Government* (Morgantown: Bureau for Government Research, West Virginia University, 1957), 1–2.

16. West Virginia Code, 8-6.

17. Ibid., 8-6; Elkins, *Municipal Home Rule in West Virginia,* 37–39.

18. Davis, et al., *West Virginia State and Local Government,* 432.

19. Harold J. Shamberger, *County Government and Administration in West Virginia* (Morgantown: Bureau for Government Research, West Virginia University, 1952), 19–21.

20. Brisbin, et al., *West Virginia Politics and Government,* 142–143.

21. West Virginia Code, 8-12.

22. Brisbin, et al., *West Virginia Politics and Government,* 159–160.

23. Ibid., 148–149.

24. Ibid., 148–149.

25. Ibid., 160–161.

26. West Virginia Code, 7-1-3i, 7-1-3j; Brisbin, et al., *West Virginia Politics and Government,* 64–65.

27. West Virginia Code, 7-1-4, 8-11-4.

28. Davis, et al., *West Virginia State and Local Government,* 221–224.

29. West Virginia Code, 8-12-10, 7-1-1 to 7-1-11.

30. William S. Reece, "Local Government Finance and Its Implications for Economic Development." In *West Virginia in the 1990s: Opportunities for Economic Progress,* ed. Robert Jay Dilger and Tom S. Witt (Morgantown: West Virginia University Press, 1994), 158, 254.

31. West Virginia Code, 8-12-3a; 7-12-1 to 7-12-16; 13-2C-1 to 13-2C-21; 31-19-1 to 31-19-21; 5B-2B-1 to 5B-2B-9.

32. Ibid., 7-20-1 to 7-20-10.

33. Davis, et al., *West Virginia State and Local Government,* 29.

34. Reece, "Local Government Finance and Its Implications for Economic Development," 290–291.

35. Ibid., 291, 312.

36. Brisbin, et al., *West Virginia Politics and Government,* 155.

37. Reece, "Local Government Finance and Its Implications for Economic Development," 298–299.

38. Davis, et al., *West Virginia State and Local Government,* 29–30, 444, 460–462.

39. West Virginia Code, 11-8-26.

40. U.S. Bureau of the Census, *Census of Governments,* 4, Government Finances (Washington, D.C.: U.S. Government Printing Office, 1992).

41. Ibid., 63–64.

42. West Virginia Code, 8-5.

43. Davis, et al., *West Virginia State and Local Government,* 69–73, 454.

44. West Virginia Code, 6-9A-1 to 6-9A-7.

45. Advisory Commission on Intergovernmental Relations. *State Laws Governing Local Government Structure and Administration* (Washington, D.C.: ACIR, 1993), 20–21.

46. Brisbin, et al., *West Virginia Politics and Government,* 161.

47. Kenneth A. Klase, "Meeting Fiscal Challenges in the 1990s: Local Government Fiscal Trends in West Virginia," *West Virginia Public Affairs Reporter* 11 (spring 1994), 2–8.

48. Kenneth A. Klase and Gerald M. Pops, "County Conflict in West Virginia," *West Virginia Public Affairs Reporter* 15 (spring 1998): 2–7.

49. L. Christopher Plein and David G. Williams, "Local Government Finance in West Virginia," *West Virginia Public Affairs Reporter* 13 (fall 1996): 2–8.

WISCONSIN

Stephen E. C. Hintz

Home rule in Wisconsin has been established both constitutionally and statutorily for more than sixty years. In comparison with municipalities in most other states, Wisconsin municipalities come out well in their degree of freedom from interference by the state. However, in recent years, two areas of potential challenge to home rule have emerged. First, the prominent role that state government plays in financing local government, particularly public education, has encouraged the legislature to consider extending its authority over municipalities in a piecemeal way. Second, proposals to deal with urban land development issues suggest further limitations on municipal planning and zoning authority.

Governmental Setting

Wisconsin, long known as America's Dairyland, was the home of the Progressive movement, led by Fighting Bob La Follette, and of Sen. Joseph McCarthy. The state is a mix of urban and rural populations, progressive and conservative ideas, and populist and business-oriented policies. Although the state has the Milwaukee metropolitan region of over one million people, nearly 60 percent of the population lives in communities of fewer than 50,000 persons.

During the Progressive era (1901–1946), Wisconsin was a national leader among states in eliminating corruption in government, adopting pathbreaking social legislation, and using state resources to benefit its people. Although Progressivism is not an identifiable political force today, its legacy is still seen in the political culture of Wisconsin. The progressive income tax, introduced in 1908, is relied upon more heavily than in most states. Open-government laws are extremely stringent, and Wisconsin citizens value clean government. Historically, they have expected a high level of government services and strong public education.[1] Snow removal is important! Participation in local government has been encouraged by the presence of many governmental units (more than 2,300) and elected officials and very large legislative boards, especially at the county level. Voter participation is above the national average. During the past thirty years, however, state political and business leaders have become increasingly concerned about Wisconsin's image as a high-tax state.

There are 190 cities, 395 villages, and 72 counties in Wisconsin. In addition, there are 1,265 town governments, covering all of the unincorporated areas of the state. Ten Indian tribes have reservations, and although they have sovereign status with regard to state and local law, the tribes can and do enter into intergovernmental agreements with state and local governments.[2] Wisconsin has 377 special purpose districts, most of which are natural resource (168) and housing and community development (177) districts.[3]

Local government in Wisconsin is defined by state statute. Cities and villages, as incorporated areas, are subject to the provisions of municipal home rule. Although cities and villages are governed under both individual and uniform statutes, there are more similarities than differences between them. Towns, as unincorporated areas, are not covered by home rule provisions and can perform only those functions that are set forth explicitly in the statutes. In this chapter, *municipalities* refers to cities and villages.

Home Rule in Wisconsin

Historical Development

The statehood constitution of 1848 granted the legislature the power to issue charters of incorporation to municipalities. By 1899, spurred by efforts to eliminate favoritism and inconsistency in municipal charters, general charter law had replaced special charters of incorporation, and in 1921 all special charters were repealed with the exception of Milwaukee's.

Progressive efforts to remove municipalities from legislative control were launched in 1903 with the support of Gov. Robert M. La Follette. When in 1912 the Wisconsin Supreme Court declared the 1911 home rule statute void, home rule supporters began to campaign for a home rule amendment to the constitution, which was passed in 1924. By 1933 the legislature had completed revising the state municipal statutes. Rather than confronting a city with a long list of responsibilities, the statutes charged it with acting "for the government and good order of the city, for its commercial benefit, and for the health, safety, and welfare of the public." Thus, home rule is established by both the state constitution and the state statutes.[4]

Definition of Home Rule

The state constitution, as amended in 1933, says that

cities and villages organized pursuant to state law may determine their local affairs and government, subject only to this constitution and to such enactments of the legislature of statewide concern as with uniformity shall affect every city or every village. The method of such determination shall be prescribed by the legislature.[5]

Thus, the issue is which responsibilities are "local affairs" and which are of "statewide concern." The Wisconsin Supreme Court recognized as early as 1952 that some issues fell into both categories and that the test of "paramount interest" would have to be used, as ultimately determined by the courts.[6]

If a matter were wholly or primarily of statewide concern, then the constitutional home rule amendment would not apply. The state legislature could deal with such issues by delegating limited authority to municipalities or by prohibiting any local legislative action, free of any limitation contained in the constitutional home rule amendment. On the other hand, if a subject were wholly or primarily a local matter, a charter ordinance could be adopted by the municipality under the constitutional home rule amendment.

Localities have asserted their constitutional home rule sparingly, for two reasons. First, the courts have declared most legislation falling into the mixed category to be matters of paramount state concern.[7] Second, statutory law has been interpreted liberally in favor of municipalities. The statutory language for home rule is found in Chapter 62 of the Wisconsin State Statutes. According to this statute, "[f]or the purpose of giving to cities the largest measure of self-government compatible with the constitution and general law, it is hereby declared that ss 62.01 to ss 62.26 shall be liberally construed in favor of the rights, powers, and privileges of cities to promote the general welfare, peace, good order and prosperity of such cities and inhabitants thereof." Chapter 62 also states that the powers of the city "shall be limited only by express language." The Wisconsin Supreme Court held that in the absence of state legislation, local governments could exercise powers of government not expressly enumerated in the statutes.

In contrast to constitutional home rule, statutory home rule allows municipalities to adopt legislation on matters of statewide concern as long as the legislation complements and does not conflict with state legislation.[8] However, it is very clear that the legislature has the authority to take away the ability of municipalities to regulate certain subjects under statutory home rule.[9]

The legislative authority to withdraw statutory powers has been clarified further by the Wisconsin Supreme Court in what Claire Silverman, assistant legal counsel for the League of Wisconsin Municipalities, calls "a blow to municipal home rule by allowing preemption to be implied rather than express." The court adopted a four-part test to determine whether statutory home rule has been withdrawn: whether the legislature has expressly withdrawn municipalities' power to act; whether the ordinance logically conflicts with state legislation; whether the ordinance defeats the purpose of the state legislation; and whether the ordinance goes against the spirit of the state legislation. Increasingly, the courts have found in favor of legislative preemptions of the authority of municipalities to regulate in certain areas.[10]

Structural Features

Since 1921 Wisconsin municipalities have been legally defined by general statute, rather than by special charter. There are four classes of cities, determined by population size. A city's responsibilities and procedures are defined in part by its class. The use of classes was necessary both to comply with the "uniformity" clause of the state constitution and to recognize the varied circumstances of cities with different populations. Cities of the first class must have a population of 150,000 or more. Only Milwaukee is a first-class city, and the class, in effect, serves as a special charter for Milwaukee. Madison is large enough to be a city of the first class but is content not to assume the statutory requirements of first-class cities; it remains by choice a second-class city, even though it exceeds the second-class population range of 39,000 to 149,999. Third-class cities are defined as cities with a population of 10,000 to 38,999, and fourth-class cities as being under 10,000. In addition to Madison, twenty-three other cities eligible to move to a higher class have chosen not to do so. There are virtually no differences in authority between second- and third-class cities, and only a few differences between third- and fourth-class cities. Interestingly, 35 percent of Wisconsin villages are large enough to meet the requirement of 1,000 residents to become a city, including ten large enough to be third-class cities, but they choose to remain under the village statute (Chapter 61), which has no classes.[11]

The statutes give cities three specific options on the form of government: mayor-council, manager-council, and commission.[12] Of the 190 cities, 10 operate under the manager-council form, 180 under the mayor-council form, and none under the commission form, a form not seen in the state since 1959. Seventy-five of the mayor-council cities have established by charter ordinance or simple ordinance the position of administrator, although this position is not mentioned as a municipal officer in the statutes.[13] The home rule statute also grants municipalities the option of establishing other forms of government of their own choosing, as long as it is done by charter ordinance.[14] No municipalities have exercised this option other than to make minor changes, such as designating the council president as the "mayor" in a council-manager city, since the state statutes make no provision for a mayor in council-manager cities.

Villages, depending on size, normally have a board of trustees with three to seven members, including the village president as one trustee. The village president must be directly elected at large. A president does not have the same powers as a mayor and votes along with the other trustees. Villages also may adopt the statutorily defined manager option by charter ordinance or the administrator option.[15] There are eight village managers and sixty-eight village administrators in the state.

The state statute defines the various municipal officers but then provides latitude about which positions are required and how they are to be filled. Ultimately, a city must have an elected mayor (unless it has a manager under Wisconsin Statute, Chapter 64, which makes no reference to a mayor); an elected or appointed clerk, treasurer, attorney, and assessor; and an appointed police chief and fire chief. Positions can be combined, and the attorney and assessor positions can be filled on a contractual basis. The formation of committees, boards, and commissions is largely at the discretion of the municipality, except when it chooses to provide certain services that have statutorily defined governance procedures, such as public libraries and zoning regulations.[16]

Police and fire service governance constitutes the major exception to home rule in the structuring of government. Cities, with the exception of municipalities with fewer than 4,000 people, are required to establish five-member police and fire commissions. The commissions appoint and dismiss the chiefs, approve the appointments of other officers by the chiefs, and deal with disciplinary matters. Some commissions have optional powers that enable them to be responsible for departmental policy and budget.[17]

One of clearest cases pitting the polar positions of "local interest" and "statewide concern" against one another arose out of a police and fire issue. The City of Eau Claire sought to cross-train some of its police officers as firefighters. The police officers had completed their training by the time the firefighters union challenged the public safety officer concept on the grounds that the state statutes recognized police officer and firefighter as separate occupations. The city argued that under the constitutional home rule amendment it had the authority to structure its own organization for delivering local services. The state supreme court in 1989 ruled that the legislature had clearly spoken of separate city police and fire departments. In fact, the state statute discussing city police and fire departments declares that it is the legislative intent that the section be "construed as enactment of statewide intent."[18]

In order for incorporation as a municipality to occur, four steps must take place. First, at least 50 residents must petition for incorporation. Second, the circuit court must determine that the proposed city meets the population, area, and population-density requirements set forth in the statutes. The population requirement for village status is 150 persons for isolated communities and 2,500 persons for communities in metropolitan areas. For incorporation as a city, there must be at least 1,000 persons in isolated areas and at least 5,000 persons in metropolitan areas. The third step is that the state Department of Administration must determine that the proposed incorporation meets specified geographic requirements, is financially able to provide a sufficient level of services, does not impose an undue burden on any portions of the township not proposed for incorporation, and "will not substantially hinder the solution of governmental problems affecting the metropolitan community."[19] Finally, the incorporation petition must be approved by the town voters.

Since 1970 there have been only seventeen successful incorporations. The small number is due primarily to limited initiatives, but it is instructive to note that successful incorporations appear to require at least the tacit approval of the dominant contiguous city in a metropolitan area. The one exception to these rules resulted from special legislation that allows "townships with more than five thousand people adjacent to a city of the first class with an equalized evaluation in excess of $20 million" to accept a petition signed by at least 100 persons and to go straight to an incorporation referendum, bypassing the circuit court and the Department of Administration. Although this special legislation was designed to apply to only one town, two towns became cities under this provision.[20]

From the perspective of the cities, the relatively stringent requirements for incorporation are beneficial and are recognition by the state of the need to grant the existing cities some control over the evolving governmental structure of the metropolitan areas. Incorporation initiatives are essentially efforts by urban townships to prevent any further annexation by adjacent cities.

Annexation laws are the other side of the coin. Just as it is difficult for townships to incorporate, it is equally difficult for municipalities to carry out annexation procedures. Annexation requires the consent of the residents being annexed as well as the governing body of the annexing municipality. And in most cases, the parties to be annexed give their consent only when there is a clear need for a sewer or source of treated water. The statutes recognize three methods of annexation. Direct annexation occurs when a number of electors equal to 50 percent of voters in the last gubernatorial election *and* the owners of 50 percent of acreage *or* owners representing 50 percent of the equalized assessed valuation petition for annexation. Second, a referendum on annexation can be called for by a petition signed by electors at least equal to 20 percent of the voters in the last gubernatorial election *and* the owners of 50 percent of the real property, either in area or assessed value. The municipality then has the option of accepting or rejecting the request, except in certain sewer-related situations. Finally, a city, upon two-thirds vote of its governing body, can petition the circuit court for an annexation referendum. The court will grant the petition unless electors at least equal to a majority of township voters in the last gubernatorial election *or* the owners of more than half of the real property in assessed value sign a petition objecting to the move. If the referendum is conducted, a majority vote determines the outcome.[21]

The annexation laws are not favorable to cities. The only resources that they have are water and wastewater treatment facilities, and the only time that town residents seek annexation is when their wells and septic systems fail or people want to develop vacant land. Even under these circumstances, a request for annexation is the last resort, because towns usually attempt to negotiate water and wastewater treatment service without being annexed, and over the years, many towns have been successful. In the landmark case *Town of Hallie v. City of Eau Claire,* the U.S. Supreme Court ruled that Eau Claire had to extend sewer treatment if asked but could require the petitioners to be annexed to the city. This case was a major victory for cities.[22] But in 1997 the State Interagency Land Use Council recommended that annexation not be a requirement of sewer service extension. Even more troubling to municipalities was its recommendation that the extraterritorial zoning and plat approval authority of cities and villages be exercised by joint planning boards with equal town and city or village representation.[23]

Cities and villages do have extraterritorial zoning and subdivision platting authority, but with substantial restrictions attached. Extraterritorial authority in unincorporated areas extends three miles for cities of the first, second, and third classes and one and one-half miles for fourth-class cities and for villages. A comprehensive extraterritorial zoning ordinance requires approval from a joint city-town committee, and platting is subject to the approval of both the town board and the municipal council or board. Municipalities can own property beyond their boundaries.[24]

Counties are the oldest unit of government in Wisconsin; three counties were established in 1818, when Wisconsin was still part of the Michigan Territory. Since 1985 Wisconsin's seventy-two counties have possessed "administrative home rule," or the authority to "exercise any organizational or administrative power, subject only to the constitution and any enactment of the legislature which is of statewide concern and which uniformly affects every county."[25] Administrative home rule provides counties with some control over nonstatutory positions and operations. However, since most county department heads, ranging from sheriff to coroner, are defined by statute as elected positions, the impact of administrative home rule has been relatively modest. Counties can decide whether to have an elected executive or an appointed administrator. If they choose neither, a county officer is designated as the administrative coordinator, a position without appointment authority. The size and composition of the county board have been contentious issues since statehood. Currently, the statute sets upper limits on the size of the board, depending on the population of the county, with the exception of Milwaukee County, which can set its own limit. Wisconsin county boards are notoriously large, ranging from seven to thirty-nine supervisors, with an average of twenty-five.

Functions of Local Government

Functional Responsibilities

Wisconsin has maintained a tradition of multifunctional units of local government, using special districts only sparingly. The most significant districts covering more than one jurisdiction are several metropolitan sewer districts. Housing and community development authorities constitute most of the urban special-use structures.

Cities and villages have substantial discretion over the nature and level of services to provide. They are charged by statute with the "management and control of the [municipal] property, finances, highways, navigable waters, and the public service, and shall have the power to act for the government and good order of the [municipality], for its commercial benefit, and for the health, safety, and welfare of the public."[26] Municipalities are obligated to provide police and fire protection, although they may contract for these services. Customarily, municipalities provide water and sewer service, trash collection and recycling, road maintenance, parks, planning and zoning, library services, inspection services, and permits for various activities. Most larger municipalities are extensively involved in economic development and redevelopment activities. Some municipalities provide recreational programming; others use services provided by school recreation departments. Public transportation, an option, is provided by twenty-four larger urban municipalities, either independently or as part of a transit authority.[27] A handful of municipalities own hospitals.

Although the statutes grant considerable latitude to municipalities on which services to provide, once the municipality chooses to offer the service, specific statutory rules must be followed. For example, municipalities have the option of establishing a plan commission and developing a comprehensive plan, adopting zoning regulations, and creating a public library. But if they provide these services, and all but the smallest municipalities do, they are subject to rules that are considered to have statewide implications. A municipality with a library must establish a library board with personnel and budgeting responsibilities. A municipality with zoning must establish a board of zoning appeals. Although many of the statutory requirements are procedural, there are state rules on group home density and location, historic preservation, and wetlands.

Most services provided by county governments are mandated by the state. The tasks performed by the clerk, sheriff, district attorney, circuit court judges, clerk of courts, register of deeds, coroner, and surveyor illustrate the traditional role of county government. Historically, counties have provided services for persons with financial, social, and developmental needs. These human services constitute the bulk of county expenditures. Counties are responsible for public health activities, although they may be shared with municipal health departments. Many counties operate nursing homes and facilities for developmentally disabled persons. Counties also have planning and zoning and road maintenance responsibilities in unincorporated areas.

The relationships between counties and municipalities are determined by statute, by long-standing practice, and by regional imperatives, and these relationships vary throughout the state. For example, city-county public safety buildings and city-county hospitals are mentioned in the statutes. Milwaukee County is responsible for the major parks, the regional public health facility, and mass transit in the metropolitan area. Outagamie County operates the public museum. Several counties operate landfill and recycling facilities for cities, villages, and towns.

Interlocal cooperation varies substantially, depending on function, location, and historical relationships. Mutual aid agreements among police and fire departments are common. Formal agreements on shared services, although permitted by statute, are considerably less common. In recent years, the most notable initiatives have been the establishment of a seven-municipality fire department and a two-municipality police department. School districts and municipalities often share specialized equipment.[28]

Administrative Discretion

For most operations, municipalities do not chafe under restrictions imposed by the state. Municipalities have fairly broad latitude to define positions and to establish recruitment and compensation standards and practices. Only cities of the first class (Milwaukee) are required to have a civil service system and a retirement system for all officers and employees, although almost all cities and most villages have a retirement program of some kind. Police officers, firefighters, assessors, building inspectors, and public health officers are required by state statute to have minimum training. Relations with employees belonging to recognized bargaining units are governed by the Municipal Employment Relations Act, which provides for binding arbitration in the event of an impasse. Contracting and purchasing rules are spelled out in the statutes but are not excessively restrictive.

Economic Development

Wisconsin municipalities have wide latitude in conducting development activities. They are given considerable authority by statute to conduct urban redevelopment projects, including condemning property and establishing redevelopment corporations.

Municipalities also can create tax incremental finance districts in areas that are blighted, in need of rehabilitation or conservation, or suitable for industrial sites.[29] The concept behind a tax incremental district is that new investment in the designated area will raise the assessed valuation there and that the additional tax revenue resulting from this investment will be used exclusively to pay for public infrastructure improvements in that district. Between the inception of tax incremental districts in 1976 and 1995, 849 districts were created, and the total assessed valuation rose from $29 million in 1977 to $3.8 billion in 1995. More than half of the investment in districts consisted of commercial property.[30] The state monitors the manner in which the districts are established but does not make decisions about the nature of the project.

Municipalities can issue industrial development revenue bonds for certain kinds of private investment. The range of allowable investment is fairly broad, but the state Department of Development must certify that the amount of the bond is available to the municipality.

Municipalities also are permitted to buy and sell land and buildings for industrial development purposes.[31] Municipalities cannot grant tax abatements on local property taxes.

Fiscal Autonomy of Local Governments

Local Revenues

Wisconsin is a relatively high tax and expenditure state. It raises substantial revenues at the state level that are spent at the local level, especially for public education, which receives two-thirds of its funding from the state. The state also limits the sources of revenue that local government units can tap. The revenue mix varies considerably by municipality because of the progressive state aid formula, which is discussed in a later section.

Historically, and today, the property tax is the mainstay of local government revenue (see Table 1). Other than the hotel/motel room tax and the little used wheel tax, municipalities have only the property tax as a local source of tax revenue. The income tax is the exclusive possession of the state, as is the sales tax, with the exception of the 0.5 percent county option. Other local revenues come from user fees, fines, permits, licenses, and gifts.

Over the years, the legislature has exempted various categories of property from taxation: utilities; organizations providing services that government might otherwise have to provide, such as cemeteries, colleges, and libraries; organizations providing for the common good, such as churches, YM/WCAs, and youth organizations; merchants' and manufacturers' inventories; manufacturers' machinery and equipment; and motor vehicles. In each instance, the state initially sought to reimburse

Table 1. Municipal Sources of Revenue, 1986 and 1996, as Percentage of Total Revenue

Revenue source	Milwaukee		Other cities		Villages	
	1986	1996	1986	1996	1986	1996
Property taxes	29.4%	22.7%	32.0%	36.6%	31.7%	36.0%
Special assessment	5.8	5.2	8.0	9.8	8.3	12.2
State aid	41.9	46.3	37.8	30.9	36.4	29.3
Other (including federal assistance)	8.2	7.7	4.8	2.9	3.1	1.3
Fees/charges	8.6	9.5	9.4	11.6	10.7	12.2
Miscellaneous	6.1	8.5	8.0	8.2	9.8	9.0

Source: The Wisconsin Taxpayer 66 (September 1998), 6–7.

communities for the loss of their property tax base, but not always at full value.

The limitation on property tax levies and on municipal expenditures is a very touchy subject at this time. Currently, municipalities are not subject to property tax or spending limits, but counties and school districts are. Under the expenditure restraint program, municipalities receive additional state aid if they do not increase their annual expenditure by more than 3 percent. In 1999, the highest tax rate was $15.56 per $1,000 of value and the state average was $8.52 per $1,000 for cities; for villages, the state average was $6.21 per $1,000.[32]

Municipalities have substantial latitude in the issuance of public debt, as long as it is for a public purpose. The state constitution limits indebtedness of municipalities to 5 percent of equalized assessed valuation of property. Excluded from the constitutional limitation are borrowing financed by revenue bonds and short-term borrowing in anticipation of revenue. Most general obligation borrowing must be repaid within twenty years, although there are some expenditure types for which the repayment period is fifty years. The debt limitation does not appear to have imposed serious hardships on municipalities. For municipalities with more than ten thousand people, the general obligation debt ranged from 0.72 percent to 4.04 percent in 1993.[33]

Cities and villages are not required to conduct referenda on borrowing for most projects that are enumerated in the statutes, unless within thirty days of passage of the borrowing resolution a petition calling for a referendum is submitted with signatures equal to at least 10 percent of the last vote for governor. Municipal governing bodies on their own volition may submit a proposal to borrow for a referendum.

Local Expenditures

Municipal expenditures vary according to the types and levels of service provided, with larger municipalities, not unexpectedly, spending more in gross terms and per capita than smaller municipalities (see Table 2). For example, the larger cities are likely

Table 2. Municipal Expenditures as a Percentage of Total Expenditures, 1997

Function	Cities	Villages
General government	9.4%	11.2%
Public safety	30.9	24.5
Public works	24.8	33.2
Health and human services	2.6	0.4
Libraries, parks, and recreation	9.2	8.1
Housing, development, and conservation	7.8	5.0
Debt service	15.3	17.5

Source: Wisconsin Department of Revenue, 1997 Summary of Revenues and Expenditures. (Madison: Department of Revenue, 1998).

to have full-time fire departments rather than volunteer departments, health departments separate from the county, and more extensively staffed police departments.

State Government Grants-in-Aid to Localities

State aid to municipalities constitutes a major source of discretionary revenue. Originally, the sharing of state taxes was designed to replace the revenue that municipalities lost when the state passed a major property tax exemption. For example, when utility property was declared exempt from the local property tax and the state assessed the property and collected the tax, 85 percent of the state collections were distributed to the municipalities in which the utilities were located. However, the portion returned did not always equal the property tax lost. For example, the state began to replace only 50 percent of the revenue that municipalities lost to the machinery and equipment exemption. For many years, however, this approach worked quite well, but disparities among municipalities eventually grew to the point that some municipalities had no or very low property taxes. In 1972 the system for distributing shared taxes was changed to reflect the relative wealth of the community rather than the amount of property exempted from the local tax. The current shared revenues program has three parts: a per capita appropriation ($25–$30); revenues based on a formula that considers locally raised revenue and the per capita equalized value of taxable property, called aidable revenues; and a public utility payment. It is the aidable revenues part that equalizes the share of state aid received by municipalities. In 1991 a tax rate disparity, or expenditure restraint, program began which provides additional shared revenue to municipalities that keep annual operating budget increases within a set limit as a fiscal incentive.[34]

State-shared revenues constitute a significant source of municipal funding. Shared revenues in recent years have ranged from less than 10 percent of property tax revenues in property-rich communities to over 150 percent in cities with a low equalized assessed valuation per capita. Shared revenues for municipalities were $1.008 billion for the 1998–1999 biennium, representing 10.1 percent of the state budget. The level of shared revenues continues to be a source of tension between state and local officials because of their fundamentally different perspectives on the revenues. In 1990 the Wisconsin Taxpayers Alliance aptly wrote, "at the state level, the payments are labeled property tax relief. Local officials regard the payments as reimbursement for loss of tax bases caused by state-enacted property tax exemptions, partial payments for state-imposed mandates or the equalization of local tax burdens by redistributing state revenues."[35] The increase in shared revenues for cities, villages, and towns from the 1988–1989 biennium to the 1998–1999 biennium was a modest 24.9 percent, in contrast to the increase of 94.4 percent for state assistance to all local government units, especially schools but also counties. This suggests legislative indifference toward if not disfavor for shared revenues to municipalities.

Unfunded Mandates

Municipal concern about unfunded state mandates has been directed primarily at recycling, pollution, and ground contamination requirements, although it is fair to say that municipalities are more concerned about federal rules, such as the Fair Labor Standards Act, the Americans with Disabilities Act, and various Environmental Protection Agency standards. Counties have been upset by requirements in the administration of various human service programs. When state-required binding arbitration brings wage awards above what municipalities want to pay, some local leaders complain that binding arbitration is an unfunded mandate. State agencies maintain consistent oversight on mandates, and the level of municipal compliance is high.

Access to Local Government

Local Elections

Primary elections for municipal offices and the nonpartisan county offices of executive and supervisor are conducted in February, and the general election in April. Elections for the parti-

san county offices—sheriff, clerk, register of deeds, coroner, treasurer, district attorney, clerk of courts—and for state and federal posts are held in the fall. Procedures for elections of officers at all levels of government are comprehensive and detailed. The tasks assigned to the county and municipal clerks leave no room for discretion. Candidates in all municipalities follow the same statutorily defined procedures and are subject to the same campaign rules, including reporting campaign contributions and expenditures to the State Elections Board. There are modest differences between villages and cities in that villages can use a caucus, rather than a primary, to select candidates for the general election. Also, the size of the municipality determines the number of signatures required to get on the ballot. Overall, however, election rules are uniform throughout the state, with the statutes providing some latitude on calling a referendum and determining the date of a special election.

Citizen Controls over Actions of Local Officials

Although the Wisconsin constitution permits the recall of members of the U.S. Congress, state officers, judges, and county officials, it is silent on recall of elected municipal officers. The state statutes, however, do provide for the recall of elected city, village, town, and school district officials. The process is initiated by a petition that states the cause of the recall and contains valid signatures equal to at least 25 percent of the votes cast in the last election for governor. The circuit court must certify that the reason for recall is stated on the petition but is not to judge the truth or falsity of the stated reason. In the recall election, the incumbent is presumed to be a candidate unless the incumbent withdraws. Other persons qualify as candidates by the regular petition process. If there are more than two candidates for a single office, a recall primary election is held.[36] Recall elections are very rare in Wisconsin municipalities. In recent years, recall efforts have been limited primarily to school districts over such issues as intradistrict boundaries or changing the high school mascot.

Elected officials also can be impeached, although impeachment is extremely rare. In cities they may be removed "for cause" by a three-quarters vote of all members of the common council. Village elective officers may be removed for "continued physical inability to perform the duties of office or gross neglect of duty" by a majority vote of all the members of the village board.[37]

Citizens can exercise the right of initiative. The state statutes contain a provision for "direct legislation" in cities and villages whereby electors equal to at least 15 percent of the votes cast in the municipality for governor in the last election can file a petition requesting that a proposed ordinance or resolution, without alteration, either be adopted by the governing body or referred to a vote of the electors. If the governing body fails to take action, then the proposal is automatically submitted to a referendum.[38] Direct legislation has been used primarily by citizens wanting to change the form of government to or from the council-manager form. It has been used sparingly during the past twenty years—perhaps no more than ten times—although there may be a modest upward trend.

The charter ordinance process also provides the option of a referendum. A charter ordinance requires a two-thirds vote of approval by the city council or village board and then a waiting period of sixty days before it goes into effect. If during this waiting period a valid petition with signatures equal to at least 7 percent of the last vote for governor is submitted, then a binding referendum must be held. Again, such referenda occur infrequently, usually in reaction to the governing body's creation of the administrator position. Finally, councils and boards can initiate advisory or binding referenda.[39]

Citizens have good access to public records and to public meetings under the state statutes, which apply uniformly to all governmental units and officials. The statutory presumption is that records and meetings shall be open to the public unless there is a compelling public interest for them not to be open. Most records and meetings about personnel can be restricted, although there is substantial case law about the balance between individual rights and the public interest.[40]

State-Local Relations

Home rule is not a general rallying cry of municipalities, and in many cases the issues that arise emerge from the concerns of individual municipalities. Nonetheless, the outcomes of the issues usually have broad implications. There are three areas in which the relationship between the state and municipalities is uneasy. The first is that of financing municipal government. The property tax in Wisconsin is called a general property tax, but over the past 125 years the scope of the tax has been narrowed to the point that it has become a tax on real property. As mentioned earlier, as the state has exempted various types of property, it has attempted to replace the lost revenue with state-shared revenue. Since 1972 state officials also have sought to redistribute the shared revenues from property-rich to property-poor communities.

Raising money at the state level and spending it at the local level creates what the Wisconsin Taxpayers' Alliance calls "fiscal schizophrenia." The governor and state legislators believe that they are doing all the revenue work and that local officials are not being responsible in holding down property taxes. Their perception does little to restrain state interest in regulating local government in a variety of ways. As the taxpayers' alliance has put it,

when state governments raise the bulk of revenues, the adage "He who has the gold makes the rules" often applies. State officials take a more active interest in local government spending because they

provide the money. Blaming local officials for waste and inefficiency, they impose mandates and cost controls on municipalities, counties and schools.[41]

To date, cost controls have been imposed on school districts and counties but not on municipalities, which may be due to the residual concept of home rule. On the other side, since local governments have few financing tools other than the local property tax and rely heavily on the state for funds, they are likely to blame the governor and legislature for inadequate funding and increased mandates.

The increasing financial pressures that municipalities face appear to have less to do with home rule issues than with two legislative decisions made in 1995. The first, and by far the more significant, was to assume responsibility for funding two-thirds of public education costs in order to provide local property tax relief. This required the legislature to find an extra $1.2 billion in the first biennium, without income or sales tax increases. Reducing the growth of shared revenues is a tempting option for the legislature. The second legislative decision was to change the assessment of agricultural property from a market-value to a use-value basis. The revenue impact of this change, now fully implemented, will be an average local tax increase of 1 to 3 percent to make up for lost property taxes. The annual revenue that will need to be made up by the largest municipalities is estimated at $85 million.

The second area is the impasse over annexation and incorporation rules. Urban areas continue to have problems with sprawl and relatively unregulated growth in the townships. Many of the town residents, and particularly town officials, are adamantly opposed to annexation to adjacent cities, thus effectively blocking any annexation attempts. Cities and villages want more authority to annex. On the other hand, towns want more authority to prevent annexation but would like the incorporation requirements to be eased. Resolution of this stalemate is not likely to occur soon, not because the state wishes to limit municipal authority and autonomy but because towns in Wisconsin carry a good deal of political clout. There are 1,265 towns in the state, each with its own government. Approximately 120 of them have populations above 2,500, and five have populations between 11,000 and 23,000. This is an issue that legislators do not wish to touch because there is no popular resolution.

Finally, a series of legislative and judicial decisions has narrowed the scope of municipal home rule. At the legislative level, various interest groups often lobby for statutes of statewide concern in order to reverse or preempt local policies. For example, the National Rifle Association was particularly active in the passage of legislation prohibiting municipal regulations on firearms unless they are the "same as or similar to, and no more stringent than" state law.[42] Another issue is whether a municipality should be able to require residency for municipal employees.

The uneasy fiscal relationship between state and local government provided the impetus for Gov. Tommy Thompson to establish, in early 2000, the Commission on State-Local Partnerships for the Twenty-First Century. The commission is charged with the Herculean challenge of evaluating and redesigning the structure of government in Wisconsin, a task well beyond determining who should raise and spend public money. At the state level, there is considerable sentiment for eliminating shared revenues altogether, but there is also recognition that such a move would require the state to assume directly some responsibilities now performed by local governments.

Municipalities in Wisconsin have had considerable statutory latitude to determine the nature and level of services to be provided and the manner in which they are provided. Even where the statutes prescribe rules for municipalities, these rules often provide options and do not impose onerous burdens, although the court's recognition of implied preemption and the legislature's moves to preempt local legislation or to permit only local legislation that strictly conforms to state statutes have narrowed home rule opportunities for municipalities. The recommendations of the commission may stimulate revisions in the state-local fiscal relationship and, to some degree, in the allocation of responsibilities, but the fundamental legal relationship between state and local government is not likely to change.

Notes

1. Ronald E. Weber, "The Social, Economic, and Historical Context of Wisconsin Politics." In *Crane and Hagensick's Wisconsin Government and Politics,* 6th ed., ed. Ronald E. Weber (New York: McGraw-Hill, 1996), 9.

2. *State of Wisconsin Blue Book 1997–1998,* sesquicentennial ed. (Madison: Wisconsin Legislative Reference Bureau, 1997), 231.

3. Ibid., 706–707.

4. James R. Donoghue, "The Local Government System of Wisconsin." In *State of Wisconsin 1968 Blue Book* (Madison: Wisconsin Legislative Reference Bureau, 1968), 109–110.

5. State of Wisconsin Constitution, Article XI, section 3 (1).

6. *Muench v. Public Service Commission,* 261 Wis. 492, 53 N.W. 2d 514 (1952).

7. Claire Silverman, "Municipal Home Rule in Wisconsin," *Municipality* 93 (October 1998), 384.

8. Ibid., 385.

9. Donoghue, "The Local Government System of Wisconsin," 110.

10. *Anchor Savings and Loan Association v. Equal Opportunities Commission,* 120 Wis. 2d 391, 355 N.W. 2d 234 (1984).

11. *Wisconsin 1997–1998 Blue Book,* 714–723.

12. Wisconsin Statutes, Chaps. 62 and 64.

13. *Thompson v. Whitefish Bay,* 257 Wis. 151, 42 N.W. 2d 462 (1950).

14. Wisconsin Statutes, Chap. 64.

15. Ibid., section 61.20.

16. Ibid., section 62.09.

17. Ibid., section 62.13.

18. Ibid., section 62.13(12).

19. Ibid., section 66.016(2)(d).

20. Ibid., section 66.012. For Fitchburg, see *City of Madison v. Town of Fitchburg,* 112 w (2d) 224, 332 N.W. (2d) 782 (1989).

21. Wisconsin Statutes, section 66.021.

22. *Town of Hallie v. City of Eau Claire,* 471 U.S. 34 (1985).

23. *Planning Wisconsin: Report of the State Interagency Land Use Council,* July 1, 1996, 8–9.

24. Wisconsin Statutes, section 66.32.

25. Ibid., section 59.025.

26. Ibid., section 62.11(5).

27. *Wisconsin 1997–1998 Blue Book,* 811.

28. Wisconsin Statutes, section 66.30.

29. Ibid., section 66.435.

30. "Tax Increment Financing in Wisconsin," *The Wisconsin Taxpayer* 64 (March 1996).

31. Wisconsin Statutes, section 66.52.

32. "Municipal Property Taxes and State Aids," *The Wisconsin Taxpayer* 67 (April 1999).

33. "Wisconsin State and Local Debt," *The Wisconsin Taxpayer* 62 (November 1994).

34. "Municipal Property Taxes and State Aids," *The Wisconsin Taxpayer* 67 (April 1999).

35. "Shared Revenues," *The Wisconsin Taxpayer* 58 (July 1990), and "Municipal Property Taxes and State Aids," *The Wisconsin Taxpayer* 67 (April 1999).

36. Wisconsin Statutes, section 9.70.

37. Ibid., sections 17.12 and 17.13.

38. Ibid., section 9.20.

39. Ibid., sections 9.20 and 66.01(5).

40. Ibid., sections 19.31 to 19.37.

41. Wisconsin Taxpayers Alliance, *Focus,* October 14, 1994.

42. Wisconsin Statutes, section 66.092(2).

WYOMING

Robert A. Schuhmann

Wyoming is a large, lightly populated, rural state characterized by independent thinking and a political culture that might be described as "libertarian conservatism." Of the twenty-three counties and ninety-seven municipalities, only eight cities boast populations greater than 10,000. Of these cities, only three embrace the council-manager form of government; the remainder employ the mayor-council form. Strong local government autonomy is a relatively recent phenomenon for municipalities and a topic that continues to generate many debates. Indeed, many local officials believe that home rule has not turned out to be the gift originally intended.

Governmental Setting

Gretel Ehrlich writes, "In most parts of Wyoming, the human population is visibly outnumbered by the animal."[1] With only five people per square mile, Wyoming ranks second only to Alaska for lowest population density in the nation. Wyoming is generally characterized as a pastoral state, where a frontier spirit and rugged individualism guide both citizens and government. This environment is important in shaping the concept and use of home rule in the state.

Wyoming's tourism motto, "Like No Place on Earth," keenly describes the state's politics as well as its geography. In fact, the state's origin can be traced to a bold move that is reflective of the state's frontier spirit. In 1889, unwilling to wait for formal authorization in the form of an enabling act, territorial governor Francis E. Warren called for a constitutional convention without approval from the U.S. Congress.

Wyoming's drive for statehood reflected widespread disaffection with federal control. A particularly trenchant example of Wyomingites' disaffection was their expelling in 1877 of the Wyoming territorial justice, William Ware Peck, for "arrogance and insensitivity to local customs."[2] Prominent Wyoming historian T. A. Larson contended that Peck was "too deliberate for many people who were accustomed to having court business wrapped up in a hurry."[3]

Delegates drafted Wyoming's constitution in only twenty-five days. It was of the cut-and-paste variety, relying heavily on other states' constitutional documents, particularly those of Colorado, Pennsylvania, Montana, and Illinois.[4] This is not to say, however, that Wyoming's new constitution lacked a sense of progressiveness and planning. The state constitution included such notable legal contributions as women's suffrage, water and mining law, and a prisoner's right to humane treatment. Other radical constitutional provisions included the right of citizens to "abolish the government in any manner they may think proper." Further, the constitution gave the concept of church and state separation specific form by prohibiting the appropriation of public funds for religious organizations and prohibiting religious instruction in public schools.

After the new constitution was adopted at the convention and approved by voters with a low voter turnout, Wyoming delegate Joseph M. Carey introduced a Wyoming statehood bill in the U.S. House of Representatives.[5] After much wrangling in the House, and less in the Senate, President Benjamin Harrison signed the statehood bill on July 10, 1890. Wyoming became the forty-fourth state of the Union.

Conservatism is the hallmark of Wyoming political culture.[6] Wyoming's brand of conservatism is libertarian rather than social.[7] What this means in practice is that Wyomingites hold many traditionally conservative political values, such as fiscal constraint, while they reject any government intrusion into the moral lives of citizens on such issues as political equality for women, freedom of speech, and abortion. Their self-perceived "rugged individualism" is a reflection of their brand of conservatism: Wyomingites believe that they are more self-reliant than other Americans.[8] Historically, a higher percentage of Wyomingites have registered as Republican than have the citizens of any other state. In 1994 nearly 60 percent of voters were registered Republicans—the highest percentage of Republican registration in the nation.[9]

Among the government's most distinct features is its "citizen legislature." Citizens of Wyoming endorse the notion that legislators should, in addition to their legislative role, have "real" jobs away from the capitol, where they must earn a wage and live among their constituents. As legislators, they should make decisions without the help of large staffs.[10] In order to ensure the part-time character of the institution, Article 3, section 6 of the Wyoming Constitution states that the legislature may meet for no more than sixty days every two years (twenty of these days are set aside exclusively for budget issues). In fact, the legislative session was limited to forty days until 1972, when a constitutional amendment added a budget session, to be held in even-numbered years.

In terms of structure, the executive branch is the largest and most complex feature of Wyoming government. It is where 98 percent of all state employees work.[11] The governor is the chief executive officer but does not supervise all of state government. Four other officials—secretary of state, auditor, treasurer, and superintendent of public instruction—are also elected on a partisan ballot. These officials have their own authority, granted to them by the state constitution. Of note, Wyoming was the first state to elect a female governor, Nellie Tayloe Ross, who was inaugurated in 1925.

Wyoming's judicial branch contains four levels. Municipal courts are at the bottom, county and justice of the peace courts next, followed by district courts, and finally the state supreme court.[12] The county courts are the "work horses" of the state judicial system. In 1994 county courts disposed of 122,277 cases, including both civil and criminal misdemeanors.[13]

Wyoming has had only one constitution and one constitutional convention, a distinction that can be claimed by only eighteen other states, and a distinction that bespeaks of political stability.[14] Generally, then, Wyoming politics and political culture reflect conservatism, rugged individualism, and, according to Daniel J. Elazar, a degree of internal unity matched by few other states.[15]

Home Rule in Wyoming

Historical Development

Before the establishment of home rule in 1972, municipalities in Wyoming were required to seek specific state legislative authority to act. The local government policy environment was shaped by Dillon's Rule, which holds that state power is supreme over municipalities. State supremacy, coupled with the legislature's extremely short general session and an increasingly complex urban environment, was a powerful motivating force behind the movement for home rule.

Further complicating municipal action, the Wyoming Constitution establishes four classifications of cities according to population. Any municipal legislation passed by the state must be acceptable to all cities within a particular class. This stipulation required an individual city to lobby not only the state legislators but also other cities in the same class. In many instances, the cities in a given class could not agree on what was desirable legislation. Because of the Herculean task of gaining municipal consensus and legislative approval, much needed municipal legislation never passed.

The Wyoming Association of Municipalities in both 1967 and 1969 introduced home rule legislation without success. In 1971 the association prepared another resolution for introduction into the state senate during its legislative session. This resolution passed. Closely patterned after home rule legislation in Kansas, the Wyoming measure was modified slightly to meet the needs of several special interest groups in the state. For example, "the Wyoming branch of the International Association of Fire Fighters feared that municipalities might exempt themselves from collective bargaining statutes, so these statutes were placed beyond the reach of municipal nullification."[16] Such appeasements eliminated much of the previous organized opposition to home rule.

With little resistance, the home rule measure passed both the senate and the house and was placed on the November 1972 ballot for citizens to consider. The voters ratified the measure, and from December 12, 1972, Wyoming municipalities enjoyed increased authority to govern themselves.

Definition of Home Rule

Wyoming home rule authority applies to all incorporated municipalities in the state and is constitutionally, rather than statutorily, authorized. Thus, at least in the abstract, municipalities have the most solid home rule foundation available.

Article 13 of the state constitution sets forth the basic powers and limits of municipal corporations and, as amended, is also where home rule authority can be found. The home rule amendment is a convincing mandate from the people to cities and towns to govern themselves:

All cities and towns are hereby empowered to determine their local affairs and government as established by ordinance passed by the governing body. . . .

The powers and authority granted to cities and towns, pursuant to this section, shall be liberally construed for the purpose of giving the largest measure of self-government to cities.[17]

Accordingly, the burden is now on the state legislature and the courts to find municipal actions unlawful when they conflict with the provisions established in the amended constitution. In the past, the burden was on local governments to cajole the legislature into believing that a particular new municipal grant of power was necessary and not in conflict with state law. As such, according to the Wyoming Association of Municipalities, home rule is designed to restore "grassroots democracy" to local governments.

Structural Features

The power to affect local conditions under home rule in Wyoming is subject only to:[18]

1. Referendum when prescribed by the legislature
2. Statutes uniformly applicable to all municipalities
3. Statutes prescribing limits of indebtedness
4. Laws in effect on December 12, 1972 (the effective date of the home rule amendment) relating to the incorporation of

cities and towns, the methods by which city and town boundaries may be altered, and the procedures by which cities and towns may be merged, consolidated, or dissolved, as well as existing laws pertaining to civil service, retirement, collective bargaining, and the levying of taxes, fees, or any other charges whether or not applicable to all municipalities on the effective date of the home rule amendment.[19]

Although the constitution formally provides for the possibility of four classes of cities, Wyoming law recognizes only two: first-class cities and all other incorporated municipalities. The former are incorporated municipalities having a population of 4,000 or more that have been declared first-class cities.[20] Special privilege legislation is occasionally directed at one class or the other. For example, the legislature has passed auditing and taxing legislation that is directed at only those local governments that are bound by the Uniform Municipal Fiscal Procedures Act; only first-class cities are so bound.

Title 15 of the Wyoming Statutes allows for the adoption of one of three traditional forms of government—mayor-council, council-manager, and commission. The mayor-council form is by far the most popular. According to the Wyoming Association of Municipalities, there are only three council-manager governments in the state, and no association members currently use the commission form. The Wyoming Statutes also specify that the size of the elected body depends on the form of government and the population of the municipality. Specifically, in the commission form, there can be only two commissioners (a commissioner of finance and public property and a commissioner of streets and public improvements) and a mayor. In council-manager cities with populations above 20,000 there are nine council members; in those having a population between 4,000 and 20,000 there are seven; and in cities and towns below 4,000 there are three council members and the mayor. In the mayor-council form, a *town's* elected body consists of a mayor and four council members; a *first-class city* that adopts the mayor-council form has a mayor and a number of council members equal to the number of wards in the city, which is determined by the council itself.

Wyoming state law provides that any territory not included in an incorporated city or town, having a resident population of not less than 500, and which contains within its boundaries an area of not more than three square miles may be incorporated.[21] Any person applying for incorporation must have an accurate survey and map that shows the boundaries and the amount of land to be incorporated. Not more than forty days prior to presenting the application for incorporation to the county board of commissioners, a census must be taken of the resident population of the area under consideration showing the name of the head of household and the number of persons in that household.[22] However, no territory within one mile of an incorporated city or town may be incorporated unless the governing body

of the city or town next to the area seeking incorporation approves the proposal.[23]

After this application is signed by a majority of the electors residing within the territory, it is filed with the county board of commissioners. If, after a public hearing, the board finds all requirements have been satisfied, it appoints three inspectors, who then call an election of all qualified electors within the territory. If a majority of all the votes cast are in favor of incorporation, the incorporation is accomplished.[24]

Annexation of territory can occur at the initiative of either landowners or a governing body (as of this writing, a moratorium on government-forced annexation is in effect). In either case, at a public hearing the governing body must find that the annexation is being considered for reasons of the health, safety, and welfare of both the persons residing in the area proposed to be annexed and the citizens of the city annexing the parcel.[25] If after the hearing the governing body finds that the conditions for annexation have been met, it by ordinance annexes the territory.[26] A minimum area for annexation has not been established by state statute and is left up to the individual municipality.

Counties are a mainstay of Wyoming government. According to state statute, the commission form is the only governmental structure available to counties, and home rule is not provided for these units. The lack of county autonomy is frequently noted in the Wyoming press. For example, during a controversy over whether counties can enact their own liquor laws, the acting Laramie County attorney, Margy White, said, "unlike cities and towns, counties do not have 'home rule' and cannot make the argument that Sunday liquor hours are a local [county] control issue."[27]

A three- or five-member board of commissioners governs each county. In addition to the commissioners, who are elected to serve four-year terms, state law requires the election of an assessor, attorney, clerk, sheriff, surveyor, and treasurer.[28]

Cities have extraterritorial jurisdiction for a number of purposes, including zoning, sanitation, public health, and "the comfort and general prosperity of the city."[29] Their jurisdiction extends five miles beyond their corporate limits for the enforcement of health and quarantine ordinance and regulation, and one-half mile in all other matters excepting taxation.[30] The one-half mile jurisdiction has been interpreted by city officials to mean an extraterritorial zoning jurisdiction. Generally, however, the one-half mile zoning jurisdiction is not utilized by any city in the state, and to do so would be viewed as a highly "aggressive" move for any city to carry out.[31] The five-mile jurisdiction was tested in 1996. The Wyoming Supreme Court reaffirmed the five-mile extraterritorial jurisdiction when Fireworks Unlimited requested a permit to sell its products one-half mile outside the city limits of Riverton. The court ruled that "cities and towns in Wyoming can regulate the sales of fireworks as far as five miles outside of their city limits."[32]

Functions of Local Government

Functional Responsibilities

Cities exist to provide a variety of public improvements and services that the state is unwilling, or unable, to provide. For cities in Wyoming, this role includes providing such basic services as police and fire protection, solid waste disposal, and water and sewer service. In addition, cities perform a variety of other functions, including constructing and maintaining infrastructure, such as streets and public utilities, and regulating pool halls, bowling alleys, and shooting galleries.[33]

County governments also provide important services to citizens. As counties are the primary agents of the state, they are required to perform several duties and are authorized to carry out others. For example, counties are authorized to establish a law enforcement and judicial system (in fact, each county is required to elect a sheriff), and they are required to take care of auto licensing and to maintain basic documents and records, such as marriages, wills, mortgages, and deeds to property. In addition, counties also determine property values and collect taxes. Furthermore, as a matter of course as well as a result of citizen pressure, counties in Wyoming often establish hospitals, cemeteries, recreation programs, museums, fire and rescue services, and programs for the elderly.[34]

Wyoming statutes allow for a variety of other governing units aside from cities and counties. These special districts, approximately 550 in all, are separate entities and are considered by law as political subdivisions of the state.[35] Special districts allowed by law include solid waste, museum, conservation, water conservancy, and weed and pest districts, to name only a few.[36] These districts are governed by both elected and appointed boards, and there is no clear connection between how a governing body is constituted and the purpose assigned to the board.

The most formal mechanisms for interlocal cooperation arise under the Joint Powers Act. This act and the subsequent statutes authorize counties, municipalities, and special districts to enter into joint or cooperative agreements to manage a common undertaking, such as water, sewerage, and solid waste disposal systems.[37]

Administrative Discretion

The state gives municipal governments in Wyoming wide latitude in conducting their own administrative affairs, excepting a few standard processes and procedures, such as civil service systems for fire and police departments in cities with populations above 4,000. In addition, city and town officials must abide by conflict of interest laws in both Title 15 and Title 6 of the criminal code. Each municipality must establish rules regarding conflicts of interest and any procedures for exempting an employee under special circumstances.[38] Any municipal officer who violates these provisions is subject to criminal penalties and removal from office after a hearing.

Wyoming statutes require that each city keep a journal of its proceedings, to include the votes of elected officials, which becomes a public record.[39] In addition, twice each year (in January and July) the name, position, and gross monthly salary of each chief administrative official, assistant administrative official, and department head, elected or otherwise, must be published. The state also establishes a procedure for publishing all ordinances during and after the adoption process and requires that a certificate of the clerk and the seal of the municipality accompany all approved ordinances. These ordinances must be codified, published, and accessible to the public.[40]

Additional administrative procedures required by state law regulate the sale of public property and contracts for public improvements. Excluding contracts for professional services, all purchases must be advertised for bid if the cost exceeds $7,500.[41] Contracts for the purchase of new automobiles or trucks must be advertised regardless of the cost. Contracts must be let to the lowest bidder who is determined by the governing body to be "qualified and responsible." The city may reject all bids if it finds that none are in the public interest.[42]

Planning, zoning, and land-use controls are tools generally used by cities and towns, although state statutes allow all forms of local government to regulate development. Given the political culture of the state, it is not surprising that counties have resisted any attempt to plan or organize growth. State statutes authorize cities and towns to appoint planning commissions and for these bodies to develop master plans for the community. The governing body of any city or town may, by ordinance, manage development by dividing the territory into zoning districts and within those districts restricting the construction and use of buildings and land; restricting the height of structures and the size of yards and other open spaces; and regulating population densities. Regulations may differ from one district to another but must be uniform for each class within a district. These measures should be taken "with a view to conserving the value of buildings and encouraging the most appropriate use of land throughout the city or town."[43]

Economic Development

Title 15, Chapter 9 of the Wyoming Statutes provides municipalities with broad latitude to engage in development and redevelopment efforts. The statutes encourage municipalities to afford maximum opportunity to private enterprise in its pursuit of this type of development.[44] Municipal governing bodies have authority to levy special taxes, zone particular districts, and establish specialized organizations to carry out the development mission.

Special taxes may be assessed and the revenues funneled into special funds that can be used in a variety of ways to further development activities. Property can be acquired for redevelopment through a variety of mechanisms, including eminent domain, purchase (financed with both revenue and general obligation bonds), and leasing.

Commissions or agencies oversee development activities. The mayor, with the consent of the city council, generally appoints the members of these commissions. The commission positions are not compensated, but persons who carry out administrative activities are paid through special development funds. Indicative of the state's interest in promoting public development, Wyoming statutes allow municipalities to spend funds to advertise (and therefore further) their industrial development.[45]

There are almost no circumstances, however, under which the state will allow complete or even partial tax relief for development. This philosophy is based in Article 3, section 36 of the Wyoming Constitution, which states,

[n]o appropriation shall be made for charitable, industrial, educational or benevolent purposes to any person, corporation or community not under the absolute control of the state, nor to any denominational or sectarian institution or association.

This philosophy is given life in Title 39 (taxation and revenue), Article 1, section 305, which states that "the board [of equalization] shall not compromise or reduce the tax liability of any person owing a tax to the state of Wyoming."

Fiscal Autonomy of Local Governments

Local Revenues

Local revenues in the state are subject to a variety of constraints set forth in the Wyoming statutes. Maximum levies, classes of property, and the percent of the fair market value at which property is assessed are only a few of the items regulated. As of 1994, state law set the maximum county levy at twelve mills, city and town levies at eight mills, and special district levies at variable rates. For example, the maximum levy for hospital districts is six mills; for cemetery districts, three mills; and for museum districts, one mill. The legislature assesses property used for industrial purposes at 11.5 percent, real and personal property at 9.5 percent, and minerals and mine products at 100 percent. Although the property tax is the single largest source of local revenue for most cities in the United States, Wyoming cities are unique. Here, taxes on minerals and other mine products (for example, trona, bentonite, uranium, coal, oil, and gas) can make up the lion's share of many local governments' revenue stream. Furthermore, Wyoming is one of the few states that has no income tax of any kind—neither state nor local, personal nor corporate.

With regard to local sales tax, the state legislature plays an equally important, and restrictive, role in setting limits. Counties can levy a 1 percent sales tax for general operations (often called the "fifth penny" because the state levies four of its own),

Table 1. City and Town Revenue in Wyoming, 1997

Revenue source	Percentage of total revenue
Utility charges	44%
Sales and use tax	17
Other state revenue	8
Severance tax	5
Mineral royalties	5
Property tax	3
Other	18

Source: "Revenue Sources and Needs of Municipal Governments in Wyoming," report produced by the Wyoming Association of Municipalities, 19 January 1998.

and another 1 percent for special uses, such as facilities construction (the "sixth penny"). The fifth penny can be renewed every four years, either by the voters or by the county commissioners. Part of the fifth-penny sales tax is redistributed to cities and towns within the county based on municipality population. The facilities tax, or sixth penny, must also be approved by the voters of a county, and it can be used only to fund special projects like roads, jails, courthouses, or libraries. After the project has been completed, however, the sixth penny must be dropped. Although counties are the only local government subdivision that can formally levy a sales tax, in reality cities are a driving force behind sales tax initiatives because they make up the largest percentage of a county's population. Cities, therefore, have great informal power and can make or break a tax levy.

In addition to their 2 percent sales tax, counties and municipalities can charge a lodging tax of up to 4 percent. Revenue generated by a lodging tax can be used only to advertise and promote the local tourist industry.

The debt limits of local governments are outlined in both the state constitution and state statutes. Article 16, section 4 of the constitution maintains that "no debt in excess of the taxes for the current year shall be created by any county or city unless the proposition to create such debt shall have been submitted and approved by a vote of the people." In short, counties and cities are required to meet all obligations from current tax revenues. Furthermore, the constitution establishes an absolute county debt ceiling of 2 percent of the assessed property value of the county. This debt ceiling cannot be changed even with voter support.

City and town debt limits are set a bit higher than their county counterparts. According to Article 16, section 5, no city or town shall create any indebtedness exceeding 4 percent of the assessed value of the taxable property, except that an additional indebtedness of 4 percent may be created for sewage disposal systems. Interestingly, there is no debt limit for the establishment of municipal water systems. The constitutional convention, recognizing the potentially high cost of securing water in arid Wyoming, exempted water development from debt limit provisions.[46]

Local Expenditures

There is no standard budget format for municipalities. The state grants wide latitude to cities in this regard. Its only concern is that the budget shall be "prepared to best serve the municipality." However, each municipality is required to set forth in its budget actual revenues and expenditures of the last completed fiscal year, estimated total revenues and expenditures for the current fiscal year, and the estimated available revenues and expenditures for the ensuing budget year. In addition, a budget message must accompany each budget, outlining the municipality's financial policies and reasons for budgetary changes from the previous year.[47] Budget hearings must be held on the third Tuesday in June at 8:00 p.m.

Wyoming state law requires that an annual financial audit be conducted by an independent auditor in accordance with generally accepted auditing standards as promulgated by the American Institute of Certified Public Accountants. The audit must be completed not more than six months after the end of the fiscal year. A copy of the audit report must be forwarded to the director of the state department of audit within seven months after the end of the fiscal year. If the audit does not take place, the state can demand an audit and, if necessary, may contract with an independent auditor to perform the necessary review—to be paid for from withheld municipal grants. As a result of these safeguards, local government officials and the state see municipal bankruptcy as virtually impossible. Furthermore, there are no statutory provisions governing the process, reflecting its near impossibility.

State Government Grants-in-Aid to Localities

There is significant variability in the amount of revenue returned to individual cities and towns, but the state provides 40–60 percent of a local government's revenue. According to the state auditor's report, in fiscal 1995 the state returned $286,673,892 to localities (not including state aid to education). Of these dollars, sales and use taxes accounted for the majority, with federal mineral royalties and the state severance tax rounding out the top three contributors.

The state serves as a partner in several federally funded grant programs (for example, community development block grants). State grants to local governments are numerous and diverse and include programs such as Artists-In-Residence, Fish Wyoming, and the Trade Show Incentive Program. The State Farm Loan Board runs a grant program that is a significant source of local revenue. Grant monies from this program are available to municipalities, counties, or special districts and are funded from federal mineral royalties that are returned to the state. This state grant program funds public facilities construction, improve-

Table 2. Average City and Town Expenditures in Wyoming, 1997

Function	Percentage of total expenditures
Utility and solid waste	28%
Police and fire	18
Construction	14
Land and buildings	7
Streets and roads	7
Parks and recreation	6
Other	20

Source: "Revenue Sources and Needs of Municipal Governments in Wyoming," report produced by the Wyoming Association of Municipalities, 19 January 1998.

ment, and maintenance and the purchase of emergency vehicles. Although there is a 50 percent matching requirement, local government officials consider the program to be an extremely important source of construction dollars.

The forty-eight school districts in Wyoming compete against other units of local government for funding from the state. Education funds come from a number of different sources; among the most important are federal grants and mineral royalty payments, state and local property taxes, and revenue generated by the lease or sale of the state's School Trust Lands. According to the 1995 Statistical Report, the state alone contributed $320,417,059 to K–12 public education. In that same year, the state supreme court found Wyoming's system of funding education unfair and required the legislature to develop a new formula that would guarantee equal educational opportunities throughout the state.[48] As the system had been financed, wealthier districts were able to contribute more to the mix per pupil than poorer districts; thus, educational resource inequities existed. According to the high court ruling, a new financing scheme that defined a standard of education and equalized funding so that all students would have access to the same quality of education had to be in place by July 1, 1997.

Unfunded Mandates

Most local officials feel that the state has not imposed significant unfunded mandates. The vast majority of unfunded mandates, and those of any concern, come from the federal government. Compliance rates are high; however, so is state and local resistance. Citizens see many types of federal intrusion in local affairs as inappropriate or unnecessary.

Access to Local Government

Local Elections

Wyoming state government is known for its ease of citizen access. It is not uncommon for a citizen to call the governor's office and ask to speak to the governor *personally* to voice a complaint. Equally telling, it is also common practice for a student at the University of Wyoming to call, write, or stop by the university president's office, if for only a class-scheduling conflict. This openness is indicative of the spirit of the state and reflects how citizens believe they should be treated. Such open access exists at the local level as well.

Along with the informal aspects of citizen access to government, the state specifies in some detail more formal ways for citizens to participate in their government, such as elections at both the county and city or town level. These specifications include the offices and terms of municipal officials, their qualifications and certification, and the identification of polling places. Generally, municipal elections follow the same procedures as statewide elections, and all persons who wish to vote in local elections must be registered. Candidates running in the general election must first be nominated at the municipal primary. All offices are nonpartisan, and persons running for office must reside within the political subdivision that they will represent.

State statutes require that *first-class cities* that are not governed by the commission or council-manager form of government be divided into not less than three wards. These wards must be "compact" and as "nearly equal in population as possible."[49] *Towns,* on the other hand, have some choice in their election process. Towns can choose not to conduct their elections in the same manner as the state conducts its elections if their procedures are spelled out in a charter ordinance.

Citizen Controls over Actions of Local Officials

The citizens of any city or town operating under the commission form of government have the power of recall. However, since no towns or cities have this form of government, no residents in Wyoming cities or towns exercise recall power. The initiative power is likewise unusable. That is, in any city or town operating under the commission form of government, 10 percent of the qualified electors may propose a municipal ordinance by an initiative petition.

Referendum authority, however, is granted to all forms of local government. In order for a municipality to exercise this power, a petition must be signed by 10 percent of the registered voters in the city. This petition is then filed with the city clerk no later than ten days after the ordinance in question is first published subsequent to its adoption. If the governing body does not entirely repeal the ordinance, it must submit the question to a vote at a special election. If a majority of those voting do not reject the ordinance, it becomes effective.[50]

Except where specifically provided for in Wyoming's open-meeting and public-records laws, all government meetings and public records are open to the public. Executive sessions can be held if they meet the requirements of the act for such standard purposes as current or pending litigation, real estate transactions, and matters of employment (for example, disciplinary ac-

tions, wages, salaries, and benefits). Similarly, unless otherwise provided, records shall be open for inspection by any person at reasonable times.

State-Local Relations

Local and state governments generally are supportive of each other. Dillon's Rule, however, remains an important influence in state-local affairs. Moreover, although the constitutional provision for home rule grants municipal governments access to procedures that allow significant local flexibility, the courts have ruled counter to the spirit of the home rule provision. An analysis of municipal court cases in Wyoming reflects that the "quest for home rule remains a major challenge."[51]

The challenge of utilizing home rule is reflected in the case *Tri-County Electric Association v. City of Gillette* (1978). Here, the state supreme court upheld Dillon's Rule rather than the new home rule provisions established in the constitution. In doing so, the court argued that

[t]he legislature has practically absolute power over cities and towns. . . . A city or town can only exercise those powers expressly or impliedly conferred by constitution or statute. The legislature is therefore the well-spring of practically all the powers here in play.

In the case *Cheyenne Airport Board v. Rogers* (1985) the supreme court again relied on the concept of Dillon's Rule. In this zoning case, the court stated, "[m]unicipalities remain largely the creatures of the sovereign state and in need of specific delegations of powers." The same sentiment was again expressed in *Coulter v. City of Rawlins* (1993), whereby the Wyoming Supreme Court again maintained that "it is settled that municipal corporations are creatures of the legislature and thereby subject to statutory control."

These cases are cause for much concern among local government officials because they serve as principles for state intervention in local affairs—a subject that officials thought was put to rest in 1972. As Kathleen Hunt, general counsel for the Wyoming Association of Municipalities, notes, "municipalities are not creatures of the legislature, they are creatures of a constitutional mandate."[52] The people have spoken, but the courts do not seem to be listening. The courts and the legislature are sending mixed messages. Unfortunately, home rule remains an important, yet unclear, concept for local government in Wyoming.

Not unlike cities and towns in other states, those in Wyoming face a future anchored by tight budgetary times. Because of the state's historical reliance on mineral royalty dollars and the fact that the amounts generated by these taxes fluctuate widely, Wyoming's immediate financial future is uncertain. Moreover, the fiscally conservative Wyoming electorate is not anxious to see new taxes implemented, such as a state income tax, or to see the sales tax increased. Elected officials are therefore unlikely to offer these measures as solutions to their funding woes. When mineral extraction does not produce large numbers of tax dollars (as is the current situation), Wyoming is left with few alternative revenue streams. Thus, as the cost of providing municipal services rises, local governments must either find innovative ways to use their current budgets or—the less palatable solution—implement service cutbacks. Finding ways to maximize tax dollars is a singular challenge for local officials in Wyoming. A critical issue is whether the state should continue to rely heavily on the extractive mineral industry or should diversify the funding base through an aggressive economic development strategy—one that protects the current quality of life.

As noted earlier, the state supreme court has involved itself again in the administration of local government by finding the school financing formula inequitable and, therefore, unconstitutional. For many officials, this is another intrusion by state government into the affairs of local communities. The cost of reform is expected to total about $45 million in additional funding each year. This sum, many believe, will be a burden that citizens and local communities cannot bear. According to others, this remedy is long overdue and an inexpensive repair compared to the educational gains the state will realize. Wyomingites, regardless of where they sit on the new school financing proposal, remain suspicious of government at any level. The concept of home rule is ambiguous—the constitution says Wyoming local governments have it, the courts are less certain. During these tight budgetary times, local governments seem to have more pressing concerns to worry about than what, exactly, home rule means for them in practice.

Notes

1. Gretel Ehrlich, *The Solace of Open Spaces* (New York: Penguin Books, 1985), 6.

2. Robert B. Keiter and Tim Newcomb, *The Wyoming State Constitution* (Westport: Greenwood Press, 1993), 3.

3. T. A. Larson, *History of Wyoming* (Lincoln: University of Nebraska Press, 1978), 129.

4. Keiter and Newcomb, *Wyoming State Constitution*, 4.

5. Larson, *History of Wyoming*, 256.

6. Gregg Cawley et al., *The Equality State: Government and Politics in Wyoming* (Dubuque: Eddie Bowers Publishing, 1996), 5.

7. Ibid., 11.

8. In a 1994 public opinion poll, 73 percent of state citizens believed they were more self-reliant than other citizens of the nation. Wyoming Election Year Survey, 1994.

9. Cawley et al., *The Equality State*, 37.

10. Ibid., 46.

11. Ibid., 71.

12. Justice of the peace courts are a dying breed in Wyoming. They exist only in the nine least populated counties, where they take the place of the county courts.

13. Cawley et al., *The Equality State*, 91.

14. *The Book of the States*, vol. 32 (Lexington, Ky.: Council of State Governments, 1998), 3.

15. Daniel J. Elazar, *American Federalism: A View from the States* (New York: Harper and Row, 1984), 17–18.

16. Donald W. Berney, *Home Rule for Wyoming: Be It Ever So Humble* (Laramie: Government Research Bureau, 1972), 5.

17. Article 13, section 1(b)(d).

18. The four points were adapted from Kathleen Hunt, *Handbook for Wyoming Mayors and City Council Members* (Cheyenne: Wyoming Association of Municipalities, 1994), 5–6.

19. In Wyoming, charter ordinances exempt cities from special legislation. Article 13, section 1(c) notes that

Each city or town may elect that the whole or any part of any statute, other than statutes uniformly applicable to all cities and towns and statutes prescribing limits of indebtedness, may not apply to such town. This exemption shall be by charter ordinance passed by two-thirds (²/₃) vote of all members elected to the governing body of the city or town.

In addition, the proposed charter ordinance must be published for two weeks and does not take effect until sixty days after its final publication.

20. Wyoming Statutes, 15-1-101.

21. Ibid., 15-1-201.

22. Ibid., 15-1-202.

23. Ibid., 15-01-411.

24. Hunt, *Handbook for Wyoming Mayors and City Council Members*, 18.

25. Wyoming Statutes, 15-1-402.

26. Ibid., 15-1-406.

27. Quoted in Kerry Drake, "Cheyenne, County Conflict on Sunday Bar Hours," *Casper Star Tribune*, 19 June 1996, 1A and 10A.

28. Wyoming Statutes, 18-3-201, 301, 401, 501, 601, 701, 801.

29. Ibid., 15-3-202.

30. Ibid., 15-3-202, sections b(i) and b(ii).

31. Brian Will, city-county planner, interview by author, 10 June 1996, Laramie, Wyo.

32. Quoted in "High Court Rules in Freemont Fireworks Case," *Casper Star Tribune*, 2 July 1996, 1A.

33. Wyoming Statutes, 15-1-103.

34. Ibid., 18-6-101–18-13-101.

35. Ibid., 18-12-103.

36. Ibid., 18-11-201; 18-10-201; 11-16-103; 41-3-701; and 11-5-101, respectively.

37. Ibid., 16-1-101.

38. Ibid., 15-1-127, 128.

39. Ibid., 15-1-106.

40. Ibid., 15-1-114, 115.

41. Ibid., 15-1-113.

42. Ibid., 15-1-113.

43. Ibid., 15-1-601.

44. Ibid., 15-9-104.

45. Ibid., 15-1-111.

46. Keiter and Newcomb, *Wyoming State Constitution*, 237.

47. Wyoming Statutes, 16-4-104.

48. "Education Finance Reform Proposal Gets Finishing Touches," *Laramie Daily Boomerang*, 15 May 1997, 8A.

49. Wyoming Statutes, 22-23-103.

50. Hunt, *Handbook for Wyoming Mayors and City Council Members*, 93-94; Wyoming Statutes, 22-23-1007.

51. Kathy Hunt, "Wyoming Home Rule: A Current Status Report." Report to the Wyoming Association of Municipalities, April 19, 1994, 4.

52. Ibid., 6.

APPENDIX: HOME RULE ACROSS THE FIFTY STATES

The fifty state chapters in this reference volume present a detailed picture of the current status of home rule and local government autonomy in the United States. By themselves, the chapters make an important contribution to the knowledge about and understanding of state and local government. The individual chapters provide an abundance of useful information (many of which are not readily available elsewhere) about several aspects of local government authority. These chapters also set the many details about a state within the larger context of the state's governmental setting and the evolution of its state-local relationships. Taken together, the fifty state chapters capture what is unique about local government authority in each of the American states.

While it is important to appreciate the distinctive features of each state, it is also important to understand the diversity of those features across the fifty states. Comparative analyses of home rule in the United States, as we pointed out in the Introduction, have been few in number, and one of the main motives for conducting this national research has been to facilitate comparative analysis of home rule and local government discretionary authority. This appendix draws on the information found in each of the state chapters to create several tables that illustrate the range of variation that exists in state-local relations. Each of the tables is derived solely from the information provided by the state chapter authors, and no other source has been used to augment this data. Because not every state author gave specific details about a particular topic, it should be noted that the information on some of the following tables do not include all fifty states. We made an editorial decision to create only a select set of charts and not to provide a table for every item listed on the standard outline for the state chapters. Nevertheless, the following charts illustrate well the possibilities and value of comparative analysis.

Types of Home Rule

The key question about home rule is: do cities and counties have any? That is to say, have state governments granted or permitted their local jurisdictions some degree of discretionary choice over matters of local government organization and operation. The first set of tables (Tables A1–A3) reveals several interesting patterns about home rule among the fifty states. Tables A1 and A2 list the type of home rule as to whether it is structural, functional, fiscal, or some combination of these three basic types. The usage here follows that found in the 1993 ACIR study that was mentioned in the Introduction. The type of home rule listed for each state has been taken from the state author's description. In some cases, when the state author indicated that some degree of local government choice existed in any of the three dimensions of local government—structure, functions, and fiscal—that choice was deemed as evidence of local discretionary authority. Also, under the heading "Type(s) of home rule," if the state author offered an assessment of the particular model of home rule—Dillon's Rule, devolution of powers, legislative grant, or liberal construction—that reference has been

included on Tables A1 and A2. These two tables also list the eligibility criteria for home rule status and the legal authority for home rule in each state. Of course, for more specific information, the reader should return to the individual state chapters.

Table A3 combines the information from Tables A1 and A2 and provides both a summary of home rule status and a comparison between municipalities and counties. First, a majority of states have granted some form of home rule to their municipalities as well as to their counties, and as expected, more states permit some form of home rule for municipalities (46 states) than for counties (36 states). Furthermore, most states do not put eligibility restrictions on home rule. Second, the most frequent type of home rule for both cities and counties is structural plus functional. Recall that originally home rule was defined narrowly as permitting local citizens to select their preferred form of local government by adopting a charter. Over time, as described in the history of home rule recounted in the Introduction, states extended the concept of home rule to include local discretion over the functional responsibilities of local governments. Third, for municipalities, the trend has moved even further to include some degree of fiscal discretion, as indicated by the fact that the second most-common home rule pattern for cities adds fiscal to structural and functional. If one reviews the states where some fiscal discretion has been granted to municipalities, what one finds is that state legislatures have expanded the number of revenue sources that municipal officials may choose to levy, or have given local officials some choice in setting tax rates. Examples of this fiscal discretion are the availability of the local option sales tax and the widespread reliance on service charges and user fees at the local level. This pattern is important because previous studies have found that fiscal discretion was the least common form permitted. Finally, Table A3 offers substantial evidence that contradicts the widely held conception of Dillon's Rule as a narrow grant of authority to local governments. Instead, the numbers indicate that state governments have granted something more than mere charter writing authority to their localities.

Historically, the home rule movement not only sought to gain some degree of local choice over form of government, but home rule was also seen as a means to reduce state legislative interference in local affairs. In particular, the earliest actions taken under the banner of home rule were prohibitions on the use of "local or special privilege" legislation. Table A4, however, suggests that local privilege legislation is alive and well in a number of states. Local privilege is permitted or used in at least twenty-one states, and within the twenty-four states listed as prohibiting local privilege legislation, the state authors indicate that the prohibition is not effective in seven of these states. Similarly, of the states listed as prohibiting local legislation, thirteen states resort to the use of municipal classification as a substitute for or a bypass around the prohibition. The importance of the continued use of local privilege legislation comes from its capacity to permit the state legislature to act contrary to a general grant of discretionary authority. One possible consequence could be the abrogation of existing home rule authority.

Structural Home Rule

The most basic form of local control is the power to create a new local government. While it may have been possible for a group of people to declare themselves a town in the colonial period or in the wild west, state legislatures have established specific requirements by which a community may obtain recognition as a municipal corporation. Table A5 categorizes the states by the different conditions that must be met for incorporation. The most common requirements are a minimum population, population density, and/or some specified distance from existing municipalities. Some states have adopted distance or population requirements that make it fairly difficult to create a new city. This action takes on special significance in those states where political battles over growth and urban sprawl have emerged. Table A6 ranks by degree of difficulty the different requirement for incorporation. While it is not easy to determine just how much more

difficult one method of incorporation is over another, one can base this judgment on logic as well as on the observations made by the state chapter authors. A simple petition of local residents is clearly an easier requirement to meet than other requirements such as approval in an election, approval by a commission or a judge, obtaining state legislation, or changing the state constitution to permit a new incorporation. Variations are not large in the middle range of difficulty, and what may make a difference are the population and distance requirements. But when another jurisdiction or other governing body—for example, California's Local Agency Formation Commissions—must approve the incorporation, this procedure poses palpable burdens on those persons seeking the incorporation. Of course, when other jurisdictions perceive the proposed new city as a competitor for inhabitants or revenues, then any method that gives a hearing to these views will complicate the approval process.

Annexation is a common method by which an existing municipality may expand its territory and/or population. As pointed out in the Introduction, the power to annex has become a focal point of the battle over suburban sprawl, uncontrolled growth, and the deterioration of central cities. David Rusk has popularized the argument that one very powerful cause of central city decline is their "inelasticity," by which he means the impossibility of the central city to expand its territory via annexation.[1] Table A7 shows that states vary dramatically in the number of different methods by which a municipality may annex areas outside the corporate boundaries. The variation includes among the possible procedural steps petitions, public hearings, planning board approval, city council approval, referenda (in city and/or area to be annexed), legislative, administrative, or judicial approval, and approval by the county government. Obviously, the more methods available, the more likely groups proposing annexation have a choice of tactics. One noteworthy method involves the requirement that the annexed area be contiguous to municipal limits. The reason behind this requirement is simple: the prevention of so-called "fingers" or "enclaves"— the annexation of a highway or railway as means of reaching out to an area the city would like to annex, or the annexation of areas separated from the main body of the city. Some states, principally in the Northeast, do not allow annexation, primarily because no unincorporated land exists in the state.

Table A8 ranks annexation requirements by degree of difficulty. The easiest annexation procedure allows the city government to pass an ordinance specifying the area to be annexed— no approval by residents in the area is required nor approval of any other entity. At least seven states permit this method. Not much more difficult is voluntary annexation, where residents of an area petition a city to be admitted into the municipality. Much more difficult are methods that require various official bodies to approve the annexation, and perhaps the most difficult method of annexation requires a majority vote of the residents of the area proposed for annexation. This variation in the number and degree of difficulty of annexation methods bears on the question of home rule because the less difficult the method of annexation, the more discretion is available to the municipality.

Extraterritorality is another important structural feature of local government, and one that does not receive much attention in the professional or scholarly literature. City limits often are not the extent of a municipality's jurisdiction. Municipal governments commonly own facilities or property beyond their boundaries for purposes as diverse as airfields, landfills, and water supplies. Similarly, many cities have the power to regulate and control health hazards, product sales, road locations, subdivision platting, and nuisances up to a set distance beyond their boundaries. Table A9 offers a list of the extraterritorial jurisdiction of localities in various states, as described by the state authors. Planning and zoning authority appear to be the most common form of extraterritorality, but the acquisition, ownership, and disposal of property is also an important tool for city officials, without which it would be especially difficult to acquire water supplies. Again, extraterritorial jurisdiction is one more important form of discretionary authority that may be granted to municipal governments, and should be taken into account in any discussion of home rule.

Functional Home Rule

As discussed in the Introduction, the home rule movement, reflecting its Populist and Progressive roots, focused on obtaining for citizens the authority to select a preferred form of government. Over time, home rule also became associated with the idea of local choice in policy matters. If home rule was to offer more than immunity from inappropriate state legislative interference, then it should also confer on local jurisdictions some degree of initiative power. Furthermore, different localities, even in the same state, might wish to engage in different activities or provide different forms and levels of public services, and state government ought not to impose a single standard on all of its localities, especially in activities that were obviously "local" in nature, such as parking lots or swimming pools.

Tables A10 and A11 list the functional responsibilities assigned to municipalities and counties, as mentioned by the state chapter authors.[2] First, both types of jurisdictions clearly perform a wide range of functions beyond such traditional ones as "general government" and public safety. Second, if one examines Tables A10 and A11 in the light of the descriptions presented in the individual state chapters, the number and type of functions assigned to cities and counties have increased beyond the old traditional ones. This increase should not be a surprise—all levels of government engage in more different activities today than a hundred years ago. Third, there is little evidence that a "division of labor" now exists between municipal and county govern-

ment. That is, in more than half states, cities and counties perform or have responsibility for the same set of functions. To the extent that a functional difference exists, it is found in the area of social services, historically a function associated with county government. This growing similarity of municipal and county functions confirms the old adage about the vital importance of local government—most problems affecting the quality of life require action on the part of local government. Whether it is a big or small city, rural or urban county, local governments face similar citizen demands. Likewise, problems don't stay put, they cross local government boundaries, and this prompts demands from citizens of cities and counties for similar functional authority. Fourth, while most states have moved to broaden the range of local government functions, Connecticut, Massachusetts, New Hampshire, Rhode Island, and Vermont have abolished or drastically reduce the responsibilities of county officials. These five New England states have a history of strong township government, rather modest functional roles for county government, and little if any unincorporated areas. Consequently, county governments have seen their importance wither in this part of the country.

It would probably come as a surprise to many citizens to learn that economic development activities are considered by local officials to be the second most important function they perform (after the provision of basic services such as law and order, roads and street maintenance, and water supply and waste management). The last quarter century saw economic development become a major activity of local governments. Decreasing national government aid to state and local government and the economic shifts of the 1970s and 1980s forced states and localities to adopt new development strategies, most of which relied on a significant role for local government. State governments, as a consequence, began to empower local governments with an increasing number of policy tools by which localities could pursue local plans for community and economic development. Table A12 captures the range of economic development authority states have conferred on local governments. Local governments have been given a variety of organizational, regulatory, and fiscal policy tools, and the types of tools vary from state to state. Local governments in some states may create private or nonprofit development corporations, establish enterprise zones, and join in public-private partnerships. They may also control land use, declare areas as "blighted," "distressed," or "historic," transfer public property to private ownership, and relocate existing facilities. What is most important, given the great reluctance on the part of state legislatures to permit local governments any degree of discretion in fiscal matters, local governments in many states may abate taxes, use "own source" (that is, locally raised monies) revenues, and adopt tax increment financing for the purpose of fostering local development. Without a doubt, the new economic development authority granted to counties and municipalities greatly expands the discretion of local communities to shape their futures.

Substantial fragmentation is one of the most distinctive features of American local government. The large number of cities, counties, towns, and special districts create a pattern of jurisdictions with their own citizens, officials, preferences, and powers that do not match particular problems or resources. This fragmentation, many argue, contributes to perceived and actual inefficiencies in government, and more intergovernmental cooperation is the solution often recommended. The problem with this prescription is simply that state governments must authorize local governments to cooperate; that is, before two or more local jurisdictions may engage in a joint activity, they must possess the authority and means to act cooperatively. Table A13 lists almost two dozen different mechanisms by which local governments might cooperate. Although not every state chapter author mentioned specific forms of cooperation, nevertheless, this partial list illustrates the diversity of possible means by which local governments may cooperate. These forms range from informal mutual aid among localities (often called "good neighbor" aid) such as sending crews and trucks to help with a serious fire to joint facilities such as city-county jails to complex fiscal arrangements such as cooperative purchasing agreements or interlocal insurance pools. Unless the state government acts to encourage interlocal cooperation and to create a reasonable tool kit of policy mechanisms, local officials will be hard pressed to work collectively on commonly shared problems.

Fiscal Home Rule

Previous research on home rule and local government has found that local governments possess widest discretionary choice over their governmental structure and the least discretion over their finances. Table A14 underscores this continuing state control of local government financial management. Of the forty-six states for which there is information, twenty-eight (or 60 percent) require municipal governments to balance their budgets, and twenty-four of thirty-nine states (or 61 percent) require county governments to do so as well. Almost the same proportion (58 percent) of the states listed have established a procedure for the bankruptcy of a local government—a rare event, but one that is disastrous, as shown by past occurrences in New York City and in Orange County, California.

At the same time that states continue to be watchful over the local public purse, the states have also acted to increase the degree of local discretion over fiscal affairs. At one time, cities and counties depended almost exclusively on property taxes to provide funds to pay for local public services, but over time, state governments have enlarged the list of sources from which local governments may derive revenue. Table A15 lists the primary (largest in percentage) source of revenues for municipal govern-

ments. There are two very important patterns shown on this table. First, the property tax continues to be the primary source of local revenues only for about half of the states listed. Furthermore, of the states in which property taxes remain the primary source of funds for municipal government, property taxes now compose less than half of total local revenues. By comparison, in 1987 property taxes constituted on average 73.7 percent of a municipality's revenues.[3] Thus, this shift has been both recent and swift, and in part is related to the revolt against property taxes that began in California. Over the last decade, state governments have permitted localities to levy taxes on new sources (such as sales and income) and local governments have also expanded their use of other traditional revenue sources (such as occupancy fees and user charges). Table A15 shows that municipal governments in twenty-three states derive more revenues (in percentage terms) from a source other than the property tax. Just because local officials have more options as to sources of revenues does not mean that they will raise more revenue, more revenues sources also permits local officials to exercise more choice in what will be taxed and thus gives local officials the option to spread the burden of taxation across different types of economic activity.

Diversification of revenue sources has long been used in public finance analyses and studies of governmental decentralization as one measure of expanded local discretionary authority. Table A15 offers solid evidence that state governments over the last ten years have moved to increase the degree of choice over how local governments may raise revenues. Another indicator of the degree of state control over local government finances (and local government itself) is shown on Table A16, which lists the state limit on local government debt. Most, but not all, local governments pay for long-term projects such as capital improvements by issuing bonds backed by local tax revenues. Typically, the state government limits the amount of debt that may be contracted through the issuance of bonds to a specified percentage of the assessed valuation of taxable property in the jurisdiction. As seen on Table A16, some states impose very low limits, while others have relatively high limits. It is interesting to remember that problems related to municipal bonds and debt practices in the first half of the 1800s led to Judge Dillon's declaration that local governments were creatures of the state. Dillon thought, as we noted in the Introduction, that placing local governments under state legislative control would end the fiscal mismanagement that plagued many municipalities in that day. Using this logic, the size of debt limit imposed on municipalities can serve as another indicator of local discretion, since the higher the debt limit, the more money a municipality may borrow. In fact, one could go so far as to suggest that the debt limit measures the trust the state legislature has in the decisions of local officials.[4]

The Importance of a Comparative Approach to Home Rule

Tables A1 to A16 present substantial evidence of the diversity of home rule and local government discretionary authority across the fifty states. Home rule no longer takes the sole form of the ability to write a charter and thus to select a type of government, for example, a city manager form. Home rule encompasses substantial interstate variation in the choices accorded local officials over many different types of policy decisions. If scholarship is to be true to the core concept of home rule—"any power of self-government," then research must catalogue these powers and their degree of interstate variation. As valuable as it is to demonstrate the variety of discretionary authority available to local governments in the fifty states, it will be as important to analyze why some states have granted more home rule to their local governments, while others have not. An equally compelling question to be answered is: Does home rule and (more) local discretionary authority make a difference? Because one of the motivations for this volume has been to encourage cross-state comparisons, we invite our readers to develop their own tables and to explore more fully the similarities and differences in home rule among the American states.

We believe that these sixteen tables are illustrative of the possibilities and the utility of comparing one state's practices to those of the other states. Some of the information displayed on the tables will be of particular interest to local officials—elected and administrative. To take just one example, given the competition and the stakes in economic development activities, the state chapters may well offer officials in some states new ideas. If not new ideas, the information may provide the rationale to ask the state legislature to approve new authority in this area. In a very real sense, the fifty chapters and the accompanying tables lay the foundation for comparative learning about home rule practices across the country. We encourage our readers to consider which home rule provisions might be useful to adopt in their own state.

Finally, we believe that these tables can illuminate the role in local politics played by questions about the authority and choices available to local government officials. We encourage our readers in their capacity as citizens of their locality to be alert to proposals to augment or diminish the discretion of local officials. Changes in local authority not only affect what may happen to the locality, but the changes may also shape what and how the community can act in the future. Debates over the extent of extraterritorial jurisdiction or the use of "own source" revenues for community development may not be as exhilarating as debates over property tax assessments or street closures, but proposals about local government authority which become law govern the resolution of other issues. Home rule questions typically are discussed by city hall and county court house veterans—officials, civil servants, local reporters, and local attorneys. As a matter of practical democratic politics, home rule issues define the limits of local public action. Therefore, we invite all of our readers to learn more about home rule and to support appropriate action to insure that popular sovereignty remains a vital force in each community.

Notes

1. David Rusk, *Cities Without Suburbs,* 2d ed. (Washington, D.C.: Woodrow Wilson Center Press, 1995).

2. The assignment of specific activities to a given functional category closely parallels that used by Benton and Menzel. See J. Edwin Benton and Donald C. Menzel, "County Services: The Emergence of Full-Service Government," Chap. 5 in *County Governments in an Era of Change,* ed. by David R. Berman (Westport, Conn.: Greenwood Press, 1993).

3. Steven D. Gold, *Reforming State-Local Relations: A Practical Guide* (Washington, D.C.: National Conference of State Legislatures, 1989).

4. An alternative possibility is that the size of the debt limit may measure the degree to which the state legislature has succumbed to the lobbying of local officials.

Table A1. Municipal Government Home Rule

State	Type(s) of home rule	Municipalities eligible	Enabling authority
Alabama	None/Dillon's Rule state		
Alaska	Broad "liberal construction"	1st-class cities	State constitution
Arizona	Structural + limited fiscal	3,500+ popul.	1910 const. provision
Arkansas	Structural + functional	2,500+ popul.	1926 const. amend.
California	Broad structural + functional	All	1879 const. provision + state law
Colorado	Broad structural + functional	All	1912 const. amend.
Connecticut	Structural/Dillon's Rule state	All	1969 const. provision + 1981 law
Delaware	Functional/legislative grant	1,000+ popul.	1953 law
Florida	Structural + functional	All	1968 const. provision
Georgia	Functional	All	1954 const. amend. + 1962 & 1965 laws
Hawaii	[a]		
Idaho	Only home rule "police powers"/Dillon's Rule state	All	State constitution
Illinois	Structural + functional/broad "liberal construction"	25,000+ popul.	1970 const. provision
Indiana	Limited functional/devolution of powers	All	1980 law
Iowa	Structural + limited functional	All	1968 const. amend. + 1971 law
Kansas	Structural + functional + fiscal devolution of powers/"liberally construed"	All	1960 const. amend.
Kentucky	Structural + functional/legislative grant (almost devolution of powers)	All	1980 law + 1994 const. amend.
Louisiana	Structural + functional + fiscal/devolution of powers + broad "residual" powers	All	1974 const. provision
Maine	Structural + functional/"liberally construed" devolution of powers	All	1974 const. provision
Maryland	Structural + functional	All	1954 const. amend.
Massachusetts	Structural + functional + limited fiscal/devolution of powers	All	1966 const. amend. + Home Rule Procedures Act
Michigan	Structural + functional + fiscal "liberally construed" devolution of powers	All	1908 & 1963 const. provisions + 1909 law
Minnesota	Limited structural + functional	All	1896 const. amend. + 1896 law
Mississippi	Limited structural + functional	All	1985 law
Missouri	Structural + functional + fiscal	5,000+ popul.	1945 const. provision + 1971 const. amend.
Montana	Structural + functional "not home rule, but self-government powers"	All	1972 const. provision
Nebraska	Charter writing authority only Dillon's Rule state/"illusory home rule"	5,000+ popul.	1912 const. amend.
Nevada	None/Dillon's Rule state		
New Hampshire	None		
New Jersey	Limited structural + functional + limited fiscal/ "liberally construed"	All	1947 const. provision + 1950 law
New Mexico	Structural + functional/"liberal construction"/ "maximum local self-government"	300+ popul.	1970 const. provision
New York	Structural + functional + limited fiscal "bill of rights for local governments"	All	1938 const. provision
North Carolina	Structural/modified Dillon's Rule state		
North Dakota	Structural + functional + fiscal "maximum local self-government"	100+ popul.	1889 const. provision + 1993 law
Ohio	Structural + functional + fiscal "exercise all powers of local self-government"	All	1912 const. provision
Oklahoma	Structural		State constitution
Oregon	Structural	All	1906 const. provision
Pennsylvania	Structural	All	1968 const. provision + 1972 law
Rhode Island	Structural	All	1952 const. provision
South Carolina	Structural + functional + fiscal/"liberally construed"	All	1973 const. amend.
South Dakota	Fordham approach with few limits/devolution of powers	All	1962 const. amend.

(table continues)

(Table A1 continued)

State	Type(s) of home rule	Municipalities eligible	Enabling authority
Tennessee	Structural	All	1953 const. amend.
Texas	Structural + functional	All	1912 const. amend.
Utah[b]	Structural + functional + limited fiscal	All	1932 const. amend.
Vermont	Legislative permission to adopt form of government	All	State law
Virginia	Functional/Dillon's Rule state	All	State law
Washington	Limited structural	All	1889 const. provision + Amend. 40 + 1967 law
West Virginia	Very limited structural/Dillon's Rule state	2,000+ popul.	1936 const. amend.
Wisconsin	Limited structural + functional	All	1933 const. amend.
Wyoming	Structural + functional[c]	All	1972 const. amend.

a. Hawaii has no municipal governments, only county governments.
b. Utah supreme court stated Dillon's Rule is archaic, unrealistic, & unresponsive" (1980).
c. "Liberally construed for the purpose of giving the largest measure of self-government to cities."

Table A2. County Government Home Rule

State	Type(s) of home rule	Counties eligible	Enabling authority
Alabama	"Limited"	3 most populous counties	Special law
Alaska	Broad/"liberal construction"	All boroughs	Const. provision
Arizona	Structural + limited fiscal	500,000+ popul.	1992 const. amend.
Arkansas	Structural + functional	All	1974 const. amend.
California	Broad structural + functional	All	1911 const. amend.
Colorado	Structural/legislative grant	All	1981 const. provision
Connecticut	Counties abolished in 1960		
Delaware	None		
Florida	Structural + limited functional	All	1968 const. provision
Georgia	Functional	All	1966 const. amend.
Hawaii	Structural + limited fiscal	All	1968 const. provision
Idaho	Only "police powers" home rule/Dillon's Rule state	All	Const. provision
Illinois	Broad structural + functional/"liberal construction"	All	1971 const. provision
Indiana	Limited functional/devolution of powers	All	1980 law
Iowa	Structural + functional	All	1978 const. amend. + 1988 law
Kansas	Structural + functional + fiscal/devolution of powers/ "liberally construed"	All	1974 law
Kentucky	Structural + functional	All	1990 law
Louisiana	Structural + functional/devolution of powers/ broad "residual powers"	All	1974 const. provision
Maine	Limited fiscal[a]		1985 & 1996 law
Maryland	Structural & functional	All	1915 & 1966 const. amends.; "Express Powers Act"
Massachusetts	None (7 of 14 counties abolished)		
Michigan	Limited structural (only Wayne County has a charter)	All	State law
Minnesota	Limited structural	Ramsay County[b]	1987 law
Mississippi	Limited structural	All	1988 law
Missouri	Structural + functional + fiscal	85,000+ popul.[c]	1945 & 1971 const. amends.
Montana	Structural + functional/"residual powers"	All	1972 const. provision
Nebraska	None		
Nevada	None		
New Hampshire	None/counties have very limited functions		
New Jersey	Structural + limited fiscal	All	1947 const. + 1972 law
New Mexico	None		
New York	Structural + functional + limited fiscal[d]	All	1959 const. amend.

(table continues)

(Table A2 continued)

State	Type(s) of home rule	Counties eligible	Enabling authority
North Carolina	Modified Dillon's Rule/may choose manager form	All	
North Dakota	Structural + functional (only 3 counties have charters)	All	1985 law
Ohio	Structural	All	1933 const. amend.
Oklahoma	None		
Oregon	Structural	All	1958 const. amend.
Pennsylvania	Structural	All	1968 const. + 1972 law
Rhode Island	None (no counties exist in Rhode Island)		
South Carolina	Structural + functional + limited revenue	All	1973 const. amend.
South Dakota	Broad/Fordham plan[e]	All	1962 const. amend.
Tennessee	[not mentioned]		
Texas	None[f]		
Utah	Structural + functional + limited fiscal	All	1971 const. amend.[g]
Vermont	None (counties have minimal governing role)		
Virginia	Charter (only 3 of 95 counties)	All	State law
Washington	Limited structural[h]	All	1948 "statutory home rule" law
West Virginia	None		
Wisconsin	"Administrative" home rule	All	1985 law
Wyoming	None		

a. Maine counties are "very weak" and primarily concerned with law enforcement.
b. Only 1 of 87 counties.
c. Or Assessed property valuation of $450 million
d. In New York, 19 of 57 counties have charters.
e. In South Dakota, 2 of 66 counties have adopted charters.
f. Texas's 1933 constitutional amend. permitted county home rule, but none of the eligible counties ever adopted a charter; the 1969 amend. deleted county home rule from state constitution.
g. Upheld by 1980 Utah supreme court ruling.
h. In Washington, 5 of 39 counties have adopted charters.

Table A3. Comparison of Municipal and County Home Rule

Type	Municipal	County
Structural	9	9
Functional	4	2
Fiscal	0	1
Structural + functional	16	10
Structural + fiscal	1	3
Functional + fiscal	0	0
Structural + functional + fiscal	11	5
Broad[a]	2	2
Limited[b]	3	4
None	3	10
Counties abolished	–	3
No municipal governments	1	–
Not mentioned by state author		1

a. Includes the Fordham approach, liberal construction, and liberally construed.
b. Includes administrative home rule, charter writing only, and legislative permission.

Table A4. The Continued Use of Local Legislation

State	Local legislation permitted/used	Classification used as substitute for local laws	Local legislation prohibited
Alabama	Y	Y	N
Alaska	–	–	–
Arizona	N	Y	Y
California	–	Y	Y
Colorado	–	–	–
Connecticut	–	–	Y
Delaware	Y[a]	N	–
Florida	Y	–	–
Georgia	Y	–	–
Hawaii	N	Y	–
Idaho	Y	N	Y
Illinois	N	Y	Y
Indiana	Y	Y	Y
Iowa	N	–	Y
Kansas	Y	Y	Y
Kentucky	Y	Y	Y
Louisiana	–	–	–
Maine	–	–	–
Maryland	Y[b]	N	Y
Massachusetts	N	N	Y
Michigan	Y[c]	Y	Y
Minnesota	Y[d]	N	Y
Mississippi	Y	–	–
Missouri	Y	Y	N
Montana	N	Y	Y
Nebraska	N	Y	Y
Nevada	–	–	Y
New Hampshire	–	–	–
New Jersey	N	Y	Y
New Mexico	–	–	–
New York	–	–	–
North Carolina	Y	–	N
North Dakota	–	Y	–
Ohio	–	–	Y
Oklahoma	Y	–	–
Oregon	N	N	–
Pennsylvania	–	Y	Y
Rhode Island	Y	N	–
South Carolina	N	–	Y
South Dakota	Y	Y	–
Tennessee	Y[e]	–	–
Texas	–	Y	Y
Utah	–	Y	Y
Vermont	Y	–	–
Virginia	Y	–	–
Washington	N	–	–
West Virginia	–	–	Y
Wisconsin	–	–	Y
Wyoming	Y	Y	–

Note: A dash indicates that the state chapter author did not mention the specific item.

a. Used sparingly.

b. For two or more local governments.

c. With two-thirds vote in both legislative chambers.

d. If governing body or voters approve the special legislation before it becomes law.

e. With two-thirds vote of local governing body required.

Table A5. Incorporation: Requirements for Forming a City

States that have no laws for incorporation[a]	Connecticut, Hawaii, Massachusetts, New Hampshire, New Jersey, Pennsylvania, Rhode Island, Vermont
States with incorporation law and regulations	Alabama, Alaska, Arizona, Arkansas, Delaware, Florida, Georgia, Hawaii, Idaho, Indiana, Illinois,Iowa, Kentucky, Louisiana, Maryland, Michigan, Mississippi, Minnesota, Missouri, Montana, Nebraska, New Mexico, New York, North Carolina, North Dakota, Ohio, Oregon, South Carolina, South Dakota, Utah, Virginia, Washington, West Virginia, Wisconsin, Wyoming
A specific density is required within a set area.	Alabama, Florida, Indiana, Montana, Nebraska, Nevada, New Mexico, North Carolina, North Dakota, Ohio, South Carolina, South Dakota, Utah, Wisconsin, Wyoming
Specific locations include limitations on where new cities can be formed such as it has to be more than 5 miles from the boarders of the closest city	Alabama, Arizona, Florida, Georgia, Idaho, Montana, Ohio, South Carolina, South Dakota, Utah, Wyoming
Minimum specific population is less than 500 residents	Alabama, Georgia, Kentucky, Louisiana, Maryland, Oregon, Utah, Wisconsin, Wyoming
Minimum specific population is more than 1,000 residents	Florida, Michigan, Ohio, South Carolina, Virginia, Wisconsin
No data in chapter	California, Colorado, Delaware, Kansas, Maine, Mississippi, Oklahoma, Tennessee, Texas

a. Most of these states have no unincorporated land. Vermont has not used the laws for more than 150 years. Hawaii does not have cities.

Table A6. Methods of Incorporation by Degree of Difficulty

5 (hardest)	Constitutionally mandated commission must approve incorporation	Alaska
4	County must agree to having the disputed area turned into a city	Indiana, Maryland, Montana, Nebraska, Nevada, North Dakota, Virginia, Washington, West Virginia, Wyoming
3	State legislators must vote to approve incorporation	Florida, Georgia, Nevada, New York, North Carolina, Washington
	State agency (usually one dealing with state-local relations) must approve incorporation	California, Michigan, North Dakota, Utah, Wisconsin
	Administrative judge must approve incorporation	Arkansas, Kentucky, Louisiana, Wisconsin
	Special commissions (members mandated by state law) must approve incorporation	New Mexico, Vermont
2	Incorporation must be approved by simple majority vote (50% +1)	Florida, Illinois, Louisiana, Maryland, Missouri, Nevada, North Dakota, Oregon, South Carolina, Virginia, Washington, West Virginia, Wyoming
1 (easiest)	Residents (registered voters and land owners) must petition state	Alabama, Illinois, Indiana, Kentucky, Louisiana, Maryland, Minnesota, Missouri, Montana, Nebraska, Nevada, New Mexico, North Carolina, North Dakota, Ohio, Oregon, South Carolina, South Dakota, Virginia, West Virginia, Wisconsin, Wyoming

Table A7. Total Number of Annexations Methods Used per State

No annexation	Connecticut, Hawaii, New Hampshire, Massachusetts, New Jersey, Pennsylvania. Rhode Island, Vermont
One method of annexation	Alaska, Idaho, Illinois, Indiana, Maine, Maryland, Minnesota, Missouri, Nebraska, New Hampshire, Oklahoma, South Carolina, Texas
Two methods of annexation	Florida, Georgia, Kentucky, Michigan, Nevada, Tennessee, Virginia, Washington, West Virginia, Wyoming
Three methods of annexation	Colorado, Kansas, New Mexico, North Carolina, North Dakota, Ohio, Wisconsin
Four methods of annexation	Alabama, Delaware
Strict contiguous requirements[a]	Colorado, Delaware, Idaho, Indiana, Kansas, Maryland, Nevada, New Mexico, North Carolina, South Carolina
No data	California, Louisiana, New York, Utah, Montana, Mississippi, Pennsylvania

a. These states have strict laws how cities may annex areas. The laws that are designed to prevent enclaves may required the city and the disputed area to share common boarders. The laws designed to prevent fingers may require the approval of the connecting area between the main body of the city and the disputed area. This prevents cities from annexing a highway or the banks of a river as connecting areas, annexing highly desirable areas and bypassing less desirable areas.

Table A8. Annexation Requirements by Degree of Difficulty

6 (hardest)	All methods that need simple majority vote (in election)	Alabama, Colorado, Delaware, Florida, Illinois, Kentucky, Maryland, Missouri, Pennsylvania, Ohio, Tennessee, Washington, West Virginia
5	County must agree to have the disputed area annexed into the city	Alaska, Delaware, Maine, North Dakota, Ohio, West Virginia
4	Special commissions must approve annexation[a]	Colorado, Idaho, Indiana, Kansas, Maryland, Michigan, New Mexico,
	State legislators must vote to approve annexation	Maine, North Carolina, Virginia
	Administrative judge must approve annexation	Alabama, Virginia, Wisconsin
	State agency (usually one dealing with state-local relations) must approve annexation	New Hampshire, Virginia
3	City must pass an ordinance in conjunction with components such as public hearings.	Alabama, Delaware, Kansas, Michigan, Nebraska, Nevada, New Mexico, North Dakota, Ohio, South Carolina, Tennessee, Wisconsin, Wyoming
2	Residents must apply to be admitted to the city (voluntary annexation)	Colorado, Delaware, Florida, Georgia, Kansas, Michigan, Nevada, Minnesota, Minnesota, North Carolina, North Dakota, Ohio, Oklahoma, South Carolina, Washington, West Virginia, Wisconsin, Wyoming
1 (easiest)	City must only pass an ordinance to annex the area	Alabama, Idaho, Indiana, Kentucky, Nebraska, Ohio, Texas

a. Special commissions are created specifically for annexation proceedings. They are not a standing body or regulatory agencies. Several states have named standing bodies as special commissions; those states are not included in this category. The members of these commissions are set by individual state law, but usually include elected county and city representatives.

Table A9. Municipal Extraterritorial Jurisdiction

Type of authority	State permitting authority
Acquire/own/dispose of facilities &/or property beyond city boundaries	Alabama, Arizona, Idaho, Indiana (4 mi.), Iowa, Kansas, Louisiana, Maine, Maryland, Minnesota, Missouri, Nebraska, Nevada, New Hampshire (only through intergovernmental agreements), New Mexico, New York, North Carolina, Ohio, Oregon, Pennsylvania, Utah, Virginia, Washington, West Virginia, Wisconsin
Acquire right-of-way or other land rights	Colorado, Utah (water rights), Vermont (water supply, but may be taxed by other local jurisdiction)
Annex facilities not contiguous to city	Idaho
Condemn property/eminent domain	Colorado, Indiana (4 mi.), North Carolina, Utah
Control disorderly conduct & nuisances outside city limits	Maryland
Improve infrastructure (flood control, mass transit, river ports, utilities, water & sewer lines)	Kentucky, Louisiana
Issue industrial revenue bonds to companies outside city limits	Kansas
Planning/zoning	Alabama (5 mi. beyond corporate limits) Arizona (3 mi. within unincorporated territory) Arkansas (5 mi. beyond corporate limits, but city must have a planning commission) Iowa (2 mi. if county is not zoned; if zoned, city has only subdivision power within 2 mi. limit) Kansas (3 mi. as long as affected area is represented on city planning commission) Kentucky (subdivision regulation within 5 mi. with approval of county fiscal court) Missouri (2 mi. if area is unincorporated) Montana (from 1 to 4 mi. depending on the specific function & size of municipality) Nebraska (1, 2, or 3 mi. depending on class of city) New Mexico (5 mi. but not into a contiguous municipality) North Carolina (with county commissioners approval 2 mi. if city size is 10,000–25,000, & 3 mi. if city size is above 25,000)[a] North Dakota ($1/2$, 1, 2 mi. depending on city size)[b] Ohio (cities to 3 mi.; villages to 1 mi.) South Dakota (1 mi. limit)[c] Tennessee (most municipalities with a population of more 10,000 are entitled to a 5 mi. zone)[d] Texas (ranges from $1/2$ mi. for populations under 5,000 to 5 mi. for 100,000+ population)[e] Wisconsin (3 mi. for 1st, 2nd, & 3rd class cities, & 1 mi. for 4th class cities & villages) Wyoming (5 mi. for enforcement of health & quarantine ordinance & regulations, & for fireworks; $1/2$ mi. for all other matters)
"Police jurisdiction"	Alabama (3 mi. beyond corporate limits for Class 1–7 cities & 1 mi. for Class 8 cities; city may regulate businesses within their police jurisdiction, & may levy taxes at the city rate, but revenues must be used to pay for services within the police jurisdiction)
Prezone land slated for annexation	California
Sell water	Colorado
Utility service provision	Kentucky, Louisiana, South Carolina

*Limits on municipal extraterritorial jurisdiction	State limiting authority
Extraterritorial authority subject to the zoning regulations of the locality in which the extraterritorial power is sought to be exercised	Virginia

(table continues)

(Table A9 continued)

Limits on municipal extraterritorial jurisdiction	*State limiting authority*
Extraterritorial authority negotiated with county or other municipalities	Georgia, Idaho, North Carolina
Extraterritorial authority negotiated with other municipalities	New Hampshire, Wisconsin
No extraterritorial zoning authority	New York
No extraterritorial regulatory power	Maine
No extraterritorial jurisdiction	California, Connecticut, Delaware, Illinois, Massachusetts, New Jersey, Rhode Island
No extraterritorial jurisdiction in contiguous unincorporated areas	Oregon

a. However, 1 mi. if county is not enforcing zoning, subdivision regulations, & the state building code within prospective area.

b. City ranges are less than 5,000; above 5,000 but below 25,000; & above 25,000, & county must appoint a representative to the city planning commission).

c. Additionally any "public ground or park" that belongs to the municipality, whether it is inside or outside the corporate limits.

d. When a municipal planning commission is designated as the regional planning commission, the municipality may exercise zoning powers beyond its boundaries & within the planning region if the county is not exercising such zoning power. Zoning power to 10 mi., depending on the municipality's population.

e. Limited authority over unincorporated areas that are contiguous.

Table A10. Municipal Government Functions by Category

Responsibility and definition	*States that allow these responsibilities*
City general government (operates city officer—legislative, executive, & judicial; conduct elections; collect taxes; administer state programs; maintain city buildings; maintain records and vital statistics)	Alabama, Alaska, Arizona, Arkansas, California, Colorado, Connecticut, Delaware, Florida, Georgia, Idaho, Illinois, Indiana, Iowa, Kansas, Kentucky, Louisiana, Maine, Maryland, Massachusetts, Michigan, Minnesota, Missouri, Mississippi, Montana, Nebraska, Nevada, New Hampshire, New Jersey, New Mexico, New York, North Carolina, North Dakota, Ohio, Oklahoma, Oregon, Pennsylvania, Rhode Island, South Carolina, South Dakota, Tennessee, Texas, Utah, Vermont, Virginia, Washington, West Virginia, Wisconsin, Wyoming
City public safety (law enforcement; detention, corrections, and jail; fire protection; emergency services, ambulances, and 911 service; animal control)	Alabama, Alaska, Arizona, Arkansas, California, Colorado, Connecticut, Delaware, Florida, Georgia, Idaho, Illinois, Indiana, Iowa, Kansas, Kentucky, Louisiana, Maine, Maryland, Massachusetts, Michigan, Minnesota, Missouri, Mississippi, Montana, Nebraska, Nevada, New Hampshire, New Jersey, New Mexico, New York, North Carolina, North Dakota, Ohio, Oklahoma, Oregon, Pennsylvania, Rhode Island, South Carolina, Tennessee, Texas, Utah, Vermont, Virginia, Washington, West Virginia, Wisconsin, Wyoming
City public health (board or health; city health officer; country hospitals; mental health facilities)	Alabama, Alaska, Arizona, Arkansas, Colorado, Connecticut, Georgia, Iowa, Kansas, Louisiana, Maine, Massachusetts, Mississippi, Nebraska, Nevada, New Jersey, New Mexico, North Dakota, Ohio, Oregon, South Carolina, Tennessee, Texas, Utah, West Virginia, Wisconsin, Wyoming
City public works (build roads; dispose of solid waste; operate airports, harbors, ports, and utilities; public transportation; flood control)	Alabama, Alaska, Arizona, Arkansas, California, Colorado, Connecticut, Delaware, Florida, Georgia, Idaho, Illinois, Indiana, Iowa, Kansas, Kentucky, Louisiana, Maine, Maryland, Massachusetts, Michigan, Minnesota, Missouri, Mississippi, Montana, Nebraska, Nevada, New Hampshire, New Jersey, New Mexico, New York, North Carolina, North Dakota, Ohio, Oklahoma, Oregon, Pennsylvania, Rhode Island, Tennessee, Texas, Utah, Vermont, Virginia, Washington, West Virginia
City social services (public housing; child/adult protections; welfare; general assistance youth services; veteran services; aging services; public cemetery)	Alabama, Arizona, Arkansas, Connecticut, Georgia, Iowa, Kansas, Louisiana, Mississippi, Montana, New Jersey, New Mexico, Oklahoma, Oregon, Tennessee, Texas, Utah, Washington, West Virginia

(table continues)

(Table A10 continued)

Responsibility and definition	States that allow these responsibilities
City economic development (economic/community development corporations; industrial parks)	Alabama, Alaska, Arizona, Arkansas, California, Colorado, Connecticut, Delaware, Florida, Georgia, Idaho, Illinois, Indiana, Iowa, Kansas, Kentucky, Louisiana, Maine, Maryland, Massachusetts, Michigan, Minnesota, Missouri, Mississippi, Montana, Nebraska, Nevada, New Hampshire, New Jersey, New Mexico, New York, North Carolina, North Dakota, Ohio, Oklahoma, Oregon, Pennsylvania, Rhode Island, South Carolina, South Dakota, Tennessee, Texas, Utah, Vermont, Virginia, Washington, West Virginia, Wisconsin, Wyoming
City physical environment (plan zoning; land use control; environmental regulation; conservation and resource management)	Alabama, Alaska, Arizona, Arkansas, California, Colorado, Connecticut, Delaware, Florida, Georgia, Idaho, Illinois, Indiana, Iowa, Kansas, Kentucky, Louisiana, Maine, Maryland, Massachusetts, Michigan, Minnesota, Missouri, Montana, Mississippi, Nebraska, Nevada, New Hampshire, New Jersey, New Mexico, New York, North Carolina, North Dakota, Ohio, Oklahoma, Oregon, Pennsylvania, Rhode Island, South Carolina, South Dakota, Tennessee, Texas, Utah, Vermont, Virginia, Washington, West Virginia, Wisconsin, Wyoming
City culture and recreation (libraries; cultural activities; historical societies; parks and recreations; sporting events)	Alabama, Alaska, Arizona, Arkansas, California, Colorado, Connecticut, Delaware, Florida, Georgia, Idaho, Illinois, Indiana, Iowa, Kansas, Kentucky, Louisiana, Maine, Maryland, Massachusetts, Michigan, Minnesota, Missouri, Montana, Nebraska, Nevada, New Hampshire, New Jersey, New Mexico, New York, North Carolina, North Dakota, Ohio, Oklahoma, Oregon, Pennsylvania, Rhode Island, South Carolina, South Dakota, Tennessee, Texas, Utah, Vermont, Virginia, Washington, West Virginia, Wisconsin, Wyoming
*City public schools (manage kindergarten to 12th grade)	Alaska, Connecticut, Illinois, Kansas, Maine, Massachusetts, Tennessee, Utah, Tennessee, Texas, Vermont

Note: Hawaii does not have city governments.

Table A11. County Government Functions by Category

Responsibility and definition	States that allow these responsibilities
No county responsibilities (state has no counties or the counties have no functional responsibilities beyond boundaries for courts)	Connecticut, Massachusetts, New Hampshire, Rhode Island, Vermont
County general government (operates city officer—legislative, executive, & judicial; conduct elections; collect taxes; administer state programs; maintain city buildings; maintain records and vital statistics)	Alabama, Alaska, Arizona, Arkansas, California, Colorado, Delaware, Florida, Georgia, Hawaii, Idaho, Indiana, Illinois, Iowa, Kansas, Kentucky, Louisiana, Maine, Maryland, Michigan, Minnesota, Missouri, Michigan, Mississippi, Montana, Nebraska, New Hampshire, New Jersey, New Mexico, New York, North Carolina, North Dakota, Ohio, Oklahoma, Oregon, Pennsylvania, South Carolina, South Dakota, Tennessee, Texas, Utah, Virginia, Washington, West Virginia, Wisconsin, Wyoming
County public safety (law enforcement; detention, corrections, and jail; fire protection; emergency services, ambulances, and 911 service; animal control)	Alabama, Arizona, California, Colorado, Delaware, Florida, Georgia, Hawaii, Indiana, Illinois, Iowa, Kansas, Kentucky, Louisiana, Maine, Maryland, Minnesota, Missouri, Mississippi, Nebraska, New Jersey, New Mexico, New York, North Carolina, North Dakota, Ohio, Oklahoma, Oregon, Pennsylvania, South Carolina, South Dakota, Tennessee, Texas, Utah, Virginia, Washington, West Virginia Wisconsin, Wyoming
County public health (board or health; city health officer; country hospitals; mental health facilities)	Alabama, Alaska, Arizona, Arkansas, California, Florida, Georgia, Indiana, Iowa, Louisiana, Maryland, Mississippi, Nebraska, New Jersey, New Mexico, New York, North Carolina, North Dakota, Oklahoma, Oregon, Pennsylvania, South Carolina, South Dakota, Tennessee, Texas, Utah, Vermont, Virginia, West Virginia, Wisconsin, Wyoming

(table continues)

(Table A11 continued)

Responsibility and definition	States that allow these responsibilities
County public works (build roads; dispose of solid waste; operate airports, harbors, ports, and utilities; public transportation; flood control)	Alabama, Arizona, Arkansas, California, Colorado, Connecticut, Delaware, Florida, Georgia, Hawaii, Idaho, Indiana, Iowa, Kansas, Kentucky, Louisiana, Maine, Maryland, Michigan, Minnesota, Missouri, Mississippi, Montana, Nebraska, New Jersey, New Mexico, New York, North Carolina, North Dakota, Ohio, Oklahoma, Oregon, Pennsylvania, South Carolina, South Dakota, Tennessee, Texas, Utah, Virginia, Washington, Wisconsin, Wyoming
County social services (public housing; child/adult protections; welfare; general assistance youth services; veteran services; aging services; public cemetery)	Alabama, Arizona, Arkansas, California, Colorado, Florida, Hawaii, Indiana, Iowa, Kansas, Louisiana, Maryland, Mississippi, Montana, Nebraska, New Jersey, New Mexico, New York, North Carolina, North Dakota, Ohio, Oklahoma, Pennsylvania, South Carolina, South Dakota, Tennessee, Texas, Utah, Virginia, Washington, West Virginia, Wisconsin, Wyoming
County economic development (economic/community development corporations; industrial parks)	Alabama, Arizona, Arkansas, California, Colorado, Florida, Hawaii, Indiana, Illinois, Iowa, Kansas, Kentucky, Louisiana, Maine, Maryland, Mississippi, Nebraska, New Jersey, New Mexico, New York, North Dakota, Ohio, Oklahoma, Pennsylvania, South Carolina, South Dakota, Tennessee, Utah, Virginia, West Virginia, Wisconsin
County physical environment (plan zoning; land use control; environmental regulation; conservation and resource management)	Alabama, Alaska, Arizona, Arkansas, California, Delaware, Florida, Georgia, Idaho, Illinois, Indiana, Iowa, Kansas, Kentucky, Louisiana, Maine, Maryland, Michigan, Minnesota, Missouri, Montana, Nebraska, New Jersey, New Mexico, North Carolina, North Dakota, Ohio, Oregon, Pennsylvania, South Carolina, South Dakota, Tennessee, Virginia, Washington, Wisconsin
County culture and recreation (libraries, cultural activities, historical societies, parks and recreations, sporting events)	Alabama, Arizona, California, Colorado, Connecticut, Florida, Georgia, Hawaii, Idaho, Illinois, Indiana, Iowa, Kansas, Kentucky, Louisiana, Maine, Maryland, Mississippi, Nebraska, New Jersey, New Mexico, New York, North Carolina, North Dakota, Oregon, South Carolina, Tennessee, Texas, Virginia, Wisconsin, Wyoming
County public schools (manage kindergarten to 12th grade)	Alaska, Arizona, Maryland, North Carolina, Oregon, Tennessee, Virginia
County higher education (community colleges; vocational-technical schools)	Kansas, Missouri, New Jersey

Table A12. Economic Development Authority Available to Local Governments

Alabama. May acquire real property; sell, lease, or give away property; promote industrial, commercial, and agricultural development; become a stockholder in corporations; lend its credit and grant public monies; sell bonds to acquire property; levy special taxes to pay public indebtedness; create a public corporation (an industrial development authority).

Alaska. Organized boroughs may select 10 percent of vacant, unappropriated, and unreserved lands located within their boundaries for development; land has been used as an incentive to provide for privately built and financed housing subdivisions, construction of office space, retail space, and multiple family buildings, and to exchange for the construction of public facilities; public land may be exchanged for private lands to construct public facilities; cities may establish economic development authorities to finance and provide direction for economic development.

Arizona. Have broad development authority; nearly all have created departments of economic development; many make cash contributions to local or regional economic development organizations (limited to

$500,000 per year) and chambers of commerce; may form enterprise zones, industrial parks, and other facilities (airports, ballparks); may form an Industrial Development Authority to promote industrial development and create jobs; may have lease purchase agreements with private developers, tax increment financing, and nonprofit agencies to finance construction.

Arkansas. May establish community development corporations, industrial parks, planning and development districts, enterprise zones, and improvement districts; state guarantees county and municipal revenue bonds; may form "industrial development compacts" empowered to issue revenue bonds.

California. May create community redevelopment agencies with powers of tax increment financing and eminent domain to attack urban blight; may create enterprise zones; infrastructure financing via general obligation bonds; waiver of developer fees; subsidize public works; discount land sales; may not give property tax rebates.

(table continues)

(Table A12 continued)

Colorado. Cities exercise local control over land use, water, and transportation planning; may finance, acquire, own, lease, improve, and dispose of property to promote industry and economic development; may issue bonds for development financing; may establish a general improvement districts and business improvement districts for large commercial development or large-cost infrastructure items; may set up an urban renewal authority to encourage development with TIFs, condemnation authority, and debt financing.

Connecticut. Cities may establish an economic development commission, which may conduct research, develop plans, and coordinate local development activities; may establish convention and visitors' commissions, historic districts, foreign trade zones, and local redevelopment agencies; state provides special aid to "distressed communities," which also may create enterprise zones that grant tax abatements and deferrals.

Delaware. May set up economic development corporations, business zones, and main street development programs.

Florida. May issue revenue bonds for economic development purposes; counties may expend public monies to attract and retain businesses—including developing and improving infrastructure, issuing bonds for capital projects and industrial plants, leasing and conveying property, and making grants to private enterprises; cities and counties may establish enterprise zones that may offer tax credits and corporate and sales tax exemptions; counties may approve or disapprove issuance of revenue bonds by all entities within their borders; cities and counties may use TIFs.

Georgia. May establish a development authority in each city or county; may establish downtown development authorities for central business districts; state favors a regional development center approach, and the state uses the tax code to encourage business development (statewide job tax credit); various property tax exemptions exist, among which are a freeport exemption and a homestead exemption; counties and cities may create "community improvement districts."

Hawaii. May create assessment districts and float bonds to pay the cost of an improvement whose benefits are to be shared by the landowners of the district; state legislature can create development authorities able to override county zoning limitations and building codes; may finance low- and moderate-income housing and engage in urban renewal; primary responsibility for economic development rests at state level.

Idaho. Local governments have only a limited number of incentives—use of property tax is severely restricted by state law, and they may not offer tax exemptions or set up enterprise zones; may issue industrial revenue bonds; may use TIFs as part of an urban renewal effort; may impose an assessment fee on downtown businesses to support an improvement district.

Illinois. May create community development corporations; cities may form neighborhood redevelopment corporations; state law encourages the formation of county- or regional-level industrial development agencies; may establish enterprise zones with state approval; home rule cities may grant residential development abatements to fight urban decay, and all cities may grant abatements on annexed property; may abate any portion of property taxes on commercial and industrial property and may impose performance conditions; may use TIFs, create industrial parks, control land assembly, designate business districts, create small business incubators, and abate sales taxes through economic incentive agreements.

Indiana. May engage in planning, zoning, land-use regulation, and code enforcement; may form a redevelopment commission to oversee re-covery of blighted areas; two or more counties may form a regional planning commission to coordinate regional economic development activities; state prohibits the establishment of enterprise zones, economic development districts, and allocation areas.

Iowa. May using zoning authority, tax abatements, and tax increment financing; may provide loans and grants for development; may fund a multijurisdictional economic development organization; may offer tax abatements for ten years and TIFs up to twenty-five years.

Kansas. Cities may undertake almost any development function; may establish community development organizations, enterprise zones, and economic development banks; county governments have broad development functions but rarely undertake urban development projects within city boundaries without consent of city authorities.

Kentucky. May establish industrial parks; may undertake infrastructure improvements targeted to attract business location or expansion; may establish enterprise zones; may grant tax credits and issue industrial bonds; may create revolving loan funds and industrial development authorities; may use public office space and clerical support, issue revenue bonds, and acquire land through condemnation; industrial sites are not assessed property taxes; may establish nonprofit industrial foundations to acquire and develop industrial sites; state maintains a local government economic development fund; may use their own funds to renew blighted areas; may sponsor a main street program; and may use own funds for economic and community development without voter approval.

Louisiana. State permits exemptions from several different state and local taxes; may establish an enterprise zone with state permission.

Maine. Cities may engage in economic and community development activities and may use own source revenues for the benefit of private entities, but they may not grant tax credits; local taxes may be used to develop industrial parks, establish an enterprise zone, renew blighted areas, create a revolving loan fund bank, improve infrastructure, and develop municipal districts; cities and towns may use own source funds with a vote of the local residents; counties may not use own source funds, have no provision for a vote of citizens and are very restricted in the area of community and economic development.

Maryland. May engage in economic or community development activities; counties may grant tax credits, develop industrial parks, establish and maintain enterprise zones, revitalize blighted areas, and make infrastructure improvements targeted to economic or community development projects; cities are limited to establishment of enterprise zones, renewal of blighted areas, and improvement of infrastructure; cities and counties may use own source revenues for economic or community development projects that benefit private entities (no local referendum needed).

Massachusetts. Any city or town may create an industrial development finance authority, an economic development corporation, a redevelopment authority, or a development and industrial commission; economic opportunity areas may negotiate tax abatements.

Michigan. "Brown fields" are exempt from all taxes for up to twelve years, except sales taxes; local units may ask the state to approve "renaissance zones" that offer tax incentives; many local units have downtown development authorities, which may use TIFs.

Minnesota. Cities may organize and fund economic development activities through departments or separate economic development agencies; counties, cities, and townships may cooperate in regional development commissions; may use TIFs.

(table continues)

(Table A12 continued)

Mississippi. Municipalities may offer businesses property tax waivers for up to ten years, but exemptions for school district tax are prohibited.

Missouri. Cities may assemble an economic redevelopment plan for "blighted" areas where all real property taxes are exempt for the first ten years, then for next fifteen years, property is taxed at 50 percent; TIFs may be used; may establish economic development districts and industrial development boards, which have the power to issue revenue bonds and receive funds; cities may establish special business districts; local revenues may be used for economic and community development purposes such as tax credits, industrial parks, enterprise zones, and infrastructure development.

Montana. May create development corporations that can receive public monies, borrow from public entities, and make loans to private firms for promoting business and economic development; may create industrial parks, and may exempt the park from property taxes; may adopt urban renewal plans and projects to eliminate blight, and may use TIFs for this purpose.

Nebraska. Local governments may promote economic development through an infrastructure redevelopment fund, an optional sales tax, TIFs, and fifteen year revenue bonds; cities may create an enterprise zone.

Nevada. May not engage in development activities by absence of enabling legislation; local governments may engage in urban renewal and issue bonds; may designate historic districts; may issue revenue bonds for industrial development.

New Hampshire. Cities and towns may create industrial development authorities, but use of public funds to help businesses is prohibited, unless there is a public benefit to be gained; state prohibits enterprise zones; cities may form central business service districts, establish TIFs, and have industrial development authorities set up revolving loan funds and act as developers in certain areas.

New Jersey. Cities may create a redevelopment authority for any area in need of "rehabilitation;" may offer property tax abatements; may create an urban enterprise zone, a special improvement district, and establish a district management corporation where special district charges are considered an assessment, not a tax.

New Mexico. May use public resources to encourage local and regional development; may permit joint powers agreements to plan and support regional development projects; local and regional economic development departments may provide land, buildings, and infrastructure to support business growth and the introduction of new ventures; may have public works improvements, payments for professional service contracts for planning or implementation of local projects, and direct grants and loans, loan guarantees, and grants for public works infrastructure improvements essential to location or expansion of a qualifying business; may establish an enterprise zone and use TIFs in enterprise zones.

New York. May create an industrial development authority, which may acquire land through eminent domain, offer incentives for projects, issue revenue bonds, and set up variable repayment schedules.

North Carolina. Cities and counties may engage in activities related to community and economic development, industrial promotion, and urban renewal; counties may create special authorities to issue industrial revenue bonds, subject to approval of state Dept. of Commerce and the Local Government Commission; local governments may build and prepare sites for industrial parks; may construct, lease, and sell shell buildings, and convey property to a private company; may appropriate public monies to aid and encourage the location of manufacturing enterprises; may make property available to private developers as a part of a redevelopment project; may issue revenue bonds, but property tax abatements or special classifications are prohibited.

North Dakota. Municipalities, and to a lesser extent counties, may tax, borrow, and lend for economic development purposes; cities may establish economic development organizations, industrial parks, enterprise zones, loan or grant pools, and job training projects; cities and counties may acquire property, issue revenue bonds, and lease property to industrial, commercial, or nonprofit organizations, school districts for vocational education, or health institutions; may grant partial or complete tax exemptions for ad valorem increases in tangible property for up to five years—agricultural processing plants may obtain an extra year exemption; may use up to one mill to finance vocational or on-the-job training (60 percent majority vote required); cities may establish job development authorities and earmark up to four mills for their support; job development authorities may loan or grant funds or property, provide loan guarantees, or invest funds; cities may acquire "blighted" property through eminent domain, improve, develop, or sell the property, issue revenue bonds, and offer TIFs with a public hearing.

Ohio. Cities may abate property and other taxes, may establish enterprise zones, and may create a "community reinvestment area."

Oklahoma. Cities may use incentives and exemptions from local taxation, TIFs, and tax apportionment bonds and notes as economic development strategies; cities and counties may create industrial parks, establish and maintain enterprise zones, create revolving loan banks and funds, undertake weatherization relocation, and revitalization projects; may undertake infrastructure improvements targeted to specific community development projects; may grant tax credits (with vote of citizens).

Oregon. Have broad administrative discretion with respect to economic development; may establish urban renewal agencies; may use TIFs; substantial state level aid and assistance to local governments.

Pennsylvania. State created twelve "Keystone Opportunity Zones" that permit the use of tax abatements through credits, exemptions, waivers, and deductions to reduce taxable economic activity to zero within the zone; cities may create neighborhood investment districts (to revitalize downtowns); counties support industrial parks and create economic development entities.

Rhode Island. Cities and towns may exempt property taxes to encourage business location or retention; may establish an enterprise zone with state approval; may use local revenues in aid of economic development.

South Carolina. Municipalities may create a redevelopment commission that may contract with businesses and public entities and issue bonds to finance specific projects, may establish enterprise zones and offer tax credits for creating new jobs within the zone, and may set up industrial parks; counties may develop industrial or business projects involving land, buildings, and improvements in support of manufacturing or commercial activity, may issue revenue bonds, but require approval of the state Budget and Control Board, and may offer fee-in-lieu of taxes for qualified properties in an industrial park.

South Dakota. Municipalities may take part in economic development projects and create business improvement districts, within which the city may use funds for a variety purposes; cities may issue bonds, acquire or construct projects, enter into revenue agreements with individuals, pri-

(table continues)

(Table A12 continued)

vate corporations, or governmental bodies, or offer property tax abatements; counties may issue bonds for economic development; may offer tax incentives to encourage growth and development; may use general fund monies to assist nonprofit corporations and associations for the purpose of promoting industrial, tourist, and recreational activities; may establish an enterprise zone in areas that are economically disadvantaged and may offer special loans to these areas.

Tennessee. May create industrial parks, enterprise zones, community development organizations, and private industrial development boards by which the local government can finance projects via lending from private institutions; industrial development boards may buy property, construct buildings, and accept payment in lieu of taxes; local government borrowing for economic development requires a Certificate of Public Purpose and Necessity from the state Dept. of Economic and Community Development, and the municipality must hold a referendum or a public meeting and place the matter before the public (but not for revenue bonds).

Texas. Municipalities—and to a lesser extent, counties—may establish public-private partnerships, quasi-governmental economic development corporations, and purely public economic development programs; cities may provide direct financial assistance to fully or partially private agencies; local development may be financed through local general revenues, local hotel occupancy taxes, local option sales taxes, federal or state grants-in-aid, municipal general obligation or revenue bonds, and TIFs; cities and counties may abate certain taxes in eligible areas for up to fifteen years; cities may establish special business zones, and cities and counties may designate enterprise zones, within which local governments may offer various financial incentives and limited regulatory relief.

Utah. May establish a neighborhood redevelopment agency to stimulate local development by exercising the power of eminent domain and offering TIFs; counties may establish an enterprise zone; may use the state's Permanent Community Impact Fund.

Vermont. Towns may establish industrial parks, but few towns have any formal program for economic development; growth, whether commercial or residential, is not immediately embraced as a public good in Vermont.

Virginia. May conduct various economic and community development activities; may acquire, lease, or sell land; may regulate sewage disposal and water service, manage development in historical areas, prepare capital improvement programs, and issue bonds to finance development activities; may seek approval from the state to set up a community development authority to improve infrastructure; may adopt a main street program to revitalize downtown areas; may form nonprofit industrial development authorities and establish enterprise zones; may provide low interest loans to private businesses, give a partial exemption from real estate taxes, and issue industrial revenue bonds for nonprofit corporations.

Washington. Municipalities may develop specific plans for urban renewal; may establish foreign trade zones; may provide, in conjunction with the state, limited financing for efforts to attract private industry and support other forms of local economic development; may contract with nonprofit corporations to further economic development; may partner with private sector entities.

West Virginia. Cities may create integrated departments of development; cities and counties may participate in county and municipal development authorities and area development corporations; may acquire, lease, loan, purchase, and sell industrial and commercial projects, and finance these projects through loans and revenue bonds; may establish enterprise zones; counties may collect fees for the costs associated with capital improvements; counties can levy impact fees related to population growth and public services needs, adopt a county-wide comprehensive plan, adopt zoning and subdivision ordinances, adopt formal building permit and review systems, and provide for capital improvement programming (referendum approval could be needed).

Wisconsin. Municipalities have wide latitude in conducting development activities; may conduct urban redevelopment projects, including condemning property and establishing redevelopment corporations; cities may create TIFs in areas that are blighted, in need of rehabilitation, or are suitable for industrial sites; cities may issue industrial revenue bonds, buy and sell land and buildings, but cannot grant tax abatements on local property taxes.

Wyoming. Municipalities have broad latitude to engage in development and redevelopment efforts; cities may levy special taxes, zone particular districts, and establish specialized organizations to carry out development; special taxes may be assessed and the revenues funneled into special funds to further development; property may be acquired for redevelopment through eminent domain, purchase, and leasing; cities may form development commissions or agencies; tax abatement or relief is prohibited.

Table A13. Interlocal Cooperation

Form of cooperation	States permitting cooperation
Consolidation of services	Mississippi, Nevada, North Carolina, Pennsylvania, Virginia
Cooperative purchasing agreements/programs	Connecticut, Delaware, Hawaii, Maine, Montana, New York, Pennsylvania
Council of government	Alaska, Connecticut, Massachusetts, Ohio, Oklahoma, Pennsylvania, South Carolina, Tennessee, Utah, West Virginia
Financial incentive for interlocal cooperation	Nebraska
Informal mutual aid	Maine, Nebraska, Wisconsin
Interlocal agreements	Arizona, Arkansas, Colorado, Connecticut, Florida, Georgia, Idaho, Illinois, Indiana, Kansas, Louisiana, Michigan, Minnesota, Mississippi, Missouri, Montana, Nebraska, New Hampshire, New Jersey, New York, North Dakota, Ohio, Oklahoma, Oregon, South Carolina, Texas, Utah, Virginia, West Virginia, Wisconsin, Wyoming
Interlocal risk management	Indiana, Louisiana, Nebraska, Oklahoma
Investment of funds	Idaho
Joint equipment/facilities	Alabama, Arkansas, Delaware, Idaho, Iowa, Maryland, Massachusetts, Mississippi, Missouri, Montana, Nebraska, New Mexico, New York Ohio, Oklahoma, Oregon, South Carolina, West Virginia, Wisconsin
Joint/regional planning	Alabama, Connecticut, Florida, Illinois, Kansas, Kentucky, Maine, Maryland, Massachusetts, Minnesota, Mississippi, Nebraska, Ohio Pennsylvania, South Carolina, Utah, Virginia
Joint power agreement	Arizona, Idaho, Indiana, Iowa, Kentucky, Louisiana, Massachusetts, Minnesota, Nebraska, Nevada, New Hampshire, New Mexico, North Dakota, Tennessee, Utah, Virginia, Wyoming
Joint power authority, agency, or commission	Arizona, California, Louisiana, North Dakota, Oklahoma, Tennessee, Wyoming
Lease property or services	Maryland
Memo of understanding	California, Nebraska
Merge agencies or departments	Alabama, Mississippi, Oregon
Metropolitan district	Colorado, Connecticut, Minnesota, Oregon, Tennessee
Public authority	Alabama, Arizona, Arkansas, Delaware, Illinois, Indiana, Iowa, Maryland, Massachusetts, Michigan, Missouri, Montana, Nebraska, Nevada, New York, North Dakota, Ohio, Oklahoma, Pennsylvania, Rhode Island
Public corporations	California, Maryland, Mississippi, Nebraska, South Carolina
Regional commissions/districts	Connecticut, Minnesota, Montana, Virginia, West Virginia
Service delivery contracts	Alabama, Arizona, Arkansas, Delaware, Florida, Georgia, Idaho, Illinois, Indiana, Iowa, Kansas, Maine, Maryland, Michigan, Minnesota, Mississippi, Missouri, Montana, Nebraska, Nevada, Oklahoma, Oregon, South Carolina, Tennessee, Texas, Utah, Virginia
Special districts	Alabama, Arizona, Arkansas, California, Colorado, Connecticut, Delaware, Florida, Georgia, Illinois, Indiana, Iowa, Kansas, Kentucky, Louisiana, Maine, Maryland, Massachusetts, Michigan, Minnesota, Missouri, Montana, Nebraska, Nevada, New Hampshire, New Jersey, New Mexico, New York, North Dakota, Ohio, Oklahoma, Oregon, Rhode Island, South Carolina, South Dakota, Tennessee, Texas, Utah, Virginia, West Virginia, Wyoming
Sports authority	Arizona
Transfer authority	New York, Ohio

Table A14. Local Government Fiscal Management

State	Balanced budget reequired Municipal	Balanced budget reequired County	Bankuptcy proceedings established
Alabama	Y	Y	Y
Alaska	N	N	–
Arizona	Y	Y	a
Arkansas	N	N	–
California	N	Y	–
Colorado	Y	Y	–
Connecticut	Y	Y	Y
Delaware	–	–	N
Florida	Y	Y	–
Georgia	Y	Y	N
Hawaii	n/a	N	–
Idaho	Y	Y	–
Illinois	N	N	N
Indiana	b	–	N
Iowa	N	N	–
Kansas	N	N	N
Kentucky	N	N	Y
Louisiana	Y	Y	N
Maine	Y	Y	Y
Maryland	N	N	N
Massachusetts	Y	n/a	Y
Michigan	Y	Y	Y
Minnesota	Y	Y	Y
Mississippi	Y	Y	–
Missouri	Yc	–	–
Montana	Y	Y	Y
Nebraska	N	N	N
Nevada	Y	Y	Y
New Hampshire	N	N	N
New Jersey	N	N	Y
New Mexico	Y	Y	Y
New York	Y	Y	Y
North Carolina	Y	Y	Y
North Dakota	Y	Y	d
Ohio	e	–	Y
Oklahoma	Y	–	–
Oregon	Y	Y	–
Pennsylvania	–	–	Y
Rhode Island	Y	n/a	Y
South Carolina	Y	Y	N
South Dakota	N	N	Y
Tennessee	Y	–	N
Texas	Y	Y	Y
Utah	Y	Y	N
Vermont	N	–	–
Virginia	N	N	N
Washington	N	N	Y
West Virginia	Y	Y	N
Wisconsin	–	–	–
Wyoming	N	N	N

Note: A dash indicates that the state chapter author did not mention the specific item.
a. May be disincorporated.
b. State board of tax commissioners review and approve every local government budget.
c. Commonly unenforced.
d. City dissolved.
e. County approves.

Table A15. Primary Source of Municipal Revenue

Primary tax	State
Property tax	
76%–100%	Maine (86%), Vermont (approx. 85%), Idaho
51%–75%	Pennsylvania (68%), Connecticut (57%), New York (towns 56%), Kansas (52%)
40%–50%	Massachusetts (50%), South Carolina (50%), New York (villages 48%), New Hampshire (47%), New Jersey (44%), Oregon (42.5%)
30%–40%	Minnesota (cities above 2,500 popul. 36%), Virginia (33%), Maryland (32%)
20%–30%	Tennessee (27%), Indiana (26%), Georgia (24%)
Varies by municipality	Nebraska (36%–22%), South Dakota
% unspecified by chapter author	Illinois, Michigan, Montana, North Dakota, Rhode Island, Texas
Consumption or sales tax	Oklahoma (47%), Colorado (44.5%), Louisiana (38%), Utah (27.5%), Arizona (26%), Arkansas
Charges & user fees	Delaware (50%), Iowa (50%), Kentucky (44%), Wyoming (44%), California (41%), Washington (40%) North Carolina (39%), Alabama (35%), Ohio (34%), Mississippi (33%), Utah (30%), New York (cities 30%)
Business & commercial fees	West Virginia (42%)
State shared revenues	Alaska, Minnesota (cities with less than 2,500 popul. 34%) Missouri (34%, includes counties), Wisconsin (varies with city)

Note: Primary source of municipal revenue as a percentage of total municipal revenue.

Table A16. Debt Limits on Municipal Governments

Bonded debt limit (as % of assessed valuation)	State
0.0%	Alaska
1.75%	New Hampshire
2.0%	Idaho, Indiana
2.5%	Massachusetts (cities)
3.0%	Oregon, Rhode Island
3.5%	New Jersey
4.0%	Utah,[a] Wyoming[b]
5.0%	Iowa, Massachusetts (towns), Missouri,[c] North Dakota,[d] West Virginia, Wisconsin
6.0%	Arizona
7.5%	Maine
8.0%	North Carolina, South Carolina[e]
10%	Georgia, Kentucky, Michigan, Oklahoma,[f] Virginia
10.5%	Ohio[g]
15%	Delaware, Hawaii,[h] Maryland
15–20%	Arizona (for specified purposes)
20.0%	Alabama
28.0%	Montana
30%	Kansas, Nevada[i]
35.0%	Louisiana

Other

10 times assessed value	Vermont
Limited by voter approval & bond rating	Texas
% of its borrowing base[j]	Pennsylvania (municipalities 250%; counties 300%)
Varies with city size	Illinois, Kentucky, Nebraska[k]
Varies with purpose	California (1.5–15%), Connecticut

a. Additional 4% for water, sewer, or lights.

b. Additional 4% for sewers, no limit for water.

c. Missouri municipalities may add another 10%--for a total of 15% debt--for public improvements.

d. North Dakota can exceed debt limit with two-thirds vote.

e. South Carolina can exceed debt limit with vote.

f. Excludes revenue bonds.

g. Ohio cannot exceed 5.5% without voter approval.

h. Debt limit is on counties since Hawaii has no municipal governments.

i. Nevada charters vary from 10 to 40%.

j. Borrowing base is the average total revenues over preceding three full fiscal years.

k. Nebraska state government uses local bonding authority for state highway construction borrowing, and this makes it difficult to sort out the debt limit on municipal borrowing.

GLOSSARY

***Ad valorem* taxes**—Taxes that are imposed by a governmental authority based on the fair market value of the real and personal property in the jurisdiction. These taxes are usually levied on the basis of "mils;" a mil is 1/1000th of the assessed value of the property (which is some percentage of the fair market value, such as 40 percent). Most states have an elaborate system governing *ad valorem* property taxation by local governments that must be strictly followed.

Annexation—The expansion of municipal boundary lines to take in adjacent territory located in the unincorporated area of a county. The methods by which this expansion can occur are usually delineated by state law and are often subject to referendum approval by the voters in the area to be annexed.

Authorities—Political subdivisions of limited purpose. These entities are normally created by state law for a specific program or purpose and, while limited in scope, can have some power over other local governments. Examples include public housing authorities, park and recreation authorities, water and sewer authorities, and parking and transit authorities. Such authorities usually have an appointed board; some board members may be appointed by the governor, and some may be on the board because they are members of a participating general purpose government. Although appointed, the board is generally empowered to impose assessments, fees, or "taxes" for the service or activity provided, although use of the term "tax" may create controversy.

Bids and bidding—State law often requires that purchases by state and local government entities of a certain type or over a certain amount be subject to a competitive bidding process. This is to ensure that the public is getting the best return on its expenditures and to deter conflicts of interest on the part of government officials. Competitive bidding processes are usually set forth in detail in state law.

Board of commissioners—The name of the governing authority of a county in many states. Traditionally this board has had both legislative and executive powers, and this dual nature has led to calls for reform in county governance in many states.

Bonds—Financial instruments that allow governments to borrow money on the bond market. These bonds are often attractive to investors because the interest paid on them is not subject to state or federal income tax. The two principal types of bonds are "general obligation bonds" and "revenue bonds." General obligation bonds are secured by the full faith and credit of the political subdivision issuing them. Revenue bonds are secured only by the revenues generated by the operation of the facility or program provided.

Charter—A legal document that is the equivalent to the constitution of a city (or county), describing the powers and form of government a city or county may have. A charter can be instrumental in the creation of a city, but many cities and counties acquire charters when they cease running their affairs under general state laws. General charters are essentially local "constitutions" created by the state that apply automatically to all cities that have not requested a "special act charter" or a home rule charter. Special act charters are generally passed as "local acts" of the state legislature initially and can be amended or even repealed by the state legislature in many states.

City council—The generic name of the legislative governing authority of a city.

City/county manager—The person appointed by the city council or the county commission to manage the affairs of the city or county. This manager is supposed to be appointed on the basis of competence (education and experience) rather than political connections or favoritism, and he/she serves at the pleasure of the governing authority.

Civil service system—A system of personnel administration in which appointments to publicly funded positions are made on the basis of merit (that is, competence—based on education and experience), rather than on patronage or political connections. Employees who are part of a civil service system generally enjoy a higher level of protection from unfair decisions of government officials than those who are not part of the system.

Classes of cities—Some states employ a classification system for cities and/or counties that allows the states to differentiate between degrees of legal authority and discretion. Cities or counties of the "first class," for example, might be given a higher level of autonomy than cities or counties of the "second class" or "third class." These classifications are normally based on population or size. Many states have an elaborate system, with a different code for each type of local government. Classification is sometimes used to legislate for one city (such as the largest in the state), thereby avoiding the ban on "special local acts" that may be part of constitutional or statutory law.

Condemnation—The exercise of the power of eminent domain by a state or local government entity. The federal and state constitutions require that the power of eminent domain be exercised only for a public use or purpose and that the property owner be given "just compensation." *See also Eminent domain.*

Conflict of interest—Public officials are elected or appointed to serve the public interest. Their office is held in public trust. Any time a public official receives some special benefit or advantage not available to the public generally, it raises the potential of a "conflict of interest." Conflicts of interest include both actual and perceived conflicts. Public officials try to avoid even the appearance of impropriety.

Consolidation—The combining two or more political jurisdictions into one, generally for the purpose of achieving economies of scale. It may require a legislative enactment or referendum approval by the voters. The term is often associated with the merger of a city and a county governing authority. Partial consolidation occurs when there is a merger of the administration of one service by a city and a county.

Contract—A legal instrument entered into by two or more parties, creating legal obligations and expectations on both sides. One common type of contract in intergovernmental relations is an intergovernmental service delivery contract, in which one or more cities and/or counties agree to share or delegate certain governmental services or functions.

County vs. city services—Counties in the American governmental system are hybrids, performing a role both as an administrative arm of state government and also as a local government service delivery unit similar to a city. Historically counties provided very few "urban" or municipal-type services, but today they have become more urban-like in many of their attributes. As a consequence, competition has sometimes developed between cities and counties concerning local government service delivery. In these cases, debate has revolved around which unit is in the best position to provide which service. The traditional services performed by counties have been road and bridge construction and maintenance, law enforcement, judicial and electoral services, as well as health and welfare services.

Debt financing—The borrowing of money by state or local governments to finance certain projects or programs over time. These are usually costly items, such as major capital improvements, and they often require referendum approval by the voters.

Debt instruments—The legal documents entered into by a political subdivision to borrow money. Debt instruments include general obligation bonds, revenue bonds, industrial revenue bonds, local residential housing bonds, temporary notes, and others.

Development authorities—Political subdivisions established by law to carry out a specific purpose or activity such as downtown or urban development. *See also Authorities.*

Dillon's Rule—A rule of "strict construction" in local government law

that is taken from the 1868 ruling of Judge John Dillon in *City of Clinton v. Cedar Rapids and Missouri River Railroad Company.* The precedent-setting ruling states:

> "A municipal corporation possesses and can exercise the following powers, and no others: first, those granted in expressed words; second, those necessarily or fairly implied in or incident to the powers expressly granted; third, those essential to the accomplishment of the declared objects and purposes of the corporation—not simply convenient, but indispensable. Any fair, reasonable, substantial doubt concerning the existence of power as resolved by the course against the "municipal" corporation, and the power is denied."

"Direct democracy"—Methods by which the public can have direct access to policy makers or public policy itself, including the right to propose direct constitutional and/or statutory amendments, the right to call for special ballot initiatives, the right to recall public officials, and other methods providing for direct citizen action. The best example of direct democracy at work in the United States today is still the townhall meeting in New England.

Discretionary versus ministerial acts—In local government law a distinction is often made between decisions of public officials that are "governmental" or discretionary in nature versus decisions that are "ministerial" or administrative in nature. Public officials are generally immune from liability for decisions of the former kind, even in the case of errors of judgment, but are not immune from liability for negligence in the carrying out of "ministerial" acts.

Disincorporation—The legal process of "undoing" the incorporation of a municipality. Charter revocation, for example, is one type of disincorporation. This process usually requires referendum approval by the voters, but not always. When this occurs, the territory of the former city reverts to the status of unincorporated area of the county and from then on gets its services from the county.

Economic development districts—Special districts created by law in which special fees or taxes may be levied to support specific economic development activities; or special districts in which specific benefits or incentives are offered to encourage greater economic development activity by private enterprise. These are also known as enterprise zones.

Eminent domain—The power of the state or local government to "take" private property for public use, provided that just compensation is paid to the owner.

Enterprise revenue—Revenue obtained from special assessments, levies, or fees to support a specific type of service, such as water, electricity, gas, and wastewater treatment. This revenue is usually held separate from the main budget of the city or county.

Escheat funds—Funds derived from property that has reverted back to the state, as a result of a provision in a will or an estate.

Excise taxes—Special taxes levied on particular types of products or services, such as those imposed on certain luxury or special items.

Federal pass-through dollars—Intergovernmental transfer payments from the federal government to state or local governments that are, by law, earmarked for specific purposes.

Fiscal notes—Statements attached to proposed legislation analyzing its probable financial impact, outlining current costs, projected future costs, proposed sources of revenue, and long-term fiscal effects. Many states are requiring such notes for proposed "unfunded mandates" on local governments.

Form of government—The framework of the local government, including the membership of the governing body, terms of office, and the relationship between the legislative and executive powers. The typical forms of local government include the county commission form, the mayor-council form (strong or weak), the chief administrative officer form, and the council manager or commission manager form.

"Front foot" assessments—Tax valuations based on lineal front footage, usually of street fronts or waterfronts.

General assembly—The term used in many states to designate the state legislature.

General-obligation bonds—Bonds issued by the state or local government that are supported by the full faith and credit of the taxing jurisdiction. These bonds carry a lower interest rate than other types of bonds, because they are normally exempt from state and local income taxes. These are usually conditioned on referendum approval by the voters.

Grants-in-aid—Funds, which are earmarked for a particular use or purpose, allocated from the federal government to the state or local governments or from the state government to the local governments.

Governing authority—The generic term for the local government officials who are empowered to act on behalf of the citizens in a city, county, or other local government entity.

Home rule—The power of local self-government, or the power of local governments to deal with matters of local concern without having to turn to the state legislature for approval, as long as their actions do not contravene already defined state policies. As the sovereign, the state may carve out new areas of "state concern."

Housing codes—The set of rules and regulations adopted by the state and/or local governments that govern the construction of new homes and other buildings. These may include separate codes for air conditioning and heating, electrical, plumbing, and other items.

Historic preservation programs—Programs and services provided by state and local governments intended to promote the protection, enhancement, perpetuation, and use of historic places, properties, districts, structures, sites, and works of art. In some states the zoning regulations may freeze the dimensions or architectural style of a property for many years.

Immunity—The legal defense available to state or local government officials for official acts for which they are not liable. When local governments claim "immunity," they are claiming to act as agents of the state.

Impact-fee legislation—A type of fee imposed by some local governing authorities on developers, to try to transfer some of the cost of local government infrastructure to new residents. Costs are intended to pay for such investments as roads, sewers, drainage projects, and water lines necessary for new development. They may also be imposed to defray the cost of new police stations, school buildings, and fire stations. In many states these fees are strictly regulated by state law. Courts have sometimes required that the funds be kept in separate accounts, to ensure that the money collected is expended only in the area where the improvements have been made.

Intergovernmental relations—The manner in which two or more state and/or local subdivisions interact with each other to promote a common approach to public policy problems.

Intergovernmental revenues—Revenues received from federal, state, and/or local sources.

Interlocal service agreements or contracts—Agreements entered into between local units of governments for specific services or activities, such as law enforcement, libraries, economic development, juvenile detention facilities, mental health facilities, or any other public service, activity, or program that each jurisdiction is authorized to undertake. These agreements can take many forms; they can allow one local unit to charge customers directly for the service; they can require lump sum payments by one unit to the other; they can provide for full provision of the service; they can provide for aid in times of emergency (such as a major fire); and they can be tailored to the needs and desires of the jurisdictions affected.

Lease-purchase agreements—Agreements entered into by governments and vendors that allow the political subdivision to make lease payments over time and receive credit toward the purchase price if the government later decides to buy the property outright.

Levy—The formal term for the imposition of a tax on properties subject to taxation. This occurs after the property has been appraised or assessed by the tax assessor or appraiser. The term can also be used for the imposition of a sales tax. It also refers to the total tax obligation.

Line-item budgeting—The process used by state legislatures and local governments whereby specific amounts of money are allocated to particular categories and purposes, and each is given a "line number." Subsequent changes in the lines or between categories require a new authorization. Line-item budgeting is associated with a rigid form of budgeting, and a high level of public accountability.

Local impact statements—Similar to fiscal notes, these statements are intended to provide an objective analysis of the likely impact—financial, environmental, and otherwise—on local governments of proposed new legislation.

Local legislation—The types of laws passed by state legislatures that affect only a particular city, county, or other local government entity. Many states have abolished local legislation in favor of local "home rule."

Local-option tax—A tax authorization granted by state governments to local governments that is permissive in nature, to give local governments the discretion to adopt or not adopt a certain type of tax, such as a hotel/motel tax or a sales tax.

Merger—Another term for consolidation of units or services. A merger often requires governmental reorganization.

Mils—A unit of measurement signifying 1/1000th of a dollar. This term is generally associated with *ad valorem* taxation, to designate the tax that a person will pay on real and personal property owned. For example, if the tax rate is 5 mils, and a person's property is worth $100,000, the tax will be calculated as follows: 5 X 1/1000th X $100,000 = $500. *See* Ad valorem *taxes.*

Municipal corporations or municipalities—The formal term for cities. Most cities were originally created by the adoption of a "charter" by the state legislature, and the city was said to be "incorporated," much as a business is incorporated. Once a community becomes a "municipality," it acquires privileges and obligations described in its charter.

Nontax revenue sources—Sources of revenue for local governments other than from taxation, including fines and forfeitures, assessments and fees, and other sources.

Notice—The formal legal requirement often imposed upon state and local governments either by the state constitution or by law to give the public advance warning of major changes being proposed, such as the form of government, taxation, zoning, land use, and other matters. Methods of notice include postings, newspaper advertisements, billboards, and others.

Occupation licenses—The fee imposed by many counties and cities on businesses to help defray the cost of regulation of those businesses by the government.

Open-records/open meetings—The legal requirement often imposed upon state and local governments either by the state constitution or by law that mandates that all public meetings and all public records be open to the public and to public inspection, with certain limited exceptions (such as proposed property purchases to deter land speculation, sensitive personnel matters to protect reputations, and other limited exceptions). Special districts are often exempt from these kinds of "sunshine" laws.

Ordinances—The legal term for the laws passed by the local governing authority. These are called "acts" or "laws" at the state and federal levels.

Own-source revenue—All types of revenue that the local governing authority generates under its own authority, including property taxes, general and special sales taxes, income taxes, privilege licenses, user fees and assessments, and others.

Piggybacking—A method whereby local governments can participate in a general state and/or income tax and receive a prorated share of the money collected.

Planning and zoning—The authority of state and local governments to provide for the regulation of land use and the division of the territory of a city or county into districts in which certain uses are permitted and certain uses are prohibited. The authority to do this derives from the police power of the state, or the right of the government to provide for the public health, safety, morals, and general welfare; in many states "general welfare" has been held to include aesthetic considerations.

Police power—The authority of a governmental entity to provide for the public health, safety, morals, and general welfare.

Populist movement/reforms—The Populist movement supported the right of the "common man" and inspired the use of the initiative, referendum, and recall as well as the regulation of business and political parties. It emerged from a revolt against the domination of big business (the railroads and banks) from the 1870s to 1890s. To this day any movement that champions the rights of average citizens against some "conspiracy of wealth" is called populist. Generically, the term may also relate to provisions in charters, laws, and state constitutions that provide for public input into the decision-making process, including provisions for initiative and referendum, recall, ballot initiatives, and other changes in law or policy. *See also "Direct democracy."*

Powers—The authority vested in a state or local government entity by the state constitution or state statutory laws to act.

Preemption—The action taken by a state to provide uniform and statewide regulation of a particular field or subject area, thereby removing and/or superseding local government action in that area. Preemption eliminates "home rule" as to the subject area preempted. Sometimes a state will preempt some but not all of a particular subject area. The federal government also uses preemption in its efforts to ensure that states comply with federal programs and policies.

Privilege licenses—Also known as business licenses in some states, these are special fees and assessments levied on businesses to help defray the cost of the regulation of those businesses by the government.

Property tax—*See* Ad valorem *taxes.*

Proposition 2—The Massachusetts version of "Proposition 13," limiting local tax revenues to 2.5 percent of the total value of taxable property.

Proposition 13—The California proposition that placed constitutional limitations on the taxing authority of local governments. The "grandfather" of local property tax limitations, this proposition spawned similar constitutional restrictions in other states. These provisions limit greatly the discretion and authority of local governments to tax the citizens. They have had a significant effect on the conduct of local government in California and elsewhere.

Protest petitions—The authority provided in state law for citizens to stop the action of local governing bodies through certain legal procedures.

Public authorities—*See Authorities.*

Public records—All records generated by public employees in the conduct of state and local government business. Most of these records are subject to disclosure under open records laws, with certain limited exceptions.

Rainy day fund—Accounts established in public budgets to provide a cushion in the face of serious economic downturns or sudden revenue shortfalls. These are especially important in state and local government because most state and local budgets must be balanced.

Redevelopment—The effort to revitalize an area of a city, usually the downtown area, which has suffered from out-migration of businesses and high crime rates. Redevelopment usually requires the expenditure of funds to address the crime problem and help local residents rehabilitate their homes and attract new businesses and jobs to the area, through a variety of incentives.

Revenue bonds—Bonds that are supported by the revenues generated by the activity or service provided. These bonds are issued to finance activities that cannot or will not be supported by general obligation bonds. Revenue accruing to another activity can also be used to back revenue bonds in some cases.

Revenue sharing—A program that the federal government sponsored in the 1970s and 1980s to send money (on the basis of a formula using population and poverty levels) from Washington to local governments. Some of it bypassed the states. The money could be used for any local initiative. The practice of sending intergovernmental transfers from the federal government directly to local governments still remains in effect, but the program areas where the money can be used are very narrowly defined (such as midnight basketball).

Revolving loan fund—A fund established for the receipt and disbursement of funds on an irregular basis, and for special purposes, such as local infrastructure improvement projects.

Risk pooling—The ability of state and/or local governments to contract with one another for joint insurance coverage and wider risk sharing.

Sheriff—The chief law enforcement officer of the county in many states. The sheriff in independently elected along with other county officials. The office usually has substantial power separate from the rest of county government.

Sovereign immunity—The "common law" principle that "the King could do no wrong," this concept today means that public officials cannot normally be held liable for actions taken in the course of their duties, absent intentional wrong-doing. In order to provide redress for citizens injured by government action, many states have adopted tort claims acts and/or provided insurance coverage to abrogate the sovereign immunity principle. *See also Immunity.*

Special-act legislation—Laws passed by the state legislature that are limited in their effect to a particular jurisdiction or activity.

Special districts—Subunits of a political jurisdiction created for a specific purpose or activity. State law in many states authorizes local governments to create special districts for limited and specific purposes, such as water, sewer, and drainage. Districts can be administered by the governmental unit or by an appointed board, and can impose special fees or assessments for the service or activity provided.

State-shared revenues—Revenues that the state government shares with local governments, such as state-collected gasoline taxes, alcoholic beverage taxes, and motor vehicle license tag fees, and others.

Sunshine laws—Laws passed by the legislature to provide for open meetings and open records so that the work of the government occurs in the "sunshine"—as opposed to behind closed doors.

Supplemental levies—Additional levies and fees imposed by state and local governments to cover budget shortfalls.

Tax Increment Financing (TIF)—A method of financing economic and community development from tax revenues accruing from the net increase in the taxable value in a particular area (called a district) after the improvements and investments have been made. The revenues are held in a separate fund by the local government and are used only in the redevelopment area and to pay off debts incurred for such development.

Unfunded mandates—Regulations and requirements imposed by a higher level of government on a lower lever of government, without the requisite funds necessary to pay for them or the authority to raise the needed funds (such as an additional tax or fee). Examples include state-mandated environmental regulations, such as for water and sewer improvements; requirements to pay for mental health services; mandatory training programs; and others. Unfunded mandates have an adverse effect on local government's discretionary authority.

Unincorporated area—The area of a county that is not part of the municipal corporate limits (that is, the "incorporated" area).

Urban redevelopment—*See Redevelopment.*

User fees—The charges imposed on a citizen for a particular service, such as garbage collection, building inspection, or utility usage.

Zoning—The power of local government to establish land use districts within its jurisdiction in which certain uses are permitted and certain uses are prohibited, in order to promote the public health, safety, morals, and general welfare. The concept of zoning as a valid exercise of the police power was first approved by the U.S. Supreme Court in 1926 in the case of *Village of Euclid v. Ambler Realty Company.*